# French Warships

## *in the Age of Steam 1859-1914*

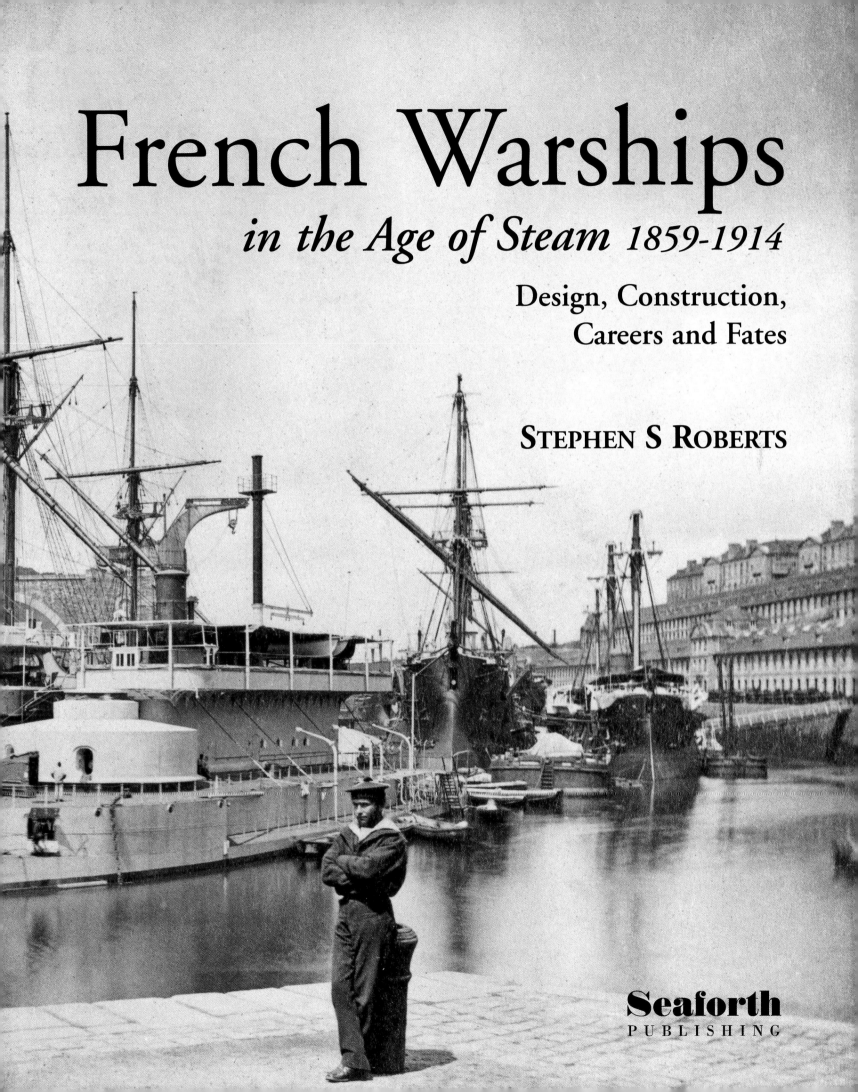

# French Warships

## in the Age of Steam 1859-1914

### Design, Construction, Careers and Fates

#### STEPHEN S ROBERTS

**Seaforth**
PUBLISHING

**Title pages:** The 2nd class coast defence ironclad *Tempête* alongside the 1st rank ironclad *Redoutable* at Brest. The 1st rank ironclad *Trident* and a 2nd rank ironclad, either *Triomphante* or *Victorieuse* (bows-on, from left to right), are in the right background. *(NHHC, NH-74894)*

Copyright © Stephen S Roberts 2021

This edition first published in Great Britain in 2021 by
Seaforth Publishing,
An imprint of Pen & Sword Books Ltd,
47 Church Street,
Barnsley
South Yorkshire S70 2AS

www.seaforthpublishing.com
Email: info@seaforthpublishing.com

*British Library Cataloguing in Publication Data*
A catalogue record for this book is available from the British Library

ISBN 978-1-5267-4533-0 (Hardback)
ISBN 978-1-5267-4534-7 (ePub)
ISBN 978-1-5267-4535-4 (Kindle)

Pen & Sword Books Limited incorporates the imprints of Atlas, Archaeology, Aviation, Discovery, Family History, Fiction, History, Maritime, Military, Military Classics, Politics, Select, Transport, True Crime, Air World, Frontline Publishing, Leo Cooper, Remember When, Seaforth Publishing, The Praetorian Press, Wharncliffe Local History, Wharncliffe Transport, Wharncliffe True Crime and White Owl.

Typeset and designed by Stephen Dent
Printed and bound in India by Replika Press Pvt. Ltd

# Contents

# Part 3.
# Towards a Modern Battle Fleet, 1897-1914

# Preface

This book is the first comprehensive listing in English of the nearly 1,350 warships that were added to the official French navy fleet list (*Liste de la Flotte*) between 1 January 1859 and World War I. (The navy's many service craft and a few other subsidiary categories are excluded.) A few ships not in the fleet lists are also covered, but as this was not a wartime period the number of such ships is small. The ships listed include everything from the largest battleships to a small armoured gunboat that looked like a floating egg (*Tortue*). For each ship the book attempts to answer three questions:

1. Why was it built or acquired?
2. What were its technical characteristics at the time it entered service?
3. What happened to it?

To answer these questions the author first consulted the remarkable monographs produced by many French authors on their nations's warships, from early authorities like Henri Le Masson (the author's mentor in 1964 and 1973) to the present day (John Jordan and Philippe Caresse produced two books in English on this period with an equivalent level of detail and authoritative sourcing). This impressive literature, largely inaccessible to monoglot English-speaking readers and no doubt to many French readers as well, is fully documented in the bibliography at the end of this volume. To fill the inevitable gaps left by multiple authors working over a period of decades the present author then turned to the French naval archives at Vincennes, first in person and then with the assistance of a very capable researcher who ended up taking over 23,000 photographs of document pages. The results of this archival work can be seen on almost every page in the book (including all references to the fleet lists) but are particularly prominent in the design histories and technical characteristics of the larger ships as well as in the entries for some particularly obscure ones.

This book serves as a sequel to two Seaforth Publishing volumes, *French Warships in the Age of Sail, 1626-1786* and *French Warships in the Age of Sail, 1786-1861*, written jointly by Rif Winfield and the present author. These two books begin with Cardinal Richelieu's self-appointment in October 1626 as *Grand maître, chef et surintendant général de la navigation et commerce de France* (or otherwise, absolute master of everything maritime) and carry through the effective end of the 'wooden walls' with the first sea trials in 1861 of the world's first ironclad battleship, France's *Gloire*. The present book begins two years earlier in 1859 to allow covering the design and construction of *Gloire* and other ships built with her, and it then takes the story forward to the outbreak of World War I in August 1914. In many ways this book forms the third volume in a trilogy that provides a complete picture of the overall development of French warships over a period of almost three centuries.

The author hopes to post in the French section of his website, www.shipscribe.com, any additions and modifications to this book that may be found by him or reported by readers after publication. Contact information for the author is provided on the 'About Shipscribe' page of that website.

# Acknowledgments

The two primary sources for this work were the large number of excellent works published by French authors, portions of which this book brings conveniently to many English-speaking readers for the first time, and the files in the archives at the Château de Vincennes in Paris. Many monographs and studies have been produced since the 1960s by French authors, some of whom in alphabetical order are Michèle Battesti, Philippe Caresse, Robert Dumas, Bernard Estival, Luc Feron, Gérard Garier, Jean Guiglini, Henri Le Masson, Jean Moulin, Gérard Prévoteaux, and Marc Saibène. Others are referenced in the Bibliography. France also has a long tradition of ship lists or *Répertoires* beginning with the *Répertoire alphabétique des bâtiments de tout rang armés et désarmés par l'État de 1800 à 1828 compris* by Baron De Lagatinerie. (The fourth and fifth supplements to this, extending to the end of 1878, were used in the present volume.) The latest of these, the *Dictionnaire des bâtiments de la flotte de guerre française de Colbert à nos jours* of Jean-Michel Roche, has been a source of copious information, as have the earlier *Répertoires* of Frank Lecalvé, Jacques Vichot, and Pierre Le Conte. The last of the eight volumes of the *Nomenclature des navires français* by Commandant Alain Demerliac, all of which are loaded with technical and historical information, was an essential source of data for this volume as its earlier volumes were for the sailing navy books. The website by Alain Clouet, *La Flotte de Napoleon III*, was of great use for that period. I gratefully acknowledge my debt to all these authors and publications and offer my apologies to any that I have inadvertently omitted from this page.

My first exposure to the archives of the French Navy was in person from the 1960s to the 1980s, and I would like to express my thanks to the former directors of the archives and library of the *Service Historique de la Marine* in Paris, Messrs. Joël Audouy and Jean-Pierre Busson, who helped me so much during my doctoral research in Paris between 1973 and 1976 and to their successors who have continued to preserve France's maritime heritage, now as part of the *Service Historique de la Défense* at Vincennes. More recently, I was extremely fortunate to make the acquaintance of Jane Winfield, the sister of Rif Winfield, my co-author for the two Age of Sail books. Jane, a long-time French resident and a professional researcher in Paris until recently, first assisted her brother and me with the sail books and then took me on as a client for this volume. Under my substantive guidance she mined the archives for basic references like the *Listes de la Flotte* and then for authoritative material on the history of the origins of the ships and on their technical characteristics, most notably the minutes of the *Conseil des travaux* and the files retired after ships were condemned (the 7DD1 series), which contained correspondence, reports, *devis d'armament*, and *devis de campagne*. She also copied several hundred ship plans from the microfilms of the 8DD1 collection. These, given their microfilm origin, were suitable for research but not for reproduction. I am enormously grateful to Jane for diligently and enthusiastically carrying out this massive amount of research at Vincennes, which essentially made this book possible.

Many of the ship drawings in this volume are from an extensive set of builder's plans widely used by modern French authors that for several years were posted online by the Service Historique de la Défense and are still available on other websites. Most of these are thought to have originated in the *Atlas de Coque*, technical documents produced for individual ships by the Navy and collections of which reside in the *Centre d'Archives de l'Armement* at Châtellerault, the *Musée de la Marine*, and in one or more port archives. For reasons of space only relatively simple general arrangement views extracted from the more complex plans in this collection can be provided here, but additional portions of these plans can be seen in some of the French monographs.

The author acquired most of the photographs and sketches in this book from two sources, the collection of the U.S. Naval History and Heritage Command in Washington, D.C., and small sellers online. He has made a diligent effort to identify the original sources of these images, including consulting websites of known image suppliers, but with indifferent success. The purchased images, many of which are postcards, mostly bear credits to sources that are unknown today, and the U.S. Navy collection contains much material purchased by naval attachés in Europe in the 1890s on some of which the credits are absent, not visible, or unknown today. It is highly unlikely that any of the photographs of uncertain or unknown origin remain in copyright, but the author offers his apologies in case his efforts have failed to turn up a holder of legitimate rights to an image presented here.

I would also like to acknowledge the information and helpful advice and support that I have received over the decades from a number of friends and correspondents, both in France and around the world, including but not limited to Henri Le Masson, Christian de Saint Hubert, Christopher C. Wright, Charles Haberlein, Norman Friedman, and John Jordan. I want particularly to thank Rif Winfield, who taught me how to produce a book like this while we worked together on the two sail volumes and who gave me encouragement and help when I started this one. I also wish to remember my late wife Sue Goetz Ross, who accompanied me on some of my research trips to France but who died long before I got the opportunity to publish my work in this book. She encouraged me in my research and, while I was in the archives, she would find a good restaurant or concert for us to enjoy together in the evening.

This publication would not have been possible without the enthusiastic co-operation and support of Robert Gardiner and Seaforth Publishing. To Rob and to the rest of the team at Seaforth, I wish to express my profound thanks. I would also like to thank the U.S. Naval Institute Press, which long ago in 1986 gave me the opportunity to edit for publication the typescript Ph.D. thesis of Theodore Ropp which it published as *The Development of a Modern Navy, French Naval Policy 1871-1904*, and which co-publishes in the United States many Seaforth Publishing titles including the three on French warships with which I am associated.

# Structure and Organisation of the Book

During the period covered by this book the French navy went through three tumultuous phases of technological innovation and political controversy. In each phase different technological, political, and strategic circumstances produced different concepts of the kind of navy France needed. This book is divided into three separate Parts corresponding to the three phases, both to keep contemporary ships together and to show the substantially different composition of the fleets built during the different phases.

From the late 1850s to the early 1880s (Part 1), despite the trauma of the 1870-1871 war, the French continued to build a fleet structured much like the old sailing fleets, with heavily-armed ships for battles in European waters, a substantial number of cruisers (initially steam frigates and corvettes) primarily for service as cruisers on distant stations and on the sea lanes, and many smaller vessels (steam avisos, gunboats, and smaller types) for local service both at home and in the colonies. This fleet however was updated with the latest technology, including iron and steel hulls and massive guns and armour in the largest ships. The period from the early 1880s to the end of the 1890s (Part 2) was dominated by a conflict (which had political as well as military overtones) between advocates of the traditional fleet and those claiming that new technology – particularly the torpedo boat – had rendered large battleships obsolete and that naval wars would be won by fast steel cruisers acting as commerce raiders. By the end of the 1890s France, having to some extent tried to follow both paths, had few new battleships (none as large as the best foreign ships) and over two hundred torpedo boats. The Fashoda crisis in 1898 revealed the inability of this navy to stand up to foreign fleets. Between the end of the 1890s and the beginning of World War I (Part 3), with the exception of a costly lapse between 1902 and 1905, opinion coalesced around a Mahanian navy consisting almost entirely of a strong battle fleet for European waters. In 1914 this fleet remained far behind those of Britain and Germany in numbers, but taken individually French warships remained among the best in the world.

Within each Part, ship type groupings are arranged in the order used in the official fleet lists for the period covered by the Part. It should be noted that this order varied between periods, reflecting changes in ideas on how the ships were to be used. For example, the ships listed in the transport category as *transports avisos* in Part 1 were moved to the aviso category in Part 2 (in 1883) as *avisos-transports*, their use as small cruising ships evidently having been found more significant than their use as cargo carriers. At the beginning of each type grouping the nomenclature used for it in the fleet lists are shown along with all subsequent changes.

Within each ship type grouping, ship classes are arranged chronologically by the year in which the first ship in the class was ordered or acquired. Each ship class listing is divided into three sections. The first section is a narrative giving the history of the design of the class or ship and providing a sense of why the ships were built the way they were. The second section contains the basic technical characteristics of the ships as built along with significant changes during service. The third section is a list of the individual ships in the class with their ship and engine builders, construction dates, entry in service, occasional career highlights, and complete end of service data. The definitions and terminology used in the second and third sections are described further below.

The coast defence battleship *Terrible* with her short but massive 420mm (16.5-inch) guns probably photographed at Villefranche in about 1890-1891. Photo by J.G., Nice. *(NHHC from ONI album of foreign warships dated about 1900, NH-88824)*

# Definitions and Terminology

## Technical Characteristics

The technical characteristics of the ships listed here are drawn where possible from the *devis d'armement*, documents prepared by shore-based naval constructors as the ship was being readied for duty and presented to and signed for by the ship's commanding officer close to the ship's full commissioning. (The term *devis* used by itself in this book refers to the *devis d'armement* or commissioning reports, other *devis*, notably the *devis de campagne* or cruise reports, are specifically identified.) Most of the data attributed in this book to *devis d'armement* up to 1885 were taken, not from the documents themselves, but from virtually identical compilations dated 1881 and 1884 (the latter extending into 1885) by the then-Secretary of the *Conseil des travaux*, naval constructor Jean-Rosier Albaret. (Paul Dislère, an earlier Secretary of the *Conseil des travaux*, produced a similar compilation in 1873 that is used for early ships not in Albaret's volumes.) The *devis* cited here for ships from 1885 were either found in the ships' disposal files in the archives (the 7DD1 series) or were so cited by French authors in their monographs. Comparable data cited in other monographs, although not credited to *devis d'armement*, most likely also came from them.

### Dimensions & tons

*Length*: Dimensions for ships up to 1885 are taken from Albaret's compilations. In these he departed from the original *devis* by standardising the length measurements to eliminate the effects of the different measurement practices used by individual dockyards and designers and make them comparable. Using all of the documents then available in the Ministry (many of which are now lost), Albaret produced two standardised length measurements, the first between the intersection of the hull with the waterline at both ends of the ship with minor adjustments, and the second from the same point at the bow to the axis of the rudder. Albaret preferred the former measurement because it included the portion of the underwater hull aft of the rudder. Because the French defined the forward and aft perpendiculars for ships with forward-raked or straight bows as being at the intersection of the bow with the waterline and at the axis of the rudder respectively, Albaret's second measurement was effectively the length between perpendiculars for such ships and is so listed here, although he did not use that term. For ships with ram or reversed bows the forward perpendicular was defined as being at the tip of the ram underwater, so the length between perpendiculars for such ships consisted of Albaret's second measurement plus the projection of the ram underwater forward of the waterline, which Albaret and we (with a + sign) have both reported. Albaret's first measurement was effectively the actual length on the waterline and is so listed here. Following tradition Albaret did not report the length overall as it was of little use to naval architects, although it was important for ship handling and docking. Length on deck (the primary gun deck) and length of keel were holdover measurements from the Age of Sail that went out of use in the 1860s. This book uses Albaret's figures for ships up to 1885, and any cases during this period in which length measurements are known to diverge from his standards are identified.

In a new template for the *devis* adopted in 1885 the measurement formerly called waterline length but defined essentially as Albaret's second measurement was renamed length between perpendiculars (pp) and redefined as the length from the forward extremity of the hull at the waterline or the tip of the ram to the axis of the rudder (a few naval constructors used the stern rather than the rudder). These variant measurements are distinguished here as (wl fwd to rudder) and (tip fwd to rudder) or (wl fwd to wl aft) and (tip fwd to stern) respectively. In addition, the overall length (oa) (*longueur du bâtiment hors tout or longueur d'encombrement*) and the actual

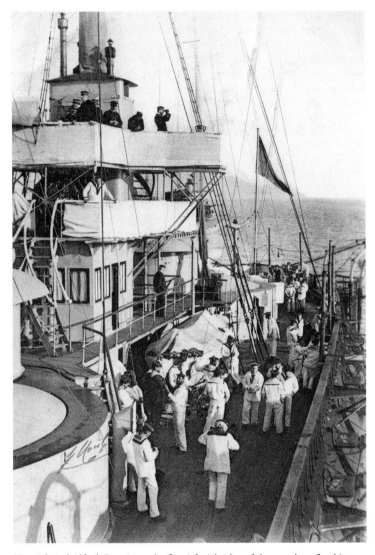

Vice Admiral Alfred Gervais on the flag (after) bridge of the squadron flagship *Formidable* observing the *Escadre de la Méditerranée* during manoeuvres. He commanded the *Escadre* in 1896. The amidships 370mm barbette is in the foreground and the after one is beyond the superstructure. The deckhouse with windows was the restroom for the flag staff. The superstructure largely obscures two battleships in line behind *Formidable*. *(Postcard by A Bougault)*

waterline length (wl) (*longueur de la flottaison en charge, en différence*) were added to the *devis* template for the first time. These changes were directed by a ministerial *circulaire* in 1885. Another *circulaire* followed on 15 February 1893 that moved the after perpendicular from the rudder post to the intersection of the load waterline with the tip of the stern, while leaving the forward perpendicular at either the waterline at the bow or the tip of the ram. For ships without a ram this made the waterline length and the length between perpendiculars essentially identical (wl/pp).

Both length and beam figures are as measured while the ship was approaching completion. If measurements were not taken figures as designed are used. The measurements of ships within a class varied somewhat, due to different construction practices in different yards, to differences in working plans, and to measurement errors (including in successive measurements of the same ship). In such cases the measurements for a representative ship are given here unless the differences are significant.

*Beam (breadth)*: During the period of this book this measurement was reported as the extreme beam of the hull taken at its widest point including the hull planking or plating (*hors bordage*). For wooden ships an older measurement called the moulded beam, taken to the outside of the frame but excluding the planking (*hors membrure*), was sometimes reported. In some ships the maximum beam occurred above or below the waterline rather than at it. A greater beam below the waterline was significant for stability calculations while a greater beam above the waterline (sometimes caused by projections like gun sponsons) was significant for handling the ship in restricted spaces. This book follows the *devis* in giving both the extreme (ext) and, if different, waterline (wl) beams.

*Displacement.* The displacements presented here are generally normal displacements, which were calculated in the *devis* from the draughts empirically observed or expected to result after a ship embarked its normal allowance of men, stores, water, and ordnance and was othewise ready for sea. (Designed displacements, based on the designed draughts, were also recorded in the *devis* and are given here if the actual ones were not available.) Many ships could also carry a surcharge of some items, primarily coal, in addition to their normal allowance, and displacements with this surcharge are reported if provided.

*Draught.* The draughts (forward, mean/amidships, and aft) in the devis correspond to the actual (normal) displacement reported in the devis or if not available to the designed displacement. Usually the keel of a ship was straight from near the bow to the rudder post, meaning that the third figure could be calculated from the other two and allowing only two, usually the mean and aft draught to be reported here. In some cases, however, the keel curved up or was cut off short of the stern. Such ships had two after draughts, an actual (real) one and a larger theoretical (*fictif*) one based on a projection of the keel line to the stern. The after draught of torpedo boats was often greatly increased by a frame protecting the screw and rudder which projected well below the line of the keel. In ambiguous cases like these the draught forward is also given when known.

*Men.* Figures up to 1885 are from Albaret who used manning documents then in the Ministry. Detailed data on the crew were not provided in the *devis d'armament*, which were technical and not administrative documents. However, these *devis* used a single number of men on board as a multiplier for calculating the weight of the provisions and water that needed to be carried, and this number is commonly cited here for ships after 1885 as the designed size of the crew. The crew allowance lists, separate documents occasionally found in the 7DD1 files, showed a wide range of crew sizes, ranging from an augmented combat crew to a reduced reserve crew, leaving it difficult to discern the crew size for which the ship was designed.

## Machinery

The data presented here on a ship's propulsion plant begin with measurements of its designed performance, including its indicated horsepower (ihp) or for turbines shaft horsepower (shp) with the corresponding rotational speed of the engines (rpm), and the rated boiler pressure in kilogrammes per square centimetre (kg/cm², 1kg/cm² being equal to 14.2233psi). The mechanical power in one indicated metric horsepower was defined as 75 kilogram-metres per second (0.986 mechanical horsepower as defined by James Watt, one mechanical horsepower being 550 foot-pounds per second). The archaic measurement of nominal horsepower (nhp) which dated back to the origins of the steam engine, also continued to be used well into this period. One nominal horsepower was redefined on 1 January 1867 as one quarter of the horsepower of 75 kilogram-metres per second that the engine was designed to develop, resulting in a reduction of the nominal horsepower ratings of most of the engines built up to that date. The fleet lists finally changed from nominal to indicated horsepower in 1891.

These data are followed here by data on steam trials, which over time were reported in increasing detail in the *devis d'armement*. The basic data supplied here include the date of the trials, the indicated horsepower and speed maintained under the conditions established for the trials, and the corresponding rotational speed of the engines and boiler pressure. Trial figures for torpedo boats were for the average on a two or three-hour run in open water (*route libre*). The results of runs on the measured mile (*base*) were also reported and are given here if better than the *route libre* figures.

Next comes a basic description of the propulsion plant, consisting of the number of screws, the number and type of the engines with the number and diameters of their cylinders and their stroke. The number and type of the boilers is also provided. The reglementary cylindrical boilers in the French navy as dictated by Navy rules existed in three varieties: high (*haut*, 3.60m diameter), medium (*moyen*, 3.48m diameter) and low (*bas*, 3.25m diameter). The diameters of the tubes and the spacing between them were the same for all three types. Boiler types proliferated with the advent of water tube boilers. The most successful ones were Belleville and Niclausse boilers and, with smaller tubes, Normand, Normand-Sigaudy, and Guyot-Du Temple models. Early Du Temple models (1891-93) featured from two to five bends (called folds) of almost 180 degrees in the water tubes which quickly accumulated scale that could not be cleaned out.

Last comes data on the amount of coal carried and the corresponding operating range, ideally at a speed of 10 knots (later increased to 14 knots). The ships were designed for a normal allowance of coal in their regular bunkers, but additional stowage was provided for an often substantial surcharge, sometimes on the deck above the regular bunkers. Estimates of the operating range (generally based on the normal coal allowance) were added to the trial data in the *devis* template in 1892.

## Armour

Armour data through 1885 are from Albaret who used documentation then available in the Ministry. Surprisingly, armour data were only added to the *devis* template in 1891, although the gap between 1885 and 1891 was easily filled by later *devis*. The section in the *devis* for armour was doubled in size in 1893, resulting in far more detail on armour schemes than can be reproduced here. One peculiarity of the armour data in the *devis* is that the thicknesses referred only to armour-quality plating and 'construction steel' and not to the regular hull plating (*platelage*) that supported the armour and in some cases also contributed to protection. Construction steel and hull plating were the same thing, regular mild steel, but they differed in that the former was considered part of the protection scheme and was included in the armour weights while the latter was considered part of the hull and was included in the hull weights. This is most significant in the case of armoured decks, whose thicknesses reported in other sources often include both the armour itself and its hull steel backing. Fortunately, the *devis* include the thicknesses of the backing as well as the armour and both are reported here for horizontal armour. The hull steel backing for vertical armour, however, is generally ignored both here and elsewhere.

Schneider began developing steel armour in place of iron armour for vertical surfaces in the late 1870s and in 1880 the navy contracted with Schneider for steel armour for the coast defence ship *Terrible*. At the same time the navy contracted for its first compound armour (iron armour with a layer of steel bonded on top), developed in Britain and made in France, for her three sisters. Through the 1880s compound armour and Schneider's steel armour were regarded as roughly equivalent. Harvey cemented (face-hardened) steel armour, invented in America, was first adopted by Schneider in the turrets of the battleship *Bouvet* in 1893, and it generally replaced both steel and compound armour soon afterwards. In the meantime iron continued to be used for decks. The purpose of armoured decks was not to prevent penetration by shells but to deflect them by bending under the impact, and a soft metal was better for this purpose than hardened steel, which would fracture rather than bend. At the end of the 1880s an extra mild steel called *métail de Saint-Jacques* was developed by Châtillon-Commentry for use in armoured decks, and the Navy made its use mandatory in 1892.

The battleship *Brennus*, flagship of the *Escadre de la Méditerranée*, in fleet gunnery practice as drawn by Fred T. Jane in 1898. (Jane's first *Fighting Ships* came out in the same year and contained many of his sketches.) In the foreground is the entire port 164.7mm battery with the guns firing individually and behind it the after single 340mm turret also firing a round. The admiral and his staff are on the after bridge with a 65mm or 47mm gun just below them adding to the noise. Jane specified that the ship was using high capacity shells. *(Black and White, 26 November 1898, page 67)*

### Armament (guns, torpedoes, and searchlights)

The armament listings here begin with the armament on board the ship at the time of its entry into service (earlier armaments as designed are reported in the narratives if significant) and all known changes affecting calibres of 100mm and above follow to the extent possible. There were far too many changes in the numbers and locations of 47mm and 37mm quick fire guns and revolving cannon to be listed here, although major changes in the configuration of this battery are shown when known. The inventories of guns carried were taken from the *devis d'armement* and *devis de campagne* where possible. The information in these sources on the model designators of the guns was compared with the tables in the official *Renseignements sur les Bouches à Feu de l'Artillerie Navale de tous Calibres & Modèles*, now in the U.S. National Archives, to ensure accuracy. Key extracts from these tables, which were officially passed to the U.S. Naval Attaché in Paris in 1919, are provided in Appendix A.

French practice regarding the designation of the calibre of their guns varied over time. Initially they showed the calibre of their guns in rounded-off centimetres (guns under 10cm were rated in millimetres), but in a decision of 6 December 1893 the Minister directed that all guns in service afloat and ashore were to be designated by their exact calibre in millimetres (most in tenths of millimetres). This change can be observed in the 'Designation' column in Appendix A. Elsewhere, however, this book uses the 1893 standards throughout, using millimetres and tenths both before and after 1893 to enhance comparability and reduce confusion.

Torpedo armaments were added to the template for the *devis d'armement* in 1885 and searchlights were added in 1891.

## Ships' Histories

### Order and construction dates

*On list.* The first annual edition of the fleet list in which the ship appeared. The annual editions were nominally dated 1 January, although there is evidence that changes before printing were occasionally made as late as early March.

*Order (Ord:).* The dates on which Paris notified the building yard that

An inspirational painting of the 24-metre submarine *Thon*, one of the twenty small *fritures*, in heavy weather by the official painter of the Ministry of Marine, R. Dumont-Duparc. The guards around the bow planes and the bow rudder are accurate according to the ship's plans, as are other key technical details. The bow, prominent here, was often submerged and invisible when the ship was at rest or underway. *(Colour postcard by LL)*

construction of the ship had been assigned to it and in some cases assigned a name to the ship. For contract-built ships, the notation '(contract)' indicates that the order date given here is instead the date on which the contract was signed or in some cases approved.

*Keel laying (K:).* Ideally these are the dates on which the ship's first keel plate was laid on the building ways (*mis sur cale*), but some may be earlier dates on which fabrication work on the ship's frames and hull plating or planking was begun by the dockyard or ordered begun by Paris (*mis en chantier*). Occasionally order dates were even reported as keel dates. Start of construction dates like these were normally not reported to Paris by contractors and are thus often missing from official records for contract ships.

*Launch (L:).* The date of entry into the water from inclined building ways or from a building dock, a physical event often accompanied by a public ceremony.

*Engine installation.* The *devis* identify the engine builder and provide the dates for the start of engine installation (*montage*) and the first dock (stationary machinery) trials. Installation of the machinery usually began soon after the ship was launched and the engines and boilers were operated in place for the first time while the ship was assembling its trial crew.

### Commissioning and entry into service dates

*Commissioning (Comm:).* The normal sequence as a ship approached completion was first for the muster list for the crew to be opened, beginning the process of manning and fitting out the ship for trials. In the 1800s Baron De Lagatinerie and his successors recorded this as the single *date armé* for the ship because their primary interest was accounting for pay for the crew which began on that date; this date was also later reported as *armé pour essais*. A more accurate term was *entré en armement pour essais* to indicate that the process was just beginning. The ship's first commanding officer was often assigned at this time. The ship would eventually receive her full trial crew and outfit, completing her *armement pour essais* and becoming fully *armé pour essais*, and trials would soon follow. The report on the trials would then be delivered (*clôture des essais*), the ship would augment her trial crew to form her full regular crew and load her combat allowance of stores in place of the trials allowance, and she would then go into full commission or *armement définitif*. (The date on which she joined the operational *escadre* to which she had been assigned was sometimes also reported as *armement définitif*.) The ship was then admitted to active service (*admis au service actif*) and accepted for service (*clôture d'armement*).

An effort has been made to provide enough of the relevant dates, where available, to clarify this confusing period in a ship's history.

*Completion (C:).* In cases where better data are lacking a generic completion date or year is given to show roughly when the ship was ready for service. This can also be necessary for ships that went into reserve instead of full commission after completion of trials.

**End of service dates**
The basic sequence of events for removing a ship from the navy was to decommission her definitively if she was in active service or 1st or 2nd category reserve, condemn her, strike her name from the *Liste de la Flotte*, and break her up (BU), either in a dockyard or by sale to a private scrapper. The main alternative to this process was to strike the ship from the main part of the fleet list but then retain her for use as a hulk in a dockyard. Lorient and Rochefort both used many old ships as coal hulks, floating warehouses, and mooring or landing hulks while Toulon used hulks primarily as floating barracks. In addition, some hulks became base ships for the torpedo boats of the *Défense mobile* or for harbour commanders and security services. Hulks were carried in the fleet lists in a section for condemned ships and were eventually transferred to a list of ships to be broken up or sold. Sales were handled by the government agency responsible for all government property, the Administration des Domaines.

Ships were struck (*rayé*) from the fleet list by a circular notice generally signed by the Minister of Marine or the Director of Matériel and promulgated in the *Bulletin officiel de la Marine*. Usually the action took effect on the date of the notice, but in some cases the notice reported a decision taken on an earlier date, which is used here. (Thus a Ministerial decision of 4 September 1900 striking the ironclads *Colbert, Trident, Richelieu* and *Turenne* and the avisos *Inconstant* and *Papin* was only promulgated in the *Bulletin officiel* in a notice dated 11 September.) Virtually all of the strikes (*radiations*) in this book were taken directly from the *Bulletin officiel*. The texts of some of these orders called them *condamnations* rather than *radiations* but all were carried in the indexes of the *Bulletin officiel* as *radiations*.

# Deck levels in a warship
Generally the terminology for the structure of a ship of the late nineteenth century is much more familiar to modern readers than the terminology for ships of the Age of Sail. The terminology for deck levels, however, remains confusing, in part because the French changed it in the middle of our period (1900). Provided here is a drawing by John Jordan which illustrates both the old and the new nomenclature for the various decks. The decks are discussed below from top to bottom following the drawing.

**Decks to 1900.**
The drawing shows a battleship of the *Charlemagne* class with the armour scheme favoured by French designers from the early 1870s to the late 1890s, a narrow but thick armoured belt between the main deck and the 1st platform deck with the main deck at the top of the belt being the ship's single heavy armoured deck and the 1st platform deck at the bottom of the belt being only a thin splinter deck. The deck arrangement, including some of its nomenclature, goes back much further into the Age of Sail.

*Teugue* and *dunette* (Forecastle and poop or quarterdeck, not shown on the drawing). Decks over the bow and stern above the *pont des gaillards*, usually short and often missing.

*Spardeck* (Shelter deck). Named for the spars once stored in sailing ships above the *pont des gaillards*, this deck in the late nineteenth century often became the lowest level in a ship's amidships superstructure. Over time several levels of *passerelles* (bridges, not shown on the drawing) rose above it.

*Pont des gaillards* (Upper deck). During the Age of Sail this was a largely open level with only a few walkways and gratings, but it was filled in during the early nineteenth century and by the 1850s was a complete deck cover-

ing the battery deck. In later ships it was often the top deck that was more or less complete.

*Pont de la batterie/pont intermédiaire* (Battery deck), formerly the upper gun deck in a two-decker and there called the *second batterie* or *second pont*. A three-decker would also have a *troisième batterie* or *troisième pont* above it. Smaller ships omitted this level.

*Pont principal* (Main deck), formerly the lower gun deck of a two- or three-decked ship of the line and called there the *première batterie* or the *premier pont*. It eventually became too low in the water to carry guns.

*Faux pont* (1st platform deck); a (mainly) continuous deck level within the ship, usually at or below the waterline and covering the machinery spaces. It was called the orlop deck during the Age of Sail.

*Plateforme de cale* (2nd platform deck). Partial decks fore and aft of the machinery spaces.

*Cale* (Hold). The level directly above the ship's keel.

**Decks 1900 onwards.**
The drawing, based on the dreadnoughts of the *Courbet* and *Bretagne* classes, shows the transformation of the hull configuration of large French warships as part of a new protection scheme introduced by Émile Bertin in the late 1890s and used in his *Patrie* class and later battleships and in most of his armoured cruisers. The two armoured decks were still the main deck and 1st platform deck but both were raised higher in the hull and they were moved further apart to allow for a much taller armour belt and to enclose a tightly-subdivided cellular layer (*tranche cellulaire*) between them. The main deck was also called the upper armoured deck (*pont blindé supérieur* or PBS) while the 1st platform deck was also called the lower armoured deck (*pont blindé inférieur* or PBI). In contrast to the older scheme, both were true armoured decks and were of roughly the same thickness.

*2e pont* (2nd deck). Equivalent to the former upper deck.

*1er pont* (1st deck). Equivalent to the former battery deck.

## Nomenclature

### Decks 1890-1900

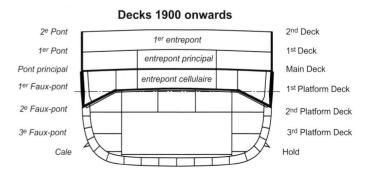

© John Jordan 2015

*Pont principal* (Main deck). Moved well above the waterline.

*1er faux pont* (1st platform deck). Moved up to the waterline with armoured slopes at the sides descending well below it. It remained the lowest of the complete decks and covered the machinery spaces.

*2e faux pont* (2nd platform deck). Partial decks fore and aft of the machinery spaces and amidships between them.

*3e faux pont* (3rd platform deck). Partial decks fore and aft of the machinery spaces, a level added in the largest ships.

*Cale* (Hold). The level directly above the ship's keel.

Interior view of the control room of the submarine *Andromaque* taken at Cherbourg in 1916-17. The commanding officer is at the periscope, two crewmen are at the dive planes, and on the deck behind the periscope is the gyro compass. By January 1918 *Andromaque* had moved to Toulon and joined the naval school for underwater navigation. *(NHHC, NH-55621)*

# Political, Diplomatic, and Naval Chronology

## 1852-1882

**1852-1870** Napoleon III controlled the government of the Second Empire, selecting and dismissing all ministers. The legislature was compliant during the 1850s, liberal reforms in the 1860s produced much political unrest but ultimately had little practical effect.

**1854-1856** The Crimean War set Russia against Britain and France in a conflict that originated in concerns about the protection of Christians in the Ottoman Empire and ended up redefining international relations in the Balkans and the Black Sea region. Steam powered warships and shell guns proved their worth.

**1857-1860** Naval operations took place in China, first with the Anglo-French seizure of Canton (1857-58) and then with the Anglo-French occupation of Peking (1859-60).

**1857 (23 Nov.)** The French Naval Programme of 1857 became law

**1858-1862** A joint French and Spanish naval expedition against the long-unfriendly Annamite court at Hué bombarded Tourane (Da Nang) in Annam and then turned to the south and occupied Saigon in Cochinchina

**1859 (May-July)** Napoleon III initiated war in Northern Italy in which France and Piedmont sought to drive Austria out of Italy. The end result was the unification of Italy in 1861.

**1861-1867** Napoleon III undertook an expedition to Mexico, purportedly to collect debts but actually to establish an empire there under the Austrian Archduke Maximilian. The Navy provided transportation and support to the French troops. In 1866, after the American Civil War ended and as the threat from Prussia became severe, Napoleon III recalled his troops. Maximilian stayed behind and was executed in 1867.

**1867-1868** The French occupied the three western provinces of Cochinchina after an insurrection, then explored the Mekong River as far as Yunnan. Its upper portion was found to be unnavigable and French attention turned to the Red River of Tonkin.

**1870 (July)** Napoleon III declared war with Prussia over a Hohenzollern candidacy for the Spanish throne. Prussia was supported militarily by the South German states.

**1870 (2 Sep.)** Napoleon III capitulated with a French army at Sedan.

**1870 (4 Sep.)** A republic was declared in place of the empire and a government of national defence was formed.

**1871 (18 Jan.)** The unified German Empire was proclaimed at Versailles.

**1871 (Feb.)** Following the capitulation of Paris on 28 January, the Germans permitted an election for a single-chamber National Assembly that was to decide whether to continue the war or make peace. The election was won by conservatives and monarchists who named Adolphe Thiers as Chief of the Executive Power (President of the Republic from August 1871).

**1871-1873** Thiers negotiated peace terms with Germany (February-March 1871), suppressed the Paris Commune (March-May 1871) and arranged for payment of the German indemnity (June 1871-July 1872).

**1871 (Nov.)** The French Naval Programme of 1872 was reported to the National Assembly.

**1873 (May)** A worldwide banking crisis triggered a recession that ultimately lasted to 1896.

**1873 (May)** The Royalist majority in the Assembly repudiated Thiers as insufficiently conservative and attempted to restore the monarchy.

When the legitimate heir made impossible demands (notably the replacement of the tricolor flag with the Bourbon fleur de lys) the monarchists bought time by making Marshal MacMahon president for seven years.

**1873 (Sep.)** The evacuation of French territory by German troops following payment of the indemnity was completed.

**1873-1874** A French merchant explored the Red River in Tonkin, and Lieutenant de vaisseau Francis Garnier with a handful of men, exceeding instructions, then attacked and took Hanoi and most of the Red River delta. Garnier was killed in an ambush and the French returned Hanoi in a treaty of 1874 with Annam which Annam evaded.

**1875-1879** Republican constitutional laws with a Senate, a Chamber of Deputies, and a seven-year president were passed in 1875. A Republican victory in the elections of February and March 1876 and the crisis of 16 May 1877 in which MacMahon forced out a ministry led to more Republican victories and MacMahon's resignation in January 1879.

**1878-1879** An economic recovery plan developed in 1878 by Minister of Public Works Freycinet (premier in 1879) responded to the recession with a large transportation development programme (primarily railways).

**1879 (Jan.)** A moderate conservative (opportunist or pragmatic) Third Republic replaced the Monarchist regime with Jules Grévy as president and with Jules Ferry dominating the government to 1885 (premier 1880-81 and 1883-85).

**1879 (June-July)** The Berlin Congress of 1879 gave France freedom of action in Tunisia, but no activity immediately followed as the public was indifferent.

**1879 (Oct.)** The Dual Alliance between Germany and Austria was concluded.

**1881 (May)** A French protectorate over Tunisia was established by the Treaty of Bardo after premier Jules Ferry, a strong advocate of colonialism, secured funds from Parliament to counter tribal raids from there into Algeria. Prolonged tension followed with Italy which had many nationals and its own ambitions in Tunisia.

## 1882-1897

**1882 (Jan.)** Speculation in bank shares produced a new market crash, further depressing the economy until 1888.

**1882 (May)** The Triple Alliance between Germany, Austria, and Italy was concluded.

**1882-1883** In April 1882 Capitaine de vaisseau Henri Rivière and a small force, exceeding his instructions, briefly took the citadel at Hanoi. When Jules Ferry became premier for the second time in February 1883 he strongly supported Rivière's actions. Rivière was killed in an ambush in May 1883, reinforcing Ferry's determination and leading to treaties (1883 and 1884) with the emperor in Hué establishing French protectorates and control over Tonkin and Annam.

**1883-1885** Continued resistance by pirates and Black Flag guerillas supported by China led to continued fighting on the Red River in Tonkin and the outbreak in 1884 of a naval war with China, the French forces being led by Vice Admiral Courbet. China recognized the French protectorate over Tonkin in June 1885.

**1883-1885** War with Madagascar led to French control of Madagascar's foreign affairs, a large indemnity, and the cession of Diego Suarez.

**1884-1885 (Feb.)** The Berlin Conference regulated colonial expansion in the Congo and Niger river basins.

**1885 (Mar.)** Ferry fell over a minor reverse at Langson during the war with China and over his policy of cooperating with Germany in colonial expansion.

**1885 (Oct.)** An election without a victor generated more political instability than usual (7 cabinets between 1885 and 1889).

**1886-1889** Gen. Georges Boulanger, leader of a Bonapartist populist movement against the Republic and for revenge against Germany, became Minister of War in January 1886. (This cabinet also included the reformist Vice Admiral Aube as Minister of Marine.) Boulanger was excluded from the government in May 1887 but gained even more mass support, and an electoral victory in January 1889 gave him an opportunity to seize power. Failing to take it, he fled into exile in April 1889.

**1887 (Feb.)** The First Mediterranean Agreement was concluded between Britain and Italy, soon joined by Austria and Spain. A second agreement (without Spain) followed in December.

**1887 (Feb.)** The Triple Alliance was renewed. It was prematurely renewed again in May 1891 in part to support Italy against France in North Africa.

**1887** Italy's commercial treaty with France expired and France refused to renew it because Italy was a member of the Triple Alliance. A bitter trade war followed, mostly to Italy's disadvantage.

**1889 (May)** The British Naval Defence Act established and funded a two-power standard for the Royal Navy.

**1891 (July)** A French squadron under Admiral Alfred Gervais visited Kronshtadt. The August Convention between France and Russia followed.

**1893 (July)** A French ultimatum to Siam over influence in the upper Mekong River region led to a small naval engagement off Bangkok.

**1893 (October)** A Russian squadron made a diplomatic visit to Toulon.

**1893 (Dec.-Jan.)** The military convention of 1892 between France and Russia was ratified, constituting a Franco-Russian Alliance against the Triple Alliance.

**1894 (Mar.)** The Spencer Programme further reinforced the British Royal Navy.

**1894 (Dec.)** The Dreyfus Affair started with the wrongful conviction of a Jewish Army officer for treason (espionage). It reached an initial peak in January 1898 with the publication of Émile Zola's *J'accuse* and then became a furious political battle between *Dreyfusards* (republicans) and anti-*Dreyfusards* (Army officers and conservative monarchists). Dreyfus was pardoned in 1899 and acquitted in 1906.

**1894-1896** The French conquered Madagascar.

**1896 (approx.)** Prices completed their recovery ending the recession.

# 1897-1914

**1898 (Mar.)** The German Reichstag passed its first Naval Law, beginning the expansion of the German Navy under Admiral Tirpitz.

**1898 (Apr.)** France obtained a lease on Kwangchow Wan (Guangzhouwan) and a sphere of influence in Yunnan, Kwangtung, and Kwangsi as part of the partition of influence in China between the imperialist powers.

**1898-1914** A swing to the left in the May 1898 elections led to a more progressive radical republic that lasted to 1914.

**1898-1905** Delcassé as French foreign minister from June 1898 isolated Germany and courted Britain.

**1898 (Sep.-Nov.)** The Fashoda Crisis between Britain and France over control of the upper Nile River ended with France being forced to recall its expedition under Army captain Marchand.

**1898 (Nov.)** A commercial treaty ended the tariff war between France and Italy and began the reconciliation of the two powers.

**1899-1902** A Ministry of Republican Defence under the moderate Republican Waldeck-Rousseau responded to the Dreyfus Affair by purging the Army and limiting the Church.

**1900 (June)** The second German Naval Law was passed, providing for a fleet of 38 battleships to be built in 20 years.

**1900 (June-Aug.)** The Boxer uprising in China and siege of the foreign legations in Peking was relieved by an international expeditionary force including French units.

**1900 (9 Dec.)** The French Naval Programme of 1900 became law.

**1902-1905** The Centre-left Radical party won the 1902 election resulting in the Combes ministry of June 1902 to January 1905. It enacted a full separation of church and state in response to the Dreyfus Affair and produced in the Navy the disruptive Pelletan ministry and in the Army under Gen. André the *affaire des fiches* (a card file that tracked the religious behaviour of Army officers).

**1904-1905** The Russo-Japanese war resulted in a decisive defeat for Russia and many lessons for naval strategists and ship designers.

**1904 (Apr.)** The Entente Cordiale was concluded between France and Britain.

**1906-1909** The radical ministry of Georges Clemenceau (June 1906 to July 1909) became known for its suppression of a series of strikes by industrial workers and civil servants. Clemenceau's Minister of Marine, Thomson, however, returned the navy to equilibrium after the disruptions of Pelletan.

**1905 (Mar.)** The first Moroccan crisis was triggered by a visit by the Kaiser to Tangier.

**1906 (Jan.-Apr.)** The Algeciras conference gave France police and financial responsibilities in an independent Morocco. From 1907 on this led to French naval involvement in Morocco.

**1906 (May)** The German Naval Law was amended to add six large cruisers and widen the Kiel Canal for larger battleships.

**1907 (Aug.)** The Anglo-Russian entente was concluded with French encouragement.

**1909 (Feb.)** Germany recognized France's 'special political interests' in Morocco.

**1909-1911** Clemenceau's successor as premier, Aristide Briand (July 1909 to March 1911), continued the pattern of political radicalism and social conservatism, but also presided over an increase in readiness of both the army and the navy led in the navy by Minister of Marine Vice Admiral Boué de Lapeyrère.

**1911 (June-Nov.)** The Second Moroccan crisis was triggered by the French entering Fez in May 1911 in response to anti-foreign disturbances and featured a visit by the German gunboat *Panther* to Agadir in July. Germany finally gave France a free hand in Morocco in exchange for territory in the Congo.

**1912 (Mar.)** A German naval bill containing further increases in the German fleet was published.

**1912 (30 Mar.)** The French Naval Programme of 1912 became law.

**1912 (July)** The Franco-Russian naval convention was concluded.

**1912 (July)** The British Admiralty decided to withdraw its battleships from the Mediterranean, and the French soon moved their modern battleships at Brest to Toulon.

**1914 (1 Aug.)** Germany and France mobilised for a war expected to last six months.

# The Triumph of Steam, 1819-1859

Steam propulsion entered the French Navy in 1818 when two 32nhp (nominal horsepower) vessels, *Voyageur* and *Africain*, were ordered to help reoccupy Senegal after the Napoleonic wars and extend French influence up the Senegal River. Domestic uses followed with a request in early 1821 for a steamer to tow the King's ships on the Charente River between Rochefort and the Île d'Aix, resulting in the construction of two 80nhp ships, *Coureur* and *Rapide*. The construction of steamers for supporting roles in European waters and for colonial service burgeoned after the 160nhp *Sphinx* was begun in 1828, but it was only in the early 1840s that the French made a serious effort to use the new technology militarily to help offset British sea power. In 1842 the French established a programme for a steam navy that would parallel the sailing navy, with 40 combat steamers including twenty steam frigates of 450 and 540nhp and twenty steam corvettes of 220nhp. Also in 1842, France began the construction of her first screw frigate, the 220nhp *Pomone*, built to a sailing frigate design to which an auxiliary steam engine had been added. Under the guidance of the Prince de Joinville, a son of the king who had chosen the navy as his career, this steam navy programme was expanded to 100 ships at the end of 1845, including 10 steam frigates and 20 steam corvettes. Joinville wanted steam frigates to be true combatants with an armament of 30 large guns and engines of 600nhp or more. In 1846 Minister of Marine, Vice Admiral Ange-René-Armand, Baron de Mackau, combined the traditional sailing fleet and Joinville's steam fleet in a single programme which was to be achieved in seven years using the navy's regular budgets plus special appropriations totalling 93 million francs. The execution of the Programme of 1846 was interrupted by the revolution of 1848, in which King Louis Philippe was overthrown and replaced by a second republic. The revolution ushered in a new period of fiscal retrenchment, which severely slowed down naval shipbuilding. However, on 11 January 1848, just before the 1848 revolution, the plans for a revolutionary fast steam two-decked line of battleship by Stanislas Charles Henri Laur Dupuy de Lôme were approved and construction of one ship was ordered. On 3 April 1848 the ship was named *24 Février* to commemorate the date of the declaration of the French Second Republic, but on 17 July 1850 after Louis Napoléon became president of the Second Republic she was renamed *Napoléon*. Her trials were regarded as a sensational success – on 30 August 1852 during a run from Toulon to Ajaccio she averaged 12.14 knots over a distance of 119 miles and reached 13 knots for short periods.

On 2 December 1851 Louis Napoléon carried out a coup d'état which gave him control of the government and made him, a year later, Emperor Napoleon III. The new regime quickly embarked on a revolutionary transformation of the battle fleet from sail to steam, which it finally codified in 1857 in a new naval programme (see Appendix F). In early 1852, the first French screw ship of the line to run trials, the converted mixed-propulsion *Charlemagne* of moderate speed, demonstrated that the large screw-propelled warship was a practical reality. At this time, the navy estimated that Britain had afloat or under construction 10 such ships compared to 3 for France. In 1852 and 1853 the new French government substantially increased the funds available to the navy for shipbuilding, and in mid-1852 the navy decided to use the funds to convert seven more ships of the line along the lines of *Charlemagne*. In justifying this programme, Minister of Marine Théodore Ducos told his senior advisory council in May 1852 that he felt France's strategy in a war with Britain should be to strike hard at British commerce while threatening a rapid, unexpected landing on the coasts of the United Kingdom. Converted ships like *Charlemagne* could make a substantial contribution with their dependable speed of around 8 knots, while fast ships of the line like *Napoléon* would be even more appropriate. The sensational success of *Napoléon* in August 1852 caused the navy to start building additional ships of the type as quickly as possible.

In October 1853 as the war clouds of the Crimean War gathered, *Napoléon* gave dramatic proof of the importance of steam by towing the three-decker sailing French flagship *Ville de Paris* up the Turkish straits against both wind and current while the British fleet had to wait for more favourable conditions. Subsequent operations reinforced the lesson that only screw steamers could be considered combatant warships. In October 1854, while preparing the list of construction work to be undertaken in 1855, the ministry of marine proposed converting to steam all 33 of its remaining sailing ships of the line in the next several years. One third of the resultant fleet was to be fast battleships like *Napoléon* (including a few fast conversions), and the remainder were to be conversions like *Charlemagne* of moderate speed. Conversions of existing ships of the line were carried out as quickly as the ships could be spared from war operations.

Following the main actions of the Crimean War, a navy commission in August 1855 drafted a formal programme for the modernization of the fleet. The key elements of its programme were a combat fleet of 40 fast battleships and 20 fast frigates and a fleet of transports large enough to transport an army of 40,000 men. While the new combat fleet was being built, the navy was to rely on a transitional fleet of screw ships converted from sail, which was to be completed as quickly as possible. In 1857 the number of transports was reduced from 94 to 72, all but 5 of the conversions of frigates to transports were abandoned, and more sailing frigates were ordered in 1858 to be converted to steam frigates instead. The final Programme of 1857 was promulgated by imperial decree on 23 November 1857.

While the wooden steam battle fleet seemed triumphant at the end of 1858, it contained the seeds of its own destruction in the form of shell guns. Explosive shells had long been fired from mortars, but these used a vertical trajectory which precluded accurate aiming. In 1821 a French artillery officer, Henri Joseph Paixhans, figured out how to fire explosive shells from regular cannon, which with their horizontal trajectory and long barrels could be accurately aimed. In 1824 the navy test-fired Paixhans's 22cm shell gun against the discarded 80-gun two-decker *Pacificateur*. The effects were terrible, the explosions tearing gaping holes in the side of the ship, and it was realised that a hit on the waterline could have sunk her. The Paixhans shell gun was ideally suited to steamers and could also be mounted on large sailing ships. In 1838 the standard armaments of sailing ships of the line were changed to include at least four 22cm and four 16cm shell guns, and this number was doubled to eight of each in 1848. The paradox of shell guns in wooden hulls that they could destroy could no longer be ignored after the battle of Sinop on 30 November 1853, in which a Russian force of six sail of the line and two frigates entered the Turkish Black Sea port and annihilated an Ottoman force of seven sailing frigates, two corvettes, and two steamers, only one steamer escaping. Four of the Russian ships of the line carried four or eight 68pdr (8-inch) shell guns each, but the other two each had complete lower batteries of twenty-eight 68pdr shell guns with only four long guns for chase fire. The Russian shells immediately set fires on the Turkish ships which their crews were unable to control in the hail of both solid shot and explosive shells that followed. The lessons of *Pacificateur* and Sinop were confirmed in the unsuccessful naval bombardment of Sevastopol when *Napoléon*, one of many ships damaged, was forced to withdraw after a shell produced a large leak in her side. In contrast, the bombardment of the forts at Kinburn exactly a year later revealed the answer to the shell gun when French armoured floating batteries proved practically impervious to the Russian shells. The battle between guns and armour had begun.

While refining the technical portion of the programme in late 1856, the navy's constructors under Dupuy de Lôme had included a clause allowing the Minister of Marine to replace ship types in the programme with others equivalent in military strength and construction cost. Dupuy de Lôme knew better than most how quickly the programme would become obsolete because, inspired by the success of the armoured batteries, he was already working on the plans for the world's first 'armoured frigates'. In

March 1858 Minister Hamelin ordered the construction of the first three of these, including *Gloire*, and simultaneously cancelled construction of two fast 70-gun ships of the line, *Desaix* and *Sébastopol*, which had not yet been laid down, and a proposed class of fast 40-gun steam wooden-hulled frigates. By October 1858 the navy had decided that the new armoured frigates were not only equivalent but superior to line of battle ships. At the same time the fast frigates in the programme gave way eventually to a series of 'armoured corvettes' in the 1860s. The Programme of 1857 remained the legal basis for the modernization of the French fleet until 1872, but the ships built under it bore little resemblance to those in the initial 1855 proposal.

# The French Navy as at 1 January 1859

The following is a complete list of the screw-propelled ships that were listed in the official French *Liste de la Flotte* dated 1 January 1859 along with the paddle and sailing ships that were launched in 1852 or later. They are shown here as listed in that document with the addition of basic hull measurements, launch, strike, and last mention (D:) dates, along with a few key career events and any changes in name. Long intervals between strike and last mention dates usually indicate harbour service. Numbers of guns and men are the reglementary (officially assigned) ones shown in the fleet list and may not reflect the actual numbers carried. Nominal horsepower figures are from the 1860 fleet list in which they first appeared. The reader is referred to *French Warships in the Age of Sail, 1786–1861*, for full details on the vessels listed here and also for the earlier paddle and sailing vessels.

**Screw Ships of the Line.**
**(A) Screw 1st Rank Ships of the Line** (*Vaisseaux à hélice de 1re rang*).
**Afloat**
*Bretagne*. 1,200nhp. 130 guns. 1,170 men. 81.000m wl x 18.080m ext. 6,873.750t disp. L: 17.2.1855. Struck 26.7.1866 at Brest, school for novices and apprentice seamen, exchanged names with her relief, *Ville de Bordeaux*, 28.1.1880. D: 1881.
*Louis XIV*. 600nhp (480 from 1867). 114 guns. 1,079 men. 63.90m deck, 63.28m wl x 17.40m ext. 5,170t disp. L: 1857. Became gunnery school at Brest c1863 and at Toulon c1866 (replaced *Montebello*) to 28.5.1872 (replaced by *Alexandre*). Struck 3.5.1880 at Toulon. D: 1882.
*Montebello*. 140nhp (110 from 1867). 114 guns. 1,063 men. 63.31m deck, 63.20m wl x 17.12m ext. 4,830t disp. L: 23.8.1852. Gunnery school at Toulon 12.4.1860 to 28.11.1865. Struck 25.7.1867 at Toulon. D: 1889.
*Souverain*. 600nhp (480 from 1867). 114 guns. 1,079 men. 63.45m deck, 62.61m wl x 17.34m ext. 5,096t disp. L: 11.1854. Engines removed 11.1876, gunnery school at Toulon 1876 to 1885 (replaced *Alexandre*, replaced by *Couronne*). Struck 8.12.1885 at Toulon. D: 1905.
*Ville de Paris*. 600nhp (480 from 1867). 114 guns. 1,079 men. 68.50m deck, 69.05m wl x 17.15m ext. 5,302t disp. L: 5.1858. Converted at Toulon to a steam transport 1867 to 1.1868 but remained in reserve. Transport 1871. Struck 7.2.1882 at Toulon. Sold 2.3.1898 at La Seyne, BU completed 7.1898.

**(B) Screw 2nd Rank Ships of the Line** (*Vaisseaux à hélice de 2e rang*).
**Afloat**
*Alexandre*. 800nhp (640 from 1867). 90 guns. 913 men. 73.38m deck, 72.03m wl x 16.25m ext. 5,292t disp. L: 27.3.1857. Engines condemned and ordered removed 20.11.1871. Gunnery school at

Toulon 28.5.1872 to 1876 (replaced *Louis XIV*, replaced by *Souverain*). Struck 22.2.1877 at Toulon. D: 1900.
*Algésiras*. 900nhp (800 from 1867). 90 guns. 913 men. 71.46m deck, 71.23m wl x 16.80m ext. 5,121t disp. L: 4.10.1855. Rebuilt as a transport in 1869-70, gaining an additional deck and a poop. School for torpedoes at Toulon 1888-1898 (replaced *Japon*, replaced by *Marceau* and *Magenta*). Struck 20.11.1901 at Toulon. School for torpedo boat engineers 1902-06. Burned accidentally 25.11.1906. D: 1907.
*Arcole*. 900nhp (800 from 1867). 90 guns. 913 men. As *Algésiras*. L: 20.3.1855. Struck 11.4.1870 at Cherbourg. D: 1872.
*Austerlitz*. 500nhp (420 from 1867). 84 guns. 883 men. 70.62m deck, 70.32m wl x 16.80m ext. 4,467t disp. L: 15.9.1852. Struck 22.7.1872 at Brest. School for boys at Brest 1876-1894 (replaced the sailing two-decker *Inflexible*, replaced by *Bretagne* ex *Fontenoy*). D: 1895.
*Duguay-Trouin*. 600nhp (420 from 1867). 82 guns. 883 men. 64.90m deck, 62.25m wl x 16.80m ext. 4,636t disp. L: 1857. Struck 22.7.1872 at Brest, renamed *Vétéran* 1872. D: 1877.
*Duquesne*. 650nhp (530 from 1867). 80 guns. 814 men. 62.84m deck, 61.40m wl x 16.88m ext. 4,566t disp. L: 2.12.1853. Struck 6.9.1867 at Brest, renamed *Veilleur* c1872. D: 1888.
*Eylau*. 900nhp (800 from 1867). 90 guns. 913 men. 69.22m deck, 68.72m wl x 16.80m ext. 5,023t disp. L: 15.5.1856. Third deck added and converted to transport at Toulon 1862 or early 1863. Struck 22.2.1877 at Toulon. D: 1905.
*Fleurus*. 650nhp (530 from 1867). 90 guns. 883 men. 62.50m deck, 62.07m wl x 16.98m ext. 4,509t disp. L: 2.12.1853. Engines condemned 21.5.67, refitted 8-9.1867 at Toulon as a headquarters ship for Saigon. In commission between 26.8.1867 and 25.5.1868 for the voyage to Indochina and then replaced the 74-gun *Duperré* there as headquarters ship. Struck 17.8.1869 at Saigon. D: 1877.
*Impérial*. 900nhp (800 from 1867). 90 guns. 913 men. As *Algésiras*. L: 15.9.1856. Struck 15.11.1869 at Toulon, renamed *Jupiter* 19.9.1870. D: 1897.
*Napoléon*. 900nhp (800 from 1867). 90 guns. 913 men. 71.46m deck, 71.23m wl x 16.80m ext. 5,120t disp. L: 16.5.1850. Struck 6.11.1876 at Brest. D: 1886.
*Navarin*. 650nhp (530 from 1867). 90 guns. 883 men. As *Fleurus*. L: 2.12.1853. Engines removed and converted at Toulon to a sailing transport 1873-74. Struck 13.7.1886 at Brest. D: 1908.
*Prince Jérôme*. 650nhp (530 from 1867). 90 guns. 883 men. 62.87m deck, 62.65m wl x 17.01m ext. 4,505t disp. L: 2.12.1853. Ex *Annibal* 24.5.1854, renamed *Hoche* 19.9.1870. Struck 6.6.1872 at Toulon, reinstated on the list 28.11.1872 as the sailing transport *Loire*. Struck 13.7.1886 at Saigon. D: 1897.
*Redoutable*. 900nhp (800 from 1867). 90 guns. 913 men. As *Algésiras*.

The former steam two-decker ship of the line *Tage* in the Penfeld at Brest around the early 1880s. She had been converted at Brest in 1875-76 to a sail transport to carry convicts to New Caledonia, and large sponsons for latrines had been added on each side amidships. She was struck in May 1884 at Brest. She was photographed by Émile Mage, who was active at Brest from 1860 to 1900. *(NHHC from ONI album of French warships, NII-75902)*

L: 25.10.1855. Struck 15.11.1869 at Brest. D: 1874.

*Tage*. 600nhp (420 from 1867). 82 guns. 883 men. 64.07m deck, 63.72m wl x 16.75m ext. 4,707t disp. L: 1857. converted to sailing transport 12.1875-10.1876 at Brest. Struck 6.5.1884 at Brest, renamed *Vétéran* 1885. D: 1896.

*Tourville*. 650nhp (530 from 1867). 82 guns. 814 men. As *Duquesne*. L: 31.10.1853. Struck 12.8.1872 at Cherbourg, renamed *Nestor* 21.8.1873. D: 1878.

*Turenne*. 600nhp (480 from 1867). 82 guns. 883 men. 64.90m deck x 16.80m ext. 4,554t disp. L: 1858. Struck 25.11.1867 at Brest, renamed *Éléphant* 1.2.1875. D: 1886.

*Ulm*. 650nhp (530 from 1867). 82 guns. 883 men. 62.50m deck, 62.30m wl x 17.06m ext. 4,493t disp. L: 13.5.1854. Struck 25.11.1867 at Brest. D: 1890.

*Ville de Nantes*. 900nhp (800 from 1867). 90 guns. 913 men. 72.55m deck, 71.76m wl. x 16.80m ext., otherwise as *Algésiras*. L: 7.8.1858. Struck 28.11.1872 at Cherbourg. D: 1887.

*Wagram*. 650nhp (530 from 1867). 90 guns. 883 men. As *Prince Jérôme*. L: 12.6.1854. Comm: 16.1.1855 (trials). Became service craft in early 1867 as a torpedo and mine trials hulk, first sunk 29.4.1867. Struck 22.7.1867, definitively sunk 3.12.1867.

**Building**

*Castiglione*. 800nhp (640 from 1867). 90 guns. 913 men. 73.97m deck, 72.99m wl x 16.28m ext. 5,137t disp. L: 4.7.1860. Struck 11.10.1881 at Toulon. D: 1900.

*Intrépide*. 900nhp (800 from 1867). 90 guns. 913 men. As *Algésiras*. Conversion to a transport (4-30pdrs) begun 6.1863. L: 17.9.1864. Condemned 8.1887, engines removed and third deck added at Toulon 1887-1889. Struck 6.12.1889 at Brest, renamed *Borda* 1890 as school hulk for the Naval Academy (*École navale*) at Brest replacing the sailing three-decker *Valmy* which had been renamed *Borda* 18.8.1863. Out of use 1912 sank accidentally 5.1913, sold and BU in place 1914-1922.

*Masséna*. 800nhp (640 from 1867). 90 guns. 913 men. As *Castiglione*. L: 15.3.1860. Struck 9.5.1879 at Toulon, renamed *Mars* 1892. D: 1906.

*Ville de Bordeaux*. 900nhp (800 from 1867). 90 guns. 913 men. As *Algésiras*. L: 21.5.1860. Struck 14.1.1879 at Brest, replaced *Bretagne* and took her name 1880 as school for novices and apprentice seamen, depot for training apprentice seamen 1884, replaced by her annex, the sailing corvette *Galathée* (*Galatée*) 1891. D: 1894. *Galathée* on sale list 1.1893.

*Ville de Lyon*. 900nhp (800 from 1867). 90 guns. 913 men. 72.00m deck, 71.37m wl x 16.75m ext., otherwise as *Algésiras*. L: 26.2.1861. Struck 28.6.1883 at Brest. D: 1885.

**(C) Screw 3rd Rank Ships of the Line** (*Vaisseaux à hélice de 3e rang*).
**Afloat**
*Bayard*. 450nhp (400 from 1867). 80 guns. 814 men. 63.55m deck, 62.30m wl x 16.28m ext. 4,230t disp. L: 1859. Struck 20.6.1872 at Cherbourg, renamed *Triton* 3.8.1876. D: 1879.

*Breslaw*. 500nhp (450 from 1867). 80 guns. 814 men. 63.54m deck, 62.30m wl x 16.28m ext. 4,289t disp. L: 1856. Struck 22.7.1872 at Brest. D: 1887.

*Charlemagne*. 450nhp (370 from 1867). 80 guns. 814 men. 60.10m deck, 59.80m wl x 16.24m ext. 4,124t disp. L: 16.1.1851. Transport 1871. Struck 7.2.1882 at Toulon. D: 1884.

*Donawerth*. 450nhp (400 from 1867). 80 guns. 814 men. As *Saint Louis*. L: 27.3.1857. Fitted as seagoing school for midshipmen 8-9.1868, renamed *Jean Bart* 20.9.1868, and served as such out of Brest until replaced by the frigate *Renommée* in 1873. Struck 13.4.1880 at Brest, renamed *Cyclope* 1886. D: 1897.

*Duguesclin*. 450nhp. 80 guns. 814 men. As *Bayard*. L: 1858. Ran aground 14.12.1859 on the point of Île Longue during speed trials in the Brest roadstead. Determined to be a total loss 17.12.1859 and ordered broken up in place 3.1.1860. Struck 20.2.1860. Refloated 6.1860 and BU. Her engines replaced earlier engines in *Jean Bart*.

*Fontenoy*. 450nhp (400 from 1867). 80 guns. 814 men. 62.46m deck, 62.27m wl x 16.28m ext. 4,051t disp. L: 2.12.1858. Engines removed and converted to sailing transport at Brest 1877-79. Struck 10.2.1892 at Brest. Renamed *Bretagne* 11.5.1894 as school for boys at Brest replacing *Austerlitz*. Replaced by *Bretagne* (ex *Mytho*) and reverted to *Fontenoy* 1.1910. Offered for sale 20.7.1911 at Brest by the Domaines with *Formidable*, *Valmy*, and others.

*Jean Bart*. 450nhp (400 from 1867). 80 guns. 814 men. 63.60m deck, 60.70m wl x 16.26m ext. 4,070t disp. L: 14.9.1852. Became seagoing school for midshipmen after refit at Brest 7-10.1864. Exchanged names with her replacement, *Donawerth*, 20.8.1868. Struck 18.1.1869 at Brest. D: 1869.

*Saint Louis*. 450nhp (400 from 1867). 80 guns. 814 men. 60.50m deck, 60.28m wl x 16.28m ext. 4,231t disp. L: 2.11.1857. Cut down 1880 and became seagoing annex to the gunnery school at Toulon (*Souverain*, *Couronne*) 1881 to 1894 (replaced *Implacable*, replaced by *Vauban* and *Calédonien*). Renamed *Cacique* 1893. Struck 26.11.1894 at Toulon. D: 1895.

*Tilsitt*. 500nhp (450 from 1867). 80 guns. 814 men. As *Breslaw*. L: 1856. Engines removed 1872. Struck 22.7.1872 at Brest, hulk there. Fitted as barracks hulk and sailed for Saigon 1.1877 to replace *Fleurus*. D: 1887.

**(D) Ironclad Frigates** (*Frégates cuirassés*). These, the first ships of the seagoing ironclad navy, are fully described in Chapter 1. Their state of completion on 1 January 1859 is shown below in the traditional 24ths.
**Building**
*Couronne*. 900nhp. 40 guns. 570 men. Building at Lorient (0.10/24 complete)

*Gloire*. 900nhp. 36 guns. 570 men. Building at Toulon (8.25/24 complete)

*Invincible*. 900nhp. 36 guns. 570 men. Building at Toulon (3.25/24 complete)

*Normandie*. 900nhp. 36 guns. 570 men. Building at Cherbourg (0.50/24 complete)

**Cruising Ships.**
**(A) Screw 1st Rank Frigates** (*Frégates à hélice de 1re rang*).
**Afloat**
*Ardente*. 800nhp (640 from 1867). 56 guns. 530 men. 74.76m deck, 73.98m wl x 14.78m ext. 3,797t disp. L: 25.5.1857. Decomm. 14.10.1862 after major machinery failure. Struck 15.11.1869 at Brest. D: 1871.

*Audacieuse*. 800nhp (640 from 1867). 56 guns. 530 men. As *Ardente*. L: 22.1.1856. Struck 11.4.1870 at Cherbourg. D: 1872.

*Foudre*. 800nhp (640 from 1867). 56 guns. 530 men. As *Ardente*. L: 2.12.1856. Struck 1.7.1872 at Rochefort, renamed *Ulloa* 1891. D: 1895.

*Impératrice Eugénie*. 800nhp (640 from 1867). 56 guns. 530 men. As *Ardente*. L: 21.8.1856. Renamed *Touraine* 19.9.1870. Engines landed 1872. Struck 8.2.1878 at Toulon. D: 1887.

*Impétueuse*. 800nhp (640 from 1867). 56 guns. 530 men. 72.21m deck, 72.00m wl x 14.72m ext. 3,773t disp. L: 15.8.1856. Struck 3.11.1869 at Cherbourg. D: 1874.

*Souveraine*. 800nhp (640 from 1867). 56 guns. 530 men. As *Impétueuse*. L: 3.6.1856. Struck 24.5.1872 at Brest. D: 1892.

*Renommée*. 200nhp (180 from 1867). 56 guns. 57.80m deck, 55.60m wl x 14.50m ext. 2,650t disp. L: c1857. Converted to a steam transport with an additional battery deck in 1.1869. Seagoing school for midshipmen at Brest 8.1873 to 9.1876 (replaced *Jean Bart* ex *Donawerth*, replaced by *Flore*). Struck 15.11.1878 at Brest. D: 1898.

**Building**
*Guerrière*. 600nhp (480 from 1867). 56 guns. 78.10m deck, 77.00m wl x 14.56m ext. 3,597t disp. L: 3.5.1860. Converted to a 1,300-ton steam transport at Lorient 1868-9 with an additional battery deck. Struck 28.5.1888 at Toulon. D: 1912.

*Pallas*. 600nhp (480 from 1867). 56 guns. 77.80m deck, 76.95m wl x 14.56m ext. 3,618t disp. L: 15.8.1860. Struck 23.10.1883 at Rochefort. Hulk offered for sale 15.9.1910 at Rochefort. D: 1910.

*Sémiramis*. 600nhp (480 from 1867). 56 guns. 77.33m deck, 75.05m wl x 14.50m ext. 3,830t disp. L: 8.8.1861. Struck 3.5.1877 at Brest. central station at Landévennec 1877-1895. BU 1895. Replaced successively by the frigate *Magicienne*, the cruiser *Aréthuse*, and the station battleship *Victorieuse*, all of which assumed her name.

*Victoire*. 600nhp (480 from 1867). 56 guns. 77.16m deck, 76.31m wl x 14.44m ext. 3,582t disp. L: 21.8.1861. Struck 13.2.1880 at Brest. D: 1882.

**(B) Screw 2nd Rank Frigates** (*Frégates à hélice de 2e rang*).
**Afloat**
*Bellone*. 200nhp (180 from 1867). 36 guns. 388 men. 56.50m deck, 53.55m wl x 14.40m ext. 2,328t disp. L: 11.8.1858. Struck 22.2.1877 at Lorient. D: 1895.

*Danaé*. 200nhp (180 from 1867). 36 guns. 388 men. 60.00m deck, 57.36m wl x 13.88m ext. 2,438t disp. L: 1856. Converted to a steam transport in 1868. Struck 18.1.1878 at Brest. D: 1879.

*Isly*. 650nhp (530 from 1867). 40 guns. 415 men. 73.40m deck, 70.00m wl x 13.24m ext. 2,675t disp. L: 19.7.1849. Struck 22.7.1872 at Brest. D: 1875.

*Pandore*. 200nhp (180 from 1867). 36 guns. 388 men. 56.80m deck, 54.40m wl x 13.76m ext. 2,341t disp. L: c1858. Converted to a steam transport in 1868. Struck 2.11.1877 at Rochefort. D: 1893.

*Zénobie*. 200nhp (180 from 1867). 36 guns. 388 men. 57.14m deck, 54.50m wl x 13.78m ext. 2,485t disp. L: c1859. Struck 7.8.1868 at Toulon. D: 1868.

**Building**
*Astrée*. 600nhp (480 from 1867). 46 guns. 77.58m deck, 76.58m wl x 14.40m ext. 3,564t disp. L: 24.12.1859. Struck 3.5.1877 at Lorient, renamed *Ponton No 2* 1913. D: 1922.

*Thémis* was laid down in 1847 as a 2nd rank sailing frigate and was lengthened and converted to steam in 1858-1862 while still on the ways. The ship was based at Toulon for nearly her entire active career, which ended in 1882. (*NHHC from ONI album of French warships, NH-74985*)

*Circé*. 600nhp (380 from 1867). 46 guns. 75.75m deck, 74.60m wl x 13.84m ext. 3,136t disp. L: 15.10.1860. Struck 22.7.1872 at Brest D: 1875.

*Flore*. 600nhp (380 from 1867). 46 guns. 76.05m deck, otherwise as *Circé*. L: 27.2.1869. Replaced *Renommée* as seagoing school for midshipmen at Brest in 1876 and served as such to 1882. *Iphigénie* took her place in 1884. Struck 18.10.1886 at Brest. D: 1901.

*Hermione*. 600nhp (480 from 1867). 46 guns. 78.75m deck, 78.30m wl x 13.88m ext. 3,550t disp. L: 15.8.1860. Converted to a steam transport with two battery decks 1868. Struck 11.5.1877 at Toulon. D: 1892.

*Junon*. 600nhp (480 from 1867). 46 guns. As *Hermione*. L: 28.1.1861. Struck 24.3.1872 at Saigon. D: 1876.

*Magicienne*. 600nhp (480 from 1867). 46 guns. 75.69m deck, 74.36m wl x 14.40m ext. 3,408t disp. L: 26.12.1861. Struck 19.4.1886 at Brest, renamed *Sémiramis* 1895, reverted to *Magicienne* 1899. D: 1900.

*Thémis*. 600nhp (480 from 1867). 46 guns. As *Magicienne*. L: 29.4.1862.

Struck 7.11.1882 at Lorient. Sold 1930, hulk burned in Lorient harbour 1.7.1931.

### (C) Screw 3rd Rank Frigates (*Frégates à hélice de 3e rang*).
**Afloat**

*Clorinde*. 180nhp (150 from 1867). 36 guns. 388 men. 51.95m deck, 51.00m wl x 13.28m ext. 1,720t disp. L: 23.5.1857. Struck 26.1.1888 at Lorient, renamed *Tibre* 26.5.1911. D: 1922.

*Pomone*. 220nhp (150 from 1867). 36 guns. 388 men. 54.77m deck, 52.00m wl x 13.30m ext. 2,010t disp. L: 20.6.1845. Struck 15.11.1862 at Lorient, reinstated 12.5.1863 as a 500-ton screw transport. Struck 3.5.1877 at Brest. D: 1887.

**Building**

*Armorique*. 400nhp (340 from 1867). 42 guns. 76.95m deck, 76.00m wl x 13.50m ext. 2,890t disp. L: 1.3.1862. Struck 8.11.1884 at Rochefort. D: 1911.

*Résolue*. 400nhp. 42 guns. 49.77m deck, 48.55m wl x 13.41m ext. 1,871t disp. L: 18.6.1863 as sailing frigate (engines cancelled), 150nhp engines assigned 1869, installed 1872, and ordered removed 16.10.1877. Replaced the sailing frigate *Isis* 9.1878 as seagoing school for seamanship and steering at Brest, became seagoing school for seamen 1884, relieved by the new *Melpomène* 15.9.1890. Struck 31.12.1890 at Rochefort. D: 1913.

### (D) Corvettes with covered batteries (*Corvettes à batterie couverte* to

1.1858, *corvettes à batterie* from 1.1862, *frégates à hélice de 3ᵉ rang* 1.1859 thru 1.1861).

**Afloat**

*D'Assas.* 400nhp (300 from 1867). 16 guns. 251 men. 63.65m deck, 61.85m wl x 10.98m ext. 1,945t disp. L: 27.4.1854. Struck 5.6.1878 at Lorient, renamed *Euphrate* 12.1893. D: 1933.

*Du Chayla.* 400nhp (300 from 1867). 16 guns. 251 men. 63.52m deck, 60.60m wl x 11.14m ext. 1,846t disp. L: 19.3.1855. Ex *Volta* 16.5.1855. Struck 4.11.1875 at Lorient. D: 1890.

**(E) Corvettes with open batteries (*Corvettes à batterie barbette* to 1.1858, *corvettes à barbette* from 1.1862, *corvettes à hélice* 1.1859 thru 1.1861).**

**Afloat**

*Laplace.* 400nhp (300 from 1867). 10 guns, 191 men. 61.75m deck, 56.72m wl x 11.40m ext. 1,467t disp. L: 3.6.1852. Struck 18.3.1879 at Brest. D: 1880.

*Phlégéton.* 400nhp (300 from 1867). 10 guns, 191 men. As *Laplace*. L: 25.4.1853. Struck 28.5.1868 at Brest. D: 1868.

*Primauguet.* 400nhp (300 from 1867). 10 guns, 191 men. As *Laplace*. L: 15.9.1852. Struck 3.5.1877 at Brest. D: 1886.

*Roland.* 400nhp (300 from 1867). 10 guns, 191 men. 54.67m deck, 52.92m wl x 10.40m ext. 1,299t disp. L: 5.9.1850. Renamed *Hortense* 14.4.1852 and *Reine Hortense* 24.4.1852 as yacht, replaced by *Comte d'Eu* and reverted to *Roland* effective 1.6.1853. Struck at Brest 2.5.1870. D: 1870.

*Reine Hortense* (*Cassard*). 320nhp (220 from 1867). 10 guns, 191 men.

---

This ship was laid down by Normand as the 1st class screw aviso *Cassard*, generally similar to *Forfait*, below, but was used as a yacht during the 1860s under the names *Jérôme Napoléon* and *Reine Hortense*. She reverted to an aviso in 1870 under the name *Kléber*. The image, undated but captioned as *Kléber*, shows her with her luxury deckhouse aft and an armament including two guns close together to starboard amidships and a smaller one aft. Her armament in 1873 was two 138.6mm No 2 MLR. *(NHHC from ONI album of French warships, NH-74808)*

64.50m deck, 63.00m wl x 10.96m ext. 919t disp. L: 20.12.1846. Ex *Patriote* effective 1.6.1853, ex *Comte d'Eu* 29.2.1848. Renamed *Cassard* 14.2.1867. Struck 8.4.1882 at Toulon, renamed *Faune* 10.1893. D: 1914/1920.

**Building**

*Cosmao.* 400nhp (340 from 1867). 10 guns, 191 men. 64.39m deck, 62.84m wl x 11.80m ext. 1,619t disp. L: 10.6.1861. Struck 29.6.1881 at Brest. D: 1882.

*Dupleix.* 400nhp (340 from 1867). 10 guns, 191 men. 66.34m deck, 63.80m wl x 11.40m ext. 1,773t disp. L: 28.3.1861. On fishery protection service off Iceland from 1876 to 1886. Struck 2.7.1887 at Cherbourg. D: 1892.

**(F) 1st Class Avisos (*Avisos de 1ʳᵉ classe*).**

**Afloat**

*Biche.* 200nhp (110 from 1867). 4 guns. 81 men. 33.85m wl x 8.71m ext. 439t disp. L: 3.9.1848. Struck 13.2.1868 at Toulon. D: 1868.

*Caton.* 260nhp (200 from 1867). 4 guns. 123 men. 56.98m deck, 54.38m wl x 9.37m ext. 892t disp. L: 1.5.1847. Struck 30.1.1874 at Toulon. D: 1875.

*Chaptal.* 220nhp. 4 guns. 123 men. 54.30m wl x 9.53m. 1,007t disp. L: 9.12 1845. Blown ashore 25.10.1862 in a storm near Vera Cruz during the Mexican operation. Engine and boilers salvaged and reused in *Linois* (1867). Struck 27.1.1863, remains sold 14.3.1863.

*Lucifer.* 200nhp (180 from 1867). 4 guns. 93 men. 51.64m deck, 49.74m wl x 8.15m ext. 820t disp. L: 24.5.1853. Struck 29.10.1874 at Cherbourg. D: 1887.

*Mégère.* 200nhp (180 from 1867). 4 guns. 93 men. 51.48m deck, otherwise as *Lucifer*. L: 19.7.1853. Converted from 3.1871 at Toulon to a 420-ton sailing transport and replaced brig *Oreste* as school for boys at Marseille. Struck 28.9.1875 at Toulon, remained on loan until replaced by cruiser *Fabert* in 1899. D: 1901.

*Sentinelle.* 120nhp (80 from 1867). 4 guns. 81 men. 35.08m deck, 34.00m wl x 8.62m ext. 457t disp. L: 29.8.1848. Struck 17.8.1869 at Toulon. D: 1877.

The 1st class screw aviso *Forfait*, designed for fleet duties, combined relatively high speed and good endurance, for which she carried a substantial barque rig. The ironclad behind her bow is *Océan*, which was flagship of the *Escadre d'évolutions* when *Forfait* served in it from 1873 until sunk in a collision in 1875. *(Private collection)*

### Building

*Cassard* (*Kléber*). 250nhp (230 from 1867). 5 guns. 136 men. 68.20m wl x 10.21m. 1,223t disp. L: 13.12.1859. Renamed *Jérôme Napoléon* 30.7.1860 as a yacht, replaced by a larger and faster ship and reverted to *Cassard* as an aviso 16.8.1866, renamed *Reine Hortense* as a yacht 14.2.1867 replacing an older ship, became *Kléber* as an aviso 19.9.1870. Struck 23.5.1879 at Toulon. D: 1891.

*Monge*. 250nhp (230 from 1867). 5 guns. 136 men. 66.60m deck, 62.40m wl x 10.40m ext. 1,154t disp. L: 19.3.1859. Lost with all hands on 4.11.1868 after leaving Saigon for Hong Kong and Japan, probably off the Annam coast in a typhoon. Off list 1869. Declared lost 1.11.1870.

*Forbin*. 250nhp (230 from 1867). 5 guns. 136 men. 63.20m deck, 61.00m wl x 10.04m ext. 1,154t disp. L: 4.5.1859. Struck 28.7.1884 at Lorient, renamed *Fournaise* 1885. D: 1896.

*Forfait*. 250nhp (230 from 1867). 5 guns. 136 men. 67.65m deck, 65.35m wl x 9.69m ext. 1,237t disp. L: 28.12.1859. Rammed and sunk 21.7.1875 by the ironclad *Jeanne d'Arc* during fleet exercises off Corsica, entire crew saved. Struck 27.8.1875.

### Small Avisos and Gunboats

(A) 2nd Class Avisos (*Avisos de 2e classe*).

#### Afloat

*D'Entrecasteaux*. 150nhp (135 from 1867). 2 guns. 65 men. 53.06m deck, 49.50m wl x 8.12m. 628t disp. L: 26.7.1858. Given 18.8.1876 to the Emperor of Annam under a commercial treaty of 15.3.1874, became *Loi Dat*. Struck 18.8.1876 (published 11.10.1876). Was unserviceable when France occupied Annam in 1884.

*Prégent*. 150nhp (135 from 1867). 2 guns. 65 men. 54.00m deck, 49.50m wl x 8.35m. 615t disp. L: 22.4.1857. Struck 29.10.1874 at Cherbourg. D: 1887.

*Renaudin*. 150nhp (135 from 1867). 2 guns. 65 men. As *Prégent*. L: 19.5.1857. Struck 8.5.1873 at Brest. D: 1879.

*Surcouf*. 150nhp (135 from 1867). 2 guns. 65 men. As *D'Entrecasteaux*. L: 16.3.1858. Struck 15.11.1878 at Brest, renamed *Charbonnier* 9.5.1885. Sunk 15.5.1902 as a gunnery target off Brest.

*Ariel*. 120nhp (100 from 1867). 2 guns. 74 men. 42.40m deck, 40.00m wl x 6.62m ext. 261t disp. L: 1.8.1848. Struck 31.7.1873 at Cherbourg. D: 1875.

*Corse*. 120nhp (100 from 1867). 4 guns. 73 men. 48.00m deck, 45.90m wl x 8.52m ext. 506t disp. Acq: 26.11.1850. Struck 31.12.1890 at Toulon. Sold 15.1.1903.

*Faon*. 120nhp (100 from 1867). 2 guns. 74 men. 41.00m deck, 40.50m wl x 6.00m. 196t disp. Acq: 7.5.1855. Training ship for the School for Piloting of the North at Saint-Servan 1865-1877 when replaced by *Crocodile*. Struck 7.5.1878 at Cherbourg. D: 1882.

*Marceau*. 120nhp (100 from 1867). 4 guns. 73 men. 43.21m deck, 39.94m wl x 7.80m ext. 450t disp. L: 19.5.1852. Struck 1.8.1871, school for boys for the merchant marine at Cette (Sète) 1871-1902, renamed *Hérault* c12.1880, replaced by *Gabès* 1902. D: 1903.

*Passe-Partout*. 120nhp (100 from 1867). 2 guns. 74 men. 39.15m deck, 37.57m wl x 6.40m ext. 238t disp. L: 26.3.1846. Struck 4.6.1868 at Toulon. D: 1870.

*Pélican*. 120nhp (100 from 1867). 2 guns. 74 men. 41.00m deck, 40.00m wl x 6.80m. 258t disp. L: 1.6.1847. Struck 21.3.1873 at Lorient, tug (service craft) 1875-1884. Sold 1885.

*Salamandre*. 120nhp (100 from 1867). 2 guns. 74 men. 35.00m wl x 6.50m. 242t disp. L: 2.10.1847. Struck 2.6.1871 at Toulon. D: 1871.

### Building

*Coëtlogon*. 150nhp (135 from 1867). 2 guns. 65 men. 56.50m deck, 54.55m wl x 8.50m ext. 672t disp. L: 4.6.1859. Struck 2.11.1877 at Rochefort. D: 1879.

*D'Estaing*. 150nhp (135 from 1867). 2 guns. 65 men. 54.20m deck, 53.00m wl x 8.40m ext. 695t disp. L: 26.5.1859. Given at Saigon to

Annam on 4.8.1876 with the gunboat *Scorpion* under a commercial treaty of 15.3.1874. Struck 4.8.1876 (published 28.9.1876).

**Lamotte-Picquet** (*La Motte-Picquet, Lamothe-Picquet*). 150nhp (135 from 1867). 2 guns. 65 men. As *Coëtlogon*. L: 18.5.1859. Struck 26.2.1881 at Lorient. D: 1892.

**Latouche-Tréville.** 150nhp (135 from 1867). 2 guns. 65 men. As *D'Estaing*. L: 16.2.1860. Struck 5.6.1886 at Toulon. D: 1887.

**Bougainville.** 120nhp (100 from 1867). 57.30m deck, 55.50m wl x 9.68m. 737t disp. L: 30.5.1859. Designed for use as a seagoing annex to the Naval Academy in *Borda* at Brest. Relieved 1889 by the transport-aviso *Allier* which assumed her name. Struck 15.10.1889 at Brest. D: 1890.

**(B) Flotilla Avisos** (*Avisos de flottille*).
**Afloat**

**Croiseur.** 60nhp (50 from 1867). 2 guns. 51 men. As *Rôdeur*. L: 31.7.1855. Struck 5.11.1868, probably at Toulon. D: 1868.

**Rôdeur.** 60nhp. 2 guns. 51 men. 36.34m deck, 35.00m wl x 6.02m ext. 175t disp. L: 5.2.1855. Struck 19.4.1866 at Toulon, ordered BU 9.1866.

**Labourdonnaye** (*La Bourdonnais*). 35nhp (25 from 1867). 2 guns. 51 men. 34.89m deck, 32.00m wl x 6.52m. 247t disp. L: 17.7.1856. Struck 10.3.1870, renamed *Mahé* 1873 as station hulk at Nossi Be. D: 1876.

**(C) 1st Class Gunboats** (*Canonnières de 1re classe*).
**Afloat**

**Aigrette.** 110nhp. 4 guns. 79 men. 45.40m deck, 43.94m wl x 7.76m. 484t disp. L: 15.5.1855. Sunk 17.8.1859 by boiler explosion off Antivari in the Adriatic. Struck 8.9.1859.

**Alarme.** 110nhp (70 from 1867). 4 guns. 79 men. 44.38m deck, otherwise as *Aigrette*. L: 3.5.1855. Struck 29.11.1871 at Saigon. D: 1872.

**Avalanche.** 110nhp. 4 guns. 79 men. As *Aigrette*. L: 26.5.1855. Struck 16.11.1866 at Saigon. D: 1867.

**Dragonne.** 110nhp (70 from 1867). 4 guns. 79 men. As *Aigrette*. L: 12.5.1855. Struck 7.3.1867 at Saigon. D: 1867.

**Éclair.** 110nhp (70 from 1867). 4 guns. 79 men. As *Aigrette*. L: 18.4.1855. Struck 20.11.1871 in French Guiana. D: 1873.

**Étincelle.** 110nhp. 4 guns. 79 men. As *Aigrette*. L: 18.3.1855. Lost 19.3.1862 (last seen 15.3.1862, 60 leagues from her destination of Mayotte, and probably lost with all hands in a cyclone in the Mozambique Channel). Struck 18.4.1864.

**Flamme.** 110nhp (70 from 1867). 4 guns. 79 men. 44.80m deck, otherwise as *Aigrette*. L: 7.5.1855. Struck 24.3.1872 at Saigon. D: 1878.

**Flèche.** 110nhp. 4 guns. 79 men. 44.38m deck, otherwise as *Aigrette*. L: 9.5.1855. Struck 11.2.1865 at Brest. D: 1883.

**Fulminante.** 110nhp. 4 guns. 79 men. As *Aigrette*. L: 20.5.1855. Struck 11.2.1865 at Brest. D: 1879.

**Fusée.** 110nhp (70 from 1867). 4 guns. 79 men. 44.38m deck, otherwise as *Aigrette*. L: 16.5.1855. Struck 5.11.1868 at Saigon. D: 1869.

**Grenade.** 110nhp (70 from 1867). 4 guns. 79 men. 44.80m deck, otherwise as *Aigrette*. L: 7.5.1855. Struck 2.5.1871 at Toulon. D: 1871.

**Mitraille.** 110nhp (70 from 1867). 4 guns. 79 men. 44.38m deck, otherwise as *Aigrette*. L: 24.5.1855. Struck 5.11.1868 at Saigon. D: 1869.
**Building**

**Comète.** 120nhp (same from 1867). 4 guns. 79 men. 75.80m deck, 73.30m wl x 8.90m ext. 820t disp. L: 29.9.1859. A unique vessel that combined the functions of gunboat and transport. Placed in reserve after completion. To Senegal and Gabon 1867-1870. Struck 1.7.1872 at Rochefort, used 1874-79 as service craft to carry convicts to the Île de Ré. D: 1880.

**(D) 2nd Class Gunboats** (*Canonnières de 2e classe*).
**Afloat**

**Arquebuse.** 90nhp. 2 guns. 59 men. 36.36m deck, 35.38m wl x 6.72m

wl. 289t disp. L: 4.5.1855. Struck 25.11.1862 at Brest. D: 1882.

**Lance.** 90nhp. 2 guns. 59 men. As *Arquebuse*. L: 1.5.1855. Grounded 22.1.1863 in the Bay of Tampico, ordered burned 24.1.1863. Struck 11.8.1863.

**Poudre.** 90nhp. 2 guns. 59 men. As *Arquebuse*. L: 30.4.1855. Struck 31.12.1864 at Brest, converted to a paddle tug of 60nhp 1864 and used to 1881. D: 1884.

**Redoute.** 90nhp. 2 guns. 59 men. As *Arquebuse*. L: 1.5.1855. Struck 25.11.1862 at Brest. D: 1879.

**Sainte-Barbe.** 90nhp. 2 guns. 59 men. As *Arquebuse*. L: 30.4.1855. Decomm. at Vera Cruz 31.7.1865, the hull being badly eaten by shipworms. Struck 31.12.1865 and BU.

**Salve.** 90nhp. 2 guns. 59 men. As *Arquebuse*. L: 4.5.1855. Struck 25.11.1862 at Brest. Reported scuttled off Brest with the paddle aviso *Podor* on 11.2.1871 with the carcasses of 550 diseased cattle from a herd assembled at Landerneau for the replenishment of Paris but both remained on the list until 1875.

**Tempête.** 90nhp. 2 guns. 59 men. As *Arquebuse*. L: 4.4.1855. Struck 15.10.1866 at Vera Cruz because of yellow fever on board and BU in place.

**Tourmente.** 90nhp (55 from 1867). 2 guns. 59 men. As *Arquebuse*. L: 4.4.1855. Struck 2.3.1868 at Brest. D: 1869.

**(E) Gun Launches** (*Chaloupes-canonnières*).
**Afloat**

**Alerte.** 25nhp (16 from 1867). 3 guns. 40 men. 31.03m deck, 30.90m wl x 6.20m. 144t disp. L: 9.5.1855. Struck 29.12.1874 at Cherbourg. D: 1884.

**Bourrasque.** 25nhp (16 from 1867). 3 guns. 40 men. As *Alerte*. L: 12.5.1855. Struck 20.6.1867 in Senegal.

**Couleuvrine.** 25nhp (16 from 1867). 3 guns. 40 men. As *Alerte*. L: 16.5.1855. Struck 16.3.1868 in Senegal.

**Meurtrière.** 25nhp (16 from 1867). 3 guns. 40 men. As *Alerte*. L: 30.5.1855. To Danube station 1857. Struck 30.4.1868 at Galatz, sold 1868.

**Mutine.** 25nhp (16 from 1867). 3 guns. 40 men. As *Alerte*. L: 23.5.1855. Pilot training ship at Saint Servan 1864-65 with three schooner masts. Struck 29.12.1874 at Cherbourg, ordered BU 1.2.1883.

**Rafale.** 25nhp. 3 guns. 40 men. As *Alerte*. L: 3.5.1855. Struck 8.11.1862 in Gabon, engine removed and put in a new iron tug at Cherbourg. Hulk sank 24.1.1865.

**Stridente.** 25nhp. 3 guns. 40 men. As *Alerte*. L: 27.5.1855. Washed ashore in a tidal wave at Rufisque, Senegal, 31.8.1859. Struck 26.12.1859, engine returned to Toulon.

**Tirailleuse.** 25nhp (16 from 1867). 3 guns. 40 men. As *Alerte*. L: 4.5.1855. Struck 24.4.1876 in Gabon.
**Building**

**Nº 1 to Nº 11.** 16nhp. 1 gun. 10 men. See the *Canonnière nº 1* class in Chapter 4.

**Transports**

**(A) Transports with battery decks** (*Transports à batterie*).
**Afloat**

**Amazone.** 250nhp (240 from 1867). 4 guns. 200 men. 72.85m deck, 71.70m wl x 14.06m ext. 3,155t disp. L: 30.3.1858. Disabled in a hurricane in the Antilles off Saint Thomas 10.10.1871, condemned 30.10.1871 at Fort de France, decomm. there 15.8.1872. Struck 15.2.1872, BU 1873.

**Entreprenante.** 250nhp (240 from 1867). 4 guns. 200 men. 78.10m deck, 77.00m wl x 14.44m ext. 4,063t disp. L: 4.11.1858. Struck 6.7.1885 at Toulon, sold to BU 18.6.1896.

**Dryade.** 250nhp (240 from 1867). 4 guns. 200 men. 72.80m deck, 71.55m wl x 14.43m ext. 2,890t disp. L: 29.12.1856. Struck 13.2.1883 at Toulon, renamed *Iéna* 1884, sold 24.12.1896, BU 1897.

*Cérès.* 200nhp (180 from 1867). 4 guns. 200 men. 71.75m deck, 70.25m wl x 13.44m ext. 3,139t disp. L: 26.3.1857. Struck 8.11.1884 at Toulon. D: 1899.

**(B) Horse Transports (*Transports écuries*, 250nhp).**
**Afloat**
*Calvados.* 200nhp (same from 1867). 4 guns. 200 men. 82.70m deck, 79.43m wl x 12.95m ext. 3,230t disp. L: 14.8.1858. Struck 5.6.1886 at Toulon. D: 1887.
*Garonne.* 200nhp (same from 1867). 4 guns. 200 men. As *Calvados*. L: 22.10.1858. Struck 2.4.1891, probably at Brest. D: 1891.
*Jura.* 200nhp (same from 1867). 4 guns. 200 men. As *Calvados*. L: 13.7.1858. Struck 18.7.1883 at Toulon. D: 1888.
**Building**
*Aube.* 200nhp (same from 1867). 4 guns. 200 men. As *Calvados*. L: 31.8.1859. Struck 22.7.1872 at Brest. D: 1877.
*Finistère.* 200nhp (same from 1867). 4 guns. 200 men. As *Calvados*. L: 1.8.1859. Struck 18.10.1886 at Lorient, sold 19.3.1921.
*Rhône.* 200nhp (same from 1867). 4 guns. 200 men. As *Calvados*. L: 18.4.1859. Struck 29.10.1874 at Cherbourg, towed to Rochefort 1876. D: 1899.

**(C) 1200-ton Transports (*Transports de 1200tx*).**
**Afloat**
*Dordogne.* 160nhp (150 from 1867). 4 guns. 150 men. 73.00m deck,

---

*Finistère* was one of six *transports écuries* designed to carry horses in addition to troops ordered in 1855 and built with two complete battery decks with small ports for light and air. The sponson amidships housed the latrines for the troops She was photographed in the Penfeld at Brest around the early 1880s by Émile Mage. *(NHHC from ONI album of foreign warships dated about 1900, NH-88813)*

71.00m wl x 12.88m ext. 2,750t disp. L: 14.6.1855. Engines removed 2-9.1883 at Toulon, hospital at Diego-Suarez 1885. Struck 24.2.1892 at Diego-Suarez. D: 1893.
*Durance.* 160nhp (150 from 1867). 4 guns. 150 men. As *Dordogne*. L: 16.7.1855. Struck 12.8.1872 at Cherbourg. D: 1875.
*Gironde.* 160nhp (150 from 1867). 4 guns. 150 men. As *Dordogne*. L: 30.5.1855. Wrecked 9.2.1867 at Kingston, Jamaica. Struck 25.4.1867.
*Isère.* 160nhp. 4 guns. 150 men. As *Dordogne*. L: 27.8.1855. Blown onto a rock in the harbour of Amoy 17.5.1860 and lost. Struck 17.8.1860.
*Loire.* 160nhp (150 from 1867). 4 guns. 150 men. As *Dordogne*. L: 15.6.1855. Struck 12.8.1872 at Cherbourg, renamed *Dromadaire* 5.2.1873. D: 1877.
*Marne.* 160nhp (150 from 1867). 4 guns. 150 men. As *Dordogne*. L: 16.4.1855. Struck 15.9.1878 at Brest. D: 1894.
*Meurthe.* 160nhp. 4 guns. 150 men. As *Dordogne*. L: 3.5.1855. Struck 14.5.1866 at Saigon. D: 1872.
*Meuse.* 160nhp (150 from 1867). 4 guns. 150 men. As *Dordogne*. L: 24.11.1855. Raised by a deck 8.1862-7.1865 at Brest. Struck 29.6.1881 at Lorient. D: 1904.
*Nièvre.* 160nhp (150 from 1867). 4 guns. 150 men. As *Dordogne*. L: 26.10.1855. Raised by a deck 3-9.1865 at Cherbourg. Struck 29.11.1871 at Cherbourg after running aground. D: 1874.
*Rhin* (150 from 1867). 160nhp. 4 guns. 150 men. As *Dordogne*. L: 27.8.1855. Raised by a deck 4.1869-7.1870 at Brest and given the 230nhp engines of *Allier* (1861). Struck 5.6.1886 at Brest. D: 1910.
*Saône* (150 from 1867). 160nhp. 4 guns. 150 men. As *Dordogne*. L: 17.4.1855. Struck 24.5.1872 at Cherbourg. D: 1875.
*Seine* (150 from 1867). 160nhp. 4 guns. 150 men. Iron hull. 78.29m deck, 72.71m wl x 11.80m ext. 2,150t disp. L: 10.12.1856. Sunk

29.8.1882 during torpedo trials in Laninon Bay, refloated. Struck 8.11.1884 at Brest. D: 1885.

*Yonne* (150 from 1867). 160nhp. 4 guns. 150 men. As *Dordogne*. L: 12.11.1855. Struck 24.2.1885 at Lorient. D: 1914/18.

### (D) 900-ton Transports (*Transports de 900tx*).
**Afloat**

*Adour*. 120nhp (110 from 1867). 2 guns. 117 men. Iron hull. 71.45m deck, 69.10m wl x 10.25m ext. 2,089t disp. L: 31.5.1856. Converted to floating workshop 1872 at Brest. Struck 26.2.1886 at Haïphong. D: 1905.

*Ariège*. 120nhp (110 from 1867). 2 guns. 117 men. Iron hull. As *Adour*. L: 31.7.1856. Struck 13.5.1895, offered for sale 15.11.1895 at Brest with the fishery protection craft *Ablette* and 20.1.1896 with the former gunboat *Poulmic* but minimums not met.

*Mayenne*. 120nhp (110 from 1867). 2 guns. 117 men. Iron hull. 78.35m deck, 71.98m wl x 10.44m ext. 1,841t disp. L: 18.9.1857. Transferred 30.8.1876 to the Empire of Annam under a commercial treaty of 15.3.1874. Struck 1.9.1876 (published 11.10.1876).

*Sèvre*. 120nhp (110 from 1867). 2 guns. 117 men. Iron hull. As *Mayenne*. L: 22.6.1857. Driven aground by the Raz Blanchard, a strong tidal current between France and the Channel Islands, and lost 6.2.1871. Struck 14.8.1871.

### (E) 300-ton Transports (*Transports de 300tx*).
**Afloat**

*Loiret*. 100nhp (90 from 1867). 2 guns. 44 men. 59.40m deck, 57.52m wl x 9.08m ext. 1,139t disp. L: 15.9.1856. Struck 31.12.1881 at Rochefort (published 4.1.1882). D: 1883.

*Somme*. 100nhp (90 from 1867). 2 guns. 44 men. As *Loiret*. L: 15.10.1856. Struck 27.6.1872 at Brest. D: 1887.

### (F) 200-ton Transports (*Transports de 200tx*).
**Afloat**

*Zélée*. 60nhp. 2 guns. 39 men. 31.90m x 8.77m. 540t disp. L: 1854. Struck 31.12.1863 at Lorient. D: 1887.

### Floating Batteries
Exceptionally, full details of this pre-1859 class are provided in Chapter 2. These ships had no clear place in the structure of the fleet as defined in 1857, and in the 1859 fleet list they were shown here after the transports and before the paddle steamers.

### (A) floating batteries (*Battéries flottantes*).
**Afloat**

*Dévastation*. 225nhp (150 from 1867). 18 guns. 282 men. L: 17.4.1855. Struck 9.5.1871 at Toulon. D: 1872.

*Tonnante*. 225nhp (150 from 1867). 18 guns. 282 men. L: 17.3.1855. Struck 31.8.1871 at Toulon. D: 1874.

*Lave*. 225nhp (150 from 1867). 18 guns. 282 men. L: 26.5.1855. Struck 9.5.1871 at Toulon. D: 1873.

*Foudroyante*. 225nhp (150 from 1867). 18 guns. 282 men. L: 2.6.1855. Struck 29.11.1871 at Cherbourg. D: 1875.

*Congrève*. 225nhp (150 from 1867). 18 guns. 282 men. L: 1.6.1855. Struck 13.5.1867 at Brest. D: 1868.

### Paddle Steamers (1852 and later)
Paddle steamers remained on the fleet list in large numbers in 1859, but after the Crimean War they were no longer considered to have any serious military value. They continued to be built during the 1850s and afterwards in small numbers for colonial and specialized services. Paddle steamers ordered or acquired after 1 January 1859 (mostly for colonial use) are listed with full details later in this volume.

### (A) Paddle Corvettes (*Corvettes à roues*).
*Aigle*. 500nhp (same from 1867). 2 guns. 180 men. 83.00m deck, 82.00m wl, 76.80m keel x 10.50m ext. 2,047 tons disp.

L: 23.12.1858. 14.24 knot paddle yacht designed by Dupuy de Lôme for the Emperor. Used by Napoleon III in 1860 and 1865 and by Empress Eugénie in 1869 to inaugurate the Suez Canal. Renamed *Rapide* 31.5.1873 but saw no further service. Struck 29.1.1891, sold 6.10.1891.

### (B) Paddle 2nd Class Avisos (*Avisos de 2e classe à roues*).
*Chamois*. 150nhp (130 from 1867). 2 guns. 64 men. 40.70m deck, 39.80m wl, 38.65m keel x 6.30m ext. 334 tons disp. Purch: 7.5.1855, ex *Daim*. Struck 15.11.1878. D: 1878.

*Casabianca*. 160nhp (140 from 1867). 2 guns. 78 men. 56.49m deck 53.01m wl, 47.01m keel x 9.00m ext. 979 tons disp. L: 15.8.1859. Served in French Guiana. Struck 3.5.1877. D: 1884.

### (C) Paddle Flotilla Avisos (*Avisos de flottille à roues*).
*Marabout*. 60nhp. 2 guns. 44 men. 44.65m deck, 42.00m wl x 6.00m ext. 238 tons disp. L: 1.7.1852. Struck 31.12.1864 at Brest, renamed *Soute* 12.1869 as coal hulk. D: 1871.

*Oyapock*. 20nhp. 2 guns. 25 men. 22.00m x 5.06m. 96 tons disp. L: 3.5.1852. Struck 31.12.1864 in French Guiana. D: 1865.

*Serpent*. 25nhp. 2 guns. 25 men. 42.30m deck, 40.40m wl x 5.00m. 161 tons disp. L: 20.1.1852. Struck 18.11.1863 in Senegal. D: 1865.

*Grand Bassam*. 40nhp (30 from 1867). 2 guns. 25 men. 34.35m deck, 33.50m wl x 5.60m moulded, 5.72m ext. 206 tons disp. L: 1.7.1852. Struck 16.3.1868, probably in Senegal. D: 1868.

*Basilic*. 30nhp (25 from 1867). 2 guns. 25 men. 42.30m deck, 40.40m wl x 5.00m wl/ext. 161 tons disp. L: 26.9.1854. Struck 3.6.1873, probably in Senegal.

*Akba*. 20nhp. 2 guns. 25 men. 20.30m deck, 20.00m wl x 4.80m. 48 tons disp. L: 15.4.1854. Struck 26.12.1859 at Gorée, Senegal.

*Économe*. 25nhp (20 from 1867). 2 guns. 25 men. 24.00m wl x 4.10m wl & ext. 69 tons disp. L: 3.4.1855. Struck 7.11.1873 at Cayenne. D: 1874.

*Surveillant*. 25nhp (20 from 1867). 2 guns. 25 men. As *Économe*. L: 3.4.1855. Struck 13.2.1868 at Cayenne.

*Dialmath*. 60nhp. 2 guns. 44 men. 41.75m deck, 40.00m wl x 7.12m wl, 7.16m ext. 340 tons disp. L: 14.8.1855. Struck 16.5.1865 in Gabon.

*Podor*. 60nhp. 2 guns. 44 men. As *Dialmath*. L: 14.8.1855. Struck 10.11.1864 at Brest. Reported scuttled off Brest with the gunboat *Salve* on 11.2.1871 with the carcasses of 550 diseased cattle from a herd assembled at Landerneau for the replenishment of Paris but both remained on the list until 1875.

*Africain*. 60nhp (50 from 1867). 2 guns. 44 men. 41.75m deck, 40.00m wl x 7.12m wl, 7.16m ext. 376 tons disp. L: 15.4.1858. Struck 19.2.1878, barracks hulk at Dakar, Senegal 1878-1879. D: 1879.

*Arabe*. 60nhp (50 from 1867). 2 guns. 44 men. As *Africain*. L: 15.4.1858. Struck 20.5.1879, renamed *Africain* 1879, barracks hulk in Senegal 1879-1881, reverted to *Arabe* 1881 (*Espadon* became *Africain*) and barracks hulk in the upper river in Senegal 1881-1882. Off list 1882.

*Crocodile*. 20nhp (15 from 1867). 2 guns. 25 men. 21.20m deck, 20.00m wl x 4.80m. 80 tons disp. L: 2.1.1858. Struck 25.3.1869 in Senegal.

*Griffon*. 20nhp (15 from 1867). 2 guns. 25 men. As *Crocodile*. L: 4.1.1858. Struck 25.3.1869 in Senegal.

*Abeille*. 100nhp (75 from 1867). 2 guns. 64 men. 51.12m deck, 49.82m wl, 48.87m keel x 7.38m ext. 578 tons disp. L: 22.10.1858. Struck 26.11.1868, disposal suspended and chosen 26.12.1868 as hulk for the new torpedo school at Boyardville, not on the fleet list. Traded names 27.2.1871 with the former screw aviso *Lutin* (1861), school closed 2.4.1871 and both hulks BU 3-5.1871.

*Étoile*. 100nhp (75 from 1867). 2 guns. 64 men. As *Abeille*. L: 30.12.1858. Struck 20.4.1878. D: 1879.

*Archer*. 20nhp. 2 guns. 25 men. 24.82m deck, 24.00m wl x 5.00m wl &

ext. 91 tons disp. L: 5.1859. Struck 1.3.1866, barracks hulk in Senegal 1866-1871. D: 1871.

*Pionnier*. 20nhp (15 from 1867). 2 guns. 25 men. As *Archer*.
L: 18.5.1859. Struck 31.10.1872 in Gabon. D: 1873.

## Sailing Ships (1852 and later)

Like paddle steamers, sailing vessels remained on the fleet list in large numbers in 1859 but were not considered to have any serious military value. The few that were launched or acquired in 1852 or later are shown here. Sailing vessels ordered or acquired after 1 January 1859 (all of which were small) are listed with full details later in this volume.

### (A) 1st Rank Corvettes (*Corvettes de 1er rang*).

*Cornélie*. 22 guns. 254 men. 43.00m wl, 40.2m keel x 11.80m moulded, 12.00m ext. 1,192 tons disp. K: 9.1849. L: 6.11.1858. Struck 17.8.1869. Refitted at Toulon from 10.1873 and restored to the main list 1.1875 as the training corvette (*corvette école*) attached to the school for seamanship and to the school for novices and apprentice seamen (*Bretagne*) at Brest. Relieved by *Favorite* 1879. Struck again 9.5.1879. D: 1909.

*Cordelière*. 22 guns. 254 men. As *Cornélie*. K: 26.4.1850. L: 12.6.1858. Struck 10.3.1870 at Gabon, out of service there 10.1876.

*Favorite*. 22 guns. 254 men. As *Cornélie*. K: 30.7.1849. L: 14.5.1870. While under construction was reclassified as a 600-ton transport 1.1864, as a corvette transport 1.1873, and back to a *corvette à voiles* 1.1879. Replaced *Cornélie* 1878 as seagoing school for seamanship and steering and served to 1884. Refitted as a stationary training corvette at Brest 1-2.1887. Condemned and struck 10.2.1892, on sale list at Brest 1.1.1893, BU 1893.

### (B) 1st Rank Brigs (*Bricks de 1er rang*).

*Zèbre*. 12 guns. 117 men. 33.00m deck, 32.50m wl, 29.75m keel x 9.60m moulded, 9.80m ext. 542 tons disp. K: 26.5.1848. L: 4.11.1854. Construction suspended 1851-1853 and 1855-1857. Struck 8.11.1866 at Lorient. D: 1896.

*Euryale*. 12 guns. 117 men. As *Zèbre*. K: 31.10.1849. L: 11.11.1863. Construction suspended 1853-1862, completed 1863-1864 as 250-ton transport on plans by E. Boden. Wrecked 5.3.1870 on Starbuck Island in the Pacific. Struck 20.6.1870.

*Beaumanoir*. 12 guns. 117 men. As *Zèbre*. K: 19.1.1850. L: 2.12.1853. Converted to transport with three masts 11.1878 to 3.1879. Struck 23.10.1883 at Cherbourg. D: 1904.

*Chevert*. 12 guns. 117 men. As *Zèbre*. K: 4.1850. L: 26.11.1863. Construction suspended 1855-1862, completed 1863-1864 as 250-ton transport on plans by E. Boden. Off main list 1872 and to harbour service at Papeete, decomm. and out of use 1.8.1873.

### (C) Schooners (*Goëlettes*) (*bâtiments de flottille*).

*Île d'Énet*. 13 men. 18.40m oa, 17.82m deck, 16.67m keel x 5.28m moulded, 5.44m ext. 95/60 tons. L: c7.1853. Decomm. at Cayenne 23.5.1862. Struck 8.11.1862.

*Bombe*. 2 guns. 21 men. 24.00m deck, 23.40m wl, 22.43m keel x 6.10m moulded, 6.24m ext. 183 tons disp. L: 18.4.1855. Ex Crimean War sailing bomb vessel, listed as a schooner 1858-1859. Struck 21.10.1859. Converted to sailing water barge *Citerne Nº5* at Cherbourg in 5-9.1860 (her four sisters, struck earlier, were already citernes). On service craft list at Cherbourg as *Citerne Nº5* 1.1865, then converted to sailing hoy *Bugalet Nº2* at Cherbourg in 1865, renamed *Fort* 1.1866, and in use at Cherbourg until 1920.

*Sakalave*. 20 men. L: 4.1855 (built at Nossi-Bé, probably ex-mercantile). Annexe to the hulk (ex transport) *Indienne* at Mayotte. Struck 16.11.1860. Back in service 25.3.1864 as a station ship (service craft) at Mayotte, out of service and off list 1.1869.

*Entreprenant* was one of several brigs like *Zèbre* ordered during the 1840s and later re-rigged with three masts as transports or training ships. *Entreprenant*, begun at Rochefort in 1846 and launched and commissioned in 1849, was converted to a 250-ton transport with three masts at Rochefort between February and December 1868. She was downgraded to a service craft at Rochefort in 1881 and is shown here at Algiers in around 1885. Reduced to a torpedo-boat depot hulk at Bastia in April 1887, she was struck on 2 August 1887 and remained in use until broken up in 1909. *(NHHC from ONI album of French warships, NH-74954)*

*Laborieuse*. 2 guns. 14 men. 21.5m oa, 20.00m deck, 18.8m keel x 5.75m moulded, 5.84m ext. 113 tons disp. L: 20.6.1855. Struck 1.8.1871 at Cayenne.

*Pourvoyeuse*. 2 guns. 14 men. As *Laborieuse*. L: 20.6.1855. Condemned 22.2.1874 at Cayenne and out of commission 1.1875. D: 1880.

*Vigilante*. 2 guns. 14 men. As *Laborieuse*. L: 20.6.1855. Wrecked 24.2.1869 on the Roches Noires of Îlet La Mère near Cayenne. Struck 2.6.1870.

### (D) Cutters (*Cutters*) (*bâtiments de flottille*).

*Alcyon* (*Alcyone*). 2 guns. 20 men. 17.80m oa, 16.90m deck, 16.25m wl, 14.68m keel x 5.10m. 78 tons disp. L: 24.12.1858. Built for fishery protection on the Granville station. Replaced by *Sainte Barbe* 1891. Struck 16.5.1892, sold 8.1892 to M. Muselet of La Rochelle.

### (E) Transports (*Transports*).

*Orione*. 420 tons burthen. 2 guns. 41 men. Russian merchant ship captured 11.7.1854 and comm. 1.6.1855. Decomm. 17.6.1868 at Cherbourg. Struck 31.1.1870. D: 1883.

*D'Zaoudzi*. 60 tons burthen, 100 tons disp. 31 men. Merchant ship built at London 1852, purchased at Réunion 10.1855 and comm. 13.10.1855. Station ship 1860-1864, probably at Réunion. Struck 29.10.1864 and transferred to colonial account of Sainte-Marie de Madagascar.

*Calédonienne*. 60 tons burthen. 2 guns. 37.5m oa, 32.70m wl, 25.4m keel x 7.06m moulded, 7.30m ext. 245 tons disp. L: 12.5.1858. To *goëlette* from *transport* 1.1874. Struck 3.2.1883 at New Caledonia. The schooners *Perle* and *Gazelle* in Chapter 7 were built to the same plans.

# Part One

---

# The Traditional Fleet Updated
# 1859-1882

During the period from the end of the 1850s to the early 1880s the French remained largely faithful to the traditional structure of the fleet inherited from the age of sail while updating it to respond to rapid changes in technology. The main elements of this traditional structure were large heavily-armed ships for battles in European waters, cruisers (initially frigates and corvettes) primarily for service on distant stations and on the sea lanes, and smaller ships (initially brigs and avisos) and flotilla craft for local service both at home and in the colonies. These categories dominated the Programme of 1846, the last for a primarily sailing fleet, the Programme of 1857, which opened the period of this book, and the Programme of 1872, officially a revision of the 1857 programme that added armoured coast defence ships and fast cruisers to the traditional force while recognizing the need for austerity resulting from the traumatic defeat a year earlier in the Franco-Prussian War. The traditional force structure was retained in updates of the 1872 programme in 1879 and 1881, and although alternative views of the composition of the fleet were advocated, especially after 1878, none came close to adoption during this period.

Technology, however, changed some ship types practically beyond recognition, and also created others. The most extreme transformation was that of capital ships. Over these two decades a battle raged between guns and armour, in which ever more powerful guns (in the French case, rifled breechloading weapons of increasing sizes) led to ever thicker armour and vice versa. The *Gloire* of 1859 was designed for a main battery of thirty-six 164.7mm guns on her sides which were completely covered by thin armour plating, while the *Marceau* of 1880 ended up with a main battery of four 340mm guns in armoured barbettes and narrow bands of very thick side armour along the waterline. When the drive towards larger guns was abandoned at the end of the 1870s after reaching 420mm (16.5 inches) it was replaced by continuous qualitative improvements. The Model 1875-79 370mm gun introduced slow-burning powder and a longer bore that gave projectiles greater velocities and penetrating power, and these principles were then applied to the families of Model 1881 and Model 1884 guns that included most calibres then in use. Armour manufacturers fought back, introducing more effective compound and steel armour in place of wrought iron armour soon after 1880. The effects of technology on cruising ships, with a few exceptions, were much less dramatic. They received improved compound engines and artillery, but experiments with large guns on cruisers were abandoned and in 1882 most cruisers were still slower than battleships and still had wooden hulls and no armour. Technology also generated new weapons, beginning in 1860 with the ram (included in all subsequent battleship designs and also generating a new category of coast defence ships) and continuing in the mid-1870s with the torpedo and small experimental craft to carry it.

During the entire period covered by this book the French Navy was involved in no major fleet actions against European powers, although its wooden steam fleet reached Venice in 1859 during Napoleon III's war against Austria and its ironclads cruised in the southern Baltic in August and September 1870 to blockade Prussian forces there. Its other main operations between 1859 and 1882 were tied to France's efforts to extend her influence overseas, in China (1857-1860), Cochinchina (1858-1863), Mexico (1861-67), Tonkin (1873-4), and Tunisia (1881-2). Many ships served in these operations but none was specially built for them.

The Navy generally escaped political and press controversy during Napoleon III's Second Empire and the early years of the Third Republic. The Emperor had a majority in the legislature and selected and dismissed all of his ministers, and there were only three Ministers of Marine between 1855 and 1870. The political situation became intense after Napoleon III surrendered to the Prussians at Sedan on 2 September 1870 and the Third Republic was declared in Paris two days later, but the main struggle during the 1870s between the Royalists who wanted to restore the monarchy and the Republicans who wanted a true republic had little effect on the Navy except for frequent changes in ministers (twelve changes between 1870 and 1882). The navy's main problems at this time were economic. The costs of the war and the punitive indemnity payments to Germany (paid off in 1873) forced Minister of Marine Pothuau to accept a reduction of 29 million francs in the budget as voted for 1872 (147.6 millions) compared to the original 1871 budget. The general fiscal distress was greatly prolonged by the world banking crisis of 1873 which triggered a recession that lasted in France to 1896. Fiscal austerity limited the scope of the navy's Programme of 1872 on which construction activity into the early 1880s was based. The resignation of a monarchist cabinet in December 1877 finally put the republican parties in charge of the Third Republic.

In November 1878, a year after the republican success, the young deputy Étienne Lamy delivered a highly critical report on the Navy's 1879 budget and thereby injected the navy into politics and press polemics. The report lambasted massive waste within all parts of the naval establishment and suggested that the nation was not getting its money's worth out of battleships and would do better, after ensuring the defence of its coasts, to invest in fast strongly-armed commerce-raiding cruisers. Lamy's report prompted an outbreak of articles in the press on maritime topics, previously of interest only to specialists, that drew attention to the views of those who earlier in the 1870s had advocated alternatives to the battleship. In 1882 Rear Admiral Théophile Aube, then second in command of the *Escadre d'Évolutions* and the father of what soon became known as the *Jeune École*, wrote in the *Revue des Deux Mondes* that the day of the battleship navy was over and that it was giving place to a new navy centred on commerce raiding by cruisers and industrial warfare conducted by torpedo boats and defensive gunboats. The consensus on the traditional fleet structure was broken.

# Chapter One

# Squadron Ironclads, 1859-1882

**(A) Squadron Ironclads (*Cuirassés d'escadre*).**
Originally *Frégates cuirassées*. *Magenta* and *Solférino* to *Vaisseaux cuirassés* and the others to *Frégates cuirassées de 1er rang* in the 1.1865 fleet list. All to *Cuirassés de 1er rang* 1.1873 and *Cuirassés d'escadre* 1.1880.

### The Programme of 1857
In October 1854 the Minister of Marine, Admiral of France Ferdinand Alphonse Hamelin, proposed converting to steam all 33 of France's remaining sail ships of the line in the next several years. One third of the resultant fleet was to be fast battleships (*vaisseaux rapides*) like *Napoléon*, designed in 1848 by naval constructor Stanislas Charles Henri Laur (or Laurent) Dupuy de Lôme (known to his family as Henri). The remainder were to be mixed sail and steam conversions of moderate speed (*vaisseaux mixtes*) like *Charlemagne*. In August 1855 a navy commission, formed at the Emperor's direction to examine the responses, drafted a formal programme for the modernization of the fleet. The key elements of its programme were a combat fleet of 40 fast battleships and 20 fast frigates and a fleet of transports large enough to transport an army of 40,000 men. While the combat fleet was being built, the navy would rely on a transition fleet of screw ships converted from sail that was to be completed as soon as possible. The Emperor referred the plan to the *Conseil d'Etat* in January 1857 for its review. The final programme, which provide for the expenditure of 235 million francs over 14 years beginning in 1858, was promulgated by imperial decree on 23 November 1857. While refining the technical portion of the programme in late 1856, Dupuy de Lôme had included a clause allowing the Minister of Marine to replace ship types in the programme with others equivalent in military strength and construction cost. The Programme of 1857 remained the legal basis for the modernization of the French fleet to the end of the 1860s, but with technology advancing rapidly the ships built under it bore little resemblance to those in the initial 1855 proposal. The full programme as promulgated and as modified through 1869 is in Appendix F.

### The advent of the seagoing ironclad
The success under enemy fire on 17 October 1855 of three French floating batteries in the reduction of the Russian forts at Kinburn in the Crimea provided conclusive validation of the idea of using iron armour to protect ships against artillery. In four hours the three batteries (*Dévastation*, *Lave*, and *Tonnante*, listed in Chapter 2) fired over 3,000 projectiles at the Russian fortifications, and although hit a total of over 120 times in a hail of return fire they suffered practically no damage and only two men killed and 22 injured by lucky hits. Many naval officers, naval constructors, civilian inventors, and even Emperor Napoleon III himself quickly turned their creative attention to the application of iron armour to seagoing battleships.

The generally conservative *Conseil des travaux de la marine* (the navy's senior technical advisory board) advised Minister of Marine Hamelin on 13 January 1857 'to tackle resolutely the question of armoured ships and to suspend all new construction of warships in which the sides are not protected from the ravages of the new artillery.' The main technical problem was the configuration of the armoured side including the attachment of the armour, and in October a proposal by naval constructor Camille Audenet for an iron hull coated with a layer of wood that supported the armour using wooden bolts, was tried at Vincennes and proved successful. (It was used in *Couronne*, below.)

On 1 January 1857 Dupuy de Lôme was named the navy's Director of Materiel, responsible among many other things for the design and construction of the navy's ships. He already had many successes to his credit in addition to the *Napoléon* of 1848, and he enjoyed the full confidence of the Emperor. He turned immediately to the development of a 'fast and armoured frigate', and the success with armour at Vincennes in October 1857 allowed him to proceed to the detailed calculations needed to produce the design that became *Gloire*. Dupuy de Lôme started with a design he had submitted on 7 November 1856 for an updated *Napoléon* lengthened by 5.39m, with finer lines forward, and able to carry 96 guns on two decks and then produced an entirely new design for *Gloire* in which the upper gun deck was deleted and the sides fitted with armour able to resist the 164.7mm rifles then entering service. The new ship was also given a straight bow reinforced by the armour belt and suitable for ramming. Minister of Marine Hamelin took the revolutionary design and its author straight to the Emperor for approval. The *Conseil des travaux* got to see it 'for information' on 8 June 1858, over a month after the ship was laid down.

---

**GLOIRE Class.** *Frégates cuirassées*. Broadside ironclads with wooden hulls and straight bows. One funnel, three masts, a light barquentine rig in *Gloire*, then ship rigged and from 1864 barque rigged. Designed by Dupuy de Lôme.

On 4 March 1858 Minister Hamelin ordered the construction of three armoured frigates of 900nhp, two at Toulon and one at Lorient. The two ships at Toulon were named on 8 March 1858. A fourth ship was added at Cherbourg on 3 September 1858 in anticipation of the 1859 building programme and named on 24 September 1858 along with the iron-hulled ship at Lorient (see *Couronne*, below). Plans by Dupuy de Lôme for *Gloire* were approved by Hamelin on 20 March 1858 and were also used for *Invincible* and *Normandie*. The engines of *Gloire* were ordered from the Forges et Chantiers de la Méditerranée (FCM) by a contract approved on 4 June 1858. The engines of *Invincible* were ordered with those of the iron-hulled *Couronne* (below) from Mazeline by a contract approved on 4 June 1858, but they were reassigned as replacement engines for the 90-gun two-decker *Napoléon* and new engines for *Invincible* were ordered from FCM by a contract approved on 18 May 1860. The engines of *Normandie* were ordered from Mazeline by a supplement approved on 22 September 1858 to Mazeline's contract for the machinery of *Couronne*. The 900nhp engines in these ships were like those of the 90-gun two-decker *Algésiras* (a *Napoléon* with updated machinery laid down in 1852) with some modifications. *Normandie*'s engines were reused in the 1870s in the coast defence ship *Tonnerre*.

*Gloire* began to go into commission (*ouverture de campagne/préparation d'armement*) on 26 December 1859 while still incomplete and ran preliminary trials in June 1860 and official trials on 20-21 August 1860, reaching 13.5 knots. She escorted Napoleon III to Algiers in September 1860 and was the only escort able to remain with the imperial yacht *Aigle* during a storm on the return trip. She then ran comparative trials with *Algésiras* beginning on 12 November 1860 and ending with a trial report dated 30 March 1861. During her trials *Gloire* was criticized for rolling more than a ship of the line in calm seas, for shipping a lot of water over the bows in rough seas, and above all for the low height of her battery above the water of only 1.88m. Otherwise she was declared to be a masterpiece.

Because of rapid changes in technology the armaments of these ships changed dramatically during their first few years, the calibres of the guns increasing and their numbers decreasing. The 164.7mm rifles initially fitted in these ships were muzzle-loaders. *Gloire* received an experimental 164.7mm breech-loading rifle on 4 September 1861 and then ran experimental gunnery trials in March 1862 with 17 breech-loading 164.7mm rifles on one side and 17 muzzle-loading 164.7mm rifles on the other side. The breech-loaders were clear winners, and in 1863 *Gloire* received a complete armament of 34 breech-loading 164.7mm rifles. However, neither the 164.7mm rifles nor the 50pdr (194mm) smoothbores carried

Outboard profile and plan of the upper deck of the ironclad frigate *Gloire*. These plans were submitted by Dupuy de Lôme in connection with a change to a barque rig and approved by Minister Chasseloup-Laubat on 22 January 1864. The side armour is complete from end to end both on the waterline and on the battery deck. The conning tower and navigating bridge are just before the mizzen mast. The ship had no axial fire, directly ahead or astern. *(Vice Admiral François Edmond Pâris, Souvenirs de marine conservés, 1882 and later, reproduced by him from the Mémorial du Génie maritime)*

by *Normandie* in 1865 could penetrate the armour on *Gloire* and the other early ironclads, and the new Model 1864 artillery was developed with calibres up to 274.4mm to defeat this armour. In 1867-68 all three ships were rearmed with six or eight 240mm/17.5 M1864 guns in the battery and from two to six 194mm/18 M1864 guns as shown below. *Gloire* was originally given a light barquentine rig, but received a full rig during the winter of 1860-61 except that her bowsprit was a plain pole. All were re-rigged as barques in 1864.

**Dimensions & tons:** (*Gloire*) 80.39m oa, 77.40m deck, 77.89m wl x 16.82m ext. 5,617t disp. Draught: 7.28m fwd, 8.38m aft. Men: 570. Height of battery (*Gloire*, 1869) 2.03m.

**Machinery:**

(*Gloire* and *Invincible*): 900nhp (800 from 1867), 2,500ihp designed at 50rpm. Trials (*Gloire*, 1869) 2,537ihp = 12.8kts at 50.8rpm. 1 screw. 1 horizontal engine by FCM with return connecting rods and 2 cylinders of 2.08m diameter and 1.27m stroke. 8 tubular boilers with superheaters. 500-682t coal.

(*Normandie*): 900nhp (800 from 1867). Trials 3,253ihp = 13.3kts at 53.48rpm. 1 engine by Mazeline (reused in *Tonnerre*). 8 boilers.

**Armour:** (iron)

Side: Belt at waterline 120mm iron on 800mm wood backing (full length of ship). Height from 2m below the wl to 0.5m above.

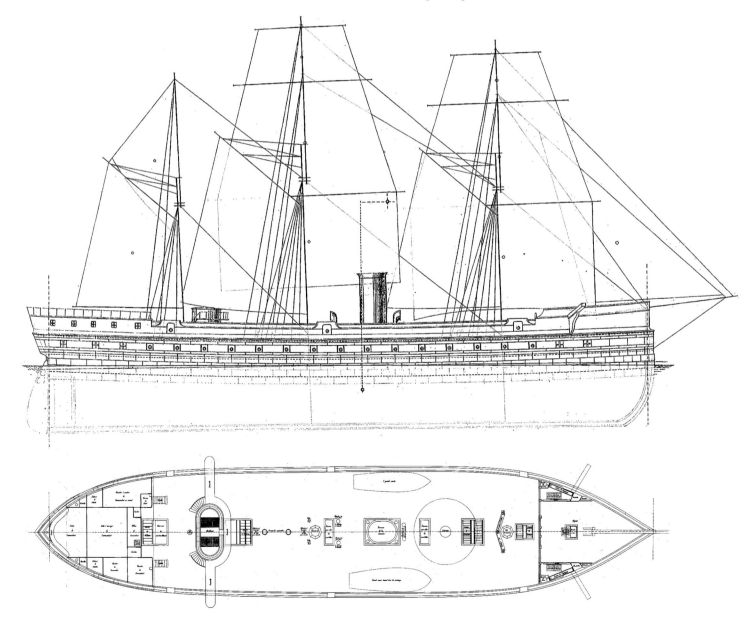

Guns: Broadside battery 110mm iron on 660mm wood backing (full length of ship).

Deck: 10mm plating on 100mm wood.

Conning tower located just forward of the mizzen mast.

**Guns:**

(1859) 36 x 164.7mm/16.7 M1858 MLR (34 in the battery, 2 on the upper deck).

(1864, *Gloire*, and 1865, *Invincible*) 32 x 164.7mm/16 M1858-60 BLR (28 in the battery, 4 on the upper deck).

(1865, *Normandie*) 12 x 50pdr 194mm/16.4 smoothbores, 12 to 16 x 164.7mm rifles (probably M1858-60 BLR).

(1867, *Gloire*) 6 x 240mm/17.5 M1864 in the amidships portion of the battery, 2 x 194mm/18 M1864 on the upper deck, one forward and one aft.

(1868, *Normandie*) 8 x 240mm/17.5 M1864, 6 x 194mm/18 M1864.

(1869 and 1876, *Gloire*) 6 x 240mm in the battery, 4 x 194mm on the upper deck.

*Gloire* Toulon Dyd/F.C. Méditerranée, Marseille.

On list 1.1859. Ord: 4.3.1858. K: 5.1858. L: 24.11.1859.
  Comm: 26.12.1859 (trials). C: late 1860.

Began sea trials 20.8.1860. Escorted Napoleon III to Algiers 9.1860. Ship and gunnery trials continued through 6.1862. In reserve after 1871. Struck 27.12.1879, for disposal at Brest 1879-1882, BU 1883.

*Invincible* Toulon Dyd/F.C. Méditerranée, Marseille.

On list 1.1859. Ord: 4.3.1858. K: 5.1858. L: 4.4.1861.
  Comm: 6.4.1861 (trials). C: mid-1862.

Manned for trials 6.3.1862, trials at Toulon from 19.4.1862. In commission in reserve later in 1862, active 3.1863 and left Toulon for Cherbourg 29.6.1863. Struck 12.8.1872, hulk at Cherbourg 1872-1873, for disposal 1873-1877, BU 1875-77.

*Normandie* Cherbourg Dyd/Mazeline, Le Havre.

On list 1.1859. Ord: 3.9.1858. K: 14.9.1858. L: 10.3.1860.
  Comm: 2.7.1860 (trials), 13.5.1862 (full).

Manned for trials 11.1861, trials at Cherbourg from 3.12.1861. Left Cherbourg for Mexico 21.7.1862. Struck 1.8.1871 at Toulon. BU 1871.

---

**COURONNE.** *Frégate cuirassée.* Broadside ironclad with an iron hull and a straight bow. One funnel, three masts, ship then barque rig. Designed by Audenet.

On 16 April 1858 Dupuy de Lôme wrote that his wooden-hulled *Gloire* should not be the exclusive model for all three of the ships ordered on 4 March 1858 but that other types of construction should also be considered. He proposed using the plans of *Gloire* for the second ship at Toulon, but for the ship at Lorient he recommended the iron-hulled design of naval constructor Camille Audenet, which incorporated his armour design that had shown the way forward in the Vincennes trials of October 1857. Audenet, like Dupuy de Lôme an expert in iron ship construction, produced a design for an iron-hulled 40-gun, 900nhp frigate with dimensions similar to *Napoléon* and *Gloire*. The engines for this ship were ordered from Mazeline by a contract approved on 4 June 1858. Audenet's plans were approved by the *Conseil des travaux* on 8 June 1858 and new plans signed by Audenet on 21 July 1858 were approved by Minister of Marine Hamelin on 1 September 1858. The ship was named on 24 September 1858.

As in the other early ironclads her armaments changed frequently during the 1860s, especially after the advent of the Model 1864 guns. *Couronne* was decommissioned in 1881 at Toulon and converted to a gunnery school ship in 1881-85 by the Mouraille enterprise on plans by and under the direction of naval constructor Victor Louis Félix Cousin. The armour and two boilers were removed (leaving her with 600nhp), a full iron spardeck

and poop were added giving her a second battery deck, and a full scale barque rig was fitted. She was recommissioned in February1885 for trials which ended in June. She then functioned as the Navy's primary gunnery school ship, including short exercises at sea, until 1909, and then lasted as a hulk until 1933.

**Dimensions & tons:** 81.85m deck, 80.00m wl x 16.70m ext. 6,004t disp. Draught: 7.14m fwd, 8.69m aft. Men: 570. Height of battery (1869) 1.88m.

**Machinery:** 900nhp (800 from 1867), 2,900 designed. Trials (1862) 2,913ihp = 12.66kts. 1 screw. 1 horizontal engine with return connecting rods and 2 cylinders of 2.08m diameter and 1.27m stroke. 8 tubular boilers. 650t coal.

**Armour:** (iron)

Side: Belt at waterline 100mm wrought iron on 100mm teak backing on 40mm closely-spaced iron slats on 250mm teak on 10mm hull plating

Guns: Broadside battery 80mm iron on 100mm teak backing on 40mm closely-spaced iron slats on 280mm teak on 10mm hull plating.

Deck: 25mm plating on 100mm wood.

**Guns:**

(1861) 10 x 50pdr 194mm/16.4 SB and 26 x 164.7mm/16.7 M1858 MLR in the battery, 4 x 164.7mm M1858 MLR on the upper deck (changed to 22cm 223.3mm/10.5 MLR converted shell guns in 1864).

(1865) 14 x 194mm/18 M1864 in the battery, 4 x 164.7mm rifles (probably 164.7mm/19.2 M1864) on the upper deck.

(1869) 8 x 240mm/17.5 M1864 in the battery, 4 x 194mm/18 M1864 on the upper deck at the ends. By 1878 also had 2 x 12pdr (121mm/17) bronze and 12 x 37mm revolving cannon.

(1881 as school ship) 3 x 240mm, 3 x 194mm, and 3 x 164.7mm in the lower battery, 16 x 138.6mm in the upper battery, 3 x 100mm on the upper deck.

(later as school ship) 3 x 164.7mm, 15 x 138.6mm, and 14 x 65mm in the batteries, plus 1 x 90mm, 2 x 47mm, and 5 x 37mm on the upper deck.

*Couronne* Lorient Dyd-Caudan/Mazeline, Le Havre.

On list 1.1859. Ord: 4.3.1858. K: 14.2.1859. L: 28.3.1861.
  Comm: 11.10.1861 (trials). C: 4.1862.

Manned for trials 2.2.1862, trials at Lorient from 18.3.1862. To Cherbourg from Lorient 16.4.1862, in commission in reserve there 22.7.1862. Active in the Mediterranean by 5.1865. Ended last tour in the *Escadre d'évolutions* 1879. Converted to school for gunnery 1881-85, replaced *Souverain* 6.1885 as the school for gunners, renamed school for gunners and helmsmen in 1889, reverted to school for gunnery in 1899, all at Toulon. Replaced by *Tourville* (ex *Gironde*) 1909, decomm. 1.9.1909. Off main list 1910 but retained on harbour service as a barracks ship for the central workshop of the fleet and later as a hulk attached to the workshop at Toulon 1910-1933. Sold 25.10.1933 to M. Bonturi, BU 1934 at La Seyne.

---

*Napoléon I^er*

The building programme for the year 1859, outlined by Dupuy de Lôme on 30 October 1858, included four armoured frigates, of which one (*Normandie*) had been ordered in advance at Cherbourg in September 1858 as a third sister of *Gloire* to get work started right away. In October 1858 Minister of Marine Hamelin ordered constructors in the ports to submit plans for the other three armoured frigates (one each at Cherbourg, Brest, and Lorient), but on 26 April 1859 the *Conseil des travaux* rejected all eight of the designs received. On 10 June 1859 Dupuy de Lôme recommended that Hamelin approve the Council's April rejections with the exception of a design by naval constructor Paul Marie Étienne Picot de Moras which he felt was 'very good'. It included 56 guns on two decks, a wooden hull, engines of 1,200nhp for a speed of 13.5 knots, and a removable ram on the bow. The Council's only criticisms had been its excessive dimensions (91m x 17.88m) and the removable nature of the ram. Dupuy de Lôme proposed sending the plan back to Picot de Moras for revisions along the lines recommended by the Council and added that 'We can then build the ship at Cherbourg to either of his plans.' The Council on 30 August 1859 again returned Picot de Moras' plan to him for revision but Hamelin had already decided to limit 1859 ironclad construction to two ships. On 22 March 1860 the *Moniteur de la Flotte* reported in its unofficial section that the start of construction had been announced of a *vaisseau blindé* at Cherbourg that would have a length of 100 metres, an iron ram of 10 metres, an engine of 1,200nhp, and that would be named *Napoléon I^{er}*; this appears to have been a belated and mistaken reference to Picot's ship.

---

*MAGENTA* Class. *Frégates cuirassées.* Two-decker broadside ironclads with wooden hulls and ram bows. One funnel, three masts, barquentine rig with pole bowsprit, increased to barque 1864 and to ship with full fixed bowsprit 1869. Designed by Dupuy de Lôme. To *vaisseaux cuirassés* 1.1865 and *cuirassées de 1^{er} rang* 1.1873.

In his report to Minister of Marine Hamelin on 10 June 1859 Dupuy de Lôme wrote that he would have been willing to use plans of a modified *Gloire* for the remaining ironclads of the 1859 programme but he was dissuaded by alarming news from England, where a panic engineered by the Admiralty, Parliament, and the media had stirred up concern over the new French ironclads. In May the British had ordered a ship, *Warrior*, designed to outclass the French ships in both speed and armament. She had an iron hull and thirty-eight 68pdr guns on one long deck. Dupuy de Lôme therefore adopted the idea of wooden-hulled ships with two covered batteries and increased speed and range that was included in several of the 1859 design submissions including that of Picot de Moras and produced the design for the 1,000nhp *Magenta* class with two battery decks and a 14,000kg bronze ram. The ship had a complete armour belt from end to end, but the armoured portion of the two battery decks above it was only about 45m long with armoured bulkheads at the ends; the wooden bow and stern beyond the bulkheads were unprotected. On 15 June 1859 Hamelin ordered two ships built to this design, one at Brest and one at Lorient. On 1 July 1859 Dupuy de Lôme proposed and Hamelin approved naming the ships *Magenta* and *Solférino* after victories just won by Napoleon III in Italy and calling them *vaisseaux cuirassés*, Dupuy de Lôme explaining that they had two covered batteries without an armed upper deck and thus fell between frigates and ships of the line. However, the orig-

---

The ironclad frigate *Solférino* photographed by Rideau, a photographer at Cherbourg, between her arrival there from Lorient at the end of September 1863 for trials and the 1864 order to rig all ironclads as barques, probably carried out in her case before her departure in July 1864 for the Mediterranean. Eleven guns are visible in the lower battery and twelve in the upper battery. By 1869 she was ship-rigged and the lower battery was empty. Her large eagle figurehead, originally brightly gleaming, is here painted the same colour as the rest of the ship making it nearly invisible. *(NHHC, NH-43641)*

inal designation of *frégates cuirassées* was restored on 18 July 1859 because of their relatively small number of guns and because foreign equivalents were being called frigates. The plans for the ships received final approval on 2 December 1859 and their engines were ordered from Mazeline by a contract signed on 27 April 1860.

The two ships were identical in appearance except for a giant eagle figurehead on *Solférino* (painted black after about 1864). *Magenta* received hull sheathing (*soufflage*) between September 1867 and May 1868. Technology advances caused the batteries of these ships to decline from 52 to 14 guns by the end of the 1860s. The 52-gun armament shown below was assigned on 4 January 1864 and fitted to both ships. The smaller armaments shown below as assigned in 1866 and early 1868 may not have been fitted. On 7 December 1868 the class was assigned a 14-gun armament that was fitted to both ships in 1869 of ten 240mm in the upper battery and four 194mm on the upper deck, the lower battery being vacant.

**Dimensions & tons:** (*Magenta*) 91.96m oa, 84.53m deck, 86.10m wl x 17.34m ext (18.30m after sheathing 1868). 7,058t disp. Draught: 7.03m fwd, 8.63m aft. Men: 706 without flag. Height of lower battery 1.60m.

**Machinery:** 1,000nhp (900 from 1867) and 3,600ihp designed at 51.50rpm and 1.80kg/cm$^2$ boiler pressure. Trials (*Magenta*, 1869) 4,019ihp = 12.89kts. 1 screw. 1 engine with return connecting rods and 2 cylinders of 2.102m diameter and 1.30m stroke. 8 cylindrical boilers. 625-800t coal. Range 2,900nm @ 8kts or 1,350nm @ 12.5kts.

**Armour:** (iron)
Side: Belt at waterline 120mm iron on 830mm wood backing (full length of ship). Height from 1.5m below to 1.6m above the waterline.
Guns: Two broadside batteries 120mm iron on 670mm wood backing over a length of 45 metres with armoured transverse bulkheads at the ends.
Deck: 110mm wood, plating not recorded.
Conning tower: 100mm, just aft of the funnel.

**Guns:**
(1861) 26 x 164.7mm M1858 rifles in the lower battery, 24 x 164.7mm M1858 in the upper battery, and 2 x 164.7mm M1858 on the upper deck (all probably MLR).
(1864, both) 16 x 50pdr 194mm/16.4 SB and 10 x 164.7mm rifles in the lower battery, 24 x 164.7mm in the upper battery, 2 x 22cm 223.3mm/10.5 MLR converted shell guns on the upper deck. (The 164.7mm were probably 164.7mm/16 M1858-60 BLR).
(1865, *Magenta*) Lower battery unchanged. 4 x 240mm/17.5 M1864 and 4 x 194mm/18 M1864 in upper battery, 4 x 194mm and 2 x 22cm 223.3mm/10.5 MLR converted shell guns on the upper deck.
(Assigned 20.10.1866) Lower battery disarmed. 6 x 240mm/17.5 M1864 and 12 x 194mm/18 M1864 in the upper battery, 4 x 240mm on the upper deck.
(Assigned 13.2.1868) 6 x 240mm in the upper battery, 2 x 240mm and 2 x 194mm on the upper deck.
(5.1868, *Magenta*) 6 x 240mm in the upper battery, 4 x 240mm on the upper deck.
(1869, both) 10 x 240mm/17.5 M1864 in the upper battery, 4 x 194mm/18 M1864 on the upper deck. The guns of *Magenta* were soon upgraded to M1870, but *Solférino* was inactivated in 1871 with M1864 guns. By1875 *Magenta* had added one 12pdr (121mm/17) bronze and five 4pdr (86.5mm/11) bronze for her landing party and boats.

*Magenta* Brest Dyd/Mazeline, Le Havre.
On list 1.1860. Ord: 15.6.1859. K: 22.6.1859. L: 22.6.1861.
  Comm: 18.9.1861 (trials), 2.1.1863 (full).
Embarked her machinery 12.1861, manned for trials 22.5.1862. Joined the division of armoured ships at Cherbourg 1863. Left Cherbourg for Vera Cruz, Mexico 3.1.1867 to cover the return of French troops. Destroyed 31.10.1875 at Toulon when she caught fire and her after magazine blew up almost three hours later. Struck 31.12.1875.

*Solférino* Lorient Dyd/Mazeline, Le Havre.
On list 1.1860. Ord: 15.6.1859. K: 24.6.1859. L: 24.6.1861.
  Comm: 18.12.1861 (trials), 25.8.1862 (full).
Left Lorient for Cherbourg 17.4.1863. Joined the division of armoured ships at Cherbourg 1863, to the Mediterranean 1865. Artillery and rig modified 9.1868 to 7.1869. To 3rd category reserve at Cherbourg 18.4.1871 and not again active except for a transit to Brest 8.1878. Struck 21.7.1882, ordered BU 27.11.1882, BU completed at Brest 14.8.1884.

---

**Ironclad conversions**

On 31 October 1859 the Conseil des travaux examined a 'project for the conversion of the ship of the line *Ville de Lyon* into an armoured ship' by naval constructor Pierre Armand Guieysse and decided not to pursue it. Other designs for armoured conversions that the *Conseil des travaux* rejected at around this time were the conversion of the sailing two-decker *Jemmapes* to a slow armoured battery and ram for the defence of Cherbourg (first discussed 12 January 1858 and finally rejected 25 January 1859), and the conversion of the sailing three-decker *Valmy* to an armoured frigate (5 July 1859).

**Updated programme, 1860.**

Napoleon III was very favourably impressed with the performance of *Gloire* when she escorted him to and from Algiers in September 1860 and decided upon his return to accelerate his naval building programme based on this new type. On 22 September 1860 Dupuy de Lôme submitted a report to Minister of Marine Hamelin which updated the Progamme of 1857 in light of the new technology and laid out a building programme for immediate implementation. Fourteen of the 40 fast steam battleships in the 1857 programme and 6 armoured frigates were afloat or building leaving a requirement for 20 more armoured frigates, plus another ten requested by a coast defence commission on 24 May 1860. Building all 30 at once was beyond France's capabilities, and Dupuy de Lôme on 22 September 1860 called for immediately beginning 10 (9 wood and 1 iron). This programme also called for 11 floating batteries (6 wood and 5 iron) to reach the 20 called for by the coast defence commission and 6 ships of new types for the overseas stations including 2 small frigates with 22 guns (the *Vénus* class), 2 open-battery corvettes with 16 guns, and 2 transports of 400 tons.

---

*PROVENCE* **Class.** *Frégates cuirassées.* Broadside ironclads with wooden hulls and straight bows. One funnel, three masts, barque rig. Designed by Dupuy de Lôme.

Dupuy de Lôme returned to the design of *Gloire* as the starting point for the new class. He responded to the main criticism of that ship by increasing the height of the battery above the waterline from the inadequate 1.88m to 2.25m, more than suggested by anyone else including the Emperor. He also modified the bow for improved seakeeping and increased the thickness of the armour at the waterline from 120mm to 150mm in response to recent trials of 164.7mm rifles while keeping the 110mm protection of the battery. The weight of the additional armour was offset by using some weight saved in the engines and by raising the bottom edge of the belt from 2.10m below the waterline to 1.80m. The ten ships were ordered on 16 November 1860, their plans were approved on 19 November 1860, and they were named on 29 December 1860. Encouraged by a new Minister of Marine, Count Prosper de Chasseloup-Laubat, Dupuy de Lôme soon increased their nominal horsepower from the 900 of *Gloire* to the 1,000 of *Magenta* and their designed speed from 13.6 to 14.0 knots to keep up with potential British competition.

The engines for seven ships (including the iron-hulled *Héroïne*, below) were ordered from the Forges et Chantiers de la Méditerranée and Mazeline by contracts signed on 27 November 1861, while the other three ships were engined by the Navy's engine factory at Indret. Conventional horizontal simple expansion two-cylinder engines based on those of *Algésiras* with steam introduced directly into each cylinder were begun for *Provence, Flandre, Guyenne, Surveillante,* and *Héroïne,* but the French then learned that the British *Warrior* had achieved 14.3 knots on trials and resolved to increase the designed speed of the other five to 14.5 knots by adding a third cylinder to their engines. All five received horizontal engines with three cylinders of the same diameter, and in *Gauloise* and *Revanche* the steam was introduced simultaneously into all three cylinders (simple or single expansion). However, in *Savoie, Magnanime,* and *Valeureuse* it entered the middle cylinder and from there expanded into the other two, making these three engines an early form of compound (double expansion) machinery, a type that soon replaced the original simple expansion engines. *Provence* ran her speed trials 14 February 1865, *Savoie* ran hers from 7 May to 9 June 1866,

and *Magnanime* followed between 19 April 1866 and 15 May 1866.

The class was designed with 34 guns but, as Dupuy de Lôme later wrote, 'with the thought of reducing this figure when larger guns were available.' In fact, the armament of the class fell from 34 to 12 guns before the end of the 1860s. By 1870 most had eight 240mm/17.5 M1864 in the battery and four 194mm/18 M1864 on the upper deck. There were nine positions on the upper deck for the four 194mm guns: two forward behind a bulkhead with ports for both ahead and broadside fire, one in the extreme stern with three ports, and three on each side above the 240mm battery.

**Dimensions & tons:** (*Provence*) 82.90m oa, 80.00m deck, 78.85m wl x 17.06m ext, 17.00 wl. 5,810t disp. Draught: 7.00m fwd, 8.40m aft. Men: 580-594. Height of battery (*Provence*, 1865) 2.22m.

**Machinery:** 1,000nhp (900 from 1867) and 3,600ihp designed at 55.0rpm and 1.80kg/cm² boiler pressure. Trials (*Flandre*, 5.1865) 3,537ihp = 14.34kts at 53.9rpm and 1.601kg/cm² boiler pressure. 1 screw. 1 simple expansion or compound engine with return connecting rods and 2 or 3 cylinders (see above), all of 2.10m diameter and 1.30m stroke. 8 high rectangular tubular boilers each with 4 furnaces as in *Flandre,* or 10 rectangular tubular boilers of which 4 had 3 furnaces and 6 had 4 as in *Provence.* 575t coal (*Provence*). Range with 575t coal 3,730nm @ 10kts.

**Armour:** (iron)
Side: Belt at waterline 150mm iron on 750mm wood backing

---

Inboard profile and upper deck and battery deck plans of the *Flandre* type ironclad frigate showing the armament carried by many of the class after about 1870. This included eight 240mm/17.5 M1864 guns in the battery and four 194mm/18 M1864 guns on the upper deck, far fewer the 34 guns she carried when completed but with much greater penetration capability. Note also the alternate gun positions on the upper deck including two behind a transverse bulkhead in the forecastle and one in the stern for axial fire, the two conning positions (one in the conning tower amidships and one on the poop), the two-cylinder machinery, and the heavy wooden hull structure. (*Aide-Mémoire d'Artillerie navale, 1878*)

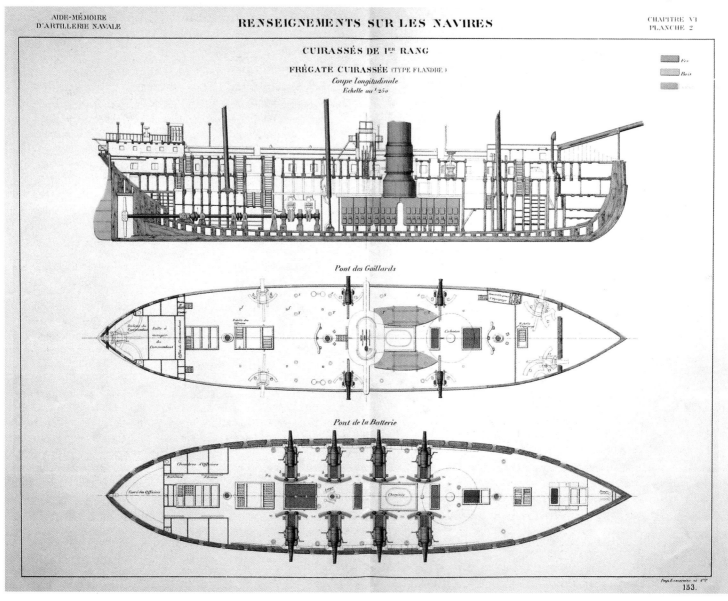

Guns: Broadside battery 110mm iron on 610mm wood backing.

Deck: 10mm plating on 100mm wood.

Conning tower: 100mm, just aft of the funnel.

**Guns:**

(Design) 34 x 16 M1858 battery, 4 x 16 M1858 gaillards

(1865, *Provence* and *Flandre*) 10 x 50pdr 194mm/16.4 SB and 22 x 164.7mm/19.2 M1864 rifles in the battery, 2 x 22cm 223.3mm/10.5 MLR converted shell guns on the upper deck. In *Flandre* and perhaps others two of the 164.7mm rifles were on the upper deck.

(1866-67, *Valeureuse* and *Revanche*, probably *Magnanime* and *Savoie*) 8 x 240mm/17.5 M1864 battery, 1 x 194mm/18 M1864, 6 x 164.7mm M1858 (MLR in *Valeureuse*) upper deck.

(late 1867, *Gauloise*, *Guyenne*, and probably *Surveillante*) 4 x 240mm/17.5 M1864 and 6 x 194mm/18 M1864 in the battery and 1 x 194mm/18 M1864 and 6 x 164.7mm M1858 on the upper deck.

(1868, *Flandre*) 4 x 240mm and 6 x 194mm in the battery, 4 x 194mm on the upper deck. These were upgraded to M1870 guns around 1875.

(1869-70, *Provence*, *Flandre*, *Guyenne*, *Savoie*, *Magnanime* and *Surveillante*) 8 x 240mm/17.5 M1864 in the battery and 4 x 194mm/18 M1864 on the upper deck. In some or all the 194mm guns could fire forward from under the forecastle and aft from under the poop. This was the standard armament for the class by 1.1869. In 7.1870 *Surveillante* also had 5 x 4pdr (86.5mm/11) bronze, *Savoie* had 1 x 12pdr (121mm/17) bronze and 5 x 4pdr bronze, *Guyenne* had 1 x 12pdr bronze and 4 x 4pdr bronze. In *Surveillante* the big guns were upgraded to M1870 around 1873 and a decision of 2.1.1880 directed the replacement of the 12pdr (121mm) guns on her upper deck with 138.6mm M1870 guns.

(1875, *Valeureuse* and *Revanche*) 8 x 240mm/19 M1870, 1 x 194mm/19.8 M1870, 6 x 164.7mm M1858-60, 1 x 12pdr (121mm/17) bronze, 5 x 4pdr (86.5mm/11) bronze. In 1882 the light artillery of *Valeureuse* was 1 x 12pdr (121mm/17) bronze, 2 x 4pdr (86.5mm/11) bronze mountain, 6 x 37mm revolving cannon.

(1875-77, *Provence*, *Gauloise* and *Guyenne*) 8 x 240mm/19 M1870 in the battery, 4 x 194mm/19.8 M1870 on the upper deck, one 12pdr (121mm/17) bronze and four 4pdr (86.5mm/11) bronze (*Guyenne* had 5 x 4pdr.). *Gauloise* also had 8 x 12pdr (121mm/17) bronze in the battery, probably on shipboard mounts.

(1876-78, *Savoie*, *Magnanime*, and *Revanche*) 8 x 240mm/19 M1870 in the battery, 3 x 194mm/19.8 M1870 and 2 x 138.6mm/21.3 M1870 on the upper deck, also 1 x 12pdr (121mm/17) bronze, 4 x 4pdr (86.5mm/11) bronze (boat) except 3 x 12pdrs and no 4pdrs in *Revanche*.

*Provence* Toulon Dyd/F.C. Méditerranée, Marseille (2 cylinders).

On list 1.1862. Ord: 16.11.1860. K: 3.1861. L: 29.10.1863. Comm: 25.2.1864 (trials), 1.2.1865 (full).

Joined the *Escadre d'évolutions* at Toulon 2.1865. Ended last Mediterranean tour 1879 as flagship of the Levant Division. Struck 3.5.1886, for disposal at Toulon 1886-1893, used as a gunnery target, sold and BU 1893.

*Flandre* Cherbourg Dyd/Mazeline, Le Havre (2 cylinders).

On list 1.1862. Ord: 16.11.1860. K: 28.1.1861. L: 21.6.1864. Comm: 20.2.1865 (trials), 5.1865 (full).

Visited Plymouth, England with *Magenta* 6.1865, then joined the division of armoured ships at Cherbourg. Left Cherbourg for Vera Cruz, Mexico 3.1.1867 to cover the return of French troops. Mostly in reserve at Cherbourg after 1871. Struck 12.11.1886, BU 1887.

*Surveillante* Lorient Dyd/Indret (2 cylinders).

On list 1.1862. Ord: 16.11.1860. K: 28.1.1861. L: 18.8.1864. Comm: 13.5.1867 (trials), 21.10.1867 (full).

Fitted as flagship at Lorient 10.1867, then in 3.1868 joined the division of armoured ships at Cherbourg. Ended last tour in the *Escadre*

*d'évolutions* 1881. Struck 13.5.1887 at Brest, central ship for the reserve at Cherbourg 1887-1896 (converting 1887-1889, see also *Poursuivante* & *Reine Blanche*), repair hulk for the reserve 1896-1897, designated for conversion to coal hulk 1897 but BU 1898.

*Guyenne* Rochefort Dyd/Indret (2 cylinders).

On list 1.1862. Ord: 16.11.1860. K: 11.2.1861. L: 6.9.1865. Comm: 15.4.1867 (trials), 6.11.1867 (full).

Trials off the Île d'Aix 20.8.1867. At Cherbourg 1868 with the division of armoured ships. Ended last tour in the *Escadre d'évolutions* 1877. Struck 19.10.1882, for disposal at Toulon 1882-1887, BU 1887.

*Savoie* Toulon Dyd/F.C. Méditerranée, Marseille (3 cylinders, compound).

On list 1.1862. Ord: 16.11.1860. K: 3.1861. L: 29.9.1864. Comm: 25.3.1865 (trials), 9.11.1866 (full).

Full power trials 16.6.1866. Joined the division of armoured ships at Cherbourg 22.7.1867. Ended last tour in the *Escadre d'évolutions* 1878. Struck 19.11.1888, BU 1889.

*Magnanime* Brest Dyd/Mazeline, Le Havre (3 cylinders, compound).

On list 1.1862. Ord: 16.11.1860. K: 27.2.1861. L: 19.8.1864. Comm: 1.11.1865 (trials), 7.7.1866 (full).

Joined the division of armoured ships at Cherbourg in 1866, left Cherbourg with *Flandre* and *Magenta* for Vera Cruz, Mexico, 3.1.1867 to cover the return of French troops. Ended last tour in the *Escadre d'évolutions* 1877. Struck 19.6.1882, for disposal at Brest 1882-1885, BU 1885.

*Valeureuse* Brest Dyd/Indret (3 cylinders, compound).

On list 1.1862. Ord: 16.11.1860. K: 13.5.1861. L: 18.8.1864. Comm: 27.2.1867 (trials), 25.3.1867 (full).

Commissioned into the division of armoured ships at Cherbourg 1867, to the Mediterranean 11.1867. Ended last tour in the *Escadre d'évolutions* 1876. Struck 26.2.1886, for disposal at Brest 1886-1887, BU 1888.

*Gauloise* Brest Dyd/Mazeline, Le Havre (3 cylinders, simple).

On list 1.1862. Ord: 16.11.1860. K: 21.1.1861. L: 26.4.1865. Comm: 12.4.1867 (trials), 5.12.1867 (full).

At Cherbourg 1868 with the division of armoured ships. Ended last tour in the *Escadre d'évolutions* 1879. Struck 23.10.1883, for disposal at Cherbourg 1883-1886, BU 1886.

*Revanche* Toulon Dyd/F.C. Méditerranée, Marseille (3 cylinders, simple).

On list 1.1862. Ord: 16.11.1860. K: 3.1861. L: 28.12.1865. Comm: 16.4.1867 (trials), 12.8.1867 (full).

Left Toulon for the Île d'Aix 12.8.1867, then back to Toulon to join the *Escadre d'évolutions* there. Ended last tour in the *Escadre d'évolutions* 1883. Annex to *Provençale* (station hulk or *stationnaire* at Toulon) 1888-1891, central ship for the *Défense mobile* in Algeria 1891-1892. Struck 10.1.1893. BU 1893.

---

*HÉROÏNE. Frégate cuirassée.* Broadside ironclad with an iron hull. One funnel, three masts, barque rig. Designed by Dupuy de Lôme.

Although the *Conseil des travaux* had recommended in 1859 using iron hulls in the new armoured fleet to the greatest extent possible, only one of the ten *Provence* class ships was built to the *Provence* design modified for construction in iron. That ship, *Héroïne*, was laid down on the slip at Lorient vacated by the iron-hulled *Couronne*. (The slip was at Caudan, a much-used annex across the Scorff river from the main dockyard.) Her engines were ordered from Mazeline by a contract signed on 27 November 1861. Except for her hull structure she was virtually identical to the rest of the *Provence* class.

**Dimensions & tons:** 80.00m deck, 80.08m wl x 17.13m ext, 17.06m wl.
   5,969t disp. Draught: 7.77m fwd, 8.27m aft. Men: 580-594.
   Height of battery (1867) 2.12m.

**Machinery:** 1000nhp (900 from 1867) and 3,600ihp designed at
   51.5rpm and 1.80kg/cm$^2$ boiler pressure. Trials (7.1865) 3,066ihp =
   12.57kts at 53.20rpm and 1.349kg/cm$^2$ boiler pressure. 1 screw.
   1 horizontal simple expansion engine with return connecting rods and
   2 cylinders of 2.10m diameter and 1.30m stroke. 8 high rectangular
   tubular boilers (4 with 5 furnaces each and 4 with 4). 536t coal.
   Range 3,330nm @ 10kts.

**Armour:** (iron)

Side: Belt at waterline 150mm iron on 380mm wood backing on 20mm
   hull plating

Guns: Broadside battery 110mm iron armour on 380mm wood backing
   on 20mm hull plating

Deck: 16mm plating on 90mm wood.

Conning tower: 100mm.

**Guns:**

(1865) 10 x 50pdr 194mm/16.4 SB and 22 x 164.7mm/19.2 M1864
   rifles in the battery, 2 x 22cm 223.3mm/10.5 MLR converted shell
   guns on the upper deck. Two of the 164.7mm rifles may have been on
   the upper deck.

(1867) 8 x 240mm/17.5 M1864 battery, 1 x 194mm/18 M1864,
   6 x 164.7mm M1858 (perhaps MLR) upper deck

(1876) 8 x 240mm/19 M1870 (battery), 3 x 194mm/19.8 M1870 (2 on
   the upper deck and 1 under the forecastle) 2 x 138.6mm/21.3 M1870
   (upper deck), 1 x 12pdr (121mm/17) bronze, 4 x 4pdr (86.5mm/11)
   bronze (boat). In 1883 the small guns were 3 x 12pdr bronze and
   6 x 4pdr bronze.

(1893) 8 x 240mm, 3 x 194mm, 8 x 138.6mm (upper deck),
   2 x 47mm/40 M1885 QF, 10 x 37mm

*Héroïne* Lorient Dyd-Caudan/Mazeline, Le Havre (2 cylinders).

On list 1.1862. Ord: 16.11.1860. K: 10.6.1861. L: 10.12.1863.
   Comm: 1.4.1864 (trials), 7.6.1865 (full).

Left Cherbourg for Toulon 3.1.1867 and joined the *Escadre d'évolutions*
   there. Ended last tour in the *Escadre d'évolutions* 1883. Struck
   10.1.1893 and engines removed, at Toulon destined for Dakar 1893-
   1894, sent there under sail with a full ship rig 1-2.1894, in Senegal as
   a floating workshop 1894-1895 and as central ship for the local station
   at Dakar 1895-1901. She retained her eight 240mm battery guns and
   was also assigned duty as a floating fort 1.1898 to 1.1901. Scuttled off
   Dakar 29.12.1901 after an epidemic of yellow fever.

---

*OCÉAN* **Class.** *Frégates cuirassées de 1er rang.* Central battery ironclads with
four upper deck barbettes, wooden hulls, iron upper works outside the battery, and ram bows. One funnel, three masts, barque rig. Designed by
Dupuy de Lôme.

By mid 1864 two of the ten units of the *Provence* class were running trials,
the other eight were progressing, and some capacity was opening up in the
dockyards. However, France, with 16 armoured frigates in service or building, still had a long way to go to reach the 40 ships of the line (now
armoured frigates) called for by the 1857 programme. Dupuy de Lôme
therefore began design work on a third generation of armoured frigates.
Reflecting the rapid advances in technology since the *Provence* class was
designed, the new generation had armour on the waterline thick enough to
resist 240mm guns but less armour elsewhere, used iron for the unprotected ends of the wooden hulls to reduce the risk of fire, and responded to
the shift to end-on combat tactics by redistributing the heavy guns to
obtain strong axial (fore and aft) fire and by retaining the strong ram introduced in the *Masséna* class.

In late 1864 Dupuy de Lôme completed a preliminary design for a new

The ironclad frigate *Marengo* in her original configuration with a full barque rig,
possibly during trials or while in 1st category reserve at Toulon in 1872-75. She
was then out of service at Cherbourg until 1880 when she emerged resembling her
sister *Océan*, below. This class introduced four barbette turrets on the upper deck
providing some axial fire in addition to four large guns in the battery below and
between them. *(NHHC from ONI album of French warships, NH-74929)*

type of 1st rank armoured frigate with a central battery and a 20,000kg
bronze ram armed with 16 guns. Bypassing the *Conseil des travaux* once
again, he discussed the design directly with Minister of Marine Chasseloup-
Laubat and Emperor Napoleon III. The Emperor signed the preliminary
design on 1 December 1864, and the new construction programme promulgated on 15 January 1865 by Chasseloup-Laubat ordered laying down in
the ports three 1st rank armoured frigates (two of wood and one of iron),
one 2nd rank armoured frigate, three armoured corvettes, and three
armoured coast defence ships. On 8 April 1865 the three new 1st rank
frigates were named *Océan*, *Marengo*, and *Friedland* and the 2nd rank frigate
was named *Suffren*. The lone 2nd rank frigate was deferred on 24 May 1865
and *Suffren* was reordered as a 1st rank *Océan*-class ship a year later on 26
April 1866. The armoured corvettes became the *Alma* class and the coast
defence ships the *Cerbère* class.

Dupuy de Lôme's plans for the *Océan* class were approved on 10
February 1865 and 21 March 1865. The ships were initially to have a two-
level central citadel around the funnel, the lower enclosed level containing
four 240mm and four 194mm guns and the upper level open on top
having four 240mm guns in barbette mountings at the corners. There were
also to be four 164.7mm guns on the battery deck outside the lower citadel,
and all of the guns were to be of the new Model 1864. The upper level of
the citadel was soon replaced by four individual open-topped circular
barbettes with 150mm armour above the corners of the lower citadel.
Under pressure from foreign competition the French in 1868-69 decided
first to give the enclosed battery a uniform armament of eight 240mm
guns, then to replace six of the 240mm guns with four of the new
274.4mm guns, then to replace the remaining two 240mm guns with
smaller guns, and finally to omit them altogether, giving an armament as
built of four 274.4mm guns in the battery, four 240mm guns in the
barbettes, and (imitating the newer *Richelieu*) six 12pdr guns (bronze
Army-type 121mm field guns on naval carriages) on the upper deck aft of
the barbettes. They received a barque rig, a reduction from the full ship rig
of the earlier ironclads that was applied to the earlier ships as well.

The sides of the barbettes consisted of an inner metal cylinder of 15mm
iron plating, then a 300mm layer of teak tied to the inner cylinder by
20mm bands of iron, all entirely covered on the outside by curved 150mm
armour plates. Inside the inner cylinder was a rotating platform carrying
the gun. The barbettes were called 'fixed towers with rotating platforms' or
'fixed turrets'. It should be noted that the French were able to use this type
of mounting because they used breech-loading guns, it would have been

impossible with muzzle-loaders. *Océan* was 300 tons overweight when launched and in 1872 several options were under consideration for saving weight by reducing or removing some of the barbette armour.

The main change to this class after completion was the replacement in 1876-80 of the improvised battery of Army 12pdr (121mm) bronze rifles with new Navy 138.6mm rifles in all three ships. Subsequent changes were mostly to the rig, the light battery, and the torpedo armament.

*The characteristics are based on a devis for* Suffren *dated 19.8.1873, with comparable hull measurements for* Océan *from a devis dated 15.7.1870.*

**Dimensions & tons:**
(*Suffren*) 92.19m oa, 88.70m wl (+2.75m ram), 86.92m pp (wl fwd to rudder) x 17.51m ext, 17.31 wl including 0.07m sheathing (*soufflage*) added 8.1873. 7,604t disp. Draught: 8.29m mean, 9.12m aft. Men: 750.
(*Océan*) 92.52m oa, 88.60m wl (+2.89m ram), 86.78m pp (wl fwd to rudder) x 17.56m ext including 0.12m sheathing. 7,749t disp. 8.44m mean draught.

**Machinery:** 1,000nhp and 3,800ihp designed at 62rpm and 1.80kg/cm² boiler pressure. Trials (*Suffren*, 7.1873) 4,181ihp = 14.30kts at 63.92rpm and 2.00kg/cm² boiler pressure. 1 screw. 1 compound engine with return connecting rods and 3 cylinders of 2.10m diameter

---

The ironclad frigate *Océan* as updated with a light barquentine rig, small-calibre guns including in the main and mizzen tops, and Bullivant anti-torpedo nets. The port low down in the bow contains a torpedo tube. She was placed out of service at Cherbourg in 1875 and underwent a complete refit at Brest in 1879 for service in the Mediterranean and again in 1884-85 for service in the north. Note the paddle dockyard tug on the left. *(NHHC from ONI album of French warships, NH-74948)*

and 1.30m stroke. 8 high rectangular tubular boilers. 540t coal. Range 3,000nm @ 10kts.

**Armour:** (iron)
Side: Belt at waterline 200mm amidships, 200mm fwd, 180mm aft. Height from 2.14m below the wl to 0.66m above.
Guns: Central battery 160mm sides, 120mm bulkheads. Barbettes 150mm (armour probably removed in the 1870s).
Deck: 10mm plating on 80mm wood (11mm on 110mm in *Marengo*, 20mm on 90mm in *Suffren*).
Conning tower: none

**Guns:**
(1870, *Océan*) 4 x 274.4mm/15.4 M1864 (later 274.4mm/18 M1870) in the battery, 4 x 240mm/17.5 M1864 (later 240mm/19 M1870) in barbette turrets, 10 x 12pdr (121mm/17) bronze on the upper deck, and 4 x 4pdr (86.5mm/11) bronze.
(1872, *Marengo*) 4 x 274.4mm/18 M1870 in the battery, 4 x 240mm/17.5 M1864 (later 240mm/19 M1870) in barbette turrets, and 4 x 12pdr (121mm/17) bronze on the upper deck.
(1873, *Suffren*) 4 x 274.4mm/15.4 M1864 (later 274.4mm/18 M1870) in the battery, 4 x 240mm/17.5 M1864 (later 240mm/19 M1870) in barbette turrets, and 5 x 12pdr (121mm/17) bronze.
(1876, *Océan*) 4 x 274.4mm, 4 x 240mm, 6 x 138.6mm/21.3 M1870 on the battery deck forward of the central battery, 2 x 65mm/15 bronze landing, 8 x 37mm revolving cannon. In 1886 her light armament was 2 x 65mm/16 M1881 landing, 1 x 47mm, and 12 x 37mm revolving cannon.
(1880, *Marengo*) 4 x 274.4mm, 4 x 240mm, 7 x 138.6mm/21.3 M1870 (6 in the battery and one under the forecastle). In 1886 *Marengo* also had 2 x 65mm/16 M1881 landing and 12 x 37mm, and in 1887 she added 1 x 47mm boat and landing.

(c1880, *Suffren*) 4 x 274.4mm, 4 x 240mm, 6 x 138.6mm/21.3 M1870, 1 x 12pdr (121mm/17) bronze. In 1890 her light armament was 2 x 65mm/16 M1881 landing, 10 x 37mm, along with 4 torpedo tubes.
(1892, *Suffren*) 4 x 274.4mm, 4 x 240mm, 6 x 138.6mm, 2 x 65mm/50 M1891 QF, 2 x 47mm/40 M1885 QF, 1 x 47mm boat, 16 x 37mm.

*Océan* Brest Dyd/Schneider, Creusot (engines designed by Mathieu).
On list 1.1866. Ord: 15.1.1865. K: 18.4.1865. L: 15.10.1868.
    Comm: 8.12.1869 (trials), 11.7.1870 (full).
In the *Escadre du Nord* 9.1870, joined the *Escadre d'évolutions* at Toulon 17.6.1871. Reboilered and rearmed 1878-79 at Brest, reboilered again at Brest 1886 (boiler pressure increased to 2.36kg/cm²). In 1891 became school for gunners at Toulon, then school for apprentice torpedo boat seamen there. Struck 26.11.1894, for sale at Toulon 1894-1895.

*Marengo* Toulon Dyd/F.C. Méditerranée, Marseille (engines designed by Louis Édouard Lecointre).
On list 1.1866. Ord: 15.1.1865. K: 20.2.1865. L: 4.12.1869.
    Comm: 1.7.1870 (trials), 1.5.1872 (full).
Trials delayed by the 1870 war. Joined the *Escadre d'évolutions* (in 1st category reserve) after trials in the Mediterranean 1872. Struck 24.12.1894. Sold 7.3.1896, BU 1896-97 at Cherbourg.

*Suffren* Cherbourg Dyd/Indret.
On list 1.1867. Ord: 26.4.1866. K: 6.1866. L: 26.12.1870.
    Comm: 15.1.1873 (trials). C: 8.1873.

Towed to Brest by *Solférino* 2.1.1871 after launching, returned to Cherbourg after the war. To 1st category reserve after trials 5.8.1873, placed in full commisson 1.3.1876 in the 2nd detached division (*2e division détachée*) of the *Escadre d'évolutions* at Cherbourg after a refit there. Reboilered 1882-83 (boiler pressure increased to 2.25kg/cm²). Struck 15.7.1897 at Brest.

---

**FRIEDLAND.** *Frégate cuirassée de 1er rang.* Central battery ironclad with two upper deck barbettes, an iron hull, and a ram bow. One funnel, three masts, barque rig. Designed by Dupuy de Lôme and Lemoine.

The three 1st rank armoured frigates ordered on 15 January 1865 included one of iron, *Friedland*, at Lorient where she would follow the iron *Héroïne* on the ways at Caudan. Naval constructor Nicolas Marie Julien Lemoine was ordered on 18 February 1865 to convert Dupuy de Lôme's plans of *Marengo* for construction in iron. Lemoine found it necessary to increase the length by 8m and the displacement by more than 1,000 tons. The ram was no longer separate but was integrated into the hull. His first plans, for

---

The ironclad frigate *Friedland* as completed with a barque rig. She was planned as an iron-hulled version of the *Océan* class but emerged with major differences including an armament based on the later *Colbert* and *Trident* with only two barbettes and a long six-gun battery behind them. *(NHHC from ONI album of French warships, NH-74919)*

an '1st rank armoured frigate (iron hull) with a central battery and a ram, armed with 12 large calibre guns and 4 ordinary 30pdr rifles', was signed by Lemoine on 19 July 1865 and approved by Dupuy de Lôme acting for Minister of Marine Chasseloup-Laubat on 4 October 1865. The start of construction was postponed until December 1866 and additional delays (including the 1870 war) pushed the ship's launching back to 1873 and commissioning to 1876. In the interval many changes were made, the most important being the substitution for the armament of the *Océan* class of an exclusively 274.4mm armament like that in the later *Colbert* class, with six guns in a lengthened central battery and two in barbette half-turrets. Unlike *Colbert* no guns were fitted in the bow or stern, but like her *Friedland* was fitted with eight of the new 138.6mm guns instead of the Army bronze 12pdrs (121mm) of the earlier ships. The six 274.4mm guns in the battery had ports 10m apart and with sills 3.3m (10ft 10in) above the waterline.

Modifications after completion were limited to the increase of her light battery, the addition of torpedo tubes, and the reduction of her rig to a barquentine with military tops. Her mainmast was removed in 1895.

*The characteristics are based on a devis dated 22.2.1876.*
**Dimensions & tons:** 99.50m oa, 95.66m wl (+3.05m ram), 93.96m pp (wl fwd to rudder) x 17.44+0.24m sheathing ext, 17.10+0.24m wl. 8,824t disp. Draught: 8.306m mean, 9.06m aft. Men: 700.
**Machinery:** 1,000nhp and 3,800ihp designed at 65rpm and 1.80kg/cm² boiler pressure. Trials (4.1876) 4,428ihp = 13.30kts at 65.10rpm and 2.139kg/cm² boiler pressure. 1 screw. 1 horizontal compound engine with return connecting rods and 3 cylinders of 2.10m diameter and 1.30m stroke. 8 high rectangular tubular boilers. 628t coal. Range 3,330nm @ 10kts.
**Armour:** (iron)
Side: Belt at waterline 200mm amidships and fwd, 180mm aft, all on 100mm teak, 33mm of iron lattice work, another 280mm of teak and then 20mm of hull plating.
Guns: Central battery 160mm sides. Guns on upper deck probably unprotected.
Deck: 11mm plating on 120mm wood.
**Guns:**
(1876) 8 x 274.4mm/18 M1870 (6 in the battery, 2 on upper deck in unarmoured half-turrets), 8 x 138.6mm/21.3 M1870 (3 on each side and 1 at each end) on the upper deck (subsequently moved to the battery deck forward of the battery armour). 8 x 37mm revolving cannon added 1878.
(1884) 2 tubes for 356mm torpedoes added. Two more added in 1891.
(1885) The light battery consisted of 1 x 90mm/22 M1881 boat, 2 x 65mm/16 M1881 landing, and 14 x 37mm.
(1895) The light battery was augmented to 20 x 47mm or 37mm.

*Friedland* Lorient Dyd-Caudan/Indret (engines designed by Victorin Sabattier).
On list 1.1866. Ord: 15.1.1865. K: 2.12.1866. L: 25.10.1873. Comm: 1.5.1875 (trials). C: 2.1876.
To reserve after trials, to full commission 20.6.1877 in the northern division of the *Escadre d'évolutions* after refit at Brest, to the Mediterranean 1878. Reboilered 1883 (boiler pressure increased to 2.25 kg/cm²). Mainmast removed 1895. Considered 1898 for conversion to *garde-côte convoyeur de torpilleurs*. To *cuirassé garde-côtes offensif* 1.1899. Struck 10.10.1904, for sale at Toulon 1904-1905.

---

**RICHELIEU.** *Frégate cuirassée de 1er rang.* Central battery ironclad with four upper deck barbettes and a gun under the forecastle, a wooden hull, iron upper works outside the battery, and a ram bow. One funnel, three masts, ship rig (reduced to a barque in 1876). Designed by Dupuy de Lôme and Berrier-Fontaine.

When it came time to design the next 1st rank ironclad in 1868 the French navy had just experienced in the trials of the ram *Taureau* the remarkable improvement in manoeuvrability that could be provided by twin screw propulsion. (The ship could rotate within her own length by running her screws in opposite directions.) The recent battle of Lissa had persuaded many that the ram was the essential weapon in naval combat, and twin screws would clearly improve its effectiveness. Naval constructor Jean-Baptiste Louis Félix Marc Berrier-Fontaine therefore modified Dupuy de Lôme's design for *Océan* to produce a similar ship with twin screws. His initial plans, dated 21 August 1868, included 240mm guns in both the battery and the barbettes and retained the armour, speed, and coal supply of the original *Océan* design with an increase of only 186 tons. On the same day Dupuy de Lôme as Director of Materiel recommended the plans to a new Minister of Marine, Admiral Charles Rigault de Genouilly, who approved them, ordered construction of the ship at Toulon, and assigned her name. But it was then decided to put 274.4mm guns in the battery, and on 24 September 1868 the Ministry informed Toulon that the battery armament would be four 274.4mm and two 240mm guns. This was soon changed again, and the plans that were approved on 21 November 1868 included an increase in length from 87.84m to 98.14m and in displacement from 7,373 tons to 8,400 tons. The increased size permitted increasing the length of the central battery from 18.88m to 30.70m and carrying six 274.4mm guns in the battery, four 240mm in the barbettes, and four 12pdrs (121mm) on deck. The lengthened battery also provided protection to the engines as well as the boilers. The armour was unchanged, and in April 1873 Toulon proposed recycling the iron armour from deleted floating batteries to make it. The upper works at the ends were built of 12mm iron hull plating. The only significant changes made after she was laid down were the addition in July 1870 of a 240mm gun under the forecastle and a fifth 12pdr on deck.

Supports for 37mm revolving cannon were installed during her 1876-1879 commission. The ship then underwent repairs, completed post-repair speed trials on 3 November 1880, and was placed in reserve on 12 November 1880. During the night of 29-30 December 1880 she caught fire, capsized and sank in 10.75m of water at Toulon. She was raised on 27-31 March 1881 in a huge salvage effort and drydocked on 2 April 1881. Her hull was found not to have been distorted by the fire, her propulsion machinery was untouched, and she was handed over to the dockyard on 11 June 1881 for reconstruction. She was recommissioned for trials on 1 September 1882, definitively on 10 October 1883, and rejoined the fleet on 7 November 1883. During her reconstruction the medium calibre battery of ten Army 12pdr bronze guns was replaced in 1881 with eight Navy 138.6mm guns, and on 9 June 1882 ports were ordered added fore and aft for launching Whitehead torpedoes. Her rig was reduced to a barquentine and later a fore and aft rig only, first with a single armed top on each mast and then with double tops, the bottom one armed. Bullivant nets were fitted in 1885; with them deployed her maximum speed in trials of the installation was 4 knots.

*The characteristics are based on a devis dated 11.2.1876.*
**Dimensions & tons:** 103.150m oa, 98.70m wl (+2.67m ram), 96.77m pp (wl fwd to rudder) x 17.440m+0.200m sheathing ext, 17.240m+0.200m wl. 8,790.877t disp. Draught: 8.227m mean, 8.799m aft. Men: 750.
**Machinery:** 1,000nhp and 4,400ihp designed at 80rpm and 2.250kg/cm² boiler pressure. Trials (26.1.1876) 4,240ihp = 13.22kts at 84.38rpm and 2.086kg/cm² boiler pressure, (30.10.1883) 4,108.2ihp = 13.39kts at 83.12rpm, (18.5.1886) 3,491.8ihp = 12.522kts at 78.965rpm. 2 screws. 2 horizontal compound engines with return connecting rods with 3 cylinders of 1.650m diameter and 0.850m stroke, steam being introduced into the middle cylinder. 8 high reglementary rectangular boilers. 654t coal. Range with 654t coal 3,700 miles @ 10kts.
**Armour:** (iron)
Side: Belt at waterline 200m amidships, 200mm fwd, 160mm aft. Height from 2.08m below the wl to 0.72m above.

The ironclad frigate *Richelieu* as completed with a ship rig. She was a wooden-hulled ship with four barbettes like *Océan*, a battery lengthened for six guns, and a gun under the forecastle. She caught fire and was nearly destroyed in 1880. When she re-emerged after repairs in 1883 she had a larger rectangular funnel like that of *Friedland*. (NHHC from ONI album of French warships, NH-74902)

Guns: Central battery 160mm sides, 100mm transverse bulkheads. Guns on upper deck probably unprotected.
Deck: 11mm plating on 110mm wood.
Conning tower: 100mm
**Guns:**
(1876) 6 x 274.4mm/18 M1870 (in the battery), 5 x 240mm/19 M1870 (4 in fixed half turrets above the battery corners and 1 under the forecastle), 10 x 12pdr (121mm/17) bronze (on upper deck, 6 forward intended for saluting and 4 aft). Also 2 or 3 *mitrailleuses* on the upper deck forward and 1 x 12pdr (121mm/17) bronze and 5 x 4pdr (86.5mm/11) bronze for the boats.
(1877) The 6 x 12pdr (121mm/17) on the upper deck forward were moved down to the forward battery for use in combat. 2 x 138.6mm/21.3 M1870 were added aft to provide stern fire in combat from the admiral's gallery. They were normally carried on the upper deck above and if needed for combat would be lowered through a hatch aft of the mizzen mast. A Hotchkiss revolving cannon was sent to the ship for trials in 6.1877 and provisionally mounted aft to port. The commission that conducted the tests of the Hotchkiss proposed assigning six guns of this type to the vessel, 4 at the ends of the ship (including 2 at the ends of the stern gallery and 2 on the forecastle) and 2 amidships. The installation of *mitrailleuses* in the tops protected by steel plates would complete the defence against boats and torpedo attacks. During 1878, 8 revolving cannon were embarked and 16 posi-

tions (8 on each side) installed for them to defend the ship against torpedo launches.
(1879-80) The entire armament was landed 6.1879. The ten bronze 12pdrs were removed and 4 x 138.6mm were embarked. These plus the two already on board were installed in the forward battery, with two of them to be moved to the upper deck aft in wartime. Metal hoods were added to protect the crews of the 240mm barbette turrets. Two positions for revolving cannon were installed in the fore top and one in a boat. In 1880 mountings for revolving cannon were installed in the ship's five cutters (but not in the larger 11.5-metre pinnace) and armoured shelters were installed in the tops.
(1883, after reconstruction) 6 x 274.4mm/18 M1870, 5 x 240mm/19 M1870, 8 x 138.6mm/21.3 M1870 (6 in the forward battery, 2 on the upper deck aft). Also 1 x 90mm bronze or steel, 2 x 65mm bronze or steel landing, and 12 Hotchkiss revolving cannon on deck and in the tops.
(1887) Light battery changed to 2 x 65mm/16 M1881 steel landing, 1 x 47mm revolving cannon (for the pinnace), and 18 x 37mm revolving cannon. Added 4 launchers for 356mm M1880 (4.42m) torpedoes above water on the sides. (1889) Add 2 x 47mm/40 M1885 QF. (1892) Add 4 more 47mm QF.

*Richelieu* Toulon Dyd/Indret (engines designed by Charles Louis Jaÿ).
On list 1.1869. Ord: 21.8.1868. K: 1.12.1868. L: 3.12.1873.
    Comm: 1.4.1875 (trials), 11.2.1876 (full).
Machinery installed 28.5.1874 to 26.4.1875. Flagship of the *Escadre d'évolutions* at Toulon 1876. Burned and sank 29-30.12.1880, repaired and returned to full commission 10.10.1883. Employed 9.1885 for trials of Bullivant anti-torpedo nets. Reboiled in 1886 (First lit off 15.4.1886) with 8 Mourraille boilers (also 2.25kg/cm²). Decomm. at Toulon 23.1.1896. To *cuirassé garde-côtes offensif* 1.1899. To 2nd cat-

egory special reserve in the special group of *garde-côtes offensifs* 20.7. 1899. Struck 4.9.1900 (published 11.9.1900), barracks hulk at Toulon 1900-1909. Sold 30.12.1909 to Dutch breakers, towed out of Toulon 17.1.1911 by the Dutch tug *Roodzee*, cast adrift in a storm in the Bay of Biscay, went ashore in the Scilly Isles 2.1911, refloated and taken to the Netherlands to BU.

---

**COLBERT** Class. *Frégates cuirassées de 1er rang.* Central battery ironclads with two upper deck half turrets and guns under the forecastle and on the stern, wooden hulls, iron upper works outside the battery, and metal rams. One funnel, three masts, ship rig. Designed by Sabattier.

These were the last French 1st rank armoured ships with wooden hulls. They were ordered on 5 August 1869 on the plans of *Richelieu* as they existed on 26 April 1869 and naval constructor Victorin Gabriel Justin Épiphanès Sabattier, the successor of Dupuy de Lôme as Director of Materiel after the latter retired on 10 June 1869, undertook to produce the new drawings. However, so many changes were made that a new class resulted. It was soon decided that for rigged squadron battleships the disad-

The ironclad frigate *Trident*. She and her sister *Colbert* had their guns in two barbettes, a long battery with six guns, and a gun under the forecastle, prominent here. Another large gun was soon added aft. (*NHHC from collection of Rear Admiral Ammen C. Farenholt, previously ONI, NH-66098*)

vantages of twin screws outweighed the advantages because of the danger of fallen rigging fouling twin screws, and single screws were specified. In addition the belt at the waterline was increased to 220mm amidships and forward to resist 274.4mm guns and the deck plating was increased to 15mm. The weight of the additional armour was offset by savings in the machinery and by removing the after two barbettes and fitting a uniform armament of 274.4mm guns, six in the battery and two in the remaining two upper deck barbettes. The armament also included one 240mm gun under the forecastle, four 138.6mm guns on the sides and two 138.6mm guns aft on central pivots. Sabattier's plans for *Trident* were approved on 28 October 1869, but they continued to be modified by Sabattier and by naval constructor Charles Frédéric Peschart d'Ambly. By October 1871 the ships had a complete 220mm belt 2.80m wide and rising only 1.00m above the waterline. They had a central battery with 160mm armour that was 31m long with 120mm transverse bulkheads at the ends. The redoubt contained four 320mm guns, two per side. On the upper deck there were two barbettes that were 2.3m high and had 160mm armour, each with a 320mm gun. The total armament of the ship at this time was six 320mm and four 12pdr (121mm) guns.

After the *Conseil des travaux* on 18 October 1871 decided on the technical characteristics of the new 1st rank ironclads to be built under the Programme of 1872 (below) it attempted on 27 October to incorporate some of the new features into the two ships whose construction had just been begun. The Council decided to retain the belt and central battery as

they were but arm the battery with six 274.4mm guns. The upper deck would have two 'half turrets' 1.4m high with 160mm armour on the outboard sides in place of the barbettes (saving 140 tons), each with a 274.4mm gun, and there would also be one 240mm gun under the fore-castle and six 138.6mm guns. The boilers, which had been protected by the central battery, had to be moved forward, putting the front end of the boiler rooms 6m in front of the forward bulkhead of the battery. Deck armour of 50mm was added over this space. Finally the Council raised the top of the belt from 1.0m to 1.3m above the waterline and stated that the bottom edge should not be more than 1.5m below the waterline.

In 1877 while *Colbert* was running trials further changes were made in the armament of *Trident*. A second 240mm gun was added on deck at the stern and the six 138.6mm guns on deck were moved below to the battery deck forward of the central battery. These changes were retrofitted to *Colbert* in 1881. Originally ship rigged, the two ships were soon reduced to barques and later to barquentines with armed tops.

*The characteristics are based on a devis for* Trident *dated 18.11.1878, with hull measurements for* Colbert *based on a devis dated 2.7.1877.*

**Dimensions & tons:**
(*Trident*) 101.80m oa, 97.90m wl (+3.10m ram), 96.00m pp (wl fwd to rudder) x 17.72m ext, 17.56m wl including 0.20m sheathing. 8,814t disp. Draught: 8.20m mean, 8.88m aft. Men: 774.
(*Colbert*) 101.12m oa, 97.82m wl (+3.10m ram), 96.02m pp (wl fwd to rudder) x 17.74m ext including 0.20m sheathing, 8,617t disp, 8.11m mean draught and 8.69m aft.

**Machinery:** 1,200nhp and 4,000ihp designed at 65rpm and 2.25kg/cm$^2$ boiler pressure. Trials (4.1878) 5,083ihp = 14.216kts at 71.05rpm and 2.474kg/cm$^2$ boiler pressure. 1 screw. 1 horizontal compound engine with return connecting rods, 3 cylinders of 2.10m diameter and 1.29m stroke. 8 high rectangular tubular boilers. 560t coal. Range 3,100nm @ 10kts.

**Armour:** (iron)
Side: Belt at waterline 220mm amidships and fwd, 160mm aft. Height from 1.30m below the wl to 1.40m above.
Guns: Central battery 160mm sides, 120mm transverse bulkheads. Guns on upper deck probably unprotected.
Deck: 15mm plating on 90mm wood.

**Guns:**
(1877, *Colbert* as completed) 8 x 274.4mm/18 M1870 (6 in the battery, 2 in half turrets on the upper deck), 1 x 240mm/19 M1870 under the forecastle, and 6 x 138.6mm/21.3 M1870 on the upper deck (4 sides, 2 aft). 8 x 37mm Hotchkiss added 28.6.1878.
(1878, *Trident* as completed) 8 x 274.4mm/18 M1870 (6 in the battery, 2 in half turrets on the upper deck), 2 x 240mm/19 M1870 under the forecastle and on the stern, 6 x 138.6mm/21.3 M1870 on the battery deck forward of the central battery, 8 x 37mm Hotchkiss, plus 5 x 4pdr (86.5mm/11) mountain rifles and 1 x 12pdr (121mm/17) bronze rifle for the boats. The stern 240mm was added 13.2.1878 and the 2 x 138.6mm already there were moved to the battery along with the four on deck forward.
(1881, *Colbert*) Added 1 x 240mm/19 M1870 aft and moved the 138.6mm down into the battery as in *Trident*, added 6 x 37mm.
(1888, *Trident*) Light artillery consisted of 12 x 37mm, plus 2 x 65mm/16 M1881 landing and 1 x 47mm revolving cannon for the boats, along with 6 x 356mm torpedo tubes.
(1890, *Colbert*) Light artillery consisted of 16 small guns (65mm, 47mm and 37mm) along with 4 x 356mm torpedo tubes (two on each beam).
(1894, *Trident*) Light artillery consisted of 2 x 65mm, 7 x 47mm, and 18 x 37mm.

*Colbert* Brest Dyd/Indret (engines designed by Joseph Joëssel).
On list 1.1870. Ord: 5.8.1869. K: 4.7.1870. L: 16.9.1875.
   Comm: 5.9.1876 (trials), 6.6.1877 (full).

In the northern division of the *Escadre d'évolutions* 1877-78, then became flagship of the vice admiral commanding the *Escadre d'évolutions* at Toulon 10.1879. To *cuirassé garde-côtes offensif* 1.1899. Struck 4.9.1900 (published 11.9.1900), barracks hulk for mobilisation crews at Toulon 1900-1909. Sold 1910 at Toulon to BU.

*Trident* Toulon Dyd/Indret (engines designed by Joseph Joëssel).
On list 1.1870. Ord: 5.8.1869. K: 19.4.1870. L: 9.11.1876.
   Comm: 1.10.1877 (trials), 18.11.1878 (full).
Became flagship of the rear admiral second in command of the *Escadre d'évolutions* at Toulon 12.1878. Reboilered 1886 (4 'Chevalier Grenier' boilers, pressure 2.25kg/cm$^2$) and 1894 (8 Mouraille boilers, same pressure). Considered 1898 for conversion to *garde-côte convoyeur de torpilleurs*. To *cuirassé garde-côtes offensif* 1.1899. Struck 4.9.1900 (published 11.9.1900), barracks hulk for mobilisation crews at Toulon 1900-1909, renamed *Var* 1904. Sold 1910 at Toulon to BU.

———————

**The fall of the Second Empire and beginnings of the Third Republic.**
Emperor Napoleon III and his army surrendered at Sedan on 2 September 1870 and the French Third Republic was proclaimed two days later. On 8 February 1871 a National Assembly was elected to decide the issue of peace or continued war with the Germans, and on 17 February it made Adolphe Thiers the chief executive of the French republic. Thiers selected Vice Admiral Louis Pierre Alexis Pothuau as his Minister of Marine. The decision of the Assembly on 1 March 1871 to sue for peace and allow German entry into Paris triggered the uprising of the Paris Commune, which was not suppressed until the end of May. In the Treaty of Frankfort, signed on 10 May 1871, the French lost the northern part of Lorraine and practically all of Alsace and engaged to pay an indemnity of five billion francs. German occupying forces remained in France until it was paid, leaving on 16 September 1873. In the meantime the monarchist majority in the National Assembly rebelled against Thiers on 24 May 1873 and took control of the government, although the inflexibility of the Bourbon heir to the throne on matters such as retention of the tricolour flag prevented the restoration of the monarchy.

**The Programme of 1872.**
On 19 August 1871 National Assembly member Daniel Ancel reported to the Assembly on a version of the Navy's 1871 budget that had been updated during 1871. He noted that ever since 1857 the Navy's ship construction programme had been guided by the Programme of 1857 and that as of 1 January 1870, 416 ships of the types in the programme had been completed of the 439 called for. He then informed the members that he had suggested to Minister of Marine Pothuau that, following the disas-trous 1870-71 war, it was time to develop a new programme. Pothuau had agreed that revision was imperative and told Ancel that he intended to refer a new programme to the *Conseil d'Amirauté* and report the results to the National Assembly when presenting the 1872 budget. On 4 August 1871 Pothuau had referred to the *Conseil d'Amirauté* a report of the Director of Materiel proposing a new composition of the fleet. The Council examined this programme and made its recommendations on 29 August 1871. On 14 September 1871 Pothuau referred the programme to the *Conseil des travaux* asking it to develop technical specifications for the ship types that were to enter into the composition of the new fleet.

The final programme was duly described in the ministry's preliminary note to the 1872 budget dated November 1871 and it along with the tech-nical specifications for the ships was circulated to the ports on 13 November 1871. The programme contained only 157 ships compared to the 439 in the Programme of 1857. Many of the reductions resulted from the deletion of the numerous sailing ships and ships with mixed sail and steam propulsion that were in the old programme and that were now obsolete, but the programme also effectively abandoned any attempt to compete with Britain in numbers of 1st class battleships and eliminated the large fleet of transports favoured by Napoleon III while expanding the role of coast defence forces to include offensive operations against Germany and stressing the commerce raiding function of cruisers if needed against Britain. New ships were to be made technically equal to their most perfected analogues in rival navies but without seeking superiority. The full programme is in Appendix F.

The 1872 budget (submitted in December 1871) stated that despite the financial emergency created by the war and the indemnity it was absolutely necessary to lay down, even if only to work on them moderately in 1872, two 1st rank ironclads, one 2nd rank ironclad, 2 armoured monitors, two fast unarmoured frigates, four 2nd class avisos (wooden), one large iron transport, and two gunboats. Of these were actually begun under this budget one 1st rank ironclad, the two monitors (coast defence ships), the two frigates (in the form of one 1st class and one 2nd class cruiser), the four avisos, the two gunboats, and two instead of one transports. No more new ships were funded until the 1875 budget.

———

*REDOUTABLE*. *Cuirassé de 1er rang*. Central battery ironclad with two upper deck half turrets and guns under the forecastle and on the stern, a steel and iron hull, and a ram bow. One large funnel amidships, three masts, ship rig. Designed by de Bussy.

On 18 October 1871 the *Conseil des travaux* approved specifications for 1st rank ironclads that included an iron hull 90m long, a speed of 14 knots, a central battery with six 240mm guns on a lower level behind armour and four 274.4mm guns on an upper level in open armoured barbette mountings with axial fire plus one 240mm gun under the forecastle. Minister of Marine Pothuau reversed the armament, putting six 274.4mm guns in the battery and five 240mm guns on the upper deck, and then on 14 November 1871 forwarded the specifications to the ports and asked the naval constructors there to submit designs.

The *Conseil des travaux* considered seven designs on 21 June 1872 and liked the arrangement of the artillery in the design of naval constructor Marie Anne Louis de Bussy, which provided axial fire from the battery guns as well as the barbette guns by deeply recessing the hull sides forward and aft of the battery. De Bussy's plan after re-examination by the Council on 15 July 1872 and 5 November 1872 had the following characteristics: steel and iron hull, 95m long, speed 14.5 knots, the central battery specified by the Council and Minister Pothuau but with the four 240mm guns on the upper deck in pairs on two turntables behind 1.4m high armoured parapets, one turntable per side, to maximise axial fire. The 240mm gun under the forecastle was deleted. The design thus provided axial fire directly forward from six heavy guns (two battery and four barbette) and astern to within 15 degrees of the axis by six guns. *Redoutable* was heralded as France's first steel battleship because her hull had steel frames and beams and steel shell plating except for iron for most of the underwater plating.

Although the Council was ready to accept this design on 5 November 1872, de Bussy then proposed major changes to it. He felt that the 274.4mm gun would soon be regarded as insufficient and proposed replacing the six 274.4mm guns in the battery with four 305mm guns of a new steel model and the four 240mm guns on the upper deck with two 274.4mm guns. This would reduce axial fire from six to four guns but enhance the ability to perforate armour. It also allowed shortening the battery and deleting the rotating platforms on the upper deck, the single guns there being on simpler mountings in 'half turrets' with vertical bulkheads or parapets only on the outboard sides. Using the saved weight de Bussy increased the maximum thickness of the belt from 220mm to 300mm (220mm at the ends), the battery armour from 160mm to 240mm and the transverse battery bulkheads from 120mm to 150mm. The Council proposed deleting the armour on the parapets for the two guns on the upper deck, leaving only thin plating. Because the steel 305mm gun had not yet been developed (it never was) the armament of this design became four 274.4mm/18 M1870 guns in the battery, two 320mm/19.3

M1870 guns on the upper deck, and some 138.6mm/21.3 M1870 guns on deck. De Bussy's plans dated 22 October 1872 were approved by Minister Pothuau on 14 November 1872.

The month in which the ship's construction began was variously reported as December 1872, January 1873, and July 1873, the last probably being her keel laying. The design of *Redoutable* was definitively approved on 14 November 1873. However, in July 1875, when construction of the hull was already well advanced, the maximum belt armour was increased from 300mm to 350mm. In July 1872 the Council had suggested using two independent engines, one to provide economical steaming at low speeds and the other to be coupled for higher speeds, a complex arrangement resembling that also used in the contemporary *Duquesne* and *Duguay-Trouin* class cruisers. After more changes a contract was signed on 1 June 1874 with Creusot for compound engines consisting of three independent groups of two cylinders each driving the single propeller shaft.

The crew roster (*livre de bord*) was opened on 1 August 1878, making the ship in commission for trials from that date even though some of the artillery and all of the rig had not yet been installed. The ship went into full commission (*armement définitif*) on 31 December 1878 after machinery trials but before turning and sailing trials. The commissioning report (*devis d'armement*) was completed on 8 February 1879.

As built the ship had a uniform main battery of eight 274.4mm guns with four in the battery, two above it instead of the planned 320mm guns, one added under the forecastle and one on the stern plus six 138.6mm guns. The four 274.4mm guns fitted on the upper deck and one of those in the battery were originally M1870 guns with iron tubes, M1870/75 guns with the intended steel tubes were fitted on the upper deck in 1879-80 after the ship's trials in accordance with the ship's design and the gun in the battery was replaced at Toulon in May 1886. The 274.4mm/19.75 M1875 No 2 guns in the battery were built especially for the ship and were the only four guns of this type built. The 274.4mm/19.75 M1870/75 No 1 guns were also unique to the ship. A protective shield in front of the after gun was proposed by the ship's commander in 1882 and added in 1884-85, and at the end of 1886 protective shields were fitted in front of the 274.4mm guns above the battery. Originally ship rigged, she was reduced to a barque in 1883 and to a barquentine in 1886 and lost her bowsprit in 1888.

**Overhaul at Toulon, 1893-94.** Between September 1893 and June 1894 the entire rig was replaced with two military masts and the first preliminary stage of a two stage rearmament ordered on 22 November 1892 was carried out. Seven of the 274.4mm guns were replaced with 274.4mm/28.5 M1881 guns and the after 274.4mm gun was replaced with a Model 1884 gun, all on the existing mountings (which limited them to reduced charges). Creusot was tasked with converting the existing three compound engines to triple expansion. A single high pressure cylinder replaced the middle engine and fed steam into the smaller cylinder of the two end engines, which thus became intermediate pressure cylinders in the new triple expansion system, and then into the existing low pressure cylinders and condensers of those engines. At low speed steam could be routed from the boilers directly to the end engines, which would operate as compound engines. Laborious trials (mostly caused by problems with the new high pressure cylinder) finally yielded a maximum sustained speed of 14.5 knots with a short burst at 15 knots.

**Overhaul at Toulon, 1898.** Between January and April 1898 Toulon carried out the second and definitive stage of the ship's rearmament. The work included new mountings for the three 274.4mm/28.5 M1881 guns on the upper deck and the similar gun under the forecastle and replacing the four 274.4mm guns in the battery with four 240mm/30 M1884 guns on new M1896 mountings. It also included replacement of the six 138.6mm/21.3 M1870 guns on the upper deck with six 100mm/26.2 M1881 QF guns, redistribution of the light artillery, addition of an armoured conning tower, and removal of all but two of the 37mm guns and the two forward torpedo tubes. The two after tubes followed in 1900 just before the ship left for the Far East.

*The characteristics are based on a devis dated 8.2.1879.*

**Dimensions & tons:** 100.70m oa, 96.67m wl (+3.68m ram), 95.00m pp (wl fwd to rudder) x 19.76m ext and wl. 8,858t disp (9,430t full load). Draught: 7.28m mean, 7.80m aft. Men: 700.

**Machinery:**

(Original) 1,500nhp and 6,000ihp designed at 72rpm and 2.25kg/cm² boiler pressure. Trials (12.1878) 6,071ihp = 14.668kts at 69.50rpm and 2.378kg/cm² boiler pressure. 1 screw. 3 compound (Woolf) engines with return connecting rods and two cylinders of 1.38m and 2.16m diameter and 1.25m stroke driving the single propeller shaft. 8 high rectangular tubular boilers. 492t coal. Range 2,840nm @ 10kts.

(1894) Engine converted to triple expansion by replacing the middle engine with one HP cylinder and converting the HP cylinders of the other two engines to IP cylinders. 8 new cylindrical return-flame boilers operating at 8.5kg/cm² boiler pressure.

**Armour:** (iron)

Side: Belt at waterline 350mm amidships, 220mm fwd, 230mm aft. Height from 1.52m below the wl to 1.28m above.

Guns: Central battery 300mm sides. 150mm or more on the transverse bulkheads. Guns on upper deck unprotected (18mm plating on sides of half turrets above the battery, 17mm plating on stern barbette).

Deck: flat 60mm fore and aft of the battery, 50mm forward, 40mm stern.

Conning tower: 30mm sides, 10mm top, replaced 1898 with one with 60mm special steel plus 20mm plating.

**Guns:**

(1879) 4 x 274.4mm/19.75 M1875 No 2 steel in the battery (built specially for the ship), 4 x 274.4mm/19.75 M1875 No 1 steel on the upper deck of which 2 were in half turrets over the battery, one under the forecastle and one on deck aft), 6 x 138.6mm/21.3 M1870 (one each side forward of the battery and two aft), plus 8 x 37mm Hotchkiss revolving cannon (added by decision of 28.6.1878).

**Torpedoes:** 4 tubes on the sides above water, two forward and two aft.

(1890) 4 x 274.4mm, 4 x 274.4mm, 6 x 138.6mm, 2 x 65mm, 8 x 47mm/40 M1885 QF, 1 x 47mm revolving cannon, and 16 x 37mm revolving cannon.

(1895 after first stage of rearmament) 4 x 274.4mm/28.5 M1881 in the battery, 3 x 274.4mm/28.5 M1881 upper deck at the sides and under the forecastle, 1 x 274.4mm/30 M1884 upper deck aft (all 274.4mm on existing mountings), 6 x 138.6mm/21.3 M1870 on the upper deck, 2 x 65mm, 14 x 47mm QF, 1 x 47mm revolving cannon, 6 x 37mm/20 M1885 QF, 14 x 37mm revolving cannon.

(1898 after second stage of rearmament) 4 x 240mm/30 M1884 on M1896 mountings in the battery, 4 x 274.4mm/28.5 M1881 on original mountings on the upper deck, 6 x 100mm/26.2 M1881 QF on the upper deck, 4 x 65mm/50 M1891 QF, 15 x 47mm QF, 2 x 37mm.

The 1st rank ironclad *Redoutable* in the Brest dockyard. The coast defence ship *Tempête* is behind her with only her tiny black funnel visible just before *Redoutable*'s pilot house. *Redoutable* was notable for multiple reasons, including her mostly steel hull and the tumblehome in the sides that provided axial fire from the guns in the central battery. *(NHHC from ONI album of French warships, NH-74893)*

The forward two torpedo tubes were removed, and the other two followed in 1900.

*Redoutable* Lorient Dyd/Schneider, Creusot.
On list 1.1873. K: 18.7.1873. L: 18.9.1876. Comm: 1.8.1878 (trials), 31.12.1878 (full).
Budget 1872. Trials completed 28.1.1879. Left Lorient for Toulon 24.2.1879, joined the *Escadre d'évolutions* 3.1879. Reboilered 1885-86, overhauled 1893-94 and 1897-98. Left Toulon 8.1900 for the Far East as the flagship for a vice admiral in response to the Boxer Rebellion in China. Joined the international force at Taku on 29.9.1900. Mostly inactive at Saigon from 1.1903. Struck 9.3.1910. Sold 17.8.1911 at Saigon, BU in a mud dock at the arsenal there in 1912.

---

### *Décuirassement* of the main battery

In 1871 proposals began to be made to concentrate armour on the waterline and deck and delete armour protection for the guns. On 27 October 1871 the Director of Materiel proposed a major redesign of *Colbert* and *Trident* in which the armour of the central battery and of the upper deck guns would be deleted, the belt strengthened to 270mm, a 50mm armoured deck added over the machinery, and the armament changed to eleven unprotected 274.4mm guns, 6 in the battery and 5 on the upper deck. The *Conseil des travaux* rejected the idea for 1st rank ironclads but accepted a similar proposal for the 2nd rank *Victorieuse* and *Triomphante*, which was not implemented. The idea was presented again on 26 January 1872 as part of an effort to improve the stability of *Colbert* and again rejected.

On 5, 8 and 12 November 1872, immediately after giving final approval to de Bussy's design for *Redoutable*, the Council's progressive president, Vice Admiral Philippe Victor Touchard, proposed removing all protection for the guns except a very strong transverse bulkhead to provide protection to the battery during head-on combat. Citing the design just submitted by the young Louis Émile Bertin for a corvette with a cellular waterline, he said that in such a ship all the large guns should be placed on the centreline on the upper deck able to fire to both sides. By a tied vote, Touchard breaking the tie, the council voted to submit the idea to Minister of Marine Pothuau along with specifications for an ironclad like *Redoutable* with the new configuration.

On 20 October 1873 a new Minister of Marine, Vice Admiral Charles Marius Albert de Dompierre d'Hornoy, charged the Council, now with a more conservative president (Vice Admiral Baron Didelot), to draft specifications for new battleships which were to have 'defensive strength notably greater than that of similar vessels then afloat or building'. He asked for two sets of specifications for 1st rank ironclads, one with and one without a central battery, and the Director of Materiel (Sabattier) provided sketches of each. (He also asked for specifications for a 2nd rank battleship, but only without a central battery.) The Council produced the specifications on 21 November 1873. The ironclad with the battery was basically a *Redoutable* with an extra 800 tons, a maximum belt thickness of 350mm (300mm at the ends), a 240mm battery, and a 50mm (on average) armoured deck that was now complete from end to end. The armament was four 320mm guns (a new calibre that was to exist by the time the ship was ready for them) in the battery with axial fire, two 274.4mm guns on top of the battery without protection except against small arms fire, and six or eight 138.6mm on the upper deck or on the forecastle. The ironclad without a central battery had the same hull dimensions, tonnage, armament, and the machinery as the design with the battery. The weight of the armour was also the same, but the omission of the battery allowed substantially increasing the maximum thickness of the belt and deck armour. All of the large guns were to be on the upper deck without protection, the four 320mm guns being in barbettes.

A majority of the council accepted these two alternative specifications as responsive to Minister Dompierre d'Hornoy's tasking. However, the president and three other members, while agreeing with the other conclusions of the report, demurred against the principle of *décuirassement* of the main artillery, 'a principle with which, until better informed and knowing what the British were doing, they could not be associated.' The design with the central battery was developed by de Bussy into the *Dévastation* class while the other design was set aside, but only temporarily as it contained many aspects of the design for the next ironclad, *Amiral Duperré*.

### Four new 1st rank ironclads planned, 1873-1877

The Programme of 1872 called for a second 1st rank ironclad in addition to *Redoutable* to be begun during 1872 but this did not occur. The January 1874 fleet list and the 1875 budget submission (also compiled in January 1874) added one new unnamed 1st rank ironclad at Toulon which became *Foudroyant*. The January 1875 fleet list added two more, *Dévastation* at Lorient and *Duguesclin* by contract, and the 1876 budget submission (May 1875) added an unnamed ship at Brest while omitting the name of the contract ship. The January 1876 fleet list dropped the contract ship. The 1877 budget submission (March 1876) showed *Dévastation* as to be 17% built at the beginning of 1877, the unnamed contract ship at 20%, and the unnamed Brest ship at 0%. The January 1877 fleet list added *Amiral Duperré*, which was probably the unnamed contract ship in the previous budgets and the *Duguesclin* of the January 1875 fleet list. The 1878 budget (also January 1877) showed the Brest ship at 2% at the beginning of 1878. *Amiral Baudin* probably took her place under the name *Infernal* in the 1879 budget (April 1878).

---

*DÉVASTATION* Class. *Cuirassés de 1er rang*. Central battery ironclads with two upper deck half turrets and guns under the forecastle and on the stern, a steel and iron hull, and a ram bow. Two funnels abreast amidships. *Dévastation* completed with three wooden masts and a full ship rig as in *Redoutable*, *Courbet* completed with three steel masts with armed tops and a schooner rig. Designed by de Bussy.

The *Conseil des travaux* examined de Bussy's design for the new 1st rank central battery ironclad on 16 March 1875. He was able to reduce the draught aft from 8.40m to 7.80m and he increased the belt to 400mm amidships, but the 18.40m width of the battery was insufficient to allow manoeuvring the 320mm guns and the Council ordered it to be increased to 19.50m. The armament was four 320mm M1870 guns in the battery, two 274.4mm/18 M1870M guns in half turrets above them, and eight 138.6mm/21.3 M1870 guns. The Council specified that the two forward 138.6mm guns should be under the forecastle. The Council also considered it indispensable to have the armoured deck inside as well as outside the central battery at the cost of a reduction in its overall thickness. Finally the shallower draught aft made it harder to get the rudder to function properly and to protect it, and the Council insisted on the replacement of the single screw with twin screws. In the modified design examined by the Council on 4 January 1876 the maximum belt armour was reduced to 380mm and the deck consisted of 60mm of armour plate on 20mm deck plating. *Dévastation* and *Courbet* (named *Foudroyant* until 1885) were begun to plans signed by de Bussy on 3 May 1876 and approved by Minister of Marine Vice Admiral Martin Fourichon on 11 May 1876. The ships were later given 340mm/18 M1875 guns in the central battery instead of the 320mm guns and an additional two 274.4mm/18 M1870M guns at the ends, the forward one replacing the two 138.6mm that the Council had placed under the forecastle and the after one replacing in May 1880 a 240mm gun that had previously been put there.

The trials of *Dévastation* began in late 1881 and she was placed in full commission on 15 July 1882. The combination of twin screws, a single rudder, and a flat bottom made her a challenge to steer, in contrast with *Redoutable* which with a single screw acting directly on a single rudder had an excellent reputation for holding a course and turning in tight circles. On the other hand *Dévastation* was an excellent gun platform. It was found to be very difficult to manoeuvre the 340mm guns in her battery, but this

The 1st rank ironclad *Dévastation* as completed with a full ship rig, which was soon reduced. She and her near sister *Courbet* were essentially improved versions of *Redoutable*. The central battery and the tumblehome of the sides of the ship are particularly evident here. *(NHHC from ONI album of French warships, NH-74911)*

problem was solved by adding hydraulic mountings between December 1882 and June 1883. *Courbet* was nearly identical to *Dévastation* except for some conspicuous details in appearance, including more dramatically curved bulwarks on the forecastle, a circular unarmoured barbette or tub for the after gun extending over the sides, and slightly raked funnels in each of which a pair of uptakes projected slightly above the casing. She also was completed with a later model of 340mm guns than her near sister. *Courbet* was commissioned for trials on 1 August 1885, began receiving her guns in December, and was placed in full commission on 1 October 1886 before the end of her trials which continued to March 1887. *Dévastation* was completed with a full ship rig but was soon reduced to a barque. In 1887 the wood masts of *Dévastation* were replaced with steel, most of the yardarms were removed, the bowsprit was replaced with a light pole, and each mast was fitted with two military tops. *Courbet* completed with this rig, although her tops were lower.

**Overhaul of *Courbet* at Toulon, 1897.** Between April and June 1897 the boilers of *Courbet* were replaced with others of the same type, the shields on the guns in the half-turrets were replaced with vertical plates in front of them, the conning tower was replaced with one with 80mm armour, and the Bullivant nets and the forward pair of torpedo tubes was removed. A full rearming planned for 1898 at Toulon was deferred after Lockroy replaced Besnard as minister and the ship was sent instead to Brest with the other old battleships at Toulon in September 1898.

*Dévastation* ceased to operate with the main fleet in mid-1897 because of her need for modernization. This, which included new boilers and a new armament, was scheduled to begin in 1900 at Toulon. She was instead sent to Brest in 1898 and her middle mast and bowsprit were removed there in October, the mast being replaced with a ventilator. She was placed in reserve there in October 1899 to await the completion of *Courbet*'s reconstruction.

**Overhaul of *Courbet* at Brest, 1899-1900.** *Courbet* was modified at Brest between September 1899 and December 1900. Her bowsprit and main-mast were removed and the other two masts were replaced with military masts each with two tops. The three 274.4mm guns on the upper deck were replaced with three 240mm/40 M1893 guns with new shields, and the 274.4mm gun under the forecastle was replaced with a 138.6mm/30 M1881/84 QF gun.

**Overhaul of *Dévastation* at Brest, 1900-1902.** The ship's long-awaited modifications finally began at Brest in May 1900 and were completed in March 1902. Work included replacing some of her belt armour with plates that were thinner but just as effective, replacing much of the wooden super-structure decks with metal, and replacing the foremast with a military mast and the mizzen mast with a pole mast with a searchlight platform but no fighting tops. The four 320mm guns in the battery were replaced with four 274.4mm M1893 guns and the four 274.4mm and six 138.6mm guns on the upper deck were replaced with two 240mm M1893-96 in the half turrets and ten 100mm M1891 and M1892. She was also given new Belleville boilers.

The rearmaments of these two ships were planned and first approved in early 1897 to be done at Toulon. At that time *Courbet* was to have had her 340mm battery guns replaced with 274.4mm/25 M1893 guns and *Dévastation* was to have had her 320mm battery guns replaced with 274.4mm M1875 guns taken from the deck positions on *Courbet*. After the ships were moved to Brest the programme was curtailed, and the 340mm battery guns of *Courbet* were left in place while *Dévastation* received the 274.4mm/25 M1893 that were to have gone to *Courbet*. It made little difference as neither ship had much service life left. *Dévastation* was recommissioned for trials on 10 March 1902 but never went back into full commission for operational service, and *Courbet* left the Escadre du Nord for the last time in March 1903.

*The characteristics are based on a devis for* Dévastation *dated 25.7.1882.*

**Dimensions & tons:** 100.52m oa, 96.39m wl (+3.75m ram), 94.44m pp (wl fwd to rudder) x 20.45m wl (21.26m over the battery). 10,096t disp (full load). Draught: 7.808m mean, 8.10m aft. Men: 721.

**Machinery:** 1,500nhp and 6,000ihp designed at 72rpm and 4.133kg/cm² boiler pressure. Trials (*Dévastation*, 23.3.1882) 8,350ihp = 15.17kts at 77.95/77.4rpm (stbd/port), 4.62kg/cm² boiler pressure. 2 screws. 2 vertical compound (Woolf) engines with 3 cylinders of 1.55m (1) and 2.00m (2) diameter and 1.00m stroke. (Steam entered the smaller middle cylinder and exhausted to the two larger ones.) 12 elliptical boilers. 574t coal. Range 3,100nm @ 10kts. In 1902 *Dévastation*'s machinery was replaced by 2 vertical triple expansion engines and 12 Belleville boilers.

**Armour:** (iron)
Side: Belt at waterline 380mm amidships, 220mm fwd, 300mm aft.

The 1st rank ironclad *Courbet* alongside the citadel at Brest following her reconstruction in that port in 1899-1900. Two long 240mm/40 M1893 guns were placed on top of the central battery and a third on the stern, but the old short 340mm/21 M1881 guns in the battery were retained. This photo was originally attached to the technical characteristics document for the ship. (*Feuille signalétique for the ship*)

Height from 1.95m below the wl to 0.85m above.
Guns: Central battery 240mm sides, 300mm bulkheads. Guns on upper deck unprotected.
Deck: flat 60mm amidships and ends.
Conning tower: original shelter replaced 1897 (*Courbet*) and 1901 (*Dévastation*) with one with 60mm special steel plus 20mm plating

**Guns:** (*Dévastation*)
(1884) 4 x 340mm/18 M1875 in the battery, 4 x 274.4mm/18 M1870M on the upper deck (2 in half turrets, 1 under the forecastle and 1 on deck aft), 6 x 138.6mm/21.3 M1870M (one each side forward of the battery and two per side aft of it), 8 x 37mm Hotchkiss revolving cannon (increased to 16 in 1882-83). **Torpedoes:** 4 tubes for 356mm torpedoes on the sides above water, two forward and two aft (although the forward pair were unusable because of the bow wave from the ram). **Searchlights:** 4 x 40cm, replaced with 4 x 60cm 1882-83.
(1889-90) The 4 x 340mm/18 M1875 in the battery were replaced with 4 x 320mm/25 M1870-81 and 4 x 47mm and 2 x 37mm revolving cannon were added.
(1896) 4 x 320mm, 4 x 274.4mm, 6 x 138.6mm, 2 x 65mm, 6 x 47mm/40 M1885 QF, 1 x 47mm revolving cannon for the pinnace, 20 x 37mm revolving cannon.
(1902) 4 x 274.4mm/25 M1893 in the battery, 2 x 240mm/40 M1893-96 in the half turrets above it, 10 x 100mm/45 M1891 & 1892 (8 on the upper deck near the battery, one aft and one under the forecastle), 14 x 47mm QF, 2 x 37mm/20 M1885 QF in the tops. The ship also had an allowance of 6 x 47mm QF and 2 x 37mm QF for the boats and landing force. The two forward torpedo tubes were removed.

**Guns:** (*Courbet*)
(Original) 4 x 340mm/21 M1881 (2 tubed and 2 not tubed) in the battery, 4 x 274.4mm/19.75 M1875 No 1 (2 in half turrets on top of the battery, 1 under the forecastle and 1 on deck aft, although the latter two were still M1870 in 1884), 6 x 138.6mm/30 M1881 BLR, 2 x 65mm landing M1881, 1 x 47mm revolving cannon for the pinnace, 18 x 37mm revolving cannon. **Torpedoes:** 5 tubes for 356mm torpedoes (two forward and two aft on the sides and one in the stern, all above water).
(1894) 4 x 340mm/21 M1881, 4 x 274.4/19.75 M1875M, 10 x 138.6mm/30 M1881/84 QF, 2 x 65mm/16 M1881 landing, 14 x 47mm/40 M1885 QF, 1 x 47mm revolving cannon for the pinnace, 18 x 37mm/20 M1885 QF, 7 x 37mm revolving cannon.

(1897) The upper tops on the fore and mizzen masts and the lower main
top were disarmed, deleting 8 x 37mm, and the forward two torpedo
tubes were deleted.

(1900, after rearmament) 4 x 340mm/21 M1881, 3 x 240mm/40
M1893, 11 x 138.6mm/30 M1881/84 QF, 2 x 65mm/16 M1881
landing, 16 x 47mm QF, 2 x 37mm QF, 8 x 37mm revolving cannon,
3 torpedo tubes.

*Courbet* Toulon Dyd/Indret.

On list 1.1874. K: 19.7.1875. L: 27.4.1882. Comm: 1.8.1885 (trials),
1.10.1886 (full).

Budget 1875. Originally named *Foudroyant*, renamed *Courbet* 24.6.1885
(published 25.6), 14 days after the death of the admiral who had led
the China campaign. Ready for sea (*mis sur rade*) 22.4.1886. Assigned
to the *Escadre d'évolutions* at Toulon 1.11.1886. Trials completed
18.3.1887. Reboilered 1897. Artillery modified 2.1898. To Brest
9.1898, rebuilt 9.1899 to 12.1900, remained at Brest until placed in
reserve there 1904. Decomm. 21.10.1908. Struck 5.2.1909, sold
25.7.1910 to BU.

*Dévastation* Lorient Dyd-Caudan/Indret.

On list 1.1875. K: 20.12.1875. L: 19.8.1879. Comm: 10.6.1880 (trials),
15.7.1882 (full).

Budget 1876. Trials fall 1881 to 3.1882. Left Brest for Toulon 20.1.1885,
arrived and joined the *Escadre d'évolutions* 31.1.1885. Mainmast
removed 12.1898 at Brest. Reboilered 1901. Struck 5.2.1909, annex to
the 2nd depot for sailors of the fleet (*dépôt des équipages de la flotte*) at
Brest 1909-1910, school for engineers 1910-1911, annex to
*Châteaurenault* and school for boatswains at Brest 1911-1912, definitively out of service 4.1913 and towed first to Landévennec and then
to Lorient for use in torpedo trials scheduled for 7.1914. Used as a
prison hulk at Lorient for prisoners of war from 10.1914 to 1919.
Sold 5.1921 to a Paris firm which resold her to a firm in Hamburg,
Germany. Towed out of Lorient by the Germans on 7.5.1922 with the
hulk of *Tonnerre* to BU in Hamburg but went hard aground on the
way out of Lorient. Finally refloated in an epic salvage operation
4.1927 and beached near Port Louis where she was BU.

*N* (unnamed) Brest Dyd.

Budget 1876 (delayed to 1878, then replaced by *Amiral Baudin*).

---

**AMIRAL DUPERRÉ.** *Cuirassé de 1er rang.* Ironclad battleship with four
barbettes (two abreast forward and two on the centreline behind them),
iron armour, a steel and iron hull, and a ram bow. Two funnels abreast,
three masts, schooner rig. Designed by Sabattier.

A 1st rank ironclad to be built by contract appeared on the fleet list for the
first time in January 1875 with the name *Duguesclin*, which was soon reassigned to a 2nd rank ironclad. The contract ship remained in the
programme without a name until, just after the construction contract was
signed, she appeared in the January 1877 fleet list named for Guy Victor
Duperré, Amiral of France and Minister of Marine three times between
1834 and 1843. She was the first French 1st rank ironclad to be built by
contract.

The origins of *Amiral Duperré* probably go back to the *décuirassement*
discussions of 1871 and 1872. At that time it was proposed to concentrate
all of the armour of 1st rank ironclads on the waterline and armoured deck
and delete the armour protection for the guns. The main guns would all be
on the upper deck in open unarmoured barbettes. On 20 October 1873
Minister of Marine Dompierre d'Hornoy charged the *Conseil des travaux* to
draft two sets of specifications for 1st rank ironclads, one with and one
without an armoured central battery, using sketches provided by Sabattier,
the Director of Materiel. On 21 November 1873 the Council approved
specifications for both types in which most characteristics were the same

including the weight of the armour. In the alternative specifications the
elimination of the central battery armour allowed increasing the maximum
thickness of the belt armour to 480mm from 350mm and the average
thickness of the armoured lower deck to 60mm from 50mm. The large
guns were all on the upper deck, the four 320mm guns being mounted in
open barbettes with two amidships on the centreline and two side by side
forward of the funnel with axial fire forward. One 274.4mm was mounted
on a forecastle and one on a poop. The only protection for these guns was
thin plating forming a shield (*masque*) or barbette. Six 138.6mm were also
placed on the upper deck, forecastle, or poop as space was available. The
ship was to have a complete *entrepont* (deck level) above the armour belt
with a height of 2.35m to help give the guns above it the specified height
above the water (7.15m for the amidships barbette guns).

While the specifications for the central battery ship were turned into the
design of the *Dévastation* class and examined several times by the *Conseil des
travaux*, the Council never saw a design for a barbette ship based on the
alternative specifications. Director of Materiel Sabattier, however, needed a
design for the contract ship in the budgets and produced one for a barbette
ship that was quite similar to the 1873 specifications. He made three important changes: he included narrow (1.80m wide) but thick (300mm) bands
of armour around the barbettes for the big guns, he omitted the 274.4mm
guns at the ends along with the poop, and he put a large battery of 138.6mm
guns in the *entrepont*, restoring it to its traditional function as a gun battery
deck. Even with the restored barbette armour he was able to provide thicker
belt armour than in the specifications, 550mm maximum instead of the
480mm specified and the 350mm in the latest central battery design.

Sabattier signed a full set of plans for a 1st rank ironclad with barbettes
on 8 March 1876. He presented a later set of plans to Minister of Marine
Fourichon with a minute dated 5 August 1876 explaining his ideas behind
it. The ship needed the maximum possible belt armour to prevent penetrations by heavy artillery that could sink the ship and substantial deck
armour (neglected in ships before *Redoutable*) to protect the underwater
portion of the ship including the machinery and magazines from plunging
fire. For the guns, foreign powers were turning to heavily armoured
enclosed turrets, which were admirably suited to protect the guns and their
crews but which made it hard for gun captains to see the target and fire at
the most opportune time. 'From this point of view, the French "armoured
turret", which consists of a highly mobile gun in a barbette with a large arc
of fire, has always been preferred by the majority of our officers.... While
the crews and the guns are less well protected, on the other hand the blows
will be better delivered.' Sabattier's memorandum carefully assessed the use
of a partial belt and unarmoured ends with cellular subdivision as the
British were doing but opted for the complete belt instead.

Sabattier asked Minister of Marine Fourichon to approve the design so
that contract negotiations could begin, and Fourichon did so on 5 August
1876. Both officials followed the practice of Sabattier's predecessor, Dupuy
de Lôme, and did not refer the personal work of the Director of Materiel
to the *Conseil des travaux* for its opinion. Some of the changes made to de
Bussy's *Dévastation*, however, also appeared in this ship, notably the adoption of twin screws. The contract for the hull and armour was signed on
4 December 1876 and approved on 7 December 1876.

*Amiral Duperré* entered service with three masts, the foremast of steel
and the other two of wood, each with a topmast and one small square yard
and rigged for a fore and aft sail, plus a two-piece bowsprit. On
18 November 1884 Minister of Marine Vice Admiral Alexandre Louis
François Peyron approved new steel tubular masts for the main and mizzen
and double tops for all 3 masts, and on 11 February 1885 he ordered installation of a 164.7mm/30 light (*léger*) M1884 gun under the forecastle in
place of the single 37mm revolving cannon there and a new single-piece
bowsprit to accommodate it. On 13 December 1888 the breech blew off
the amidships 340mm gun during an exercise in the Mediterranean killing
6 men. On 11 March 1889 (two days before his death) Minister of Marine
Vice Admiral Constant Louis Benjamin Jaurès directed replacing the three
340mm/18 M1875 guns in the side and amidships barbette turrets with

The 1st rank ironclad *Amiral Duperré* after being re-rigged in 1885. She was essentially an equivalent to the *Dévastation* type with her main battery in open-topped barbettes on deck instead of in a heavily armoured central battery. This, combined with her narrow but thick waterline armour belt, set the pattern for future French battleships, although her armour was still made of iron. *(NHHC from Farenholt collection, previously ONI, NH-66056)*

three 340mm/21 M1881 guns. This was done during a refit from December 1890 to February 1892 that also included new boilers. In January 1894 the fourteen 138.6mm BL guns in the battery were replaced with fourteen 100mm QF guns, and by January 1895 a 340mm/21 gun had taken the place of the 340mm/18 gun in the after barbette turret.

In his cruise report dated 15 October 1897 the ship's commander wrote that the rate of fire of the big guns was 'desperately slow', between 7 and 15 minutes per round with 10 minutes a safe average. One pump served the pressurized water mechanism that pointed and loaded all four guns. The guns could not be moved simultaneously, they had to be loaded on the centreline, and their mechanisms broke down frequently. The 164.7mm gun in the bow loaded slowly (2 minutes) and its field of fire and those of the battery 100mm guns were slight.

**Proposed overhauls.** A plan by Besnard's Ministry dated 4 May 1897 for modifications to the older battleships specified for *Amiral Duperré* the replacement of the boilers with water tube boilers, removal of the amidships 340mm barbette turret, installation of four 164.7mm M1893

QF guns in an armoured redoubt, and removal of four 100mm guns from the battery. It also included a new conning tower with 60mm special steel plus 20mm plating which had already been fabricated. On 8 August 1898 the Ministry asked Brest for a proposal for modifications to the ship, which was then being transferred there from Toulon, and on 15 February 1899 it also directed the replacement of the 164.7mm gun under the forecastle by two 100mm guns taken from the battery. On 18 May 1899 Brest reported that the battery for the 164.7mm guns could not be installed on the upper deck as in *Amiral Baudin* because the forward pair of 340mm barbettes obstructed lines of fire forward and that the redoubt would have to be put on the battery deck directly under the forward barbettes. However, to preserve the trim of the ship the forward barbettes with the 164.7mm battery under them would have to be moved 11.5m aft. The archives contain a sketch plan by Émile Bertin, chief of the *Section technique*, dated 7 August 1900 with an even more ambitious reconstruction plan, showing the ship with single guns (probably 305mm) in new enclosed turrets at each end, four guns (probably 164.7mm) in a battery amidships with two more in small turrets on top, and four guns (probably 138.6mm) in the bow and two in the stern. On 28 March 1901 the Ministry asked Brest to prepare plans for a refit in which the amidships barbette was to be removed, in part to lighten the ship and get the armoured deck above the waterline, but no other changes to the armament were to be made. Brest produced the refit plan on 14 August 1901 and Minister of Marine Jean Marie Antoine de Lanessan approved it on 28 November 1901, but ultimately the only part of the refit that was carried out was the removal of the mainmast. In

Photograph of a model of a proposed reconstruction of *Amiral Duperré* attached to a 55-page report from the Direction of Naval Construction at Brest dated 18 May 1899, written by naval constructor Bahon in response to a ministerial dispatch of 8 August 1898. The proposal involved removing the amidships 340mm barbette and moving the forward pair of barbettes back, which was ultimately considered to be not worth the cost.

1903 it was proposed to convert *Amiral Duperré* to a gunnery school ship with two 340mm and smaller new model guns to replace *Couronne*, but this also was not pursued.

*The characteristics are based on a devis dated 21.4.1883.*

**Dimensions & tons:** 101.60m oa, 96.97m wl (+4.57m ram), 94.36m pp (wl fwd to rudder) x 20.40m ext, 20.30m wl. 11,086t disp. Draught: 8.20m mean, 8.43m aft. Men: 712.

**Machinery:**
(Devis 21.4.1883): 1,500nhp and 7,500ihp designed at 70.0rpm and 4.133kg/cm² boiler pressure. Trials (21.12.1882) 7,357ihp = 14.325kts at 73.897rpm and 4.268kg/cm² boiler pressure, (19.2.1887) 5,958.55ihp = 13.367kts at 68.84rpm. 2 screws. 2 vertical compound engines with 3 cylinders of 1.55m (1) and 2.00m (2) diameter and 1.00m stroke. 12 high cylindrical return flame boilers. 693t coal. Range 2,850nm @ 10kts.
(Devis 9.5.1892): 8,125ihp designed at 78rpm and 4.250kg/cm² boiler pressure. Trials (29.3.1892) 7778.65ihp = 14.098kts at 74.7rpm. 12 new elliptical tubular return-flame boilers.

**Armour:** (iron)
Side: Belt at waterline 550mm amidships tapering to 250mm fwd and aft. Height from 2.05m below the wl to 0.41m above.
Guns: Barbettes 300mm, hoods 15mm steel (in 1895), ammunition tubes five layers of 20mm plating.
Deck: flat 60mm iron amidships and ends on 150mm wood and 20mm steel plating.
Conning tower: originally a 30mm kiosk on the bridge containing a compass and voice tubes but without room for enough personnel, later 40mm steel.

**Guns:**
(1883) 4 x 340mm/18 M1875 in barbette turrets on the upper deck, 14 x 138.6mm/21.3 M1870 in the battery, 1 x 90mm/22 M1881, 2 x 65mm/15 bronze landing, 12 x 37mm revolving cannon of which one was under the forecastle. **Torpedoes:** 4 tubes for 356mm M1880 torpedoes (2 on the sides and 2 aft). **Searchlights:** 2 x 60cm.
(1887) 4 x 340mm, 1 x 164.7mm/28 M1881 No 2 (light model, under the forecastle), 14 x 138.6mm, 2 x 65mm/16 M1881 steel landing, 18 x 37mm revolving cannon. 4 torpedo tubes. 4 x 60cm searchlights.
(1892) 4 x 340mm (3 x 340mm/21 M1881 short (*court*) model and 1 x 340mm M1875/18), 1 x 164.7mm, 14 x 138.6mm, 2 x 65mm/50 M1891 QF, 2 x 65mm/16 M1881 steel landing, 2 x 47mm/40 M1885

QF, 18 x 37mm revolving cannon, 16 x 37mm/20 M1885 QF. 4 torpedo tubes (updated). 6 searchlights.
(1895) 4 x 340mm/21 M1881 (turrets), 1 x 164.7mm, 14 x 100mm QF (battery), 2 x 65mm QF, 2 x 65mm landing, 6 x 47mm QF, 16 x 37mm QF, 18 x 37mm revolving cannon. 4 tubes for M1885 torpedoes.
(1901) 4 x 340mm (turrets), 1 x 164.7mm, 14 x 100mm QF, 2 x 65mm, 12 x 47mm, 8 x 37mm revolving cannon. 4 torpedo tubes of old model without protection.

*Amiral Duperré* F.C. Méditerranée, La Seyne/FCM, Marseille (engines designed by Orsel).
On list 1.1875. Ord: 4.12.1876 (contract, approved 7.12.1876). K: 1877. L: 11.9.1879. Comm: 1.5.1881 (trials), 17.4.1883 (full).
Budget 1876. On list 1.1875 as *Duguesclin*, 1.1877 as *Amiral Duperré*. Machinery installed 2.11.1879 to 11.5.1881. Commissioned for trials 1.5.1881 with 99 men, in trials 20.11.1882. Joined the *Escadre d'évolutions* at Toulon 22.4.1883. Boilers repaired 1886-1887, new boilers by FCM installed 23.1.1892. At Toulon until 1898 when reassigned with other old battleships to the *Escadre du Nord*, to reserve at Brest early 1901, back to Toulon 11.1903 for dockyard work, decomm. at Toulon 20.9.1905. Struck 13.8.1906, condemned 21.12.1906 for use as a target. Sunk as target c31.8.1908, refloated, sunk again c26.9. 1908 in the rade de la Badine near Hyères, wreck to Domaines for sale 24.11.1908, sold 27.4.1909 to M. Giardino of Marseille to BU.

**Monster guns**
On 14 April 1877 Minister of Marine Fourichon asked the *Conseil des travaux* for its advice on whether France should compete in the race of ever increasing calibres for large guns and how large would be enough. The Navy's largest gun was then the 50-ton 340mm gun. The Council examined the matter on 1 May 1877 and noted that an 81-ton gun had been fired in England, a 100-ton gun had been tried in Italy, Armstrong was building a 160-ton gun, and Krupp was said to be working on a 220-ton gun. The Council reported that it saw no other weapon that could offset the importance of large guns (the torpedo, by deterring ramming, simply enhanced it) and felt France needed to keep up. It noted that on 20 November 1876 the Inspector General of Artillery had proposed to Minister Fourichon to build guns of at least 100 tons. It noted that the heaviest armour then in preparation was 610mm and it recommended as a reasonable objective a gun of around 120 tons and 440mm bore (probably a 17.6-inch gun with a 2,420 pound projectile), which could penetrate up to 780mm armour with a direct hit and 630mm with an oblique hit.

*AMIRAL BAUDIN* Class. *Cuirassés de 1er rang.* Battleships with three centreline barbettes, steel armour, a steel and iron hull, and a ram bow. One funnel, two light military masts (one heavy in *Formidable*), no sails. Designed by Godron.

The 1878 budget (submitted in January 1877) carried over one unnamed battleship at Brest from the 1876 and 1877 budgets and added one new unnamed battleship at Lorient. The 1879 budget (April 1878) showed these as *Infernal* at Brest and *Formidable* at Lorient, both to be begun during 1879. The 1880 budget (January 1879) showed them as *Amiral Baudin* at Brest and *Formidable* at Lorient, to be 7.8% and 12.1% built at the start of 1880.

In a circular of 19 January 1878 Minister of Marine Pothuau, who had returned to the Ministry in December 1877, sent to the ports general specifications for a new 1st rank ironclad with a request that constructors send designs. The ship was to have 75-ton or 100-ton guns with single guns in barbettes or twin guns in enclosed turrets, both with 550mm of armour. The maximum belt thickness was also to be 550mm with armour either tapering towards the ends or replaced there with a cellular structure. Speed was to be 14.5 knots with twin screws, and sails were to be omitted. The *Conseil des travaux* examined seven designs on 30 July 1878 and chose the only one with its guns in barbettes. (The others had four 100-ton guns in two enclosed turrets). This design, by naval constructor Charles Alexandre Paul Godron, had three 100-ton guns in barbettes on the centreline. Some felt that the torpedo had reduced the value of the ram and of head-on artillery fire and restored the importance of broadside fire. Godron's design also included a complete armour belt with an armoured deck on top and a strong secondary battery of twelve 138.6mm guns. The Council objected to the 50cm height above the water of the top of his belt and stated that it had to be increased to at least 90cm before it could be accepted. Minister Pothuau approved the Council's selection of Godron's design for further development on 7 September 1878 and on 20 September charged him to prepare a new design with specified changes. Godron signed his revised design on 6 November 1878 and on 13 December 1878 Sabattier

The battleship *Amiral Baudin* in her original configuration before the addition of 164.7mm guns in sponsons near the ends of the ship in 1892-93. The masthead tops in her early-model military masts were accessed in the old manner via external ratlines. This photo was received by ONI in 1891. *(NHHC from Farenholt collection, previously ONI, NH-66054)*

presented it to Pothuau, noting that its hull dimensions were nearly the same as the British *Inflexible* but its upper works were much larger giving more space for a flag and the crew, the height above the water of its guns was 8.35m against 3.35m for the British ship, and it had a substantial 138.6mm secondary battery. Minister Pothuau approved it and sent it to Brest and Lorient on 13 December 1878 with instructions to begin construction. On 16 December 1878 the ministry's Directorate of Materiel informed the Directorate of Artillery that 100-ton guns would be needed for these ships.

The Directorate of Artillery was then developing the 75-ton 420mm Model 1875 steel gun for use in the *Indomptable* class coast defence ships and also as a step towards producing a 100-ton gun. Construction of steel guns was in its infancy, however, and so many problems were encountered in the production of the 75-ton gun that the Navy abandoned the attempt to build the 100-ton gun. By August 1880 the decision had been made to replace the 100-ton guns in the *Baudin* class with an entirely new type of gun, the 370mm 28 calibre 75-ton Model 1875-79. This, the only Model 1875-79 gun produced, was the Navy's first large gun in which an early type of slow-burning powder and a longer bore combined to produce less stress on the breech while accelerating the projectile to greater velocities and penetrating power than the old black powder Model 1875 guns could provide. The first drawings for this gun were approved on 30 August 1880 and plans for the turrets and ammunition tubes of *Amiral Baudin* were

approved on 9 September 1880. Eight guns of this type were ordered, four from Saint-Chamond for *Formidable* and four by a contract of 26 January 1881 from Schneider at Creusot for *Amiral Baudin*, including one spare for each ship. The weapons built by the two foundries differed considerably in their details, with the result that *Formidable* got guns weighing 76.28 tons while those of *Amiral Baudin* weighed only 72.58 tons. The 370mm Model 1875-79 gun proved to be an interim step to a large family of Model 1881 guns designed on the same principles but with numerous refinements. In another retreat from monster guns the largest Model 1881 gun was a 340mm 28.5 calibre 52-ton weapon. On 30 June 1881 Minister of Marine Vice Admiral Georges Charles Cloué decided to stop the construction of the 370mm guns ordered from Creusot and replace them with new 340mm M1881 guns. This 340mm gun was used in the next four battleships, but the decision on the Creusot contract was eventually rescinded and on 26 June 1882 the firm of Joseph Farcot at Saint Ouen received a contract for the hydraulic equipment and rotating platforms for the 370mm guns of both *Formidable* and *Amiral Baudin*.

The *Baudin* class also introduced steel armour into the French battle line. Schneider at Creusot had specialized in steel armour since the mid-1870s claiming that it would be lighter and stronger than the compound armour (iron armour with a layer of steel bonded on top) then being introduced by the British and by other French firms. Schneider developed a hammering process to counter the main weakness of steel, its inherent brittleness. In 1880 the Navy gave Schneider a contract for steel armour for the coast defence ship *Terrible* to encourage further development and on 31 May 1882 it approved a contract with Schneider for armour for belt and barbettes for the coast defence ship *Furieux*. On 7 July 1882 the Navy began negotiations with that firm for steel armour for the belts of the two *Baudins*, and the contract was approved on 6 September 1882. Compound armour was supplied by Châtillon-Commentry for the barbettes in both ships. Despite a major success by Schneider's steel armour in competitive trials at La Spezia at the end of 1882, compound and steel armour continued to be considered roughly equivalent until the introduction of nickel steel at the end of the 1880s and the Harvey face hardening process in the early 1890s. Iron continued to be used for deck armour, where softness was a virtue, until the introduction of extra mild steel in the early 1890s.

Indret proposed using engines practically identical to those of *Dévastation* for *Amiral Baudin*, and Minister of Marine Cloué approved the order probably in early May 1881. Engines for *Formidable* were ordered from Schneider by a contract signed on 18 October 1880 and approved on 5 November 1880.

The ships were designed with two slender steel military masts with armed tops supported and accessed by means of external rigging that limited the arcs of fire of some of the guns and had to be dismantled when clearing for action. On 19 October 1886 the *Conseil des travaux* examined a proposal from the *Escadre d'évolutions* to use tripod masts with command platforms in battleships, and the Council recommended instead steel masts of large diameter with spiral staircases and ammunition hoists on the inside, armed tops and command platforms, and no external rigging. On 8 February 1887 it examined a proposal from Lorient for changes to *Formidable* that included two of the new military masts, but the 38-ton weight of the mast was unacceptable and the Council retained only the forward new military mast, along with the original thin mainmast. Brest made no similar proposal for *Amiral Baudin* and she retained her original rig. The two ships, which had different boiler installations, could also be distinguished by their funnels, *Formidable* having one that looked much larger than that of her sister because it was taller and its outer casing rose all the way to the top instead of partway up.

On 15 August 1889 the Commander in Chief of the *Escadre de la Méditerranée* reminded Minister of Marine Vice Admiral Jules François Émile Krantz that he had conducted trials on both *Amiral Baudin* and *Formidable* that had shown that the 138.6mm guns could not be manned at the same time as the 370mm guns. He had placed sheep where the 138.6mm gun crews would be located and they were thrown onto the deck by the blast

from the big guns and some received internal injuries. He felt that currently the secondary battery could be used only intermittently and that if the secondary battery were to be enlarged locations had to be found where its guns would be protected against blast effects. To resolve this problem the size of the gun ports was reduced (at the end of 1889 in *Formidable*).

As of 1 October 1895 the 370mm guns in *Formidable* could fire once every 7 minutes. Her 164.7mm BLR and 138.6mm BLR could fire about one round per minute. By April 1903 installation of new ways of opening the breech and loading the gun by hand had speeded up the rate of fire of the main battery in *Formidable* from 7m50s with the old hydraulic system to 3m20s.

**Updated secondary batteries, 1890-93.** Concerned over the lack of axial fire from these ships, Minister of Marine Senator Édouard Barbey on 28 January 1890 directed that four sponsons be added near the ends of each ship for 164.7mm guns and that the single 138.6mm guns in the bow and stern be replaced by two 47mm QF guns. The change was made to *Formidable* between October 1891 and October 1892 giving her a secondary battery of four 164mm M1884 and ten 138.6mm M1881 slow-fire breech loaders. *Amiral Baudin* entered the Toulon Dockyard on 24 October 1892 for a refit that ended in June 1893. By then quick fire guns were available, and she received four 164.7mm QF and ten 138.6mm QF, along with the necessary modifications to the magazines and hoists for their munitions. The commander of *Formidable* resisted the conversion of her guns to quick fire, arguing in part that the battery, already completely unprotected against raking fire, especially with the enormous openings of the new 164.7mm sponsons, would be even more vulnerable if it contained hoists loaded with munitions. In August 1895 Minister of Marine Vice Admiral Armand Louis Charles Gustave Besnard directed that the change in *Formidable*'s artillery be made as soon as possible after *Brennus* joined the *Escadre de la Méditerranée*, but it would also be necessary to remove some of the excess weight on the ship which was bringing the top of her belt and her armoured deck unacceptably close to the waterline.

**Overhauls, 1896-1899.** A study by Toulon in May 1896 just after Vice Admiral Besnard became Minister indicated that the only way to make a significant impact on the excess weight in *Formidable* was to modify the main artillery. Under the final version of this plan, applied to both ships, the amidships 370mm barbette and the 164.7mm sponsons near the ends of the ships were removed and an armoured redoubt was added on each side amidships each containing two casemates for the 164.7mm guns displaced from the battery. Two 138.6mm guns was also to be deleted. Both ships were also to receive new elliptical boilers of the types originally installed. Work on *Formidable* was already underway at Toulon in November 1896

The battleship *Formidable* after modernization, with the amidships barbette replaced with a casemate containing the four 164.7mm guns that had previously been in hull sponsons. During construction she received a later-model military foremast in which the tops were accessed by a spiral ladder inside the larger-diameter mast. Her early-model military mainmast was cut down during her 1896-99 modernization. *(Postcard by Ed Revin, Villefranche)*

and she test fired her new guns in August 1897. Work on *Amiral Baudin* began after the ship was transferred from Toulon to Brest in 1897. She had been scheduled since 25 April 1896 to receive updated military masts, and on 13 August 1897 Brest proposed giving her as a foremast the military mast that they were removing from the cruiser *Isly* and replacing the upper part of the existing mainmast with a simple pole. Her funnel was also raised 2.50m. The forward military mast of *Formidable* was left essentially unchanged but her mainmast was reduced as in *Amiral Baudin*. Time was needed to produce the armour for the new 164.7mm redoubts, it was fitted in *Amiral Baudin* at Brest at the end of 1898 and in *Formidable* there in early 1899. Each redoubt was armoured on the front, rear, and outboard side, though the inboard side and the top and bottom were unprotected.

This was intended to be the first phase of a two phase modernization, the second phase replacing the remaining two 370mm guns and their barbettes with two 305mm guns in single turrets and upgrading the four 164.7mm to M1893 guns. Minister of Marine Besnard however on 23 June 1897 had the second phase deleted from a refit programme then being drafted and on 31 January 1898 the Director of Materiel informed the Director of Artillery that it would not happen for six years. The second phase was absent from a report from the naval staff approved by Minister of Marine Lanessan on 27 July 1899. The possible replacement of the 370mm guns in both ships by 305mm guns was mentioned again in 1901 but was not pursued.

*The characteristics are based on a devis for* Amiral Baudin *dated 1.2.1889.*
**Dimensions & tons:** 104.650m oa, 100.40m wl (+4.00m ram), 98.000m pp (wl fwd to rudder), 102.00m pp (tip fwd to rudder) x 21.240m ext & wl. 11,910.705t disp. Draught: 8.244m mean, 8.46m aft. Men: 517.

**Machinery:**
(*Amiral Baudin*) 2,000nhp and 8,000ihp designed at 77rpm and 4.250kg/cm² boiler pressure. Trials (22.8.1888) 8,236.1ihp = 15.22kts at 74.12rpm and 4.379kg/cm² boiler pressure. 2 screws. 2 vertical compound engines with 3 cylinders of 1.55m (1) and 2.00m (2) diameter and 1.00m stroke. 12 elliptical boilers. 700t coal. Range 4,228.5nm @ 10.685kts. Reboiled 1898 with 12 new Indret elliptical boilers operating at 4.100kg/cm² pressure.
(*Formidable*) 8,500ihp designed at 80rpm and 4.250kg/cm² boiler pressure. 2 screws. 2 vertical compound engines with 3 cylinders of 1.57m (1) and 2.02m (2) and 1.00m stroke. 12 elliptical boilers, reboilered 1897.

**Armour:**
Side: Belt at waterline (steel) 550mm amidships, 360mm fwd, 350mm aft. Height from 1.60m below the wl to 0.90m above.
Guns: Barbettes (compound) 400mm with 30mm hoods. Added 1898-99: Armoured redoubts for four 164.7mm guns on upper deck (special steel) 100mm.
Deck (iron): flat 100mm over machinery, 80mm elsewhere, both on 20mm hull plating.
Conning tower: Original shelter replaced 1898 by one with 60mm special or chrome steel plus 20mm plating with an 80mm traverse.

**Guns:**
*Original armament*
(1889, *Amiral Baudin*) 3 x 370mm/28.5 M1875-79 (barbette turrets), 12 x 138.6mm/30 M1881 BLR (on the battery deck, 10 on the sides, 1 in the bow, 1 in the stern), 2 x 65mm/16 M1881 landing, 4 x 47mm/40 M1885 QF, 1 x 47mm revolving cannon, 14 x 37mm revolving cannon. **Torpedoes:** 6 tubes for 356mm M1880 and M1885 torpedoes above water on the armoured deck (2 side forward, 2 side amidships forward of the mainmast, 2 in the stern). **Searchlights:** 4 x 60cm.
(1890, *Formidable*) Same except light armament of 5 x 47mm/40 M1885 QF (the 5th in the lower foretop), 1 x 47mm revolving cannon, and 12 x 37mm revolving cannon. In 1891 her light armament was 8 x 47mm QF, 1 x 47mm revolving cannon, and 16 x 37mm revolving

cannon. A searchlight was tested in a battery port and was successful, raising the number on board to six.
*Updated secondary batteries, 1891-93*
(1891, *Formidable*) Battery deck reconfigured with 4 sponsons 10-12.1891. 3 x 370mm, 4 x 164.7mm/30 M1884 BLR (in sponsons at ends of battery), 10 x 138.6mm M1881/30 BLR (on sides in battery), 2 x 65mm/16 M1881 landing, 12 x 47mm QF (including two in the former 138.6mm gun ports in the bow and stern), 1 x 47mm revolving cannon for the pinnace, 18 x 37mm revolving cannon, and 6 torpedo tubes
(1893, *Amiral Baudin*) Battery BLR guns converted to QF at Toulon between 10.1892 and 6.1893: 4 x 164.7mm/30 M1884 QF (in sponsons) and 10 x 138.6mm/30 M1884 QF (on the sides). In 1897 her light armament was 12 x 47mm QF, 1 x 47mm revolving cannon, 6 x 37mm/20 M1885 QF, 14 x 37mm revolving cannon, with 6 x 60cm searchlights
*Modernization, 1897-1899.*
(1898, *Amiral Baudin*) 2 x 370mm/28.5 M1875-79 (barbette turrets); 4 x 164.7mm/30 M1884 QF (in armoured redoubts amidships), 8 x 138.6mm/30 M1884 QF (battery), 2 x 65mm landing, 16 x 47mm QF (2 at ends of battery, 4 in lower forward top, 2 at the after end of the armoured battery), 6 x 37mm QF, 1 x 37mm Maxim (experimental). **Torpedoes:** 4 tubes for 356mm M1885 and M1887 torpedoes (the two forward tubes were removed). **Searchlights:** 6 x 60cm.
(1898, *Formidable*) 2 x 370mm/28.5 M1875-79, 4 x 164.7mm/30 M1884 QF (redoubts), 8 x 138.6mm/30 M1881 QF (battery), 12 x 47mm QF, 18 x 37mm revolving cannon. She retained the forward pair of torpedo tubes and lost the amidships pair. In 1903 her light armament was 18 x 47mm QF and 2 x 37mm/20 M1885 QF (for the boats). The forward torpedo tubes were in the bow wave and could not be used while underway, they were removed in 1906.

*Amiral Baudin* Brest Dyd/Indret (engines designed by Joseph Joëssel).
On list 1.1879. Ord: 13.12.1878. K: 1.2.1879. L: 5.6.1883. Comm: 1.5.1888 (trials), 21.1.1889 (full).
Budget 1879. Machinery installed 22.9.1884 to 12.1.1887. From Brest to Toulon 5-15.2.1889 to join the *Escadre d'évolutions*. Refit 24.10.1892-1.7.1893 (138.6mm guns converted to QF). Left Toulon for Brest 12.7.1897 and administratively decomm. there 1.1.1898. New Indret boilers first lit off 19.4.1898. Recomm. 15.4.1898 (trials), 23.5.1898 (full). Returned briefly to Toulon but reassigned to the *Escadre du Nord* and returned to Brest 21.9.1898. To 2nd category reserve at Toulon 9.3.1902, commissioned to replace *Couronne* during her reboilering but back to normal reserve at Toulon 7.11.1904. To special reserve at Toulon 25.4.1907, decomm. there 15.5.1908. Struck 6.5.1909, replaced *Var* (ex *Trident*) as barracks hulk for mobilisation crews at Toulon 1909-1910. Condemned 31.10.1910, offered for sale 1.8.1911 by the Domaines with *Magenta, Pascal, Milan,* and smaller vessels including torpedo boats and submarines and sold to M. Benédic to BU.

*Formidable* Lorient Dyd/Schneider, Creusot (engines designed by Mathieu).
On list 1.1879. Ord: 13.12.1878. K: 10.1.1879. L: 16.4.1885. Comm: 29.12.1888 (trials), 25.5.1889 (full).
Budget 1878 (delayed to 1879). Engines ordered 18.10.1880. From Lorient to Toulon 3-12.1.1889 for trials. Trial results approved 4.5.1889, became flagship of the *Escadre d'évolutions* and the *Escadre de la Méditerranée*. Armament modified 1-8.1897 at Toulon, redoubt armour fitted and rig reduced 2.1899 at Brest. Condemned 6.11.1908. Struck 9.2.1909, central service ship at Landévennec 1909-1910, offered for sale 20.7.1911 at Brest by the Domaines with *Valmy* and others and sold that date to BU.

---

## The Republican Third Republic

In the elections of October 1877, the liberal republican majority in the Chamber of Deputies wrested control of the government away from the conservative monarchists who had dominated it since the resignation of Thiers in 1873. This ushered in a series of moderately conservative republican governments that followed an opportunistic policy of avoiding either the socialist or monarchist extremes, an approach that endured despite much political instability and frequent cabinet changes to 1895. The republican victory led to an immediate revival of the old liberal demand for general reform of the navy. On 21 November 1878 the Budget Committee's reporter on the Navy's 1879 budget, Etienne Lamy, undertook a thorough examination of the whole naval situation, demanding reforms in the naval administration and asserting that a coast defence and cruiser force was cheaper than a high-seas fleet. The novelty of Lamy's report was not the charge against the naval administration but the entry of the Budget Committee into the field of naval strategy. This wholesale criticism from the usually passive Budget Committee created a considerable sensation, and an impressive Parliamentary Mixed Commission was appointed in 1879 to look into the charges. Including the Minister of Marine, it had no less than 33 members. By linking battleships with the fallen Empire Lamy tacitly associated big ships with political conservatism, and French liberals soon came to identify the navy's battleships and the admirals who advocated them with monarchist opposition to a democratic republic and to see smaller ships with their junior commanders as truly republican. In the elections of 1881 several of the members of the Mixed Commission were defeated, and the new Chamber never bothered to appoint new ones or to call the Commission together again. Lamy, beaten in the elections of 1881, left politics entirely at the age of 38 for a career as Secretary to the French Academy.

## The Programme of 1879

The aging of the fleet and the rapid advance of technology made it impossible to wait for the new Mixed Commission to finish its investigation, and on 27 June 1879 Minister of Marine Vice Admiral Jean Bernard Jauréguiberry tasked the *Conseil d'Amirauté* to review the Programme of 1872 and adjust it for the period through 1885. This process was facilitated by the relative clarity of the French diplomatic horizon. Tension with Germany had nearly disappeared, Italy was occupied in disputes with Austria, and the republicans in power in France favoured cooperation with England. The navy could therefore follow the line of least resistance and simply update the programme rather than reconsider France's entire naval policy. In a five-day discussion ending on 16 August 1879 the *Conseil d'Amirauté* made few changes to the programme and simply replaced the table of planned construction in the 1872 programme with a new one containing updated designations and numbers for the period through 1885. One significant change was the addition to the programme of torpedo boats, which were absent from the original 1872 listing. These included the existing small torpedo boats and four proposed larger ones that evolved into the *Condor* class torpedo cruisers. The full programme is in Appendix F.

## The Programme of 1881

The 1879 programme was received with indifference by Parliament while the Minister of Marine continued to receive questions from the ongoing Mixed Commission. He also had to consider proposals for new ship types like armoured gunboats to respond to the German *Vepr* class, larger torpedo vessels capable of seagoing operations, and transports carrying torpedo boats to a theatre of action. On 26 Feb 1881 Minister Cloué directed the *Conseil d'Amirauté* to draft a new fleet programme and to establish a new rational classification of the ships that France already had afloat or building. On 6 May 1881 the *Conseil d'Amirauté* adopted a programme that still closely resembled the 1872 programme but had no completion or expiration date and that included the three new types. The orders to build the eight armoured gunboats and four large torpedo vessels

(the *Condor* class) were given on the same day in August 1882. The Programme did not include *éclaireurs d'escadre*, a special type of aviso with high speed and excellent seagoing qualities that were to scout for the fleet while avoiding combat, because at that time too few of them existed to warrant creating a separate category for them in the programme. The full programme is in Appendix F.

---

*HOCHE. Cuirassé d'escadre.* Battleship with two single turrets on the centreline at the ends and two single barbettes on the sides amidships in a lozenge arrangement, compound armour, a steel and iron hull, and a ram bow. One funnel, two heavy military masts, no sails (as completed). Designed by Huin.

In January 1879 two new unnamed 1st rank battleships (*cuirassés de 1er rang*) were included in the 1880 budget to be begun during that year, one at Lorient and one at Toulon. In January 1880 two more ships, all now called squadron battleships (*cuirassés d'escadre*), were added in the 1881 budget, one at Brest and one by contract, for a total of four new ships.

On 10 April 1879 Minister of Marine Jauréguiberry asked the *Conseil des travaux* to formulate its ideas on 1st rank battleships before he proceeded with plans to build new ones. In sessions on 30 April and 7 May 1879 the Council opted to resist the trend towards larger battleships and set a limit of 9,000 tons with a length of 90m and mean draught of 8m. It repeated its strong preference of 30 July 1878 (when it selected the design for *Amiral Baudin*) for 100-ton guns, with two in centreline barbettes in the 9,000-ton ship. The ship would also have at least ten 138.6mm guns and six revolving cannon. The Council also repeated its strong preference for a complete armour belt with a maximum thickness of 450mm and a complete armoured deck with an average thickness of 80mm. To avoid detracting from these the barbette armour would be limited to 300mm. The Council felt that a speed of 14.5 knots with forced draught was sufficient but increased the range under steam to 3,300nm at 10 knots because the ship was to have no sails but only two signal masts. The ship was also to have two launchers for Whitehead torpedoes on each side. Minister Jauréguiberry sent these specifications to the ports on 16 May 1879.

Almost a year later, on 8 April 1880, the *Conseil des travaux* examined eight designs and selected one by naval constructor Charles Ernest Huin. Now repudiating monster guns, it asked Huin to replace the two 100-ton guns, which were to be of a 450mm type yet to be developed, in his proposal with two 340mm guns on the centreline and two 274.4mm on the sides, all in barbette turrets. This lozenge arrangement allowed bringing three guns to bear in any direction and became a favourite layout for the French. Minister Jauréguiberry in returning the design to Huin on 28 May 1880 specified that the main artillery was to be composed of 340mm guns in barbettes (number not specified) and set the following additional specifications: length overall not over 101m, beam on the waterline 19.66m, maximum draught 7.95m, displacement 10,350 tons, top of the armoured belt 80cm above the waterline, 80mm armour on the deck, 400mm on the barbettes, and 220mm on their ammunition tubes.

**First Design.** On 20 June 1880 Lorient forwarded Huin's new design. This almost certainly included a lines plan and a general arrangement plan entitled 'Design for a 1st rank battleship carrying 4 guns of 34cm and 14 guns of 14cm' that are now in the 7DD1 file for *Hoche* in the archives at Vincennes. These were signed by Huin on 19 June 1880 and marked as 'seen' by de Bussy, the senior naval constructor at Lorient, but they do not bear any indication of ministerial approval. The four 340mm barbettes are laid out in the lozenge suggested by the *Conseil des travaux* and the 138.6mm guns are on the battery deck, six on each side and one at each end. The design has one funnel and two masts with a schooner rig and single tops. The hull measured 96.00m between perpendiculars and 98.00m on the waterline (the ram below the waterline would have added another 3m) with a waterline beam of 19.66m, a mean draught of 7.95m, and a displacement of 10,350.432 tons. This design bears a striking resemblance to the design as of 1883-84 with four 340mm guns to which *Marceau*, *Neptune*, and *Magenta* were ultimately built and much time and effort would have been saved if the French had simply proceeded with it in 1880.

**Second Design.** On 6 July 1880 Huin signed and Lorient sent to Paris revised lines and general arrangement plans, and on 17 July 1880 six revised detailed interior arrangement plans were signed and sent. Some or all of these plans, now in the 8DD1 files at Vincennes, bear the title 'Design for a 1st rank battleship carrying 3 guns of 34cm and 18 guns of 14cm'. One can speculate that Minister Jauréguiberry back in May had intended to add one 340mm gun amidships and not two on the sides, and that he had Huin revise his June design accordingly. Jauréguiberry approved the first two of these plans on 22 July 1880 and referred the six detailed plans to the *Conseil des travaux*, which on 10 August 1880 made only trivial changes to them.

On 3 August 1880 Minister Jauréguiberry instructed Lorient to start

construction of a 1st rank battleship that he named *Hoche*. Some steel frames and longitudinals had already been fabricated for *Hoche* by 19 August 1880. Lorient forwarded revised interior arrangement plans on 20 August 1880 and again on 22 September 1880. On 11 September 1880 the ministry wrote to Lorient about a change in the composition of the artillery, and four days later Lorient forwarded a new general arrangement plan reflecting that change. On 23 September 1880 the ministry's Directorate of Materiel advised the Directorate of Artillery that the composition of the artillery was three 34cm guns, eighteen 14cm guns, and six 37mm revolving cannon. The register of correspondence shows no additional changes to the design, and on 7 October 1880 three more ships were ordered begun or contracted for, *Hoche* having already been ordered in early August, and the Ministry sent a complete set of plans to Lorient with instructions to forward it to Brest, presumably for use in building *Neptune*. The new characteristics were reported by the journal *Le Yacht* on 20 November 1880 and again (for *Marceau*) on 22 January 1881. At that time the total length was 100m (97m on the waterline), the beam 19.30m, the displacement 9,865 tons, the mean draught 8.00m and the belt armour 450mm, while the speed remained 14.5 knots with 6,000ihp.

**Third Design.** On 24 November 1880 Minister Cloué asked for the advice of the *Conseil des travaux* regarding observations by a French squadron of some British and Austrian battleships (HMS *Alexandra*, *Temeraire*, *Monarch*, and *Thunderer* and the Austrian *Custozza*) operating in the Adriatic. The foreign ships all showed a strong emphasis on axial (fore and aft) fire, while the newest French ships with their three big guns on the

The battleship *Hoche* at Villefranche soon after arriving in the Mediterranean for operational service in January 1891. The ship took part in manoeuvres off Corsica in June 1891. Her towering superstructure with its two tall military masts dominated her low ends and earned her the nickname 'Grand Hotel'. The large white flag with five blue dots over her after turret is the 2nd Substitute signal flag. This photo, taken by ND, was received by ONI on 1 June 1891. *(NHHC, NH-88809)*

centreline could only bring one gun to bear forward and one aft, and none if that gun were disabled. On 4 January 1881 the majority on the Council recommended replacing the middle 340mm gun in the four ships just beginning construction with two 274.4mm guns placed on the sides, thus returning to the armament it had previously recommended on 8 April 1880. On 31 January 1881 Minister Cloué proposed mounting two 340mm guns on the centreline and two 274.4mm on the sides, all in barbettes, and he approved this armament in June 1881. However, the design with three 340mm guns did not have enough displacement to support the revised armament, and on 19 July 1881 the *Conseil des travaux* approved a modified design for *Magenta* with the beam increased by 0.46m to provide the additional displacement provided the length was also increased. *Hoche* was more difficult, because the frames and beams already fabricated for her were made of steel, which at that time was very difficult to alter, preventing an increase in her beam. On 6 September 1881, when approving the modified plans for the other three ships, Minister Cloué instructed Lorient to lengthen the hull of *Hoche* and give her the same armament as the others (two 340mm and two 274.4mm). The modified *Hoche* would have a length of 100.40m between perpendiculars, a displacement of 10,636 tons, and would be 1.80m longer and 0.46m narrower than the modified *Magentas*.

Back on 25 March 1881 Indret had proposed supplying engines like those in *Amiral Baudin* (these in turn being based on *Dévastation*) for *Hoche* and *Neptune*. On 17 February 1882 the ministry decided not to use the *Baudin* engines and on 24 February 1882 it asked for a new engine design and higher pressure boilers to increase the designed speed to 16 knots. Designs were submitted on 26 May 1882 by Indret for *Hoche* and *Neptune*, on 26 June by FCM for *Marceau*, and on 1 July by Schneider for *Magenta*. After many design changes the plans for the machinery of *Neptune* were approved on 10 May 1883 and contracts were awarded for the engines of *Marceau* and *Magenta* on 23 April 1883 and 4 August 1884 respectively.

**Fourth (Turret) Design.** On 2 August 1882 Minister of Marine Jauréguiberry decided to build a new battleship, *Brennus*, at Lorient to a entirely different design by de Bussy that put its main guns in enclosed turrets low in the ship rather than in barbettes carried higher up. On 17 August 1882 he instructed Lorient to have Huin see if, without changing the displacement or trim of *Hoche*, it would be possible to replace the two 340mm barbettes at the ends with two single 340mm turrets. Huin designed a turret with 400mm armour on the turret and 350mm on its base and reported that if the 274.4mm barbettes also had 400mm armour there would be no weight change. The turrets needed to be one deck level lower than the barbettes that they replaced, however, giving the ship low ends. On 4 November 1882 Minister Jauréguiberry approved a preliminary design of enclosed turrets for *Hoche*, *Magenta* and *Neptune*. The contract-built *Marceau* seems not to have been included in this project. The plans of *Hoche* signed by Huin on 16 May 1883 included all changes to that date. These, approved by Minister of Marine Senator Charles Marie Brun (a former naval constructor who assisted in the design of the submarine *Plongeur* in 1860) on 4 June 1883, show 340mm turrets on ends that had been cut down a deck, 274.4mm barbettes high up on the sides, and a rig of three schooner masts with armed tops. On 17 August 1883 Huin wrote that a return to barbettes for the 340mm guns would require too many changes to the ship's structure which was already well advanced. (This return to barbettes was made at around this time for the other two ships.) Huin later proposed deleting the middle mast and replacing the circular funnel with an oblong one to clear the axial sight lines from the navigating bridge, a change also made in the contemporary *Brennus* design. Compound belt armour was supplied by Saint-Chamond while compound turret and barbette armour and iron deck armour were supplied by Marrel Frères.

On 19 October 1886 the *Conseil des travaux* examined a proposal from the *Escadre d'évolutions* to use tripod masts with command platforms in

battleships, and the Council recommended instead steel masts of large diameter with spiral staircases and ammunition hoists on the inside, armed tops and command platforms, and no external rigging. Huin completed plans for fitting two of these heavy military masts on 12 May 1887 and Minister of Marine Barbey approved them on 10 June 1887. The combination of low ends and a towering superstructure amidships surmounted by a large funnel and two high military masts earned her the nickname *Le Grand Hôtel*.

**Overhaul 1894-1895.** *Hoche* was ordered on 20 March 1894 and 12 June 1894 to move to Brest from Toulon to convert her 138.6mm battery to QF guns. The original intent was to convert all eighteen guns, but it was found that this would increase the excess weight of the ship to 566 tons and weight reductions were imposed. She was placed in 2nd category reserve on 23 September 1894, her eighteen 138.6mm/30 M1881 BLR were replaced with twelve 138.6 M1884 QF, the military mainmast was replaced with a pole mast, and the superstructure including the *donjons* (round galleries) over the turrets and barbettes was lightened. The ship was recommissioned for trials on 20 April 1895, the refit was completed on 29 April 1895, and she returned to full commission on 10 May 1895 and joined the *Escadre du Nord*.

**Overhaul 1898-1900.** *Hoche* was sent to Cherbourg on 21 July 1898 for a refit ordered on 30 July 1898 to plans of the senior naval constructor there, André Simon Eugéne Dupont, to replace her 8 worn out cylindrical Admiralty-type boilers with 16 new Belleville water tube boilers. To use the boilers with the ship's older engines their operating pressure of 16kg/cm² was reduced to 11 kg/cm² and the high pressure cylinders of the engines were reduced from 1.14m to 0.89m diameter. Belleville reported that the boilers would not work well with the ship's large single funnel and two new funnels side by side were fitted. The superstructure was further reduced to save more weight, including moving four 138.6mm guns from their casemates to unprotected positions on the upper deck, the rig was further lightened, and a conning tower built for *Furieux* was installed in place of the two old conning towers on the battleship. Boiler installation began on 18 January 1899, the new boilers were first lit off on 19 March 1900, and speed trials on 21 August 1900 produced a speed of 15.95 knots. The ship participated in a naval review at Cherbourg for President Loubet on 19 July 1900 and rejoined the fleet on 11 January 1901.

These overhauls were intended to be followed by another in which four

The battleship *Hoche* in the Atlantic during the later 1890s following her 1894-95 refit during which her after military mast was replaced with a lighter pole mast. Here her low bow is awash even in a practically calm sea. She is being conned from the bridge aft of the funnel atop the massive superstructure. *(NHHC from ONI album of foreign warships dated about 1900, NH-88816)*

twin turrets with 164.7mm guns were to replace the two 274.4mm barbettes on the side. By 1904 it was clear that this upgrade would never take place.

*The characteristics are based on a devis dated 21.1.1891.*

**Dimensions & tons:** 105.615m oa, 102.475m wl (+ 3.140m ram), 100.400m pp (wl fwd to rudder) x 19.752m ext (above wl, 20.374m at the bridge), 19.660m wl. 11,103.918t disp. Draught: 8.262m mean, 8.554m aft. Men: 626.

**Machinery:**
(Original) 11,876ihp designed (four engines at 2,925ihp each and 176ihp for the circulating pumps) at 90rpm and 6.200kg/cm$^2$ boiler pressure. Trials (25.7.1890) 10,912.37ihp = 15.92kts at 83.56rpm and 6.255kg/cm$^2$ boiler pressure. 2 screws. 4 vertical compound engines with 2 cylinders of 1.140m and 1.980m diameter and 1.000m stroke. 8 cylindrical direct-flame boilers. 610t coal.
(1900) 11,000ihp designed at 84rpm and 16kg/cm$^2$ boiler pressure. Trials (21.8.1900) 10,981ihp = 15.955kts at 85.25rpm and 14.775kg/cm$^2$ boiler pressure. 2 screws. 4 vertical compound engines with 2 cylinders of 0.890m and 1.980m diameter and 1.000m stroke. 16 Belleville boilers. 552t coal (normal), 600t (actual). Range 2,725.9nm @ 10.326kts.

**Armour:**
Side: Belt at waterline (compound) 450mm amidships, 290mm fwd, 300mm aft. Height from 1.50m below the wl to 0.80m above (designed). Side above belt forward (compound) 80mm.
Guns: 340mm turrets (compound) 350mm, 320mm fixed bases. 274.4mm barbettes (compound) 350mm with 60mm hoods.
Deck (iron): flat 80mm on 20mm hull plating.
Conning towers: 40mm forward (chrome steel), 30mm aft (hardened steel). Armour in 1900 was as in 1895 except for a new forward conning tower with 60mm (special steel) on 20mm plating and no after conning tower.

**Guns:**
(1891) 2 x 340mm/28.5 M1881 (enclosed turrets fore and aft), 2 x 274.4mm/28.5 M1881 (barbette turrets on sides), 18 x 138.6mm/30 M1881 BLR (14 in the battery, 2 forward and 2 aft on the shelter deck), 2 x 65mm/16 M1881 landing, 8 x 47mm/40 M1885 QF, 1 x 47mm revolving cannon, 12 x 37mm revolving cannon.
**Torpedoes:** 5 tubes for 356mm Whitehead torpedoes (4 side and one in the extreme stern, all above water).
(1895) 2 x 340mm, 2 x 274.4mm, 12 x 138.6mm/30 M1881 QF (8 in the battery and 4 in casemates at the corners of the superstructure), 4 x 65mm/50 M1888 QF, 2 x 65mm/16 M1881 landing, 9 x 47mm QF, 1 x 47mm revolving cannon, 10 x 37mm revolving cannon.
**Torpedoes:** 5 tubes above water (4 side and 1 in the stern), all for 356mm (4.99m) torpedoes (M1885 except M1887 for the two amidships tubes). **Searchlights:** 5 x 60cm.
(1900) 2 x 340mm, 2 x 274.4mm, 12 x 138.6mm QF (8 in battery, 4 unprotected on gaillards), 4 x 65mm QF, 2 x 65mm landing, 14 x 47mm QF, 4 x 37mm/20 M1885 QF. **Torpedoes:** 3 tubes for 356mm M1887 and M1887SR torpedoes above water (2 amidships and 1 in the stern). **Searchlights:** 5 x 90cm. The remaining torpedo tubes were landed in June 1906.

*Hoche* Lorient Dyd/Indret.
On list 1.1.1881. Ord: 3.8.1880. K: 8.1881. L: 29.9.1886. Comm: 15.7.1889 (trials), 12.1.1891 (full).
Budget 1880. Machinery installed from 15.9.1888 to 8.7.1889. Manned for trials 4.2.1890, arrived at Brest for trials 7.2.1890, official trials 7.1890 to 1.1891. Trial report 21.2.1891 and ship left for Toulon the same day. Arrived 28.1.1891 and joined the *Escadre de la Méditerranée*. Armament modified, superstructure reduced, and after military mast removed at Brest 1894-95. Struck uncharted rocks at Quiberon 13.5.1898 but unlike the dreadnought *France* in 1922 survived and

went into reserve at Brest for repairs 25.5.1898. Upon completion sent to Cherbourg for reboilering and other modifications that were completed at the end of 1900. To Toulon 1.1.1903, to special reserve there 1.5.1909. Decomm. 28.10.1909, decomm. completed 1.1.1910. Struck 13.6.1911 and handed over to the Domaines 6.7.1911 for sale. A proposal of 21.2.1912 to use her as a target ship in place of *Fulminant* caused her to be withdrawn from sale, towed out by *Jules Michelet* and sunk as a target 2.12.1913 on the first pass by *Jaureguiberry* and *Pothuau* 13nm off Pointe Ste. Marguerite, Hyères, during tests of a new fire control system.

--------------------------------

## *MARCEAU, NEPTUNE,* and *MAGENTA.*

The 1881 budget (submitted in January 1880) raised the number of new battleships potentially funded from two to four. On 7 October 1880 Minister of Marine Cloué ordered the Brest and Toulon dockyards each to begin construction of one ship and ordered the Machinery Commission (the *Commission permanente des machines et du grand outillage*) to begin negotiations with the Forges et Chantiers de la Méditerranée (FCM) for construction of a third. He named them *Neptune, Magenta,* and *Marceau* respectively.

**First design.** The second design described above for *Hoche* with three 340mm and eighteen 138.6mm guns was the first design for these ships. Brest began to lay down the lines for *Neptune* on 3 November 1880 and Toulon began work on *Magenta* on 15 January 1881. The contract for the hull of *Marceau* was signed on 27 December 1880 and approved on 11 January 1881, FCM being notified on 14 January 1881. However, on 31 January 1881 Minister Cloué suspended the orders to the dockyards to prepare to build *Neptune* and *Magenta* and asked Lorient to develop new plans. Brest reported that work on *Neptune* had stopped on 3 February.

**Second Design.** On 19 July 1881 the *Conseil des travaux* examined a design by Huin for a modified *Magenta* and approved it subject to an increase of the length by 1.80m to 97.70m to allow carrying more weight, the suppression of one of the three signal masts, and deletion of the two 138.6mm guns on the upper deck (the last two changes do not seem to have been made). This design was essentially the same as the third design for *Hoche,* above, except for the hull dimensions. On 25 July 1881 the ministry advised Lorient of its provisional approval of these plans, and on 26 July 1881 it advised the ports that they would get them in the second half of August. Huin explained on 4 August 1881 that he had added a cylindrical section amidships that increased the displacement by 263 tons and then refined the lines at the ends costing 56 tons, giving a new displacement of 10,583 tons. The plans as delivered lengthened the hull 2.70m amidships to 98.6m between perpendiculars (101.6m including the ram) and widened it 46cm to 20.12m on the waterline. They included a main battery of two 340mm and two 274.4mm guns, all in barbettes, twenty 138.6mm guns including two on the upper deck forward and two in the bow below them, 20 Hotchkiss 37mm guns, four torpedo tubes (two amidships and two aft) and three light schooner-rigged masts with armed tops along with a bowsprit and a jib sail. Maximum belt armour was 450mm with 400mm on the barbettes and 80mm on the deck. Lorient forwarded the plans to the Ministry on 29 August 1881 and the Ministry forwarded them to Toulon on 3 September 1881 and to Brest on 6 September 1881. Work on *Neptune* officially resumed on 12 September 1881. Minister Cloué gave his final approval for the new plans for *Marceau, Neptune,* and *Magenta* on 9 November 1881.

On 5 September 1881 Minister Cloué ordered the Machinery Commission to negotiate with FCM to modify the contract for the construction of *Marceau* in accordance with the new plans. The new contract was signed on 16 January 1882 and approved and FCM notified of the approval on 24 January 1882. *Marceau* officially began construction on 27 January 1882 under the supervision of naval constructor Opin.

**Third (Turret) Design.** On 28 June 1882 Brest and Toulon were urged to press ahead with the construction of their ships. However, the redesign of *Hoche* that began in August 1882 to use turrets rather than barbettes for the 340mm guns again disrupted the construction of *Neptune* and *Magenta*, although not the contract-built *Marceau*. Brest and Toulon both received indications in late 1882 that these changes also applied to *Neptune* and *Magenta* but received no plans or other information that they could act on until, after Brest wrote in June 1883 that 'we demand instantly notification of the new arrangements', the ministry responded on 22 June 1883 that Minister Brun had charged Huin to see if it would be possible to install on *Magenta* and *Neptune* a system of fixed turrets (i.e. barbettes) that were better protected against small guns and musketry than the current barbette turrets. As this would take a long time, and to avoid leaving Brest idle for the rest of 1883, it suggested that Brest complete *Neptune* on the plans approved for *Hoche* and that Toulon await the result of Huin's study for *Magenta*, which was not as far along. Huin on 25 July 1883 completed provisional plans for *Neptune* with turrets as in *Hoche* and they were approved on 28 July 1883 and sent to Brest. On 30 August 1883 the naval constructors charged with the construction of *Neptune* and *Magenta*, Émile Bertin at Brest and Gaston Clauzel at Toulon, simultaneously wrote to the ministry stating that since October and November 1882, when they had first heard of the change to enclosed turrets, very little work had been accomplished on their ships and that the little that had been done had used the plans of 6 September 1881. Both constructors then stated that there would no problem if the ministry retracted the decision to use turrets, cancelled the plans of 28 July 1883, and returned to the four barbette turrets on the upper deck in the 6 September 1881 plans.

**Fourth Design.** Matters took a new turn on 17 September 1883 when Minister of Marine Peyron ordered Huin to study the possibility of replacing the planned two 340mm and two 274.4mm guns in the barbettes with four 340mm guns. Huin reported on 12 October that with offsetting weight reductions changing to four 340mm guns would produce a surcharge of only 4 tons. The offsetting reductions included reducing the number of 138.6mm guns to seventeen, reducing the height of the belt by 10cm, and removing one of the three signal masts. The side barbettes would be moved 3.512m aft to maintain trim. Huin concluded that there was no reason not to make the change. Naval constructor Opin supervising the work at La Seyne completed plans for *Marceau* with four 340mm and seventeen 138.6mm guns on 23 June 1884 which Minister Peyron approved on 4 August 1884. Huin wrote on 25 August 1884 that the adoption of four 340mm guns in a new type of barbette with central loading designed by Canet, then a senior engineer at FCM, would actually increase the weight margin in the design to 137 tons while retaining the original height of the belt and that stability and trim would not be noticeably affected. Someone wrote in the margin of this note, 'This is too good to be true!' The design to which these three ships were built thus ultimately ended up strongly resembling Huin's first design for the class of 19 June 1880.

The armour in *Marceau* and *Neptune* was mostly compound, while the belt and barbette armour in *Magenta* was steel, ordered from Schneider in part to encourage that firm to continue the development of steel armour. At that time the capabilities of both compound and steel armour were regarded as roughly equal. Hammered steel by Schneider was selected for the barbettes of *Neptune* instead of the compound steel offered by other vendors purely because of price.

On 28 March 1886 Minister of Marine Vice Admiral Hyacinthe Laurent Théophile Aube suspended the construction of four battleships, *Neptune*, *Magenta*, *Brennus*, and *Charles Martel* (the last two had also been suspended on 27 January 1886). *Marceau* escaped probably because she was further advanced and was being built by contract. *Neptune* was launched in May 1887, possibly to clear the ways for the cruiser *Isly*, and construction resumed on both battleships in late 1887, but nearly two years of construction time was lost for each of them.

**Modifications during construction.** These ships were originally designed with three masts and a schooner rig. In late 1885 this rig was replaced in the most advanced ship, *Marceau*, with two slender military masts with two tops on each mast. These masts, similar to those in *Amiral Baudin*, were of only 0.90m diameter and their tops were accessed by climbing the external rigging or by ascending a vertical ladder inside the mast. On 19 October 1886 the *Conseil des travaux* examined a proposal from the *Escadre d'évolutions* to use tripod masts with command platforms in battleships, and the Council recommended instead steel masts of large diameter with spiral staircases and ammunition hoists on the inside, armed tops and command platforms, and no external rigging. On 9 July 1887 Toulon submitted to the *Conseil des travaux* a proposal for large diameter masts for *Magenta*. This was rejected on 2 August 1887 but a revised version was approved by the Council on 5 January 1888. A proposal from Brest for a rig for *Neptune* consisting of two heavy military masts and no sails was first considered by the *Conseil des travaux* on 23 May 1888 and a revised version was approved by the Council on 11 December 1889.

Many more changes were made to *Neptune* and *Magenta* between the late 1880s and the time they entered service in the early to mid 1890s. These included the addition of a high flying bridge between the two masts with vertical plating below it to protect against blast from the side barbettes (September 1888), the substitution of a conning tower with 200mm armour for the original shelter with 30mm armour (February 1889), and the addition of a breakwater on deck forward (March 1890). In *Magenta* the increase to 6 torpedo tubes on the battery deck was approved by the *Conseil des travaux* on 15 January 1888 and the addition of six 60cm searchlights was approved on 31 July 1888; the other ships also received this equipment. On 1 July 1890 the Council approved a proposal from Brest to modify the secondary battery of *Neptune* from the sixteen in the battery and one in the bow in *Marceau* to twelve in the battery (eight in the forward battery and four in the after one) and four in the superstructure with one 65mm gun in the bow. On 25 June 1891 Toulon suggested making essentially the same change in *Magenta* but without the gun in the bow. The *Conseil des travaux* on 12 August 1891 approved this arrangement, the ship ending up with six guns in the forward battery and another six in the after one. The 138.6mm guns in *Neptune* were updated to QF in mid-1892 during the delay in trials caused by problems with the steam admission slide valves of the four engines, and the secondary battery of *Magenta* was also converted to quick fire 138.6mm guns before the ship entered service.

A last major improvement was made to *Magenta* but not to *Neptune* when Minister of Marine Barbey ordered on 30 September 1891 that the form of the bow be modified to reduce the size of the bow wave. The slope of the bow was decreased, reducing the distance from the tip of the ram to the waterline from 3m to 1.50m and making the bow above the waterline more vertical. The inward-sloping bow of *Neptune* created a huge bow wave along the length of the ship and scooped green water onto the forward deck, while the modified *Magenta* experienced neither of these problems.

**Proposed modernization.** On 2 March 1899 Minister of Marine Édouard Lockroy ordered the *Section Technique* to study a modernization of *Marceau*, *Magenta*, and *Neptune* that would include replacement of the boilers with water tube boilers, converting or modifying the engines, reducing the superstructures, and completely transforming the armament. On 5 June 1900 the *Conseil des travaux* examined a design by the *Section Technique* that focused on *Neptune* because she was the most overweight. It involved removing nearly all of the superstructure and the two military masts, replacing the fore and aft 340mm guns with 305mm guns in enclosed turrets, replacing the beam 340mm guns and the 138.6mm guns with eight 164.7mm guns (6 in casemates and 2 in turrets), and fitting two light masts (the forward one with a fire control top, the after one for signals). The Council asked for changes including placing the 164.7mm guns in four twin turrets and the provision of a military foremast with the usual armed top and searchlight platform, Minister of Marine Lanessan approved its findings on 5 July 1901. The *Section technique* produced the revised study on 18 July 1901. Four days later the Chief of the Naval General Staff criticised this project for producing ships whose slight military value was not worth the high cost of their modernization. Lanessan resubmitted the design to the *Conseil des travaux* which on 5 November 1901 approved it again, arguing that the three ships could form a homogeneous division capable of operating in the first line at a cost of 22 million francs for all three against 36 millions for a single *République* class battleship. On 24 December 1901 Lanessan again referred the matter to the Council, stating that the costs would be even higher than previously estimated, but the Council on 18 February 1902 insisted that the refits should proceed. The declining influence of the now very conservative *Conseil des travaux* and the advent in 1902 of Camille Pelletin as Minister of Marine put an end to major modernization schemes for older battleships.

---

*MARCEAU. Cuirassé d'escadre.* Battleship with four barbettes in a lozenge arrangement, compound armour, a steel and iron hull, and a ram bow. One funnel, two light military masts, no sails. Designed by Huin.

On 7 October 1880 Minister of Marine Cloué ordered that negotiations be opened with the Forges et Chantiers de la Méditerranée at La Seyne to build a new battleship which he named *Marceau*. Her history before and during construction is given above along with that of her two half-sisters, *Neptune*, and *Magenta*. Compound belt armour was supplied by Marrel,

---

The battleship *Marceau*, probably in the mid-1890s with her rig as completed with two tall slender military masts. Both masts were shortened in the late 1890s. (*NHHC, NH-64097*)

compound barbette armour by Saint-Chamond, and iron deck armour by Saint-Étienne.

**Overhaul 1892-93.** *Marceau* had constant problems from the very beginning with leaks in the tubes in her Admiralty type cylindrical boilers, and in mid-1892 she entered the dockyard at Toulon to have her boilers completely retubed. (Her secondary battery was also converted to QF guns during this overhaul.) Post repair trials began in December 1892 and the ship became operational on 29 March 1893.

*Marceau* continued to have problems with her boiler tubes after the 1892 retubing. It was noted that she had been constructed before ships were fitted with means of producing fresh water for their boilers and had to resort to sea water as replacement feed water within two days of steaming at 12 knots or more after leaving port. The provision of large evaporators and reserve feed tanks was put on the list for her next major refit, as was the replacement of her fire tube boilers with Niclausse water tube boilers. This would be the first use of Niclausse boilers by the Navy in a large ship and the Navy wanted to try them first in an older one.

The external rigging on the slender military masts fitted to *Marceau* in 1885 limited the arcs of fire of the side 340mm guns and had to be dismantled when clearing for action. In June 1895 *Marceau*'s commander proposed reducing the height of the masts to make the external rigging unnecessary, and between then and 1900 the masts were shortened from 19.70m to 14.60m (fore) and 11.40m (aft) with access to the tops provided by vertical ladders on the sides of the masts.

**Overhaul 1900-1902.** The boilers of *Marceau* reached the end of their service life in January 1900 and Minister of Marine Lanessan decided at the beginning of 1900 to proceed with changing them. The ship was placed in reserve on 26 July 1900 and commenced refit at La Seyne on 30 August

1900, receiving sixteen new Niclausse boilers that had been ordered on 6 July 1898. The higher boiler pressure of 11 kg/cm² provided to the compound engines by these boilers required reducing the diameter of the HP cylinder to 1.28m. During the refit the Bullivant nets were removed and the light artillery was modified. The Niclausse boilers were first lit off on 28 May 1902 with the first static trials of the machinery plant two days later. The boilers proved to be troublesome, they had to be completely retubed in mid-1903, and trials ended inconclusively with the ship being put into reserve in February 1904.

*Marceau* never returned to active service in the fleet and her underway service was limited to torpedo launching exercises as a school ship in the Salins d'Hyères roadstead from 1906. These, however, made her the only one of her four half sisters to remain on the list into World War I, when she was put to use as a depot ship for submarines and torpedo boats at Malta, Corfu, Brindisi, and briefly after the war at Bizerte. As of 1921 her engines had operated for only 1,033 hours since their 1903 overhaul.

In 1900 the rate of fire of *Marceau*'s 340mm guns was one round every 3m30s and the rate of the 138.6mm guns was 3 rounds per minute. The bow 138.6mm gun could be fired at speeds up to 15 knots, when the ports had to be closed because of the bow wave.

*The characteristics are based on a devis dated 20.4.1891.*

**Dimensions & tons:** 103.620m oa, 100.600m wl (+3.00m ram), 98.600m (wl to rudder), 101.600m pp (tip fwd to rudder) x 20.232m ext (above wl), 20.120m wl. 10,850.405t disp. Draught: 8.138m mean, 8.181m aft. Men: 647.

**Machinery:**
(original) 12,030ihp designed at 90rpm and 6.000kg/cm² boiler pressure. Trials (12.2.1891) 11,168.95ihp = 16.194kts at 87.845rpm. 2 screws. 2 vertical compound engines with 3 cylinders of 1.580m (1) and 2.020m (2) diameter and 1.000m stroke. 8 cylindrical direct flame boilers. 610t coal. Range (designed) 2,900nm @ 10kts.
(1904) 12,000ihp designed at 90rpm and 13kg/cm² boiler pressure (11kg/cm² at the engines). Trials (13.1.1904) 12,462.8ihp = 16.437kts at 94.4625rpm and 12.1kg/cm² boiler pressure. 2 screws. 2 vertical compound engines with 3 cylinders of 1.230m and 2.020m diameter and 1.000m stroke. 16 Niclausse boilers. 600t coal (normal), 685.100t (actual). Range 4,030.2nm @ 9.29kts.

**Armour:**
Side: Belt at waterline (compound) 450mm amidships, 230mm fwd, 300mm aft. Height from 1.50m below the wl to 0.80m above (designed).
Guns: Barbettes (compound) 350mm, hoods 40mm special steel by Saint-Chamond on 20mm ordinary plating.
Deck (iron): flat 80mm on 20mm hull plating.
Conning tower (iron): 120mm.

**Guns:**
(1891) 4 x 340mm (2 x 340mm/28.5 M1884 and 2 x 340mm/28.5 M1881 not tubed, barbette turrets), 17 x 138.6mm/30 M1884 BLR (16 battery, 1 at same level in bow, with 2 empty ports in the captain's cabin aft to which guns on the side aft could be moved, suppressed 1901), 4 x 65mm/50 M1888 QF, 2 x 65mm/16 M1881 landing, 12 x 47mm/40 M1885 QF, 1 x 47mm revolving cannon for the pinnace, 8 x 37mm revolving cannon. **Torpedoes:** 6 tubes for 356mm torpedoes (2 in the forward battery, 2 on the armoured deck amidships, and 2 on the armoured deck aft, all above water).
(1892) Between May and December 1892 the 17 x 138.6mm guns were replaced with 17 x 138.6mm/30 M1884 QF. By 1897 1 x 47mm/25 M1885 light (*léger*) QF had been added for the steam pinnace and one experimental 37mm Maxim had been embarked.
(1904) 4 x 340mm/28.5 M1881/84 (turrets), 17 x 138.6mm QF (battery), 4 x 65mm QF, 2 x 65mm landing, 14 x 47mm/40 M1885 heavy QF, 2 x 37mm/20 M1885 light QF, 1 x 37mm Maxim. **Torpedoes:** 6 tubes for 356mm M1885 and M1887 torpedoes (2 in the forward

battery, 2 on the armoured deck amidships, and 2 on the armoured deck aft). **Searchlights:** 6 x 60cm.
(1909) As a school ship she retained only 4 x 340mm, 4 x 47mm QF, and 1 x 65mm landing gun used as a line throwing gun. By 1911 the 340mm guns were without munitions and the 47mm were for saluting, for training apprentice torpedomen and helmsmen, and as fog signals.
(1914) The large calibre guns were landed in 9.1914, parts of their mountings remained in place.
(1915) 2 x 65mm QF, 2 x 47mm QF (for the steam launches), One 65mm landing gun was installed by ship's company on the cover of the after barbette for anti-aircraft fire.

*Marceau* F.C. Méditerranée, La Seyne/FCM, Marseille (engines designed by Orsel).
On list 1.1881. Ord: 27.12.1880 (contract). K: 28.11.1882.
  L: 24.5.1887. Comm: 27.1.1890 (trials), 14.3.1891 (full).
Budget 1881. Construction begun 27.1.1882. Engines ordered 23.4.1883. Machinery installed 28.2.1888 to 21.11.1889. Trials began 9.1890, fully manned for trials 17.1.1891, official trials 2-3.1891. Left Toulon for Ajaccio 29.4.1891 to join the *Escadre de la Méditerranée*. The 138.6mm guns replaced 1893 with M1881 QF. Topmasts shortened 1895. Station ship at Crete 9-11.1896, replaced by *Wattignies*. In a short-lived training division (*division d'instruction*) 1898-99 with *Magenta, Neptune,* and *Calédonien*. School for torpedoes 1899-1900 (replaced *Algésiras,* replaced by *Magenta*). Refitted with new Niclausse boilers, new HP cylinders for the engines, and other hull and machinery changes 1900-1902. Recomm. late 1906 to serve as school for apprentice torpedo boat seamen at the Salins d'Hyères. Relieved *Magenta* as school for torpedo boat seamen at Toulon 1907-10, then school for electricians 1911-12 and school for torpedomen 1912-1914. Converted in late 1914 to a repair ship for torpedo vessels and submarines. At Malta, Corfu and Brindisi during the war, command ship for the *1re escadrille de sous marins* at Brindisi 1.1918. To Bizerte 12.1918 and condemned there 5.7.1919. Struck 1.10.1920. Sold 30.9.1921 to M. Saglia. Left Bizerte 17.1.1922 under tow by the tug *Marius Chambon* to be BU at Toulon but broke tow in a storm, went ashore east of Bizerte, and lingered into the 1930s slowly being BU there.

***

**NEPTUNE.** *Cuirassé d'escadre.* Battleship with four barbettes in a lozenge arrangement, compound armour (steel on the barbettes), a steel and iron hull, and a ram bow. One funnel, two heavy military masts, no sails. Designed by Huin.

On 7 October 1880 Minister of Marine Cloué ordered the dockyard at Brest to begin construction of a new battleship which he named *Neptune*. Her history before and during construction is given above along with that of her two half-sisters, *Marceau,* and *Magenta.* Her compound belt armour was supplied by Châtillon et Commentry and her steel barbette armour by Schneider.

Soon after commissioning for trials it was realized that *Neptune* would not make the designed 16.5 knots trial speed because of unsuitable propellers, but replacements were never provided. A note dated 3 February 1898 proposed lightening the after top, which like the fore top had two levels, the lower one being for 47mm guns and small arms and the upper one just for small arms. The note argued that advances in light artillery had made the upper level useless. The upper level was removed at about this time, with the searchlight being lowered to the roof of the lower level. The fore top retained both levels.

**Proposed overhaul.** *Neptune*'s original cylindrical boilers, although similar to those of *Marceau,* gave no trouble during trials or in service. Few tubes needed replacement, which was just as well as replacement was impossible because the nearby watertight bulkheads lacked doors. The ship made do by plugging the ends of the few tubes that developed leaks. In 1898 it was

The battleship *Neptune* at Brest in the mid-1890s with her two-level masthead
tops as completed. The ironclad *Suffren* of 1870 is in the background. Both ships
have early model Bullivant anti-torpedo nets. *(NHHC from ONI album of French
warships, NH-74911-A)*

proposed to replace these boilers, which in 1899 were expected to reach the
end of their service life in July 1900. Sixteen Belleville boilers were ordered
on 9 November 1898 and Indret began work on modifications to the
engines to accommodate the higher boiler pressure (12kg/cm$^2$) from the
new boilers. They were to be converted to triple expansion. The new boilers
required two new funnels on the centreline. The Ministry on 7 January
1901 sent plans to Brest with instructions to develop detailed plans that
allowed for a second phase involving modernizing the armament.
In January 1902 *Neptune* was declared unusable in case of mobilisation
because of the poor condition of her boilers. By 1903 the new boilers were
ready but Indret had problems manufacturing the new high pressure cylinders. The ship moved from Brest to Cherbourg in 1905 to be modified, but
Cherbourg advised that money spent on the ship would be wasted.
No work was done and the boilers that had been sent to Cherbourg for the
ship were sent back to Brest in 1910. Their fate is unknown.

*The characteristics are based on a devis dated 23.12.1892.*

**Dimensions & tons:** 103.700m oa, 100.720m wl (+2.980m ram),
101.700m pp (tip fwd to rudder) x 20.228m ext (above wl, 21.340m
outside beam turrets), 20.212m wl. 10,983.283t disp.

Draught: 8.216m mean, 8.477m aft. Men: 684 including 34 officers.

**Machinery:** 11,084ihp designed at 95rpm and 6.200kg/cm$^2$ boiler pressure. Trials (18.6.1892) 10,929.2ihp = 16.013kts at 87.125rpm and
6.210kg/cm$^2$ boiler pressure. 2 screws. 2 groups of two vertical compound engines each with direct connecting rods and 2 cylinders of
1.010m and 1.910m diameter and 1.000m stroke, 2 engines coupled
on each shaft, one of which could be disconnected at low speeds.
8 cylindrical direct flame boilers. 600t coal (normal), 620t (actual).
Range (designed) 2,900nm @ 10kts.

**Armour:**

Side: Belt at waterline (compound) 450mm amidships, 170mm fwd,
300mm aft. Total height 2.28m.

Guns: Barbettes (hammered steel) 350mm with 60mm hoods.

Deck (iron): flat 80mm.

Conning tower (hammered steel): 120mm.

**Guns:**

(1891) 4 x 340mm/28.5 M1884 (turrets), 16 x 138.6mm/30 M1884 QF
(12 in the battery, 4 at the corners of the flying bridge), 5 x 65mm/50
M1888 QF, 2 x 65mm/16 M1881 landing and line-throwing, 8 x
47mm/40 M1885 QF (4 more added 1894), 1 x 47mm revolving
cannon, 8 x 37mm revolving cannon. **Torpedoes:** 5 tubes for 450mm
M1889 and M1890 torpedoes above water on the battery deck (1 aft
in the captain's cabin, 2 in the centre of the battery forward of the
midships turrets, and 2 at the forward end of the battery).

**Searchlights:** 7 x 60cm.

*Neptune* Brest Dyd/Indret (engines designed by Charles Delevaque).
On list 1.1881. Ord: 7.10.1880. K: 17.4.1882. L: 7.5.1887.
   Comm: 15.5.1891 (trials), 1.12.1892 (full).
Budget 1881. Construction begun 12.9.1881. Machinery installed
   1.1889 to 4.4.1891. Manned for trials 21.9.1891. Assigned to the
   *Escadre de la Méditerranée* on 2.12.1892. Left Brest 26.12.1892,
   arrived Toulon 9.1.1893 and joined the *Escadre*. In a short-lived training division 1898-99 with *Magenta*, *Marceau*, and *Calédonien*, then
   sent to Brest and on 1.12.1899 placed in 2nd category reserve.
   Decomm. 11.1901. Left Brest 5.7.1905 for Cherbourg to be refitted
   but refit cancelled. Decomm. 1.6.1907. Condemnation proposed
   27.2.1907 with *Terrible* and *Fulminant*. Struck 4.2.1908, retained as
   target at Cherbourg 1908-1912. Used as target Nov-Dec 1912 for
   trials by the Army of projectiles loaded with Planclastite (a mixture of
   nitrogen peroxide and carbon bisulphide). Sunk in shallow water in
   one of these trials, refloated 4.4.1913 and towed to drydock by the
   service craft *Buffle*. To the Domaines 11.7.1913 for sale, sold
   24.10.1913 to M. Arthur Hanse-Trouvé of Boulogne-sur-Mer to BU.

---

**MAGENTA.** *Cuirassé d'escadre.* Battleship with four barbettes in a lozenge
arrangement, steel armour, a steel and iron hull, and a ram bow. One funnel, two heavy military masts, no sails. Designed by Huin.

On 7 October 1880 Minister of Marine Cloué ordered the dockyard at
Toulon to begin construction of a new battleship which he named
*Magenta*. Her history before and during construction is given above along
with that of her two half-sisters, *Marceau,* and *Neptune.* Her steel belt and
barbette armour was supplied by Schneider.

   During trials it was noted that when turning *Magenta* was quick to heel
and slow to recover. It was found that successive modifications during
construction had made her stability worse than in either *Marceau* or
*Neptune*, although her excess weight of 252 tons was less than in those ships.
Several plans for modifying the upper works were proposed, but the only
visible action actually taken was, during a period in reserve from August to
December 1897, the replacement of the after military mast with a plain
signal mast, the removal of two of the 138.6mm guns in the battery, and
the movement of two guns in the forward battery forward one position.

**Proposed overhaul.** *Magenta* was placed in 2nd category reserve in June
1900 for an overhaul that was to include fitting new water tube boilers and
modifying the engines to accommodate the higher pressure of the new
boilers. New Belleville boilers were ordered on 14 August 1901, probably
requiring two funnels, but in the meantime the existing boilers were
retubed and the ship was assigned to the school for torpedo boat seamen,
making occasional sorties into the Hyères roadstead. Schneider delivered
the parts for the new engines in 1907 but there was no longer any question
of doing the work. The Belleville boilers were reassigned in 1909 to the
port facilities at Diego Suarez in Madagascar.

*The characteristics are based on a devis dated 21.3.1894.*
**Dimensions & tons:** 103.620m oa, 100.600m wl (+1.500m ram),
   101.700m pp (tip fwd to rudder) x 20.236m ext (0.80m above wl)
   (21.360m outside amidships turrets), 20.120m wl. 10,850.785t disp.
   Draught: 8.149m mean, 8.3805m aft. Men: 653.
**Machinery:** 12,000ihp designed at 90rpm and 6kg/cm$^2$ boiler pressure.
   Trials (25.7.1893) 10,705.45ihp = 16.205kts at 87.28rpm. 2 screws.
   2 groups of 2 vertical compound engines each with 2 cylinders of
   1.060m and 2.020m diameter and 1.000m stroke, 2 engines coupled
   on each shaft, one of which could be disconnected at low speeds.
   8 cylindrical direct flame boilers. 600t coal (normal), 615t (actual).
**Armour:**
Side: Belt at waterline (steel) 450mm amidships, 320mm fwd, 300mm
   aft.
Guns: Barbettes (steel) 350mm.

The battleship *Magenta* before replacement of the after military mast with a pole
in 1897. Her bow was originally designed as that of *Neptune* but was redesigned
during construction to make it less wet underway. *(NHHC from ONI album of
foreign warships dated about 1900, NH-88811)*

Deck (iron): flat 80mm.
Conning tower: 150mm including plating.
**Guns:**
(1894) 4 x 340mm/28.5 M1881 (turrets), 16 x 138.6mm/30 M1884 QF
   (12 in the battery, 4 at the corners of the flying bridge), 6 x 65mm/50
   M1888 QF, 18 x 47mm/40 M1885 QF, 6 x 37mm/20 M1885 QF,
   4 x 37mm revolving cannon. **Torpedoes:** 3 tubes for 450mm M1889
   and M1892 torpedoes (2 in the battery and one aft in the admiral's
   salon). **Searchlights:** 6 x 60cm. 2 more 37mm revolving cannon were
   soon added on the platform of the forward barbette.
(1898) 4 x 340mm (turrets), 14 x 138.6mm (10 battery, 4 flying bridge),
   6 x 65mm, 14 x 47mm QF, 6 x 37mm QF, 2 x 37mm revolving cannon, 1 x Maxim.
(1903) Same but 3 x 37mm QF removed. An above-water 356mm tube
   was added on the deck below the battery for the school, along with
   three 356mm and two 381mm torpedoes.

*Magenta* Toulon Dyd/Schneider, Creusot.
On list 1.1881. Ord: 7.10.1880. K: 18.1.1883. L: 19.4.1890.
   Comm: 1.7.1892 (trials), 29.10.1893 (full).
Budget 1880. Construction begun 15.1.1881. Engines ordered 4.8.1884.
   Installation of engines completed 5.6.1892. Manned for trials
   1.1.1893, first underway trials in April, official trials 6-9.1893. Left
   Toulon 20.11.1893 to join the *Escadre de la Méditerranée*. In a short-
   lived training division 1898-99 with *Neptune, Marceau,* and
   *Calédonien.* Relieved *Marceau* as school for torpedo boat seamen at
   Toulon 1.6.1900, relieved by her 1.7.1907. Decomm. 28.10.1907 and
   14.2.1908, condemnation proposed 31.10.1908. Struck 6.5.1909,
   replaced *Colbert* as barracks hulk for mobilisation crews at Toulon
   1909-1910. To the Domaines 1911 for sale, offered for sale 1.8.1911
   by the Domaines with *Amiral Baudin, Pascal, Milan,* and smaller vessels including torpedo boats and submarines and sold to M. Bénédic.

---

**BRENNUS** (i) **Class.** *First design. Cuirassés d'escadre.* Battleships with two
turrets *en echelon* on top of a central citadel, a steel hull with unarmoured
ends, and a ram bow. Two funnels (initially four), two military masts, no
sails. Designed by de Bussy.

The 1882 budget (submitted in January 1881) included two new unnamed *cuirassés d'escadre* to be begun during 1882, one at Lorient and one at Toulon. The ships were ordered on 25 November 1881, were delayed to the 1883 budget in March 1882, and were named *Brennus* and *Charles Martel* on 7 December 1882.

On 10 March 1882 the ministry asked for a preliminary design for a new squadron battleship. De Bussy presented a design dated 3 May 1882 with plans dated 6 May 1882. His design broke radically with recent French practice by adopting enclosed armoured turrets instead of barbettes and a partial instead of complete armour belt that left the ends without heavy armour protection. (Six of the seven designs submitted for the *Amiral Baudin* class in 1878 also had four guns in two enclosed turrets but the one with barbettes was selected instead.) The result was a ship that resembled the British *Inflexible* more closely than any other French design. The ship's four 340mm guns, in two twin turrets arranged *en echelon* with the guns at 4.50m above the waterline, could all fire directly forward, directly astern, and on both broadsides. Of the eight 138.6mm guns (four of which were in open twin mountings) four could fire directly forward and aft and two others could come close to the axis, while six could fire on each beam.

De Bussy's concentrated the protection in his design in a 2.60m high layer the entire length of the ship between one armoured deck 1.60m below the waterline and one 1.00m above it. The amidships part of this layer, 50.8m long, was the heavily armoured citadel, with a maximum of 440mm armour on its sides and on its curved transverse bulkheads. The turrets were above it on bases that were a full deck level high, both turrets and bases with 300mm armour. The armour at the ends was light, with 75mm on the lower armoured deck, 16mm on the upper one, and sides 150mm thick above the waterline and unarmoured below it. The main protection for the ends was a cellular layer subdivided into many small compartments filled with 500 tons of coal briquettes.

De Bussy chose triple screws with three engines for his design because one screw was not enough once sails had been abandoned and ships with two screws had been found not to steer well. Three screws gave both redundancy and good steering, and the centre engine was also well protected against torpedoes. (The French used triple screws in their battleships and large cruisers from 1892 to 1905 for similar reasons.) He chose a very high 17-knot speed so that the fast but lightly protected Italian *Italia* and *Lepanto* could not run from the better protected French ship in an engagement. For the boilers he used a complex scheme adopted by the *Conseil des travaux* on 22 February 1882 for a fast ram that was never built. This scheme required four funnels on the centreline, the two middle ones being for six cylindrical return flame boilers capable of generating 4,560ihp to give 13.5 knots with moderate forced draught for normal steaming, and the other two for 18 direct flame locomotive boilers, 12 served by the forward funnel and 6 by the after one, that could add 5,890ihp to produce 10,450ihp for 17 knots (and more in short bursts). The locomotive boilers were of a type used in torpedo boats, but they would not fatigue as they did in torpedo boats because their firing rate would be much more conservative.

De Bussy, aware of the ingrained French preference for open barbettes, commented that the general nature of the design would not be altered if the 340mm guns were mounted instead in pairs in two barbettes with the same armour, but although these guns would be carried higher at 6.50m above the water he argued strongly against barbette mountings because their increased vulnerability and other disadvantages would not be offset by the 'pretended advantage' of better visibility for the gun crews.

The *Conseil des travaux* examined de Bussy's design between 27 and 30 May 1882 and was deeply divided on several issues. The system of protection, with the central citadel, partial belt amidships, and lightly armoured cellular ends was accepted by nine votes to five but the question of turrets or barbettes for the main armament generated a tie, broken by Minister of Marine Jauréguiberry's decision on 29 July 1882 in his approval of the Council's report to proceed with de Bussy's turrets. Only a handful of specific changes to the design came out of these sessions: the height of the main guns above the waterline was raised from 4.5m to 5.0m, the

maximum thickness of the belt was increased from 440mm to 450mm, and the armour on the turret and their bases was increased from 300mm to 400mm.

Minister Jauréguiberry made his decision in principle to build the ships on 2 August 1882 and on 8 August 1882 he formally ordered the Lorient and Toulon dockyards to begin them immediately. One significant change was made to the design at this time when Jauréguiberry directed the use of 12 cylindrical boilers instead of the two different sets of boilers in the original design, simplifying the propulsion plant and reduced the number of funnels to the middle two. He approved a hull lines plan on 6 September 1882 which was sent to Lorient with several other hull plans during the next three days. De Bussy followed with detailed plans signed by himself and Minister of Marine Jauréguiberry on 29 November 1882 and with more on 30 December 1882. On 21 April 1883 Lorient was ordered to hasten work on its ship.

*First design* (turret ship). Data from the 5.1882 design with changes through 12.1882 including the simplification of the propulsion plant in 9.1882.

**Dimensions & tons:** 105.000m wl/pp x 19.360m ext and wl. 9,742t disp. Draught: 7.55m mean, 8.00m aft. Men: 500.

**Machinery:** 10,350ihp (3 x 3,450ihp) at 6kg/cm² boiler pressure. Speed 17kts. 3 screws. 3 vertical compound engines. 12 cylindrical Admiralty cylindrical boilers in four groups of three. 900t coal. Range 5,000nm @ 10kts.

**Armour:** (compound or steel depending on contractor selected)
Side: Belt at waterline amidships within the citadel 450mm including curvilinear transverse bulkheads. Ends outside the citadel 150mm above the waterline, unprotected below the waterline.
Guns: Turrets 400mm including fixed bases.
Decks: Upper deck at top of citadel, 100mm within citadel, 16mm at ends. Lower deck at bottom of citadel, 20mm within citadel (a splinter deck), 75mm at ends.

**Guns:** 4 x 340mm in twin enclosed turrets *en echelon* amidships, 8 x 138.6mm (including 4 in 2 open twin mountings), 8 x 37mm revolving cannon in the tops and more on the upper deck.

**Torpedoes:** 2 tubes on top of the citadel near the supports for the main turrets, one on each side.

---

*BRENNUS* (i) **Class.** *Second design.* *Cuirassés d'escadre.* Battleships with four barbettes in a lozenge arrangement, a steel hull, and a straight bow. One funnel, two masts with armed tops, schooner rig. Designed by Huin.

The 1883 budget (submitted March 1882) contained a third new battleship to be built by contract and the 1884 budget (March 1883) added a fourth to be built at Brest. Neither of these ships was in the 1885 budget (February 1884).

The decision to break with barbette ships with complete waterline belts taken by a majority in the *Conseil des travaux* and Minister Jauréguibery in May 1882 was far from unanimous, and majority opinion soon turned against this decision. On 29 June 1883 a new Minister of Marine, Senator Charles Marie Brun, in view of the plan to lay down a new ship at Brest under the 1884 budget, asked the *Conseil des travaux* if some modifications should be made to the plans for *Brennus* or if it would be preferable to build the new ship on other plans. On 17 July, motivated primarily by concern over the vulnerability of the lightly armoured cellular ends, the Council decided that the new ship at Brest should not be built on the *Brennus* design but that a new design should be developed on lines very similar to those of *Marceau* but with the 17 knot speed of de Bussy's design. The Brest ship and its design, however, were not proceeded with for budgetary reasons.

The *Conseil des travaux* could not extend this recommendation to *Brennus* and *Charles Martel* because Minister had not specifically posed that question. On 18 September 1883 another new Minister, Vice Admiral

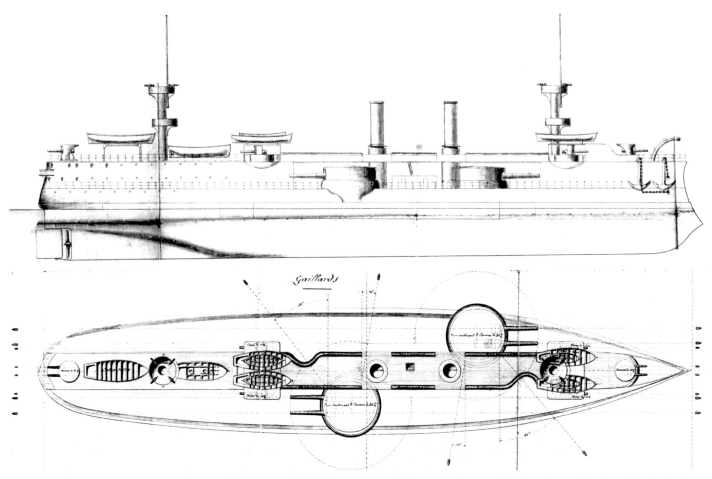

Outboard profile and upper deck plans of the battleships *Brennus* and *Charles Martel* of the central citadel type drawn by Louis De Bussy, chief of the *Service technique des Constructions navales* and designer of the ship. The deck plan was approved by Minister Jauréguiberry on 29 November 1882, both plans were also dated 30 December 1882. The three screws are abreast of each other. The turret ships would have been built to this design. *(SHM/SHD, 8DD1-58)*

Peyron, did so by asking the Council whether from a technical perspective it would be appropriate to build *Brennus* and *Charles Martel* to the plans originally adopted or if it would be better to abandon those plans and follow those of *Marceau*. Anticipating the answer, on the same date Peyron suspended the contracts for components for the ships. On 23 October 1883 the *Conseil des travaux* advised that *Brennus* and *Charles Martel* should be built to the plans of *Marceau* but without the changes recommended in July for the Brest ship because there was not time to wait for completely new plans. It asked, however, for modifications to the current *Marceau* design including a straight bow (the woes later experienced by *Neptune* with her sloping ram bow having already been anticipated), finer lines aft to be obtained by lengthening the after part of the ship, and an armament of four 340mm guns in barbettes with 350mm armour as just proposed for *Marceau* and her half sisters. On 27 October 1883 Minister Peyron asked Lorient to have Huin develop these modified *Marceau* plans for *Brennus*.

On 17 November 1883 Lorient forwarded initial plans signed on that date by Huin. He increased the length between perpendiculars of the *Marceau* design from 98.60m to 105.50m by moving the forward perpendicular nearly to the tip of the bow and lengthening the stern about 4.60m to refine the lines there. He increased the secondary battery to seventeen 138.6mm guns and lengthened the thick part of the belt to cover the magazines. On 28 November 1883 the Inspector of the *Génie maritime*, Jules Marielle, recommended a few changes to Huin's plans including

restoring a small ram attached to the straight bow like that in the original *Brennus* plans. Lorient sent the modified plans to Paris on 8 December and Marielle advised Minister Peyron on 12 December 1883 that they could be approved.

**Revised second design.** On 22 Jan 1884 Lorient sent a second series of modified *Marceau* plans for *Brennus* signed on that date by Huin. Minister Peyron referred them to Marielle on 30 January 1884 and eventually to the *Conseil des travaux* on 4 March 1884. The Council noted that the beam 340mm guns could not fire ahead or astern without endangering the end turrets and recommended moving the axis of each gun out about 1m and putting a shield of vertical plating fore and aft of it to protect the upper decks and the end turrets from their blast. It also noted that the conning tower was badly placed amidships aft of the 3m wide cylindrical funnel, and since there was nowhere else to put it the Council recommended flattening and lengthening the funnel, widening the front of the conning tower, and (to save weight) changing its shape to a trapezoid with a shorter back. It also recommended providing a steering station where the helmsman's view was not obstructed by the funnel. It accepted Huin's additional 138.6mm guns but asked that two ports be added to the stern so two of them could fire aft if needed. The full Council added a requirement for a peacetime ship control station given the poor position of the conning tower and the complete absence of superstructure forward of the funnel. Lorient was informed on 12 March 1884 that Minister Peyron had accepted the plans proposed by Huin for *Brennus* with some reserves. Huin signed and forwarded his final set of plans on 8 May and 31 July 1884.

Major forgings for *Brennus* including the stempost and sternpost were ordered from the navy's foundry at Guérigny on 1 December 1884, Lorient submitted on 9 December 1884 a lines plan and calculations of displacement and stability, and the start of both ships' construction was probably ordered on 2 January 1885. On 6 March 1885 Minister Peyron ordered a reduction in the deck armour from 80mm to 70mm.

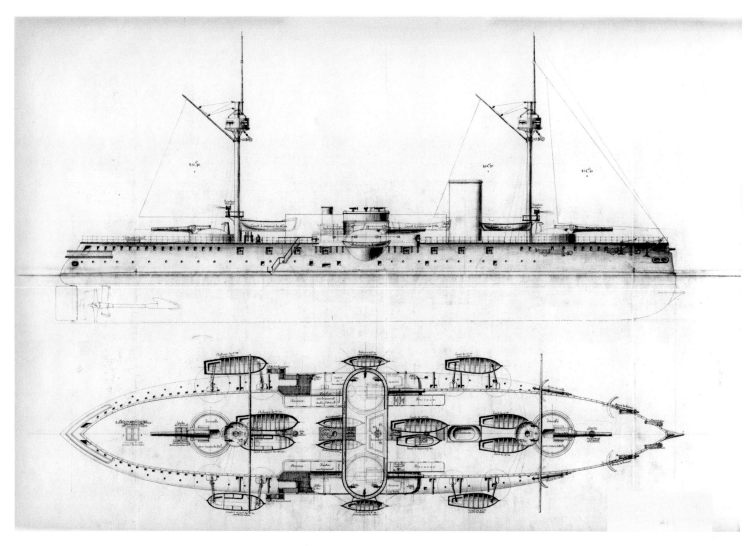

Outboard profile and upper deck plans (*plan d'ensemble*) of the battleships *Brennus* and *Charles Martel* of the 'modified *Marceau*' type, signed by naval constructor Huin at Lorient on 31 July 1884. These plans were prepared in accordance with a ministerial dispatch of 12 March 1884 that approved an earlier version of the design but directed some changes to it. *(SHM/SHD, 8DD1-58)*

On 20 January 1886 Huin wrote to the new Minister of Marine, Rear Admiral Aube, that the lines had been laid out, nearly all of the material necessary for construction of the two ships had been ordered, and work on the hulls was just underway, at about half a hundredth for each. The engines had not yet been ordered although it was planned to order one from Indret soon as Indret needed work. On 27 January 1886, when work on *Brennus* was in full activity, Aube suspended the two ships *sine die* and ordered work stopped.

*Second design* (barbette ship, improved *Marceau*).
**Dimensions & tons:** 107.60m wl (+1.60m ram), 105.50m pp (wl fwd to rudder) x 20.25m ext, 20.12m wl. 10,649.5t disp. Draught: 8.00m mean, 8.30m aft. Men: 450.
**Machinery:** 6.00 kg/cm² boiler pressure. Speed 16.4kts. 2 screws. 8 cylindrical direct-flame boilers. 600t coal. Range 2,900nm @ 10kts.
**Armour:** (compound or steel depending on contractor selected)
Side: Belt at waterline 450mm amidships, 300mm fwd and aft. Height from 1.50m below the wl to 0.65m above.
Guns: Barbettes 350mm with hoods.
Deck: 80mm amidships and ends (reduced to 70mm in 1885).
**Guns:** 4 x 340mm/28.5 M1881 long in barbette turrets (2 at ends, 2 on sides), 17 x 138.6mm (1 in the bow and 16 on the sides, probably 138.6mm/30 M1881), 14 x 37mm Hotchkiss revolving cannon.
**Torpedoes:** 3 tubes for 356mm M1880 (4.42m) torpedoes (1 in the stern and 2 on the sides aft of the barbettes, all on the armoured deck below the battery deck).

*Brennus* (i) Lorient Dyd.
On list 1.1883. Ord: 25.11.1881. K: 2.1.1885. Suspended 27.1.1886.
Budget 1882 (delayed to 1883). Named 7.12.1882. Final plans approved 12.3.1884, start of construction probably ordered 2.1.1885. Suspended 27.1.1886 with the lower part of the hull from forward frame 16 to after frame 17 (the middle of the boiler room to the middle of the engine room) on the ways, more of the lower hull assembled, and fabrication of 482 tons of material completed with another 801 tons less advanced, and 1,323 tons in storage. Another 213 tons were given to other ships. Resumed to a new design using some of these materials in 1887.

*Charles Martel* (i) Toulon Dyd.
On list 1.1883. Ord: 25.11.1881. K: 1885. Suspended 27.1.1886.
Budget 1882 (delayed to 1883). Named 7.12.1882. Barely begun when suspended 27.1.1886, not resumed. Materials used in various later ships at Toulon, notably *Carnot* and *Bouvet*.

*N* (Unnamed) Contract
Budget 1883 (delayed to 1884). Not in the 1885 budget.

*N* (Unnamed) Brest Dyd
Budget 1884. Not in the 1885 budget.

# Chapter Two

# Station and Coast Defence Ironclads, 1859-1882

## I. STATION IRONCLADS

### (A) Station Ironclads.

Originally *Corvettes cuirassées*, to *Cuirassés de 2ᵉ rang* in the 1.1873 fleet list, *Cuirassés de stations* 1.1880, *Cuirassés de croisière* 1.1885, *Cuirassés de station* 1.1891, *Cuirassés de croisière* 1.1892.

### Station flagships

In the early 1860s the squadrons maintained by European powers on distant stations were headed by large wooden steam frigates. The advent of armoured frigates led to a desire to introduce armoured ships overseas, but armoured frigates like *Gloire*, which had taken the place of ships of the line, were too large and expensive to send outside of Europe and also lacked features like a full sail rig and copper hull sheathing needed for long cruises far from supporting bases. The result was a decision to build armoured corvettes, later called 2nd rank ironclads (*cuirassés de 2ᵉ rang*), of a size equivalent to the latest wooden steam frigates and with a full sail rig and powerful artillery behind armour. The British showed the way to building smaller cruising ironclads by ordering in 1862 the ironclad corvette *Favourite* and the ironclad sloops *Enterprise* and *Research*.

*BELLIQUEUSE. Corvette cuirassée.* Central battery ironclad with a wooden hull, wooden upper works, and a ram bow. One funnel, three masts, barque rig. Designed by Dupuy de Lôme.

On 5 September 1863 Minister of Marine Chasseloup-Laubat approved plans by Dupuy de Lôme for France's first armoured corvette and ordered Toulon to lay down the ship. A vessel smaller than the armoured frigates and designed for overseas cruising, she had a complete 150mm wrought iron armour belt from the battery deck down to 1.5m below the waterline and 120mm side armour above it amidships over the guns with armoured transverse bulkheads. She was initially designed for twelve 164.7mm guns (then the largest rifled type available) in a 23-metre long central battery and two 164.7mm guns on the upper deck to provide axial fire. Following the introduction of Model 1864 artillery she was completed with four 194mm/18 M1864 and four 164.7mm/19.2 M1864 guns in the battery and two 164.7mm/19.2 M1864 guns on the upper deck (one in the bow, the other in the stern). Like the *Magenta* class she carried a bronze ram at the bow, and like *Magenta* the unarmoured portions at the ends of her hull were made of wood and vulnerable to fire. Her designed speed was 12 knots.

*Belliqueuse* was undocked 7 June 1866 at Toulon following completion of sheathing the hull. She was an excellent sea boat, steered remarkably well, and had comfortable accommodations, although under sail she was slow and handled poorly.

*The characteristics are based on a devis dated 8.12.1869.*

**Dimensions & tons:** c74.5m oa, 69.85m wl (+2.70m ram), 69.85m pp (wl fwd to rudder) x 14.00+0.12m sheathing ext and wl. 3,776t disp. Draught: 6.433m mean, 6.883m aft. Men: 360.

**Machinery:** 500nhp (450 from 1867) and 1,800ihp designed at 66rpm and 15.94kg/cm² boiler pressure. Trials (4.1866) 1,207ihp = 10.88kts at 63.3rpm and 0.987kg/cm² boiler pressure. 1 screw. 1 horizontal simple expansion engine *type Algésiras modifié* with return connecting rods and 2 cylinders of 1.54m diameter and 0.928m stroke. 4 high rectangular tubular boilers with superheaters. 318t coal. Range 2,810nm @ 10kts.

**Armour:** (iron)
Side: Belt at waterline 150mm amidships and ends. Height from 1.69m below the wl to 0.09m above (designed 1.22m to 0.56m).
Guns: Battery amidships 120mm, armoured transverse bulkheads.
Deck: 10mm plating on 110mm wood.

**Guns:**
(1869) 4 x 194mm/18 M1864 and 4 x 164.7mm/19.2 M1864 in the battery, 2 x 164.7mm/19.2 M1864 on the upper deck (one in the bow and one in the stern). Inside the battery on each side one 164.7mm gun was forward of the funnel and two 194mm guns with a 164.7mm gun between them were aft of it.
(1876) 4 x 194mm/19.8 M1870 and 4 x 164.7mm/19.2 M1864 (battery), 5 x 138.6mm/21.3 M1870 on the upper deck. 4 x 37mm Hotchkiss revolving (revolver) cannon were soon added.

*Belliqueuse* Toulon Dyd/F.C. Méditerranée, Marseille.
On list 1.1864. Ord: 5.9.1863. K: 13.12.1863. L: 6.9.1865.
Comm: 4.12.1865 (trials), 30.10.1866 (full).
Departed for the Pacific station 22.12.1866, returned to Brest 25.5.1869 after circumnavigating the globe and decomm. 22.6.1869. In commission 15.11.1869 to 29.6.1871 including war service and from 15.5.1872 to 20.5.1874 for the China station replacing *Alma*. Struck 3.5.1886, for disposal at Toulon 1886-88. Used as target for experiments with shells filled with melinite (a high explosive containing picric acid). Sold 1889 at Toulon to BU.

*ALMA* **Class.** *Corvettes cuirassées.* Central battery ironclads with two upper deck barbettes, a wooden hull, iron upper works, and a ram bow. One funnel (two abreast in *Thétis* and *Jeanne d'Arc*), three masts, barque rig. Designed by Dupuy de Lôme.

While *Belliqueuse* was under construction ideas on the role of ironclads in future combat changed. Even before the battle of Lissa the French became convinced that future combat would be head on rather than on the broadside, with the ram and axial fire from heavy guns being the determining factors. The result was the replacement of the 1st rank *Magenta* and 2nd rank *Belliqueuse* types of ironclads by the 1st rank *Océan* and the new 2nd rank *Alma* classes.

On 15 January 1865 Minister of Marine Chasseloup-Laubat ordered the ports to lay down four armoured frigates (the *Océan* class), three armoured corvettes, and three armoured coast defence ships. On 8 April 1865 four new armoured corvettes were named *Jeanne d'Arc, Alma, Reine Blanche*, and *Thétis*, a fourth ship (*Reine Blanche*) having been added at Lorient during January. By the end of 1865 a fifth ship had been added at Cherbourg and Rochefort had been brought into the programme with orders for two more ships. Plans by by Dupuy de Lôme were approved on 28 March and 20 April 1865. They included a bronze ram and upper works outside the battery made of 15mm iron plating. Paul Dislère, the secretary of the *Conseil des travaux*, recalled in around 1874 that the idea behind these ships was to provide strong fire directly ahead by means of guns placed in barbettes with their mechanisms and crews protected by armour. The orig-

The ironclad corvette *Alma* as completed with a barque rig. The ship has probably just completed coaling from the lighter alongside. Photo by He. Aunouse. *(NHHC, NH-74999)*

inal design of *Alma* thus included two superimposed redoubts. One, the battery itself, contained four 194mm guns, the other, a very narrow redoubt on the upper deck with an open top, enclosed the funnel and the command post and carried at its four corners 164.7mm guns. But it was soon feared that having four guns in a small uncovered space offered too dangerous a target for explosive projectiles, and it was found necessary to move all the way to the sides of the ship the guns whose blast in their original positions would have swept the deck from amidships to the ends of the ship. It was then decided to put them, now 164.7mm M1864 guns, into four individual barbettes over the corners of the lower armoured battery. This lower battery was only 11.50m long on the sides compared to 23m in *Belliqueuse*. As of November 1867 the design also included four 12pdr (121mm) bronze rifles on the upper deck for the boats. While the new ship had the same speed, range, and displacement (3,390 tons instead of 3,370 tons) as *Belliqueuse*, it differed in the substitution of iron for wood in the unprotected ends, a feature retained in all later 2nd rank ironclad designs. Subsequent design changes such as the addition of more watertight bulkheads to defend against ramming increased the weight of the ship, and considering also that the 164.7mm gun was no longer adequate, on 12 March 1868 it was decided to omit the after two barbettes and arm the forward pair with 194mm guns. The battery as completed was thus four 194mm guns in the battery, two 194mm guns in the barbettes, and four

12pdrs on the upper deck. The engines were all built to a single design by Dupuy de Lôme.

In service they steered extremely well and their power of their barbette guns was much appreciated, but their speed was a bit low and the battery guns were hard to handle and were submerged in even moderately heavy weather.

*The characteristics are based on a devis for* Jeanne d'Arc *dated 6.5.1879.*

**Dimensions & tons:** 72.2m oa, 70.57m wl (+3.07m ram), 69.07m pp (wl fwd to rudder) x 14.00+0.08m sheathing ext, 13.86+0.08m wl. 3,771t disp. Draught: 6.49m mean, 7.09m aft. Men: 313.

**Machinery:** 450nhp and 1,800ihp designed at 70rpm and 1.80kg/cm² boiler pressure. Trials (*Jeanne d'Arc*, 1.1869) 1,884ihp = 12.333kts at 69.3rpm and 2.30kg/cm² boiler pressure. 1 screw. 1 horizontal compound engine with return connecting rods and 3 cylinders of 1.60m diameter and 0.85m stroke. 4 low rectangular tubular boilers with steam dryers (superheaters). 258t coal. Range 2,580nm @ 10kts. Twin funnels side by side in *Thétis* and *Jeanne d'Arc* and single funnel in others.

**Armour:** (iron)

Side: Belt at waterline 150mm amidships and ends. Height from 1.61m below the wl to 1.13m above.

Guns: Central battery 120mm sides above belt with 130mm to 100mm transverse bulkheads. Barbettes 100mm.

Deck: 10mm plating on 70mm wood (20mm on 70mm in *Alma, Reine Blanche*, and *Thétis*).

**Guns:**

(1869) 4 x 194mm/18 M1864 in the battery, 2 x 194mm/18 M1864 in barbette turrets (fixed towers with rotating platforms), 4 x 12pdr (121mm/17) bronze MLR field guns on the upper deck, 2 or 4 x 4pdr (86.5mm/11) bronze MLR.

(1874-1883) The 194mm guns were upgraded to M1870 during the mid-1870s, some ships including *Armide* and *Atalante* added 2 more 12pdr (121mm/17) bronze. 4 x 37mm Hotchkiss revolving cannon were added by decision of 28.6.1878. In 1881 the light armament of *Alma* was 2 x 65mm/15 bronze landing and 4 x 37mm revolving cannon, in 1883 *Atalante* had 2 x 65mm/15 bronze landing and 12 x 37mm Hotchkiss.

(1884, *Reine Blanche*) 6 x 194mm, 4 x 100mm, 4 x 37mm, 2 x 4pdr (86.5mm/11) bronze.

(1885, *Montcalm* and *Thétis*) 6 x 194mm/19.8 M1870 Nº 2, 4 x 90mm/22 M1881, 2 x 65mm landing, 8 x 37mm.

*Alma* Lorient Dyd/C.A. de l'Océan (ex Mazeline), Le Havre.
On list 1.1866. Ord: 15.1.1865. K: 1.10.1865. L: 25.11.1867. Comm: 24.8.1868 (trials). C: 5.1869.
Final trials 21.4.1869 at Lorient. Decomm. at Brest 9.7.1869 and wood sheathing fitted over armour there. Recomm. 31.3.1870 and sent to the China station, where she blockaded the German corvettes *Hertha* and *Medusa* in Japan. Decomm. 6.2.1873. In commission 13.10.1873 to 30.12.1875 for service in the *Escadre d'évolutions* (1st division). Received torpedo equipment at Cherbourg 1875-76. Struck 12.11.1886, hulk at Cherbourg 1886-1893. Sold 5.1893 to BU.

*Jeanne d'Arc* Cherbourg Dyd/Indret (engines designed by Victorin Sabattier).
On list 1.1866. Ord: 15.1.1865. K: 5.1865. L: 28.9.1867. Comm: 9.3.1868 (trials). C: 4.1869.
Decomm. at Brest 12.5.1869 after trials. In commission 12.4.1870 to 15.11.1870 for war service in the *Escadre du Nord*. In commission 18.1.1871 to 1.1.1876 for service in the *Escadre d'évolutions* (1st division). Saw no overseas station duty. Struck 28.6.1883, for disposal at Brest 1883-1885.

*Thétis* Toulon Dyd/F.C. Méditerranée, Marseille (engines designed by Louis Édouard Lecointre).
On list 1.1866. Ord: 15.1.1865. K: 18.7.1865. L: 22.8.1867. Comm: 1.5.1868 (trials). C: 1.1869.
Named 8.4.1865. Trials off Toulon 25.2.1869, departed Toulon for Brest 8.3.1869, decomm. 17.4.1869. Full commission 12.6.1870, operated in the Baltic 1870 with the *Escadre du Nord*. Joined the *Escadre d'évolutions* (2nd division) at Toulon 1871. Decomm 17.3.1876 and reboilered 1876. Departed for the Pacific 8.10.1885 but lost her screw and had to return to Lorient under sail. Sent to Noumea 1888 as station ship and annex to the aviso *Loyalty* serving the governor of the colony. Struck 1.5.1895, initially was to be ceded to the colonial service at New Caledonia but was sold c1897 to the Établissements Ballande and BU 1900 at Sydney.

*Reine Blanche* Lorient Dyd/Indret (engines designed by Victorin Sabattier).
On list 1.1866. Ord: 1.1865. K: 1.10.1865. L: 10.3.1868. Comm: 15.4.1869 (trials). C: 9.1869.
Trials 21-22.6.1869, decommissioned 21.10.1869. Full commission 19.7.1870 to 20.11.1870, made war cruise to the Shetland Islands. In commission 18.7.1871 to 16.2.1876 for service in the *Escadre d'évolutions* (2nd division) at Toulon. Reboilered 1876. Rammed 3.7.1877 by *Thétis* and run ashore at La Badine (Hyères) to prevent sinking, refloated 6.7.1877 and repaired at Toulon. First overseas station cruise was to the Pacific beginning 1.1884. Struck 12.11.1886, hulk at Cherbourg 1887-1889, barracks hulk 1889-1893, then BU.

*Montcalm* Rochefort Dyd/F.C. Méditerranée, Marseille (engines designed by Louis Édouard Lecointre).

On list 1.1866. Ord: 8.10.1865. K: 26.10.1865. L: 16.10.1868. Comm: 15.7.1869 (trials). C: 10.1869.
Named *Indienne* when ordered, renamed *Montcalm* 25.3.1867. Arrived at Brest 14.10.1869 for official trials, left Brest for Cherbourg 5.1.1870 and then for Toulon and the *Escadre de la Méditerranée* 24.2.1870. War cruises in the North Sea and Atlantic 1870-71, decomm. 1.8.1871. In commission 1.11.1873 to 6.6.1876 for the China station replacing *Belliqueuse*. Struck 2.4.1891 at Cherbourg.

*Atalante* Cherbourg Dyd/C.A. de l'Océan (ex Mazeline), Le Havre.
On list 1.1866. K: 6.1865. L: 9.4.1868. Comm: 1.4.1869 (trials). C: 6.1869.
Decomm. at Brest 11.7.1869. In commission 4.3.1870 to 6.11.1870, with the fleet off Helgoland 8.1870. Recomm. at Cherbourg 18.1.1871 and decomm. at Lorient 17.8.1871. In commission 1.7.1872 to 19.12.1874 for the Pacific station and from 1.12.1875 to 9.6.1878 for the China station replacing *Montcalm*. Reboilered 1880. Station hulk at Saigon 6.1885. Replaced 1887 by the sail transport *Loire* (formerly screw battleship *Prince Jérôme*). Struck 2.2.1887, for sale in Cochinchina 1887-1890, sank from neglect at Saigon 10.1890 and wreck abandoned.

*Armide* Rochefort Dyd/Schneider, Creusot (engines designed by Dupuy de Lôme).
On list 1.1866. K: 26.10.1865. L: 12.4.1867. Comm: 5.11.1868 (trials). C: 2.1869.
Decomm. 8.6.1869 at Brest after trials. In full commission 20.7.1870 to 18.11.1870 for war service in the Baltic. Recomm. 12.1.1871 to blockade the German cruiser *Arcona* at Lisbon, then to the *Escadre d'évolutions* (1st division) until decomm. 28.10.1873. In commission 23.8.1874 to 23.12.1875 for service in the *Escadre d'évolutions* (2nd division). Comm. 20.11.1877 for the China station replacing *Atalante*. Struck 19.10.1882, for disposal at Toulon 1882-1886. Cast adrift 24.3.1886 off Golfe-Juan near Villefranche as target ship for 6 battleships armed with 240mm and 340mm guns and for torpedo boats, kept afloat by empty barrels. Sold 1886 at Toulon, BU 1887.

........................................

*LA GALISSONNIÈRE. Corvette cuirassée.* Central battery ironclad with two upper deck barbettes, a wooden hull, iron upper works, and a ram bow. One funnel, three masts, ship rig. Designed by Dupuy de Lôme.

While the seven *Alma* class ships were under construction it was realized that their speed was not as high as was needed, and in 1869 it was decided to give all ships the largest guns they could carry, which for 2nd rank ironclads meant replacing 194mm guns with 240mm guns. Dupuy de Lôme therefore produced a new design in which the speed could be increased and 240mm guns could be embarked. The rest of the characteristics were to be as *Alma*, but the length of the battery had to be increased from 11.50m to 15m to accommodate the handling of the larger guns and the designed displacement rose from the 3,700 to 3,800 tons of the *Alma* type to 4,155 tons (and even more in service). In addition, since it was important to retain the limited draught of the *Alma* class for operations in some overseas areas, and since the diameter of the single screw could not be increased, it was decided to fit twin screws. The ship was initially ordered on 21 April 1867 to use a 430nhp engine originally planned for the transport *Corrèze*, her construction was postponed on 16 May 1867, probably for budgetary reasons, and finally reinstated on 13 July 1868.

She proved successful in service except for some shortcomings under sail. Her name was sometimes rendered as *Lagalissonnière*.

*The characteristics are based on a devis dated 5.10.1878.*
**Dimensions & tons:** 79.74m oa, 78.12m wl (+3.12m ram), 76.32m pp (wl fwd to rudder) x 14.75+0.16m sheathing ext, 14.70+0.16m wl. 4,654t disp. Draught: 6.723m mean, 7.223m aft. Men: 391.
**Machinery:** 500nhp and 2,000ihp designed at 92rpm and 2.25kg/cm²

boiler pressure. Trials (10.1878) 2,194ihp = 12.69kts at 89.4/91.1rpm (port/stbd), 2.344kg/cm² boiler pressure. 2 screws. 2 horizontal compound engines with return connecting rods and 3 cylinders of 1.20m diameter and 0.70m stroke. 4 high rectangular tubular boilers. 355t coal. Range 3,240nm @ 10kts.

**Armour:** (iron)

Side: Belt at waterline 150mm amidships and ends. Height from 1.75m below the wl to 0.85m above.

Guns: Central battery 120mm sides, 130mm to 100mm transverse bulkheads. Barbettes 120mm.

Deck: 10mm plating on 80mm wood.

**Guns:**

(1874) 6 x 240mm/19 M1870 (4 in the battery, 2 in barbette turrets), 4 x 12pdr (121mm/17) bronze on the upper deck, and 4 x 4pdr (86.5mm/11) bronze.

(1878) 6 x 240mm, 6 x 12pdr (121mm/17) bronze on the upper deck, 4 x 37mm Hotchkiss revolving cannon, and 4 x 4pdr (86.5mm/11) bronze boat.

(1881) 6 x 240mm, 6 x 100mm on the upper deck, 2 x 65mm landing, 4 x 37mm (8 x 37mm in 1883).

*La Galissonnière* (*Lagalissonnière*) Brest Dyd/Indret (engines designed by Camille Audenet).

On list 1.1868. Ord: 21.4.1867 and 13.7.1868. K: 22.6.1868. L: 7.5.1872. Comm: 20.4.1874 (trials), 18.7.1874 (full).

Cruised around the world from 5.10.1874 to 19.3.1877, serving along the way as Pacific station flagship. Reboilered 1883. Struck 24.12.1894, for sale at Cherbourg 1894-1902.

--------

*VICTORIEUSE* **Class.** *Corvettes cuirassées.* Central battery ironclads with two upper deck barbettes, a wooden hull, iron upper works, and a ram bow. One funnel, three masts, ship rig. Designed by Sabattier.

As in the case of the 1st rank ironclad *Richelieu*, the use of twin screws in *La Galissonnière* gave rise to numerous objections and in response the two armoured corvettes begun in 1869 were given single screws. The armament and armour remained as in *La Galissonnière*. The two ships were designed by the new Director of Materiel, Victorin Sabattier, who replaced Dupuy de Lôme on 10 June 1869. The plans were approved on 28 October 1869. Their construction was much delayed during the 1870-1871 war giving rise to proposals for changes. On 27 October 1871 the *Conseil des travaux* accepted a radical redesign of the ships proposed by Sabattier that included deleting the central battery, moving the four battery guns to unprotected positions on the upper deck, and strengthening the belt and deck armour, but this *décuirassement* of the ships was not implemented. Instead the armament was updated on 27 November 1871, one 194mm gun being added under the forecastle, and six 138.6mm guns replacing four 12pdrs (121mm) on the upper deck. The armour belt around the hull was also moved up somewhat in response to an expected increase in draught.

*The characteristics are based on a devis for* Victorieuse *dated 25.10.1878.*

**Dimensions & tons:** 81.62m oa, 77.97m wl (+3.12m ram), 76.45m pp (wl fwd to rudder) x 14.72+0.16m sheathing ext, 14.60+0.16m wl. 4,595t disp. Draught: 6.695m mean, 7.17m aft. Men: 433.

**Machinery:** 575nhp and 2,400ihp designed at 88rpm and 2.31kg/cm² boiler pressure. Trials (*Victorieuse*, 8.1877) 2,379ihp = 12.87kts at 84.3rpm and 2.195kg/cm² boiler pressure. 1 screw. 1 horizontal compound engine with return connecting rods and 3 cylinders of 1.65m diameter and 0.85m stroke. 4 reinforced high rectangular tubular boilers. 340t coal. Range 3,100nm @ 10kts.

--------

The 2nd rank (station) ironclad *Victorieuse* as completed with a ship rig. The photo was taken at Algiers on 8 July 1886 while she was a unit of the *Escadre de la Méditerranée*. The ship in the right background is the aviso *Actif*, then serving as station ship at Algiers. (*NHHC, NH-74935*)

**Armour:** (iron)

Side: Belt at waterline 150mm amidships and ends. Height from 2.18m below the wl to 0.64m above.

Guns: Central battery 120mm sides, transverse bulkheads 130mm at the bottom and 100mm at the top. Barbettes 120mm.

Deck: 10mm plating on 80mm wood.

**Guns:**

(1878/80) 6 x 240mm/19 M1870 (4 in the battery, 2 in turrets), 1 x 194mm/19.8 M1870 under the forecastle and 6 x 138.6mm/21.3 M1870 on the upper deck (2 forward of the turrets and 4 evenly spaced abaft them) plus 4 x 37mm Hotchkiss revolving cannon. Also 1 x 12pdr (121mm/17) bronze field and 4 x 4pdr (86.5mm/11) bronze mountain guns for the boats.

(1882, *Victorieuse*) 6 x 240mm, 1 x 194mm, 6 x 138.6mm, 2 x 65mm landing, 4 x 37mm.

(1886, *Victorieuse*) 6 x 240mm, 1 x 194mm, 4 x 138.6mm, 2 x 90mm/22 M1881, 2 x 65mm landing, 8 x 37mm, and 1 torpedo tube.

*Victorieuse* Toulon Dyd/Indret (engines designed by Joseph Joëssel).
On list 1.1870. K: 5.8.1869. L: 18.11.1875. Comm: 1.11.1876 (trials). C: 11.1877.

To reserve 14.11.1877 after trials. Commissioned 10.9.1878 for the Pacific station. Reboiled 1886. Condemned 5.1897 as a *cuirassé* and converted at Brest to a *convoyeur de torpilleurs* and central ship for the *Défense mobile* for Bizerte 6.1897 to 4.1898 (sea trials). Concept abandoned after Lockroy replaced Besnard as Minister 6.1898. Struck 8.3.1900, renamed *Sémiramis* same date, central ship for the reserve at Landévennec 1900-1904. BU 1904.

*Triomphante* Rochefort Dyd/Indret (engines designed by Joseph Joëssel).
On list 1.1870. K: 5.8.1869. L: 28.3.1877. C: 6.5.1879.

To reserve after trials. To the Pacific station 10.1880. Reboiled 1888. Struck 7.7.1896 (published 8.7.1896), central ship for the naval division at Saigon (replacing *Loire*) 1896-1903, sold and BU 1903.

### 2nd rank ironclads in the Programme of 1872

As part of its effort as directed by Minister of Marine Pothuau on 14 September 1871 to produce technical specifications for all of the ship types that were to enter into the composition of the fleet under the Programme of 1872, the *Conseil des travaux* on 25 October 1871 discussed specifications for 2nd rank ironclads. Based on the previous deliberations of the *Conseil d'Amirauté* and a report of Director of Materiel Sabattier to Minister Pothuau the Council noted that the main purpose of 2nd rank ironclads was service on foreign stations but that they could also be useful as auxiliaries to squadrons of 1st rank ironclads. Most members felt that the 2nd rank ironclad was too imperfect a concept, weak in all forms of warfare, to warrant building in quantity, but they split on the issue of their specifications. The *Conseil d'Amirauté* had imposed a cost limit of 4 million francs, which the *Conseil des travaux* equated with a displacement of 4,000 tons. A minority on the Council wanted to design the best ship possible within this tonnage limit, while a majority wanted to design a ship having the nautical and military qualities indispensable for this type of ship and then calculate the resulting displacement.

The majority called for a ship with an iron hull, ram bow and a waterline length not over 76m. There was to be a complete armour belt with a maximum thickness of 220mm and a 50mm armoured deck over the portions of the machinery that extended beyond the battery. The ship would have a central battery with two 240mm guns, one on each side behind 160mm armour. Above it were two more 240mm guns on barbette mountings behind semi-circular parapets (half-turrets) with 160mm armour, one on each side with axial fire, along with six 138.6mm guns. The speed was 14 knots, the displacement was estimated at 4,700 tons and the cost at 4.4 million francs. Minister Pothuau transmitted these specifications on 25 November 1871 for study together with the minority's specifications, below.

In doing so he made some changes, including increasing the length to 78m, displacement to 4,934 tons, reducing the speed to 12.6 knots, and specifying Belleville boilers. The armament was to be seven 240mm of which four were in the central battery, two in barbette half turrets, and one either fore or aft. The new displacement was 4,930 tons. These specifications with their central battery were the starting point for the design of *Condé*, below.

The minority chose to stay within the cost limit of 4 million francs by *décuirassement* of the main armament, specifically by deleting the armoured central battery. The result was a somewhat smaller (72m) ship without a ram and with armour only on the waterline (220mm maximum) and on the deck over the machinery and magazines (50mm). Four 240mm guns were in unarmoured barbettes on the upper deck amidships, two on each side 8m apart, with extreme tumblehome for axial fire, along with six 138.6mm guns. The speed was 13 to 14 knots, the displacement was estimated at 4,250 tons and the cost 4 million francs. In transmitting these specifications to the ports Minister Pothuau set the speed at 13 knots and changed the armament to four 240mm, one 194mm (either fore or aft), and six 138.6mm, all unprotected. The new displacement was 4,300 tons. The use of barbettes for the entire main battery reappeared in the later *Turenne* and *Vauban* classes, although their barbettes were armoured.

---

*CONDÉ. Cuirassé de 2ᵉ rang.* Central battery ironclad with two upper deck half turrets and a gun under the forecastle, an iron hull, and a ram bow. Three masts, ship rig. Designed by Lagane (FCM La Seyne).

On 25 November 1871 Minister Pothuau asked the ports for designs for 2nd rank ironclads in accordance with the two sets of specifications just decided on by the *Conseil des travaux* on 25 October 1871 as modified by himself. The Council on 28 June 1872 examined four designs based on the two sets of specification and selected two for further work, one by naval constructor Godron and one by former naval constructor Antoine Jean Amable Lagane, now working for the Forges et Chantiers de la Méditerranée. Lagane's design had an armament of seven 240mm, four 138.6mm and six *mitrailleuses*, the main guns being in a central battery and in barbette towers. The ship had a length of 77m and beam of 16.12m. The Council wanted it lengthened amidships by about 3m, the power of the engines increased from 3,000ihp to 3,560ihp, speed increased to 13.5 knots, the coal supply increased from 400 to 520 tons for a range of 3,000nm at 10 knots, the 138.6mm battery increased from 4 to 6 guns, and the crew increased from 300 to 350 men. It estimated the new displacement at 5,200 tons. On 8 March 1873 the Director of Materiel forwarded Lagane's revised design to the Council which examined it on 21 March. Lagane had made all the changes but at the expense of lengthening the ship by 8m instead of 3m and widening it by 0.28m. Its new displacement was 5,677 tons. The *Conseil des travaux* took exception to the growth in size and cost of this design and asked, as it had in 1871, whether is was wise to propose to Minister Pothuau an expense that was now 7 million francs for a ship whose military role was difficult to define, which would be obsolete before even being laid down, and which in sum was no more than a reproduction of an old type.

Although the design process thus stalled in 1873, the Ministry made budgetary preparations to build the ship. A new *cuirassé de 2ᵉ rang* appeared on the fleet list in January 1874 without a name. The 1875 budget (submitted in January 1874) showed a new unnamed *cuirassé de 2ᵉ rang* as to be built by contract with 30% to be done during the year. The new ship was carried on the list in January 1875 as *Condé* to be built by contract. The 1876 budget (May 1875) showed her, still unnamed, as not begun and to be 20% built during the year. However, the navy then dropped the project, and the ship was not in the 1877 budget (March 1876).

*The characteristics are based on the design examined by the Conseil des travaux on 21 March 1873.*

**Dimensions & tons:** 88m oa, 85m wl and pp x 16.40m ext. 5,677t disp. Draught: 6.30m mean, 6.80m aft. Men: 350.

**Machinery:** 3,560ihp. 520t coal. Belleville boilers.
**Armour:**
Side: Belt at waterline 220mm amidships, 160mm at ends. Height from
1.99m below the wl to 0.91m above.
Guns: Central battery 160mm sides, 120mm transverse bulkheads, half-
turrets 160mm.
Deck: 50mm over the portion of the machinery that extended beyond the
battery, unprotected (probably 10mm) elsewhere.
**Guns:** 7 x 240mm (probably 4 in battery, 2 in elliptical half turrets above
it, and 1 forward), 6 x 138.6mm, 6 *mitrailleuses*

*Condé* Contract (to be F.C. Méditerranée).
Budget 1875 (delayed to 1876, then cancelled)

### 2nd class ironclads without central batteries
On 20 October 1873 Minister of Marine Dompierre d'Hornoy charged the
*Conseil des travaux* to draft specifications for new 2nd rank ironclads. While
for 1st rank ironclads he had asked for alternative specifications, with and
without a central battery, for 2nd rank ironclads he asked only for specifications for a ship without a central battery. The Council examined the matter
on 21 November 1873 immediately after examining the two sets of specifications for 1st rank ironclads. The Council recommended a ship with an
iron hull including steel where advantageous covered with wood up to the
top of the belt and sheathed with copper outside the wood. It would have
a length between perpendiculars of 81m (from the rudder post to the bow
at the waterline) plus the usual ram forward, a maximum draught of 7.30m,
and a maximum displacement of 5,600 tons. The armament would be three
240mm guns on the centreline, two new model 194mm guns under the
forecastle and on the stern, six to eight 138.6mm guns on the battery deck
that could all be moved to one side, and probably some *mitrailleuses*. This
arrangement would allow bringing nearly the entire battery to bear on one
side while retaining some fire ahead and astern, broadside fire being more
important in small scale engagements overseas than in European fleet
actions. Protection would consist of a complete armour belt with its top
1.50m above the waterline and a maximum thickness of 300mm plus a
complete deck with an average thickness of 50mm and with at least 60mm
over the machinery. The guns placed on the upper deck would be protected
only by a shield or a barbette made of light plating. The ship would have a
full ship rig, a single screw, and a speed of 13 knots. As in the preceding
discussion of 1st rank ironclads, the president and three other members,
while agreeing with the other conclusions of the report, indicated that they
did not want to be associated with the principle of *décuirassement* of the
main artillery that had been applied to this design. One member (naval
constructor Amédée Paul Théodore Mangin) also took exception to the iron
hull with a covering of wood and copper as used in the British *Inconstant*,
arguing that the British were having a lot of corrosion problems with it and
that it would be better to use a composite hull (wood hull planking on an
iron frame) with the copper sheathing attached to the wood hull.
On 28 April 1874 naval constructor Charles Alexandre Paul Godron at
Lorient, who had already produced a design that had been well received by
the Council on 28 June 1872, was ordered to develop plans for a 2nd rank
ironclad in accordance with the specifications adopted by the *Conseil des
travaux* on 21 November 1873. Godron's design was examined by the
*Conseil des travaux* on 6 July 1875 and found to depart too much from the
specifications to be recommended to the Minister of Marine, now Rear
Admiral Marquis Louis Raymond de Montaignac de Chauvance, although
the Council called it very remarkable. On 26 July 1875 Minister
Montaignac de Chauvance asked Godron to develop a design based on the
1873 specifications but with some changes. The main guns on the upper
deck were to be protected by modest armour (at least 100mm) on their
barbettes. The belt armour was to cover only two thirds of the length of the
ship, ending in transverse bulkheads of the same thickness and with
armoured decks under the waterline from there to the ends. To accommodate these changes the displacement could be increased to 6,000 tons.

Godron completed this, his third station ironclad design since 1872, on
2 February 1876. It had a length of 86m between perpendiculars and
90.80m maximum, a maximum beam of 16.60m, and a displacement of
6,012 tons. The Council on 2 May 1876 found it to be the best of the three
presented to it but rejected it because Godron used the British bracket
frame iron hull structure which the Council felt did not sufficiently
support the upper deck where the main battery was located and because he
did not meet the thickness of armour specified for the armoured deck.

⸻

*TURENNE* Class. *Cuirassés de 2ᵉ rang.* Ironclads with four upper deck barbettes (two abreast forward and two on the centreline behind them),
a wooden hull, iron upper works and a ram bow. One funnel, three masts,
full ship rig. Designed by Sabattier.

Following the rejection of Godron's latest design Sabattier offered his own
design that was essentially a reduced version of his 1st rank *Amiral Duperré*.
(Much of the work was probably done by naval constructor Alfred François
Lebelin de Dionne.) The design included a complete armoured belt and a
main battery on the upper deck in four armoured barbettes arranged as in
the larger ship. The weight saved by eliminating the central battery in the
earlier 2nd rank ironclads allowed thickening the main belt, fitting a
complete 50mm armoured deck, and giving 100mm of armour to the tubes
for passing ammunition to the barbettes. The battery on the sides containing the 138.6mm guns was unprotected. The design as of 1880 included
only one 194mm gun, which was under the forecastle, but a second
194mm gun was apparently added aft during construction to provide some
stern fire because the after 240mm barbette was masked by the mizzen mast
and its rigging. The funnels in the two ships consisted of two uptakes
within a single outer casing, in *Turenne* the outer casing rose to the top of
the uptakes giving her the appearance of a single large funnel while in
*Bayard* the outer casing ended well below the top of the uptakes giving her
the appearance of two small funnels close together inside a common enve-
lope. A noteworthy feature of this class was the reversion to wooden hulls
while all other 2nd rank ironclad designs since 1871 including the *Vauban*
class, below, used iron. Concern over the corrosion problems experienced
by the British in sheathed iron hulls may have persuaded the French not to
risk using the new system in all four of their new station battleships.

*The characteristics are based on a devis for* Turenne *dated 24.7.1882.*
**Dimensions & tons:** 81.22m wl (+2.22m ram), 78.78m pp (wl fwd to
rudder) x 17.25+0.20m (wood sheathing over belt) ext and wl. 6,363t
disp. Draught: 7.491m mean, 8.091m aft. Men: 430.
**Machinery:** 850nhp and 4,000ihp designed at 88rpm and 4.133kg/cm²
boiler pressure. Trials (*Turenne*, 16.6.1882) 4,158.8ihp = 14.15kts at
84.125rpm and 4.244kg/cm² boiler pressure. 2 screws. 2 vertical compound engines with 3 cylinders of 1.28m (1) and 1.60m (2) diameter
and 0.75m stroke. 8 high cylindrical boilers. 425.9t coal. Range
3,300nm @ 10kts.
**Armour:** (iron)
Side: Belt at waterline 250mm amidships, 180mm fwd, 160mm aft.
Height from 1.99m below the wl to 0.91m above.
Guns: Barbettes 200mm.
Deck: 50mm amidships and ends.
**Guns:**
(1881) 4 x 240mm/19 M1870M (turrets), 2 x 194mm/19.8 M1870
(under forecastle and poop), 6 x 138.6mm/21.3 M1870 (battery),
1 x 12pdr (121mm/17) bronze rifle
(1883, *Bayard* and 1885, *Turenne*) 4 x 240mm, 2 x 194mm,
6 x 138.6mm, 2 x 65mm landing, 12 x 37mm Hotchkiss revolving
cannon. Add 4 x 47mm by 1890.

*Turenne* Lorient Dyd/Schneider, Creusot.
On list 1.1875. Ord: 20.11.1876. K: 1.3.1877. L: 16.10.1879.
C: 4.2.1882.

Budget 1876. Trials 1881-82, then to reserve. To full commission 1884 as a division flagship in the augmented Far East Squadron (*Escadre*), then flagship of the Far East naval division 1885-1889, out of commission by 4.1890. In 2nd category reserve 1891-95, then out of commission. Struck 4.9.1900 (published 11.9.1900), for sale at Cherbourg 1900-1901.

*Bayard* Brest Dyd/Schneider, Creusot.
On list 1.1877. K: 19.9.1876. L: 27.3.1880. C: 22.11.1882.
Budget 1877. Trials 1882, then to reserve. Full comm. 1883, flagship of the *Division navale du Tonkin* and then the *Escadre de l'Extrême-Orient* under Vice Admiral Courbet during the Franco-Chinese war of 1883-85. Brought Courbet's remains back to France 8.1885. Active in the *Escadre de la Méditerranée occidentale et du Levant* 1889-92. To the Far East 1893 as flagship of the Far East naval division, then became a division flagship in the augmented Far East Squadron (*Escadre*) 1898-1899. Struck 26.4.1899, base hulk at Port Courbet in Ha Long Bay (*Baie d'Along*) in Tonkin 1899-1901, hulk 1901-1904, BU 1904.

---

**VAUBAN Class.** *Cuirassés de 2ᵉ rang.* Ironclads with four upper deck barbettes (two abreast forward and two on the centreline behind them), iron armour, an iron and steel hull covered with a double layer of wood, and a ram bow. One funnel, two tall masts, full brig rig. Designed by Sabattier and Lebelin de Dionne.

This class introduced to French 2nd class battleships the steel and iron hulls that had figured in several unbuilt French 2nd rank battleship designs since 1871. It used a version of the copper on wood sheathing system similar to

The 2nd rank (station) ironclad *Bayard* as completed with a ship rig. Provisions in casks are being taken aboard from lighters alongside her bow. The large cargo transport *Européen* is in the left background. (*NHHC, NH-74875*)

the updated one used by the British in the iron-hulled *Swiftsure*. It also obtained stern fire from the after 240mm barbette gun by adopting a brig (2-masted) rig instead of the usual ship (3-masted) rig, moving the after barbette aft of the mainmast, and giving the stern above water a radically downward sloping shape (although it was still possible to fit an admiral's stern walk). In this respect it emulated the British 'Great Brig', HMS *Temeraire* of 8,540 tons, a first class ironclad that was also given a brig rig to get stern fire from a barbette gun and was, according to Oscar Parkes 'the largest vessel ever handled under two masts'. Plans for *Duguesclin* were signed by naval constructor Lebelin de Dionne at Rochefort on 30 November 1876 and approved by Minister of Marine Fourichon on 26 December 1876. The design was also credited to Sabattier, who was Director of Materiel at the time.

*Vauban* in 1887 had two masts with a 2.60m bowsprit and a full brig rig with 2,156.89 sq.m. of sail. The rig of *Duguesclin* was reduced to 431.46 sq.m. by 1889 and the rig of *Vauban* was ordered reduced on 9 May 1889. The sails of *Duguesclin* had been removed by 1893 and *Vauban* had only 295 sq.m. left in 1898. *Vauban* had four 40cm searchlights in May 1889, although Minister of Marine Barbey had directed on 29 September 1887 that all armoured ships and large combatant ships should have four 60cm searchlights. On 27 October 1893 the ministry directed the study of some changes to *Duguesclin* including replacing the 194mm gun under the bow with a 164.7mm M1881 Nº 2 light (*léger*) gun, the purpose being to lighten the bow. The boilers of *Vauban* were ordered replaced with new ones of the same type on 8 April 1896 and were first lit off on 29 March 1897. On 5 February 1898 while preparing to leave for the Far East Squadron *Vauban* was ordered fitted with two additional 138.6mm guns in the battery but without additional ammunition supplies.

*The characteristics are based on a devis for* Vauban *dated 21.5.1887, the armour is from an 1898 devis.*
**Dimensions & tons:** 84.700m oa, 81.550m wl (+2.850m ram), 81.90m pp (tip fwd to rudder) x 17.26+0.19m sheathing ext, 17.440m wl

The 2nd rank (station) ironclad *Vauban* as completed with a towering brig rig. The ship moved from Cherbourg to Toulon in March 1886 and visited Ajaccio and Mers el Kebir during summer manoeuvres in June 1886. She then served as station ship at Piraeus, where this photograph was probably taken, from June 1887 to May 1889. *(NHHC, NH-74916)*

(18.600m designed outside turrets). 6,207.591t disp. Draught: 7.389m mean, 8.139m aft. Men: 500.

**Machinery:** 850nhp (*Duguesclin*) / 800nhp (*Vauban*) and 4,000ihp designed (changed to 4,307.84ihp after technical analysis) at 88rpm and 4.25kg/cm² boiler pressure. Trials (*Vauban*, 21.4.1885) 4,589.37ihp = 14.32kts at 92.125rpm and 4.250kg/cm² boiler pressure. 2 screws. 2 vertical compound engines with 3 cylinders of 1.280m (1) and 1.600m (2) diameter and 0.750m stroke. 8 high cylindrical boilers. 450t coal. Range 2,380.5nm @ 12.817kts.

**Armour:** (iron)

Side: Belt at waterline 250mm amidships, 180mm fwd, 150mm aft. Height from 1.60m below the wl to 1.25m above (designed).

Guns: Barbettes (iron) 200mm.

Deck: 50mm.

Conning towers: 30mm, one of 25mm for the admiral added in *Vauban* 1890.

**Guns:**

(1886): 4 x 240mm/19 M1870M (barbette turrets), 1 x 194mm/19.8 M1870 (under the forecastle), 6 x 138.6mm/21.3 M1870 (battery), 2 x 65mm landing, 12 x 37mm revolving cannon. **Torpedoes:** 2 tubes for 356mm M1880 (4.42m) torpedoes (on the sides at the forward end of the battery deck). **Searchlights:** 2 x 40cm (*Duguesclin* in 1889 had 2 x 47mm and only 10 x 37mm. By 1893 she had added 4 more 47mm.)

(1898, *Vauban*) 4 x 240mm/19 M1870M, 1 x 194mm/19.8 M1870 Nº 1, 8 x 138.6mm/21.3 M1870M (battery), 2 x 65mm/16 M1881 steel landing, 6 x 47mm/40 M1885 QF, 12 x 37mm Hotchkiss revolving cannon. **Torpedoes:** 2 tubes for 356mm torpedoes M1885 and M1880. **Searchlights:** 4 x 60cm.

*Vauban* Cherbourg Dyd/Indret (engines designed by Joseph Joëssel).

On list 1.1878. Ord: 13.11.1876. K: 1.8.1877. L: 3.7.1882. Comm: c1885 (trials), 9.3.1886 (full).

Budget 1876 (delayed to 1877). Machinery installed 20.10.1882 to 7.4.1884. Trials 3-4.1885. Left Cherbourg for Toulon 15.3.1886 and operated with the *Escadre d'évolutions* until 29.6.1886. Active in the *Division navale du Levant* and the *Escadre de la Méditerranée occidentale et du Levant* from 8.6.1887 to 26.8.1892. Seagoing annex to the school for gunnery in *Couronne* at Toulon 2.8.1894 to 5.2.1895

(replaced *Saint Louis/Cacique*, replaced by *Calédonien*).
Recommissioned 1.1898 as flagship of the newly augmented Far East Squadron (*Escadre*). This squadron was reduced back to a division in early 1899 and the division commander then transferred his flag to *D'Entrecasteaux*. At Saigon with a Lieutenant de vaisseau in command from 19.5.1899 to 1904. Struck 12.9.1905, central ship for the 2nd flotilla of torpedo vessels of the China Sea at Hongay in Indochina 1905-1910, central ship for submarines at Saïgon 1910-1914, was at Rach-Dua (Vung Tao) 1910-1911. Struck from subsidiary military use 21.5.1914. Proposal from Saïgon dated 5.9.1919 to sell her and *Styx* approved by the ministry 9.10.1919.

***Duguesclin*** Rochefort Dyd/Indret (engines designed by Joseph Joëssel).
On list 1.1878. K: 3.1877. L: 7.4.1883. Comm: 1.1.1886 (trials). C: 6.1887.
Budget 1877. Construction reassigned from Lorient to Rochefort c1876. Machinery installed 5.1883 to 8.9.1884. From Rochefort to Brest for trials 10-13.4.1886, trials 6.1886, to reserve 28.7.1886 and docked for bottom repairs. Comm. again for trials 27.4.1887, to reserve 7.7.1887. From Brest to Toulon with reduced crew 13.2.1888 and to 2nd category reserve there 25.3.1888. Full commission at Toulon 20.3.1889 and active with the *Escadre de la Méditerranée occidentale et du Levant* from 23.3.1889 to 1.1.1893. To 2nd category reserve at Toulon 9.2.1893, to 3rd category reserve (out of service) 25.10.1894, decommissioned 1.9.1903. Saw no overseas station duty. Struck 10.10.1904, sold 3.8.1905 at Toulon to M. Cerrutti of Genoa to BU.

### Later Station Ironclads. *Cuirassés de 2e rang*

The 1878 budget (submitted in January 1877) included two new unnamed *Cuirassés de 2e rang* to be begun during the year, one at Brest and one at Lorient. They were not in the 1879 budget (April 1878). The 1880 budget (January 1879) included two new unnamed *Cuirassés de 2e rang*, one at Cherbourg and one at Rochefort. On 27 May 1879 the *Conseil des travaux* approved new specifications for a 2nd rank ironclad with a wooden hull (in box below). The new ships were not in the 1881 budget (January 1880) but a design by Godron was approved on 25 May 1880 and after revisions again on 9 November 1880. The 1882 budget (January 1881) included two new unnamed *Cuirassés de station*, one at Cherbourg and one at Brest. They were also shown in the 1883 and 1885 budgets and the Cherbourg ship was also shown in the 1886 budget (March 1885) before being dropped. The *Conseil des travaux* examined one final design for a *cuirassé de 2e rang* by naval constructor Théodore Jean Maurice Marchal on 27 March 1888 while examining four designs for 1st class armoured cruisers (one of which was also by Marchal) and thanked him for his interesting study saying it could be consulted when it was necessary to draft specifications for a new *cuirassé de croisière*.

*Specifications adopted by the Conseil des travaux on 27 May 1879.*
**Dimensions & tons:** 85m max. 6,500t disp (raised to 6,600t). Draught: 7.40m max. Men: 500. Wooden hull up to the battery deck with steel above it, copper sheathing, ram bow. Three masts with full rig.
**Machinery:** Speed 14.5kts (forced draught). 1 screw. 1 engine. 4 cylindrical or oblong boilers operating at 4 atmospheres. Range 2,800nm @ 10kts.
**Armour:**
Side: Belt, end to end, 280mm or 300mm maximum (250mm average) from 1.50m below the waterline to 15cm or 20cm above.
Guns: Barbettes (iron) 250mm average.
Deck: 70mm average end to end, about 20cm below the waterline.
**Guns:** 1 x 274.4mm M1875 No 1 and 2 x 240mm M1870 in barbette turrets (the 274.4mm aft and the 240mm abreast forward with axial fire forward and aft), 12 x 138.6mm in the battery, 6 x 37mm revolving cannon, 2 launchers for Whitehead torpedoes, 1 torpedo boat of 15-16 metres.

*N* (Unnamed) Lorient, then Cherbourg Dyds
Budgets 1878 (Lorient), 1880, 1882, 1883, 1885, and 1886 (all Cherbourg)

*N* (Unnamed) Brest and Rochefort Dyds
Budgets 1878 (Brest), 1880 (Rochefort), 1882, 1883, and 1885 (all Brest)

## II. COAST DEFENCE IRONCLADS

### (A) Early Coast Defence Ironclads.
Originally *Garde-côtes cuirassés*, to *Garde-côtes cuirassés de 3e classe* in the 1.1873 fleet list except *Onondaga* to *Monitor*, all to *Garde-côtes cuirassés de 2e classe* 1.1874, to *Garde-côtes cuirassés* 1.1880, and to *Cuirassés gardes-côtes* 1.1892.

#### Rams and ram bows
The ancient idea of the use of ramming in naval combat saw new life in 1840 when Lieutenant de vaisseau Nicolas Hippolyte Labrousse declared that the advent of steam propulsion once again made it possible. He recommended giving all naval combatant vessels ram bows. On 4 July 1849 the *Conseil des travaux*, lukewarm to Labrousse's approach, stated that rams should be specialized vessels with impenetrable armour and no guns or masts. During the Crimean War naval constructor Victor Charles Eudore Gervaize proposed an iron ram without guns and on 5 February 1855 Minister of Marine Senator Théodore Ducos invited the ports to study the matter. On 21 July 1858 Labrousse recommended adding to the armoured frigates that were to be built a heavy iron ram bow with a steel tip. This time his ideas were welcomed as restoring offensive power to ships whose artillery was powerless against the new armour, and Dupuy de Lôme incorporated a large metal ram bow in his *Solférino* and *Magenta*. However, on 25 January 1859 the *Conseil des travaux* once again advised that 'one should only arm with ram bows and use as rams new ships that were totally specialized.' The American Civil War gave new impetus to the defensive employment of naval rams, but the increase in the power of naval artillery made it necessary to armour them.

***TAUREAU.*** *Garde-côtes cuirassé.* Coast defence ironclad with a single open barbette, a wooden hull, iron upper works, and a heavy bronze ram. One funnel, two light pole masts, no sails. Designed by Dupuy de Lôme.

France's first armoured coast defence ship (excluding floating batteries) was ordered by Minister of Marine Chasseloup-Laubat on 5 September 1863 under the designation of *batterie à hélice et à tour pour la défense des rades* (screw turret ship for the defence of roadsteads). She was listed as a *Bâtiment spécial* in the January 1864 *Liste de la flotte* because no suitable category then existed and was then classed as *Garde-côtes cuirassé (monitor)* in January 1865, *Garde-côtes cuirassé de 1re classe* in January 1866 (this ship only), and *Garde-côtes cuirassé* in January 1868.
Dupuy de Lôme's plans for *Taureau* were approved on 9 September 1863 and she was named 3 October 1863. *Taureau* seems to have been designed and ordered exclusively as a fast ram with relatively shallow draught to conceal itself near the coast. As built her ram was a 11-ton bronze cone fixed firmly to the hull with its point 2.50m below the waterline. Guns were included as a concession to conventional ideas, but in the original design the two 240mm guns were in a fixed turret able to fire only dead ahead to prepare the way for the ram strike, leaving the ship's commander without the option of engaging instead in a gunnery duel. As built *Taureau* consisted basically of an armoured raft with a deck about 70cm above the waterline supporting a two level armoured tower, the lower level containing the helm and the action station of the commander directing the attack,

the upper level containing a single 240mm gun on a rotating platform inside a wooden ring (barbette) protected by 120mm iron plating that fired over the top of the tower. A metal shell with curved sides rose above the armoured hull, one of its functions being to prevent boarding although it made handling the anchors very difficult. The speed was high for its day, over 12.50 knots on trials, and manoeuvrability was outstanding with two screws, a large rudder, a short hull and shallow draught. She could turn in place by going ahead on one of her screws and astern on the other. However, she steered and rolled badly at sea.

*The characteristics are based on a devis dated 20.7.1873.*

**Dimensions & tons:** c64m oa, 59.97m wl (+3.20m ram), 59.92m pp (wl fwd to rudder) x 14.50m ext and wl. 2,718t disp. Draught: 5.356m mean, 5.411m aft. Men: 150.

**Machinery:** 500nhp (480 from 1867) and 1920ihp designed at 82rpm and 1.80kg/cm² boiler pressure. Trials (8.1866) 1,796ihp = 12.58kts at 82rpm and 1,860kg/cm² boiler pressure. 2 screws. 2 horizontal simple expansion engines with return connecting rods and 2 cylinders of 1.20m diameter and 0.648m stroke. 8 low reglementary boilers. 171t coal. Range 1,260nm @ 10kts.

**Armour:** (iron)

Side: Belt at waterline 150mm amidships and ends. Height from 1.85m below the wl to 0.35m above.

Guns: Turret 120mm.

Deck: 50mm plating on 120mm wood.

**Guns:** (1873) 1 x 240mm/17.5 M1864 in an open barbette turret.

**Taureau** Toulon Dyd/Indret (engines designed by Victorin Sabattier).
On list 1.1864. Ord: 5.9.1863. K: 5.10.1863. L: 10.6.1865.
      Comm: 19.8.1865 (trials). C: 8.1866.

The coast defence ironclad *Bouledogue* at Lorient early in her career. Behind her is an ironclad, probably of the *Alma* class and probably under refit, and and a small paddle aviso in reserve or under refit is on the far right. *(Musée de la Marine)*

Full power trials 8.1866. From Toulon 5.8.1867 to Cherbourg, decomm. there 3.10.1867. To 1st category reserve 16.7.1870 and to full comm-ission 20.7.1870 for wartime Channel service, to 3rd category reserve (out of commission) 26.3.1871, and mostly in reserve except for brief trials afterwards. Struck 25.10.1890, sold 11.8.1891 to BU.

---

**CERBÈRE Class.** *Garde-côtes cuirassés.* Coast defence ironclads with a sin-gle enclosed turret, a wooden hull, iron upper works, and a conical bronze ram. Two funnels abreast (one funnel in *Tigre*), two light pole masts, no sails. Designed by Dupuy de Lôme.

Dupuy de Lôme developed the design for this class from that of *Taureau* but with gun power no longer subordinate to the ram. The gun mounting consisted of two turrets, a rotating one on top of a fixed one, and both protected by 180mm armour. The turret on top contained the guns and rotated on a roller path on the top of the smaller-diameter fixed turret. Even though the designed displacement compared to *Taureau* was increased by just over 1,000 tons the 50mm deck armour in *Taureau* had to be reduced to 15mm plating in the new class to save weight. The advances in gunnery also made heavier belt armour necessary. The first three ships were ordered on 15 January 1865 and named 8 April 1865 as part of a third group of armoured ships to help fulfil the Programme of 1857 and the fourth, *Tigre*, was ordered in January 1867. Plans by Dupuy de Lôme were approved on 1 August 1865 and 15 February 1866. Further changes were made during construction including extending the armour over some unprotected areas and substituting Model 1870 for lighter Model 1864 guns.

In 1873 and 1874 the *Commission des défenses sous-marines* conducted experiments to determine how to make the best use of the new Whitehead torpedo, for which France had just signed a contract with Whitehead on 5 April 1873. To investigate possible employment on large ships two fixed submerged torpedo tubes were fitted to *Tigre*, one on each side of the stem. Trials began at Brest in the summer of 1874. The main lesson from these

trials was that it would be dangerous to launch torpedoes underwater from large ships at speeds greater then 5 knots because the launching ship would have to slow down or even stop to avoid running down its own torpedo. Slowing down during an engagement was inadmissible for tactical reasons, and the commission reported on 24 February 1875 that the proper platforms for torpedoes were specially-designed small ships and boats.

*The characteristics are based on a devis for* Bélier *dated 28.2.1874.*

**Dimensions & tons:** c72m oa, 66.44m wl (+3.45m ram), 65.43m pp (wl fwd to rudder) x 16.00+0.14m sheathing ext and wl. 3,589t disp. Draught: 5,661m mean, 5,826m aft. Men: 147.

**Machinery:** 530nhp and 2,120ihp designed at 88rpm and $1.80kg/cm^2$ boiler pressure. Trials (*Bélier*, 7.1872) 1,921ihp = 12.37kts at 90.1/89.2rpm (stbd/port), $1.836kg/cm^2$ boiler pressure. 2 screws. 2 horizontal simple expansion engines with return connecting rods and 2 cylinders of 1.202m diameter and 0.70m stroke. 6 low reglementary boilers. 187t coal. Range 1,800nm @ 10kts.

**Armour:** (iron)
Side: Belt at waterline 220mm amidships and ends. Height from 1.70m below the wl to 0.50m above.
Guns: Turret (fixed and rotating parts) 180mm.
Deck: 15mm on 250mm wood (20mm on 250mm in *Bouledogue*, 20mm on 150mm in *Tigre*).

**Guns:** (1873-74) 2 x 240mm/17.5 M1864 (M1870 in *Bouledogue* and in others later) in mobile enclosed turret. *Tigre* and *Bouledogue* also had 1 x 4pdr (86.5mm/11) bronze mountain while in 1876 *Cerbère* also had 4 x 37mm revolving cannon.

*Cerbère* Brest Dyd/Schneider, Creusot (engines designed by Mathieu).
On list 1.1867. Ord: 15.1.1865. K: 14.9.1865. L: 23.4.1868. Comm: 20.9.1869 (trials). C: 7.1870.
In 7-8.1870 cruised to Cherbourg and Le Havre, then back to Brest. Full commission at Brest 12.12.1870, decomm. at Cherbourg 16.4.1871. Occasionally commissioned thereafter in 1st category reserve or trials status. Struck 12.11.1886, for disposal at Cherbourg 1886-1887, BU 1887 at Cherbourg.

*Bélier* Cherbourg Dyd/C.A. de l'Océan (ex Mazeline), Le Havre.
On list 1.1867. Ord: 15.1.1865. K: 15.9.1865. L: 29.8.1870. Comm: 10.6.1872 (trials). C: 1.1874.
Taken to Brest 1.1871 while completing, returned to Cherbourg after the war. Commissioned for trials four times between 1872 and 1878 without ever going into full commission, decom. 1.11.1878. Struck 8.7.1896, sold 17.12.1896 to BU. On 25.10.1897 some powder left on board exploded during scrapping and almost completely destroyed the ship.

*Bouledogue* Lorient Dyd/Indret (engines designed by Dupuy de Lôme).
On list 1.1867. Ord: 15.1.1865. K: 5.12.1865. L: 26.3.1872. Comm: 16.4.1873 (trials). C: 10.1873.
Entire career at Lorient, where she was in commission from 16.4.1873 to 19.4.1875. Annex of the central ship for the *Défense mobile* at Lorient, 1886-90, central ship for the *Défense mobile* 1890-95. Collided with and sank *Torpilleur nº 69* in the harbour at Lorient 31.7.1895, the torpedo boat was returned to service. Struck 24.4.1896, sold 21.3.1897 to M. Pittle of Brest and BU in the dockyard.

*Tigre* Rochefort Dyd/Indret (engines designed by Victorin Sabattier).
On list 1.1868. Ord: 1.1867. K: 1.4.1867. L: 9.3.1871. Comm: 20.7.1874 (trials). C: 9.1874.
To Brest 9.1874, to 1st category reserve 15.9.1874 and fitted for trials of torpedo tubes, recomm (trials) 1.12.1874, decomm. 17.6.1875 and to 2nd category reserve. Spent rest of career at Brest. Struck 10.2.1892, for disposal at Brest 1892-1893.

---

***ROCHAMBEAU.*** *Garde-côtes cuirassé.* Purchased American casemate ironclad with wooden hull. One funnel, two masts, schooner brig rig. Designed by Webb.

This large casemate ironclad was built during the American Civil War by William H. Webb to his own design, which called for an armament of four 381mm (15in) Dahlgren muzzle-loading smoothbores and twelve 279.4mm (11in) Dahlgren MLSB. The contract with the U.S. Navy for her construction was signed 3 July 1862 with the ship to be delivered in 15 months. Instead the ship was launched after the end of the war and was sold back to her builder in place of delivery as authorized by an Act of Congress of 2 March 1867. In April 1867 during an intense diplomatic crisis between France and Prussia over the status of Luxembourg the British press published a rumour that Prussia would purchase *Dunderberg* and *Onondaga* (Bismarck had in fact shown some interest), and Emperor Napoleon III of France on 27 April 1867 ordered the French consul-general in New York to buy them. The purchase was completed on 3 May 1867 for 14,554,171 francs of which 10,216,343 francs were for *Dunderberg*. The ship ran trials at New York on 12 June 1867 with French Navy observers who were satisfied with the results, including a speed in smooth water of 13.9 knots. The ship left New York on 19 July 1867 with an American delivery crew under a French commander and with Webb embarked and arrived at Cherbourg on 3 August. The French took her over on 6 August, commissioned her on 7 August, and took her out for two hours of trials on 9 August. She was renamed *Rochambeau* on 15 August 1867. Naval constructor Augustin Auvynet at Cherbourg completed plans on 28 October 1867 for a total reworking of her internal arrangements to meet French Navy standards for stowage of stores, these were examined by the *Conseil des travaux* the next day and approved by Minister of Marine Rigault de Genouilly on 25 November 1867. Her engine was also completely disassembled and refurbished. Her American smoothbores were replaced with French rifled breechloaders. Based on experience during the transit from New York the light portion of the stern overhanging aft of the rudder was cut off (shortening the ship several feet), the main rudder was replaced, and the rest of the stern was strengthened. A small auxiliary rudder was retained. She was in commission for post-repair trials from 18 March 1868 to 31 July 1868 and was then returned to reserve. Between August and December 1868 she was docked to replace the armour plates and the wooden ram at the bow with a single-piece cast iron ram. In 1869 parts of the battery deck, which was made of pine and unable to support the circular tracks of the large French guns, were replaced with oak. (Webb had not been able to acquire oak when he was building the ship.)

Recommissioned for the Franco-Prussian War, she sailed from Cherbourg on 25 August 1870 to join the fleet, which she did on 8 September northeast of Kiel after much difficulty in bad weather. She continued to suffer in bad weather but proved useful in coastal waters because of her shallow draught and remained with the fleet until it returned to Cherbourg at the end of September. She was disposed of in a postwar purge of the oldest ironclads that included the *Gloire*-class ironclads *Normandie* and *Invincible* and the seven surviving floating batteries of the *Dévastation* and *Palestro* classes. Minister of Marine Pothuau hesitated to write her off because of her cost, but the insufficiently aged wood used by Webb was decaying and the *Conseil d'Amirauté* concurred in her disposal.

*The characteristics are based on two devis dated 18.5.1868 and 25.7.1870.*

**Dimensions & tons:** 114.95m oa, 108.90m at the level of the armour knuckle, 107.40m pp (forward perpendicular to rudder) x 22.15m ext (above wl), 21.00m wl. 7849.289t disp. Draught: 6.50m mean, 6.75m aft. Men: 600 (1870)

**Machinery:** 1,300nhp and 5,200ihp designed (1,000nhp and 4,000ihp before 1869) at 55.810rpm and $1.80kg/cm^2$ boiler pressure. Trials (23.6.1868) 4,657.27ihp = 15.030kts at 59.33rpm and $1.1266kg/cm^2$ boiler pressure. 1 screw. 1 horizontal engine with return connecting rods and 2 cylinders of 2.54m diameter and 1.14m stroke. 8 return-flame tubular boilers (the two smaller forward ones being for auxiliary machinery). 540t coal (theoretical bunker capacity 735t).

**Armour:** (iron)

Side: Belt at main deck 89mm amidships and 63.5mm ends, lower edge at 1.5m below load waterline 63.5mm.

Guns: Casemate 114mm (solid plating).

Decks: 19mm plating on casemate deck and main deck. The main deck aft of the casemate was to have had 89mm armour at the casemate to 63.5mm at the stern according to the 1862 design but this was not fitted.

Conning tower: 305mm in twelve 25.4mm layers. The French later reported the conning tower armour as 250mm iron.

**Guns:**

(1868) 4 x 274.4mm/15.4 M1864 (at the corners of the battery with both axial and broadside ports), 10 x 240mm/17.5 M1864 (8 on the sides and 2 at the ends of the battery).

(1869) While in reserve, 1 x 240mm rifle was added on a central pivot at the forward end of the upper deck. Also had 1 x 12pdr (121mm/17) bronze field gun and 4 x 4pdr (86.5mm/11) bronze mountain guns.

*Rochambeau* Webb, New York/Etna Iron Works (engines designed by John Roach).

On list 1.1868. K: 28.9.1862. L: 22.7.1865. Comm: 7.8.1867 (French trials), 18.5.1868 (after alterations).

Decomm. 1.8.1868 after trials. Recomm. 8 July 1870 for war service with the *Escadre du Nord*, back in Cherbourg 29.9.1870. To 2nd category reserve 9.11.1870, moved to Brest 2-3.1.1871, to 3rd category reserve (out of commission) 24.1.1871, and fully decommissioned 7.3.1871. Struck 15.4.1872, BU at Brest 1872-74.

---

*ONONDAGA. Garde-côtes cuirassé.* Purchased American monitor with two turrets and an iron hull. One funnel, no masts. Designed by Quintard. To *Garde-côtes cuirassé* (*monitor*) 1.1873, *Garde-côtes cuirassé de 2e classe* (*monitor*) 1.1874, *Batterie flottante cuirassée* (*monitor*) 1.1880, *Garde-côtes cuirassé* 1.1881, and *Cuirassé garde-côtes offensif* 1.1901.

The hull and engines of this classic American Civil War monitor were built by George W. Quintard of New York to his designs under a contract of 26 May 1862. Each of the two turrets as of 23 February 1864 contained one 15-inch (381mm) Dahlgren MLSB and one 150pdr 8-inch (203mm) Parrott MLR, an arrangement that both Admiral Dahlgren and the French vigorously criticised because the big Dahlgren smoothbore took four times as long to load as did the Parrott rifle. She had an active Civil War career in the James River in 1864 and 1865 and was decommissioned on 8 June 1865. A special law of 2 March 1867 authorized the resale of the ship to her builder and subsequent sale overseas. The French purchased her with *Dunderberg* on 3 May 1867. Handed back to Quintard by the USN on 12 July 1867, she was towed out of New York for France by a chartered steamer on 31 July 1867 but soon had to turn back when the pumps failed in bad weather. She was towed out again on 2 September 1867 by the French station flagship *Thémis* escorted by the steam corvette *Phlégéton* and arrived at Halifax five days later to winter over and repair her boilers. Towed out of Halifax on 15 June 1868 by the transport *Européen* escorted by the aviso *Volta*, she arrived at Brest on 2 July 1868.

*Onondaga* completed a refit for French use in June 1869. The French found that her armour was attached in a bizarre manner with 120mm of iron armour attached directly to the 30mm hull plating and 250mm of oak attached outside of it behind a 20mm exterior iron skin. They speculated that instructions from Admiral Dahlgren had been misunderstood – while such a system might work against round shot it would be disastrous against explosive shells. They rearranged this covering in the usual manner, placing a 300mm layer of teak directly on the hull plating as backing for the 120mm of iron armour which had the 20mm skin on top of it. They also

redistributed the internal arrangements of the ship and fitted a new Joëssel rudder, which along with moving the propellers further forward and changing their direction of rotation solved the problem of the ship's poor steering. The American smoothbore guns had been left in America but their mountings remained on board, and the French adapted them for 240mm/17.5 M1864 breechloading rifles. (The port shutters had to be removed because of the length of the French guns.) In steam trials in November 1869 only three of the four boilers were lit off, a previous trial having shown that the boilers generated more power than was necessary to operate the ship's two engines.

Unlike *Rochambeau*, *Onondaga* saw no war service in 1870. In October 1889 she received four new boilers from Jollet and Babin at Nantes with an operating pressure of 1.80kg/cm². In 1900 her commander wrote that 'The *Onondaga* was never a ship intended to keep the seas, her nautical qualities are therefore almost nil; moreover, she is old now, but as she is she can still render great services: in the defence of a pass, with her four guns of 240mm and her small artillery she represents a force all the more serious that it is almost invisible.' In 1900 the interval between rounds from the main guns was reported as six minutes. After decades in reserve or harbour service her iron hull and her engines were still in good condition when she was struck in 1904.

*The characteristics are based on a devis dated 22.11.1870 and a feuille signalétique dated 29.10.1900.*

**Dimensions & tons:** 69.60m oa and wl, 67.75m pp (wl fwd to rudder) x 15.60m ext. 2,592t disp. Draught: 3.805m mean, 3.855m aft. Men: 100 (96 including 6 officers in 1900).

**Machinery:** 250nhp (150 from 1874) and 600ihp designed at 100rpm and 1.70kg/cm² boiler pressure. Trials (11.1869) 614ihp = 7.072kts at 107rpm and 1.750kg/cm² boiler pressure, (9.1.1875) 773.35ihp = 7.45kts at 110.9rpm. 2 screws. 2 horizontal simple expansion engines with return connecting rods (back-acting engines) each with two independent cylinders of 0.762m diameter and 0.457m stroke, two cylinders acting on each propeller shaft. 4 Martin boilers with vertical tubes. 178t coal. Range 720nm @ 7.1kts.

**Armour:** (iron)

Side: Belt at waterline 120mm armour on 20mm plating and 300mm teak, all on two layers of 15mm hull plating.

Guns: Turrets 300mm (laminated, 10 plates).

Deck: 50mm in two layers.

Conning tower on forward turret: 250mm (laminated, 10 plates), roof 50mm.

**Guns:**

(1870) 4 x 240mm/17.5 M1864 on the original American mountings.

(1878) 4 x 240mm/19 M1870, 6 x 37mm revolving cannon. On 19.8. 1878 all coast defence ships were assigned two towed torpedoes and a torpedo launch carrying two torpedoes, although in 1900 *Onondaga* had no torpedo equipment.

(1900) 4 x 240mm, 6 x 47mm/40 M1885 QF (2 on the forward turret and 4 on the after turret), 6 x 37mm revolving cannon (2 on deck forward, 2 by the funnel, and 2 on deck aft)

*Onondaga* Continental Iron Works, Greenport, New York/Morgan Iron Works.

On list 1.1868. K: 28.5.1862. L: 29.7.1863. Comm: 24.3.1864 (American), 1.9.1867 (French, for trials as delivered).

Refitted at Brest 6.1868 to 6.1869 with trials from 5.1869 to 11.1869. Decomm. 25.11.1869, recomm 17.7.1870, decomm. 1.4.1871, in commission for trials 23.10.1874 to 24.1.1875. In 4.1898 ran underway trials while central ship for the *Défense mobile* at Saint-Malo. Struck 2.12.1904, sold 4.1905 at Brest for 127,550 francs and towed to Cherbourg to BU.

---

## (B) 2<sup>nd</sup> class Coast Defence Ironclads (*Garde-côtes cuirassés de 2<sup>e</sup> classe*).

To *Garde-côtes cuirassés* in the 1.1880 fleet list and to *Cuirassés gardes-côtes* 1.1892.

### Coast defence ship design 1869-1871

On 8 June 1869 the *Conseil des travaux* examined some British documents it had just received on armoured ships without masts and used them in part to consider the question of coast defence ships to follow the *Cerbère* class. The documents showed that the British, who had imitated French designs in creating coast defence ships with armour of 230mm to 280mm on the sides and 200mm on the turret, had just increased the armour in a new ship (probably *Glatton*). The Council also recommended other changes, including using an iron hull with watertight compartments and moving closer to the pure monitor type. On 24 September 1869 Minister of Marine Rigault de Genouilly asked the naval constructors in the ports to suggest designs for new coast defence ships of the monitor type, built of iron, with a single turret on a central breastwork, and with speed and steaming range as in *Cerbère*. On 26 April 1870 the Council rejected a design by naval constructor Nathaniel Villaret, and on 26 July 1870 it considered three more by naval constructors Paulin Masson, Émile Ernest Clément, and de Bussy, rejecting the first and asking for major modifications to the other two in accordance with specifications that it provided. These included an armament of two 320mm guns in one turret, belt and turret armour of 300mm, and a 60cm freeboard. The war then intervened delaying further action.

On 10 November 1871 the *Conseil des travaux* as directed by Minister Pothuau on 14 September 1871 established technical specifications for the coast defence ships that were to enter into the composition of the new fleet of the Programme of 1872. Its guiding principles were that coast defence ships needed to be able to fulfil not only a defensive role on French coasts but an offensive role on enemy coasts. They therefore needed to have sufficient seaworthiness and habitability to make significant transits at sea. However, an examination of the geographic areas in which they were likely to conduct offensive operations showed that their draught should not exceed 5.10m, which would limit their speed to 10 knots. To get a speed of 13 knots it would be necessary to increase draught to 6.80m. Since it was absolutely necessary to have shallow draught coast defence ships and fast coast defence ships the Council created two classes differing only in draught and speed, the shallow draught ones being 2<sup>nd</sup> class and the fast ones 1<sup>st</sup> class. The main difference was that the 1<sup>st</sup> class ships were to have a maximum speed of 13 knots and be able to cover 1,500nm at a reduced speed of 10 knots, their maximum draught being 6.80m, while in the 2<sup>nd</sup> class ships the draught was limited to 5.20m but the speed needed only to be 10 knots and the coal supply needed to provide for a range of only 750nm. The specifications common to both classes were iron hulls, ram bows, and a monitor configuration with a low freeboard (of 80cm for the 2<sup>nd</sup> class, 90cm for the 1<sup>st</sup> class) and an armoured breastwork about 40m long set back from the sides of the ship that carried a single rotating turret with two large guns. They were to have a complete armour belt with a maximum thickness of 300mm and turret armour of 300mm with 350mm around the gun ports. The deck was to have 50mm armour. The armament was to be two 274.4mm guns in the turret and four 12pdr (121mm) bronze guns on the flying deck to defend the ship against boats or torpedo craft. The turret was to have an internal diameter of 8.80m to allow the use of a gun calibre over 274.4mm (specifically the 320mm mentioned in 1870) and to allow for a fixed conning tower on top. They were to have one screw and complements of 150 men (160 for the 1<sup>st</sup> class).

After deciding on these specifications the Council again reviewed the July 1870 proposals from de Bussy and Clément. It liked many of de Bussy's ideas but it asked him to rework his design and resubmit it in the separate competitions to be conducted for the two classes of coast defence ships under the new specifications.

———

***TEMPÊTE* Class.** *Garde-côtes cuirassés de 2<sup>e</sup> classe.* Breastwork monitors with one twin turret, a steel and iron hull, and a ram bow. 1 small funnel, 1 light mast, no sails. Designed by de Bussy.

On 30 July 1872 the *Conseil des travaux* examined four designs for 2<sup>nd</sup> class coast defence ships submitted in accordance with its specifications of 10 November 1871 as forwarded to the ports by Minister Pothuau on 29 November 1871 and approved the one by de Bussy, signed on 1 July 1872, which was a modified version of a design examined by the Council in 1870 and 1871. De Bussy used Bessemer steel in the hulls, and to protect the screw and rudder while getting an adequate flow of water to the propeller he used vaulted stern lines like those in *Rochambeau*. Other features of the design were inspired by the British coast defence ships *Glatton* and *Rupert*, particularly the former. Minister Pothuau approved the plans on 19 August 1872.

The horizontal dimensions of the hull and the armament of the second-class *Tempête* type and the first-class *Tonnant* type were virtually identical. However, the extra metre of draught in the first-class type gave them space for more powerful propulsion machinery. The freeboard aft was 0.70m, the armoured breastwork rose 2.40m above the waterline, and the superstructure was only 2.50m wide but had a wider hurricane deck on top. The turret of *Tempête* could make one rotation in 55 seconds. Firing rate was one round every three minutes when returning to the loading position after each shot or one minute and 33 seconds using ready-service ammunition. Her turning circle at 10 knots was 150m with not over two degrees of heel, and despite her low freeboard she consistently got superior evaluations for seakeeping and steering.

*The characteristics are based on a devis for* Tempête *dated 10.5.1883.*

**Dimensions & tons:** 78.60m oa, 75.57m wl (+3.03m ram), 73.57m pp (wl fwd to rudder) x 17.60m ext and wl. 4,869.2t disp. Draught: 5.414m mean, 5.40m aft. Men: 164.

**Machinery:** 425nhp and 1,754ihp designed at 4.133kg/cm² boiler pressure. Trials (*Tempête*, 11.1879) 2,193ihp = 11.676kts at 95.7rpm and 4.125kg/cm² boiler pressure. 1 screw. 3 horizontal engines with return connecting rods and cylinders of 0.90 and 1.36m diameter and 0.60m stroke arranged end to end and driving the single propeller shaft. 4 reglementary cylindrical boilers (*Tempête*), 4 high return flame cylindrical boilers by Indret (*Vengeur*). 164.6t coal.

**Armour:** (iron)
Side: Belt at waterline 330mm amidships, 250mm fwd, 300mm aft. Height from 0.886m below the wl to 1.114m above (designed for 1.20m to 0.80m). Breastwork 333mm forward, 300mm middle, 270mm aft.
Guns: Turret 300mm.
Deck: 50mm amidships and ends on 120mm teak on 10mm plating. This protection was on the deck of the breastwork and, beyond the breastwork, on the top deck of the hull just above the waterline.
Conning tower: 250mm (on top of the turret).

**Guns:**
(1883, *Tempête*) 2 x 274.4mm/19.75 M1875 N° 1 (turret), 4 x 100mm (at corners of hurricane deck, replacing the 4 x 12pdrs in the original design). Had no torpedo tubes but later in her career carried 18 torpedoes as central ship for the Défense mobile.
(1883, *Vengeur*) 2 x 340mm/18 M1875, 4 x 100mm.
(1900, *Tempête*) 2 x 274.4mm, 4 x 47mm/40 M1885 QF (from *Carnot*, replacing the 100mm guns in the corners of the hurricane deck), 4 x 37mm Hotchkiss revolving cannon (on the sides of the hurricane deck between the QF). Also three 40cm Mangin searchlights.
(1900, *Vengeur*) 2 x 340mm (turret), 6 x 47mm QF and 6 x 37mm revolving cannon (all on hurricane deck). Also 3 x 60cm searchlights.

*Tempête* Brest Dyd/Indret.
On list 1.1873. K: 26.12.1872. L: 18.8.1876. Comm: 8.8.1879 (trials). C: 3.1880.

Budget 1872. Machinery installed 12.7.1877 to 9.1.1879. Trial results approved 26.3.1880, to reserve at Brest. In full commission 15.4.1883 to 16.8.1883. Reboilered 1896-97 with medium return flame cylindrical boilers made at Nantes by the Chantiers de la Loire, arrived at Bizerte 25.7.1897 from Brest as central ship for the *Défense mobile*. Ordered back to Toulon 30.12.1905 for disposal, decomm. 15.2.1906. Struck 26.4.1907 and machinery condemned. Used as a target during all of 1908 and sank off Porquerolles 20.3.1909 in bad weather after hits from battleships *Justice* and *Gaulois*. Wreck for sale 1909-1911, finally sold 21.12.1912 by the Administration des Domaines with the wreck of the battleship *Iéna* to Lazare Nicolini of Toulon. Salvage operations were interrupted 1.8.1914, resumed 18.9.1915 and continued through the mid-1920s. In 1959 some remaining armour plate and the two 274.4mm guns were recovered.

**Vengeur** Cherbourg Dyd/Indret (engines designed by Joseph Joëssel).
On list 1.1874. K: 8.12.1874. L: 16.5.1878. Comm: 15.1.1882 (trials), 30.5.1882 (full).
Budget 1875. Arrived at Toulon from Brest 11.7.1882 and put into reserve. In commission in the *Escadre d'évolutions* at Toulon 1884-85, then to Cherbourg from Toulon 25.3.1885 and to reserve. Struck 20.6.1905. Sold 1906 at Cherbourg to BU.

----

**TONNANT.** *Garde-côtes cuirassé de 2ᵉ classe.* Coast defence ironclad with two centreline barbettes, iron armour, a steel and iron hull, and a ram bow. One funnel, one mast, no sails. Designed by de Bussy and Marchegay.

*Tonnant* was ordered in 1875 as the third ship of de Bussy's *Tempête* class. In early 1876 Minister of Marine Montaignac de Chauvance ordered the *Conseil des travaux* to recommend modifications to be made to 2ⁿᵈ class coast defence ships with the primary purpose of increasing the protection of the decks and increasing the speed, without changing the displacement but suppressing if appropriate the armoured breastwork. The Council understood these instructions to be limited to ships already under construction. On 10 March 1876 it recommended an armament of two 320mm guns in a turret of reduced diameter (7.30m) and configured in two levels like that in *Tigre* to keep the axis of the guns high (4.80m) above the water. Deck protection would be increased to 80mm including plating over the machinery and 70mm elsewhere. The breastwork would be suppressed and a complete unarmoured level 1.70m high would be added to the hull above the existing monitor deck. Any remaining tonnage would be used to increase engine power and speed, although the Council did not consider this important in a 2ⁿᵈ class coast defence ship. On 26 October 1876 Minister of Marine Fourichon ordered Rochefort to design a turret of reduced diameter with two steel 320mm guns for *Tonnant*, and naval constructor Edmond François Émile Marchegay completed the design on 8 June 1877. He moved the conning tower from the turret to the superstructure forward of the funnel and gave it 30mm armour.

Following the acceptance of the conversion design for *Furieux* (below) on 9 July 1878, Rochefort proposed to make similar modifications to *Tonnant*. Marchegay produced a design that was signed and forwarded by Rochefort on 31 August 1878 and approved by Minister of Marine Pothuau on 24 September 1878. The approval of a similar conversion design for *Furieux* was felt to render referral of the *Tonnant* design to the *Conseil des travaux* unnecessary. Marchegay moved the two 340mm guns from the single turret to two barbettes, suppressed the breastwork, and used that tonnage to increase the deck thickness from 50mm to 80mm and the maximum belt thickness from 330mm to 450mm. Because the engines and the after end of the underwater hull had already been built it was not possible to change from one screw to two as had been done in *Furieux*. The barbette armour in Marchegay's proposal was 450mm but it was quickly changed to 400mm by Minister of Marine Jauréguiberry on 12 April 1880 and again reduced (saving 24 tons) on 24 December 1880 after measure-

ments taken when the ship was launched showed her hull already 42 tons overweight with another 6.2 tons of additions planned. The new configuration of the hull above the waterline was based on the *Bélier* type but unlike in *Furieux* it retained the low monitor stern of the turret ship design. A contract for iron armour with Saint-Chamond (also called the *Compagnie des Hauts-fourneaux*) was approved on 27 June 1879. Soon after *Furieux* was given longer 21-calibre 340mm guns the ministry informed the artillery technical service on 18 June 1881 that there was no reason to consider modifying the length of the guns in *Tonnant*. On 7 March 1882 the *Conseil des travaux* approved replacing the planned wooden signal mast with a solid steel mast with a top armed with two 37mm revolving cannon, and the Council agreed in around 1889 to raise this by 3m. When fully commissioned in August 1885 the ship had a surcharge of 247 tons, mostly in the engines and boilers.

*Tonnant* was never considered for modernization. In July 1901 her 340mm guns were at Ruelle for modifications, and they were never reinstalled. On 3 April 1902 her boilers were reported to be unsafe to operate above 2.25 kg/cm² pressure, about half the intended rating, and it was then found that her turret hydraulic mechanism would not operate at that reduced pressure, making the ship unserviceable. Cherbourg reported this situation to Minister of Marine Camille Pelletan on 20 July 1902, and on 31 July 1902 Pelletan ordered her decommissioned and prepared for condemnation.

*The characteristics are based on a devis dated 8.3.1885.*
**Dimensions & tons:** 78.60m oa (tip of ram to tip of stern), 75.85m wl (+2.75m ram), 73.85m pp (wl fwd to rudder) x 17.80m ext, 17.72m wl. 5,091.3t disp. Draught: 5.636m mean, 5.636m aft. Men: 163.
**Machinery:** 425nhp and 1,700ihp designed at 95rpm and 4.132kg/cm² boiler pressure. Trials (22.4.1885) 1994.04ihp = 11.561kts at 94.2rpm. 1 screw. 1 horizontal compound (Woolf) engine with return connecting rods and 3 cylinders of 1.36m diameter (all three) and 0.70m stroke for the two low pressure cylinders and 0.50m for the high pressure middle cylinder. 4 high reglementary cylindrical boilers. 165t coal.
**Armour:** (iron)
Side: Belt at waterline 450mm amidships, 340mm fwd and aft. Height from 1.74m below the wl to 0.26m above (designed for 1.35m to 0.65m).
Guns: Barbettes 340mm.
Deck: 80mm amidships and ends.
Conning tower (steel): 30mm with 20mm roof (cylindrical, placed on the bridge)
**Guns:**
(1885) 2 x 340mm/18 M1875 (barbette turrets), 4 x 37mm revolving cannon. **Torpedoes:** 2 tubes proposed 1886 but not fitted. **Searchlights:** 2 x 40cm Mangin proposed 1888, probably not fitted.
(1889) 2 x 340mm, 8 x 37mm revolving cannon.
(1898) 4 x 47mm replaced 4 x 37mm revolving cannon at the corners of the shelter deck.

*Tonnant* Rochefort Dyd/Indret (engines designed by Joseph Joëssel).
On list 1.1875. K: 12.2.1875. L: 16.10.1880. Comm: 1.1.1885 (trials), 3.8.1885 (full).
Budget 1876. Machinery installed 11.4.1882 to 12.1882. Probably fully manned for trials 8.3.1885, moved from Rochefort to Cherbourg 15-17.3.1885 escorted by *Travailleur*. Trials 4.1885. Left Cherbourg 4.8.1885 for Toulon and put into reserve. Commissioned 23.3.1886, left Toulon for Cherbourg 2.4.1886 and to reserve. In commission for a coastal cruise between 17.6.1889 and 31.7.1889. Administratively decomm. 1.1.1890, in reserve 2ⁿᵈ category 18.7.1891. Full commission 10.7.1893 to run trials, back to 2ⁿᵈ category reserve 5.8.1893. Decomm. 1.9.1902. Struck 24.10.1902, for sale at Cherbourg 1902-1903, sold 2.4.1905.

----

## (C) 1st class Coast Defence Ironclads (*Garde-côtes cuirassés de 1re classe*).

To *Cuirassés d'escadre* in the 1.1880 fleet list and to *Garde-côtes cuirassés* 1.1884. 4 *Caïman* back to *Cuirassés d'escadre* 1.1885, then back to *Garde-côtes cuirassés* 1.1891. All to *Cuirassés gardes-côtes* 1.1892.

*TONNERRE* **Class.** *Garde-côtes cuirassés de 1re classe.* Breastwork monitors with one twin turret, a steel and iron hull, and a ram bow. One funnel (large in *Tonnerre*, smaller in *Fulminant*), one light mast, no sails. Designed by de Bussy.

On 9 August 1872 the *Conseil des travaux* examined three designs for 1st class coast defence ships submitted in accordance with its specifications of 10 November 1871 as forwarded to the ports by Minister of Marine Pothuau on 29 November 1871. It approved the one by de Bussy, signed on 29 July 1872, which was a modified version of a design examined by the Council in 1870 and 1871. De Bussy's latest design was simply his 2nd class coast defence ship with the armoured deck raised 10cm to obtain the height above the waterline of 90cm in the specifications. He then increased on the ratio of 1.25 to 1 all the vertical dimensions of the hull, obtaining a draught of 6.50m and displacement of 5,584 tons. He retained the vaulted stern lines of the 2nd class design and the Council recommended that this innovation be limited to the slower 2nd class ships until validated by experience. Minister Pothuau, however, approved the plans on 19 August 1872 without alteration. Émile Bertin in 1906 described them as copies of HMS *Glatton* but without the breastwork extending all the way to the sides and related that *Tonnerre* during a port turn at full speed would have capsized if the helmsman had not taken rudder off in time. The space between the breastwork and the side was then filled in by a light structure in both ships. The rate of fire from the big guns in *Tonnerre* was estimated in 1900 as one round every 7-8 minutes.

*The characteristics are based on a devis for* Tonnerre *dated 30.3.1878 with machinery data for* Fulminant *from a devis of unknown date.*

**Dimensions & tons:** 78.600m oa (end to end, ram to extension of poop), 75.60m wl (+3.00m ram), 73.60m pp (wl fwd to rudder) x 17.60m ext and wl. 5,588t disp. Draught: 6.421m mean, 6.639m aft. Men: 190.

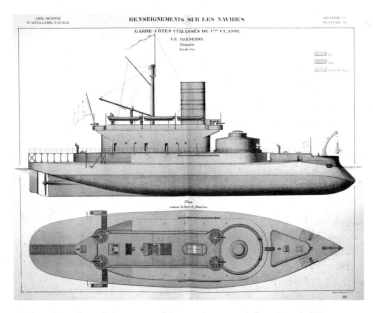

Outboard profile and plan views of the 1st class coast defence ironclad *Tonnerre*. The turret contains two 274.4mm Model 1875 steel guns while the corners of the spardeck hold four steel 100mm guns, for which 12pdr 121mm bronze guns were substituted before completion. (*Aide-Mémoire d'Artillerie navale, 1878*)

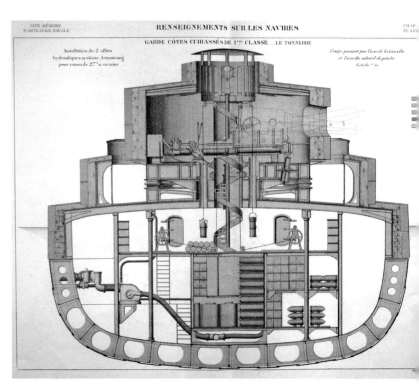

Cross section through the axis of the turret and the axis of the left gun port of the 1st class coast defence ironclad *Tonnerre* showing the installation of the ship's two hydraulic Armstrong mountings for steel 274.4mm/19.75 Model 1875 No.1 guns and the associated mechanisms. The plan also shows the fixed conning tower with its steering wheel on the top of the turret, the spiral ladder from the conning tower through the turret itself to the magazine below the turret, the shell and powder hoists, the steel hull structure, and the thick wooden backing behind the iron armour. (*Aide-Mémoire d'Artillerie navale, 1878*)

**Machinery:**
*Tonnerre* (from the ironclad *Normandie*): 850nhp and 3,400ihp designed at 60rpm and 2.25kg/cm² boiler pressure. Trials (1.1878) 4,166ihp = 14.070kts at 63.6rpm and 2.243kg/cm² boiler pressure. 1 screw. 1 horizontal simple expansion engine with return connecting rods and two cylinders of 2.085m diameter and 1.27m stroke. 8 reinforced high rectangular tubular boilers. 291t coal. Range 2,100nm @ 10kts.
*Fulminant* (new): 850nhp and 3,500ihp designed at 4.133kg/cm² boiler pressure. Trials (11.1.1881) 4,516ihp = 13.882kts at 76.83rpm and 4.39kg/cm² boiler pressure. 1 screw. 1 horizontal compound engine with return connecting rods and 3 cylinders of 1.77 and 2.05m diameter and 1.20m stroke. 8 high cylindrical boilers. 281.6t coal. Range 2,070nm @ 10kts.

**Armour:** (iron)
Side: Belt at waterline 330mm amidships, 250mm fwd, 300mm aft. Height from 1.51m below the wl to 0.89m above. Breastwork 333mm amidships, 300mm ends.
Guns: Turret 300mm, 350mm at gun ports.
Deck: 50mm amidships and ends on 120mm wood on 10mm plating, location as in *Tempête*.

**Guns:**
(1878, *Tonnerre*) 2 x 274.4mm/19.75 M1875 Nº 1 (enclosed turret), 4 x 12pdr (121mm/17) bronze (corners of the flying deck).
(1880, *Fulminant*) 2 x 274.4mm/19.75 M1875 Nº 1, 4 x 100mm (corners of the flying deck), 4 *mitrailleuses*.
(1900, both) 2 x 274.4mm/19.75 M1875 Nº 1, 6 x 47mm/40 M1885 QF, 2 x 37mm/20 M1885 QF, plus 1 x 65mm used for line throwing. Two of the 47mm QF replaced six 37mm revolving cannon that were previously carried. Also 4 x 60cm Mangin searchlights.

*Tonnerre* Lorient Dyd/engine from *Normandie* reconditioned by F.C. Méditerranée.
On list 1.1873. K: 8.1873. L: 16.9.1875. Comm: 15.9.1877 (trials), 1.4.1878 (full).
Budget 1872. Arrived at Brest 22.6.1878 and placed in reserve, to Toulon 1882. In commission in the *Escadre d'évolutions* at Toulon 1884-85, then to reserve at Cherbourg. In commission in the *Division cuirassé du Nord* and the *Escadre du Nord* 1891-94. Reboiled 3.1900. Struck 12.12.1905, retained as target at Brest 1905-1906 and at Lorient 1906-1914, for sale at Lorient 1920-1922.

*Fulminant* Cherbourg Dyd/Schneider, Creusot.
On list 1.1874. K: 24.2.1874. L: 20.8.1877. Comm: 12.8.1880 (trials). C: 1.1881.
Budget 1875. Named 20.2.1874. Full power trials 1.1881, then to reserve. To full commission 29.4.1885 and moved from Cherbourg to Toulon, returned to Cherbourg 1886. Badly damaged by striking rock 26.2.1887 in the Chenal du Four off Brest while en route Toulon and remained at Brest. In commission in the *Division cuirassée du Nord* and the *Escadre du Nord* 1891-94. Reboiled 1893-94 (first lit off 3.3.1894). Struck 14.3.1908, retained as target at Brest and assigned as such to the *Escadre de la Méditerranée* 21.6.1909. Sank 20.2.1911 after use as target, raised seven days later. To the Domaines at Toulon 4.11.1912 for sale, sold 21.12.1912 to Frank Rijsdijk's of Holland. Towed out 4.1913 to BU at Rotterdam.

---

**FURIEUX.** *Garde-côtes cuirassé de 1re classe.* Coast defence battleship with two centreline barbettes, steel armour, a steel and iron hull, and a ram bow. One funnel, one mast, no sails. Designed by de Bussy.

On 12 February 1875 Minister of Marine Montaignac de Chauvance ordered the construction at Cherbourg of a copy of *Fulminant* (*Tonnerre* class) that had been named *Furieux* on 26 January 1875. She was one of several ships then building (including *Tonnant* and probably *Vengeur* but not *Fulminant*) that were then to carry steel 320mm guns instead of steel 274.4mm guns in their turrets.

On 21 October 1875 Minister Montaignac de Chauvance ordered the *Conseil des travaux* to propose changes to new 1st class coast defence ships that were still to be laid down. Recent gunnery trials against armoured decks and data on the Brazilian monitors *Javary* and *Solimões* then building in France suggested a need to increase their offensive and defensive strength without changing displacement and cost. The Director of Materiel, Sabattier, suggested for 1st class coast defence ships increasing offensive power by adding a second turret and suppressing the breastwork and increasing defensive power by increasing deck thickness. On 25 February 1876 the Council examined what could be done without changing the current displacement or hull dimensions. Its recommendations, similar but not identical to those it gave for 2nd class coast defence ships on 10 March 1876 (above), included an armament of two 320mm guns in a single turret of reduced diameter (7.30m) and configured in two levels like that in *Tigre* to keep the axis of the guns high (4.80m) above the water. Deck protection would be increased to 70mm including plating and a splinter deck would be added over the machinery. The breastwork would be suppressed and a complete deck level 1.70m high would be added to the hull above the existing monitor deck. Astern fire would be obtained each side of the superstructure as in *Tonnerre*, requiring reducing the width of the superstructure to 2.00m. In June 1877 naval constructor Marie Pierre Henri Félix Carlet at Cherbourg, probably responding to a directive from Minister of Marine Fourichon in late 1876 similar to that for *Tonnant* (above), designed a turret of reduced diameter with hydraulic controls by Farcot. There was not enough clearance for the guns to fire together directly astern as in *Tonnerre*, but singly they could get within five degrees of the axis.

On 7 August 1877 the *Conseil des travaux* examined an early design by Sabattier for the larger *Indomptable* class which had a single large gun

mounted forward and vigorously criticised the large blind arc aft that left the stern of the ship vulnerable. On 24 August 1877 Minister of Marine Vice Admiral Albert Auguste Gicquel des Touches suspended construction of *Furieux* and on 7 September he asked de Bussy, the original designer of *Furieux* then serving at Lorient, to redesign her. De Bussy submitted his first revised design on 4 November. In December 1877 it was decided to change radically the disposition of the artillery and replace the single armoured turret with two single barbettes on the centreline forward and aft. This led to the adoption of twin screws to accommodate an ammunition hoist on the centreline for the after gun, which in turn required a complete redesign of the stern. De Bussy delivered revised designs on 17 February and 16 May 1878. On 20 May 1878 the Director of Materiel, Sabattier, presented de Bussy's latest design (signed 15 May 1878) to Minister of Marine Pothuau who referred it on 25 May to the *Conseil des travaux*.

The Council discussed the new design for *Furieux* on 25 June 1878. It noted that the overall purpose of the redesign had been to modify the configuration of the upper works and imitate to a certain degree what had been done on the large coast defence ships (the *Indomptable* class) that now carried two 75-ton guns in two barbettes. The new design suppressed the armoured breastwork, replaced the heavy single turret with two open barbettes, and reconfigured the entire hull and superstructure above the armour belt. These changes allowed increasing the belt armour from 33cm to 50cm, the deck armour from 60mm to 80mm (90mm near the sides), and giving the barbettes 45cm armour. The two 340mm guns were carried 6.30m above the water instead of 4.89m for the two 274.4mm guns of *Tonnerre* and both guns had 270° arcs of fire, one aft and one forward. Speed, range and steering remained the same, but the single engine of *Tonnerre* was replaced with two engines with two screws. The designed draught, however, was 10cm more than *Tonnerre*, reducing the height of the belt above the waterline from 90cm to 80cm. The Council concluded that the many improvements were significant but that they were dearly bought at the expense of sea-going qualities, which it predicted based on stability calculations and the new hull configuration would be inferior to those of a new ship designed in one go. However, the Council provided some technical recommendations on the design in case the money already spent on *Furieux* could not be abandoned. Minister of Marine Pothuau was not impressed with the Council's suggestion to start over and on 9 July 1878 approved de Bussy's design and sent the plans to Cherbourg with instructions to press the work as actively as possible. Naval constructors de Maupeou d'Ableiges, Garnier and Finot were successively put in charge of her construction and authored numerous modifications to her plans during construction.

On 14 March 1881 the ministry sent Cherbourg a plan for installing a lengthened 340mm gun in a barbette. It later specified that *Furieux* would get 340mm 21-calibre Model 1875 guns with a small (not enlarged) powder chamber. This was one of four 340mm/21 guns that the French designed in 1881, including two M1875 and two M1881. The other three all had an enlarged chamber. *Furieux* also got steel armour. Schneider at Creusot had specialized in steel armour since the mid-1870s and in 1880 the Navy gave Schneider a contract for steel armour for the coast defence ship *Terrible* to encourage further development. On 31 May 1882 it approved a contract with Schneider for steel armour for the belt and barbettes of *Furieux*. A contract for iron deck armour with the *Compagnie des Hauts-Fourneaux* at Saint-Chamond followed on 31 August 1882. Before the contracts were awarded the maximum belt and barbette armour thicknesses were reduced from 500mm to 450mm and 400mm respectively to take advantage of the expected greater strength of steel and because it was already apparent that the ship would be overweight.

In May 1885 the incomplete ship was found to be already 325 tons overweight, increasing her draught by 31cm and decreasing the height of her belt above the waterline by the same amount. The *Conseil des travaux* recommended removing the four 100mm guns that were to be placed at the corners of the superstructure, reducing the armour on the conning tower from 30mm to 6mm, and reducing the number of rounds for each big gun

The coast defence ironclad *Furieux* during a visit to Portsmouth, England, by the *Escadre du Nord* from 19 to 26 August 1891 following a diplomatic visit to Kronshtadt. The blue flag at her masthead is the signal flag for the letter 'M'. Photo by Symonds, Portsmouth. *(NHHC, NH-64446)*

from 80 to 40. To improve seakeeping it also recommended filling in the space between the ship's two deckhouses to produce a single structure with a full shelter deck amidships. Despite her overweight condition the Navy on 23 December 1885 approved the installation of two torpedo tubes just above the waterline amidships, on 2 March 1886 the Council approved adding electric lighting to the ship, and on 30 November 1886 it approved adding Bullivant nets. In 1893 the ship was found to be 420 tons overweight with only 20cm of the belt above the waterline instead of the designed 80cm. The Council on 16 January 1894 recommended removing the Bullivant nets still on board, reducing the ammunition for the big guns from 34 to 30 rounds each, and deleting the torpedo armament. More importantly, it wanted to raise the top of the belt of *Furieux* to 50cm above the waterline by cutting off the bottom 55cm of her side armour. (Such a partial *décuirassement* of both *Furieux* and *Requin*, both at Cherbourg, had been under consideration since late 1892.) Even though the surcharge remained substantial, it also wanted to install a new conning tower with 160mm armour.

**Modernization, 1901-1904.** On 31 May 1896 Émile Bertin, the head of the new *Section technique des constructions navales*, wrote that the proposal to remove some armour was risky and that it made more sense to restore the height above water of the belt to the 80cm on her original plans by removing nearly the entire excess weight. This could be accomplished and the ship modernized by replacing the 340mm guns, whose rate of fire was reported in 1895 as one round every 8-10 minutes, with two modern 240mm guns. The boilers would be replaced with water tube boilers of the same power, the engines converted to triple expansion, the coal supply

would be reduced from 331 to 266 tons (which would not cost any endurance because of the more efficient propulsion plant), and the torpedo armament and Bullivant nets suppressed as already decided. This would save 443.2 tons and reduce the excess weight to a mere 27.6 tons. Until this could be accomplished Bertin recommended doing nothing to the ship. On 18 August 1896 Minister of Marine Besnard asked Cherbourg for a definitive study for this modernization, and two 240mm M1893-96 guns were ordered from Ruelle on 14 October 1896.

On 26 January 1897 Minister Besnard approved an overhaul plan for *Furieux* and the four ships of the *Indomptable* class. Besnard approved Cherbourg's general design on 9 November 1897. The conversion of the engines of *Furieux* was ordered from Indret in May 1898, new Belleville boilers in two sets with two new centreline funnels were ordered on 31 August 1898, and new turrets for the two 240mm guns were ordered on 26 April 1899. Final plans by naval constructor Georges Guyot for the reconstruction were dated 24 April 1899. On 5 March 1900 Minister of Marine Lanessan ordered Cherbourg to proceed with the reconstruction, but it only began after the completion of the reconstruction of *Requin* on 1 October 1901. It then proceeded slowly, the ship being used by the dockyard to keep its workers busy between higher priority jobs. *Furieux* decommissioned on 23 November 1901 and boiler installation started in July 1902. The ship began dock trials on 29 March 1904 and sea trials on 12 July 1904. The ship went back into normal reserve on 1 January 1905 after completing trials and was never placed in full commission after her reconstruction.

At some point after 1905 her funnel caps were simplified and the inner casings of the funnels were substantially raised. This may have occurred during 1908 when she was temporarily given tall spars for wireless experiments. *Furieux* had the only 240mm guns in the fleet of a model after 1893 and in February 1909 Cherbourg was notified that such a gun was needed for the gunnery trials against the hulk of *Iéna*. The dockyard was asked to indicate its preference between sending the ship to Toulon or dismounting a gun with its cradle and loading them on a coastal transport ship no later than 1 April 1909. Instead *Furieux* left Cherbourg for Brest on 15 September 1909 with both turrets intact and was decommissioned at Brest on 2 May 1913.

*Furieux* was ordered sold 31 December 1913. The sale was scheduled for 27 August 1914 but the war intervened. She was among several ships proposed in May 1916 for use in trials of explosions against ships' hulls, the others including *Carnot, Charles Martel,* and *Indomptable.* Brest was ordered on 8 December 1916 to proceed with the trials against *Furieux,* suspending dynamometers along the hull in the vicinity of the blasts. The trials were carried out using compressed air bottles from condemned 450mm M1897 torpedoes and concluded in September 1917. It was then proposed to remove parts of her deck and some of her armour plates to send to Dunkirk for use as bombardment shelters. A photo taken in the Brest dockyard c1919 shows her afloat but extensively dismantled. Efforts to sell her began in October 1920 and a sale to Frank Rijsdijk's of Holland with *Charles Martel* was agreed to, but on 17 December 1920 she sank at her moorings at l'Aber-Wrac'h in the Brest roadstead voiding the sale. The wreck was ordered on 1 February 1921 to be sold in place and was offered for sale on 26 April 1921 but attracted no bidders. Brest reported on 3 July 1923 that she had been sold to the Société anonyme des Chalumeaux E. Royer at Lyon for 1,000 francs. She appeared in the fleet list for the last time in January 1924 as a wreck. Eugène Royer had invented in 1922 an oxyacetylene torch that could be used underwater to remove wrecks, which he apparently used on the wreck of *Liberté* but not on *Furieux.* The wreck was sold again on 22 August 1928 to André Crestois, a Parisian entrepreneur, this time for 40,000 francs. Crestois does not seem to have done any work on *Furieux,* although in 1939 he attempted to salvage the treasure ship *Télémaque* of 1790 at Quillebeuf sur Seine. A final sale offering on 3 October 1930 also failed. A wreck marked on Admiralty charts near the position of *Furieux*'s last moorings has been ascertained to be that of *Furieux;* its condition today is unknown.

*The original characteristics are based on a devis dated 28.5.1888.*

**Dimensions & tons:** 77.542m oa, 74.930m wl, 75.155m pp (tip fwd to rudder) x 17.714m ext (1.516m below wl), 17.650m wl. 6,018.875t disp. Draught: 6.861m mean, 7.181m aft. Men: 195. As of 1906 (rebuilt): 5,723.449t. Draught 6.545m mean, 6.711m aft (actual).

**Machinery:**
(1886) 1,000nhp and 4,704ihp designed at 88rpm and 5.00kg/cm² boiler pressure. Trials (21.5.1887) 4931.38ihp = 13.927kts at 89.25rpm. 2 screws. 2 vertical compound engines with 3 cylinders of 1.280m (1) and 1.600m (2) diameter and 0.750m stroke. 8 high cylindrical boilers. 300t coal.
(1904) 18kg/cm² boiler pressure (11kg/cm² at the engines). Full power trials (23.8.1904) 5,250ihp = 14.345kts at 91.062rpm. 2 vertical triple expansion engines converted from compound by Indret with 3 cylinders of 0.84m, 1,22m, and 1.97m diameter (the smallest one being in the middle). 8 Belleville boilers.

**Armour:**
Side: Belt at waterline (steel) 450mm amidships, 330mm fwd, 390mm aft. Height from 1.50m below the wl to 0.80m above (designed).
Guns:
(1886) Barbettes (steel) 400mm with 15mm hoods.
(1904) Turrets (steel) 200mm, bases 160mm.
Deck (iron): 90mm (80mm inboard) amidships and ends.
Conning tower:
(1886) 30mm (reduced to 6mm before completion).
(1904) 80mm.

**Guns:**
(1888) 2 x 340mm/21 M1875 (barbette turrets), 4 x 47mm/40 M1885 QF, 10 x 37mm revolving cannon. **Torpedoes:** 2 tubes for 356mm M1880 torpedoes (above water amidships). **Searchlights:** 2 x 60cm. 2 x 65mm/50 M1888 QF were added on after superstructure c1892.

*Furieux* at Brest in 1919 after destructive testing and partial stripping during the war. The top of the after turret is on the after deck and the gun (probably sent to the front) and both funnels are missing. She is in the background of a photo of the acquired coastal cargo ship USS *Bella,* which carried construction supplies between Brest and the U.S. Naval Air Station at Pauillac (Gironde) and other American stations in France. *(NHHC, NH-56666)*

(1901) 2 x 240mm/40 M1893-96 (enclosed turrets), 4 x 100mm/26.2 M1881 QF (converted), 12 x 47mm 40cal M1885 QF, 3 x 37mm/20 M1885 QF for the boats. Four Sautter Harley searchlights.

*Furieux* Cherbourg Dyd/Indret (engines designed by Joëssel).
On list 1.1875. Ord: 12.2.1875. K: 15.6.1875. L: 21.7.1883. Comm: 10.11.1886 (trials). C: 7.1887.
Budget 1876. Named 12.2.1875. Machinery installed 24.8.1883 to 10.5.1886. Trials began 19.3.1887, to 2nd category reserve 1.7.1887, reserve without category 11.1887 for post trial work. Full commission 28.5.1888 for a coastal cruise lasting to 1.7.1888. Again in full commission 15.2.1890 and to the *Division cuirassée du Nord* and the *Escadre du Nord* 22.2.1890. Returned to Cherbourg 20.6.1895 and back to reserve. Decomm. 23.11.1901 for reconstruction, boilers first lit off 19.3.1904, recomm. for trials 24.5.1904, trials report signed 29.8.1904, to normal reserve 1.1.1905. Moved from Cherbourg to Brest 15-16.9.1909. One of three coast defence ships assigned in 1909-10 to act as base ships for torpedo boat flotillas (the other two being *Bouvines* at Cherbourg and *Amiral Tréhouart* at Toulon.). To special reserve 10.4.1912, decomm. 2.5.1913. Struck 27.11.1913, ordered sold 31.12.1913. See above for the sequel.

---

***INDOMPTABLE* Class.** *Garde-côtes cuirassés de 1re classe.* Coast defence battleships with two centreline barbettes, compound and steel armour, a steel and iron hull (steel in *Requin*), and a ram bow. Two funnels abreast each containing two uptakes, two tripod masts with armed tops. Designed by Sabattier.

The 1876 budget (submitted in May 1875) provided for beginning two new unnamed *garde-côtes cuirassés de 1re classe,* one at Toulon and one by contract. The 1877 budget (March 1876) showed these still not begun and added a third at Rochefort. The 1878 budget (January 1877) showed the first two as to be 4% and 25% built as of January 1878, the Rochefort ship not begun, and added one more unnamed ship by contract. The 1879 budget (April 1878) listed *Caïman* at Toulon as to be 8% complete at the beginning of 1879, *Indomptable* at Lorient to be 12% complete, *Requin* by contract to be 20% complete, and *Terrible* at Brest to be 10% complete.

On 26 June 1877 Minister of Marine Gicquel des Touches submitted to the *Conseil des travaux* a design for a coast defence ship by Victorin Sabattier, the Director of Materiel, with one 100-ton or two 50-ton guns in a single barbette forward armoured with 50cm plates, with 60cm belt armour and 90mm deck armour, and with a speed of 14 knots. The Minister asked the Council if Sabattier's design would meet the specification for a coast defence ship and produce one superior to *Tonnerre.* He did not ask its opinion of the specifications themselves, and the minutes of the Council contain a comment that if the council had been asked for them it could not have agreed on them as it was deeply split on the matter.

The Council examined the design on 7 August 1877. It noted that the hull below the top of the belt was practically identical to that of *Tonnerre* when immersed an additional 30cm but that the hull above the belt was arranged completely differently. There was no armoured breastwork and the upper deck was a full 3m above the waterline. On the upper deck at 22m aft of the forward perpendicular was a single armoured barbette turret with a single 44cm 100-ton gun mounted 6.35m above the waterline. The Council noted that the armour met the Minister's specifications and commented that there did not then exist a ship this strongly protected. The Council found, however, that the design, which provided for 14 knots with forced draught, did not meet the specification of 14 knots in normal service, and it recommended increasing the speed to 14.5 knots on trials. It also found that the 100 degree blind arc aft that resulted from the choice of a single turret excessively degraded the defensive strength of the after part of the ship and recommended looking for ways to reduce this vulnerability.

In October 1877 the Navy's Artillery Directorate produced the first drawings for a 75-ton 420mm 21-calibre Model 1875 steel gun. Probably influenced by the comments of the Council and by the fact that France had no 100-ton gun, Sabattier changed his design to include barbettes at both ends armed with these 75-ton guns. Plans for one of the new ships, *Requin*, were approved by Minister of Marine Gicquel des Touches on 31 October 1877 and plans by Sabattier for another, a single ship with different stern lines and stern armour, *Caïman*, were approved by Minister of Marine Pothuau on 5 July 1878. The contract for the hull of *Requin* with the Anciens Établissements Bichon Frères was signed at the end of August 1878 and approved on 3 September 1878 (the firm became the Société Anonyme des Chantiers et Ateliers de la Gironde in 1882) and the contract with FCM for her engines was signed at the end of January 1879 and approved on 5 February 1879. On 5 November 1878 sketch designs for barbette mountings for the 420mm 75-ton guns were submitted by the Farcot firm. A contract with Saint-Chamond for compound belt armour for *Requin* was approved on 21 June 1880 (Marrel supplied the compound barbette armor) and compound belt armour was supplied by Châtillon et Commentry for *Caiman* and by Marrel Frères for *Indomptable*. Exceptionally Schneider received a contract for steel armour for the belt and barbettes of *Terrible* on 30 July 1880, in part to enable that firm to continue development of steel armour.

As some predicted the 420mm steel gun proved hard to fabricate. In successive redesigns the calibre of the gun went from 20 to 21 to 22. One of the guns was built at 21 calibres to use a tube whose tip was defective and another was built with the same length to give one ship matching guns. Additional ruptures occurred at the end of the defective tube and the two 21-calibre guns were shortened to 19.35 calibres. These short guns were used to arm *Terrible*. The other three ships received 22-calibre guns.

*The original characteristics for this class are based on a devis for* Terrible *dated 27.7.1887 with hull measurements for* Caïman *from a devis dated 25.1.1889.*

**Dimensions & tons:**
(1887, *Terrible*) 88.250m oa, 84.810m wl (+2.950m ram), 82.800m pp (wl fwd to rudder), 85.750m pp (tip fwd to rudder) (2.010m rudder to stern) x 17.780m ext (below wl), 17.520m wl. 7,767.238t disp. Draught: 7.744m mean, 8.088m aft. Men: 373. *Terrible* as lightened/rearmed 1900: 7,517.305t disp. Draught: 7.542m mean, 8.0555m aft.
(1889, *Caïman*) 87.736m oa, 84.761m wl (+2.975m ram), 82.805m pp (wl fwd to rudder), 85.780m pp (tip fwd to rudder) (1.956m rudder to stern) x 17.780m ext (below wl), 17.540m wl. 7,638.778t disp. Draught: 7.360m mean, 7.660m aft. Men: 317. *Caïman* as lightened/rearmed 1904: 7,206.722t disp. Draught: 7.008m mean, 7.322m aft.

**Machinery:** 1,200nhp and 6,000ihp designed (plus 60 or 80hp for the ventilators) at 90rpm and 4.150kg/cm² boiler pressure. Trials (*Indomptable* 26.8.1886) 6605.5ihp = 14.808kts at 88.470rpm, (*Requin* 15.3.1889, Brest) 6,503.24ihp = 15.04kts at 91.20rpm. 2 screws. 2 vertical compound engines with 3 cylinders of 1.400m (1) and 1.700m (2) diameter and 0.900m stroke. 12 cylindrical boilers (high reglementary M1875 Indret type). 394t coal (*Caïman*). Range with 394t coal 1,678.9nm @ 10.963kts.

**Armour:**
Side: Belt at waterline (compound except steel in *Terrible*) 500mm amidships, 300mm fwd, 300mm aft (lower edge aft 200mm, height 1.350m). *Caïman* same except for armour in stern: 300mm aft (lower edge 300mm, height 0.780m). Total height 2.220m.
Guns: Barbettes (compound except steel in *Terrible*) 450mm on 30mm plating, 17mm hoods (later 30mm on the sides and 15mm on the tops.
Deck (iron): flat, 80mm near centreline and 80mm outboard (60mm outboard in *Indomptable*), all on 16mm hull plating.
Conning tower: Lightly protected circular commander's shelter on the lower bridge just forward of the funnels.

**Guns:**
(1886, *Indomptable, Caïman*) 2 x 420mm/22 M1875 (barbette turrets), 4 x 100mm/26.2 M1881 (shelter deck), 2 x 65mm/16 M1881 steel landing, 2 x 47mm/40 M1885 QF, 16 x 37mm revolving cannon. Also 1 x 90mm/22 M1881 boat (soon replaced with a 47mm revolving cannon) and 1 x 4pdr (86.5mm/11) bronze mountain. **Torpedoes:** 4 tubes above water on the sides. In 1889 *Requin* had M1880 (4.42m) and M1885 torpedoes and in 1891 *Indomptable* had M1885 torpedoes. **Searchlights:** 4 (2 centreline, 2 sides), 2 more later added on tops.
(1887, *Terrible, Requin*) 2 x 420mm/19.35 M1875 (barbette turrets), 4 x 100mm/26.2 M1881 (shelter deck), 2 x 65mm, 2 x 47mm/40 M1885 QF, 10 x 37mm revolving cannon, 1 x 47mm revolving cannon. **Torpedoes:** 4 tubes for 356mm M1880 torpedoes above water on the sides. **Searchlights:** 4, later 6.
(1892-93) 4 x 100mm QF (same model converted in all).
(1896, *Caïman*) 2 x 420mm, 4 x 100mm QF, 1 x 65mm, 6 x 47mm QF, 6 x 37mm/20 M1885 QF (in upper tops), 16 x 37mm revolving cannon. **Torpedoes:** 4 tubes for 356mm M1885 and M1887 torpedoes. **Searchlights:** 6 x 60cm.

On 3 June 1879 the *Conseil des travaux* decided that traditional coast defence ships had lost their rôle in coastal defence to fixed, mobile, and automatic torpedoes, torpedo boats, and small heavily-armed gun launches. It felt that the existing 1st class coast defence ships might still be useful as annexes to squadrons of battleships. The *Conseil d'Amirauté* in its Programme of 1879, replicated in the January 1880 fleet list, moved them to the category of *Cuirassés d'escadre* while leaving the 2nd class ships as *Garde-côtes cuirassés*. Two years later in the Programme of 1881 the *Conseil d'Amirauté* moved the 1st class ships back to the coast defence category but they retained their classification as *cuirassés d'escadre* in the fleet lists until 1891.

While the French had no illusions about the ability of the former coast defence ships to function as squadron battleships the British, more accustomed than the French to low freeboard first class battleships, saw them, and particularly the four *Indomptables,* as a potential threat. Norman Friedman in his *British Battleships of the Victorian Era* found that the *Indomptable* class was one of the key influences behind the design of HMS *Collingwood*, a low freeboard first class battleship with barbette-mounted guns at each end that set the pattern for the classic British predreadnought battleship. The commander of *Indomptable* in January 1887, however, saw his ship as a coast defender with a specific mission, writing after successful machinery trials that he found that this type, 'built to respond to the large Italian battleships, was as successful as possible'.

**Modernization, 1897-1902.** As early as 1887 the commander of *Terrible* reported that his ship was 600 tons over her designed weight, and all four

The coast defence ironclad *Caïman* at Toulon in her original configuration
showing her 420mm (16.5-inch) guns with shields over the breeches and loading
stations and her fully encased funnels. *(NHHC from ONI album of French
warships, NH-74962)*

ships were soon found to be at least 500 tons too heavy. This brought the
top of the belt dangerously close to the waterline and reduced stability. The
monster 420mm guns designed in the late 1870s also drew criticism, in
1891 the commanders of *Indomptable* and *Terrible* estimated that the
average interval between rounds from the 420mm gun was about
8 minutes. In 1890 the Maritime Prefect at Toulon recommended that they
be replaced by newer guns that were both lighter and more powerful. On
2 February 1891 Minister of Marine Barbey asked Toulon to study ways to
rearm the ships, and on 12 September 1891 Toulon recommended replacing them with 305mm/45 M1887 guns in the existing barbettes. More
studies followed, but on 10 February 1893 the ministry's Artillery
Directorate told the Minister of Marine, now Vice Admiral Adrien
Barthélemy Louis Rieunier, that a 340mm/35 gun (the 42-calibre gun in
*Brennus* shortened) was a better choice and on 1 May 1893 the Minister
approved ordering three of them for *Requin* at Cherbourg and adjourned
the rearmament of the remaining three ships of the class at Toulon.

The ministry's Matériel Directorate soon resumed planning to rearm
the three ships at Toulon, this time with the new 305mm/40 M1893 gun.
As in *Requin* the upgrade was to include new water tube boilers and the
conversion of the compound engines to triple expansion. On 18 March
1896 Rear Admiral Chauvin, the Chief of the Naval General Staff,
objected to these plans, arguing that the refits of these aging ships should
be limited to removing unneeded weights and installing replacement
cylindrical boilers that already existed in storage at Toulon. In August he
added that no 305mm guns were available and none would be for three
years. In response the Matériel Directorate shifted to 274.4mm guns for
the three Toulon ships, used the existing replacement boilers, and
renounced alterations to the engines. In November or December 1896 the
navy gave one of the pairs of new 274.4mm turrets to *Requin* at
Cherbourg, which was to receive a more comprehensive reconstruction,
and reassigned *Requin's* 340mm guns to *Terrible* at Toulon. On 26 January
1897 Minister of Marine Besnard approved an overhaul plan that was
implemented in five phases. *Furieux* at Cherbourg (see above) was also
part of this plan.

**(1) *Indomptable* and *Caïman* reboilered and lightened at Toulon 1897.**
Twelve replacement cylindrical boilers were installed, in *Indomptable*
during the first half of 1897 and in *Caïman* during the second half of 1897.
The outer funnel casing was lowered around 4m, exposing the tops of the
two uptakes in each funnel as in the other two ships of the class. The
forward tripod mast was retained but the mainmast was suppressed.

**(2) *Terrible* reboilered and lightened at Toulon 11.1898-1.1899.** Twelve
replacement cylindrical boilers were installed between November 1898 and
January 1899. The two metal tripod masts were replaced with simple
wooden poles, a conning tower and its communications tube, both with
60mm armour on 20mm plating, replaced the old charthouse, and a new
charthouse was built in front of the conning tower.

**(3)** *Requin* **modernized at Cherbourg 1898-1902.** On 9 September 1897 and 9 December 1897 Besnard's ministry asked Cherbourg for plans for a comprehensive overhaul of the only ship of the class there, and on 28 October 1898 it gave general approval to the project presented by naval constructor Gaston Denis Alexandre Tréboul. The overhaul was completed in April 1902. It included replacement of the 420mm guns with the first set of the new 274.4mm guns in enclosed turrets, the installation of Niclausse water tube boilers with two new funnels on the centreline, and the conversion of the engines to triple expansion.

**(4)** *Indomptable* **and** *Caïman* **rearmed and lightened at Toulon 1898-1903.** These two ships returned to the Toulon dockyard in to have their 420mm guns and barbettes replaced with 274.4mm guns in enclosed turrets. In addition the forward military mast was replaced by a wooden pole, a conning tower with a circular pilot house on top replaced the old shelter for the commander, and two 100mm guns were added to the four-gun secondary battery on the shelter deck. *Indomptable* also had the bottom 50cm of the after end of the belt armour replaced with wood to lighten the stern, a change not applicable to the different stern configuration in *Caïman*. This second overhaul of *Indomptable* lasted from 1898 to 1902 and that of *Caïman* lasted from 1899 to 1903.

**(5)** *Terrible* **rearmed at Toulon 15.11.1899-1.5.1900.** This ship returned to the Toulon dockyard to have her 420mm guns replaced with the 340mm/35 guns originally intended for *Requin* under an installation contract with Saint-Chamond dated 7.4.1897. The 420mm guns were removed in November 1899, their platforms were removed 19 December 1899 and reinstalled after modifications on 26 February 1900, the 340mm guns were placed on them in April 1900, and heavily armoured *masques frontaux* were fitted to the long guns.

*The characteristics for the refits are based on devis for* Indomptable *dated 17.8.1897,* Caïman *dated 14.4.1898,* Terrible *dated 28.9.1900,* Requin *dated 6.5.1902,* Indomptable *dated 2.12.1902 and* Caïman *dated 16.8.1904.*

**Dimensions & tons:**
(1902, *Requin*) 88.203m oa, 84.770m wl (+2.950 ram), 87.720m pp (tip fwd to wl aft) x 17.820m ext (above wl), 17.600m wl. 7,049.573t disp. Draught: 7.115m mean, 7.608m aft. Men: 346.

**Machinery:**
(1897-98, *Indomptable* and *Caïman*) 12 cylindrical return-flame boilers from Mouraille replacing the original Creusot boilers, 4.250kg/cm² boiler pressure (4.150kg/cm² at the engines). Trials (*Caïman*, 19-20.11.1897) 4,887.2ihp = 13.38kts at 84.2rpm.
(1900, *Terrible*) Reboiled with 12 Indret return-flame cylindrical boilers

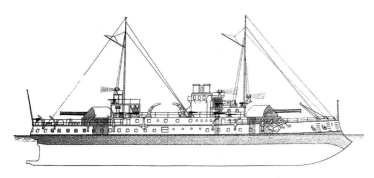

A rough outboard profile of the coast defence ironclad *Terrible* after the installation by Saint Chamond of two 340mm/35 Model 1893 guns on her existing barbettes. No photograph of her with these guns has been located. Her commander (P. de Jonquières) recorded in the *feuille signalétique* that contained this drawing that she had less military value than the similar *Indomptable, Caïman* and *Requin,* which had undergone a complete reconstruction and had a powerful main battery well protected in enclosed and balanced turrets. (*Feuille signalétique for the ship dated 1 May 1905*)

(4.250kg/cm²). Trials (13.2.1899) 4,238.76ihp = 13.5kts at 79.6rpm (natural draught, forced draught ventilators removed)
(1902, *Requin*) 6,130ihp designed at 91rpm and 15kg/cm² boiler pressure (12kg/cm² at the engines). 2 screws. 2 vertical triple expansion engines with 3 cylinders of 0.880m, 1.300m, and 1.920m diameter and 0.900m stroke. 12 Niclausse boilers (4 large principal aft and 8 small auxiliary forward). 480t coal.

**Armour:**
Guns: (*Terrible*) Original 450mm + 30mm iron barbettes retained but guns fitted with 504mm frontal shields made up of 7 layers of 72mm special steel. (*Requin, Indomptable* & *Caïman*) 274.4mm turrets (homogeneous steel) 270mm with 210mm fixed bases.
Deck: (*Requin*) 80mm extra mild steel on 16mm hull plating.
Conning tower (special steel): 136mm behind 20mm plating in *Requin*, 60mm plus 20mm plating in others.

**Guns:**
(1897-98, *Indomptable* and *Caïman*) 2 x 420mm/22 M1875 (barbette turrets), 4 x 100mm/26.2 M1881 QF (converted) (shelter deck), 6 x 47mm QF, 6 x 37mm QF, 6 x 37mm revolving cannon (no 37mm QF and 12 x 37mm revolving cannon in *Indomptable*). **Torpedoes:** 2 tubes for 356mm M1887 torpedoes (on sides above water, other two removed). **Searchlights:** 5 x 60cm..
(1900, *Terrible*) 2 x 340mm/35 M1893 (barbette turrets), 4 x 100mm/26.2 M1881 QF (shelter deck), 10 x 47mm QF, 3 x 37mm QF, 1 x 37mm Maxim. **Torpedoes:** removed. **Searchlights:** 4 x 60cm Sautter.
(1902, *Requin*) 2 x 274.4mm/40 M1893-96 (enclosed turrets), 6 x 100mm/26.2 M1881 QF (converted) (shelter deck), 10 x 47mm QF, 3 x 37mm QF (boats). **Torpedoes:** removed. **Searchlights:** 4 x 60cm Bréguet.
(1902-04, *Indomptable* and *Caïman*) 2 x 274.4mm/40 M1893-96 (enclosed turrets), 6 x 100mm/26.2 M1881 QF (converted) (shelter deck), 10 x 47mm QF, 4 x 37mm QF (the 37mm later being removed from the bridges but retained for the boats). **Torpedoes:** 2 tubes for 356mm M1887 torpedoes (on sides above water, landed 1905). **Searchlights:** 4 x 60cm Mangin.
(1919, *Requin*) 2 x 274.4mm (turrets), 6 x 100mm (shelter deck), 4 x 47mm.

*Indomptable* Lorient Dyd/Schneider, Creusot (engines designed by Mathieu).
On list 1.1878. K: 5.12.1877. L: 18.9.1883. Comm: 10.11.1885 (trials). C: 10.1886.
Budget 1877 (delayed to 1878). Construction reassigned from Rochefort to Lorient c1877. Machinery installed 3.6.1884 to 20.2.1885. Manned for trials 15.6.1886, left Lorient for Brest 22.6.1886, official trials 7-9.1886. From Brest to Toulon 23-31.10.1886. Two short cruises with the *Escadre d'évolutions* between 16.11.1886 and 3.12.1886, then to 1st category reserve 20.1.1887 and 2nd category reserve 1888. Part of the *Division* (or *Escadre*) *de réserve* at Toulon 1891 to 1895. Reboilered 1-2.1897 (trials 2-3.7.1897), rearmed 1898-1902. Never recommissioned, in normal reserve at Toulon and from 1906 at Cherbourg. Struck 3.8.1910, mooring hulk at Rochefort 1910-1914, still hulk there 1920-1927. Sold 1927 to BU.

*Terrible* Brest Dyd/Schneider, Creusot.
On list 1.1878. K: 10.12.1877. L: 29.3.1881. Comm: 15.7.1886 (trials). C: 6.1887.
Budget 1878. Construction reassigned from contract to Brest c1877. Launch advanced to clear the slip for *Neptune*. Machinery installed 17.9.1882 to 16.2.1884. Official trials 2-5.1887, to 2nd category reserve 22.6.1887 after trials. To full commission at Brest 23.1.1888, left Brest for Toulon 12.2.1888, to 2nd category reserve there 13.4.1888. Part of the *Division* (*Escadre*) *de réserve* at Toulon 1891 to 1897, to reserve 2e category 10.9.1897, new boilers installed from 15.11.1898 to 15.1.1899 (first lit off 21.1.1899), assigned to the

A row of coast defence battleships in reserve at Cherbourg. From left to right are *Valmy*, *Caïman*, *Indomptable*, and *Furieux*. Note the different configurations of the sterns of *Caïman* (a single ship) and *Indomptable* (configuration shared with *Terrible* and *Requin*). *(Postcard by LL)*

*Division des gardes-côtes* 20.1.1899 in place of *Caïman*, and recomm. 23.1.1899. Active until 10 Nov 1899. Rearmed 1899-1900, artillery trials 10.7.1900 mostly satisfactory, to 2nd category reserve 1.8.1900, no subsequent service except machinery trials 4-5.6.1903 and 1-2.12.1904. Demoted from normal to special reserve at Toulon 1906 when her three sisters were sent from there to Cherbourg. Struck 8.4.1908, sale planned for 7.10.1908 but instead converted to target for the fleet 6.7.1909 at Toulon. Heavily damaged by gunfire (300 rounds fired) 28.8.1909 and capsized and sank two days later. Wreck listed for sale 1909-1911 and as sunk 1912-1914.

*Caïman* Toulon Dyd/F.C. Méditerranée, Marseille (engines designed by Orsel).
On list 1.1878. K: 16.8.1878. L: 21.5.1885. Comm: 1.8.1887 (trials). C: 10.1888.
Budget 1876 (delayed to 1877). Machinery installed 20.9.1885 to 25.4.1887. Trials off Îles d'Hyères 3-6.1888, then mobilized for manoeuvres, then more trials 9-10.1888. To 2nd category reserve after trials 16.10.1888. Full commission 21.12.1888, replaced *Indomptable* in the *Escadre d'évolutions* 25.1.1889. To 2nd category reserve 1890. Part of the *Escadre de réserve* at Toulon 1892 to 1897. Reboiled 5-10 1897 (first lit off 13.10.1897, trials in November). In the *Division des gardes-côtes* 1898-99, then to 2nd category reserve and rearmed 1899-1903. Normal reserve at Toulon and from 1906 at Cherbourg. Decomm. 1909. Struck 20.2.1911, condemned 22.3.1911, mooring hulk at Rochefort 1910-1914, still hulk there 1920-1927, sold 1928 at Rochefort to BU.

*Requin* Bichon frères, later C.A. Gironde, Bordeaux-Lormont/F.C. Méditerranée, Marseille.
On list 1.1879. Ord: 3.9.1878. K: 15.11.1878. L: 13.6.1885. Comm: 1.12.1888 (trials). C: 6.1889.
Budget 1876 (delayed to 1877). Machinery installed 15.12.1885 to 25.11.1886. Arrived at Rochefort incomplete 17.12.1886 from Bordeaux and continued to Brest 23.12.1886 for completion including installation of armour and guns, decommissioning there 7.1.1887. Official trials at Brest 3-5.1889, then to 2nd category reserve 9.7.1889. Commissioned (full) 1.3.1890 at Brest for the *Division navale cuirassée du Nord* and the *Escadre du Nord*. Replaced in the division by *Valmy* on 30.7.1895, then in 2nd category reserve at Cherbourg 8.8.1895 for repairs. Decomm. after 22.10.1897 for modernization (boilers installed 7.1899). Comm. for trials 10.10.1901, comm. at Cherbourg 22.4.1902, arrived at Toulon 18.5.1902 and to normal reserve 6.8.1902. Back to Cherbourg and in reserve there 1.9.1906. Returned to Toulon 2.10.1909 to replace *Descartes* as a seagoing annex to the school for gunnery in *Tourville* (ex *Gironde*) at Toulon and in the Hyères roadstead. Replaced by *Charlemagne* and to special reserve at Bizerte 15.10.1913, reverted from *navire-école* to *cuirassé garde-côtes* 1.1914 and restoration to service as such directed by the Minister. Reactivated at Bizerte 8-10.1914 to defend the Suez Canal and helped save it by repulsing a Turkish advance on Ismalia 3.2.1915. Conducted coastal bombardments along the Palestine coast throughout 1917. At Port Said 11.1917-3.1918 repairing damage from actions off the Wadi el Hesi north of Gaza, spent most of 1918 in the canal. Left Port Said for Toulon 17.12.1918, gunnery school ship there to 7.1919. Decomm. 1.8.1919 at Toulon (completed 20.8.1919). Struck 21.6.1920. Sold 2.5.1921 with *Bruix* and *Torpilleur n° 269* to the Société du Matériel Naval du Midi to BU.

**Later Coast Defence Ships.** *Garde-côtes cuirassés de 1re classe.*

The 1880 budget (submitted in January 1879) included two new *garde-côtes cuirassés de 1re classe*, one at Brest and one by contract, to be advanced to 2% by the end of the year. They were not in the 1881 budget (January 1880).

On 10 April 1879 Minister of Marine Jauréguiberry asked the opinion of the *Conseil des travaux* on the types of ships to have in the future fleet for coast defence. The Council responded on 3 June 1879 that if the creation of the existing types of coast defence ships might at one time have had a reason it no longer did given the availability of fixed, mobile, and automatic torpedoes, torpedo boats, and small gun launches (*chaloupes-canonnières*) armed with heavy guns like *Tromblon* and *Épée*. The Council felt that it could no longer define what the rôle of a traditional coast defence ship should be and therefore that neither 1st class nor 2nd class coast defence ships should be included in the composition of the fleet and specifically that no more new ones should be built. The *Conseil d'Amirauté* retained the category of coast defence ships in both the Programme of 1879 and that of 1881 but did not suggest the construction of new ones of the traditional types.

*N* (Unnamed) Brest Dyd
Budget 1880. Not in the 1881 budget.

*N* (Unnamed) Contract
Budget 1880. Not in the 1881 budget.

---

## (D) Floating Batteries (*Batteries flottantes*).

To *Batteries flottantes cuirassées* in the 1.1873 fleet list.

*DÉVASTATION* Class (1854). *Batteries flottantes.* Broadside ironclad floating batteries with wooden hulls. Two small funnels abreast, three masts. Designed by Guieysse. Although the pioneering *Dévastation* class was built before 1859 full details on it are included here for readers' convenience.

At the outbreak of the Crimean War Napoleon III, wanting to attack Russian fortifications but realizing that wooden ships of the line could not withstand fire from Russian shell guns, ordered the resumption of a project for an armoured floating battery with an iron hull that had been dropped in 1847. After trials showed that thick armour plates on a heavy wood backing could resist projectiles, naval constructor Pierre Armand Guieysse completed a design for steam floating batteries armed with twelve 30pdrs No 1 (164.7mm/16.5) smoothbores on 25 July 1854 and Minister of Marine Ducos on 28 and 29 July ordered the construction of 10 wooden-hulled floating batteries (4 at Brest, 2 at Rochefort, 2 at Lorient, and 2 at Cherbourg). By contracts approved on 28 August 1854 armour was ordered from Schneider and from Petin Gaudet for five or ten batteries, and five 150nhp engines were ordered from Schneider with an option to add five more prior to 15 September 1854. However, the Navy found that French industry could not produce armour for ten batteries and suggested to the British on 15 August that they take on the construction of five of them. For that purpose he gave the British copies of the plans for the ships, which the British used to build their *Aetna* class. On 1 September 1854 the French reduced their programme to five ships, which were named on 13 October 1854. New plans for a steam floating battery armed with sixteen 50pdrs were signed by naval constructor Pierre Thomeuf at Lorient on 25 October 1854. During construction boiler power was increased to 225nhp but the official rating remained 150nhp and speed trials were disappointing.

*Lave* began to go into commission for trials (forming her crew) before she was launched. She, *Dévastation*, and *Tonnante* were towed to the Black Sea in about 45 days in August and September 1855 and proved the value of armour during the bombardment of the Russian forts at Kinburn on 17 October 1855. *Foudroyante* and *Congrève* were scheduled for use in the

Baltic, but operations there were over before they were ready and they stayed at Cherbourg. *Tonnante* originally had three masts with square sails on the fore and main, but the rig was severely reduced after the Crimean War.

*The characteristics are based on a devis for Tonnante dated 1855.*

**Dimensions & tons:** 53.00m oa, 52.35m deck x 13.55m ext. 1,604t disp. Draught: 2.50m fwd, 2.80m aft. Men: 282. Height of battery 0.90m.

**Machinery:** 225nhp (150 from 1867) and 430ihp designed at 120rpm. Trials (*Dévastation*) 457ihp = 4.4kts at 115rpm. 1 screw. 1 high pressure (5.1 atmospheres) engine with direct connecting rods and 2 cylinders of 0.6m diameter and 0.6m stroke. 6 locomotive boilers that took their feed water from the sea. No condenser. 100t coal.

**Armour:** (iron)
Side: Belt at waterline 110mm.
Guns: Battery 100mm.

**Guns:**
(1855) *Battery deck* 16 x 50pdr 194mm/16.4 SB. *Upper deck* 2 x 18pdr SB or 12pdr SB carronades.
(1866, *Dévastation* as school ship) *Battery deck* 6 x 194mm. *Upper deck* 2 x 240mm, 3 x 164.7mm M1860, 1 x 22cm 223.3mm/10.5 MLR converted shell gun.

*Dévastation* Cherbourg Dyd/Schneider.
Ord: 28.7.1854. K: 5.9.1854. L: 17.4.1855. Comm: 25.4.1855 (trials).
Left Cherbourg 10.8.1855 for the Crimea under tow by the paddle frigate *Albatros*. In the Adriatic 6-7.1859. Annex to the school for gunnery in *Louis XIV* at Toulon 1866 (see armament above). Struck 9.5.1871 at Toulon. BU 1872.

*Tonnante* Brest Dyd/Schneider.
Ord: 28.7.1854. K: 5.9.1854. L: 17.3.1855. Comm: 23.4.1855 (trials).
Left Brest 30.7.1855 for the Crimea under tow by the paddle frigate *Darien*. In the Adriatic 6-7.1859. Struck 31.8.1871, BU at Toulon 1872-1874.

*Lave* Lorient Dyd/Schneider.
Ord: 28.7.1854. K: 20.8.1854. L: 26.5.1855. Comm: 18.5.1855 (trials).
Left Lorient 6.8.1855 for the Crimea under tow by the paddle frigate *Magellan*. In the Adriatic 6-7.1859. Struck 9.5.1871, BU at Toulon 1872-1873.

*Foudroyante* Lorient Dyd/Schneider.
Ord: 28.7.1854. K: 20.8.1854. L: 2.6.1855. Comm: 4.6.1855 (trials).
Intended for Baltic operations but not sent. Struck 29.11.1871, for disposal at Cherbourg 1873-1875, BU 1874.

*Congrève* Lorient Dyd/Schneider.
Ord: 28.7.1854. K: 4.9.1854. L: 1.6.1855. Comm: 2.6.1855 (trials).
Intended for Baltic operations but not sent. Struck 13.5.1867 at Brest. BU 1868.

---

*PALESTRO* Class. *Batteries flottantes.* Broadside ironclad floating batteries with wooden hulls. Two funnels abreast, two masts, schooner rig. Designed by Dupuy de Lôme.

These four vessels were built as replacements for the *Dévastation* class of 1854 because of fears that the 1854 ships would deteriorate because they had been built hurriedly with poor wood. On 20 September 1858 Minister of Marine Hamelin ordered Cherbourg to prepare plans for new hulls to receive the armour and engines of the 1854 batteries, the new batteries to be designed more specifically for the defence of roadsteads and coasts. The resulting plans, along with the proposal to reuse the armour of the 1855 ships, were rejected by the *Conseil des travaux* on 29 March 1859, partly because the Council felt that 120mm armour (as in *Gloire*) was necessary. On 8 April 1859 Dupuy de Lôme presented specifications for the new ships which included sixteen 164.7mm rifles, 2.70m draught, 7.5 knots speed, armour as *Gloire*, and decks protected against 32cm mortar shells. He then drafted plans that featured the smallest tonnage compatible with 120mm armour, reduced length to reduce the target offered by the ship, finer lines to increase speed, and twin screws and altered stern lines to improve manoeuvrability. The resulting *Palestro* class fell somewhat short of the initial requirements with only 12 guns and a draught of 3.00m. The *Conseil des travaux* approved these plans in May 1859 and recommended that construction be assigned to the dockyards, but with the dockyards fully occupied, Dupuy de Lôme on 11 May 1859 proposed two sets of plans, one with a wooden hull to be built by Lucien Arman at Bordeaux and one with an iron hull to be built by the Forges et Chantiers de la Méditerranée (FCM) at La Seyne. Hamelin selected the wooden version, and one battery, *Paixhans,* was ordered from Arman by a contract of 20 May 1859 approved on 1 June 1859. Minister of Marine Hamelin on 5 July 1859 approved ordering three more. These (*Saigon, Peiho,* and *Palestro,* in the original renderings of their names) were ordered from Arman by a supplemental contract approved on 18 July 1859 and named on 27 July 1859. The high-pressure engines for all four ships were ordered from FCM by a contract signed on 9 September 1859. Construction was delayed by a series of design modifications, and *Paixhans* and *Palestro* were further delayed by late delivery of their armour (which had to be reordered in October 1860) and a fire in the shipyard's warehouses in January 1862.

Trials were mediocre, mainly because of steering difficulties. When examined at Rochefort for recommissioning in 1867 they were found to be in bad condition, and they were disposed of at the same time as the *Dévastation* class that they were to have replaced.

**Dimensions & tons:** 47.50m deck, 46.40m wl?, 42.70m keel x 14.04m ext. 1,563t disp. Draught: 3.06m fwd, 3.22m aft. Men: 212. Height of battery 0.98m.
**Machinery:** 150nhp. 580ihp = 7.50kts. 2 screws. 2 high pressure engines. 40t coal.
**Armour:** (iron)
Side: Belt at waterline 120mm
Guns: Battery 110mm.
Deck: Light plating
**Guns:** 12 x 164.7mm/19.2 M1864. Later reduced to 10 x 164.7mm.

*Paixhans* Lucien Arman, Bordeaux/F.C. Méditerranée, Marseille.
On list 1.1860. Ord: 1.6.1859 (contract). K: 24.5.1859. L: 9.9.1862. Comm: 1.1.1863 (trials). C: 7.1863.
Fitted out at Rochefort 2-7.1863 by David Cazelles, then to 2nd category reserve 13.7.1863 and to 3rd category reserve 16.4.1864. Comm. at Rochefort 13.9.1870, to 3rd category reserve (out of commission) 14.11.1870. Struck 21.8.1871 at Rochefort. BU 8.1871-2.1872.

*Palestro* Lucien Arman, Bordeaux/F.C. Méditerranée, Marseille.
On list 1.1860. Ord: 18.7.1859 (contract). K: 24.5.1859. L: 9.9.1862. Comm: 1.9.1862 (trials). C: 6.1863.
Began to commission for trials about a week before launching. Fitted out at Rochefort 3-7.1863 by David Cazelles, then to 2nd category reserve 6.6.1863 and to 3rd category reserve (out of commission) 7.4.1864. Comm. at Rochefort 8.9.1870, back to 3rd category reserve 10.11.1870. Struck 21.8.1871 at Rochefort. BU 8.1871-1.1872.

*Peï-ho* Lucien Arman, Bordeaux/F.C. Méditerranée, Marseille.
On list 1.1860. Ord: 18.7.1859 (contract). K: 20.7.1859. L: 25.5.1861. Comm: 15.7.1861 (trials). C: 10.1862.
To Rochefort 5.1861 for fitting out, fully manned for trials 5.10.1861. Back at Rochefort from Bordeaux with the paddle steamer *Solon* 24.3.1862. Fitted out at Rochefort from 3.1862 by Louis Marc Willotte. To 2nd category reserve 24.3.1864, then to 3rd category reserve 1.2.1865. Struck 15.11.1869 at Rochefort. BU 4.1870 to 10.1871.

*Saïgon* Lucien Arman, Bordeaux/F.C. Méditerranée, Marseille.
On list 1.1860. Ord: 18.7.1859 (contract). K: 20.7.1859. L: 24.6.1861. Comm: 10.10.1861 (trials). C: 11.1862.
To Rochefort 28.6.1861 for fitting out. Back at Rochefort from Bordeaux 4.2.1862. Fitted out at Rochefort 4-11.1862 by Louis Marc Willotte. To 2nd category reserve 1.1.1863. Caught fire 15.11.1863 and sank in the Charente River, refloated 30.11.1863, decomm. 1.1.1864, repairs completed 3.1864 and in 3rd category reserve. Comm. at Rochefort 13.9.1870, decomm. and to 3rd category reserve 22.11.1870. Struck 21.8.1871, embarkation hulk at Rochefort 1871-1883 (cut down 1-4.1872), for disposal 1883-1884, BU 1884.

---

**REMPART Class** (not built). *Batteries flottantes.* Ironclad floating batteries with iron hulls and low ends. Designed by Lemoine.

On 24 May 1860 a commission on coast defences acknowledged that it was impossible to build some needed forts and that it was necessary to use floating batteries instead. It recommended building eleven more floating batteries to give France a total of twenty for the defence of her main military and commercial ports (the nine already built or in hand were the five *Dévastation* class and the four *Palestro* class). On 3 October 1860 Minister of Marine Hamelin asked the *Conseil des travaux* to draft specifications for the new batteries. The Council on 30 October insisted on iron hulls to make the units more durable during long periods in reserve but felt that otherwise the characteristics of the *Palestro* class left little to be desired except that the height of the battery should be increased from 1.20m to 1.45m. The armament was to be fourteen 164.7mm rifles. Minister Hamelin sent these characteristics to the ports on 16 November 1860 and decided to build five iron-hulled ships in the dockyards (*Rempart* and *Réveil* at Cherbourg, *Indomptable* and *Courageuse* at Lorient, and one unnamed at Brest) and six by contract.

The Navy realized that the offensive use of floating batteries as in the Crimea was impracticable against England and that the main function of the ships would be defence of French coasts and ports. For this the ships needed shorter batteries than the full-length ones in the *Dévastation* and *Palestro* classes to reduce the target they offered and to add the ability to fire forward and aft. Napoleon III also wanted the ships to be as small and as inexpensive as possible. On 30 April 1861 the *Conseil des travaux* examined plans from five naval constructors and Lucien Arman of Bordeaux and selected the design of naval constructor Nicolas Lemoine, who had put the guns in a battery with the ends cut off and replaced with removable sheet metal bulwarks, allowing fire in all directions. The Council asked for some modifications, including increasing the armament from six to ten guns. Lemoine produced new plans on 19 and 24 June 1861 and they were approved by the Council on 9 July 1861 and by Minister of Marine Chasseloup-Laubat on 20 July 1861. Eleven ships were ordered to them on 14 August 1861. In early November the orders were redistributed, *Rempart* going to Cherbourg, *Indomptable* and *Courageuse* to Lorient, *Réveil* to Brest, three *Implacable* class to Ernest Gouin at Nantes, and four *Embuscade* class to Lucien Arman at Bordeaux. The programme was then curtailed for budgetary reasons by the cancellation of the four dockyard ships on 28 November 1861.

---

**IMPLACABLE Class.** *Batteries flottantes.* Ironclad floating batteries with iron hulls and low ends. One funnel, two masts. Designed by Lemoine.

These ships were ordered from Ernest Gouin at Nantes by a contract signed on 13 September 1861. The final plans for this class by Nicolas Lemoine, which followed his July 1861 preliminary design, were dated 3 February 1862 and retained the low ends in his original design along with temporary bulwarks that could be erected for transits at sea. Their high pressure engines were ordered from Schneider with those of the *Embuscade* class by a contract signed on 10 October 1862. Their designed armament remained nine 164.7mm rifles. The designed height of their battery above the water was 1.45m; in service it was 1.32m. Later the armament of these ships was upgraded to 194mm guns, probably in 1867 when *Imprenable* was ordered upgraded. In 1870 *Opiniâtre* and *Implacable* had four 194mm in the battery and two 164.7mm on deck.

In March 1868 Lemoine offered a design for converting the *Arrogante* class batteries into turret ships and another design to enlarge their gun ports for bigger guns. In November and December 1868 he offered plans for installing larger guns on *Arrogante* including a 240mm aft. In April 1869 naval constructor Godron and artillery captain Mallat offered a design to give *Arrogante* and *Imprenable* an armament of three 240mm rifles, and by August 1869 *Arrogante* had received three 240mm guns in the battery and four 12pdrs (121mm) on deck.

**Dimensions & tons:** 44.08m deck, 44.00m wl x 14.76m ext, 14.58m wl. 1,440t disp. Draught: 2.64m fwd, 2.94m aft. Men: 200. Height of battery in service 1.32m.

**Machinery:** 150nhp (120 from 1867) and 480ihp designed at 80rpm (engines) and 160rpm (screws) and 1.55kg/cm$^2$ boiler pressure. Trials (*Opiniâtre*, 1865) 457ihp = 6.98kts, (*Arrogante*, 7.1876) 374ihp = 5.92kts at 65.75rpm and 1.175kg/cm$^2$ boiler pressure. 2 screws, 1 rudder. 2 geared engines each with direct connecting rods and one cylinder of 0.86m diameter and 0.75m stroke. 4 special type direct flame boilers. 38t coal. Range 272nm @ 5.9kts.

The floating battery *Opiniâtre* as a support hulk for the *Défense Mobile* at Cherbourg. Torpedo boats *no 320* and *no 301* are identifiable on the left, *no 315* and *no 316* on the right. *(Postcard by F.C. Cherbourg)*

**Armour:** (iron)
Side: Belt at waterline 120mm on 400mm wood on 12mm iron hull
Guns: Battery 110mm on 400mm wood on 12mm iron hull.
Deck: 10mm plating on 120mm wood.

**Guns:**
(1866) 4 x 164.7mm/19.2 M1864, 5 or 6 x 164.7mm M1858-60.
(1869, *Arrogante*) 3 x 240mm/17.5 M1864 in the battery and 4 x 12pdr (121mm/17) bronze on deck.
(by 1870, *Opiniâtre* and *Implacable*) 4 x 194mm/18 M1864 in the battery and 2 x 164.7mm M1858 on the upper deck
(1870s, *Implacable* as school ship) 2 x 240mm/19 M1870, 2 x 194mm/19.8 M1870, 1 x 194mm/18 M1864, 1 x 164.7mm M1860, 2 x 164.7mm/19.2 M1864, and 6 x 138.6mm/21.3 M1870, all in the battery, and on the upper deck 1 x 22cm 223.3mm/10.5 MLR converted shell gun and 1 x 12pdr (121mm/17) bronze.

*Implacable* Ernest Gouin, Nantes/Schneider, Creusot.
On list 1.1.1862. Ord: 9.1861 (contract). K: 1.10.1861. L: 21.1.1864. Comm: 10.7.1864 (trials). C: 1.1866.
To reserve 1.1.1866 after trials. Recomm. 29.10.1867, to Brest from Lorient, decomm. 26.4.1868. Comm (trials) 8.8.1868, decomm. 31.8.1868. Comm. 17.7.1870, decomm. 1.11.1870. Recomm. 24.5.1871 and to Toulon from Brest as seagoing annex to the school for gunnery there, in successively *Louis XIV, Alexandre,* and *Souverain*, until decomm. 12.8.1877 (replaced *Dévastation*, replaced by *Arrogante*). Again seagoing annex to the school for gunnery in *Souverain* 3.4.1879 to 1880 after sinking of *Arrogante*. School for engineers 3.6.1880 to 1881. Struck 30.12.1884, annex to the school for engineers at Toulon 1884-1907, torpedo calibration and test platform 1907-1908. BU 1908.

*Opiniâtre* Ernest Gouin, Nantes/Schneider, Creusot.
On list 1.1862. Ord: 9.1861 (contract). K: 10.3.1862. L: 23.3.1864.
  Comm: 10.1.1865 (trials). C: 1866.
To reserve after trials. Recomm. 23.10.1867 (trials), to Brest from
  Lorient, decomm. 17.9.1868. Recomm. 17.7.1870, to Cherbourg
  11.1870, and decomm. there 9.4.1871. Designated 25.6.1881 to
  replace *Faon* as central ship for the *Défense mobile* at Cherbourg.
  Barracks for the *Défense mobile* 1883. Struck 19.3.1885, hulk for the
  *Défense mobile* and its successors at Cherbourg from 1885 to 1911,
  sold 1912 to BU.

*Arrogante* Ernest Gouin, Nantes/Schneider, Creusot.
On list 1.1862. Ord: 9.1861 (contract). K: 20.3.1862. L: 26.6.1864.
  Comm: 25.1.1865 (trials). C: 1.1866.
Decomm. 1.1.1866, recomm. 29.10.1867 to test a 240mm gun at
  Lorient, decomm. 16.5.1868, recomm. 10.8.1868, decomm.
  9.12.1869. Comm. 20.7.1870, moved from Lorient to Brest to defend
  that port, decomm. 1.12.1870. Recomm.10.6.1876 and to Toulon
  1876 escorted by the paddle steamer *Euménide*, decomm. 5.9.1876.
  Comm. 5.7.1877 as seagoing annex to the school for gunnery in
  *Souverain* at Toulon, replacing *Implacable*. Swamped and sank in a
  squall 19.3.1879 at La Badine, Hyères, raised 10.5.1879, decomm.
  31.5.1879 and repaired. Struck 30.12.1884, annex of the central ship
  for the reserve at Toulon 1884-1896, service of the reserve 1896-1898.
  Sunk as fleet gunnery target off Cape Cépet (Saint Mandrier) 9.1898.
  Sold 1899.

........................................

*EMBUSCADE* Class. *Batteries flottantes.* Ironclad floating batteries with
iron hulls and high ends. One funnel, two masts. Designed by Lemoine.

These ships were ordered from Lucien Arman at Bordeaux by a contract
signed on 13 September 1861. They were to have been built to the same
plans as the *Implacable* class, but objections were raised that they needed to
be able to operate in outer roadsteads as well as inner harbours and needed
to match the increase in the armour thickness of the latest French ironclad
frigates. Minister of Marine Chasseloup-Laubat had Lemoine prepare
revised plans but these were rejected by the *Conseil des travaux* on 7 January
1862. The Minister then had the plans for the Arman ships modified with
the height of battery raised to 2m and armour increased to 140mm. In
addition the ends of the ships were raised to improve seaworthiness and the
hull was shortened and widened, causing the number of guns to be reduced
from ten to eight 164.7mm rifles including four M1864 guns. The resulting plans by Nicolas Lemoine for these ships were dated 30 January 1862.
Their engines were ordered from Schneider with those of the *Implacable*
class by a contract signed on 10 October 1862. The height of the battery
above the water in the *Embuscade* class was recorded in service as 1.40m,
barely more than that of the *Implacable* class.

Construction of *Imprenable* was suspended June 1866 for consideration
of a plan by Jean-Baptiste Pastoureau-Labesse, the naval constructor on
leave serving as director of Arman's Chantiers et Atéliers de l'Océan at
Bordeaux, to convert her to a monitor with a turret with two 240mm guns.
Orders were instead given March 1867 to fit her existing gun ports for
194mm guns. Installation of machinery was completed in the 1st semester
of 1867 at Bordeaux and she was launched in December. The original eight
164.7mm guns were replaced with four 194mm guns, for which all of the
gun ports including those forward and aft had been modified. The ship
transited from Bordeaux to Lorient 27-29 August 1868 escorted by *Isère*
and under her own power, making up to 7 knots at times. Except for fitting
the masts, the work remaining to be done at Lorient would not delay final
machinery trials. The other three ships of the class still had this armament
of four 194mm guns in 1870.

In November 1868 Lemoine offered plans for installing an armament in
*Imprenable* probably like the one he proposed at the same time for

*Arrogante* with a 240mm gun aft. In March 1869 Godron at Lorient
proposed the installation of three 240mm guns in *Imprenable* and
*Arrogante*, two forward able to pivot to the sides and one aft. On 27 April
the *Conseil des travaux* directed installing two 194mm guns instead of one
240mm aft in *Imprenable*, and it reaffirmed this directive on 26 October
1869. After waiting for the trials of *Arrogante* the battery of *Imprenable*,
including two 12pdr (121mm) bronze rifles on the upper deck, was
installed between May and early August 1870. A cruise report dated
29 November 1871 for *Imprenable* covering the period 29 November 1870
to 15 March 1871 reported that the forward ports, although lowered 13cm,
were not large enough for the 240mm guns. It also reported that with
8 furnaces lit the average speed on a transit from Le Hâvre to Cherbourg
was 5.5 knots in a calm with 62rpm and 5 knots into the wind. The extra
weight from the modifications (which also included adding two months of
provisions and one month of water) was not well balanced and caused the
ship to trim down by the bow.

*The characteristics are based on a devis for* Imprenable *dated 9.8.1870.*
**Dimensions & tons:** 39.65m deck, 39.50m wl x 15.80m ext, 15.60m wl.
  1,614.940t disp. Draught: 3.620m fwd, 3.520m mean, 3.420m aft.
  (With the heavy guns forward *Imprenable* trimmed by the bow,
  draught for *Embuscade* on 13.8.1870 was 3.449m mean and 3.644m
  aft.) Men: 180. Height of battery in service 1.40m.
**Machinery:** 150nhp (120 from 1867) and 480ihp designed at 80rpm
  (engines) and 130rpm (screws) and 1.74kg/cm² boiler pressure.
  Trials (*Imprenable*, 15.10.1868) 411.642ihp = 5.516kts at 113.294rpm
  (screws) and 1.53kg/cm² boiler pressure; (*Protectrice* c1870) 409ihp =
  7.40kts, (*Embuscade*, 8.1870) 220ihp = 8.51kts at 116.4rpm. 2 screws,
  1 rudder. 2 horizontal geared engines each with direct connecting rods
  and one cylinder of 0.86m diameter and 0.75m stroke. Gear ratio
  about 0.61 to 1. 4 special type direct flame boilers. 80t coal plus 50t in
  bags. Range 670nm @ 8.5kts.
**Armour:** (iron)
Side: Belt at waterline 140mm on 400mm wood on 10mm iron hull
Guns: Battery 110mm on 400mm wood on 10mm iron hull.
Deck: 10mm plating on 120mm wood.
**Guns:**
(1866) 4 x 164.7mm/19.2 M1864, 4 x 164.7mm M1860.
(1870, *Imprenable*) 2 x 240mm/17.5 M1864 able to fire through ports
  forward and on the sides in the battery and 2 x 194mm/18 M1864 in
  after ports plus 2 x 12pdr (121mm/17) bronze on the upper deck.
(1870, others) 4 x 194mm/18 M1864 in the battery and no guns on
  deck.

*Embuscade* Lucien Arman, Bordeaux/Schneider, Creusot.
On list 1.1862. Ord: 9.1861 (contract). K: 25.2.1862. L: 18.11.1865.
  Comm: 22.1.1866 (trials). C: 9.1866.
Fully manned 6.9.1866, towed to Lorient 10.1866 by *Coligny*, decomm.
  29.9.1867. Recomm. 22.10.1867, to Cherbourg from Lorient,
  decomm. 25.12.1867. Artillery modified 1868. In commission in
  reserve 22.7.1870, full commission 24.7.1870, sent back to Bordeaux
  and then to Rochefort where she decomm. 16.11.1870. Struck
  28.1.1885, central ship for the *Défense mobile* and its successors at
  Rochefort 1885-1914, hulk 1920-1929, landing hulk (*ponton
  d'accostage*) 1929-1939. Sold 1945 to BU.

*Refuge* Lucien Arman, Bordeaux/Schneider, Creusot.
On list 1.1862. Ord: 9.1861 (contract). K: 25.2.1862. L: 1.5.1866.
  Comm: 1.10.1866 (trials). C: 10.1867.
Decomm. 22.9.1867, recomm. 27.10.1867, to Brest from Lorient 1868,
  decomm. 26.4.1868, comm 31.8.1868 (trials), in reserve 17.9.1868.
  In commission at Brest 10.7.1870, to 3rd category reserve there
  25.11.1870. Struck 5.7.1884, central ship for the *Défense mobile* at
  Brest 1884-1889, school for engineers 1889-1894. For sale 1894-1895,
  hull was still in the Penfeld at Brest in 6-7.1940. BU 1945?

*Protectrice* Lucien Arman, Bordeaux/Schneider, Creusot.
On list 1.1862. Ord: 9.1861 (contract). K: 25.2.1862. L: 8.12.1866. Comm: 1.1.1867 (trials). C: 8.1867.
Decomm. 18.9.1867, recomm. 27.10.1867, to Brest from Lorient 1867, decomm. 1.1.1868. Comm. 22.7.1870, sent to Le Havre 1870 to protect that port, ran into a pier there and sank 1.1871, salvaged, decomm. 19.3.1871. Used for gunnery trials 1872, was the last armoured floating battery on the fleet list as such 1.1889. Struck 9.8.1889 at Cherbourg, BU 1890.

*Imprenable* Lucien Arman, Bordeaux/Schneider, Creusot.
On list 1.1862. Ord: 9.1861 (contract). K: 25.2.1862. L: 18.12.1867. Comm: 1.2.1868 (trials). C: 2.1868.
Construction suspended 6.1866, probably resumed 3.1867. Arrived at Lorient from Bordeaux 29.8.1868. Trials at Lorient 29.12.1868. Full commission 9.8.1870 at Lorient. To Cherbourg from Lorient c1870, decomm. there 4.4.1871 and not recomm. Assigned to torpedo calibration service at Cherbourg 31.5.1881 and moored in the roadstead there. Struck 7.3.1882, hulk for the torpedo service at Cherbourg attached to the paddle steamer *Coligny* 1882-1886, torpedo calibration workshop for the *Défense mobile* 1886-1914 (housed over 1892), hulk for launching torpedoes 1926-1939. Sold 1939 to BU.

---

## (E) Armoured Sectional Floating Batteries (*Batteries flottantes démontables*).

To *Batteries flottantes cuirassées* in the 1.1873 fleet list, *Batteries flottantes démontables* 1.1874, and *Batteries cuirassées démontables* 1.1875, to *Batteries flottantes cuirassées* 1.1885 with the larger ships.

*BATTERIE N° 1* Class. *Batteries flottantes démontables.* Sectional ironclad floating batteries with a casemate forward on a barge-style hull with two ports in the front and none on the sides. Iron hulls, two funnels abreast aft. Designed by Dupuy de Lôme.

On 3 May 1859 France declared war on Austria which had invaded Piedmont in northern Italy. On 24 May 1859 Napoleon III, in the field commanding French forces, telegraphed a request for Dupuy de Lôme to prepare two floating batteries for use on rivers having one 12pdr rifle forward, drawing only one metre of water, with a length not over 24m, and protected by iron armour against field artillery. They were to destroy bridges in the rear of Austrian forces while the French army attacked from the front. Dupuy de Lôme replied that it would take 60 days to build them and get them to the theatre of war. Napoleon III approved Dupuy de Lôme's plans and on 31 May ordered that five be ordered from the Forges et Chantiers de la Méditerranée. In response to these instructions, Minister of Marine Hamelin on 10 June 1859 ordered the immediate construction of the five armoured floating batteries and, because of the need for haste, he accepted the offer of the Forges et Chantiers de la Méditerranée La Seyne to build them (including their engines) at cost plus 12 percent without a formal contract. The batteries were designed by Dupuy de Lôme to carry two 240mm BLR, but these were not ready and older 164.7mm (30pdr) rifles were used. The 50mm armour was designed to be proof against Austrian 12cm (12pdr) field guns (their largest). The vessels consisted of 14 sections which were bolted together with bands of rubber in between; they could be dismantled in 45 hours and reassembled in 87 hours. 32 rail cars were needed to transport one battery with its equipment. Names were proposed on 12 June 1859 but it was decided instead to use only numbers.

The industrial effort to produce these craft was remarkably successful although they saw no action. On 2 December 1859 it was reported that the first one had been delivered on 4 July 1859, only 35 days after Napoleon

III ordered them, and the other four had followed on 25 August 1859, but *Nos 1-3* are also listed as commissioned on 8 July 1859 and decommissioned on 21 July. *Batterie n° 1* was embarked on the former paddle frigate *Cacique* on 7 July 1859 in sections and transported to Genoa. She arrived by rail at Sampierdarena just west of Genoa on 8 July 1859, the day on which the armistice of Villafranca was signed. Sent back to France still in sections, she was assembled at Toulon on 6 August 1859 in 87 hours, launched on 10 August, tried successfully in the harbour on 11 August, disassembled on 26-27 August in 30 hours, and put in storage at Mourillon. The others were sent directly to storage. All five were sent from Toulon to Paris in August 1870 (having initially been routed to Strasbourg for use on the Rhine but then diverted), and they were assembled at the Claparède yard at Saint Denis and participated in the siege as part of the flotilla of Capitaine de vaisseau Thomasset.

**Dimensions & tons:** 21.94m on deck x 7.00m hull, 7.70m outside armour. 142t disp. Draught: 1.00m fwd, 1.10m aft. Men: 30.
**Machinery:** 32nhp (24 from 1867). Trials 95ihp = 4.21kts. 2 screws, 2 rudders. 2 engines each with direct connecting rods and 1 cylinder. 2 boilers with 2 funnels. 6t coal (24 hours).
**Armour:** (iron)
Side: Belt at waterline 50mm. on 300mm backing,
Guns: Battery 50mm.
**Guns:**
(1859) 2 x 164.7mm rifles firing forward.
(1870) 2 x 138.6mm.

*Batterie n° 1* F.C. Méditerranée, La Seyne/FCM, Marseille.
On list 1.1861. Ord: 10.6.1859. Begun 1.6.1859. Delivered 5.7.1859. First comm: 8.7.1859.
Decomm. 21.7.1859. Assembled and launched 6-10.8.1859, disassembled 26-27.8.1859. Assembled and launched 24.8.1870-2.9.1870 at Claparède & Cie., Saint Denis. Decomm. 16.2.1871 after the armistice. Seized by the Paris Communards 18.3.1871, sunk by Government artillery or scuttled at Saint Denis 4 or 5.1871. Struck 10.7.1871.

*Batterie n° 2* F.C. Méditerranée, La Seyne/FCM, Marseille.
On list 1.1861. Ord: 10.6.1859. Begun early 6.1859. Delivered and first comm: 8.7.1859.
Decomm. 21.7.1859. Assembled briefly in 1867, then assembled and launched 24.8.1870-2.9.1870 at Claparède & Cie., Saint Denis. Decomm. 16.2.1871 after the armistice. Seized by the Paris Communards 18.3.1871, not used and recovered by Government forces at Paris 27.5.1871. Struck 3.7.1871, BU 1872 at Cherbourg.

*Batterie n° 3* F.C. Méditerranée, La Seyne/FCM, Marseille.
On list 1.1861. Ord: 10.6.1859. Begun early 6.1859. Delivered and first comm: 8.7.1859.
Decomm. 21.7.1859. Assembled and launched 21.8.1870-25.8.1870 at Claparède & Cie., Saint Denis. Hit a piling of the Pont Notre-Dame in Paris 8.2.1871 and sank. Decomm. 16.2.1871. Refloated probably after Government forces retook the city in May 1871. Struck 3.7.1871, BU 1872 at Cherbourg.

*Batterie n° 4* F.C. Méditerranée, La Seyne/FCM, Marseille.
On list 1.1861. Ord: 10.6.1859. Begun early 6.1859. Delivered 7.1859. First comm: 24.8.1870 at Paris.
Assembled and launched 24.8.1870-2.9.1870 at Claparède & Cie., Saint Denis. Decomm. 16.2.1871 after the armistice. Seized by the Paris Communards 18.3.1871, not used. Scuttled 5.1871 at Saint Denis. Struck 10.7.1871.

*Batterie n° 5* F.C. Méditerranée, La Seyne/FCM, Marseille.
On list 1.1861. Ord: 10.6.1859. Begun early 6.1859. Delivered 7.1859. First comm: 24.8.1870 at Paris.

One of the five sectional ironclad floating batteries of the *No 1-5* type of 1859 assembled on the Seine by Claparède at Saint Denis in August-September 1870 for the defence of Paris. All but *No 5* were afloat by 2 September, with *No 3* ahead of the others on 25 August. The design for these vessels was based on specifications by Napoleon III for craft he needed for his 1859 Northern Italy campaign. *(Illustrated London News, 10 September 1870, page 273)*

Assembled and launched 24.8.1870-12.9.1870 at Claparède & Cie., Saint Denis. Decomm. 16.2.1871 after the armistice. Seized by the Paris Communards 18.3.1871 and placed in service, renamed *Commune* 4.1871. Retaken 27.5.1871 near the Pont de la Concorde by Government forces, name reverted to *Batterie flottante démontable No 5.* Struck 29 10.1874, hulk at Cherbourg 1874 to 1875, floating workshop 1876-1896, coal hulk for the *Défense mobile* and its successors 1896-1914, for sale at Cherbourg 1920-1922, sold 1923 at Cherbourg to BU.

---

*BATTERIE No 6* **Class.** *Batteries flottantes démontables.* Sectional ironclad floating batteries with a casemate amidships on a low monitor-style hull with two ports on each beam and two forward. Iron hull, two funnels abreast aft. Designed by Dupuy de Lôme.

In 1864 war with Prussia seemed inevitable and Napoleon III decided to complete his force of armoured river floating batteries with a new improved series for operations on the Rhine. Six of these were ordered under a contract of 29 March 1864 and numbers were assigned to them as names on 12 April 1864. Again designed by Dupuy de Lôme, they had 80mm armour and increased dimensions to support it. The armoured casemate was moved back with its after bulkhead amidships and had two ports facing forward and two ports on each side, allowing both guns to be engaged in any of these directions. For shipping by rail these batteries could be broken down into 17 sections, of which 5 were for the armoured casemate. One battery could be assembled in 7 days, two simultaneously in 8 days. As in 1859 the Forges et Chantiers de la Méditerranée at La Seyne built them rapidly, delivering the first one on 29 May and the others within the 70 days in the contract. They also provided the engines, which were designed by Jules Orsel. The designed armament, specified by the Emperor, was two Army 12pdr (12cm) field guns, but the Navy felt these were not powerful enough. The Navy wanted to substitute 30pdr 164.7mm rifles but there was not room for them in the casemate and they ultimately settled on 138.6mm M1864 rifles. Once disassembled after trials they joined the 1859 group in storage at Lagoubran, Toulon, until called to service in 1870.

**Dimensions & tons:** 27.00m oa, 26.45m wl, 25.75m pp (wl fwd to rudder) x 9.00m ext outside armour, 8.14m hull. 292t disp. Draught: 1.70m mean, 1.70m aft. Men: 40.

**Machinery:** 50nhp (40 from 1867) designed at 220rpm and 5.68kg/cm² boiler pressure. Trials (5.1867) 92ihp = 5.37kts at 5.68kg/cm² boiler pressure. 2 screws. 1 rudder. 2 horizontal engines with direct connecting rods, each with 1 cylinder of 0.35m diameter and 0.30m stroke. 4 special type return flame boilers with 2 funnels. 12t coal.

**Armour:** (iron)
Side: Belt at waterline 80mm on 350mm backing. Height from 0.50m below the wl to 0.20m above.
Guns: Battery 80mm sides and bulkheads.
**Guns:** 2 x 138.6mm rifles.

*Batterie no 6* F.C. Méditerranée, La Seyne/FCM, Marseille.
On list 1.1865. Begun 1.4.1864. Delivered 29.5.1864.
First comm: 19.12.1870.
Probably began assembly 30.5.1864 and launched c6.6.1864 for trials, then disassembled and put into storage at Toulon Lagoubran. Briefly assembled again 1868. Shipped to Cherbourg where assembly begun 19.12.1870 and vessel launched 31.12.1870 for the defence of Le Havre. Foundered 5.1.1871 at sea 30 miles from Le Havre while being towed there from Cherbourg by the paddle corvette *Coligny.* Struck 10.7.1871.

*Batterie no 7* F.C. Méditerranée, La Seyne/FCM, Marseille.
On list 1.1865. Begun early 4.1864. Delivered 31.5.1864.
First comm: 9.11.1870.
Assembled briefly in 1867, then began assembly at Toulon in early 11.1870 and launched 9.11.1870 for the defence of Lyon. Foundered 15.11.1870 at sea between Toulon and the mouth of the Rhône River while en route from Toulon to Lyon. Struck 10.7.1871.

*Batterie no 8* F.C. Méditerranée, La Seyne/FCM, Marseille.
On list 1.1865. Begun early 4.1864. Delivered 2.6.1864.
First comm: 30.1.1871.
Assembled briefly in 1867, then began assembly at St. Nazaire in early 1.1871 and launched in late 1.1871 for the defence of the Loire. Decomm. there 21.3.1871. Disassembled 1875 and put into storage at Lorient. Struck 26.1.1886, assembled and converted to torpedo calibration workshop at Lorient 1886-1913, sold 1913 at Lorient to BU.

*Batterie no 9* F.C. Méditerranée, La Seyne/FCM, Marseille.
On list 1.1865. Begun 4.1864. Delivered 4.6.1864.
First comm: 16.11.1870.
Assembled briefly in 1867, then began assembly at Toulon in early 11.1870 and launched 16.11.1870. Intended for the defence of the Loire but not sent there. Decomm. at Toulon 12.5.1871, disassembled 1873 and to storage. Struck 11.2.1888 at Toulon, reportedly converted to coal barge but not listed as such and sold 1889 to BU.

*Batterie no 10* F.C. Méditerranée, La Seyne/FCM, Marseille.
On list 1.1865. Begun 4.1864. Delivered 6.6.1864.
First comm: 29.1.1871.
Assembled briefly in 1867, then began assembly at St. Nazaire in early 1.1871 and launched in late 1.1871 for the defence of the Loire. Decomm. there 21.3.1871. Disassembled 1875 and to storage at Lorient. Struck 6.4.1888 at Lorient. Sold 1889 to BU.

*Batterie no 11* F.C. Méditerranée, La Seyne/FCM, Marseille.
On list 1.1865. Begun 4.1864. Delivered 8.6.1864.
First comm: 9.11.1870.
Assembled briefly in 1867, then began assembly at Toulon in early 11.1870 and launched 9.11.1870. Intended for the defence of Lyon but not sent there. Decomm. at Toulon 12.5.1871, disassembled 1873 and to storage. Struck 11.2.1888 at Toulon, reportedly converted to coal barge but not listed as such and sold 1889 to BU.

# Chapter Three

# Cruisers, 1859-1882

The three classes of cruisers that first appeared in the January 1874 *Liste de la Flotte* are used to organise this chapter. Although the conversions of the last sail frigates to steam were ordered in 1858 before the period of this book, full details on two classes (*Magicienne* and *Circé*) that served as station flagships into the 1880s and were cited as models for the *Dubourdieu* class of 1879 are included here for readers' convenience.

## (A) 1st Class Cruisers (*Croiseurs de 1re classe*).

Before the 1.1874 fleet list these were listed as *frégates* (3 ranks) except *Vénus* and *Minerve* which were *Corvettes à batterie* from 1.1862 to 1.1871. To *croiseurs à batterie* 1.1880, *croiseurs de station à batterie* 1.1891, 2 *Duquesne* to *Croiseurs de 1re classe* 1.1892 and 4 *Iphigénie* to *Croiseurs de 2e classe* 1.1892.

*MAGICIENNE* Class (1858). *Frégates à hélice de 2e rang.* Large cruising ships with covered and open batteries, wooden hulls, and knee bows. One funnel, three masts, ship rig. Designed by Sochet, converted by de Roussel.

These ships were begun as 50-gun 2nd rank sailing frigates similar to the *Amazone* class to plans by naval constructor Prix Charles Sochet that were approved on 24 January 1845. They were among nine frigates still on the ways that were selected in 1858 to be lengthened to receive large engines of 600nhp. Their engines were ordered from the Forges et Chantiers de la Méditerranée by a contract approved on 4 June 1858. They were lengthened by about 22m on the ways and converted on plans by naval constructor Anselme de Roussel. The *Conseil des travaux* approved these plans on 26 January 1858 but with the recommendation that, because of the vulnerability of their machinery, the ships should be used in wartime as transports and in peacetime as station cruisers with a reduced armament. Installation of their machinery was completed in September 1862 and May 1863 respectively.

Dimensions & tons: 75.69m deck, 74.36m wl x 14.40m ext. 3,408t disp. Draught: 3,408 tons disp. Draught 6.38m mean. Men: 415.
Machinery: 600nhp (480 from 1867), engines as in *Pallas* and *Guerrière*. *Thémis*: 1,920ihp designed at 55rpm and 1.80kg/cm² boiler pressure. Trials (11.1879) 1,675ihp = 11.56kts at 54.84rpm and 1.884kg/cm² boiler pressure. 1 screw. 1 horizontal engine with return connecting rods and 2 cylinders of 1.75m diameter and 1.06m stroke. 6 low rectangular tubular boilers. 469.1t coal. Range 3,070nm @ 10kts.
Guns:
(*Magicienne*, 1862) *Battery deck* 24 x 164.7mm M1858 MLR;
   *Upper deck* 4 x 164.7mm M1858 MLR;
(*Thémis* 1865) *Battery deck* 24 x 164.7mm rifles;
   *Upper deck* 4 x 164.7mm rifles.
(*Thémis*, 1867) *Battery deck* 18 x 30pdrs Nᵒ 1, 8 x 164.7mm rifles;
   *Upper deck* 6 x 164.7mm rifles.
(*Thémis*, 1872) *Battery deck* 12 x 164.7mm M1864-6 BLR;
   *Upper deck* 6 x 164.7mm M1858-60 MLR.
(*Magicienne*, 1879) *Battery deck* 16 x 138.6mm M1870 BLR;
   *Upper deck* 4 x 138.6mm M1870 BLR, 4 Hotchkiss
(*Thémis*, 1879) *Battery deck* 12 x 138.6mm; *Upper deck* 6 x 138.6mm

M1870 BLR and 4 Hotchkiss, plus 1 x 12pdr bronze and 4 x 4pdr bronze for the boats.

*Magicienne* Toulon Dyd/Forges et Chantiers de la Méditerranée.
K: 26.6.1845. Conversion start: 10.1859. L: 26.12.1861. Comm: 8.1.1862 (trials). C: 9.1862.
Flagship of the Pacific station 1876-78 and the Antilles station 1880-82. Struck 19.4.1886, on harbour service list at Brest as a floating barracks 1886-1895, renamed *Sémiramis* and became central ship for the reserve at Landévennec 1895. Replaced by *Aréthuse* 1899 and name reverted to *Magicienne*, on sale list 1.1900. Sold to BU 1900.

*Thémis* Toulon Dyd/Forges et Chantiers de la Méditerranée.
K: 4.1847. Conversion start: 1858. L: 29.4.1862. Comm: 21.11.1862 (trials). C: 12.1862.
Flagship of the South Atlantic station 1877-79 and the Far East station 1879-81. Struck 7.11.1882, on harbour service list at Lorient as a mooring and storage hulk there 1883-1914 and as a hulk 1920-1929. Sold 1930, burned in Lorient harbour 1.7.1931.

---

*CIRCÉ* Class (1858). *Frégates à hélice de 2e rang.* Large cruising ships with covered and open batteries, wooden hulls, and knee bows. One funnel, three masts, ship rig. Designed by Hubert, converted by Vidal.

These ships were begun as 50-gun 2nd rank sailing frigates similar to the *Artémise* class to plans by naval constructor Jean-Baptiste Hubert dating from 1826 but with an updated armament. In March 1858 these two frigates on the ways at Rochefort were each allocated half of a four-cylinder 900nhp engine built there for the ship of the line *Intrépide* which was completed as a transport with a two-cylinder 900nhp engine. Plans by Charles Marie Brun for dividing the engine (originally designed by Victorin Sabattier) were approved by the *Conseil des travaux* on 30 March 1858, and plans by naval constructor Albin Abraham Vidal for converting the ships, initially reviewed in April 1858, were approved on 28 September 1858. They were lengthened by about 22m on the ways. *Circé* was completed promptly, but *Flore* languished until 1870 and in 1886 became the last traditional French frigate (other than *Vénus* and *Minerve*) to complete a tour as a flagship on an overseas station.

Dimensions & tons: 75.75m (*Flore* 76.05m) deck, 74.60m wl x 13.84m ext. 3,136t disp. Draught: 6.20m mean. Men: 415.
Machinery: 480nhp (380 from 1867). *Flore*: 1,520ihp designed at 48rpm and 1.80kg/cm² boiler pressure. Trials (3.1870) 1,465ihp = 12.49kts at 51.99rpm. 1 hoisting screw. 1 horizontal trunk engine with two cylinders of 1.913m diameter (equivalent to ordinary cylinders of 1.7m diameter) and 1.00m stroke. 8 rectangular tubular boilers with short furnaces. 360.4t coal. Range 2,220nm @ 10kts.
Guns:
(*Circé*, 1866) *Battery deck* 12 x 30pdrs Nᵒ 1, 14 x 164.7mm rifles;
   *Upper deck* 4 x 30pdrs Nᵒ 1;
(*Circé*, 1868) *Battery deck* 18 x 164.7mm M1860 BLR;
   *Upper deck* 4 x 164.7mm M1858-60 MLR.
(*Flore* 1870) *Battery deck* 12 x 164.7mm M1864-6 BLR;
   *Upper deck* 4 x 164.7mm M1864-6 BLR.
(*Flore*, 1873) *Battery deck* 12 x 164.7mm M1864-6 BLR;

*Upper deck* 6 x 138.6mm Nº 1 M1864 MLR.

(*Flore* 1876 as school ship) *Battery deck* 12 x 138.6mm M1870 BLR; *Upper deck* 2 x 138.6mm M1870 BLR and 17 x 12pdr bronze, plus 1 x 4pdr bronze boat.

(*Flore*, 1883) *Battery deck* 18 x 138.6mm M1870 BLR; *Upper deck* 4 x 138.6mm M1870 BLR, 3 x 100mm, 8 revolving (revolver) cannon.

*Circé* Rochefort Dyd (including engines).
K: 24.4.1847. Not launched as sail.
Conversion began: 1858. L: 15.10.1860. Comm: 12.11.1862 (trials). C: 11.1862.
Struck 22.7.1872, on harbour service list at Brest as hulk 1872-74, on disposal list 1.1875. BU 1875.

*Flore* Rochefort Dyd (including engines).
K: 26.7.1847. Not launched as sail.
Conversion began: 1860. L: 27.2.1869. Comm: 1.2.1870 (trials). C: 7.1870.
Flagship of the Pacific station 1870-82, then to reserve. Designated in June 1876 to replace *Renommée* as seagoing school for midshipmen at Brest and so served from 9.1876 to 1882, including as flag of the flying training division 1879-81. Flagship of the Indian Ocean station 1882-83 and the North Atlantic station 1884-86. Struck 18.10.1886, on disposal list at Brest 1886-1888, harbour flagship and school for seamanship at Brest 1888-1899, on sale list 1.1900. Sold for BU 1901.

---

*VÉNUS* Class. *Corvettes à batterie.* Large cruising ships with covered and open batteries, wooden hulls, and knee bows. One funnel, three masts, ship rig. Designed by Compère-Desfontaines.

On 22 September 1860 Dupuy de Lôme submitted a report to Minister of Marine Hamelin which updated the Programme of 1857 in the light of the adoption of armour, and laid out a building programme for immediate implementation. This called for beginning 10 armoured frigates, 11 floating batteries, along with 6 ships of new types for the overseas stations including 2 small frigates with 22 guns (*frégates de croisière*), 2 open-battery corvettes with 16 guns, and 2 transports of 400 tons. The small frigates were to serve as a station flagships in place of the old large frigates which were expensive to man. Minister Hamelin on 27 September 1860 decided to proceed with the two frigates and on 16 November 1860 he sent to the ports specifications and asked the naval constructors in the ports to submit designs for them. On 4 June 1861 the *Conseil des travaux* examined seven designs and gave conditional approval to the design of naval constructor Théophile Zéphirin Compère-Desfontaines, which was the one whose construction would require the lowest expenditures. Revised plans were completed on 24 July 1861 and approved on 13 August 1861 by the *Conseil des travaux*. On 26 August 1861 Minister of Marine Chasseloup-Laubat approved the plans of Compère-Desfontaines and signed a dispatch to Brest ordering the immediate start of work on *Minerve* and *Vénus*, whose construction had been announced on 26 November 1860 as part of the building programme for 1861. Their engines were ordered from Schneider by a contract signed on 6 December 1861 and were designed by the contractor. The design provided for an armament of twenty-two 164.7mm MLR. Although designed as small frigates a change in the way ships were classified caused them to appear on the 1.1862 fleet list as *corvettes à batterie* (corvettes with covered batteries) and they were joined as such by one 3rd rank screw frigate still under construction, *Armorique*.

*The characteristics are based on a devis for* Vénus *dated 7.3.1879.*
**Dimensions & tons:** 72.60m wl, 75.20m pp (wl fwd to rudder) x 13.08m ext and wl. 2,750t disp. Draught: 5.88m mean, 6.51m aft. Men: 412.
**Machinery:** 500nhp (430 from 1867), 1,720ihp designed at 60rpm and 1.80kg/cm² boiler pressure. Trials (*Vénus*, 11.1865) 1,500ihp =

12.57kts at 60.32rpm and 1.171kg/cm² boiler pressure. 1 screw. 1 horizontal simple expansion engine with return connecting rods and 2 cylinders of 1.60m diameter and 0.96m stroke. 6 low rectangular tubular boilers. 319.8t coal. Range 2,240nm @ 10kts.

**Guns:**
(c1865-1866) *Battery deck* 10 x 164.7mm/16.7 MLR and 8 x 30pdrs Nº 1 (164.7mm/16.5) smoothbores; *Upper deck* 4 x 164.7mm/16.7 MLR (4 x 30pdrs Nº 1 in *Minerve*).
(c1872-75, both) *Battery deck* 12 x 164.7mm/16 M1858-60 BLR; *Upper deck* 4 x 140mm/17.45 M1858-60 Nº 1 MLR (2 forward and 2 amidships). In 1878-79, *Vénus* also had 4 x 4pdr (86.5mm/11) bronze boat and 2 x 37mm revolving cannon.
(1882-83) *Battery deck* 12 x 138.6mm M1870 (short); *Upper deck* 4 x 138.6mm M1870 (long). *Vénus* also had 1 x 90mm/22 bronze, 2 x 65mm landing, 6 x 37mm revolving cannon, *Minerve* also had 2 x 65mm landing, 5 x 37mm revolving cannon.

*Vénus* Brest Dyd/Schneider, Creusot.
On list 1.1862. Ord: 26.8.1861. K: 5.9.1861. L: 27.12.1864. Comm: 22.7.1865 (trials), 7.10.1865 (full).
Left Brest for the Pacific 8.12.1865. Flagship of the Levant naval division 1883-1886. Struck 10.12.1886, mooring hulk at Rochefort 1886-1909. Sold 5.10.1909 to BU.

*Minerve* Brest Dyd/Schneider, Creusot.
On list 1.1862. Ord: 26.8.1861. K: 5.9.1861. L: 10.7.1865. Comm: 20.3.1866 (trials), 11.7.1866 (full).
To the Indian Ocean 9.1866. Armament slightly modified 1870 while in reserve. Complete refit at Brest 1877-1882. Flagship of the Antilles station 1882-84 and the North Atlantic station 1886-88. Struck 26.10.1888 and engines removed, sent from Brest to Gabon c1890 for use as hospital hulk, for disposal 1895-1896 and to be ceded to the colonial service at Gabon, accidentally burned 1897 and wreck ceded to the colony.

---

**1st class cruiser design 1869-1871**

The January 1869 fleet list included eighteen large and medium-sized steam screw frigates afloat and one (*Flore*) still building along with five covered battery corvettes including *Vénus, Minerve,* and *Armorique*. With this large inventory and with armoured corvettes taking their place as station flagships, the French during the 1860s saw little need to build more large cruising ships and attention focused on smaller open-battery corvettes. However, Confederate commerce raiding during the American Civil War had caused both the Union and British navies to build a few very large and very fast cruisers (the American *Wampanoag* type and the British *Inconstant*) to hunt down raiders. The French were more likely to be raiding commerce than protecting it, but they realized at the end of the decade that they would need some cruisers able to stand up to or outrun the new large foreign ships.

On 10 August 1869 the *Conseil des travaux* selected the following specifications for a fast cruiser to follow the *Infernet* and *Sané* class open-battery corvettes (below). They were to have a 16-knot speed, the smallest possible dimensions possible for either a commerce raiding vessel or for a scout attached to a fleet, and an armament of three 164.7mm M1860 and two 138.6mm guns. The Council accepted an innovative 1,838-ton design from Normand for a successor to his *Châteaurenault* and a larger more conventional design by naval constructor Arthur François Alphonse Bienaymé subject to additional work, but no action was taken on either. On 28 February 1870 Minister of Marine Rigault de Genouilly circulated to the ports a new set of specifications increasing the armament to at least six 164.7mm guns. The ship was to have chase guns under a forecastle, and because of a need for high sides he suggested that consideration be given to making this a covered-battery corvette. Only one design was received before the war interrupted work. This, by Lebelin de Dionne, had a displacement of 4,770 tons, almost as much as *Inconstant* (5,212 tons), and was armed with twelve 164.7mm guns (well under the armament of *Inconstant*). The Council examined it on 13 December 1870 after evacuating to Bordeaux, was alarmed by its size and comparatively weak armament, and opted to wait for more projects before proceeding. Between September and November 1871 it received three more proposals for 1st class cruisers based on the 28 February 1870 specifications. In the meantime it received instructions on 14 September 1871 from Minister of Marine Pothuau to produce specifications for all of the ship types that were to enter into the composition of the fleet under the Programme of 1872, and it used the proposals before it on 16 December 1871 to develop new specifications for 1st class cruisers.

---

**DUQUESNE Class.** *Croiseurs de 1re classe.* Large cruisers with covered and open batteries, iron hulls with wooden sheathing, and ram bows. Two funnels, three masts, ship rig. Designed by Lebelin de Dionne.

The specifications set by the *Conseil des travaux* on 16 December 1871 for 1st class cruisers included a speed of 17 knots, a range of 5,000nm at 10 knots, an iron hull sheathed in wood and coppered, a full sail rig, and

The 1st class cruiser *Tourville*, probably in North Africa. She was active in the occupation of Tunisia in 1881 and transited the Suez Canal in 1883 and 1884 at the ends of a deployment to the Far East. *(NHHC from Farenholt collection, previously ONI, NH-66097)*

an estimated displacement of 4,800 tons. A cruiser needed a specialized armament that included one or two large guns capable of firing long range shots dead ahead to summon a fast liner or merchant ship to stop, numerous medium-sized guns in a covered battery to sustain an engagement with a similar enemy ship, and a few guns aft in case of need to retreat. The Council recommended four 164.7mm M1864 guns capable of both axial and broadside fire and six 138.6mm guns (then in development), all on the upper deck, and a covered battery of eight to ten more guns like the 138.6mm. Minister of Marine Pothuau specified an iron hull sheathed in wood and copper, changed the armament to five 164.7mm M1864 and four 138.6mm on the upper deck, with one of the 164.7mm under the forecastle and the other four in half turrets with axial fire, plus another twelve 138.6mm guns in the battery, raised the estimated displacement to 5,424 tons, and then transmitted the specifications to the ports on 23 January 1872 with a request that they submit designs. The Council protested the increase in tonnage in the 'official' design and offered the thought that the immediate creation of 1st class cruisers of this size did not present advantages that justified the high cost involved. On 13 August 1872 the Council examined designs by five naval constructors and selected that of Alfred François Lebelin de Dionne with the condition that he increase the beam somewhat to improve stability. The Council wanted the 6,600ihp machinery to consist of two separate engines on one propeller shaft, the after one providing speeds up to 10-11 knots and the forward one being coupled for higher speeds. Lebelin's plans were approved by Minister of Marine Pothuau on 13 February 1873. The original armament on the plans was seven 164.7mm/19.2 M1864 and two 138.6mm/21.3 M1870 on the upper deck and eighteen more 138.6mm in the battery. The final

armament with 194mm guns (below) was fixed on 11 May 1876 after several intervening changes.

The two ships retained their full ship rig throughout their careers due to their intended use overseas. The funnels of *Tourville* were both taller and wider than those of her sister, and on both ships the after funnel was made telescopic to allow use of the mainsail. The complicated engines consumed 'frightful' amounts of coal and lubricant and constantly broke down, while the rectangular boilers were outmoded when installed and could not provide the economies allowed by the use of compound machinery. The engines of *Tourville* were rebuilt between 26 October 1879 and 5 January 1881 but continued to break down frequently.

*Duquesne* underwent major machinery work in 1893-94. Her HP cylinders were reduced in diameter from 1.65m to 1.40m and the LP cylinders were rebored to 2.303m. She got twelve new cylindrical boilers operating at 4,250 kg/cm$^2$, but these had less grate area than the old boilers and developed only half as much steam and 5,000ihp instead of the original 7,200 or more. Minister of Marine Besnard on 15 July 1896 approved a modernization scheme for *Tourville* that included lengthening the ship 5.50m to improve the lines aft, new twin-screw machinery of 9,750ihp and 17.5 knots, and a new armament, but the unprotected ship was not considered worth the high cost and the change was limited to her artillery. The deep draught of these ships and their unreliable machinery made them unsuitable for cruising on overseas stations, and *Duquesne* was in commission for only seven years while *Tourville* was active for only four.

*The characteristics are based on a devis for* Duquesne *dated 8.7.1879 with machinery data for* Tourville *from a devis of 4.7.1879.*

**Dimensions & tons:** 99.64m wl (+1.65m ram), 101.58m pp (wl fwd to rudder) x 15.56m ext, 15.43m wl. 5,824t disp. Draught: 7.143m mean, 8.093m aft. Men: 551.

**Machinery:** .

(*Duquesne*): 1,700nhp and 7,200ihp designed at 80rpm and 2.25kg/cm$^2$ boiler pressure. Trials (9.1878) 8,611.3ihp = 16.858kts at 80.76rpm and 2.490kg/cm$^2$ boiler pressure. 1 screw. 3 horizontal compound engines with return connecting rods, each with cylinders of 1.65m and 2.30m diameter and 1.00m stroke, and each acting on the single propeller shaft through cranks spaced 120 degrees apart. 12 high rectangular tubular boilers. 726.9t coal. Range 6,680nm @ 10kts.

(*Tourville*): 1,700nhp and 7,200ihp designed at 78rpm and 2.25kg/cm$^2$ boiler pressure. Trials (1.1878) 7,466.8ihp = 16.898kts at 76.4rpm and 2.582kg/cm$^2$ boiler pressure. 1 screw. 2 horizontal engines with return connecting rods, each with 4 cylinders, two of 1.42m, two of 2.05m diameter, and all of 1.00m stroke. In each engine the two HP and two LP cylinders were connected to common rods. The two engines drove the single propeller shaft through cranks spaced 180 degrees apart. 12 high rectangular tubular boilers. 726.9t coal. Range 7,570nm @ 10kts.

**Guns:**

(1879, *Duquesne*) 7 x 194mm/19.8 M1870 (6 on the upper deck in half turrets (sponsons) and 1 under the forecastle, 14 x 138.6mm/21.3 M1870 in the battery, 6 x 37mm Hotchkiss, plus 1 x 12pdr (121mm/17) bronze and 4 x 4pdr (86.5mm/11) bronze for the boats. She got 8 more 37mm in 1886.

(1879, *Tourville*) 7 x 194mm, 14 x 138.6mm, 4 x 37mm. She got another 4 x 37mm and 2 x 65mm landing in 1883.

(1894, *Duquesne*) 7 x 164.7mm (heavy) M1881 QF, 14 x 138.6mm/30 M1881 QF, 4 x 47mm/40 M1885 QF, 14 x 37mm plus in *Tourville* 2 x 65mm.

**Duquesne** Rochefort Dyd/Indret (engines designed by Joëssel).
On list 13.2.1873. K: 18.6.1873. L: 11.3.1876. Comm: 20.1.1878 (trials). C: 12.1878.
Budget 1872. Machinery installed 16.7.1877 to 14.2.1878. Trials 20.5.1878. To 2$^{nd}$ category reserve 10.12.1878 after trials. To full comm. 20.6.1879 for experimental operations with the fleet. To 2$^{nd}$

category reserve 23.9.1879, reserve without category 1.11.1879, and 3$^{rd}$ category reserve after modifications 1.1884. In full commission 21.12.1885 for service on the Pacific station. Struck 4.12.1901, retained provisionally at Cherbourg 1901-1907, sold 2.3.1908 to M. Guilhaumon to BU.

**Tourville** F.C. Méditerranée, La Seyne/FCM, Marseille (engines designed by Orsel).
On list 1.1874. Ord: 7.1873 (contract). K: 23.2.1874. L: 24.2.1876. Comm: 17.8.1876 (trials). C: 3.1878.
Budget 1875. Machinery installed 25.2.1876 to 1.9.1876. To 2$^{nd}$ category reserve 5.3.1878 after trials. To full comm. 4.7.1879 for operations with the fleet, back to 2$^{nd}$ category reserve 7.10.1879 for extensive machinery work. To full comm. 15.1.1881 for the occupation of Tunisia, recommissioned 25.5.1883 for the China station. Struck 4.12.1901, retained for experiments with coal transfer systems. To the Domaines 8.6.1903 for sale, sold 20.11.1903 to M. Cousin to BU.

*N* (Unnamed) Contract.
Budget 1875. A third ship, unnamed and to be built by contract, was carried in the 1.1874 fleet list and in the 1875 budget but then disappeared from both.

———————

*IPHIGÉNIE. Croiseur de 1$^{re}$ classe, Croiseur à batterie* (1880). Large cruiser with covered and open batteries, a wooden hull with iron deck beams and beam shelves, and a clipper bow. One funnel, three masts, ship rig. Designed by Valin.

On 2 February 1877 Minister of Marine Fourichon forwarded to the ports his specifications for new cruisers, and on 13 June 1877 his successor, Vice Admiral Gicquel des Touches, forwarded to the *Conseil des travaux* three designs by naval constructors Romain Léopold Eynaud, Jules Victor Charles Chaudoye, and Pierre Gaston Hermann Valin that had been submitted by the ports. Unlike Minister Pothuau with *Duquesne* in 1872, Fourichon wanted 1$^{st}$ class cruisers designed primarily to navigate under sail for the purpose of giving officers and crews the practical education that formed true seamen, and secondarily to respond to the needs of distant stations. Specifications included a wooden hull, a displacement of about 3,000 tons, a speed under steam of 12 knots, a covered battery, and quarters for a flag officer and staff. The armament was to be eight to ten 164.7mm guns in the battery and two or three 194mm guns on the upper deck. The frigate *Flore* was suggested as a model but with the height of battery above the water and length increased. The Council noted that these ships would have very mediocre military value and would be subject to attack by even small enemy cruisers, putting the embarked admiral in 'a very critical situation'. It concluded that if Minister Gicquel des Touches persisted in the intention to build ships to the specifications of his predecessor the design of naval constructor Romain Léopold Eynaud could be chosen because it was a bit smaller, but noted that all three designs more or less met the specifications. The Minister proceeded with the designs of both Valin for *Iphigénie* and Eynaud for *Naïade*.

The armament on the plans dated 14 October 1877 for Valin's *Iphigénie* was four 164.7mm on the upper deck and twelve 138.6mm guns in the battery, although ten 164.7mm could be carried in the battery instead of the 138.6mm guns if the coal supply were reduced. Two 138.6mm guns were removed from the planned armament in the battery in 1880 and other changes followed. Installation of her machinery took over a year, the delay being to wait for the trials of *Naïade* which had the same design machinery except that the engines of *Naïade* was simple (single) expansion while those of *Iphigénie* were compound.

On 16 October 1883 *Iphigénie* was ordered converted into a seagoing school for midshipmen, and the conversion took place between the end of trials on 27 February 1884 and going into full commission on 16 August 1884. The conversion included a reduction in armament as indicated below. She continued the tradition begun in 1864 in *Jean Bart* of providing a year of experience at sea under sail to student officers leaving the Naval Academy. As a school ship she was crowded and conditions on board were unsanitary, although habitability was improved somewhat in 1896. She made 18 cruises between 1884 and 1900, after which she was replaced by *Duguay-Trouin* (ex transport *Tonkin*) and struck in 1901.

*The characteristics are based on a devis dated 3.10.1884.*

**Dimensions & tons:** 74.53m wl, 73.20pp x 14.235m ext, 14.20m wl. 3399.9t disp. Draught: 6.443m mean, 6.993m aft. Men: 500.

**Machinery:** 550nhp and 2,240ihp designed at 4.133kg/cm² boiler pressure. Trials (4.2.1884, natural) 2,467.57ihp = 13.348kts at 82.86rpm and 4.644kg/cm² boiler pressure. 1 screw. 1 horizontal compound engine with return connecting rods and 3 cylinders of 1.37m (1) and 1.68m (2) diameter and 0.90m stroke. 6 medium reglementary cylindrical boilers. 435.3t coal. Range 5,200nm @ 10kts. The operating pressure of the boilers was reduced to 3.250kg/cm² in 1892, and in 1894 they were replaced with four new ones operating at 4.25kg/cm².

The covered battery cruiser *Naïade* photographed in 1893 by the Detroit Photographic Co. As flagship of the *Division navale volante et d'instruction* (Flying and training naval division) she was in New York during 1893 but was not part of the April 1893 Columbian Naval Review. In the background are the Hudson River piers of the New York, Lake Erie & Western Railroad with coal barges and tugs. (Library *of Congress, LC-D4-21140*)

**Guns:**
(1883) 2 x 164.7mm/21 M1870 on the forecastle, 18 x 138.6mm/21.3 M1870 (2 on the poop, 4 on the upper deck sides, and 12 in the battery), all M1870, plus 10 x 37mm revolving cannon.
(1884 as school ship) 8 x 138.6mm on the upper deck, 2 x 100mm/26.5 M1875 on the forecastle, plus 10 x 37mm Hotchkiss and 2 x 65mm landing.
(1886) 6 x 138.6mm, 2 x 100mm, 8 x 37mm, 2 x 65mm landing. In 1890 the two 100mm guns were upgraded from M1875 to M1881, two 37mm revolving cannon were replaced with 2 x 37mm/20 M1885 QF, and one 356mm torpedo tube was installed in the battery.
    (1896) 4 x 138.6mm, 2 x 100mm, 8 x 37mm, 2 x 65mm, one torpedo tube .

*Iphigénie* Brest Dyd/Claparède, Saint Denis.
On list 1.1878. K: 23.8.1877. L: 8.9.1881. Comm: 15.5.1883 (trials). C: 2.1884.

Budget 1878. Machinery installed 18.1.1882 to 15.2.1883. Full power trials 29.1.1884 (2,782ihp = 14.14kts), then to 3rd category reserve 27.2.1884 to be fitted as school ship. Full commission as seagoing school for midshipmen 16.8.1884. Caught fire at Toulon 3.3.1887, taken into drydock and partially flooded to put out the fire, repairs completed 5.5.1887. To *Croiseur de 3e classe* 1.1897, still as seagoing school for midshipmen. Replaced by *Duguay-Trouin* (ex *Tonquin*) and decomm. 14 August 1900. Struck 4.12.1901, retained for possible use at the civilian *École professionnelle de Bordeaux*. To the Domaines 30.8.1904 for sale, sold 19.1.1905 to M. Pitel.

*NAÏADE. Croiseur de 1ʳᵉ classe, Croiseur à batterie* (1880). Large cruiser with covered and open batteries, a wooden hull with iron deck beams and beam shelves, and a clipper bow. One funnel, three masts, ship rig. Designed by Eynaud.

On 10 July 1877 the *Conseil des travaux* reported that a design of Eynaud best met the specifications of Minister of Marine Fourichon for a cruiser intended primarily for use as a sail training ship and secondarily as a flagship on foreign stations. Ministers of Marine Gicquel des Touches on 27 July 1877 and Vice Admiral Albert Edmond Louis baron Roussin on 30 November 1877 modified the design to increase the strength of the machinery, to replace M1858/60 guns with M1870 guns, and to change the structure of the hull to use iron instead of wood deck beams and beam shelves and to add watertight bulkheads. The armament in the modified plans approved on 4 February 1878 was four 164.7mm on the upper deck (two forward and two aft) and ten 138.6mm in the battery. The embrasured ports giving both axial and broadside fire to the upper deck guns were identical to those of the British cruiser *Boadicea*, whose plans the English had given to the French at Toulon. The design also included two torpedo launchers on carriages, normally stowed in the ports forward of the battery guns but with firing positions in chase ports forward and stern ports aft. An order from Minister of Marine Jauréguiberry dated 15 May 1880 added six 138.6mm guns including four M1870M guns on the upper deck. Trials of the machinery were difficult and were completed on 11 May 1883 only after many modifications. The replacement of the twelve M1870 guns with M1870M guns was planned in 1892 to standardise the armament but it was not carried out.

*The characteristics are based on a devis dated 10.8.1883.*

**Dimensions & tons:** 72.53m wl, 74.86m pp (wl fwd to rudder) x 14.15m ext and wl. 3,527t disp. Draught: 6.688m mean, 7.188m aft. Men: 496.

**Machinery:** 600nhp and 3,300ihp designed at 90rpm and 4.133kg/cm² boiler pressure. Trials (6.7.1882) 2,412.2ihp = 13.865kts at 81.83rpm and 3.920kg/cm² boiler pressure. 1 screw. 1 horizontal simple expansion engine (direct introduction of steam into each cylinder) with return connecting rods and 3 cylinders, all of 1.40m diameter and 0.90m stroke. 8 low reglementary cylindrical boilers. 503t coal. Range 5,810nm @ 10kts. Boilers replaced in 1892 by 8 return-flame Belleville boilers operating at 4.25kg/cm².

**Guns:**

(1881) 4 x 164.7mm/21 M1870 (2 forecastle and 2 poop), 16 x 138.6mm/21.3 M1870 (battery), two torpedo tubes above water.

(1883) 2 x 164.7mm (forecastle), 18 x 138.6mm (2 x 138.6mm/21.3 M1870M on the poop, 4 x M1870M and 12 x 138.6mm/21.3 M1870 in the battery), 10 x 37mm.

(1886-94) In 1886 the two 164.7mm were replaced with 164.7mm/28 M1881 Nᵒ 2 (light) guns and moved down a deck to under the forecastle. In 1890 2 x 65mm and 1 x 47mm were added, and in 1894 3 x 37mm/20 M1885 QF were added for training use.

*Naïade* Toulon Dyd/Claparède, Saint Denis.

On list 1.1878. Ord: 24.1.1878. K: 25.2.1878. L: 6.1.1881. Comm: 6.1882 (trials). C: 6.1883.

Budget 1878. To 2ⁿᵈ category reserve 9.8.1882 for modifications to the machinery, commissioned for trials again 20.2.1883. Trials completed 11.5.1883 (2,829ihp = 13.63kts), to 2ⁿᵈ category reserve 1.6.1883. Full commission 10.8.1883 to replace *Flore* in the Indian Ocean, relieved by *Nielly* 1886. Struck 1.12.1899, sold 29.3.1900 to M. Pitel at Brest to BU.

---

*ARÉTHUSE. Croiseur de 1ʳᵉ classe, Croiseur à batterie* (1880). Large cruiser with covered and open batteries, a wooden hull with steel deck beams and beam shelves, and a ram bow. One funnel, three masts, ship rig. Designed by Bienaymé.

This ship originated as a large open-battery cruiser roughly the size of the 2ⁿᵈ class cruiser *Duguay-Trouin*. It was proposed by naval constructor Arthur François Alphonse Bienaymé on his own initiative. Minister of Marine Pothuau referred his design on 8 February 1878 to the *Conseil des travaux* which examined it on 26 March 1878. Bienaymé's ship had a wooden hull of a special pattern with steel reinforcements that he had developed (he also used it in *Lapérouse* and *Rigault de Genouilly* but with iron), a displacement of 3,184 tons, dimensions of 82.55m length (tip of the ram to the rudder post) and 13.30m beam, a speed of 16 knots, and an armament, all on the upper deck, of six 194mm and twelve 138.6mm guns. The Council felt that a ship of this size should have a covered battery and recommended deleting two of the 194mm guns and moving most or all of the 138.6mm guns to the battery, which in turn would require raising the upper deck some 30cm. It invited Bienaymé to revise his design.

Minister of Marine Pothuau on 6 April 1878 sent to the ports new specifications for a 1st class covered-battery cruiser that were very similar to the Council's recommendations for Bienaymé's ship. These included a length between perpendiculars not over 83m, an armament of four 194mm or six 164.7mm guns on the upper deck and twelve 138.6mm guns in the battery, a speed of 16 knots, and accommodations for a flag officer. He also included a new specification, that the highest parts of the machinery were to be at least 30cm below the waterline. In July 1878 Minister Pothuau forwarded to the Council six designs including a revised one from Bienaymé, and on 13 August 1878 the Council picked two, Bienaymé's with a wooden hull and another with a steel hull. It observed that were no conclusive facts nor prolonged experience showing that iron or steel hulls covered with wood presented any serious problems but it still felt that it was preferable to stay with wooden hulls for ships no longer than these.

The hull was of wood construction with steel longitudinal beam shelves, whose strength allowed omitting the inner hull planking. The bow had a ram. The original armament was four 194mm/19.8 M1870 guns in sponsons on the upper deck and twelve 138.6mm guns in the battery. Minister of Marine Jauréguiberry decided on 5 May 1882 that this armament would make the ship overweight and ordered the 194mm guns replaced with 164.7mm/28 M1881 Nᵒ 1 (heavy) guns. But on 10 November 1882 Jauréguiberry, thinking that a small amount of excess weight was better than an insufficient armament, ordered Toulon to plan for installing an armament of four 164.7mm and twenty-two 138.6mm guns like the one he had just assigned to *Dubourdieu*. Plans were approved on 27 July 1883 for this armament (of the twenty-two 138.6mm/21.3 M1870 guns, twenty were in the battery while one was on the forecastle and one on the poop). But this increased artillery created a need for 118 more men while reducing the space available for their berthing and provisions. In late 1885 the replacement of the 138.6mm M1870 guns with M1881 guns was under consideration but the *Conseil des travaux* on 16 February 1886 recommended leaving the armament unchanged and in any case not reducing the number of 138.6mm guns. The design also called for four torpedo launchers in the battery, two forward in the unarmed chase ports, one to starboard in port Nᵒ 7 (the middle one), and one to port in port Nᵒ 8, but they were not embarked.

*The characteristics are based on a devis dated 27.5.1885.*

**Dimensions & tons:** 83.00m wl (+1.30m ram), 84.00m pp (wl fwd to rudder) x 13.61m ext, 13.60 wl. 3,587.6t disp. Draught: 6.127m mean, 6.877m aft. Men: 464.

**Machinery:** 800nhp and 3,360ihp designed at 96rpm and 4.250kg/cm² boiler pressure. Trials (2.4.1885) 4,175ihp = 15.57kts at 91.3rpm. 1 screw. 1 horizontal compound engine with return connecting rods and 3 cylinders, one small middle cylinder of 1.61m diameter and 0.80m stroke and two large ones also of 1.61m diameter but of 0.95m stroke. 8 medium reglementary cylindrical boilers. There were also two small boilers operating at 8kg to superheat the steam before admission into the small high-pressure cylinder. 477.8t coal. Range 5,100nm @ 10kts.

**Guns:**

(1885) 4 x 164.7mm/28 M1881 N° 1 (heavy) on the upper deck in half turrets (sponsons), 22 x 138.6mm/21.3 M1870 (20 in the battery, 1 on the forecastle and 1 on the poop), 8 x 37mm Hotchkiss, and 2 x 65mm landing.

(1892) 4 x 164.7mm on the upper deck, 16 x 138.6mm in the battery, 2 x 65mm, 4 x 47mm/40 M1885 QF, 8 x 37mm. The 138.6mm on the forecastle and poop were ordered removed on 7.8.1890 and the four after battery guns were ordered removed on 8.5.1891 to make room for an officers wardroom.

*Aréthuse* Toulon Dyd/Indret (engines designed by Joëssel).
On list 1.1878 (unnamed). K: 11.2.1879. L: 14.9.1882.
    Comm: 1.1.1884 (trials), 5.5.1885 (full).
Budget 1879. Full power trials 2.4.1885 (4,171ihp = 15.57kts). Comm. for a diplomatic mission to Morocco, then to reserve. Left Toulon for

---

The covered battery cruiser *Aréthuse* photographed by the Detroit Publishing Co. at the Columbian Naval Review in the Hudson River in 1893. The ships assembled in Hampton Roads in March 1893 and then moved to New York where the naval parade took place on 27 April 1893. At that time *Aréthuse* was flagship of the North Atlantic naval division. The ship behind her stern is USS *Bennington*. *(Library of Congress, LC-D4-5506)*

the West Africa station 7.9.1886 and then served as flagship of the South Atlantic and the Atlantic stations to 1890. Struck 1.12.1899, renamed *Sémiramis* 1899, central ship for the reserve at Landévennec 1899-1900 (then had only four 37mm guns). Name reverted to *Aréthuse* after being replaced as *Sémiramis* by ex-*Victorieuse* in 1900. Offered unsuccessfully for sale 12.1.1900, sold 21.2.1901 to M. Morice, BU 1904 at Brest.

---

**Future 1st class cruisers, 1878**

On 8 February 1878 Minister of Marine Pothuau, after referring to the *Conseil des travaux* the design by naval constructor Bienaymé that became *Aréthuse*, also asked the Council to report its opinion on the types of cruisers that should be built in the future. In addition, considering that cruisers of the *Tourville* type were too expensive to replicate and, assuming that the navy would be limited for the time being to two of them, he asked for the Council's advice on whether there was reason to build covered-battery cruisers that were less fast and less expensive. The Council examined the matters on 26 March 1878. It defined the true commerce raiding cruiser of the future as a covered battery ship of 3,000-3,200 tons, moderate length, and high on the water, a speed of 16 knots with forced draught and a range of 4,000nm at 10 knots. The artillery would consist of four 194mm guns in half turrets or six 164.7mm M1870 guns on the upper deck and at least twelve 138.6mm guns in the battery for broadside combat. It noted that, after setting aside eight old frigates, the navy had only two covered-

The covered battery cruiser *Dubourdieu* off the Mare Island Navy Yard in June 1891. She was drydocked there between 30 June and 23 July 1891 to repair damage to the structure of the sternpost around the propeller shaft. Photo by William H. Topley. *(NHHC, NH-71239)*

battery cruisers and that there was therefore reason to lay down some more.

This discussion introduced a new issue for the design of unarmoured cruisers, their protection. The Council noted that in the fleet before the advent of armour designers generally tried to place the engines and boilers of combatant ships below the waterline, and it noted that the same would seem to apply to current unarmoured cruisers. It pointed to the experience of the aviso *Bouvet* in 1870 whose exposed machinery was disabled by a shell from the Prussian aviso *Meteor* in an engagement off Cuba. While the protection of machinery could not be absolute without armour, the Council recommended that the top of the machinery in future covered-battery cruisers be 30cm below the waterline, that it be under a platform deck covered in part with light metal plating, and that it be surrounded in the vicinity of the waterline by coal bunkers installed so that the horizontal layer of coal under the platform deck was consumed last. For smaller open-battery cruisers the protection of the machinery could be less rigorous, but the machinery should still be kept below the waterline and protected by a platform deck and coal bunkers.

---

**DUBOURDIEU Class.** *Croiseurs à batterie.* Large cruiser with covered and open batteries, wooden hulls with iron deck beams and beam shelves, and clipper bows. One funnel, three masts, ship rig. Designed by Valin.

While discussing the Programme of 1879 on 16 August 1879, the *Conseil d'Amirauté* noted that France had three large cruisers, *Flore*, *Duquesne*, and *Tourville*. (The fleet list for 1879 showed ten with only three, *Flore*, *Magicienne*, and *Thémis*, fully active.) Before 1885 the 3 covered-battery cruisers of the *Aréthuse* type would also be completed, but this number was absolutely insufficient because the construction of combat ships without masts left the navy needing large cruisers for instruction in long voyages under sail. The Council could not recommend using the *Aréthuse* type as station flagships because it did not have the right armament to engage ships like the British *Shah* and the German *Leipzig*. The Council therefore proposed building between now and 1885 four covered-battery cruisers of about 3,600 tons displacement (a modified *Thémis* type) to serve on three foreign stations and assigning the *Aréthuse* type to the flying squadron for training duty. The four new ships were to have a full sail rig and powerful artillery.

*Dubourdieu* and *Capitaine Lucas* were both designed by naval constructor Valin. Valin lengthened his design for *Iphigénie* by 4.20m to provide room for six more guns in the battery and more powerful machinery. The 1881 budget (submitted in January 1880) included two ships, one at Cherbourg and one at Rochefort, and the 1882 budget (January 1881) added a second ship at Rochefort for a total of three. All data in this entry apply to *Dubourdieu* (at Cherbourg), the only one built, except as indicated.

In accordance with the deliberations of the *Conseil d'Amirauté* in August 1879 the original armament of *Dubourdieu* was four 164.7mm/21 M1870 guns on the upper deck (two under the forecastle and two under the poop for axial fire) and twenty 138.6mm/21.3 M1870 in the battery. An order from Ministe of Marine Jauréguiberry dated 10 November 1882 moved the 164.7mm guns to sponsons (half-turrets) like those in *Aréthuse* on the sides of the upper deck, added two more 138.6mm guns in the stern, and replaced the M1870 guns with M1881 guns. On 9 March 1883 the sponsons were ordered enlarged to provide 70-degree arcs of fire, on 8 July 1884 the 164.7mm guns were ordered mounted on Vavasseur central pivots and the sponsons strengthened to receive them, and on 5 November 1885 the hull sides were ordered reinforced to withstand axial fire from them. An order of 19 June 1885 added two torpedo tubes in the battery. These changes, however, made the ship overweight, and on 20 July 1886 Minister of Marine Aube ordered the removal of ten of the 138.6mm guns in the battery. The ship entered service with the armament shown below. The shields on the 164.7mm guns were removed in 1894. The original design called for machinery of 2,500ihp, which was later increased to 2,800ihp and then to 3,150ihp by enlarging the cylinders.

The construction of Valin's *Capitaine Lucas* at Rochefort was supervised by Eynaud, whose plans to provide seven watertight bulkheads as called for in her design were under discussion Feb 1881. She was carried in the 1881 budget as to be advanced from 5% to 14% built during that year and in the 1882 budget to be advanced from 9% to 15% (this budget also showed a second covered-battery cruiser to be begun at Rochefort and carried to 1%). On 4 August 1881 the *Conseil des travaux* summarily rejected a design by Émile Bertin for a steel-hulled 1st class cruiser with a cellular layer at the waterline on top of a submerged armoured deck, but Minister of Marine Cloué suspended work on the wooden *Capitaine Lucas* in August 1881 and his successor as Minister in the Gambetta cabinet, Capitaine de vaisseau Auguse Gougeard, ordered the construction instead of Bertin's steel cruiser that became *Sfax* using the funds budgeted for *Capitaine Lucas*. *Sfax* duly appeared in the 1883 budget at Brest to be taken from 7% to 31%, while the two Rochefort ships were deleted.

**Dimensions & tons:** (design) 73.97m wl, 77.30m pp (wl fwd to rudder) x 14.28m ext, 14.20 wl. 3354.7t disp. Draught: 6.20m mean, 6.965m aft. Men: 422.
**Machinery:** 600nhp and 2,800ihp (natural) and 3,150ihp at 88rpm and 4.250kg/cm² boiler pressure. Speed 14kts. Trials (9.9.1886) 13.91kts. 1 screw. 1 horizontal compound engine with return connecting rods and 3 cylinders of 1.40m and 1.74m diameter and 0.95m stroke. 6 cylindrical boilers. 400t coal. Range 4,780nm @ 10kts.
**Guns:** 4 x 164.7mm/28 M1881 Nº 1 (heavy) in sponsons on the upper deck, 12 x 138.6mm/30 M1881 BLR (10 in the battery and 2 aft), 1 x 47mm, 10 x 37mm revolving cannon, 2 x 65mm landing, 2 x 356mm torpedo tubes (sides above water).

*Dubourdieu* Cherbourg Dyd/Schneider, Creusot.
On list 1.1881. Ord: 24.12.1879. K: 6.9.1880. L: 6.12.1884.
   Comm: 15.6.1886 (trials). C: 12.1887.
Budget 1881. Named 20.8.1880. Full power trials 9.9.1886 (13.91kts), then to reserve. Comm. again for trials 6.6.1887, problems found on first run 16.7.1887 and to 3rd category reserve 10.8.1887 and after more trials to 2nd category reserve 22.12.1887. Commissioned 18.11.1889 to replace *Duquesne* on the Pacific station, but ruptures of two pistons brought her back to Cherbourg on 15.2.1890. Left again for the Pacific 10.4.1890 and, except for a period in reserve from July 1893 to March 1895, cruised overseas nearly continuously until decomm. 9.5.1899 and condemned 10.11.1899. Struck 1.12.1899, sold 19.5.1900 at Lorient to M. Degoul to BU.

*Capitaine Lucas* Rochefort Dyd.
On list 1.1881 only. Work begun 10.1880.
Budget 1881. On 16.8.1881 Minister of Marine Cloué ordered work stopped on *Capitaine Lucas*. On 20.8.1881 Rochefort responded to a question from Minister Cloué of the same date asking how much material had already been expended on *Capitaine Lucas* by reporting that 130,000 francs worth of oak had been used for the keel, stem and

sternpost, which had been cut but not erected, and for some frames. No other materials had been used and no contracts had been let for the metallic parts of the hull. The ministry wanted to use the wood in *Dubourdieu* but Cherbourg reported on 26.8.1881 that the hull of that ship was completely erected. In response to orders from Minister Cloué dated 26.8.1881 and 12.11.1881 Rochefort proceeded to dismantle the hull. The total spent on the ship was 131,092.35 francs and as of 28.1.1882 she no longer existed.

*N* (Unnamed) Rochefort Dyd
Budget 1882. Not in the 1883 budget (submitted in March 1882).

---

### Reduction in the cruiser programme, 1881

While discussing the Programme of 1881 on 6 May 1881, the *Conseil d'Amirauté* noted that it had reduced the number of covered and open-battery cruisers from 18 of each in the 1879 programme to 12 of each in the 1881 programme, which it felt to be sufficient. It also noted that Britain was beginning to build armoured cruisers (*Imperieuse* and *Warspite*) and that France would probably have to follow suit and define a new ship of type between and combining station battleships and large cruisers. In the meantime there were fourteen covered-battery cruisers afloat or under construction in the January 1881 fleet list, more than the twelve in the new programme.

---

### (B) 2nd Class Cruisers (*Croiseurs de 2e classe*).

Before the 1.1874 fleet list these were *Corvettes à barbette*. To *Croiseurs à barbette* 1.1880. *Duguay-Trouin* and the *Lapérouse/Villars* classes to *Croiseurs de 1re classe* 1.1885 and others to *Croiseurs de 2e classe*, *Duguay-Trouin* and the *Lapérouse/Villars* classes to *Croiseurs de station de 1re classe* 1.1891 and others to *Croiseurs de station de 2e classe* 1.1891, *Duguay-Trouin* to *Croiseur de 2e classe* 1.1892 and others including *Lapérouse* and *Villars* classes to *Croiseurs de 3e classe* 1.1892.

**Repeat *COSMAO* Class.** *Corvette à barbette.* Cruiser with an open battery, a wooden hull, and a clipper bow. One funnel, three masts, ship or barque rig. Designed by Courbebaisse.

In 1855 a *Commission supérieure* formed by Minister of Marine Hamelin on 27 July 1855 to propose a new organisation of the fleet decided that it would include 30 1st class steam corvettes of the *Phlégéton* type (400nhp), 30 1st class avisos similar to *Chaptal* (220nhp), and 30 2nd class avisos similar to *Corse* (120nhp). One result of this restructuring was that all 2nd class corvettes smaller than 300nhp, including *Chaptal*, were reclassified as 1st class avisos and the larger corvettes were merged into a single corvette category (soon called simply 'corvettes') covering ships in the 300-400nhp range. On 16 October 1855 the *Conseil des travaux* proposed specifications for these three types of cruising ships, recommending for the corvettes an increased armament of six 22cm Nº 1 shell guns and eight 30pdr Nº 1 long guns along with increased length and displacement and other adjustments. In 1856 the first two corvettes of the new type, *Cosmao* and *Dupleix*, were ordered to different plans. In 1861 a third, *Decrès*, was added. She was built to the plans by naval constructor Émile Marie Victor Courbebaisse that had been approved for *Cosmao* on 1 October 1856. Her first rearmament was directed on 23 April 1869 and her second on 2 July 1873. For the 1873 rearmament the gun platforms at both ends were enlarged and the one aft raised.

*The characteristics are based on a devis dated 1.8.1870*
**Dimensions & tons:** 64.45m deck, 62.90m pp (wl fwd to rudder,

2.457m from rudder to forward sternpost) x 11.82m ext and wl. 1,772.522t disp. Draught: 5.134m mean, 5.804m aft. Men: 194

**Machinery:** 400nhp (340 from 1867) and 1,360ihp designed at 65rpm and 1.8kg/cm² boiler pressure. Trials (5.8.1867) 1,478.32ihp = 12.04kts at 67.042rpm. 1 screw. 1 horizontal compound engine with 3 cylinders of 1.600 diameter and 0.750m stroke. 4 low reglementary boilers. 278t coal.

**Guns:**

(1862) 4 x 164.7mm rifles, 6 x 30pdrs Nº 1 (164.7mm/16.5) smooth-bores.

(1870) 2 x 164.7mm/19.2 M1864 (fore and aft on platforms), 4 x 138.7mm/16.5 M1858-60 Nº 2 MLR, 4 x 4pdr (86.5mm/11) bronze mountain.

(1873) 1 x 164.7mm M1858-60/16 BLR (pivot, forward), 9 x 138.6mm/16.5 M1860 Nº 2 MLR (1 on pivot aft, 8 on sides), 4 x 4pdr (86.5mm/11) bronze mountain.

(1878) The 1 x 138.6mm M1860 MLR aft replaced with 1 x 138.6mm/13.5 M1864 BLR, 2 x 4pdr.

(1885) 8 x 138.6mm M1870 BLR (1 forward and 1 aft on platforms, 3 on each side), 1 x 65mm landing, 8 x 37mm revolving cannon.

*Decrès* Lorient Dyd/Indret (engines designed by Sabattier).

On list 1.1862. K: 23.10.1861. L: 10.9.1866. Comm: 1.5.1867 (trials). C: 8.1867.

Machinery installed 13.9.1866 to 1.8.1867. Decomm. 20.8.1867 after trials. Recomm. 20.7.1870 for war service. Cruised in the Baltic and in the Channel 3.8.1870 to 12.3.1871, then in the Far East 2.8.1873 to 11.2.1876. Struck 25.6.1890, coal hulk at Rochefort 1890-1909 (converting 1890-1896). To Domaines for sale 31.3.1909, sold c1910 to BU.

---

**CASSARD (*DESAIX*).** *Corvette à barbette.* Cruiser with an open battery, a wooden hull, and a clipper bow. One funnel, two masts, schooner rig. Designed by Normand.

By a supplement signed on 3 December 1861 to Augustin Normand's contract of 16 November 1860 for the aviso *Talisman* (see below) the Navy ordered a 1st class aviso like *Jérôme Napoleon* (ex *Cassard*) which was given the name *Cassard*. On 24 May 1862 Minister of Marine Chasseloup-Laubat asked Normand to enlarge the new *Cassard* and increase the size of her machinery to give her the maximum speed suitable for her intended military service as a fast corvette. Mazeline produced a plan for installing in the ship a 3-cylinder 450nhp low-pressure engine like the one in the transport *Loiret*, and Normand then produced a new plan for the ship that called for hull dimensions of 78.00m x 10.60m and a displacement of 1600 tons. Normand's plans were approved on 30 June 1863 and a modification to the contract was signed on 31 July 1863 to alter her hull. Another modification was signed on 8 April 1864 to further enlarge the vessel. On 14 August 1864 it was proposed to substitute the new *Cassard* for the smaller and slower *Jérôme Napoléon* as a yacht, and in October the Emperor directed that she be put at the disposition of Prince Napoléon. The engines for the ship were ordered by a contract signed on 23 December 1864 by Mazeline under the new name of that firm after merging with Arman of Bordeaux, Chantiers et Ateliers de l'Océan. On 3 July 1865 Normand completed plans to complete her as a yacht, and another modification to the contract was signed on 22 December 1865. By a new contract signed on 24 November 1865 a new ship, *Coquette* (renamed *Château-Renaud* in March 1867, later rendered *Châteaurenault*) was ordered from Normand to replace the second *Cassard* as a cruiser. The former yacht retained her yacht deckhouse and light rig when renamed *Desaix* and converted back to a cruiser in the early 1870s.

**Dimensions & tons:** 79.55m wl x 10.62m ext and wl. 1,684t disp. Draught: 5.47m aft. Men: 159.

**Machinery:** 450nhp and 1,800ihp designed at 92rpm and 2.25kg/cm² boiler pressure. Trials (8.1866) 1,443ihp = 14.21kts at 84.5rpm and 2,025kg/cm² boiler pressure. 1 screw. 1 horizontal compound engine with return connecting rods and 3 cylinders of 1.42m diameter and 0.80m stroke. 4 low rectangular tubular boilers. 306.0t coal. Range 3,880nm @ 10kts.

**Guns:**

(1866 as yacht) 4 x 12pdr (121mm/17) bronze.

(by 1880) 7 x 12pdr (121mm/17) bronze (2 forecastle, 1 aft, 4 sides), 1 x 4pdr (86.5mm/11) bronze, 2 x 37mm revolving cannon.

(c1882) 4 x 100mm (including one forward and one aft), 1 x 65mm landing, 4x 37mm revolving cannon.

*Cassard* (*Desaix*) Augustin Normand, Le Havre/C.A. de l'Océan (ex Mazeline), Le Havre.

On list 1.1862. Ord: 12.1861 (contract). K: 1.1.1862. L: 20.2.1866. Comm: 16.8.1866 (trials). C: 1.9.1866.

Listed as a 250nhp 1st class aviso with *Talisman* 1.1862-63 and as a 400nhp *corvette à barbette* from 1.1864. Renamed *Jérôme Napoleon* 16.8.1866 when commissioned for trials and now rated at 450nhp, out of naval commission three days later on 19.8.1866. Expedition to the Arctic Ocean with Prince Jérôme Napoléon 1867-68. Renamed *Desaix* 19.9.1870. Sank *Lézard* as a target during towing torpedo trials at Toulon 1877. *Éclaireur d'escadre* 1.1881, *Croiseur de 2e classe* 1.1885, *Croiseur de station de 2e classe* 1.1891, *Croiseur de 3e classe* 1.1892. School ship at Toulon 1891. Struck 10.8.1894, sold 21.12.1894 at Toulon to BU.

---

**CHÂTEAURENAULT.** *Corvette à barbette.* Cruiser with an open battery, a wooden hull, and clipper bow. One funnel, three masts, barque rig. Designed by Normand.

After *Cassard* (above) was taken over as an imperial yacht Minister of Marine Chasseloup-Laubat decided on 1 October 1864 to order the construction by Normand of an identical open-battery corvette with the dimensions fixed for *Cassard* on 8 April 1864. The contract was signed on 24 November 1865 and 15 December 1865 and Normand was notified on 3 January 1866. Originally named *Coquette*, the ship was renamed *Château-Renaud* 18 March 1867 which was rendered as *Châteaurenault* after January 1877. Minister Chasseloup-Laubat assigned her six 164.7mm guns on 15 November 1866 but soon changed this to five 164.7mm/19.2 M1864 guns, one forward of the foremast and four on the sides. In 1869 while the ship was completing it was decided to replace this armament with three 194mm guns on rotating mountings as in *Infernet*, below, but she was judged to be too light to carry these heavy guns and she reverted to the previous assigned armament in February 1870. She was again rearmed between two Levant cruises at Toulon between 23 July and 28 August 1875 in accordance with directives from Minister of Marine Montaignac de Chauvance dated 28 June and 31 July 1875.

*The characteristics are based on a devis dated 31.3.1879.*

**Dimensions & tons:** 85m oa, 78.60m wl, 79.90m pp (wl fwd to rudder) x 10.72m ext and wl. 1,879t disp. Draught: 4.91m mean, 5.81m aft. Men: 210.

**Machinery:** 450nhp and 1,800ihp designed at 90rpm and 1.80kg/cm² boiler pressure. Trials (8.2.1870) 1,701.7ihp = 14.27kts at 80.2rpm and 1.988kg/cm² boiler pressure. 1 screw. 1 horizontal compound engine with return connecting rods and 3 cylinders of 1.45m diameter and 0.80m stroke. 4 low rectangular tubular boilers. 314.7t coal. Range 4,500nm @ 10kts.

**Guns:**

(1870) 5 x 164.7mm/19.2 M1864 (1 on a platform forward, 4 on the sides).

(1875) 7 x 138.6mm/21.3 M1870 (on the upper deck, one on a pivot forward, 6 on sides between the funnel and the mizzen mast, none aft).

(1882-86) Added 1 x 65mm landing and 2 x 37mm in 1882, 2 more 37mm in 1885 and 4 more in 1886 for a total of eight.

(1887) 6 x 138.6mm/21.3 M1870, 2 x 100mm/26.5 M1875, 1 x 65mm landing, and 4 x 37mm as modified for fishery protection duty.

*Châteaurenault* Augustin Normand, Le Havre/C.A. de l'Océan (ex Mazeline), Le Havre.

On list 1.1866. Ord: 24.11.1865 (contract). K: 19.11.1866. L: 20.7.1868. Comm: 1.9.1869 (trials). C: 3.1870.

Ex *Coquette* 18.3.1867. Machinery installed 1.9.1868 to 29.9.1869. To 3rd category reserve 16.3.1870 after trials. To 1st category reserve 20.7.1870 and to full commission 26.7.1870. Departed Brest 28.1.1871 for North America and the Antilles. Reboilered at Lorient 5.1878 with Indret boilers (1.80kg/cm²). Stern rebuilt at Lorient mid-1881 to 7.1882. Reboilered with FCM boilers (2.36kg/cm²), artillery changed, and bridge rebuilt at Lorient between 12.1885 and 10.1886. The ship then moved to Brest where a forecastle was added in 11.1886 for fishery protection duty. Decomm. 7.10.1891. Struck 16.5.1892, hulk at Cherbourg reserved for future use 1892-1894, renamed *Onglet* late 1895 and reserved for the defence of the passes through the Cherbourg breakwater, storage hulk 1899-1902, for sale 1902-1903.

---

*INFERNET* **Class.** *Corvettes à barbette.* Cruisers with open batteries, wooden hulls, straight bows (except for a clipper bow in *La Clocheterie*), and raked pointed sterns. One funnel, three masts, barque rig. Designed by Bienaymé.

Commerce raiding by Confederate cruisers during the American Civil War, particularly by *Alabama* which met her end off Cherbourg, created a sensation in naval circles. Admirals Richild Grivel, Philippe Victor Touchard, and other experts advocated the construction of cruisers of moderate cost with wooden hulls but of high speed for commerce raiding, which they felt should be a fundamental element in French naval strategy. On 19 October 1864 Minister of Marine Chasseloup-Laubat sent to Toulon and Brest specification developed by the Directorate of Materiel for a *corvette à vapeur à grande vitesse* (a fast steam corvette) and invited naval constructors there to submit plans. It called for an armament of four or six large-calibre guns including one on a pivot at each end. The ships were to have machinery of 450nhp capable of producing a speed of 14 knots and enough coal to maintain that speed for seven days. They were also to have a rig that, while moderate, would allow them to cruise under sail. A design by naval constructor Arthur François Alphonse Bienaymé was approved pending numerous modifications by the *Conseil des travaux* on 9 June 1865 and again on 15 May 1866, the final plans being approved on 10 January 1867. The second design resulting from this competition was naval constructor Dutard's *Sané* class, below. *La Clocheterie* was the only ship in either the *Infernet* or *Sané* classes with a clipper bow, the others having straight bows, and she was also the only one built at Cherbourg.

These two classes were at the centre of a debate as to whether French cruising ships should be fast commerce raiders like the Confederate *Alabama* with a few large guns or more general purpose ships with more smaller guns. The *Infernet* and *Sané* types were designed for an interim armament directed by Minister of Marine Chasseloup-Laubat on 9 September 1865 of six 164.7mm (30pdr Nº 1) rifles of which two were on pivots placed one before the foremast and one abaft the mizzen mast, the four others on the sides. On 30 April 1867 Minister of Marine Rigault de Genouilly directed that *Infernet* be armed with three large 194mm guns on the centreline on rotating platforms, and this armament was also planned for *Sané*. It was assigned to *Dupetit-Thouars* on 30 April 1868. These platforms, resembling turrets without sides, were replaced on 26 November 1868 by rotating gun mountings with 3mm thick metal shields. *Infernet*, the only one of the class to see service during the Franco-

Prussian War, sailed from Brest with her three large guns on 26 January 1871 a day after entering full commission but encountered heavy winds 800 miles west of Cape Finisterre and, encumbered by the weight of her artillery, 'behaved so badly in the heavy seas, the rolling motions being so violent and the vessel embarking so much water, that she was obliged to return to port for modifications that appeared urgent.' Minister Fourichon on 15 February 1871 ordered the 194mm guns removed and assigned *Infernet* and *Sané* a battery of smaller guns (one 164.7mm and eight 138.6mm). *Infernet* eventually recommissioned with this armament in 1873, but on 17 April 1871 the Minister of Marine, now Vice Admiral Pothuau, ordered *Sané* fitted with three of the next largest guns, the 164.7mm, similarly mounted on the centreline on rotating mountings with metal shields. The change from the 194mm guns reduced the weight of the armament from 79 tons to 54 tons. The same armament was then assigned to *Dupetit-Thouars* on 4 June 1871 and to *La Clocheterie* on 10 October 1871. *Sané's* trials with this armament on 29 March 1872 were declared to be successful, but comparative trials between the rearmed *Infernet* and *Sané* that ended in January 1873 with a final trial on 9 May 1873 revealed problems with this configuration such as the restricted field of fire of the amidships gun, which made this armament weak for a ship of her size. Armaments with larger numbers of smaller guns, mostly 138.6mm weapons, began to be assigned to this class in 1873 when *La Clocheterie* was assigned a battery of ten 138.6cm guns on 21 August 1873. The *Conseil des travaux* on 8 December 1874 opposed fitting half turrets (sponsons) on ships like *Infernet* that did not have sufficiently high upper works, but at least three of these ships had their broadside 138.6mm guns re-mounted in sponsons between 1882 and 1885, increasing their arcs of fire to 130 degrees from the 30 degrees allowed by ports cut in the bulwarks.

The engines of *Dupetit-Thouars* were like those of *Infernet* and were of the familiar Indret type with reverse connecting rods and 3 cylinders with direct introduction of steam into the central cylinder after passing through the steam jackets of the end cylinders. Her displacement increased between 1877 and 1882 by 23 tons because of the creation of half-turrets for the 138.6mm guns on the sides and the addition of Hotchkiss revolving cannon on the upper deck, along with four more in the fore and main mast tops. Installation of new boilers by MM Imbert frères of Saint-Chamond identical to the original boilers was completed and the boilers were first lit off on 31 August 1881. In a later refit new boilers, also identical, were first lit off on 18 November 1890.

*The characteristics are based on a devis for* Dupetit-Thouars *dated 12.2.1877.*

**Dimensions & tons:** 81.85m oa (85.93m in *La Clocheterie*), 80.65m wl, 78.92m pp (wl fwd to rudder) x 10.89m ext and wl. 1,963t disp. Draught: 4.85m mean, 5.70m aft. Men: 206.

**Machinery:** 450nhp and 1,800ihp designed at 90.25rpm and 2.25kg/cm² boiler pressure (1.702kg/cm² at engines). Trials (*Dupetit-Thouars*, 6.9.1875) 2,018ihp = 15.076kts at 94.07rpm and 2.380kg/cm² boiler pressure, (*D-T* with new boilers by Indret 12.8.1882) 1,875.5ihp = 14.435kts at 91.025rpm, (*D-T* 17.10.1894 with 4 new boilers *type bas renforcé* taken from *Duguay-Trouin*) 1,689.2ihp = 13.36kts at 87.82rpm and 2.239kg/cm² boiler pressure. 1 screw. 1 horizontal compound (Wolff) engine with return connecting rods and 3 cylinders of 1.45m diameter and 0.80m stroke (steam introduced into the middle cylinder). 4 reinforced reglementary low rectangular tubular boilers with superheaters. 330t coal. Range 6,010nm @ 10kts. The engine of *Champlain* was built at Brest to Audenet's design for the engines of *Dupetit-Thouars*, *La Clocheterie*, and *Fabert* but using parts from the salvaged engine of the two-decker *Duguay-Trouin*.

**Guns:**

*3 x 194mm*

(1870, *Infernet*) 3 x 194mm on central pivot mountings with 3mm metal shields.

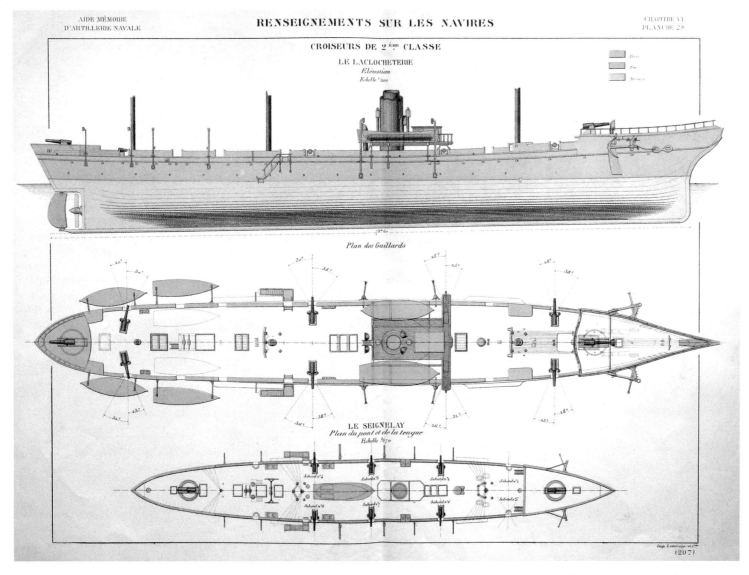

CROISEURS DE 2ᵐᵉ CLASSE
LE LACLOCHETERIE
*Élévation*
*Echelle 1/200*

*Plan des Gaillards*

LE SEIGNELAY
*Plan du pont et de la teugue*
*Echelle 1/70*

Outboard elevation and plan of the upper deck and forecastle of the 2nd class cruiser *La Clocheterie* of the *Infernet* class along with a smaller deck view of the 2nd class cruiser *Seignelay* of the *Sané* class. On 21 August 1873 *La Clocheterie* was assigned an armament of ten 138.6mm M1870 guns with eight on the sides on broadside mountings (two hidden here under the bridge wings) and one on the forecastle and one on the poop on central pivot mountings. On 5 July 1875 *Seignelay* was assigned eight 138.6mm M1870 guns, six on the sides and two on platforms fore and aft. (*Aide-Mémoire d'Artillerie navale, 1879*)

### 1 x 164.7mm, 7 to 9 x 138.6mm

(1873, *Infernet*) 1 x 164.7mm/19.2 M1864 (pivot forward), 8 x 140mm/17.45 M1858-60 Nº 1 MLR (sides).

(1874, *Champlain*) 1 x 164.7mm/19.2 M1864 (pivot forward), 8 x 138.6mm/21.3 M1870 Nº 1 (sides).

(1877, *Infernet*) 1 x 164.7mm/19.2 M1864 (pivot forward), 7 x 138.6mm/21.3 M1870 (6 on the sides and 1 on a platform aft). Light armament by 1882 was 2 x 37mm revolving cannon and 1 x 65mm landing.

(1878, *Champlain*) 1 x 164.7mm/19.2 M1864 (*pivot sur tourelle fixe* AV), 9 x 138.6mm/21.3 M1870 (8 in side ports and 1 on a platform aft, the stern gun added following trials), plus 3 x 4pdr (86.5mm/11) bronze.

### 10 x 138.6mm

(1874, *La Clocheterie*) 10 x 138.6mm/21.3 M1870 (1 forecastle, 8 on the sides, 1 on a short poop deck or platform aft), plus 2 x 4pdr (86.5mm/11) bronze mountain.

(1877, *Dupetit-Thouars*) 10 x 138.6mm/21.3 M1870, 3 x 4pdr (86.5mm/11) bronze mountain rifles. By 1886 her light armament was 1 x 65mm landing and 8 x 37mm.

(1884, *Champlain*) 10 x 138.6mm (1 x 138.6mm/21.3 M1870M on pivot on new forecastle, 8 x 138.6mm/21.3 M1870 in new sponsons on sides, 1 aft), 1 x 65mm landing, 8 x 37mm.

(1894, *Dupetit-Thouars*) 10 x 138.6mm/21.3 M1870 (1 on forecastle, 8 on sides in half turrets (sponsons), 1 on stern), 1 x 65mm/16 M1881 steel landing, 9 x 37mm revolving cannon. The fore and aft 138.6mm had shields that were cumbersome and gave little protection. Also had 2 x 40cm searchlights.

### 8 x 138.6mm

(1885, *Infernet*) 8 x 138.6mm/21.3 M1870 (1 at each end, 6 in new sponsons on the sides), 1 x 65mm landing, 8 x 37mm revolving cannon (including 2 for tops and boats).

(1885, *La Clocheterie*) 8 x 138.6mm, 6 x 37mm revolving cannon, plus 1 x 65mm landing and 2 x 4pdr (86.5mm/11) bronze. In 1887 while fitting out for fishery protection duty at Cherbourg two more 138.6mm guns were removed (leaving 6) and the two forward and aft were replaced with M1870M guns.

*Infernet* Brest Dyd/Indret (engines designed by Victorin Sabattier).
On list 1.1867. Ord: 29.10.1866. K: 3.12.1866. L: 27.5.1869.
    Comm: 17.9.1870 (trials), 25.1.1871 (full).

Machinery installed 7.1869 to 24.1.1870. Sent from Brest towards New York 26.1.1871 to hunt German packets but forced by heavy weather to return to Brest and lighten her armament. Decomm. at Brest 14.5.1872, recomm. 23.10.1872 and arrived at Toulon 10.12.1872 for service in the *Escadre d'évolutions*. Left Toulon for the Pacific 20.1.1874. Reboilered at Cherbourg 1882. Forecastle lengthened and the side 138.6mm guns remounted in sponsons while out of commission at Lorient 19.7.1884-15.2.1885. Struck 10.8.1891, for sale at Cherbourg 1891-1892, four attempts to sell failed due to falling prices for metals, contract with M. Guilhaumon to dismantle the machinery and break up the hull in the dockyard on the Navy's account approved 30.8.1892, proceeds reported 4.11.1893.

***Champlain*** Brest Dyd/Brest Dyd (engines designed by Camille Audenet).
On list 1.1868. Ord: 5.1.1867. K: 10.1.1867. L: 4.10.1872.
    Comm: 22.7.1874 (trials). C: 4.1875.
Trials 3.1875, then to 3rd category reserve at Brest 2.4.1875. To full commission 26.1.1878 and left Brest for Toulon and service in the *Escadre d'évolutions*. Left Toulon 2.1.1879 for the China station. Reboilered, forecastle extended, and broadside 138.6mm guns re-mounted in sponsons while out of commission at Lorient 1883. Struck 11.4.1893. Sold 12.10.1893 at Lorient to BU, being BU in the commercial port there 5.1894.

***La Clocheterie*** (*Laclocheterie*) Cherbourg Dyd/Indret (engines designed by Camille Audenet).
On list 1.1868. Ord: 5.1.1867. K: 1.4.1868. L: 20.8.1872.
    Comm: 5.7.1874 (trials). C: 9.1874.
To 3rd category reserve 27.9.1874 for modification of artillery, full commission 25.7.1875 and sent to the Far East. Reboilered at Cherbourg 1884-85 (first lit off 19.2.1885). On 17.3.1885 the after end of the main condenser ruptured while the machinery was being adjusted, the ship was towed into the shallow passage into the Charles X basin and sank there, refloated 30.3.1885 and left for the Far East 20.4.1885. Fitted for fishery protection duty while at Cherbourg 1887-88, receiving a spardeck and having her forecastle enclosed and superstructure amidships enlarged. Reboilered again 7.1890 with the boilers of *Decrès*. Struck 10.8.1894 but was needed for another Newfoundland patrol and was re-established on the list 19.10.1894. Struck again 26.4.1899, sold 4.1901 at Lorient to M. Raguet to BU in the naval dockyard.

***Dupetit-Thouars*** Brest Dyd/Indret (engines designed by Camille Audenet).
On list 1.1868. Ord: 7.3.1867. K: 27.3.1867. L: 27.8.1874.
    Comm: 16.7.1875 (trials), C: 9.1875.
Named 7.3.1867. Machinery installed 15.12.1874 to 14.7.1875. Trials 6.9.1875, then to 3rd category reserve 27.9.1875. To full commission 1.1.1877. Left Brest for the Antilles 28.2.1877. Reboilered 1881. Recomm. 3.7.1882 for the South Atlantic, returned to Brest 2.5.1885 and to reserve 23.5.1885. Recomm. 4.3.1886 to form part of the torpedo boat trials division (*division navale d'expérience des torpilleurs*). To reserve 13.8.1886. Recomm. 7.2.1887 for the same service, soon out of comm. Reboilered again 11.1890 with boilers from *Duguay-Trouin* (contract of 19.7.1890). Comm. 1.10.1894 for the Indian Ocean. Struck 26.4.1897, renamed *Oléron* 8.1897, mooring hulk at Rochefort 1897-1914 (converting 1897-1899), hulk there 1920. Sold 10.5.1920 to BU.

--------

**SANÉ Class.** *Corvettes à barbette.* Cruisers with open batteries, wooden hulls, straight bows, and raked pointed sterns. One funnel, three masts, barque rig. Designed by Dutard.

The second design approved following the request of 19 October 1864 from Minister of Marine Chasseloup-Laubat to the ports to submit plans for fast steam corvettes was by naval constructor Louis Dutard. His design

was approved on 30 July 1866 after modifications. They differed little from the *Infernet* group, both classes having an unusual pointed stern based on the early armoured frigates, but the hull above the waterline aft in *Infernet* was fuller, offsetting the weight of the bow and providing extra displacement aft, while *Sané* had to have ballast added in her narrow stern to balance the ship and then pitched badly because of the lack of buoyancy aft. The early history of their armaments paralleled that of the *Infernet* class. After the idea of carrying three large guns on the centreline (first 194mm and then 164.7mm weapons) was abandoned, Minister of Marine Dompierre d'Hornoy on 16 June 1873 gave *Sané* one 164.7 M1864 gun on a central pivot forward and six 138.6 M1870 guns, but this modification was deferred on 21 August 1873 because of difficulties with the recoil of the M1870 guns. Soon afterwards Minister Dompierre d'Hornoy on 23 September 1873 directed for *Seignelay* an armament of six 138.6mm/21.3 M1870 guns including one on the forecastle, one on a platform aft, and four on the sides. Minister Dompierre d'Hornoy on 13 March 1874 directed the same armament for *Fabert*. His successor, Minister Montaignac de Chauvance on 25 June 1874 gave *Sané* one 164.7mm M1860 gun and five 138.6mm/21.3 M1870 guns in place of her three 164.7mm guns, but on 28 July 1874 he accepted Toulon's recommendation of two 138.6mm/21.3 M1870 guns on central pivots on existing platforms fore and aft (the amidships platform being removed) and four 138.6mm/21.3 M1870 guns on the sides.

*The characteristics are based on a devis for* Seignelay *dated 10.12.1875.*
**Dimensions & tons:** 81.51m oa, 79.84m wl, 78.80m pp (wl fwd to rudder) x 11.015m ext and wl. 1,943t disp. Draught: 4.84m mean, 5.52m aft. Men: 206.
**Machinery:**
(*Seignelay*): 450nhp and 1,800ihp designed at 90rpm and 4.133kg/cm$^2$ boiler pressure. Trials (6.1875) 1,804ihp = 14.47kts at 86.7rpm and 3.956kg/cm$^2$ boiler pressure. 1 screw. 1 horizontal compound engine with return connecting rods and 3 cylinders, one of 1.30m and two of 1.60m diameter, all of 0.80m stroke. 6 medium cylindrical boilers. *Seignelay*'s engines were built by the Forges et Chantiers de la Méditerranée at Marseille to plans by Orsel.
(*Sané* and *Fabert*): Had engines like those in the *Infernet* class built at Indret and 4 tubular boilers of 2.25kg/cm$^2$ pressure. 336t coal. Range 6,140nm @ 10kts.
**Guns:.**
*3 x 164.7mm*
(1871, *Sané*) 3 x 164.7mm on central pivot mountings on platforms on the centreline with metal shields.
*6 x 138.6mm*
(1875, *Sané*) 6 x 138.6mm/21.3 M1870 (2 on platforms fore and aft and 4 on the sides). By 1888 her light armament was 1 x 65mm landing and 8 x 37mm. *Seignelay* and *Fabert* briefly carried 6 x 138.6mm before adding two more.
*8 x 138.6mm*
(1875, *Seignelay* and 1877, *Fabert*) 8 x 138.6mm (1 forecastle, 1 aft, and 6 sides), plus 3 x 4pdr (86.5mm/11) bronze boat (2 in *Fabert*). By 1887 the light armament of *Seignelay* was 8 x 37mm, of which 6 were Hotchkiss revolving cannon. By 1890 the light armament of *Fabert* was 1 x 65mm, and 6 x 37mm

***Sané*** Toulon Dyd/Indret (engines designed by Victorin Sabattier).
On list 1.1868. Ord: 3.9.1866. K: 13.9.1866. L: 9.4.1870.
    Comm: 6.11.1871 (trials). C: 2.4.1872.
Not launched 9.4.1869 as some documents indicate. Machinery installed 7.5.1870 to 11.7.1871. Manned for trials 29.3.1872, to reserve after trials. Full commission 10.11.1872, attached to the *Escadre d'évolutions* as a *répétiteur* (signal relay ship) and for comparative trials with *Infernet*, to 3rd category reserve 30.5.1873 for modifications to artillery and decomm. 14.6.1873. Recomm. 30.3.1875 and sent to the Antilles.

The 2<sup>nd</sup> class cruiser *Seignelay* at Toulon early in her career. The 138.6mm guns on the forecastle and poop are visible as are two of her broadside guns. *(NHHC from ONI album of French warships, NH-74991)*

To *Éclaireur d'escadre* 1.1881, *Croiseur de 2<sup>e</sup> classe* 1.1885. Reboilered and broadside 138.6mm guns re-mounted on sponsons 1885. Reboilered again at Rochefort 1890. Struck 13.12.1892, hulk at Rochefort 1892-1893, coal hulk at Rochefort 1893-1899 (converting 1893-1896), coal hulk at Brest 1899-1909, coal and torpedo calibration hulk at Brest 1909-1913, renamed *Ponton n<sup>o</sup> 1* 1910, for sale at Brest 1913-1914.

*Seignelay* Toulon Dyd/F.C. Méditerranée, Marseille (engines designed by Jules Orsel).
On list 1.1867. Ord: 3.9.1866. K: 12.9.1866. L: 5.2.1874.
    Comm: 20.10.1874 (trials). C: 2.1875.
Caught fire 6.6.1874 while completing, fire contained by flooding the dock. Trials 1.1875. To 2<sup>nd</sup> category reserve 21.2.1875 after trials for modifications to artillery, in full commission 20.11.1875 and left Toulon for the Pacific 17.12.1875. To *Éclaireur d'escadre* 1.1881, *Croiseur de 2<sup>e</sup> classe* 1.1885. Reboilered at Toulon 1886. Grounded off Jaffa 26.4.1891, refloated 1.5.1891 and towed to Toulon. Struck 16.5.1892 and sold 8.1892.

*Fabert* Rochefort Dyd/Indret (engines designed by Camille Audenet).
On list 1.1869. K: 1.3.1868. L: 1.8.1874. Comm: 20.7.1875 (trials).
    C: 12.1875.
To 3<sup>rd</sup> category reserve c19.12.1875. In full commission 25.10.1877 and sent to the Indian Ocean. Reboilered 2.1885 at Rochefort. Broadside guns re-mounted in sponsons at Cherbourg 1890. Received new bridge 1893, reboilered again 1893-94. Struck 25.11.1899, replaced aviso *Mégère* as school for boys at Marseille 1899, school closed, sold 8.1903 at Marseille to BU.

## 2nd class cruisers in the Programme of 1872.
As part of its effort as directed by Minister of Marine Pothuau on 14 September 1871 to produce technical specifications for all of the ship types that were to enter into the composition of the fleet under the Programme of 1872, the *Conseil des travaux* on 16 December 1871 established specifications for 2<sup>nd</sup> class cruisers. Armament (all on the upper deck) was to be four 164.7mm M1864 guns in half turrets and four 138.6mm guns in ordinary ports. Other specifications were a substantial sail area, a speed of 16 knots, an iron hull with wood and copper sheathing, and an estimated displacement of 2,532 tons. Minister Pothuau added one 164.7mm gun under the forecastle and then transmitted the specifica-tions to the ports on 23 January 1872 with a request that they submit designs. The total displacement was now estimated at 2,880 tons.

---

*DUGUAY-TROUIN. Croiseur de 2<sup>e</sup> classe.* Cruiser with an open battery, an iron hull with wooden sheathing, and a ram-shaped (inverted) bow. Two funnels, three masts, ship rig. Designed by Eynaud.

On 13 August 1872 the *Conseil des travaux* examined designs for 2<sup>nd</sup> class cruisers by five naval constructors and selected that of naval constructor Romain Léopold Eynaud. Eynaud, who did not think it advisable to get axial fire from the sponsons on the sides, added a fifth 138.6mm gun on the stern to provide axial fire aft similar to that forward from the 164.7mm gun under the forecastle. (The Council wanted the design to include axial fire from the sponsons and to delete the fifth 138.6mm gun but the the gun was retained.) His hull lines, including the inverted bow shaped like a ram but not reinforced for ramming and the configuration of the stern, were inspired by the experimental aviso *Renard* but were less extreme and avoided the weaknesses of that ship. Eynaud tried to get as much of the machinery as possible below the waterline, including by using low rather than high profile boilers. The Council wanted the power of the machinery increased to 3,520ihp and for it to include two separate engines, the after one providing speeds up to 10-11 knots and the forward one being coupled for higher speeds as in the 1<sup>st</sup> class cruisers. Minister Pothuau approved Eynaud's plans on 10 March 1873 and the ship was begun, but a later Minister, Dompierre d'Hornoy, then asked for changes on 21 December 1873 and only approved the final plans on 1 May 1874. The engines were of the same design as those of *Duquesne* but smaller, and unlike those in the larger ship gave little trouble in service although they had the same voracious appetite for coal. The boilers were in two boiler rooms each with its own funnel, the after one being thinner and telescopic to allow use of the mainsail. Forced draught was ordered omitted on 25 September 1877. Her 164.7mm guns were upgraded from M1864 to M1870 during construction.

Her barque rig was strengthened in December 1882. The larger rig harmed her stability, however, and after her coal supply was ordered reduced to 456 tons on 20 January 1883 the ship was ordered on 24 June 1884 to revert to her previous rig, which she retained to the end of her active career. She underwent significant changes at Cherbourg between 1 November 1885 and 15 September 1887 after returning from service in the 1884 war with China including a reduction ordered on 31 May 1886 from a 194mm to a 164.7mm main battery. In 1887 the ship was reboilered with 8 high model boilers designed for 4.25 kg/cm² (fires first lit on 29 July 1887), requiring reducing the diameter of the HP cylinders to 1.10m and giving a trial speed on 11 April 1888 of 15.78 knots at 4,804ihp. She handled badly under sail but well under steam except for rolling badly.

*The characteristics are based on a devis dated 23.5.1882.*
**Dimensions & tons:** 88.00m wl (+0.00m ram), 90.15m pp (wl fwd to rudder) x 13.205m ext, 12.905m wl. 3,662.1t disp. Draught: 5.635m mean, 6.72m aft. Men: 311.
**Machinery:** 900nhp and 3,500ihp designed at 90rpm and 2.25kg/cm² boiler pressure. Trials (26.12.1878) 3,804.2ihp = 15,538kts at 87.27rpm and 2.22kg/cm² boiler pressure. 1 screw. 3 horizontal compound engines with return connecting rods, each with cylinders of 1.25m and 1.74m diameter and 0.85m stroke, and each acting on the single propeller shaft through cranks spaced 120 degrees apart. 8 low reinforced rectangular tubular boilers. 575.2t coal. Range 6,500nm @ 10kts (but only 3,000nm @ 10kts in practice).
**Guns:**
(1878) 5 x 194mm/19.8 M1870 (4 in half-turrets/sponsons, 1 under the forecastle), 5 x 138.6mm/21.3 M1870 (4 on the sides, 1 aft on a very short poop deck), 2 Hotchkiss (4 in 1881). The 194mm and 138.6mm were listed as M1870M in 1881.

The 2nd class cruiser *Duguay-Trouin* early in her career. Her original ship rig was reduced to a barque by 1879. The second funnel was thinner and telescopic to allow use of the mainsail. *(NHHC from ONI album of French warships, NH-74933)*

(1881) The 194mm and 138.6mm M1870 guns were replaced in 1880-81 with M1881 guns of the same calibre but with a lengthened tube.

(1888) 5 x 164.7mm heavy M1881 (the half-turrets for the 4 on the sides being reconfigured), 5 x 138.6mm/21.3 M1870 (the four on the sides being moved further apart to improve their firing arcs), 2 x 65mm, 4 x 47mm, 5 x 37mm, and 2 tubes for M1885 torpedoes. The large guns received 4mm thick shields, but those on the forward two 138.6mm guns were soon removed as they interfered with handling the sails.

*Duguay-Trouin* Cherbourg Dyd/Indret.
On list 10.3.1873. Ord: 10.3.1873. K: 29.4.1873. L: 31.3.1877. Comm: 26.7.1878 (trials). C: 2.1879.
Budget 1872. Named 10.3.1873. Machinery installed 11.10.1877 to 31.5.1878. Manned for trials 28.11.1878. To 2nd category reserve 1.2.1879 after trials. Full commission 11.5.1882 for operations with the fleet. Sent in 1893 to the Pacific, then to the Far East. Struck 25.11.1899 in Cochinchina, retained provisionally 1899-1901, renamed *Vétéran* 25.5.1900, towed after alterations to Rach Dua (Vung Tao) 30.3.1901 as central ship for the 1st flotilla of torpedo boats, replacing *Cimeterre*. Central ship for the *Défense mobile* and basing centre at Rach Dua 1901-1910. To the Domaines 7.1910 for sale, sold at Saigon 12.9.1911.

---

*VILLARS* Class. *Croiseurs de 2e classe.* Cruisers with open batteries, wooden hulls with iron deck beams and beam shelves, and ram bows. One funnel, three masts, ship rig. Designed by Sabattier.

On 8 March 1875 Minister of Marine Montaignac de Chauvance referred to the *Conseil des travaux* two designs for 2nd class cruisers produced according to new specifications intended to augment the artillery while holding to moderate displacements, resulting in some reduction in speed. One design was prepared in the office of the Director of Materiel, Sabattier, while the other was produced by naval constructor Bienaymé who in the mid-1860s had designed the *Infernet* class. The Council examined them on 28 May 1875. On 27 April 1875 the Council had examined the question of cruiser size and armaments, and these two ships at about 2,260 tons fell between one type defined by the Council with 2,000 tons and 15 knots and one with 2,500 tons and 15.5 knots. Overall the two designs were very similar. Both had six guns on each side plus two forward and one aft and Sabattier assigned 138.6mm M1870 guns to all fifteen positions. The

Council wanted a somewhat heavier armament for ships of this size and asked for six 164.7mm M1858-60 (hopefully to be replaced with a new lightweight 164.7mm gun) and nine 138.6mm/21.3 M1870 guns. Sabattier proposed two options for mounting the two chase guns, one putting them on top of the forecastle on central pivots in the usual manner and the other putting them under it with embrasures cut away as done by the British to give them axial fire. The Council recommended using embrasures in Sabattier's ships and the usual placement on top of the forecastle in Bienaymé's ships to compare the two, which was done. The tops of the boilers and the surface condenser in Sabattier's design rose up to the waterline and were vulnerable despite the partial protection provided by coal bunkers on the sides. Recalling that the machinery of the aviso *Bouvet* had been disabled by the Prussian aviso *Meteor* in an engagement off Cuba in 1870, a majority in the Council proposed covering the sides amidships for a length of 28m and height of 2m over the machinery in both designs with 30mm metal plating at a cost of 26 tons.

Neither the side plating nor the Council's proposed armament was accepted and the ships were built as designed with fifteen 138.6mm guns, although in Sabattier's ships the stronger 138.6mm/21.3 M1870M with a short tube was substituted for the original M1870 during construction. The difference was noted favourably by the commander of *Villars* in 1885, although others felt that the 138.6mm gun was weak for ships of this size. The second pair in Sabattier's quartet was built to modified plans with a slightly larger load displacement. All four ships had single funnels but that of *Forfait* with her Marseille-built boilers was larger than those of the others.

*The characteristics for the three Cherbourg-built ships are based on a devis for* Villars *dated 20.1.1882 and those for the Toulon-built* Forfait *are based on a devis dated 1.9.1879.*

**Dimensions & tons:**
(Cherbourg ships) 74.27m wl (+0.27m ram), 76.27m pp (wl fwd to rudder) x 11.60m ext and wl. 2,419.3t disp. Draught: 5.313m mean, 5.813m aft. Men: 269.
(*Forfait*) 79.400m oa, 74.18m wl (+0.41m ram), 76.16m pp (wl fwd to rudder) x 11.618m ext and wl. 2,321t disp. Draught: 5.134m mean, 5.761m aft. Men: 264.

**Machinery:**
(*Villars, Magon, Roland*) 650nhp and 2,700ihp forced draught and 2,160ihp natural designed at 95rpm and 4.133kg/cm² boiler pressure. Trials (*Villars*, 10.6.1881) 2943.64ihp = 14.605kts at 98.75rpm and 4.34kg/cm² boiler pressure. 1 screw. 1 horizontal compound engine with return connecting rods and 3 cylinders of 1.50m (1) and 1.60m (2) diameter and 0,55m stroke for the small cylinder and 0.76m for the large cylinders. 6 cylindrical boilers, medium type. 334.7t coal. Range 4,810nm @ 10kts.
(*Forfait*): 650nhp and 2,160ihp natural draught designed at 84rpm and 4.133kg/cm² boiler pressure. Trials (16.12.1880) 2,960.87ihp = 14.715kts at 89.070rpm. 1 screw. 1 horizontal compound engine with return connecting rods and 3 cylinders of 1.440m (1) and 1.670m (2) diameter and 0.800m stroke. 6 cylindrical boilers, medium type. 330t coal. Range 4,800nm @ 10kts.
(*Forfait*, new boilers 1888): 2,700ihp designed at 90rpm and 4.250kg/cm² boiler pressure. Trials (20.7.1888, forced) 2,942.1ihp = 14.733kts at 91.58rpm. 6 cylindrical boilers, medium type (Indret Model 1880). 370t coal.

**Guns:** (1879) 15 x 138.6mm/21.3 M1870M (2 under the forecastle, 12 on sides, 1 on platform aft), 2 x 37mm Hotchkiss revolving cannon, 2 x 4pdr (86.5mm/11) bronze mountain guns or 1 x 65mm landing. The 37mm battery was soon increased, *Forfait* having 8 x 37mm revolving cannon in 1892.

*Villars* Cherbourg Dyd/Indret (engines designed by Joëssel).
On list 1.1875. K: 9.7.1875. L: 21.8.1879. C: 1881 (trials). C: 7.1881.
Budget 1876. Named 12.2.1875. Full power trials 10.6.1881 (2,885ihp =

14.6kts), to 2nd category reserve 10.7.1881. In full commission 20.1.1882 for the Far East. Struck 8.7.1896. Sold 17.12.1896 at Cherbourg to BU.

*Forfait* Toulon Dyd/F.C. Méditerranée, Marseille (engines designed by Orsel).
On list 1.1877. K: 2.11.1876. L: 6.2.1879. Comm: 1.9.1879 (trials). C: 4.1880.
Budget 1877. Named 27.3.1876. Machinery installed 28.5.1879 to 15.10.1879. Full power trials 9.3.1880, to 2nd category reserve 21.4.1880, more trials on 14.8.1880 with new screw and on 13-16.12.1880. In full commission 3.10.1881 to replace *La Clochèterie* in the Indian Ocean, returned 1886. New boilers by the Cie. de Fives-Lille installed 11.6.1888. Second cruise 1892-96 in the Far East. Struck 26.4.1897, mooring hulk at Rochefort 1897-1914 (converted 1897-1899), still hulk there 1920, sold to BU 1920.

*Magon* Cherbourg Dyd/Indret (engines designed by Joëssel).
On list 1.1877. K: 18.4.1876. L: 9.8.1880. C: 1.7.1882 (trials). C: 9.1882.
Budget 1877. Named 27.3.1876. Construction begun 18.4.1876. Full power trials 31.8.1882 (2,957ihp = 14.63kts), to 2nd category reserve 9.9.1882. Full commission c12.1884, left Cherbourg 31.12.1884 for the Far East. Struck 19.12.1895, sold 17.7.1896 at Brest to M. Gordais to BU.

*Roland* Cherbourg Dyd/Indret (engines designed by Joëssel).
On list 1.1878. Ord: 13.11.1876. K: 2.7.1877. L: 14.10.1882. C: 25.3.1884 (trials). C: 8.1884.

The open battery cruiser *Roland* photographed on 6 September (*7bre*) 1886 at Algiers. Her seven starboard 138.6mm guns are visible in an embrasure under the forecastle and in six small sponsons along the side, and the single pivot mounting aft can also be made out. (*NHHC from ONI album of French warships, NH-74816*)

Budget 1878. Named 29.1.1877, sometimes spelled *Rolland* which technically was correct as she was named for Rear Admiral Pierre-Nicolas Rolland (1761-1825), commander of the 74-gun *Romulus* in combat off Toulon on 13.2.1814. Construction begun 8.5.1877. Full power trials 15.7.1884 (2,825ihp = 14.32kts), to 2nd category reserve 1.8.1884 and 3rd category reserve 5.11.1884. To full commission 21.1.1885 for the Far East. Struck 19.5.1897, sold 5.11.1898 at Lorient to M. Degoul to BU.

*N* (Unnamed) Toulon Dyd
Budget 1878. This unnamed 2nd class cruiser was not in the 1879 budget.

———

*LAPÉROUSE* Class. *Croiseurs de 2e classe.* Cruisers with open batteries, wooden hulls with iron deck beams and beam shelves, and ram bows. One funnel, three masts, ship rig. Designed by Bienaymé.

Naval constructor Bienaymé's design for the *Lapérouse* class was generally very similar to Sabattier's for the *Villars* class, but Bienaymé's design had a midships cross section with a higher deadrise in the floor (V-shape) than Sabattier's. This raised the foundations of the low reglementary boilers in the original design pushing the tops of the boilers to about 15cm above the waterline. Cylindrical boilers would rise even higher, but less of the boiler surface would be vulnerable, and cylindrical boilers were adopted in both designs. Another result was that the upper deck and the sides were about 30cm higher in Bienaymé's ship, giving the guns greater command but also making the hull heavier. The hull lines at the ends were also a bit sharper, similar to those of Bienaymé's *Infernet*, making the ships slightly faster than Sabattier's. The two chase guns were on top of the forecastle. *D'Estaing* had a tall single funnel while the other three had a shorter double funnel (two uptakes close together extending above a low single outer casing). The machinery in these ships was regarded as successful, reliably outrunning other ships when necessary. Only *D'Estaing* was reboilered, receiving a new identical set built by Indret in 1894. In *Nielly* the aging original boilers

The open battery cruiser *Lapérouse* photographed on 2 August 1886 at Algiers. The guns in this ship were arranged in the same manner as those of *Roland*, above, except that the foremost guns were on the forecastle rather than under it. The ram-shaped bow was also more extreme. *(NHHC from ONI album of French warships, NH-74975)*

were kept in service by reducing their operating pressure to 3.50kg/cm$^2$ in 1895 and 3.00kg/cm$^2$ in 1900.

*The characteristics are based on a devis for* Lapérouse *dated 10.5.1880 with machinery data for* D'Estaing *from a devis dated 8.5.1881.*

**Dimensions & tons:** 79.50m wl (+1.21m ram), 81.75m pp (wl fwd to rudder) x 11.40m ext and wl. 2,.319.7t disp. Draught: 5.292m mean, 5.792m aft. Men: 264.

**Machinery:** (*Lapérouse* and 2 sisters) 650nhp and 2,160ihp designed at 88rpm and 4.133kg/cm$^2$ boiler pressure. Trials (*Lapérouse*, 12.1879) 2,661.3ihp = 15.15kts at 90.08rpm and 4.366kg/cm$^2$ boiler pressure. 1 screw. 1 horizontal compound engine with return connecting rods and 3 cylinders of 1.38m and 1.70m diameter and 0.85m stroke. 6 cylindrical boilers, medium type. 317.1t coal. Range 4,980nm @ 10kts.

**Machinery:** (*D'Estaing*) 650nhp and 2,160ihp designed at 90rpm and 4.133kg/cm$^2$ boiler pressure. Trials (*D'Estaing*, 15.3.1881) 3,034.2ihp = 15.308kts at 93.125rpm and 4.770kg/cm$^2$ boiler pressure. 1 screw. 1 horizontal compound engine with return connecting rods and 3 cylinders of 1.44m and 1.67m diameter and 0.80m stroke). 6 cylindrical boilers, medium type. 315.1t coal. Range 4,800nm @ 10kts.

**Guns:**

(1881) 15 x 138.6mm/21.3 M1870 (2 on the forecastle, 12 on sides in small sponsons on the upper deck, and 1 on a platform aft), 2 x 37mm Hotchkiss, 3 x 4pdr (86.5mm/11) bronze boat. The number of 37mm Hotchkiss was increased in 1882-84 to 8 in *Lapérouse* and *d'Estaing*, 7 in *Nielly*, and 10 in *Primauguet*

(1892, *Primauguet*) 10 x 138.6mm, 1 x 65mm, 10 x 37mm.

*Lapérouse* Brest Dyd/Schneider, Creusot (engines designed by Mathieu).

On list 1.1875. K: 23.6.1875. L: 5.11.1877. C: 6.10.1879 (trials). C: 3.1880.

Budget 1876. Full power trials 22.12.1879 (2,660ihp = 15.15kts), to 2nd category reserve 7.3.1880 and 3rd category reserve 7.8.1881. In full commission 1.12.1884 for the Far East station. Modified 1890 for a Newfoundland cruise by enclosing her forecastle and adding a spardeck around the funnels and an enclosed shelter for the bridge watch. Broke her moorings and driven ashore 31.7.1898 while waiting to coal in the anchorage at Fort Dauphin, Madagascar (her chains may have been struck by a submerged wreck dislodged by an unusually heavy swell). General Gallieni and his staff were on board, all hands were saved as were the guns and provisions. Struck 14.12.1898, sale authorized 6.9.1899, sold 15.1.1901 to Casim Olla.

*D'Estaing* Brest Dyd/F.C. Méditerranée, Le Havre.

On list 1.1877. K: 4.8.1876. L: 16.10.1879. C: 1.9.1880 (trials). C: 4.1881.

Budget 1877. Named 17.7.1876. Full power trials 15.3.1881 (3,034ihp = 15.3kts), to 2nd category reserve 1.4.1881 and 3rd category reserve 7.8.1881. Commissioned for trials 1883 and left Brest 31.12.1883 to join Rear Admiral Courbet in the Far East. Struck 2.5.1901. Sold 20.8.1901 at Brest to M. Guilhaumon to BU.

*Nielly* Brest Dyd/Schneider, Creusot (engines designed by Mathieu).

On list 1.1877. K: 16.8.1876. L: 25.5.1880. C: 1.1.1881 (trials). C: 3.1881.

Budget 1877. Named 17.7.1876. Full power trials 10.3.1881 (2,921ihp=15.22kts), to 2nd category reserve 26.3.1881 and 3rd category reserve 7.8.1881. In full commission 22.8.1884 for the Far East. Struck 18.1.1902. To the Domaines 24.5.1902 for sale, sold 25.9.1902 to M. Pitel and BU at Brest.

*Primauguet* Rochefort Dyd/Schneider, Creusot (engines designed by Mathieu).

On list 1.1877. K: 10.1.1877. L: 27.9.1882. Comm: 1883 (trials), 14.11.1883 (full).

Budget 1877. Originally named *Monge* after a cruiser lost with all hands in a typhoon in 1868 but renamed *Primauguet* 15.9.1882 just before launching to avoid adverse effects on crew morale. Full power trials 27.10.1883 (2,922ihp = 15.36kts). Commissioned 14.11.1883 for transit from Rochefort to Toulon, then to 2nd category reserve 5.12.1883. Recomm. 15.12.1884 for the Far East. Received major work to her boilers, engines, bridgework and rig in 1889-90 after a long cruise. Another refit was ordered on 11.1.1897 after her return to Rochefort from the Indian Ocean using six medium cylindrical boilers in storage at Brest but it was suspended 6.1898. Struck 13.2.1901, sale adjourned 20.11.1901 and ship used as a mooring hulk to 1906, sold 9.2.1907 to MM Lhermitte and Brunelat of Brest.

## Future 2nd class cruisers, 1878
The *Conseil des travaux* on 26 March 1878 provided some specifications for possible successors to the *Villars* and *Lapérouse* classes. Open-battery cruisers like these were not suitable for primary use as commerce raiders and needed less ambitious characteristics than the larger covered-battery cruisers, including a displacement of around 2,000 tons, a speed of 16 knots with forced draught, and protection of machinery limited to keeping it below the waterline and surrounding it with a platform deck and coal bunkers. The armament, all on the upper deck, would be four 164.7mm M1870 guns in half turrets and six 138.6mm guns. Technical improvements were thus to focus on reduction of displacement, a different composition of the artillery, and better placement of the machinery. The Council, however, pointed out that, under the Programme of 1872 France still needed some 1st class covered-battery cruisers but had enough 2nd class open-battery cruisers, and none of the latter appeared in the next several budgets.

## (C) 3rd Class Cruisers (*Croiseurs de 3e classe*).
Before the 1.1874 fleet list these were *Avisos de 1re classe*. To *Avisos d'escadre* 1.1880 and *Éclaireurs d'escadre* 1.1881. *Rigault de Genouilly* cl. and *Desaix* to *Croiseurs de 2e classe* 1.1885 and others to *3e classe*, *Rigault de Genouilly* cl. to *Croiseurs de station de 2e classe* 1.1891 and others to *Croiseurs de station de 3e classe* 1.1891, all to *Croiseurs de 3e classe* 1.1892.

### 1st class avisos, 1855-1856
In 1855 a *Commission supérieure* formed by Minister of Marine Hamelin on 27 July 1855 to propose a new organisation of the fleet included in it 30 1st class steam corvettes of the *Phlégéton* type (1850, 400nhp), 30 1st class avisos similar to *Chaptal* (1845, 220nhp), and 30 2nd class avisos similar to *Corse* (1842, 120nhp). On 16 October 1855 the *Conseil des travaux* developed specifications for the three types of cruising ships including the new 250nhp 1st class avisos. The first four ships designed to the new specifications for 1st class avisos were *Monge* and *Forbin*, ordered from the Brest dockyard in October 1855, and *Forfait* and *Cassard*, ordered from Normand in May 1856, all to different designs. On 2 July 1856 the specifications for the 1st class avisos were modified to enhance performance under sail so the ships could operate on the foreign stations as well as with the fleet.

*TALISMAN. Aviso de 1re classe.* Small cruiser with an open battery, a wooden hull, and a clipper bow. One funnel, three masts, barque rig. Designed by Normand.

On 16 October 1860 Minister of Marine Hamelin directed that a contract be negotiated with Augustin Normand for a 250nhp screw aviso on his design similar to a 1,223-ton ship ordered from him in 1856 as the aviso *Cassard* and completed in 1860 as the yacht *Jérôme Napoléon*. The 1856

design by Normand with Adrien Joyeux and Victor Legrand did not follow the navy's specifications, but the navy recognized that the ship would probably be an excellent sea boat and that it should be a 'veritable clipper' with very good speed under sail and sufficient speed under steam. The contract for the replacement ship was approved on 16 November 1860 and the name *Talisman* was assigned to her on the same date. The engines were ordered from Mazeline by a contract signed on 8 February 1861. Normand's plans dated 15 September 1861 were approved on 16 November 1861.

**Dimensions & tons:** 68.60m deck, 68.52m wl x 10.25m ext and wl. 1,334t disp. Draught: 3.53m fwd, 4.83m aft. Men: 154.
**Machinery:** 250nhp (230 from 1867) and 920ihp designed at 85rpm and 1.800kg/cm² boiler pressure. Trials (8.1863) 800ihp = 12.38kts at 79.1rpm and 1.653kg/cm² boiler pressure. 1 hoisting screw. 1 horizontal simple expansion engine with return connection rods and 2 cylinders of 1.25m diameter and 0.70m stroke. 2 low rectangular tubular boilers. 271.3t coal. Range 3,250nm @ 10kts.
**Guns:**
(1863) 2 x 164.7mm rifles, 4 x 12pdr (121mm/17) bronze MLR.
(1875) 6 x 138.6mm/21.3 M1870 (2 on platforms forward and aft, 4 on sides).

*Talisman* Augustin Normand, Le Havre/Mazeline, Le Havre.
On list 1.1861. Ord: 16.10.1860. K: 4.1861. L: 24.9.1862. Comm: 2-3.1863 (trials), 9.1863 (full).
Arrived at Cherbourg 28.2.1863 under tow from the builder. Left Cherbourg 27.9.1863 with the division of armoured ships acting as a *mouche* or scout on a cruise to the Canary Islands. Left Toulon 8.1865 for the Pacific station, returned to Cherbourg 13.11.1868 and decommissioned. In commission 26.2.1870 to 18.5.1872 for the Antilles and Newfoundland station and from 20.2.1875 to 24.1.1878 for the China station. Conducted a scientific expedition exploring the sea bottom in the Sargasso Sea in the Atlantic in 1883. Struck 7.7.1893, replaced *Guêpe* in Tunisia 1895-1898 as central ship for the *Défense mobile* at Bizerte 1896-1898, then used as a repair hulk at Bizerte 1898-1901, a hulk for the *Défense mobile* at Bizerte 1901-1905, and a support hulk for the 5th flotilla of torpedo vessels of the Mediterranean at Oran 1905-1908. For sale in Algeria 1908-1909.

*HAMELIN Class. Avisos de 1re classe.* Small cruisers with open batteries, wooden hulls, and clipper bows. One funnel, three masts, ship rig. Designed by Pastoureau-Labesse.

Between May 1864 and March 1865 three dockyards began work on five new 1st class avisos. On 31 January 1865 Minister of Marine Chasseloup-Laubat approved plans for a modified *Monge* by naval constructor Jean-Baptiste Pastoureau-Labesse, who had designed the original *Monge*. *Lhermitte* was named for Vice Admiral baron Lhermitte, the rendering of her name as *L'Hermitte* often encountered in contemporary sources thus being technically incorrect.

*The characteristics are based on a devis for* Volta *dated 22.5.1874.*
**Dimensions & tons:** 67.5m oa, 62.20m wl, 63.50m pp (wl fwd to rudder) x 10.36m ext, 10.35m wl. 1,300.7t disp. Draught: 4.406m mean, 4.856m aft. Men: 159.
**Machinery:** 250nhp and 1,000ihp designed at 90rpm and 1.800kg/cm² boiler pressure. Trials (*Volta*, 10.1867) 1,066ihp = 12.94kts at 91.15rpm and 1.795kg/cm² boiler pressure. 1 screw. 1 horizontal compound engine with return connecting rods and 3 cylinders of 1.25m diameter and 0.70m stroke. 2 high rectangular tubular boilers (only *Lhermitte* had superheaters in the base of the funnel). 234.5t coal. Range 3,290nm @ 10kts.
**Guns:**
(1866, *D'Estrées, Limier* and *Volta*) 1 x 164.7mm M1860 on a double

pivot fwd, 4 x 138.7mm/16.5 M1858-60 Nº 2 MLR sides, 4 x 4pdr
   (86.5mm/11) bronze mountain, 2 espingoles
(1867, *Hamelin*, *Volta*) 1 x 164.7mm M1860 fwd, 5 x 140mm/17.45
   M1858-60 Nº 1 MLR sides and aft
(1868, *D'Estrées* and *Volta*) 2 x 164.7mm M1858-60 (one forward on a
   platform and one aft), 4 x 140mm/17.45 M1858-60 Nº 1 MLR sides,
   1 x 4pdr (86.5mm/11) bronze (2 in *D'Estrées* in 1873), 2-4 espingoles.
(1869, *Hamelin*) 2 x 164.7mm M1858-60 on pivots, 2 x 138.7mm/16.5
   M1858-60 Nº 2 MLR sides, 1 x 4pdr (86.5mm/11) bronze mountain
(1873, *Lhermitte*, *D'Estrées*) 1 x 164.7mm M1864-66 (M1860 in
   *D'Estrées*) fwd, 4 x 138.7mm/16.5 M1858-60 Nº 2 MLR sides,
   1 x 4pdr (86.5mm/11) bronze mountain.
(1874-1880, *Volta* (1874), *Hamelin* (1876), *D'Estrées* (1880))
   1 x 164.7mm fwd, 5 x 138.6mm (4 sides, 1 on a central pivot aft),
   1 x 4pdr (86.5mm/11) bronze mountain (*Volta*)
(1874-1886, *Limier* (1874), *Volta* (1875), *Hamelin* (1876), *D'Estrées*
   (1886)) 6 x 138.6mm/21.3 M1870 (1 on forecastle on central pivot,
   4 sides, 1 aft on a platform), 1 x 4pdr (86.5mm/11) bronze.

*Hamelin* Lorient Dyd/Indret (engines designed by Victorin Sabattier).
On list 1.1865. K: 6.5.1864. L: 16.9.1866. Comm: 1.5.1867 (trials).
   C: 6.1867.
Decomm. 16.8.1867 after trials, in reserve 1868-9. In commission
   9.5.1870 to 1.4.1873 for the Pacific station and from 1.4.1876 to
   10.8.1878 for the South Atlantic station. Grounded in the Min River
   in China 16.7.1884 near the beginning of the Sino-French war,
   refloated. Struck 12.7.1887 at Toulon, in Corsica as a basing post for
   torpedo boats at Ajaccio 1887-1894 (converted at Toulon 1887-1888),
   same at Bonifacio 1894-1910, then probably BU.

*Limier* Brest Dyd/Brest Dyd (engines designed by Victorin Sabattier).
On list 1.1865. K: 7.3.1865. L: 21.12.1866. Comm: 5.5.1867 (trials),
   5.6.1867 (full).
Comm. for the *Escadre du Nord* 5.6.1867, decomm. at Cherbourg
   3.6.1870. In commission for trials 22.7.1870 and in full commission
   3.8.1870 to 31.1.1873 for service in the Levant and with the *Escadre
   d'évolutions*. In commission 1.12.1875 to 20.7.1878 for the Pacific
   station. Struck 28.10.1887, hulk at Lorient 1887-1888, mooring hulk
   1888-1893, coal and mooring hulk 1893-1914, floating barracks
   1920-1922, hulk 1922-1929, landing hulk 1929 to 7.1931. May have
   been BU during World War II.

*D'Estrées* Cherbourg Dyd/Indret (engines designed by Victorin Sabattier).

The 1st class aviso *Limier* during the mid-1880s, probably at Algiers. Note the
138.6mm gun on its central pivot mounting on the forecastle. *(NHHC from ONI
album of French warships, NH-74840)*

On list 1.1865. K: 15.11.1864. L: 24.1.1867. Comm: 27.5.1867 (trials).
   C: 8. 1867.
Decomm. 28.8.1867 and to reserve. In commission 7.12.1867 to
   24.11.1869 for the Antilles. To 1st category reserve 20.7.1870 and in
   full commission 26.7.1870 to 8.4.1871 for wartime service in the
   Atlantic and the North Sea. In commission 1.1.1873 to 18.4.1875 for
   the China station. Struck 2.4.1891.

*Lhermitte* Lorient Dyd/Indret (engines designed by Victorin Sabattier).
On list 1.1865. K: 19.10.1864. L: 4.6.1867. Comm: 5.7.1867 (trials),
   C: 10.1867.
Ran trials 3.9.1867, decomm. 11.10.1867 and to reserve. To full comm.
   at Lorient 16.7.1870, decomm. at Toulon 3.4.1871. In commission
   1.7.1873 for the Pacific station. Wrecked 29.6.1874 on the reefs of
   Wallis Is., Oceania, crew less two lost took refuge ashore and were rescued 7.1874. Administratively decomm. 29.8.1874. Struck 7.12.1874,
   natives of Wallis authorized 25.11.1875 to dismantle the wreck.

*Volta* Cherbourg Dyd/Indret (engines designed by Victorin Sabattier).
On list 1.1865. K: 15.11.1864. L: 4.6.1867. Comm: 28.8.1867 (trials).
   C: 11.1867.
At Réunion in the Indian Ocean 1.1869. Decomm. 1.1.1872. In commission 1.5.1874 to 3.9.1876 for the China station and the Pacific
   station. Reboilered 1882-83, then left Cherbourg 26.2.1883 to relieve
   *Kersaint* on the China station. Flagship of Vice Admiral Courbet during the Battle of Foochow on 23.8.1884. Again reboilered 1887 for a
   cruise to New Caledonia. Struck 16.5.1892, for disposal at Cherbourg
   1892-1893, BU there 1894.

---

**LINOIS.** *Aviso de 1ʳᵉ classe.* Small cruiser with an open battery and a
wooden hull. One funnel, three masts, barque rig. Designed by Daymard.

This ship was designed to receive the engines and boilers of *Chaptal* that
were recovered after that ship was wrecked 25 October 1862 near Vera
Cruz. *Chaptal* had just received new engines in 1861 which were of the
same type as those in *Algésiras*, although smaller. The first design for the
new ship were examined by the *Conseil des travaux* on 22 December 1863.
A new design by naval constructor Victor André Daymard was first examined on 10 January 1865 and approved with changes on 4 April 1865.
Minister of Marine Rigault de Genouilly on 17 February 1868 invited
Toulon to study the installation forward on *Linois* of a gun on a platform,
imitating what had been done on *D'Estrées* and *Volta* except with a
138.6mm vice a 164.7mm gun. *Linois* was completed with this gun on a
small forecastle.

*The characteristics are based on a devis dated 24.8.1877.*
**Dimensions & tons:** 60.80m wl, 62.07m pp (wl fwd to rudder) x 9.80m
   ext and wl. 1,169t disp. Draught: 4.26m mean, 4.86m aft. Men: 141.
**Machinery:** 220nhp (180 from 1867) and 720ihp designed at 70rpm and
   1.549kg/cm² boiler pressure. Trials (7.1875) 720ihp = 11.48kts at
   76.25rpm. 1 screw. 1 horizontal simple expansion engine with return
   connection rods and 2 cylinders of 1.20m diameter and 0.70m stroke.
   2 low rectangular tubular boilers. 197t coal. Range 2,400nm @ 10kts.
**Guns:**
(1868) 2 x 138.6mm/13.5 M1864 (1 on a forecastle, 1 aft), 4 x
   140mm/17.45 M1858-60 Nº 1 MLR (sides), 2 x 4pdr (86.5mm/11)
   bronze boat. By 1877 the two M1864 138.6mm guns had been
   replaced by M1870 guns.
(1882) 5 x 138.6mm/13.5 M1864, 1 x 4pdr (86.5mm/11) bronze mountain, 4 x 37mm.

*Linois* Toulon Dyd/F.C. Méditerranée, Marseille (engines designed by
   Dupuy de Lôme).
On list 1.1866. K: 18.7.1865. L: 31.10.1867. Comm: 11.6.1868 (trials).
   C: 2.1869.

Ran trials 28.12.1868, decomm. 1.2.1869. In commission 1.4.1870 to 22.6.1873 for the China and the Cochinchina stations. In commission 10.8.1877 to 1879 in the Mediterranean. Listed with 4 boilers in 1879, reboilered 1880-82 with 5 Imbert boilers made at Saint-Chamond of 1.80 kg/cm². To *Aviso de stations* 1.1880, and to *Croiseur de 3ᵉ classe* 1.1885. Struck 31.12.1890, for sale at Toulon 1890-1891.

---

*BOURAYNE* Class. *Avisos de 1ʳᵉ classe.* Small cruisers with open batteries, wooden hulls, straight bows, and raked pointed sterns. One funnel, three masts, barque rig. Designed by Pastoureau-Labesse and Dupuy de Lôme.

The design for these ships as a modified *Monge* was prepared by Jean-Baptiste Pastoureau-Labesse, approved on 13 August 1867, and modified by Dupuy de Lôme after Pastoureau-Labesse left the service for industry in August 1868. The design included the shift to a few large guns in cruising ships that was also evident in the larger *Infernet* and *Sané* classes of open-battery corvettes The 1867 budget included one ship at Cherbourg and one at Lorient. The 1868 budget added four more, one under the extraordary budget and three under the regular budget. The 1869 budget showed these six as *Kerguélen, Kersaint, Vaudreuil, Duchaffault,* and two unnamed at Brest, and added another four, of which one ended up being built at Brest and three by contract. The three contract ships were the first ones to be completed. The two ships assigned to Cherbourg were modified during construction and became a separate class, below.

The initial armament of the *Bourayne* class, asssigned by Minister of Marine Chasseloup-Laubat on 5 January 1867, was one 194mm gun on a rotating platform and probably two 164.7mm guns. In July 1868 Minister of Marine Rigault de Genouilly ordered the 194mm gun to be placed insteaed on an iron rotating mounting with a shield (*masque*). In March 1869 the armament of all 1ˢᵗ class avisos then under construction was set at one 194mm rifle and two 164.7mm/19.2 M1864 guns, but the armament of the *Bourayne* type was reset on 5 October 1869 to one 194mm gun, two 140mm Nᵒ 1, and one 138.7mm Nᵒ 2. The 194mm gun was changed to a 164.7mm after the 1870 trials of *Infernet* showed that it was too heavy for ships of this size and because it was also considered to be too long. In 1873 the armament of *Bourayne* was updated to one 164.7mm gun without a shield and five 138.6mm M1870 guns, four on the sides and one aft on a central pivot. The 164.7mm gun was on a pivot just forward of a tripod foremast that was set well aft of the bow to augment the gun's field of fire. This eventually became the configuration of the *Bourayne* type, although in May 1874 *Vaudreuil* still had one 194mm gun and three 138.6mm guns and her commander wanted to add two more 138.6mm guns. The two Cherbourg ships, listed separately below as the *Duchaffault* class, had the same hull as the *Bourayne* type but their guns were arranged differently and their machinery was slightly more powerful.

*The characteristics are based on a devis for* Bourayne *dated 8.3.1877.*

**Dimensions & tons:** 65.0m oa, 62.28m wl, 62.68m pp (wl fwd to rudder) x 10.42m ext and wl. 1,296.2t disp. Draught: 4.33m mean, 4.915m aft. Men: 154.

**Machinery:** 230nhp and 920ihp designed at 92rpm and 1.80kg/cm² boiler pressure (2.066 kg/cm² in *Ducouëdic*). Trials (*Bourayne,* 4.1870) 960ihp = 12.04kts at 92.1rpm and 1.80kg/cm² boiler pressure. 1 screw. 1 horizontal compound engine with return connecting rods and 3 cylinders of 1.10m diameter and 0.70m stroke. 2 low rectangular tubular boilers with steam dryers (superheaters). 186.7t coal. Range 2,950nm @ 10kts.

**Guns:**
(1869-71, *Bourayne, Segond, Dayot, Kersaint, Ducouëdic,* and *Vaudreuil*) 1 x 194mm/18 M1864 forward, 3 x 140mm/17.45 M1858-60 Nᵒ 1 MLR (2 x Nᵒ 1 and 1 x 138.7mm/16.5 M1858-60 Nᵒ 2 MLR in *Ducouëdic,* 3 x 12pdr (121mm/17) bronze in *Segond*).
(1871, *Bourayne,* also *Dayot* and *Kersaint*) 1 x 164.7mm forward,

The 1ˢᵗ class aviso *Bourayne* at Algiers, probably in the mid-1880s. The ship was designed to carry a 194mm gun forward, which required stepping the foremast well aft of the bow and reinforcing it with tripod legs. In this image the gun forward is a much smaller 138.6mm weapon, one of six carried. *(NHHC from ONI album of French warships, NH-74990)*

3 x 140mm/17.45 M1858-60 Nᵒ 1 MLR.
(1873-77, all) 1 x 164.7mm/19.2 M1864 forward, 5 x 138.6mm/21.3 M1870 (4 side and 1 aft). Several also had 1 x 4pdr (86.5mm/11) bronze mountain rifles. *Vaudreuil* was credited with 1 x 100mm in 1875 and *Ducouëdic* had 2 x 37mm Hotchkiss in 1878.
(1880-88, all) 6 x 138.6mm/21.3 M1870. *Kersaint* also had 1 x 4pdr (86.5mm/11) bronze mountain rifle and 2 x 37mm Hotchkiss in 1880, By 1889 most had received between 2 and 8 x 37mm revolving cannon, and from 1884 several added 1 x 65mm landing.

*Bourayne* Ernest Gouin, Nantes/Schneider, Creusot (engines designed by Mathieu).
On list 1.1868. K: 19.11.1867. L: 29.5.1869. Comm: 1.6.1869 (trials). C: 7.1870.
Commissioned 1.6.1869 at Nantes, arrived at Toulon 23.3.1871, decomm. there 4.4.1871. In commission 2.10.1871 to 16.10.1874 for the Cochinchina and the China stations. In commission 10.2.1877 to 1879 for the Indochina station. Struck 27.6.1889, hulk at Lorient 1889-1890, coal and mooring hulk 1890-1914, floating barracks 1920, hulk 1922-1929, landing hulk 1929, to the Domaines for sale 10.7.1929.

*Segond* Ernest Gouin, Nantes/Schneider, Creusot (engines designed by Mathieu).
On list 1.1868. K: 19.11.1867. L: 24.5.1869. Comm: 1.6.1869 (trials). C: beginning 1870.
Comm. at Nantes 1.6.1869, left Lorient 22.6.1870 for the Levant division, on the China station 1871-72, decomm. at Lorient 1.2.1873. In commission 5.1.1877 to 1879 for the Pacific station. Reboilered 1881-82. Struck 26.11.1894, school for engineers at Brest 1894-1896. BU 1896.

*Dayot* Ernest Gouin, Nantes/Schneider, Creusot (engines designed by Mathieu).
On list 1.1868. K: 19.11.1867. L: 15.4.1869. Comm: 24.6.1869 (trials). C: 4.1870.
Comm. at Nantes 24.6.1869, decomm. at Lorient 5.4.1871. Conversion to a mortar vessel reportedly considered 1870. In commission 27.8.1874 to 7.10.1877 for the Pacific station. Reboilered 1882-83. Blown ashore 22.2.1888 by a typhoon in the harbour at Tamatave and lost there. Struck 21.4.1888.

*Ducouëdic* Brest Dyd/Brest Dyd (engines designed by Victorin Sabattier).
On list 1.1868. K: 28.4.1867. L: 30.3.1869. Comm: 4.9.1870 (trials),
C: 12.1870.
To 3rd category reserve at Brest 16.12.1870, in commission at Brest
18.1.1871 to 5.4.1871, provisionally commissioned 22.6.1871 and
transported and guarded prisoners from the Paris Commune at Brest
from 19.6.1871 to 23.9.1871. In full commission 1.10.1871 to
1.11.1874 for the Indian Ocean and the East Africa stations.
Reboiled 1877-78 (2.25kg/cm$^2$), in commission 5.8.1878 to 1881
for the Indochina and Cochinchina stations. Struck 25.1.1889, mooring hulk at Rochefort 1889-1896, coal hulk 1896-1914, for sale 1920.

*Kersaint* Lorient Dyd/Indret (engines designed by Victorin Sabattier).
On list 1.1868. K: 24.1.1868. L: 7.9.1869. Comm: 17.8.1870 (trials).
C: 9.1870.
Left Cherbourg 4.1871 for Iceland fishery patrol duty, decomm. at
Cherbourg 29.12.1871. In commission 22.2.1872 to 31.10.1875 for
the Antilles and Newfoundland station. Struck 16.12.1884, for dispos-
al at Cherbourg 1884-1886. Last shown in the fleet list 1.1886. Sold
1903 at Cherbourg to BU.

*Vaudreuil* Lorient Dyd/Indret (engines designed by Victorin Sabattier).
On list 1.1868. K: 24.1.1868. L: 26.8.1870. Comm: 1.3.1871 (trials).
C: 3.1871.
In commission 1871 to 5.4.1874 for the Pacific station and from
20.1.1878 to 1880 for the South Atlantic station. Reboiled 1882.
Struck 27.6.1889, coal hulk at Lorient 1889-1898, coal depot and
mooring hulk 1898-1914. Moved to the left bank of the river for
dredging 30.12.1915, moved back 18.1.1916, condemned 25.7.1917
and BU by the sailors of the Directorate of the Port and German prisoners.

*Hugon* Brest Dyd/Indret (engines designed by Joseph Joëssel).
On list 1.1868. K: 10.11.1867. L: 6.8.1872. Comm: 1.4.1873 (trials).
C: 9.1873.
Manned for trials 11.6.1873. In reserve without category 12.9.1873,
commissioned again for trials 18.4.1874, decomm. and to 3rd category
reserve 20.5.1874. In commission 15.7.1877 to 1880 for the China,
the New Caledonia, and the Pacific stations. Reboiled 1880 and
1887. Struck 31.7.1895, for sale at Lorient 1895-1896.

*Beautemps-Beaupré* Brest Dyd/Indret (engines designed by Joseph
Joëssel).
On list 1.1868. K: 19.11.1867. L: 4.7.1872. Comm: 18.11.1874 (trials).
C: 3.1875.
Decomm. at Brest 1.3.1875 after trials. In commission 12.10.1877 to
1880 for the Pacific and the New Caledonia stations. Retired
11.12.1896, coal hulk in Corsica 1898-1909, for sale in Corsica 1909-
1910.

---

**DUCHAFFAULT Class.** *Avisos de 1re classe.* Small cruisers with open batteries, wooden hulls, clipper bows, and raked pointed sterns. One funnel,
three masts, barque rig. Designed by Pastoureau-Labesse, Dupuy de Lôme,
and Cousin.

These ships were built to the design by Jean-Baptiste Pastoureau-Labesse
and Dupuy de Lôme for the *Bourayne* class with additional modifications by
Victor Louis Cousin. On 5 January 1867 Minister of Marine Chasseloup-
Laubat ordered Cherbourg to begin work on a 1st class aviso and on 10
January 1867 he ordered Indret to submit a design for a 230nhp engine for
the ship. On 11 February 1867 Cherbourg forwarded a design for a modified *D'Estrées*. On 11 July 1867 Minister of Marine Rigault de Genouilly
ordered the start of construction of the hull and engine and assigned the
name *Kerguélen* to the ship. Similar directives were probably given for
*Duchaffaut,* the other ship of the *Bourayne* class assigned to Cherbourg. In

1872-73 these two ships were modified to bring them closer to the new
types of 1st class avisos then envisaged, with the result that while having the
same hull as the *Bourayne* class they had a short forecastle and poop added,
their battery was arranged differently with the guns at the ends on a forecastle and a poop and the guns on the sides located further forward than in the
original group in sponsons extending over the sides. Their engines were relocated within the hull and their cylinders were enlarged slightly, and they also
had a normally placed and rigged foremast instead of the tripod. A notice
dated 12 May 1887 corrected the spelling of the name *Duchaffaut,* and the
name was rendered as *Duchaffault* in fleet lists beginning in 1888.

The initial armament of the *Kerguélen* class, asssigned on 5 January
1867, was two 194mm guns on turret (barbette) mountings and probably
two 164.7mm. In November 1868 Minister of Marine Rigault de
Genouilly ordered the 194mm guns to be placed on rotating iron mountings with shields (*masques*). On 25 March 1869 the armament of all 1st
class avisos then under construction was set at one 194mm rifle and two
164.7mm rifles. In June 1871 a recommendation from Brest was approved
to fix the armament of the *Kerguélen* class at one 164.7mm/19.2 M1864
gun and five 138.6mm/13.5 M1864 guns including one aft on a pivot. The
arrangement of these guns was specified by Minister of Marine Pothuau on
25 April 1872 as one 164.7mm/19.2 M1864 amidships on a double pivot
capable of pivoting quickly to either side and five 138.6mm guns including two in half turrets or sponsons extending only slightly over the sides
and one aft. On 21 July 1873 a proposal from Cherbourg was approved to
change this to four 138.6mm/21.3 M1870 guns in half turrets, two
138.6mm/13.5 M1864 guns on central pivots, one on a forecastle and one
aft on a platform, and two 138.6mm M1864 guns on broadside mountings. On 30 October 1873 Minister of Marine Dompierre d'Hornoy
approved a request from Cherbourg to upgrade the two pivots to M1870
guns and omit the two broadside mountings because the ships could not
carry eight of the newer weapons.

*The characteristics are based on a devis for* Duchaffault *dated 28.10.1874.*
**Dimensions & tons:** 65.16m oa, 62.17m wl, 62.67m pp (wl fwd to rudder) x 10.42m ext, 10.39m wl. 1,289.3t disp. Draught: 4.257m mean,
4.807m aft. Men: 154.
**Machinery:** 250nhp and 1,000ihp designed at 92 rpm and 2.25kg/cm$^2$
boiler pressure. Trials (*Duchaffault*, 10.1874) 1,214ihp = 12.72kts at
101.25rpm and 2,351kg/cm$^2$ boiler pressure. 1 screw. 1 horizontal
compound (Woolf) engine with return connecting rods and 3 cylinders of 1.20m diameter and 0.70m stroke. 2 reinforced low rectangular
tubular boilers with steam dryers (superheaters). 223.6t coal. Range
3,700nm @ 10kts.
**Guns:**
(1874, both) 6 x 138.6mm/21.3 M1870 (1 forecastle, 1 on a platform
aft, and 4 in half turrets on the sides), 1 x 4pdr (86.5mm/11) bronze
mountain. (1878, *Kerguélen*) Add 2 x 37mm revolving cannon. (1884,
*Duchaffault*) Add 5 x 37mm revolving cannon.
(1889, *Duchaffault*) 6 x 138.6mm/21.3 M1870, 1 x 65mm landing,
6 x 37mm.

*Duchaffault* (*Duchaffaut*) Cherbourg Dyd/Indret (engines designed by
Camille Audenet).
On list 1.1868. K: 17.8.1868. L: 17.10.1872. Comm: 10.9.1874 (trials).
C: 10.1874.
On the Indochina station 1875-78. Reboiled 1888-89. Struck
17.11.1896, converting to a steam coal hulk at Toulon 1.1897, coal
hulk at Bizerte 1898-1907, sold and BU at Bizerte 1907.

*Kerguélen* Cherbourg Dyd/Indret (engines designed by Camille Audenet).
On list 1.1868. K: 17.8.1868. L: 19.9.1872. Comm: 1.11.1874 (trials).
C: 1.1875.
Machinery installed 22.4.1873 to 7.1.1874. Comm. 1.11.1874, to 3rd
category reserve 17.1.1875. Comm. 10.11.1878, left Cherbourg for
the China station 28.12.1878, returned 8.6.1881. In 1883 the forecas-

The 1st class aviso *Duchaffault* (erroneously spelled *Duchaffaut* before 1888), probably in the early or mid-1880s. She and *Kerguélen* were begun at Cherbourg to the plans of the *Bourayne* class but were modified in 1872-73 to add a small forecastle carrying a 138.6mm pivot gun, move the foremast forward to its normal position, and delete the tripod legs. *(NHHC from ONI album of French warships, NH-74851)*

tle was lengthened 2.5m. Struck 2.2.1894. school for stoking and repair hulk for the reserve at Lorient 1894, school for stoking and harbour flagship there 1898, barracks hulk 1905. Ordered delivered to Domaines 29.11.1912, for sale 1912-1913 with *Torpilleur Nº 232* and *Batterie Nº 8*. Sold 6.10.1903 at Lorient.

---

*HIRONDELLE. Aviso de 1re classe.* Small cruiser (ex yacht) with an open battery, a wooden hull, a clipper bow, and a large poop. One funnel, two masts (later three), schooner rig. Designed by Normand.

In 1868 Napoleon III decided to build on his personal account a yacht to be used at Biarritz where the Imperial family spend its Septembers. As was his custom, he wanted to use it to experiment with innovations in shipbuilding and marine machinery, and he gave the contract to Augustin Normand who had recently produced a very fast yacht, the *Grille*, for the King of Prussia. Normand designed her to the Emperor's specifications, which included a draught limited to 4m to enter the river at Biarritz, a speed of 16 knots, a two-day coal supply along with oil fuel, twin screws and high pressure machinery. Dupuy de Lôme was charged with oversight of the project, which he delegated to naval constructor Guesnet. The trials were a great success, the twin screws providing great manoeuvrability and the novel propulsion plant delivering a speed of 16.41 knots, making her the fastest yacht for the next decade. Unfortunately Napoleon III never got to enjoy her because of the international crisis that led to the fall of his Second Empire in August 1870.

*Hirondelle* was mobilized in August 1870 and at the end of the war was formally taken over by the Navy and added to the fleet list as a 1st class aviso. Her 450nhp exceeded the limits for that type, but she could comfortably carry only a light armament of one 138.6mm or two 100mm guns. The *Conseil des travaux* examined plans by naval constructor de Maupeou d'Ableiges for her conversion for naval use on 3 October and 19 December 1871. The machinery was converted to compound in 1874-75 by adding to each engine two small HP cylinders placed above the original cylinders which now functioned as LP cylinders.

*The characteristics are based on a devis dated 13.6.1876.*
**Dimensions & tons:** 79m oa, 76.65m wl, 76.30m pp (wl fwd to rudder)

x 9.25m ext and wl. 1,162.0t disp. Draught: 3.810m mean, 4.06m aft. Men: 114.
**Machinery:**
(Original): Trials (3.1870) 2,124.8ihp = 16.41kts at 119.65rpm and 4.190kg/cm² boiler pressure. 2 vertical engines, each with 2 cylinders of 1.00m diameter and stroke 0.60m. 6 Belleville boilers with horizontal tubes, designed pressure 5.00kg/cm².
(1874-75) Engines converted by addition of HP cylinders and boilers replaced. 450nhp (430 in 1878-83) and 1,720ihp designed at 130 to 135rpm and 4.00kg/cm² boiler pressure. Trials (5.1876) 1,916ihp = 15.573kts at 134.23rpm and 4.537kg/cm² boiler pressure. 2 screws. 2 vertical compound engines each composed of 4 cylinders, 2 large of 0.50m and 1.00m diameter and 0.60m stroke with 2 small superposed on them sharing the same piston rod. 4 special tubular cylindrical return flame boilers. 146.1t coal. Range 3,440nm @ 10kts.
**Guns:**
(as yacht) 2 x 4pdr (86.5mm/11) bronze M1858.
(10.1870) 2 x 138.6mm.
(1873-75) 1 x 138.6mm in the waist on a double pivot mounting that could traverse to sponsons on either side, 1 x 12pdr (121mm/17) bronze.
(1881) 2 x 100mm, 4 x 37mm revolving cannon.

*Hirondelle* Augustin Normand, Le Havre/C.A. de l'Océan (ex Mazeline), Le Havre (engines designed by Cody).
On list 1.1871. Ord: 20.1.1868 (contract). K: 1.7.1868. L: 15.5.1869. Comm: 10.8.1869 (trials), 12.7.1870 (full).
Trials 21-24.3.1870, to 1st category reserve 26.4.1870, in full commission 12.7.1870 to 19.7.1871. In commission for trials 15.2.1873 to 1.8.1873. After changes to the engines commissioned for trials 13.9.1875 and to full commission 26.5.1876 in the northern division of the *Escadre d'évolutions*, then in the Mediterranean. Reboilered 1890. To *Aviso* 1.1874, *Aviso de stations* 1.1880, and to *Croiseur de 3e classe* 1.1885. Condemned 11.12.1896, hulk for the orphanage and school for sons of fishermen at Martigues near Marseille 1896-1914. For sale at Toulon 1920-1927, BU 1928.

---

### 3rd class cruisers in the Programme of 1872

As part of its effort as directed by Minister of Marine Pothuau on 14 September 1871 to produce technical specifications for all of the ship types that were to enter into the composition of the fleet under the Programme of 1872, the *Conseil des travaux* on 5 January 1872 established specifications for 1st class avisos, which soon became 3rd class cruisers. The Council stated that 1st class avisos needed to be able to act as scouts for the fleet, as cruisers in European waters, and to serve on foreign stations. They thus needed high speed and good nautical qualities under sail, while their artillery could be relatively modest and a shallow draught was not necessary. It recommended a speed of 15 knots, armament of six 138.6mm, a wooden hull with iron deck beams and beam shelves, a large sail area, and a range of 3,000nm at 10 knots. The displacement was estimated at 1,450 tons. Minister Pothuau modified the armament to two 164.7mm guns on double pivots able to fire from sponsons on either side and four 138.6mm guns and transmitted the specifications to the ports on 16 February 1872 with an invitation to submit designs.

---

*RIGAULT DE GENOUILLY* Class. *Croiseurs de 3e classe.* Small cruisers with open batteries, wooden hulls with iron deck beams and beam shelves, and ram bows. One funnel, three masts, ship later barque rig. Designed by Bienaymé.

On 29 October 1872 the *Conseil des travaux* examined designs for 1st class avisos by six naval constructors and selected that of naval constructor Bienaymé subject to several modifications. The council considered

The 3rd class cruiser *Rigault de Genouilly* with her original boilers and funnel. She opened her career with a cruise to the Caribbean and North America in 1882-84, followed immediately by cruises to the Far East 1884-85 and the eastern Mediterranean in 1885-86 despite a boiler explosion at Keelung in November 1884. *(NHHC from ONI album of French warships, NH-74987)*

Bienaymé's modified design on 28 January 1873. Instead of mounting the two 164.7mm guns on double pivots Bienaymé put them on central pivots, and the 138.6mm gun on the forecastle was also put on a central pivot. Bienaymé's plans were approved by Minister of Marine Dompierre d'Hornoy on 20 June 1873. The designed armament of two 164.7mm/19.2 M1864 guns and four 138.6mm guns was changed to eight 138.6mm guns in 1873. The engines were of the same complex design as those of *Duquesne* and *Dupetit-Thouars* but smaller; they functioned well but were hard to maintain in the crowded engine room. The original six cylindrical boilers were of a type designed especially for these two ships.

After one boiler on *Rigault de Genouilly* exploded in November 1884 the operating pressure was reduced in 1885 to 3.70kg/cm². In *Rigault de Genouilly* the boilers were replaced in 1886-89 by 8 Belleville boilers operating at 12kg/cm² served by a larger funnel. In *Éclaireur* the original boilers were removed and repaired in 1888-9, the funnel casing being raised, and finally replaced in 1896 by 6 return-flame Belleville boilers operating at 4.25kg/cm².

*The characteristics are based on a devis for* Éclaireur *dated 4.10.1879.*
**Dimensions & tons:** 71.90m wl (+0.70m ram), 73.80m pp (wl fwd to rudder) x 10.80m ext and wl. 1,769t disp. Draught: 4.688m mean, 5,249m aft. Men: 195.
**Machinery:** 500nhp and 2,000ihp designed at 100rpm and 4.133kg/cm² boiler pressure. Trials (*Éclaireur*, 5.1879) 2,436.6ihp = 15.00kts at 103.475rpm and 4.425kg/cm² boiler pressure. 1 screw. 1 horizontal compound engine composed of 3 groups of 2 cylinders with return connecting rods, 1 large and 1 small, of 0.90m and 1.36m diameter

and 0.60m stroke. Each group drove one of three cranks on the shaft spaced 120° apart. 6 cylindrical boilers. 194t coal. Range 3,130nm @ 10kts.
**Guns:**
(1879) 8 x 138.6mm/21.3 M1870 (1 on the forecastle offset slightly to starboard to clear the rigging, 6 x 138.6mm sides, 1 x 138.6mm on poop), 2 x 37mm Hotchkiss, 2 x 4pdr (86.5mm/11) bronze boat.
(1883-1897) *Rigault de Genouilly* received 3 more 37mm in 1883 and three more in 1886 for a total of eight, while *Éclaireur* got one more in 1883 for a total of four and two more by 1897. By 1897 both ships also had 1x 65mm.

***Rigault de Genouilly*** Brest Dyd/Indret (engines designed by Joëssel).
On list 1.1874. K: 31.7.1873. L: 19.9.1876. Comm: 15.6.1878 (trials). C: 11.1878.
Budget 1875. To 3rd category reserve at Brest after trials 8.11.1878, decomm. 1.12.1878. In full commission 10.3.1882 for service in the Antilles. Renamed *Amiral Rigault de Genouilly* 25.3.1895. Struck 3.2.1899, renamed *Rumengol* 1899, coal hulk at Brest 1899-1914, condemned as such 16.6.1914, then at Landévennec where in 1918 she served as a storage depot for the U.S. Navy's base at Brest. Reported sold 14.6.1919, although still listed for sale at Brest 1920-1922.

***Éclaireur*** Toulon Dyd/Indret (engines designed by Joëssel).
On list 1.1874 (unnamed). K: 5.5.1874. L: 30.8.1877. Comm: 15.11.1878 (trials). C: 7.1879.
Budget 1875. To 2nd category reserve 29.7.1879. In full commission 15.7.1881 to replace *Dayot* on the Pacific station. Struck 4.11.1902. To the Domaines 29.1.1903 for sale, sold at Lorient 22.3.1904 to M. Guilhaumon to BU.

*N* (Unnamed) Cherbourg Dyd
Budget 1876. To have been carried to 15% in 1876 but not in the 1877 budget.

# Chapter Four

# Avisos, Special Ships, and Gunboats, 1859-1882

## I. AVISOS

### (A) Screw 2nd Class Avisos (*Avisos de 2e classe*).

To *Avisos* in the 1.1874 fleet list, *Avisos de stations* 1.1880, *Avisos de 1re classe* 1.1885, *Avisos de station de 1re classe* 1.1891, and *Avisos de 1re classe* 1.1892.

#### Precursors, 1855-1858

In 1855 a *Commission supérieure* formed by Minister of Marine Admiral of France Ferdinand Alphonse Hamelin on 27 July 1855 to propose a new organisation of the fleet included in it 30 1st class steam corvettes of the *Phlégéton* type, 30 1st class avisos similar to *Chaptal*, and 30 2nd class avisos similar to Normand's highly successful screw postal packet *Napoléon* (acquired by the navy in 1850 as the second-class aviso *Corse*). On 16 October 1855 the *Conseil des travaux* developed specifications for the three types of cruising ships including the new 2nd class avisos. It recommended building some with wood hulls for use overseas and some with iron hulls for use near French ports. It provided specifications for the wooden hulled ships, increasing the length and displacement somewhat compared to *Corse*. The old 120nhp engines of *Corse* now provided only 9 knots, new 120nhp engines would provide 10 knots, but this was still too slow for operations with the fleet and the Council recommended 150nhp for 11.80 knots (possibly over 13 knots with steam and sail). For the iron-hulled 2nd class avisos no new specifications were necessary and it would suffice to copy *Corse*. Between 1855 and 1857 four very similar pairs of wooden-hulled 150nhp 2nd class avisos were ordered, *Surcouf* and *D'Entrecasteaux* at Rochefort to plans by naval constructor Louis François Octave Vésigné, *Prégent* and *Renaudin* from Lucien Arman's yard at Bordeaux to plans by naval constructor Marie Pierre Henri Félix Carlet, *Lamotte-Picquet* and *Coëtlogon* at Cherbourg to revised plans by Vésigné that were approved by the *Conseil des travaux* on 16 March 1858, and *D'Estaing* and *Latouche-Tréville* at Toulon to plans by naval constructor Louis Dutard, who was told to follow Vésigné's revised plans.

---

#### Repeat *LAMOTTE-PICQUET* Class. *Avisos de 2e classe.* 150nhp screw avisos with wooden hulls and clipper bows. One funnel, three masts, barque rig. Designed by Vésigné.

In 1859-1860 seven more ships were ordered from private shipbuilders to Vésigné's plans for *Lamotte-Picquet* and *Coëtlogon*. The construction of the first five of these was ordered by Minister of Marine Hamelin on 28 October 1859 and they were named on 26 December 1859. They were ordered from four different shipbuilders by contracts signed on 18 November 1859 (25 November 1859 for *Curieux*). The engines of *Diamant, Lutin, Lynx,* and *Tancrède* were ordered from the Forges et Chantiers de la Méditerranée (FCM) by a contract approved on 18 May 1860 while those of *Curieux* were ordered from Mazeline by a contract signed on 27 April 1860. The last two ships, *Adonis* and *Amphion*, were ordered from Lucien Arman's yard in Corsica by a contract signed on 16 November 1860 and approved on 27 November 1860 after the navy tried unsuccessfully to turn down the petition for the order from Arman, who was a deputy in the *Corps legislative*, on the grounds that the Navy lacked personnel to supervise work in private yards, particularly in Corsica.

The engines for these two ships were ordered from FCM by a contract signed on 23 November 1860. Dimensions varied slightly, and those given here are representative of the class. This type was described as a little longer than *Latouche-Tréville* but with a little less displacement.

The hulls of *Lynx* and *Tancrède* were badly built (*Tancrède* suffering from green wood and tropical humidity) and the boilers of *Lynx* were in bad condition, leading to their rapid demise, while the early end of *Lutin* may have been caused by nearly continuous overseas service (from February 1862 to October 1867 except for the first half of 1865). The engines of *Lutin* were reused in *Boursaint* (1872), those of *Tancrède* went into *D'Entrecasteaux* (1856), and those of *Lynx* went into *Bruat* (1867).

**Dimensions & tons:** 56.50m deck, 54.55m wl x 8.50m ext. 672t disp. Draught: 2.62m fwd, 3.82m aft. Men: 65.

**Machinery:**

(all but *Curieux*): 150nhp (135 from 1867), 400ihp designed. Trials (*Adonis*) 546ihp = 11.3kts at 107rpm and 2.69kg/cm$^2$ boiler pressure, (*Diamant*) 360ihp = 9.8kts at 90rpm. 1 screw. 1 horizontal simple expansion engine with return connecting rods and 2 cylinders of 0.93m diameter and 0.54m stroke. 2 low rectangular tubular boilers. 100t coal. Range 1,700nm @ 10kts.

(*Curieux*): 150nhp (135 from 1867). Trials 448ihp = 11.3kts at 97rpm and 1.76kg/cm$^2$. 1 screw. 1 horizontal simple expansion engine with 2 cylinders of 0.95m diameter and 0.50m stroke. 2 low rectangular tubular boilers. 100t coal.

**Guns:**

(1861-62) 2 x 16cm shell (*canons-obusiers*). All but *Adonis* and *Amphion* completed thus.

(1863-65) 4 x 12pdr (121mm/17) bronze field MLR. *Adonis* and *Amphion* as completed, *Lutin* and *Lynx* rearmed.

(1866, *Diamant, Amphion*) 1 x 164.7mm M1858-60 MLR, 2 x 12pdr (121mm/17) bronze MLR.

(1867 *Diamant, Amphion*) 2 x 138.6mm No 1 MLR, 2 x 12pdr (121mm/17) bronze field MLR.

(1872, *Adonis, Curieux*) 4 x 138.6mm No 2 MLR.

(1874, *Adonis*) 1 x 138.6mm, 1 x 12pdr (121mm/17) bronze.

(1875, *Diamant*) 1 x 164.7mm pivot, 1 x 138.6mm pivot on deck forward.

*Curieux* Émile Cardon, Honfleur/Mazeline, Le Havre.
On list 1.1860. Ord: 28.10.1859. K: c6.1860. L: 13.12.1860. Comm: 13.2.1861 (trials). C: 6.1861.
At Réunion in the Indian Ocean 11.1863, returned to Brest from the Antilles and Newfoundland 8.10.1869. Struck 14.2.1879 at Brest. BU 1879.

*Diamant* Lucien Arman, Bordeaux/F.C. Méditerranée, Marseille.
On list 1.1860. Ord: 28.10.1859. K: 15.12.1859. L: 8.5.1861. Comm: 1.8.1861 (trials). C: 15.10.1861.
Left Lorient for the Pacific 23.12.1861. Struck 7.5.1878, for disposal at Rochefort 1878-1879. BU 1879.

*Lutin* Lucien Arman, Bordeaux/F.C. Méditerranée, Marseille.
On list 1.1860. Ord: 28.10.1859. K: 15.12.1859. L: 25.4.1861. Comm: 1.8.1861 (trials), 3.10.1861 (full).
To Rochefort 6.1861 for completion by Louis-Marc Willotte.

Full commission 3.10.1861, left Rochefort 16.1.1862 for Montevideo. Returned to Rochefort 30.10.1867. Struck 13.2.1868. BU begun 5.1868, then suspended and retained as hulk not on the fleet list. Traded names 27.2.1871 with the former paddle aviso *Abeille* (1858) which was the hulk at the torpedo school at Boyardville, school closed 2.4.1871 and both hulks BU 3-5.1871.

*Lynx* Moulinié & Labat, Bordeaux/F.C. Méditerranée, Marseille.
On list 1.1860. Ord: 28.10.1859. K: 1.12.1859. L: 10.5.1861.
  Comm: 16.10.1861 (trials). C: 12.3.1862.
Towed to Rochefort 5.1861 for completion. Left Rochefort for the Indian Ocean 27.9.1862, returned and decommissioned 1.12.1865. Struck 21.6.1866 at Rochefort. BU completed 9.8.1866.

*Tancrède* Bichon frères, Bordeaux-Lormont/F.C. Méditerranée, Marseille.
On list 1.1860. Ord: 28.10.1859. K: 1.12.1859. L: 25.5.1861.
  Comm: 17.10.1861 (trials). C: 5.1862.
Towed from Bordeaux to Rochefort 13.12.1861 by the tug (service craft) *Boyard*. To the China station 1862, returned to Bordeaux 8.10.1865. Struck 21.6.1866 at Rochefort. BU 11.1866 to 1.1867.

*Adonis* Lucien Arman, Ajaccio/F.C. Méditerranée, Marseille.
On list 1.1861. Ord: 27.11.1860 (contract). K: 1860. L: 15.1.1863.
  Comm: 18.7.1863 (trials). C: 10.1863.
To Vera Cruz 15.10.1863. Transported and guarded prisoners from the Paris Commune at Brest 1.6.1871 to 20.2.1872. Struck 27.3.1883, embarkation hulk at Rochefort 1883-1893, mooring hulk 1893-1907, sold 1907 to BU.

*Amphion* Lucien Arman, Ajaccio/F.C. Méditerranée, Marseille.
On list 1.1861. Ord: 27.11.1860 (contract). K: 1860. L: 9.5.1863.
  Comm: 12.10.1863 (trials). C: 10.1863.
To Mexico 1863. Wrecked 21.4.1866 at Vera Cruz. Struck 11.6.1866.

———

*CUVIER. Aviso de 2e classe.* 120nhp screw aviso with an iron hull and a clipper bow. One funnel, two masts, schooner-brig rig (later schooner). Designed by Mangin.

On 16 October 1855 the *Conseil des travaux* recommended building some screw 2nd class avisos with iron hulls for use near French ports in addition to those with wood hulls for use overseas. In 1859 the navy had five of these 120nhp iron screw avisos, *Passe-Partout* (1846), *Salamandre* (1847), *Pélican* (1847), *Ariel* (1848), and *Faon* (acquired 1855). *Cuvier*, the first one added to this group after the 1855 recommendation, was designed by naval constructor Amédée Paul Théodore Mangin as a modified version of *Pélican*, which had been ordered in 1845 as a platform for conducting experiments with different screw propellers. *Pélican* tested over 100 different screw propellers before being assigned to general service. *Cuvier* was ordered along with seven paddle avisos (the *Espadon*, *Protée*, and *Phaéton* classes) from Ernest Gouin, who after 1856 operated the former Guibert yard at Nantes, by a contract approved on 12 September 1859. All eight vessels in this contract had iron hulls and most were used mainly for colonial service. Their names were assigned on 11 November 1859.

**Dimensions & tons:** 41.50m wl x 7.02m ext (above wl), 6.82m wl.
  341t disp. Draught: 2.56m fwd, 3.16m aft. Men: 75.
**Machinery:** 120nhp (100 from 1867) and 400ihp designed at 89rpm and 1.80kg/cm² boiler pressure. Trials (6.1872) 364.9ihp = 10.82kts at 88.71rpm and 1.796kg/cm² boiler pressure.1 screw. 1 horizontal sim-ple expansion trunk engine with two cylinders of 1.00m diameter and 0.50m stroke. 1 high rectangular tubular boiler. 61.0t coal.
**Guns:** (1871) 2 x 4pdr (86.5mm/11) bronze mountain MLR on boat carriages.

*Cuvier* Ernest Gouin, Nantes/Indret.
On list 1.1860. Ord: 1.7.1859. K: 10.1859. L: 15.9.1860.

Comm: 21.4.1861 (trials). C: 4.1861.
Cruised to the west coast of Africa 1862-63 and Réunion and Madagascar 1863-66. *Bâtiment de flottille* 1.1869, *Aviso de flottille* 1.1874, *Aviso de 2e classe* 1.1885, *Aviso de station de 2e classe* 1.1891, *Aviso de 2e classe* 1.1892. Struck 5.11.1892. Hull damaged 3.12.1892 in a test explosion of an 80kg charge of nitrocellulose. For sale at Brest 1892-1893.

———

*ACTIF. Aviso de 2e classe.* 120nhp screw aviso with an iron hull and a clipper bow. Two funnels (later one), two masts, schooner-brig rig. Designed by John Scott & Co.

On 17 February 1860 Minister of Marine Hamelin approved the proposal of the *Conseil des travaux* to order for trial purposes from John Scott & Co. of Greenock an iron ship of their design equipped with a high pressure steam engine similar to the one that Scott had placed in the British vessel *Thetis* and which had been recommended by naval constructor Armand Forquenot for its fuel economy. The engine had six cylinders, of which two operated at high pressure and four at low pressure. The ship was ordered from Scott by a contract signed on 3 July 1860. The original two tubular boilers with superheaters were replaced by three Belleville boilers with horizontal tubes in the 1860s, a single special type tubular boiler designed and built by Joseph Joëssel at Indret in July 1878, and four Belleville boilers in July 1888.

**Dimensions & tons:** 41.48m deck, 40.84m wl x 6.80m ext and wl.
  391t disp. Draught: 2.80m fwd, 3.60m aft. Men: 75.
**Machinery:** 120nhp (100 from 1867) and 400ihp designed at 7.00kg/cm² boiler pressure. Trials (8.6.1870) 419.2ihp = 10.405kts at 97.00rpm and 7.41kg/cm² boiler pressure. 1 screw. 1 vertical com-pound (Woolf) engine composed of 6 cylinders, 2 small high pressure and 4 large low pressure of 0.31m and 0.61m diameter respectively and 0.61m stroke. The high pressure cylinders were vertical and the low pressure inclined to either side in two groups of three, each group operating a single crank arm. See text for boilers. 53.0t coal. Range 1,380nm @ 10kts.
**Guns:** (1867 and 1880) 2 x 4pdr (86.5mm/11) bronze mountain MLR on boat carriages.

*Actif* Scott, Greenock (engines by builder).
On list 1.1861. Ord: 17.2.1860. K: summer 1860. L: autumn 1861.
  Comm: 20.1.1862 (trials). C: 1.1862.
Operated on the French coasts and in the Mediterranean. *Bâtiment de flottille* 1.1869, *Aviso de flottille* 1.1874, *Aviso de 2e classe* 1.1885, *Aviso*

The 2nd class aviso *Actif* photographed on 18 October (8bre) 1885 during her assignment as station ship at Algiers from 1885 to 1892. *(NHHC from ONI album of French warships, NH-74804)*

*de station de 2ᵉ classe* 1.1891, *Aviso de 2ᵉ classe* 1.1892. Struck 7.5.1892 at Rochefort and converted to a 400ihp tug (service craft). Still at Rochefort 2.8.1919, not listed in the 1920 fleet list.

---

**BOUVET (i) Class.** *Avisos de 2ᵉ classe.* 150nhp screw avisos with wooden hulls, iron deck beams and beam shelves, and clipper bows. One funnel, three masts, barque rig. Designed by Vésigné with modifications by de Lacelle and Robiou de Lavrignais.

These three ships were built to the plans of naval constructor Vésigné for *Lamotte-Picquet* as modified by naval constructors Eugène Gaston de Lacelle and Alexandre Auguste Gustave Robiou de Lavrignais. The latter signed the plans for *Bouvet* and *Guichen*, neither constructor is mentioned in connection with *Bruat*. The engines of *Bruat* came from the *Lynx* of 1861. *Bouvet* carried the armament originally intended for the class. She fought a famous but inconclusive action with the Prussian gunboat *Meteor* off Havana on 9 November 1870 in which her machinery was disabled by a hit on a superheater in the base of her funnel, she retired under sail while *Meteor*'s crew tried to clear the fallen rigging that had fouled her screw.

*The characteristics are based on a devis for* Bruat *dated 26.5.1877.*
**Dimensions & tons:** 62.15m oa, 54.34m wl, 55.86m pp (wl fwd to rudder) x 8.56m ext (above wl), 8.40m wl. 761.3t disp. Draught: 3.536m mean, 3.906m aft. Men: 88.
**Machinery:**
(*Bouvet* and *Guichen*): 150nhp. Trials (*Bouvet*) 634ihp = 12.7kts at 100 rpm; (*Guichen*) 10.5kts at 94.1rpm. 1 screw. 1 compound engine with return connecting rods and 3 cylinders of 1.10m diameter and 0.5m stroke. 2 boilers with steam dryers (superheaters). 103t coal. Range 1,400nm @ 10kts.
(*Bruat*, taken from *Lynx*) 150nhp (135 from 1867) and 540ihp designed at 109rpm and 1.80kg/cm² boiler pressure. Trials (5.1877) 557.6ihp = 10.766kts at 108.2rpm and 1.912kg/cm² boiler pressure. 1 screw. 1 horizontal simple expansion engine with return connecting rods and 2 cylinders of 0.932m diameter and 0.54m stroke. 2 low rectangular tubular boilers. 101.2t coal. Range 1,400 or 2,000nm @ 10kts.
**Guns:**
(1866-70, *Bouvet*) 1 x 164.7mm M1858-60 pivot aft, 2 x 12pdr (121mm/17) bronze MLR.
(1867-75, *Guichen*) 1 x 164.7mm M1860 pivot, 1 x 138.6mm/13.5 M1864 (1867) pivot forward.
(1869-75, *Bruat*) 2 x 138.6mm, 2 x 12pdr (121mm/17) bronze.
(1875, *Bruat*) 3 x 138.6mm (1 on deck forward, 2 on sides aft of mainmast), 1 x 100mm on deck aft.
(1880, *Guichen*) 2 x 138.6mm, 1 x 100mm pivot.
(1882, *Bruat* and 1885, *Guichen*) 2 x 138.6mm, 2x 100mm.

**Bouvet** Rochefort Dyd/Indret (engines designed by Victorin Sabattier).
On list 1.1864. K: 2.10.1863. L: 24.5.1865. Comm: 18.6.1866 (trials). C: 6.1866.
Wrecked 17.9.1871 in a gale on the south coast of Haiti, crew saved. Struck 4.12.1871.

**Guichen** Rochefort Dyd/Indret (engines designed by Victorin Sabattier).
On list 1.1864. K: 2.10.1863. L: 19.10.1865. Comm: 6.11.1866 (trials). C: 12.1866.
Machinery installed 15.3.1866 to 15.8.1866. Left Lorient for Tahiti 22.1.1867. Struck 19.11.1888, hulk at Toulon 1888-1889, coal hulk 1889-1901, renamed *Mineur* 1895, for sale at Toulon 1901-1902.

**Bruat** Rochefort Dyd/F.C. Méditerranée, Marseille (engines designed by Dupuy de Lôme).
On list 1.1867. K: 1.9.1866. L: 15.10.1867. Comm: 6.9.1869 (trials). C: 10.1869.
At Alexandria, Egypt, 11.1869, cruised in the Indian Ocean and Pacific

1871-74. Struck 31.5.1886, torpedo calibration hulk at Rochefort 1886-1912, mooring hulk 1912-1914, for sale 1920.

---

**RENARD.** *Aviso de 2ᵉ classe.* 150nhp screw aviso with a wooden and iron hull built on Arman's mixed hull system and with Béléguic's experimental lines and long inverted (ram-shaped) bow. One funnel, three masts, barquentine rig. Designed by Béléguic.

This experimental aviso was designed by Capitaine de frégate Eugène Corentin Béléguic in accordance with hydrodynamic theories that he had developed. He wanted a ship that could maintain high speed even into heavy seas without taking water over the bow, that could carry a large long-range gun on the bow, and that could carry a large coal supply for extended operations. His ship had a spectacular 9m long *étrave inversée* or inverted (ram shaped) bow and the rest of the hull had pronounced concave sides above the waterline (sloping inward and then back out). The bow resembled a ram but was not reinforced for ramming, its purpose being to improve speed and seakeeping qualities. Many later French ships had ram-shaped bows that were not reinforced for ramming and in a few cases *Renard* was cited specifically as the inspiration. Arman's mixed wood and iron hull structure consisted of wooden hull planking on wooden frames that were spaced more widely than normal, with iron and wood reinforcements including diagonal iron straps on the side planking, iron deck beams, iron beam shelves, and an iron keelson. (Other Navy ships built on Arman's system were the aviso *Surcouf* and the transport *Dordogne*.) The lines plans for *Renard* were signed by Arman, the builder, on 3 October 1863 and accepted 'for trial purposes' by the ministry on 7 January 1864. Additional plans were signed by Arman on 20 October 1864 and accepted on 10 November 1864. In 1885 *Renard* was lost with all hands in high winds in the Red Sea, and the reduced stability associated with inward-sloping hull sides may have been a factor.

*The characteristics are based on a devis dated 23.4.1867.*
**Dimensions & tons:** 71.15m wl (+1.80m ram), 70.50m pp (wl fwd to rudder), 60.65m on deck x 8.40m ext (below wl), 7.80m wl. 814t disp. Draught: 3,605m mean, 4.48m aft. Men: 92.
**Machinery:** 150nhp (135 from 1867) and 540ihp designed at 98rpm and 1.80kg/cm² boiler pressure. Trials (3.1873) 548ihp = 11.49kts at 95.0rpm. 1 screw. 1 horizontal simple expansion engine with return connecting rods and 2 cylinders of 0.95m diameter and 0.50m stroke. 2 low rectangular tubular boilers. 146.4t coal. Range 2,770nm @ 10kts.
**Guns:** (1867) 4 x 12pdr (121mm/17) bronze field on the sides, one pair just forward of the funnel and one forward of the mizzen mast. (1884) Add 2 x 37mm.

**Renard** C.A. de l'Océan (Arman), Bordeaux-Bacalan/C.A. de l'Océan (ex Mazeline), Le Havre.
On list 1.1865. Ord: 12.2.1864 (contract). K: 20.4.1864. L: 19.1.1866. Comm: 1.2.1866 (trials). C: 25.7.1866.
Moved to Rochefort 1.1866 for fitting out. Operated with the division of armoured ships in the North 1866-67 and with the *Escadre d'évolutions* in the Mediterranean 1867-69. Reboilered 1872-73. Major repairs 1875-76. Reboilered 1883-84. Sent to Obock 1.1885 as station ship. Lost with all hands 3.6.1885 in a typhoon while transiting from Obock to Aden. Struck 2.10.1885.

---

**BRUIX.** *Aviso de 2ᵉ classe.* 150nhp screw aviso with a wooden hull and a clipper bow. One funnel, three masts. Designed by Brassens.

This second experimental aviso was designed by Raymond Brassens, who in 1862 patented a scheme for building ships with two screws, two sternposts, and three keels. He first used this structure in the diminutive *Souris*, which the Emperor bought as a yacht in 1862 and transferred to the Navy as a *bâtiment de flottille* (q.v.) in 1865. Brassens then designed *Bruix* with two screws and two side keels in addition to the usual keel on the centre line as a larger-scale implementation of his ideas. She was too big for Brassens to build in his own yard so he had her built at Arman's yard. The work was supervised by naval constructor Louis Auguste Silvestre du Perron, who also supervised the construction of the experimental *Renard*, above. *Bruix* was struck in 1876 after relatively short service and converted into a steam coal lighter, retaining her engines.

*The characteristics are based on a devis dated 3.1868.*

**Dimensions & tons:** 56.09m pp x 9.14m wl. 759t disp. Draught: 2.95m mean, 3.18m aft.

**Machinery:** 150nhp and 540ihp designed at 105rpm. Trials (27.12.1867) 482ihp = 9.29kts at 2.48kg/cm$^2$ boiler pressure. 2 screws. 2 vertical simple expansion engines each with 2 cylinders of 0.70m diameter and 1.0m stroke. 4 boilers. 143t coal. Range 1,340 miles at maximum speed.

**Guns:** (1868) 1 x 164.7mm M1860 pivot, 2 x 138.6mm/13.5 M1864 (1867) including one on a pivot.

*Bruix* C.A. de l'Océan (Arman), Bordeaux-Bacalan/Indret (engines designed by Victorin Sabattier).
On list 1.1866. K: 15.4.1865. L: 25.3.1867. Comm: 14.4.1867 (trials). C: 14.3.1868.
Left Lorient 15.3.1868 for Brazil and the Plata. Struck 7.12.1876, hulk at Rochefort 1876-1877, steam coal hulk (service craft) 1877-1880, for disposal 1880-1882.

───────

**BOURSAINT.** *Aviso de 2e classe.* 150nhp screw aviso with a wooden hull and a ram bow. One funnel, three masts, barque rig (later barquentine). Designed by Vésigné and Marchegay.

Initially designed by naval constructor Vésigné (who left the service in 1866) as a modified *Bruat* and then by naval constructor Edmond François Émile Marchegay, she was altered during her long construction period as were the last three 1st class avisos of the contemporary *Bourayne* class. The alterations of *Boursaint* included a forecastle and a ram bow. Her engines came from *Lutin* (1861).

*The characteristics are based on a devis dated 8.5.1877.*

**Dimensions & tons:** 63.70m oa, 59.72m wl, 61.48m pp (wl fwd to rudder) x 8.54m ext (above wl), 8.40m wl. 763.6t disp. Draught: 3.338m mean, 3.858m aft. Men: 88.

**Machinery:** (taken from *Lutin*) 150nhp (135 from 1867, re-rated 150 in 1875) and 600ihp designed at 92rpm and 2.311kg/cm$^2$ boiler pressure. Trials (2.1874) 679.5ihp = 11.516kts at 97.6rpm and 2.180kg/cm$^2$ boiler pressure. 1 screw. 1 horizontal compound engine with return connecting rods and 3 cylinders of 1.10m diameter and 0.50m stroke. 2 low rectangular tubular boilers. 104.4t coal. Range 2,040nm @ 10kts.

**Guns:**
(1872) 1 x 164.7mm/19.2 M1864 (pivot amidships), 2 x 138.6mm/13.5 M1864 (1867) (one on a pivot on the forecastle, one on the stern with ports on both sides).
(1882) 1 x 138.6mm/21.3 M1870 (on deck amidships), 2 x 100mm/26.5 M1875 (on the forecastle and the stern), 4 x 37mm revolving cannon.

*Boursaint* Rochefort Dyd/Indret (engines designed by Victorin Sabattier).
On list 1.1869. K: 3.1868. L: 20.8.1872. Comm: 1.12.1873 (trials). C: 7.1874.
Decomm. 1.3.1874 after trials, in commission 19.4.1877 to 7.7.1878 for service in the *Escadre d'évolutions*. Reboilered 1881-82. Struck 7.5.1892.

───────

## 2nd class avisos in the Programme of 1872

As part of its effort as directed by Minister of Marine Pothuau on 14 September 1871 to produce technical specifications for all of the ship types that were to enter into the composition of the fleet under the Programme of 1872, the *Conseil des travaux* on 5 January 1872 established specifications for 2nd class avisos. These included a speed of 12 knots, draught aft of 3.60m, an armament of one 164.7mm M1864 gun and two 138.6mm guns, sizeable sail area, a crew of 90 men, and coal for a range of 3,000nm at 9 knots. The estimated displacement was 800 tons and the bow was to be sloped back in its upper part. Two types of hull structures were to be considered, the now usual wooden hull with iron deck beams and beam shelves and one favoured by Normand with crossed diagonal wood hull planking on wood frames and with iron deck beams but no beam shelves. This system of *bordages croisés* was introduced in Britain in 1830 by Oliver Lang and was first used by Normand in 1857 in his highly successful yacht for the king of Prussia, *Grille*.

The Council asked the Minister to use the term *Canonnières de station* (station gunboats) for these rather than the term *Avisos de 2e classe* because the Council's new specifications merged two types, 2nd class avisos and gunboats (*canonnières*). It intended for the new ships both to operate militarily near coasts and in large rivers and to keep the seas on overseas stations in company with 1st class avisos. For inshore work the ships needed a larger gun like the 164.7mm M1864 along with 138.6mm guns and a draught (3.50m to 3.60m maximum) that was relatively restrained but was still deep enough for navigation under sail. In return a reduction in speed to about 12 knots had to be accepted. Minister Pothuau transmitted these specifications to the ports on 16 February 1872 with some modifications and asked for designs. He set the armament at one 164.7mm gun amidships on a central pivot with wide arcs of fire on either side and two 138.6mm guns, one on the forecastle and one aft.

Minister Pothuau rejected the Council's vision of a single type of *canonnières de station* for overseas use by retaining the classification of *Avisos de 2e classe*. This and the eventual replacement of 164.7mm guns with 138.6mm guns on the 2nd class avisos meant that French overseas stations would need both small avisos and new gunboats of the *Crocodile* and later types. The 2nd class avisos soon became simply *avisos* when the 1st class avisos were promoted to 3rd class cruisers in 1874.

───────

**BOUVET** (ii) Class. *Avisos de 2e classe,* to *Avisos* (1874). 175nhp screw avisos with wooden hulls, iron deck beams and beam shelves, and ram bows. One funnel, three masts, barque rig. Designed by Marchegay.

On 29 October 1872 the *Conseil des travaux* examined designs for 2nd class avisos by five naval constructors and selected that of naval constructor Edmond François Émile Marchegay with some changes, including the substitution of a M1864 164.7mm gun for the M1860 gun in his design. Marchegay feared that the 138.6mm gun on the short forecastle would fatigue the ship's structure so he also gave it a *poste de mer* where it could be secured for sea on the centreline forward of the funnel with ports on both sides. The Council argued that this type of ship was destined to operate on coasts and in large rivers and would not have as much need for axial fire forward as 1st class avisos, and it suggested permanently mounting the forward 138.6mm in Marchegay's *poste de mer* and placing a lighter gun on the forecastle. Marchegay's plans were used for a pair of 2nd class avisos begun at Rochefort at the end of 1872. Their final designed armament was one 164.7mm/19.2 M1864 gun, two 138.6mm/21.3 M1870 guns, and one 100mm gun, but the 164.7mm gun was replaced by a 138.6mm gun before completion. The engines were probably built at Indret.

*The characteristics are based on a devis for* Parseval *dated 27.12.1880.*

**Dimensions & tons:** 59.97m wl (+0.12m ram), 60.98m pp (wl fwd to rudder) x 8.555m ext, 8.535m wl. 859.2t disp. Draught: 3.402m mean, 3.942m aft. Men: 114.

**Machinery:** 175nhp and 700ihp designed at 100rpm and 4.133kg/cm$^2$

boiler pressure. Trials (*Parseval*, 12.1880) 803.8ihp = 12.053kts at 106.33rpm and 4.133kg/cm² boiler pressure. 1 screw. 1 horizontal compound engine with return connecting rods and 3 cylinders of 0.96m and 1.10m diameter and 0.50m stroke. 2 medium type cylindrical boilers. 111t coal. Range 2,200nm @ 10kts.

**Guns:**
(1877, *Bouvet*) 3 x 138.6mm (2 on the sides just forward of the bridge and one on a centreline pivot between the after two masts), 1 x 100mm (on the forecastle)
(1880, *Parseval*) same except the gun on the forecastle was a 138.6mm instead of a 100mm.

*Bouvet* Rochefort Dyd.
On list 1.1873. K: 16.12.1872. L: 23.5.1876. Comm: 5.6.1877 (trials). C: 7.1877.
Budget 1872. Decomm. 10.8.1877 after trials. Recomm. 22.1.1878 for the Levant Division. Grounded at Zanzibar 28.12.1889, refloated with British help and arrived back under tow 12.5.1890 at Toulon, where she was judged unserviceable. Struck 2.4.1891.

*Parseval* Rochefort Dyd.
On list 1.1873. K: 16.12.1872. L: 7.5.1879. C: 10.1879.
Budget 1872. To Cochinchina 1880. Renamed *Amiral Parseval* 25.3.1895. Struck 22.11.1898, for sale at Toulon 1898-1899, reserved as gunnery target for the *Escadre de la Méditerranée* 1899-1900.

———

**BISSON Class.** *Avisos de 2ᵉ classe*, to *Avisos* (1874). 175nhp screw avisos with wooden hulls including three layers of crossed wooden planking on wooden frames with iron deck beams but no beam shelves, and ram bows. One funnel, three masts, barque rig. Designed by Sabattier.

———

The aviso *Parseval* at Algiers on 12 December (Xᵇʳᵉ) 1886. The pronounced rake of her masts and funnel was carried over from some avisos of the late 1850s, notably Vésigné's *Lamotte-Picquet* type, and Béléguic's experimental *Renard*. (NHHC from ONI album of French warships, NH-74881)

For a pair of 2ⁿᵈ class avisos to be ordered from Normand in 1873, Director of Materiel Victorin Gabriel Justin Épiphanès Sabattier produced a design developed from Vésigné's *Boursaint*, which had been launched the previous year at Rochefort. It used a hull structure developed by Normand that included three layers of planking, two diagonal thin layers crossing each other on the inside and a single thicker longitudinal layer on the outside. This hull form was lighter and stronger than the conventional single layer of longitudinal planking but was more expensive to build and nearly impossible to repair. This and the *Chasseur* class which followed, virtually identical except for the hull structure, had a short forecastle and shorter poop deck. Sabattier's plans for the *Bisson* type were approved and construction of first two was ordered on 12 February 1873. Their original designed armament was one 164.7mm M1860 gun on a central pivot, two 138.6mm/21.3 M1870 guns, and one 100mm gun on the forecastle but the 164.7mm gun was replaced by a 138.6mm gun before completion.

*The characteristics are based on a devis for* Dumont d'Urville *dated 10.1.1880.*

**Dimensions & tons:** 59.45m wl (+0.40m ram), 61.05m pp (wl fwd to rudder) x 8.73m ext, 8.724m wl. 851.4t disp. Draught: 3.653m mean, 4.278m aft. Men: 108.

**Machinery:** 175nhp and 700ihp designed at 100rpm and 4.133kg/cm² boiler pressure. Trials (*Dumont d'Urville*, 28.6.1879) 1,081.8ihp = 13.004kts at 107.3rpm and 4.217kg/cm² boiler pressure. 1 screw. 1 horizontal compound (Woolf) engine with return connecting rods and 2 cylinders of 0.92m and 1.50m diameter and 0.60m stroke. 2 cylindrical boilers. 154.5t coal. Range 3,560nm @ 10kts.

**Guns:**
(1880) 4 x 138.6mm on the centreline (1 on the forecastle, 1 forward of the bridge, 1 between the after two masts, and 1 on the poop). In *Dumont d'Urville* one of these (probably on the forecastle) was a 100mm gun.
(1884) In *Bisson* three 138.6mm guns were replaced with M1870 guns, the forward 138.6mm was replaced with a 100mm QF, a position for 1 x 65mm landing gun was added on the upper deck, and 5 x 37mm

revolving cannon were added. In *Dumont d'Urville* 3 x 37mm revolving cannon were added.

***Bisson*** Augustin Normand, Le Havre/Claparède, Saint Denis.
On list 12.2.1873. Ord: 3.3.1873 (contract). K: 1.4.1873. L: 27.10.1874. Comm: 6.12.1875 (trials), 1.3.1876 (full).
Budget 1872. Trials 1.1876. Left Cherbourg for Toulon and the *Escadre d'évolutions* 12.5.1876. Decomm. 16.1.1892. Struck 18.8.1892, designated for conversion at Cherbourg to coal hulk or lighter 1892-1899, coal hulk 1899-1902, for sale 1902-1903.

***La Bourdonnais*** Augustin Normand, Le Havre/Claparède, Saint Denis.
On list 12.2.1873. Ord: 3.3.1873 (contract). K: 1.4.1873. L: 20.5.1875. Comm: 28.6.1876 (trials), 1878 (full).
Budget 1872. To the Antilles 1878. While at anchor at Sainte Marie de Madagascar on 21.2.1893 was blown onto the reefs of Îlot Madame by a storm. Struck 17.3.1893 under name *Labourdonnais*. Wreck sold 8.9.1893.

***Hussard*** Augustin Normand, Le Havre/Claparède, Saint Denis.
On list 1.1877. Ord: 10.4.1876 (contract). K: 20.4.1876. L: 27.8.1877. Comm: 20.12.1878 (trials), 21.7.1879 (full).
Budget 1877. Trials 2.1879, to the Pacific station 1879. Reboilered 1888. Struck 24.4.1896, school for stoking at the school for engineers at Brest 1896-1899. Replaced by *Voltigeur* 9.1899, sold 23.12.1899 to

---

The aviso *Hussard* photographed by the Detroit Publishing Co. in the Hudson River in New York during the Columbian Naval Review in 1893. The naval parade was on 27 April 1893. *(Library of Congress, LC-D4-21128)*

M. Pitel. (*Ponton nº 1* was the former sailing brig *Hussard* at Lorient, not this ship.)

***Dumont d'Urville*** Augustin Normand, Le Havre/Claparède, Saint Denis.
On list 1.1877. Ord: 10.4.1876 (contract). K: 20.4.1876. L: 5.3.1878. Comm: 5.1879 (trials), 1.1880 (full).
Budget 1877. Originally named *Lancier*, renamed 3.1.1879. Machinery installed 16.8.1878 to 16.4.1879. Trials 6.1879. In the Antilles 1880. Struck 9.8.1897. Sold 10.2.1898 at Rochefort.

---

**CHASSEUR Class.** *Avisos.* 175nhp screw avisos with wooden hulls, iron deck beams and beam shelves, and ram bows. One funnel, three masts, barque rig. Designed by Sabattier.

For a pair of 2nd class avisos to be built at Brest in 1874 Sabattier produced a design virtually identical to that of *Bisson* except that the Brest ships used a conventional hull structure with a single layer of longitudinal hull planking. There were also some differences in the machinery including the use of Belleville boilers. *Chasseur* initially had cylindrical boilers operating at 10 kg/cm² pressure but these proved more prone to failures than the Bellevilles in *Voltigeur*.

*The characteristics are based on a devis for* Voltigeur *dated 3.9.1880.*
**Dimensions & tons:** 59.10m wl (+0.46m ram), 61.00m pp (wl fwd to rudder) x 8.71m ext. 910.2t disp. Draught: 3.597m mean, 4.122m aft. Men: 116.
**Machinery:** 175nhp and 700ihp designed at 100rpm and 7.022kg/cm² boiler pressure. Trials (*Voltigeur*, 29.5.1880) 998.63ihp = 12.483kts at 110.1rpm and 7.179kg/cm² boiler pressure. 1 screw. 1 horizontal com-

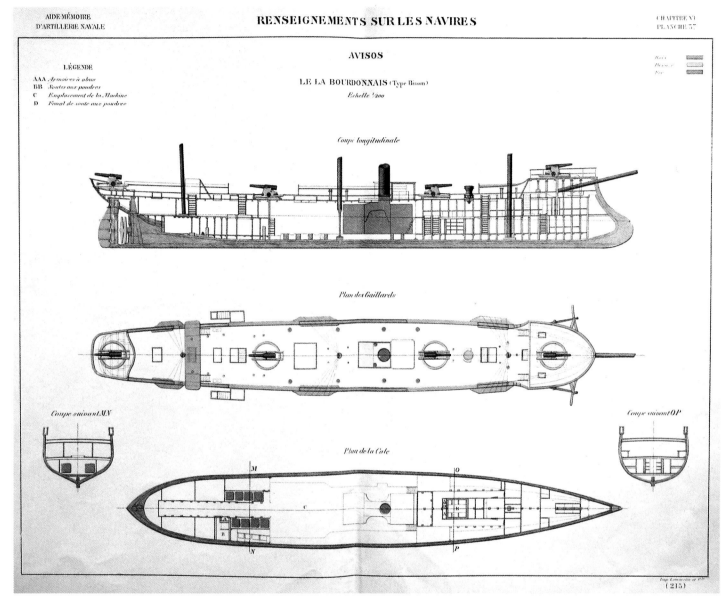

AVISOS

LE LA BOURDONNAIS (Type Bisson)

Echelle 1/200

LÉGENDE

AAA  Armoires à obus
BB   Soutes aux poudres
C    Emplacement de la Machine
D    Fanal de soute aux poudres

Coupe longitudinale

Plan des Gaillards

Coupe suivant MN

Plan de la Cale

Coupe suivant OP

(215)

Inboard profile and plans of the upper deck and hold of the aviso *La Bourdonnais* of the *Bisson* class. The ship had four 138.6mm M1870 guns on central pivot mountings nearly equally spaced along the centreline from one on the forecastle to one on a small platform on the stern. (*Aide-Mémoire d'Artillerie navale, 1879*)

pound engine with return connecting rods and 3 cylinders of 0.96m (1) and 1.10m (2) diameter and 0.50m stroke. 6 Belleville boilers. 145.0t coal. Range 3,380nm @ 10kts.

**Guns:** (1880) 4 x 138.6mm on the centreline (1 on the forecastle, 1 forward of the bridge, 1 between the after two masts, and 1 on the poop).

*Chasseur* Brest Dyd/Indret (engines designed by Joëssel).
On list 1.1874 (unnamed). K: 16.11.1874. L: 13.6.1878. Comm: 6.1879 (trials), 27.7.1879 (full).
Budget 1875. To the Pacific station 1879. Struck 6.11.1893, for sale at Brest 1893-1894.

*Voltigeur* Brest Dyd/Indret (engines designed by Joëssel)
On list 1.1874 (unnamed). K: 16.11.1874. L: 12.7.1878. Comm: c3.1880 (trials), 3.9.1880 (full).
Budget 1875. Machinery installed 1.8.1879 to 6.1.1880. Trials 4-5.1880. To the Levant 1881. Struck 17.6.1899, school for stoking and engine operation at the school for engineers at Brest 1899-1904.

*N* (Unnamed) Toulon Dyd
Budget 1877. This additional aviso, class unknown, was not in the 1878 budget.

———————

### (B) Screw Flotilla Avisos (*Avisos de flottille à hélice*), 120 50nhp (1867 rating).

To *Bâtiments de flottille à hélice* in the 1.1865 fleet list, *Avisos de flottille* 1.1874, *Avisos de 2e classe* 1.1885, *Avisos de station de 2e classe* 1.1891, *Avisos de 2e classe* 1.1892, and *Avisos* (classes omitted) 1.1909.

*VIGIE. Aviso de flottille à hélice.* 60nhp screw aviso with an iron hull and a clipper bow. One funnel, two masts, schooner-brig rig. Designed by Mangin.

This vessel was ordered from Gustave & Arnaud-Frédéric Bichon (Bichon Frères) at Bordeaux by a contract signed on 23 September 1859 as an addition to the programme of one screw (*Cuvier*) and seven paddle iron-hulled avisos (*Espadon*, *Protée*, and *Phaëton* classes) ordered earlier in the month from Ernest Gouin at Nantes. Designed by naval constructor Amédée Paul Théodore Mangin, *Vigie* duplicated the 60nhp iron *Rôdeur* of 1855, which had been assessed to be 'perfect' for her assigned duties of coast guard and fishery protection service on the coasts of southern France and Algeria because of her slight draft, low cost of operation, and relatively high speed. (The measurements of *Rôdeur* were 36.34m deck, 35.00m wl x 6.02m ext. 175 tons disp. Draught: 1.60m fwd, 2.20m aft.) The name *Vigie* was assigned on 11 November 1859. Her engines were ordered from the Forges et Chantiers de la Méditerranée by a contract approved on 18 May 1860.

**Dimensions & tons:** 37.15m deck, 35.00m wl x 6.16m ext. 240t disp. Draught: 2.10m fwd, 2.84m aft. Men: 51.
**Machinery:** 60nhp (50 from 1867). Trials (1867) 73ihp = 8.50kts. 1 screw. 2 cylinders. 1 boiler. 50t coal.
**Guns:** 2 x 4pdr (86.5mm/11) bronze mountain MLR.

*Vigie* Bichon frères, Bordeaux-Lormont/F.C. Méditerranée, Marseille.
On list 1.1860. Ord: 28.9.1859 (contract). K: 11.1859. L: 3.12.1861. Comm: 1.4.1862 (trials). C: 5.1862.
Supported submerged trials of the submarine *Plongeur* at Rochefort 1864, otherwise served primarily on fishery protection duty. Reboilered 9-11. 1867. Struck 8.4.1881, for disposal at Toulon 1881-1884. BU 1885.

───────────

## PURCHASED VESSELS, 1858-1860. *Avisos de flottille à hélice.*

*Peï-Ho.* This ship, requisitioned by the French on 7.12.1858 and named *Peï-Ho*, sometimes described as a screw aviso of 70 or 90nhp, never appeared as such on the *Liste de la Flotte* and is believed to be the paddle aviso of 40nhp that first appeared on that list for 1.1860 under the name *Shamrock*. See the listing for *Shamrock* in Chapter 7 for full details.

*Norzagaray.* Screw *aviso de flottille*, ex mercantile. This new American steamer was inspected by the French at Manila on 14 and 16.4.1859, found in good condition and purchase was recommended 17.4.1859. Purchased 4.1859 at Manila, previous name retained. Commissioned or recommissioned 1.4.1860. On fleet list 1.1861.

**Dimensions & tons:** Length 44m. Men: 30. **Machinery:** 50nhp. Informal trials 9.25kts at 63rpm. 1 screw. 1 vertical engine with direct connecting rods and 2 fixed inverted cylinders. 2 tubular return-flame boilers. (The cylinders and the steam chest were above the deck.)
**Guns:** 2, including 1 x 12pdr (121mm/17) bronze.

Was in service in Indochina on 7.5.1859, and as tender to the flagship *Du Chayla* was the French participant in the second attack on the Taku forts on 27.6.1859. Commissioned or recommissioned 1.4.1860. Replacement boilers ordered 24.3.1863 at Whampoa, delivered five months late on 15.2.1864. Decomm. 1.3.1864, hull found irreparable 24.7.1866, engine to be retained. Struck 6.8.1866 at Saigon.

*Alon Prah.* Screw *aviso de flottille*, ex mercantile. Rigged as schooner-brig. May have been built at Bordeaux in 1857-1858. Owned by a Bordeaux company and named after the founder of the then-current Burmese dynasty, she arrived at Mandalay 5.1859 to be offered for sale to the king and carrying around 20 French emigrants to set up a silk factory there and a Roman Catholic emissary. Purchased 11.1.1860 by the French Navy in the Far East. Commissioned 10.4.1860. On fleet list 1.1861.

**Dimensions & tons:** 32.11m x 7.22m. 113 tons burden. Draught 3.20m to 3.50m. Men: 45-50. **Machinery:** 80nhp (60 from 1867). **Guns:** 2.

Listed 1.6.1860 at Manila, erroneously as a paddle aviso. Decomm. 1.10.1864, recomm. 1.4.1867, decomm. 1.5.1868 at Saigon. Struck 11.5.1869, floating guard post in Cochinchina (Saigon) 1869-1879. BU 1879 at Saigon.

───────────

*ARGUS. Avisos de flottille à hélice.* 60nhp screw aviso with an iron hull. Two masts. Designed by Mangin.

On 3 February 1860 Minister of Marine Hamelin approved the construction of an aviso of the *Rôdeur* type to conduct experiments with the water tube boilers of Julien-François Belleville. The Navy had previously tested Belleville boilers in the *corvette mixte Biche* (a small iron-hulled corvette with a weak steam engine) in 1855-56, but *Argus* received a new model with horizontal tubes instead of the earlier vertical tubes. Mangin's plans for *Argus* differed from the *Rôdeur* type only enough to permit installation of the different boilers. The hull of the ship was ordered from Durenne at Asnières-sur-Seine by a contract signed on 17 February 1860, her engines were ordered from Gouin's factory at Paris by a contract signed on 30 March 1860, and two Belleville boilers were ordered from the Belleville firm at Saint Denis by a contract signed on 2 April 1860. Lieutenant Camille Fleuriot de Langle may have been assigned as early as 25 March 1860 as her prospective commander. In January 1861 he was following in Paris the trials of the Belleville boilers that were being built at Saint Denis for the ship, and he was promoted to Capitaine de frégate in August 1861. *Argus* received a Lagrafel boiler in 1875 and new trials in 1877 produced 176ihp and 8.93 knots.

**Dimensions & tons:** 37.20m deck, 35.00m wl x 6.12m ext. 239t disp. Draught: 2.10m fwd, 2.90m aft. Men: 50.
**Machinery:** 60nhp (50 from 1867), 160ihp designed at 120rpm and 5.00kg/cm² boiler pressure. Trials (1871) 80ihp = 6.57kts. Trials (27.2.1877) 176.4ihp = 8.93kts at 110.5rpm and 3.3538kg/cm² boiler pressure. 1 screw. 1 horizontal simple expansion direct-acting trunk engine with two cylinders of 0.704m diameter and 0.394m stroke. Reboilered in 1871 with 2 Belleville boilers and in 1877 with 1 Lagrafel type boiler modified by Joëssel. 38.1t coal. Range 930nm @ 10kts.
**Guns:** (1872-75) 2 x 4pdr (86.5mm/11) bronze mountain MLR on boat carriages.

*Argus* Durenne, Asnières-sur-Seine/Ernest Gouin, Paris.
On list 1.1861. Ord: 3.2.1860. K: 3.1860. L: 26.11.1860. Comm: 5.1862.
Served primarily on fishery protection and pilot training duty. Left Cherbourg for Concarneau 29.5.1862. Seagoing school for pilots at the School for Piloting of the West at La Rochelle from 1868 with the pinnace *Mesquer* as annex, but unreliable experimental boilers caused her to be replaced frequently by *Chamois*, *Pélican*, or *Phoque*. Permanently replaced 1880 by the gunboat *Oriflamme*. Struck 6.5.1884 and BU.

───────────

*ÉLAN. Aviso de flottille.* 80nhp screw aviso with an iron hull and a clipper bow. One funnel, two masts, schooner-brig rig (later schooner). Designed by Du Buit.

The 1877 budget had two unnamed *avisos de flottille* to be built by contract (probably *Élan* and *Cigale*), and the 1878 budget had three (probably adding *Mouette*). The plans of *Élan* were signed by Paul Du Buit, the senior engineer at F.C. Méditerranée, Le Havre-Graville, on 23 August 1878. They were inspired by Normand's 40.5-metre 120nhp iron-hulled *Faon*, one of three steam packets launched in 1847-48 under a law of 4 August 1844 for postal service on the Calais-Dover route and whose plans were based on the British pioneering 120nhp screw steamer *Fairy* which attained speeds as high as 13 knots. After the cross-channel postal service was turned over to contractors the Navy purchased *Faon* from the Ministry of Finance on 7 May 1855. *Faon* served as school ship for the School for Piloting of the North from 1865 to 1877. *Élan* took her place at Brest from her completion in 1878 until her relief by *Chamois* in 1907.

*The characteristics are based on a devis dated 29.7.1878.*
**Dimensions & tons:** 39.60m wl, 40.70m pp (wl fwd to rudder) x 6.24m ext (above wl), 6.17m wl. 236.7t disp. Draught: 2.116m mean, 2.306m aft.
**Machinery:** 80nhp. 350ihp designed at 145rpm and 4.133kg/cm² boiler pressure. Trials (13.7.1878) 351.5ihp = 12.045kts at 155.23rpm and

2536. - L'Aviso *Elan*, Bateau de Pilotage

The seagoing training ship for pilots *Élan*, classed as a flotilla aviso. She served at the school for piloting at Saint Servan from 1878 to 1907. Behind her stern is a *Gloire* class armoured cruiser. *(Postcard by H. Laurent, Port Louis)*

4.282kg/cm² boiler pressure. 1 screw. 1 vertical compound engine with 2 cylinders of 0.58m and 1.00m diameter and 0.50m stroke. 1 tubular cylindrical boiler. 30.8t coal. Range 1,640nm @ 10kts.

**Guns:** (1878) 2 espingoles. (1887) 2 x 47mm (wartime only)

*Élan* F.C. Méditerranée, Le Havre-Graville.

On list 1.1878. Ord: 3.3.1877 (contract). K: 19.9.1877. L: 18.4.1878. Comm: 17.7.1878 (trials). C: 7.1878.

Budget 1877. Seagoing school for piloting at Saint Servan from 7.1878 in place of *Crocodile* to 1907 when replaced by *Chamois*. Struck 24.3.1910.

---

***MOUETTE.*** *Aviso de flottille.* 80nhp screw aviso with a galvanised iron hull and a clipper bow. One funnel, two masts, schooner-brig rig. Designed by Du Buit.

Ordered as an exact copy of *Élan* from the same builder. The contract was dated 30 September 1878 and the original plans were signed by Du Buit on 13 October 1878. On 24 November 1878 Cherbourg forwarded a letter in which the commander of *Élan* reported some imperfections in his ship, and it was decided to lengthen *Mouette* by 2m forward of the pilot house. The contract modification was dated 13 January 1879 and the lengthened plans were signed on 24 January 1879 and approved by Minister of Marine Jauréguiberry on 4 March 1879. She served primarily on fishery protection duty in the Channel and after 1898 as station ship at Constantinople. In September 1908 it was proposed to send her to Indochina with *D'Iberville*, the former to be assigned to the Governor General and *Mouette* to be a yacht for the King of Cambodia. *D'Iberville* was sent as planned but the cost of the repairs to *Mouette* was excessive and on 19 February 1909

Toulon was informed that she would not be sent to Indochina. Du Buit's third and last ship for the navy was *Ibis*, described in Chapter 10.

*The characteristics are based on a devis dated 21.2.1880.*

**Dimensions & tons:** 41.60m wl, 42.70m pp (wl fwd to rudder) x 6.235m ext (above wl), 6.159m wl. 259.523t disp. Draught: 2.130m mean, 2.310m aft. Men: 71.

**Machinery:** 80nhp and 350ihp designed at 145rpm and 4.133kg/cm² boiler pressure. Trials (14.12.1879) 417.5ihp = 11.82kts at 154.03rpm and 4.40kg/cm² boiler pressure. 1 screw. 1 vertical high pressure compound engine with 2 cylinders of 0.58m and 1.00m diameter and 0.50m stroke. 1 cylindrical return tube boilers. 33.600t coal. Range 1,470nm @ 10kts.

**Guns:**

(1879) 4 x 4pdr (86.5mm/11) bronze rifled mountain guns.

(1882) 2 x 4pdr (86.5mm/11) bronze rifled mountain guns, 2 x 37mm revolving cannon.

(1887) 2 x 65mm/16 M1881 landing, 2 x 37mm revolving cannon.

(1902) 2 x 37mm Hotchkiss revolving cannon.

*Mouette* F.C. Méditerranée, Le Havre-Graville/FCM, Le Havre (engines designed by Raymond Cody).

On list 1.1879. Ord: 30.9.1878 (contract). K: 20.1.1879. L: 14.11.1879. Comm: 10.12.1879 (trials), 21.2.1880 (full).

Budget 1878. Machinery installed 15.11.1879 to 1.12.1879. On the North Sea fishery station, later the Channel and North Sea station, 1880-1895, mainly for fishery protection. Modified 1898 to serve as station ship at Constantinople (additional deckhouse, yacht fittings and boats). Replaced by *Jeanne Blanche* 1908, returned to Toulon 17.7.1908, decomm. there 1.4.1909. Struck 9.3.1910, sold 30.12.1910

---

*VOLAGE. Aviso de flottille.* 100nhp screw aviso with a wooden hull and a clipper bow. One funnel, three masts, barquentine rig. Designed by Finaz.

The design for this small wooden-hulled aviso was based on Normand's *Corse* of 1842 as lengthened 3.50m by naval constructor Joseph Marie Finaz at Toulon. She was used on the local stations of Tahiti and the Society Islands.

*The characteristics are based on a devis dated 12.6.1882.*
**Dimensions & tons:** 47.90m wl, 49.68m pp (wl fwd to rudder) x 9.35m ext (above wl), 8.42m wl. 506.3t disp. Draught: 3.195m mean, 3.67m aft. Men: 78.
**Machinery:** 100nhp. 400ihp designed at 130rpm and 4.25kg/cm$^2$ boiler pressure. Trials (2.6.1882) 401.2ihp = 10.76kts at 132.2rpm and 3.99kg/cm$^2$ boiler pressure. 1 high cylindrical boiler. 77.4t coal. Range 2,500nm @ 10kts.
**Guns:** (1882) 2 x 90mm in sponsons on the sides, 4 x 37mm Hotchkiss revolving cannon.

*Volage* Toulon Dyd.
On list 1.1881. K: 7.10.1880. L: 1.12.1881. C: 6.1882.
Budget 1882. At Tahiti 1882-85 and 1888-91. Grounded and lost 9.7.1891 on the reefs of Marokau Atoll in the Tuamotu Archipelago in French Polynesia. Struck 25.8.1891.

———————

*CHIMÈRE. Aviso de flottille.* 50nhp screw aviso with a wooden hull, iron deck beams and beam shelves, and a clipper bow. One funnel, two masts, schooner rig with one square yard on the foremast. Designed by de Maupeou d'Ableiges.

This small wooden-hulled vessel was designed specifically for hydrographic missions by naval constructor Gilles Louis de Maupeou d'Ableiges and operated by the *Ingénieurs Hydrographiques*.

*The characteristics are based on a devis dated 3.5.1882.*
**Dimensions & tons:** 36.60m wl, 37.83m pp (wl fwd to rudder) x 6.20m ext (above wl), 6.10m wl. 226.7t disp. Draught: 2.197m mean, 2.385m aft. Men: 60.
**Machinery:** 50nhp. 180ihp designed at 145rpm and 4.25kg/cm$^2$ boiler pressure. Trials (16.1.1882) 201.2ihp = 9.435kts at 158.1rpm and 4,278kg/cm$^2$ boiler pressure. 1 screw. 1 vertical compound engine with 3 cylinders of 0.32m (2) and 0.75m (1) diameter and 0.35m stroke. 1 tubular cylindrical boiler. 34.2t coal. Range 1,470nm @ 9.5kts.
**Guns:** (1882) 2 x 4pdr (86.5mm/11) bronze.

*Chimère* Rochefort Dyd.
On list 1.1881. K: 10.1880. L: 27.7.1881. C: 4.1882.
Budget 1882. Conducted summertime hydrographic operations in Corsica 1884-85 and in Tunisia in 1887, later based at Lorient and performed hydrographic work on the west coast of France. Replaced by *Utile* in 1908 because her repairs were no longer worth the cost. Struck 4.2.1908 and to the Domaines for sale. Sold or BU 1908.

———————

## (C) Small Screw Flotilla Avisos (*Avisos de flottille à hélice*), 40-25nhp (1867 rating).

To *Bâtiments de flottille à hélice* in the 1.1865 fleet list and *Avisos de flottille* 1.1874. *Étincelle* and *Fourmi* became *chaloupes à vapeur* 1.1884 and *Marabout* and *Loyalty* became *Avisos de 3ᵉ classe* 1.1885, *Avisos de station de 3ᵉ classe* 1.1891, and *Avisos de 3ᵉ classe* 1.1892.

*SYLPHE* **Class.** *Avisos de flottille.* 10nhp fishery protection steam launches with iron hulls and rounded bows. One tall, thin funnel, two masts, schooner rig. Designed by Mangin.

The hydrographic ship *Chimère*, classed as a flotilla aviso, at Toulon. She was operated by the Hydrographic Service. *(Postcard by A. Bougault)*

Plans for an iron-hulled steam launch (*chaloupe à vapeur*) of a modified *Rôdeur* type for fishery protection duty on the French coast were signed by Amédée Paul Théodore Mangin on 12 July 1860 and submitted on 30 July 1860. Two of these 15nhp vessels were ordered from Lucien Arman by a contract signed on 5 August 1860. They were to have been built at Arman's yard at Paris, but his main yard was at Bordeaux and the little craft were built there. Each had a fish tank forward of the engine room that was used for purposes including studies of shellfish.

**Dimensions & tons:** 20.67m deck, 20.00m wl x 4.62m ext. 75t disp. Draught: 1.32m fwd, 1.92m aft. Men: 15.
**Machinery:** 15nhp (10 from 1867) Trials (*Sylphe*) 38ihp = 6.41kts. 1 screw. 1 vertical engine with 1 cylinder. 1 boiler. 10-11.5t coal.
**Guns:** (1862, *Favori*) 2 espingoles. (*Sylphe* 1875) none.

*Sylphe* Lucien Arman, Bordeaux/Mazeline, Le Havre.
On list 1.1861. Ord: 8.1860 (contract). K: 9.1860. L: 22.7.1861. Comm: 1.1.1862 (trials). C: 1.1862.
Arrived at Lorient from Bordeaux 1.4.1862 and was completing fitting out at Lorient in late June. Carried out fishery protection and hydrographic duties along the French coast from Toulon to Cherbourg and Rouen. Struck 9.4.1878, for disposal at Brest 1878-1879, BU 1879.

*Favori* Lucien Arman, Bordeaux/Mazeline, Le Havre.
On list 1.1861. Ord: 8.1860 (contract). K: 9.1860. L: 5.8.1861. Comm: 9.1.1862 (trials). C: 1.1862.
Arrived at Toulon 14.3.1862 from Bordeaux via the Canal du Midi. Struck 19.2.1878, barracks hulk at Marseille 1878-1884, for sale at Marseille 1884-1887, sold 1887 to BU.

---

## PURCHASED VESSELS, 1863-1866. *Avisos de flottille.*

*Gia-Dinh.* On 24.2.1863 the governor of Cochinchina reported to Minister of Marine Chasseloup-Laubat that he was in urgent need of small river steamers for resupply missions in the interior and was proceeding to buy two iron screw river avisos, *Magnet* and *Sycée*, at Hong Kong. They were purchased from Mr. D. Lapraik at Hong Kong by naval constructor Philippe Frédéric Korn by a contract dated 14.3.1863. The governor initially gave the names *Bien-Hoa* to *Magnet* and *Saïgon* to *Sycée*, then renamed *Saïgon* to *Gia-Dinh* as the navy already had a *Saïgon,* and then swapped the names of the two vessels. *Gia-Dinh* ex *Magnet* was built at Whampoa, China, by Couper & Cie. with an engine from Glasgow and was new when purchased. Comm: 4.4.1863. On list 1.1864.

**Dimensions & tons:** 28.96m wl x 4.88m. Draught: 1.68m aft.
**Machinery:** 35nhp, c100ihp. 1 screw. 1 high pressure engine with two oscillating cylinders, one vertical cylindrical boiler, 1.76kg/cm². 5 days coal.
**Guns:** 1 or 2 small.

Decomm. 14.5.1864 and given to King Norodom of Cambodia on 30.5.1864, the day of his coronation as puppet king of Cambodia under Siamese hegemony and French protection. Refitted at Saigon c10.1864. The Ministry of Marine became aware of the transfer in 1.1866. Struck effective 31.12.1865.

*Bien-Hoa.* *Sycée* was the other iron screw river aviso purchased from Mr. D. Lapraik at Hong Kong by naval constructor Korn by a contract dated 14.3.1863. *Bien-Hoa* ex *Sycée*, unlike the new *Gia-Dinh* ex *Magnet,* needed some repairs before delivery. Comm: 26.4.1863. On list 1.1864.

**Dimensions & tons:** 24.38m x 4.42m. Draught: 1.68m. Men: 29, to 50 in 1869 and 51 in 1875.
**Machinery:** 30nhp (25 from 1868), c100ihp. 1 screw. 1 high pressure engine. 6 days coal
**Guns:** unknown.

Decomm. 31.7.1863. Transfer to Cambodia approved 24.10.1866. Struck 2.11.1866 and off the list. Transfer cancelled 11.4.1867, recomm. 15.6.1867, back on the list 1.1868. Given to the Emperor of Annam as a yacht with the aviso *D'Entrecasteaux* on 18.8.1876 under a commercial treaty of 15.3.1874. Struck 18.8.1876 (published 11.10.1876).

*Yahou.* Purchased 1865-6, possibly built in 1859. On list 1.1867. Comm: 15.8.1867.

**Dimensions & tons:** 25.60m x 5.71m. 48t, 54t, or 80t disp. Draught: 1.7m. Men: 26. **Machinery:** 20nhp (1867), c80ihp. **Guns:** none.

Participated in 1866 in the Mexican campaign. Called *Youyou* in 1.1867, also called *Yalou*. Refitted at Lorient 8.1867. Wrecked at Grand Bassam, Ivory Coast, 19.6.1869. Struck 14.4.1870.

---

*SOURIS.* *Bâtiment spécial, Bâtiment de flottille* (1866). 25nhp experimental steam schooner. Designed by Brassens. Purchased.

This wooden-hulled craft was one of several marine technology experiments supported by Napoleon III under his household budget and then sold to the Navy. She was designed and built in 1861-62 by Raymond Brassens, who in 1859 had patented a scheme for building a ship with two sternposts side by side and two screws. His design had three keels, two extending to the bow from the two sternposts and the centre one extending from the bow back to the aftermost hull frame between the sternposts. *Souris*, which had two screws, was built at Brassens' yard at Quinsac near Bordeaux and was probably a prototype of his invention which he sold to the Emperor after testing. The aviso *Bruix*, designed by Brassens and built by Arman at Bordeaux in 1865-67, also had three keels and two screws and was a larger-scale application of his ideas. Purchased by the Navy in April 1865 and refitted at Cherbourg, *Souris* was described as a yacht and annex to the yachts of the imperial family. Called a steam schooner, *Souris* had a mere 93 sq.m. of sail.

*The characteristics are based on a devis dated 5.1866.*
**Dimensions & tons:** 19.40m deck, 18.50m pp x 3.91m wl. 53.16t disp. Draught: 1.50m mean, 1.80m aft. Men: 10.
**Machinery:** 25nhp (20nhp from 1867), c80ihp. 1 geared engine with 2 cylinders, 2 screws, 70 rpm (engine), 105rpm (screws). 1 boiler. 5.0t coal.
**Guns:** (1866) None.

*Souris* Brassens, Quinsac, Gironde/Brassens? (engines designed by Dietz).
On list 1.1865. K: end 1861. L: c4.1862. Comm: 1.6.1862 (trials). C: 6.1862.
Left Le Havre under tow by *Dauphin* 26.8.1862 for Biarritz for presentation to the Emperor. *Bâtiment spécial* 1.1865 as *Annexe des Yachts Impériaux*, became annex to *Chamois* 16.4.1865, to *bâtiment de flottille à hélice* 1.1866, from Cherbourg to Rochefort account 7.11.1868 for hydrographic service. Struck 21.12.1876, BU 1877 at Toulon.

---

*MARABOUT.* *Bâtiment de flottille.* 20nhp screw colonial aviso with an iron hull. 1 mast, schooner rig. Designed by Audenet.

This small iron screw aviso for colonial service was built at a private yard at Nantes (probably Jollet & Babin, who had just taken over the yard of Ernest Gouin) to a design by naval constructor Camille Audenet.

*The characteristics are based on a devis dated 9.5.1871.*
**Dimensions & tons:** 28.10m deck, 27.37m wl, 27.58m pp (wl fwd to rudder) x 5.70m ext (above wl), 5.66m wl. 107.620t disp. Draught: 1.382m mean, 1.792m aft. Men: 19.
**Machinery:** 20nhp. 80ihp designed at 4.133kg/cm² boiler pressure. 1 screw. 1 vertical simple expansion engine with 2 cylinders of 0.30m diameter and 0.23m stroke. 2 tubular cylindrical boilers. 15.8t coal.

**Guns:** (1871) 4 *espingoles* (53mm).

*Marabout* Nantes/Indret (engines designed by Charles Louis Jaÿ).
On list 1.1870. K: 8.3.1870. L: 24.9.1870. Comm: 29.9.1870 (trials),
    20.4.1871 or 9.5.1871 (full).
Machinery installed 30.9.1870 to 4.11.1870. Ran trials at Nantes.
    Decomm. in Cayenne 12.4.1872, recomm. at Saint-Louis (Sénégal)
    4.6.1872 under the informal name *Tirailleuse-Marabout*, decomm. at
    Gabon 16.11.1876 and name reverted to *Marabout*. Wrecked 1885 or
    early 1886 in the Ogoué in Gabon. Struck 26.1.1886.

---

*LOYALTY. Aviso de flottille.* 25nhp screw colonial aviso with a wooden hull
and a straight bow. One funnel, two masts, schooner rig. Designed by
Mort's Dock, Australia.

This vessel was built at Sydney, Australia, in 1879 for the government of
French New Caledonia in response to an order from Minister of Marine
Pothuau dated 24 May 1878. The contract was signed by Mr. Franck,
director of Mort's Dock & Engineering Company, who both designed and
built the small vessel. The French expected her to make 9 knots, but no
speed was indicated in the contract and she fell well short of that figure and
also had high coal consumption. The report for her 1891-1893 cruise
(dated 11 February 1893) stated that she 'constituted all by herself the
entire New Caledonia local station'. She was too small to transport either
personnel or cargo and the small amounts she sometimes carried displaced
the commander and the crew from their quarters.

*The characteristics are based on the manuscript contract for the vessel.*
**Dimensions & tons:** 29.00m oa, 27.43m wl, x 4.72m (interior).
    105t disp. Draught: 2.00m mean, 2.50m aft. Men: 27 (36 including
    3 officers in 1897).
**Machinery:** 25nhp, 90ihp (maximum) at 4.5kg/cm² boiler pressure. Trials
    76.80ihp (natural draught) = 7.6kts at 125rpm. 1 screw. 1 compound
    high pressure engine with 2 cylinders of 0.3427m and 0.661m diame-
    ter and 0.381m stroke. 1 cylindrical tubular boiler.
**Guns:** 2 x 4pdr (86.5mm/11) bronze. By 1891 had 2 x 37mm revolving
    cannon, 1 on each side forward)

*Loyalty* Mort's Dock, Sydney (with engine).
On list 1.1879. Ord: 23.12.1878. K: 1879. L: 1879. Comm: 9.10.1879.
Arrived at Nouméa 4.11.1879 as station ship for New Caledonia.
    Ordered decommissioned 18.4.1896 for budgetary reasons and offered
    gratis to the Colonial Ministry, who accepted 28.1.1897. Struck
    4.8.1897, received by the local colonial administration 3.1898.

---

**PURCHASED VESSEL, 1879.** *Aviso de flottille*

*Étincelle.* Ex *Ondiwaga*, purchased at Constantinople 1879 to serve the
French ambassador and initially classed as an *aviso de flottille*. On list
1.1880. Successively annex at Constantinople to *Pétrel*, *Lévrier*, *Flèche*,
*Étoile*, *Bombe*, and *Mouette*.

**Dimensions & tons:** 31t disp. Men: 5. **Machinery:** 14nhp, 200ihp.
    **Guns:** probably none.

At Constantinople 1880-1895, then annex to other ships there to 1902.
    To *chaloupe à vapeur* 1.1884. Sold 14.12.1902 to the builder of
    *Mascotte*, which replaced her. Off list 1902.

---

*FOURMI. Aviso de flottille.* Steam launch. Probably designed by builder. To
*chaloupe à vapeur* 1.1884.

This small craft, hardly larger than a ship's boat and probably designed by
her builder, was probably intended as an annex or tender to the hydrographic ship *Chimère*, which was built at the same time.

**Dimensions & tons:** 20t disp.
**Machinery:** 80ihp.
**Guns:** probably none.

*Fourmi* Dyle et Bacalan, Bordeaux-Bacalan.
On list 1.1882. K: 1881. L: 1881. C: 1881.
Budget 1882. Listed in 1.1882 as an annex to *Chimère* and in reserve at
    Rochefort, then in commission at Rochefort 1883-1885. Struck
    10.12.1886, for disposal at Rochefort 1886-1887.

---

# II. SPECIAL SHIPS

## (A) Special Screw Vessels (*Bâtiments spéciaux à hélice*).

This category appeared the end of the regular portion of the
*Liste de la Flotte* for screw ships from 1.1861 (for *Plongeur*)
to 1872 and later also included *Tortue*, *Puebla*, *Taureau*
(1864 only) and *Souris* (1865 only). *Dix Décembre* (*Ampère*),
which was navy manned and on naval signal lists for many
years, is also listed here although she was never on the navy's
fleet list because she was owned by the Ministry of Finance.

*PLONGEUR. Bâtiment spécial.* Experimental submarine with an iron hull
and operated by compressed air. Designed by Bourgois and Brun. Called a
*Garde-côte porte-torpille submersible.*

Capitaine de vaisseau Siméon Bourgois, concerned that the invention of
the ironclad battleship had given the advantage to offensive forces,
presented Minister of Marine Hamelin on 24 November 1858 a memorandum describing a submarine that would restore the ability of defensive
forces to protect French harbours and ports and break any blockades of
them. (Bourgois also saw uses for his submarine in cross-channel offensive
operations like those envisioned in 1805 for the Boulogne Flotilla.) The
fundamental novelty of Bourgois's submarine was that it was driven by
compressed air, which in turn made it unusually large, the size of a small
aviso, to contain the bulky air tanks. On 11 February 1859 Hamelin
invited the naval constructors in each port to submit proposals for building Bourgois's invention. Of the three complete projects submitted, the
*Conseil des travaux* on 23 August 1859 selected for further work the only
one that stayed close to Bourgois's concept, that of Charles Marie Brun, a
naval constructor at Rochefort. Brun had known Bourgois from when the
two worked together on experimental screw propellers in the aviso *Pélican*
in the late 1840s. Brun's final plans were approved by the Council on
24 January 1860, construction of a *bateau sous-marin* by the Rochefort
dockyard was ordered on 6 February 1860, the boat was named *Plongeur*
on 17 February 1860, and she appeared on the fleet list in January 1861
under the new category *bâtiments spéciaux à hélice*.

    The hull of riveted metal plates 8mm thick was mostly occupied by
23 tanks, most measuring 7.24m x 1.12m, for the compressed air that
drove the engine. These had a total capacity of 147m³ and were tested to
18 kg/cm². The compressed air was designed to last for 2 hours. The tanks
were pressurized by a compressor installed on the harbour service craft
*Cachalot*. The crew worked in a 22-metre long corridor along the centreline between the compartments containing most of the air tanks. These
compartments also served as ballast tanks, the space around the tanks being
flooded to submerge the boat and being blown with compressed air to
surface. The air that drove the engine exhausted into the space occupied by
the crew after expanding in the cylinders, giving the crew a constant supply
of fresh air and maintaining pressure within the boat. The boat carried
212.89 tons of ballast, of which 34 tons were rigged for quick release in case
of an emergency. She was intended not to go below 12 metres, partly to
avoid giving the crew decompression sickness and partly because the effi-

ciency of the compressed air engine decreased rapidly as immersion increased due to back pressure on the exhaust system.

The boat began trials on the surface in June 1863 and in September 1863 a series of submerged trials was conducted in a drydock at Rochefort. Trials resumed in February 1864 after Bourgois returned from duties with the fleet, with *Plongeur* being towed on 11 February 1864 by the aviso *Vigie* to the protected waters at the mouth of the Charente, followed by the support craft *Cachalot*. The boat steered and manoeuvred well, but it was found to be nearly impossible to control the horizontal stability of the boat (depth and trim) when diving or underwater. This was blamed on the control mechanisms, on the decision to use the same compartments for both ballast and trim tanks, and on the fact that the weight of the boat decreased as the compressed air was released. (The ultimate answer, horizontal bow planes, was suggested but not pursued.) In addition her endurance of 5 miles at 4 knots, 5.7 miles at 3.8 knots, and 7.5 miles at 2.4 knots, was clearly insufficient for meaningful military use. Underway trials ceased after February 1864 and, although Brin's successor Alfred François Lebelin de Dionne and others conducted static experiments in 1864 to 1865 with solutions to the control problems, she was placed out of service 20 January 1867 and condemned as a submarine on 15 February 1872.

The hull of *Plongeur*, however, was in good condition and was converted into a 434-ton steam water barge at Rochefort on plans by the naval constructor Courbebaisse which were referred to the *Conseil des travaux* on 11 September 1871 and approved by it on 28.11.1871. Conversion began in March 1872, she was re-launched on 3 December 1873, but fitting out lasted into 1882. Her capacity was 190 tons of fresh water. A new 2-cylinder engine of 30nhp and 120ihp was built from the engines of the gun launches (*chaloupes-canonnières*) *Lance* and *Obus* that had been recovered after those vessels went out of service in Gabon. This engine was replaced December 1898 to 1899 at Rochefort with the 520ihp engine of *Torpilleur nº 74* (although she continued to be listed at 120ihp in the fleet lists through January 1914 and was listed at 300ihp in 1920). The internal arrangements and superstructure were modified at Rochefort in 1903 and

Inboard profile and horizontal section of the submarine boat (*bateau sous-marin*) *Plongeur* of Capitaine de vaisseau Bourgois and naval constructor Brun. The large cylindrical objects that take up most of the space within the boat are compressed air tanks. The crew worked in the walkway down the centreline. (*Vice Admiral Pâris, Art naval, 1867 and Forest and Noalhat, Les bateaux sous-marins historique, 1900*)

she was also fitted for towing. She was reassigned to Toulon 27 May 1927 when the dockyard at Rochefort was closed, towed to Toulon by the transport *Loiret* in July 1927, and was in service there on 21 August 1927 supplying water to ships undergoing torpedo training in the Salins d'Hyères roadstead.

**Dimensions & tons:** 42.50m pp x 6.00m. 420t disp (surfaced), 453.20t (submerged). Draught: 2.86m surfaced. Men: 12.
  Reserve buoyancy: 7.3%
**Machinery:**
(surfaced) 80hp designed at 12kg/cm$^2$ air pressure. Speed 5kts surfaced for 2 hours (7nm) designed. Trials (surfaced): 3.5kts over a distance of 965 metres. 1 screw. 1 compressed air engine with 4 single-expansion cylinders of 0.32m diameter and 0.32m stroke, pairs of cylinders arranged in inverted V form.
(submerged): 80hp. Speed 4kts for 2 hours (6nm).
**Torpedoes:** One 4.5m long spar for an electrically-fired torpedo (never fitted).

*Plongeur* Rochefort Dyd.
On list 1.1861. K: 6.1860. L: 18.5.1863. Comm: 1.11.1863 (trials). C: 11.2.1864.
Dock trials 8.6.1863, underway trials in the Charente 10.6.1863 (sank because of a broken porthole, crew saved), diving trials in a dock 5.9.1863. Comm. in reserve 2nd category 1.11.1863 for sea trials, underway for trials at sea 11.2.1864 supported by the aviso *Vigie* and the service craft *Cachalot*, dove to 9.2m depth 18.2.1864. To 3rd category reserve (out of commission) 16.4.1864 after trials ended and fully decomm. as submarine 20.6.1867. Struck 15.2.1872, steam water barge (*citerne à vapeur*) at Rochefort 1872-1927 and at Toulon 1927-1935. Condemned at Toulon as unserviceable 27.12.1935, to the Domaines 1935 for sale, sold by them 26.5.1937.

―――――――

*TORTUE. Bâtiment spécial.* Experimental screw armoured gunboat with one gun inside an egg-shaped hull covered with metal plating. Two small funnels side by side. Probably designed by Arman.

The emperor ordered this experimental 'screw craft with a carapace' under his household budget. The plans were signed by Arman at Bordeaux on 23 September 1861 and press reporting suggests he was also the inventor and designer. She was built at Bordeaux and taken to Cherbourg in 1861

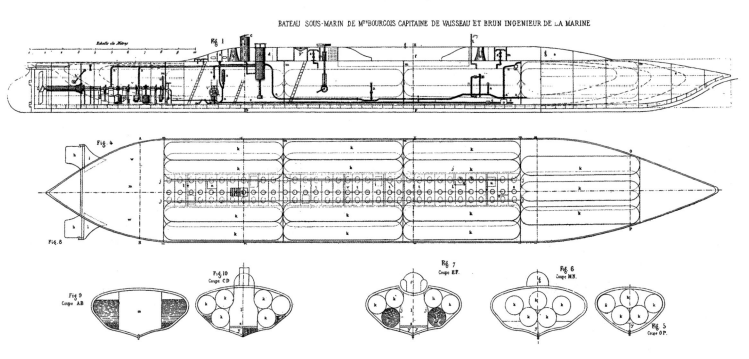

BATEAU SOUS-MARIN DE Mʳ BOURGOIS CAPITAINE DE VAISSEAU ET BRUN INGENIEUR DE LA MARINE

for completion. On around 15 February 1862 the Emperor directed the Navy to take charge of the vessel, which it did at her moorings at St. Cloud (Paris) on 24 March 1862. On 16 April 1862 she was reported to have arrived at Asnières sur Seine after experiencing steering difficulties. By decision of 17 April 1862 the Navy retained the name *Tortue* for the vessel, and assigned her to Cherbourg. The navy manned her as an iron gunboat (*canonnière en fer*) from 2 April to 12 August 1862, then took her out of service at Cherbourg in 1862 or 1863 and put her in covered storage with the *Canot de l'Empereur* (the ceremonial barge on display for many years in the *Musée national de la Marine* at Paris). A plan provided by Arman on 24 September 1864, a photograph of her hauled out in storage at Cherbourg, and several press reports show her with an egg-shaped hull and two small funnels spaced wide apart abreast amidships with a probable personnel access hatch aft of them and a gun hatch on the centreline forward of them. No details have been found about the armour. On 27 August 1866 Minister of Marine Chasseloup-Laubat ordered Cherbourg to proceed with the condemnation of *Tortue*. Cherbourg forwarded the condemnation paperwork to Paris on 17 September 1866, noting that 'this vessel in its current form does not appear susceptible of rendering any service, while her engine could be usefully employed by installing it on one of the floating water barges (*citernes flottantes*) of the Port of Cherbourg.' The vessel was struck on 16 November 1866 and Cherbourg was ordered to break her up. The products of the scrapping were reported back to Paris on 12 May 1868. Her engine went into the Cherbourg water barge *Amphore*, which was listed as a *citerne à voiles* in the January 1867 fleet list and as a *citerne à hélice* of 10nhp in the January 1868 fleet list. This service craft last appeared in the January 1907 fleet list, by which time she was rated at 40ihp.

**Dimensions & tons:** 15m hull excluding rudder x 5.00m amidships x 1.70m *creux* (3.10m in the redoubt amidships) of which 1.30m below the waterline. 61.500t disp. Draught 1.40m mean, 1.60m aft.
**Machinery:** 1 engine, 2 screws. 1 rudder.
**Guns:** 1 x 164.7mm M1858-60 BLR on a sliding mount in the bow.

*Tortue* Arman, Bordeaux-Paludate.
On list 1.1863. K: 10.1860. L: c2.1861. C: 1861/2 (trials) at Cherbourg. Comm: 2.4.1862.
To naval custody 24.3.1862 in the Seine near St. Cloud, having fitted out and run trials earlier for the Imperial household at Cherbourg. Decomm. 12.8.1862. Struck 16.11.1866. BU c1867 at Cherbourg.

---

*PUEBLA. Bâtiment spécial.* Experimental screw steam launch (river yacht) with open seating for the passengers. One funnel aft, no masts. Designed by Dupuy de Lôme.

On 12 March 1863 Napoleon III returned to an idea he had first had in 1852 of obtaining a small yacht for harbours and rivers, and he entrusted her construction to Dupuy de Lôme. He planned to use her for excursions along the Seine from his summer palace at Fontainebleau, and he offered her to the Empress who named her *Puebla*. She was essentially a large decked steam launch without masts or sails, with the machinery and its funnel near the stern, and with a canopy spread from there to near the bow. The deck was planked with teak and open seating was provided along the sides under the canopy for the passengers. Napoleon III used her to test several technical innovations including a steel hull and a vertical two-cylinder engine coupled to twin screws by conical bronze gears that acted as variable-pitch propellers. The machinery was designed by Raymond Cody, chief engineer for her builder, Mazeline, who was almost exclusively an engine builder. She was launched into the Vauban basin at Le Havre and taken to Asnières for acceptance trials conducted by Dupuy de Lôme. Her twin screws gave the craft great manoeuvrability and good speed but Cody's gearing was not a great success.

**Dimensions & tons:** 18.50m deck, 18.00m wl x 3.75m. 17.5t disp. Draught: 0.80m mean, 0.90m aft. Men: 10.
**Machinery:** 12nhp (or 10nhp) at 200rpm and 5 atmospheres of boiler pressure. Speed 8.62kts. 2 screws. 1 vertical geared engine with 2 cylinders. 1 boiler.
**Guns:** none.

*Puebla* François Mazeline, Le Havre (including engines).
On list 1.1864. Ord: 24.4.1863 (contract). K: 5.1863. L: 31.7.1863. Comm: 10.7.1863 (trials). C: 7.8.1863.
Classed as *Annexe des Yachts Impériaux* 1.1864 to 1.1869, to *Bâtiments de flottille* 1.1870. Not used in the defence of Paris in 1870, sold 17.3.1871 to the Ministry of Public Works. Seized 18.3.1871 at winter moorings at the Île aux Cygnes by the Paris Commune but not used by them. Decomm. by the Navy as of 1.4.1871. Retaken by government forces 24.5.1871 and returned to the Navy 2.9.1871 by the Ministry of Public Works. Out of service to 1875. Described as a *bateau de rivière* 1.1874 and 1.1875. Off main list during 1875, assigned 27.8.1875 to the Direction des Constructions Navales as an annex to the tug *Navette*, served as a tug at Cherbourg 1875-1885, reboilered 1880. Condemnation and replacement as a tug by *Chevrette* (ex *Torpilleur*

---

Exterior details and details of the bow of the experimental armoured river gunboat *Tortue*. The author of the article that included these drawings, Frédéric Bernard, pointed out that the rounded structure was intended to cause all the projectiles that hit it to ricochet while its iron covering prevented penetration. 'This ship, of small dimension, is intended to act on rivers. With its small draught of water it could on occasion effectively protect the establishment of troops on a bridge and on the shore provide powerful assistance to a landing by sweeping the beach before the arrival of boats loaded with troops.' He added that 'this steamer reflected the greatest honour on our skilled shipbuilder M. Armand of Bordeaux, whose genius has already endowed the navy with innovations of immense importance.' The gun is at the top of the opening in the bow. At the time of publication, the vessel was scheduled to run trials in the presence of Napoléon III. (*La Semaine des enfants, 2 November 1861, also in the Journal pour tous, 1861, page 352.*)

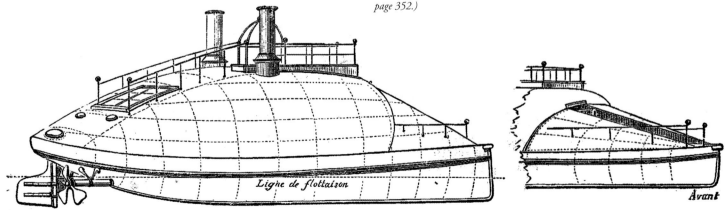

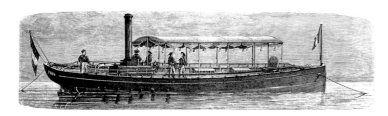

The river yacht *Puebla*, designed for the Empress. The vessel was completed in the Vauban basin at Le Havre and left there on 7 August 1863 for Asnières where she was received by her designer Dupuy de Lôme. In his additional trials there she steered perfectly and could turn around in 2.5 to 3 times her length. She was built at Mazeline's works under the direction of M. Lelaidier, inventor of a new variable pitch propeller. The engine and boiler were in the open, and there was nothing under the deck except for the rudder mechanism, the coal bunkers, two beds for the crew, and the shafts for the two screws. A canopy covered the deck, and the steering wheel was under the after end so the emperor himself could steer aided by the boat's commander stationed at the tiller in the stern. (*L'Illustration, Journal Universel, 5 September 1863, page 176*)

n[o] 3) proposed by Cherbourg 21.12.1884. Retired 28.1.1885 as service craft, for disposal 1885-1886, BU 1886-87.

---

**DIX DÉCEMBRE (*AMPÈRE*).** Screw cable-layer (ex collier) with an iron hull and a straight bow. One tall funnel between main and mizzen masts, three masts, schooner rig. Acquired and owned by the Ministry of Finance, operated by the Navy.

This ship was built in 1861 as the British collier *Commerce* to carry coal from Shields on the Tyne to London and merchandise back to Shields. In 1863 the *Administration des Lignes Télégraphiques* of the French Ministry of Finance needed a ship to help connect Algeria and France by telegraph cable and purchased *Commerce* for conversion to a cable ship. She was named *Dix Décembre* for the date on which the future Emperor Napoleon III was elected president of the short-lived French Second Republic. The ship was the property of the Ministry of Finances and thus never appeared on the Navy's *Liste de la Flotte*, but she was manned and maintained by the Navy according to arrangements formalised in orders from Minister of Marine Chasseloup-Laubat dated 18 January and 23 February 1866. The ship was commissioned with a naval crew in early July 1863 and taken to Cherbourg where the naval dockyard fitted her with two cable tanks in the hold and a deckhouse for the commanding officer and the telegraph engineer. She was then sent back to the Thames where the contractor for the cable operation, Siemens, Halske, & Co., installed the cable handling machinery and loaded the cable. *Dix Décembre* left England in December 1863 for the Mediterranean with 130 miles of cable on board. Cable laying was still in its infancy and several attempts starting in January 1864 to lay an Oran-Cartagena cable failed with the cable breaking each time. *Dix Décembre*, however, went on to a long and productive cable laying career in the Mediterranean and then along the French Atlantic and Channel coasts. She was renamed *Ampère* in September 1870 after the fall of the Second Empire and was joined in 1873 by a second cable ship, *Charente*, a converted Navy transport (q.v.) that unlike *Ampère* was navy property and remained on the *Liste de la Flotte* for the entire period of her loan to the Ministry of Finance from 1873 to 1932.

The original boiler of *Dix Décembre* was landed and overhauled in November 1864, having suffered greatly from the overload needed to operate the cable laying gear and from the continuous operation of that equipment during cable operations. It was landed again in early 1868 and replaced on 9 July 1868 with the boiler of the aviso *Passe Partout*, which had seen little use since it was installed on that ship in 1862. This boiler was in turn replaced in 1878 with one from Cail (Paris).

*The data are based on two devis dated 17.7.1868 and 19.1.1871.*
**Dimensions & tons:** 52.40m deck, 51.40m wl (stem to sternpost) x 8.00m ext, m wl. 754.347t disp. Draught: 3.20m mean, m aft. Men: 69 & 75.
**Machinery:** 65nhp and 260ihp at 66rpm. Speed 9.9kts. 1 vertical engine with 2 cylinders of 0.866m diameter and 0.660m stroke. 1 boiler. 55t coal. Reboilered 1868 with tubular boiler of 1.356kg/cm$^2$ (later 1.500kg/cm$^2$) built by Peyruc in 1862 and taken from the aviso *Passe Partout*. The boiler pressure could be increased to 1.80kg/cm$^2$ to operate the cable raising equipment without also operating the propulsion machinery.
**Guns:** none.

*Dix Décembre* T. & W. Smith, North Shields/engine by R. & W. Hawthorn, Newcastle upon Tyne, 1860.
Completed 3.1861. Purchased 7.1863. Comm: 5.7.1863.
Boiler overhauled 11.1864, replaced 5-7.1868 and again in 1878 as noted above. Renamed *Ampère* 9.1870. The Ministry of Finances requested a replacement for her on 22.2.1899 because of the age of her engine and wear to her hull and took her out of service for those reasons later in 1899. She was condemned in 1900 at Le Havre and last appeared on navy signal lists in January 1901. (Navy manning reportedly ended earlier, in 1889.) The aviso transport *Vaucluse* was suggested as a replacement but the Navy could not spare her from transport duty and the Ministry of Finances returned *Ampère* to service. She received new cable gear in 1907 and maintained Anglo-French cables in the Channel until she was scrapped in 1925.

---

# III. GUNBOATS

## (A) 2nd Class Gunboats (*Canonnières de 2ᵉ classe*).

To *Bâtiments de flottille* as *Canonnières transformées en bâtiments de flottille, 2ᵉ categorie* in the 1.1880 fleet list, then to *Canonnières de flotille, 2ᵉ categorie* 1.1883 and to to *Canonnières* 1.1884.

### Gunboat characteristics, 1858.

During the Crimean War the French built two types of gunboats designed specifically for coastal offensive and defensive operations, a 1st class of almost 500 tons and a 2nd class of about 300 tons. Both, like the similar British gunboats, gave bad results, the 1st class having neither speed nor seagoing qualities and the 2nd class having an unbalanced rig, excessively fragile high pressure engines, and extremely bad seagoing characteristics, on occasion rolling dangerously. On 10 March 1858 Minister of Marine Hamelin charged the *Conseil des travaux* to review both the French and British experience and recommend characteristics for future gunboats if they were needed. The Council examined the issue on 25 May 1858 at a time when gunboats were being rejected for coastal use in favour of armoured floating batteries and 2nd class avisos were preferred to 1st class gunboats for overseas use. For 2nd class gunboats the Council recommended the existing type, about 280 tons, 2.50m mean draught, the original two-gun armament concentrated forward, a light three-masted schooner rig, and coal for two or three days steaming. The matter was then dropped for a year and a half.

---

**DÉCIDÉE Class.** *Canonnières de 2ᵉ classe.* 2nd class gunboats with wooden hulls and rounded bows. One funnel, two masts, schooner-brig rig. Designed by Aurous.

On 12 December 1859 Minister of Marine Hamelin sent to the ports specifications for a small gunboat intended not only for coastal use in European waters but for crossing the ocean and operating in African and American

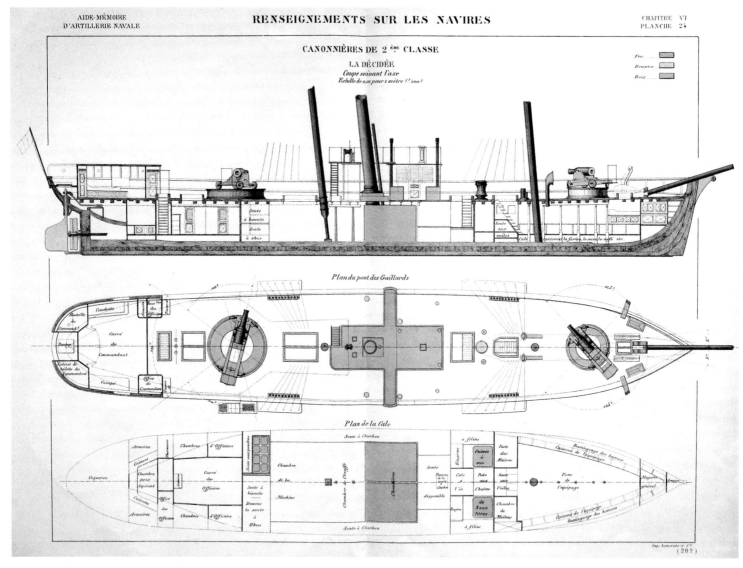

AIDE-MÉMOIRE
D'ARTILLERIE NAVALE

RENSEIGNEMENTS SUR LES NAVIRES

CHAPITRE VI
PLANCHE 24

CANONNIÈRES DE 2.ème CLASSE

LA DÉCIDÉE
*Coupe suivant l'axe*
*Échelle de 0,01 pour 1 mètre (¹⁄₁₀₀)*

*Plan du pont des Gaillards*

*Plan de la Cale*

Inboard profile and upper deck and hold plans of the 2nd class gunboat *Décidée*. The ship had two 138.6mm M1864-67 guns, the apparent difference in their sizes on the plan being due to the forward one being on a short carriage and the after one on a long carriage. (*Aide-Mémoire d'Artillerie navale*, 1879)

rivers. The Minister specified dimensions and draught as in the Crimean gunboats, an armament of two 164mm M1858 guns able to fire forward and to the sides, no armour belt or shield, a speed of at least 8 knots, one screw, and a substantial sailing rig. The Council examined designs responding to these specifications on 3 April 1860. These were closer to the Crimean 1st class gunboats than to the 2nd class because of the need to replace the high pressure engines of the latter with medium pressure engines and the need to augment the endurance and rig for longer range operations. Acknowledging that the weaknesses of the earlier types, notably in rolling and in poor steering, could not be completely eliminated in vessels of this type, it selected the design of naval constructor Jules Aurous. and on 1 October 1860 Minister Hamelin approved revised plans by Aurous and assigned names to the four ships. The Council reviewed more modifications to the design between November 1860 and July 1861. A flat bottom and two lateral false keels permitted the ships to beach themselves and remain high and dry for the duration of a low tide but, as the Council anticipated, they were heavy rollers and hard to steer at sea. The engines were ordered from Schneider by a contract signed on 7 June 1861.

**Dimensions & tons:** 39.56m deck, 38.84m wl x 6.72m ext and wl.

359t disp. Draught: 2.10m fwd, 2.58m aft. Men: 59.

**Machinery:** 60nhp (50 from 1867) and 160ihp designed at 66rpm (engine) and 140rpm (screw) and 1.80kg/cm² boiler pressure. Trials (*Décidée*) 184ihp = 8.19kts, (*Pique*, 4.1863) 173ihp = 8.82kts at 57.9rpm (engine) and 123.3rpm screw with 1.513kg/cm² boiler pressure. 1 screw. 1 horizontal geared engine with direct connecting rods and 2 cylinders of 0.683m diameter and 0.65m stroke. Gear ratio 1 to 2.13. 2 special type return flame boilers. 30.1t coal. Range 690nm @ 8.1kts.

**Guns:**

(1863) 2 x 164.7mm M1858 MLR.

(1870-81) 2 x 138.6mm N° 1 or M1864 (1867) on pivots on platforms, 1 x 4pdr bronze.

(1870, *Surprise* and 1873, *Tactique*) 2 x 12pdr (121mm/17) bronze field guns, 1 x 4pdr (86.5mm/11) bronze on the poop.

*Pique* Toulon Dyd/Schneider, Creusot.
On list 1.1861. Ord: 4.1860. K: 7.1861. L: 16.10.1862.
  Comm: 27.1.1863 (trials). C: 2.1863.
Trials completed 18.7.1863 and sent to Mexico. Struck 13.11.1886, coal hulk at Madagascar (Nossi-Bé) 1886-1887, for sale at Madagascar 1889-1895, sold 1895 to BU.

*Décidée* Toulon Dyd/Schneider, Creusot.
On list 1.1861. Ord: 4.1860. K: 9.1861. L: 11.12.1862.
  Comm: 12.2.1863 (trials). C: 2.1863.

Left 9.1863 for the station of Brazil and the Plata. Struck 8.11.1884, for disposal at Toulon 1884-1885. BU 1885.

*Surprise* Toulon Dyd/Schneider, Creusot.
On list 1.1861. Ord: 4.1860. K: 3.1862. L: 19.2.1863.
  Comm: 1.10.1863 (trials). C: 10.1863.
In Senegal and Gabon 1864. Struck 5.11.1885, renamed *Kep* 1885, station hulk (*ponton stationnaire*) at Haiphong 1885-1887. Replaced 4.1887 by *Nagotna*, sold 13.9.1887 to BU.

*Tactique* Toulon Dyd/Schneider, Creusot.
On list 1.1861. Ord: 4.1860. K: 6.1862. L: 19.3.1863.
  Comm: 1.10.1863 (trials). C: 10.1863.
Departed Toulon 1.2.1864 for Mexico. Struck 28.1.1886 at Buenos Aires. BU 1886.

---

*DILIGENTE. Canonnière de 2e classe.* 2nd class gunboat with a wooden hull. One funnel, two masts, schooner-brig rig. Designed by Lemoine.

In discussion the design for what became the *Décidée* class on 3 April 1860, the *Conseil des travaux* felt that it would be useful to protect the forward part of 2nd class gunboats with transverse armour shields. Minister of Marine Hamelin, when ordering the construction of the unprotected *Décidée* class, also asked the Council for specifications using the new idea. On 12 June 1860 the Council recommended a single 164mm M1858 gun with an armour shield or *masque* 5m from the bow and extending down to the keel to protecting the gunboat as well as the gun while fighting head on. The top part of the shield would be 100mm thick and the bottom part 90mm. The unprotected part of the bow would be low and filled with cork. Other specifications were a speed of 8 knots, coal for 5 days, and a 2.10m draught. The Council estimated the gunboat's displacement at 250 tons. On 20 November 1860 the Council selected a design by naval constructor Nicolas Marie Julien Lemoine, which it approved on 11 May 1861 after modifications. The design was used for a single ship, *Diligente*. The 100mm armoured shield was composed of nine plates of wrought iron and weighed 24 tons. The engines were ordered from Schneider by a contract signed on 10 October 1862 and Minister of Marine Chasseloup-Laubat approved a contract with Mariel frères for nine armour plates on 17 August 1863. Finer lines forward helped increase her speed to 9 knots, but her autonomy was poor. *Diligente* was the model for the *Aspic* class, below, with which she was sometimes listed.

**Dimensions & tons:** 37.40m deck, 36.80m wl x 6.50m ext, 6.36m wl. 283t disp. Draught: 2.20m fwd, 2.38m aft. Men: 59.
**Machinery:** 50nhp (40 from 1867) and 160ihp designed at 80rpm (engine) and 130rpm (screw) and 1.99kg/cm² boiler pressure. Trials (2.1865) 135ihp = 9.03kts at 83rpm (engine) and 137.4rpm (screw) with 1.829kg/cm² boiler pressure. 1 screw. 1 horizontal geared engine with direct connecting rods and 2 cylinders of 0.56m diameter and 0.60m stroke. Gear ratio 2 to 3. 1 special type boiler. 21.6t coal. Range 590nm @ 9kts.
**Armour:** 100mm bulwark forward shielding gun.
**Guns:**
(1864) 1 x 164.7mm M1858 MLR forward. Also had 2 x 4pdr (86.5mm/11) bronze in 1870.
(1875 or before) 1 x 138.6mm, 2 x 12pdr (121mm/17) bronze.

*Diligente* Lorient Dyd/Schneider, Creusot.
On list 1.1862. K: 21.5.1861. L: 2.9.1864. Comm: 1.12.1864 (trials). C: 3.1865.
Left Lorient for Mexico 2.7.1865. Struck 15.11.1878, guard station for the breakwater (*poste de la digue*) at Toulon 1879-1884, barracks hulk at Marseille 1884-1892. BU 1893.

---

*KENNEY* Class. *Canonnières de 2e classe.* 2nd class gunboats with wooden hulls and rounded bows. One funnel, two masts, lugger rig. Designed by Verny.

These ships were ordered on 2 September 1862 and built in an occupied Chinese yard using engines of Crimean War-vintage gunboats whose hulls had worn out. This action was taken in part because it was felt that 2nd class gunboats could not safely make the voyage from France to China. Their plans, by the French naval constructor in charge at Ningpo, François Léonce Verny, were similar to other 2nd class gunboats but had lower upper works and a lighter rig as they were intended for river operations and not to go to sea. The plans were signed by Verny at Brest on 2 October 1862 and approved by Minister of Marine Chasseloup-Laubat on 11 October 1862. They were given names of French officers killed during the Taiping Rebellion. Their short service was due to the poor quality of wood available and, it was said, to the tendency of the Chinese workers to steal nails and other metal fasteners.

**Dimensions & tons:** 36.04m deck, 35.38m wl x 6.72m ext. 253t disp. Draught: 1.94m fwd, 2.14m aft. Men: 59.
**Machinery:**
(*Kenney* and *Bourdais*): 90nhp (55 from 1867) at 180rpm. Speed 8.4kts. 1 screw. 1 engine with 2 cylinders of 0.44m diameter and 0.4m stroke.
(*Le Brethon* and *Tardif*): 90nhp (55 from 1867) at 120rpm. Speed 8.4kts. 1 screw. 1 horizontal high pressure (5 atmosphere) engine with direct connecting rods and 2 cylinders of 0.46 m diameter and 0.4 m stroke, 1 boiler.
**Guns:** (1864) 1 x 164.7mm rifle, 2 x 12pdr (121mm/17) bronze MLR.

*Kenney* Ningpo (engine by Charbonnier et Bourguignon from *Poudre*).
On list 1.1863. Ord: 2.9.1862. K: 5.2.1863. L: 31.10.1863.
  Comm: 1.12.1863 (trials). C: 12.1863.
Decomm. at Saigon 3.4.1865, could not be repaired. Struck 7.7.1868 at Saigon. BU 1869.

*Bourdais* (*Commandant Bourdais*) Ningpo (engine by Charbonnier et Bourguignon from *Redoute*).
On list 1.1863. Ord: 2.9.1862. K: 25.4.1863. L: 20.5.1864.
  Comm: 18.6.1864 (trials). C: 6.1864.
Struck 7.7.1868 at Saigon. BU 1869.

*Le Brethon* (*Lebrethon*) Ningpo (engine by Gouin from *Salve*).
On list 1.1863. Ord: 2.9.1862. K: 20.7.1863. L: 17.9.1864.
  Comm: 9.11.1864 (trials). C: 11.1864.
Originally named *Aigrette*, renamed *Lebrethon* 25.9.1863. Commissioned at Shanghai. Participated in the Korean expedition of October 1866. Struck 19.4.1869 at Saigon and sold to BU.

*Tardif* Ningpo (engine by Gouin from *Arquebuse*).
On list 1.1863. Ord: 2.9.1862. K: 15.11.1863. L: 14.12.1864.
  Comm: 26.1.1865 (trials). C: 1.1865.
Originally named *Aventure*, renamed *Tardif* 25.9.1863. Struck 7.7.1868 at Saigon, replaced lorcha *Donaï* as lightship (*bateau-feu*) 30.7.1869.

---

*ASPIC* Class. *Canonnières de 2e classe.* 2nd class gunboats with wooden hulls and straight bows. One funnel, two masts, schooner-brig rig. Designed by Lemoine.

These gunboats were repeats of *Diligente* enlarged to carry more coal and stores for greater autonomy. When sent to Mexico in 1865 Nicolas Lemoine's *Diligente* with her gun removed was an excellent sea boat, needing only a higher bow, but her coal supply had to be reduced to 2.5 days and she could not carry the provisions and water in the original specifications. On 1 August 1865 the *Conseil des travaux* reviewed her reports and recommended that future gunboats be lengthened to carry the supplies needed for a longer campaign. Lemoine then prepared a new design with increased length and sail area. The Council approved the design on 27 March 1866, on 26 April 1866 Minister of Marine Chasseloup-Laubat ordered construction of four gunboats, and on 22 May 1866 he approved Lemoine's plans for a modified *Diligente*. A contract with Schneider for the engines was approved on 30 May 1866 and a contract with Châtillon for the armour plates was approved on 11 June 1866.

Although brand new, *Couleuvre* underwent at Cherbourg a transformation to allow her to navigate from France to Cochinchina. According to plans dated 8 September 1867 a full sized permanent poop replaced the original after deckhouse and a temporary rudder and an additional keel were fitted for the voyage. Upon arrival in Cochinchina the additional keel was removed and the rudder was replaced with the original river rudder. All four were sent to the Far East. In contrast to their predecessors their seagoing qualities were completely satisfactory, but their speed fell to 8 knots.

*The characteristics are based on a devis for* Frelon *dated 30.7.1867.*

**Dimensions & tons:** 39,890m deck, 39.40m wl, 39.56m pp (wl fwd to rudder) x 6.58m ext, 6.440m wl. 283.982t disp. Draught: 2.100m mean, 2.200m aft. (The displacement of *Couleuvre* for the trip to China was 310t at 2.253m mean draught including the 30pounder in the hold.) Men: 40.

**Machinery:** 50nhp (40nhp from 1867) and 160ihp designed at 80rpm (engine) and 130rpm (screw) and 4.32kg/cm² boiler pressure. Trials (*Frelon*, 9.1866) 146ihp = 8.00kts at 81.5rpm (engine) and 131.87rpm (screw) with 1,790kg/cm² boiler pressure. 1 screw. 1 horizontal geared engine with direct connecting rods and 2 cylinders of 0.56m diameter and 0.60m stroke. Gear ratio 80 to 130. 1 boiler. 39.8t coal. Range 1,070nm @ 8.2kts.

**Armour:** Armoured bulwark forward shielding gun.

**Guns:** 1 x 164.7mm M1858 (forward). On the transit to Cochinchina the 164.7mm (30pdr) gun was placed in the hold and 2 x 4pdr (86.5mm/11) bronze mountain guns were mounted on the upper deck.

*Aspic* Lorient Dyd/Schneider, Creusot (engines designed by Mathieu).
On list 1.1867. K: 26.4.1866. L: 11.8.1866. Comm: 13.8.1866 (trials). C: 9.1866.
Left Cherbourg for Cochinchina 12.9.1867. Wrecked 13.1.1877 off the small coastal port of Manh-Son in northern Annam. Struck 29.4.1877.

*Couleuvre* Lorient Dyd/Schneider, Creusot (engines designed by Mathieu).

A 2nd class gunboat, either *Scorpion* or *Frelon*, at Lorient in August 1866 during trials. Note the transverse bulkhead forward to protect the vessel's single big gun, not present in this view.

On list 1.1867. K: 28.5.1866. L: 11.8.1866. Comm: 13.8.1866 (trials), C: 9.1866.
Machinery installed late 7.1866 to 8.1866. To reserve after trials 1.10.1866. Recommissioned (full) 13.5.1867. Ordered to China 7.6.1867. Transited from Lorient to Cherbourg 2-4.8.1867, then left Cherbourg for Cochinchina 12.9.1867 and arrived Saigon 29.4.1868. Repaired 1875 to 4.1878, then replaced *Flamme* as a lightship at Cangiou Point near the mouth of the Saigon River with machinery ashore, hull deteriorated rapidly. Struck 24.2.1882, for disposal in Cochinchina 1882-1887, BU at Saigon.

*Frelon* Lorient Dyd/Schneider, Creusot (engines designed by Mathieu).
On list 1.1867. K: 28.5.1866. L: 11.8.1866. Comm: 13.8.1866 (trials), C: 9.1866.
Machinery installed 7.1866. Recommissioned 19.5.1867 (full). Left Cherbourg for Cochinchina 12.9.1867. Returned to Toulon 7.1874 via Mayotte. Struck 15.11.1878, guard station for the breakwater at Toulon 1879-1888, for sale 1888-1889.

*Scorpion* Lorient Dyd/Schneider, Creusot (engines designed by Mathieu).
On list 1.1867. K: 5.1866. L: 13.8.1866. Comm: 13.8.1866 (trials). C: 9.1866.
Left Cherbourg for Cochinchina 12.9.1867. Struck 4.8.1876 (published 28.9.1876), given to the King of Annam on that date with the aviso *D'Estaing* under a commercial treaty of 15.3.1874. Was at Tourane (Da Nang) in 1883 in bad condition.

––––––––––––

## (B) 1st Class Gunboats (*Canonnières de 1ʳᵉ classe*).

Newer ones to *Canonnières de stations* in the 1.1880 fleet list. *Chacal* class to *Bâtiments de flottille* as *Canonnières transformées en bâtiments de flotille, 1ʳᵉ categorie* 1.1880, then to *Canonnières de flotille, 1ʳᵉ categorie* 1.1883. All to *Canonnières* 1.1884.

**CHACAL Class.** *Canonnières de 1ʳᵉ classe.* 1st class gunboats with wooden hulls and straight bows. One tall funnel, two tripod masts, schooner-brig rig. Designed by Dupuy de Lôme.

On 5 January 1867 Minister of Marine Chasseloup-Laubat decided to build eight new gunboats to the design of *Diligente* modified to increase the armament. They were designed for service in European waters, although after the 1870 war some also served on overseas stations. In previous gunboats ordinary methods had been used to train the guns, but the new class used platforms rotating on central pivots. The artillery was initially set at one 194mm gun on a rotating platform forward of the foremast and two 12pdr (121mm/17) bronze field guns. (It was changed on 2 January 1869 to one 194mm gun as before, a single 12pdr on a pivoting platform aft, and two 4pdr (86.5mm/11) bronze mountain guns.) The speed was increased to 10 knots. To get this speed in shallow draft hulls required the use of twin screws, and high pressure engines with Belleville boilers were also adopted. The most conspicuous features were two tripod masts not supported by rigging and a very tall thin funnel. These changes led to an increase in displacement to 455 tons causing the ships to be classified as 1st class gunboats. Plans by Dupuy de Lôme were approved on 7 June 1867. With their shallow draught and full lines they retained the poor seagoing qualities of some of their predecessors, with extreme rolling, pitching that caused the bow to embark huge amounts of water and practically stop the ship, and erratic steering under sail.

The original high pressure engines and Belleville boilers caused constant problems and eventually had to be replaced. *Chacal*'s machinery trials at Toulon lasted for an abnormally long time. The engines had problems with metal fouling and overheating of the liners and seals, which the engine builders blamed on the novel Belleville boilers providing steam that was either too dry or too saturated depending on the circumstances. Ultimately the boilers were replaced in 1874-75 in all eight ships and the engines were also replaced in the four ships built at La Seyne with engines by Farcot and Son at Saint-Ouen. In the mid-1870s the platform with the heavy bulwark forward for the 194mm gun was replaced with a platform for a 138.6mm gun, and later a forecastle was fitted. *Étendard* received a charthouse and transverse bridge in 1886, and a poop in 1888 for hydrographic service.

*The characteristics are based on a devis for* Gladiateur *dated 27.3.1875 with machinery data for the FCM ships from two devis for* Léopard *dated 29.7.1870 and 8.4.1881.*

**Dimensions & tons:** 45m oa, 44.20m wl, 43.70m pp (wl fwd to rudder) x 7.40m ext and wl. 482t disp. Draught: 2.49m mean, 2.79m aft. Men: 70.

**Machinery:**

(FCM ships) 60nhp and 240ihp designed at 135rpm and 6kg/cm² boiler pressure. Trials (11.2.1870) 258.59ihp = 9.28kts at 144/138.80 rpm (stbd/port). 2 screws. 2 horizontal engines with direct connecting rods and 2 cylinders of 0.326m diameter and 0.300m stroke. 2 Belleville boilers. 38t coal.

(FCM ships re-engined) 65nhp and 260ihp designed at 160rpm and 4.4kg/cm² boiler pressure. Trials (6.7.1875) 277.58ihp = 9.6kts at 164/165.25 rpm. 2 screws. 2 vertical Woolf high-pressure engines with 2 cylinders of 0.365m and 0.655m diameter and 0.396m stroke. 1 tubular return-flame high-pressure boiler. 41t coal.

(Bordeaux ships) 60nhp and 240ihp designed at 135rpm and 6.0kg/cm² boiler pressure. Trials (*Étendard*, 4.10.1869) 273.70ihp = 9.394kts at 145.88rpm; (*Gladiateur*, 3.1875 with new boilers) 215ihp = 9.59kts at 139.7rpm and 4.66kg/cm² boiler pressure. 2 screws. 2 horizontal simple expansion engines with direct connecting rods and 2 cylinders of 0.32m diameter and 0.30m stroke. 1 Belleville boiler, replaced by 2 cylindrical return-flame boilers of 5.25kg/cm² pressure built at Indret. 58.6t coal. Range 1,570nm @ 9.6kts.

**Guns:**

(1870-71) 1 x 194mm (on rotating platform forward surrounded by a 9.5-ton bulwark with passages for the anchor chains), 1 x 12pdr (121mm/17) bronze aft, 2 x 4pdr (86.5mm/11) bronze. In 1875 *Gladiateur* had a 164.7mm gun forward instead of the 194mm.

(1879-81) 1 x 138.6mm/21.3 M1870 pivot (after end of a new forecastle), 1 x 100mm M1870-75 (aft), 2 x 37mm Hotchkiss revolving cannon aft. The two big guns in *Étendard* got steel shields in 1884. *Hyène* added 1 x 4pdr (86.5mm/11) bronze or 1 x 65mm landing gun in 1887.

(1887, *Étendard*) All guns were landed in 1887 when she was fitted for hydrographic work except for a 4pdr line-throwing gun. In 1890 she had 2 x 4pdr (86.5mm/11) bronze guns for the boats.

*Chacal* F.C. Méditerranée, La Seyne/FCM, Marseille (engines designed by Louis-Édouard Lecointre).
On list 1.1868. K: 10.9.1867. L: 11.4.1868. Comm: 22.6.1868 (trials). C: 7.1869.
Decomm. 16.7.1869, in comm. 7.10.1869 to 1.1.1870 for more trials and 21.7.1870 to 11.11.1870 for war operations in the Middle East. Out of comm. 1871-1881 except engines and boiler replaced 11.1874 to 5.1875 at Toulon, then in comm. 11.5.1875 to 24.7.1875, probably for trials. To Tunisia 1881 and then operated in the Mediterranean through 1890 with a visit to Obock and Aden in 1884. Struck 31.7.1888 at Nossi-Bé, for sale 1888-1895.

*Hyène* F.C. Méditerranée, La Seyne/FCM, Marseille (engines designed by Louis-Édouard Lecointre).
On list 1.1868. K: 18.9.1867. L: 23.5.1868. Comm: 21.7.1870 (trials). C: 7.1870.
Left Toulon for Sicily 2.8.1870. Decomm. 16.11.1870 after war service in the Mediterranean. Engines and boiler replaced 1874 to 9.1874 at Toulon, then recomm. 12.8.1874 for more Mediterranean service.

The 1st class gunboat *Hyène* at Toulon showing her tall thin funnel and two tripod masts. (*NHHC from ONI album of French warships, NH-74810*)

Forecastle modified 1884 and sent to Tonkin. Struck 23.4.1889, light-ship at the mouth of the river leading to Haïphong (probably replacing *Léopard*) 1889-1893, for sale at Haïphong 1893-1894.

*Jaguar* F.C. Méditerranée, La Seyne/FCM, Marseille (engines designed by Louis-Édouard Lecointre).
On list 1.1868. K: 27.9.1867. L: 13.6.1868. Comm: 1.2.1870 (trials). C: 4.1870.
Decomm. 1.4.1870, probably after trials. In comm. for war service in the Mediterranean 21.7.1870 to 26.11.1870. Engines and boiler replaced 3.1874 to 1.1875 at Toulon, then in commission 1.1.1875 to 1.3.1875, probably for trials. To Senegal 2.1880 but towed home 1881 with engine failure. In Tunisia 1882-83, left for Indochina 8.3.1884. Struck 22.8.1888, for sale at Saigon 1888-1889.

*Léopard* F.C. Méditerranée, La Seyne/FCM, Marseille (engines designed by Louis-Édouard Lecointre).
On list 1.1868. K: 14.10.1867. L: 4.7.1868. Comm: 1.1.1870 (trials). C: 2.1870.
Machinery installed 5.7.1868 to 13.1.1870. Decomm. 1.2.1870, probably after trials. In comm. for war service in the Mediterranean 21.7.1870 to 22.12.1870 (sent to the Levant). New engines installed 2.7.1874 to 11.3.1875 at Toulon, then in commission 25.2.1875 to 16.5.1875, probably for trials. In Tunisia 1881, then left for Saigon 13.9.1881. Struck 17.11.1886, hulk in Tonkin 1886-1887, replaced a junk as a lightship at the mouth of the river leading to Haïphong 1887-1889. Probably replaced by *Hyène*.

*Gladiateur* C.A. de l'Océan (Arman), Bordeaux-Bacalan/C.A. de l'Océan (ex Mazeline), Le Havre (engines designed by Amédée Mangin).
On list 1.1868. K: 10.12.1867. L: 5.8.1868. Comm: 15.8.1868 (trials). C: 5.1869.
Arrived at Lorient 12.1868 for trials and fitting out. Decomm. 11.5.1869 at Lorient. No 1870-71 war service. Reboilered 1874 to 3.1875 at Lorient, then in commission 1.3.1875 to 8.5.1877 for overseas service. Annex of the school for engineers at Toulon 16.8.1880, to Tunisia 1881. Struck 31.12.1890, coal hulk at Toulon 1890-1902 (converted 1890-1892). Sold 1902 at Toulon to BU.

*Oriflamme* C.A. de l'Océan (Arman), Bordeaux-Bacalan/C.A. de l'Océan (ex Mazeline), Le Havre (engines designed by Amédée Mangin).
On list 1.1868. K: 10.1867. L: 17.8.1868. Comm: 16.9.1868 (trials). C: 10.1869.
Decomm. 1.10.1869. Comm. 7.9.1870, active on the Seine in late 1870, decomm. at Lorient 8.4.1871. Reboilered 1873 to 4.1874 at Lorient,

then in comm. 1.4.1874 to 27.12.1876 as station ship in the Bidassoa. Served as seagoing school for pilots at the School of Piloting of the West at La Rochelle in place of *Argus* 1880-82 and after that school closed in Senegal 1882-84. Struck 30.12.1884, mooring hulk at Rochefort 1884-1900, guard hulk 1900-1902. Sold 1902 to BU.

*Étendard* C.A. de l'Océan (Arman), Bordeaux-Bacalan/C.A. de l'Océan (ex Mazeline), Le Havre (engines designed by Amédée Mangin).
On list 1.1868. K: 10.12.1867. L: 17.8.1868. Comm: 10.10.1868 (trials). C: 10.1869.
Machinery installed 1.10.1868 to 25.10.1868. Launch also reported as 3.9.1868. Arrived at Lorient from Bordeaux 15.1.1869. Decomm. 17.10.1869. In comm. 25.8.1870 to 8.4.1871, active on the lower Seine from Rouen with *Oriflamme* and *Alerte* 12.1870 to 31.1.1871. Out of commission 1871-1881. Reboilered 1874 to 12.1874 at Lorient (new Indret boilers installed 15.12.1874). Transferred from Lorient to Toulon and cruise on Tunisian coast 1881-82. Major repairs 1883-84. Mission to Obock from Toulon 19.3.1884 to 4.11.1884. Hydrographic mission on Tunisian coast 25.4.1885 to 1.11.1885. Hydrographic missions off Corsica 26.4.1887 to 14.11.1887 and 19.5.1888 to 20.12.1888. Decomm. 30.7.1891. Struck 7.5.1892 at Toulon, sold 1892 to BU.

*Fanfare* C.A. de l'Océan (Arman), Bordeaux-Bacalan/C.A. de l'Océan (ex Mazeline), Le Havre (engines designed by Amédée Mangin).
On list 1.1868. K: 12.11.1867. L: 24.8.1868. Comm: 10.10.1868 (trials). C: 8.1869.
Decomm. 1.9.1869 at Lorient. No 1870-71 war service. Reboilered 1874 to 1.1875 at Lorient. To Tunisia 1881, then left for Cochinchina 15.9.1881. Struck 25.10.1890, for sale at Saigon 1890-1891.

---

### Gunboats in the Programme of 1872
In his report to Minister of Marine Pothuau on the composition of the fleet the Director of Material included no gunboats in the main part of the fleet but placed a group of 32 *canonnières* at the end of his list, presumably as flotilla craft. The *Conseil d'Amirauté* considered these *canonnières* a powerful and economical reserve of floating artillery and moved them to the group of ships intended for the attack and defence of the coast. On 14 November 1871 the *Conseil des travaux* developed for this category characteristics for *chaloupes-canonnières* (gun launches, essentially small craft with one oversized gun like the British *Staunch*), but the Director of Materiel felt that, in view of certain contingencies outside Europe, it was necessary for the fleet to include a class of seagoing armed vessels with a draught notably less than the 3.60m of the new 2nd class avisos. Equating the *chaloupes-canonnières* with British gunboats, he said it was necessary to create a gun vessel. The *Conseil des travaux* on 23 January 1872 therefore established specifications a new type of gunboat to replace the *Chacal*, *Décidée*, and *Aspic* classes, combining the essential characteristics of the *chaloupe-canonnière* with the ability to cross the ocean safely. An order from Minister of Marine Pothuau dated 19 February 1872 asked the ports to produce designs for a ship with a composite wood and iron hull (instead of the wood hull specified by the Council), a maximum draught aft of 2.40, one screw, a speed of 10 knots, a range of 2,400nm at 7 knots, a substantial sail area, and an estimated displacement of 451 tons. The armament was to consist of one 194mm gun behind the foremast and one 12pdr forward and one aft, both on raised centreline platforms. On 19 November 1872 the Council examined five designs based on the 19 February 1872 specifications and rejected all of them. A design by naval constructor Victor André Daymard was good enough for the Council to invite him to revise it, but it was overtaken by Bertin's design for *Crocodile*.

---

***CROCODILE* Class.** *Canonnières de 1re classe.* 1st class gunboats with composite hulls including two longitudinal layers of teak planking (oak below the waterline) on iron frames, iron deck beams and beam shelves, and ram bows. One funnel, three masts, barque rig (later barquentine). Designed by Bertin.

On 18 December 1872 naval constructor Émile Bertin submitted a design for a 1st class gunboat. He later wrote that the vessel was intended for local service in France, not for distant navigation. The *Conseil des travaux* examined the design on 14 January 1873 and Minister of Marine Pothuau sent it back to Bertin on 23 January 1873 asking him to make the changes requested by the Council. These changes included a less extreme form of the inverted ram-shaped bow (*étrave renversée*), a change from two to three masts, and lowering the 194mm gun. The bow had a small 270kg bronze ram but Bertin later stated that its main role was not ramming but reducing pitching and reducing resistance to propulsion. On 26 February 1873 Pothuau asked the *Conseil des travaux* to examine Bertin's revised design. The Council approved his plan on 11 March 1873 subject to several final changes, one of which involved the mounting of the after 12pdr gun. Pothuau approved the plans on 9 April 1873. Four more ships were added to the list in January 1874. The 1875 budget also included an unnamed sister to be built by contract, she was not in the 1876 budget. *Lionne* was the first to run trials with disappointing results. She was later re-rigged with two masts and a full brig rig, a change not made to the three Cherbourg ships.

*The characteristics are based on a devis for* Lynx *dated 31.7.1878.*
**Dimensions & tons:** 43.00m wl (+0.40m ram), 44.24m pp (wl fwd to rudder) x 7.30m ext and wl. 471t disp. Draught: 2.50m mean, 2.92m aft. Men: 77.
**Machinery:** 100nhp and 400ihp designed at 120rpm and 4.212kg/cm$^2$ boiler pressure. Trials (*Lynx*, 6.1878) 423ihp = 10.38kts at 126.0rpm and 4.25kg/cm$^2$ boiler pressure. 1 screw. 1 compound engine with return connecting rods and 2 cylinders of 0.7515m and 1.2015m diameter and 0.45m stroke. 2 special cylindrical boilers, 53.9t coal. Range 1,110nm @ 10kts.
**Guns:**
(c1875, *Crocodile* and *Lionne*) 1 x 194mm/18 M1864 on a central pivot between the funnel and the mainmast, 2 x 12pdr (121mm/17) bronze on central pivots, one on the forecastle and one on the poop.
(1877, *Crocodile*) 1 x 194mm, 2 x 100mm.
(1878, *Lynx*) 2 x 138.6mm, 2 x 100mm.
(c1894, *Lynx* and *Lutin*) 2 x 100mm guns upgraded to M1875M.

*Crocodile* Cherbourg Dyd.
On list 1.1874. K: 22.4.1873. L: 16.6.1874. Comm: 24.5.1875 (trials), 26.8.1875 (full).
Budget 1872. Named 9.4.1873. Seagoing school for piloting at Saint Servan 1877-78 between *Faon* and *Élan*. To the Granville station 1878-82 and to service off Newfoundland 1883. Struck 7.3.1894, floating electricity plant at Lorient 1894-1896, for sale 1896-1897, replenishment hulk for the *Défense mobile* at Concarneau 1898-1899, same at la Trinité-sur-mer 1899-1900, torpedo boat station at la Trinité 1901-1914, floating barracks at Lorient 1920-1922, hulk 1922-1929, landing hulk 1929-1939. Still afloat at Lorient 10.1943.

*Lionne* Bichon frères, Bordeaux-Lormont.
On list 1.1874. K: 9.1873. L: 4.5.1874. Comm: 6.9.1874 (trials).
Budget 1872. Construction reassigned from Brest to contract c1873. On the Channel and North Sea station 1880-83, to Tonkin 1884. Struck 16.2.1888, for sale at Cherbourg 1888-1889.

*Lutin* Cherbourg Dyd.
On list 1.1874 (unnamed). K: 3.3.1874. L: 2.8.1877. Comm: 15.3.1878 (trials). C: 5.1878.
Budget 1875. Named 11.4.1874. Decomm. 10.5.1878 after trials. To the China station 1881. Ceded 16.1.1897 to Cambodia for use as a yacht. Struck 8.3.1897. Burned accidentally 23.3.1903 and destroyed at Port Dayot.

The gunboat *Lionne* at Algiers on 26 December 1886, re-rigged with two masts. At this time she was probably returning from Tonkin, where the shield around her bow gun would have been necessary. The ram-shaped bow in this class was replaced in later classes with more conventional bows. (*NHHC from ONI album of French warships, NH-74992*)

*Lynx* Cherbourg Dyd.
On list 1.1874 (unnamed). K: 3.3.1874. L: 19.2.1878.
   Comm: 15.5.1878 (trials). C: 7.1878.
Budget 1875. Named 11.4.1874. Saigon 1878, from Madagascar and decomm. 1896. Struck 3.2.1899. Sold for BU at Cherbourg.

*N* (Unnamed) Contract
Budget 1875, not in the 1876 budget.

*Milan* Rochefort Dyd.
On list 1.1875 only.
Budget 1876, not in 1877 budget. Cancelled 1875.

*Vautour* Rochefort Dyd.
On list 1.1875 only.
Budget 1876, not in 1877 budget. Cancelled 1875.

———————

*ASPIC* Class. *Canonnières de 1re classe, Canonnières de stations* (1880). 1st class (station) gunboats with composite hulls including two longitudinal layers of teak planking on steel frames, iron deck beams and beam shelves, and straight bows. One funnel, three masts, barquentine rig. Designed by Bertin.

On 8 October 1878 Minister of Marine Pothuau ordered Cherbourg to have Émile Bertin draw up a new design for a composite gunboat for distant stations. In this directive Pothuau specified the replacement of the ram-shaped bow (*étrave renversée*) with a straight bow (*étrave droite*). Bertin's design for a modified *Lynx* largely duplicated that ship, giving the new ship a straight bow while retaining the same total length and underwater lines forward of *Lynx*. Bertin signed the design on 16 November 1878 and Cherbourg forwarded it two days later. Bertin and his superiors at Cherbourg acknowledged that the *étrave renversée* in *Lynx* had encountered some criticism in service but felt that the change to a straight bow would notably reduce her seakeeping qualities by adding to her weight forward. The hull structure was the same as in *Lynx* except for some lightening of frames and beams amidships where *Lynx* had been designed to carry a heavy 194mm gun. On 26 November 1878 Minister Pothuau approved the design for use in the construction of *Vipère* and *Aspic* at Rochefort and ordered construction to begin. The contract with Claparède for the engines for both ships was dated 22 December 1879. An increase in hull weight just before the *mise en rade* (completion of fitting out) in September 1881 was largely due to items added to the hull at the last

moment for the installation of two 138.6mm guns, particularly the bronze and wood tracks on which they rotated.

*The characteristics are based on a devis for* Aspic *dated 10.9.1881.*
**Dimensions & tons:** 42.87m wl, 44.40m pp (wl fwd to rudder) x 7.30m ext and wl. 476.283t disp. Draught: 2.721m mean, 3.171m aft. Men: 77.
**Machinery:** 100nhp and 400ihp designed (plus 20ihp for the circulating pump) at 120rpm and 4.15kg/cm² boiler pressure. Trials (*Aspic*, 25.7.1881) 435.2ihp = 10.304kts at 120rpm and 4.29kg/cm² boiler pressure. 1 screw. 1 horizontal compound engine with return connecting rods and 2 cylinders of 0.75m and 1.20m diameter and 0.45m stroke. 2 special cylindrical direct flame boilers, 52.4t coal. Range 1,080nm @ 10kts.
**Guns:**
(1881) 2 x 138.6mm/21.3 M1870 (on upper deck on centreline pivots, 1 between the funnel and the mainmast and one between the main and mizzen masts), 2 x 100mm/26.5 M1870 (1 on the forecastle, 1 on the low poop).
(c1894, *Aspic* and *Vipère*) 2 x 100mm guns upgraded to M1875M.

*Aspic* Rochefort Dyd/Claparède, Saint Denis.
On list 1.1879. Ord: 26.11.1878. K: 4.1879. L: 2.10.1880.
   Comm: 1.7.1881 (trials), 1.9.1881 (full).
Budget 1878. Laid down 20.10.1879. Machinery contract approved 13.1.1880, machinery installed 19.3.1881 to 15.6.1881. To Tunisia 1881, the Levant 1882, and Tonkin 1883. Struck 9.4.1906. Sold 20.10.1906 at Saigon to Chinese merchants from Saigon and Cholon.

*Vipère* Rochefort Dyd/Claparède, Saint Denis.
On list 1.1879. K: 4.1879. L: 12.2.1881. Comm: 1881 (trials), 2.1882 (full).
Budget 1878. To Tunisia 1881-82, and Tonkin 1883. Struck 4.12.1905, for sale at Saigon 1905-1907, central service ship for the submarine station at Saïgon 1907-1909, for sale at Saigon 1909-1910.

———————

*CAPRICORNE* Class. *Canonnières de stations*. Station gunboats with wooden hulls including three layers of crossed wooden planking on wooden frames with iron deck beams but no beam shelves, and clipper bows. One funnel, three masts, barquentine rig. Designed by Bertin and Normand.

These gunboats were a development of Bertin's *Aspic* class built by Normand and using Normand's hull structure of wooden frames and three layers of hull planking, including two thin diagonal layers crossing each other on the inside and a single thicker longitudinal layer on the outside. The straight bow in the *Aspic* class was also replaced with a clipper bow. Normand signed the contract on 13 October 1879.

*The characteristics are based on a devis for* Sagittaire *dated 8.12.1882.*
**Dimensions & tons:** 44.67m wl, 45.67m pp (wl fwd to rudder) x 7.35m ext and wl. 485.8t disp. Draught: 2.934m mean, 3.328m aft. Men: 80.
**Machinery:** 100nhp and 400ihp natural draught designed at 120rpm and 4.150kg/cm² boiler pressure. Trials (*Sagittaire*, 5.7.1883) 663.5ihp forced draught = 12.166kts at 142.75rpm and 4.74kg/cm² boiler pressure. 1 screw. 1 horizontal compound engine with return connecting rods and 2 cylinders of 0.75 and 1.20m diameter and 0.45m stroke. 2 special cylindrical direct flame boilers, 67.1t coal. Range 1,380nm @ 10kts.
**Guns:** (1882) 2 x 138.6mm/21.3 M1870 (on centreline pivots, 1 between the funnel and the mainmast and 1 between the main and mizzen masts), 2 x 100mm/26.5 M1870-75 (1 on the forecastle and 1 on the poop), 2 x 37mm revolving cannon on a rotating platform. In *Sagittaire* the 100mm guns were upgraded to M1875M in 1890.

*Capricorne* Augustin Normand, Le Havre.
On list 1.1880. K: 1.11.1879. L: 24.4.1882. C: 25.8.1883.

Budget 1879. To the Indian Ocean 1883. Struck 17.8.1906. Sold 18.1.1907 at Diégo-Suarez to BU.

*Sagittaire* Augustin Normand, Le Havre/Claparède, Saint Denis.
On list 1.1.1880. K: 1.11.1879. L: 8.10.1881. Comm: 24.7.1882 (trials), 21.11.1882 (full).
Budget 1879. Engine installed 14.12.1881 to 1.7.1882. Left Cherbourg 1.1883 to take Savorgnan Brazza to the Congo for his third exploring expedition. In the South Atlantic 1883-84 and the Far East 1884-86. Struck 24.4.1896, suction dredge at Rochefort 1896-1908, hopper barge 1908-1914, for sale at Lorient 1920.

---

## Gunboats in the Programmes of 1879 and 1881

The Programme of 1872 had included 32 screw gunboats (some of them gun launches) among the ships intended for coastal defence and attack in European waters. In the Programme of 1879 the newer gunboats built since 1872 were reclassed as station gunboats, reflecting their actual use alongside the avisos there. The two types were retained as station avisos and gunboats in the 1881 programme. The older gunboats and all of the gun launches (*chaloupes-canonnières*, demoted in 1874 to flotilla craft) were relegated in 1879 to a coast defence category that was declared to be obsolete and not to be reproduced, and in 1881 the older gunboats were included with the gun launches among the many types of flotilla craft.

---

*LION* **Class.** *Canonnières de stations.* Station gunboats with composite hulls including two longitudinal layers of teak planking on steel frames, steel deck beams and beam shelves, and clipper bows (*étraves élancées*). One funnel, three masts, barquentine rig. Designed by Bertin and Normand.

In this class, still based on Bertin's *Aspic*, Normand shifted from his wooden hull as in *Capricorne* to a composite hull as in *Aspic* but spaced the steel frames further apart than usual and reinforced the planking with steel bands. *Lion* and *Scorpion* were ordered first, then Minister of Marine Jauréguiberry on February 1882 ordered *Comète* and *Météore* to be built to the plans of *Lion*, which had just been approved. The engines of the four ships were ordered from Claparède by a contract of 1 May 1882, delivery dates were between 10 May 1883 for *Comète* and 10 February 1884 for *Scorpion*.

*The characteristics are based on a devis for* Lion *dated 2.3.1885.*
**Dimensions & tons:** 44.95m wl, 46.35m pp (wl fwd to rudder) x

The gunboat *Lion*, typical of the French gunboats built in the early 1880s. The main battery of two 138.6mm guns was on the upper deck behind the bulwarks along the deck edge while the second battery of two 100mm guns was on the forecastle and poop. (*NHHC, NH-74993*)

7.565m ext and wl. 503.4t disp. Draught: 2.93m mean, 3.28m aft. Men: 78.
**Machinery:** 100nhp and 420ihp natural draught designed at 120rpm and 4.15kg/cm$^2$ boiler pressure. Trials (*Lion*, 16.2.1883) 601.8ihp forced draught = 11.80kts at 141.12rpm and 3.800kg/cm$^2$ boiler pressure. 1 screw. 1 horizontal compound engine with return connecting rods and 2 cylinders of 0.75m and 1.20m diameter and 0.45m stroke. 2 special cylindrical direct flame boilers, 66.4t coal. Range 1,365nm @ 10kts.
**Guns:** (1885) 2 x 138.6mm (on centreline pivots, 1 between the funnel and the mainmast and one between the main and mizzen masts), 2 x 100mm (1 on the forecastle and 1 on the poop).

*Lion* Augustin Normand, Le Havre/Claparède, Saint Denis.
On list 1.1882. Ord: 10.1881 (contract). K: 1.6.1882. L: 9.4.1884. Comm: 27.1.1885 (trials), 12.2.1885 (full).
Budget 1884. Machinery ordered 1.5.1882 and installed 17.4.1884 to 5.8.1884. Arrived Cherbourg 2.12.1884 for trials. Trials 2.1885. Left Cherbourg 3.3.1885 for Haiphong. Struck 9.5.1904. Sold 23.10.1907 at Saigon.

*Scorpion* F.C. Méditerranée, Le Havre-Graville/Claparède, Saint Denis.
On list 1.1882. Ord: 10.1881 (contract). K: 1.6.1882. L: 20.9.1884. Comm: 5.1885 (trials), 4.6.1885 (full).
Budget 1884. Machinery ordered 1.5.1882 and installed 25.9.1884 to 12.12.1884. To Cherbourg for trials 19.1.1885. Trials 5-6.1885. Left Cherbourg 8.6.1885 for the Indian Ocean. Decomm. 12.7.1902 at Lorient. Struck 17.1.1905, intended as hulk for the post for torpedo boats at Le Rocher (near Longeville-sur-Mer) 1906-1914 but never sent there, used to train naval constructors in 1905 and rig removed for training use ashore 4.1908. Floating barracks at Lorient 1920-1922, hulk 1922-1929, landing hulk 1929-1939. May have been sunk during the aerial bombardment of Lorient at the end of 1943. Wreck sold 1947 for BU at Lorient.

*Comète* Cherbourg Dyd/Claparède, Saint Denis.
On list 1.1882. Ord: 16.3.1882. K: 1882. L: 16.2.1884. Comm: 15.6.1884 (trials), 10.10.1884 (full).
Budget 1883. Machinery ordered 1.5.1882 and installed 4.3.1884 to 24.5.1884. Trials 7-8.1884. Left Cherbourg for Saigon 23.10.1884. In reserve at Saigon 1904. Struck 24.2.1909. Ceded 24.2.1909 by the Ministry of Colonies to King Sisowath in Cambodia for use as a yacht replacing *Lutin*.

*Météore* Cherbourg Dyd/Claparède, Saint Denis.
On list 1.1882. Ord: 16.3.1882. K: 1882. L: 3.1.1885. Comm: c5.1885 (trials), 21.7.1885 (full).
Budget 1883. Machinery ordered 1.5.1882 and installed 21.1.1885 to 1.4.1885. Trials 7.1885. Left Cherbourg for the Levant 25.7.1885. Machinery broke down in Indian Ocean 5.10.1898, towed back to Toulon by *Utile*. Struck 8.9.1899. Sold 30.7.1900 at Toulon to Marius Martin.

---

*GABÈS.* *Canonnière de stations.* Station gunboat with composite hull including two longitudinal layers of teak planking on steel frames, iron or steel deck beams and beam shelves, and a straight bow. One funnel, three masts, barquentine rig. Designed by Bertin and Eynaud.

Although ordered with the *Lion* class, *Gabès* was built to working plans drawn by naval constructor Romain Léopold Eynaud who based them on the previous ships built at Rochefort, *Aspic* and *Vipère*. Plans for *Gabès* marked *type Vipère modifié* were signed by naval constructor Alfred Rabourdin at Rochefort on 24 July 1882 and approved on 17 November 1882 by Minister of Marine Jauréguiberry. The main difference between *Gabès* and the other gunboats built around this time was that her engines came from Indret and not Claparède. The Indret engines weighed 75 tons

476 — Le " Gabès " Aviso transport

The gunboat *Gabès*, mis-captioned as an aviso-transport. She had the vertical stem preferred for gunboats by the Rochefort dockyard. *(Postcard by A. Bougault)*

instead of 80 tons, operated at a higher pressure, and had a higher rotational speed and slightly smaller cylinders. They consumed a little more coal at top speed but were more economical at low speeds. Compared to *Vipère* she was slightly shorter and wider. The available plans of the two ships also show a slight lowering of the platform deck in *Gabès* to give a little more headroom inside the upper part of the hull. *Sirius*, also to have been built at Rochefort, would presumably have been as *Gabès*. *Étoile*, which replaced *Sirius* in the budgets, was also initially described as of the *Gabès* type, although as built she was very different.

**Dimensions & tons:** 41.00m pp x 7.50m ext. 466t disp. Draught: 2.67m mean, 3.12m aft.
**Machinery:** 424ihp at 131rpm. 10.5 knots. 1 screw 1 horizontal compound engine with return connecting rods and 2 cylinders. 2 special cylindrical direct flame boilers.
**Guns:** 2 x 138.6mm, 2 x 100mm, 2 x 37mm revolving cannon.

*Gabès* Rochefort Dyd/Indret.
On list 1.1882. K: 3.1882. L: 28.2.1884. Comm: 5.6.1884 (trials), 27.8.1884 (full).
Budget 1883. Left Rochefort 24.8.1884 for Montevideo to relieve *Sagittaire* on the South Atlantic station. Struck 25.5.1900 at Rochefort, selected 1901 to replace *Hérault* (ex *Marceau*) at the school for boys (*École Bousquet*) at Cette (Sète) which trained boys in engineering. Replaced 1951 by the passenger ship *Gouverneur Général Lépine* and BU at Sète.

*Sirius* Rochefort Dyd.
Budget 1883. Replaced in the 1884 budget (drafted c1882) by *Étoile*, below.

*ÉTOILE. Canonnière de stations* (1880). Station gunboat with composite hull including two longitudinal layers of wood planking on iron frames, iron deck beams and beam shelves, and a clipper bow. One funnel, three masts, barquentine rig. Designed by Chaudoye.

Called on her plans a 'gunboat for the service of the rivers of the Plata', *Étoile* was designed by naval constructor Jules Victor Charles Chaudoye working as part of de Bussy's *Service technique des constructions navales*. Chaudoye signed her plans on 25 April 1882 and they were approved by Minister of Marine Jauréguiberry on 28 April 1882. The ship was composite-built like the *Aspic* class. Probably for river service, the bulwarks between the forecastle and poop were full height, with the guns being moved to fire through ports in them rather than being mounted on pivots and firing over them.

*The characteristics are based on the ship's design.*
**Dimensions & tons:** 45.50m wl, 45.50m pp (wl fwd to rudder) x 7.50m ext and wl. 448.2t disp. Draught: 2.40m mean, 2.55m aft. Men: 77.
**Machinery:** 100nhp and 450ihp designed at 200rpm and 6.20kg/cm$^2$ boiler pressure. Speed 10kts. 2 screws. 2 vertical compound engines with 2 cylinders of 0.322m and 0.646m diameter and 0.36m stroke. 2 special cylindrical direct flame boilers (steel with corrugated furnaces), 47.4t coal. Range 1,050nm @ 10kts.
**Guns:** 2 x 138.6mm (1 stowed on the centreline between the funnel and the mainmast and one between the main and mizzen masts), 2 x 100mm (1 on the forecastle and 1 on the poop).

*Étoile* Lorient Dyd.
On list 1.1883. K: 9.11.1882. L: 26.3.1885. C: 9.1885.
Budget 1884 (see *Sirius*, above). Named 4.1882. Construction reassigned from Rochefort to Lorient 1882/83. On the South Atlantic station 1885-89, at Obock 1890-95. Ceded to colonial service 1.10.1898 while inactive at Toulon. Struck effective 1.1.1899 (published

27.2.1899) and handed over to the Colonial Ministry by order of General Gallieni. Activated at Toulon 2.1899 for service in Madagascar.

───────────

## (C) Gun Launches (*Chaloupes-canonnières*).

Grouped under *Canonnières* to 1.1872, under *bâtiments de flottille* from 1.1873.

*CANONNIÈRE Nº 1* **Class.** *Chaloupes-canonnières.* Screw gun launches with one gun behind a bulwark forward and a wooden hull. One funnel, one removable mast and cutter rig. Designed by Dupuy de Lôme.

On 22 December 1858 Minister of Marine Hamelin ordered ten wooden-hulled steam gun launches built on an urgent basis for use on rivers and lakes in the Northern Italian campaign. They were to carry one rifled gun behind an armoured bulwark and were to be able to pass through the locks in French canals and be disassembled for transportation. They were given rudders at both ends. The first one was to be delivered assembled for trials on 25 March 1859, the second was to be delivered dismantled for transportation on 30 May 1859, and the others were to follow at a rate of two per week. Plans by Dupuy de Lôme were approved on 22 December 1858, and the gunboats (including engines) were ordered from the Forges et Chantiers de la Meditérranée at La Seyne by a contract dated 24 December 1858 and approved on 7 January 1859. Iron armour plating and wood screws to fasten it were ordered for these gunboats from Schneider by a contract approved on 24 January 1859. The numerical designations were promulgated on 17 January 1859. The design specified a 24pdr gun but a 30pdr M1858 was ultimately mounted, incurring a weight surcharge.

*Nº 1* left Toulon on 5 June 1859 for Genoa under tow by the paddle corvette *Berthollet* and arrived on 7 June 1859. Ordered back to Toulon, she left Genoa on 14 June 1859 under tow by the paddle frigate *Cacique* and arrived on 15 June 1859. She then left Toulon for the Adriatic on 18 June 1859 under tow by the paddle corvette *Catinat*. After calling at Messina on 23-25 June 1859 the pair encountered a storm off Taranto on 26 June 1859 and because of enormous rolling the gunboat sheltered at Santa Maria de Leucca. Underway again on 29 June 1859, she called at Antivari on 30 June to 1 July 1859 and arrived at Possini on 3 July 1859. There the gunboat coaled, embarked her gun, and carried out test firing. She left Possini on 8 July 1859 and arrived off Venice on 9 July 1859, the gun during this transit being re-embarked in the 90-gun *Redoutable*. Mission complete, the gunboat left Venice on 13 July 1859 and after multiple stops arrived at Toulon on 3 August 1859.

*Nos 6* to *10* were commissioned as a group under a single commanding officer in May 1859, completed in June, transported by rail from Genoa to Lake Garda in July, and assembled at Desenzano beginning in August 1859 by the Toulon naval constructor Auguste Émile Boden. They were to have participated in an attack on the fortress of Peschiera on Lake Garda, but the armistice of Villafranca intervened on 11 July 1859 and on 27 July Napoleon III informed the Navy that he intended to give these five vessels, fully fitted out, to the King of Sardinia (Piedmont). They were duly transferred later in 1859 and four of them became part of the new Italian navy in March 1861.

On 7 September 1865 *Canonnières Nos 1* to *5* were struck from the fleet list on the grounds that they had been in use for a long time as dockyard service craft and could not reasonably be restored to military use. They were to be inscribed on the list of service craft (an action taken on 1 October) and the choice of their names was left to their Maritime Prefects.

*The characteristics are based on a devis for* Canonnière nº 1 *dated 4.6.1859.*
**Dimensions & tons:** 26.10m oa, 24.70m wl & deck x 4.90m wl. 99.384t disp. Draught: 1.58m mean, 1.70m aft. Men: 26.
**Machinery:** 16nhp and 45ihp designed at 210rpm and 5.8 atmospheres boiler pressure (4.8 atmospheres or 4.96kg/cm² at the engine). Trials

8kts at 200rpm and 4 atmospheres boiler pressure, 8.35kts at 250rpm and 5 atmospheres. 1 screw. 1 vertical high pressure engine with 1 cylinder of 0.350m diameter and 0.300m stroke and no condenser. 1 boiler. 2 rudders (1 fore, 1 aft). 10t coal.
**Armour:** Bulwark forward shielding gun.
**Guns:** 1 x 164.7mm rifle M1858 (30pdr Nº 1).

*Canonnière nº 1* F.C. Méditerranée, La Seyne.
On list 1.1859. Ord: 22.12.1858. K: 12.1858. L: 10.3.1859.
    Comm: 16.3.1859, C: 5.1859.
Engine installed 3-4.1859. From Toulon to the Adriatic 18.6.1859. From Toulon to Brest 6.1861 and assigned to towing dredging barges at Brest 12.1861. Struck 7.9.1865, to service craft list 1.10.1865, tug *Poulmic* (12nhp/50ihp) at Brest 1865-1895, condemned 24.9.1895 after inspection, for sale 1895-1896, offered for sale 20.1.1896, sale successful and BU 1896.

*Canonnière nº 2* F.C. Méditerranée, La Seyne.
On list 1.1859. Ord: 22.12.1858. K: 1.1859. L: 4.1859.
    Comm: 3.5.1859, C: 5.1859.
From Toulon to the Adriatic 18.6.1859. To Rochefort 6.1861. Struck 7.9.1865, to service craft list 1.10.1865, tug *Précieuse* (12nhp) at Rochefort 1865-1876 when replaced by *Mousquet*. BU 3.1876.

*Canonnière nº 3* F.C. Méditerranée, La Seyne.
On list 1.1859. Ord: 22.12.1858. K: 1.1859. L: 10.4.1859.
    Comm: 16.4.1859, C: 5.1859.
From Toulon to the Adriatic 18.6.1859. To Lorient 3.1863. Struck 7.9.1865, to service craft list 1.10.1865, tug *Va et Vient* (12nhp/50ihp) at Lorient 1865-1908 (assigned to the Commission de Gâvres 1894-1908), hulk at Lorient 1908-1914, Sold 1919 to BU.

*Canonnière nº 4* F.C. Méditerranée, La Seyne.
On list 1.1859. Ord: 22.12.1858. K: 1.1859. L: 20.4.1859.
    Comm: 23.4.1859, C: 5.1859.
From Toulon to the Adriatic 18.6.1859. To Rochefort c1860. Struck 7.9.1865, to service craft list 1.10.1865, tug *Modeste* (12nhp) at Rochefort 1865-1881, for disposal 1881-1882, BU 1883.

*Canonnière nº 5* F.C. Méditerranée, La Seyne.
On list 1.1859. Ord: 22.12.1858. K: 1.1859. L: 20.4.1859.
    Comm: 23.4.1859, C: 5.1859.
From Toulon to Genoa 5.6.1859 for the *Flottille de l'intérieur de l'Italie*. From Toulon to Brest 20.4.1862-7.5.1862 via the Canal du Midi. Annex to hulk *Uranie* at Brest 1.12.1862. Struck 7.9.1865, to service craft list 1.10.1865, tug *Minou* (12nhp/50ihp) at Brest 1865-1904. Used as personnel transport shuttling between the school ship *Borda* and the shore. Also used in 1874 to test an above-water tube for launching a torpedo on the broadside. (The results were favourable, but the experiment also demonstrated that the shock of the torpedo entering the water during a broadside launch could throw it out of alignment and off course.) For sale at Brest 1904-1905, BU 1905.

*Canonnière nº 6* F.C. Méditerranée, La Seyne.
On list 1.1859. Ord: 22.12.1858. K: 1.1859. Comm: 21.5.1859,
    C: 6.1859. L: c8.1859.
From Toulon to Genoa 28.6.1859 for the *Flottille de canonnières du lac Majeur* and assembled on Lake Garda. Transferred to Sardinia 10.8.1859 as *Frassineto*, decomm. 20.8.1859, off list 1859. In service with the Italian Navy 17.3.1861, ceded to the *Società per le Ferrovie dell'Alta Italia* (Upper Italian Railways) 1867. Struck (Italian) 13.12.1878.

*Canonnière nº 7* F.C. Méditerranée, La Seyne.
On list 1.1859. Ord: 22.12.1858. K: 1.1859. Comm: 21.5.1859,
    C: 6.1859. L: c8.1859.
From Toulon to Genoa 28.6.1859 and assembled on Lake Garda.

Transferred to Sardinia 10.8.1859 as *Sesia*, decomm. 20.8.1859, off list 1859. Sunk by accident in Italian hands 8.10.1860.

*Canonnière nº 8* F.C. Méditerranée, La Seyne.
On list 1.1859. Ord: 22.12.1858. K: 1.1859. Comm: 21.5.1859, C: 6.1859. L: c8.1859.
From Toulon to Genoa 28.6.1859 and assembled on Lake Garda. Transferred to Sardinia 10.8.1859 as *Torrione*, decomm. 20.8.1859, off list 1859. In service with the Italian Navy 17.3.1861. Struck (Italian) 3.12.1878.

*Canonnière nº 9* F.C. Méditerranée, La Seyne.
On list 1.1859. Ord: 22.12.1858. K: 1.1859. Comm: 21.5.1859, C: 6.1859. L: c8.1859.
From Toulon to Genoa 28.6.1859 and assembled on Lake Garda. Transferred to Sardinia 10.8.1859 as *Castenedolo*, decomm. 20.8.1859, off list 1859. In service with the Italian Navy 17.3.1861. Struck (Italian) 1867.

*Canonnière nº 10* F.C. Méditerranée, La Seyne.
On list 1.1859. Ord: 22.12.1858. K: 1.1859. Comm: 21.5.1859, C: 6.1859. L: c8.1859.
From Toulon to Genoa 28.6.1859 and assembled on Lake Garda. Transferred to Sardinia 10.8.1859 as *Pozzolengo*, decomm. 20.8.1859, off list 1859. In service with the Italian Navy 17.3.1861. Struck (Italian) 1867.

———

**CANONNIÈRE Nº 11 (*GUÊPE*).** *Chaloupe-canonnière.* Screw gun launch with one gun behind a bulwark forward and a wooden hull. One funnel, one removable mast and cutter rig. Designed by Augustin Dupouy.

The construction of one gun launch with a wooden protective bulwark forward on plans by Capitaine de vaisseau Augustin Dupouy was ordered on an urgent basis from Lucien Arman at Bordeaux by a contract approved on 17 December 1858. The vessel was to be delivered on 13 March 1859, the Navy providing the engines and armour to be placed on the bulwark. Her engine was added in a supplement to the contract with the Forges et Chantiers de la Méditerranée for *Nos 1-10* when that contract was approved on 7 January 1859. She was designated *Nº 11* on 17 January 1859. She was designed to be capable of being dismantled for transportation. She received considerable press attention during a visit to Paris in April 1859.

**Dimensions & tons:** 26.40m wl/pp x 6.34m wl. 127t disp. Draught: 1.25m fwd, 1.80m aft. Men: 18.
**Machinery:** 16nhp (12 from 1867) at 200rpm. 1 screw. 1 high pressure engine (5.8 atmospheres) with 1 cylinder of 0.35m diameter and 0.30m stroke and no condenser. 1 boiler. 10t coal.
**Armour:** 120mm iron on wooden bulwark forward shielding gun.
**Guns:** 1 x 164.7mm M1858 (30pdr Nº 1) MLR.

*Canonnière nº 11* (*Guêpe*) Lucien Arman, Bordeaux/F.C. Méditerranée, Marseille.
On list 1.1859. Ord: 17.12.1858 (contract). K: 12.1858. L: 3.1859. Comm: 5.3.1859 (trials). C: 28.4.1859.
Commissioned at Cherbourg, on public display at Paris late 4.1859. From Toulon to the Adriatic 15.6.1859, back at Toulon 2.8.1859. Tested a spar torpedo 1865-66 with a 3kg explosive at the end of a 4-metre spar. Named *Guêpe* 1.1.1867. Struck 15.1.1878, tug (service craft, 12nhp) at Toulon for use at Saint-Mandrier 1878-1887, central ship for the *Défense mobile* in Tunisia 1887-1896 (assigned 1887, sent there 1888), replaced by *Talisman* and for sale 1896-1897, sold 1.1898 in Tunisia.

———

**CANONNIÈRE Nº 12 (*ARC*) Class.** *Chaloupes-canonnières démontables.* Screw sectional gun launches (Type 1859) with one gun behind a bulwark

*Chaloupe-canonnière nº 11* (later named *Guêpe*) built at Bordeaux, commissioned at Cherbourg, and taken to Grenelle in April 1859 for display to the Parisian public. The publicity stated that the protective bulkhead for the gun had 12cm of iron on a heavy wood backing, the breech loading gun was rifled on a new system, and its projectiles weighed 48 *livres*. The gun was reinforced by steel bands made by the firm of Petin et Gaudet. The crew was 12 men including the commander and the speed was 8.5 knots. The galley was in the bow as indicated by the smoking galley chimney. *(Monde illustré, 23 April 1859, page 268)*

forward and an iron hull. One funnel, one removable mast and schooner rig. Designed by Dupuy de Lôme.

On 15 October 1859 Minister of Marine Hamelin directed the construction of 20 gun launches (including their engines) for an expedition to China, and they were designated *chaloupes-canonnières Nos 12-31* on 21 October 1859. Plans by Dupuy de Lôme were approved on 17 October 1859 and the launches were ordered from the Forges et Chantiers de la Méditerranée (FCM) by an official order dated 15 October 1859 followed by a contract dated 3 November 1859 that was approved on 26 December 1859. Their layout and appearance were generally similar to the wooden-hulled *Canonnière Nº 1* type. They had low hulls with a single arched deck above the waterline, higher amidships than at the ends, with level bulwarks from end to end (the forward part being removed before firing the gun) and a rudder at each end. The gun was on a wheeled carriage forward behind a thick wooden transverse bulkhead that extended down to the keel. These vessels were never supposed to go to sea so there was no stowed position for the gun. The engine, boiler and funnel were aft of amidships and a single mast was stepped forward of amidships. It could be raised when not in combat and spread a single lug or schooner sail and a jib. In the tropics these launches were normally covered end to end by a large cloth canopy.

For shipping to the Far East they were disassembled into 15 rail-transportable sections, although these were of fairly large size and took up a lot of space because of their shape. The large transports *Weser*, *Européen*, and *Japon* were purchased in England to ship them and the merchantmen *Louise*, *Léonie*, and *Pomone* were hired for the same purpose. The first transport ships carrying French troops arrived off the coast near Shanghai on 1 May and were then sent to Chefoo in the north to disembark. The gun launches were assembled and launched at Chefoo by the Toulon constructor Arthur François Alphonse Bienaymé. These were sent south to Cochinchina in 1861-62 except for one that went to the Yangtse. The surviving units received names on 1 January 1867. Plans for configuring *Carabine* and others of this type as transport gunboats (*canonnières transports*) were signed by naval constructor Jean Rosier Albaret at Saigon on 26 June 1869.

*The characteristics are based on an undated devis for* Arc.
**Dimensions & tons:** 26.50m oa, 24.70m deck, 25.20m wl, 25.54m pp

(wl fwd to rudder) x 4.90m ext and wl. 88.9t disp. Draught: 1.426m mean, 1.69m aft. Men: 26.

**Machinery:** 16nhp (12 from 1867) and 48ihp designed at 200rpm and 4.0kg/cm² boiler pressure. Trials (16.2.1860) 57.0ihp = 7.564kts at 209rpm and 3.00kg/cm² boiler pressure. 1 screw. 1 vertical engine with 1 cylinder of 0.35m diameter and 0.30m stroke and no condenser. 2 special tubular boilers. 10.5t coal. Range 150nm @ 7kts.

**Guns:** 1 x 164.7mm M1858 (30pdr N° 1).

***Canonnière n° 12 (Arc)*** F.C. Méditerranée, La Seyne/FCM, Marseille.
On list 1.1860. Ord: 15.10.1859. K: 10.1859. L: 1.1860. C: 1.1860. L: 8.1860 at Chefoo. Comm: 19.8.1860.
Launched 1.1860 and in commission from 23.1 to 18.3.1860, probably for class trials. Left for Chefoo (Zhifu, now Yantai), China, 4.1860 in transport *Japon*. In the Peï-Ho Flotilla 12.1860, to Cochinchina 1862. Foundered 14.10.1873 in a storm while under tow by the aviso *D'Estrées* (1867) after leaving Saigon 11.10.1873 for Tourane (Da Nang). Struck 8.12.1873.

***Canonnière n° 13 (Carabine)*** F.C. Méditerranée, La Seyne/FCM, Marseille.
On list 1.1860. Ord: 15.10.1859. K: 11.1859. C: 2.1860. L: 9.1860 at Chefoo. Comm: 6.10.1860.
Left for Chefoo 3.1860. Participated in the Anglo-French exploration of the Bohai Bay 1861. To Cochinchina c1862. Struck 23.4.1889 at Haiphong and sold to BU.

***Canonnière n° 14 (Sainte Anne)*** F.C. Méditerranée, La Seyne/FCM, Marseille.
On list 1.1860. Ord: 15.10.1859. K: 11.1859. C: 2.1860. To storage at Toulon 3.1860.

Remained at Toulon 1860. In service 1861 at Saint-Mandrier. Comm: 11.5.1865. To Cayenne 16.10.1865. Struck 20.6.1872 at Cayenne and BU.

***Canonnière n° 15 (no name)*** F.C. Méditerranée, La Seyne/FCM, Marseille.
On list 1.1860. Ord: 15.10.1859. K: 11.1859. C: 2.1860. L: 9.1860 at Chefoo. Comm: 4.10.1860.
Left for Chefoo 3.1860. Participated in the Anglo-French exploration of the Bohai Bay 1861 under Lieutenant Kenney. Grounded in the bay of the Ta-Tsing River 7.8.1861, refloated by the next tide. To the Yangtse 1862. Sunk 14.10.1863 at Shanghai by boiler explosion. Struck 26.1.1864. She had unofficially carried the name *Étoile* on the Yangtse in 1862-63 but this was repudiated by all authorities in 1864.

***Canonnière n° 16 (Casse-tête)*** F.C. Méditerranée, La Seyne/FCM, Marseille.
On list 1.1860. Ord: 15.10.1859. K: 11.1859. C: 2.1860. L: 9.1860 at Chefoo. Comm: 19.9.1860.
Left for Chefoo 3.1860. In the Peï-Ho Flotilla 12.1860, to Cochinchina early 1861. Sunk 7.5.1867 in the Mekong River by boiler explosion while aiding the merchantman *Saint Vincent de Paul*. Her commander was unable to make his orders heard over the noise of steam from the boiler and had the safety valve closed. Struck 22.7.1867.

***Canonnière n° 17 (no name)*** F.C. Méditerranée, La Seyne/FCM, Marseille.
On list 1.1860. Ord: 15.10.1859. K: 11.1859. C: 3.1860. L: 12.1860 at Chefoo. Comm: 13.1.1861.
Left for Chefoo 4.1860 in merchantman *Pomone*. Foundered 6.2.1861 while under tow by the aviso *Écho* from Chefoo to Saigon. Struck 25.4.1861.

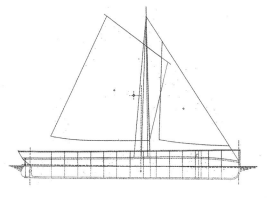

Inboard profile and upper deck plan with an inset mast and sail plan for the 20nhp wooden-hulled screw *chaloupes canonnières* (gun launches) of the *N° 12-31* type destined for the expedition to China. The plans were signed by Dupuy de Lôme and approved by Minister of Marine Hamelin on 17 October 1859. The protective transverse bulkhead (which rises only to the height of the rail) and the downward-sloping deck can be seen forward, while the rigging plan shows the mast in its raised position. (*Atlas du Génie Maritime, French collection, plate 589*)

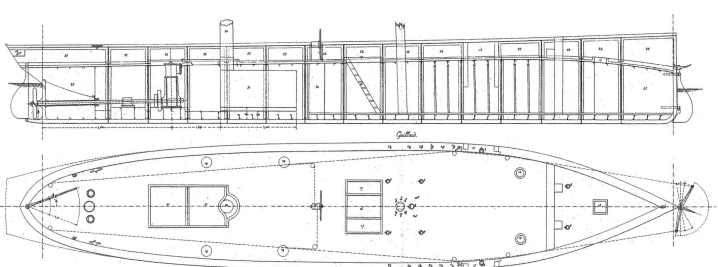

*Canonnière n° 18* (*Cimeterre*) F.C. Méditerranée, La Seyne/FCM, Marseille.

On list 1.1860. Ord: 15.10.1859. K: 11.1859. C: 3.1860. L: 8.1860 at Chefoo. Comm: 20.8.1860.

Left for Chefoo 4.1860 in transport *Japon*. In the Peï-Ho Flotilla 12.1860. To Cochinchina early 1861. Struck 7.8.1870 in Indochina.

*Canonnière n° 19* (*Coutelas*) F.C. Méditerranée, La Seyne/FCM, Marseille.

On list 1.1860. Ord: 15.10.1859. K: 11.1859. C: 3.1860. L: 4.1861 at Chefoo or Saigon. Comm: 19.5.1861.

Left for Chefoo 4.1860 in transport *Européen*. To Cochinchina c1862. Struck 21.4.1885, for disposal in Cochinchina 1885-1888. BU 1889.

*Canonnière n° 20* (*Dague*) F.C. Méditerranée, La Seyne/FCM, Marseille.
On list 1.1860. Ord: 15.10.1859. K: 11.1859. C: 3.1860. L: 12.1860 at Chefoo. Comm: 17.1.1861.

Left for Chefoo 4.1860 in merchantman *Pomone*. To Cochinchina 1861-62. Struck 24.12.1878, for sale at Saigon 1878-1879, sold 1879 to BU.

*Canonnière n° 21* (*Sainte Marie*) F.C. Méditerranée, La Seyne/FCM, Marseille.

On list 1.1860. Ord: 15.10.1859. K: 11.1859. L: 2.1860. C: 3.1860. Comm: 28.6.1860 at Toulon, decomm. 13.9.1860.

Remained at Toulon 1860. Served the hospital at Saint-Mandrier 1861-67. To Cayenne 12.6.1867 in transport *Amazone*, comm. 1.10.1867. Struck 2.4.1872 at Cayenne. BU 1872.

*Canonnière n° 22* (*Épée*) F.C. Méditerranée, La Seyne/FCM, Marseille.
On list 1.1860. Ord: 15.10.1859. K: 11.1859. C: 3.1860. L: 8.1860 at Chefoo. Comm: 22.8.1860.

Left for Chefoo 4.1860 in transport *Japon*. In the Peï-Ho Flotilla 12.1860. To Cochinchina early 1861. Sunk 25.1.1867 near Mytho by boiler explosion. Struck 18.3.1867.

*Canonnière n° 23* (*Espingole*) F.C. Méditerranée, La Seyne/FCM, Marseille.

On list 1.1860. Ord: 15.10.1859. K: 11.1859. C: 3.1860. L: 12.1862 at Saigon. Comm: 1.1.1863.

Remained at Toulon until sent to Saigon late 1862. Struck 24.12.1878, for sale at Saigon 1878-1879.

*Canonnière n° 24* (*Fauconneau*) F.C. Méditerranée, La Seyne/FCM, Marseille.

On list 1.1860. Ord: 15.10.1859. K: 11.1859. C: 3.1860. L: 1861 at Chefoo or Saigon. Comm: 25.6.1861.

Left for Chefoo 4.1860 in transport *Européen*. To Cochinchina 1861-62. Struck 7.8.1870 at Saigon and sold to BU.

*Canonnière n° 25* (*no name*) F.C. Méditerranée, La Seyne/FCM, Marseille.

On list 1.1860. Ord: 15.10.1859. K: 11.1859. C: 3.1860. L: 1861 at Chefoo or Saigon. Comm: 23.5.1861.

Left for Chefoo 4.1860 in transport *Européen*. Arrived at Saigon 13.4.1861 and immediately assembled. Sunk 3.3.1862 at Rach Dam by a 'criminal' boiler explosion shortly after leaving Mytho while carrying a company of soldiers. Fifty-two men were killed or wounded, and a commission of enquiry found that the explosion was due to sabotage instigated by the mandarins of the province of Vinh Long. In response the French and Spanish captured Vinh Long on 22.3.1862. Struck 16.10.1863.

*Canonnière n° 26* (*no name*) F.C. Méditerranée, La Seyne/FCM, Marseille.

On list 1.1860. Ord: 15.10.1859. K: 11.1859. C: 3.1860. L: 7.1860 at Chefoo. Comm: 26.7.1860.

An unidentified *chaloupe-canonnière* in Cochinchina, probably of the *N° 12* class or later. She is moored near a river bank and is presumably in transit with her mast raised, sail furled, and canvas awning deployed. *(Private collection)*

Left for Chefoo 3.1860 in transport *Weser*. Participated in the capture of Beitang 1.8.1860 during the initial landing there against the Taku Forts and Peking. In the Peï-Ho Flotilla 12.1860. Sank 28.1.1861 off Annam while under tow by the transport *Rhône* from Woosung to Saigon. Struck 25.4.1861.

*Canonnière n° 27* (*Faulx*) F.C. Méditerranée, La Seyne/FCM, Marseille.
On list 1.1860. Ord: 15.10.1859. K: 11.1859. C: 3.1860. L: 7.1860 at Chefoo. Comm: 27.7.1860.

Left for Chefoo 3.1860 in transport *Weser*. To Cochinchina 1861-62. Struck 24.12.1878, for sale at Saigon 1878-1879. BU 1879.

*Canonnière n° 28* (*Flamberge*) F.C. Méditerranée, La Seyne/FCM, Marseille.

On list 1.1860. Ord: 15.10.1859. K: 11.1859. C: 3.1860. L: late 1862 at Saigon. Comm: 21.1.1863.

Remained at Toulon until sent to Saigon 1862. Served in Cochinchina. Struck 21.4.1885, for disposal in Cochinchina 1885-1888.

*Canonnière n° 29* (*Fleuret*) F.C. Méditerranée, La Seyne/FCM, Marseille.
On list 1.1860. Ord: 15.10.1859. K: 11.1859. C: 3.1860. L: 6.1861 at Chefoo or Saigon. Comm: 14.7.1861.

Left for Chefoo 4.1860 in transport *Européen*. To Cochinchina 1861-62. Struck 1.3.1878 at Saigon. BU 1886.

*Canonnière n° 30* (*Framée*) F.C. Méditerranée, La Seyne/FCM, Marseille.
On list 1.1860. Ord: 15.10.1859. K: 11.1859. C: 3.1860. L: 12.1860 at Chefoo. Comm: 24.1.1861.

Left for Chefoo 4.1860 in merchantman *Pomone*. To Cochinchina 1861-62. Struck 5.6.1891, for sale at Saigon 1891-1895.

*Canonnière n° 31* (*Glaive*) F.C. Méditerranée, La Seyne/FCM, Marseille.
On list 1.1860. Ord: 15.10.1859. K: 11.1859. C: 3.1860. L: 7.1860 at Chefoo. Comm: 1.8.1860.

Left for Chefoo 3.1860. To Cochinchina early 1861. Struck 21.4.1885, for disposal in Cochinchina 1885-1888.

---

**CANONNIÈRE N° 32 (HACHE) Class.** *Chaloupes-canonnières démontables.* Screw sectional gun launches (type 1862) with one gun behind a bulwark forward and an iron hull. One funnel, one removable mast and schooner rig. Designed by Dupuy de Lôme.

The first eight were ordered from the Forges et Chantiers de la Méditerranée by a contract dated 30 April 1862 and approved 17 May 1862 for an expedition to Cochinchina. Dupuy de Lôme's plans for this 1862 type (approved 20 March 1862) essentially reproduced his 1859 type

(*Nos 12-31*) but the new ships were to be 1.55m longer, 0.02m wider, and 6 tons heavier than the old ships. They were also to have machinery of 60ihp and 8.00 knots instead of 48ihp and 7.00 knots. They were divided into 16 sections each for shipping instead of the 15 sections of the 1859 type. The plans were signed by naval constructor Charles Louis Marie Layrle. All eight had been completed by the time one of them, *Javeline*, ran trials in October 1862, and all eight were shipped to Saigon in 1863. One additional boat was added later, perhaps in November 1863, and ended up at Nouméa. They were very similar in appearance to the *Canonnière n° 12 (Arc)* group of 1859. The vessels were all assigned names effective 1 January 1867, Cochinchina being notified on 10 December 1866 and Toulon on 19 December 1866.

*The characteristics are based on an undated devis for* Hache.

**Dimensions & tons:** 26.30m wl, 26.84m pp (wl fwd to rudder) x 4.90m ext and wl. 94.5t disp. Draught: 1.42m mean, 1.47m aft. Men: 26.

**Machinery:** 20nhp (15 from 1867) and 48ihp designed at 200rpm and 4.0kg/cm$^2$ boiler pressure. Trials (*Javeline*, 10.10.1862) 76.8ihp = 7.982kts at 206.5rpm and 4.085kg/cm$^2$ boiler pressure. 1 screw. 1 vertical high pressure engine with 1 cylinder of 0.35m diameter and 0.30m stroke and no condenser. 2 special tubular boilers.

**Guns:**

(1863) 1 x 164.7mm M1858-60. Later only 1 x 12pdr (121mm/17) bronze in some, some also had 1 x 4pdr bronze mountain aft.

(1879) 1 x 30pdr smoothbore canon-obusier forward (was a M1827 in *Sagaïe*), 1 x 4pdr bronze mountain gun on the stern on a pivoting boat carriage. All armed thus except for *Hallebarde* and *Massue*, on detached duty in Tonkin with 1 x 138.6mm M1858-60 rifle, and *Harpon* serving the governor of Cochinchina with only 6 *espingoles*. *Massue* also had 1 x 47mm and 1 x 37mm.

(1888) *Sagaïe* modified to receive a 90mm gun in place of her 30pdr but remained in reserve.

*Canonnière n° 32 (Hache)* F.C. Méditerranée, La Seyne/FCM, Marseille (engines designed by François Bourdon).

On list 1.1863. Ord: 30.4.1862 (contract). K: 3.1862. C: 1862. To Saigon 2.1863. L: 5.1864. Comm: 14.5.1864.

Carried to Indochina 6.2.1863 by merchantmen *Sansonnet* and *Étoile*. To Tonkin 1882. Struck 17.11.1886, hulk in Tonkin 1886-1888. Sold c1889.

*Canonnière n° 33 (Hallebarde)* F.C. Méditerranée, La Seyne/FCM, Marseille (engines designed by François Bourdon).

On list 1.1863. Ord: 30.4.1862 (contract). K: 1862. C: 1862. To Saigon 3.1863. L: 6.1866? Comm: 20.6.1866.

Carried to Cochinchina 26.3.1863 by merchantman *Napoleon III*. Towed from Cochinchina to Tonkin 13.6.1875 by *Duchaffault*. Struck 29.6.1880 at Haiphong after damaged in grounding 4.1880 and sold to BU.

*Canonnière n° 34 (Harpon)* F.C. Méditerranée, La Seyne/FCM, Marseille (engines designed by François Bourdon).

On list 1.1863. Ord: 30.4.1862 (contract). K: 1862. C: 1862. To Saigon 2.1863. L: 9.1863. Comm: 16.9.1863.

Carried to Cochinchina 2.2.1863 by merchatman *Étoile*. Struck 21.4.1885, for disposal in Cochinchina 1885-1888.

*Canonnière n° 35 (Javeline)* F.C. Méditerranée, La Seyne/FCM, Marseille (engines designed by François Bourdon).

On list 1.1863. Ord: 30.4.1862 (contract). K: 1862. L: 28.8.1862. C: 13.8.1862 (trials completed). To Saigon 5.1863. L: 11.1866?. Comm: 1.11.1866.

Carried to Cochinchina 4.5.1863 by merchantmen *Auguste* and *Gustave*. Annex to *Duperré* 1.1866. Towed from Cochinchina to Tonkin by *Drac* 2.9.1883. Boiler unusable 8.1885 and decomm. at Thuan An. Struck 12.7.1887, to be BU, for disposal at Haiphong 1887-1890.

*Canonnière n° 36 (Massue)* F.C. Méditerranée, La Seyne/FCM, Marseille (engines designed by François Bourdon).

On list 1.1863. Ord: 30.4.1862 (contract). K: 1862. C: 1862. To Saigon 3.1863. L: 11.1866?. Comm: 9.11.1866.

Carried to Cochinchina 26.3.1863 by merchantman *Napoleon III*. At Saigon 20.7.1863. Annex to *Duperré* 12.1866. Ran onto a tree trunk and sank 2.10.1876, refloated. To Tonkin 1880. Struck 11.2.1887 at Haiphong and sold to BU.

*Canonnière n° 37 (Mousqueton)* F.C. Méditerranée, La Seyne/FCM, Marseille (engines designed by François Bourdon).

On list 1.1863. K: Ord: 30.4.1862 (contract). 1862. C: 1862. To Saigon 2.1863. L: 6.1866. Comm: 20.6.1866.

Carried to Cochinchina 6.2.1863 by merchantman *Sansonnet*. Assembled 25.7.1863, out of service at Saigon 1865-66. Annex to *Duperré* 20.6.1866. Towed to Tonkin 29.7.1883 by *Triomphante*. Struck 23.4.1889, retained 1889-1890 for eventual use as a lighthouse in Tonkin.

*Canonnière n° 38 (Sagaïe)* F.C. Méditerranée, La Seyne/FCM, Marseille (engines designed by François Bourdon).

On list 1.1863. K: Ord: 30.4.1862 (contract). 1862. C: 1862. To Saigon 1.1863. L: 28.7.1863. Comm: 16.9.1863.

Carried to Cochinchina 27.1.1863 by merchantman *Christoph Colomb*. Assembled 16.9.1863, assigned to river postal and transport service 1864. In 1894 was the last of the 16-section *Hache* type gun launches left on the list. Struck 10.8.1894, central ship for the *Défense mobile* at Saïgon 1894-1897 (there since 1893), replaced by *Cimeterre*, sold 17.2.1898.

*Canonnière n° 39 (Yatagan)* F.C. Méditerranée, La Seyne/FCM, Marseille (engines designed by François Bourdon).

On list 1.1863. K: Ord: 30.4.1862 (contract). 1862. C: 1862. To Saigon 2.1863. L: 11.1863. Comm: 23.11.1863.

Carried to Cochinchina 1863 by merchantman *Étoile*. In Tonkin by 6.1883. Boiler unusable 8.1885 and decomm. Struck 23.4.1889 at Haiphong and sold there.

*Canonnière n° 40 (Caïman)* F.C. Méditerranée, La Seyne/FCM, Marseille (engines designed by François Bourdon).

On list 1.1864. K: 1863?. C: 1865?. L: 1865? Comm: 12.1.1865.

Decomm. 1.3.1865 at Cherbourg and remained there disassembled until sent to Nouméa 1867 in the 2-decker *Fleurus*. L: 2.1868. Recomm. 10.2.1868. Ceded 23.5.1871 to the Penitentary Service at New Caledonia and renamed *Foa*. Decomm. 1.7.1871 at Nouméa, off list 1871.

———

*ARBALÈTE* **Class.** *Chaloupes-canonnières.* Screw gun launches with one gun behind a bulwark forward and a wooden hull. One funnel, one mast, schooner rig. Designed by Dupuy de Lôme.

These vessels were ordered by a foreign government from the Forges et Chantiers de la Méditerranée, but conditions in 1866 made delivery impossible and the navy took them over. They were built to Dupuy de Lôme's plans for the iron-hulled type of gun launches and their engines were designed by former naval constructor Louis Édouard Lecointre, now with the Forges et Chantiers de la Méditerranée, and built at Marseille. Because they had wooden hulls they could not be disassembled into sections, but they could transit the French canals. One was towed to Dakar, the others remained in France, three being associated with fishery protection duty in the Bidassoa River at Hendaye on the Spanish border. Photos of *Javelot* there show a hull and rig essentially the same as the iron sectional *chaloupes-canonnières*

*The characteristics are based on an undated devis for* Boutefeu.

**Dimensions & tons:** 25.50m deck, 24.97m wl, 25.40m pp (wl fwd to

rudder) x 4.90m ext and wl. 104.4t disp. Draught: 1.63m mean.
Men: 26.

**Machinery:** 12nhp (1867) and 48ihp designed at 200rpm and
4.00kg/cm² boiler pressure. Trials (*Dard*, 23.5.1867) 55.6ihp =
6.555kts at 202rpm and 3.382kg/cm² boiler pressure. 1 screw.
1 vertical engine with 1 cylinder of 0.35m diameter and 0.30m stroke
and no condenser. 2 special high pressure tubular boilers. 7.4t coal.
Range 112nm @ 7kts.

**Guns:**

(1867-68) 1 x 164.7mm M1858 with four firing positions, two forward
and two aft. *Boutefeu* also had 3 x 4pdr (86.5mm/11) bronze mountain
(1870-75) 1 x 138.6mm Nº 1 or M1864 (1867), *Épieu* also had 1 x 4pdr
(86.5mm/11) bronze.
(1886, *Javelot*) 2 x 37mm Hotchkiss, one to port and one to starboard.

*Arbalète* F.C. Méditerranée, La Seyne/FCM, Marseille.
On list 1.1867. K: early 1866. L: 29.8.1866. Comm: 24.4.1867.
Refitted at Toulon 7-8.1876, then towed to Dakar by *Finistère* and to
Gabon by *Loiret*. Local unofficial name from 1.1877 *Arbalète
Marabout*. Out of commission 1881, annex to *Africain* 1882-84 at
Saint-Louis de Sénégal. Struck 16.2.1886 (published 1.3.1886), proba-
bly at Dakar.

*Biscaïen* F.C. Méditerranée, La Seyne/FCM, Marseille.
On list 1.1867. K: early 1866. L: end 8.1866. Comm: 1.5.1867 or
28.4.1867.
Saw no further service as a gunboat after decommissioning on 1.8.1867.

---

The *chaloupe-canonnière Javelot* in the Bidassoa River at the Navy's post at
Hendaye on the Spanish border where she was station ship from 1886 to 1901
and a hulk until 1910. She is moored by chains both fore and aft, indicating a
semi-permanent mooring. (*Postcard by A. Villatte, Tarbes*)

Struck 28.7.1878, tug (service craft, 12nhp/50ihp) at Toulon 1878-
1891 (converted 1878-79), sold 1891 to BU.

*Boutefeu* (*Boute-feu*) F.C. Méditerranée, La Seyne/FCM, Marseille.
On list 1.1867. K: 6.6.1866. L: end 8.1866. Comm: 1.5.1867.
Decomm. at Toulon 31.5.1867, recomm. 27.4.1868 or 16.5.1868,
arrived at Lorient 14.6.1868 with *Flambant* and assigned to service in
the arsenal, decomm. 20.6.1868. To the Loire Flotilla at Saint Nazaire
11.1870. Back to Lorient 14.3.1871. Ordered to Paris 2.4.1871 to
fight the Commune, left 24.4.1871 via Le Havre. Towed back to
Rochefort by *Oise* 10.1876. Struck 28.6.1878, tug (service craft,
12nhp/50ihp) at Rochefort 1878-1893 (also served as annex to
*Messager* at Boyardville), Sold 1893 to BU.

*Dard* F.C. Méditerranée, La Seyne/FCM, Marseille.
On list 1.1867. K: 6.6.1866. L: 24.8.1866. Comm: 1.5.1867 or
29.4.1867.
Examined the navigability of the Rhone at Arles 5.1867, then out of
commission at Toulon 7.1867 to 3.1868, To Brest from the
Mediterranean 1.1871 (transited the canals 11-12.1870, served in the
Loire Flotilla, and then sent to Brest to guard Communard prisoners).
Decomm. at Rochefort 24.3.1871. Sank 16.12.1874 at sea while under
tow by *Travailleur* to Socoa near Hendaye. Struck 16.12.1874.
Replaced by *Épieu*.

*Épieu* F.C. Méditerranée, La Seyne/FCM, Marseille.
On list 1.1867. K: 6.1866. L: 29.8.1866. Comm: 1 or 9.5.1867.
Decomm. 29.5.1867. To Bordeaux from the Mediterranean 1.1871.
From Rochefort to the Bidassoa 19.6.1875. Struck 3.11.1885, prob-
ably at Hendaye. A design by naval constructor Édouard Guillaume for
a new vessel to replace her (27m x 4.6m, 76 tons) was approved by the
*Conseil des travaux* on 19.10.1886 but instead her never-used sister
*Javelot* became the replacement.

Les Pyrénées   Hendaye   Le « Javelot » et les Etablissements de la Marine

A. Villatte, éditeur, Tarbes

*Flambant* F.C. Méditerranée, La Seyne/FCM, Marseille.

On list 1.1867. K: 19.7.1866. L: 1.9.1866. Comm: 1.5.1867.

Decomm. at Toulon 31.5.1867, recomm. 27.4.1868 or 16.5.1868, arrived at Lorient 14.6.1868 with *Boutefeu* and assigned to service in the arsenal, decomm. 27.6.1868. To the Loire Flotilla at Saint Nazaire 11.1870. Ordered to Paris 2.4.1871 to fight the Commune, left via Le Havre 24.4.1871 with *Boutefeu* and *Mutine*. From Cherbourg to Brest 10.1878 and to Rochefort 6.6.1879. Struck 28.11.1879, for disposal at Rochefort 1879-1880.

*Fronde* F.C. Méditerranée, La Seyne/FCM, Marseille.

On list 1.1867. K: 6 or 7.1866. L: end 8.1866 or start 9.1866. Comm: 3.5.1867.

Out of commission at Toulon 1867-69. To Saint Nazaire from the Mediterranean 1.1871, served in the Loire Flotilla. Decomm. at Rochefort 24.3.1871, local service there from 1874. Struck 31.1.1880, hulk for the rear guard (*bâtiment d'arrière-garde*) at Rochefort 1880-1884. BU 1885.

*Javelot* F.C. Méditerranée, La Seyne/FCM, Marseille.

On list 1.1867. K: 6.1866. L: 29.8.1866. Comm: 3.5.1867.

Out of commission at Toulon except for trials 1867-85. Left Toulon for Bordeaux via the Canal du Midi 17.1.1886, replaced sister *Épieu* as station ship in the Bidassoa River (at Hendaye) in late 1886. Struck 2.5.1901, station hulk in the Bidassoa 1901-1910, for sale there 1910-1911.

*Mousquet* F.C. Méditerranée, La Seyne/FCM, Marseille.

On list 1.1867. K: 6 or 7.1866. L: end 8.1866 or start 9.1866. Comm: 1.5.1867.

To Bordeaux from the Mediterranean 1.1871. Struck 9.3.1876, tug (service craft, 12nhp) at Rochefort 1876-1887 (converted between 12.1875 and 3.1879), BU 9.1887.

*Pertuisane* F.C. Méditerranée, La Seyne/FCM, Marseille.

On list 1.1867. K: 6 or 7.1866. L: end 8.1866. Comm: 1.5.1867.

Saw no further service as a gunboat after decommissioning on 31.5.1867. Also reported decom. 29.8.1867 after trials and hauled out at Toulon. Struck 28.7.1878, tug (service craft, 12nhp/50ihp) at Toulon 1878-1891, taken out of service 21.2.1891, then sold to BU.

---

*BAÏONNETTE* (*BAYONNETTE*) **Class.** *Chaloupes-canonnières démontables.* Screw sectional gun launches (type 1867) with one gun behind a bulwark forward and an iron hull. One funnel, one removable mast. Designed by Dupuy de Lôme.

These vessels were ordered from Clément et Paul Claparède & Cie. at Saint Denis (Paris) in 1867, still on Dupuy de Lôme's 1859 plans. The builder also used Dupuy de Lôme's design for the single cylinder engines. These vessels were similar in structure and appearance to the 1859 and 1862 types but were slightly shorter than either and reverted to 15 sections. All but two sent to Senegal in 1869 were active at Paris in 1870 and 1871, four of these were then sent to New Caledonia and two to Saigon while two remained at Brest. By 1874, before being sent to New Caledonia, *Caronade* was modified by the addition of a section that increased her length to 26.31m and her displacement to 94.33 tons. *Estoc* was similarly modified at Saigon during 1874 and *Escopette* in early 1875, both without authorization from Paris. Their modification reduced their draught by 30cm and provided a badly needed expansion of the crew's accommodations.

*The characteristics are based on a devis for* Escopette *dated 6.10.1874 and on devis for* Rapière *and* Caronade, *both dated 1874.*

**Dimensions & tons:** 24.80m wl (bow to rudder) x 4.90m wl. 86.823t disp. Draught: 1.426m mean, 1.691m aft. Men: 24.

**Machinery:** 12nhp and 48ihp designed at 200rpm and 4kg/cm² boiler pressure. Speed 6.7kts to 7.9kts. 1 screw. 1 vertical engine with 1 cylinder of 0.350m diameter and 0.300m stroke. 2 tubular boilers. 10t coal. Range 370 miles at full speed.

**Guns:**

(1868) 1 x 164.7mm/19.2 M1864 BLR. In 1868 *Lance* and *Obus* had only 1 x 12pdr bronze. Some had 1 x 4pdr (86.5mm/11) bronze mountain aft

(1874, *Caronade*, *Escopette*, *Estoc*, *Perrier*) 1 x 164.7mm canon-obusier SB. In 1874 *Escopette*, *Caronade*, and *Rapière* had only 1 x 12pdr bronze rifle.

*Baïonnette* (*Bayonnette*) Claparède & Cie., Saint Denis.

On list 1.1868. K: 1867. C: 1867. Comm: 25.8.1870 at Saint Denis and L: 9.1870.

From Cherbourg to Paris 8-9.1870, crew soon reassigned to forts. Seized 18.3.1871 at winter moorings at the Île aux Cygnes by the Paris Commune and used by them until retaken late 5.1871. To New Caledonia and recomm. at Nouméa 6.11.1872. Out of commission there 1875, hulk 1878 following inspection as *Rapière*. Struck 28.4.1882 and sold to BU (still listed 1.1883).

*Caronade* Claparède & Cie., Saint Denis.

On list 1.1868. K: 1867. C: 1867. L: 1.7.1868 at Cherbourg. Comm: 1.7.1868.

Machinery installation completed 28.8.1868. In reserve at Cherbourg 1868. From Cherbourg to Paris and refitted 8-9.1870, comm. at Saint Denis, crew soon reassigned to forts. Seized 18.3.1871 at winter moorings at the Île aux Cygnes by the Paris Commune but not used by them, retaken 28.5.1871. Refitted at Cherbourg 10.1874, transported to New Caledonia by the merchantman *Nouveau St. Michel*. Station ship at Nouméa 9.7.1875. Struck 7.3.1883 at Nouméa and sold to BU.

*Claymore* Claparède & Cie., Saint Denis.

On list 1.1868. K: 1867. C: 1867. Comm: 24.8.1870 at Saint Denis and L: 9.1870.

To Cherbourg in sections by rail 1868 and stored there 1868-69. From Cherbourg to Paris 8-9.1870, crew soon reassigned to forts. Seized 18.3.1871 at winter moorings at the Île aux Cygnes by the Paris Commune and used by them until retaken at the Quai des Tuileries 24.5.1871 and recommissioned that day by government forces. To Brest 1872 to guard Communard prisoners. Off main list 1876, tug at Brest (12nhp/50ihp) and assigned to the Naval Academy 1876-1902. Condemned 1902 and sold 1903 to BU.

*Escopette* Claparède & Cie., Saint Denis.

On list 1.1868. K: 1867. C: 1867. Comm: 25.8.1870 at Saint Denis and L: 9.1870.

Launched 1867, machinery installed 1868, to Cherbourg in sections by rail 1868. First commissioned 1870 and left Cherbourg 30.8.1870 for Paris. Decomm. 2.1871 after the armistice. Seized 18.3.1871 at winter moorings at the Île aux Cygnes by the Paris Commune and used by them until sunk c5.1871 under the second arch of the Point du Jour viaduct between Billancourt et Auteuil. Refloated 8.1871, arrived Cherbourg 1.2.1872 and hauled out for refitting. Cochinchina asked for two *canonnières démontables* 18.1.1873. Loaded in sections on merchantman *Boréal* 12.1873 and transported to Saigon via Nouméa, launched at Saigon 7.12.1874. Sank immediately 15.9.1877 in 8 metres of water after striking an uncharted rock while en route from Saigon to Baria. Struck 20.12.1877, but recovered and repaired 12.1877-4.1878 and strike annulled 3.4.1878. Struck 13.12.1886, sold at Saigon 5.11.1888 to Sung Seng.

*Estoc* Claparède & Cie., Saint Denis.

On list 1.1868. K: 1867. C: 1867. Comm: 23.8.1870 at Saint Denis and L: 9.1870.

From Cherbourg to Paris 8-9.1870. Decomm. 2.1871 after the armistice. Seized 18.3.1871 at winter moorings at the Île aux Cygnes by the Paris

Commune and used by them until sunk 12.5.1871 by government artillery at Meudon or Sèvre. Refloated 8.1871. Transported by merchantman *Boréal* to Saigon via Nouméa 12.1873, refitted at Saigon 2.1875. Sank accidentally 2.9.1883 off Cape Padaran while under tow by the aviso-transport *Drac*. Struck 1.10.1883.

*Lance* Claparède & Cie., Saint Denis.
On list 1.1868. K: 1867. To Cherbourg 1867, L: 6.1868, Comm: 1.7.1868.
Towed to Dakar 10.8.1868-4.9.1868 by *Gorgone* and to Gabon 1869 by *Volta* for river service, arriving 6.2.1869. Decomm. 1.7.1871. Struck 24.3.1872. Engine recovered and reused with that of *Obus* in submarine *Plongeur* when she was converted to a steam water barge.

*Obus* Claparède & Cie., Saint Denis.
On list 1.1868. K: 1867. To Cherbourg 1867, L: 12.1867. Comm: 2.1.1868.
Sections embarked in *Meuse* 2.1.1868 for Senegal, re-launched 12.1868 in Gabon for river service. Hauled ashore there 5.1871 after springing a leak, decomm. 1.6.1871. Struck 24.3.1872. Engine recovered and reused with that of *Lance* in submarine *Plongeur* when she was converted to a steam water barge.

*Perrier* Claparède & Cie., Saint Denis.
On list 1.1868. K: 1867. C: 1867. L: 12.1869 or 1.1.1870 at Cherbourg. Comm: 29.8.1870 at Saint Denis and L: 9.1870.
Temporarily afloat at Cherbourg 9-10.1869 for comparative trials with *Sabre*. From Cherbourg to Paris 8-9.1870, crew soon reassigned to forts. Seized 18.3.1871 at winter moorings at the Île aux Cygnes by the Paris Commune and used by them until retaken late 5.1871 near the Pont de la Concorde. Transported in 1874 to New Caledonia with *Caronade* by the merchantman *Nouveau St-Michel*. Refitted at Nouméa 1.6.1875. Struck 6.9.1886, for disposal at Nouméa 1886-1887, sold 1887 at Nouméa to BU. (Her name was consistently rendered in fleet lists as *Perrier* although the correct spelling for the old weapon was *Pierrier*.)

*Rapière* Claparède & Cie., Saint Denis.
On list 1.1868. K: 1867. C: 1867. L: . Comm: 24.8.1870 at Saint Denis and L: 9.1870.
To Cherbourg in sections by rail 1868. From Cherbourg to Paris 8-9.1870 and commissioned, crew soon reassigned to forts. Seized 18.3.1871 at winter moorings at the Île aux Cygnes by the Paris Commune but not used by them, retaken 28.5.1871. Transported to New Caledonia in 1872 by merchantman *France*, refitted in Nouméa 10-11.1872. Inspected 26.3.1877 while hauled out and hull plating found thin in many places. Struck 13.7.1880, for disposal at New Caledonia 1880-1884.

*Sabre* Claparède & Cie., Saint Denis.
On list 1.1868. K: 1867. C: 1867. L: . Comm: 24.8.1870 at Saint Denis and L: 9.1870.
To Cherbourg in sections by rail 1868. Temporarily afloat 9-10.1869 for comparative trials with *Perrier*. From Cherbourg to Paris 8-9.1870, crew soon reassigned to forts. Seized 18.3.1871 at winter moorings at the Île aux Cygnes by the Paris Commune and used by them until retaken at the Quai des Tuileries 24.5.1871 and recommissioned that day by government forces. Listed as in commission from 1.7.1871, ordered to Le Havre with *Claymore* 25 8.1871, decomm. at Brest 5.10.1871 and used by the port to guard Communard prisoners. Off main list when Brest informed 30.3.1876 that she was downgraded to harbour service. Tug (12nhp/50ihp) at Brest and supporting the professors of the Naval Academy 1876-1895. Condemned 1895, sold 6.10.1895 to M. Morice.

---

*MITRAILLEUSE* Class. *Chaloupes-canonnières.* Screw gun launches with one large gun forward and an iron hull. One funnel, no masts. Designed by Farcy. Purchased.

Lieutenant de vaisseau Jérome Eugène Farcy was an advocate for small launches with large guns. His first proposals to the Navy were rejected by the *Conseil des travaux* on 2 June 1863 and 3 May 1864. In Britain in 1867 the designer George Rendel of the Armstrong firm developed a new type of 'flatiron' gunboat with a single battleship gun (initially a 9in (229mm) 12-ton muzzle loader) on a small hull displacing 164 tons. Their purpose was to augment fortifications with mobile floating artillery and to help defend nearby coasts. The first of these, HMS *Staunch*, was launched in December 1867 and attracted much international attention. The French naval attaché in London, Commandant Pigeard, reported details of the new type to Paris, the *Conseil des travaux* on 2 June 1868 decided to explore it, and Minister of Marine Rigault de Genouilly on 11 June 1868 asked the ports to develop plans, resulting in the designs for *Épée* and *Tromblon*, below. However, Farcy took Rendel's concept to the extreme and put an equivalent French gun (240mm) on a much smaller steel hull (45 tons), producing a vessel that was often called an *affût flottant,* or floating gun carriage. The tiny vessel had a ram-shaped inverted bow to improve seakeeping and was considered unsinkable because it contained 84 watertight cylinders. The hull form featured longitudinal troughs in which the screws ran efficiently and which also gave the vessel great stability. The *Conseil des travaux* rejected two more proposals from Farcy on 5 January and 20 April 1869, feeling that Farcy's vessel was too lightly built and preferring a larger seagoing version, but in April 1869 the Emperor intervened and ordered one Farcy gunboat under his personal household budget, which was built by Clément and Paul Claparède at St. Denis. The trials of this vessel in mid-1869 reportedly displayed the 'striking' superiority of this type as an *affût flottant* over the existing river gun launches, with its shorter length, shallower draught, and heavier gun. A second Farcy gunboat was also begun, reportedly under an order from the Danish navy. The first, commonly called the *Canonnière Farcy* and named *Révolver* after the war, was requisitioned for war service in August 1870, and the second was purchased by the Navy and named *Mitrailleuse* in December 1869 and taken over on 24 January 1870, in time to appear in the January 1870 fleet list. In 1871 the Danes ordered a replacement vessel to the same design that served as their *Drogden* until 1904.

*The characteristics are based on an undated devis for* Mitrailleuse.
**Dimensions & tons:** c16.4m oa, c15.90m wl, 15.15m pp (wl fwd to rudder) x 4.66m ext and wl. 45.0t disp. Draught: 1.00m mean, 1.00m aft. Men: 16.
**Machinery:** 10nhp and 44ihp designed. Speed 6.8kts. 2 screws. 2 vertical engines, each with 1 cylinder of 0.196m diameter and 0.14m stroke and no condenser. 1 special tubular cylindrical boiler. 3.0t coal and water.
**Guns:**
(1870, both) 1 x 240mm.
(10.1870, *Mitrailleuse*) 1 x 194mm.
(1872) 1 x 164.7mm/19.2 M1864, 2 x 4pdr (86.5mm/11) bronze mountain on the after deck.

*Révolver* Claparède & Cie., Saint Denis.
On list 1.1872. K: 6.5.1869. L: 6.1869. C: 9.1869.
Ordered by Napoleon III in April 1869 under his personal household budget. Successfully tried at Paris, Honfleur, and Cherbourg between 19.7.1869 and 7.9.1869 and purchased by the Emperor on 20.1.1870. Requisitioned 8.1870 and active in the Seine and Marne 10.1870 to 1.1871. Seized 18.3.1871 at winter moorings at the Île aux Cygnes by the Paris Commune and commissioned by them under the name *Liberté*. Purchased and renamed *Révolver* 6.1871 after recovery by the government but not commissioned. Hauled out and put into storage at Cherbourg 5.3.1872. Transported from Toulon to Ha Long Bay (*Baie*

The *Canonnière Farcy*, later the Navy's *chaloupe-canonnière Révolver*, employed in early September 1870 in the defence of the Seine and the Marne against the Germans. The drawing makes it clear why Farcy's boats were described as floating gun carriages. The gun is a 240mm breechloading rifle. (*La Guerre illustrée, 7 September 1870, p. 108*)

d'Along) in Tonkin between 20.2.1884 and 23.3.1884 by the transport *Bien-Hoa*, offloaded 9.4.1884 by sheer legs mounted on the flagship *Bayard*. Struck 23.4.1889, probably at Haiphong. Used briefly as a lightship, then sold 1890.

**Mitrailleuse** Claparède & Cie., Saint Denis.
On list 1.1870. K: 1869. L: 1869. Comm: 1.8.1870 (trials). C: 5.1871.
Ordered by the Danish navy and purchased by the French Navy 10.12.1869. Commissioned for the Flotille de Seine 1.8.1870 she was towed from Cherbourg to Le Havre, but en route the tow line snagged on the muzzle of the 240mm gun, the vessel heeled over, and the gun fell into the sea. Decomm. 25.8.1870, gun replaced at Cherbourg with a 194mm gun. Ordered to Paris 2.4.1871 to fight the Commune, recomm. 4.4.1871 at Cherbourg, and arrived in Paris 29.4.1871. Decomm. 11.7.1871. Into storage at Cherbourg 7.1872. Transported from Toulon to Ha Long Bay (*Baie d'Along*) in Tonkin 20.2.1884 to 23.3.1884 by the transport *Bien-Hoa*. Struck 23.4.1889 in Tonkin.

---

**Gun launches, 1869-1871**
As noted above, Minister Rigault de Genouilly on 11 June 1868 invited the ports to submit designs for gun launches (*chaloupes-canonnières*), which the French now defined as vessels like the British Rendel gunboats of very small dimensions carrying one gun of very large calibre and protected mainly by their small size and mobility. In addition to port and coastal defence the Council assigned these vessels a third mission of acting as an artillery train for an offensive by a continental army, which required a notable increase in size. The *Conseil des travaux* examined these submissions on 2 and 23 February 1869 and selected those by naval constructors Charles Ernest Huin and Jean Baptiste Louis Félix Marc Berrier-Fontaine for further work. The Huin project was examined again after modifications on 8 June 1869 while the Berrier-Fontaine design was last examined on 26 October 1869, but the war then interrupted work.

On 14 September 1871 Minister of Marine Pothuau directed the Council to determinine characteristics for ship types that were to enter into the composition of the new fleet of the Programme of 1872 then being developed by the *Conseil d'Amirauté*. In his proposal to the *Conseil d'Amirauté* the Director of Material included no gunboats in the main part of the fleet but placed a group of 32 *canonnières* at the end of his list, presumably as flotilla craft. The *Conseil d'Amirauté* considered these *canonnières* a powerful and economical reserve of floating artillery and moved them to the group of ships intended for the attack and defence of the coast. On 14 November 1871 the *Conseil des travaux* recommended specifications for these *chaloupes-canonnières*. It once again passed over the concept of small *affûts flottants* like

Farcy's craft and returned to the larger seagoing Huin and Berrier-Fontaine designs of 1869, recommending additional changes to bring them in line with the new specifications. These included an armament of one 240mm and one 12pdr (121mm) gun, a crew of 24 men, a speed of 8 knots and a range of 600 miles at that speed, high pressure machinery, Belleville boilers, and twin screws. Both designs were recommended for Ministerial approval once these changes were made. *Chaloupes-canonnières* did not, however, became part of the new fleet, being displaced by larger *canonnières* of the *Crocodile* type, and although trials in 1875 were generally satisfactory neither the *Épée* nor the *Tromblon* type was repeated.

---

***ÉPÉE.*** *Chaloupe-canonnière.* Screw gun launch with one large gun forward, a steel and iron hull, and a straight bow. Two very tall funnels abreast, one pole mast, no spars or sails. Designed by Huin and Challiot. Called a *Bâtiment de flottille à hélice, canonnière* in January 1873, to *chaloupe-canon-nière* January 1874.

Huin's 1869 design was modified in early 1872 by naval constructor Jean Paul Challiot in Huin's absence. The *Conseil des travaux* approved the plans on 5 March 1872 and Minister of Marine Pothuau approved them on 20 March 1872. The gun crew was protected by a hood of 10mm plating over the gun. A report on trials at sea during 1875 stated that she rolled considerably but not dangerously and could navigate along the coast with an escort but would need to be ready to shelter in an inlet in case of a storm. Her appearance was dominated by two strikingly tall strictly vertical funnels side by side aft of amidships and a single pole mast barely taller than the funnels. The low hull was surmounted by a tall bulwark set in from the sides all the way around the vessel, and a curved fixed shield covered the big gun forward.

*The characteristics are based on a devis dated 11.7.1874.*
**Dimensions & tons:** 24.60m wl, 24.20m pp (wl fwd to rudder) x 7.50m ext and wl. 185.2t disp. Draught: 1.66m mean, 1.81m aft. Men: 24.
**Machinery:** 45nhp and 180ihp designed at 180rpm and 8.6kg/cm² boiler pressure. Trials (22.2.1874) 181.9ihp = 8.6kts at 189.2rpm and 7.55kg/cm² boiler pressure. 2 screws. 2 vertical compound engines each with 2 cylinders of 0.228m and 0.500m diameter and 0.30m stroke. 2 Belleville boilers. 20.3t coal. Range 460 miles.
**Guns:** (1874) 1 x 240mm forward on a fixed mounting, 1 x 12pdr (121mm/17) bronze aft.

*Épée* Lorient Dyd.
On list 1.1873. K: 7.1872. L: 23.9.1873. Comm: 7.1.1874 (trials). C: 3.1874.
Career at Lorient, mostly in reserve. Struck 6.11.1895. Sold 3.5.1896 at Lorient for use as a landing platform by the harbour steamers of Port Louis.

---

***TROMBLON.*** *Chaloupe-canonnière.* Screw gun launch with one large gun forward, a steel and iron hull, and a ram bow. One funnel, no masts. Designed by Berrier-Fontaine. Called a *canonnière* when added to the list on 15 January 1873, to *chaloupe-canonnière* January 1874.

In November 1871 the *Conseil des travaux* examined Berrier-Fontaine's 1869 design and asked for some modifications, but instead of doing so Berrier-Fontaine produced a new design which displaced 216 tons instead of 154 tons. The Council rejected this design on 16 April 1872 but on 30 July 1872 approved a revision of Berrier-Fontaine's original design. Minister of Marine Pothuau approved the plans on 15 January 1873. In appearance she resembled a much enlarged version of Farcy's craft with a low hull and high bulwarks forming a ram-shaped inverted bow and a similarly inverted stern, a single tall and slightly raked funnel, and no mast. The widest part of the hull was near its bottom, it tapered in up to the waterline and then back out.

A collection of coastal craft from an unidentified source including from left to right a 1st class coast defence torpedo boat (*N° 63*), the *chaloupe-canonnière* (gun launch) *Tromblon*, the 1st class coast defence ship *Bélier*, and a fishery protection cutter.

*The characteristics are based on a devis dated 12.9.1875.*

**Dimensions & tons:** 24.10m wl (+1.60m ram), 23.50m pp (wl fwd to rudder) x 7.44m ext, 6.44m wl. 189.5t disp. Draught: 1.86m mean, 1.92m aft. Men: 24.

**Machinery:** 75nhp and 180ihp designed at 180rpm and 7.00kg/cm² boiler pressure. Trials (20.8.1875) 219.1ihp = 9.10kts at 171.25rpm and 7.321kg/cm² boiler pressure. 2 screws. 2 vertical compound engines each with 2 cylinders of 0.225m and 0.500m diameter and 0.30m stroke. 2 tubular cylindrical boilers. 20.1t coal. Range 670 miles.

**Guns:** (1875) 1 x 240mm forward on a fixed mounting, 1 x 12pdr (121mm/17) bronze aft.

*Tromblon* Toulon Dyd.

On list 15.1.1873. K: 30.3.1874. L: 1.1875. Comm: 20.5.1875 (trials).

Career at Toulon, mostly out of commission. Struck 11.8.1898. Sunk 21.10.1898 as target for the Peyras battery at La Seyne-sur-mer near Toulon.

---

**CANONNIÈRES DÉMONTABLES.** *Chaloupes-canonnières.* Screw sectional gun launches with one large gun forward.

The 1876 and 1877 budgets (submitted in May 1875 and March 1876)

included four *canonnières démontables* to be built by contract. The Minister on 9 March 1876 referred a design for a *chaloupe-canonnière* (not *démontable*) by naval constructor Aurous to the *Conseil des travaux* which examined it on 4 April 1876. These were to be *affûts flottants* like Farcy's *Mitrailleuse*, not larger craft like *Épée* and *Tromblon*. Aurous sought to carry a large calibre gun on the smallest possible hull and retained the 240mm gun and dimensions of Farcy's craft. The design was not sectional, but it did include watertight compartments including some for the coal, water, and munitions. Aurous also prepared a version with a 274.4mm gun with the characteristics shown below that the Council preferred to the 240mm design. The Council rejected both versions of the design, pointing to technical shortcomings and repeating its statement of 14 November 1871 that the construction of vessels of this type was not urgent and that it was more appropriate to experiment first with larger craft able to operate offensively against enemy coasts as well as defensively, as was then being done with *Épée* and *Tromblon*. In case Minister of Marine Fourichon wanted to proceed with one, however, it suggested some changes to the larger one which would increase its size somewhat. The *canonnières démontables* were not in the 1878 budget (submitted in January 1877).

**Dimensions & tons:** 18.00m x 5.50m. 68t disp. Draught: 1.10m.

**Machinery:** . 6.5kts. 40nhp to 60nhp and 1.8t coal in the variant with the 240mm gun.

**Guns:** 1 x 240mm forward on a fixed mounting.

*N, N, N, N* (4 unnamed) Contract

Budget 1876 (delayed to 1877, then cancelled).

# Chapter Five

# Torpedo Boats, 1859-1882

## (A) Torpedo Boats (*Bateaux Torpilleurs*)

*Bateaux torpilleurs* (under *Bâtiments de Flottille*) in the 1.1876 fleet list, *Bateaux torpilleurs pour le service de la Défense mobile* 1.1880, *Torpilleurs Garde-Côtes de 1re classe et 2e classe* and *torpilleurs-vedettes* (torpedo launches) 1.1883, and *Torpilleurs de 1re et 2e classe* and *torpilleurs-vedettes* 1.1885.

*TORPILLEUR Nº 1. Bateau torpilleur.* A large 38-metre boat with two submerged torpedo tubes (one forward and one aft), one torpedo spar, two funnels abreast, and a straight bow. Designed by the Directorate of Matériel To *Torpilleur de 1re classe* January 1883 (*Torpilleur garde-côtes* in 1883-1884).

As part of the process directed by Minister of Marine Pothuau on 14 September 1871 of determining the types of ships to be in the future fleet (the Programme of 1872) the *Conseil des travaux* on 21 November 1871 developed specifications for 'torpedo carrying boats' (*bateaux porte-torpilles*) or spar torpedo boats, using as starting points two designs by naval constructor Émile Ernest Clément that had been referred to it on 11 October 1871. The Council had previously discussed *bateaux porte-torpilles* in 1868 and 1870. Clément's preferred design was a 113-ton, 18-metre vessel with a submerged spar above the keel extending a 30kg charge 6m from the bow and with armour protection. The Council recommended reducing the displacement to 70-80 tons and omitting the armour, using 10mm steel plating for protection against small arms only.

On 26 March 1872 the Council reviewed a new design by Clément and asked that construction of the hull begin immediately and that full details on the engine and boilers be referred back to it for review after its recommended changes were incorporated. Clément's boat was not built, but his design was the starting point for the one produced by the Directorate of Matériel for *Torpilleur nº 1* that was approved on 16 December 1874. This was a much longer vessel (38m) notable for including two tubes for Whitehead automobile torpedoes in addition to a spar. The vessel was built by Claparède at Saint Denis on the Seine just outside of Paris, who also designed the propulsion machinery. The contract provided that the boat would be rejected if she failed to make 15.7 knots, but the Director of Materiel concluded that she would be an effective military machine at a speed of 14 knots and Minister of Marine Pothuau accepted her.

**Dimensions & tons:** 38.67m wl, 38.00m pp (wl fwd to rudder) x 4.20m wl (4.00m on deck). 95t disp designed, 101.4t as completed, 103.52t trials. Draught: 1.25m fwd, 2.60m aft under propeller guard (1.67m mean trials). Men: 9.
**Machinery:** 800ihp designed at 400rpm and 8.25kg/cm² boiler pressure. Speed 17kts. Trials: 740ihp = 14.37kts at 367rpm for 2 hours, reached 15.42kts on two measured mile runs. 2 screws with a rudder aft of each screw. 2 vertical compound engines each with 3 cylinders of 0.31m (1) and 0.38m (2) diameter and 0.33m stroke. 2 locomotive boilers. 10t coal.
**Torpedoes:**
(1877) 2 submerged torpedo tubes for 356mm (4.40m) Whitehead torpedoes, one in the bow and one aft, plus 1 torpedo spar that extended a 50kg charge 7m in front of the bow. The Whitehead torpedoes were ejected from their tubes by steam from the boat's boiler acting on a piston.

(1883 as aviso) 1 torpedo spar offset to the side and, on the centreline, one trainable tube for a 3.75-metre torpedo. **Guns:** 2 x 47mm.

*Torpilleur nº 1* Claparède & Cie., Saint Denis.
On list 1.1876. Ord: 12.7.1875 (contract). K: 25.9.1875. L: 1876. Trials: 3.1877-5.1878.
Trials at Cherbourg. Suffered from problems with her torpedo tubes and boilers. Accepted 17.5.1878. The operating pressure of her boilers was reduced in 1881 to 6kg/cm² and her speed fell to 11kts. Condemnation proposed 28.4.1883 but retained as an aviso for the defence of the Cherbourg roadstead. Decomm. 15.5.1883. To *Isard*, *aviso de flottille*, 30.5.1883, *Aviso de 3e classe* 1.1885. Struck 3.10.1885, *service de la défense fixe at Cherbourg* 1885-1889, condemned as service craft 25.7.1889, BU 1889 at Cherbourg.

---

*TORPILLEUR Nº 2. Bateau torpilleur.* Experimental programme. 21-metre boat with one torpedo spar and a slightly inclined bow. Designed by Baron at Rochefort.

This vessel was built at the Rochefort dockyard in accordance with propositions presented on 17 March 1875 by the *Commission permanente des défenses sous-marines pour la défense des rades et des estuaires*. She was designed by naval constructor Jean Baron.

**Dimensions & tons:** 22.42m wl (wl fwd to wl aft), 21.00m pp (wl fwd to rudder) x 3.50m ext. 32.498t disp. Draught: 1.18m fwd, 1.27m amidships, 1.36m aft. Men: 8.
**Machinery:** 100ihp designed at 480rpm and 8.25kg/cm² boiler pressure. Speed 13kts designed. Trials 11kts. 1 screw. 1 vertical simple expansion engine with 2 cylinders of 0.35m diameter and 0.25m stroke. 1 locomotive boiler. 3.2t coal.
**Torpedoes:** 1 torpedo spar.

*Torpilleur nº 2.* Rochefort Dyd/F.C. Méditerranée.
On list 1.1876. Ord: 1875. K: 21.9.1875. L: 3.1876. Trials: 31.7.1876-7.1878.
Budget 1877. Trials at Rochefort. Suffered from insufficient stability and constant boiler casualties. Made only 11 knots. Never left Rochefort. After long and mediocre trials the navy gave up on using her as a torpedo boat, accepted her 7.1878, and instead used her in 11.1878 to develop the spar torpedo designed by naval constructor Eusèbe Victor Vincent de Paul Desdouits. Struck 14.12.1880 and named *Vergeroux*, tug at Rochefort 1880-1895, annex to *Dives* (fixed defences) 1895-1899, condemned 31.5.1899, sold 20.4.1900 at Rochefort to M. Saugerac of Paimboeuf.

---

*TORPILLEUR Nº 3. Bateau torpilleur.* Experimental programme. 20-metre boat with one fixed torpedo tube on deck forward, one large funnel, and a straight bow. Designed by Claparède. To *Torpilleur (garde-côtes) de 2e classe* 1.1883.

This boat was designed and built by Claparède & Cie. at Saint Denis in accordance with the propositions of 17 March 1875 of the *Commission Permanente des Défenses Sous-Marines pour la défense des rades et des estuaires*. The contract was signed on 12 July 1875 and approved on 28 July 1875.

Her machinery had no condenser, the spent steam being sent up the funnel and makeup feed water being taken from the sea.

*Torpilleur nº 3* was delivered at Cherbourg in December 1876 but on 10 August 1877 her trial commission reported that she had been unable to exceed 12 knots while the contract called for an average of 14 knots with rejection if 13 knots were not reached. On 24 August 1877 Minister of Marine Gicquel des Touches decided to accept her even so, in recognition of the fact that this was the first attempt in France to reach high speeds with small vessels. She was also a good sea boat. She was accepted on 27 August 1877 and proved most useful in the development of the first French torpedo tube that launched torpedoes above water by compressed air (a bronze tube mounted on deck on the starboard side of the vessel developed by naval constructor Gilles Louis de Maupeou d'Ableiges). She was delivered to the *Défense mobile* at Cherbourg in March 1880 and served with it until March 1883, when she was judged unsuitable for combat because of her low speed. In October 1882 de Maupeou produced a study on the use of heavy oil (mineral oil) to heat the boilers of torpedo boats and in January 1883 *Torpilleur nº 3* was taken to the Forges et Chantiers de la Méditerranée at Le Havre to be fitted with that system for trials. On 30 May 1883 she was reclassified as an *aviso de flottille* for her new role and named *Chevrette*. Trials at Le Havre in August 1884 showed that oil fuel functioned well but was far from being economical. *Chevrette* returned to Cherbourg under tow with fires lit in September 1884 and continued to test oil fuel and ways to burn it. By a decision of 25 May 1885 she was

struck from the first part of the fleet list, inscribed as a service craft, and ordered to be fitted as a tug to replace *Puebla*, then being broken up at Cherbourg. After being hauled out on 5 July 1887, however, she was found unsuitable for such use, and she was also found to be too badly corroded to be refloated without repairs.

**Dimensions & tons:** 20.62m oa, 20.00m pp x 3.00m ext & wl. 28t disp (38t during trials). Draught: 1.10m fwd, 2.30m aft under propeller guard (*sous crosse*). Men: 8.

**Machinery:** 285ihp designed at 400rpm and 8.25kg/cm$^2$ boiler pressure (300ihp at 365rpm). Speed 14kts. Trials 12.32kts at 376rpm. 1 screw. 1 engine with 2 cylinders of 0.31m diameter and 0.25m stroke. 1 direct-flame locomotive boiler. 4.0t coal. Range 100.7nm @ full speed.

**Torpedoes:** 1 381mm torpedo tube forward, replaced with a torpedo spar c 1879.

*Torpilleur nº 3* Claparède & Cie., Saint Denis.
On list 1.1876. Ord: 12.7.1875 (contract). K: 1875. L: 1876. Trials: 12.1876-7.1877.
Budget 1877. Delivered 12.1876. Tested Maupeou torpedo tube from 7.1878. To *aviso de flottille* and named *Chevrette* 30.3.1883. Used for trials of oil fuel 1884-87. Listed as *Aviso de 3ᵉ classe* 1.1885. Struck 25.5.1885, rated as tug (service craft) at Cherbourg 1885-1887. Unserviceable 7.1887, BU at Cherbourg 1887-88.

---

*Torpilleur nº 4*, or according to Yarrow's caption, 'Torpedo Steamer, built for the French Government. Speed 20 miles an hour.' Note the complex spar torpedo mechanism. She was one of Yarrow's few failures. *(Steam launches and torpedo boats by Yarrow & Co., ca. 1888, NHHC, NH-70392)*

*TORPILLEUR Nº 4. Bateau torpilleur.* Experimental programme. Yarrow 22-metre boat with one torpedo spar, one funnel, and a straight bow. This boat was ordered from Yarrow & Co. at Poplar on the Thames, a well known English builder of fast small craft, in accordance with the proposi-

tions of 17 March 1875 of the *Commission Permanente des Défenses Sous-Marines pour la défense des rades et des estuaires*. Accepted 28.3.1876 by the French naval attaché in London, she was the first of the experimental boats to enter service. Her machinery had no condenser, the spent steam exhausting into the funnel to produce forced draught. By 1879 the French realized that she had two fatal flaws: an absolute lack of stability despite the addition of 3 tons of ballast (the movement of multiple crew members from one side to the other risked capsizing her), and an insufficient supply of water to the boiler (exhausted after 45 minutes at 13 knots). She was described as *un bâtimet complètement raté*, or a total failure.

**Dimensions & tons:** 22.77m wl (wl fwd to wl aft), 22.03m pp (wl fwd to rudder) x 3.00m ext (above wl), 2.66m wl. 18t disp (26.5t at draughts shown). Draught: 0.70m fwd, 1.17m amidships, 1.68m aft. Men: 8.
**Machinery:** 13kts designed at 350rpm and 8.69kg/cm² boiler pressure. Trials (21.3.1876 at Blackwall) 13.27kts at 337 rpm. 1 screw. 1 vertical engine with 2 cylinders of 0.279m diameter and 0.356m stroke. 1 locomotive boiler.
**Torpedoes:** 1 torpedo spar (planned).

*Torpilleur nº 4* Yarrow, UK.
On list 1.1876. Ord: 10.5.1875 (contract). K: 1875. L: 1875. Trials: 12.1875-3.1876.
Budget 1877. Trials at Cherbourg. Judged unusable even for dockyard service, sale first proposed 12.1879. To *torpilleur-vedette* January 1883. A note dated 24.4.1883 ruled that she was definitively condemned, whatever her use, and declared her 'unseaworthy'. Struck 30.5.1883, hull sold 27.10.1883, machinery condemned 15.12.1883 and sold c8.1884. She is commonly shown as having been retained on the main fleet list as an aviso, converted at Cherbourg for service in Congo, and renamed *Djoué*, but *Djoué* (described in Chapter 10 under 3rd class avisos) was in fact a different screw vessel specially built with the paddle steam launch *Licona* for the 1884 Brazza expedition to the Congo.

---

*TORPILLEURS Nᵒˢ 5–6. Bateaux torpilleurs.* Experimental programme. Thornycroft 19.7-metre boats with two torpedo spars, one funnel, and a straight bow. To *torpilleurs-vedettes* 1.1883.

These two torpedo launches were ordered from another leading English builder of fast small craft, John I. Thornycroft & Co. at Chiswick on the Thames, also in accordance with the propositions of 17 March 1875 of the *Commission Permanente des Défenses Sous-Marines pour la défense des rades et des estuaires*. On their delivery voyage the two boats steamed directly from Dover to Cherbourg rather than hugging the coasts. The trials commission for the two boats considered the trials results to be very satisfactory, leading to further orders, but in service the boats were found to be practically unusable because the crews could not live on board (the headroom in the crew quarters and engine room was only 1.50m) and movement of the two torpedo spars was impeded by nearby objects. Thornycroft's spars pivoted to allow attacks on the sides as well as on the bow, but the French soon altered the boats to attack only in front, where they could best resist the effects of an explosion, in the process altering the armament to one non-pivoting spar. On 3 March 1877 one of these boats chased down and sank the towed hulk *Bayonnaise* with her spar torpedo.

**Dimensions & tons:** 20.37m wl (wl fwd to wl aft), 19.65m pp (wl fwd to rudder) x 2.59m ext (above wl), 2.39m wl. 12.206t disp (16.5t fully loaded). Draught: 0.37m fwd, 0.70m amidships, 1.03m aft, 1.41m aft under propeller guard. Men: 8.
**Machinery:** 220ihp designed at 412rpm and 8.43kg/cm² boiler pressure. Speed 18kts. Trials (*Nº 5*) 197ihp = 17.81kts at 422rpm and 7.5kg/cm² boiler pressure for 2 hours, best measured mile 210ihp = 18.34kts at 431rpm; (*Nº 6*) 18kts for 2 hours, best measured mile 19.18kts. 1 screw. 1 compound engine with 2 cylinders of 0.254m and

0.489m diameter and 0.267m stroke. 1 locomotive boiler. 1.20t coal.
**Torpedoes:** 2 torpedo spars, each mounted on a pivot, soon reduced to one non-pivoting spar.

*Torpilleur nº 5* Thornycroft, Chiswick, UK.
On list 1.1876. Ord: 9.5.1875 (contract). K: 7.1875. L: 1875. Trials: 7-8.1876.
Budget 1877. Trials at Cherbourg. Conducted comparative boiler trials, then school for stoking 1878. Out of commission 1880-86. Struck 3.6.1887. BU 1888 at Cherbourg.

*Torpilleur nº 6* Thornycroft, Chiswick, UK.
On list 1.1876. Ord: 9.5.1875 (contract). K: 7.1875. L: 1876. Trials: 7-8.1876.
Budget 1877. Trials at Cherbourg. School for stoking 1876, to the school for torpedoes at Boyardville 1882 as a school ship, then to the *Défense mobile* at Rochefort. Struck 30.5.1888. Used by the *Direction de la défense sous-marine* at Rochefort. Rochefort informed Paris 13.9.1888 that she would be used as a harbour ferry and for pilot training, and to avoid confusion would henceforth be called *Lupin*. Sale proposed 8.10.1889, sold 21.5.1890 at Rochefort.

---

*TORPILLEUR Nº 7. Bateau torpilleur.* Experimental programme. 14.6-metre boat with one torpedo tube in the bow above the water and a straight bow. Designed by Jubal and Clément at Brest. To *torpilleur-vedette* January 1883.

This boat was built at the Brest dockyard in accordance with the propositions of 17 March 1875 of the *Commission Permanente des Défenses Sous-Marines pour la défense des rades et des estuaires*. She was designed by Mécanicien Principal Jubal or Juhel with naval constructor Clément. Her first Belleville boiler consumed too much coal and was replaced in July 1877 by another of the same type but heavier. The trial results of May 1878 were regarded as unsatisfactory, primarily because of the boiler. She had a torpedo tube mounted in the bow just above the waterline that was initially operated by steam. It was first inclined to get a submerged torpedo run, then mounted horizontally to launch above the water. In August 1877 steam was replaced by compressed air to launch faster torpedoes. Trials in 1887 at the end of her career as a torpedo boat showed that this tube, located 32cm above the waterline, was essentially unusable because of the ingress of water during firing, and moving it up to the deck or replacing it with a spar was not possible because of the impact on stability. Her hull and machinery were then still in good condition because she had spent most of her time hauled out at Brest except for rare torpedo launching trials, and she lasted to 1910 as a service craft.

**Dimensions & tons:** 14.76m wl (wl fwd to wl aft), 14.60m pp (wl fwd to rudder) x 2.80m ext (above wl), 2.78m wl. 14.724t disp, later 18t, then (7.1877) 22.49t. Draught: 0.77m fwd, 1.045m amidships, 1.32m aft. Men: 10.
**Machinery:** 105ihp designed at 500rpm and 9kg/cm² boiler pressure. Speed 14kts. Trials (22.5.1878) 136ihp = 9.45kts at 428rpm, best speed 10.17kts. 1 screw. 1 compound engine with 2 cylinders of 0.226 and 0.377m diameter and 0.160m stroke. 1 Belleville boiler.
**Torpedoes:** 1 torpedo tube projecting forward from the bow just above the waterline (with three 5.85m torpedoes), soon replaced with a torpedo spar.

*Torpilleur nº 7* Brest Dyd/F.C. Méditerranée.
On list 1.1876. Ord: 1875. K: 1875. L: 1876. C: 1876.
Budget 1877. Struck 10.5.1887, renamed *Compagnon* 1887, annex to *Chimère* 1887-1892 (initially for a hydrographic survey of the Chenal du Four to the west of Brest, between the mainland and Ouessant), school for stoking at the school for engineers at Brest, condemned 10.5.1909, for sale 1909-1910, sold 1910 at Brest to BU.

### Torpilleurs nᵒˢ 8–64.

The torpedo boats ordered between 1877 and 1881 (*Nᵒˢ 8-64*), presented here in numerical order, fall into the following groups, each with small differences between successive orders. The groups are:

(1) Three large boats of over 30 metres (*Nᵒˢ 26-28*), one from each of the three French builders
(2) Twelve boats of 26 metres built by Thornycroft (*Nᵒˢ 8-19*)
(3) Nine 27-metre boats built by Normand (*Nᵒˢ 20-21, 41-42, 47-49,* and *54-55*)
(4) Nine 27-metre boats built by Claparède (*Nᵒˢ 22-23, 37-40,* and *51-53*)
(5) Eleven 27-metre boats built by Forges et Chantiers de la Méditerranée at La Seyne (*Nᵒˢ 24-25, 33-36, 43-46* and *50*).
(6) Four torpedo launches (*vedettes*) built by Thornycroft (*Nᵒˢ 29-30* and *58-59*) and two copies built by FCM (*Nᵒˢ 56-57*)
(7) Two torpedo launches built by Yarrow (*Nᵒˢ 31-32*)
(8) Five improved versions of Normand's *Nᵒ 27* (*Nᵒˢ 60-64*), followed in 1883 by orders for ten more.

---

**TORPILLEURS Nᵒˢ 8–19.** *Bateaux torpilleurs.* Thornycroft 26-metre type with one torpedo spar, one funnel offset to starboard, and a straight bow. To *Torpilleurs* (*garde-côtes*) *de 2ᵉ classe* 1.1883 and *Torpilleurs de 3ᵉ classe* 1.1890.

The first six were ordered by a contract dated 13 March 1877, the rest were added by a modification to that contract dated 9 July 1877. All had a small funnel offset to one side to allow manoeuvring the single torpedo spar, which was of the type that the French retrofitted to *Nᵒˢ 5-6*. They also had a strong buffer projecting from the bow to protect the boat in the event of a collision with the target, a forerunner of the *tampon de choc* on many later French torpedo craft. All of the boats were still active in 1893 and able to make an average of 13.9 knots at 268rpm with a maximum of 15 or 16 knots. They proved to be good sea boats for their size, but the trials commission noted that, while they were 'very remarkable', the trial speeds had been accomplished by extreme firing of the boilers, severely stressing them and requiring elite personnel.

**Dimensions & tons:** 26.62m wl (wl fwd to wl aft), 26.40m pp (wl fwd to rudder) x 3.26m ext (above wl), 2.93m wl. 26.630t disp. Draught: 0.48m fwd, 0.82m amidships, 1.47m aft. Men: 10.
**Machinery:** 300ihp designed at 360rpm and 8.43kg/cm² boiler pressure. Speed 18kts. Trials: 18.28kts to 19.46kts on the measured mile (*Nᵒˢ 8-13*), 18.30kts to 19.72kts (*Nᵒˢ 14-19*). 1 screw. 1 vertical compound engine with 2 cylinders of 0.324m and 0.530m diameter and 0.305m stroke. 1 locomotive boiler. 1.60t coal. Range 35.5nm @ full speed.
**Torpedoes:** 1 torpedo spar. *Nᵒ 10* entered service with two mobile Maupeou torpedo tubes on the sides while *Nᵒ 16* was similarly fitted a few months after delivery. By around 1890 *Nᵒ 19* and perhaps others had torpedo tubes instead of the spar.

*Torpilleur nᵒ 8* Thornycroft, Chiswick, UK.
On list 1.1878. Ord: 13.3.1877. K: 1877. L: 1878. Trials: 5-6.1878.
*Défense mobile* at Cherbourg 1879-92 and Lorient 1893-96. Received a Du Temple boiler 1889. Struck 26.12.1896, hull for sale at Lorient 1896-1898.

*Torpilleur nᵒ 9* Thornycroft, Chiswick, UK.
On list 1.1878. Ord: 13.3.1877. K: 1877. L: 1878. Trials: 5-6.1878.
*Défense mobile* at Brest 1880-95. Sunk 6.6.1889 in collision with a fishing vessel in the entrance strait (*Goulet*) at Brest, refloated. School for stoking 1885-95. Struck 29.11.1895, school for stoking at the school for engineers at Brest 1895-1899. Sold 28.12.1899.

*Torpilleur nᵒ 10* Thornycroft, Chiswick, UK.
On list 1.1878. Ord: 13.3.1877. K: 1877. L: 1878. Trials: 5-6.1878.

*Défense mobile* at Cherbourg 1878-92, Lorient 1893-96. Struck 18.8.1896, hull for sale at Lorient 1896-1898.

*Torpilleur nᵒ 11* Thornycroft, Chiswick, UK.
On list 1.1878. Ord: 13.3.1877. K: 1877. L: 1878. Trials: 5-6.1878.
*Défense mobile* at Cherbourg 1879-92, Lorient 1893-95. Struck 14.3.1895, hull for sale at Lorient 1895-1897.

*Torpilleur nᵒ 12* Thornycroft, Chiswick, UK.
On list 1.1878. Ord: 13.3.1877. K: 1877. L: 1878. Trials: 5-6.1878.
*Défense mobile* at Cherbourg 1879-92, Lorient 1893-94. Struck 26.11.1894. For disposal at Lorient (hull to be BU) 1894-1897.

*Torpilleur nᵒ 13* Thornycroft, Chiswick, UK.
On list 1.1878. Ord: 13.3.1877. K: 1877. L: 1878. Trials: 5-6.1878.
*Défense mobile* at Cherbourg 1879-92, Lorient 1893-95. Struck 19.12.1895, hull for sale at Lorient 1895-1896.

*Torpilleur nᵒ 14* Thornycroft, Chiswick, UK.
On list 1.1878. Ord: 9.7.1877. K: 1877. L: 1878. Accepted at Cherbourg: 31.10.1879.
*Défense mobile* at Cherbourg 1879-92, Rochefort 1893-94. Tested a Guyot du Temple boiler 1880. Struck 15.1.1894, tug (service craft) *Économe* for the use of the *Défense mobile* at Rochefort 1894-1898. Condemned 1898, sold 24.10.1898 to M. André Giraud of Rochefort.

*Torpilleur nᵒ 15* Thornycroft, Chiswick, UK.
On list 1.1878. Ord: 9.7.1877. K: 1877. L: 1878. Accepted at Cherbourg: 31.10.1879.
*Défense mobile* at Brest 1880-94. Struck 15.5.1894. Engine used in the sawmill in the dockyard for many years, hull BU 1894.

*Torpilleur nᵒ 16* Thornycroft, Chiswick, UK.
On list 1.1878. Ord: 9.7.1877. K: 1877. L: 1878. Accepted at Cherbourg: 31.10.1879.
*Défense mobile* at Brest 1880-94. Boiler accident while underway 3.1883, school for stoking at Brest from 1883. Struck 15.5.1894. BU 1895 at Brest.

*Torpilleur nᵒ 17* Thornycroft, Chiswick, UK.
On list 1.1878. Ord: 9.7.1877. K: 1877. L: 1878. Accepted at Cherbourg: 31.10.1879.
*Défense mobile* at Brest 1880-95. Received a Du Temple boiler 1889 (13kg/cm²). Struck 29.11.1895, for sale at Brest 1895-1896.

*Torpilleur nᵒ 18* Thornycroft, Chiswick, UK.
On list 1.1878. Ord: 9.7.1877. K: 1877. L: 1878. Accepted at Cherbourg: 31.10.1879.
*Défense mobile* at Brest Brest 1880-97. Struck 26.4.1897. Sold 29.6.1897 to Decout-Lacour.

*Torpilleur nᵒ 19* Thornycroft, Chiswick, UK.
On list 1.1878. Ord: 9.7.1877. K: 1877. L: 1878. Accepted at Cherbourg: 31.10.1879.
*Défense mobile* at Brest 1880-95. Received two unsuccessful Trépardoux boilers 1889 with two funnels. Struck 22.6.1895. Offered for sale 4.10.1895 and 15.11.1895, Sold 16.11.1895 to M. Troussey.

---

**TORPILLEURS Nᵒˢ 20–21.** *Bateaux torpilleurs.* Normand 27-metre type (1877 batch) with one torpedo spar, two funnels abreast, and a straight bow. To *Torpilleurs* (*garde-côtes*) *de 2ᵉ classe* 1.1883 and *Torpilleurs de 3ᵉ classe* 1.1890.

When the order for *Nᵒˢ 8 to 13* was given to Thornycroft in early 1877 the Navy also wanted to give three French builders a chance at torpedo boat construction, each being given an order for two 27-metre torpedo boats. These firms were Normand at Le Havre, Claparède at Saint Denis, and the

Forges et Chantiers de la Méditerranée (FCM) at their main yard at La Seyne near Toulon. Normand was invited to compete on 11 March 1877, agreed to do so on 17 March, sent in his proposal on 23 March and followed it with his complete plans and data sheets on 6 June. A dispatch of 24 June directed the purchase of the six *canots-torpilleurs*, and the contracts with the three firms were signed in July. The French-built boats were about a metre longer than the Thornycrofts, which they otherwise resembled. The Normand pair and three subsequent annual batches through *Nᵒ 55* all had successful trials and in service (mostly at Cherbourg) were always judged to be excellent. Their seagoing qualities were remarkable, *Nᵒ 55* easily surviving the squall that sank the 35-metre *Nᵒ 110* in 1896.

**Dimensions & tons:** 27.36m wl (wl fwd to wl aft), 27.00m pp (wl fwd to rudder) x 3.28m ext, 3.24m wl. 30.20t disp (33.15t to 35.68t on trials). Draught: 0.64m fwd, 0.91m amidships, 1.83m aft under propeller guard.

---

The 27-metre *Torpilleur nᵒ 20*, the Navy's first torpedo boat built by Augustin Normand, photographed at Villefranche in about 1890 following her 1884-86 refit in which two boilers were installed in place of the original single boiler. *Torpilleur nᵒ 74* appears behind her along with several others. (*NHHC from ONI album of foreign warships dated about 1900, NH-88786*)

**Machinery:** 500ihp designed at 320rpm and 8.43kg/cm² boiler pressure. Speed 18kts. Trials (*Nᵒ 20*) 498ihp = 18.80kts at 318rpm, best measured mile 19.78kts. 1 screw. 1 vertical compound engine (Woolf system) with 2 cylinders of 0.32m and 0.52m diameter and 0.38m stroke. 1 locomotive boiler. 3.00t coal. Range 250nm @ 10kts.

**Torpedoes:** 1 torpedo spar on the bow offset to starboard.

*Torpilleur nᵒ 20* Augustin Normand, Le Havre.
On list 1.1878. Ord: 16.7.1877. K: 1878. L: 30.7.1878. Trials: 9-11.1878.
*Défense mobile* at Cherbourg 1878-95. Reboilered with two du Temple boilers 1884-86, raising the centre of gravity. Assigned to the *Défense mobile* at Rochefort 1895, while en route with *Torpilleur nᵒ 119* capsized in a beam swell 18.5.1895 near the Île d'Aix. Wreck refloated. Struck 2.6.1896, hull reported sold 3.4.1896 but listed for sale at Rochefort 1896-1898.

*Torpilleur nᵒ 21* Augustin Normand, Le Havre.
On list 1.1878. Ord: 16.7.1877. K: 1878. L: 18.11.1878. Trials: 2-3.1879.
*Défense mobile* at Brest from 1880. New locomotive boiler 11.1892. Struck 5.3.1896.

---

**TORPILLEURS N<sup>os</sup> 22–23.** *Bateaux torpilleurs.* Claparède 27-metre type (1877 batch) with one torpedo spar, two funnels abreast, and a straight bow. To *Torpilleurs (garde-côtes) de 2<sup>e</sup> classe* 1.1883 and *Torpilleurs de 3<sup>e</sup> classe* 1.1890.

The initial design by Claparède & Cie. of Saint Denis, just outside Paris, for a 27-metre torpedo boat included a bow with a ram and a spar torpedo, but both of their boats were built with straight bows. The three-cylinder compound engines in the Claparède and FCM boats had one high pressure cylinder in the middle that exhausted simultaneously into two low pressure cylinders on each side of it.

**Dimensions & tons:** 27.25m wl (wl fwd to wl aft), 27.00m pp (wl fwd to rudder) x 3.55m ext (above wl), 3.30m wl. 30.58t disp (34t trials). Draught: 0.54m fwd, 0.85m amidships, 1.59m aft.
**Machinery:** 500ihp designed at 320rpm and 8.43kg/cm$^2$ boiler pressure. Speed 18kts. Trials (*N<sup>o</sup> 23*) 18.96kts at 342rpm, best measured mile 20.11kts at 353rpm. 1 screw. 1 compound engine with 3 cylinders of 0.40m (1) and 0.32m (2) diameter and 0.38m stroke. 1 locomotive boiler. 3.00t coal. 250nm @ 10kts.
**Torpedoes:** 1 torpedo spar.

*Torpilleur n<sup>o</sup> 22* Claparède & Cie., Saint Denis.
On list 1.1878. Ord: 16.7.1877. K: 1877. L: 1878. Trials: 9.1878.
*Défense mobile* at Cherbourg 1880-1901. Tested D'Allest system of oil firing 1891. Struck 14.6.1901, hull and boiler for sale at Cherbourg 1901-1902.

*Torpilleur n<sup>o</sup> 23* Claparède & Cie., Saint Denis.
On list 1.1878. Ord: 16.7.1877. K: 1877. L: 1878. Trials: 12.1878.
Trials at Cherbourg, then *Défense mobile* at Brest 1880-97. Struck 3.5.1898, BU at Brest.

**TORPILLEURS N<sup>os</sup> 24–25.** *Bateaux torpilleurs.* F.C. Méditerranée, La Seyne 27-metre type (1877 batch) with one torpedo spar, one funnel, and a straight bow. To *Torpilleurs (garde-côtes) de 2<sup>e</sup> classe* 1.1883 and *Torpilleurs de 3<sup>e</sup> classe* 1.1890.

The well-established Forges et Chantiers de la Méditerranée (FCM) at La Seyne near Toulon was the third recipient of orders in 1877 for two 27-metre torpedo boats. The trials of their two boats were considered very successful.

**Dimensions & tons:** 27.44m wl (wl fwd to wl aft), 27.32m pp (wl fwd to rudder), 26.00m pp x 3.60m ext (above wl), 3.30m wl. 31.474t disp (33t to 36t trials). Draught: 0.43m fwd, 0.80m amidships, 1.71m aft under propeller guard.
**Machinery:** 500ihp designed at 320rpm and 8.43kg/cm$^2$ boiler pressure. Speed 18kts. Trials 438ihp = 18.275kts at 319.5rpm (*N<sup>o</sup> 25*), best measured mile 19.27kts (*N<sup>o</sup> 24*). 1 screw. 1 compound engine with 3 cylinders of 0.42m (1) and 0.35m (2) diameter and 0.35m stroke. 1 locomotive boiler. 2.30t coal. Range 250nm @ 10kts.
**Torpedoes:** 1 torpedo spar. (*N<sup>o</sup> 24* c1897) 2 torpedo tubes added aft, one on each side.

*Torpilleur n<sup>o</sup> 24* F.C. Méditerranée, La Seyne.
On list 1.1878. Ord: 16.7.1877. K: 1877. L: 1878. Trials: 5-7.1878.
*Défense mobile* at Toulon 1880-1902. Attached to the school for torpedoes (*Algésiras*) 1897-1900 when she received two above-water torpedo tubes. Struck 16.4.1903, for sale at Toulon 1903-1904.

*Torpilleur n<sup>o</sup> 25* F.C. Méditerranée, La Seyne.
On list 1.1878. Ord: 16.7.1877. K: 1877. L: 1878. Trials: 7.1878.
*Défense mobile* at Toulon 1880-93. Transported to Saigon 1893. To *Torpilleur colonial n<sup>o</sup> 1-S* (Saigon) 1901. Struck 17.5.1904, sold at Saigon 1904 to BU.

**TORPILLEUR N<sup>o</sup> 26.** *Bateau torpilleur.* F.C. Méditerranée, La Seyne experimental large type with one submerged bow torpedo tube and a ram bow. To *Torpilleurs (garde-côtes) de 1<sup>re</sup> classe* 1.1883 and *Torpilleurs de 2<sup>e</sup> classe* 1.1890.

In November 1877 the Navy ordered three large boats longer than 30 metres (the *trois grands*, *N<sup>os</sup> 26-28*) on an experimental basis. Of these the Normand boat, *N<sup>o</sup> 27*, was the most successful.

**Dimensions & tons:** 34.76m wl (wl fwd to wl aft) (+0.56m ram), 34.20m pp (wl fwd to rudder) x 3.64m ext (above wl), 3.368m wl. 44.277t disp. Draught: 0.51m fwd, 0.765m amidships, 1.70m aft under propeller guard. Men: 11.
**Machinery:** 500ihp designed at 320rpm and 8.43kg/cm$^2$ boiler pressure. Speed 18kts. Trials 18.43kts at 310rpm, best measured mile 19.23kts at 328rpm. 1 screw. 1 compound engine with 3 cylinders of 0.42m (1) and 0.35m (2) diameter and 0.35m stroke. 1 locomotive boiler.
**Torpedoes:**
(Original) Ram-shaped bow (*étrave renversée*) that opened to expose 1 submerged tube for 381mm Whitehead torpedoes launched by steam (Claparède system as in *Torpilleur no 1*). **Guns:** 2 x 37mm, the first guns mounted on a French torpedo boat.
(Modified) Straight bow with 2 tubes, one on each side, for torpedoes launched by compressed air.

*Torpilleur n<sup>o</sup> 26* F.C. Méditerranée, La Seyne.
On list 1.1878. Ord: 12.11.1877. K: 1878. L: 1878. Trials: 11.1878-7.1879.
*Défense mobile* at Toulon 1880-1901. Struck 8.8.1901, renamed *Écouvillon* 1901 as service craft, annex to the gunnery school at Toulon as target tug 1901-1910. Restored to the regular fleet list 1.1911 as annex to the *station de sous-marins* at Toulon 1910-1913. Struck 4.4.1913 (as *Écouvillon*), sold 1914 at Toulon to BU.

**TORPILLEUR N<sup>o</sup> 27.** *Bateau torpilleur.* Normand experimental large type with one submerged bow torpedo tube, one funnel, and a ram bow. To *Torpilleurs (garde-côtes) de 1<sup>re</sup> classe* 1.1883 and *Torpilleurs de 2<sup>e</sup> classe* 1.1890.

*N<sup>o</sup> 27* was considered very successful and served as a model for the 33-metre type, below. After her 1887-89 modifications *N<sup>o</sup> 27* was sent from Toulon to Cherbourg and completed the trip in 9 days and 3 hours including port calls instead of the 20 to 25 days needed by the smaller boats.

**Dimensions & tons:** 33.00m wl (wl fwd to wl aft) (+0.84m ram), 31.80m pp (wl fwd to rudder) x 3.30m ext (above wl), 3.263m wl. 44.056t disp. Draught: 0.62m fwd, 0.90m amidships, 1.85m aft under propeller guard. Men: 12.
**Machinery:** 500ihp designed at 320rpm and 8.43kg/cm$^2$ boiler pressure. Speed 18kts. Trials 18.34kts at 335rpm, best measured mile 19.42kts. 1 screw. 1 compound engine with 2 cylinders of 0.32m and 0.52m diameter and 0.38m stroke. 1 locomotive boiler. 3.00t coal.
**Torpedoes:**
(1879) 1 submerged torpedo tube in the ram bow, steam operated, converted to compressed air 1880.
(1887-89) 1 torpedo spar forward, 1 rotating twin tube mount aft for lengthened 356mm 4.42m torpedoes with a 60kg charge instead of the normal 42kg. This compromised stability and the spar was removed, the superstructures were lowered by 10cm, and the torpedo tubes were moved to fixed mountings amidships.

*Torpilleur n<sup>o</sup> 27* Augustin Normand, Le Havre.
On list 1.1878. Ord: 12.11.1877. K: 1878. L: 7.3.1879. Trials: 4-7.1879.
*Défense mobile* at Brest 1880-86, Toulon 1887-1903, attached to the

school for torpedoes (*Algésiras*) 1897-1900. Struck 16.4.1903, for sale at Toulon 1903-1904.

---

***TORPILLEUR Nº 28.*** *Bateau torpilleur.* Claparède experimental large type with one submerged bow torpedo tube and a ram bow. To *Torpilleurs (garde-côtes) de 1ʳᵉ classe* 1.1883 and *Torpilleurs de 2ᵉ classe* 1.1890.

The original boiler of *Nº 28* was replaced twice, first with one originally intended for *Nº 60*, (13kg/cm² boiler pressure), and then with an experimental Oriolle boiler ordered for her on 8 January 1896 (9.25kg/cm² boiler pressure). The two replacement boilers produced trial speeds of 15.27 knots and 15.15 knots respectively. One or more of these boiler installations included two funnels abreast.

**Dimensions & tons:** 35.42m wl (wl fwd to wl aft) (+0.70m ram), 34.50m pp (wl fwd to rudder) x 3.66m ext (above wl), 3.375m wl. 43.897t disp. Draught: 0.53m fwd, 0.815m amidships, 1.630m aft under propeller guard. Men: 11.
**Machinery:** 500ihp designed at 8.43kg/cm² boiler pressure. Speed 18kts. Trials 17kts, best measured mile 20kts at 352rpm. 1 screw. 1 compound engine with 2 cylinders. 1 locomotive boiler.
**Torpedoes:**
(Original) 1 submerged torpedo tube in the ram bow (Claparède type as in *Torpilleur no 1*).
(1ˢᵗ change) 2 conjoined tubes for 356mm torpedoes forward, trainable over an angle of 115º.
(2ⁿᵈ change) 2 fixed tubes in the bow (the torpedoes being loaded from between the funnels)
(3ʳᵈ change) 2 conjoined tubes aft as in *Nº 27* (replacing the bow tubes).

*Torpilleur no 28* Claparède & Cie., Saint Denis.
On list 1.1878. Ord: 20.9.1877. K: 1878. L: 1879. Trials: 6.1879.
*Défense mobile* at Brest 1880-86 (boiler accident 3.1883). *Défense mobile* at Toulon 1887-1908, attached to the school for torpedoes (*Algésiras*) 1899-1902. Struck 19.10.1908, retained at Toulon as gunnery target 1908-1909, for sale 1909-1911. Offered for sale 1.8.1911 by the Domaines at Toulon with *Amiral Baudin, Magenta, Pascal, Milan,* and smaller vessels.

---

### The *Défenses mobiles*
On 11 December 1877 Minister of Marine baron Roussin ordered the creation of coastal *défenses fixes et mobiles* to support coastal mining units and torpedo boats. In the late 1870s Cherbourg was the main French torpedo boat base. New boats were brought there from Le Havre, Saint Denis, and Britain to fit out, commission, and run acceptance trials, and then to join the *Défense mobile* or mobile coastal defence unit there. Personnel were also trained there for nascent *défenses mobiles* at Brest and Lorient. By 1879 there was a plan for enlarging the *défenses mobiles* of French ports and harbours that required a total of 55 torpedo boats, and to provide these, and to recognize the importance of this new type of ship the *Conseil d'Amirauté* on 16 August 1879 added 50 torpedo boats to the Programme of 1879 that it was then drafting. Cherbourg was also the focal point for research and development to improve torpedo boat technology, and the thirteen torpedo boats in the *Défense mobile* there in 1879-1880 were constantly underway conducting trials of all kinds.

---

***TORPILLEURS Nᵒˢ 29–30.*** *Bateaux torpilleurs.* Thornycroft torpedo launches (1878 batch) with two torpedo launch frames amidships, one funnel, and a straight bow. To *torpilleurs-vedettes* 1.1883.

These two torpedo launches, slightly smaller than Thornycroft's *Nᵒˢ 5-6*, were ordered as prototypes for the *torpilleurs embarquables*, of which the navy wanted to give two to each battleship. They were Thornycroft's hulls

100-101 and were ordered right after the British 2ⁿᵈ class torpedo boats *Nᵒˢ 51-62* (yard hulls 82-93) and six larger Dutch boats. They made their careers at Toulon embarked on the converted transport *Japon* and then on the specially-built *Foudre* (see Chapter 9) during her first commission. The practical speed of *Nº 29* very quickly fell to 11 knots. *Nᵒˢ 56-57* were near copies by a French builder while *Nᵒˢ 58-59* were built to a later Thornycroft design.

**Dimensions & tons:** 19.20m wl (wl fwd to wl aft), 18.30m pp (wl fwd to rudder) x 2.28m ext (above wl), 2.04m wl. 7.67t disp (9.5t trials, 12.5t full load). Draught: 0.20m fwd, 0.58m amidships, 0.98m aft. Men: 12.
**Machinery:** Designed at 620rpm and 8.80kg/cm² boiler pressure. Speed 17kts (14.5kts actual). Trials (*Nº 29*) 16.20kts at 622rpm. 1 screw. 1 compound engine with 2 cylinders of 0.178m and 0.280m diameter and 0.203m stroke. No condenser. 1 locomotive boiler. 0.5t coal. Could steam for 4 hours with 1 ton of coal.
**Torpedoes:** 2 torpedo launch frames (*tubes carcasses*) amidships of a type developed by Thornycroft for 356mm (4.42m) torpedoes, one frame on each side amidships.

*Torpilleur no 29* Thornycroft, Chiswick, UK.
On list 1.1879. Ord: 1.4.1878. K: 1878. L: 1879. Trials: 9.1879.
Trials at Cherbourg, then to *Défense mobile* at Toulon 1880-97. Reboiled 12.1887 with an Imbert locomotive boiler. Struck 4.8.1897 after a collision. Sold 1901 at Toulon to BU.

*Torpilleur no 30* Thornycroft, Chiswick, UK.
On list 1.1879. Ord: 1.4.1878. K: 1878. L: 1879. C: 10.1879.
Trials at Cherbourg, then to *Défense mobile* at Toulon 1880-1903. Reboiled 1900-01 with an Imbert locomotive boiler. Struck 16.4.1903, for sale at Toulon 1903-1904.

---

***TORPILLEURS Nᵒˢ 31–32.*** *Bateaux torpilleurs.* Yarrow 27-metre type (1878) with two torpedo launch cages two funnels abreast, and a straight bow. To *Torpilleurs (garde-côtes) de 2ᵉ classe* 1.1883 and *Torpilleurs de 3ᵉ classe* 1.1890.

The French returned to Yarrow for two 27-metre torpedo boats. They had a rudder forward as well as the usual one aft. Unlike the original French Yarrow boat (*No 4*) their trials were very satisfactory.

**Dimensions & tons:** 27.00m oa, 26.21m wl x 3.30m ext (above wl), 3.00m wl. 27t disp (light). Draught: 0.55m fwd, 0.84m amidships, 1.41m aft.
**Machinery:** 500ihp designed at 430rpm and 9.14kg/cm² boiler pressure. Speed 19kts. Trials (*Nº 32*) 19.97kts at 472rpm. 1 screw. 1 compound engine with 2 cylinders of 0.317m and 0.546m diameter and 0.305m stroke. 1 locomotive boiler. 3.5t coal (could take 7.5 tons in sacks on deck).
**Torpedoes:**
(1879) 2 torpedo launch cages of the Yarrow 'skeleton' type.
(1885) 2 conjoined Maupeou tubes inside the bow.

*Torpilleur no 31* Yarrow, UK.
On list 1.1879. Ord: 17.6.1878. K: 1878. L: 1879. Trials: 7-10.1879.
*Défense mobile* at Brest 1880-93, Lorient 1894-97, then back to Brest. Struck 2.5.1901, sold 1901.

*Torpilleur no 32* Yarrow, UK.
On list 1.1879. Ord: 17.6.1878. K: 1878. L: 1879. C: 10.1879.
*Défense mobile* at Brest 1880-93, Lorient 1894-97, then back to Brest. New locomotive boiler by the Chantiers de la Loire 5.1889. Struck 27.11.1900, hull and machinery for sale at Brest 1900-1901.

---

## Torpilleurs Nos 33-55

As soon as the trial results for the first French built torpedo boats (*Nos 20-25*) were known the decision was made in November 1878 to order more with the same general characteristics (*Nos 33-42*). More repeat orders for this 27-metre type followed (*Nos 43-49* and *Nos 50-55*). Within this group each builder continued to develop its technology in successive orders.

---

**TORPILLEURS Nos 33–36.** *Bateaux torpilleurs.* F.C. Méditerranée, 27-metre type (1878 batch) with two torpedo tubes inside a raised bow, two funnels abreast, and a straight bow. To *Torpilleurs (garde-côtes) de 2e classe* 1.1883 and *Torpilleurs de 3e classe* 1.1890.

In contrast with the Claparède boats of this type, these FCM boats had their torpedo tubes under the forecastle and had a large dome over their engines.

**Dimensions & tons:** 27.44m wl (wl fwd to wl aft), 27.32m pp (wl fwd to rudder), 26.00m pp x 3.60m ext (above wl), 3.30m wl. 31.47t disp (33t to 36t trials). Draught: 0.43m fwd, 0.80m amidships, 1.71m aft under propeller guard.
**Machinery:** 500ihp designed at 320rpm and 8.43kg/cm² boiler pressure. Speed 18kts. Trials (*No 33*) 445ihp = 18.56kts at 317.16rpm, best measured mile 19.05kts at 325.4rpm. 1 screw. 1 compound engine with 3 cylinders of 0.42m (1) and 0.35m (2) diameter and 0.35m stroke. 1 locomotive boiler. 2.30t coal. 250nm @ 10kts.
**Torpedoes:** 2 bow tubes under the forecastle for 381mm M1876 (5.85m) torpedoes. **Guns:** 2 x 37mm added later.

*Torpilleur no 33* F.C. Méditerranée, La Seyne.
On list 1.1879. Ord: 18.11.1878. K: 1878. L: 1879. C: 1.1880.
*Défense mobile* at Toulon 1880-1906. Struck 17.8.1906, for sale at Toulon 1906-1908.

*Torpilleur no 34* F.C. Méditerranée, La Seyne.
On list 1.1879. Ord: 18.11.1878. K: 1878. L: 1879. C: 10.1879.
*Défense mobile* at Toulon 1880-1903 (at Bizerte 1892). Struck 16.4.1903, for sale at Toulon 1903-1904.

*Torpilleur no 35* F.C. Méditerranée, La Seyne.
On list 1.1879. Ord: 18.11.1878. K: 1878. L: 1879. C: 9.1879.
*Défense mobile* at Toulon 1880-1906. Struck 17.8.1906, for sale at Toulon 1906-1907, retained as gunnery target 1907-1909, torpedo target (*but pour lancements de torpilles*) 1909-1912, for sale 1912-1914, Sold 1915 at Toulon to BU.

*Torpilleur no 36* F.C. Méditerranée, La Seyne.
On list 1.1879. Ord: 18.11.1878. K: 1878. L: 1879. C: 10.1879.
*Défense mobile* at Toulon 1880-1906. Struck 17.8.1906, for sale at Toulon 1906-1907, retained as gunnery target 1907-1909, torpedo target 1909-1912, for sale 1912-1914, Sold 1914 at Toulon to BU.

---

**TORPILLEURS Nos 37–40.** *Bateaux torpilleurs.* Claparède 27-metre type (1878 batch) with two torpedo tubes on top of the bow, one funnel offset to starboard, and a straight bow. To *Torpilleurs (garde-côtes) de 2e classe* 1.1883 and *Torpilleurs de 3e classe* 1.1890.

These Claparède 27-metre boats and their later *Nos 51-53* had torpedo tubes and one funnel instead of the spar torpedo and two funnels in *Nos 22-23*.

**Dimensions & tons:** 27.25m wl (wl fwd to wl aft), 27.00m pp (wl fwd to rudder) x 3.55m ext (above wl), 3.30m wl. 30.58t disp (34t trials). Draught: 0.54m fwd, 0.86m amidships, 1.69m aft.
**Machinery:** 500ihp designed at 320rpm and 8.43kg/cm² boiler pressure. Speed 18kts. Trials (*No 39*) 538ihp = 20.79kts at 355.82rpm. 1 screw. 1 compound engine with 3 cylinders of 0.40m (1), 0.32m (2) diameter and 0.38m stroke. 1 locomotive boiler. 3.00t coal. 250nm @ 10kts.

**Torpedoes:** 2 bow tubes on top of the forecastle for 381mm M1876 (5.85m) torpedoes.

*Torpilleur no 37* Claparède & Cie., Saint Denis.
On list 1.1879. Ord: 18.11.1878. K: 1878. L: 1880. Trials: 1-7.1881.
To Toulon for trials 1880 via inland waterways. Boiler rejected after first round of trials 8.1880 to 1.1881. *Défense mobile* at Toulon 1880-1903. Was the first French warship to enter the old port at Bizerte (1.4.1887) and Lake Bizerte (16.5.1889). Struck 8.5.1903, for sale at Toulon 1903-1904.

*Torpilleur no 38* Claparède & Cie., Saint Denis.
On list 1.1879. Ord: 18.11.1878. K: 1878. L: 1880. Trials: 1-7.1881.
*Défense mobile* at Rochefort 7.1880 to 1886, Toulon 1886-1901. Struck 8.8.1901, for sale at Toulon 1901-1902.

*Torpilleur no 39* Claparède & Cie., Saint Denis.
On list 1.1879. Ord: 18.11.1878. K: 1878. L: 1880. Trials: 5-10.1881.
*Défense mobile* at Rochefort 1.1881 to 1886, Toulon 1886-92. Transported to Saigon 12.1892 by *Shamrock*. To *Torpilleur colonial no 2-S* (Saigon) 1901. Struck 9.9.1903, for sale at Saigon 1903-1907.

*Torpilleur no 40* Claparède & Cie., Saint Denis.
On list 1.1879. Ord: 18.11.1878. K: 1878. L: 1880.
Trials: 11-12.1881.
*Défense mobile* at Rochefort 1881-97. Sunk 28.3.1890 in collision with the service craft *Boutonne* (a dockyard tug used to transport prisoners) in the roadstead of the Île d'Aix, raised and repaired. Struck 19.5.1897, off list 1897. Sold 1904 at Rochefort to BU.

---

**TORPILLEURS Nos 41–42.** *Bateaux torpilleurs.* Normand 27-metre type (1878 batch) with two bow torpedo tubes, two funnels abreast, and a ram bow. To *Torpilleurs (garde-côtes) de 2e classe* 1.1883 and *Torpilleurs de 3e classe* 1.1890.

These boats had ram bows as in *No 27*, a feature dropped in the later *Nos 47-49*.

**Dimensions & tons:** 27.36m wl (wl fwd to wl aft), 27.00m pp (wl fwd to rudder) x 3.28m ext (above wl), 3.24m wl. 30.20t disp (33.15t to 35.68t on trials). Draught: 0.64m fwd, 0.91m amidships, 1.81m aft under propeller guard.
**Machinery:** 500ihp designed at 320rpm and 8.43kg/cm² boiler pressure. Speed 18kts. Trials (*No 42*) 19.88kts at 324.51rpm. 1 screw. 1 vertical compound engine (Woolf system) with 2 cylinders of 0.32m and 0.52m diameter and 0.38m stroke. 1 locomotive boiler. 2.30t coal. Range 250nm @ 10kts.
**Torpedoes:** 2 bow tubes for 381mm M1876 (5.85m) torpedoes.

*Torpilleur no 41* Augustin Normand, Le Havre.
On list 1.1879. Ord: 18.11.1878. K: 1878. L: 27.11.1879. Trials: 2-3.1880.
Trials at Brest, then *Défense mobile* at Lorient 1880-87 and Rochefort 1887-99. Tested a Petit et Godard tubular boiler. Struck 20.10.1899.

*Torpilleur no 42* Augustin Normand, Le Havre.
On list 1.1879. Ord: 18.11.1878. K: 1878. L: 27.12.1879. Trials: 2-3.1880.
Trials at Brest, then *Défense mobile* at Lorient 1880-97 and Rochefort 1897-99. Struck 20.10.1899, school for stoking (*école de chauffe*) at Rochefort 1899 to 12.1901, sold 2.1902 at Rochefort to BU.

---

**TORPILLEURS Nos 43–46.** *Bateaux torpilleurs.* F.C. Méditerranée, La Seyne 27-metre type (1879 batch) with one torpedo spar, one funnel, and a straight bow. To *Torpilleurs (garde-côtes) de 2e classe* 1.1883 and *Torpilleurs de 3e classe* 1.1890.

These boats were ordered by a modification (*acte additionel*) to the contract for *N<sup>os</sup> 33-36* that also included *N<sup>o</sup> 50*.

**Dimensions & tons:** 27.55m wl (wl fwd to wl aft), 27.30m pp (wl fwd to rudder), 26.00m pp x 3.60m ext (above wl), 3.30m wl. 31.47t disp (33t to 36t trials). Draught: 0.43m fwd, 0.80m amidships, 1.71m aft under propeller guard.

**Machinery:** 500ihp designed at 320rpm and 8.43kg/cm² boiler pressure. Speed 18kts. Trials (*N<sup>o</sup> 43*) 471.2ihp = 19.46kts at 333.3rpm. 1 screw. 1 compound engine with 3 cylinders of 0.42m (1) and 0.35m (2) diameter and 0.35m stroke. 1 locomotive boiler. 2.30t coal. 250nm @ 10kts.

**Torpedoes:** 1 torpedo spar. *N<sup>o</sup> 44* later received side launch devices or dropping gear (*pinces-tenailles*) for 356mm torpedoes.

*Torpilleur n<sup>o</sup> 43* F.C. Méditerranée, La Seyne.
On list 1.1880. Ord: 10.2.1879. K: 1878. L: 1879. C: 4.1880.
*Défense mobile* at Toulon 1881-92. Transported to Saigon 12.1892 by *Shamrock*. To *Torpilleur colonial n<sup>o</sup> 3-S* (Saigon) 1901. Struck 3.5.1904. Sold 1905 at Saigon to BU.

*Torpilleur n<sup>o</sup> 44* F.C. Méditerranée, La Seyne.
On list 1.1880. Ord: 10.2.1879. K: 1878. L: 1879. C: 6.1880.
*Défense mobile* at Toulon 1881-85. Transported to Formosa with *Torpilleur n<sup>o</sup> 50* by *Mytho* 1.1885, then taken to Saigon 6.1885 by *Gironde*. To *Torpilleur colonial n<sup>o</sup> 4-S* (Saigon) 1901. Struck 5.12.1908, for sale at Saigon 1908-1910.

*Torpilleur n<sup>o</sup> 45* F.C. Méditerranée, La Seyne.
On list 1.1880. Ord: 10.2.1879. K: 1878. L: 1879. C: 6.1880.
*Défense mobile* at Toulon 1881-82. Transported to Tonkin 5.1883 by *Annamite*. Lost 28.3.1885 in a storm while being towed by *Châteaurenault* from the Pescadores to Ning Po. Struck 18.6.1885.

*Torpilleur n<sup>o</sup> 46* F.C. Méditerranée, La Seyne.
On list 1.1880. Ord: 10.2.1879. K: 1878. L: 1879. C: 6.1880.
*Défense mobile* at Toulon 1881-82. Transported to Tonkin 6.1883 by *Mytho*, then to Thuan An 9.1883 by *Saône*. Lost 30.4.1885 when the tow line broke in a squall while being towed by *D'Estaing* off the Pescadores. Struck 18.6.1885.

———————

*TORPILLEURS N<sup>os</sup> 47–49. Bateaux torpilleurs.* Normand 27-metre type (1879 batch) with one torpedo spar, two funnels abreast, and a straight bow. To *Torpilleurs (garde-côtes) de 2<sup>e</sup> classe* 1.1883 and *Torpilleurs de 3<sup>e</sup> classe* 1.1890.

These boats and *N<sup>os</sup> 54-55* had hull lines slightly different from *N<sup>os</sup> 20-21* and *N<sup>os</sup> 41-42* but were otherwise similar.

**Dimensions & tons:** 27.46m wl (wl fwd to wl aft), 27.04m pp (wl fwd to rudder) x 3.28m ext (below wl), 3.24m wl. 30.20t disp (33.15t to 35.68t on trials). Draught: 0.64m fwd (keel line projected), 0.91m amidships, 1.83m aft under propeller guard.

**Machinery:** 500ihp designed at 320rpm and 8.43kg/cm² boiler pressure. Speed 18kts. Trials (*N<sup>o</sup> 49*) 19.10kts at 313rpm, best measured mile 19.77kts at 324rpm. 1 screw. 1 vertical compound engine (Woolf system) with 2 cylinders of 0.32m and 0.52m diameter and 0.38m stroke. 1 locomotive boiler. 3.00t coal. Range 250nm @ 10kts.

**Torpedoes:** 1 torpedo spar.

*Torpilleur n<sup>o</sup> 47* Augustin Normand, Le Havre.
On list 1.1880. Ord: 10.2.1879. K: 1878. L: 13.4.1880. C: 6.1880.
*Défense mobile* at Lorient 1880-86 and Rochefort 1886-96. Struck 2.6.1896, hull for sale at Rochefort 1896-1898.

*Torpilleur n<sup>o</sup> 48* Augustin Normand, Le Havre.
On list 1.1880. Ord: 10.2.1879. K: 1878. L: 10.6.1880. C: 7.1880.

*Défense mobile* at Lorient 1880-98. Struck 28.6.1898, hull for sale at Lorient 1898-1904.

*Torpilleur n<sup>o</sup> 49* Augustin Normand, Le Havre.
On list 1.1880. Ord: 10.2.1879. K: 1878. L: 20.7.1880. C: 8.1880.
*Défense mobile* at Lorient 1880-1901 and Brest 1901-1902. Struck 7.11.1902, hull retained at Brest as gunnery target 1902-1909, for sale 1909-1910.

———————

*TORPILLEUR N<sup>o</sup> 50. Bateau torpilleur.* F.C. Méditerranée, La Seyne 27-metre type (additional 1879 boat) with two bow torpedo tubes, two funnels abreast, and a straight bow. To *Torpilleurs (garde-côtes) de 2<sup>e</sup> classe* 1.1883 and *Torpilleurs de 3<sup>e</sup> classe* 1.1890.

This boat was ordered with *N<sup>os</sup> 43-46* but had torpedo tubes instead of their torpedo spar.

**Dimensions & tons:** 27.44m wl (wl fwd to wl aft), 27.32m pp (wl fwd to rudder), 26.00m pp x 3.60m ext (above wl), 3.30m wl. 31.47t disp (33t to 36t trials). Draught: 0.43m fwd, 0.80m amidships, 1.71m aft under propeller guard.

**Machinery:** 500ihp designed at 320rpm and 8.43kg/cm² boiler pressure. Speed 18kts. Trials 454ihp = 18.84kts at 320.5rpm. 1 screw. 1 compound engine with 3 cylinders of 0.42m (1) and 0.35m (2) diameter and 0.35m stroke. 1 locomotive boiler. 2.30t coal. 250nm @ 10kts.

**Torpedoes:** 2 bow tubes for 381mm M1876 (5.85m) torpedoes.

*Torpilleur n<sup>o</sup> 50* F.C. Méditerranée, La Seyne.
On list 1.1880. Ord: 10.2.1879. K: 1878. L: 1879. C: 2.1880.
*Défense mobile* at Toulon 1880-85. Transported to Formosa with *Torpilleur n<sup>o</sup> 44* by *Mytho* 1.1885, transported to Saigon 6.1885 by *Nive*. Struck 22.11.1898, annex to the school for stoking at Saigon while on sale list 1898-1900, service ship for fixed defences (controlled mines) 1900-1905, renamed *Circuit* 1901, for sale at Saigon 1905-1906, sold 6.1906 at Saigon to BU.

———————

*TORPILLEURS N<sup>os</sup> 51–53. Bateaux torpilleurs.* Claparède 27-metre type (1879 batch) with two torpedo tubes inside the bow, one funnel, and a straight bow. To *Torpilleurs (garde-côtes) de 2<sup>e</sup> classe* 1.1883 and *Torpilleurs de 3<sup>e</sup> classe* 1.1890.

These boats were ordered by an *acte additionel* to the contract for *N<sup>os</sup> 37-40*. Their torpedo tubes were inside the bow rather than on top of it as in the earlier boats.

**Dimensions & tons:** 27.25m wl (wl fwd to wl aft), 27.00m pp (wl fwd to rudder) x 3.55m ext (above wl), 3.30m wl. 30.58t disp (34t trials). Draught: 0.54m fwd, 0.86m amidships, 1.69m aft.

**Machinery:** 500ihp designed at 320rpm and 8.43kg/cm² boiler pressure. Speed 18kts. Trials (*N<sup>o</sup> 53*) 426ihp = 19.66kts at 347.97rpm, best measured mile 20.21kts. 1 screw. 1 compound engine with 3 cylinders of 0.40m (1), 0.32m (2) diameter and 0.38m stroke. 1 locomotive boiler. 3.00t coal. 250nm @ 10kts.

**Torpedoes:** 2 tubes inside the bow for 381mm M1876 (5.85m) torpedoes.

*Torpilleur n<sup>o</sup> 51* Claparède & Cie., Saint Denis.
On list 1.1880. Ord: 10.2.1879. K: 1878. L: 3q.1880.
Trials: 10.1880-8.1881.
*Défense mobile* at Rochefort 1880-97. Struck 8.3.1897.

*Torpilleur n<sup>o</sup> 52* Claparède & Cie., Saint Denis.
On list 1.1880. Ord: 10.2.1879. K: 1878. L: 3q.1880. Trials: 8.1881.
*Défense mobile* at Rochefort 1882-86 and Toulon 1886-91. Transported to Saigon 1891. To *Torpilleur colonial n<sup>o</sup> 5-S* (Saigon) 1901. Struck 15.12.1903, for sale at Saigon 1903-1907.

*Torpilleur nᵒ 53* Claparède & Cie., Saint Denis.
On list 1.1880. Ord: 10.2.1879. K: 1878. L: 3q.1880. Trials: 5-6.1882.
Delivery for trials at Cherbourg delayed by grounding in the Seine
  9.1880, re-launched 4q.1881 after repairs. *Défense mobile* at Lorient
  1883-99 and Brest 1899-1901. Struck 8.8.1901, renamed *Enclume*
  8.1901, annex to the school for engineers at Brest 1901-1907,
  condemned 3.1907, replaced by *Torpilleur nᵒ 89*, and BU.

---

**TORPILLEURS Nᵒˢ 54–55.** *Bateaux torpilleurs.* Normand 27-metre type
(1880 batch) with two torpedo tubes inside a raised bow, one funnel, and
a straight bow. To *Torpilleurs (garde-côtes) de 2ᵉ classe* 1.1883 and *Torpilleurs
de 3ᵉ classe* 1.1890.

These boats had torpedo tubes and one funnel instead of the spar torpedo
and two funnels in the earlier Normand 27-metre boats. The funnel and
the dome over the engine were offset from the centreline to permit
handling the torpedoes.

**Dimensions & tons:** 27.46m wl (wl fwd to wl aft), 27.04m pp (wl fwd
  to rudder) x 3.28m ext (below wl), 3.24m wl. 30.20t disp (33.15t to
  35.68t on trials). Draught: 0.64m fwd (keel line projected), 0.91m
  amidships, 1.83m aft under propeller guard.
**Machinery:** 500ihp designed at 320rpm and 8.43kg/cm² boiler pressure.
  Speed 18kts. Trials (*Nᵒ 55*) 515ihp = 19.833kts at 342.2rpm. 1 screw.
  1 vertical compound engine (Woolf system) with 2 cylinders of 0.32m
  and 0.52m diameter and 0.38m stroke. 1 locomotive boiler. 3.00t coal.
  Range 250nm @ 10kts.
**Torpedoes:** 2 bow tubes for 381mm M1876 (5.85m) torpedoes.

*Torpilleur nᵒ 54* Augustin Normand, Le Havre.
On list 1.1881. Ord: 6.12.1880. K: 1878. L: 1882. Trials: 9-12.1882.
*Défense mobile* at Cherbourg 1883-93 and Rochefort 1893-96. Struck
  17.11.1896, school for stoking at Rochefort 1896-1900, sold 1900 to
  BU.

*Torpilleur nᵒ 55* Augustin Normand, Le Havre.
On list 1.1881. Ord: 6.12.1880. K: 1878. L: 1882. Trials: 10-12.1882.
*Défense mobile* at Cherbourg 1883-91 and Rochefort 1891-96. Struck
  17.11.1896, school for stoking at Rochefort 1896-1898, engine
  ordered removed 8.6.1898 for use in tug *Lama*, condemned
  31.5.1899, sold 1899 to BU.

---

**TORPILLEURS Nᵒˢ 56–57.** *Bateaux torpilleurs.* F.C. Méditerranée, La
Seyne torpedo launches (1881) with two torpedo tubes on top of the bow,
one funnel, and a straight bow. To *torpilleurs-vedettes* 1.1883.

These torpedo launches were built to plans drafted by the Navy based on
Thornycroft's plans for *Nᵒˢ 29-30*. They were somewhat heavier than the
Thornycroft boats and somewhat slower. Like the other early *vedettes* they
made their careers at Toulon embarked on the transport *Japon* and then on
*Foudre* during her first commission.

**Dimensions & tons:** 19.20m oa, 18.40m wl x 2.33m ext (above wl),
  2.04m wl. 7.67t disp (11.1t trials, 12.5t full load). Draught: 0.35m
  fwd, 0.70m amidships, 1.05m aft. Men: 12.
**Machinery:** Designed at 620rpm and 9.126kg/cm² boiler pressure
  (originally 8.43kg/cm²). Speed 17kts (14.5kts actual). Trials (*Nᵒ 57*)
  14.60kts at 568rpm. 1 screw. 1 compound engine with 2 cylinders of
  0.2095m and 0.3429m diameter and 0.203m stroke. No condenser.
  1 locomotive boiler. Could steam for 4 hours with 1 ton of coal.
**Torpedoes:** 2 tubes, one on each side on deck forward, for 356mm
  (4.42m) torpedoes, originally launched by steam and later by a powder
  charge (*tubes-bélier* or impulse tubes).

*Torpilleur nᵒ 56* F.C. Méditerranée, La Seyne.
On list 1.1881. Ord: 15.2.1881. K: 1881. L: 1882. Trials: 7.1882.

Trials at Toulon. Struck 9.3.1910. Sold 1910 at Toulon to BU.
*Torpilleur nᵒ 57* F.C. Méditerranée, La Seyne.
On list 1.1881. Ord: 15.2.1881. K: 1881. L: 1882. Trials: 8.1882.
Trials at Toulon. Struck 3.5.1904. Sold 1904 at Toulon to BU.

---

**TORPILLEURS Nᵒˢ 58–59.** *Bateaux torpilleurs.* Thornycroft torpedo
launches (1881 batch) probably with two torpedo tubes on the bow, two
funnels, and a ram bow. To *torpilleurs-vedettes* 1.1883.

These torpedo launches were Thornycroft's hulls 137-138 and were ordered
right after the British 2ⁿᵈ class torpedo boats *Nᵒˢ 76-95* (yard hulls 117-
136) which they probably resembled. While the hull dimensions and
machinery were the same as in Thornycroft's earlier *Nᵒˢ 29-30* their upper
works were quite different, including a torpedo launching system in the
bow instead of side dropping gear, ram bows, and a prominent conning
tower for the helmsman aft that reappeared in the torpedo launches built
for *Foudre* in the 1890s.

  Their original torpedo launching system consisted of two steam-oper-
ated impulse tubes in the bow in which steam from the boiler drove a
piston that expelled the torpedo. This system allowed the torpedo to be
discharged while the boat was running at full speed, but it required that the
tubes be sloped downward to facilitate expelling the torpedo and it added
weight forward, causing the boat to bury her bow in anything but a flat
calm. The French probably soon replaced the steam launching system with
powder charges as they did in *Nᵒˢ 56-57*. Like the four other French
*vedettes*, *Nᵒˢ 58-59* made their careers at Toulon embarked on the transport
*Japon* and then on *Foudre* during her first commission.

**Dimensions & tons:** 19.20m wl (wl fwd to wl aft) (+0.60m ram),
  18.30m pp (wl fwd to rudder) x 2.285m ext (above wl), 2.04m wl.
  7.67t disp (9.5t trials, 12.5t full load). Draught: (trials) 0.20m fwd,
  0.58m amidships, 0.98m aft. Men: 12.
**Machinery:** Designed at 620rpm and 8.80kg/cm² boiler pressure
  (originally 8.43kg/cm²). Speed 17kts (14.5kts actual). Trials (*Nᵒ 59*)
  16.92kts at 648.27rpm. 1 screw. 1 compound engine with 2 cylinders
  of 0.2095m and 0.3429m diameter and 0.203m stroke. No condenser.
  1 locomotive boiler. 0.50t coal in the bunkers + 0.025t in the furnace.
  Could steam for 4 hours with 1 ton of coal.
**Torpedoes:** 2 tubes, one on each side on deck forward, for 356mm
  (4.42m) torpedoes, launched by steam (impulse tubes) and probably
  later by a powder charge.

*Torpilleur nᵒ 58* Thornycroft, Chiswick, UK.
On list 1.1881. Ord: 16.8.1880. K: 11.1880. L: 1881. C: 9.1881.
Trials at Cherbourg. Struck 30.7.1903, for sale at Toulon 1903-1904.

*Torpilleur nᵒ 59* Thornycroft, Chiswick, UK.
On list 1.1881. Ord: 16.8.1880. K: 11.1880. L: 1881. C: 9.1881.
Trials at Cherbourg. Loaned 2-3.1903 to the Prince of Monaco for
  oceanographic work. Escorted, then towed by *Torpilleur nᵒ 103*, on
  25.3.1903 during her return she capsized under tow during the night
  off Cavalaire east of Hyères (4 dead). Struck 26.5.1903. Wreck found
  8.3.1978.

---

**Torpedo boat categories, 1881-1883**
The next boat, *Nᵒ 60*, was a new type, even larger than the *trois grands* of
November 1877 on which she was based. She was listed as a *bateau
torpilleur pour le service de la Défense mobile* (torpedo boat for service with
the mobile coastal defence force) with all the other torpedo boats when she
first appeared on the fleet list in 1.1881, but she was the only one also
described as a *torpilleur de haute mer* (seagoing torpedo boat). *Nᵒˢ 61-64*
joined her under these listings in 1.1882. In the 1.1883 fleet list the
*Batiments torpilleurs* (torpedo vessels) were reorganized into multiple
groupings, including *Torpilleurs éclaireurs* (torpedo scouts, the *Condor*

class), *Torpilleurs avisos* (torpedo avisos, the *Bombe* class), and three classes of *Torpilleurs garde-côtes* (coast defence torpedo boats), of which the first class consisted only of *Nº 1* (because of her size), *Nᵒˢ 26-28* (the *trois grands*), and *Nᵒˢ 61-68*. The second class included the other torpedo boats before *Nº 60* and the third class consisted of the six torpedo launches or *vedettes* plus the small *Nᵒˢ 4-7*. *Torpilleur nº 60* thus marked the coming of age of the French torpedo boat and was the first of the 300 torpedo boats between 33 and 38 metres in length that the French ordered for mobile coastal defence units (the *défenses mobiles*) between 1880 and 1904.

### *TORPILLEURS Nᵒˢ 60–64*. 33-METRE TYPE, 1ST SERIES, 1880 & 1881 ORDERS. *Torpilleurs garde-côtes de 1re classe* (from 1.1883) and *Torpilleurs de 1re classe* (from 1.1885). Normand 33-metre torpedo boats with two torpedo tubes inside the bow, two funnels abreast, and a straight bow. To *Torpilleurs de 2e classe* 1.1890.

*Nᵒˢ 60–64* were repeats with improvements of Normand's *Nº 27*, the most successful of the *trois grands* of November 1877. Normand's *Projet de bateau torpilleur à grand rayon d'action* was approved by the *Conseil des travaux* on 11.5.1880 subject to some additional studies of stability and internal arrangements. *Nᵒˢ 60–64* had straight bows and vertical sides at the

waterline, the sides angled in from an extreme beam of 3.28m to produce a deck 2.45m wide. They had two funnels abreast on the sides, tall and thin on all except *Nº 61* whose funnels were short and thick. (Her funnels turned the smoke around and vented it out of the side of the boat in an effort to reduce visibility.) *Nº 60* made 20.62 knots on trials with the boiler forced to 9.5kg/cm² pressure and made 19.27 knots at the rated 8.43kg/cm² boiler pressure. They were excellent sea boats, demonstrated when *Nᵒˢ 62-64* transited to Toulon for service in 1884, when *Nº 61* went from Cherbourg to Toulon and back to participate in Mediterranean exercises in 1886, and again when both *Nº 61* and *Nº 60* made the same voyage in 1887. *Nᵒˢ 65–74* in Chapter 11 were near sisters ordered in 1883. With *Nᵒˢ 26-28* they became *Torpilleurs de 2e classe* in the 1890 fleet list.

**Dimensions & tons:** 33.75m wl (wl fwd to wl aft) (+ 0.84m ram in *Nᵒˢ 60-61* only), 33.00m pp (wl fwd to rudder) x 3.28m ext (below wl), 3.26m wl. 46.1t disp (42.9t on trials for *Nº 60*, 45.04t to 46.26t for the others). Draught: 0.81m fwd (keel line projected), 1.10m amidships, 1.95m aft under propeller guard. Men: 11.
**Machinery:** 500ihp designed at 325rpm and 8.43kg/cm² boiler pressure. Speed 20kts Trials (*Nº 60*) 20.62kts at 322.3rpm and 9.5kg/cm² boiler pressure. The others made between 20.14kts and 20.55kts on trials. 1 screw. 1 compound engine with 2 cylinders of 0.32m and 0.52m diameter and 0.38m stroke. 1 locomotive boiler. 8.380t coal. Range 67 hours @ 12kts.
**Torpedoes:** 2 bow tubes for 381mm M1876 (5.85m) torpedoes. Torpedoes originally launched by compressed air and later by powder charges.

The 33-metre *Torpilleur nº 63*, probably photographed at Le Havre. She served in the *Défense mobile* at Toulon from 1884 to 1895 followed by similar service at Algiers and Oran. The large steam cruiser in the background may be flying American flags. Candidates include USS *Lancaster*, *Quinnebaug* and *Kearsarge*. *(NHHC from ONI album of foreign warships dated about 1900, NH-88794)*

French "Torpilleur" 1st Class.
Register, No. 4880.

The 33-metre *Torpilleur nº 64*, probably photographed by Normand immediately after completion at Le Havre in the fall of 1884. She was delivered at Cherbourg and then spent her entire career in the Mediterranean. *(NHHC from ONI Register 4880, NH-88795)*

*Torpilleur nº 60* Augustin Normand, Le Havre.
On list 1.1881. Ord: 5.11.1880. K: 1880. L: 31.3.1882. Trials: 7-8.1882.
*Défense mobile* at Cherbourg 1882-93, at Dunkirk 1895. Tested a Petit et Godard tubular boiler 12.1888. Struck 1.12.1904, for sale at Cherbourg 1904-1905.

*Torpilleur nº 61* Augustin Normand, Le Havre.
On list 1.1882. Ord: 31.10.1881. K: 1881. L: 12.6.1883. Trials: 3.1884.
*Défense mobile* at Brest 1884-1904. Collided with and sank *Torpilleur nº 83* near Brest 11.1896, repaired. Struck 15.11.1904, for sale at Brest 1904-1905.

*Torpilleur nº 62* Augustin Normand, Le Havre.
On list 1.1882. Ord: 31.10.1881. K: 1881. L: 4.8.1883. Trials: 5-10.1883.
*Défense mobile* at Toulon 1884-1900 (in Corsica 1895-96), then to reserve. Designated escort for submarines (*convoyeur de sous-marins*) 10.1902. Replaced by *Torpilleur nº 140* in 3.1907. Struck 6.3.1908. Sold 1908 at Toulon to BU.

*Torpilleur nº 63* Augustin Normand, Le Havre.
On list 1.1882. Ord: 31.10.1881. K: 1881. L: 9.3.1883. Trials: 3.1884.
*Défense mobile* at Toulon 1884-95, Algiers 1896-98, Oran 1899-1900. Struck 18.12.1900, for sale at Toulon 1900-1902.

*Torpilleur nº 64* Augustin Normand, Le Havre.
On list 1.1882. Ord: 31.10.1881. K: 1881. L: 10.4.1883. Trials: 10.1884.
*Défense mobile* at Toulon from 1884, then to Corsica. Sunk 4.6.1886 in collision with *Torpilleur nº 66* in four metres of water off Corsica, refloated. Struck 25.8.1900, for sale at Toulon 1900-1904.

# Chapter Six

# Transports, 1859-1882

## (A) Colonial Transports (*Transports pour les colonies*).

To *Grands transports* in the 1.1880 fleet list, *Transports de 1ʳᵉ classe* 1.1885, and *Transports* 1.1909. All had two covered batteries.

### Transports in the Programme of 1872

The Programme of 1872 deleted the large force of troop transports that was in the Programme of 1857, initially to support military operations in Europe by Napoleon III, in favour of a smaller number of transports, primarily to maintain communications with the colonies and carry cargoes along French coasts. As part of its effort as directed by Minister of Marine Pothuau on 14 September 1871 to produce technical specifications for all of the ship types that were to enter into the composition of the fleet under the Programme of 1872, the *Conseil des travaux* on 25 November 1871 reviewed specifications it had developed before the war for troop transports. On 20 July 1869 the Council had concluded that a single transport should carry both men, horses, and materiel rather than having different types of transports for each, resulting in specifications for a large (115-metre) ship with an iron hull and with two covered batteries. On 2 August 1870 the Council had reviewed nine designs without finding any fully satisfactory, a decision that it reaffirmed on 25 November 1871. On 16 January 1872 the Council examined the question of large transports in a different context, developing specifications for transports to assign to the Cochinchina service. It decided to replicate the hull structure and interior arrangements of the British troopship *Euphrates* with some modifications. The ship was to have an iron hull, capacity for 800 passengers, 950 tons of coal to cover 8,000 miles at a speed of 9.5 knots, a maximum speed of 13 knots, and moderate sail area.

---

*ANNAMITE. Transport pour les colonies.* Colonial transport with wooden hull frames and hull and deck planking, iron hull frames and deck beams, and a straight bow. One funnel, three masts, ship rig. Designed by Cazelles.

On 18 October 1872 the *Conseil des travaux* examined six designs for transports for the Cochinchina service produced in response to its specifications of 16 January 1872, and that of naval constructor David Jules Frédéric Cazelles with internal arrangements by naval constructors Bertin and Thomas Garnier was recommended to Minister of Marine Pothuau and approved on 25 November 1872. (Bertin developed an innovative ventilation system for these ships.) Cazelles's design was based not on the Council's specifications but on his own experiences on transport runs to Cochinchina. Most significantly he designed the hull with wooden inner and outer hull planking because he felt that on long voyages iron hulls fouled too rapidly and were less healthy for the many people on board. His ship had a hybrid double hull that alternated frames of iron and wood, the iron frames supporting the iron deck beams and the wood frames supporting both inner and outer wooden hull planking. The decks had wooden planking. The Council accepted his composite design for the first ship provided some diagonal wooden reinforcements were added to the hull, although it maintained its preference for iron hulls for later ships.

Concerns arose almost immediately about the strength of this structure with the result that the exterior hull planking was thickened several times beginning in 1873, making the ship 215 tons overweight and causing her intended sister *Mytho* to be redesigned with more iron. The contract for the machinery was dated 17 August 1874. The first launch attempt on

21 August 1876 failed, and during the otherwise successful second attempt the ship broke loose and struck the opposite side of the basin. The ships of this type could carry over 1,000 troops or other passengers, or part of the troop spaces could be fitted for horses.

*The characteristics are based on a devis dated 6.9.1877.*

**Dimensions & tons:** 103.80m wl, 105.32m pp (wl fwd to rudder) x 15.38m ext, 15.32m wl. 5,623.6t disp. Draught: 6.769m mean, 7.192m aft. Men: 243.

**Machinery:** 650nhp and 2,640ihp designed at 66rpm and 4.00kg/cm² boiler pressure. Trials (18.7.1877) 2,350.3ihp = 13.121kts at 67.4rpm and 4.020kg/cm² boiler pressure. 1 screw. 1 vertical compound engine with 3 cylinders of 1.40m (1) and 1.86m (2) diameter and 1.00m stroke. 8 low cylindrical boilers. 701.5t coal. Range 6,570nm @ 10kts.

**Guns:**

(1877) 2 x 138.6mm on the upper deck just forward of the long poop, 5 x 4pdr (86.5mm/11) bronze boat.

(by 1893) 2 x 138.6mm, 3 x 90mm, 10 x 37mm revolving cannon.

*Annamite* Cherbourg Dyd/Schneider, Creusot.

On list 1.1873. Ord: 25.11.1872. K: 12.12.1872. L: 5.9.1876. Comm: 15.5.1877 (trials), 6.9.1877 (full).

Budget 1872. Machinery installed 19.10.1876 to 23.4.1877. First trials (under sail) 8.8.1877. Last regular Indochina voyage 1895. Decomm. at Toulon 27.3.1896 and relieved *Tonquin* as barracks ship for unassigned personnel (*bâtiment caserne pour les isolés*). Struck 6.11.1896, barracks hulk at Toulon 1896-1909, for sale 1909-1910. Sold 1911 at Toulon to BU.

---

*MYTHO. Transports pour les colonies, Grand transport* (1880). Colonial (large) transport with iron frames, outer hull plating, and deck beams and wooden inner hull and deck planking. One funnel, three masts, ship rig. Designed by Cazelles and Delaitre.

*Mytho* was ordered at the same time as *Annamite* to the same plans but was much modified by naval constructors Cazelles and Pierre Delaitre during construction to correct defects in the first ship and was launched after *Tonquin* and *Shamrock*. As modified all of her hull frames were iron and her outer hull shell was also iron rather than wood. She still had inner hull planking and decks of wood. Her engine was displayed at the 1878 *Exposition Universelle*, gaining its builder, Schneider, a top prize but delaying its installation in the ship. She was the only one of the eight transports with an inclined two-piece bowsprit rather than a horizontal pole.

*The characteristics are based on a devis dated 3.3.1880.*

**Dimensions & tons:** 103.20m wl, 105.20m pp (wl fwd to rudder) x 15.406m ext, 15.302m wl. 5,653t disp. Draught: 6.441m mean, 6.866m aft. Men: 311.

**Machinery:** 650nhp and 2,640ihp designed at 66rpm and 4.00kg/cm² boiler pressure. Trials (*Mytho*, 19.2.1880) 2,614ihp = 13.248kts at 75.75rpm and 4,240kg/cm² boiler pressure. 1 screw. 1 vertical compound engine with 3 cylinders of 1.40m (1) and 1.86m (2) diameter and 1.00m stroke. 8 low cylindrical boilers. 707.1t coal. Range 6,240nm @ 10kts.

**Guns:**

(1880) 2 x 138.6mm on the upper deck just forward of the long poop,

5 x 4pdr (86.5mm/11) bronze boat.
(by 1893) 2 x 138.6mm, 3 x 90mm, 4 x 37mm revolving cannon.

*Mytho* (later *Bretagne, Armorique*) Cherbourg Dyd/Schneider, Creusot.
On list 1.1873. Ord: 25.11.1872. K: 17.2.1873. L: 11.3.1879.
   Comm: c1879 (trials), 3.3.1880 (full).
Budget 1872 (late addition). Machinery installed 22.3.1879 to
   2.11.1879. Out of commission 1886 to 1891. Last regular Indochina
   voyage 1894. Extensive internal damage from heavy rolling in bad
   weather off Morocco 11.1908, not worth repairing. Sale planned but
   instead designated 23.9.1909 to replace *Bretagne* (ex *Fontenoy*) as
   school for boys at Brest. Towed into Brest 15.11.1909, engines
   removed but boilers retained for harbour service. Retired as *Mytho* and
   renamed *Bretagne* 1.1910 as school for apprentice seamen and boys at
   Brest. Ship renamed *Armorique* c1.1913 and name of school shortened
   to school for apprentice seamen 4.8.1913. Students and instructors
   evacuated 18.6.1940 to Plymouth, England in the battleship *Paris* as
   the Germans approached Brest. Towed in early 1942 to Landévennec
   and used as a base ship for *kriegsfischkutters* (armed fishing trawlers)
   until scuttled in late 8.1944. Wreck sold 10.1950 to the firm 'Moyen'
   but proved unsalvageable. Funnel and foremast blown up during the
   1950s as hazards to navigation, hull remains on the bottom at
   Landévennec.

The large transport *Tonquin*, one of eight built between 1872 and 1884 to serve
the expanding colony in Indochina. She became the seagoing school for
midshipmen *Duguay-Trouin* in 1900. *(NHHC from ONI album of French warships,
NH-74899)*

**Transports 1874-1877**
The 1875 budget (submitted January 1874) added an unnamed transport
to be built by contract, and this new contract transport appeared on the
January 1874 fleet list without a name and on the January 1875 list as
*Tonquin*. The 1876 budget (May 1875) added a second unnamed ship,
both still to be begun. Both *Tonquin* and the unnamed ship were among
those cancelled during 1875 and did not appear on the January 1876 fleet
list. Both ships were on the January 1877 fleet list with the names *Tonquin*
and *Shamrock*.

*TONQUIN* Class. *Transports pour les colonies, Grands transports* (1880).
Colonial (large) transports with all-iron hulls except for wood planking on
the iron decks. One funnel, three masts, ship rig. Designed by Cazelles and
Bertin.

The design for this class by Cazelles and Bertin included internal arrangements by naval constructor François Opin. The ships were described as a
modified *Mytho* type, although they were launched before her. They had
iron double hulls in which both the outer and inner hull plating were made
of iron. *Shamrock* was completed at Cherbourg after launching at Graville.
The contract for the engines of both ships was dated 5 February 1877.
Modifications of *Duguay-Trouin* (ex *Tonquin*) in 1900 as a school ship for
midshipmen included the addition of a sizeable bridge and removal of the
characteristic sponsons amidships for the troops' latrines. (*Gironde* lost her
sponsons in 1909 when she became *Tourville*, the others kept theirs.) In
1905 the masts of *Duguay-Trouin* were replaced with those of the cruiser
*Sfax*, which were single-piece metal poles (*mâts à pible*), her bridge was
enlarged, and pairs of casemates with 138.6mm guns were added on each
side of the upper deck aft of the mainmast. In 1908 she received a mix of

boilers taken from the aviso transport *Meurthe,* the wooden cruiser *d'Estaing,* and the armoured cruiser *Dupuy de Lôme. Shamrock* was one of three large transports permanently disabled or lost during the Morocco operation of 1907-08.

*The characteristics are based on a devis for* Tonquin *dated 15.7.1879.*
**Dimensions & tons:** 102.80m wl, 105.20m pp (wl fwd to rudder) x 15.42m ext, 15.34m wl. 5,637.7t disp. Draught: 6.417m mean, 6.612m aft. Men: 311.
**Machinery:** 650nhp and 2,640ihp designed at 66rpm and 4.133kg/cm² boiler pressure. Trials (*Tonquin,* 27.4.1880) 2,655ihp = 13.285kts at 68.27rpm and 4,375kg/cm² boiler pressure. 1 screw. 1 vertical compound engine with 3 cylinders of 1.40m (1) and 1.86m (2) diameter and 1.00m stroke. 8 low cylindrical boilers. 966.5t coal. Range 8.530nm @ 10kts.
**Guns:**
(1879) 2 x 138.6mm on the upper deck just forward of the long poop, 5 x 4pdr (86.5mm/11) bronze boat.
(1882) 5 revolving cannon to replace the 4pdrs. 3 x 90mm were added to *Shamrock* (not *Tonquin*) by 1893.
(1900, *Duguay-Trouin*) 2 x 138.6mm on the upper deck just forward of the bridge, 6 x 100mm, 4 x 47mm QF, and some 37mm revolving cannon.
(1905, *Duguay-Trouin*) 6 x 138.6mm on the upper deck (four added in pairs of casemates forward of the long poop), 4 x 100mm, 8 x 47mm QF.

***Tonquin*** (or *Tonkin,* later *Duguay-Trouin, Moselle*) F.C. Méditerranée, La Seyne/FCM, Le Havre (engines designed by Raymond Cody).
On list 1.1877. Ord: 7.8.1876. K: 23.12.1876. L: 15.10.1878. Comm: 26.3.1879 (trials), 15.7.1879 (full).
Budget 1875 (delayed to 1876). Installation of machinery begun 1.11.1878. Out of commission 1886 to 1892. Last regular Indochina voyage 1892. Barracks ship at Toulon from 24.6.1895 until replaced by *Annamite* 3.1896. Assigned 21.12.1899 as seagoing school for midshipmen, replacing *Iphigénie.* Renamed *Duguay-Trouin* 23.5.1900, in full commission 1.8.1900. Carried out twelve annual cruises between 1900 and 1912. Replaced 10.1912 as seagoing school by armoured cruiser *Jeanne d'Arc* and moved to Landévennec in October awaiting implementation of an order of 11.6.1912 to convert her to replace the last *Borda* (ex *Intrépide*) as the Naval Academy (*École navale*) until buildings ashore were completed. The full conversion was abandoned, but she received some furnishings from *Borda* and replaced her on 15.9.1913. The Naval Academy was closed at the outbreak of World War I and the ship, which still had its engines, was ordered converted to a hospital ship on 4.8.1914 and was designated as such 10.8.1914. She was still in commission as a *transport hôpital* in 1.1922. She was condemned on 18.2.1922 and designated on 26.6.1922 as a barracks hulk for the school for engineers and stokers at Toulon although still listed as a hospital ship. Renamed *Moselle* on 21.7.1922 effective 1.9.1922. Off main list 1925 (condemnation pending), condemned 18.2.1927 as a seagoing ship, and continued to be used as a hulk for the school for engineers at Toulon until 1936. The school moved to Saint-Mandrier and the ship was handed over 12.9.1936 to the Domaines for disposal. Sold 26.1.1937 to M. Van-Ocker to BU, BU begun 26.5.1937.

***Shamrock*** F.C. Méditerranée, Le Havre-Graville/FCM, Le Havre (engines designed by Cody).
On list 1.1877. Ord: 6.4.1876. K: 20.9.1876. L: 17.4.1878. Comm: c1879 (trials), 19.10.1880 (full).
Budget 1876 (delayed to 1877). Last regular Indochina voyage 1893. Lost her screw and irreparably damaged her propeller shaft in bad weather 1.1908 during the Morocco operation. Not repaired, designated 10.1911 to replace the frigate *Guerriere* as barracks and storage ship for

veteran sailors at Toulon, instead off main list 1913 and became a barracks and repair hulk for the school for engineers at Toulon 1913-1914. Reactivated 22.3.1915 without propulsion but with functioning boilers, towed out of Toulon 11.4.1915 and arrived 28.4.1915 at Mudros to serve as repair and base ship for French forces there. Later served at Corfu, Cephalonia, and Itea (near Delphi), then towed back to Mudros 8.6.1918 as base ship and water distillation plant for submarines guarding against a Turkish sortie. In reserve 1920 and in special reserve 1922-24 as a repair ship (*bâtiment atelier*) without engines at Toulon. Condemned 24.8.1924, for sale at Toulon. Struck 18.4.1925. To Domaines 20.4.1925, sold 27.4.1926 to BU.

*N* (Unnamed) Rochefort Dyd
Budget 1877, not in the 1878 budget.

———

***BIEN-HOA* Class.** *Transports pour les colonies, Grands transports* (1880). Colonial (large) transports with iron hulls except for wooden deck planking. One funnel, three masts, ship rig. Designed by Cazelles and Noël.

The 1879 budget included one new transport to be built by contract, the second was added in the 1880 budget. They were designed by naval constructors Cazelles and Charles Joseph Noël with internal arrangements by naval constructor Jean Casimir Duplaa-Lahitte specifically as hospital ships (*transports hôpitaux*) for the Cochinchina service. Noël signed a design for *Vinh-Long* and *Bien-Hoa* (modified *Shamrock* and *Tonquin* type) at Le Havre on 27 December 1877 and Minister of Marine Pothuau approved it on 6 February 1878. The engines of both ships were included in the contract of 5 February 1877 for the engines of the *Shamrock* class. Like that class they had iron double hulls. They could be distinguished from the others by the open galleries that ran all the way around the stern on the upper deck aft.

**Dimensions & tons:** 105.000m pp x 15.300m wl (moulded). 5775.453t disp (designed). Draught: (designed) 6.300m mean, 6.510m aft.
**Machinery:** 650nhp and 2,825ihp designed at 66rpm. Trials: 12.73kts (*Bien-Hoa*) and 13.12kts (*Vinh-Long*). 1 screw. Engines and boilers as *Tonquin* class.
**Guns:**
(1882) 2 x 138.6mm on the upper deck just forward of the long poop, 5 x 4pdr (86.5mm/11) bronze boat.
(by 1893) 2 x 138.6mm, 3 x 90mm, 5 x 37mm revolving cannon (7 in *Bien-Hoa*).

***Vinh-Long*** Bichon frères, Bordeaux-Lormont/F.C. Méditerranée, Le Havre (engines designed by Cody).
On list 1.1879. Ord: 6.2.1878 (contract 29.4.1878 approved 7 May 1878). K: 7.5.1878. L: 4.1.1881. Comm: 9.8.1882 (trials?), 9.2.1883 (full).
Budget 1879. Last regular Indochina voyage 1894. Reboilered 1912 and to reserve. Recommissioned as a transport 2.8.1914. Ordered converted to hospital ship on 14.4.1916 using medical equipment transferred from the mercantile *Canada* in a restructuring of the hospital ship fleet and declared operational 26.4.1916. (She had two red crosses on each side of her hull during the war while her two sisters also serving as hospital ships had none.) Still rated as a *Transport hôpital,* she burned off San Stefano in the Sea of Marmara 16.12.1922 after a cigarette ignited some movie films while on her twenty-first voyage from Toulon to Constantinople after the end of the war. Of the 505 aboard, 451 were rescued by USS *Bainbridge* (DD-246) and taken to Constantinople and the Panamanian merchantman *Stuyvesant* received 40 more. The burned-out hulk sank the next day. Struck 12.2.1923.

***Bien-Hoa*** F.C. Méditerranée, Le Havre-Graville/FCM, Le Havre (engines designed by Cody).
On list 1.1879. Ord: 6.2.1878. K: 16.9.1878. L: 6.10.1880.

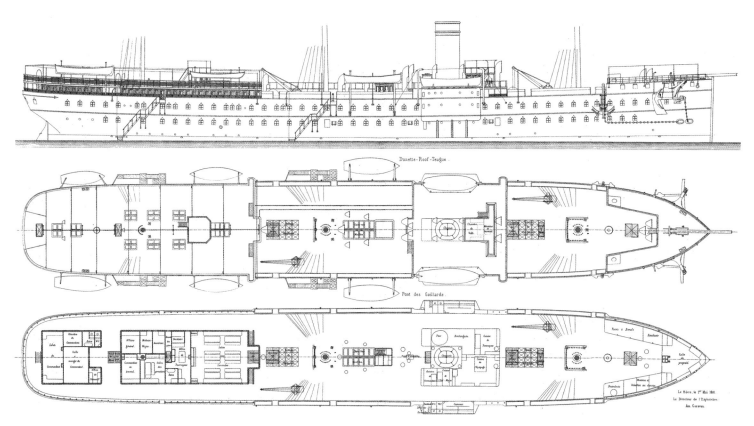

Outboard profile, a plan at the level of the forecastle and poop decks, and a plan of the upper deck of the 'hospital transport' *Bien-Hoâ*, produced by the Forges et Chantiers de la Méditerranée at Le Havre and signed there on 1 May 1881 by the director of the yard, A. Cazavan. The promenade around the recessed cabins all the way around the poop was a recognition feature of this ship and her sister, *Vinh-Long*.

---

Comm: 7.2.1881 (trials?), 12.6.1882 (full).

Budget 1880. Reboilered by Fraissinet at Marseille 1889-90. Last regular Indochina voyage 1891. Converted 1897-98 to a squadron transport for munitions, interrupted by a run to China in 1898, designated 24.3.1899 as a munitions transport and replenishment ship for the *Escadre de la Méditerranée* and became a depot for explosives in the Toulon/La Seyne area. All munitions were landed 9.1909. Restored as a transport and boilers repaired 10.1911 to replace *Vinh-Long*, which needed new boilers, in the Morocco naval division. Served as a transport in the Gallipoli operation until ordered on 14.6.1915 to be converted to a hospital ship for the same operation. Used as a hospital transport until decommissioned 1922. Condemned 1.7.1923, for sale at Toulon 1923-1924, barracks hulk at Toulon 1924-1929 (including for submarines), and hulk for submarines 1929-1936. Replaced 1936 by *Rhin* (ex *Tourville* ex *Gironde*), sold 2.10.1936 to the Société du matériel naval du Midi to BU.

---

**NIVE Class.** *Grands transports.* Large transports with iron hulls except for wooden deck planking. One funnel, three masts, ship rig. Designed by Cazelles and Opin.

The 1881 budget included one new transport to be built by contract, the second was added in the 1882 budget. They were designed by Cazelles and Opin with internal arrangements by Piaud, Champenois, Beausire and de Maupeou d'Ableiges in *Nive* and Dudebout and Champenois in *Gironde*. A modified *Bien-Hoa* type, they were designed specifically as troopships (*transports de troupes*) with expanded facilities to carry horses as well as men. Plans for *Nive* by the Société Nouvelle des Forges et Chantiers de la

Méditerranée under a contract of 20 September 1880 were approved by Minister of Marine Jauréguiberry, on 21 September 1880 and plans for *Gironde* by Bichon Frères under a contract of 20 September 1880 were also approved by Minister Jauréguiberry on 21 September 1880. Their hulls were very similar to those of the *Tonquin* and *Bien-Hoa* classes except that their iron double hulls became single hulls halfway up the sides of the ship. The engines of *Nive* were built at Marseille on the model of the engines of *Annamite* and had higher coal consumption than the engines built for several sisters at Graville. Her engines were reliable but her boilers developed leaks that frequently required the use of sea water to make up for the lost feed water. The engines of *Gironde* were identical to those of the *Shamrock* and *Bien-Hoa* classes. The horse stalls in the two batteries of *Nive* were replaced with regular passenger berthing in July 1893. These two large transports could be distinguished from the other six by the absence of any open galleries on the upper deck aft, giving the appearance of a longer poop.

On 25 March 1890 the *Conseil des travaux* examined a proposal to convert *Gironde* to a *transport d'escadre*, meaning that she would accompany the fleet and carry and launch small torpedo boats if needed. The Navy decided to build a new ship for this mission (which became *Foudre*) rather than convert one, and *Gironde* was designated instead on 10 August 1891 as a fleet replenishment ship for torpedo supplies (*ravitailleur d'escadre pour le matériel de torpillerie*), although she was still shown in the fleet list as a *transport d'escadre*. The 3rd class cabins in the lower battery were removed to create a large open space and the 2nd class cabins in the upper battery had their furnishings removed, allowing the ship to stock 250 torpedoes on special cradles, minesweeping equipment and explosive charges. She was fitted out but was never commissioned in this role.

*The characteristics are based on a devis for* Nive *dated 29.1.1884.*

**Dimensions & tons:** 101.80m wl, 105.20m pp (wl fwd to rudder) x 15.39m ext, 15.36m wl. 5,619.9t disp. Draught: 6.185m mean, 6.385m aft. Men: 300.

**Machinery:** 650nhp and 2.640ihp designed at 70rpm and 4.133kg/cm² boiler pressure. Trials (*Nive*, 16.1.1884) 2,743.3ihp = 13.737kts at 71.15rpm. 1 screw. 1 vertical compound engine with 3 cylinders of

1.40m (1) and 1.86m (2) diameter and 1.00m stroke. 8 low cylindrical boilers. 885.4t coal. Range 8,000nm @ 10kts.

**Guns:**

(1884, *Nive*) 2 x 138.6mm on the upper deck just forward of the long poop, 5 Hotchkiss 37mm revolving cannon.

(1890, *Gironde*) 2 x 138.6mm/21.3 M1870 on upper deck just forward of the long poop, 3 x 90mm/22 M1881 (later had four), 2 x 65mm, 10 x 37mm revolving cannon.

(1909, *Gironde/Tourville*, as gunnery school) 2 x 164.7mm/40 M1893, 2 x 164.7mm/40 M1893-96 (which had optical sights), 4 x 138.6mm (in the lower battery for loading drills), 2 x 100mm on the bridge, some 65mm for landing exercises, and 8 x 47mm QF.

*Nive* F.C. Méditerranée, Le Havre-Graville/FCM, Marseille.
On list 1.1881. Ord: 11.6.1880 (contract 20.9.1880). K: 5.10.1880. L: 7.5.1883. Comm: 1.10.1883 (trials), 5.3.1884 (full).
Budget 1881. Out of commission at Toulon 13.5.1887 to 14.1.1892. Last regular Indochina voyage 1895. Reboilered 1898. Sortied from Casablanca during the Morocco operation because of bad weather 31.12.1907, through navigational errors struck the Cocktomb rock five miles south of the city 1.1.1908 and lost. Struck 4.5.1908, wreck sold 9.6.1908 to M. Leudrat of Casablanca to BU. BU completed 5.1909.

*Gironde* (later *Tourville*, *Rhin*) Bichon frères, Bordeaux-Lormont/F.C. Méditerranée, Le Havre.
On list 1.1881. Ord: 11.6.1880 (contract 20.9.1880). K: 2.1881. L: 13.2.1884. Comm: c1884 (trials), 25.3.1885 (full).
Budget 1882. Last regular Indochina voyage 1887 (she made only three round trips). In reserve from 1887 to 1908 with two short breaks in 1892 and 1893. Listed as squadron transport (*transport d'escadre*) 1.1891 and converted during that year (see above). Reboilered in 1905. Hastily converted to a hospital ship for the 1908 Morocco operation, listed as a *transport* with the others 1.1909. Designated 23.1.1909 to replace *Couronne* as school for gunnery at Toulon and renamed *Tourville* 1.7.1909. Decomm. 1.8.1914 and training guns removed. Recomm. 12.1914 and sent to Malta as French base ship there, particularly for submarines. Replaced *Shamrock* at Corfu 21.1.1917, returned to Toulon 16.8.1919. In reserve as a repair ship 3.1920, used as transport from 10.1920, listed as a hospital transport 1.1922 and between 3.1.1922 and 5.10.1923 carried out medical transport voyages between France, the Eastern Mediterranean and the Black sea. To reserve at Toulon 5.10.1923, still listed as a hospital transport 1.1924. Renamed *Rhin* and attached to the school for apprentice gunners 26.11.1924 (notified 18.2.1925). Trained reserve officers 1925-27, pierside hospital ship 1927-33. Officially listed as a transport to 1936 but definitively out of commission 1933 and used as a floating barracks for the training division. Off main list 1936 and listed with the declassified ships. Seized intact by the Germans at Toulon 27.11.1942 and moved to the quai Noël as a barracks ship. Sunk there by allied air bombardments 7.3.1944 and 24.4.1944, raised and BU 1948.

———————

## (B) Horse Transports (*Transports écuries*), 500nhp.

To *Grands transports* in the 1.1880 fleet list and *Transports de 2e classe* 1.1885.

### Transports écuries

French horse or cavalry transports (literally stable transports, *transports écuries*) were designed to carry in addition to personnel several hundred horses in two battery decks (*entreponts*) illuminated through small ports and equipped with a ventilation system. They were initially part of the effort of Napoleon III to build a large force of transports to support military operations in European waters. Three classes were built, the 250nhp

*Jura* class in 1855 (*Jura*, *Calvados*, *Garonne*, *Rhône*, *Finistère*, and *Aube*), and the two classes listed here, the 300nhp *Ardèche* class and the 500nhp *Sarthe* class.

———————

*SARTHE* **Class.** *Transports écuries.* 1,500-ton (first two 1,530-ton), 500nhp horse transports with wooden hulls and knee bows. One funnel, three masts, ship rig. Designed by Guesnet.

On 28 October 1859 Minister of Marine Hamelin ordered two *transports-écuries* similar to the *Jura* and *Calvados* of 1855 from Cherbourg and two from Rochefort. On the same date the Director of Naval Construction wrote that the Minister had ordered him to prepare to lay down ten new ships of this type, including the four at the two dockyards and six to be ordered from private firms (the *Ardèche* class, below). The four dockyard ships were increased to 500nhp, making them a separate class and causing them to be described as high-speed cavalry transports (*transports-écuries à grande vitesse*). They were intended for service to the Far East. Plans for the ships by naval constructor Achille Antoine Guesnet were approved by Minister Hamelin and sent to the ports on 23 March 1860 and their names were approved on 4 April 1860. *Tarn* was probably added to the class in 1860, and plans by Louis Dutard for modifications to her stern were approved on 28 September 1860. All five engines were probably built at Indret. The designed armament for the class was four old but lightweight 16cm smoothbore shell guns (*obusiers*). *Corrèze* completed long after the others. This and the *Ardèche* class introduced the large sponsons amidships for latrines for troops and the crew that were also prominent features of the large *Annamite* type transports. All five were built up aft at Toulon in 1871-73 by the addition of a poop deck and roundhouse.

**Dimensions & tons:** 87.20m deck, 82.00m wl x 13.52m ext and wl. 3,607t disp. Draught: 5.85m fwd, 6.55m aft. Men: 211.
**Machinery:** 500nhp (430 from 1867) and 1,720ihp designed at 62rpm and 1.80kg/cm² boiler pressure. Trials (*Tarn*, 15.4.1865) 1,634ihp = 14.0kts at 64.0rpm and 1.579kg/cm² boiler pressure. 1 screw. 1 horizontal simple expansion engine with return connecting rods and two cylinders of 1.655m diameter and 0.95m stroke. 6 high rectangular tubular boilers. 583.0t coal. Range 3,720nm @ 10kts.

**Guns:**

(1863) 4 x 16cm shell.

(1872-74) 2 x 138.6mm No 1 (No 2 in *Tarn*) on the upper deck.

*Sarthe* Cherbourg Dyd/Indret.
On list 1.1861. Ord: 28.10.1859. K: 8.4.1860. L: 25.11.1862. Comm: 9.7.1863 (trials). C: 10.1863.
Departed Cherbourg for Indochina 21.10.1863. Struck 11.12.1896, for sale at Toulon 1896-1900, barracks hulk 1900-1909, for sale 1909-1910. Sold 1911 to BU. Reportedly renamed *Vem* in 1901 but remained *Sarthe* in the fleet lists through 1910.

*Aveyron* Cherbourg Dyd/Indret.
On list 1.1861. Ord: 28.10.1859. K: 5.7.1860. L: 3.9.1864. Comm: 6.7.1865 (trials). C: 10.1865.
Supported the evacuation of Mexico in early 1867, began service to Indochina 1.1871. Driven by high winds onto the wreck of a merchant ship (*Mekong*, lost in 1877) off Cape Guardafui on 21.8.1884. Could not be saved and was burned by her crew, who with 254 passengers were rescued by passing merchant ships. Struck 8.11.1884.

*Creuse* Rochefort Dyd/Indret.
On list 1.1861. Ord: 28.10.1859. K: 11.4.1860. L: 29.8.1863. Comm: 1.5.1864 (trials). C: 9.1864.
At Saigon 31.7.1865, probably on first voyage there. Struck 2.4.1891 and BU.

*Corrèze* Rochefort Dyd/Indret.
On list 1.1861. Ord: 28.10.1859. K: 1.9.1861. L: 23.5.1868.

Comm: 16.4.1869 (trials). C: 6.1869.

Arrived at Brest from Rochefort 11.6.1869, began service to Indochina 1.1871. Hospital ship at Diego Suarez 1885. *Transport à voiles* 1.1890 to replace *Dordogne* at Diego-Suarez. Engines removed at Toulon 1889-92. Struck 5.2.1892 and sent back to Diego-Suarez under sail, hospital hulk at Diego-Suarez 1892-1895, for sale 1895-1896, BU 1896.

*Tarn* Toulon Dyd/Indret.

On list 1.1861. K: 8.1860. L: 10.12.1863. Comm: 2.9.1864 (trials). C: 9.1864.

Left for Mexico 5.1865, began service to Indochina 19.5.1868. Struck 4.11.1889, barracks hulk at Toulon 1889-1905 (for unassigned personnel from 1900 and also for colonial troops from 1902), BU 1905.

---

## (C) Horse Transports (*Transports écuries*), 300nhp.

Orne to *transport pour le matériel et le service des stations* in the 1.1880 fleet list and *Transport de 2ᵉ classe* 1.1885.

*ARDÈCHE* Class. *Transports écuries*. 1,200-ton, 300nhp horse transports with wooden hulls and knee bows. One funnel, three masts, ship rig. Designed by Guesnet.

On 28 October 1859 the Director of Naval Construction wrote that Minister of Marine Hamelin had ordered him to prepare to lay down ten new *transports-écuries* similar to *Jura* and *Calvados*, including six to be ordered from private firms. He proposed to order three hulls from Arman, one from Bichon Frères, and one from Moulinié, all at Bordeaux, plus one from Ernest Gouin at Nantes. The five ships at Bordeaux were ordered from the three shipbuilders by contracts signed on 18 November 1859, and the single Nantes ship was ordered by a contract signed on 25 November 1859. The Director of Ports asked Achille Antoine Guesnet to modify his plans for the *Jura* type based on experience with them, and on 25 November 1859 Minister Hamelin approved Guesnet's new plans (type *Ardeche*, based on *Rhône*), which were a little longer and wider. The names for the ships were recommended on 26 December 1859. The engines for all six ships were ordered from Schneider by a contract signed on 3 February 1860. With their two battery decks they could carry 440 horses and 400 cavalry personnel.

**Dimensions & tons:** 86.13m deck, 80.33m wl x 13.00m ext. 3,200t disp. Draught: 5.40m fwd, 6.00m aft. Men: 200.

**Machinery:** 300nhp (230 from 1867) and 920ihp designed at 58rpm and 1.55kg/cm² boiler pressure. Trials (*Orne*, 15.5.1875) 1,011.8ihp = 10.10kts at 65.0rpm. 1 screw. 1 horizontal simple expansion engine with return connecting rods and two cylinders of 1.31m diameter and 0.90m stroke. 4 low rectangular tubular boilers, 260.1t coal. Range 1,850nm @ 10kts.

**Guns:**

(1862) 4 x 16cm shell.

(1872-77) 4 x 138.6mm Nº 1 on the upper deck, 1 x 4pdr (86.5mm/11) bronze boat.

*Ardèche* Lucien Arman, Bordeaux/Schneider, Creusot.

On list 1.1860. Ord: 18.11.1859. K: 31.1.1860. L: 4.12.1861. Comm: 1.4.1862 (trials).

Departed Rochefort (Île d'Aix) 7.8.1862 for Toulon and Mexico. Modified 1869 with additional superstructure and sponsons for latrines amidships and a light forecastle. Struck 11.11.1875, hulk at Toulon 1875-1877, artillery storage hulk 1877-1886, for disposal 1886-1887, sold 1887 to BU.

*Drôme* Lucien Arman, Bordeaux/Schneider, Creusot.

On list 1.1860. Ord: 18.11.1859. K: 1859. L: 25.10.1862. Comm: 11.2.1863 (trials). C: 5.1863.

Departed Rochefort 30.6.1863 for Cherbourg and Mexico. Struck 22.7.1872, hulk at Brest 1872-1874, for disposal 1874-1875, BU 1875.

*Var* Lucien Arman, Bordeaux/Schneider, Creusot.

On list 1.1860. Ord: 18.11.1859. K: 31.1.1860. L: 12.12.1863. Comm: 25.3.1864 (trials). C: 4.1864.

Departed Bordeaux 7.4.1864 to fit out at Rochefort, departed Rochefort (Île d'Aix) 22.8.1864 for Mexico. Struck 31.12.1879, for disposal at Toulon 1879-1883, at Rochefort 1883-1886, at Toulon 1886-1887. Never used as hulk. Sold 1896 to BU.

*Allier* Ernest Gouin, Nantes/Schneider, Creusot.

On list 1.1860. Ord: 25.11.1859. K: 1859. L: 11.12.1861. Comm: 3.7.1862 (trials). C: early 1863.

Arrived at Lorient 30.6.1862 from St. Nazaire under tow by *Montezuma*. Departed Cherbourg for Mexico 3.9.1862. Not renamed *Dragon* 3.1.1865 as sometimes reported, was still named *Allier* in late 1.1866 when she called at Martinique with a battalion of zouaves who mutinied when put ashore. Struck 26.11.1868 (published 27.11.1868) at Brest, probably BU 1869. Engines transferred to *Rhin* of the *Loire* class (listed in the Preamble) 1869.

*Eure* Moulinié & Labat, Bordeaux/Schneider, Creusot.

On list 1.1860. Ord: 18.11.1859. K: 16.12.1859. L: 16.4.1862. Comm: 22.5.1862 (trials). C: 8.1862.

Arrived at Rochefort 4.1862 for fitting out, departed Rochefort 12.8.1862 for Cherbourg and Mexico. Struck 22.7.1872, hulk at Brest 1872-1874, for disposal 1874-1877, BU 1877.

*Orne* Bichon frères, Bordeaux-Lormont/Schneider, Creusot.

On list 1.1860. Ord: 18.11.1859. K: 12.1859. L: 26.9.1862. Comm: 1.1.1863 (trials). C: 3.1863.

Departed Bordeaux 2.1863 to fit out at Brest. Departed Brest 28.7.1863 for five years in the Far East. Struck 5.6.1891 at Rochefort, BU 1891.

---

## (D) 2350/2500/2300-ton Transports (*Transports de 2350/2500/2300tx*).

*EUROPEEN*. *Transport de 2,350tx.* 2,350-ton cargo transport with a steel hull and a clipper bow. One funnel, three masts, ship rig. Purchased.

On 20 April 1855 Scott & Co. of Greenock, Scotland, launched the steel-hulled passenger and cargo ship *European* (their hull 23) for the short-lived European & Columbian Steam Navigation Co. Her sister, *Columbian*, was launched by William Simons of Glasgow on 17 March 1855. Reorganized as the European & Australian Royal Mail Company, the firm was wound up in 1858 and its ships went to the Royal Mail Steam Packet Company. *Columbian* was sold in 1859 to the P&O Line.

On 2 November 1859 Minister of Marine Hamelin ordered that a commission be sent to Britain to buy three steamers to transport to China as many as possible of the 20 screw chaloupes cannonnieres (*Nᵒˢ 12-31*) that were under construction for a forthcoming China expedition. The purchase contract for *European* was concluded with the Royal Mail on 14 November 1859 and the purchase was completed on 18 November 1859. The three steamers retained the French versions of their mercantile names. *Européen* could carry 850 tons of cargo.

**Dimensions & tons:** 93.20m deck, 89.14m wl x 11.90m ext. 3,747t disp. Draught: 5.70m fwd, 6.30m aft. Men: 119.

**Machinery:** 500nhp (400 from 1867). Trials (1872): 1,206ihp = 11.25kts. 1 screw. 1 vertical engine with 2 cylinders of 1.83m diameter and 0.905m stroke. 6 boilers. 600-645t coal.

**Guns:** (1860) 4, (1875) 2 x 138.6mm Nº 2 on the upper deck.

The large transport *Européen* at Algiers about 1885. Unlike the big Cochinchina transports she was primarily a cargo carrier. *(NHHC from ONI album of French warships, NH-74878)*

*Européen* Scott, Greenock.
On list 1.1860. K: 1854. L: 24.4.1855. Comm: 25.12.1859 at Glasgow.
Departed Lorient for Toulon 27.1.1860 and then carried four *chaloupes cannonnieres* to Chefoo, China. To *Grand transport* 1.1884, to *Transport de 2e classe* 1.1885. Central ship for the *Défense mobile* at Toulon and annex to *Japon* 1887 (made trips to Salins d'Hyères and back). Commissioned 20.9.1891 to replace *Loire* as barracks hulk at Saigon. Struck 2.4.1895, coal hulk in Cochinchina 1895-1905, munitions depot 1905-1907, for sale at Saigon 1907-1911, BU 1911.

———

**WESER.** *Transport de 2,500tx.* 2,500-ton cargo transport with an iron hull and a clipper bow. Two funnels, three masts, full rig. Purchased.

*Weser* was built by Palmer Bros. & Co., Jarrow-on-Tyne, England, for the North German Lloyd in 1858. She was one of the first four ships built for this firm, the others being her sister *Hudson* by Palmer along with *Bremen* and *New York* by Caird, Greenock. *Weser*'s engines were the largest direct-acting engines built to that date. There were accommodations for 70 first, 100 second, and 450 third class passengers. She sailed from Bremen on her maiden voyage to New York on 4 December 1858 but had to put back to Cork for repairs after being damaged by heavy seas. She sailed from Cork on 6 March 1859 and arrived in New York on 18 March 1859. She started her third and last Bremen-Southampton-New York voyage on 1 July 1859. *Weser*'s sister *Hudson* was launched on 12 June 1858 and started her maiden voyage on 11 September 1858. With *Hudson* and *Weser* the North German Lloyd planned to despatch a ship from each side of the Atlantic every fortnight, but after only one voyage *Hudson* burned out in dock at Bremerhaven on 2 November 1858. Palmer's bought the wreck, towed her back to their yard, and rebuilt her with new engines and with one funnel

removed. *Hudson* re-entered commercial service as *Louisiana* in 1862 and was scrapped in 1894. *Weser* was sold back to Palmer's soon after Palmer's bought the burned-out wreck of her sister.

On 2 November 1859 Minister of Marine Hamelin ordered that a commission be sent to Britain to buy three steamers to transport to China as many as possible of the 20 screw *chaloupes cannonnieres* (N$^{os}$ *12-31*) that were under construction for a forthcoming China expedition. The purchase contract for *Weser* was concluded on 17 November 1859 and the purchase was completed on 24 November 1859.

**Dimensions & tons:** 106.68m deck, 99.8m wl/pp x 12.1m. 4,000t disp (2,266grt). Men: 150.
**Machinery:** 746nhp. Speed 10kts. 1 screw. 1 engine with 2 cylinders of 2.29m diameter. 4 boilers with 24 furnaces. 1,000t coal.
**Guns:** (1860) 4.

*Weser* Palmer Bros., Jarrow/Palmer.
On list 1.1860. K: 1857. L: 21.10.1858. Comm: 17.12.1859.
Arrived at Toulon from Lorient 10.2.1860 and then carried two *chaloupes cannonnieres* to Chefoo, China. Wrecked 16.1.1861 at the mouth of the Mekong River 27 miles southwest of Vung Tau, 400 passengers and most of the crew being rescued by the paddle aviso *Shamrock*. Struck 25.4.1861.

———

**JAPON.** *Transport de 2,300tx.* 2,300-ton cargo transport with a steel hull and a clipper bow. One funnel, three masts, full rig. Purchased.

On 6 October 1857 the Caird shipbuilding firm at Greenock, Scotland, launched the steel hulled passenger ship *Prinzessin von Joinville* (their hull 57) for the Hamburg Brazilianische Packetschiffahrt Gesellschaft of Hamburg. This company closed while the ship was building and she was registered as *Japan* by Henry F. Tiarks, a merchant banker of London, on 20 November 1858. *Japan* could carry 900 tons of cargo at a draft of 6.25m and had two enclosed decks (*entrepots*).

On 2 November 1859 Minister of Marine Hamelin ordered that a commission be sent to Britain to buy three steamers to transport to China as many as possible of the 20 screw *chaloupes cannonnieres* (*Nos 12-31*) that were under construction for a forthcoming China expedition. The purchase contract for *Japan* was concluded on 3 December 1859 and the purchase was completed on 5 December 1859.

*Japon* was ordered on 25 November 1879 to be fitted as a transport for torpedo boats, and plans for embarking torpedo launches on this ship were drafted in 1880. She was fitted to carry France's six *torpilleurs-vedettes*, *Nos 29-30* and *56-59*, and was attached to the torpedo school at Toulon in 1884 where she served as a torpedo school and depot ship. Ultimately replaced by *Foudre*, she was converted in 1898 to a collier and fitted with Temperley equipment that allowed her to transfer coal to ships of the fleet while underway at ten knots. She could carry 2,500 tons of coal in addition to her own supply. Already very old, she remained in this role only to 1902.

**Dimensions & tons:** 100.00m deck, 94.50m wl x 12.30m ext, 12.20m wl. 4,017t disp. Draught: 5.20m fwd, 5.80m aft. Men: 150.
**Machinery:** 400nhp (300 from 1867) and 1,200ihp designed at 50rpm and 1.55kg/cm$^2$ boiler pressure. Trials (9.6.1869) 1,671.4ihp = 12.41kts at 52.11rpm and 1.593kg/cm$^2$ boiler pressure. 1 screw. 1 vertical simple expansion engine with 2 cylinders of 1.788m diameter and 1.062m stroke. 4 high rectangular tubular boilers with steam dryers (superheaters). 729.5t coal. Range 7,290nm @ 10kts.
**Guns:** (1860) 2, (1871) 2 x 138.6mm/13.5 M1864 (1867), plus 1 x 4pdr (86.5mm/11) bronze boat by 1877.

*Japon* Caird & Co, Greenock.
On list 1.1861. L: 10.10.1857. Comm: 19.1.1860.
Arrived at Toulon from Brest 1.3.1860 and then carried three *chaloupes cannonnieres* to Chefoo, China. Special duty at Toulon and the Salins d'Hyères as seagoing school for torpedo boats 1880-84, as school for automobile torpedoes 1884-88, and as annex to the school for torpedoes (*Algésiras*, which replaced *Japon* in 1888) 1891-92, during which time she was capable of carrying vedette torpedo boats. Classification changed to *bâtiment spécial* from *transport* 1.1884, *transport de 2e classe* 1.1889, *école des torpilles* 1.1892, and *transport de 2e classe* 1.1893. Central ship for the *Défense mobile* at Toulon 1896. Converted 1898 to collier for Mediterranean Fleet (mainmast removed and fitted with Temperley system for coaling ships underway). Struck 22.11.1902, for sale at Toulon 1902-1903. BU at Marseilles 1903 (broke in half during demolition).

---

## (E) 1000-ton Transports (*Transports de 1000tx*).
To *Transports* in the 1.1909 fleet list

*CHARENTE. Transport de 1000tx.* 1,000-ton cargo transport with an iron hull, a short forecastle and bridge island, a long poop, and a clipper bow. One funnel, three masts. Purchased.

This merchant ship was purchased in Britain by the French on 11 August 1862, probably upon completion. She served as a cable layer on loan to the Ministry of the Interior from 1873 to 1932.

*The characteristics are based on a devis dated 1.1867.*
**Dimensions & tons:** 69.70m oa, 64.68m pp x 9.65m wl ext. 1,618t disp. Draught: 4.50m mean. Men: 55.
**Machinery:**
(1862) 1 screw. 1 vertical 2 cylinder engine of 150nhp (200nhp British) and 450ihp. 2 boilers (British).
(1866) Re-engined with 1 engine of 120nhp and 480ihp with 2 cylinders. Boilers also replaced. Trials (5.1.1867) 367ihp = 9.76kts. 180t coal.
**Guns:**
(1862) 2 x 18pdr carronades.

(1864) 4 x 12pdr (121mm/17) Nº 3 bronze.

*Charente* W. Pile, Jr., Monkwearmouth, yard no. 6.
On list 1.1863. L: 29.5.1862. Comm: 24.8.1862.
Arrived at Cherbourg 14.8.1862, left for Toulon 31.8.1862. Collided with the steam 2-decker *Fleurus* in the Straits of Gibraltar 31.8.1862, repaired by 6.1863. Engine replaced 1865-66 at Toulon, recomm. 12.1866. Converted to cable layer 1873 and loaned to the Ministry of the Interior's *Administration des lignes télégraphiques* 8.1873 (LF1.1.1874) but retained on the fleet list until 1.1914. Back on main list as *bâtiment spécial* 1.1884, to *transport de 3e classe* 1.1885. Returned to the navy and struck 26.1.1932.

---

*BIÈVRE. Transport de 1000tx.* 1,000-ton cargo transport with an iron hull and a forecastle and bridge island but no poop. One funnel, two masts, schooner-brig rig. Purchased.

The British *Norseman,* owned by C. M. Webster of Sunderland, was purchased for war service by the French in Britain in early August 1870 soon after completion and first commissioned at Cherbourg 5 August 1870. British records show a purchase date of 26 August 1870.

*The characteristics are based on a devis dated 12.1870.*
**Dimensions & tons:** 62.00m deck, 60.94m wl, 58.21m pp x 8.88m wl. 1,867t disp. Draught: 5.20m mean. Men: 34.
**Machinery:** 150nhp (125 from 1878) and 500ihp designed. 7.5kts to 8kts (9.5kts sail and steam). 1 screw. 1 vertical engine with 2 cylinders of 1.00m diameter and 0.93m stroke. 2 boilers, 84t coal.
**Guns:** (1870) 1 x 4pdr (86.5mm/11) bronze mountain on boat carriage.

*Bièvre* T. R. Oswald, Pallion (Sunderland), yard no. 92.
On list 1.1871. L: 3.1870. Comm: 5.8.1870.
Refitted at Cherbourg 12.1870. To *transport de matériel* 1.1874, *transport pour le matériel et le service des stations* 1.1880, and *Transport de 3e classe* 1.1885. Wrecked 6.10.1885 near Lorient in the Graser on a rock between Larmor and the Île de Groix because of a compass error. Struck 14.11.1885. Wreck sold 1900 for BU.

---

## (F) 900-ton Transports (*Transports de 900tx*).
To *transports de matériel* in the 1.1874 fleet list, *transports pour le matériel et le service des stations* 1.1880, and *Transports de 3e classe* 1.1885.

*MOSELLE. Transport de 900tx.* 900-ton cargo transport with an iron hull, a flush deck with a small island amidships, and a clipper bow. One funnel between the main and mizzen masts, three masts, and a barque rig. Purchased.

The British *Elizabeth Jane,* an iron-hulled 160nhp mixed-propulsion (auxiliary screw) merchant ship completed in 1857 by J. & G. Thompson, Govan, Scotland, (their hull 31) was purchased by the French Navy on 25 May 1859 as a cargo transport (*transport de matériel*). She had no passenger accommodations. Until then sailing gabarres had been used for this purpose. The name *Moselle* was recommended for this ship on 27 May 1859. The French liked her enough to build two copies in the early to mid-1860s, *Vienne* and *Isère*, and the *Caravane* of the early 1870s was also based on the plans of *Moselle*.

**Dimensions & tons:** 63.70m deck, 62.20m wl x 9.40m ext. 1,971t disp. Draught: 4.80m fwd, 5.00m aft. Men: 48.
**Machinery:** 120nhp (100 from 1867). Trials: 525ihp = 9.05kts at 58.7rpm and 2.38kg/cm$^2$. 1 screw. 1 vertical engine with 2 cylinders of 1.12m diameter and 0.786m stroke. 2 boilers. 151-190t coal.
**Guns:** 2 x 4pdr (86.5mm/11) bronze mountain MLR.
(1867) 2 *espingoles*.

*Moselle* J. & G. Thompson, Govan.
On list 1.1860. L: 11.12.1856. Comm: 26.5.1859.
In commission 1859-71, inactive 1872-76, reactivated 11.1876 for
    service on the French coasts. Struck 9.2.1887.

---

**Repeat *MOSELLE* Class.** *Transport de 900tx.* 900-ton cargo transports
with an iron hull, a flush deck, and a clipper bow. One funnel forward of
the mizzen mast, three masts, barque rig. Designed by Lemoine.

These two cargo transports were built to the plans of the British-built
*Moselle*, above, as adapted by naval constructor Nicolas Lemoine. The
construction contract for *Vienne* (yard no. 263) was dated 4 April 1862.
Her original engines were built by the Forges et Chantiers de la
Méditerranée to British plans by James Jack. They were found to be too
complex and too heavy (513kg/ihp instead of 300 for ordinary engines),
and they were replaced in 1872 with engines built at Indret to plans of the
Chantiers & Ateliers de l'Océan (formerly Mazeline).

*The characteristics are based on a devis for* Isère *dated 20.6.1868.*
**Dimensions & tons:** 66.5m oa, 62.50m wl, 61.44m pp (wl fwd to
    rudder) x 9.43m ext, 9.28m wl. 1517.0t disp. Draught: 4.06m mean,
    5.00m aft. Men: 54.
**Machinery:**
(*Vienne*, original): 160nhp (150 from 1867) and 600ihp designed.
    Trials: 565ihp = 8.37kts at 62.5rpm and 2.58kg/cm² boiler pressure.

---

The 900-ton (later 3rd class) transport *Vienne*, missing at sea since 10 December
1903. The card was mailed in 1904, soon after the loss. She was a coastal transport
that normally carried cargo between naval dockyards and bases in France and
North Africa. *(Postcard by A. Bougault)*

1 screw. 1 vertical compound engine with 4 cylinders (2 high pressure
    and 2 low pressure, the former being on top of the latter and connect-
    ed to the same connecting rods) of 0.50m and 1.00m diameter and
    0.75m stroke. 1 Belleville boiler with horizontal tubes operating at
    6kg/cm. 116t coal.
(*Vienne*, replacement): 150nhp and 600ihp designed. Trials: 532ihp =
    9.5kts. 1 screw. 1 vertical compound Woolf engine with 2 cylinders of
    0.82m and 1.45m diameter and 0.90m stroke. 2 boilers (3.1kg/cm²
    pressure).
(*Isère*): 160nhp (140 from 1867) and 560ihp designed at 65rpm and
    1.8kg/cm² boiler pressure. Trials (15.3.1872) 449.6ihp = 9,197kts at
    64.12rpm and 1,349kg/cm² boiler pressure. 1 screw. 1 vertical com-
    pound Woolf engine with return connecting rods and 3 cylinders of
    1.20m diameter and 0.60m stroke. 1 high rectangular tubular boiler.
    130.1t coal.
**Guns:**
(1864, *Vienne*) 2 x 12pdr (121mm/17) bronze.
(1868, *Isère*) 2 x 164.7mm *canons-obusiers*.
(1872-73, both) 2 x 138.6mm Nº 2 M1858. Only one in *Isère* in 1881
(1883, *Isère*) 2 x 65mm/16 M1881 landing. No guns by 1908.

*Vienne* F.C. Méditerranée, La Seyne/FCM, Marseille (to British plans).
On list 1.1863. K: 4.1862. L: 19.10.1863. Comm: 6.7.1864 (trials).
    C: 7.1864.
Initially operated mainly along the French coast. Engine and boilers
    replaced 1.1872 to 11.1873 at Lorient by François Duchesne (see
    machinery, above). Reboilered 1882-83 at Toulon (4.0kg/cm², trials
    7.51kts at 78rpm). Left Rochefort 10.12.1903 for Oran and Toulon,
    disappeared with all hands 11-12.12.1903 in a storm in the Bay of
    Biscay. Struck 1.4.1904.

*439. — La "Vienne" Transport de 3ᵉ class· disparu depuis le 10 Décembre 1903.*

*A. Bougault* ↤→

*Isère* Lorient Dyd/Indret (engines designed by Victorin Sabattier).
On list 1.1864. K: 13.7.1863. L: 25.4.1866. Comm: 1.11.1866 (trials). C: 4.1867.
Decomm. 16.4.1867, recomm. 12.5.1868 for the Far East. Otherwise operated mainly along the French coast. Reboiled 1872-74 (2.25kg/cm²). Delivered the Statue of Liberty to Bedloe's Island at New York from France 19.6.1885. Reboilered 1894. Engines and boilers replaced 1904-1908 (800ihp, 10.8kts, 13kg/cm² Niclausse boiler) but the refit was unsuccessful and the hull was worn out. Decomm. at Rochefort 12.1909. Struck 22.5.1911, coal hulk at Rochefort 1911-1914, listed as hulk there 1920-1927 but towed by tug *Renne* (1918) from Rochefort to Lorient 4.1924. Reappears on list as landing hulk at Lorient 1.1934. In use in 1940 as a landing hulk on the right bank of the mouth of the Scorff River and became one of the landing hulks used between 6.1940 and 3.1941 by German submarines returning from patrol. Damaged by aerial bombardments 13.2.1943 and scuttled by the Germans in the Lorient roadstead at Sainte Catherine. Not refloated, eventually cut down to permit construction of a pleasure boat marina at Locmiquélic.

---

*OISE. Transport de 900tx.* 900-ton cargo transport with iron hull, a small forecastle, a combined bridge island and poop, and a straight bow. One funnel, two masts, brig rig. Purchased.

The British merchantman *Hypatia,* owned by Robert Hough of London, was purchased for war service by the French in early August 1870 soon after completion. British records show a sale date of 17 August 1870.

*The characteristics are based on a devis dated 8.1874.*
**Dimensions & tons:** 64.60m pp x 9.26m wl. 2,080t disp. Draught: 5.20m mean. Men: 34.
**Machinery:** 150nhp and 600ihp designed. Trials 423ihp = 9.07kts at 56rpm and 2.38kg/cm2 boiler pressure. 1 screw. 1 vertical engine with 2 cylinders of 1.0m diameter and 0.935m stroke. 2 boilers. 174t coal.
**Guns:** (1874) 1 x 4pdr (86.5mm/11) bronze mountain.

*Oise* T. R. Oswald, Pallion (Sunderland), yard no. 93.
On list 1.1872. L: 4.1870. Comm: 5.8.1870 (trials), C: 9.12.1870.
Arrived at Cherbourg 5.8.1870, first commissioned 9.12.1870 for coastal service. Reboilered 1883-84. Lost 25.2.1885 when she broke in half during a cyclone in the harbour of Tamatave. Struck 16.4.1885.

---

*CARAVANE. Transport de 900tx.* 900-ton cargo transport with an iron hull, a forecastle, a poop, and a straight bow. One funnel forward of the mizzen mast, three masts, barque rig. Designed by Willotte.

Naval constructor Louis Marc Antoine Émile Willotte designed this coastal transport as an enlargement of *Moselle.* Willotte's design was examined by the *Conseil des travaux* on 23 November 1869 and 18 January 1870 and the plans were approved by Minister of Marine Rigault de Genouilly on 27 January 1870. Construction began in April 1870. As directed by Minister of Marine Pothuau on 14 September 1871 the *Conseil des travaux* on 30 January 1872 examined the question of specifications for future *transports de matériel* and decided that the plans of *Caravane* could be used without any modification unless problems arose during her trials.

*The characteristics are based on a devis dated 17.9.1879.*
**Dimensions & tons:** 64.24m wl, 64.90m pp (wl fwd to rudder) x 9.44m ext, 9.20m wl. 1,713.5t disp. Draught: 4.298m mean, 5.398m aft. Men: 39.
**Machinery:** 150nhp and 600ihp designed at 75rpm and 3.104kg/cm² boiler pressure. Trials (11.9.1879) 677.3ihp = 10.10kts at 78.0rpm and 3.115kg/cm² boiler pressure. 1 screw. 1 vertical compound engine with 2 cylinders of 0.82m and 1.45m diameter and 0.90m stroke. 2 cylin-

drical boilers by Randolph, Elder & Co. 148.7t coal. Range 1,800nm @ 10kts.
**Guns:** (1879) 2 x 12pdr (121mm/17) bronze on the upper deck, also listed with 2 x 4pdr (86.5mm/11) bronze and with 2 x 37mm.

*Caravane* Lorient Dyd/Indret.
On list 1.1871. K: 15.11.1870. L: 3.10.1876. Comm: 14.8.1877 (trials). C: 9.1879.
Put in service 1879 with the navy's *Service des transports réguliers* (scheduled transport service) for use on the French coasts with *Moselle* and *Oise.* Sunk 23.10.1900 in collision with the Japanese steamer *Yamaguchi Maru* (2,038 tons net) in the Inland Sea of Japan. Struck 8.11.1900.

---

## (G) 400-ton Transports (*Transports de 400tx*).

To *transports pouvant faire le service d'avisos* in the 1.1874 fleet list, *transports avisos* 1.1875, *transports pour le matériel et le service des stations* 1.1880, *transports avisos* 1.1883, and moved to aviso category as *Avisos-transports* 1.1884.

*INDRE* Class. *Transports de 400tx.* 400-ton small transports with wooden hulls and clipper bows. One funnel aft of the mainmast, three masts, barque rig. Designed by Huin.

For overseas service France needed vessels that could serve both as avisos and as small transports. They needed speed and armament approaching those of 1st class avisos plus cargo capacity of several hundred tons. Taking inspiration from the 300-ton transports *Loiret* and *Somme* of 1856, naval constructor Charles-Ernest Huin produced plans for two ships that were approved on 7 January 1862. *Cher* was named and her construction was ordered on 24 November 1862. Four more ships were ordered to this design on 23 March 1868 and named on 9 April 1868. These six ships formed one class despite the gap in time between the first two and last four.

*The characteristics are based on a devis for* Seudre *dated 20.10.1873.*
**Dimensions & tons:** 70.90m oa, 63.78m wl x 10.32m ext and wl. 1,531.2t disp. Draught: 4.204m mean, 4.904m aft. Men: 84.
**Machinery:** 150nhp and 600ihp designed at 92rpm and 2.221kg/cm² boiler pressure. Trials (*Seudre,* 26.10.1873) 678.7ihp = 10.89kts at 95.83rpm and 2.250kg/cm² boiler pressure. 1 screw. 1 horizontal compound engine with return connecting rods and 3 cylinders of 1.10m diameter and 0.50m stroke. 2 low reinforced rectangular tubular boilers. 168.8t coal. Range 2,700nm @ 10kts.
**Guns:**
(1871, *Dives*) 2 x 138.6mm N° 2; (1873, *Seudre*) 2 x 138.6mm N° 1 M1858-60 (1 forward and 1 aft), 4 x 12pdr (121mm/17) bronze field, amidships on sides. Add 1 x 4pdr (86.5mm/11) bronze
(1872-74, *Cher, Vire, Rance, Indre*) 6 x 138.6mm N° 1 M1858 MLR. *Cher* and *Rance* also had 1 x 4pdr (86.5mm/11) bronze mountain, *Vire* added 1 x 37mm Hotchkiss in 1881 and added 1 x 65mm/16 M1881 landing and three more 37mm in 1887.
(1874-85, *Indre, Rance, Dives*) 4 x 138.6mm/13.5 M1864 (1867). *Indre* and *Rance* added 1 x 4pdr (86.5mm/11) bronze boat 1878-80, *Indre* replaced this with 2 x 37mm in 1883, and *Indre* and *Dives* added 1 x 65mm landing and two more 37mm in 1885.
(1889, *Seudre*) 4 x 138.6mm, 2 x 90mm, 1 x 65mm landing.

*Indre* Lorient Dyd/Indret (engines designed by Victorin Sabattier).
On list 1.1863. K: 25.9.1862. L: 13.12.1864. Comm: 22.5.1865 (trials). C: 8.1865.
Decomm. 17.6.1869. Recomm. 1.11.1869, at Réunion in early 1872, decomm. 11.8.1872. In commission 1.3.1874 to 8.9.1878 for Indochina. Reboilered 1878-80. Struck 2.4.1891, hulk for fixed defences at Lorient 1891-1914, navigation security station at the

The 400-ton transport *Vire*, photographed at Algiers 10 December 1885, probably while en route home from Tahiti. By this time she was classed as an aviso-transport, indicating her dual role overseas as both an armed vessel and a cargo carrier. *(NHHC from ONI album of French warships, NH-74978)*

entrance to the passes at Port Louis during the 1914-18 war. Towed from Lorient to Brest at the end of the war, for sale at Brest 1920-1921. Struck a second time 14.5.1921. Sold 11.1928 to Mr Bache-Villier for 152,300 francs. BU at Lorient 1944.

*Cher* Cherbourg Dyd/Indret (engines designed by Dupuy de Lôme).
On list 1.1863. Ord: 24.11.1862. K: 15.1.1863. L: 25.5.1865.
    Comm: 18.9.1865 (trials). C: 4.1866.
Decomm. 21.5.1870. Comm. 5.3.1872, On summer fishery protection
    duty off Iceland 1872, in New Caledonia 1873-76, decomm.
    15.6.1876. Reboilered 1876-77. Wrecked 10.1.1885 on Île Contrariété

The aviso-transport *Allier* at Algiers on 1 September (*9bre*) 1886, probably photographed by Geiser like many other photos taken here at this time. Her funnel was shorter than those of her sisters. She became a Naval Academy training ship a few months later. *(NHHC from ONI album of French warships, NH-74979)*

in New Caledonia. Struck 19.3.1885. Wreck discovered 1968.

*Rance* Lorient Dyd/Indret (engines designed by Charles Louis Jaÿ).
On list 1.1869. Ord: 23.3.1868. K: 13.4.1868. L: 14.6.1870.
    Comm: 17.8.1870 (trials). C: 8.1870.
At New Caledonia 1871-74, decomm. 17.8.1874. In commission
    15.10.1874 to 27.10.1877 for Réunion. Reboilered at Rochefort
    1877-78. Struck 19.11.1881, BU at Rochefort 1882.

*Dives* Brest Dyd/Indret (engines designed by Victorin Sabattier).
On list 1.1869. Ord: 23.3.1868. K: 14.5.1868. L: 23.7.1870.
    Comm: 18.9.1871 (trials). C: 10.1871.
At Réunion 1872-75, decomm. 1.5.1875. In commission 1.3.1876 to
    5.4.1878 for the South Atlantic. Reboilered and artillery modified
    1883-85. Struck 7.1.1890, hulk for fixed defences at Rochefort 1890-
    1912, mooring hulk 1912-1914, for sale at Rochefort 1920.

*Vire* Lorient Dyd/Indret (engines designed by Charles Louis Jaÿ).
On list 1.1869. Ord: 23.3.1868. K: 5.4.1868. L: 24.2.1872.
    Comm: 1.10.1872 (trials). C: 10.1872.
Decomm. 1.1.1873. Recomm. 1.6.1873 for New Caledonia and the
    Pacific Station, decomm. 1879. Reboilered 1880-81 and 1886-87.
    Struck 5.8.1892 and BU.

*Seudre* Rochefort Dyd/Indret (engines designed by Victorin Sabattier).
On list 1.1869. Ord: 23.3.1868. K: 27.6.1868. L: 20.7.1872.
    Comm: 15.9.1873 (trials). C: 20.10.1873.
On the Pacific station 1873-75 and New Caledonia 1875-. Reboilered
    1883. Struck 5.6.1891, mooring hulk at Rochefort 1891-1898
    (converting 1891-1896), for sale 1898-1899.

---

***ALLIER* Class.** *Transports avisos.* Small transports with wooden hulls, iron deck beams and beam shelves, and clipper bows except *Romanche* with three layers of crossed wooden planking, probably on wooden frames with iron deck beams but no beam shelves. One funnel just aft of the mainmast, three masts, barque rig. Designed by Sabattier.

Plans by Sabattier for the next class of transport avisos were approved on 6 March 1875. The 1877 and 1878 budgets had another ship of this type to be begun at Brest, the funds were probably used for *Romanche*. *Romanche* was the largest ship to date to use Normand's system of crossed layers of hull planking as in the *Bisson* class avisos and *Capricorne* class gunboats.

*The characteristics are based on a devis for* Allier *dated 1.11.1878 with machinery data for* Drac *from a devis dated 21.12.1880.*
**Dimensions & tons:** 62.67m wl, 64.17m pp (wl fwd to rudder) x
    10.50m ext and wl. 1,659.8t disp. Draught: 4.608m mean, 5.318m
    aft. Men: 99.
**Machinery:**
(*Allier* and others): 175nhp and 700ihp designed at 100rpm and
    4.133kg/cm² boiler pressure (150nhp in *Romanche*, 190nhp in *Scorff*).
    Trials (*Allier*, 9.11.1878) 624.3ihp = 9.28kts at 82.98rpm and
    3,931kg/cm² boiler pressure. 1 screw. 1 horizontal compound engine
    with return connecting rods and 3 cylinders of 0.90m (1) and 1.10m
    (2) diameter and 0.50m stroke. 2 cylindrical boilers, medium type.
    260.3t coal. Range 2,870nm @ 10kts.
(*Drac* and others): 175nhp and 650ihp designed at 90rpm and
    4.133kg/cm² boiler pressure. Trials (*Drac*, 23.11.1879) 689.2ihp =
    10.935kts at 89.53rpm and 4,204kg/cm² boiler pressure. 1 screw.
    1 horizontal compound engine with return connecting rods and two
    cylinders of 0.92m and 1.50m diameter and 0.60m stroke. 2 cylind-
    rical boilers, medium type. 182t coal. Range 2,500nm @ 10kts.
**Guns:** (1878) 6 x 138.6mm/21.3 M1870 (1 on the forecastle, 4 on the
    sides amidships, 1 on the stern).

*Allier* Lorient Dyd/Indret (probably).
On list 1.1875. K: 22.3.1875. L: 19.3.1878. Comm: 15.10.1878 (trials).
C: 11.1878.
Budget 1876. At New Caledonia 1878-82, Iceland 1882-83, Réunion
1883-84, and New Caledonia 1884-86. Converted 3-8.1887 for use as
a seagoing annex to the Naval Academy in *Borda* at Brest. Took the
name of her predecessor, *Bougainville*, 6.3.1890. Reboilered 1891.
Replaced by the small cruiser *D'Estrées* 1912, out of commission
1.6.1912, reverted to *aviso* 1.1913. Struck 10.5.1920.

*Nièvre* Cherbourg Dyd.
On list 1.1875. K: 13.4.1875. L: 15.10.1878. Comm: 28.6.1880 (full).
Budget 1876. Named 12.2.1875. Running trials 1.1880. Commissioned
at Cherbourg 6.1880, at Réunion 1880-83. Struck 16.6.1905.

*Drac* Toulon Dyd.
On list 1.1877. K: 11.5.1876. L: 5.12.1878. C: 12.1880.
Budget 1876. Running trials 1.1880, then in Cochinchina and Tonkin
1880-85. Struck 10.8.1894, for sale at Lorient 1894-1903. Sold
3.1903 at Lorient to BU.

*Romanche* Augustin Normand, Le Havre/Claparède.
On list 1.1878. K: 20.3.1878. L: 15.12.1879. C: 1881.
Budget 1877 (delayed to 1878). Construction reassigned from Brest to
contract c1877. In reserve 1.1882. At Punta Arenas 11.1882 for the
transit of Venus, then off Iceland 1883-84 and in the Indian Ocean
1884-86. Struck 9.10.1899, service ship for the reserve at Toulon
1899-1910.

*Saône* Toulon Dyd.
On list 1.1878. K: 12.2.1877. L: 15.1.1880. C: 1880.
Budget 1877. In reserve 1.1881, then in Tunisia 1881-83 and Tonkin
1883-85. Struck 4.3.1895, school for apprentice seamen at Brest 1895-
1907, for sale 1907-1908, central service ship for the 1st flotilla of
torpedo vessels of the Atlantic (*1re flottille de torpilleurs de l'Océan*)
1908-1911, replaced *Navarin* as central service ship for the torpedo
vessels of Brest 1911-1913, for sale 1913-1914.

*Scorff* Lorient Dyd.
On list 1.1880. K: 31.5.1879. L: 27.9.1882. C: 1883.
Budget 1881. In reserve 1.1884. In the Indian Ocean 1884-85 and Tahiti
1885-88. Struck 22.11.1898, coal hulk at Rochefort 1899-1914
(converted 1898-1899), still hulk there 1920.

---

***POURVOYEUR.*** *Transports avisos.* Small transport with a wooden hull
with iron deck beams and beam shelves and a clipper bow. One funnel, two
masts, brig rig. Designed by Sabattier.

Sabattier designed this diminutive transport aviso for service in French

The *transport-aviso Romanche*. She was the only one of her six-ship class to be built
by contract instead of in a dockyard and was built with Normand's complex hull
structure of three crossed layers of wooden hull planking on wooden frames.
*(NHHC from ONI album of French warships, NH-74977)*

Guiana. The engine has the same specifications as that of *Drac*, above, but
her hull dimensions were all smaller and she had only two masts.

*The characteristics are based on a devis dated 30.4.1879.*
**Dimensions & tons:** 54.85m wl, 56.52m pp (wl fwd to rudder) x 9.40m
ext and wl. 1,022.6t disp. Draught: 3.563m mean, 3.743m aft.
Men: 77.
**Machinery:** 175nhp and 700ihp designed at 100rpm and 4.133kg/cm$^2$
boiler pressure. Trials (3.1879) 715ihp = 10.79kts at 99.16rpm and
3.950kg/cm$^2$ boiler pressure. 1 screw. 1 horizontal compound engine
with return connecting rods and 2 cylinders of 0.92m and 1.50m
diameter and 0.60m stroke. 2 cylindrical boilers, medium type.
152.4t coal. Range 3,100nm @ 10kts.
**Guns:** (1879) 2 x 100mm on the upper deck.

*Pourvoyeur* Lorient Dyd.
On list 1.1878. K: 2.3.1877. L: 31.7.1878. C: 3.1879.
Budget 1878. In French Guiana 1879-84 and French Congo and Gabon
1885-89. Struck 10.9.1900, *Défense mobile* at Diégo-Suarez
(Madagascar) 1900-1901, central ship for the Navy at Diégo-Suarez
1901-1906.

# Chapter Seven

# Paddle Steamers and Sailing Vessels, 1859-1882

While construction of large paddle steamers for military use and all sailing vessels larger than schooners stopped soon after the end of the 1840s, construction of smaller types, mostly for colonial use, continued during the 1850s. These ships are listed summarily in the Preamble and in full detail in *French Warships in the Age of Sail, 1786-1861*. In early 1859 Minister of Marine Hamelin, struck by the multiplicity of paddle aviso types that had been created, ordered the *Conseil des travaux* to pick among them for future construction. The Council on 24 February 1859 retained the *Casabianca* (160nhp), *Étoile* (100nhp), *Podor* (60nhp), *Serpent* (30nhp), and *Guet N'Dar* (20nhp) types and discarded the *Grand Bassam* (40nhp), *Économe* (25nhp), *Oyapock* (20nhp), and *Crocodile* (20nhp) types. In 1859 (listed below) the *Espadon* class was ordered to the *Podor* type, the *Phaéton* class to the *Serpent* type, and the *Protée* class to the *Guet N'Dar* type. After that no more paddle avisos were built for military use until 1870.

By 1870 the vessels of the 1850s needed replacement and production of new paddle avisos resumed, again almost exclusively for colonial service. According to Commandant de Balincourt, who commanded one of them (the *Cigogne* of 1886), the new vessels fell into three categories: (1) The large and comfortable ones like *Pétrel, Pluvier, Albatros,* and *Mésange* of 500 to 600 tons and 80 to 100nhp (reduced 1867 nhp ratings) with a high freeboard and usable at sea in equatorial regions as well as in the larger rivers; (2) the minuscule and uncomfortable vessels like *Oyapock* and *Cigogne* of 130 to 200 tons and 40nhp with very shallow draft for use in the arroyos of Gabon and French Guyana; and (3) a hybrid type consisting of *Cigale, Écureuil, Pingouin,* and *Alcyon* (both 1884) of about 300 tons and 55 to 70ihp which did not turn out well, the last of them being used only in desperation after lying for several years in reserve in the dockyards after completion. In the meantime, sailing vessel construction was limited primarily to a few schooners for the colonies and various small types for fishery protection.

---

## I. PADDLE STEAMERS

### (A) Paddle 1ˢᵗ Class Avisos (*Avisos de 1ʳᵉ classe à roues*).
220-200nhp in the 1.1860 fleet list, 200-120nhp from 1867. To *Bâtiments de flottille à roues* in the 1.1873 fleet list, *Avisos de flottille à roues* 1.1874.

**PURCHASED VESSEL, 1860.** *Aviso de 1ʳᵉ classe à roues.* 220nhp paddle aviso.

*Écho.* Originally the mercantile *Peiho* built in New York in 1859 for P. S. Forbes. According to the *New York Times* of 2.4.1859, 'The new steamship *Peiho* was this afternoon taken on the Great Balance Dock for the purpose of receiving her first suit of copper. She is intended for the China trade, and will sail for Hong Kong about the middle of the month.' Purchased by the French in the Far East c3.1860 for 200,000 piastres and named *Saïgon*, probably because the China station already had a *Peï-Ho* (see *Shamrock,* below). Quickly renamed *Écho,* probably to avoid confusion with an armoured floating battery that had been ordered from Arman on 18 July 1859 and named *Saïgon* on 27 July 1859. Commissioned 26.3.1860, probably as *Écho.* Shown as *Écho,* at Chusan, on a list of the 'naval forces stationed in the China seas as of 1.6.1860'. She first appeared on the fleet list as *Écho* 1.1861 and was never listed there as *Saïgon.*

**Dimensions & tons:** 70.10m x 9.75m. 1,113 tons (gross). Men: 30. **Machinery:** 220nhp, 700ihp. **Guns:** 1.

Grounded 13.6.1865 in the Saigon River and lost. Decomm. 8.7.1865 at Saigon. Struck 21.9.1865.

---

*TRAVAILLEUR. Aviso de 1ʳᵉ classe à roues.* 200nhp large paddle tug with an iron hull and a clipper bow. One funnel, two masts, schooner-brig rig. Designed by Denis de Senneville.

This large paddle steamer was designed by naval constructor Henri Paul Ernest Denis de Senneville and built on ways Nᵒ 5 at the Lorient dockyard. The beam outside her paddle boxes was 15.48m. She was rated as a 1ˢᵗ class paddle aviso and not as a service craft, but she spent most of her time towing large navy ships between the dockyards and on other coastal support missions. In 1880-82 she conducted scientific expeditions exploring the sea bottom in the Mediterranean and the Atlantic. Two other 200nhp tugs, *Robuste* and *Utile,* appeared on the fleet list in January 1861 but were moved to the service craft list when that portion of the list was established in January 1865. Five smaller tugs were also moved off the main list to the service craft list at the same time: *Milou* (1863, 40nhp), *Patient* (1863, 30nhp), *Caniche* (1864, 25nhp), and *Balaguier* and *Mourillon* (1861, 15nhp).

*The characteristics are based on a devis dated 9.1870.*
**Dimensions & tons:** 47.70m pp x 8.82m wl. 860t disp. Draught: 3.75m mean, 4.06m aft. Men: 85.
**Machinery:** 200nhp (150 from 1867). Trials 526ihp = 9.7kts at 20rpm. Paddles 7.00m diameter. Beam engine, 2 cylinders of 1.416m diameter and 1.70m stroke. 2 boilers. 136t coal.
**Guns:** (1866) 4 x 4pdr (86.5mm/11) bronze. (1870) 4 x 12pdr (121mm/17) bronze. (1881) add 2 x 37mm.

*Travailleur* Lorient Dyd.
On list 1.1864. K: 28.1.1863. L: 31.10.1864. Comm: 5.11.1864 (trials), 1.8.1865 (full).

The 1ˢᵗ class paddle aviso *Travailleur,* built at Rochefort. She spent most of her time towing large navy ships along the French coast between the navy's dockyards and on other coastal missions. Her funnel and mainmast were further aft and the rake greater than shown here. (*V. Vattier d'Ambroyse (Ch.-F. Aubert), Le Littoral de la France, quatrième partie, de la Rochelle à Hendaye, Paris, 1887, Page 407*)

Comm: 5.11.1864 for initial trials and transit to Rochefort where she was completed and fitted out at Rochefort 12.1864 to 6.1865 by Denis de Senneville. In constant service, mostly on the French coast and often as a tug, station ship at Rochefort 1871-90. To *aviso à roues* 1.1874, *aviso de flottille à roues* 1.1884, and *aviso de 1re classe* from 1.1885. Struck 3.5.1890 (replaced by *Castor*), hulk at Rochefort 1890-1893. Sold 1895 at Rochefort to BU.

---

*ESTAFETTE. Aviso de 1re classe à roues.* 120nhp paddle aviso with an iron hull. Two vertical masts without bowsprit, topsail schooner rig. Purchased.

This vessel was purchased in 1867 during construction in Britain and arrived at Cherbourg on 30 December 1867. Her hull and engines were designed by her builder, Jones Quiggin, who had profited from building blockade runners during the American Civil War but had fallen on hard times by 1867. Named *Tiger* by her builder, she was renamed *Estafette* by the French on 6 January 1868. The beam outside her paddle boxes was 13.49m. Her English topsail schooner rig was replaced with a full brig rig at Martinique in May 1876.

*The characteristics are based on a devis dated 15.4.1878.*
**Dimensions & tons:** 45.38m wl, 45.50m pp (wl fwd to rudder) x 7.05m ext. 511.8t disp. Draught: 2.603m mean, 2.563m aft. Men: 49.
**Machinery:** 120nhp (1867). 410ihp designed at c27rpm and $1.41\text{kg/cm}^2$ boiler pressure. Trials (30.12.1867) c480ihp = 10.25kts at 30.33rpm. Articulated paddles 4.88m diameter. 2 beam engines each with one cylinder, one to port and one to starboard and capable of being made independent. Cylinders 1.02m diameter and 1.44m stroke. 2 low reinforced rectangular tubular boilers. 67.8t coal.
**Guns:** (1878) 1 x 4pdr (86.5mm/11) bronze mountain, 2 *espingoles*. (1882) 2 x 4pdr (86.5mm/11) bronze, 2 x 37mm.

*Estafette* Jones Quiggin & Co., Liverpool.
On list 1.1868. K: c5.1867. L: Autumn 1867. Comm: 12.1.1868 (trials), C: 5.1868.
Newfoundland patrol 1868-70, Guadeloupe station 1871-76, Antilles 1878-84 with a visit to Senegal in 1880. Re-rigged as a brig 1876. *Aviso de 2e classe* 1.1885. Struck 24.4.1886 at Rochefort, BU there 1888.

---

## (B) Paddle 2nd Class Avisos (*Avisos de 2e classe à roues*).
200-120nhp in the 1.1860 fleet list, 140-80nhp from 1867. To *Bâtiments de flottille à roues* in the 1.1873 fleet list, *Avisos de flottille à roues* 1.1874.

*ALECTON* Class. *Avisos de 2e classe à roues.* 120nhp paddle avisos with a wooden hull and iron frames, deck beams and beam shelves, and a straight bow. One funnel, two masts, brig rig. Designed by Mangin.

On 24 February 1859 the *Conseil des travaux* had recommended adopting the *Étoile* type (100nhp, 1858) for use on the Danube, although it was noted that the *Étoile* type was not large enough for this duty. The *Alecton* class was the result. They were designed by Amédée Mangin as a modified *Étoile* type with engines designed by Philip Taylor. The hulls were ordered from the Forges et Chantiers de la Méditerranée (FCM) at La Seyne by a contract signed on 30 November 1859, their names were assigned on 26 December 1859, and their engines were ordered from FCM by a contract signed on 11 May 1860. Two more units of this type slightly modified, *Pétrel* and *Antilope*, were launched in 1872. They were originally listed as *Avisos de flottille à roues* and became *Avisos de 2e classe à roues* 1.1862.

**Dimensions & tons:** 50.92m deck, 49.92m wl x 7.38m ext. 592-632t disp. Draught: 2.54m fwd, 2.60m aft. Men: 64.
**Machinery:** 120nhp (80 from 1867) and 320ihp designed at 24rpm and

$1.80\text{kg/cm}^2$ boiler pressure. Trials (*Magicien*, 18.6.1877) 508.7ihp = 9.773kts at 28.874rpm. Paddles 5.50m diameter. 1 simple expansion engine with two oscillating cylinders on Penn's system of 1.11m diameter and 1.19m stroke. 1 high rectangular tubular boiler. 72.0t coal. Range 880 miles at maximum speed.
**Guns:**
(1867, *Alecton*) 4 x 4pdr (86.5mm/11) bronze mountain.
(1868, *Castor*) 2 x 12pdr (121mm/17) bronze.
(1870, *Magicien*) 2 x 12pdr (121mm/17) bronze MLR, 2 x 4pdr (86.5mm/11) bronze mountain.

*Alecton* F.C. Méditerranée, La Seyne/FCM, Marseille.
On list 1.1860. Ord: 30.11.1859. K: 1859. L: 29.1.1861.
Comm: 24.6.1861 (trials). C: 6.1861.
Served three tours in French Guiana and Guadalupe between 1861 and 1878. Struck 10.8.1883, for disposal at Lorient 1883-1887.

*Castor* F.C. Méditerranée, La Seyne/FCM, Marseille.
On list 1.1860. Ord: 30.11.1859. K: 1.3.1860. L: 23.2.1861.
Comm: 9.9.1861 (trials). C: 9.1861.
To *Aviso de 2e classe* 1.1885. Served in the Mediterranean, the Antilles, and West Africa. Struck 19.4.1886, tug (service craft) at Toulon (80nhp/400ihp, out of service) 1886-1889 and at Rochefort 1889-1894 (station ship and tug at Arcachon near Rochefort 1890-1894). Condemned 7.1894, sold 18.9.1894 to BU.

*Magicien* (ex *Pollux* 1859) F.C. Méditerranée, La Seyne/FCM, Marseille.
On list 1.1860. Ord: 30.11.1859. K: 3.1860. L: 11.4.1861.
Comm: 1.12.1861 (trials). C: 12.1861.
To *Aviso de 2e classe* 1.1885. Served on the Danube 1862-68 and then in the West Indies and Senegal to 1883. Decomm. 12.1883 at Rochefort and used there as a station ship, at Bastia 1.1887 and in reserve at Toulon 19.8.1887. Struck 17.12.1889, for sale at Toulon 1889-1890.

---

## (C) Large Paddle Flotilla Avisos (*Avisos de flottille à roues*), 200-135nhp (1867 rating).
To *Bâtiments de flottille à roues* in the 1.1873 fleet list, *Avisos de flottille à roues* 1.1874, *Avisos de 1re classe* 1.1885, *Aviso de station de 1re classe* 1.1891, and *Avisos de 1re classe* 1.1892. Flotilla avisos were 100-20nhp in the 1.1860 fleet list, 75-15nhp from 1867.

*VIGILANT. Aviso de flottille à roues.* 160nhp paddle aviso with a wooden hull and iron deck beams and beam shelves, and a schooner-brig rig. Designed by Lemoine and Eynaud.

This vessel was built at Rochefort to the plans of Nicolas Lemoine's *Casabianca* (1858) slightly modified by naval constructor Romain Léopold Eynaud for use on the Cayenne station.

*The characteristics are based on a devis dated 23.8.1884.*
**Dimensions & tons:** 55.14m wl, 55.40m pp (wl fwd to rudder) x 9.625m ext, 9.58m wl. 1,054.5t disp. Draught: 3.24m mean, 3.33m aft. Men: 79.
**Machinery:** 160nhp, 720ihp designed at 100rpm (engine) and $4.25\text{kg/cm}^2$ boiler pressure. Trials (12.4.1884) 682ihp = 9.63kts at 72.0rpm (engine), $4.21\text{kg/cm}^2$ boiler pressure. Paddles 5.20m diameter. 1 vertical compound geared engine with 2 cylinders of 0.87m and 1.43m diameter and 0.50m stroke. 2 low cylindrical boilers. 158.4t coal. Range 1,940nm @ 9.6kts.
**Guns:** (1884) 2 x 90mm, 4 Hotchkiss.

*Vigilant* Rochefort Dyd/Indret.
On list 1.1882. K: 5.9.1881. L: 3.9.1883. Comm: 23.8.1884.

Budget 1883. Machinery installed 15.11.1883 to 15.5.1884. First comm. 8.1884, to French Guiana. Returned to Rochefort in 1888 and not recommissioned. Struck 7.5.1892. Sold 19.7.1892 to M. Péron of Rochefort to BU.

_____

## (D) Paddle Flotilla Avisos (*Avisos de flottille à roues*), 120-50nhp (1867 rating).

To *Bâtiments de flottille à roues* in the 1.1873 fleet list, *Avisos de flottille à roues* 1.1874, *Avisos de 2ᵉ classe* 1.1885, *Avisos de station de 2ᵉ classe* 1.1891, and *Aviso de 2ᵉ classe* 1.1892, *Avisos* (classes omitted) 1.1909.

*ESPADON* Class. *Avisos de flottille à roues.* 80nhp paddle avisos with iron hulls. One funnel, two masts, brig rig (later schooner-brig). Designed by Sabattier.

On 24 February 1859 the *Conseil des travaux* recommended adopting the *Podor* type of 1854 for use in the lower portions of the Senegal River but recommended increasing the engine power from 60 to 80nhp without increasing draught or length. The best way to accomplish this was to shift to iron hulls, and the *Espadon* class was the result. They were designed by Victorin Sabattier as a modified *Podor* type and their engines were also designed by Sabattier. The beam outside their paddle boxes was 12.23m. These ships were among eight ordered from Ernest Gouin by a contract approved on 12 September 1859. Their names were assigned on 11 November 1859. All three were in commission for trials as of January 1861 but did not immediately enter service.

**Dimensions & tons:** 42.25m deck, 40.00m wl x 7.17m ext. 318-379t disp. Draught: 1.49m fwd, 2.09m aft. Men: 44.
**Machinery:** 80nhp (70 from 1867 and 60 from 1885) and 280ihp designed at 34rpm and 1.80kg/cm² boiler pressure. Trials (*Espadon*, 21.12.1860) 253.8ihp = 8.274kts at 33.39rpm and 2.51kg/cm2 boiler pressure. Paddles 4.06m diameter. 1 simple expansion engine with two oscillating cylinders of 0.90m diameter and 0.90m stroke. 1 low rectangular tubular boiler. 73.8t coal. Range 740miles at maximum speed.
**Guns:**
(1867, *Archimède* and 1870, *Espadon*) 2 x 4pdr (86.5mm/11) bronze mountain MLR.
(1873, *Phoque*) 4 x 4pdr (86.5mm/11) bronze mountain.

*Espadon* Ernest Gouin, Nantes/Indret.
On list 1.1860. Ord: 1.7.1859. K: 10.1859. L: 4.6.1860.
    Comm: 1.7.1863 (full).
Trials 1860 (not commissioned). To reserve at Lorient 15.1.1861. Full comm. 1.7.1863 and to Senegal, stayed there except for a refit at Rochefort in 1874-76. Struck 29.6.1880, barracks hulk at Saint Louis, Senegal, and annex to the hospital there 1880-1883, renamed *Africain* 1881, BU 1883.

*Phoque* Ernest Gouin, Nantes/Indret.
On list 1.1860. Ord: 1.7.1859. K: 10.1859. L: 6.6.1860.
    Comm: 22.7.1861 (full).
Trials 1860 (not commissioned). Out of commission after trials 6.1860. Full comm. 22.7.1861. Service between Saint Nazaire and Brest 1861, fishery protection in the Channel 1863, hydrography on the French coast 1867, torpedo school at Boyardville 1875. Annex to the transport *Messager*, the torpedo school at Rochefort, 1879-84. Struck 9.7.1886.

*Archimède* Ernest Gouin, Nantes/Indret.
On list 1.1860. Ord: 1.7.1859. K: 10.1859. L: 1.8.1860.
    Comm: 22.7.1861 (full).
Trials 1860 (not commissioned). To Senegal 1862 and stayed there except for a reboilering in 1866-67 and a major refit in 1874-75, both at

Lorient. Became annex to the hospital at Saint-Louis du Senegal 1878. Infected with yellow fever and scuttled c1881. Struck 29.7.1881, for disposal in Senegal 1881-1882. Sold 8.1883 to BU.

_____

## PURCHASED VESSELS, 1859-1860. *Avisos de flottille à roues.*

*Lily.* Paddle *aviso de flottille*, ex mercantile. Built c1857-58. In service 3.1858 under the French flag in the river at Canton, probably chartered. Purchased 6.1859 and armed. On fleet list 1.1860. Commissioned or recommissioned 1.4.1860.

**Dimensions & tons:** unknown. Men: 30-44. **Machinery:** 90nhp (60 from 1867). **Guns:** 4.

Listed on the China station 1.11.1859. Listed 1.6.1860 as performing river service at Saigon. Refitted in 1860, 1864, and at Saigon in 1870. Out of commission there 1871-75. Struck 31.5.1875 at Saigon, sold 1876 to BU.

*Kien-Chan.* Paddle *aviso de flottille*, ex mercantile *Toey Wan*. An English steamer chartered at Hong Kong by the American Minister to China in 1859 to take him up the river to Peking, instead she witnessed the ill-fated second assault by the British and French (in *Norzagaray*) on the Taku forts on 27.6.1859 and then assisted in it. Purchased 15.3.1860 by the French. Commissioned 20.3.1860. On fleet list 1.1861.

**Dimensions & tons:** unknown. Men: 30-44. **Machinery:** 80nhp (60 from 1867). **Guns:** 2, later 4.

Hospital ship in the mouth of the Pei Ho river in northern China for the attack on the Taku forts 7.1860, station ship there 1860-61. Boiler unserviceable 1861, explored the Pei Ho bay under sail. Boiler replaced or repaired 1862. At Shimonoseki, Japan, 7.1863, and again 9.1869 when a fort fired on her. Participated in the capture and evacuation of Kang hoa island (Ganghwa do), Korea, 10-11.1866. Struck 30.10.1873, for disposal at Saigon 1873-1876. BU there 1876.

*Déroulède.* Paddle *aviso de flottille*, ex mercantile *Tahn Wan* or *Than Wan* built in 1852. Purchased 15.3.1860 at Hong Kong or Manila. Commissioned 1.4.1860 in China. On fleet list.1.1861.

**Dimensions & tons:** unknown. Men: 30-44. **Machinery:** 90nhp (60 from 1867). **Guns:** 2, later 3.

In constant commission until 1867, participated in the Korean expedition of 10.1866. Struck 31.12.1867, decomm. 10.3.1868. Either BU at Saigon 1868 or sold with the schooner *Mirage* at Shanghai 25.3.1868.

*Hong Kong.* Paddle *aviso de flottille*, ex mercantile *Hong Kong*. Purchased 28.3.1860 in the Far East. Commissioned 1.4.1860. On fleet list 1.1861.

**Dimensions & tons:** unknown. Men: 30. **Machinery:** 90nhp. **Guns:** 2.

Replaced in the division by the gunboat *Le Brethon*. Struck 18.12.1865 and sale ordered by Paris, decomm. 1.3.1866 at Woosung. Sold 6.1866 to Mr. Jenkins of Shanghai.

*Ondine.* Paddle *aviso de flottille*, ex mercantile. Launched at Hong Kong 4.1.1859. Purchased 2.12.1860 for 254,659 francs from the Hong Kong merchant Douglas Lupruck, for whom she had been built. She was bought to replace the chartered *Rose*, a vessel of the same type 'leased very expensively' that was carrying mail between Hong Kong and Canton under the command of a French naval officer on 1.6.1860 but was never formally commissioned or carried in the *Liste de la Flotte*. Hull made of teak, schooner rigged. The beam outside her paddle boxes was 10.15m. Commissioned 1.9.1861. On fleet list 1.1862.

**Dimensions & tons:** 42.20m x 5.90m. 70 tons. Men: 36-44.

Launch of the Colonial Administration's paddle aviso *Laprade* into the Seine from Claparède's shipyard at Saint Denis on 15 January 1880, just upriver from the point where the canal behind the yard emptied into the Seine. The spectators assembled on the river bank and on the stern of another ship also building for the government. At that time there were no paved roads along the Seine here and temporary launch ways like these could be dug to launch ships into the river. *Laprade* was acquired by the Navy in July 1884 from the Colonial Administration and is listed in Chapter 10. (*L'Illustration, 31 January 1880, page 80*)

**Machinery:** 70nhp (50 from 1867), 10 to 11kts, oscillating cylinders.
**Guns:** 2 carronades.

Participated in the occupation of Cochinchina 1860-63 (flagship for the capture of Vinh Long on 22.2.1862), then became yacht for the naval commander there. Decomm. 1.6.1870 at Saigon. Struck 12.2.1871 with instructions to send her engine to France.

———————

*PÉTREL* Class. *Avisos de flottille à roues.* 80nhp paddle avisos with wooden hulls with three layers of crossed wooden planking, probably on wooden frames with iron deck beams but no beam shelves, and with straight bows. One funnel, two masts, schooner-brig rig. Designed by Mangin.

These two ships were lightly modified variants of the *Alecton* class of 1859, above, with Normand's system of crossed wooden hull planking. Amédée Mangin's plans for these *Antilope* type ships were dated 9 March 1870 and approved 28 March 1870.

**Dimensions & tons:** 49.97m wl x 7.67m ext. 566t disp. Draught: 2.62m mean, 2.62m aft. Men: 66.
**Machinery:** 80nhp, 350ihp at 4.0kg/cm². Speed 9.96kts. Paddles 5.9m diameter. 1 compound engine with 2 inclined cylinders of 0.96m and 1.56m diameter and 1m stroke. 1 tubular boiler. 86t coal. Range 1,770 miles at full speed.
**Guns:** (1873). 2 x 12pdr (121mm/17) bronze field. (1879) 4 x 4pdr (86.5mm/11) bronze.

*Pétrel* Augustin Normand, Le Havre/Schneider, Creusot (engines designed by Mathieu).
On list 1.1871. K: 2.5.1870. L: 10.5.1872. Comm: 1.11.1872 (trials). C: 1.1873.
Decomm. 26.1.1873 after trials, in full comm. 5.6.1873. In Senegal 1873, decomm. at Toulon 6.8.1874. Recomm. 10.1.1875, station ship at Constantinople from 1875 to the end of her career. Reboilered 1882 and rated at 120nhp from 1885. Retired 11.12.1896, for sale at Toulon 1896-1898. Target ship at Toulon 1897, sunk 24.3.1898 off Toulon by gunfire from *Carnot, Marceau, Brennus,* and *Jaureguiberry.*

*Antilope* Augustin Normand, Le Havre /Schneider, Creusot (engines designed by Mathieu).

On list 1.1871. K: 2.5.1870. L: 9.7.1872. Comm: 1.11.1872 (trials). C: 7.1.1873.
Decomm. 26.1.1873 after trials, in full comm. 15.3.1873. In Cochinchina by 1875 and through at least 1879. Struck 6.5.1884, guard hulk for the rear guard at Lorient 1884-1911, for sale 1911-1912.

———————

*ÉCUREUIL. Avisos de flottille à roues.* 70nhp paddle aviso with an iron hull and a straight bow. One funnel, two masts, schooner rig. Designed by Sabattier and Penelle.

The design of this vessel is credited to Director of Materiel Sabattier and naval constructor Claire Émile Penelle, who probably did most of the work and finished it after Sabattier's retirement. *Écureuil* replaced *Castor* in Senegal in 1881 and went out of service at Rochefort in 1886.

*The characteristics are based on a devis dated 4.7.1881.*
**Dimensions & tons:** 46.00m wl, 46.20m pp (wl fwd to rudder) x 7.40m ext and wl. 328.7t disp. Draught: 1,305m mean, 1.32m aft. Men: 38.
**Machinery:** 70nhp, 280ihp designed at 4.25kg/cm² boiler pressure. Trials (2.7.1881) 334.1ihp = 9.614kts at 32.0rpm and 4.181 kg/cm² boiler pressure. Paddles 4.50m diameter. 1 compound engine with 2 oscillating cylinders of 0.70m and 1.20m diameter and 1.00m stroke. 1 tubular cylindrical boiler, special type. 51.8t coal. Range 1,150nm @ 9.2kts.
**Guns:** (1881) 2 x 4pdr (86.5mm/11) bronze, 2 *espingoles.*

*Écureuil* Dyle et Bacalan, Bordeaux-Bacalan.
On list 1.1880. K: 9.1879. L: 3.2.1881. C: 4.7.1881.
Budget 1881. Active in Senegal 1881-85. Struck 3.5.1898, retained at Rochefort as gunnery target for the *Escadre du Nord* 1898-1900, same at Brest 1900-1901, for sale at Brest 1901-1909, retained provisionally at Brest 1909-1914. (The *Écureuil* struck on 27.2.1920 and sold at Rochefort was probably the ex-Spanish trawler of 1916 that served at Verdon near Bordeaux.)

———————

*PLUVIER* Class. *Avisos de flottille à roues.* 100nhp paddle avisos with wooden hulls with three layers of crossed wooden planking and iron deck beams, probably on wooden frames and without beam shelves, and with clipper bow. One funnel, two masts, schooner-brig rig. Designed by Sabattier.

*Pluvier* photographed by Dr. Édouard Hocquard, who took passage in her at the end of 1885 from Haiphong to Hué and Saigon. (*Hocquard, 'Trente mois au Tonkin', in Le Tour du Monde, nouveau Journal des voyages, 1st semester 1889*)

The paddle 2nd class station aviso *Alouette* at Saigon during a visit there by a Russian squadron between 15 and 19 March 1891. Behind her is the Russian gunboat *Koreyets* (*Korea*). The French ships were full-dressed with large signal flags to celebrate an exchange of diplomatic notes between France and Russia that soon became the Franco-Russian alliance.

The hulls of these ships used Normand's three layers of wooden planking, two thin interior layers crossing at 45° relative to the waterline and one thicker exterior layer longitudinal. Both vessels went to Cochinchina upon completion.

*The characteristics are based on the design for* Alouette.
**Dimensions & tons:** 50.18m wl, 50.10m pp (wl fwd to rudder) x 7.50m ext and wl. 486.3t disp. Draught: 2.00m mean. Men: 40.
**Machinery:** 100nhp, 420ihp designed at 4.25kg/cm² boiler pressure. Paddles 4.80m diameter. 1 compound engine with 2 cylinders of 0.80m and 1.30m diameter and 1.20m stroke. 1 high cylindrical boiler. 80.0t coal.
**Guns:** (Design) 3 Hotchkiss in circular enclosures on the upper deck. (In service) 2 x 90mm, 2 Hotchkiss.

*Pluvier* Cherbourg Dyd.
On list 1.1881. Ord: 16.2.1880. K: 1.3.1880. L: 10.8.1881. C: 1882.
Budget 1882. Named 16.2.1880. Construction begun 20.2.1880. To Cochinchina 1882. Struck 6.11.1896, for sale in Cochinchina 1896-1898.

*Alouette* Lorient Dyd.
On list 1.1881. K: 12.4.1880. L: 3.5.1882. C: 7.1882.
Budget 1882. In Cochinchina by 1885. Struck 20.3.1905, central service ship for the submarine station at Saïgon 1905-1909, for sale at Saigon 1909-1910.

---

**ALBATROS.** *Aviso de flottille à roues.* 100nhp paddle aviso with a galvanised iron hull and a clipper bow. One funnel, two masts, schooner-brig rig. Designed by Sabattier.

Designed as a repeat of the *Pétrel* type with less draught.

*The characteristics are based on a devis dated 22.8.1882.*
**Dimensions & tons:** 54.22m wl, 54.18m pp (wl fwd to rudder) x 7.70m ext and wl. 585.6t disp. Draught: 2.585m mean, 2.685m aft. Men: 68.
**Machinery:** 100nhp, 400ihp designed at 26rpm and 4.15kg/cm² boiler pressure. Paddles 5.90m diameter. 1 compound engine with 2 cylin-

ders of 0.96m and 1.56m diameter and 1.20m stroke. 1 special tubular cylindrical boiler. 74.1t coal. Range 1,800nm @ 10kts.
**Guns:** (1882) 2 x 90mm.

*Albatros* Claparède & Cie., Saint Denis.
On list 1.1881. K: 1880. L: 29.10.1881. C: 8.1882.
Budget 1881. To Dakar 1882. In Gabon 1885. Stationnaire at Lorient 1887. Replaced *Goéland* in Congo 1891. Wrecked 29.11.1891 in the bay of Batah, Gabon. Struck 31.12.1891 (published 22.1.1892).

---

**HÉRON Class.** *Avisos de flottille à roues.* 100nhp paddle avisos with iron hulls. Two masts, schooner-brig rig. Designed by Sabattier and modified by Claparède.

These ships were built to the design of *Albatros* modified by their builder, Claparède. Both were ordered and named in October 1881.

*The characteristics are based on a devis for* Héron *dated 18.10.1883.*
**Dimensions & tons:** 54.30m wl, 54.38m pp (wl fwd to rudder) x 7.70m ext and wl. 526.6t disp. Draught: 2.636m mean, 2.701m aft. Men: 67.
**Machinery:** 100nhp, 400ihp designed at 26rpm and 4.25kg/cm² boiler pressure. Trials (*Héron*, 6.10.1883) 482.2ihp = 10.271kts at 26.55rpm. Paddles 5.60m diameter. 1 compound engine with with direct connecting rods and 2 inclined cylinders of 0.96m and 1.56m diameter and 1.20m stroke. 1 tubular cylindrical boiler. 86.4t coal. Range 1,900nm @ 10kts.
**Guns:** (1883) 2 x 90mm, 2 Hotchkiss.

*Goéland* (*Goéland*) Claparède & Cie., Saint Denis.
On list 1.1882. Ord: 10.1881. K: 1881. L: 4.7.1883. C: 1883.
Budget 1883. To Senegal 1883. Out of service 1891 at Lorient. To French Guiana 1898, back in Senegal by 1903. Struck 13.7.1911, for sale at Dakar 1911-1912, lighter 1912-1914.

*Héron* Claparède & Cie., Rouen-Petit Quévilly.
On list 1.1882. Ord: 10.1881. K: 6.1882. L: 4.1883. C: 10.1883.
Budget 1883. In Senegal by 1886. Struck 18.5.1899, for sale at Lorient 1899-1900.

---

**MÉSANGE Class.** *Avisos de flottille à roues.* 100nhp paddle avisos with wooden hulls with crossed layers of wooden planking, probably on wooden frames with iron deck beams and without beam shelves, and with clipper bows. One funnel, two masts, schooner-brig rig. Designed by Sabattier.

These vessels were designed as modified versions of *Alouette* and *Pluvier* using Normand's system of crossed wooden hull planking. The two built by Normand were ordered and named in October 1881.

*The characteristics are based on a devis for* Mésange *dated 1.4.1884.*
**Dimensions & tons:** 53.80m wl, 53.82m pp (wl fwd to rudder) x 7.50m ext and wl. 612.0t disp. Draught: 2.214m mean, 2.229m aft. Men: 70.
**Machinery:** 100nhp, 420ihp designed at 36rpm and 4.25kg/cm² boiler pressure. Trials (*Mésange*, 18.3.1884) 501.8ihp = 10.015kts at 38.187rpm. Paddles 4.334m diameter. 1 compound engine with direct connecting rods and 2 inclined cylinders of 0.80m and 1.32m diameter and 1.20m stroke. 1 tubular cylindrical boiler. 79.4t coal. Range 1,360nm @ 10kts.
**Guns:** (1884) 2 x 90mm, 2 Hotchkiss.

*Mésange* Cherbourg Dyd.
On list 1.1882. K: 8.1881. L: 10.5.1883. C: 4.1884.
Budget 1883. In Gabon by 1886. Struck 18.5.1899, floating guard station at Rochefort 1899-1907, mooring hulk 1907-1914, hulk 1920-1927.

*Ardent* Augustin Normand, Le Havre.
On list 1.1882. K: 18.1.1882. L: 18.8.1883. C: 4.8.1884.

75. SÉNÉGAL — DAKAR - L'Aviso "Goëland"

Collection Galamet, Dakar

The paddle flotilla aviso *Goëland* at Dakar, Senegal during her second period of service there that began in 1903. She was one of the large and comfortable type of colonial paddle steamers (600 tons and 100nhp) that was usable at sea as well as in the larger rivers and that generally found constant employment. Struck in 1911, *Goëland* was the last survivor of her type in active service. *(Postcard by Galamet, Dakar)*.

Budget 1883. To Senegal 1884. Struck 1.4.1904. Sold at Lorient 20.2.1905 to BU.

*Brandon* Augustin Normand, Le Havre.
On list 1.1882. K: 1882. L: 31.12.1883. C: 1884.
Budget 1883. To Cochinchina 1884, decommissioned at Cherbourg 1888, to Senegal 1889. Struck 18.5.1899. Sold 1899 at Cherbourg to BU.

---

## (E) Small Paddle Flotilla Avisos (*Avisos de flottille à roues*), 40-25nhp (1867 rating).

To *Bâtiments de flottille à roues* in the 1.1873 fleet list, *Avisos de flottille à roues* 1.1874, *Avisos de 3ᵉ classe* 1.1885, *Avisos de station de 3ᵉ classe* 1.1891, and *Avisos de 3ᵉ classe* 1.1892.

***PHAËTON* Class.** *Avisos de flottille à roues.* 50nhp paddle avisos with iron hulls. Designed by Sabattier.

On 24 February 1859 the *Conseil des travaux* had recommended adopting the *Serpent* type of 1851 for use in the upper portions of the Senegal River but recommended increasing the engine power by 10 or 20nhp without increasing draft or length. An increase of beam, however, was acceptable and was adopted along with iron hulls. They were designed by Victorin

Sabattier as a modified *Serpent* type. These ships were among eight ordered from Ernest Gouin by a contract approved on 12 September 1859. Their names were assigned on 11 November 1859. They were in commission for trials as of January 1861. The beam outside their paddle boxes was 11.65m.

**Dimensions & tons:** 40.00m wl x 7.15m ext. 241t disp. Draught: 1.24m aft. Men: 44.
**Machinery:** 50nhp (40 from 1867) and 200ihp. Trials (*Phaëton*) 8.5kts at 39rpm. Paddles 3.5m diameter. 2 oscillating cylinders of 0.80m diameter and 0.65m stroke.
**Guns:** (1864, *Phaëton*) 2 x 4pdr (86.5mm/11) bronze mountain MLR.

*Phaëton* (*Phaëton*) Ernest Gouin, Nantes/Indret.
On list 1.1860. Ord: 1.7.1859. K: 10.1859. L: 19.7.1860. Comm: 1.3.1864 (full).
Trials c1860 (not commissioned). In reserve at Lorient 10.1.1861. Full comm. 1.3.1864 and to Senegal. Second tour there from 1872 to 1876. Struck 19.2.1878, barracks hulk in Senegal 1878-1879, sold or BU 1879.

*Sphinx* Ernest Gouin, Nantes/Indret.
On list 1.1860. Ord: 1.7.1859. K: 10.1859. L: 18.7.1860. Comm: 1.3.1864 (full).
Trials c1860 (not commissioned). In reserve at Lorient 10.1.1861. Full comm. 1.3.1864. In Senegal by 1.1867, ended her career there in 1872. Struck 31.1.1873 at Saint-Louis de Senegal.

---

***PROTÉE* Class.** *Avisos de flottille à roues.* 25nhp paddle avisos with iron hulls. Designed by Sabattier.

On 24 February 1859 the *Conseil des travaux* had recommended adopting the *Guet N'Dar* type for use in the marshes of the Senegal River and in French Guiana as replacements for the *Économe* class of 1855, and the *Protée* class was the result. The hulls and engines were designed by Sabattier as a modified *Guet N'Dar* type. These ships were among eight ordered from Ernest Gouin by a contract approved on 12 September 1859. Their names were assigned on 11 November 1859. They were in commission for trials as of January 1861. *Pygmee* was fitted with articulated paddles in 1862. The beam outside their paddle boxes was 8.20m.

**Dimensions & tons:** 25.05m deck, 24.00m wl x 5.00m ext. 125t disp. Draught: 1.34m fwd, 1.34m aft. Men: 25.
**Machinery:** 25nhp (20 from 1867) and 59ihp. Trials (*Pygmée*) 8.8kts at 38rpm. Paddles 3m diameter. 2 oscillating cylinders of 0.60m diameter and 0.5m stroke. 1 boiler. 18t coal.
**Guns:** 2 x 4pdr (86.5mm/11) bronze mountain MLR.

*Protée* Ernest Gouin, Nantes/Indret.
On list 1.1860. Ord: 1.7.1859. K: 10.1859. L: 19.6.1860. Comm: 1.5.1864 (full).
Trials 8.1860 (not commissioned). In reserve at Lorient 10.1.1861. Full comm. 1.5.1864 and to Senegal 20.7.1864, then career in Gabon. Decomm. 1.6.1868 (lost?). Struck 15.6.1868.

*Pygmée* Ernest Gouin, Nantes/Indret.
On list 1.1860. Ord: 1.7.1859. K: 10.1859. L: 21.6.1860. Comm: 18.9.1861 (full).
Trials 1860 (not commissioned). In reserve at Lorient 11.1.1861. Full comm. 18.9.1861. To Senegal 20.7.1864, decomm. there 16.6.1868. Recomm. and sent to Gabon. Decomm. there 6.10.1872. Struck 8.5.1873.

——————

**PURCHASED VESSEL, 1859.** *Aviso de flottille à roues.*

*Shamrock* (ex *Peï-Ho*). Built in 1858 by William Roos at Hong Kong. Requisitioned by the French on 7.12.1858 and named *Peï-Ho*. Renamed *Shamrock* before 1.1860, probably to avoid confusion with an armoured floating battery that had been ordered from Arman on 18 July 1859 and named *Peï-Ho* on 27 July 1859. Communications being slow, she continued to be referred to as *Peï-Ho* up to 2.1861 as indicated below. *Peï-Ho* was sometimes recorded as a screw steamer of 70 or 90nhp. This *Peï-Ho* never appeared on the *Liste de la Flotte* and *Shamrock* first appeared in it in 1.1860.

**Dimensions & tons:** 30.33m x 5.49m. 105 tons gross (74t net). Draught: 2.35m. Men: 36. **Machinery:** 40nhp (30 from 1867). **Guns:** 1.

*Peï-Ho* participated in the capture of Saigon 17.2.1859 and became station ship there 17.2.1859. *Shamrock* appeared on the fleet list in 1.1860, was refitted in 4.1860, and was commissioned or recommissioned on 1.4.1860. *Peï-Ho* was listed 1.6.1860 as a paddle aviso performing river service at Saigon under the command of Lieutenant de vaisseau Rieunier, a future admiral. She was part of the *Division Navale des mers de Chine* in 8.1860 and part of the naval force in Cochinchina on 1.9.1860. *Shamrock* saved the crew and passengers of the large transport *Weser* after she ran aground in the mouth of the Mekong River 16.1.1861. *Peï-Ho* appears for the last time in 2.1861 on a list of ships in service in Indochina. *Shamrock* participated in the relief of Saigon on 25.2.1861 and the capture of Mytho on 12.4.1861 and Vinh Long on 22.2.1862. She was refitted again in 9.1863, and was out of commission at Saigon 1868-75. Struck 31.5.1875 at Saigon, BU there 1876.

——————

*SERPENT.* *Aviso de flottille à roues.* 30nhp paddle aviso with an iron hull. Designed by naval constructor Camille Audenet.

This ship used an engine built at Rochefort in 1852 to a design by Victorin Sabattier for the paddle aviso *Grand Bassam*. After that vessel was condemned in 1868 the engine was reused in the new *Serpent*. The beam outside her paddle boxes was 9.92m.

*The characteristics are based on a devis dated 6.1873.*
**Dimensions & tons:** 40.00m pp x 5.70m wl. 236t disp. Draught: 1.50m mean, 1.77m aft. Men: 36.
**Machinery:** 30nhp. Trials (20.1.1872) 149ihp = 6.83kts at 32rpm and 2.69 kg/cm$^2$ boiler pressure. Paddles 3.91m diameter. 1 engine with 2 oscillating cylinders of 0.7m diameter and 0.8m stroke. 1 boiler. 30t coal. Range 680 miles at maximum speed.
**Guns:** (1873) 2 x 4pdr (86.5mm/11) bronze mountain.

*Serpent* Ernest Gouin, Nantes.
On list 1.1871. K: 6.3.1870. L: 2.2.1871. C: 5.1871.
In French Guiana 1872-78. Struck 21.12.1879 (published 13.2.1880).

——————

**CYGNE Class.** *Avisos de flottille à roues.* 40nhp paddle avisos with iron hulls. Designed by Daymard.

Two ships were planned of which one was not built. The design for use in Senegal was by naval constructor Victor André Daymard. Their builder, Jollet & Babin, took over the Ernest Gouin yard at Nantes in 1869.

*The characteristics are based on a devis for Cygne dated 5.1875.*
**Dimensions & tons:** 43.23m pp x 7.21m wl. 297t disp. Draught: 1.20m mean, 1.35m aft.
**Machinery:** 40nhp. Trials (*Cygne*, 21.5.1874) 176ihp = 6.57kts. Paddles 3.60m diameter. 77t coal. Range 1,530 miles at maximum speed.
**Guns:** (1875) 4 x 4pdr (86.5mm/11) bronze mountain.

*Cygne* Jollet & Babin, Nantes.
On list 1.1872. K: 1873. L: 8.8.1873. Comm: 1.10.1873 (trials).
Ran trials at Nantes, then to Senegal 1873. Became barracks hulk and renamed *Africain* 1883. Struck 22.1.1884, barracks hulk in Senegal to 1895, wreck for sale in Senegal 1895-1896.

*Cigale.*
On list 1.1872 only (40nhp), finally built in 1877-78 with a larger engine (below).

——————

**RÔDEUR Class.** *Avisos de flottille à roues.* 30nhp paddle avisos with iron hulls. Designed by Sabattier.

Three ships were planned of which two were not built. The 1875 budget (submitted January 1874) had three unnamed *avisos à vapeur de flottille* to be built by contract. The 1876 budget (May 1875) had two of these, *Rôdeur* 50% built and another to be begun by contract. *Rôdeur* and *Furet* were named during 1874 but only *Rôdeur* was proceeded with. Sabattier's plans were approved on 15 February 1875 and the contract for *Rôdeur* was approved on 10 May 1875. *Rôdeur* was built for service at Cayenne and was a slightly enlarged version of the *Économe* and *Surveillant* built in 1855 for service there. Doubts arose as to whether she could safely cross the Atlantic for reasons of stability, freeboard and fuel capacity and she was not sent there.

*The characteristics are based on the launch report and the contract for the vessel.*
**Dimensions & tons:** 25.00m pp (stempost to sternpost) x 4.83m (outside planking). 121.570t disp. Draught 1.59m mean. Men: 17.
**Machinery:** 30nhp, 120ihp at 110rpm. Paddle. Vertical compound engines with 2 cylinders of 0.400m and 0.640m diameter and 0.500m stroke. Gearing to paddles 1 to 2.75.
**Guns:** 1.

*Rôdeur* Jollet & Babin, Nantes.
On list 1.1874. Ord: 18.4.1875 (contract). K: 1875. L: 1.4.1876. Comm: 25.4.1876 (trials). C: 9.1876.

Budget 1875. Completed steam trials at Nantes 5.7.1876. Intended for French Guiana but instead lay in reserve at Lorient 9.1876 to 2.1878 and at Cherbourg from 12.1878. Struck 29.6.1880, tug (service craft, 30nhp/120ihp) at Rochefort 1880-1913 (annex to the Défense Mobile 1887-1895), for sale 1913-1914, struck 6.1.1914 as tug, hulk 'ex gunboat' used as mooring point for water barges 1920-1927. Handed over to the Société Goldenberg at Rochefort under a contract dated 5.11.1927.

*Furet* Contract.
On list 1.1874 and 1.1875. Budget 1875. Cancelled 1875. Not in the 1877 budget (submitted March 1876).

*N* (Unnamed) Contract.
On list 1.1874, not 1.1875. Budget 1875. Cancelled 1874. Not in the 1876 budget.

---

**CIGALE.** *Avisos de flottille à roues.* 55nhp paddle aviso with an iron hull and a straight bow. One funnel, two masts, schooner-brig rig (later schooner). Designed by Daymard.

A replica of *Cygne* also designed by Daymard for service in Senegal but with a somewhat larger engine.

*The characteristics are based on a devis dated 26.3.1880.*
**Dimensions & tons:** 42.95m wl, 43.23m pp (wl fwd to rudder) x 7.23m ext and wl. 305.0t disp. Draught: 1.229m mean, 1.229m aft. Men: 65.
**Machinery:** 55nhp, 225ihp designed at 120rpm (engine) 38.7rpm (paddles) and 4.133kg/cm$^2$ boiler pressure. Trials (20.3.1880) 219ihp = 8.32kts at 90.11rpm (engine), 30.03rpm (paddles), 4.475kg/cm$^2$ boiler pressure. Paddles 3.94m diameter. 1 vertical compound geared engine with 2 cylinders of 0.43m and 0.77m diameter and 0.50m stroke. 1 tubular cylindrical boiler. 55.5t coal. Range 1,290 miles at full speed.
**Guns:** (1880) 1 x 4pdr bronze.

*Cigale* T. H. Dubigeon & Fils, Nantes.
On list 1.1878. K: 6.1877. L: 5.1878. Comm: 15.8.1878 (trials), C: 5.1879.
Budget 1877. Ran trials at Nantes. Active in Senegal 1881 to 1890, then in reserve there. Retired 11.12.1896, for sale in Senegal 1896-1897.

---

**OYAPOCK.** *Aviso de flottille à roues.* 40nhp paddle aviso with a wooden hull and iron deck beams and beam shelves and with a clipper bow. One funnel, two masts, schooner-brig rig. Designed by Sabattier.

On 10 January 1880 French Guiana asked for an aviso to replace *Serpent* and provided some guidance on characteristics. The vessel was designed by Sabattier. On 23 March 1880 Minister of Marine Jauréguiberry instructed the Machinery Commission (the *Commission permanente des machines et du grand outillage*) to negotiate with Jollet & Babin of Nantes a contract for a paddle aviso and named the aviso *Maroni*. The contract was approved on 21 May 1880. The name was changed to *Oyapock* on 15 September 1880.

*The characteristics are based on a devis dated 1.7.1881.*
**Dimensions & tons:** 34.63m wl, 35.22m pp (wl fwd to rudder) x 5.57m ext (above wl) (9.03m outside the paddle boxes), 5.52m wl. 205.692t disp. Draught: 1.918m mean, 2.120m aft. Men: 25.
**Machinery:** 40nhp and 160ihp designed at 115rpm (engine) and 41.8rpm (paddles) and 4.25kg/cm$^2$ boiler pressure. Trials (1.7.1881) 207.57ihp = 9.53kts at 113.74rpm (engine) and 41.36rpm (paddles). Paddles 3.400m diameter. 1 vertical compound engine with 2 cylinders of 0.420m and 0.680m diameter and 0.500m stroke. 1 special tubular cylindrical boiler. 26.2t coal including 1.2t wood. Range 930nm @ 9.5kts.
**Guns:** (1881) 2 x 4pdr (86.5mm/11) bronze. (1888) 2 x 37mm QF

*Oyapock* Jollet & Babin, Nantes.
On list 1.1881. K: 15.5.1880. L: 13.4.1881. Comm: 1.7.1881.
Budget 1881. Name changed from *Maroni* 15.9.1880. Engine installed 15.4.1881 to 21.5.1881. Boilers installed 21.5.1881. To French Guiana 9-11.1881. Struck 13.3.1893. Sold 8.6.1893.

---

**BASILIC.** *Aviso de flottille à roues.* 25nhp paddle aviso with a wooden hull with crossed layers of wooden planking, probably on wooden frames with iron deck beams and without beam shelves. Clipper bow. One funnel, two masts, schooner-brig rig (later schooner). Designed by Normand.

On 23 August 1880 Minister of Marine Jauréguiberry ordered the Machinery Commission to negotiate a contract for a paddle flotilla aviso for Gabon and named her *Basilic*. A contract with Normand for design and construction of the ship was approved on 17 November 1880, and on 31 December 1880 he was authorized to lengthen the hull by 2m to 30m. She was needed to replace *Marabout*, which drew too much water and lacked speed. This, the smallest paddle aviso built after 1870, rendered excellent service on the Ogowe and other rivers and in the arroyos of Gabon. By early 1893 the hull was eaten by white ants and seaworms, and on 11 June 1893 the governor at Libreville reported that *Basilic* could no longer light fires in her boiler without danger and asked that the ship be decommissioned. She was to be replaced by *Cigogne*.

*The characteristics are based on a devis dated 1.8.1882.*
**Dimensions & tons:** 30.14m wl, 30.10m pp (wl fwd to rudder) x 5.06m ext (above wl), 5.06m ext (above wl, 8.624m outside the paddle boxes), 5.01m wl. 112.913t disp. Draught: 1.315m mean, 1.365m aft. Men: 28.
**Machinery:** 25nhp and 110ihp designed (excluding the circulating pump) at 130rpm and 5.0kg/cm$^2$ boiler pressure. Trials (15.7.1882) 131.4ihp = 9.20kts at 138rpm (engines), 34.5rpm (paddles), 4.99kg/cm$^2$ boiler pressure. Paddles 3.90m diameter. 1 horizontal compound geared engine with 2 cylinders of 0.32m and 0.52m diameter and 0.38m stroke. Gear ratio 4 to 1. 1 tubular cylindrical return flame boiler. 16.0t coal. Range 860nm @ 9.2kts.
**Guns:** (1882) 2 revolving cannon (2 positions on the upper deck and four on the paddle boxes, forward and aft).

*Basilic* Augustin Normand, Le Havre.
On list 1.1881. K: 17.2.1881. L: 15.4.1882. Comm: 1.8.1882.
Budget 1881. Engine installed 25.2.1882 to 15.4.1882. Arrived at Dakar 8.1882 en route Gabon. Decomm. 1.7.1893. Struck 15.12.1893, sold at Gabon 4.3.1894 to the Cie. des Chargeurs Réunis.

---

# II. SAILING VESSELS

## (A) Schooners (*Goëlettes, bâtiments de flottille*).

**Repeat CALÉDONIENNE Class.** *Bâtiments de flottille (Goëlettes).* Schooners with wooden hulls. Designed by Pastoureau-Labesse.

In September 1857 Minister of Marine Hamelin approved the plans of naval constructor Jean-Baptiste Pastoureau-Labesse for a schooner for French Oceania. At the same time he decided to build her at Brest, and on 21 September 1857 he named her *Calédonienne*. This vessel (listed in the Preamble) was begun on 25 September 1857, launched on 12 May 1858, and commissioned for the first time on 6 September 1858. She was first classified as a 60-ton transport, then (from 1873) as a schooner. Two sisters were ordered to the plans of *Calédonienne* in late 1859 but were classified as schooners from the beginning. (Their measurements, below, differed slightly from those of *Calédonienne*.) A second *Perle* was built to the same design in 1875 and lasted until 1892.

**Dimensions & tons:** 38.00m oa, 33.00m wl x 7.32m ext. 245t disp. Draught: 2.96m fwd, 3.16m aft.

**Guns:** 2 x 12cm carronades.

*Perle* Arnaud, François, & Charles Chaigneau, Bordeaux-Lormont.
On list 1.1860. Ord: 25.11.1859 (contract). K: 1.12.1859. L: 20.6.1860. Comm: 20.11.1860.

Towed from Lormont to Lorient 13.8.1860 by *Goéland* for fitting out. Sailed from Lorient for Réunion 2.2.1861. Wrecked 13.5.1863 on Platte Island in the Seychelles while aiding another vessel, crew rescued by *Lynx*. Struck 11.8.1863.

*Gazelle* Arnaud, François, & Charles Chaigneau, Bordeaux-Lormont.
On list 1.1860. Ord: 25.11.1859 (contract). K: 12.1859. L: 1860. Comm: 1.9.1860.

Commissioned at Lorient, to New Caledonia 1861. Struck 3.2.1883 in New Caledonia.

----

## PURCHASED VESSELS, 1860. *Bâtiments de flottille (Goëlettes)*

*Aurore.* Mercantile schooner built at Salem, Mass., and purchased 3.1860 in French Guiana from a merchant named Fabius. Comm: 1.4.1860. On list 1.1861.

**Dimensions & tons:** 21.50m deck, 20.50m wl x 5.80m ext. 150t (capacity 84 or 68 tons). Draught 1.80m fwd, 2.80m aft. Men: 13. **Guns:** (1861) 2.

Struck 7.3.1867, out of service 24.7.1867.

*Fine.* Mercantile (?) schooner built in New Caledonia and purchased in late 1860. On list 1.1861. Comm: 1.1.1861.

**Dimensions & tons:** 20 men. **Guns:** 2.

Decomm. 5.10.1869 at Nouméa. Struck 20.11.1871.

*Mirage.* Mercantile schooner purchased in China 6.1860 and fitted (at Shanghai?) as a *goélette-citerne*. On list 1.1861. Comm: 1.11.1861.

**Dimensions & tons:** 20 men. **Guns:** 1.

Decomm. 16.12.1867 in China. Struck 30.1.1868, sold with the steamer *Déroulède* at Shanghai 25.3.1868.

----

***BELETTE*** Class. *Bâtiments de flottille (Goëlettes)* Schooners with wooden hulls. Designed by naval constructors Alfred François Lebelin de Dionne and Charles Marie Hippolyte Auxcousteaux.

These schooners were similar to *Pourvoyeuse*, *Vigilante*, and *Laborieuse* of 1855.

*The hull data are based on a devis for* Belette *dated 3.7.1876.*

**Dimensions & tons:** 20.58m wl, 20.80m pp (wl fwd to rudder) x 6.01m ext (above wl), 5.88m wl. 130.2t disp. Draught: 2.80m mean, 3.15m aft. Men: 20.

**Guns:** 4 *espingoles*.

*Belette* Rochefort Dyd.
On list 1.1866. K: 7.8.1865. L: 3.4.1866. Comm: 1.3.1867.
Served primarily at Saint Pierre de Terre-Neuve. Struck 3.2.1883, probably at Cherbourg.

*Levrette* Rochefort Dyd.
On list 1.1866. K: 7.8.1865. L: 3.4.1866. Comm: 1.3.1867.
Served mainly at Ste-Marie de Madagascar, probably as a pilot boat. Struck 3.2.1883.

----

***TOPAZE.*** *Bâtiments de flottille (Goëlettes)* Schooner with wooden hull and 2 masts. Designed by builder.

*Topaze* was built to resupply penitentiaries on small offshore islands in French Guiana and was fitted to transport cattle. On 17 March 1870 Minister of Marine Rigault de Genouilly directed the Machinery Commission to contract for the design and construction of a *goélette clipper* for service in French Guiana. A contract was signed by Chaigneau frères of Bordeaux on 15 April 1870 and approved by the Minister on 26 April 1870, when the name was also assigned. She was accepted on 14 October 1870.

*The hull data are based on a devis dated 8.5.1871.*

**Dimensions & tons:** 33.00m oa, 30.060m deck, 30.050m wl/pp x 7.365m ext, 7.345m wl. 229.792t disp. Draught: 2.30m mean, 2.60m aft. Men: 18.

**Guns:** 2 *espingoles*. Had no guns in 1871.

*Topaze* Chaigneau frères, Bordeaux-Lormont.
On list 1.1871. K: 5.5.1870. L: 10.9.1870. Comm: 8.11.1870.
Still at Bordeaux when *devis d'armement* signed 5.1871. To French Guiana 1871 and spent entire career there as supply ship for the prisons on the Îles du Salut and the Îlet la Mère except for a brief return to Rochefort in 1878 to be immersed in fresh water. Decomm. at Cayenne 25.4.1882. Struck 3.2.1883, loaned to the colony, returned to the navy 24.7.1884, sold 17.2.1885.

----

***ÉMERAUDE.*** *Bâtiments de flottille (Goëlettes)* Schooner with wooden hull and 2 masts. Probably designed by builder.

*Émeraude* was built for general service in French Guiana and served there as a station ship.

*The hull data are based on a devis dated 20.2.1874.*

**Dimensions & tons:** 29.95m wl, 30.30m pp (wl fwd to rudder) x 7.36m ext and wl. 259.5t disp. Draught: 2.47m mean, 2.77m aft. Men: 16.

**Guns:** 2 *espingoles*.

*Émeraude* Nantes (probably Jollet & Babin).
On list 1.1874. K: 6.1873. L: 11.1873. Comm: 5.1.1874 (trials). C: 2.1874.
Ran trials at Nantes. Station ship at French Guiana 1874-81. Struck 21.4.1882. BU 1883 at Cayenne.

----

## PURCHASED VESSEL, 1873. *Bâtiments à voiles (Goëlettes)*

*Mésange.* 1 ship (purch 1873 at Papeete). On list 1.1874. K: . L: . Comm: 1.8.1873 at Papeete.

**Dimensions & tons:** unknown. Men: 22. **Guns:** 2.

Wrecked 13.8.1877 in the bay at Hanavave on Fatu Hiva in the Marquises. Struck 16.11.1877.

----

***PERLE.*** *Bâtiments à voiles (Goëlettes).* Schooner with a wooden hull.

This was the fourth schooner built to Pastoureau-Labesse's design for the *Calédonienne* of 1857, the second (another *Perle*) and third having been built in 1860 as shown above. Her building time was unusually long as she was fitting out afloat from 1876 to 1882 and was only commissioned in 1883 after being used for scientific research in 1882 at Concarneau by Senator Charles Philippe Robin, director of the Laboratory of Marine Zoology there.

**Dimensions & tons:** 270t disp. Men: 22, later 31 including 1 officer.
**Guns:** 2.

*Perle* Brest Dyd.
On list 1.1875. K: 17.4.1874. L: 2.7.1875. C: 1883.
Struck 10.2.1892. Offered for sale 28.7.1892.

*CANADIENNE* Class. *Bâtiments à voiles (Goëlettes)* Schooners with wooden hulls. Designed by builder.

Designed and built by A. Cantin at Montreal. *Évangéline* was named on 22 August 1876.

*The hull data are based on a devis for* Canadienne *dated 14.8.1881.*
**Dimensions & tons:** 26.23m wl, 26.50m pp (wl fwd to rudder) x 7.20m ext (above wl), 7.15m wl. 195.8t disp. Draught: 2.69m mean, 3.15m aft. Men: 22.
**Guns:** none listed.

*Canadienne* Cantin, Montreal.
On list 1.1876. K: c1876. L: 1876. Comm: 14.6.1876.
Commissioned at Saint Pierre, off Newfoundland. Struck 28.11.1883.

*Évangéline* Cantin, Montreal.
On list 1.1876. K: c1876. L: 1876. Comm: 14.6.1876.
Commissioned at Saint Pierre, off Newfoundland. Struck 28.11.1883.

*AORAÏ* Class. *Bâtiments à voiles (Goëlettes).* Schooners with wooden hulls. Designed by builder.

Designed and built by William Bell & Co, San Francisco, for French Oceania (Papeete).

**Dimensions & tons:** 75t disp. Men: 22 including 1 officer.
**Guns:** 2.

*Aoraï* William Bell & Co, San Francisco.
On list 1.1879. K: 1878. L: 1878. Comm: 1878.
Struck 19.4.1892.

*Orohéna* William Bell & Co, San Francisco.
On list 1.1879. K: 1878. L: 1878. Comm: 25.6.1878 at Papeete.
Struck 3.5.1890, hulk and lighter at Tahiti 1890-1893. Sold 20 October 1893 to M. Martin, merchant at Papeete.

*NU-HIVA* Class. *Bâtiments à voiles (Goëlettes).* Schooners with wooden hulls. Designed by builder.

On 12 July 1880 the commander of French Oceania ordered a commission to San Francisco to identify firms there that could design, build, and deliver to Papeete two schooners of 40 to 50 tons that would be suitable for service in the Tuamotu Archipelago. Five firms submitted proposals, and on 11 November 1880 the Ministry asked the French consul at San Francisco to contract with one of them, Turner and Rundle (Matthew Turner), for the two vessels. The contract was dated 29 January 1881. The two schooners arrived at Papeete, one on 22 April and the other on 22 May 1881, were then fitted out and entered service in October 1881.

**Dimensions & tons:** 21.95m x 6.10m. 42t disp. Men: 15, later 22 including 1 officer.
**Speed:** 10 knots on trials at San Francisco 22.3.1881.
**Guns:** 2.

*Nu-Hiva* Turner & Rundle, San Francisco.
On list 1.1881. K: 1880. L: 1881. Comm: 10.1881.
Accepted at Tahiti 15.6.1881. Struck 26.11.1894, reported 11.5.1895 as sold at Tahiti to a local merchant.

*Taravao* Turner & Rundle, San Francisco.

On list 1.1881. K: c1880. L: 1881. Comm: 10.1881.
Struck 3.5.1898, for sale at Tahiti 1898-1900.

## (B) Cutters (*Cutters*).

### PURCHASED VESSEL, 1866. *Bâtiment de flottille (Cutter)*

*Martin Pêcheur.* Cutter at Rochefort acquired and placed in service 1866 as a fishery protection ship (*garde-pêche*) fitted with a fish tank (*vivier*). On list 1.1867 as a cutter.

**Dimensions & tons:** unknown. **Guns:** probably none.

Sometimes called *Vivier n⁰ 1.* Struck 18.1.1869, guard hulk at Rochefort 1869-1875.

*GUETTEUR. Bâtiment à voiles (Cutter)* Cutter with a wooden hull. Designed by Finot.

On 18 December 1871 Minister of Marine Pothuau decided to build at Cherbourg two new cutters to replace some that would soon be retired from service, and he requested a design based on the best models available. Naval constructor Henri Édouard Finot at Cherbourg based his design on the successful fishery protection cutter *Alcyone* of 1858 with minor modifications to the dimensions to obtain the necessary displacement. Finot's design, used to build *Guetteur*, was examined and approved by the *Conseil des travaux* on 4 June 1872.

*The hull data are based on a devis dated 10.10.1879.*
**Dimensions & tons:** 18.20m deck, 16.78m wl, 17.05m pp (wl fwd to rudder) x 5.55m ext and wl. 86.3t disp. Draught: 2.36m mean, 2.80m aft. Men: 16.
**Guns:** (designed) 2 x 4pdr (86.5mm/11) bronze mountain guns, 4 *espingoles.*

*Guetteur* Cherbourg Dyd.
On list 1.1873. K: 6.7.1872. L: 29.3.1873. Comm: 1.5.1873. C: 5.1873.
Struck 31.12.1885.

## (C) Lorchas (*Lorchas, bâtiments de flottille*).
Lorchas were sailing craft built in China and Indonesia with a largely European-style hull built of camphor wood or teak, a square poop, a junk rig with Cantonese or other Chinese-style batten sails, and a small bowsprit. They varied widely in configuration and characteristics but on average at this time they were about 29-30m long and 6.7m wide. Six armed lorchas purchased at Macao, probably never on the fleet list, participated in the relief of Saigon in February 1861.

### PURCHASED VESSELS, 1861-1862 (Named). *Bâtiments de flottille (Lorchas).*
*Donaï.* Purchased 11.1861. Comm: 25.11.1861. On fleet list 1.1865.
16 men (32 in 1868). 3 masts. No guns in 1867.
Converted to lightship 1866 and listed as such 1867-1869. Decomm. 10.3.1869. Struck 31.5.1869.

*Soïrap.* Purchased 11.1861 or built 1861. Comm: 25.11.1861 (listed as a *canonnière à hélice* on some muster rolls, probably in error). On fleet list 1.1865.
16 men. 3 masts.
Decomm. 10.10.1864, recomm. 12.9.1868, decomm. 10.5.1869. Struck 22.7.1872.

*Vaïco.* Purchased 11.1861. Comm: 25.11.1861 (listed as a *canonnière à hélice* on some muster rolls, probably in error). On fleet list 1.1865.
16 men (22 in 1868). 3 masts.

Decomm. 12.9.1868. Struck 5.11.1868.

*Espérance.* Purchased 1861. Never on fleet list.
30 men. 3 masts. 2 guns.
Boarded and burned near Mytho on the Nhat Tao canal by forces of the Vietnamese resistance leader Nguyen Trung Truc 10.12.1861.

*Amphitrite.* Purchased at the end of 1861. Comm: 1.1.1862. On fleet list 1.1865.
30 men (16 in 1865). 3 masts. 4 guns.
Decomm. 26.5.1867. Struck 29.7.1867.

*Jacaréo.* Purchased at the end of 1861. Comm: 1.1.1862. On fleet list 1.1865.
30 men (16 in 1865). 3 masts. 4 guns.
Decomm. 17.9.1866. Struck 26.11.1866.

*Saint Joseph.* Purchased at the end of 1861. Comm: 1.1.1862. On fleet list 1.1865.
30 men (16 in 1865). 3 masts. 4 guns.
Decomm. 3.3.1865. Struck 25.5.1865.

*Mandarine.* Purchased at the beginning of 1862. Comm: 26.2.1862. Never on fleet list.
30 men. 3masts. 2 guns.
Decomm. 13.7.1862.

---

### PURCHASED VESSELS, 1861-1862 (Numbered). *Bâtiments de flottille (Lorchas)*

All bought at Macao. Characteristics unknown except crew size: 16 men (22 in 1868 except 41 in *Lorcha nº 4* and 45 in *Lorcha nº 10*). 3 masts.

*Lorcha nº 1.* K: 1862. L: 1862. Comm: 14.7.1862. On list 1.1865. Decomm. 16.7.1868. Struck 10.9.1868.

A typical Chinese merchant lorcha employed in the river at Canton in 1857. The lorcha was a vessel with a junk rig on a European-style hull and was developed around 1550 in Macau, then a Portuguese colony in China, primarily to counter Chinese pirates. The hull made the lorcha faster and able to carry more cargo than the normal junk while the junk rig was easier to handle, permitting a smaller crew than did European rigs. The lorcha sailed faster than traditional pirate ships and British traders began to use it after the First Opium War between Britain and China (1839-42). It figured prominently in the Second Opium War (1856-60), in which France also participated. *(Illustrated London News, 14 March 1857, front page)*

*Lorcha nº 2.* K: 1862. L: 1862. Comm: 29.7.1862. On list 1.1865. Decomm. 1.9.1866. Struck 16.11.1866.

*Lorcha nº 3.* K: 1861. L: 1861?. Comm: 25.11.1861. On list 1.1865. Decomm. 10.5.1869. Struck 22.7.1869.

*Lorcha nº 4.* K: 1862. L: 1862. Comm: 14.6.1862. On list 1.1865. Decomm. 12.5.1869. Struck 15.11.1869.

*Lorcha nº 5.* K: 1862. L: 1862. Comm: 22.8.1862. On list 1.1865. Decomm. 10.6.1863. Struck 10.9.1868.

*Lorcha nº 6.* K: 1862. L: 1862. Comm: 29.7.1862. On list 1.1865. Decomm. 1.10.1864. Struck 20.9.1867.

*Lorcha nº 7.* K: 1862. L: 1862. Comm: 10.6.1862. On list 1.1865. Decomm. 26.3.1869. Struck 22.7.1872.

*Lorcha nº 8.* K: 1862. L: 1862. Comm: 18.8.1862. On list 1.1865. Decomm. 1.7.1863. Struck 5.11.1868.

*Lorcha nº 9.* K: 1862. L: 1862. Comm: 1.10.1862. On list 1.1865. Decomm. after 31.12.1868. Struck 11.5.1869, floating guard post at Saigon 1869-1872.

*Lorcha nº 10.* K: 1862. L: 1862. Comm: 10.6.1862. On list 1.1865. Decomm. 15.2.1869. Struck 22.7.1872.

---

### (D) Sail Transports (*Transports*).

#### PURCHASED VESSELS, 1859-1860. *Transports.*

*Ménagère.* Ex mercantile *Adéline* acquired 5.1859 and comm. 11.5.1859. On list 1.1860.

**Dimensions & tons:** dimensions unknown. 420 tons burthen. Men: 41. **Guns:** 2.

Decomm. 9.11.1866. Struck 31.10.1867 at Brest. Reappears on harbour service list at Brest 1.1876, coal hulk 1876-1888, BU 1889. *Ménagère, Abondance,* and *Truite* may have been sisters laid down as merchant vessels at Toulon 1.1859 and completed 5.1859; a Navy memo of 6.5.1859 stated that Minister of Marine Hamelin had just authorized their acquisition at Marseilles and selected their Navy names.

*Abondance.* Ex mercantile *Lahore* acquired 5.1859 and comm. 11.5.1859. On list 1.1860.

**Dimensions & tons:** dimensions unknown. 420 tons burthen. Men: 41. **Guns:** 2.

Arrived at Venice 30.5.1859 under tow by *Algésiras* with coal for the French naval division there. She was one of 16 vessels that were wrecked on 22.9.1866 in the harbour of Saint-Pierre in a storm. Struck 13.12.1866. Wreck sold and BU there.

*Truite.* Ex mercantile *Gange* acquired 5.1859 and comm. 11.5.1859. On list 1.1860.

**Dimensions & tons:** dimensions unknown. 420 or 460 tons burthen. Men: 41. **Guns:** 2.

Arrived at Venice 30.5.1859 under tow by *Algésiras* with coal for the French naval division there. Decomm. 1.12.1866 at Toulon. Condemned 26.8.1872, for sale at Toulon 1872-1873, station hulk in French Guiana 1873-1893 (sent there 1874), dépôt 1893-1898, sank 1898 from deterioration.

*Bonite.* Ex mercantile *Mogador*, built 1851, lengthened and changed from 2-masted brig to 3-masted barque 1856. Purchased 11.1859 from Charles

Van Cauwenberghe of Dunkirk, comm. 18.11.1859 and named 23.11.1859. On list 1.1860.

**Dimensions & tons:** dimensions unknown. 292 tons gross (242 tons before lengthening). Men: 36. **Guns:** 2.

Sailed from Cherbourg for New Caledonia 10.2.1860, arrived 25.7.1860 and spent entire career there. Struck 1.7.1872 at Nouméa.

*Ressource.* Ex mercantile *Brasiliero* built at Nantes, purchased 14.6.1860 and comm. 25.7.1860. On list 1.1861.

**Dimensions & tons:** dimensions unknown. 200 tons, 31 men.

Wrecked 12.11.1861 on the Chilean coast. Struck 6.5.1862.

---

*DORADE. Transport.* Purchased while building.

Mercantile clipper ship purchased on the ways in January 1860 under a contract signed on 25 December 1859 and completed for the Navy.

**Dimensions & tons:** 35.90m deck x 8.40m ext. 480t disp (300 tons burthen). Draught: 3.67m mean. Men: 30.
**Guns:** 4 x 12pdr carronades.

*Dorade* Gustave Guibert, Bordeaux.

On list 1.1861. K: 1859. L: 28.2.1860. Comm: 21.5.1860.
Struck 10.2.1873, barracks hulk (*poste caserne*) at Saigon 1873-1874, for disposal 1874-1876, then BU there.

---

## ROCHEFORT SERVICE CRAFT. *Transports.*

Rochefort with its dockyard some 12 miles up the Charente River and even farther from its roadstead near the Île d'Aix had an unusually varied collection of service craft, some of which including the following were large enough to be used on occasion as coastal transports.

*Messager.* Chatte or transport brig *Charente* begun at Rochefort 5.1837, launched 11.1.1838, and commissioned as a service craft on 2.4.1838. Designed by Émile Étinennez, probably sister to *Touvre* below. Renamed *Messager* 3.11.1862.

**Dimensions & tons:** 21.18m (deck?), 21.10m wl x 6.61m. 150 to 187t disp. Draught: 2.17m mean, 2.73m aft. Men: 13 including 1 officer or master.

On list 1.1865. Decomm. 10.9.1869. Comm. 15.3.1872 as a *transport de 100tx armé au materiel* (100-ton cargo transport). Stationary school for torpedoes at Boyardville near Rochefort 1875-1884 and school for submarine defences there 1884-1886. Struck 9.7.1886, hulk for the rear guard at Rochefort 1886-1887, floating guard station 1887-1899, replaced 1899 by *Mésange* and BU.

*Touvre.* Chatte or transport brig begun at Rochefort 8.1836, launched 20.5.1837 and in service as a service craft in 6.1837. Designed by Émile Étinennez, probably sister to *Charente* above.

**Dimensions & tons:** 21.64m (deck?), 21.14m wl x 6.61m. 125t disp. Draught: 2.14m mean, 2.76m aft. Men: 13 including 1 officer or master.

On list 1.1865. During the 1860s operated between Rochefort and Cherbourg, Brest, Lorient, Bordeaux, and Toulon as a 1st category service craft. Commissioned 1.8.1870, coasting operations included a call at Falmouth 1.1872. Decomm. at Brest 30.11.1872. Listed as *transport de 100tx armé au Materiel* 1.1873. School for boys at Brest 1874-75. Struck 19.2.1878, hulk at Brest 1878-1893, security post 1893-1897, hulk 1897-1900.

*Marie.* Transport brig from Brest commissioned at Rochefort as a service craft on 28.7.1853. She may have been the 80-ton *gabare de port* named *Marie* of the *Victoire* type launched at Brest 24.4.1830 (see *Express* below).

**Dimensions & tons:** 70 tons burthen. Men: 13.

On list 1.1865. Decomm. at Rochefort 11.7.1869 and inactive until struck. Struck 1.7.1872, hulk at Rochefort 1872-1874, torpedo trials 1874-1877, bugalet (a Breton type of hoy) 1877-1880, for disposal as a schooner 1880-1882.

*Express* (*Exprès*). Transport brig *Victoire* from Brest commissioned at Rochefort as a service craft on 2.8.1853, renamed *Express* (sometimes rendered as *Exprès*) 3.9.1862, and called a coastal transport of the port of Rochefort. Promoted to the main part of the fleet list in 1.1865 as a sail transport. May originally have been the 80-ton *gabare de port* named *Victoire* launched at Brest 24.4.1830.

**Dimensions & tons:** 150 tons (70t burthen). Men: 13.

On list 1.1865. Left Rochefort for Bordeaux 30.1.1863, operated on this route until decomm. at Rochefort 14.7.1869, then inactive until struck. Struck 26.10.1874 after use as a torpedo target.

*Île de Ré.* Schooner commissioned at Rochefort as a service craft on 9.6.1850 replacing or converted from a chasse-marée dating from 1824 that had served there from 1844 to 1848. The dimensions below are for the 1824 ship, which was designed by Alphonse Levesque.

**Dimensions & tons:** 15.50m hull, 15.00m wl x 4.68m moulded. 73t. Draught 2.27m mean, 2.45m aft.

On list 1.1865. Sailed for Brest from Rochefort 8.6.1865, having operated between the two ports since at least 1862. Decomm. 6.5.1868 at Cherbourg and recomm. there ten days later. Struck 12.8.1872, bugalet at Cherbourg 1872-1888, for sale 1888-1889.

---

## (E) Small Fishery Protection Vessels etc. (*Petits Garde-pêche &a, 1.1872*).

Fishery protection vessels first appeared on the *Liste de la Flotte* in January 1865, that list containing the first 26 vessels listed below (through *Garde-pêche nº 6R*). Many of these had previous names as indicated. The letter suffixes for the numbered vessels stood for Cherbourg (CH), Lorient (L), and Rochefort (R). Most were removed from the main part of the list in the January 1897 fleet list and listed *pour ordre* (for the record) with service craft because they were under commercial operation. They disappeared from the fleet list altogether in 1908, being moved to a separate non-naval listing that is not reported here. The 15nhp screw *avisos de flottille Sylphe* and *Favori* of 1861 and the cutter *Martin Pécheur* of 1867 were also fishery protection craft and were fitted with fish tanks (*viviers*), compartments open to the sea in which fish could be kept alive. A *chaloupe pontée* was a decked launch.

*Annexe.* 6 tons. Purchased from M. Béléguic, builder at Dourarnenez c1859 and commissioned 21.5.1859 at Brest. On list 1.1865 as a schooner (*garde-pêche annexe*) at Brest. Listed as cutter (*garde-pêche annexe*) at Cherbourg 1869-1872, classed as *garde-pêche* 1873-1892. Struck 13.6.1892, fishery protection *chaloupe* at Brest 1892-1897, hulk 1897-1898, for sale 1898-1899 as *Annexe* (*Gorréguer*).

*Écureuil.* May have been the *Écureuil Nº 2* that went out of service in Senegal in 1859. On list 1.1865 as a cutter (*garde-pêche annexe*) at Brest. (There were two cutters at Brest named *Écureuil* in this fleet list, the one not on fishery protection duty is listed in the Preamble.) Renamed *Furet* 1865, classed as *garde-pêche* 1873. Struck 8.5.1873, for disposal at Brest 1873-1874.

*Esméralda*. 29 tons, 9 men. Built at Brest 1854. On list 1.1865 as a schooner (*garde-pêche annexe*) at Brest. Classed as *garde-pêche* 1873-1892. Struck 13.6.1892, steam pump (*pompe à vapeur*, ex cutter) at Brest 1892-1893.

*Éveil*. Built at Brest and commissioned 11.2.1842 as a *transport péniche*. On list 1.1865 as a *péniche* (*garde-pêche annexe*) at Lorient. At Brest 1867 and at Cherbourg 1868-1872. Struck 2.8.1872.

*Gabrielle*. On list 1.1865 as a schooner (annexe) at Guadeloupe. At Lorient 1868-1872. Struck 4.1.1872.

*Lutin*. 11 tons, 5 men. Built at Lorient in 1864 (begun 3.1864) to plans by Augustin Marie Samuel Auvynet. Dimensions: 10.90m oa, 9.03m wl, 8.88m pp x 3.65m ext. Draught: 1.40m mean, 1.60m aft. 10.5 tons. On list 1.1865 as a cutter (*garde-pêche annexe*) at Lorient. Renamed *Loutre* c1.1866, classed as *garde-pêche* 1873. Struck 18.8.1896, sold at Lorient 9.1.1897.

*Scorff*. On list 1.1865 as a *chaloupe* (*garde-pêche annexe*) at Lorient. Struck 22.7.1872, powder vessel (*poudrière*, variously described as a *péniche*, *chaloupe*, and *gabare*) 1872-1914, renamed *Pulvérin* 1879, sold 1914.

*Unité*. 15 tons, 6 men. Commissioned at Brest 23.3.1858. On list 1.1865 as a schooner (*garde-pêche annexe*) at Brest. To Cherbourg 1869, classed as *garde-pêche* 1873-1886. Struck 12.11.1886, for sale at Cherbourg 1886-1887.

*Garde-pêche nº 1 CH*. 14 tons, 6 men. Launched at Cherbourg 21.10.1858 to plans by Victor Pierre Legrand. On list 1.1865 as a cutter (*garde-pêche annexe*) at Cherbourg. Renamed *Canard* 1866. Struck 7.7.1896.

*Garde-pêche nº 2 CH*. Launched at Cherbourg 22.12.1858 as *Gazelle nº 1*. Dimensions: 13.6m oa, 12.3m pp x 4.07m. c50 tons. On list 1.1865 as a cutter (*garde-pêche annexe*) at Cherbourg. Also called *Vivier nº 2*. Renamed *Colibri* 1866. At Brest 1872 and Cherbourg 1873. Struck 24.5.1878, lighter at Cherbourg 1878-1884.

*Garde-pêche nº 3 CH*. Designed and built by Émile Cardon at Honfleur 1856-57 as *Marie*. Dimensions: 14.5m oa, 12.8m wl x 4.85m ext. Draught 2.09m mean, 2.26m aft. c50 tons. On list 1.1865 as a cutter (*garde-pêche annexe*) at Cherbourg. Renamed *Sarcelle* 1866, classed as *garde-pêche* 1873-1886. Struck 12.11.1886, for sale at Cherbourg 1886-1887, sold to Gaston Le Houiller and still in service 1.1893.

*Garde-pêche nº 4 CH*. Designed and built by Émile Cardon at Honfleur 1856-57 as *Emmanuel* and was a sister to *Marie* above. On list 1.1865 as a cutter (*garde-pêche annexe*) at Cherbourg. Renamed *Emmanuel* 1866, classed as *garde-pêche* 1873-1882. Struck 19.6.1882, for disposal at Cherbourg 1882-1884.

*Garde-pêche nº 5 CH*. 14 tons, 9 men. Previously named *Ramier*, built at Cherbourg in 1858. On list 1.1865 as a cutter (*garde-pêche annexe*) at Cherbourg. Renamed *Ramier* 1866, classed as *garde-pêche* 1873-1892. Struck 13.6.1892.

*Garde-pêche nº 6 CH*. 14 tons, 9 men. Acquired 9.1855 at Calais and named *Gazelle nº 2*. Dimensions: 11.72m oa, 10.75m pp x 3.45m. Draught 1.52m mean, 1.87m aft. c28 tons. On list 1.1865 as a cutter (*garde-pêche annexe*) at Cherbourg. Renamed *Macreuse* 1866, classed as *garde-pêche* 1873-1896. Struck 7.7.1896.

*Garde-pêche nº 1L*. 21 tons, 9 men. Built at Lorient 1857 as *Elisa*. On list 1.1865 as a *péniche* (*garde-pêche annexe*) at Lorient. Renamed *Bler* 1.1866. Struck 18.8.1896, sold at Lorient 9.1.1897.

*Garde-pêche nº 2L*. 21 tons, 8 men. Built at Lorient 1854 as *Souveraine*.

21 tons. On list 1.1865 as a *péniche* (*garde-pêche annexe*) at Lorient. Renamed *Noyallo* 1.1866. Off main list 1896 and listed *pour ordre*, with service craft at Lorient 1.1897 under commercial operation 1.1898, on special fisheries list 1908 to 1914 at Auray.

*Garde-pêche nº 3L*. Commissioned at Brest 1.8.1859 as *Amélie*. On list 1.1865 as a *chaloupe* (*garde-pêche annexe*) at Lorient. Renamed *Amélie* 1866. Struck 22.7.1872, station vessel in the Bono (near Quiberon) 1872-1873, annexe to *Chamois* at Rochefort 1873-1875, station *péniche* annexe to *Euménide* at Lorient 1875-1876, *péniche* out of commission at Lorient 1876-1884.

*Garde-pêche nº 4L*. Built at Lorient 1859 as *Levrette*. On list 1.1865 as a *péniche* (*garde-pêche annexe*) at Lorient. Renamed *Trinité* 1866. Struck 22.7.1872, sold 1873 to BU.

*Garde-pêche nº 5L*. Built at Lorient 1852 as *Eugénie*. On list 1.1865 as a *péniche* (*garde-pêche annexe*) at Lorient. Renamed *Eugénie* 1866. Struck 5.11.1868.

*Garde-pêche nº 6L*. 21 tons, 8 men. In service as *Étoile* 4.1858 at Auray. On list 1.1865 as a *péniche* (*garde-pêche annexe*) at Lorient. Renamed *Pénerf* 1866. Off main list 1896 and listed *pour ordre* with service craft at Lorient 1.1897, under commercial operation 1.1898, for sale at Lorient 1899-1900 and replaced by a steam *Pénerf*.

*Garde-pêche nº 1R*. Launched 11.1854 at Rochefort as *Active nº 2*, became *Garde-pêche nº 1R* in 1858. Schooner-rigged. On list 1.1865 as a *chaloupe pontée* (*garde-pêche annexe*) at Rochefort. Renamed *Loubine* 15.2.1866. Off main list 1872 at Rochefort and on loan to the life-saving station (*Société de sauvetage*) 1872-1896.

*Garde-pêche nº 2R*. 26 tons, 7 men. Launched 22.3.1855 at Rochefort as *Furet* to plans by Bernard Charles Chariot, became *Garde-pêche nº 2R* in 6.1858. Dimensions: 12.88m oa x 3.83m ext. Draught 1.45m mean, 1.50m aft. 27 to 30 tons. 2 masts. 2 guns. On list 1.1865 as a *chaloupe pontée* (*garde-pêche annexe*) at Rochefort. Renamed *Congre* 15.2.1866. Struck 26.12.1896, for sale at Brest 1896-1897.

*Garde-pêche nº 3R*. Launched 5.1857 at Rochefort as *Surprise nº 1*, became *Garde-pêche nº 3R* in 1858. On list 1.1865 as a *chaloupe pontée* (*garde-pêche annexe*) at Rochefort. Renamed *Rouget* 15.2.1866. Struck 1.7.1872.

*Garde-pêche nº 4R*. 26 tons, 9 men. Launched 16.9.1858 at Rochefort as *Surprise nº 2*, became *Garde-pêche nº 4R* in 1858. 27 tons. On list 1.1865 as a *chaloupe pontée* (*garde-pêche annexe*) at Rochefort. Renamed *Turbot* 15.2.1866. Off main list 1895 and listed with service craft at Rochefort as a *garde-pêche* 1.1896 with *Active* (*garde-pêche*) and *Barbue* and *Fauvette* (*chaloupes pontées*). *Turbot* and *Active* listed *pour ordre* with service craft at Rochefort 1.1897, *Turbot* moved to regular service craft list with *Barbue* and *Fauvette* as *chaloupe pontée* (instead of *garde-pêche*) 1.1898, stationnaire à l'île d'Aix 1898-1905, for sale at Rochefort 1906-1907 (with *Fauvette*).

*Garde-pêche nº 5R*. Launched 26.8.1859 at Rochefort. Dimensions: 12.44m deck x 3.66m ext. Draught 1.38m mean, 1.76m aft. 23 tons. 2 masts. On list 1.1865 as a *chaloupe pontée* (*garde-pêche annexe*) at Rochefort. Renamed *Barbue* 15.2.1866. Struck 1.7.1872, *péniche* annexe du stationnaire de la rade at Rochefort 1872-6, *péniche* 1876-1887, *chaloupe pontée* (like *Active* and *Fauvette*) 1887-1910. This or another *Barbue* listed as steam service craft (no horsepower shown) 1911-1914 and for sale at Rochefort 1920.

*Garde-pêche nº 6R*. Launched 30.5.1860 at Rochefort to plans by Firmin Joffre. Dimensions: 12.45m oa, 11.00m wl x 3.10m ext. Draught 1.35m mean, 1.65m aft. 17.7 tons. On list 1.1865 as a cutter (*garde-*

*pêche annexe*) at Rochefort. Renamed *Grondin* 15.2.1866, classed as *garde-pêche* 1873-1881. Struck 26.2.1881 as a cutter, hulk at Sables-d'Olonne 1881-1882, Rochefort 1882-1883, in the channel that separates the Île d'Oléron from the continent 1883-1888 (out of commission 1886), and unassigned hulk 1888-1890.

*Bécassine*. 8.5 tons, 6 men. On list 1.1867. 8.5 tons. *Péniche* at Cherbourg 1.1867, classed as *garde-pêche* 1873-1891. Struck 29.12.1891, for sale at Cherbourg 1891-1893.

*Mesquer*. On list 1.1867. *Péniche* at Lorient 1.1867. To Rochefort 1.1873. Struck 28.11.1883.

*Zéphyr*. 35 tons, 7 men. On list 1.1867. Launched in 1863 and also known as *Vivier nº 3*. Cutter at Cherbourg 1.1867, at Rochefort 1.1872, classed as *garde-pêche* 1873-1896. Struck 7.7.1896, school for fisheries at Boulogne 1896-1914, BU or sold 1919.

*Saintonge*. On list 1.1872. Chaloupe at Rochefort, built by Claparède & Cie., Saint Denis. Struck 1.7.1872.

*Ablette*. On list 1.1874. Built at Brest in 1844, at Brest 1.1874. Measured 12.96m wl (bow to rudder) x 4.08m ext., 25 tons, draught 1.60m. Struck 22.6.1895, offered for sale in usable condition at Brest 4.10.1895, 15.11.1895 and 20.1.1896 but minimums not met.

*Barbillon*. 12 tons, 5 men. On list 1.1875 at Rochefort, to Lorient 1.1876. Struck 24.2.1892.

*Bergeronnette*. 7 tons, 9 men. On list 1.1879. At Toulon 1879-1892. Described 1892 as a *balancelle*. Struck 7.5.1892, lighter at Bastia for torpedo boats 1891-1897, sold at Bastia 3.7.1897 for 160 francs.

*Morbihan*. 5 men. On list 1.1879. At Lorient 1879-1896. Off main list 1896 and listed *pour ordre* with service craft at Lorient 1.1897, under commercial operation 1.1898-1.1907, not listed 1.1908.

*Courrier*. Built by Augustin Normand at Le Havre under a contract of 13.10.1879. Launched 1879 and completing when first listed 1.1880. On list 1.1880 as a *garde-pêche* à voiles, but was actually a cutter identical to *Pilotin* built for postal service between Gabon and São Tomé and Príncipe. Left Le Havre for Gabon under a merchant captain after running lights added 6.1880. Struck 16.11.1880 and turned over to colonial authorities in Gabon but still navy-manned 1888.

*Lamproie*. 9 tons, 8 men. On list 1.1881. At Lorient 1881-1896. Off main list 1896 and listed *pour ordre* with service craft at Lorient 1.1897, under commercial operation 1.1898, on special fisheries list 1908 at Auray, for sale at Lorient 1909-1911.

*Saumon*. 10 tons, 8 men. On list 1.1881. At Lorient 1.1881-1896. Off main list 1896 and listed *pour ordre* with service craft at Lorient 1.1897, under commercial operation 1.1898, on special fisheries list 1908 to 1912 at Auray.

*Dorade*. 5 tons, 5 men. On list 1.1882. At Rochefort 1882-1895. Off main list 1895 and listed as *garde-pêche* with service craft 1.1896. Struck 2.6.1896.

*Rouget*. On list 1.1882. At Rochefort 1882-1893. Struck 23.5.1893.

*Furet*. 10 tons, 9 men. On list 1.1882. Building 1.1882, at Toulon 1883-1896. Off main list 1896 and listed *pour ordre* with service craft at Toulon 1.1897, under commercial operation 1.1898-1.1907 (less

1.1903 and 1.1904), on special fisheries list 1908 to 1910 at Étang de Berre, for sale at Toulon 1911-1912.

---

*PILOTIN*. *Garde-pêche*. Schooner with a wooden hull for fishery protection and pilot training. One mast, schooner rig. Designed by Normand.

This schooner was attached to the school for piloting at Saint Servan. She was under commercial operation by January 1897 and off the fleet list for that reason in January 1908.

*The hull data are based on a devis dated 15.6.1878.*
**Dimensions & tons:** 14.31m wl, 14.03m pp (wl fwd to rudder) x 4.13m ext (above wl), 4.07m wl. 40t disp. Draught: 1.75m mean, 2.12m aft. Men: 8.
**Guns:** probably none.

*Pilotin* Augustin Normand, Le Havre.
On list 1.1879. K: 14.1.1878. L: 6.5.1878. C: 6.1878.
Annex to *Élan* at the school for piloting at Saint Servan 1878-83 (relieved *Colibri*, replaced by *Mutin*). Off main list 1896 and listed *pour ordre* with service craft at Brest and under commercial operation 1.1897, on special fisheries list 1908 to 1914 at Douarnenez.

---

*HARENG* Class. *Garde-pêche*. Schooners [cutter below] with wooden hulls for fishery protection and pilot training. One mast, topsail schooner rig, the second pair may have been yawl rigged. Designed by Normand.

Normand built the first pair in 1881 for regular fishery protection duty. The second pair appeared in the 1883 budget (submitted March 1882) for construction by contract and were built for the school for piloting at Saint Servan. These four ships remained in navy hands on the regular fleet list after the other fishery protection vessels were relisted in 1897-1898 as service craft and under commercial operation.

*The hull data are based on a devis for Mutin dated 10.8.1883.*
**Dimensions & tons:** 16.49m wl, 16.74m pp (wl fwd to rudder) x 4.84m ext (above wl), 4.71m wl. 55t disp. Draught: 1.62m mean, 2.19m aft. Men: 9.
**Guns:** probably none.

*Hareng* Augustin Normand, Le Havre.
On list 1.1881. K: 1881. L: 1881. C: 1882.
Rated cutter (*cotre*) 1.1908. Struck 1.7.1910, for sale at Cherbourg 1910-1911.

*Sardine* Augustin Normand, Le Havre.
On list 1.1881. K: 1.3.1881. L: 24.12.1881. C: c1882.
Struck 20.4.1904.

*Mutin* Augustin Normand, Le Havre.
On list 1.1883. K: 4.1.1883. L: 24.5.1883. C: 8.1883.
Budget 1883. Annex to *Élan* at the school for piloting at Saint Servan 1883-1914 (replaced *Pilotin*) and 1919-24 and to *Ancre* 1924-25. *Cotre* 1.1908. Renamed *Sylphe* 1925. Still listed 1.1936. Retired 1937.

*Railleur* Augustin Normand, Le Havre.
On list 1.1884. K: 15.10.1883. L: 14.3.1884. C: 1885.
Budget 1883. Annex to *Élan* at the school for piloting at Saint Servan 1884-1914 and 1919-24 and to *Ancre* 1924-27. *Cotre* 1.1908. Condemned 24.3.1937, hulk at Brest 1937-1939.

# Part Two

---

# The Fleets of the *Jeune École*, 1882-1897

During the 1880s and 1890s all navies had to adjust to fundamental technological challenges, above all the torpedo. In France this adjustment involved heated polemics in the press and in Parliament by partisans of the *Jeune École* (literally 'Young School') favouring torpedo boats as replacements for the *mastodontes* (mastodon battleships) while much of the navy and its civilian supporters defended the battleship as the only lasting form of sea power. In January 1886 Rear Admiral Aube, the naval leader of the *Jeune École*, became Minister of Marine and promptly stopped work on all battleships under construction. After exercises at sea showed that when faced by operational realities some of the more extreme *Jeune École* theories failed to meet expectations, he resumed some battleship construction work in 1887 without giving up his *Jeune École* ideas. By the end of the 1880s the views of the *Jeune École* had been adopted by the political left and, as Minister of Marine Barbey found in 1890, any attempt to build large battleships triggered withering partisan attacks in a legislature torn by a constant series of political crises culminating in the Panama scandal (1892-1893) and the Dreyfus Affair (1894-1906). The result was that by the end of 1897 the French had over 200 torpedo boats built or on order while their few new battleships had steadily decreased in size. Battleships of 14,000 tons were rejected under political pressure in 1890 in favour of 12,000-ton ships and further reductions followed to 11,000 tons in 1892 and a remarkable 8,700 tons in 1895. At the same time the British continued the series production of battleships of 14,800 and 13,000 tons, leading to a French qualitative as well as quantitative inferiority.

Naval planners also had to adjust to changes in the diplomatic and strategic situation. During the 1880s the alliance system in Europe that ultimately led to World War I began to take shape. The 1879 alliance between Germany and Austria was followed by the Triple Alliance between Germany, Austria, and Italy in 1882. The French had not forgotten the potential threat from Italy's large fast battleships against French coasts, and new concerns were aroused by the early renewal of the Triple Alliance in 1887, a bitter trade war lasting to 1895 that began when France refused to renew its commercial treaty with Italy because of her Triple Alliance membership, and the start of Italian development in 1888 of La Maddalena in northern Sardinia as a naval base following their 1887 naval manoeuvres. In late 1890 Minister of Marine Barbey asked his new *Conseil supérieur de la Marine* for a new naval programme focused exclusively on the Triple Alliance. The resulting programme included a largely traditional fleet of 24 battleships and 36 cruisers in European waters and another 34 cruisers for the overseas stations, with most of the *Jeune École*'s torpedo boats being assigned to coast defence along with 17 coast defence battleships. Two updates to the 1890 naval programme followed in 1894 and 1896, but the three programmes had little practical effect as Parliament had not been consulted about them and refused to be bound by them. Diplomacy began to produce a response to the Triple Alliance when, following a July 1891 visit of a French naval squadron to Kronshtadt, a convention was concluded between France and Russia in August 1892 and a military convention between the two Powers was completed in January 1894. The long economic recession ended when prices finally recovered in 1896, creating the possibility of larger budgets.

French ships benefited from many technological advances during the 1880s and 1890s. Improved artillery construction methods made possible the introduction of large and medium-sized *Modèle* 1887 guns with much longer bores (which otherwise would have suffered from barrel 'droop'), resulting in improvements in range, accuracy, and penetration. These longer guns used new slow-burning and smokeless powders ('Powder B' or *poudre blanche*) and in successive modifications during the 1890s (*Modèle* 1893 and 1896 variants) they received firing chambers with greater volumes optimized for the new powders. Also introduced were projectiles for medium calibre guns containing high explosives (melinite) and quick-firing medium calibre guns up to 164.7mm. Small (37mm and 47mm) rapid fire guns came into general use in the early 1880s, along with the need to protect ships against them. Face-hardened steel armour became available for battleships when French firms began licensing the Harvey process in 1893. Cruisers beginning with Émile Bertin's *Sfax* of 1882 acquired protective armoured decks, in some cases with cellular layers above them or armour on the sides, and battleships began to receive thin side protection above the main armour belt and over secondary batteries for protection against both melinite-filled shells and small calibre gunfire. Finally, Minister of Marine Aube in 1886 ordered construction of the first practical French submarine, *Gymnote*, and two more experimental boats followed during the 1890s.

The Navy's few combat operations during this period were all associated with France's efforts to extend her influence and ultimately her empire overseas. The most extensive were the primarily riverine operations between 1882 and 1885 to establish control over Tonkin and Annam. The Tonkin operation also led to a short maritime war with China in 1884-5 led by Vice Admiral Courbet, for which the Far East Naval Division was temporarily expanded to a Squadron (*Escadre*). The French also engaged in riverine combat in Madagascar in 1883-5 and 1895. Several classes of river gunboats were built for Tonkin between 1881 and 1886 and two classes were built for Madagascar in 1894-5, but such colonial activity remained on the periphery of overall French naval planning.

# Chapter Eight

# Battleships and Coast Defence Ships, 1882-1897

## I. BATTLESHIPS

### (A) Battleships (*Cuirassés d'escadre*).

#### Suspension and resumption of battleship construction, 1886-87

On 7 January 1886 Rear Admiral Hyacinthe Laurent Théophile Aube, the leader along with journalist Gabriel Charmes of the *Jeune École* that advocated among other things building torpedo boats in place of battleships, became Minister of Marine. On 27 January 1886 he suspended *Brennus* and *Charles Martel* (see Chapter 1) *sine die* and ordered work on them stopped. He then deleted funding for them from the draft 1887 budget, submitted on 16 March 1886. On 28 March 1886 Aube (who had become a vice admiral on the 17th) also suspended the construction of *Neptune* and *Magenta*, although he had funded them in the draft 1887 budget. Aube then conducted a series of tests of the ideas of the *Jeune École* regarding *torpilleurs autonomes* (with the 33-metre type) and *bateaux canons* (with *Gabriel Charmes*), finding that when faced by operational realities each fell seriously short of theoretical expectations. While not renouncing the theories of the *Jeune École* he included in his draft budget for 1888, submitted on 23 March 1887, funding for a full year's work during 1888 on *Neptune*, *Magenta*, and *Brennus*. In the meantime *Neptune* was launched in May 1887, possibly to clear the slip for the cruiser *Isly*. Aube left the ministry on 17 May 1887 and was replaced as Minister at the end of the month by Senator Édouard Barbey, who held the office until 4 December 1887. Construction resumed on *Neptune* and *Magenta* in late 1887.

#### New technologies

The advent in the late 1870s and early 1880s of small rapid fire guns like the 37mm Hotchkiss revolving cannon (also known as a revolver cannon) and 37mm and 47mm Hotchkiss QF guns presented two new problems to ship designers: how to protect against them and where to mount them. On 6 January 1885 the *Conseil des travaux* discussed how to protect guns in open barbettes and their crews against fire from these guns, particularly plunging fire from those high up in tops on masts, and recommended a thick cover over the rotating platform with a raised roof over the loading gear at the breech of the gun and an armoured position for the gun pointer. On 19 October 1886 the *Conseil des travaux* examined a proposal from the *Escadre d'évolutions* to use tripod masts with command platforms in battleships, and the Council recommended instead steel masts of large diameter containing spiral staircases and ammunition hoists, with enclosed tops for small rapid fire guns as well as for command platforms. These versatile but heavy structures became distinctive features of French battleship and cruiser designs for the next several years. Finally the advent in the mid-1880s of projectiles for medium calibre guns containing high explosives based on picric acid (melinite for the French, lyddite for the British) made it necessary to provide protection for secondary batteries, which had previously been unprotected.

#### Battleship specifications of 1887 (i)

On 10 June 1887 Minister of Marine Barbey asked the *Conseil des travaux* to recommend the general design parameters for a future battleship. The Council, in a marathon series of seven sessions ending on 26 July 1887, specified the artillery, protection, speed, and range of action for such a ship. A battleship's main battery needed to be able to penetrate 45 to 50cm of steel armour at 1,000m distance. The Council rejected 100-ton monster guns and selected the latest of the new types of smaller guns with a higher

initial velocity and a higher rate of fire, the 52-ton 340mm Model 1884 gun. The new ship should have at least three in either enclosed turrets or in barbette mountings (the latter with two abreast forward). With foreign navies now using 152mm guns for secondary batteries it was necessary to increase from the traditional 138.6mm gun to the new 164.7mm Model 1884 gun, of which the new ship should have at least ten. If the main battery was in turrets the height of the secondary guns above the waterline could be as low as 3.50m provided that at least half of them were notably higher. The ship should have one or two of the new heavy military masts, a good torpedo armament, and one 14-knot torpedo-capable vedette boat.

For protection the Council clung to the traditional French scheme of a complete end-to-end belt 2m high, of which 50cm was above the waterline, with a protective deck on top and a splinter deck underneath. It included cofferdams with small compartments along the sides behind the belt and above it, the latter being behind 12cm side armour. Maximum thicknesses were 45cm steel or compound armour for the belt (less at the ends), 80mm (including hull plating) for the primary deck, and 15mm for the splinter deck. The main guns were to have 45cm armour and barbettes were to have protection for pointers and loading gear equivalent to that given by enclosed turrets. Experiments with melinite shells against the old armoured corvette *Belliqueuse* showed that the secondary battery needed 12cm of armour. This battery was to be mounted in a citadel amidships with 12cm armour covering the entire height of the hull from the belt to the upper deck and with 12cm transverse bulkheads at the ends. Secondary guns in other locations were to receive the same protection.

A speed of 18 knots at forced draught was specified to match the big Italian battleships and the steaming range was set at 4,000nm at 10 knots. The Council calculated that this design could be achieved without a major increase in displacement over *Hoche* and the previous *Brennus* design and therefore set a maximum of 11,000 tons. The Council also felt that the ram bows of French battleships were way too long, creating huge bow waves and reducing speed and seakeeping qualities, and insisted that the ram should project only slightly from the bow.

---

***BRENNUS*** (ii). *Cuirassé d'escadre*. Battleship with two centreline main battery turrets (a twin forward and a single aft) and four single secondary battery turrets on the sides on top of a central citadel, a steel hull, and a straight bow. Two funnels, one military and one pole mast (after 1895 modifications). Designed by Huin.

On 27 August 1887 Minister of Marine Barbey transmitted to the ports the specifications for a *cuirassé d'escadre* produced by the *Conseil des travaux* on 26 July 1887 and asked them to submit designs. On 1 September 1887 Lorient sent to the ministry a statement of the state of *Brennus* at the time work was stopped. In early October Barbey asked Huin, the senior constructor at Lorient, if it would be possible to meet most of the August specifications while retaining the underwater portions (*oeuvres vives*) of the hull which had already been fabricated and in some cases laid on the building ways. Huin reported to the Maritime Prefect on 11 October that it would be possible to modify the design for the suspended *Brennus* to satisfy nearly completely the new specifications while using the work already done and added that the yard needed the work as soon as possible. Lorient forwarded Huin's report to Paris on 18 October and proposed resuming work. The Ministry replied on 26 October that for the moment resumption of work could not be authorized but asked Huin to continue his study

The battleship *Brennus* in her original configuration with heavy funnels, two military masts, and a high complete flying deck between them. In June 1894 she was found to have a catastrophic lack of stability and was extensively lightened in 1895. *(Musée de la Marine)*

of a redesigned *Brennus*. Huin submitted his proposal for the modification of *Brennus* on 6 December 1887, Barbey referred it to the *Conseil des travaux* on 9 December 1887 for examination, and on 15 December 1887 a new Minister, Deputy François Césaire de Mahy, called Huin and Saglio to Paris to participate in the discussion. On 24 December 1887 the *Conseil des travaux* examined designs for the transformation of *Brennus* from both Huin and naval constructor Laurent François Maurice Terré, then serving at Paris.

Huin's design for a modified *Brennus* had three 340mm guns in turrets (one twin and one single) patterned on those of *Hoche*, ten 164.7mm guns of which four were in armoured redoubts in the superstructure above the turrets and six were in a central citadel in the hull, and one military mast between the two funnels with the conning tower at its base. It measured 105.50m length between perpendiculars (the same as the suspended *Brennus*), 20.2m beam, 10,673 tons displacement, and 12,538ihp. Terré put his secondary battery in a central citadel with four barbette turrets on top, allowing four to fire forward and four aft, an arrangement that the Council felt was both better and lighter than Huin's. Huin was present during the Council's deliberations and proposed changes to respond to the Council's criticisms. He adopted Terré's arrangement of the secondary battery, the increase to two military masts, the placement of the conning tower forward of the funnels rather than between them, an increase in power to 13,500ihp, and Belleville boilers. He lengthened the bow by 3m to give it finer lines. He had reduced the armour on both turrets from 45cm to 40cm to stay under the weight limit, he restored the forward turret (but not the after one) to 45cm at the cost of reducing the maximum belt thickness from 45cm to 40cm. Only 17.5 knots could be guaranteed rather than the 18 knots in the August 1887 specifications. The changes added 104 tons to the design, which were compensated by lengthening the hull amidships by two frames (about 1 metre each). The Council accepted Huin's modified project because in most respects it closely followed the August 1887 programme, because it would give France a powerful battleship as early as possible, and because none of the designs received for completely new ships was entirely satisfactory. Minister de Mahy approved Huin's design in principle on 31 December 1887 and authorized resuming work on the ship while confirming the cancellation of *Charles Martel*. The discussion of detailed plans continued to the end of May 1888.

Contracts for main belt armour were approved on 1 October 1889 with Marrel Frères for lot D, Saint-Chamond for lot E, Schneider for lot F (steel), and Châtillon et Commentry for lot G. Saint-Chamond was authorized on 16 November 1889 to substitute steel for compound in Lot E but apparently supplied compound as did Marrel and Châtillon. Contracts were then approved on 27 November 1890 with Châtillon et Commentry for armour for the forward turret and with Marrel for the after turret. Contracts were approved on 17 June 1891 with Châtillon et Commentry for steel armour for the central citadel (Lot K) and with Marrel for the thin steel side armour above the belt (Lot L). Finally a contract was approved on 23 September 1891 with Saint-Étienne for four armoured 164.7mm turrets. Iron deck armour was ordered on 8 March 1889 from the Navy's forge at Guérigny (Forges de la Chaussade).

Huin probably showed the 28.5-calibre 340mm M1884 gun on his design for *Brennus*, but on 4 July 1888 plans were approved for a much longer 42-calibre 340mm M1887 gun with a higher initial velocity, and this gun was used in subsequent design work. Her engines were the first triple expansion engines built at Indret for a large ship. A fifth torpedo tube aft in the Admiral's cabin on early plans was deleted before completion in 1894 and a sixth in the bow between the hawse pipes was deleted even earlier. Several suggestions to add a small ram to the bow were rejected because the lengthened bow was not strong enough for ramming. On 19 December 1890 the artillery directorate reported that the 164.7mm guns would be converted to QF guns using metal powder casings, requiring increasing the diameter of the turrets, although only slow-firing BL guns were available when the ship was completed in 1894.

On 17 June 1894 the usual stability trials conducted upon completion of fitting out revealed a catastrophic lack of stability. With the turrets trained on the beam and crew lined up on the rail, the ship heeled 28 degrees and the casemate 164.7mm guns dipped below the water for half of their length. She could not right herself because of the wide armour shelf that was now 20cm below the waterline. The ship moved from Lorient to Brest and began trials in this condition, but the trials were soon suspended. On 17 October 1894 Brest submitted a proposal for lightening the ship which was discussed by the *Conseil des travaux* on 30 October 1894. It concluded that there was 412 tons of excess weight, mostly high in the ship. Huin took much of the blame for this situation, though in many cases the reasons for his actions were acknowledged to be well founded.

Minister of Marine Deputy Félix Faure ordered on 15 November and 8 December 1894 numerous steps to remedy the problems which Brest further developed in subsequent studies. These included cutting back the superstructure projections above the turrets and to the sides, lowering the superstructure by deleting the deck linking the forward and after bridges, replacing the military mainmast with a simple pole mast, and removing the heavy funnel tops and cutting down the outer casings of the funnels. The armour shelf was filled in with a light timber caisson covered with steel plating so it would not prevent the ship from righting itself. The opportunity was also taken to replace the original M1887 164.7mm secondary battery guns with the M1893 QF model. A second stability trial on 22 December 1895 was considered successful. There was no remedy, however, for the fact that the turrets were not balanced and when they were trained on the beam the upper edge of the main armour belt was level with the water, and for future battleships the French insisted on balanced turrets. Gunnery trials during her transit from Brest to Toulon in January 1896 showed that the rate of fire of the 340mm guns was 1 round every 4 minutes.

On 27 February 1906 Vice Admiral Touchard, the commander of the *Escadre de la Méditerranée* recommended lightening the ship again to allow her to carry adequate amounts of fuel and ammunition. He proposed removing several superstructure decks, and it was later also proposed to replace the military mast with a pole. Discussions dragged on until Minister of Marine Alfred Picard on 10 April 1909 ordered Toulon to do only the work that could be done without delaying the completion of the current overhaul, which he defined on 7 July 1909 as the removal of the forward half of the forward upper bridge including the pilot house (an open steering position was to be retained on this level) and trimming back the overhang of the top of the conning tower. Equipment for hand-loading the 340mm guns to improve rates of fire was installed between early 1909 and January 1911 but it is not known whether test firings were ever conducted. All additional work on the ship was stopped at the end of 1911 when the 1912 naval programme listed her as to be struck in 1913.

*The characteristics are based on a devis dated 1894 for the ship as completed at Lorient and on a devis dated 18.1.1896 for the ship as lightened at Brest.*

**Dimensions & tons:** 114.446m oa, 114.181m wl, 110.300m pp (wl fwd to rudder) x 20.620m ext (above wl), 20.416m wl. As designed: 10,983.243t disp, Draught: 7.876m mean, 8.000m aft (actual), 8.189m (keel line projected). Actual in 1894: 11,395.083t disp, Draught: 8.108m mean, 8.335m aft (actual), 8.524m (keel line projected). Men: 667. Actual in 1896: 11,370.694t disp, Draught: 8.094m mean, 8.600m aft (keel line projected).

**Machinery:** 13,486ihp (13,500ihp) max designed at 90rpm and 17kg/cm$^2$ boiler pressure (12kg/cm$^2$ at the engines). Trials (9.1.1896) 13,950.3ihp = 17.107kts at 91.905rpm and 15.689kg/cm$^2$ boiler pressure. 2 screws. 2 vertical triple expansion engines with direct connecting rods and 4 cylinders of 1.140m (1), 1.650m (1) and 1.920m (2) diameter and 1.100m stroke. 32 Belleville boilers. 701.500t coal (610t normal, only 250t coal was actually embarked in 1894). Range (1896) 2,805nm @ 11.860kts.

**Armour:**
Side: Belt at waterline (compound and Creusot steel) 400mm amidships, 300mm fwd, 300mm aft, all on 30mm plating. Total height amidships 2.100m of which 0.24m above wl. Side above belt (steel) 100mm on 25mm plating, height 1.200m.
Guns: Main turrets including fixed bases (compound) 455mm forward turret, 405mm after turret, both on 30mm plating. Secondary turrets (steel) 100mm on 20mm plating. Citadel for secondary guns (steel) 100mm sides and ends on 20mm plating. 20mm internal splinter bulkheads.
Decks: Armoured deck (iron) 60mm on 20mm hull plating outside the citadel, 50mm on 20mm hull plating within it (totals 80mm and 70mm). Deck at top of citadel 20mm reinforcement plating on 20mm regular plating.
Conning tower: (hammered and laminated steel) 120mm on 20mm plating.

**Guns:**
(1894) 3 x 340mm/42 M1887 (2 *à corps court* [short body] in twin turret forward and 1 *à corps long* [long body] in single turret aft, both on centreline), 10 x 164.7mm/45 M1887 (4 in single turrets and 6 in the citadel on the sides amidships), 4 x 65mm/50 M1891 QF, 2 x 65mm/16 M1881 boat and landing, 14 x 47mm/40 M1885 QF, 1 x 47mm revolving cannon (for the boats), 14 x 37mm.
**Torpedoes:** 4 tubes for 450mm M1889 torpedoes above water.
**Searchlights:** 6 x 60cm.
(1896) Same as in 1894 except the 164.7mm were upgraded to M1893 special QF, the 47mm revolving cannon was deleted, and many small guns and one searchlight were repositioned.
(1900) 3 x 340mm, 10 x 164.7mm, 4 x 65mm QF, 14 x 47mm, 2 x 37mm (for the boats), and possibly 2 x 65mm landing. The four torpedo tubes were landed 4.1906 and 2 x 47mm were landed 10.1909.

*Brennus* Lorient Dyd/Indret (engines designed by Garnier).
On list 1.1888. Ord: 31.12.1887. K: 2.1.1889. L: 17.10.1891. Comm: 16.12.1893 (trials) and 1.8.1895 (trials after lightening), 9.1.1896 (full).
Budget 1888. Machinery installed 1.12.1891 to 12.1.1894 (8.5.1894 for the port engine). Boilers first lit off 12.1.1894. Manning complete for trials 25.7.1894, left Lorient 2.8.1894 for Brest to run trials. Began underway trials 5.9.1894 but then suspended them pending lightening the ship. Underway trials resumed 21.8.1895. Began to go into full commission 25.12.1895, final trial successful 9.1.1896 and placed in full commission (*armement définitif*) same date. Admitted to active service (*admis au service actif*) 11.1.1896 to replace *Formidable* as flagship of the *Escadre de la Méditerranée*. Accepted for service (*clôture d'armement*) 20.1.1896. From Brest to Toulon 20-26.1.1896. Vice Admiral Gervais shifted his flag from *Formidable* to *Brennus* 1.4.1896. The destroyer *Framée* crossed her bow and was sunk 10-11.8.1900. *Brennus* was relieved by *Saint Louis* as flagship of the *Escadre de la Méditerranée* on 30.9.1900, but she remained popular because of her spacious flag accommodations and usually had a flag embarked while in the *Escadre*'s reserve and training divisions. To normal reserve

The battleship *Brennus* transiting the canal at Bizerte early in her career after lightening, possibly on 14 May 1896 when she and *Redoutable* were the first large French warships to pass through it and enter Lake Bizerte. The lightening included the replacement of the after military mast with a pole. *(Postcard by ND)*

25.8.1907 for overhaul and additional superstructure reductions. Recommissioned 15.11.1909 as flagship of a new division of torpedo boat schools at Toulon in which *Marceau* was the school for torpedo boat seamen. Machinery and standard gunnery trials 6-7.1910, then intermittent local operations through 9.1911 including to the Salins d'Hyères. Relieved by *D'Entrecasteaux* 1.1.1912 and to special reserve 1.2.1912. Definitively decommissioned 1.4.1914 (with *Charles Martel*, *Carnot*, and *Masséna*), decommissioning completed 25.6.1914 and handed over to port authorities. Barracks hulk for mobilisation crews at Toulon 6.1914. In 1915 her three 340mm guns, along with four similar guns from *Valmy* and *Jemmapes* and two spare guns, were removed and sent to Ruelle to be re-bored as 400mm M1915 howitzers for use on the front. Condemned 22.8.1919. Struck 30.10.1919, for sale at Toulon 1920-1921. Taken off sale and handed over 13.1.1921 as part payment to the firm breaking up *Liberté* (Boursier, Borrely and Sidensner). BU at Toulon 1922.

---

### Battleship specifications of 1887 (ii)

The designs for new ships produced in response to the specifications of July 1887 were reviewed by the Council on 24 January 1888. None was found satisfactory and two designers including Huin (whose design closely resembled his original *Brennus* modification project) were asked to revise their plans. The revisions were examined a year and a half later, on 30 July 1889. The Council's staff recommended accepting Huin's *Brennus*-type design with additional changes but the Council itself decided that with the increasing use of 340mm main battery guns and melinite explosives since July 1887 it was necessary to conduct some experiments and then draft a new set of specifications.

### Battleship specifications of 1890 with 340mm guns

Senator Édouard Barbey returned to the Ministry for a second time on 10 November 1889 and asked for new specifications for battleships, which the *Conseil des travaux* developed between 10 and 24 December 1889. The report to the Council by its drafting committee opened with a statement that the laying down by Britain of 14,000-ton battleships (the Naval Defence Act had just been passed) obliged France to follow suit. Barbey's brand new *Conseil supérieur de la Marine*, established by a decree of 5 December 1889, felt that the real threat was not the British but the large fast battleships that Italy had just concentrated at La Maddalena at the north end of Sardinia. Given the size of the threats the drafting committee did not start with a limit on displacement but instead formulated specifications for a battleship that would yield nothing to the foreign battleships that might oppose it. Barbettes mountings for the main battery and unprotected batteries for secondary guns as in the *Marceau* and earlier types would no longer suffice because of the advent of QF guns and melinite explosives. The committee strongly opposed twin turrets as in *Brennus* for both operational and vulnerability reasons and instead adopted a main battery of four single turrets, for which it felt the best arrangement was a lozenge as in *Marceau*. Four of the new 340mm Model 1887 guns in four enclosed turrets would be too heavy even for a 14,000-ton ship, but the penetration capabilities of the Model 1887 guns were so much better than those of previous models that the 274.4mm Model 1887, which also had a more rapid rate of fire and was easier to handle, would be ample for all but the forward turret, producing a main battery of one 340mm M1887 and three 274.4mm M1887 guns. The committee also adopted the 138.6mm gun for the secondary battery on the grounds that there was not much different between its performance and that of the 164.7mm gun against the 13cm armour used by the British on their latest secondary batteries. (Not mentioned was the additional fact that a quick fire 138.6mm gun was available while a quick fire 164.7mm gun had not yet been developed.) It placed eight of these guns in single turrets like those in *Dupuy de Lôme* and *Chanzy* on the sides and two more in the bow and stern, an arrangement that it preferred to the citadel with turrets in *Brennus*. The protection

scheme was to be as in earlier French battleships with a two-metre high complete belt with a maximum thickness of 45cm and a 90mm (including 20mm plating) deck on top. Also specified were two military masts with QF guns in the tops and propulsion with either two or three screws. Consulted on these specifications during the meetings, the *Conseil supérieur* demanded two 340mm guns instead of one, which was offset by the deletion of the 138.6mm guns in the bow and stern producing an armament of two 340mm, two 274.4mm, and eight 138.6mm guns. The speed was to be 17 knots at natural draught with the possibility of jets of steam in the funnels producing a higher speed for a few instants. (This did not match the 18 knots of which the Italian ships were thought to be capable.) The displacement of the resulting ship was calculated by different members at between 13,500 and 14,300 tons, which both Councils limited to 14,000 tons.

Minister Barbey sent these specifications to the ports on 4 January 1890, his only change being to make twin screws mandatory. The two Councils, however, by ignoring tonnage limits had put the Minister in a difficult position politically. Barbey soon faced a firestorm of opposition in the Chamber of Deputies and in the press from the partisans of the *Jeune École* to *mastodantes*, battleships in any form but particularly 14,000-ton ones. He drew back and asked Director of Material Bienaymé to look for ways to reduce the displacement by giving up some of the specifications. On 18 January 1890 Bienaymé confirmed that the existing specifications would result in a 14,000-ton ship and reported that replacing the two 340mm guns with two 274.4mm guns would save 2,000 tons. On 23 January 1890 Barbey issued another directive to the ports that asked the designers to provide second designs with a main battery of four 274.4mm guns and with the displacement reduced to 11,000 tons in parallel with the designs requested on 4 January 1890. The budget for 1891 was submitted on 22 February 1890 with three new battleships.

The *Conseil des travaux* examined the designs received from four naval constructors in reponse to the two directives on 12 June 1890. The responses to the original specifications of 24 December 1889 fell into the low 13,000-ton range, that of Huin measuring 13,273 tons and that of Saglio measuring 13,036 tons. None completely met the specifications but the Council invited two of the authors, Huin and Saglio, to modify their submissions and gave them lists of desired corrections. Turning to the designs limited to 11,000 tons (Huin's measured 11,204 tons) and with four 274.4mm guns, the Council stated that to meet that limit the authors had had to cut much more deeply into various design elements than the specifications of 23 January 1890 allowed, most notably the armour protection and the weight margin, and it summarily rejected all of the 11,000-ton designs.

### The Programme of 1890

The renewal in February 1887 of the Triple Alliance between Germany, Austria, and Italy drew new attention to the threat to French coasts from fast Italian battleships operating from La Maddalena, and naval scares followed in the French Parliament and press in both 1888 and 1889. In 1888 the Budget Commission for the first time in a decade advocated a French 'two-power' standard against the two principal navies of continental Europe (Germany and Italy), and in 1889 France experienced a full scale big-navy agitation with public opinion demanding a greater naval force, although primarily for coast defence. The navy responded in 1889 with summer manoeuvres focused on the problem, after which Minister Barbey asked his new *Conseil supérieur*, which had replaced the *Conseil d'Amirauté* on 21 October 1890 for handling issues relating to strategy and fleet structure, what should be the regular composition of a fleet (*armée navale*), a squadron (*escadre*), and a division in a battle fleet focused entirely on the Triple Alliance. Of the three other fleets in the Programme of 1872, the transport fleet disappeared completely, the coast defence fleet was assigned a strictly defensive role to free the battle fleet for offensive operations, and the station fleet was given the older cruisers that were useless elsewhere (although replacements were provided for). The programme contained no commerce-raiding cruisers and no funds for overseas coaling stations. The battle fleet was to remain on the defensive against Germany but fall with all its might on the Italians. The Council concluded on 22 November 1890 that the division was the basic tactical unit of the battle fleet and should consist of 3 battleships, 3 squadron cruisers (1 first, 1 second, and 1 third class), 1 *contre-torpilleur* or torpedo cruiser, and 5 seagoing torpedo boats. The squadron should consist of two divisions and have in addition 2 cruisers, one commercial resupply ship, and one torpedo boat transport. The navy's combat fleet would consist of four squadrons, which would thus have 24 battleships (the number then in the fleet including those building) supported by 84 warships of different types (32 cruisers, 8 *contre-torpilleurs*, 40 seagoing torpedo boats, and 4 torpedo boat transports). The squadron cruisers (see Chapter 9) would be of three types, the large ones of the *Jean Bart* type, the 2nd class of an enlarged *Davout* type, and the 3rd class of an enlarged, improved, and above all stronger *Forbin* type. The coast defence fleet consisted of ships already existing, while the station fleets were to be led by 8,000-ton protected cruisers instead of station battleships whose number was to be twice that of the number of stations so they could be periodically relieved. The Director of Materiel with the Chief of the Naval General Staff and the director of the Minister's cabinet then converted this guidance into a full naval programme which he reported on 18 March 1891 and in a revised form on 2 July 1891. The final July 1891 version is included in Appendix F along with the other French naval programmes. Approval by Parliament was never sought nor received and the annual battles over the budget left it consistently underfunded.

---

*CHARLES MARTEL* (ii). *Cuirassé d'escadre.* Battleship with four single main battery turrets in a lozenge layout (two centreline turrets at the ends and two on the sides amidships) and eight single secondary battery turrets on the sides. Two funnels, two military masts. Designed by Huin.

On 4 July 1890 Director of Materiel Bienaymé reported to Minister Barbey that the *Conseil des travaux* on 12 June 1890 had identified Huin's 13,273-ton design and the one by Saglio as suitable for further work but that once the Council's suggestions were incorporated the displacement of Huin's design would approach 14,000 tons. On the other had the Council, reflecting the views of many flag officers, firmly rejected the armament of four 274.4mm guns as inadequate and wanted greater penetration power for two of the guns on the new battleships. To accomplish this while restraining displacement Bienaymé and the Director of Artillery proposed using a new 305mm gun that was in development. It could pierce 45cm armour at twice the range that the 274.4mm gun could. A ship thus armed would displace 11,800 tons. On 14 August 1890 Barbey directed Huin and Saglio to proceed with the changes to their original designs that the Council had requested on 12 June 1890 but also directed the replacement of the two 340mm guns with two of the new 305mm Model 1887 guns. He set the armour for the 305mm turrets at 40cm and for the 274.4mm turrets at 35cm.

By making these reductions himself Barbey relieved the Council of responsibility for them, and when it reviewed the two revised designs on 29 August 1890 it concentrated on ensuring that the designs responded to the changes it had requested in June and met Barbey's August directive. It approved Huin's design dated 12 August 1890, now measuring 11,882 tons, subject to a few final changes including lowering the point of the ram from 1.5m to 2.5m below the waterline, changing the funnel casings from rectangular to circular, and adding four 47mm QF guns for a total of 12. It also preferred the single-piece 138.6mm turret developed by Saglio and adopted by Huin to the two-part model in *Dupuy-de-Lôme* in the specifications. The torpedo tube battery at this time was four on the sides and one just added in the bow. On 10 September 1890 Barbey directed Brest to begin construction of a battleship that would carry the name *Charles Martel*. The ship's physical keel laying followed on 1 August 1891.

The belt armour was ordered in four lots, one of hammered steel from

Schneider and three of compound metal from Marrel Frères, Saint-Chamond and Châtillon et Commentry. About two thirds of the belt was compound and one third steel. This was the first use of nickel steel in belt armour in France. Schneider had just developed this alloy, which it demonstrated in competitive trials at Annapolis in 1890, but it could not make enough to fill the navy's needs. The thin steel side armour above the belt and over the cofferdam was supplied by Marrel. Schneider also contracted for the engines and boilers on 26 August 1891 and the turrets and their machinery on 17 February 1892.

As early as August 1891 concerns arose that the ship would be overweight. In 1893 the design of the superstructure was modified to reduce its weight and also reduce the target that it provided to enemy high explosive shells. Two small redoubts placed under the longitudinal bridge, one forward and one aft, whose only purpose was to accommodate two 47mm guns each, were suppressed, the guns being relocated. The Admiral's smoking gallery was suppressed, to be replaced in this function by the deck aft of the Admiral's cabins on either side of the after 305mm turret. The flare locker was also suppressed, the flares being stowed elsewhere. With the structures under the longitudinal bridge (flying deck) thus being eliminated, the bridge was lowered to 4m above the deck and the conning tower was also lowered. The foremast was reduced in height to match the after mast. Brest's plan for the ship had a torpedo tube in the stern firing aft; this had been suppressed in *Brennus* and *Jauréguiberry* and was now suppressed in this ship too. In December 1895 the reserve margin was calculated at 46.313 tons, well under the 350 tons in Huin's original design but considered acceptable in this late stage of construction. As built the two military masts were identical, with an observation platform above the bridges surmounted in order by a top armed with 47mm guns, a top with 37mm guns (although the forward top received no guns), and a searchlight platform.

*The characteristics are based on a devis dated 30.7.1897.*
**Dimensions & tons:** 121.594m oa, 119.684m wl, 115.506m pp (tip fwd to rudder) x 21.714m ext (21.678 at beam turrets), 21.654m wl. 11,879.995t disp. Draught: 7.999m mean, 8.289m aft. Men: 647 without flag, 694 with.
**Machinery:** 13,500ihp designed at 95rpm and 15kg/cm² boiler pressure (12kg/cm² at the engines). Trials (5.5.1897) 14,997.33ihp = 18.128kts at 96.494rpm and 12.625kg/cm² boiler pressure. 2 screws. 2 vertical triple expansion engines with 3 cylinders of 1.130m, 1.700m, and 2.680m diameter and 1.100m stroke. 24 Lagrafel et d'Allest water tube boilers built by Fraissinet & Cie. 657t coal. Range (c1905) 2,340nm @ 10kts with 638t coal.
**Armour:**
Side: Belt at waterline (compound for plates 1-24, hammered steel plates 25-46, plates 1 and 2 being in the bow and 45 and 46 in the stern) 450mm amidships, 350mm fwd, 310mm aft. Total height amidships 2.000m of which 0.58m above normal load waterline. Side above belt (steel) 100mm on 20mm plating, height amidships 1.193m.
Guns: Four main turrets (hammered steel) 370mm with 320mm fixed bases (forged steel), both on 30mm plating. 138.6mm turrets (steel) 100mm with 100mm fixed bases (forged steel), both on 20mm plating.
Decks: Armoured deck (iron) 70mm on centreline, 100mm outboard, both on 20mm hull plating. Splinter deck 25mm hull plating.
Conning tower (steel): 230mm on 30mm plating.
**Guns:**
(1897) 2 x 305mm/45 M1887 (single turrets at ends) 2 x 274.4mm/45 M1887 (single turrets on sides), 8 x 138.6mm/45 M1891(2) QF (single turrets on sides), 4 x 65mm/50 M1891 QF, 2 x 65mm/16 M1881 landing, 18 x 47mm/40 M1885 QF, 5 x 37mm/20 M1885 QF.
**Torpedoes:** 4 tubes for 450mm M1892 torpedoes (2 submerged and 2 above water). **Searchlights:** 6 x 60cm.
(1906) 2 x 305mm, 2 x 274.4mm, 8 x 138.6mm, 4 x 65mm, 2 x 65mm

landing, 18 x 47mm QF, 2 x 37mm QF (for the boats). **Torpedoes:** 2 submerged tubes. The two above water tubes were removed 14.6.1906.

*Charles Martel* Brest Dyd/Schneider, Creusot.
On list 1.1891. Ord: 10.9.1890. K: 1.8.1891. L: 29.8.1893.
     Comm: 10.1.1896 (trials), 20.2.1897 (full).
Budget 1891. Engine contract 26.8.1891. Machinery installed 24.1.1894 to 24.9.1895, boilers first lit off 28.5.1895. Trials at Brest.5.1896 to 2.1897. Attached temporarily to the *Escadre du Nord* 14.9.1896 to 16.10.1896 for the visit to Cherbourg of the Tsar. From Brest to Toulon in full commission 8-15.3.1897, more trials 5-6.1897, admitted to active service 20.7.1897. Joined the *Escadre de la Méditerranée* at Toulon 2.8.1897, division flag embarked from 26.9.1897 to 1.5.1902, then operated with reserve divisions of the *Escadre de la Méditerranée* until reassigned with *Masséna* to training duty at Toulon 4.1908. Transferred to Cherbourg, then Brest, 11.1909. To normal reserve at Cherbourg 1.3.1912 and special reserve there 1.7.1912. Moved to Brest 7.4.1913 and moored at Landévennec. Definitively decommissioned 1.4.1914 (with *Brennus*, *Carnot*, and *Masséna*), decommissioning complete 9.5.1914 and handed over to port authorities at Brest as a barracks hulk, which was briefly used in late 1914 for German prisoners before they could be transferred ashore. Eight boilers were removed during the war for use in new *Aurochs* class patrol tugs. The 274.4mm guns were landed on 6.9.1916 and converted to railway guns, the 305mm were converted at Ruelle to 370mm M1915 mortars, and the 138.6mm guns became mobile land artillery in 1916.

The battleship *Charles Martel*, probably after arriving at Cherbourg from Toulon in October 1909. She is wearing the uniform bluish-grey paint scheme adopted in 1908 in place of the traditional two-tone black and 'wet canvas' (*toile moullée*) scheme. The card was mailed in 1913. *(Postcard by P.B. Cherbourg)*

Condemned 8.1919, Struck 30.10.1919. Sold 20.12.1920 at Brest to Frank Rijsdijk' Scheepssloperij, Dordrecht, Holland and towed to Hendrik Ido Ambacht to BU.

———

**CARNOT (ex *LAZARE CARNOT*).** *Cuirassé d'escadre.* Battleship with four single main battery turrets in a lozenge layout and eight single secondary battery turrets on the sides. Two funnels, one military and one pole mast (after 1896 modifications). Designed by Saglio.

The design history of Saglio's *Carnot* was essentially the same as that of Huin's *Charles Martel* up to 29 August 1890, when the *Conseil des travaux* approved both designs subject to some final revisions. For *Carnot*, the Council asked for the removal of the shelters overhanging the main battery turrets whose purpose was to provide access to the latter through the turret roofs. (These were probably similar to the overhanging structures in Huin's early designs for *Brennus* and *Charles Martel*.) A distinctive feature of Saglio's design was that the upper works were set well back from the curved hull sides to produce a steady gun platform, a feature also evident in de Bussy's *Masséna*. The torpedo battery at this time was two tubes in the bow firing forward, two on the sides, and a fifth in the stern. On 10 September 1890 Minister Barbey approved Saglio's new design with some reservations and ordered a ship of the type built at Toulon under the name *Lazare Carnot*. On 20 October 1890 Toulon forwarded the design of Saglio modified in response to Barbey's directive of 10 September 1890. The steel belt was supplied by Schneider and Saint-Chamond, each delivering two lots, Saint-Chamond also supplied steel armour for all the turrets and Marrel Frères iron deck armour. In early 1891 the engines were assigned to Indret. They were to be as those in *Brennus* except that the rotational speed was to be increased from 90 to 96rpm at maximum power with forced draught, raising the power of the two engines at forced draught from 13,020 (13,486 including auxiliaries) to 15,440ihp. The funnels were of unequal

Collection P. B., Cherbourg

The battleship *Carnot*, shown between 1903, when the bulwarks on the upper foretop under the searchlight were deleted, and 1905 when the round position for the admiral below the lower foretop was removed. *(Postcard by ND)*

size, the wider rectangular forward one serving two thirds of the boilers. Static machinery trials were completed on 3 January 1896 but underway trials were delayed until the hull was ready. It then became clear that the ship was overweight and of questionable stability and the bridgework and military masts were substantially reduced, the foremast being lightened and the after military mast being removed altogether and replaced with a light pole. The designed light armament of four 65mm QF on the fore and aft superstructures, eight 47mm QF on the main bridge and in the tops, and eight 37mm revolving cannon was also altered as commissioned.

On 6 December 1897 Minister of Marine Vice Admiral Armand Louis Charles Gustave Besnard directed that flag facilities be removed from the ship, and she served her entire career as a private ship. The conspicuous cylindrical observation post for the admiral around the base of the foremast was not removed until October 1905. Curiously the ship steered better after it was removed. During gunnery exercise in August 1907 excessive motion during recoil was noted in the forward 305mm turret. This were traced to weaknesses in the foundation low in the ship on which the pivot column (*fût-pivot*) of the turret rotated, and similar problems were also found under the after 305mm turret. Further examination during repairs in 1908 (which involved pulling the turrets) showed that some rivets in this structure were loose and others were missing altogether. Repairs were completed in May 1909 and the ship returned to full commission on 5 October 1909. During 1911 similar signs of fatigue appeared in the foundations of the 274.4mm turrets but these were satisfactorily remedied and the ship continued to operate with the fleet until going into normal reserve at Brest on 7 May 1913 and special reserve on 11 November 1913 preparatory to disposal. One reason that the turret problems had not been discovered earlier was that as of 1908 the forward 305mm turret had fired only 36 rounds with full combat charges while the after turret had fired only 44.

*The characteristics are based on a devis dated 25.6.1897.*

**Dimensions & tons:** 117.000m oa, 115.160m wl, 114.000m pp (tip fwd to rudder) x 21.500m ext & wl (22.500m outside turrets). 12,146.337t disp. Draught: 7.973m mean, 8.317m aft. Men: 654 including 32 officers (1900).

**Machinery:** 15,000ihp designed (including 504ihp for the air, circulating, and feed pumps) at 96rpm and 15kg/cm² boiler pressure (12kg/cm² at the engines). Trials (29.12.1896) 16,344.31ihp = 17.865kts at 106.025rpm and 13.544kg/cm² boiler pressure. 2 screws. 2 vertical triple expansion engines with 4 cylinders of 1.140m (1), 1.650m (1), and 1.920m (2) diameter and 1.100m stroke. 24 Lagrafel et d' Allest water tube boilers. 724t coal (700t normal). Range 3843.4nm @ 11.50kts.

**Armour:**

Side (steel): Belt at waterline 450mm amidships, 350mm fwd, 240mm aft. Total height amidships 2.000m of which 0.40m above normal load waterline. Side above belt 100mm on 20mm plating, height 2.500m (probably less except in bow).

Guns (steel): Four main turrets 370mm with 320mm fixed bases. 138.6mm turrets 100mm on 20mm plating.

Decks: Armoured deck (iron) 70mm on 20mm hull plating. Splinter deck 20mm plating.

Conning tower (steel): 230mm on 20mm plating.

**Guns:**

(1897) 2 x 305mm/45 M1887 (single turrets at ends), 2 x 274.4mm/45 M1887 (single turrets on sides), 8 x 138.6mm/45 M1891(2) QF (single turrets on sides), 4 x 65mm/50 M1891 QF, 2 x 65mm/16 M1881 landing, 16 x 47mm/40 M1885 QF, 5 x 37mm/20 M1885 QF, 3 x 37mm revolving cannon. **Torpedoes:** 2 submerged tubes for 450mm M1892 torpedoes. (2 above-water tubes were deleted on 7.7.1896 during trials to save weight.) **Searchlights:** 6 x 60cm.

(1900) 2 x 305mm, 2 x 274.4mm, 8 x 138.6mm, 4 x 65mm QF, 18 x 47mm, 2 x 37mm (for the boats). **Torpedoes:** 2 submerged tubes.

*Carnot* Toulon Dyd/Indret.

On list 1.1.1891. Ord: 10.9.1890. K: 14.7.1891. L: 12.7.1894. Comm:
  17.3.1896 (trials), 1.3.1897 (full).

Budget 1891. The ceremonial first rivet was driven on 8.8.1891 by
  President of the Republic Sadi Carnot, grandson of Lazare Carnot who
  had organized the victory in 1793 of the revolutionary French republic
  and for whom the ship was named. The official keel laying followed
  two days later. She was renamed *Carnot* on 7.7.1894 after the assassi-
  nation of President Carnot to remember them both. Machinery
  installed 2.1895 to 27.12.1895 when the boilers were first lit off. Trials
  5.1896 to 4.1897. Admitted to active service 25.6.1897 and joined the
  *Escadre de la Méditerranée* 25.6.1897. Reassigned to the north in 1900,
  to the Mediterranean in 1901, to the North in 1904, and to the
  Mediterranean in 1907. In normal reserve at Toulon for repairs to turret bases 8.12.1907 to 7.6.1909. To the north again 1910, to normal
  reserve at Brest 2.5.1913. Definitively decommissioned 1.4.1914 (with
  *Brennus*, *Charles Martel*, and *Masséna*), decommissioning completed
  9.5.1914 and handed over to port authorities at Brest as a barracks
  hulk, including for German prisoners. 274.4mm guns removed 1916,

the 305mm and 138.6mm were also removed. Some boilers used in
new *Aurochs* class patrol tugs. Struck 30.10.1919, sold by the
Domaines at Brest on 8.4.1920 to Frank Rijsdijk' Scheepssloperij,
Dordrecht, Holland. Overtaken by a storm 6.1920 while under tow to
Hendrik Ido Ambacht, capsized and sank.

————

**JAURÉGUIBERRY.** *Cuirassé d'escadre.* Battleship with four single main
battery turrets in a lozenge layout and four twin secondary battery turrets
on the sides. Two funnels, two military masts. Designed by Lagane (FCM
La Seyne).

In its session of 12 June 1890 in which the *Conseil des travaux* examined
designs for 13,000-ton and 11,000-ton battleships from four constructors
it also examined a single design of 11,597 tons by Amable Lagane, shipyard
director at the Forges et Chantiers de la Méditerranée at La Seyne. It criticised this design for several reasons including the location of the main guns
too far from the centre of the ship, the use of electricity to operate the main
turrets, and the use of twin turrets for the secondary battery. On 23 July
1890 Minister of Marine Barbey asked Lagane to revise his plans with

---

Outboard profile and overhead view (*plan d'ensemble*) of the battleship
*Jauréguiberry*, built at La Seyne on plans by the director of the yard, Lagane. The
undated plan by the Forges et Chantiers de la Méditerranée carries the names of
Lagane and the Navy's control officer, Opin. The small calibre artillery carried at
this time included 4 x 65mm M1891 QF guns (on the amidships bridge at the

shelter deck level), 12 x 47mm QF guns (4 on the lower forward bridge, 4 on
the after bridge, and 4 in two lower tops), 4 x 37mm QF guns (in two upper
tops), and 8 x 37mm revolving cannon (2 in the upper forward bridge, 2 in the
after bridge, and 4 in two upper tops). there were also 2 x 65mm M1881
landing guns.

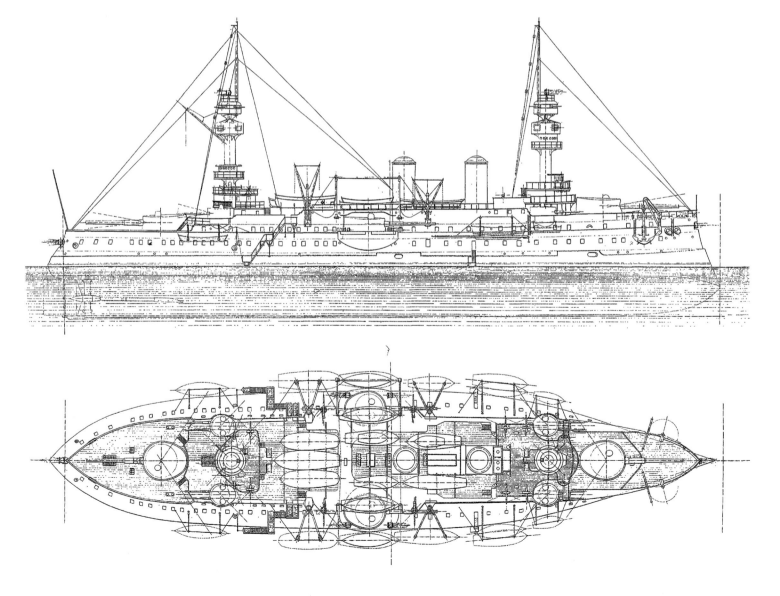

305mm guns at the ends and informed the Council that he was ready to accept electric drive for the turrets and twin mounting for the secondary battery if the technical details were satisfactory. With these issues thus removed from further discussion, the Council examined Lagane's revised design on 21 October 1890. The ship was shorter and wider than the other four ships built at this time, and the Council again objected to the fact that her 305mm guns were too close to the ends of the ship. The Council also provided a list of detailed changes that needed to be made if the Minister decided to proceed with the ship, including the replacement of the 356mm torpedoes in the design with the new 450mm torpedoes. Minister Barbey sent the design back to Lagane for revision on 5 November 1890. After reviewing the revised plans *Inspecteur général du génie maritime* Peschart-D'Ambly advised Minister Barbey on 16 January 1891 that they could be accepted with a few exceptions. On 22 January 1891 Barbey ordered the Machinery Commission (the *Commission permanente des machines et du grand outillage*) to contract with FCM for construction of a battleship with the name *Jauréguiberry*, and the contract was signed on 8 April 1891 and approved on 15 April 1891.

The steel belt was supplied by Schneider and Saint-Chamond. The engines were built at FCM's engine facility in the Menpenti district of Marseille. The boiler installation was identical to that of *Carnot* except that each funnel served half of the boilers. Completion was delayed by a serious boiler explosion on 9 June 1896 at the end of the final steam trials which was ascribed to design and manufacturing faults in the tubes of the Lagrafel et d'Allest boilers. Final steam trials were repeated in January 1897. Gunnery trials showed that if the 138.6mm guns in the twin turrets were fired separately the first gun fired would throw off the aim of the second, and it was recommended that they be fired simultaneously. The ship's first commander liked the twin mountings, however, because of their high location and the quick response of their electric drive. In 1898 the ship's commander noted that the main and medium artillery could be trained and elevated either by electricity or manually and that it was possible to shift between them nearly instantaneously. The time between rounds for the main battery was 1.5 minutes without danger (3 minutes with all safety procedures), and the hoists for the 138.6mm guns could supply 10 rounds per minute.

*The characteristics are based on a devis dated 8.6.1897.*
**Dimensions & tons:** 111.054m oa, 109.700m wl, 108.525m pp (tip fwd to rudder) x 22.150m ext & wl (22.860m over beam turrets). 11,818.000t disp (designed), 11,889.042t (normal, updated in devis), 12,080.755t (with surcharge). Draught: (normal) 8.1388m mean, 8.5208m aft. Men: 650.
**Machinery:** 14,200ihp designed at 97rpm maximum and 15kg/cm² boiler pressure (12kg/cm² at the engines). Trials (27.5.1896) 14,411.9ihp = 17.67kts at 96.71rpm and 13.064kg/cm² boiler pressure. 2 screws. 2 vertical triple expansion engines with 3 cylinders of 1.100m, 1.630m, and 2.465m diameter and 1.120m stroke. 24 Lagrafel et d'Allest boilers built by FCM. 700t coal. Range 3,568.625nm @ 12.15kts.
**Armour:**
Side (steel): Belt at waterline 450mm amidships, 300mm ends. Total height amidships 2.000m. Side above belt 100mm on 20mm plating, height amidships 1.200m.
Guns (steel): Four main turrets 370mm with 370mm max fixed bases. 138.6mm turrets 100mm on 20mm plating with 80 to 120mm fixed bases, the 80mm on 16mm plating.
Decks: Armoured deck (iron) 70mm on 20mm plating. No splinter deck below the deck but unlike the four ships ordered in 1890 and 1892 had a cellular layer above it.
Conning tower (steel): 250mm, covered with 45mm plating.
**Guns:**
(1897) 2 x 305mm/45 M1887 (single turrets at ends), 2 x 274.4mm/45 M1887 (single turrets on sides), 8 x 138.6mm/45 M1891(2) QF (twin turrets on sides), 4 x 65mm/50 M1891 QF, 2 x 65mm/16 M1881

landing, 12 x 47mm/40 M1885 QF, 5 x 37mm/20 M1885 QF, 7 x 37mm revolving cannon. **Torpedoes:** 6 tubes for 450mm M1889 torpedoes (4 above water and 2 submerged). **Searchlights:** 8 x 60mm.
(1907) 2 x 305mm, 2 x 274.4mm, 8 x 138.6mm, 4 x 65mm QF, 14 x 47mm. **Torpedoes:** 2 submerged tubes. The above-water tubes were removed in 1906.
(1917) All artillery removed 2-20.3.1917 except 2 x 65mm QF and 2 x 47mm QF (the latter fitted for AA fire).

*Jauréguiberry* F.C. Méditerranée, La Seyne/FCM, Marseille.
On list 1.1891. Ord: 8.4.1891 (contract). K: 23.4.1891. L: 27.10.1893. Comm: 30.1.1896 (trials), 24.3.1897 (full).
Budget 1891. Machinery installed 10.1894 to 24.10.1895. Trials 2.1896-2.1897 with some continuing into 4.1897. Accepted for service in the *Escadre de la Méditerranée* 15.5.1897, joined it in Golfe Juan two days later. To *Escadre du Nord* 1.4.1904, from 2.1907 alternated between the North and the Mediterranean. Seagoing annex to the gunnery school in *Tourville* (ex *Gironde*) at Toulon 1913 to 8.1914. Designated in war plans of 6.1914 to lead a special division that was to escort convoys carrying troops from North Africa to France. Active in the Dardanelles 28.3.1915 to 19.6.1915, took one mortar hit aft. Part of a French force that rescued 4,200 Armenians from the Turks at Musa Dagh near Antiochia in 9.1915 and evacuated them to Port Said. Taken off fleet service 30.10.1915 and reassigned to the protection of the Suez Canal, partly because of her low speed and partly because of increased U-boat activity to which she would be highly vulnerable. She remained at Port Said from 1.1916 to 2.1919 except for a visit to Malta for maintenance 11-12.1916. Attacked by a submarine 26.11.1916. Torpedo tubes verified in good condition at Malta 12.1916, ordered not to manoeuvre them because of sand in the canal. 'Excellent ship able easily to make 15 knots. Hull excellent.' Light artillery removed early 1917 to arm new patrol vessels and ship placed in reserve as a base ship and repair ship for the small French vessels at Port Said. Returned to Toulon 6.3.1919, decommissioned 30.4.1919, and joined *Saint Louis* as barracks hulk for the school for engineers and stokers. Struck 21.6.1920 and continued that service until replaced by the armoured cruiser *Jules Michelet* in 1932. For sale by the Domaines 1932. Condemned 1933. Sold 23.7.1934 to the Société du Matériel Naval du Midi to BU.

----

*BOUVET. Cuirassé d'escadre.* Battleship with four single main battery turrets in a lozenge layout and eight single secondary battery turrets on the sides. Two funnels, two military masts. Designed by Huin.

On 28 January 1891, after *Charles Martel* had been ordered from Brest but before she had been laid down, Minister Barbey informed the ports that the 1892 draft budget called for two battleships and that these would be built to the plans of either *Carnot* or *Charles Martel* unless a naval constructor could come up with something better. He then asked Huin to develop a new design derived from *Charles Martel* that took into consideration the comments made about it after the Minister had approved the plans and the trials with melanite projectiles then underway at Gâvres. The *Conseil des travaux* examined four designs on 31 July 1891 including the improved *Charles Martel* by Huin dated 30 May 1891, and asked for changes. Huin submitted a modified design on 31 October 1891, noting that the changes requested by the Council added a considerable amount of weight and that as the tonnage and the tonnage margins could not be changed he had adopted the suggestion of the Council that new metals (special steel) be adopted for the armour of the turrets allowing reductions in its thickness. The Council examined Huin's modified design on 29 December 1891 and asked for more changes, notably the addition of a 40mm armoured splinter deck (including 10mm plating) below the main armoured deck instead of the unarmoured platform deck that Huin favoured. In his revised design submitted on 26 March 1892 Huin adopted triple screws with three engine rooms abreast in the after part of the ship (as already adopted in *Masséna*), an arrangement adopted in part to limit the height of the vertical triple expansion engines and keep them behind the belt and below the newly-added splinter deck. *Bouvet* was ordered to Huin's still-evolving design in April 1892.

On 26 May 1893 Schneider was asked to modify the 305mm and 274.4mm turret designs of *Masséna* for M1893 instead of M1887 guns, and this probably applied to *Bouvet* as well. The 305mm M1893 gun existed in both 45-calibre and 40-caliber versions, the earlier longer gun probably being used in the single turrets of *Bouvet* and *Masséna* and the later shorter one which also had a slightly enlarged chamber in the twin turrets of the *Charlemagne* class. Special steel armour for the 305mm turrets was ordered from Schneider in July 1893 and steel belt armour was ordered from Marrel Frères at around the same time. In August 1893 Schneider asked permission to use cemented steel armour for the 305mm turrets instead of the homogeneous special (nickel) steel in his contract. The navy approved his request, resulting in the first use in France of the new Harvey cemented (face-hardened) steel armour, for which Schneider had just obtained the licence earlier in the year. The 274.4mm turrets received special steel armour by Saint-Chamond and the 138.6mm turrets received special steel armour from Châtillon et Commentry. The armoured decks in *Bouvet* and *Masséna* were made of extra mild steel instead of iron. This material was developed by Châtillon et Commentry and was sometimes called *métail de Saint-Jacques* after the plant at Montluçon where it was

developed, the Navy made its use mandatory in new designs in 1892. Decks required softer armour than did vertical surfaces because they would normally be struck highly obliquely. The enclosed tops on the masts in the original design were replaced with larger open tops during construction in 1896, causing the deletion of some 37mm guns.

The superstructure was lightened between May and November 1907. Modifications included suppressing the forward upper bridge, fitting a pilot house in front of the conning tower, removing the longitudinal bridge connecting the transverse bridge amidships with the after superstructure, lowering the stowage of the boats outboard of the fore funnel, and lowering the outer casing of the fore funnel to the same level as that of the after funnel. The change to the funnels was made to increase the field of view of the Barr and Stroud rangefinder newly fitted on top of the conning tower.

*Bouvet* capsized and sank very quickly during the maritime assault on the Bosporus on 18 March 1915. For many years her loss was attributed to a mine, but recent research indicates that she was in fact sunk by a shell from a shore battery that struck the handling room under the starboard 274mm turret.

*The characteristics are based on a devis dated 9.3.1898.*
**Dimensions & tons:** 122.599m oa, 121.005m wl, 117.900m pp (tip fwd to rudder) x 21.40m ext and wl. 12,205.3t disp (designed), 12,052.4t (normal with flag). Draught: (designed) 7.995m mean, 8,000m aft.

---

Outboard profile and overhead view (*vue extérieure*) of the battleship *Bouvet*, built on the plans of naval constructor Huin. The plans were dated on 25 January 1898 at Lorient by the naval constructor in charge of the ship, Lejeune. The small calibre artillery carried at this time included 8 x 100mm/45 M1891(2) guns (2 on the lower forward bridge, 2 on the after bridge, and 4 on the flying bridge

amidships), 12 x 47mm/40 M1885 heavy QF guns (4 in foretop, 4 in after top, 2 on the upper (navigating) bridge forward, and 2 on the after bridge), 5 x 37mm QF guns (4 on the flying bridge amidships and 1 on the after bridge), and 3 x 37mm revolving cannon (on the lower bridge forward in front of the conning tower). There were also 2 x 65mm landing guns.

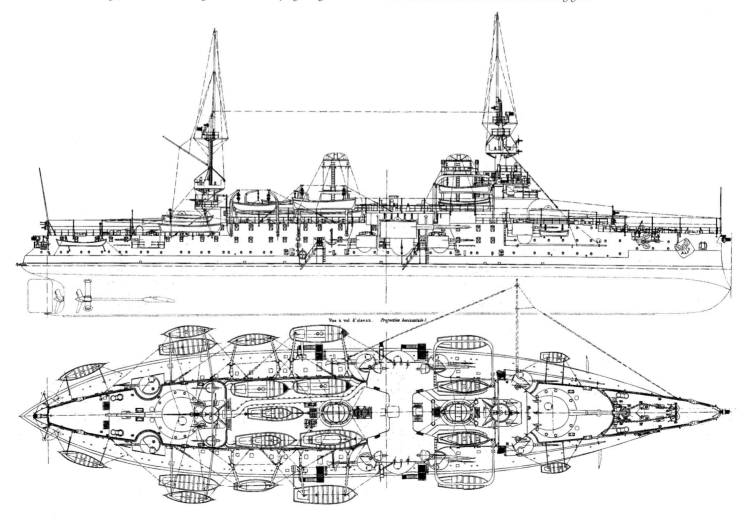

Men: 622 (692 with flag).

**Machinery:** 14,000ihp designed at 120rpm and 17kg/cm² boiler pressure (13kg/cm² at the engines) to give 17kts. Trials (mid-1898) 15,462ihp and 18.188kts. 3 screws. 3 vertical triple expansion engines with 3 cylinders of 0.930m, 1.430m, and 2.200m diameter and 0.840m stroke. 32 Delaunay Belleville boilers built by Indret. 777t coal (normal). Range with 777t coal 2,450nm @ 10kts; with 1,000t coal 3,154nm @ 10kts.

**Armour:**

Side: Belt at waterline (special steel) 400mm amidships, 300mm fwd, 260mm aft. Total height amidships 2.00m of which 0.50m was above the waterline (submerged by a 3 degree heel). Side above belt (steel) 80mm on 20mm plating, height amidships 1.19m (submerged by a 10 degree heel).

Guns: Four main turrets (cemented steel for the 305mm turrets, special steel for the 274.4mm turrets) 370mm with 310mm fixed bases. 138.6mm turrets and bases (special steel) 100mm. 100mm gun shields (special steel) 72mm.

Decks: Armoured deck (extra mild steel) 70mm on 20mm plating. Splinter deck (mild steel, also called boiler steel) 30mm on 10mm hull plating.

Conning tower (special steel): 320mm maximum front, 300mm minimum sides plus 20mm plating.

**Guns:**

(1898) 2 x 305mm/45 M1893 (single turrets at ends), 2 x 274.4mm/45 M1893 (single turrets on sides), 8 x 138.6mm/45 M1891(2) QF (single turrets on sides), 8 x 100mm/45 M1891(2) (2 on the lower bridge forward, 4 on the flying bridge amidships, and 2 on the after bridge), 2 x 65mm/16 M1881 landing, 12 x 47mm/40 M1885 QF, 5 x 37mm/20 M1885 QF, 3 x 37mm revolving cannon. **Torpedoes:** 4 tubes for 450mm M1892 torpedoes (2 above water and 2 submerged). **Searchlights:** 6 x 60cm.

(1906) 2 x 305mm, 2 x 274.4mm, 8 x 138.6mm, 6 x 100mm (2 forward deleted), 14 x 47mm. **Torpedoes:** 2 submerged tubes

*Bouvet* (A1) Lorient Dyd/Indret.

On list 1.1893. Ord: 3.4.1892. K: 16.1.1893. L: 27.4.1896. Comm: 15.7.1897 (trials), 1.10.1898 (full).

Budget 1892 (designated A). Installation of engines begun 15.10.1896. Fully manned and equipped for trials 5.3.1898, transited from Lorient to Toulon with her trial crew 9-20.3.1898 and began trials there, the hasty movement being due to the Fashoda crisis. Principal trials 4-7.1898. Admitted to active service 27.7.1898. Trial results approved and placed in full commission 1.10.1898, joining the *Escadre de la Méditerranée* in a division with *Masséna* and *Brennus*. Moved to the *Escadre du Nord* 4.10.1909 and back to the *Escadre de la Méditerranée* 16.10.1912. In 1914 was in the *Division de complément* of the *1re Armée navale*. Sunk by Turkish artillery in Dardanelles 18.3.1915. Struck 19.5.1915.

----

*MASSÉNA. Cuirassé d'escadre.* Battleship with four single main battery turrets in a lozenge layout, eight single secondary battery turrets on the sides, and a prominent ram-shaped bow. Two funnels, two military masts. Designed by de Bussy (A.C. Loire).

When Minister Barbey on 28 January 1891 called for plans for the two battleships of the 1892 budget, one submission came from the Ateliers et Chantiers de la Loire at Saint Nazaire. Marie-Anne-Louis de Bussy had joined this firm as *conseiller technique* after he retired as *Inspecteur général du génie maritime* in October 1889, and he guided the preparation of the new battleship design. De Bussy felt that low freeboard hulls with rounded sides like those he had given *Furieux* and *Jemmapes* could both save weight and provide a stable gun platform, and in *Masséna* he combined this type of hull with a tall narrow superstructure on the centreline supporting the guns and other fittings needed for a 1st class battleship. (*Carnot* had a

similar layout.) He extended the low hull with a long ram-shaped (inverted) bow, although the *Conseil des travaux* made him moderate it. He had also favoured vaulted sterns that were hollowed out above the screws in his previous designs including *Tonnerre* and *Tempête* and gave *Masséna* one also. Finally he adopted triple rather than twin screws. The *Conseil de travaux* examined the A.C. Loire design on 31 July 1891 and noted that the project had three main advantages over the others already adopted including triple screws, a thick splinter deck (30mm) over the engines, boilers, and magazines, and a low displacement. It summarized the advantages of triple screw plants as having three engine rooms instead of two for greater protection against a hit, using vertical triple expansion engines small enough to fit under a splinter deck, using engines with higher rotational speeds and thereby lighter weight, and the ability to run on only the centre engine at low speeds to save fuel, thereby achieving a significant reduction in displacement. The Council felt that triple screws, although untested, could be accepted provided the company guaranteed to achieve the speed of 17 knots using natural draught. It considered the splinter deck to be a laudable innovation, but the reductions in displacement gave up too much and the Council asked for adjustments. A.C. Loire submitted the revised design on 28 October 1891 and the Council approved it on 29 December 1891, asking only that some 100mm QF guns be added to the armament.

Work probably commenced in late 1892, the keel laying coming somewhat later. On 26 May 1893 Schneider was asked to modify the 305mm and 274.4mm turret designs for M1893 instead of M1887 guns. The steel belt armour was supplied by Schneider and Saint-Chamond, the steel armour for the 305mm turrets came from Marrel Frères, that for the 274.4mm and 138.6mm turrets was from Châtillon et Commentry, and these two firms also supplied the extra mild steel deck while Schneider provided the light side armour above the belt. The rig of *Masséna* was altered during construction to include large armed 'Schwartz' tops on her masts. Following her builder's practice, she was launched with engines and boilers installed. Machinery trials began on 9 November 1896 for the centre engine and the after boiler room, on 17 December 1896 for the port engine and the forward boiler room, and on 19 December 1896 for the starboard engine and the middle boiler room.

Underway trials showed that the ship steered badly. With three screws in a vaulted stern the single rudder, even after being enlarged during trials, could control the ship's movements only with difficulty. The vaulted stern also pounded violently in bad weather. *Bouvet* and later French naval ships that used triple screws had more conventional stern hull lines and did not encounter these problems. The tall strictly vertical sides of *Masséna*'s central superstructure also made her unusually sensitive to cross winds, while the long inverted bow produced a huge bow wave when steaming at high speeds into heavy seas.

*The characteristics are based on a devis dated 18.7.1898.*

**Dimensions & tons:** 117.120m oa, 116.785m wl, 112.647m pp (rip fwd to rudder) x 20.310m ext (above wl), 20.282m wl. 11,923.551t disp (designed), 12,316.175t (normal). Draught: (designed) 7.730m mean, 8.166m aft (real), 8.430m aft (keel line projected). Men: 611 including 32 officers without flag, an additional 83 including 14 officers with.

**Machinery:** 13,500ihp designed at 120rpm and 15kg/cm² boiler pressure (12 kg/cm² at the engines). Trials (27.1.1898, forced) 13,374ihp = 16.973kts at 125.3rpm. (Reached 14,021ihp on forced draught trials on 27.1.1898 but speed was not measured.) 3 screws. 3 vertical triple expansion engines with 4 cylinders of 0.89m (1), 1.32m (1), and 1.54m (2) diameter and 0.84m stroke. 24 Lagrafel et d'Allest water-tube boilers. 875t coal (normal). Range with 875t coal 3,755nm @ 10kts; with 1,070t coal 4,592nm @ 10kts.

**Armour:**

Side (steel): Belt at waterline 450 mm amidships, 350mm at ends. Total height 2.00m. Side above belt 100mm on 20mm plating, height 1.20m.

Guns: Four main turrets (special steel) 370mm with 320mm fixed bases.

138.6mm turrets (special steel) 100mm.
Decks: Armoured deck (extra mild steel) 70mm on 20mm hull plating.
  Splinter deck 40mm hull plating (2 x 20mm layers).
Conning tower (compound): 330mm front, 280mm sides and rear, plus
  20mm plating.
**Guns:**
(1898) 2 x 305mm/45 M1893 (single turrets at ends), 2 x 274.4mm/45
  M1893 (single turrets on sides), 8 x 138.6mm/45 M1891(2) QF (single turrets on sides), 8 x 100mm/45 M1891(2) QF (shields on shelter
  deck), 2 x 65mm/16 M1881 landing, 12 x 47mm/40 M1885 QF, 5 x
  37mm/20 M1885 QF, 3 x 37mm revolving cannon. (The ship initially
  had 9 x 37mm QF including 8 in the upper tops but on 1.6.1897 the
  four in the upper foretop were ordered to be replaced with a rangefinder.) **Torpedoes:** 4 tubes for 450mm M1892 torpedoes (2 above
  water and 2 submerged). Another submerged pair forward was deleted
  on 24.9.1896 during construction. **Searchlights:** 6 x 60cm.
(1906) 2 x 305mm, 2 x 274.4mm, 8 x 138.6mm, 8 x 100mm,
  2 x 65mm, 14 x 47mm, 37mm QF (for the boats).
  **Torpedoes:** 2 submerged tubes.

*Masséna* (A2) A.C. Loire, Saint Nazaire/ACL, Saint Denis.
On list 1.1893. Ord: 18.5.1892. K: 9.1892. L: 24.7.1895.
  Comm: 18.4.1897 (trials), 21.5.1898 (full).

The battleship *Masséna* at Toulon, probably in the post-1908 uniform bluish-grey
paint scheme. The rounded hull sides are typical of the later designs of Louis de
Bussy, both as a naval constructor and as technical counsellor at the Ateliers et
Chantiers de la Loire. *Torpilleur no 347* is alongside. *(Photo postcard by A. Noyer,
Paris)*

Budget 1892 (designated B). Machinery installation completed 11-12.
  1896. Ship delivered 17.4.1897 and moved to Brest where she was
  commissioned the next day for trials. Trials at Brest 4.1897 to 5.1898.
  Designated 25.5.1898 to replace *Hoche* as flagship of the *Escadre du
  Nord*, but joined the *Escadre de la Méditerranée* 22.10.1898 in response
  to the Fashoda crisis. Flagship of the *Escadre du Nord* 15.1.1900 to
  21.10.1901 and 1.4.1903 to 1.1907. Attached to the division of gunnery schools at Toulon 18.4.1908, became its flagship 1.10.1908.
  Reviewing ship with President Fallières embarked for a naval review on
  4.9.1911 that paraded 19 French battleships. To normal reserve
  1.1.1912. Boiler accident in forward boiler room 6.1.1913 ended her
  active career, to special reserve 1913. Definitively decommissioned
  1.4.1914 (with *Brennus, Charles Martel*, and *Carnot*), decommissioning
  completed 25.6.1914 and handed over to port authorities. Hull
  stripped and guns and superstructure removed. Struck 27.3.1915.
  Towed from Toulon 28.8.1915 via Bizerte to Mudros, arriving
  19.9.1915. Scuttled 7.11.1915 with the passenger ship *Saghalien* as a
  breakwater to shelter the French landing zone at Sedul-Bahr in the
  Dardanelles. Remains sold 3.1923 for salvage to Mr. Jost.

---

**Bertin's 1890-91 battleship designs**
Émile Bertin returned from detached duty in Japan in May 1890 and soon
replaced as deputy director of naval construction at Toulon naval constructor Victor Saglio, the designer of *Lazare Carnot*, who on 13 October 1890
was named director of the navy's engine building plant at Indret. When
Toulon forwarded to Paris Saglio's final revision to the *Carnot* design on
20 October 1890 Bertin attached to it his own proposal for a radical change
to the ship's protection scheme. This was not pursued and Bertin then

submitted a complete design containing his ideas. He proposed an alternative protection scheme in which the main armoured deck, instead of being flat on top of the upper edge of the main armoured belt, was just above the waterline at the centreline and angled down near the sides to join the belt at its lower edge. Bertin's idea was that a shell to penetrate to the ship's vitals would have to pass through both the belt and the angled portion of the deck instead of just the belt. The level above this deck became a complete cellular layer of small watertight compartments where current French ships had only narrow cofferdams running along the sides. After meeting the belt at its lower edge Bertin's armoured deck continued down vertically to become a torpedo defence bulkhead.

On 25 November 1890 the *Conseil des travaux* firmly rejected Bertin's design. He resubmitted his *Carnot* design when on 28 January 1891 Minister Barbey called for designs for two battleships that were in the 1892 budget. It was one of the four designs examined by the *Conseil des travaux* on 31 July 1891 in response to that call. The Council stated that this was little more than Bertin's November 1890 design with the addition of a light belt above the main belt and rejected it, asserting that the traditional protection in *Charles Martel* and Saglio's *Carnot* was far superior. It saw merit only in the anti-torpedo protection but felt that any superiority of this over the current system of multiple watertight bulkheads did not justify the increased weight.

Bertin's ability to implement his ideas fully had been hampered by the 12,000-ton size limit then in effect, and he then submitted a design that he had previously developed without any tonnage restriction. It measured 13,631 tons and 132m in length, and had a main battery of four 305mm guns in two twin turrets. The Council examined this design on 8 December 1891 and acknowledged that the armour scheme in the design provided better protection from gunfire for the vitals of the ship below the waterline than the scheme in ships then building but rejected out of hand the twin main battery turrets as contrary to the principles of the French navy, feared that the displacement would be unacceptable, and claimed that the great length of the ship would hamper its manoeuvrability. Ironically twin main battery turrets were adopted six months later by the Minister for the *Charlemagne* class, a version of the torpedo bulkhead reappeared a few years later in Bertin's *Henri IV* of 1896 (although Bertin did not include one in his later *Patrie* class), and his new protection system became standard in the French navy beginning with his *Patrie* class of 1901. The British introduced a similar system in HMS *Majestic* in 1893 that became standard in subsequent British battleships, although the ends of the British ships were largely unprotected.

---

## CHARLEMAGNE Class. *Cuirassés d'escadre*. Battleships with two twin centreline main battery turrets. Two funnels, two military masts. Designed by Thibaudier.

On 25 June 1892 Minister of Marine Deputy Godefroy Cavaignac informed the *Conseil des travaux* that he wanted to start work on designs for the eventual construction of new battleships. None was in the 1893 budget submitted in March 1892 but more were needed to comply with the building programme just completed by the *Conseil supérieur* (the Programme of 1890). The Minister, now probably Deputy Auguste Laurent Burdeau, guided by Director of Materiel Bienaymé who provided a sketch illustrating the proposed secondary battery, directed that, in order to obtain the greatest tonnage reduction possible while retaining an armament a bit superior to that of *Carnot* and *Charles Martel*, the main battery would consist of two 305mm guns in one twin turret forward and two 274.4mm guns in one twin turret aft. He added that these could be barbette turrets if that would lead to weight savings allowing a uniform calibre for the main battery. The secondary battery would be ten 138.6mm QF in a battery and six 100mm QF in the superstructure. He specified an unusual anti-torpedo boat battery of eighteen 65mm QF, fourteen 37mm QF, and six 37mm revolving cannon which was not retained. The protection would be analogous to that in *Bouvet* and *Masséna*, although he asked

if it would be possible to abandon the armour at the extreme bow and stern. as the British were doing. The maximum belt armour would be 40cm as would be the armour on both turrets. Deck thicknesses would be 90mm upper and 40mm lower (both including plating). Speeds would be at least 17 knots at natural draught and 18 knots at forced draught. Range with normal coal would be 4,000nm at 10 knots and with surcharge 6,000nm at 10 knots. He urged the council to do whatever was necessary to reduce the cost and the duration of construction.

The Council reviewed these specifications on 2 August 1892. It calculated the weight of the Minister's ship as about 10,600 tons. It reluctantly adopted the two twin turrets instead of four single turrets for weight savings and to free up the sides for secondary guns but insisted on 305mm guns in both turrets. Anticipating the problem experienced with *Brennus* in 1894 it wanted balanced turrets that would not cause the ship to heel when the guns were trained on the beam, and it preferred barbette mountings if they could be balanced as well as enclosed turrets. It followed the Minister in putting the 138.6mm QF secondary battery in casemates or shields, the weight of secondary turrets as in the five 1890-1892 battleships being prohibitive in the new design. It paid a lot of attention to protecting the ship against British 6-inch guns when engaging head-on which it considered a likely scenario. It included a 220mm transverse bulkhead just forward of the casemates, doubled the forward bulkheads of the forward casemates to 150mm, and added 50mm of armour to the forward part of the forward 305mm turret. It insisted on a full length armour belt on the grounds that damaged ends could endanger stability. The ship was to have triple screws, Belleville boilers, and two military masts. The council's final estimated displacement was 11,500 tons. When transmitting these specification to the ports on 25 August 1892 Minister Burdeau limited the displacement to 11,000 tons and made some reductions in the protection to make this possible, including eliminating the Council's extra protection for the secondary battery against raking fire and reducing the transverse bulkhead to 150mm.

On 20 June 1893 the *Conseil des travaux* reviewed six designs (a seventh followed on 25 July 1893). Of these one by naval constructor Jules César Claude Thibaudier completely satisfied the specifications and needed only minor alterations, while one by the Société de la Loire (designer of *Masséna*) was a close runner-up. In designing his ship Thibaudier was heavily inspired by the lines of *Bouvet*. He also found room for two more 100mm guns. Thibaudier's design was approved on 2 August 1893. Minister Faure agreed to add a third ship, *Gaulois*, when the *Conseil supérieur* agreed to his two corsairs, *Guichen* and *Châteaurenault*. While Thibaudier probably did the best he could with 11,200 tons, the ships suffered from poor stability, poor habitability, a narrow armour belt whose top was often below the waterline, an absence of side armour between the belt and the secondary casemates, and an inadequate steaming range.

Some sources state that the three ships had main belts made of the new Harvey cemented (face-hardened) steel, but the fact that the thickness of the belt amidships was identical to that in *Bouvet* and that Schneider only acquired the first French licence to the Harvey process in 1893 suggests that like *Bouvet* they had the earlier homogeneous nickel steel. The belt armour for the two ships at Brest was provided by Saint Chamond and Marrel and that of Saint Louis came from Schneider and Châtillon et Commentry. The guns and turrets for all three ships were delivered late (October 1898 for *Gaulois*, April 1899 for *Charlemagne*, and September 1899 for *Saint Louis*), forcing them to run trials without their main armaments. *Saint Louis*, built at Lorient, differed in many details from her two sisters, which were built at Brest in succession on the same slip and were virtually identical. Most visibly, in *Saint Louis* the longitudinal flying bridge aft of the second funnel was omitted and the after superstructure was lowered to regular deck heights. The six 47mm guns in the hull were located differently, the two 47mm guns in the forward structure were mounted a deck higher, the two 37mm guns were mounted on the navigating bridge instead of the shelter deck amidships, and the searchlight arrangement was different. She was the only one of the three that was fitted to carry an admiral and his staff. Finally the special steel portion of the belt in the bow was longer, extending back to the front of the fore turret rather than changing to cemented armour aft of the hawsepipes. The special steel portion of the belt aft was the same length in all three ships but in *Saint Louis* it was slightly thinner in the stern. *Saint Louis* was the last French battleship with its main turrets resting on hydraulic pivots, the two others still had pivots but supported most of the weight of the main turrets on roller paths.

Concerns over the stability of the three ships were raised by an episode on 30 May 1913 when *Charlemagne* during post-refit turning trials at Brest heeled a startling 34 degrees while turning at a speed of 16 knots. This concern was magnified by experiences during the Dardanelles campaign of 1915 culminating in the capsizing of *Bouvet* in less than a minute after an underwater hit in March 1915. *Gaulois* underwent a corrective reconstruction at Toulon between 16 April 1915 and 8 June 1915 while *Saint Louis* followed at Lorient between November 1915 and May 1916. *Charlemagne* was scheduled to receive these modifications at Bizerte in early 1917 but was instead removed from service. The modification consisted of fitting a caisson or *soufflage* of timber and thin steel from the top edge of the armour belt to just below the waterline. Its function was to dampen rolling and offset the effects of the hull's tumblehome in damaged condition; it offered no anti-torpedo protection. To compensate for the 130 tons of weight added by the caissons in *Gaulois*, the forward and after superstructures were much reduced, the light artillery reduced, and the platforms on the foremast removed. In *Saint Louis* the platforms on both masts were removed, the masts and superstructures were lightened, and most of the flying bridge around the funnels was removed.

**Dimensions & tons:** 117.700m oa (117.650m in *Saint Louis*), 116.200m wl (+1.300m ram), 117.500m pp (tip fwd to stern) x 20.300 ext (below wl), 20.264m wl (20.260m in *Saint Louis*). 11,287.323t disp (designed, *Charlemagne*), 11,415t (normal, *Charlemagne*). Draught: (designed) 7.900m mean, 8.400m aft. Men: 692 including 32 officers without flag, add 58 officers and men for flag. *Saint Louis* rated at 758 men.

**Machinery:** 14,200ihp designed (natural draught) at 125rpm and 17kg/cm$^2$ boiler pressure. Designed speed 17kts. Trials (*Charlemagne*, 16.6.1898) 18.136kts, (*Gaulois*, 10.9.1898) 15,162ihp = 18.024kts,

Outboard profile and overhead view (*plan d'ensemble*) of the battleship *Charlemagne* built at Brest on the plans of M. Thibaudier. The plans were probably signed by T. Garnier, Director of Naval Construction there in 1897-99. The drawing style emphasizes the ship's six searchlights, two in sponsons in the bow, two on the admiral's stern gallery, and two on the mastheads. The small calibre artillery carried at this time included 8 x 100mm/45 M1893 guns (2 on the lower bridge forward, 4 on the flying bridge amidships, and 2 on the after bridge), 20 x 47mm/40 M1885 guns (8 in the lower platforms of the military masts, 4 in the corners of the forward and aft superstructures, 6 in the hull sides on the battery deck, and 2 on the same level in the admiral's gallery), and 2 x 37mm QF guns (on the shelter deck just aft of the second funnel, or on the navigating bridge in *Saint Louis*). There were also 2 x 65mm M1881 field guns for the landing party, and three of the 47mm guns could be used in the pinnaces.

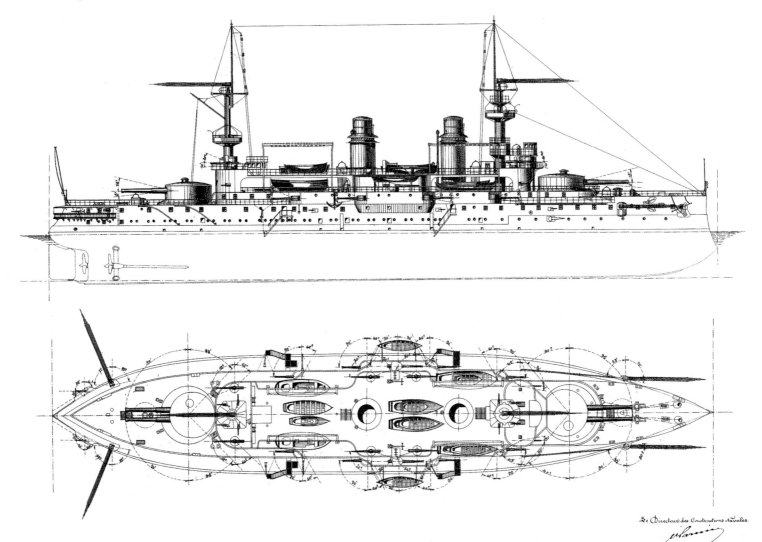

A photo of the battleship *Saint Louis* dated 1900 originally attached to the technical characteristics document for the ship. Although of the same class, she was built in a different dockyard and differed in many details from her sisters *Charlemagne* and *Gaulois*, particularly in the after superstructure. Three of her four main battery guns appear to be at maximum elevation. *(Feuille signalétique for the ship)*

---

(*Saint Louis*, 24.8.1900) 17.84kts. 3 screws. 3 vertical triple expansion engines, those in *Charlemagne* with 4 cylinders of 0.92m (1), 1.35m (1), and 1.53m (2) diameter and with 0.80m stroke, those in *Gaulois* with 4 cylinders of 0.91m (1), 1.34m (1), and 1.56m (2) diameter with 0.76m stroke, and those in *Saint Louis* with 3 cylinders of 0.93m, 1.43m, and 2.20m diameter and 0.84m stroke. 20 Delaunay-Belleville boilers. 638t coal (normal), 1,102t (surcharge) + 50t oil. Range 4,000nm @ 10kts.

**Armour:**
Side: Belt at waterline (special steel) 400mm amidships, 320mm fwd, 300mm aft (280mm aft in *Saint Louis*). Height 2.04m from 1.54m below the wl to 0.50m above. Side above belt (hammered or special steel) 55mm, height amidships 1.04m. Transverse bulkhead forward 150mm.

Guns: Main turrets (special steel) 320mm max with 270mm fixed bases. Redoubt/casemates (hammered or special steel) 55mm sides with 54mm gun shields. Two open mounts on 3rd deck had 72mm fixed and 55mm mobile shields.

Decks: Armoured deck (extra mild steel) 70mm on 20mm hull plating. Splinter deck 40mm hull plating (2 x 20mm layers).

Conning tower (special steel): 326mm max.

**Guns:**
(1899) 4 x 305mm/40 M1893 (twin turrets fore and aft), 10 x 138.6mm/45 M1893 QF (8 in casemates on the upper deck and 2 in shields on the shelter deck above them), 8 x 100mm/45 M1893 (2 on the lower bridge forward, 4 on the flying bridge amidships, and 2 on

the after bridge), 2 x 65mm/16 M1881 landing, 20 x 47mm/40 M1885 QF, 2 x 37mm/20 M1885 QF. Three of the 47mm guns could be used in the pinnaces. **Torpedoes:** 4 tubes for 450mm M1892 torpedoes (2 above water and 2 submerged). **Searchlights:** 6 x 60cm (2 at the mastheads and 4 in the hull. In *Charlemagne* and *Gaulois* two of the latter were on the sides near the ends while in *Saint Louis* two were on the sides amidships, 1 was in the bow and 1 was in the stern.)

(1906) Same except the two above-water torpedo tubes were removed from all three ships.

(4.1915, *Gaulois*) 2 x 100mm (forward bridge) and 6 x 47mm guns removed.

*Henri IV* (A3) Contractor not selected.

Budget 1894 (not funded). The largest of several contract-built ships included in the 1894 budget (submitted 5.1893) with the stipulation that no funds were to be spent on them during 1894. None was contracted for and the 1895 budget (3.1894) deferred most of them indefinitely. By then A3 was named *Henri IV*. The other similarly ephemeral ships in the 1894 budget (all unnamed) were the 2nd class cruisers E5, E6 and G3, the seagoing torpedo boat N12, the 2nd class torpedo boats Q1 to Q4, the 2nd class aviso U1, and the *chaloupes à vapeur* X2 and X3.

*Charlemagne* (A4) Brest Dyd/Schneider, Creusot.

On list 1.1894. Ord: 30.9.1893. K: 2.7.1894. L: 17.10.1895. Comm: 15.10.1897 (trials), 12.9.1899 (full).

Budget 1894. Machinery installed 17.11.1896 to 17.11.1897. Official machinery trials 4.-7.1898, results approved 15.10.1898. Main battery guns delivered 4.1899. Left Brest 21.9.1899 to join the *Escadre du Nord* at Cherbourg, then proceeded to Toulon 18-24.1.1900 and joined the *Escadre de la Méditerranée*. In *Escadre du Nord* 4.10.1909 to 25.9.1912, then to reserve at Brest. Returned to Toulon 7.1913 and served as seagoing annex to the gunnery school in *Tourville* (ex *Gironde*) at Toulon 23.7.1913 to 8.1914, replacing *Requin*. Arrived at

Toulon 17.9.1917 from war service in the Eastern Mediterranean because of a shortage of coal for the fleet, ordered converted to a depot ship for propellent and explosives and 138.6mm guns removed. Decomm. at Toulon 1.11.1917, struck from the first part of the *Liste de la Flotte* 14.3.1918 with the provision that her machinery be maintained in an operational state. Struck 21.6.1920. Handed over in 1921 in part payment to the firm salvaging *Liberté* (Sidensner, Boursier & Borrely), resold by them to Vincenzo Rizzo and towed to Savona, Italy, to BU.

*Saint Louis* (A5) Lorient Dyd-Caudan/Indret.
On list 1.1894. Ord: 30.9.1893. K: 25.3.1895. L: 8.9.1896.
    Comm: 15.11.1898 (trials), 1.9.1900 (full).
Budget 1894. Machinery installed 18.12.1897 to 24.11.1898. Main battery guns delivered 9.1899. Manning for trials completed 10.1.1900, left Lorient 15.2.1900 to run trials at Brest. At naval review at Cherbourg 19.7.1900. Official machinery trials 7-8.1900. Left Brest 15.9.1900 to join the *Escadre de la Méditerranée* at Toulon, flagship 1.10.1900 to 24.2.1904. Flagship of the *Escadre du Nord* 4.10.1909 to 11.11.1911 and 15.4.1912 to 14.3.1913. Rammed and sank submarine *Vendémiaire* during exercises west of Cherbourg 8.6.1912. In early 1914 was flagship of the *Division de complément* of the *1re Armée navale* at Toulon. War service in the Eastern Mediterranean. To special reserve 2.3.1917 at Bizerte for maintenance and because of a shortage of coal for the fleet, decomm. 20.4.1917 four days after her 305mm guns were landed. Moved to Toulon 1.1919 and to reserve there with reduced crew 8.2.1919. Struck 21.6.1920, hulk for the school for engineers and stokers at Toulon 1921-1929. Replaced 19.10.1929 by *Jules Michelet* and towed to Brégaillon. Ordered 26.4.1931 to be turned over to the Domaines for sale, condemned 1.7.1931, sold definitively 8.5.1933 to Pierre Slisenwiez, director of the Banque de Provence, to BU.

*Gaulois* (A7) Brest Dyd/A.C. Loire, Saint Denis.
On list 1.1896. Ord: 22.1.1895. K: 6.1.1896. L: 6.10.1896.
    Comm: 15.1.1898 (trials), 15.1.1899 (full).
Budget 1895. Machinery installed 12.5.1897 to 9.3.1898. Official machinery trials 7-9.1898. Main battery turrets installed 10.1898, the 138.6mm guns followed in early 1899, and the main battery was accepted 10.1899. To Cherbourg 10.1899 and to Toulon 1.1900 with *Charlemagne* to join the *Escadre de la Méditerranée*. Special mission to Annapolis, Maryland, to represent France at the dedication of a statue of Rochambeau near the White House in Washington, DC. Spent most of her career in the Mediterranean except for 8.1909 to 10.1912 when all three ships were assigned to Brest. In early 1914 was in the *Division de complément* of the *1re Armée navale*. Beached to prevent sinking after hit by shell in the Dardanelles 18.3.1915. Torpedoed 27.12.1916 by *UB-47* on the starboard side abreast the after 305mm turret in the Aegean en route to Salonica, capsized and sank in about half an hour. All but four of the crew were saved by the requisitioned trawlers *Roche Bonne* and *Marie Rose* which came alongside the sinking battleship and by the destroyer *Dard*.

---

### The Programme of 1894

In 1894 Minister of Marine Faure, responding to a suggestion by the Budget Committee of 1893 for a 'compromise programme' containing something for everyone and in reaction to the fact that execution of the Programme of 1890 was seriously in arrears, asked the *Conseil supérieur* to update the Programme of 1890, which it did between 5 and 11 December 1894. The programme remained directly focused on the Triple Alliance despite England's renewed activity and France's new military agreements with Russia. The Council regretted that it could not include a number of battleships equal to the 29 of the Triple Alliance because of production limitations and retained the 24 battleships of the 1890 programme. The main differences from the 1890 programme were a requirement that all

1st class cruisers be armoured (the new ones to be more powerful, better protected and faster than *Dupuy de Lôme* and the 1st class protected cruisers being demoted to the 2nd class), the addition of two specialized commerce raiding cruisers (*Guichen* and *Châteaurenault*), and the deletion from the programme of torpedo boat transports and supply transports. The coast defence fleet reflected a decision of the Council on 16 December 1892 to use *aviso-torpilleurs* as leaders for groups of torpedo boats. The other features of the 1890 programme, including the total numbers of battleships and cruisers and the entire station fleet, remained intact. The full programme is in Appendix F. While preparing this programme the naval staff began developing the system of alpha-numeric designators for ships to be built under the programme that was thereafter used in both programmes and budgets and that are shown in this book. *Bouvet*, then building, was thus designated squadron battleship (*cuirassé d'escadre*) A1.

---

### MINISTER BESNARD'S 8,700-TON SQUADRON BATTLESHIP A6.

*Cuirassé d'escadre.* Small battleship with two single centreline main battery turrets, a secondary battery in casemates on the upper deck, a raised forecastle, and one military mast. No designs prepared.

During the debates on the 1895 budget on 12 March 1895 a new Minister of Marine, Vice Admiral Armand Besnard, renounced large battleships costing 27 to 28 million francs in favour of battleships of 7,000 or 8,000 tons costing 17 to 18 million francs that he said would be fast enough and able to fight the enemy's 'monsters'. Besnard was known for his republican views and for his connections with Aube, who promoted him to flag rank, although in his support of foreign station fleets and new cruisers for them and most of his other policies he remained a thorough traditionalist. He claimed that the four *Jemmapes*-type ships formed the most homogeneous and dangerous squadron that one could meet at sea, invulnerable with few upper works, powerful guns, good secondary armaments, and a small turning circle for using the ram, still a most important weapon. Édouard Lockroy, a leader of the *Jeune École* faction in parliament who was soon to become Minister, cheered this declaration. A new battleship designated A6 of about the same size as *Tréhouart* was proposed for construction by contract in the 1896 budget (submitted May 1895) and moved to a dockyard when the Budget Commission on 13 July 1895 struck most of the overseas station ships from that budget and cancelled credits for them on 24 October 1895.

On 1 August 1895 Minister of Marine Besnard asked the *Conseil des travaux* to examine draft specifications for a battleship which the Director of Materiel, then naval constructor Jules Omer Lemaire, probably assisted by naval constructor Alphonse Hauser, the chief of his new *Section technique des constructions navales* (established on 9 July 1895), had drafted at his direction. The note of 30 July 1895 by Lemaire that forwarded the draft stated that Besnard had given him the following requirements orally: a speed of 17 knots under natural and very near 18 knots under moderately forced draught, a range of 4500nm at 10 knots in trials and 4000nm in service, a main armament of two 305mm M1893 as in *Bouvines* and a secondary battery of six 138.6mm M1893 and four 100mm guns. The advent of Harvey face-hardened steel made possible notable reductions in armour thicknesses and weights compared to *Bouvines*. After developing the detailed specifications and after agreement with the Chief of the Naval General Staff, the Director of Artillery, and the Chief of Submarine Defences, Lemaire concluded that the displacement should not exceed a maximum limit of 8,700 tons.

The Council examined the specifications on 24 August 1895. The ship was essentially an enlarged *Bouvines*. It had two 305mm M1893 guns in the same locations and the same heights above the water as did *Bouvines* and a secondary battery of six 138.6mm M1893 in redoubts or casemates on the upper deck between the main turrets and four 100mm M1891 guns in the superstructure. Like the earlier ship it had one military mast and twin screws. It was protected by the standard French complete armour belt with the principal armoured deck on top, although it added the second deck (in this case of 34mm hardened steel) at the bottom of the belt that had been introduced in *Masséna*, *Bouvet*, and *Charlemagne*

The *Conseil des travaux* did its own calculations and concluded that it was unlikely that an 8,700-ton ship with these characteristics could contain machinery large enough to guarantee 18 knots at forced draught. It would probably need at least another 180 tons. Since the 8,700-ton limit was firm and nothing else in the specifications seemed safe to reduce the Council softened the speed requirements to say that designers should get as close to 18 knots forced and 17 knots normal as the displacement limit of 8,700 tons would permit.

*The characteristics are based on the specifications produced by the Conseil des travaux on 24 August 1895.*

**Dimensions & tons:** 8,700t disp. (max). Men: 414. One military mast with two armed tops.

**Machinery:** 18kts moderately forced if possible. 2 screws. 2 engines. Multi-tubular boilers. Range 4,500nm (trials), 4,000nm (in service) @ 10kts.

**Armour:**

Side: Belt at waterline (Harvey cemented, to 0.50m above the waterline) 280mm amidships to 240mm forward and 200mm aft. Side above belt 75mm including plating (height 1m, more in bow) with cofferdam behind it. Transverse bulkhead forward 150mm.

Guns: Main turrets (Harvey cemented) 300mm on 240mm bases. Casemates 120mm over the guns and 60mm between them (150mm over the foremost guns). Shields for 100mm guns 54mm.

Decks: Armoured deck at top of belt 75mm including 20mm plating. Splinter deck at bottom of belt 34mm hard steel (2 x 17mm layers)

Conning tower (Harvey cemented) 240mm.

**Guns:** 2 x 305mm M1893 (in balanced turrets fore and aft), 6 x 138.6mm M1893 (in redoubts as in *Charlemagne* and *D'Entrecasteaux* on the upper deck between the turrets, two forward, two aft, and two amidships), 4 x 100mm M1891 (on the superstructure, 2 forward and 2 aft, but not above the 138.6mm), 8 x 47mm QF, 4 x 37mm QF.

**Torpedoes:** Two underwater tubes on the sides, with space reserved for two above water behind the 75mm armour. **Searchlights:** six.

Matters stood here when Besnard left office on 28 October 1895 and Deputy Édouard Lockroy began a first short term as Minister on 1 November 1895. Lockroy lost no time in making Émile Bertin his Director of Materiel on 13 November 1895, Hauser remaining chief of the *Section technique*. Around the end of 1895 the name *Henri IV* was transferred from the deferred full-sized A3 to the smaller A6.

---

**HENRI IV.** *Cuirassé d'escadre*. Monitor-type battleship with tall centreline superstructure, two single centreline main battery turrets and a single centreline turret for one of its seven secondary guns. Two funnels, one military and one pole mast. Designed by Bertin. To *Cuirassé garde-côtes* 1.1909.

Neither Lockroy nor Bertin wanted to proceed with Besnard's unimaginative A6. Bertin noted that with the height of her armoured hull one eighth of that required by her beam and without a cellular layer this *Tréhouart empiré* (worsened) was also dangerous. Lockroy, however, was unwilling to increase her displacement above the 8,700 tons in the budget. Bertin, a specialist in ship stability since the 1870s, felt that there were two ways to design a battleship so that it would not capsize too easily, either with a narrow and tall armoured hull as in HMS *Majestic* and his design that became *Patrie*, or with a wide and low hull as in monitors. (In 1906 he called them respectively *cuirassés-croiseurs* and *cuirassés-monitors*, quickly adding that *Patrie* was no more a cruiser than its predecessors and *Henri IV* was not a monitor or *garde-côtes*.) Given the impossibility of getting the 14,000-ton displacement needed for the first option, he chose the monitor option. Lockroy and Bertin agreed on the main lines of the radically new design on 27 February 1896, and work on it probably began earlier on 18 January 1896. Bertin called his ship a *cuirassé à grande stabilité initiale*

*genre monitor*, a battleship with great initial stability of the monitor type, that consisted of a low-freeboard monitor hull surmounted by a tall superstructure running down the centreline that completely defended the bow against the seas when running into them but remained narrow enough so as not to lose the benefits for stability of the low freeboard hull on the sides and stern. It would remedy the main weakness of all French battleships since *Amiral Duperré* and many foreign ships, which was that if their light upper works were destroyed they would lose stability when the top of their armour belt went under the water and would then capsize. (Bertin was known to call existing French battleships *chavirables*, or prone to capsizing.) He argued that his design combined the extreme stability of monitors, which would not change as long as the armour was intact, with capabilities of steaming into heavy seas and habitability qualities that were typical of cruisers. However, he kept the main armoured deck at the top of the belt rather than at its lower edge as he was advocating for high-freeboard battleships. Bertin's first design was for a 7,600-ton 16-knot monitor-type ship (she was listed at 7,000 tons in the January 1896 fleet list). This design had one twin 305mm turret on the low after deck, two 305mm mortars on the centreline forward and superfiring aft, and eight 164.7mm guns including six in a redoubt amidships and two in the hull sides forward. In early 1896 Bertin enlarged this design to an 8,950-ton 17-knot ship with a revised armament of two single 274.4mm turrets on the centreline, one forward and one aft, and seven 138.6mm guns, six in the amidships redoubt and one superfiring aft. He insisted that his ship was a *cuirassé d'escadre* and not a coast defence ship, and she was duly classed as such in fleet lists through 1908.

The Minister, now Vice Admiral Besnard in his second and longer term, submitted the specifications for Bertin's enlarged design to the *Conseil des travaux* on 22 May 1896 and it examined them on 9 June 1896. The Council found the speed of 17 knots inadequate because many foreign ships were being designed for 18 knots, the armament of two 274.4mm guns inadequate because although some foreign ships had main battery guns smaller than 305mm, none had only two of them, and also found the protection of the upper works inadequate. It also thought that the quick roll of an excessively stable hull might make it a poor gun platform. On 4 July 1896 Besnard ordered the construction of the ship at Cherbourg. He then sent Bertin's complete design to the Council, which complained on 25 July 1896 that none of its recommendations had been taken. As before it was willing to see the ship built as a one-time experiment if its recommendations were taken but otherwise opposed it, although it made some detailed recommendations in case Minister Besnard insisted on proceeding with it. Bertin had had strained relations with the *Conseil des travaux* since the 1870s, and from this point on they simply got worse. The plans for the lines and weights of the ship were signed by Bertin on 31 July 1896 and approved by Besnard and sent to Cherbourg on 1 August 1896. The engines were ordered from Indret on 8 October 1896.

One innovation in this design was the use of a superfiring turret, in this case a single 138.6mm turret firing over the after 274.4mm turret. This gun was originally in a shield, but it became possible to substitute a turret when a change was made in September 1897 from Lagrafel et d'Allest boilers to lighter Niclausse boilers. As of 1906 this gun was restricted from firing aft of the beam for fear of blast effects on the 274.4mm turret captain's hood, experiments having been conducted with sheep. Another innovation was to carry the lower armoured deck down in a semi-circle at the side of the ship to join the double bottom and form an early type of torpedo defence. Her commander wrote in 1906 that the primary armoured deck, not being under superstructure or behind side armour, was directly exposed to the fire of the enemy. He also noted that the operating range of *Henri IV* was superior to that of all of the other battleships then in service and was essentially that of a cruiser.

On 13 May 1896 Besnard changed the battleship A3 at Brest, which Lockroy had intended to build to Bertin's 14,000-ton design, to a 9,000-ton *cuirassé d'escadre* analogous to *Henri IV*. The idea was dropped and in early 1897 A3 became the 12,000-ton *Iéna*.

*The characteristics are based on a devis dated 7.10.1903.*

**Dimensions & tons:** 109.800m oa, 108.000m wl, 108.000m pp (tip fwd to stern) x 22.200m ext & wl. 8,948.381t disp. (designed), 8958.870t (normal, updated in the devis), 9,263.162t (with coal surcharge). Draught: 6.850m mean, 7.000m aft (actual), 7.100m aft (keel line projected). Men: 462 including 26 officers. Freeboard aft 0.90m.

**Machinery:** 11,500ihp designed at 125rpm and 20kg/cm² boiler pressure (17/cm² at the engines). Trials (23.6.1903) 11,316.58ihp = 17.289kts at 124.75rpm and 17.844kg/cm² boiler pressure. 3 screws. 3 vertical triple expansion engines with 3 cylinders of 0.830m, 1,240m, and 1.840m diameter and 0.720m stroke. 12 Niclausse boilers (8 large and 4 small). 725t coal normal (max capacity 1,053t). Range with normal coal (725t) 4,303nm @ 10kts; with 1,015t coal 6,020nm @ 10kts.

**Armour:**

Side: Belt at waterline (cemented except special steel at extreme bow) 280mm amidships, 180mm ends. Total height amidships 2.193m of which 0.900m above wl. Side above belt (special steel) covering the deck above the belt and the sides of the 138.6mm gun redoubt above it 100mm upper edge, 70mm lower edge, all on 15mm hull plating.

Guns: Main turrets (cemented) 270mm max with 210mm fixed bases. Turret for after 138.6mm gun (special steel) 85mm with 102mm fixed base. Shields for two 138.6mm guns (special steel) 72mm. Casemates for four 138.6mm guns 80mm sides.

Decks: Armoured deck (extra mild steel) 60mm on 20mm hull plating at ends (including on the low stern), 30mm on 20mm hull plating behind the side armour above the belt. Splinter deck 32mm special steel. This splinter deck curved down to form an anti-torpedo bulkhead before joining the inner bottom.

Conning tower (special steel): 190mm.

**Guns:** 2 x 274.4mm/40 M1893-96 (single turrets fore and aft), 7 x 138.6mm/45 M1893 QF (1 in turret aft, 4 in armoured redoubt on the battery deck, 2 in shields on the upper deck), 2 x 65mm/16 M1881 landing, 12 x 47mm/40 M1885 QF, 2 x 37mm/20 M1885 QF. **Torpedoes:** 2 submerged tubes for 450mm M1892 torpedoes. **Searchlights:** 6 x 60cm.

*Henri IV* (A6) Cherbourg Dyd/Indret (engines designed by Lhomme). On list 1.1896. Ord: 4.7.1896. K: 15.7.1897. L: 23.8.1899. Comm: 16.12.1902 (trials), 21.9.1903 (full).

Budget 1896. Machinery installed 7.2.1901 to 11.1.1902 when the boilers were first lit off. Trials 4-6.1903. Assigned to *Escadre du Nord* 15.9.1903 replacing *Valmy*. Moved from Cherbourg to the Mediterranean in 1909, arriving at Bizerte 10.10.1909. Collided with the destroyer *Dard* 13.12.1909 cutting off the destroyer's bow back to the bridge (she survived). War service in the Dardanelles in 1915 and as base ship for transports at Taranto in 1917-18. Decomm. 1.8.1918, assigned 10.9.1919 to replace *Amiral Tréhouart* at the new school for radiomen at Toulon. Struck 21.6.1920, struck again 15.1.1921. Sold 22.6.1921.

---

The battleship *Henri IV* in the pre-1908 two-tone paint scheme, although the caption uses her post-1908 classification of 'coast defence battleship' which better matched both her capabilities and her employment. The low monitor-type hull that her designer, Émile Bertin, used to get sufficient stability is readily apparent in this view, as is her single superfiring 138.6mm turret. *(Postcard by H. Laurent, Port-Louis)*

## The Programme of 1896

In 1896 Minister of Marine Besnard asked the *Conseil supérieur* for another update of the building programme. The Council did so in sessions of 17, 18, and 21 December 1896. This time the programme took Britain somewhat into account while retaining the primary focus on the Triple Alliance. The main feature of this revision was a strengthening of forces in Europe at the

473. - Le *Henri IV*, Garde-Côtes Cuirassé

expense of the station fleets. The Minister felt it was necessary, in order to gain acceptance of the considerable expenditures on the European fleet, to reduce to a strict minimum spending on the station fleets, whose importance was not generally appreciated outside the Navy. The Council, regretting having to accept this reduction, which it felt to be prejudicial to both French political action overseas and the maritime education of the Navy's officers, cut from the station fleets six of the ten armoured cruiser flagships, six of twelve 2nd class cruisers and seven of twelve 3rd class cruisers. These savings were used to provide an additional four battleships as replacements for those in the four European squadrons (*escadres*) and to provide cruisers and other ships for a fifth squadron built around the nine most modern coast defence ships. The number of torpedo vessels for the *escadres* (*contre-torpilleurs* of the *Hallebarde* type and 150-ton *torpilleurs d' escadre*, formerly *torpilleurs de haute mer*) was increased to 30 of each, both numbers reflecting one for each of the 24 battleships plus six replacements. The number of *avisos-torpilleurs* acting as leaders in the coast defence fleet was reduced from 30 to 20.

### The Programme of 1898
With the clouds of the colonial rivalry with Britain gathering that led to a war scare in France in February and March and to the Fashoda crisis later in the year, the *Conseil supérieur* on 17 January 1898 addressed a question from Minister Besnard as to whether it wanted to adopt a proposal of two of its members to increase from 12 to 24 the number of armoured cruisers for European waters. The additional armoured cruisers were intended solely and specifically for commerce raiding against Britain. The council decided unanimously to raise the number to 18, which raised the number for the navy as a whole from 19 to 25. By five votes to four it also upheld the view expressed by the *Conseil de travaux* on 10 December 1897 that protected cruisers, with sizeable displacements, nothing but an armoured deck and cellular layer to protect their vitals, and no protection for the gun battery, no longer fulfilled the conditions necessary for a combat ship and that future cruisers smaller than armoured cruisers should be of the smaller *estafette* (dispatch) type. Both programmes are in Appendix F.

### Minister Lockroy's *cuirassé-croiseur*
The advent of melinite explosives and other issues persuaded Lockroy during his first ministry that sizeable displacement was needed for a balanced battleship. As a disciple of the *Jeune École* he also believed that speed was a form of protection that allowed refusing or accepting combat. He wrote that if we do not adopt the solutions of Britain (HMS *Magnificent*, *Renown*) and Italy (*Ammiraglio di Saint Bon*) we should at least look for new ones. Lockroy convened the *Conseil des travaux* and posed the question if something should be done about recent developments and it agreed. He planned to convene the *Conseil supérieur* later but ran out of time. Although the political opposition to large ships was even stronger than before, Lockroy accepted in early April 1896 the displacement of 14,000 tons and initiated the study of a new solution, a *cuirassé genre croiseur* (a cruiser type battleship) or *cuirassé-croiseur* (battleship-cruiser) that was two knots faster than battleships, would have two 305mm guns in single turrets and fourteen 164.7mm guns of which six were in single turrets. As soon as he returned to office Minister Besnard abruptly stopped the study of the *cuirassé-croiseur* that had begun in April.

Upon his return to the Ministry in June 1898 Lockroy took up again the *cuirassé-croiseur*. He asked the *Conseil supérieur* 'Have any new facts occurred that would cause a significant change in the characteristics of our combat vessels?' The options were to augment displacement to 14,000 or 15,000 tons without changing anything else or to use the progress in industry that had produced cemented armour to develop a combatant ship that combined the qualities of a battleship and those of a cruiser into a single type that would form a powerful homogeneous fleet to fight both near the coasts and also on the high seas. Lockroy and Bertin seem to have first considered in 1898 a *cuirassé-croiseur* of 13,500 tons and 21 knots armed with four 240mm and sixteen 164.7mm guns, but the specifications forwarded by Lockroy to the *Conseil supérieur* on 23.9.1898 were for a

*croiseur cuirassé de 1er rang* of 14,800 tons and 21 knots armed with four 305mm guns in two twin turrets and sixteen 164.7mm guns in eight twin turrets. It would have been protected at the waterline by a belt of 140-160mm instead of 300mm while the upper works were armoured with 100mm armour instead of 80mm. This was essentially Bertin's *Patrie* with protection traded off for speed.

The *cuirassé-croiseur* was mentioned in one form or another in budget reports and Parliamentary discussions, but it was definitively dropped when Deputy Jean Louis de Lanessan replaced Lockroy as Minister in June 1899. De Lanessan and Bertin refocused on Bertin's 14-15,000-ton battleship that was three knots slower but better protected and on the Programme of 1900 of which it was part. However, Lockroy, back in Parliament, did not give up and during the debates on the Programme of 1900 he asked instead for the construction under the ordinary budget of 6 *cuirassés-croiseurs* and a 250 million franc loan to build six more along with 20 of Normand's *contre-torpilleurs* and 50 of Laubeuf's submersibles. The French never built a *cuirassé-croiseur*, but it was represented abroad by Cuniberti's *Vittorio Emmanuele* and the Japanese *Tsukuba*.

---

# II. COAST DEFENCE SHIPS

## (A) Coast Defence Battleships.
Classed as *Cuirassés d'escadre* in the 1.1890 fleet list, *Gardes-côtes cuirassés* 1.1891, and *Cuirassés garde-côtes* from 1.1892.

### Coast defence battleship intended to serve as the centre of action for a group of torpedo boats
On 25 January 1887 the *Conseil des travaux* examined detailed specifications referred to it by Minister of Marine Aube for a *garde-côtes cuirassé destiné à servir de centre d'action à un groupe de torpilleurs*. Aube envisioned a ship of not over 6,500 tons and 95m in length with a speed of at least 16 knots. Its two 34cm guns would be mounted either in a single turret as in *Fulminant* or in two centreline barbettes as in *Furieux*. Its maximum belt armour would be 35cm with deck armour of 50mm and a 5mm splinter deck. It would have one military mast with an armed top. Its special facilities to support torpedo boats included magazines and workshops to store and repair 24 torpedoes, air compressors for them, two evaporators and auxiliary boilers to make fresh water, cargo handling gear to embark and disembark torpedoes and replenish the torpedo boats with fresh water and coal, and temporary accommodations for the officers and men of three torpedo boats. The Council felt it was better not to put the two guns in the same turret and opted for the two barbettes, but as the ship seemed likely to fight head on supporting an attack by the torpedo boats or their withdrawal, it wanted the two barbettes abreast. It also suggested considering turrets as in *Hoche* instead of barbettes, increasing the armoured deck to 70mm, enlarging the main boilers and deleting the auxiliary boilers, and adding a torpedo armament and possibly a second military mast. These changes would increase the displacement to 6,600 tons.

Aube sent these specifications to the ports on 17 February 1887 but it was not until 7 February 1888, with Vice Admiral Jules François Émile Krantz as Minister of Marine, that the Council examined the eight designs received in response to it. Two, by Huin and naval constructor Séverin Edmond Bayssellance, were worth additional work, but one senior council member challenged the concept of a combatant ship being used to store munitions and supplies, especially delicate items like torpedoes, and did not feel that a coast defence battleship could fill this function. The Council concluded its report with the statement that it did not think the concept of a coast defence ship acting as the centre of action for torpedo boats to be a happy one and advised that it should not be put into practice. No ship was specially built for this purpose, but a number of existing coast defence ships were fitted with stowage for spare torpedoes for torpedo boats.

---

*JEMMAPES* **Class.** *Cuirassés garde-côtes.* Coast defence battleships with two single centreline main battery turrets, a low flush deck, and a ram bow. Two funnels, one military foremast, and a diminutive pole mast aft. Designed by de Bussy.

The renewal in February 1887 of the Triple Alliance that associated Italy with Germany and Austria revived concerns in the French Parliament over the threat that fast Italian battleships if based at La Maddalena could pose to French coasts. French mobilisation exercises at Toulon produced a naval scare in Italy and in February 1888 Germany engineered a British naval visit to Genoa to show support for the Italians. Minister of Marine Krantz included one small coast defence battleship (*Tréhouart*, later *Amiral Tréhouart*), and one small armoured cruiser (*Charner*, later *Amiral Charner*) in the regular budget for 1889 (submitted in June 1888). Some in Parliament thought more should be done about the Italian threat, and although Krantz announced his intention to ask for supplementary credits the leftist deputy (and future Minister of Marine) Jean Louis de Lanessan on 8 July 1889 interpolated the Minister on how he planned to remedy the inadequacy of the navy for coast defence, and he was followed on the last day of the session, 16 July 1889, by a leader of the right in the Chamber, Jules Delafosse, who protested when Krantz reported that a 58 million franc credit awaited only the approval of the Minister of Finance. The Chamber then bypassed its usual procedures and voted for the construction of three more *Tréhouart*s and 44 torpedo boats. This resulted in a law of 22 November 1889 that created an extraordinary budget for 1890. The 44 torpedo boats became four torpedo avisos similar to *Léger*, ten seagoing torpedo boats of the *Agile* and *Avant Garde* types, and thirty 54-ton 34-metre Normand-designed coast defence torpedo boats, although money ran out after 21 of the larger 36-metre type were ordered instead (*Nos 147-149* and *152-169*). Of the four coast defence battleships thus funded, *Jemmapes* and *Valmy* were built to the original design for the type and *Tréhouart* (the original name ship for the class) and *Bouvines* were built to a modified design.

On 15 November 1888 de Bussy sent Minister of Marine Krantz a note on the newly-completed coast defence ship *Furieux*, which he had designed in 1878 and which in June 1888 had conducted a month-long cruise along the northern French coast. Krantz responded on the same date by inviting de Bussy to draft a design for a coast defence battleship derived from *Furieux* that would have the same scale of artillery, protection, draught and coal capacity as the earlier ship but with a speed with natural draught of

16 instead of 14 knots and using modern Belleville boilers. She was to be inscribed on the fleet list as *Tréhouart*. On 14 February 1889 de Bussy delivered a design with lengthened hull lines and reduced beam and draught which raised the designed displacement to 6,595 tons from the 6,019 tons of *Furieux* as completed. He replaced the barbettes in *Furieux* with two single turrets for far more powerful 340mm/42 M1887 guns that were copies of the after turret in *Brennus*, added four 100mm guns, and provided one military mast like the two in *Hoche*. The bow was suitable for ramming and the stern was vaulted (hollowed out underneath). The design inherited nothing from the 1887 design for a torpedo boat mother ship and had no features for supporting torpedo boats. The *Conseil des travaux* approved de Bussy's proposal on 26 February 1889 as being faithful to the Minister's instructions. The plans for a *garde-côtes cuirassé type Furieux modifié (Jemmapes et Valmy)* were completed on 2 July 1889 and approved by Minister Krantz on 6 July 1889. Both ships were named on 29 November 1889 and the contract for their construction was signed on 18 December 1889 and approved on 26 December 1889. The engines were designed by the builder and built at Saint Denis. On 3 October 1890 the Navy accepted the shipbuilder's proposal to award half of the belt armour of *Jemmapes* and probably also *Valmy* to Schneider (steel) and half to Saint-Chamond (compound), and the two firms also split the deck armour while Saint-Chamond got the contract for the turret armour a year later.

The Bullivant nets were suppressed in both ships by an order of 28 April 1894. In 1898 the rate of fire of the main guns was one round every 5 minutes; this was speeded up between 1900 and 1902 by adding equipment for hand loading. The commanding officer of *Jemmapes* reported in January 1896 that the low bow was badly protected against the sea and that at speeds over 13 knots it created a bow wave that over 15 knots became an almost insurmountable barrier, any additional coal burned beyond that point being almost totally wasted.

*The characteristics are based on a devis for* Jemmapes *dated 25.2.1896 and one of the same date for* Valmy.

**Dimensions & tons:** 89.600m oa, 89.350m wl, 86.535m pp (tip fwd to rudder) x 17.500m ext (above wl), 17.480m wl. 6,579.477t disp. Draught: 6.7073m mean, 7.4373m aft. Men: 299.

**Machinery:** 1,875nhp and 8,400ihp designed at 108rpm and 15kg/cm² boiler pressure (12kg/cm² at engines). Trials (*Jemmapes*, 13.10.1894) 9,118.0ihp = 15.682kts at 111.125rpm and 14.262kg/cm² boiler pressure; (*Valmy*, 15.5.1895) 8,911.6ihp = 15.916kts at 110.69rpm and 13.108kg/cm² boiler pressure. 2 screws. 2 horizontal triple-expansion engines with 3 cylinders of 0.790m, 1,220m, and 1.900m diameter and 1.00m stroke. 16 Lagrafel et d'Allest boilers. 350.840t coal. Range with 335 tons of coal 2,667nm @ 10.924kts.

**Armour:**
Side: Belt at waterline (hammered steel to port, compound to starboard) 460mm amidships, 310mm fwd, 410mm aft. Total height amidships 1.90m.
Guns: Main turrets 450mm (compound) with 400mm fixed bases (forged steel). 100mm gun shields (hammered steel) 80mm.
Decks (special mild steel): 70mm on centreline amidships and aft, 60mm forward, 100mm outboard, all on 20mm hull plating.
Conning tower (laminated steel): 80mm on 20mm plating

**Guns:**
(1896) 2 x 340mm/42 M1887 (turrets), 4 x 100mm/45 M1891(2) QF (at corners of shelter deck), 1 x 65mm/16 M1881 landing, 6 x 47mm/40 M1885 QF, 8 x 37mm/20 M1885 QF. **Torpedoes:** 2 above water tubes for 450mm M1889 torpedoes. **Searchlights:** 5 x 60cm.
(c1907) 2 x 340mm. 4 x 100mm, 10 x 47mm, 2 x 37mm. **Torpedoes:** tubes removed in 1906. The 65mm landing gun was retained as a line throwing gun.

*Jemmapes* A.C. Loire, Saint Nazaire/ACL, Saint Denis.
On list 1.1890. Ord: 18.12.1889. K: 26.12.1889. L: 27.4.1892.

The coast defence battleship *Valmy* as built except that her pole mast on the after superstructure has been lengthened. *Tréhouart* and *Bouvines* were also initially to have been built to this design. The tilted yard and masthead spars suggest she may be in official mourning. (*NHHC, NH-64201*)

Comm: 19.1.1894 (trials), 4.3.1895 (full).
Budget 1890 (extraordinary). Machinery installed 5.1892-3.7.1893.
Arrived Brest from Saint Nazaire 24.12.1893 for trials. Official
machinery trials 5.1894-1.1895, machinery accepted 31.1.1895. Joined
the *Escadre du Nord* 16.3.1895. In normal reserve at Cherbourg 1902,
left Cherbourg for Brest 20.9.1909 and Brest for Rochefort 9.12.1909,
decomm. there 22.3.1910. Struck 3.8.1910, mooring hulk at Rochefort
1910-1914, hulk there 1920-1927. Ceded to the Société Goldenberg in
a contract dated 5.11.1927, being BU at Rochefort 1.1929.

*Valmy* A.C. Loire, Saint Nazaire/ACL, Saint Denis.
On list 1.1890. Ord: 18.12.1889. K: 1889. L: 6.10.1892.
Comm: 12.1894 (trials), 14.8.1895 (full).
Budget 1890 (extraordinary). Machinery installed 11.1892 to 15.3.1894.
Machinery accepted 13.8.1895 after trials, trial results approved and
entered into full commission 14.8.1895 to replace *Requin* in the
*Escadre du Nord*. In reserve from 1903. To Brest 1-2.9.1909 and on
11.10.1909 was ordered decommissioned as soon as possible. Struck
1.7.1910, offered for sale 20.7.1911 at Brest by the Domaines with
*Formidable* and others.

---

**BOUVINES.** *Cuirassé garde-côtes.* Coast defence battleship with two single
centreline main battery turrets, a long forecastle, and a ram bow. Two
funnels, one military foremast, and a full-height pole mast aft. Designed by
de Bussy and Opin.

*Bouvines* was one of three sisters to *Tréhouart* ordered under the extraordinary budget for 1890 to be built by contract. She was named on 29 November 1889 and the contract for her construction was signed on 18 December 1889 and approved on 26 December 1889. For the original design of all four ships see the *Jemmapes* class, above. On 4 September 1890 the Director of Mateiral, Bienaymé, asked the office under naval constructor Godron that supervised work by contract to submit a design for modifications of the internal arrangements of *Bouvines* to allow her to embark a rear admiral. On 11 November naval constructor Opin supervising work at FCM La Seyne submitted such a plan. Opin wrote that adding an admiral to *Bouvines* could not be done without a nearly total revision of the internal arrangements of the ship and even some of its fundamental structures. He decided to take advantage of this situation to correct some of the deficiencies in the design, including the rounded lines of the ends which had no other purpose than to save weight, the low bow that would be constantly wet preventing the use in many circumstances of the bow gun, and the habitability of the ship which left much to be desired. His solution included the substitution of 305mm/45 guns for the 340mm/42 guns, following the example of *Carnot* and *Charles Martel*, the weight saved making possible the addition of a shelter deck above the upper deck from forward of the after turret to 9m before the forward turret where it sloped down to the original upper deck as a breakwater, and even adding two 164.7mm/45 guns in half turrets at the after end of the shelter deck. He put the four 100mm guns of the original design in a redoubt forward. The modified design displaced 6,589.880 tons.

On 29 November 1890 Bienaymé asked the Chief of the Naval General Staff, Vice Admiral Vignes, about modifications to the *Tréhouart* class, and on 4 December 1890 Vignes said that he felt it was necessary to fit two ships of this type with full facilities for a rear admiral. He felt this could be done in the manner that Opin suggested. The other two ships would not be modified as their 340mm guns were already being manufactured. Bienaymé then asked Opin to complete his proposal with the necessary calculations.

Director of Materiel Bienaymé formally submitted Opin's redesign to Minister Barbey on 23 January 1891, citing the support of senior operational commanders for the new design, noting that it was the change in calibre of the main battery that had made it possible to add flag facilities to the ship, and suggesting that the forecastle added by Opin be extended to the bow and the forward turret be raised accordingly, both being made possible by reducing the armour of the main turrets as had been done in *Charles Martel* and *Carnot*. On the same date Minister Barbey approved Bienaymé's recommendation that Opin's design be submitted to the *Conseil des travaux*.

The *Conseil des travaux* examined Opin's design on 11 February 1891. It recommended adding four more 100mm QF for a total of eight instead of Opin's two 164.7mm. It supported the idea of extending the raised deck amidships to the bow, although calculations of trim and stability would need to be done, but opposed reducing the turret armour (40cm) in Opin's design, preferring to take the weight out of the reserve. It also recommended adding a signal mast aft. Opin submitted his revised design on 16 March 1891 (the shipyard director at FCM, Lagane, assisted) and the Council reviewed it again on 17 April 1891. The designed displacement was now 6,593.518 tons, the turret armour was 40cm, and the signal mast was removed. The reserve was now too low and the Council recommended reducing turret armour to 37cm, replacing the armoured redoubts around the four forward 100mm guns with 40mm armoured shields (later increased to 72mm) as for the after guns, and keeping the signal mast.

On 30 April 1891 Bienaymé recommended to Minister Barbey that *Bouvines* and *Tréhouart* be modified according to Opin's design. He reported that *Jemmapes* and *Valmy* were too far advanced to be modified and that the navy needed only two of the ships fitted with flag accommodations. Minister Barbey approved this recommendation the same day and approved the plans on 4 May 1891. Marrel Frères provided compound belt and turret armour and iron deck armour, Schneider may have provided some steel belt armour as they did for the other three vessels of this general type. The bows of all four ships were reinforced for ramming

*The characteristics are based on a devis dated 14.2.1896.*
**Dimensions & tons:** 89.650m oa, 89.382m wl, 86.500m pp (tip fwd to rudder) x 17.867m ext (above wl), 17.784m wl. 6,788.833t disp. Draught: 6.858m mean, 7.488m aft. Men: 216.
**Machinery:** 8,330ihp designed at 114rpm and 15kg/cm² boiler pressure (12kg/cm² at engines). Trials (26.6.1895) 8,865.07ihp = 16.05kts at 116.55rpm and 14.031kg/cm² boiler pressure. 2 screws. 2 horizontal (slightly inclined) triple expansion engines with 3 cylinders of 0.83m, 1.23m, and 1.86m diameter and 1.00m stroke. 16 multitubular Lagrafel et d'Allest boilers. 450t coal. Range with normal coal (457.5t) 2,068nm @ 10kts, with full coal (557.5t) 2,522nm @ 10kts.
**Armour:**
Side (compound and perhaps steel): Belt at waterline 464mm amidships, 310mm fwd, 417mm aft. Total height amidships 1.895m.
Guns: Main turrets (compound) 370mm with 320mm fixed bases.
Decks: Armoured deck (iron) 72mm at centreline thickening to 100mm at the sides of the ship, both on 20mm hull plating. Splinter deck below the armoured deck and over the machinery 6mm hull plating (the regular decks were 5mm).
Conning tower (hammered steel): 80mm.
**Guns:**
(1896) 2 x 305mm/45 M1887 (turrets at ends), 8 x 100mm/53.3 M1892 long Canet QF (4 on shelter deck, 2 on fore bridge, 2 on aft bridge), 1 x 65mm/16 M1881 landing, 4 x 47mm/40 M1885 QF, 10 x 37mm revolving cannon. **Torpedoes:** 2 tubes for 450mm M1889 torpedoes above water. **Searchlights:** 5 x 60cm.
(after 1905) 2 x 305mm, 8 x 100mm, 8 x 47mm QF, 3 x 37mm QF (for the boats). The 65mm landing gun was retained as a line throwing gun for mooring the ship. **Torpedoes:** tubes removed.

*Bouvines* F.C. Méditerranée, La Seyne/FCM, Marseille (Menpenti).
On list 1.1890. Ord: 18.12.1889. K: 30.9.1890. L: 29.3.1892.
Comm: 15.10.1894 (trials), 1.12.1895 (full).
Budget 1890 (extraordinary). Machinery installed 30.6.1892 to 21.12.1893. Official trials in summer 1895. Full comm. 1.12.1895, to Brest from Toulon 13-22.1.1896, joined the *Escadre du Nord* 1.2.1896 as flagship of its 2nd Division. Flagship of the *Division des gardes-côtes*

*de l'Escadre de la Méditerranée* 15.12.1898. Her division was attached to the *Escadre du Nord* at Cherbourg 22.7.1900. Flagship of the 2nd Division of the *Escadre du Nord* 1.9.1901 until placed in reserve 1.1.1907. Recomm. 13.4.1910 as annex to the 1st flotilla for torpedo boats and submarines at Cherbourg. To *Garde-côtes cuirassé annexe des flottilles, armé avec effectif spécial* at Cherbourg, 1.1.1911. To special reserve 1.6.1912 and decomm. 6.7.1912. Base ship for submarines 1914 and then for boarding vessels, guns removed during war. Struck 8.6.1918. Offered for sale 2.6.1920 at Cherbourg, sold 4.9.1920 to Mr. S. Francart of Enghien to BU.

---

**AMIRAL TRÉHOUART (originally *TRÉHOUART*).** *Cuirassé garde-côtes.*
Coast defence battleship with two single centreline main battery turrets, a long forecastle, and a ram bow. One funnel, one military foremast, and a diminutive pole mast aft. Designed by de Bussy and Opin.

*Tréhouart* was initially the name ship of a class of four, the original design being the one by de Bussy for a modified *Furieux* to which *Jemmapes* and *Valmy* were built. On 21 October 1890 Minister of Marine Barbey asked for a study of ways to add to her design the facilities needed to accommodate a rear admiral and his staff. The senior naval constructor at Lorient, Eynaud, submitted a preliminary report on 31 October 1890 pointing out that in the original design all officers and men were berthed on a single deck (the armoured deck) running the length of the hull, that this space

was already full with ship's company, and that a flag staff could not be added there. He concluded that it would be necessary to add a second deck level amidships between the turrets, thus raising the entire superstructure by a deck, and that an additional deckhouse would be needed at its after end for the admiral's quarters. (The resulting superstructure would resemble that of *Hoche*.) Lorient was negotiating with the boiler supplier, Belleville, to trunk the two funnels into one and free up some badly needed space. The *Conseil des travaux* reviewed Eynaud's report on 25 November 1890 and recommended that the project not be proceeded with because studies had made it clear that, if fitted with facilities suitable for an Admiral, *Tréhouart* would end up with a considerable weight surcharge and a reduction in stability from weights high in the ship that would put her at risk from a military perspective. The Council made some suggestions in case the Minister insisted, but in the meantime naval constructor Opin stationed at La Seyne had developed a much more ambitions solution to the problem for *Bouvines* (q.v.) that saved weight by replacing the 340mm guns with 305mm guns and added what became a long forecastle deck extending from the bow to the after turret. On 30 April 1891 Director of Materiel Bienaymé recommended to Minister Barbey that both *Bouvines* and *Tréhouart* be modified according to Opin's design. Although *Bouvines* and *Tréhouart* ended up being built to the same modified plans, *Tréhouart* had twelve Belleville boilers all trunked into a single funnel (probably inherited from Eynaud's design) while the three contract ships including *Bouvines* had sixteen Lagrafel et d'Allest boilers that needed the original two

Outboard profile and plan of the shelter deck (*spardeck*) of the coast defence battleship *Bouvines* built at La Seyne on plans by *Inspecteur Général du Génie Maritime* De Bussy. The plans by the Forges et Chantiers de la Méditerranée, dated 28 October 1894, carry the names of the director of the yard, Lagane, and the Navy's control officer, Dupont. The small calibre artillery carried at this time

included 4 x 47mm heavy QF guns (in the military top) and 10 x 37mm revolving cannon (2 on the platform above the conning tower which was the upper forward bridge, 2 on the lower forward bridge, 2 on the lower after bridge, and 4 at the corners of the spardeck near the 100mm guns). There was also 1 x 65mm M1881 landing gun stowed on the upper deck.

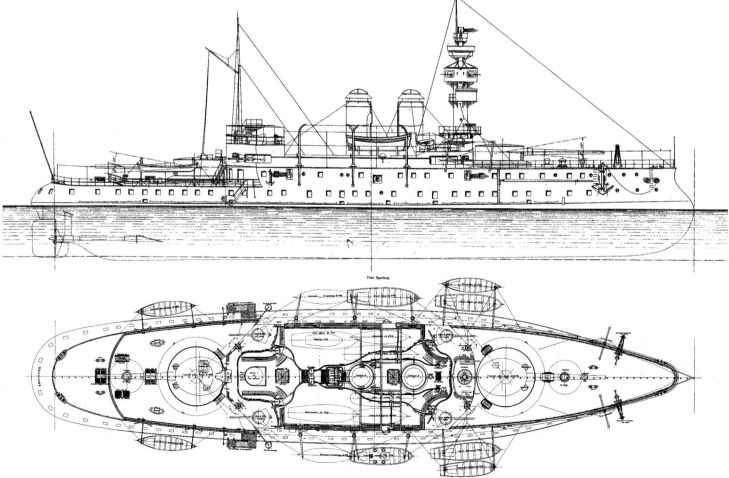

A fine view of the coast defence battleship *Amiral Tréhouart* that was originally attached to the technical characteristics document for the ship. A desire to add flag facilities to the design for *Jemmapes* and *Valmy* led to the addition of a forecastle and the many other changes seen here. *(Feuille signalétique for the ship dated May 1905)*

funnels. The armour belt was provided by three firms, Schneider (steel, amidships) and Marrel Frères and Saint-Chamond (compound, at the ends). Marrel provided the armour for the rotating parts of the turrets, the turret bases probably came from Schneider, and Guérigny supplied the iron deck armour.

The commander of *Amiral Tréhouart* reported at the end of a cruise in November 1897 that she was a good ship at sea, her speed was sufficient for a coast defence ship and she steered remarkably well. However, in the Atlantic an ocean swell on the beam produced rolls up to 35° to each side and prevented the use of the main guns which could not withstand rolls of over 15° without danger to their hydraulic mechanisms. A signal mast aft was necessary, the number of signal flag hoists was insufficient for ordinary signals and it was impossible to make long distance signals. It was unfortunate that the magazines for the 100mm QF guns were placed at the ends of the ship while the guns were near the middle. In summary *Amiral Tréhouart* met the requirements for a coast defence ship but could never be a *cuirassé d'escadre*, a function for which she had not been conceived.

*The characteristics are based on a devis dated 5.9.1896.*

**Dimensions & tons:** 89,745m oa, 89.545m wl, 89.545m pp (tip fwd to stern) x 17.882m ext (above wl), 17.825m wl. 6,778.364t disp. Draught: 6.8596m mean, 7.2739m aft. Men: 337.

**Machinery:** 8,350ihp designed at 113.5rpm and 17kg/cm² boiler pressure (12kg/cm² at engines). Trials (6.5.1896) 8,270.1ihp = 15.702kts at 112.22rpm and 15.899kg/cm² boiler pressure. 2 screws. 2 slightly inclined (3°40' off the horizontal) triple expansion engines with cylin-

ders 0.82, 1.20, and 1.92m diameter and 1.00m stroke. 12 Belleville boilers. 454.683t coal. Range with normal coal (530t) 2,705nm @ 10kts, with maximum coal (630t) 3,220nm @ 10kts.

**Armour:** (measurements in source are in cm)

Side: Belt at waterline 46cm amidships (steel), 31cm fwd (compound), 41cm aft (compound). Total height 1.9m.

Guns: Main turrets (compound) 37cm with 32cm fixed bases (hammered steel).

Decks: Armoured deck (iron) 7cm on centreline increasing progressively to 10cm at the outboard edges, all on 2cm hull plating. The profile of the deck was a shallow circular arc. Splinter deck probably as *Bouvines*.

Conning tower (special steel): 8cm plus 2cm plating.

**Guns:**

(1896) 2 x 305mm/45 M1887 (turrets at ends), 8 x 100mm/53.3 M1892 long Canet QF (4 on shelter deck, 2 on forward bridge and 2 on after bridge), 1 x 65mm/16 M1881 landing, 4 x 47mm/40 M1885 QF, 10 x 37mm revolving cannon. **Torpedoes:** 2 x 450mm tubes (above water). **Searchlights:** 5 x 60cm.

(after 1905) 2 x 305mm, 8 x 100mm, 8 x 47mm, 3 x 37mm. The 65mm landing gun was retained as a line throwing gun for mooring the ship. **Torpedoes:** tubes removed.

***Amiral Tréhouart*** Lorient Dyd/Indret (engines designed by Garnier).

On list 1.1890. Ord: 6.7.1889. K: 29.10.1889. L: 16.5.1893. Comm: 1.8.1895 (trials), 16.6.1896 (full).

Budget 1889 (delayed to 1890). Originally named *Tréhouart*, new name *Amiral Tréhouart* decided 25.3.1895 and promulgated 2.4.1895. Installation of engines began 5.3.1894, boilers first fired 16.4.1895, first static machinery trials 16.5.1895, fully manned for trials 15.10.1895. Arrived at Brest from Lorient 10.12.1895 to conduct trials. Joined the *Escadre du Nord* 29.6.1896. Alternated between Cherbourg and Brest 1901-1909. From Cherbourg to Toulon 13-28.10.1909, commissioned with a special crew 20.4.1910 for assignment as a *Garde-côtes cuirassé annexe des flottilles* supporting the 1st flotilla of torpedo vessels and submarines of the Mediterranean. To special reserve at Toulon 1.5.1912. Released from the reserve group 26.2.1914 and assigned to the school for chiefs of wireless radio posts. Replacement by *Henri IV* approved 10.9.1919. Struck 21.6.1920, replaced 15.11.1920 as prospective target for aviation bombing by ex-Austrian dreadnought *Prinz Eugen*, sold at Toulon 11.5.1921 to M. Saglia.

## (B) 1st Class Armoured Gunboats (*Canonnières cuirassées de 1re classe*).

To *Canonnières cuirassées* (without class) in the 1.1892 fleet list. These were listed with coast defence battleships and not with gunboats.

*ACHÉRON* Class. *Canonnières cuirassées de 1re classe.* Armoured gunboats with one single centreline main battery turret and a straight bow. One funnel, one pole mast. Designed by Chaudoye.

On 6 May 1881 the *Conseil d'Amirauté* adopted a fleet programme that closely resembled its 1872 and 1879 programmes but that included three new ship types that had been proposed since 1879 including armoured gunboats. (The others additions were four large torpedo craft that became

The 1st class armoured gunboat *Achéron* at Toulon, probably in 1892 after becoming station ship there in place of the sail transport *Provençale*. She was the only one of the four ships of her type to have 100mm guns in shields in sponsons on each side of the funnel. *(NHHC from ONI album of French warships, NH-74849)*

the *Condor* class torpedo cruisers and two torpedo boat transports to replace the converted *Japon*.) In 1879 the creation of light draught gunboats armed with one gun of large calibre was proposed to the Council for defence of French coasts and for the eventuality of a naval operation in the Baltic, where the Germans were known to be building vessels of the same kind which French fleets would encounter without being able to reach them because of their shallow draught. The inclusion of such vessels in the 1879 programme was set aside however because no satisfactory ships existed. In 1881 the French had more complete information and knew that the German navy already had 10 armoured gunboats of the *Wespe* class and was building others. The Council concluded that it was indispensable to create gunboats with a draught of 3m, with offensive and defensive strength at least equal to that of the German ships, and which in case of need would also be a useful complement for the defence of French coasts and ports. It included in the new programme eight of these armoured gunboats.

The German *Wespe* class armoured gunboats were designed in 1875 and eleven of them entered service between 1876 and 1881 (18 were planned). They displaced around 1,100 tons, were armed with one 305mm 22-calibre gun and had 203mm iron armour on their belts and barbettes. Their dimensions as known to the French in 1882 were 43.50m wl x 10.65m max x 3.10m draught fore and aft.

The French response took the form of two different designs, one designated 1st class with one 274.4mm gun in an enclosed turret and the other designated 2nd class with one 240mm gun in a barbette with an armoured hood. On 2 August 1882 Minister of Marine Vice Admiral Jean Bernard Jauréguiberry decided to begin construction of the eight armoured gunboats and on 5 August 1882 he allocated them to three dockyards and ordered the yards to prepare to begin their construction.

The 1st class ships were designed by naval constructor Jules Victor Charles Chaudoye then assigned to the *Inspection générale du génie*

*maritime* at Paris and also working for de Bussy's *Service technique des constructions navales.* Chaudoye's plan of the ship's hull lines and explanation of the design were dated 28 October 1882 and de Bussy recommended them for ministerial approval. They were approved and sent to Cherbourg on 30 October 1882. A contract with Claparède for the engines and boilers of all four ships was signed 23 April 1883 and approved on 23 May 1883.

The trials commission for *Achéron* reported that it was not possible to fire the 274.4mm gun directly forward or nearly so without having to fear grave damage to the deck and perhaps the hull. The various changes made between 1891 and 1900 added 70.138 tons to the ship.

*The characteristics are based on a devis for* Achéron *dated 28.2.1889.*

**Dimensions & tons:** 55.593m oa, 55.173m wl, 53.400m pp (wl fwd to rudder) x 12.302m ext (below wl), 11.923m wl. 1,721.410t disp. Draught: 3.750m mean, 3.787m aft. Men: 99.

**Machinery:** 275nhp and 1,650ihp designed including 180ihp for auxiliary machinery at 160rpm and 6kg/cm² boiler pressure (also 6kg/cm² at the engines). Designed speed 13kts. Trials (27.10.1888) 1,689.98ihp = 11.63kts at 155.875rpm. 2 screws. 2 horizontal (slightly inclined) compound engines with 2 cylinders of 0.660m and 1.140m diameter and 0.500m stroke. 4 locomotive boilers. 87.622t coal (72t normal). Range 1,800nm @ 8kts.

**Armour:**

Side (compound): Belt at waterline 200mm (entire length of ship). Total height amidships 1.00m, from 0.50m below the wl to 0.90m above.

Guns: Main turret 200mm, fixed base 200mm.

Decks: Armoured deck (iron?) flat 20mm on 30mm plating. A separate 5mm splinter layer was located immediately under the deck beams.

Conning tower: 10mm (2.4m diameter and 1.40m high with raised roof).

**Guns:**

(1882, design) 1 x 274.4mm/M1881 (turret), 2 x 100mm (upper deck in sponsons on the sides amidships), 2 x 37mm revolving cannon (positions on bridge wings and stern). **Torpedoes:** none. A third 100mm was added to the design on the stern in October 1884.

(1889, *Achéron*) 1 x 274.4mm/28.5 M1881 (turret), 3 x 100mm/26.2 M1881 (amidships sponsons and on the stern), 2 x 47mm/40 M1885 QF (bridge wings), 4 x 37mm revolving cannon (bridge deck and top). She also had a 4pdr bronze mountain rifle that was not part of her armament and that was used as a line throwing gun for mooring the ship.

(1890, *Cocyte*) 1 x 274.4mm, 2 x 100mm (upper deck in sponsons on the sides near the stern), 2 x 47mm QF (bridge wings), 4 x 37mm revolving cannon (bridge deck and top)

(1900, *Cocyte*) 1 x 274.4mm, 2 x 100mm/26.2 M1881 QF (converted 1892), 4 x 47mm QF (2 on the bridge deck and 2 on the bridge wings), 2 x 37mm QF (in the top).

(1901, *Achéron*) 1 x 274.4mm, 3 x 100mm/26.2 M1881 QF (converted 1891 to M1891 long), 4 x 47mm QF (2 added near the stern replacing the 37mm revolving cannon), 1 x 4pdr (86.5mm/11) bronze mountain rifle and 2 x 40cm searchlights. The 100mm guns received steel shields in July 1897 and the 47mm also had shields.

*Achéron* Cherbourg Dyd/Anc. Éts. Claparède, Saint Denis.

On list 1.1883. Ord: 5.8.1882. K: 4.11.1882. L: 23.4.1885.
  Comm: 10.4.1888 (trials), 2.10.1889 (full).

Budget 1884. Engine contract 23.4.1883. Machinery installed 22.9.1885 to 10.3.1886. To reserve 1.3.1889, trials resumed 25.8.1889. Left Cherbourg for Toulon 3.10.1889, arrived 2.11.1889 and to reserve the next day. Replaced the sail transport *Provençale* (1841) as station ship at Toulon 6.1.1892, then in commission for manoeuvres 7-8.1892 and back to reserve. At Bizerte 1897-1900. Reboilered 1900 at Toulon with new identical boilers by Fives-Lille, then comm. 8.1.1901 and left for Saigon 20.1.1901. Replaced *Styx* 3.1904 as central ship for the *Défense mobile* at Rach Dua (Vung Tao). Decomm. 3.10.1910 at Saigon.

Condemned 22.12.1911. Struck 6.2.1912, sold at auction on 10.12.1912 to M. Lê-Mai, a merchant of Cholon, Saigon, to BU.

*Cocyte* Cherbourg Dyd/Anc. Éts. Claparède, Saint Denis.

On list 1.1883. Ord: 5.8.1882. K: 4.11.1882. L: 13.1.1887.
  Comm: 20.1.1890 (trials). C: 7.1890.

Budget 1884. Engine contract 23.4.1883. Trial results approved 23.7.1890. To reserve at Cherbourg 1.8.1891, briefly commissioned for manoeuvres 7.1894, remained at Cherbourg until 20.1.1899 when commissioned to replace *Flamme* as stationnaire for the *Défense mobile* at Dunkirk. Moved there 19-20.2.1899. No further activity. Struck 9.3.1910, for sale at Cherbourg 1910-1911.

---

*PHLÉGÉTON* **Class.** *Canonnières cuirassées de 1re classe.* Configuration as the *Achéron* class. Designed by Chaudoye and Bosquillon de Frescheville.

When delivered in 1888 *Achéron* was found to be 85 tons overweight. Naval constructor Henri Raymond Bosquillon de Frescheville at Cherbourg proposed lengthening Chaudoye's design by 3.60m amidships for the two ships still on the ways, *Phlégéton* and *Styx,* to provide additional displacement to support the additional weight. De Frescheville submitted his design on 7 January 1889, the *Conseil des travaux* examined it on 29 January 1889, and the plans were approved on 12 February 1889. In this design the 100mm guns in the earlier ships were replaced with a single 138.6mm/30 M1881 gun on the stern. A proposal followed on 24 April 1891 for replacing this gun in both ships with ones converted to QF. The *Conseil des travaux* approved this project on 2 June 1891 and both ships were altered before completion.

*Phlégéton* was sent to Bizerte in 1901, and on 17 September 1901 Minister de Lanessan ordered the replacement of the 138.6mm/30 M1881 QF gun on her stern with a 100mm/26.2 M1881 QF gun. The change was made while in drydock in November 1902. The ship already had two 100mm/26.2 M1881 QF that had been added on the sides somewhat aft of amidships. None of the 100mm guns had shields. In 1905 Bizerte proposed adding two more 100mm QF guns and using *Phlégéton* with *Fusée* and *Mitraille,* below, to defend the entrance canal there. The change was ordered for *Phlégéton* on 19 September 1906 but the ship still had her 1902 armament when decommissioned in 1909.

*The characteristics are based on a devis for* Phlégéton *dated 11.7.1892.*

**Dimensions & tons:** 59.210m oa, 58.820m wl, 57.00m pp (wl fwd to rudder) x 12.312m ext (below wl), 11.932m wl. 1,796.079t disp. Draught: 3.612m mean, 3.7895m aft.

**Machinery:** 1,700ihp designed at 160rpm and 6kg/cm² boiler pressure. 2 screws. 2 horizontal compound engines (bases slightly inclined) with 2 cylinders of 0.660m and 1.140mm diameter and 0.500m stroke. 4 locomotive boilers. 72t coal (normal).

**Armour:** As *Achéron.*

**Guns:**

(1892) 1 x 274.4mm/28.5 M1881 (turret), 1 x 138.6mm/30 M1881 QF (converted, on the stern), 2 x 47mm/40 M1885 QF (on bridge wings), 3 x 37mm revolving cannon (6 positions provided), 2 x 37mm/20 M1885 QF (mast top). **Torpedoes:** none.

(1902, *Phlégéton*) 1 x 274.4mm, 3 x 100mm/26.2 M1881 QF (converted, 2 side and one on the stern), 4 x 47mm QF.

(1905, *Styx*) 1 x 274.4mm, 1 x 138.6mm, 4 x 47mm QF

*Phlégéton* Cherbourg Dyd/Anc. Éts. Claparède, Saint Denis.

On list 1.1883. Ord: 5.8.1882. K: 3.1885. L: 20.12.1890.
  Comm: 21.3.1892 (trials). C: 10.1892.

Budget 1884. Construction began 4.11.1882. Engine contract signed 23.4.1883 and notified 23.5.1883. Machinery installed 20.4.1891 to 2.2.1892. Manning for trials completed 20.4.1892. Trial results approved 10.1892. To 2nd category reserve at Cherbourg 1.12.1892, remained there to 1900 with short periods in commission in 1893 and

1894 for the summer manoeuvres. Recomm. 20.7.1901, left Cherbourg for Bizerte 19.8.1901 to replace the coast defence ship *Tempête*. Made frequent trips to Toulon for repairs. Began decommissioning at Bizerte 15.10.1909, crew roster closed 31.10.1909. Minister Delcassé on 8.7.1912 ordered her reserved her for military use in wartime, preventing her from being condemned. Her military mast and funnel were to be removed, her armament was to be reduced to four 47mm guns, and she was to be moored in the channel at Bizerte for use as a base by the navigation police there. She was in use there in 1916. Condemned 2.8.1916 when Paris notified Bizerte that no further military use of the ship was planned. On 27.4.1917 Paris notified Bizerte that it was looking for a ship to be beached in shallow water at Corfu as a gunnery target for light craft of the fleet and suggested *Phlégéton*, which was duly towed to Corfu during the summer of 1917.

**Styx** Cherbourg Dyd/Anc. Éts. Claparède, Saint Denis.
On list 1.1883. Ord: 5.8.1882. K: 9.1889. L: 22.8.1891.
   Comm: 1.12.1892 (trials). C: 3.1893.
Budget 1884. Engine contract 23.4.1883. Trial results approved 3.1893. To reserve after trials 20.6.1893. To full commission and assigned to Saigon 4.8.1893. Left Cherbourg for Saigon 27.8.1893. Central ship at Rach Dua (Vung Tao) 1903-04. Assisted in salvage of destroyer *Takou* 1911 at Poulo Condor Is. Hydrographic service on the Mekong River 1912-13. Struck 30.10.1919. Sold 19.12.1919 to Mr. Agliastro to BU.

---

## (C) 2nd Class Armoured Gunboats (*Canonnières cuirassées de 2e classe*).

To *Canonnières cuirassées* (without class) in the 1.1892 fleet list.

**FUSÉE Class.** *Canonnières cuirassées de 2e classe.* Armoured gunboats with one single centreline main battery barbette and a ram bow. One funnel, one or two pole masts with armed tops. Designed by Albaret.

The class was designed by naval constructor Jean Rosier Albaret, then secretary of the *Conseil des travaux* at Paris. Albaret's ship had a single internal deck (the armoured deck) with the hull sides above it curved inward and protected by a cofferdam. Albaret kept the top of the belt low to diminish as much as possible the vertical target exposed to enemy fire: its height above the waterline was 0.15m amidships and 0.45m at the ends while its depth below the waterline was 0.70m amidships, 1.50m fwd, and 0.35m aft. He studied with particular care the calibre of the main gun and determined that a new model 240mm 28.5-calibre 18-ton gun with a high initial velocity could pierce nearly 50cm of iron and would be an acceptable equivalent to the older model 305mm 22-calibre 35.9-ton gun in the German gunboats despite having a smaller projectile. He included in the design a 90mm gun on the stern and two 37mm revolver canon, stating that four more 37mm and one bow torpedo tube could be added. The Council felt the additional 37mm were not needed but that the torpedo tube was necessary. Albaret signed the revised plan of the ship's lines on 28 July 1882 and Minister Jauréguiberry approved the design in early August 1882.

On 9 August 1882 the ministry sent to Lorient the approved plan for *Grenade* and informed Rochefort that Cherbourg would send it the plan for *Mitraille* while Lorient would send its mould loft data. The machinery for *Mitraille* was ordered from Indret on 11 November 1882 and on the same day the Machinery Commission was ordered to contract for the machinery for the others. A contract with Schneider for this machinery was finally approved a year later on 28 November 1883. Cherbourg was told on 28 November 1882 that the armoured deck would be made up of two plates of 18mm and one plate of 24mm, but on 2 February 1883 the ministry informed the ports that the deck was to be reduced from 60mm to 50mm. On 19 March the *Conseil des travaux* forwarded a proposal to modify the upper works in the extreme bow of the *Flamme* type, on 2 April 1883 the

*Inspecteur général du génie maritime* advised against it and on 6 April the ministry notified the *Conseil des travaux* that it had not been adopted. However, *Flamme* was completed with a ram-shaped bow and restructured upperworks in contrast to the rounded bow of the other three. On 7 February 1884 the accepted plan for the hood over the barbette gun was forwarded to the ports, with Guérigny charged with manufacturing the two armour plates for it. The plans for the belt armour (compound and steel) were approved on 27 February 1884, and a contract with Marrel Frères for *Mitraille* was approved on 9 May 1884. Information on the slight downward inclination of the bow torpedo tubes in the class was sent to the ports on 9 February 1885 and steps were taken in March to contract for the tubes. On 3 March 1885 the *Conseil des travaux* considered a system for mounting Hotchkiss guns in masthead tops behind rotating shields proposed by Albaret at Cherbourg for *Flamme*, along with two similar systems, one for river gunboats for Tonkin and one for *Tonnant*. On 19 January 1886 Rochefort sent to Paris plans of this system as installed in *Mitraille*.

During trials in December 1885 of *Fusée*, the first ship of the class to be completed, the ship trimmed down by the bow and generated a huge bow wave. To lighten the bow the large armoured hood for the main gun was removed and the mainmast was moved aft. (Fabrication of the hood for *Grenade*, the second ship of this type at Lorient, was suspended on 22 October 1886.) The mainmast was moved aft substantially in the two Lorient ships, *Fusée* and *Grenade*, and slightly aft in the Rochefort ship, *Mitraille*, while the Cherbourg ship, *Flamme*, lacked a mainmast altogether as completed. *Fusée* steered badly and the hull lines aft in *Grenade* were modified in response, although a suggestion to change from two rudders to one was rejected. The slightly inclined bow torpedo tube planned for the class was fitted in *Fusée*, and when initial trials with it succeeded one was ordered installed in *Grenade* too. At this time the naval constructors at Lorient felt that ships of this type were most likely to be used to support torpedo boats. However, the tube was heavily criticised and the *Conseil des travaux* decided on 21 January 1890 and Minister Barbey ordered on 29 January 1890 that it should not be installed in *Mitraille* and *Flamme*. On 11 September 1902 the removal of the torpedo tubes in *Fusée* and *Grenade* was authorized on the grounds that they constituted more of a danger to the ships than an augmentation in their offensive strength.

In 1905 the replacement of the 37mm revolving cannon in *Fusée* and *Mitraille* with 47mm QF guns was planned for service at Bizerte, it was also to be done there in *Tempête*. Bizerte also proposed replacing the stern 90mm gun with three 100mm QF guns in *Fusée* and *Mitraille* and using the ships along with *Phlégéton*, above, to defend the entrance canal there.

*The characteristics are based on a devis for* Mitraille *dated 14.4.1888 with machinery data for* Grenade *from a devis dated 20.5.1889.*
**Dimensions & tons:** 50.66m oa, 50.30m wl (+0.24m ram), 48.95m pp (wl fwd to rudder) x 9.95m ext (below wl), 9.80m wl. 1,128.400t disp. Draught: 3.345m mean, 3.457m aft. Men: 93.
**Machinery:**
(*Mitraille*/Indret) 175nhp and 1,516ihp designed at 210rpm and 7kg/cm² boiler pressure. Trials (4.4.1888) 1,527.334ihp = 10.105kts at 153rpm. 2 screws. 2 vertical compound engines with 3 cylinders of 0.520m (1) and 0.740m (2) diameter and 0.420m stroke. 3 cylindrical direct flame boilers. 72.265t coal.
(*Grenade*/Creusot) 175nhp and 1,500ihp designed at 175rpm and 7kg/cm² boiler pressure. Designed speed 13kts. Trials (6.3.1889) 1,680.93ihp = 12.122kts at 192.57rpm. 2 screws. 2 vertical compound engines with 3 cylinders of 0.575m (1) and 0.790 (2) diameter and 0.450m stroke. 3 cylindrical direct flame boilers. 62t coal. Range with normal 45.8t coal 850nm @ 8kts.
**Armour:** (Creusot steel in the Lorient ships, compound in the others)
Side: Belt at waterline 200mm amidships, 240mm fwd, 150mm aft (height from 0.70m below the wl to 0.15m above) as designed; later recorded as 205mm amidships, 270mm fwd, and 160mm aft (height 0.825m of which 0.15m above the wl).

A view of the 2nd class armoured gunboat *Grenade* that was originally attached to the technical characteristics document for the ship. The sloping shield over her single 240mm gun is barely visible over the forward bulwarks and the muzzle of her single torpedo tube can be seen just over the top of the buoy to which she is moored. *(Feuille signalétique for the ship)*

Guns: Barbette 200mm front, 120mm aft. *Fusée* and probably others eventually received a 20mm shield for the 240mm gun.

Decks: Armoured deck: slightly curved to 0.45m above the waterline, 20mm on 30mm plating.

Conning tower: 10mm.

**Guns:**

(1882, design) 1 x 240mm/28.5 M1881 (fixed turret/barbette forward), 1 x 90mm/22 M1881 (on stern platform), 2 x 37mm revolving cannon. **Torpedoes:** 1 tube in the bow (added).

(1887-90) 1 x 240mm/28.5 M1881 (fixed turret/barbette forward), 1 x 90mm/22 M1881 (on stern), 4 x 37mm revolving cannon (1 on each bridge wing, 1 in each top), 1 x 4pdr (86.5mm/11) bronze mountain rifle (used as a line throwing gun). **Torpedoes:** 1 tube in the bow for 356mm M1887 torpedoes in *Fusée* and M1885 torpedoes in *Grenade*, none in *Flamme* and *Mitraille*. *Flamme*, with only 1 mast, had one 37mm on the turret hood and one in the top.

(1906, *Fusée*) Torpedo tube removed (also authorized for but probably not done in *Grenade*).

(1908, *Fusée*) The stern 90mm replaced with 3 x 100mm QF (also planned for *Mitraille* but not completed).

**Flamme** Cherbourg Dyd/Schneider, Creusot.

On list 1.1883. Ord: 5.8.1882 K: 23.8.1882. L: 29.8.1885.
    Comm: 25.2.1889 (trials). C: 6.1889.

Budget 1884. Engines installation begun 9.1885. Trial results approved 24.6.1889. In reserve after trials at Cherbourg 7.1889. To full comm. 4.1893, left Cherbourg 15.4.1893 for service in the *Défense mobile* at Dunkirk, to reserve 9.1898, replaced by *Cocyte* 1.1899 and back in reserve at Cherbourg 26.2.1899. Decomm. 25.6.1905. Struck 9.4.1906, sold to BU 28.7.1906 with *Grenade*.

**Fusée** Lorient Dyd/Schneider, Creusot (engines designed by François Joseph Barba).

On list 1.1883. Ord: 5.8.1882. K: 10.10.1882. L: 8.5.1884.
    Comm: 25.11.1885 (trials). C: 10.1887.

Budget 1884. Admitted to active service 28.10.1887 and to reserve. Full commission 20.2.1888, left for Toulon 21.2.1888, then to reserve there. To Tunisia 1904, to reserve 1.12.1908, decomm. 15.10.1909. Struck 24.3.1910, for sale in Tunisia 1910-1912, sold 24.8.1912 at Bizerte to BU.

**Grenade** Lorient Dyd/Schneider, Creusot (engines designed by Barba).

On list 1.1883. Ord: 5.8.1882. K: 10.10.1882. L: 18.10.1888.
    Comm: 15.11.1888 (trials), 21.5.1889 (full).

Budget 1884. Engine contract 19.11.1883, installation began 9.1885. Launched nearly complete after modifications to stern and addition of torpedo tube in bow based on trials of *Fusée*. Machinery installation completed 18.12.1888. Trial results approved 26.4.1889. Left Lorient for Cherbourg 21.5.1889. Gunnery trials at La Hougue 20.6.1889, then to reserve 3.7.1890 and never fully recommissioned. Definitively decomm. 25.6.1905. Struck 9.4.1906 sold to BU 28.7.1906 to M. Cousin with *Flamme*.

**Mitraille** Rochefort Dyd/Indret (engines designed by Garnier).

On list 1.1883. Ord: 5.8.1882. K: 16.4.1883. L: 3.7.1886.
    Comm: 1.12.1887 (trials), 8.4.1888 (full).

Budget 1884. Machinery installed 10.7.1886 to 4.12.1886. Commissioning deferred 24.12.1886, Rochefort authorized 3.9.1887 to begin commissioning her for trials on 20.9.1887, Rochefort requested delay 16.9.1887, granted 17.9, boiler fire on board same day, then run into by *Vigilant* 26.9.1887. Trials 1-4.1888. Left Rochefort for Toulon 27.4.1888, arrived 19.5.1888 after stopping at Port Vendres for coal and boiler repairs. In reserve at Toulon 7.6.1888 to 1904 with short periods in commission including for manoeuvres 7-8.1892. Reboilered 1895-96, post-repair trials conducted with crew of *Achéron*. To Tunisia (Bizerte) 26.9.1904. Decomm. 15.10.1909, crew roster closed 25.11.1909. Struck 24.3.1910, sale at Bizerte to M. Boccara reported 24.8.1912.

# Cruisers, 1882-1897

## Chapter Nine

**(A) Covered battery cruisers (*Croiseurs à batterie*).**

All 3 to *Croiseurs de station à batterie* in the 1.1891 fleet list and *croiseurs de 1re classe* 1.1892.

*SFAX. Croiseur à batterie.* Partially protected cruiser with main guns on the upper deck, secondary guns in a covered battery, a steel hull with wooden sheathing, and a ram bow. Two funnels, three masts, ship rig. Designed by Bertin. To *Croiseur de 2e classe* 1897.

---

The covered battery cruiser *Sfax* as completed with a full barque rig. This was later reduced to three nearly bare masts with armed tops and then to two light pole masts without tops. She was protected by a full-length armoured deck and cellular layer. *(NHHC from ONI album of French warships, NH-74873)*

In 1870 naval constructor Louis Émile Bertin introduced his first design that included a protective cellular layer (*tranche cellulaire*) at the waterline. This design, dated 16 June 1870, was one of nine for ironclad monitors and other ironclads without rigging examined by the *Conseil des travaux* on 5 July 1870. The layer consisted of a space between two decks (*entrepont*) that was divided into many small watertight compartments with all penetrations to the lower parts of the ship concentrated near the centreline. After the war Bertin revived the idea in July 1872 in a design for a small *corvette de croisière* in which the cellular layer lay on top of a 50mm armoured deck. At its outer edge was a cofferdam, a ring of even smaller compartments along the waterline, either empty or filled with material that would expand when penetrated and seal the hole. After a change in membership the Council rejected Bertin's cellular layer at the end of 1873. Bertin persisted, and as he told the story in 1906, his chance came in 1881

when Director of Materiel Sabattier fell ill and was replaced temporarily by naval constructor Lebelin de Dionne. Bertin submitted two variants of his 1873 corvette, one of which was a steel-hulled 1st class cruiser which the *Conseil des travaux* rejected on 4 August 1881 in part because work had recently started on the wooden cruiser *Capitaine Lucas.* But Lebelin de Dionne got Minister of Marine Vice Admiral Georges Charles Cloué to approve the cruiser design and suspend *Capitaine Lucas,* and after the *Conseil des travaux* made some changes the new Director of Material got the new Minister of Marine, Capitaine de vaisseau Auguste Gougeard, to order the construction of Bertin's ship using the funds budgeted for *Capitaine Lucas.* She was named *Sfax* to commemorate the naval expedition that suppressed an uprising in that Tunisian city in July 1881.

In *Sfax* Bertin's *tranche cellulaire* consisted of an armoured deck 0.750m below the waterline over the length of the ship with the edges sloping down at the sides of the ship, and many watertight compartments between this deck and the battery deck some 2.7m above it along with a row of small compartments (a cofferdam) filled with cellulose along the sides. The engines were ordered on 28 August 1883 to be increased from 84rpm to 90rpm with the cylinder diameters being reduced from 1.16m to 1.08m (HP) and 2.20m to 2.00m (LP). The armoured deck was initially to have been 38mm thick on 10mm hull plating but was reduced to 30mm to allow reinforcement of the deck beams. The bow was strengthened for ramming.

Vibrations in the after engine became apparent at 13 knots and effectively limited speed to 65rpm and 15 knots. The ship sailed poorly, and the rig, initially three square-rigged masts with 1,989 sq.m of sail, was reduced in 1888 to 1,829 sq.m with the foremast being lowered 2m. She received new screws between October 1888 and February 1889 but these were unsuccessful and the original screws were restored between August 1889 and June 1890. The bowsprit gave way to a jib boom in 1892, and the whole rig was replaced with military masts and only 359 sq.m of sail during a refit at Marseille between March 1893 and May 1894 that also included work on the armament and machinery. At Brest between August 1897 and August 1898 the fore and mizzen masts were replaced by simple wooden pole masts and the main mast was removed, the bottom being retained as a ventilating shaft. In June 1898 the boilers were replaced with 12 new ones of the same type made at Indret, and the torpedo tubes were also removed. By 1900 forced draught was no longer being used. In September 1905 the three old masts of *Sfax* were installed on the school ship *Duguay Trouin.*

**Dimensions & tons:** 96.079m oa, 90.030m wl, 91.556m pp (tip fwd to rudder) x 15.00m ext & wl. 4,561.354t disp (designed), 4,888t (act-ual), 5,023t (after 1898 refit). Draught: (designed) 6.7686m mean, 7.650m aft. Men: 470.

**Machinery:** 1,200nhp and 7,680ihp designed including 680ihp auxiliary machinery at 90rpm and 6.250kg/cm$^2$ boiler pressure. Speed 16kts. Trials (13.5.1887) 6,495ihp at 78rpm = 16.712kts at full power (forced). 2 screws. 2 horizontal compound engines with direct connecting rods and 2 cylinders of 1.08m and 2.00m diameter and 1.00m stroke. 12 cylindrical return-flame boilers. 730t coal (1,000t with surcharge). Range 4,200nm @ 10.5kts.

**Armour:**
Decks: Armoured deck (iron) 30mm flat and 28mm slopes, both on 10mm hull plating.
Guns: 8mm plating (sponsons and hull) around the 164.7mm guns.
Conning tower: 30mm.

**Guns:**
(1887) 6 x 164.7mm/28 M1881 long (upper deck, 4 in sponsons), 10 x 138.6mm/30 M1881 (battery), 2 x 65mm/16 M1881 landing, 8 x 37mm. **Torpedoes:** 5 tubes for 356mm torpedoes (2 forward, 2 side, 1 stern, all above water).
(1893-94) Main guns upgraded to 6 x 164.7mm/30 M1881 QF and 10 x 138.6mm/30 M1881 QF.
(1898) 6 x 164.7mm QF, 10 x 138.6mm QF, 2 x 65mm landing, 6 x 47mm/40 M1885 QF, 4 x 37mm QF, 6 x 37mm revolving cannon,

2 torpedo tubes on the sides (forward and stern tubes removed).

*Sfax* Brest Dyd/Indret (engines designed by Garnier).
On list 1.1882. Ord: 7.4.1882. K: 26.7.1882. L: 26.5.1884.
  Comm: 17.1.1887 (trials), 7.6.1887 (full).
Budget 1883. Machinery installed 10.10.1885 to 1.9.1886. Left Brest for Toulon 15.6.1887 and to reserve. Active in the reserve division of the *Escadre de la Méditerranée* 1891. To special reserve 20.1.1903, decomm. 13.8.1905. Struck 25.5.1906, provisionally retained at Brest as magazine for powder and munitions 1906-1909, to the Domaines 26.5.1909 for sale, sold 25.8.1910.

––––––––––

**Bertin's modified *Sfax***
On 10 July 1883 the *Conseil des travaux* approved specifications for a modified *Sfax.* The main change was an increase in speed to 18 knots, which was to be obtained by using a propulsion plant as in *Milan* consisting of four engines on two shafts and Belleville boilers. The ship was to have a complete curved armoured deck of 40mm under the waterline surmounted by a cellular layer. Bertin submitted a design which the Council examined on 20 May 1884, but it now wanted 19 knots because of the progress made in fast merchant steamers, and to get this speed it proposed to delete the cellular layer. On 9 June 1885 the Council examined three more submissions from Bertin including a revision of his 1884 design in which he increased the speed to 19 knots by further lightening the machinery and increasing its power to 11,200ihp, but the Council rejected all three. According to Bertin the rejection was simply a question of persons, ministers and directors having changed since 1882.

––––––––––

*TAGE. Croiseur à batterie.* Protected cruiser with main guns on the upper deck, secondary guns in a covered battery, a steel hull without sheathing, and a ram-shaped bow. Three funnels, three masts, ship rig. Designed by Jaÿ (A.C. Loire).

In its discussion on 20 May 1884 of Bertin's modified *Sfax* the *Conseil des travaux* stated that in view of the considerable progress in speed realized by the latest large passenger liners it wanted to give future 1st class cruisers a speed of at least 19 knots to allow them to pursue with success these fast ships. It was also willing to give up Bertin's *tranche cellulaire* to get this speed. On 19 January 1885 Minister of Marine Vice Admiral Alexandre Louis François Peyron referred to the *Conseil des travaux* a design for a large 19-knot cruiser proposed on 18 December 1884 from Charles Louis Jaÿ, a former naval constructor now a senior engineer at the Ateliers et Chantiers de la Loire. The Council evaluated it on 24 February 1885. Jaÿ designed the hull and the two triple expansion engines to produce between 19 and 20 knots with 19 on trials. In designing this machinery he used data on the British cruiser *Iris,* which had reached a speed of 18.573 knots. For protection he gave her a complete 40mm curved armoured deck surmounted by a cofferdam along the sides. The Council asked for changes including a main and secondary battery as in *Sfax* instead of Jaÿ's four 164.7mm and nine 138.6mm guns. It added 40mm of armour to the sides on the forward 12 metres of the ship and 80mm transverse bulkheads at each end of the battery to protect against raking fire. Jaÿ submitted his modified design on 15 April 1885 and the Council approved it on 26 May 1885. The contract was concluded on 3 August 1885. Trials lasted 16 months with numerous failures. The ship was originally rigged as a three-masted barque with a jib boom, but the square sails on the mainmast were replaced with a fore-and-aft rig and the mast was lowered by an order of 4 December 1889. The bow was not reinforced for ramming but the compartmentation of the hull forward could sustain some damage if it were attempted.

The ship was overhauled and rearmed at Toulon between August 1892 and April 1893 in accordance with orders of 23 July 1892 and 5 October 1892. The additional 164.7mm gun sponsons received their guns and two

The 1st class cruiser *Tage*, a covered battery cruiser originally with three masts and a barque rig, seen here after her major overhaul in 1892 and 1893 that included the removal of her mainmast and sails. She had a complete protective deck but no cellular layer. This photo was received by ONI in 1895. *(NHHC from Farenholt collection, previously ONI, NH-66092)*

138.6mm guns were landed. All 164.7mm and 138.6mm guns were replaced with M1884 QF guns. The mainmast was removed, the other masts were lowered, the sails were removed, and the mizzen mast was moved forward of the poop. The ship suffered from severe vibrations aft at high speeds (90rpm), and on 27 February 1893 the engines were limited to 87rpm. The LP cylinder, placed forward of the others, could be disconnected and the engines operated as two-cylinder compound engines; this feature was removed in 1901. The ship was overhauled for the last time at Brest between September 1899 and April 1901, the main changes being new boilers and light artillery.

**Dimensions & tons:** 124.100m oa, 119.940m wl, 118.800m pp (wl/tip fwd to rudder) x16.380m ext (below wl), 16.300m wl. 7,073.646t disp (designed), 7,600t (full). Draught: (designed) 6.950m mean, 7.500m aft. Men: 511 (of whom 250 were for the propulsion plant).

**Machinery:** 2,440nhp and 12,410ihp (forced) designed (including 1,040ihp for auxiliary machinery) at 97 rpm and 8.50kg/cm² boiler pressure. Designed speed 19kts. Trials 9,294ihp at 85.5rpm (natural draught), 12,069ihp at 92.7rpm (forced draught). 2 screws. 2 horizontal triple expansion engines with direct connecting rods and 3 cylinders of 1.090m, 1.725m, and 2.500m diameter and 1.200m stroke. 12 cylindrical return-flame boilers. 1,023t coal (856t normal). Range with 1,023t coal 4,642nm @ 12kts.

**Armour:**
Decks: Armoured deck (iron) flat 40mm, slopes 44mm amidships and 40mm ends, all on 14mm hull plating. Deck increased to 80mm over the magazines. It ran the length of the ship.
Side: Reinforced in the bow above the deck (the first 11.80m of length) by 30mm of plating on top of the regular 14mm hull plating. The steering compartment was also protected.
Guns: Transverse bulkheads 80mm at both ends of the 138.6mm gun battery.
Conning tower: 80mm.

**Guns:**
(1889) 6 x 164.7mm/28 M1881 (upper deck, 4 in sponsons), 10 x 138.6mm/30 M1881 (battery), 3 x 47mm/40 M1885 QF, 1 x 47mm revolving cannon, 12 x 37mm. **Torpedoes:** 7 tubes for 356mm torpedoes (2 forward, 4 side, 1 stern, all above water).
(1889) Ordered on 29.6.1889 and 4.12.1889 during trials to add two more 164.7mm guns in small sponsons amidships, although these positions remained without guns until 1892 due to delays in supplying the gun mountings.
(1892-93) Main guns upgraded to 8 x 164.7mm/30 M1884 QF and 8 x 138.6mm/30 M1884 QF
(1901) 8 x 164.7mm QF, 8 x 138.6mm QF, 2 x 65mm/16 M1881 landing, 14 x 47mm/40 M1885 QF, 2 x 37mm/20 M1885 QF, 4 torpedo tubes on the sides (other tubes removed 1897)

*Tage* A.C. Loire, Saint Nazaire/ACL, Nantes.
On list 1.1886. Ord: 3.8.1885 (contract). K: 8.1885. L: 28.10.1886. Comm: 1.3.1889 (trials), 20.10.1890 (full).
Budget 1885 (delayed to 1886). Construction reassigned from Rochefort to contract c1885. Contract included engines. Machinery installed 11.5.1887 to 12.7.1888. Towed to Brest just before commissioning for trials. Left Brest for Toulon 23.10.1890 and joined the *Escadre de la Méditerranée*. Refitted at Brest 1898. Reboiled 1901 with 12 new

cylindrical boilers. To special reserve 20.10.1903, to Landévennec 1904 to form a reserve group with *Sfax*. Struck 7.6.1907, provisionally retained at Brest 1907-1909, to the Domaines 3.12.1909 for sale, initial sale cancelled, finally sold to the Shipbreaking Co. of London 25.8.1910.

---

***CÉCILLE.*** *Croiseur à batterie.* Protected cruiser with main guns on the upper deck, secondary guns in a covered battery, a steel hull, and a ram-shaped bow. Three funnels, three masts, ship rig. Designed by Lagane (FCM La Seyne).

On 17 June 1885 Minister of Marine Rear Admiral Charles Eugène Galiber referred to the *Conseil des travaux* a design submitted on 8 April

1885 by Antoine Jean Amable Lagane, who had been shipyard director at the Forges et Chantiers de la Méditerranée at La Seyne since 1872. The council discussed it on 7 July 1885. Like *Tage* the new ship was designed to produce between 19 and 20 knots with 19 on trials. Lagane gave her the same armament as in *Sfax* and what he called serious defensive strength, somewhat greater than in *Tage*. Vertical protection of 40mm was fitted on the bow, a feature added by the Council to *Tage*. His protective deck was 10mm thinner at the ends than over the machinery, but the Council changed it to uniform thickness. As in *Tage* the prominent ram bow was usable only against lightly-built ships. The designed armament was six 164.7mm and ten 138.6mm guns plus a light armament of four 47mm QF and twelve 37mm. On 6 July 1889 two 164.7mm were ordered added in new sponsons amidships for a total of eight, and two more 47mm, and two more 37mm were also added. These changes were carried out at La Seyne at the end of 1889.

*Cécille* was in collision with a British merchantman that crossed her bow and sank on 25 July 1893. While she was at La Seyne for repairs to her bow between September 1893 and July 1894 the armament was upgraded to QF guns. The boilers were overhauled in 1902. Coal consumption was a

The covered battery cruiser *Cécille* at Villefranche early in her active career with the additions to her armament ordered in 1889. The 1st rank ironclad *Courbet* and the bow of *Amiral Baudin* are in background. *(NHHC from ONI album of foreign warships dated about 1900, NH-88804)*

problem for this ship, which in practice never got over 2,850nm at 10 knots with the 717 tons of coal in her bunkers. She was originally fitted with three square-rigged masts, but the square sails on the mizzen mast were gone by around 1889; those on the mainmast were removed in 1895, and the remaining yards and sails were removed soon afterwards.

**Dimensions & tons:** 122.400m oa, 117.600m wl, 115.500m pp (tip fwd to rudder) x 15.030m ext and wl. 5,790.295t disp (designed), 6,137t (full in 1900). Draught: (designed) 6.032m mean, 6.800m aft. Men: 486 (557 with flag in 1900).

**Machinery:** 1,725nhp and 10,200ihp designed at 101 rpm and 6.250kg/cm² boiler pressure. Designed speed 19kts. Trials (1&5.7.1890) 10,680ihp at 100rpm = 19,436kts. 2 screws. 4 vertical compound engines with 2 cylinders of 1.00m and 1.840m diameter and 0.920m stroke in 2 compartments, two per shaft. 6 double-ended cylindrical return-flame boilers. 717t coal (normal), 850t coal (max). Range with normal coal 2,868nm @ 10kts, with max coal 3,400nm @ 10kts.

**Armour:**

Decks: Armoured deck (iron) flat 40mm on 10mm hull plating end to end, upper slopes 90mm on 10mm hull plating, lower slopes 85mm on 15mm hull plating.

Guns: 80mm transverse bulkheads at both ends of the 138.6mm gun battery.

Conning tower: 80mm.

**Guns:**

(1889) 8 x 164.7mm/28 M1881 (1 under the forecastle, 6 in sponsons (*tourelles barbettes*) on the sides, and one on a platform aft), 10 x 138.6mm/30 M1881 (battery), 6 x 47mm/40 M1885 QF, 14 x 37mm. **Torpedoes:** 4 tubes for 356mm torpedoes (1 bow, 2 side, 1 stern, all above water).

(1893) Main guns upgraded to 8 x 164.7mm/30 M1884 QF and 10 x 138.6mm/30 M1884 QF.

(after 1900) 8 x 164.7mm QF, 10 x 138.6mm QF, 2 x 65mm/16 M1881 landing, 12 x 47mm QF, 3 torpedo tubes (bow tube removed 1898).

(1907) For use by the school for torpedo boat engineers, three torpedo tubes of different sizes (356mm, 381mm, and 450mm) were fitted on the main deck forward to starboard.

*Cécille* F.C. Méditerranée, La Seyne/FCM, Marseille (engines designed by Orsel).

On list 1.1886. Ord: 23.11.1885 (contract). K: 1.9.1886. L: 3.5.1888. Comm: 26.1.1889 (trials), 9.10.1890 (full).

Budget 1886. Contract included engines. Machinery installed 21.5.1889 to 15.1.1890. Trial results approved 9.10.1890 and joined the *Escadre de la Méditerranée*. To special reserve 9.1.1903. Decomm. 24.9.1906. Struck 27.8.1907, hulk for the school for torpedo boat engineers replacing the burned *Algésiras*, later the school for torpedomen at Toulon 1910 to 1.5.1912 in place of *Marceau*, then barracks and storage hulk for veteran seamen at Toulon replacing *Guerrière* 1912-1917. To the Domaines 15.3.1919 for sale, sold 21.7.1919 to M. Saglia.

---

## (B) 1st class cruisers (*Croiseurs de 1re classe*).

Were large *Croiseurs à barbette* before the 1.1885 fleet list.

*JEAN BART* Class. *Croiseurs de 1re classe*. Protected cruisers with main guns on the sides, secondary guns on the sides and ends, and with a ram-shaped bow. Two funnels, two military masts. Designed by Thibaudier. To *Croiseurs d'escadre de 1re classe* (*non cuirassés*) 1.1891 and back to *Croiseurs de 1re classe* 1.1892, to *Croiseurs de 2e classe* 1.1897.

On 12 June 1885 Minister of Marine Galiber forwarded to the *Conseil des travaux* specifications for a high speed 1st class open-battery cruiser which he intended to send to the ports with a request for designs. The Council examined them on 15 July 1885. The main parts of Galiber's specifications were essentially the same as those in the design by FCM for the covered-battery cruiser *Cécille* that was discussed on 7 July. The speed of 19 knots and the defensive system were the same, while the armament, sail area, and coal supply were less. The concept behind the large covered-battery cruisers beginning with *Duquesne* was that they needed some large guns on the upper deck capable of firing long range shots to stop a fast liner or to cover a retreat and numerous medium-sized guns in a covered battery to fight off commerce protection cruisers. The new specifications essentially abandoned the medium-sized battery and its deck level while retaining the other features of the large raiders. The specifications were close to the characteristics of *Jean Bart* as built except that the rig was to be three masts with a full barque rig (square sails on the mainmast and foremast) and with small guns in the tops of all three masts. The original specifications called for 3,700 tons but the Council raised this to 4,100 tons, still well under the designed 5,514 tons of *Cécille*.

Minister of Marine Galiber sent the specifications as revised by the Council to the ports on 21 July 1885. On 2 March 1886 the Council examined the eight designs that were received and approved four of them for further work. (It also expressed its opinion that barbette cruisers like these did not have sufficient protection against the seas while at high speed and asked for study of a cruiser with a shelter deck (spardeck) capable of keeping its high speed in bad weather without being invaded by the sea.) Of the four designs on 31 July 1886 it approved two with modifications, one by Thibaudier that was used to build *Jean Bart* and later *Isly* and another by Marchal that was used for *Alger*. It rejected a design by Lagane at FCM but he submitted a revision of his design which the Council approved on 15 February 1887 for *Mogador*. Thibaudier proposed for *Jean Bart* a conservative propulsion plant consisting of four horizontal compound engines (two per shaft) and cylindrical boilers. The cylindrical boilers were retained but the compound engines were replaced with two horizontal triple expansion engines.

Minister of Marine Aube's original 1887 budget submission (16 March 1886) included only two cruisers, *Tage* and *Cécille*, plus a line for 'construction not yet decided: cruisers, gunboats, torpedo boats, etc'. By the time the Budget Commission reported on 15 July 1886 the budget had acquired three more 1st class cruisers at Cherbourg, Brest, and Rochefort (*Alger*, the first *Dupuy de Lôme*, and *Jean Bart*), two 2nd class cruisers at Brest and Toulon (later deferred to the extraordinary 1887 budget as *Davout* and *Suchet*), and three 3rd class cruisers (*Surcouf*, *Forbin*, and *Troude*), along with the paddle aviso *Bengali* or a fourth sister to the 1st class screw aviso *Fulton* at Lorient, the aviso transport *Rance* at Lorient, plus the torpedo boat *Ouragan*, and the torpedo boat *N° 74* (both budgets included *N°s 75-125*).

On 4 May 1888 Minister of Marine Krantz directed the replacement of the original three masts with two military masts, for which the composition and distribution of the small artillery was modified (four 47mm QF and six 37mm were planned in 1886). On 28 January 1891 Minister Barbey directed replacement of the Model 1881 164.7mm and 138.6mm guns with Model 1891 QF guns, but the structural changes needed for the M1891 guns were too great and converted M1881 QF guns were accepted. *Isly* received this modification before entering service, *Jean Bart* was modified during a refit between May 1893 and February 1894 at Rochefort and *Alger* was also modified in 1893. The bow was not reinforced for ramming.

*Jean Bart* visited New York with *Aréthuse* and *Hussard* in 1893 for the Columbian Exposition and became the most popular of the foreign ships there because the spiral staircases in her military masts reminded visitors of the Eiffel Tower. However, the commander of *Isly* reported in 1894 that the military masts were a nuisance on a cruiser. The ship lacked the manpower to man the upper tops, which were intended for small arms fire, they suffered from vibrations, and they amplified the rolling of the ship. In early 1897 the military masts of *Jean Bart* were cut down to the level of the top of the pilot house where new armed tops were fitted and above which metal pole masts and wooden topmasts were installed. Later that year the military masts of *Isly* were replaced with simple pole masts. (One was installed in *Amiral Baudin*.) The boilers of *Jean Bart* were replaced between

17 February 1903 and 20 July 1905 with 12 Niclausse boilers operating at 13kg/cm² boiler pressure, trials produced 17.03 knots with 7.025ihp in October 1905. The replacement of the boilers of *Isly* was considered in 1910 but rejected because of cost and the ship was struck instead.

**Dimensions & tons:** 109.60m oa, 107.70m wl x 13.30m wl. 4,165t disp (4,436t full in *Jean Bart* and 4,300t full in *Isly*). Draught: 6.05m mean, 6.40m aft. Men: 331.

**Machinery:** 1,270nhp and 7,700ihp (8.100ihp in *Isly*) designed at 9.5kg/cm² boiler pressure. Speed 19kts. Trials (28.11.1891) 7,707ihp = 18.41kts (*Jean Bart*), (9.8.1893) 8.252ihp = 18.28kts (*Isly*). 2 screws. 2 horizontal triple expansion engines with 3 cylinders of 0.900m, 1.350m, and 2.100m diameter and 0.960m stroke. 8 cylindrical boilers. 750t coal (880t in *Isly*, max in both 940t). Range 7,014nm @ 10kts.

**Armour:**

Decks: Armoured deck (iron) flat 40mm on 10mm hull plating, upper slopes 90mm on 10mm hull plating, lower slopes 85mm on 15mm hull plating. Splinter deck below the armoured deck in the machinery spaces 5mm. Cofferdam along the sides above the deck (60cm wide), no cellular layer.

Guns: Shields 54mm, sponsons (chrome steel) 35mm

Conning tower: 80mm strip 1.6m high (120mm in *Isly*).

**Guns:**

(1891) 4 x 164.7mm/28 M1881 (sponsons), 6 x 138.6mm/30 M1881

---

The 1st class cruiser *Jean Bart,* photographed by the Detroit Publishing Co. at the Columbian Naval Review in the Hudson River in 1893. The naval parade was on 27 April 1893. *(Library of Congress, LC-D4-5508)*

BLR (4 in sponsons amidships, 1 under the forecastle and 1 on the poop, with the three forward pieces in *Jean Bart* being 138.6mm/30 M1884), 2 x 65mm/50 M1888 QF (never in *Isly*), 2 x 65mm/16 M1881 landing, 6 x 47mm/40 M1885 QF, 8 x 37mm/20 M1885 QF.

**Torpedoes:** 5 tubes for 356mm torpedoes on the battery deck (2 forward, 2 side, 1 stern).

(1893-94) Main guns upgraded to 4 x 164.7mm/30 M1881 QF (M1884 in *Jean Bart*) and 6 x 138.6mm/30 M1881 QF (3 forward pieces 138.6mm/30 M1884 in *Jean Bart*)

(1896-97) Forward torpedo tubes removed from *Jean Bart* leaving 3, forward and stern torpedo tubes removed from *Isly* leaving 2.

(1905, *Jean Bart*) 4 x 164.7mm, 6 x 138.6mm, 2x 65mm QF, 2 x 65mm landing, 10 x 47mm QF, 4 x 37mm QF, 3 torpedo tubes.

(1909, *Isly*) 4 x 164.7mm, 6 x 138.6mm, 12 x 47mm, no torpedo tubes.

***Jean Bart*** Rochefort Dyd/Indret (engines designed by Garnier).

On list 1.1887. Ord: 18.9.1886 and 19.11.1886. K: 9.1887. L: 24.10.1889. Comm: 5.3.1891 (trials), 5.3.1892 (full).

Budget 1887. Initial trial results approved 8.10.1891, left Rochefort 18.10.1891 with a trial crew for more trials at Toulon. Commissioned into the reserve squadron of the *Escadre de la Méditerranée* for operations 5.3.1892. Refitted 1901-1905 at Lorient with new Niclausse boilers (10.5kg/cm² pressure) and bilge keels. Wrecked 11.2.1907 in fog on an uncharted reef off the Saharan coast 80 miles north of Cap Blanc. Broke in half 23.2.1907, fully evacuated by crew 2.4.1907, wreck sold 8.4.1907 to Blandy Bros. of Las Palmas. Struck 13.4.1907. Still not fully broken up 11.3.1914.

***Dupuy de Lôme* (i)** Brest Dyd.

Budget 1887. Stopped 11.1886. *Isly* soon took her place.

*Isly* Brest Dyd/Indret (engines designed by Garnier).

On list 1.1888. Ord: 1.3.1887. K: 3.7.1887. L: 22.6.1891.
  Comm: 25.10.1892 (trials), 20.9.1893 (full).

Budget 1887 (extraordinary). Arrived at Cherbourg for active service in
  the *Escadre du Nord* 30.9.1893. Decomm. 13.3.1911. Struck
  23.11.1911, central service ship for torpedo boats at Lorient 1911-
  1913, for sale 1913-1914, sold 11.4.1914 to Willer Peterson of
  Copenhagen.

---

**ALGER Class.** *Croiseurs de 1re classe.* Protected cruiser with main guns on
the sides, secondary guns on the sides and ends, and a ram-shaped bow.
Two funnels, two military masts. Designed by Marchal. To *Croiseurs
d'escadre de 1re classe (non cuirassés)* 1.1891 and back to *Croiseurs de 1re classe*
1.1892, to *Croiseur de 2e classe* 1.1897.

Minister of Marine Galiber sent specifications for a high speed 1st class
open-battery cruiser to the ports on 21 July 1885, and on 31 July 1886 the
*Conseil des travaux* approved with modifications one by naval constructor
Théodore Jean Maurice Marchal that was used for *Alger.* Marchal used a
hull form close to that of the British cruiser *Iris* which had become famous
for making over 18 knots in trials and he used Belleville boilers as in *Milan.*
His forward 164.7mm guns were closer to the bow than were Thibaudier's
in *Jean Bart.* According to Pierre Le Conte, who recorded this series of
events in manuscript notes preserved at Brest, on 13 October 1886 a
*croiseur de 1re classe* was ordered to be built at Cherbourg to plans by
Marchal and was named *Alger.* On 29 November 1886 she was renamed
*Dupuy de Lôme,* 'the ship of that name that had been ordered at Brest
having been stopped.' On 14 February 1887 a second cruiser similar to this
*Dupuy de Lôme* was ordered at Cherbourg and on 1 March 1887 this ship
was re-ordered under the extraordinary chapter of the budget and named
*Alger.* On 8 August 1887 Cherbourg recommended suspending the
construction of *Dupuy de Lôme* to concentrate on ships whose construction
was further advanced, and on 16 August 1887 Minister of Marine Barbey
approved this action. Contracts for the materials for *Dupuy de Lôme* were
then cancelled and on 9 December 1887 (confirmed on 26 December
1887) Minister of Marine de Mahy advised that the *Dupuy de Lôme* at
Cherbourg would not be built and that a new cruiser carrying the same
name would be built at Brest.

The bow of *Alger* was lightly built and not suited for ramming. Her military masts were replaced with two pole masts in 1897 at Toulon. Her
boilers were refurbished in 1904. Her hull configuration was assessed as
inferior to that of *Isly,* the ship taking more water over the bow because of
its shape, the sponsons protruding excessively from the sides and being
damaged by the waves, and the stern pounding because of its unsupported
flare above the waterline.

**Dimensions & tons:** 109.00m oa, 105.60m wl x 13.80m wl, 16.12m
  over sponsons. 4,123t disp (4,356t full). Draught: 5.75m mean, 6.47m
  aft. Men: 399.
**Machinery:** 1,250nhp and 8,200ihp designed at 17kg/cm$^2$ boiler pressure. Speed 19kts. Trials (10.5.1892) 7,928.5ihp at 115rpm =
  19.61kts. 2 screws. 2 vertical triple expansion engines with 3 cylinders
  of 0.860m, 1.360m, and 2.060m diameter and 0.850m stroke. 24 single-furnace Belleville boilers. 618t coal (675t max). Range 6,440nm @
  10kts.
**Armour:**
Decks: Armoured deck (iron) flat 40mm on 10mm hull plating, upper
  slope 90mm on 10mm hull plating, lower slope 85mm on 15mm hull
  plating. Splinter deck below the armoured deck in the machinery
  spaces 8mm.
Guns: Shields 54mm.
Conning tower: 70mm.
**Guns:.**
(1892) 4 x 164.7mm/28 M1881 (sponsons), 6 x 138.6mm/30 M1881

(4 in sponsons, 1 under the forecastle and 1 on the poop), 2 x 65mm/
16 M1881 landing, 12 x 47mm/40 M1885 QF, 8 x 37mm/20 M1885
QF. **Torpedoes:** 5 tubes for 356mm torpedoes (2 forward, 2 side,
1 stern, all above water).
(1893) Main guns upgraded to 4 x 164.7mm/30 M1881 QF and 6 x
138.6mm/30 M1881 QF after machinery trials between 6.1892 and
1.4.1893.
(1900) 4 x 164.7mm/30 M1881 QF, 6 x 138.6mm/30 M1881 QF,
2 x 65mm/50 M1888, 2 x 65mm/16 M1881 landing, 10 x 47mm QF,
3 x 37mm QF (for the boats), 2 torpedo tubes (sides). The other three
tubes were removed in 1897, the last two followed in 1903-06.

*Dupuy de Lôme* (ii) Cherbourg Dyd.

On list 1.1887 Ord: 13.10.1886. Stopped 8.1887.

Budget 1887. Named *Alger* 13.10.1886, renamed *Dupuy de Lôme*
  29.11.1886 after the ship of that name at Brest was stopped.
  Suspended 16.8.1887, cancelled 9/26.12.1887.

*Alger* Cherbourg Dyd/Schneider, Creusot.

On list 1.1888. Ord: 14.2.1887 and 1.3.1887. K: 11.1887.
  L: 24.11.1889. Comm: early 1892 (trials). C: 6.1892.

Budget 1887 (extraordinary). Engine contract 6.6.1888. Full power trials
  5.1892, then to reserve 6.1892 for work on the machinery and conversion of the battery to QF guns. In full commission 17.4.1893 in the
  *Escadre de la Méditerranée.* Decomm. 12.10.1910 after a long Far East
  cruise. Struck 23.11.1911, for sale at Rochefort 1911-1912, mooring
  hulk at Rochefort 1912-1914, coal hulk at Lorient 1920-1929, landing
  hulk there 1929-1939, sold 1940 to BU.

---

**MOGADOR.** *Croiseur de 1re classe.* Protected cruiser with main guns on the
sides and secondary guns on the sides and ends. Three masts with armed
tops, barque rig (as of 1886). Designed by Lagane (FCM La Seyne).

Minister of Marine Galiber sent specifications for a high speed 1st class
open-battery cruiser to the ports on 21 July 1885. On 2 March 1886 the
Council examined the eight designs that were received in response and
approved four of them for further work including one by Amable Lagane,
shipyard director at the Forges et Chantiers de la Méditerranée at La Seyne
since 1872. Of these on 31 July 1886 it approved with modifications two,
one by Thibaudier that was used to build *Jean Bart* and later *Isly* and
another by Marchal that was used for *Alger.* It rejected Lagane's design
because it had only a single very high deck level between the armoured deck
and the upper deck while Thibaudier and Marchal had two, a low one
above the armoured deck for coal and stores surmounted by one of regular
height above it for the crew.

On 14 October 1886 Minister of Marine Aube submitted to Parliament
an arrangement he had concluded with seven large shipbuilding contractors for 200 million francs worth of contract work spread over 15 years of
regular budgets, of which 140 million were to provide six 1st class cruisers,
ten 3rd class cruisers, 20 *contre-torpilleurs* of the *Ouragan* type, 50 *bateaux
canons,* 100 torpedo boats, and 3 armoured coast defence ships. The
extraordinary budget for 1887 added to the regular programme three 1st,
three 2nd, and three 3rd class cruisers plus 8 *éclaireurs torpilleurs à grande
vitesse* (of which four were to be 75% built during the year and the other
four 40%), and 24 torpedo boats (*Nos 126-149*). Lagane then submitted a
revision of his design with the two deck levels which the Council approved
on 15 February 1887. The characteristics presented below are as of 15
February 1887. *Mogador* was assigned to FCM for construction to this
design under the extraordinary chapter of the budget, probably by a ministerial order of 1 March 1887, and the Machinery Commission proceeded
to negotiate a contract.

A new Minister of Marine, Barbey, took office on 30 May 1887 and
soon found that the navy was overextended financially and lacked the funds
to carry out in full Aube's cruiser program. *Alger, Isly, Davout, Suchet,*

*Lalande, Cosmao,* and *Coëtlogon* had been begun by this time and work on them proceeded, but contracts for one 1st class cruiser (*Mogador*) and one 2nd class cruiser (*Chanzy*) along with the *éclaireurs* and the 24 torpedo boats had not yet been concluded and were adjourned. At this time experiments with melinite high explosive shells were also raising doubts about the designs, soon leading to the fully armoured design of the cruiser *Dupuy de Lôme*. Between August and November 1887, however, contracts were authorized under the extraordinary budget for the *éclaireurs Coureur* (Thornycroft) and *Avant-Garde* (Normand) and for torpedo boats *Nos 126* and *127*, and during 1888 torpedo boats *Nos 128* and *129* and *éclaireurs Agile* and *Audacieux* followed. The armoured *Dupuy de Lôme*, laid down at Brest in 1887, was initially charged to the regular budget but was moved to the extraordinary budget during the first months of 1888.

**Dimensions & tons:** 107.00m pp x 13.528m wl. 4,183.595t disp.
   Draught: 5.326m mean, 6.10m aft.
**Machinery:** 8,200ihp at 125rpm designed at 9.5kg/cm² boiler pressure.
   Speed 19kts. 2 screws. 2 vertical triple expansion engines with
   4 cylinders of 1.000m (1), 1.520m (1), and 1.690m (2) diameter.
   6 double-ended cylindrical return-flame boilers as in *Cécille*.
**Armour:** As *Cécille*. The specifications called for a complete armoured
   deck of 50mm including hull plating on the flat, plus a 5mm splinter
   deck and the usual cellular layer with a belt of cofferdams along the
   sides.
**Guns:** 4 x 164.7mm (in sponsons), 6 x 138.6mm (4 on the sides, 1 under
   the forecastle, 1 aft), 4 x 47mm QF, 6 x 37mm revolving cannon,
   4 tubes for 4.42m (356mm) Whitehead torpedoes (1 bow, 2 sides, and
   1 stern).

*Mogador* F.C. Méditerranée, La Seyne.
Budget 1887 (extraordinary). Contract not concluded, adjourned in mid-
   1887 with *Chanzy* (see below) in a cutback of the cruiser programme
   and never in the fleet lists although named in the budget.

---

### New 1st and 2nd class cruiser specifications, 1887

On 10 June 1887 Minister of Marine Barbey asked the *Conseil des travaux* if there was a need to modify for future construction the specifications which had been used to build the 1st and 2nd class cruisers recently begun. In particular he wanted to know if the Council feel a need to introduce new conditions relative to speed or to the protection of personnel and material against explosive shells. The Council examined the issue on 20 July 1887 and noted the increasingly high speeds of the big transatlantic steamers, especially between Europe and the USA, which French cruisers needed to be able to catch. It also noted the recent enormous increase in the initial velocity of modern guns that gave both large ones and small QF guns unprecedented penetration power and precision. Finally it noted the experiments at Lydd in Kent County in August and September 1885 that introduced hollow shells loaded with explosives much more energetic than ordinary (black powder) charges. (The explosives were called lyddite in Britain and melinite in France.) It concluded that, while necessary, an armoured deck surmounted by a cellular layer was no longer sufficient for a cruiser and that armour covering as much of the sides as possible was also necessary.

The Council therefore drew up new specifications for both 1st and 2nd class cruisers. It felt that the adversaries that the new cruisers were likely to face were fast, well-armed protected cruisers including the British *Orlando* type belted cruisers along with auxiliary cruisers converted from the fastest commercial vessels. The 1st class cruisers were intended to take on the former while the 2nd class cruisers were to go after the latter. To accomplish these missions both types needed a speed of 20 knots and a range of 5,000nm with coal surcharge at 12.5 knots. The 1st class cruisers were to have two military masts like those in *Hoche* and no sails, the 2nd class were to retain as much sail as possible on four masts, with square sails on the foremast and small armed tops on all masts. The main battery was to be eight guns with five bearing in any direction consisting of two 194mm and

six 164.7mm guns in the 1st class and two 164.7mm and six 138.6mm in the 2nd class. They were to have side armour from below the waterline to the upper deck measuring 100mm on 20mm plating in the 1st class and 80mm on 12mm in the 2nd class, both sufficient according to the 1887 experiments with *Belliqueuse*. (According to 1888 French press accounts, Melinite shells had practically no effect on the thin iron armour on the sides of *Belliqueuse*, leaving only slight marks, but against the unarmoured portions they created 'terrible havoc'.) The ships were to have complete curved or vaulted armoured decks of 20mm on 10mm plating (1st class) and 18mm on 9mm (2nd class) with side cofferdams on top. The 1st class cruiser was also to have a cellular layer between the armoured deck and the battery or intermediate deck on which the crew was accommodated. Displacements were expected to be 6,200 tons (1st class) and 3,700 tons (2nd class) and lengths between perpendiculars 113m (1st class) and 96m (2nd class), although these were not formally specified and as customary were left to the designers to determine.

---

*DUPUY DE LÔME* (iii). Initially *Croiseur blindé* 1.1888. Armoured cruiser with two single main battery turrets on the sides amidships, six single secondary battery turrets with three at each end, complete side armour, and a long ram-shaped bow. Two funnels, two military masts. Designed by de Bussy. To *croiseur cuirassé de 1re classe* 1.1890, *Croiseur d'escadre de 1re classe (cuirassé)* 1.1891, *Croiseur de 1re classe* 1.1892, and *Croiseur cuirassé* 1.1897.

After the *Conseil des travaux* adopted specifications for 1st class cruisers on 20 July 1887 (above), Minister of Marine Barbey asked De Bussy for a design. De Bussy, as *Inspecteur général du génie maritime*, was a member of the Council, knew the specifications well, and had no doubt influenced them. In his design the two 194mm guns were on the sides a little forward of amidships overhanging the side by about 1.5m to get maximum axial fire. They were in open-topped barbettes whose armour was 100mm thick and only one metre high. The protection of these guns was completed by circular covers attached to the superstructure walkways made of 4mm chrome steel and by vertical shields 120mm thick mounted on the gun turntables and wide enough to protect the gun crew. Forward there were three 164.7mm guns, all with axial fire, one on each side in a casemate with 100mm armour on 20mm plating and a third above them on the forecastle in an open-topped barbette covered by an inclined shield of 4mm chrome steel mounted on the turntable of the gun and reinforced by 40mm armour the height of the shield covering a 60° sector. Aft were three 164.7mm guns mounted and placed in an identical manner except that the arc of fire of the barbette gun on the poop was 280 vice 240 degrees. De Bussy added two 65mm guns on the forecastle abreast of the military mast and two more on the poop. He submitted his design to Minister Barbey on 5 October 1887 and the *Conseil des travaux* approved it on 18 October 1887.

On 24 July 1888, soon after the keel was laid, the Minister, now Vice Admiral Krantz, asked Brest if the guns in barbettes could be mounted in turrets instead, and a design for the turrets by the firm of Farcot was approved by the Council on 6 April 1889. On 15 April 1889 the Ministry asked Brest to replace the four casemates with turrets and lower the centre-line turrets at both ends. The *Conseil des travaux* approved this modification on 15 October 1889, all three after turrets now being on the same level although the elevated position for the forward centreline gun was retained. The original design called for four fixed 356mm torpedo tubes, these were replaced with trainable tubes on wheels and ball joints. The extreme inverted ram-shaped bow, with armour on the sides and an armoured deck inside, was nearly 9m long. The hull side armour was of two types, steel by Marrel Frères and nickel steel by Schneider (their first), and the turrets received chrome steel armour by Saint-Étienne. The process of making forged steel was still experimental and acceptance of the hull plating was tedious because of problems with brittleness. *Dupuy de Lôme* may have been the first ship to receive the new extra mild steel deck armour developed by

The armoured cruiser *Dupuy-de-Lôme*, probably at Cherbourg just before or just after her visit to Spithead in January-February 1901 for Queen Victoria's funeral. The topmasts were lengthened in 1900, and the diagonal spar at the top of her mainmast is supporting long wire radio aerials. *(Postcard by Germain Fils aîné, St-Malo, photo Bissonnier, Cherbourg)*

Châtillon et Commentry in 1887-89 and made mandatory in the French Navy in place of iron in 1892. The design called for 14,000ihp including for auxiliaries (the air, circulating, and feed pumps) giving 20 knots.

A boiler accident in the very first underway trials in June 1892 immobilized the ship for almost a year, then it was found that the old-style cylindrical fire-tube boilers could not produce enough steam for the engines to reach their trial rpm, a problem that changing the screws several times did not remedy. In October 1893 the boilers were found to be sagging from overheating (a problem also encountered in *Fleurus*) and two more accidents claimed several victims. On 2 February 1894 former naval constructur Jules Victor Charles Chaudoye, now Director General of A.C. Loire including their boiler and machinery works at Saint-Denis, asked for all the boilers to be landed for repairs, and this process began 21 February 1894. The ship was commissioned for trials for a second time on 15 November 1894. The boilers were unable to generate the steam needed to meet the designed speed and were at risk of further sagging, causing standards to be relaxed for the final trials. *Dupuy de Lôme* was attached to the *Escadre du Nord* when commissioned in 1895 but rolled badly in a seaway and was found to have less metacentric height than designed. The novel ship had fervent advocates, including Admiral Fournier who in his *La Flotte Nécessaire* advocated building 177 ships like her, which he felt could fight a battleship like *Hoche*, catch up with or escape from a fleet, and carry out all of the roles of cruisers: scouting, commerce raiding, and overseas station service.

The boilers were replaced in 1902-06 with 16 large and 4 small Guyot-du Temple boilers built by Indret (selected in December 1901 after long discussion), rated at 18 kg/cm² but operating at 11.25kg/cm² because of limitations in the engines and the ship's piping. These boilers required three vice two funnels, and the transverse bulkhead between the former first two boiler rooms had to be deleted to accommodate the capstan. The new boilers were first fired on 5 March 1906 and produced 13,380ihp in static trials. The ship was recommissioned for trials 19 July 1906. Incomplete full power trials on 28 July 1906 produced only 12,887.5ihp and 18.268 knots at 133.87rpm and 11.142kg/cm² boiler pressure. The after military mast was replaced with a pole but the forward one was retained with lightened tops. Other deficiencies in the ship, notably its awkward anchors and its tiny conning tower, were not addressed in the refit.

*The characteristics are based on devis dated 6.1.1894, 9.5.1895, and 31.8.1906.*

**Dimensions & tons:** 113.980m oa, 113.980m wl, 113.980m pp (tip fwd

to stern) x 15.700m ext & wl. 6,405.583t disp. Draught: 7.149m mean, 8.0075m aft (8.3775m keel line projected). Men: 320 (trials), 523 (full). In 1906: 6,910.721t disp. Draught: 7.510m mean, 8.7105m aft. Men: 496.

**Machinery:**
(1895) 13,710ihp designed at 140rpm and 11.250kg/cm² boiler pressure. Trials (2.4.1895) 13,186.1ihp = 19.73kts at 137.58rpm and 11.020kg/cm² boiler pressure. 3 screws. 3 engines including 2 horizontal triple expansion engines (slightly inclined) with 3 cylinders of 0.791m, 1.222m, and 1.901m diameter and 1.000m stroke on the outboard shafts and 1 vertical triple expansion engine with 3 cylinders of 0.841m, 1.311m, and 2.043m diameter and 0.850m stroke on the centre shaft. 11 cylindrical Admiralty direct flame boilers plus 2 smaller cylindrical return flame boilers to supply auxiliary machinery. 1,112.000t coal (900t designed). Range with 900t coal 7,287nm @ 10.42kts.
(1906) Reboilered with 20 Guyot-du Temple small tube boilers built by Indret. Trials (27-28.7.1906) 12,889.5ihp = 18.628kts at 134.12rpm and 11.142kg/cm² boiler pressure. 1466.390t coal. Range 3,607.7nm @ 13.383kts.

**Armour:**
Side: Belt at waterline and entire side 100mm amidships (nickel steel) on 20mm plating, 100mm fwd, 78.5mm aft. Total height amidships 5.38m.
Guns: Turrets (chrome steel) 100mm with 100mm fixed bases, both on 20mm plating.
Decks: Armoured deck (extra mild steel) 30mm on 10mm plating. The deck curved down evenly from the wl near the centreline to meet the lower edge of the belt at 1.38m below the waterline. Cellular layer containing coal above it and 8mm splinter deck below it over the boilers, engines, and magazines.
Conning tower (steel): 100mm.

**Guns:**
(1895) 2 x 194mm/45 M1887 (turrets on sides amidships), 6 x 164.7mm/45 M1887 (turrets, 3 forward and 3 aft), 4 x 65mm/50 M1888 QF, 2 x 65mm/16 M1881 landing, 8 x 47mm/40 M1885 QF, 8 x 37mm revolving cannon. **Torpedoes:** 4 tubes for 450mm M1889 torpedoes above water. **Searchlights:** 6 x 60cm.
(1897) In 11.1897 the two after torpedo tubes were landed because their ports were so close to the waterline that they could rarely be used. Their removal was confirmed by an order of 23 June 1899.
(1900) 2 x 194mm, 6 x 164.7mm, 4 x 65mm QF, 2 x 65mm landing, 12 x 47mm QF, 2 x 37mm QF, 2 torpedo tubes (side, above water)
(1906 after reboilering) As 1900 but 4 x 37mm QF (for the boats) and only 5 x 60cm searchlights.

***Dupuy de Lôme*** (iii) Brest Dyd/A.C. Loire, Saint Denis.
On list 1.1888. Ord: 26.11.1887. K: 4.7.1888. L: 27.10.1890. Comm: 1.4.1892 (trials), 15.5.1895 (full).
Budget 1888 (later moved to the extraordinary 1887 budget). Engine contract 23.4.1888. Machinery installed 9.3.1891 to 4.12.1891 (starboard forward engine), 13.1.1892 (port middle engine), and 23.2.1892 (centre aft engine). In reserve for repairs 6.11.1893 to 15.11.1894. Assigned to the *Escadre du Nord* 6.5.1895, trial results approved 31.7.1895. Presidential visit to Kronstadt 8.1897, at Spithead 30.1.1901 to 6.2.1901. To normal reserve for reconstruction and administratively decomm. 20.9.1903. New boilers first lit off 5.3.1906. Completed commissioning for trials 19.7.1906, to normal reserve at Brest after trials 4.10.1906. Commissioned 21.9.1908 to replace *Kléber* on the Morocco station. Hull found to be in poor condition at Tangier 6.1909, ship returned to Lorient 13.9.1909, placed in special reserve 14.11.1909 and decomm. 20.3.1910 for condemnation. On 20.2.1911 the *Conseil supérieur* decided to strike her from the fleet list, but on 20.4.1911 the Navy received from the Foreign Ministry a request from Peru, which feared that Ecuador was

buying the Italian cruiser *Umbria*, to buy an armoured cruiser. The Ministry of Foreign Affairs proposed a ship of the *Montcalm* class, and the Navy proposed refitting *Dupuy de Lôme* instead. A draft purchase contract was submitted to the Minister on 21.7.1911, the ship was ready for sea trials 15.1.1912, final acceptance trials were completed 6.3.1912, and the ship was formally transferred to Peru 12.9.1912 as *Commandante Aguirre*. Off main list 1912. The Peruvians, however, lost interest after *Umbria* was sold to Haiti instead of Ecuador and made only the first of three payments on the ship. The ship remained at Lorient and was abandoned there by Peru to French caretakers 10.1914. On 4.6.1916 Paris, after discussions with Lorient, concluded that the ship could not be used in the war effort. After more negotiations the ship was formally retroceded by Peru to France 17.1.1917. On 23.6.1918 Lorient was ordered to fit her as a mooring hulk at Kergroise for use by the Americans at Lorient, but she was replaced by *Descartes* 28.8.1918 and in 10.1918 Lorient was advised that she had been sold to the Lloyd Royal Belge for use as a cargo ship. She was towed to Bordeaux in 2.1919 and converted to a cargo ship by C.A. Gironde, retaining only the centreline engine and the after boiler room and with a false bow hiding her ram. She was delivered and renamed *Peruvier* 12.1919. On her first voyage as a merchant ship beginning 1.1920 her engine and boilers failed, her cargo of coal caught fire, and on 4.3.1923 the un-repaired ship left Antwerp for breakers at Flushing.

---

***CHARNER* Class.** *Croiseurs cuirassé de 2ᵉ classe* (first three) 1.1890. Armoured cruisers with two single main battery turrets at the ends, six single secondary battery turrets on the sides, and a ram bow. Two funnels, two military masts. Designed by Thibaudier. To *Croiseurs d'escadre de 1re classe (cuirassés)* (all four) 1.1891, *Croiseurs de 1ʳᵉ classe* 1.1892, and *Croiseurs cuirassés* 1.1897.

The specifications for 2ⁿᵈ class armoured cruisers adopted by the *Conseil des travaux* on 20 July 1887 (above) were sent to the ports on 8 August 1887 with a request for designs. Four were received in response and the Council examined them on 13 March 1888. Thibaudier submitted one with a displacement of 4,168 tons, length of 104m, engines of 9,780ihp for 20 knots, armour of 80mm on the sides and 18mm on the deck, and an armament of two 164.7mm guns in barbette turrets on the forecastle and poop and six 138.6mm guns in sponsons on the sides. The Council felt that the 164.7mm guns should be on the sides with two 138.6mm moving to their places at the ends to balance weights, but it accepted his proposal as the basis for further work.

This process was interrupted when on 6 June 1888 Minister of Marine Krantz forwarded to the Council a summary study (author unknown) of a 'protected coast defence cruiser' based on the Italian *Stromboli* to which the author had added side armour. 'The *croiseur garde-côtes protégé* is intended, either to cruise by itself on the coasts or to be capable of pursuing enemy unarmoured cruisers.' The legend for a design accompanying this study described a ship larger than *Stromboli* of 4,250 tons, 100m in length, 7,000ihp and 18 knots with forced draught, a range of 2,500nm at 12 knots, armour of 120mm on the sides and 40mm on a curved deck, and an armament of two 194mm guns in turrets at the ends and six 138.6mm guns in turrets on the sides. Krantz asked the Council for specifications based on this study that could be put out for tenders. The Council on 26 June 1888 noted that the cruiser and coast defence missions were very different and hard to reconcile, the first requiring high speed and a considerable range and the second requiring a powerful armament and strong protection, and asked for more information. Minister Krantz supplied more specific guidance on 10 July 1888 and dropped the reference to a coast defence role. On 31 July 1888 the Council produced new specifications for an armoured cruiser that included a speed of 18 knots at natural draught, Belleville boilers, a range of 3000nm at 12 knots, an armoured deck of 45mm including plating except for 55mm on the parts under the

waterline and over the machinery, an 8mm splinter deck over the machinery, side and turret armour of 110mm including plating, and an armament of two 194mm and six 138.6mm guns. There were to be two military masts. The Council's sections suggested small enclosed turrets for the guns to avoid having several guns disabled by a single projectile. The full Council accepted this work by its sections but recommended that because the artillery specified by Minister Krantz was inferior to that of ships it would have to combat that the armoured deck should be increased to 60mm average, accepting the 250-ton increase. These specifications were transmitted to the ports on 10 August 1888.

On 28 December 1888 the Council examined five designs submitted in response to the 10 August 1888 specifications and approved four for further work. It pointed out that side armour of 110mm was only effective against revolver cannon and small QF guns and that a medium calibre shell loaded with explosives could penetrate it. All ammunition handling and its personnel therefore had to be kept below the armoured deck. It examined revised plans on 22 March 1889 retaining three, and on 4 June 1889 selected Thibaudier's design, which had a displacement of 4,745 tons, length of 107m, horizontal engines of 8,765ihp for 19 knots with forced draught and 7,400ihp for 18 knots with natural draught, and an armament of two 194mm and six 138.6mm guns. The armoured portion of the ship were surmounted by an unarmoured forecastle and poop that together were 75m long. Thibaudier kept the big guns at the ends because the ship had enough firepower on the sides.

*Charner* was funded in the 1889 budget, and after Parliament learned there were some building ways available *Latouche-Tréville* and *Chanzy* were provided for by a special law of 28 February 1889 that funded them under the 1890 budget. *Bruix* was funded under the regular 1890 budget at Toulon and, after being delayed, under the 1891 budget at Rochefort. These ships had one fewer decks than *Dupuy de Lôme*, the battery deck between the main and upper decks being omitted. On 9 July 1890, shortly after the start of construction, FCM proposed fitting *Latouche-Tréville* with electrically-operated balanced elliptical turrets in place of the hydraulically-operated circular turrets in the original design. The balanced elliptical turret operated by electricity was an innovation proposed by Gustave Canet who directed gun manufacturing for the Forges et Chantiers de la Méditerranée at Le Havre from 1881 to 1897. The *Conseil des travaux* was not enthusiastic about electrically-powered turrets, but as FCM was also building the battleship *Jauréguiberry* with them and the cruiser was expected to be completed before the battleship the Conseil permitted the change in order to get experience with the new equipment as soon as possible. As the first French warship with electrically-operated turrets *Latouche-Tréville* not surprisingly had considerable difficulty in service with the new technology, although her initial trials went well. The other three ships retained the usual hydraulically-operated circular turrets. In March 1892 it was decided to give *Bruix* vertical 4-cylinder engines instead of the horizontal 3-cylinder engines in her sisters. The 3-cylinder port engine was aft of the starboard engine in *Chanzy* and *Latouche-Tréville*, the longer 4-cylinder engines were side by side in *Bruix*, an arrangement repeated in *Pothuau*. The belt armour in *Bruix* was of Creusot (Schneider) hammered nickel steel while that of *Latouche-Tréville* was the first use of chrome steel made by Châtillon et Commentry after they introduced it in the Greek battleships *Hydra* and *Spetsai*. In the bow the side and deck armour came together to produce a usable ram, but its position suggested it was intended more for speed than for ramming.

*Charner* was renamed *Amiral Charner* on 25 March 1895 when the word *Amiral* was added to the names of several existing ships. The name *Chanzy* had previously been assigned to a 2ⁿᵈ class protected cruiser ordered and quickly cancelled during 1887 (see below).

**Dimensions & tons:** (*Latouche-Tréville*) 110.160m oa, 109.250m wl, 106.121m pp (tip fwd to rudder) x 14.039m ext (below wl), 13.998m wl. 4,748t disp (normal), 4,990 (full). Draught: 5.806m mean, 6.064m aft. Men: 414 including 36 officers without flag.

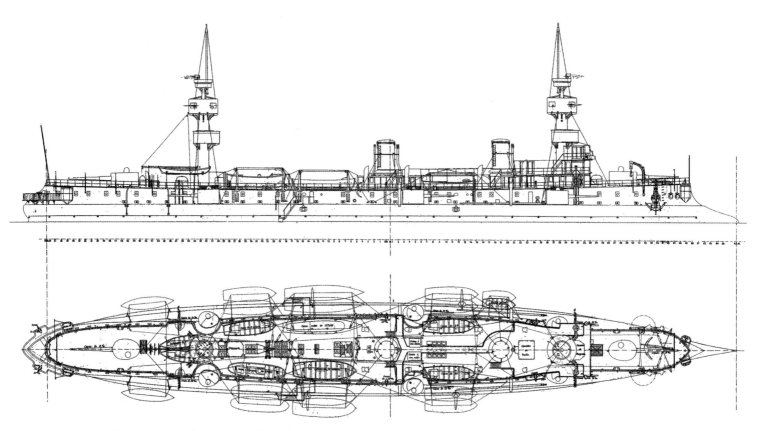

Longitudinal and overhead views (*plan du pitonnage*) of the 2nd class armoured cruiser *Latouche-Tréville*, built on the plans of M. Thibaudier. The plans by the Forges et Chantiers de la Méditerranée at Le Havre were signed at Graville on 25 October 1893 by the chief engineer there, Marmiesse. The small calibre artillery carried at this time included 4 x 65mm/50 M1891 QF guns (2 on the lower bridge deck forward and 2 on the shelter deck aft between the after turret and the mainmast), 4 x 47mm/40 M1885 QF guns (on the lower platforms of the military masts, where there were positions for 8), and 6 x 37mm revolving cannon (2 on the shelter deck abreast or abaft the foremast, 2 on the shelter deck abreast the after funnel, and 2 on the stern gallery). There were also 2 x 65mm M1881 guns for the landing force, stowed on the upper deck. *Plans de pitonnage* show small fittings including *pitons* (eye bolts through which ropes could be passed) and in the process also show many details of the exterior appearance of the ships.

**Machinery:** 1,850nhp and 8,300ihp (7,945ihp in *Chanzy*, 9,000ihp in *Bruix*) designed at 17kg/cm² boiler pressure. Designed speed 18.3kts (19kts in *Bruix*). 2 screws. 2 engines. 16 Belleville boilers. 535t coal (normal 406t). Range 4,000nm @ 10kts.

(*Charner* & *L-T*) Trials (*Charner*, 18.6.1895) 8,956ihp = 18.40kts, (*Latouche-Tréville* 23.2.1895) 8,276ihp = 18.164kts. 2 horizontal triple expansion engines with direct connecting rods and 3 cylinders of 0.780m, 1.150m, and 1.750m diameter and 1.000m stroke.

(*Chanzy*) 2 horizontal triple expansion engines with direct connecting rods and 3 cylinders of 0.800m, 1.200m, and 1.900m diameter and 0.900m stroke.

(*Bruix*) Trials (15.9.1896) 9,107ihp = 18.372kts. Was originally to have had engines as *Charner* but in 3.1892 was assigned two vertical triple expansion engines of 9,000hp with 4 cylinders including two low pressure cylinders of 1.40m diameter.

**Armour:**
Side: Belt at waterline (steel) 92mm amidships, 60mm fwd and aft. Total height amidships 3.75m, from 1.200m below the wl to 2.550m above.
Guns: 194mm and 138.6mm turrets (steel) 92mm.
Decks: Armoured deck (extra mild steel) 40mm near centreline, 50mm near sides, both on 14mm hull plating. The deck curved down evenly from 0.5m above the wl near the centreline to meet the lower edge of the belt at 1.2m below the waterline. Splinter deck over the boiler and engine rooms 8mm.
Conning tower: 92mm.

**Guns:**
(1893) 2 x 194mm/45 M1887 (turrets fore and aft), 6 x 138.6mm/45 M1887 QF (turrets on the sides), 4 x 65mm/50 M1891 QF, 2 x 65mm/16 M1881 landing, 4 x 47mm/40 M1885 QF, 6 x 37mm revolving cannon. **Torpedoes:** 4 above water tubes for 356mm torpedoes (sides). (A 5th tube in the stern in the initial design was omitted during construction.) **Searchlights:** 6 x 60cm.

(after 1905, *Bruix*) 2 x 194mm, 6 x 138.6mm, 4 x 65mm QF, 1 x 65mm landing, 3 x 37mm (for the boats). Torpedo tubes removed.

***Amiral Charner*** Rochefort Dyd/F.C. Méditerranée, Le Havre (engines designed by Laudeau).
On list 1.1890. Ord: 21.6.1889. K: 15.1.1891. L: 18.3.1893. Comm: 16.1.1894 (trials), 26.8.1895 (full).
Budget 1889 (delayed to 1890). Originally named *Charner*, renamed 25.3.1895. Engine contract 12.3.1890. Machinery installed 28.12.1892 to 5.12.1893. Trials began 6.1894. Arrived at Toulon 1.9.1895 and admitted to active service 5.9.1895 in the *Escadre de la Méditerranée*. Military masts replaced by poles at Bizerte c1913. Recommissioned 8.1914, war service in the Eastern Mediterranean. Torpedoed 8.2.1916 by *U-21* west of Beirut, sank within two minutes with only one survivor.

***Latouche-Tréville*** F.C. Méditerranée, Le Havre-Graville/FCM, Le Havre (as *Charner*).
On list 1.1890. Ord: 18.12.1889 (contract). K: 26.4.1890. L: 5.11.1892. Comm: 16.10.1893 (trials), 6.5.1895 (full).
Budget 1890 (late addition). Contract included engines. Machinery installed 9.1892 to 7.1893. To Cherbourg 9.10.1893 for trials. Trials suspended 5-12.1894 to resolve boiler combustion problems. To Brest 17.5.1895 for service with the *Escadre du Nord*, to Toulon and the *Escadre de la Méditerranée* 1.1896. Seagoing annex to the gunnery

school in *Couronne,* then in *Tourville* (*Gironde*) at Toulon 15.2.1907 to 1911 (replaced *Calédonien,* replaced by *Jules Michelet*). Serious explosion in after turret 22.9.1908. Military masts replaced by poles at Bizerte 11–12.1913. War service in the Eastern Mediterranean until placed in reserve at Corfu 12.1917. After topmast removed 8.1915. To Toulon 31.12.1918, decomm. 1.5.1919. Struck 21.6.1920. Loaned 4.9.1920 to the contractor salvaging *Liberté* – her hulk carried the generator that produced compressed air for the salvage and was moored parallel to the wreck. *Liberté* was raised 21.2.1925, the former cruiser was returned to the Navy in 1925 and sold for BU in 1926.

***Chanzy*** **(ii)** C.A. Gironde, Bordeaux-Lormont/Schneider, Creusot (engines designed by Barba).

On list 1.1890. Ord: 18.12.1889 (contract). K: 1.1890. L: 24.1.1894. Comm: 6.2.1894 (trials), 20.7.1895 (full).

Budget 1890 (late addition). Contract included engines. Machinery installed 28.10.1892 to 26.1.1894. Was essentially complete when launched, as was normal practice at this yard. To Rochefort for trials 21.2.1894, to reserve for repairs 3.12.1894, recomm. 1.5.1895, trials completed 26.6.1895. Arrived at Toulon 13.8.1895 for service in the *Escadre de la Méditerranée.* Funnel casings raised 1.8m after steam drum rupture 20.2.1900, reserve 3.5.1904. Recommissioned 15.9.1906 for the Far East. Ran onto rocks 20.5.1907 in the fog at high tide off Ballard Islet in the Chusan archipelago off Ningpo on the China coast. Attempts by *Alger, Bruix,* and *D'Entrecasteaux* to refloat her failed, wreck evacuated 30.5.1907 after stern began to sink in bad weather, crew roster closed 1.6.1907, blown up 12.6.1907. Struck 27.8.1907.

***Bruix*** Rochefort Dyd/FCM, Le Havre.

On list 1.1891. Ord: 12.9.1890. K: 9.11.1891. L: 2.8.1894. Comm: 4.5.1895 (trials), 1.12.1896 (full).

Budget 1890 (delayed to 1891). Construction reassigned c1890 from Toulon to Rochefort where she was laid down next to *Charner.* Manned for trials 15.4.1896, trials 23.7.1896–19.9.1896. Initially assigned to the *Escadre du Nord* at Brest. Military masts replaced with poles at Bizerte 4–7.1914. War service in Cameroon in late 1914 and then in the Eastern Mediterranean until placed in reserve at Salonika 31.1.1918. Reactivated 11.1918 for service in the Black Sea, returned to Toulon 8.6.1919. Struck 21.6.1920. Sold 2.5.1921 with *Requin* and *Torpilleur nº 269* to the Société du Matériel Naval du Midi.

---

***POTHUAU.*** *Croiseur de 1ʳᵉ classe.* Armoured cruiser with two single main battery turrets at the ends, secondary guns on the sides in casemates and shields, and a ram bow. Three funnels, two pole masts. To *Croiseur cuirassé* 1.1897. Designed by Thibaudier.

The Programme of 1890 called for 12 *croiseurs d'escadre de 1ʳᵉ classe* of which 11 existed. In early 1891 Minister of Marine Barbey told the *Conseil des travaux* that among the ships planned for the 1892 budget was an unnamed 1st class squadron cruiser designated C. He felt that its design should be based on the *Charner* type and asked the Council for specifications. He asked specifically if the 138.6mm battery, now of QF guns, should be mounted in enclosed turrets or simply in shields as foreign navies were doing. The Council, examining the matter on 29 May 1891, felt that since some of these guns were used in axial fire and a few moments of hits from QF guns would render the decks uninhabitable, retention of the turrets was justified. The Council after much discussion changed the two 194mm BL guns to 164.7mm QF guns, a model that did not yet exist but which was in preparation. It felt that further improvements in armour allowed reducing the side armour to 100mm including 20mm hull plating, which would still fulfill its functions of protecting the ship against projectiles from guns up to 65mm and detonating high explosive shells before they could penetrate. The deck was to be 55mm thick on the horizontal

portion and 100mm on the curved sides. The Council retained most of the other features of the *Charner* type including the two military masts, although the need to provide the flag quarters required by the Minister and to increase steaming range (in which the *Charner* design was deficient) resulted in a 5,000-ton displacement. Before sending the specifications to naval constructor Thibaudier at Rochefort to produce a design Minister Barbey restored the 194mm guns and changed the profile of the armoured deck from a circular arch as in *Dupuy de Lôme* and *Chanzy* to the polygonal form with a flat top and inclined sides that was used in most later ships.

On 10 February 1892 Minister Barbey referred to the *Conseil des travaux* a design for a *croiseur d'escadre de 1ʳᵉ classe* of an enlarged *Charner* type prepared by Thibaudier according to the Council's specifications of 29 May 1891 as modified by the Minister. Thibaudier's design was 108m long and displaced 5,066 tons. To accommodate the flag he restored the battery or intermediate deck that was present in *Dupuy de Lôme* but not in the *Charners,* although unlike in *Dupuy de Lôme* the side armour did not cover it. The Council reviewed the design on 15 March 1892 and made a few changes, but the Council's president, Vice Admiral Duperré, found her lacking compared to foreign cruisers, notably the British *Orlando* type belted cruiser. Unable to resolve this matter without redesigning the ship, the entire council less one member concluded that the specifications upon which Thibaudier had based his design were insufficient in artillery, speed, protection, and range and recommended not building the ship and instead drafting new specifications.

Minister Cavaignac decided on 6 April 1892 to proceed with the project and on 14 April 1892 ordered the Machinery Commission to negotiate for her construction. In November FCM Le Havre accepted a clause stating that no payments would be made before 1 January 1894, and in December 1892 it was decided to include in the contract the replacement of ordinary steel with special steel for the side armour. The contract was approved on 20 January 1893. The ship was given electrically-operated balanced elliptical 194mm turrets as in *Latouche Tréville.* In the meantime Thibaudier and the ministry made some adjustments to his design but without changing its length. The turrets for the 138.6mm guns were replaced by casemate and open mountings and their number was increased from six to ten. The rig was reduced to pole masts although the base of the after military mast was retained. The design was approved on 11 April 1893. The projecting bow was strengthened by 50mm of steel on each side (32mm of armour and 18mm of plating) and by the 50mm armoured deck (35mm of armour and 15mm plating), allowing the ship to attack by ramming.

On 22 February 1906 a decree was published instituting a seagoing school for gunnery practice (*École d'application de tir à la mer*) on board *Pothuau.* Gunnery training had previously been conducted at Toulon and in nearby sheltered waters on board *Couronne* and her annexes, but these no longer fulfilled modern requirements and the decree instituted an additional gunnery course at sea to follow training in *Couronne. Pothuau* had modern guns and mountings and could be spared from the fleet. In early 1914 it was proposed to move the school to *D'Entrecasteaux* because of weaknesses found in the bases of the two turrets of *Pothuau.* After active war service these turrets were pulled and she resumed service as seagoing school for gunnery practice from 1919 to 1926.

*The characteristics are based on a devis dated 10.7.1897*

**Dimensions & tons:** 113.288m oa (including the stern gallery), 113.058m wl, 113.088m pp (tip fwd to stern) x 15.354m ext & wl (17.180m outside sponsons). 5,059.555t disp. Draught: 5.947m mean, 5.732m aft. Men: 457.

**Machinery:** 10,000ihp designed at 140rpm and 17kg/cm² boiler pressure (12kg/cm² at the engines). Designed speed 19kts. Trials (19.2.1897) 10,534.33ihp = 19.120kts at 129.875rpm and 14.612kg/cm² boiler pressure. 2 screws. 2 vertical triple expansion engines with 4 cylinders of 0.930m (1), 1.350m (1), and 1.400m (2) diameter and 0.820m stroke. 18 Belleville boilers. 800t coal. Range 6,532.29nm @ 10.597kts.

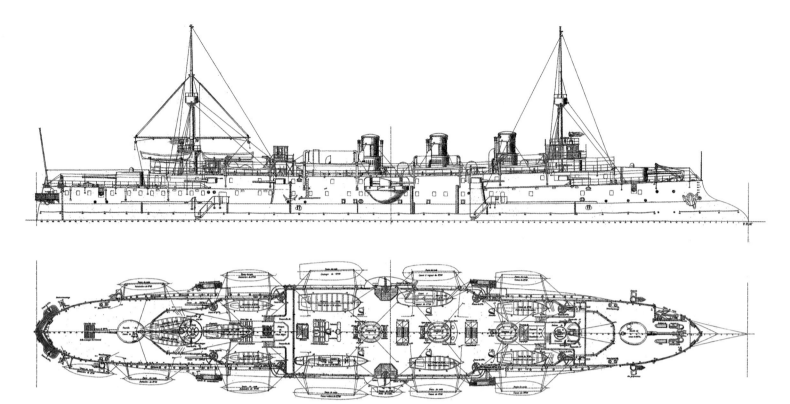

Longitudinal and overhead views (*plan de pitonnage*) of the 1st class armoured cruiser *Pothuau*, built on the plans of M. Thibaudier. The plans by the Forges et Chantiers de la Méditerranée at Le Havre were signed at Graville on 1 July 1896 by the chief engineer there, A. Coville. The small calibre artillery carried at this time included 10 x 47mm/40 M1885 QF guns (on the shelter deck directly above the 138.6mm guns), 5 x 37 mm M1885 QF guns (1 above the conning tower, 2 on the fore bridge, and 2 on a platform on the after mast), and 3 x 37mm revolving cannon (2 in the stern gallery and 1 above the conning tower). There were also 2 x 65mm M1881 landing guns.

**Armour:**

Side: Belt at waterline (steel) 60mm amidships on 20mm hull plating, 32mm fwd and 32mm aft on 18mm hull plating. Height amidships from 1.2m below the wl to 2.5m above.

Guns: 194mm turrets (steel) 180mm with 60mm fixed bases. 138.6mm guns: eight in 60mm casemates with 56mm shields, two in sponsons with 54mm fixed bases and 30mm shields.

Decks: Armoured deck (extra mild steel) flat 35mm, upper and lower slopes 85mm, all on 15mm hull plating.

Conning tower (steel): 170mm.

**Guns:**

(1897) 2 x 194mm/40 M1893 (turrets fore and aft), 10 x 138.6mm/45 QF (8 casemates of which 6 had M1893 and two M1891(2) guns plus 2 M1891(2) guns in shields on pivot mountings), 2 x 65mm/16 M1881 landing, 10 x 47mm/40 M1885 QF, 5 x 37mm/20 M1885 QF, 3 x 37mm revolving cannon. **Torpedoes:** 4 above-water tubes for 356mm M1887 torpedoes on the sides. **Searchlights:** 6 x 60mm.

(1906) 2 x 194mm, 10 x 138.6mm, 2 x 65mm landing, 12 x 47mm QF, 3 x 37mm QF (for the boats). Torpedo tubes landed by 1907. Includes 2 x 47mm added forward in 1903 in place of some 37mm to respond to complaints that the ship lacked small calibre protection forward

(1919) 194 mm guns and turrets landed leaving 10 x 138 mm and 4 x 75 mm.

(1925) 10 x 138mm M1910, 2 x 75mm M1918 AA, 1 Van Deuren 58mm trench mortar (naval variant).

*Pothuau* (D1) F.C. Méditerranée, Le Havre-Graville/FCM, Le Havre.

On list 1.1.1894. Ord: 11.1.1893 (contract). K: 25.5.1893. L: 19.9.1895. Comm: 17.8.1896 (trials), 13.7.1897 (full).

Budget 1892 (designated C, delayed to 1894). Attempted launches on 22 and 23.8.1895 failed. Machinery installed 20.9.1895 to 25.2.1896. Represented France at the Spithead review 26.6.1897-1.7.1897, then to the *Escadre du Nord* 2.7.1897. Carried French President Félix Faure to Kronshtadt 23-27.8.1897 and during fleet service carried the French President three times 1901-1904. To reserve 8.5.1904. Recomm. 17.4.1906 as seagoing school for gunnery practice and served to 7.1914. War service from 8.1914, in Cameroun 10.1914 to 7.1915, Eastern Mediterranean, Red Sea, Indochina and back 1.1916 to 9.1917 (artillery fitted for indirect fire 1-4.1916). Mainmast removed late 1917 to permit use of captive balloons, then to Corfu 11.1917 to 1.1919 as seagoing school for gunnery practice. 194mm guns and turrets removed 1919 and continued service as seagoing school for gunnery practice to 12.6.1926 when replaced by *Gueydon* and decommissioned. Struck 3.11.1927. Sold 25.9.1929 at Toulon by the Domaines to the Société du Matériel Naval du Midi to BU.

---

*D'ENTRECASTEAUX. Croiseur de 1re classe.* Protected cruiser with reinforced side plating, two single main battery turrets at the ends, secondary guns on the sides in casemates and in shields, a steel hull sheathed in two layers of teak covered with copper, and a ram-shaped bow. Three funnels in groups of two and one, two pole masts. Designed by Lagane (FCM La Seyne). To *croiseur cuirassé* 1.1897 and back to *croiseur de 1re classe* 1.1899. *Croiseur léger* in 1.3.1920.

Minister of Marine Barbey on 28 April 1891 sent to the *Conseil des travaux* draft specifications for a protected cruiser intended to carry the flag of an admiral on overseas stations and requested that the Council review them. He specified a displacement of not over 8,000 tons, a trial speed of 19 knots with moderately forced draft, and boilers of a type tested in long cruises (meaning cylindrical and not water tube boilers). The armament was to include four 240mm guns (the calibre in the old station battleships that she would replace) and eight 138.6mm QF behind shields. The primary protection was to be an armoured deck 55mm thick including hull plating on the flat portions and 65mm on the slopes with a cellular layer above it.

The hull sides between the armoured deck and the top of the cellular layer along the entire length of the ship was to have light armour of at least 60mm. The 240mm turrets were to have 300mm armour and the 138.6mm guns were to have 40mm shields. The hull was to be sheathed with wood and copper, she was to have semi-military masts with one armed top and a platform for a searchlight and spreading enough sails to provide a serious capability in case coal ran short.

The Council examined these specifications on 7 July 1891 and found that they could not be achieved on 8,000 tons. The only way to do it was to reduce the number or calibre of the main battery, but Barbey's instructions did not allow this, so the Council presented specifications with his armament of four 240mm guns and the least possible displacement. It arranged the main battery in four single turrets, two at the ends and two on the sides, and put the secondary battery in sponsons or angled ports with four able to fire in any direction. To save some weight it reduced the range to 5500nm at 10 knots and used multitubular boilers, but it still ended up with an 8,600-ton, 118m long ship. If the main battery were reduced the result would be an 8,000-ton ship with a length of 115m. Amable Lagane at FCM later produced plans of such a ship dated 15 December 1891 which had many of the features of the final *D'Entrecasteaux*.

Barbey responded to the Council in July 1891 by reducing the number of 240mm guns to two and reducing the deck to 50mm thick on the flat portions and 100mm on the slopes over the machinery and 40mm flat and 70mm slopes at the bow and stern. These changes permitted the use of cylindrical double ended boilers as in *Cécille* instead of multitubular ones while keeping the displacement within limits. The light 60mm side plating was split into 20mm plating on the side of the ship proper and another 40mm on the inner bulkhead of the cofferdam set back about 1.20m from the ship's side over the machinery. The outer layer was to detonate high explosive shell and the inner layer was to protect the ship from the resulting splinters. The armour on the main turrets was reduced to 250mm on the front halves and 210mm on the after halves, the savings allowing thicker (72mm) shields for the 138.6mm guns. She was to have a complete double hull in the machinery spaces and a maximum length of 115m. Barbey then transmitted the specifications in a circular to the ports and commercial firms on 31 July 1891 and asked for designs. Some changes followed. On 18 November 1891 Barbey notified the designers that the Model 1892 240mm gun was to be substituted for the Model 1887 gun, and on 2 March 1892 he issued a directive changing the classification of the ship to a *croiseur de 1re classe* and informed the Council that the sails were to be suppressed and the masts in the specifications were to be replaced with two military masts with two armed tops and a searchlight on each.

The Council on 29 March 1892 examined the seven projects received and recommended those of Tréboul, Raymond, and Lagane at FCM La Seyne for further work. Lagane probably scaled down his plan of 15 December 1891, which already had the Model 1892 240mm guns. The Council also asked the designers to make some more changes. It added space and weight for submerged torpedo tubes and adopted La Seyne's system of redoubts for the 138.6mm guns (asking Raymond and Tréboul to imitate it). It also used the savings from the deletion of sails and a reduction in provisions to add four more 138.6mm guns in shields on the shelter deck, and it asked the designers to study whether the 138.6mm guns could be put on two levels to provide six guns with forward axial fire and four with axial fire aft. It wanted the 240mm guns moved as far as possible from the ends, especially the bow. The length on the waterline could be increased to 120m.

On 5 November 1892 and 1 December 1892 Minister of Marine Burdeau forwarded revised designs by Tréboul and FCM La Seyne to the Council which discussed them on 31 January 1893. (Raymond's came later and was rejected.) The two were very similar (7,998 tons and 8,086 tons). Tréboul's had many good features, including the main guns being at a sufficient distance from the ends, a good installation of the 138.6mm guns, and a better boiler installation, but it also had a much less satisfactory double hull in the engine room. The La Seyne design used balanced turrets operated by electricity like those in their *Latouche Tréville* and *Jaureguiberry*, Tréboul's

design used unbalanced turrets based on those in *Brennus*. The La Seyne turrets, however, were still too close to the ends. Their double hull was more satisfactory but led to the use of less satisfactory boilers and a placement of coal bunkers that caused a less satisfactory arrangement of the 138.6mm guns. The Council concluded that both designs could be approved but advised that if only one could be used it preferred that of Tréboul.

Two ships of this type, *croiseurs de 1re classe* N and O, appeared in the 1893 budget (submitted on 10 March 1892), both to be built by contract. Both ships were deferred, N to the 1894 budget and O to the 1895 budget. With one design from a contractor already in hand the Navy proceeded with it first, and in the May 1893 submission of the 1894 budget cruiser N had become *D'Entrecasteaux*, (ex N, designed by F.C. Mediterranée).

Despite being classed as an armoured cruiser in 1897-98, *D'Entrecasteaux* was a large deck-protected cruiser with vertical side protection limited to a second layer of 10mm hull plating near the waterline reinforcing the usual 10mm layer plus 40mm of similar plating 1.20m inside the ship on the inner bulkhead of the cofferdam. The lower part of the hull was clad with two layers of teak planking 80mm and 60mm thick with an external skin of 0.9mm copper sheathing, extending from the keel to just above the lower section of the cofferdam belt. A stern torpedo tube in the design was omitted from the final design. The ram-shaped (inverted) bow had a bronze stempost and was not intended for ramming.

**Dimensions & tons:** 120.921m oa, 120.000m wl and pp x 17.850m ext and wl. 8,122.971t disp (designed). Draught: (designed) 7.160m mean, 7.520m aft (keel line projected). Men: 559 (587 with flag).

**Machinery:** 13,500ihp designed (uprated to 14,500ihp after trials) at 110rpm and 10.5kg/cm$^2$ boiler pressure. Trials (23.12.1898) 14,578ihp at 112rpm = 19.099kts. 2 screws. 2 vertical triple expansion engines with 3 cylinders of 1.10m, 1.63m, and 2.465m diameter and 1.040m stroke. 5 double-ended cylindrical return flame boilers. 960t coal (normal), 1,133.9t (max). Range with normal coal 4,729nm @ 10kts; with max coal 5,585nm @ 10kts.

**Armour:**

Decks: Armoured deck, flat 30mm over the machinery (special steel) and 20mm elsewhere (construction steel), slopes 80mm over the machinery and 50mm elsewhere (both hardened steel), all on 20mm hull plating. Cellular layer above the deck with a cofferdam along the sides.

Side: 20mm vertical plating on the side from the edge of the armoured deck below the waterline to the top of the cellular layer in two layers of 10mm plating, plus 40mm in two 20mm layers of plating about 1.20m inside the ship on the inner side of the cofferdam. Total side protection was 60mm of hull plating.

Guns: 240mm turrets (special steel) 230mm max with 175mm max fixed bases. 138.6mm casemates 54mm circular gun shields (hardened steel) and 52mm casemate faces and sides (special steel).

Conning tower (hardened steel): 230mm.

**Guns:** 2 x 240mm/40 M1893 BLR (turrets at ends), 12 x 138.6mm/45 M1893 QF (8 in casemates and 4 shielded), 2 x 65mm/16 M1881 landing, 12 x 47mm/40 M1885 QF, 6 x 37mm/20 M1885 QF (later 4, later 2 for the boats). **Torpedoes:** 4 tubes for 450mm M1892 torpedoes (2 above water and 2 submerged, all removed 1910-11). **Searchlights:** 8 x 60cm (2 at the tops of the masts soon removed leaving 6).

*D'Entrecasteaux* (C1) F.C. Méditerranée, La Seyne/FCM, Marseille.
On list 1.1894. Ord: 8.11.1893 (contract). K: 6.1894. L: 12.6.1896. Comm: 1.1.1898 (trials), 15.2.1899 (full).
Budget 1893 (designated N, delayed to 1894). Installation of machinery completed 8.7.1897, trials completed 25.1.1899. Left Toulon 6.4.1899 to replace *Vauban* on the Far East station, to reserve at Toulon 12.2.1903. Recomm. 1.9.1905 for the Indian Ocean and Far East, to reserve at Toulon 1.1.1910. Recomm. 15.11.1911, flagship of the Mediterranean school division 1.1.1912 replacing *Brennus*, replaced by

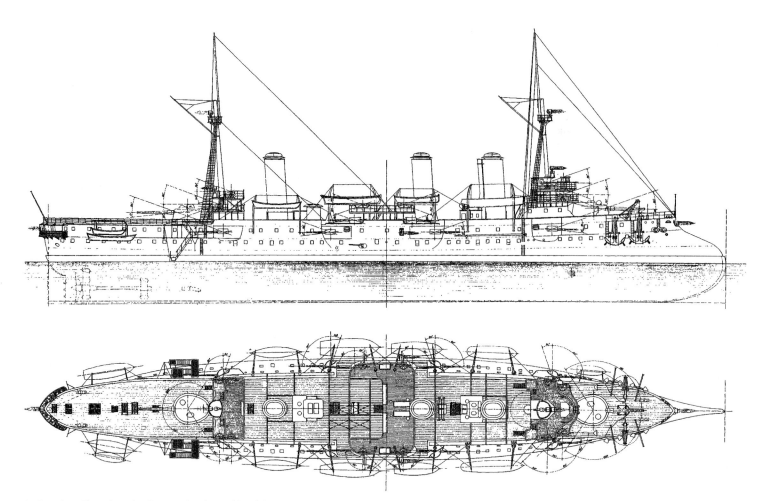

Outboard profile and overhead view (*plan d'ensemble*) of the 'armoured cruiser' *D'Entrecasteaux*, built at La Seyne on plans by M. Lagane. The undated plan by the Forges et Chantiers de la Méditerranée carries the names of the director of the yard, Lagane, and the Navy's control officer, Rampal. The small calibre artillery carried at this time included 12 x 47mm/40 M1885 QF guns (4 on the forward bridges, 4 on the after bridges, and 4 on a bridge amidships over the 138.6mm battery), and 4 x 37mm QF guns (2 on the forward bridges and 2 on the lower bridge aft). There were also 2 x 65mm M1881 landing guns (stowed in the battery).

*Suffren* 15.11.1913 and to reserve at Toulon 25.11.1913. Active in the Mediterranean 8.1914 to 7.1919, with *Requin* helped defend the Suez Canal 3.2.1915 from advancing Turkish troops. Joined the Division of schools of the Atlantic at Brest 5.9.1919 as school for seamen, helmsmen, and carpenters. Decomm. 1.6.1921, condemnation proposed 17.5.1922. Struck 27.10.1922 (as *croiseur cuirassé*) in preparation for loan to Belgium. Towed to Bruges 24.5.1923, handed over 30.5.1923 to Belgium on loan as accommodation ship for a flotilla of small German A-class torpedo boats left in Belgium by the Germans. The Belgians disbanded this flotilla 6.1926 and returned the cruiser, which was towed back to Cherbourg 4.2.1927 after it was found uneconomical to sell her at Bruges. Poland requested her 28.2.1927 and bought her 7.3.1927, Polish flag raised 30.7.1927, reportedly renamed *Król Władysław IV*, towed from Cherbourg to Gdynia 31.7 to 11.8.1927, renamed *Bałtyk* 13.8.1927. Used 9.1939 by the Poles to block the entrance to the military basin in the port of Gdynia, recovered by the Germans and used as an accommodations hulk until BU 1941-8.1942 at Danzig.

---

**JEANNE D'ARC (i).** *Croiseur de 1ʳᵉ classe.* Protected cruiser with reinforced side plating, two single main battery turrets at the ends, secondary guns on the sides in two levels of casemates, a steel hull sheathed in two layers of teak covered with copper, and a ram-shaped bow. Three evenly spaced funnels, two pole masts. Designed by Tréboul.

First class station cruiser like *D'Entrecasteaux*. The history of *Jeanne d'Arc* (budget designator O) was identical to that of *D'Entrecasteaux* (N, above)

through 31 January 1893, when the *Conseil des travaux* concluded that both designs could be approved but advised that if only one could be used it preferred that of Tréboul. On 8 February 1893 the ministry asked Tréboul to revise his design based on the Council's report of 31 January and more changes specified by Minister of Marine Vice Admiral Adrien Barthélemy Louis Rieunier on 23 February and 10 March 1893. With one design from a contractor (FCM La Seyne) already in hand, however, the Navy proceeded with it first, leaving Tréboul's design to be caught up in the budget turmoil of the mid-1890s. In the 1894 budget submission of May 1893 cruiser O was listed as designed by Tréboul and to be built by contract. The Budget Commission report of 22 June 1893 stated that 'this start of construction, provided for in the 1893 budget law, is provisionally reserved', thus postponing it to 1895. In the meantime, on 3 August 1893 the Director of Materiel, Bienaymé, asked Minister of Marine Rieunier to approve the latest revision of Tréboul's plans. Orders would then be given to the Machinery Commission to request tenders for the construction of the ship, which would be inscribed on the *Liste de la flotte* under the name *Jeanne d'Arc*.

The initial submission of the 1895 budget by Minister Auguste Alfred Lefebre on 17 March 1894 included *Jeanne d'Arc* (ex O) as a 1ˢᵗ class cruiser designed by Tréboul whose contract had not yet been let. This submission was reduced by the ministry on 21 June 1894 although *Jeanne d'Arc* was retained. On 20 October 1894 a new Minister, Deputy Félix Faure (who was soon to become President of the Republic), told Parliament that he planned to modify the 1895 budget with increased spending on new construction, and on 4 November 1894 he distributed a new list of proposed shipbuilding. In it Tréboul's *Jeanne d'Arc* was replaced by two *croiseurs grande vitesse* (*Guichen* and *Châteaurenault*) and two 3rd class station cruisers (K1 and K2).

The initial submission of the 1896 budget on 14 May 1895 reinstated Tréboul's *Jeanne d'Arc*, now designated C2 as a 1st class station cruiser and to be built at Toulon instead of by contract. However, the Budget Commission on 13 July 1895 deleted all station cruisers including Tréboul's *Jeanne d'Arc* from the budget and moved the unnamed *croiseur d'escadre* D2 from contract to the dockyards, where the cancelled station cruisers were to have been built. Tréboul's plans for *Jeanne d'Arc, croiseur protégé, chef de station* dated 2 July 1895 were signed by Minister of Marine Besnard on 21 August 1895 after the Budget Commission had cancelled the ship. The Budget Commission on 24 October 1895 reaffirmed its decision cancelling the credits for the station cruisers in the 1896 budget.

*The characteristics are from Tréboul's modified design of 31.1.1893 and the original specifications. The design was modified further in 1893-95.*
**Dimensions & tons:** 116m pp x 17.88m ext. 7,998.5t disp. Draught: 7.15m mean, 7.50m aft.
**Machinery:** 13,200ihp designed (uprated by the *Conseil des travaux* from Tréboul's 12,750ihp) at 106rpm and 10.50kg/cm$^2$ boiler pressure. Speed 19kts. 2 screws. 2 vertical triple expansion engines with 4 cylinders, the two LP cylinders being of 1.803m diameter, 1.02 m stroke. 6 cylindrical boilers. 657t coal (normal). Range (from the specifications) 5,500nm @ 10kts
**Armour:** (*figures from the specifications, others are from the 1893 design)
Decks: Armoured deck (extra mild steel) 50mm* deck including hull plating, increased to 100mm* on the slopes and over the machinery. Splinter deck located 1.20m below the armoured deck 8mm*.
Side: 20mm plating on the sides from the edge of the armoured deck below the waterline to the top of the cellular layer plus 40mm plating about 1.20m inside the ship on the inner side of the cofferdam.
Guns: 240mm turrets 250mm* max with 200mm* max fixed bases. 138.6mm redoubts/casemates 72mm (separate redoubts on the upper and shelter decks).
Conning tower: 200mm*.
**Guns:** 2 x 240mm/40 M1893, 12 x 138.6mm, 12 x 47mm QF, 4 x 37mm QF. **Torpedoes:** 8 tubes of which 5 above water, (2 on the sides forward, 2 amidships, and 1 aft) and 3 submerged (1 forward and 2 on the sides). **Searchlights:** 4 in the hull at the ends on the upper deck and probably 2 on the masts.

*Jeanne d'Arc* (i) (C2) Contract (1893-95), Toulon (1896).
Budget 1893 (designated O, delayed to 1896), suspended with other station ships in execution of decisions by the Budget Commission on 13.7.1895 and 24.10.1895.

---

**CROISEUR D'ESCADRE D2.** *Croiseur de 1re classe.* Protected cruiser with reinforced side plating, two single main battery turrets at the ends, secondary guns in one long redoubt on the sides, a steel hull without sheathing, and a ram bow. Four funnels in two groups of two, two military masts. Changed to armoured cruiser in May 1896 but no design prepared. Designed by A.C. Loire (de Bussy).

The 1896 budget submission (submitted in May 1895) introduced a 1st class *croiseur d'escadre* (unnamed, designated D2) as well as reinstating Tréboul's station cruiser *Jeanne d'Arc* (C2). This D2 was to be an 8,500-ton 20-knot 1st class protected cruiser for squadron (European) service with a battery of two 194mm and ten 138.6mm guns. Minister of Marine Besnard sent the *Conseil des travaux* draft specifications for it which it approved with revisions on 8 June 1895. On 8 August 1895 Besnard sent to the ports the final specifications. The Council wanted the main battery turrets on the sides as in *Dupuy de Lôme* to maximize axial fire but Besnard's specifications put them in the Council's alternative position at the ends.

When the Budget Commission on 13 July 1895 deleted all station cruisers including Tréboul's *Jeanne d'Arc* from the budget it moved the unnamed *croiseur d'escadre* D2 from construction by contract to construction in a dockyard, where the cancelled station cruisers were to have been built. D2 appeared at Lorient in the first budget for 1897 submitted by Minister Lockroy in February 1896. Four designs for her based on Besnard's specifications of 8 August 1895 were referred to the *Conseil des travaux* in January and February 1896 for examination. On 5 March 1896 the Chief of the Naval General Staff asked the Council to accelerate its review of the designs as it was desired to start construction of the ship as soon as possible. The Council examined the four designs on 27 March 1896 and approved one by A.C. Loire for further work. The firm had designed a hull similar to that of De Bussy's *Dupuy de Lôme*, successfully scaling it up about a third and retaining its substantial internal capacity by eliminating the difference in draught between bow and stern, as the firm had already done in *Guichen*. The 194mm guns were in single turrets 22m from the bow and 25m from the stern and the 138.6mm guns were in a redoubt 66m long between them. The machinery was arranged as in *Guichen* with the boilers in four groups, two forward of the engines and two aft of them. The design did not replicate the protection scheme of *Dupuy de Lôme* including its side armour but gave the new ship the protection scheme specified by the Navy with a protective deck and reinforced side plating based like that of *D'Entrecastaux*.

*The characteristics are for the the design of A.C. Loire as recorded on 27 March 1896.*
**Dimensions & tons:** 127.68m wl x 17.62m wl and ext. 8567 tons. Draught: 7.50m mean, 7.50m aft (actual).
**Machinery:** 15,800ihp at 120rpm. 20kts designed (forced draught). 3 screws, 3 vertical triple expansion engines with 4 cylinders of 0.800m (1), 1.10m (1), and 1.40m (2) and 1.05m stroke. 22 Lagrafel et d'Allest boilers. Coal 1,600t including 535t surcharge. Range 7,700nm @ 10kts on trials, 7,000nm in service.
**Armour:** (All thicknesses include hull plating)
Decks: Armoured deck 50mm flat, 100mm on slopes over engines and boilers from 0.80m above the waterline to 1.40m below, 40mm flat and 70mm slopes at end. A cellular layer with cofferdam was on the level above this deck.
Side: 75mm vertical plating including 15mm hull plating either on the outboard side of the cofferdam above the deck at the sides or split between 25mm there and 50mm on the inner bulkhead of the cofferdam, about 1.20m from the ship's side.
Guns: Turrets 200mm. Redoubt for 138.6mm guns (66m long) 120mm over the gun positions, 60mm between them, 150mm forward bulkhead and 80mm after bulkhead.
Conning tower: 160mm
**Guns:** 2 x 194mm (single barbette turrets fore and aft), 10 x 138.6mm (8 in an armoured redoubt on the upper deck with the guns in angled ports, 2 on the deck above them amidships with axial fire), 16 x 47mm, 8 x 37mm (of which 8 x 47mm and 8 x 37mm were in two military masts). **Torpedoes:** Two submerged tubes on the sides angled forward. **Searchlights:** Six.

On 10 March 1896 after completing its technical evaluation of the designs the Council received long awaited data from Gâvres on experiments with melinite shells which showed the concept of protection of ships in general and this kind of cruiser in particular was no longer effective. The Council on 8 May 1896 recommended major changes to be made in the protection scheme of the A.C. Loire design. It was to be given a 210mm belt on the side over the engines and boilers with a flat 40mm deck on top, retaining the original protective deck at the ends. Side plating of 115mm amidships thinning at the ends was to be provided over over the cellular layer for the length of the ship. The Council implied that these and other recommended changes were complex enough that the design should be reviewed again before final approval, but with the ship postponed to the 1897 budget no further action was immediately taken. On 31 December 1896 the Council cited this enlarged *Dupuy de Lôme* as its preferred armoured cruiser design when opposing Bertin's *Desaix*. In 1897 she was replaced in the building programme by Bertin's *croiseur d'escadre* C3 described below.

---

*JEANNE D'ARC* (ii). *Croiseur de 1re classe.* Armoured cruiser with two single main battery turrets at the ends and secondary guns on the sides in sponsons and shields. Six funnels in two groups of three, one military and one pole mast. Designed by Bertin. To *Croiseur cuirassé* 1.1897.

In 1892 Émile Bertin, now director of naval construction at Rochefort, began plans for a 22-knot armoured cruiser derived directly from those that he had recently finished at Toulon for the 14,000-ton battleship that the *Conseil des travaux* had rejected on 8 December 1891. The vertical armour in the new cruiser covered the usual waterline area, the entire cellular layer, and all of the hull forward up to the upper deck, its maximum thickness being 12cm. Trials at Toulon, probably against the old *Provence*, had shown that 138.6mm shells filled with melinite had no effect against 10cm plates and 12cm was thus considered safe. Bertin was reassigned on 4 February 1892 as director of the *École d'application du génie maritime* at Paris, interrupting the study.

In 1895 the French became alarmed about the huge 14,000-ton 22-knot British protected cruisers *Powerful* and *Terrible*. The only design the French then had in hand was Tréboul's 8,000-ton 19-knot *Jeanne d'Arc*, now planned for construction at Toulon. The Rochefort design was retrieved and judged usable. The model of boilers was changed, the engine room was

lengthened somewhat, and the underwater vertical anti-torpedo armour was deleted, making possible a 23rd knot. Armour thicknesses were adjusted to allow using Harvey cemented armour, which then could not be made less than 15cm thick. The lines drawings were not touched. In the meantime the cancellation by the Budget Commission of the station cruisers in the 1896 budget including Tréboul's *Jeanne d'Arc* had left Toulon in desperate need of work and an immediate decision was needed. The Navy got the Budget Commission to authorize increasing the tonnage of the cruiser at Toulon by 2,500 tons to 11,000 tons, and on 28 December 1895 Lockroy sent a dispatch to Toulon ordering the start of construction (*mise en chantier*) of a 9,000-ton first-class armoured cruiser named *Jeanne d'Arc* to replace the ship of the same name whose construction had been suspended by the Budget Commission. He specified that the engines and boilers were to be built at Indret and would include 3 triple expansion engines of 9,500ihp each and 24 double-ended Du Temple-Normand boilers. Very quickly the tonnage grew to over 11,000 tons and the horsepower to over 30,000ihp, requiring a change to 36 Guyot-du Temple boilers. One set of plans by Bertin was approved by Lockroy on 25 January 1896, another was signed by Bertin on 16 March 1896.

Construction of the ship started very quickly, but it was then slowed between 1 September 1896 and 1 June 1898 by the turmoil at Toulon following the discovery that *Carnot* was overweight and unstable and the ensuing personnel actions. Indret also had problems producing the engines, and the ship was launched without them. On preliminary trials on 8 November 1902 she reached around 33,000ihp at her designed rpm but made only 22 knots because the screws were thickly encrusted with marine

---

Outboard profile and overhead view (*plan d'ensemble*) of the 1st class armoured cruiser *Jeanne d'Arc* built on the plans of M. Bertin. The plans were signed at Toulon by A. Laubeuf on 15 April 1903. The small calibre artillery carried at this time included 16 x 47mm/40 M1885 QF guns (4 on the lower platform on the

mast, 2 on the shelter deck level on the forward bridge, 6 on the same level amidships and 2 aft, 6 more positions also being provided in the hull on the main deck amidships and abreast the 194mm turrets), and 4 x 37mm guns for the boats with underway positions on the upper bridge.

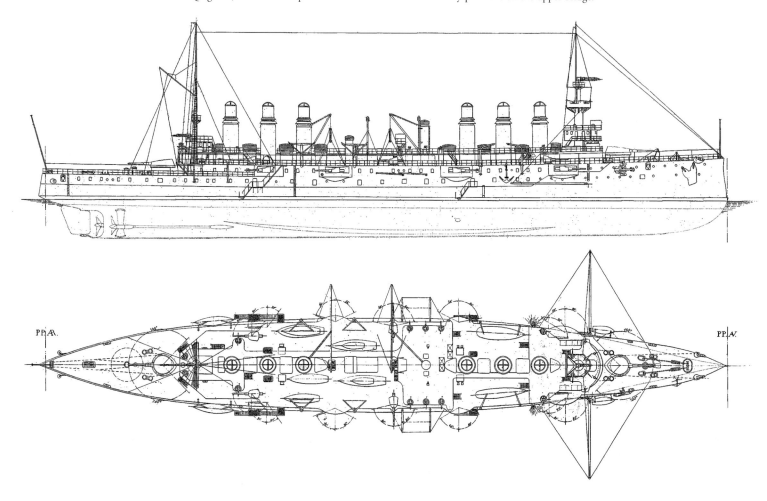

growth. On 23 January 1903 she failed to make her designed 23 knots on official full power trials, and a devis de campagne of 1908 stated that, although her designer had given up much for speed, she had never exceeded 21.7 knots despite changes to her screws, shafts, and bilge keels. She was placed in full commission in May 1903 for special missions and her final trial report was dated 12 October 1903.

**Dimensions & tons:** 147.000m oa, 145.400m wl and pp x 19.418m ext and wl. 11,329.244t disp (designed). Draught: (designed) 7.530m mean, 8.130m aft (keel line projected). Men: 651 (without flag).

**Machinery:** 33,000ihp designed (originally 28,500ihp). Designed speed 23kts. Trials (23.1.1903) 29,690.8ihp = 21.724kts at 137.85rpm max. 3 screws. 3 triple expansion engines with 4 cylinders. 36 Guyot-du Temple boilers. 1,400t coal (normal), 2,100t (max). Range with normal coal 9,000nm @ 10kts, with max coal 13,500nm @ 10kts

**Armour:**

Side: Belt at waterline (special steel) 150mm amidships, 100mm fwd, 80mm aft. Height amidships 2.21m, of which 0.70m above wl. Upper strake 80mm, height amidships 1.92m. Side above belt forward 40mm.

Guns: 194mm turrets 161mm front (cemented) with 176mm max fixed bases (special steel). Shields for all 14 of the 138.6mm guns 72mm, sponsons for 8 of the 138.6mm guns 40mm.

Lower armoured deck (extra mild steel): flat 45mm, upper slope 55mm, lower slope 45mm, all on 20mm hull plating.

Upper armoured deck (mild steel): 11mm on 7mm hull plating.

Conning tower (cemented): 138mm max.

**Guns:** 2 x 194mm/40 M1893 BLR (turrets fore and aft), 14 x 138.6mm/ 45 M1893 QF (8 in sponsons, 6 in shields), 16 x 47mm/40 M1885 QF, 4 x 37mm (for the boats). **Torpedoes:** 2 submerged tubes for 450mm M1892 torpedoes. **Searchlights:** 6 x 60cm.

*Jeanne d'Arc* (ii) (new C2) Toulon Dyd/Indret.

On list 1.1896. Ord: 28.12.1895. K: 24.10.1896. L: 8.6.1899. Comm: 1.3.1901 (trials), 19.5.1903 (full).

Budget 1896. Machinery installed 2.2.1900 to 20.2.1901. To Toulon 3.1903, took President Loubet to North Africa 12-29.4.1903, then finished trials. Left Toulon for Brest 20.5.1903 and replaced *Bruix* in the *Escadre du Nord* 1.6.1903. Left for Brest 7.2.1908 and to normal reserve. Assigned 1.5.1912 to the Division of schools of the Atlantic, she replaced *Duguay Trouin* (ex *Tonquin*) as seagoing school for midshipmen and left Brest 10.10.1912 for her first round-the-world training cruise. She returned from the second cruise 27.7.1914. Following the outbreak of war she first served in the Channel, was assigned to the Eastern Mediterranean on 15.4.1915, and served in the Caribbean in 1916-17. Recommissioned 1.8.1919, again served as seagoing school for midshipmen 1919-1928 for 9 campaigns. Replaced by *Edgar Quinet* 1928. Renamed *Jeanne d'Arc II* 1929. Struck 15.2.1933, towed to Landévennec, and condemned 21.3.1933. For sale by the Domaines 1933-1934. Sold 9.7.1934 at Brest to the Chantier du Bon Sacré at La Seyne, towed from Brest to Toulon 11.8.1934 by the tug *Abeille XXII* and BU.

---

*CROISEUR D'ESCADRE C3. Croiseur de 1re classe.* Armoured cruiser with two single main battery turrets at the ends and secondary guns on the sides in casemates and shields. Six funnels in two groups of three, one military and one pole mast. Designed by Bertin.

In February 1896 Minister of Marine Lockroy submitted a budget for 1897 that included a 1st class *croiseur d'escadre* D2 at Lorient. It is unclear whether the design for the ship at this time was the enlarged *Dupuy de Lôme* described above or Bertin's revised *Jeanne d'Arc* described here, although the latter seems a more likely choice for Lockroy. He was replaced in April by Besnard who submitted a revised 1897 budget in June that

redesignated the ship C3 and moved it to Toulon. She is shown in that budget with characteristics identical to Bertin's *Jeanne d'Arc*. Bertin, however, made a number of changes to the design including replacing the 138.6mm secondary battery with 164.7mm and 100mm guns. The resulting design as referred by Besnard to the *Conseil des travaux* had the following characteristics:

**Dimensions & tons:** 152.75m oa, 151m wl x 20.24m. 11,456t disp. Draught: 8.32m aft. Men: 626 with flag.

**Machinery:** 28,500ihp. Speed 23kts. 1,400t coal (normal), 2,100t (max). Range with normal coal 9,000nm @ 10kts, with max coal 13,500nm @ 10kts

**Armour:**

Side: Belt 150mm maximum from 1.50m below to 0.70m above the waterline. Side above belt 80mm maximum to top of cellular layer, 40mm above this forward.

Guns: 194mm turrets 200mm. Casemates 116mm on the two forward and two aft, 72mm on the two middle. Shields for guns on shelter deck 72mm.

Decks: Main armoured deck flat 0.15m above the waterline, slopes descending to 1.50m below the waterline.

Conning tower: 160mm.

**Guns:** 2 x 194mm (turrets fore and aft), 10 x 164.7mm QF (8 in casemates, 2 in shields on the shelter deck), 4 x 100mm QF (in shields on the shelter deck), 16 x 47mm QF, 6 x 37mm. **Torpedoes:** 2 submerged torpedo tubes. **Searchlights:** 6 x 60cm.

The *Conseil des travaux* examined the design on 17 March 1897 and refused to approve it because it did not either fit in the fleet programme adopted in December 1896 by the *Conseil supérieur* or conform to the specifications advocated for a long time by the *Conseil des travaux*, most recently on 31 December 1896 (the enlarged *Dupuy de Lôme*, D2, above). The Council felt that for an armoured cruiser the protection of the vitals and of the artillery was insufficient while the speed and range were excessive. Both Councils felt that 20 knots was sufficient for a *croiseur cuirassé d'escadre*, allowing it to engage cruisers while avoiding battleships. In a squadron 23-knot speeds should be reserved for small unarmoured cruisers intended to carry information rapidly to semaphores or to the main fleet while armoured cruisers maintained contact with the enemy. The design would also be unsuitable as a *croiseur corsaire*. Besides the fact that that the utility of such a ship was highly problematic, there was no point in armouring a ship whose role was chasing merchant ships. The range of 13,500nm was also excessive, 9,000nm being enough. The Council would no doubt have had a similar reaction to Bertin's *Jeanne d'Arc* had it had the opportunity to express it. As a result *Croiseur d'escadre* C3 (ex D2) was not built and was replaced in the building programme by the 9,500-ton *Dupetit-Thouars* (C3).

---

*GUICHEN.* Originally *Croiseur rapide* (No 1 in the budget) 1.1896, to *Croiseur de 1re classe* 1.1897. Protected cruiser with main guns at the ends in shields and secondary guns on the sides. Four funnels in two pairs, two (then three then two) pole masts. Designed by A. C. Loire (de Bussy). *Croiseur léger* in 1.3.1920.

The design was prepared by A. C. Loire under the overall supervision of their senior consulting engineer, Louis de Bussy. A major mission for French cruisers since the late 1860s had been commerce raiding, and the French including Minister of Marine Faure were most impressed with two specialized large, fast, but lightly armed cruisers, *Columbia* and *Minneapolis*, that the United States had started building in 1891 to hunt down fast North Atlantic liners. The second one, *Minneapolis*, was commissioned in December 1894, made 23.0 knots on trials, and could sustain nearly 20 knots at sea. On 4 November 1894 Faure distributed a new list of proposed shipbuilding under the 1895 budget in which Tréboul's station cruiser *Jeanne d'Arc* was replaced by two *croiseurs à grande vitesse* and two

3rd class station cruisers. *Minneapolis* displaced 7,505 tons on trials and around 8,133 tons in service and Minister Faure hoped to get on a displacement of 8,500 tons a French equivalent able to make 23 knots with moderate forced draught and a sustained 20 knots with natural draught. On 9 November 1894 Faure informed the president of the *Conseil des travaux*, Vice Admiral Duperré, that at his request the Directorate of Materiel and the Naval General Staff had drafted preliminary specifications for a *croiseur très rapide* whose target was enemy commerce and which, in view of the great distances between French metropolitan and colonial coaling stations, was above all to have high speed and as great a range as possible. Since there was no intention of this ship engaging large enemy cruisers, which she had the speed to evade, a moderate armament was sufficient, and since enemy auxiliary cruisers in wartime would have guns like the French 138.6mm an armoured deck and 20mm side plating to detonate melinite projectiles would provide enough protection. He asked the Council to examine the specifications promptly. On 18 December 1894 the Council produced specifications for what it then called a *croiseur corsaire* which were very similar to Faure's specifications. Faure, in one of his last official acts as Minister (he went on to become President of the Republic) communicated the results of the Council's assessment with some final changes by the Ministry to three potential builders on 15 January 1895. Two designs for

what was now called a *croiseur extra-rapide*, one by A.C. Loire and one by FCM La Seyne, were accepted with minor changes by the *Conseil des travaux* 23 July 1895, while a third design by C.A. Gironde was rejected.

*Guichen* was named on 13 September 1895 and her construction as a *croiseur rapide* was authorized on 24 October 1895. Her hull lines were derived from those of de Bussy's *Dupuy de Lôme* and *Davout* whose speed had proven to be satisfactory, though the bow lines were finer. The design included an inverted ram-shaped bow for which a straight bow was substituted. The hull structure was more rigid than in *Châteaurenault*, and the Council felt that this along with the placement of the engines amidships might make *Guichen* more resistant to vibrations at high speed. The funnels in the design were tall as in most liners and some foreign cruisers. Unlike *Châteaurenault* she had a complete shelter deck instead of a forecastle and poop with an open space in between. The boilers were in six groups, three forward of the engines and three aft. The ship was not sheathed for overseas duty and had no flag accommodations. She was designed and built with two masts, but on 3 March 1899 Minister Lockroy ordered adding a third amidships to support the Temperley system for coaling ship. This mast was broken during a replenishment from the British collier *Stilhsdale* at Chefoo on 25 June 1906 and was cut down and converted to a ventilation trunk. The Lagrafel et d'Allest boilers could not be cleaned while steaming.

**Dimensions & tons:** 133.000m oa, 133.000m wl and pp x 16.710m ext and wl. 8,281.930t disp. Draught: 7.500m mean, 7.500m aft (real). Men: 594.

**Machinery:** 24,000ihp designed at 124rpm and 15.5kg/cm² boiler pressure. Trials (10.11.1899) 25,163.177ihp at 136rpm = 23.544kts. 3 screws. 3 vertical triple expansion engines with 4 cylinders of 0.980 (1), 1.420m (1), and 1,720m (2) diameter and 1.013m stroke. 36 Lagrafel et d'Allest boilers. 1,680t coal. Range 8,430nm @ 10kts.

The 1st class cruiser *Guichen* at Brest after the addition at Toulon in February 1900 of a third mast amidships to support the shipboard portion of a Temperley Transporter coaling system. The mast ruptured during coaling operations in the Far East in June 1906 and was cut down to a ventilation trunk. *Guichen* operated with three masts at Brest and in the north from March to June 1900 and October 1901 to January 1905. The sponson amidships contained a 138.6mm gun. *(Postcard by FT Brest)*

58. - Marine Militaire. - Le " Guichen "

**Armour:**

Decks: Armoured deck (extra mild steel, with a small amount of nickel added) flat 20mm over the machinery and 15mm at the ends, upper slope 65mm over the machinery and 35mm at the ends, lower slope 35mm over the machinery and 20mm at the ends, all on 15mm hull plating.

Side: The hull at the waterline was reinforced with a layer of 10mm hardened steel 4.70m high on the regular 10mm plating with a watertight cofferdam behind it.

Guns: Shields for 164.7mm and 138.6mm guns amidships (hardened steel) 54mm, casemates for 138.6mm guns at ends (hardened steel) 40mm.

Conning tower (special steel): 160mm.

**Guns:**

(1898) 2 x 164.7mm/45 M1893 QF (fore and aft), 6 x 138.6mm/45 M1893 QF (2 in sponsons amidships and 4 in casemates fore and aft), 12 x 47mm/40 M1885 QF, 3 x 37mm/20 M1885 QF (for the boats).
**Torpedoes:** two above-water tubes for 450mm torpedoes were installed but removed just before the ship went into full commission.
**Searchlights:** 6 x 60cm.

(1915-17) 3 x 37mm replaced 1.1915 by machine guns, which were soon removed. 2 x 47mm transferred to trawlers 4.1915. 4 x 47mm converted to AA guns 8-9.1916. 6 x 47mm removed 5.1917 and 4 x 138.6mm casemate guns removed 11.1917, leaving 2 x 164.7mm, 2 x 138.6mm, and 4 x 47mm QF/AA.

*Guichen* (D'1) A.C. Loire, Saint Nazaire/ACL, Saint Denis (engines designed by Boulogne).
On list 1.1896. Ord: 9.10.1895 (contract). K: late 5.1896.
L: 26.10.1897. Comm: 10.10.1898 (trials), 9.3.1900 (full)

Budget 1895. Machinery installed 3.11.1897 to 15.9.1898. From Saint Nazaire to Toulon 4-9.12.1898 to run trials. Trials 1.1899 to 3.1900, arrived at Brest 19.3.1900. Assigned to the *Escadre du Nord* 17.4.1900 but hastily left for the Far East 23.6.1900 in response to the Boxer rebellion with some work incomplete, returned 17.10.1901. At Brest 1912-13 with the school for carpenters and sail makers embarked. During World War I patrolled in the Bay of Biscay, the English Channel, the Mediterranean, and in 1916 West Africa. On 12.9.1915 rescued 1,952 Armenian refugees from Turkish troops north of Latakia and took them to Port Said. Fitted at Brest 8.1916 to carry troops (liferafts and additional galley stoves for them were soon fitted) and from 9.1916 carried troops (including Russians and Serbs) to Salonika and then to Itea in Greece, Corfu and other Mediterranean destinations. Crew mutinied 26.5.1919 against the endless trooping duties and miserable conditions, mutiny suppressed by Senegalese troops but ship soon idled at Brest for boiler repairs. By November 1920 was central ship for the reserve at Landévennec. Decomm. 3.1921. Condemned 12.11.1921. Struck 29.11.1921. Sold 11.3.1922 at Brest to M. Bénédic.

———

*CHÂTEAURENAULT.* Originally *Croiseur rapide* (N° 2 in the budget) 1.1896, to *Croiseur de 1re classe* 1.1897. Protected cruiser with with main guns at the ends in shields and secondary guns on the sides. Four evenly spaced funnels, two pole masts. Designed by Lagane (FCM La Seyne).

The history of *Châteaurenault* through July 1895 was identical with that of *Guichen*, above. Her design was accepted with minor changes by the *Conseil des travaux* on 23 July 1895.

*Châteaurenault* was named on 13 September 1895 and her construction

Outboard profile and overhead view (*plan d'ensemble*) of the 1st class cruiser *Châteaurenault*, built on the plans of M. Lagane. The undated plan by the Forges et Chantiers de la Méditerranée at La Seyne carries the names of the director of the yard, Lagane, and the Navy's control officer, Rampal. The small calibre artillery carried at this time included 12 x 47mm/50 QF guns (2 on the lower

bridge wings forward, 2 on the forward casemates, 2 amidships above the sponsons, 4 on deck just forward of the after casemates, and 2 on the after bridge), and 3 x 37mm QF guns (1 on the stern gallery and 2 on the forward casemates). There were also 2 x 65mm M1881 landing guns stowed in the battery.

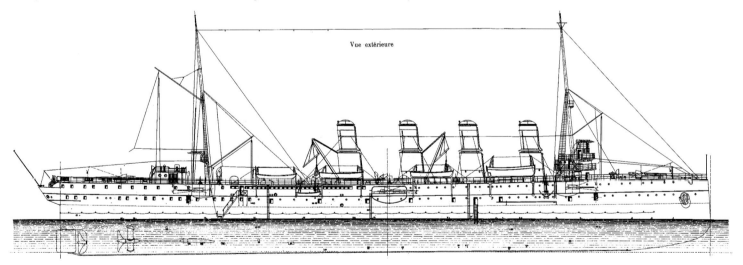

Vue extérieure

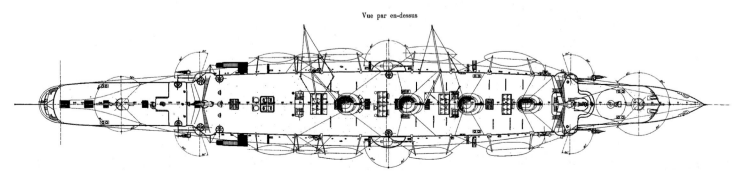

Vue par en-dessus

was authorized on 12 October 1895. In his design Lagane imitated the general appearance of large passenger liners of the period with their vertical bows and counter sterns, although she did not resemble any particular ship. Her engines were placed aft of her boilers, making possible a profile with four evenly-spaced funnels rather than the two pairs in *Guichen*, although the Council had to ask for the funnels to be increased in height. She had a long forecastle and long poop connected by tall bulkheads in between that gave her a flush-decked appearance. The ship was not sheathed for overseas duty. The contract design had 28 Lagrafel et d'Allest boilers but in November 1896 the contractor was authorized to use Normand-Sigaudy boilers instead, an option that he had included in his original design. Her trials were prolonged by pronounced vibrations between 18 and 21 knots which led to dismantling, aligning, and reassembling the propeller shafts. Replacing the three-bladed centre screw with a four-bladed one in 1904 eliminated the vibrations up to 19.5 knots, but in 1906 it was determined that the vibrations of the reciprocating engines (which as usual at this time were slightly out of balance) between 20 and 22.5 knots matched the natural resonant frequency of the after part of the hull and that the only possible remedy was to avoid these engines speeds.

**Dimensions & tons:** 139.375m oa (including the counter stern), 135.000m wl and pp x 17.000m ext and wl. 8.042.740t disp, 8,313t (full). Draught: 6.850m mean, 7.400m aft. Men: 567.

**Machinery:** 23,000ihp designed at 124rpm and 15kg/cm² boiler pressure. Speed 23kts. Trials (25.7.1902) 24,304ihp = 24.023kts. 3 screws. 3 vertical triple expansion engines with 3 cylinders of 1.050m, 1.570m, and 2.320m diameter and 1.000m stroke. 28 Normand-Sigaudy boilers (14 double-ended). 1,300t coal (normal), 1,828 tons (max). Range with normal coal 7,140nm @ 11.4kts.

**Armour:**

Decks: Armoured deck (extra mild steel) flat 20mm, upper and middle slopes 75mm over the machinery and 50mm at the ends, bottom slope 45mm over the machinery and 30mm at the ends, all on 15mm hull plating.

Side: The hull at the waterline was reinforced with a layer of 10mm hardened steel plating 4.10m high with a watertight cofferdam behind it.

Guns: Shields for 164.7mm and 138.6mm guns amidships (hardened steel) 54mm, casemates for 138.6mm guns at ends (special steel) 40mm on 14mm hull plating.

Conning tower (special steel): 160mm.

**Guns:**

(1899) 2 x 164.7mm/45 M1893 QF (fore and aft), 6 x 138.6mm/45 M1893 QF (2 in sponsons and 4 in casemates), 2 x 65mm/16 M1881 landing, 12 x 47mm/40 M1885 QF, 3 x 37mm/20 M1885 QF.

**Torpedoes:** none. **Searchlights:** 6 x 60cm.

(1915-17) 2 x 47mm landed at Brest 4.1915, 2 more landed at Bizerte 10.1915. 4 x 47mm fitted for anti-aircraft fire 1916. The casemate 138.6mm guns were ordered removed 9.1917 but the ship was lost before this could be carried out.

*Châteaurenault* (D'2) F.C. Méditerranée, La Seyne/FCM, Le Havre (engines designed by Sigaudy).

On list 1.1896. Ord: 12.10.1895 (contract). K: 23.5.1896. L: 12.5.1898. Comm: 24.10.1899 (trials), 10.10.1902 (full).

Budget 1895. Machinery installed 1.7.1898 to 19.8.1899 (26.9 for the starboard and 15.10 for the port engine). The engines suffered from excessive vibrations and trials were only completed in 7.1902. Left Toulon 30.10.1902 to relieve *D'Entrecasteaux* in the Far East. Damaged 7.11.1904 by striking an uncharted rock at Phan Rang, Cochinchina, and headed home for repairs 12.3.1905 after being relieved by *Guichen*. Recommissioned at Cherbourg 15.1.1910 for service in the Mediterranean, but en route to Toulon she ran aground in bad weather 30.1.1910 on Cape Spartel, Morocco. Refloated by *Du Chayla* and two Gibraltar tugs and towed from Gibraltar to Toulon by *Victor Hugo*.

Flagship 1911-13 for the Division of schools of the Atlantic with the school for boatswains embarked. During World War I patrolled in the English Channel, the Mediterranean, and from 2.1916 off West Africa searching for the German raider *Möwe*. From 9.1916 used to carry troops to Salonika and then to Itea in Greece. Rescued 1,200 survivors of the torpedoed transport *Gallia* 5.10.1916. Fitted 12.1916 with liferafts and a battleship galley stove for use as a transport. Torpedoed twice 14.12.1917 by *UC-38* off Cape Ducato in the Ionian Sea, except for twelve men killed in the explosion all aboard were saved by escorting trawlers and destroyers, which also sank the submarine.

---

*JURIEN DE LA GRAVIÈRE. Croiseur de 1re classe.* Protected cruiser with two main guns at the ends in shields and the others on the sides and with a steel hull sheathed in wood. Four funnels in two pairs, two pole masts. Designed by Bertin. *Croiseur léger* (light cruiser) in 1.3.1920.

The 1896 budget as submitted on 14 May 1895 included for the station fleet a 1st class cruiser similar to *D'Entrecasteaux*, Tréboul's *Jeanne d'Arc* (C2), and a 2nd class cruiser of the *Catinat* class named *Jurien de la Gravière* (E5). The Budget Commission on 13.7.1895 deleted all station cruisers including these two from the budget and cancelled credits for them on 24.10.1895. While considering station cruisers for the 1897 budget Minister Lockroy found the first of these to be too big and the second too weak. Émile Bertin agreed and noted that the excessive dimensions of *D'Entrecasteaux* made her too costly to maintain for station service. More importantly, he noted the complete absence in the French navy of high speed ships with copper sheathing for overseas service. Lockroy's 1897 budget included two 1st class station cruisers, one at Brest designated C3 and one by contract designated C'1. In April 1896 Bertin proposed to Lockroy a design for a 5,500-ton fast sheathed 1st class cruiser substantially smaller than *D'Entrecasteaux*, stating that his development of this design had been prompted by the refusal in October 1895 of credits for *Jurien de la Gravière*. While budgeted and sheathed for overseas duty, the ship would be at least as useful as a fleet scout in European waters. In 1906 Bertin wrote that his ideal fleet was a squadron of *Patrie* type battleships with *Jurien de la Gravière* type scout cruisers and small 3,000-ton dispatch vessels, his big 23-knot armoured cruisers being reserved for long-range warfare on the world's sea lanes.

Besnard replaced Lockroy at the end of April 1896 and submitted a revised budget at the end of June in which Lockroy's two first-class station cruisers were retained, now as 5,500-ton ships and listed as D2 at Lorient and D3 by contract. Besnard referred Bertin's 5,500-ton design to the *Conseil des travaux* which examined it on 20 October 1896. The Council rejected the design, questioning the range of action at 10 knots, the ability to make the engines robust enough on the weight given, and the adoption of Normand-Sigaudy boilers. It also complained that the specifications on which it was based had not been submitted to it, and stated that it felt that a ship carrying the flag of a rear admiral commanding a station fleet should be a combat ship, which this one was not. Noting, however, that Minister Besnard and the Chambers seemed intent on building the ship it recommended some changes. On 7 November 1896 Besnard ordered Bertin to incorporated these and Besnard then ordered D2 at Lorient on 20 November 1896 and the engines from Indret on 9 December 1896. D3 was not built to this design but emerged as the armoured station cruiser *Dupleix* (see Chapter 14).

*Jurien de la Gravière* suffered from high coal consumption that severely limited her range, from rolling, and from vibrations at high speed. The vibrations, attributed to light scantlings, became dangerous to her hull structure and piping at 95rpm, which unfortunately was her economical speed. She served for much of her career with the fleet, and from 1913 to the end of World War I was designated as a *répétiteur*, whose role in theory was to repeat signals and pass orders from the flagship to the rest of the fleet.

*The characteristics are based on a devis dated 6.7.1903.*

**Dimensions & tons:** 138.900m oa, 137.000m wl and pp (tip fwd to stern) x 15.040m ext (above wl, 17.100m over sponsons), 15.000m wl. 6,167.555t disp. Draught: 6.379m mean, 7.009m aft. Men: 478.

**Machinery:** 17,400ihp designed at 180rpm and 18kg/cm² boiler pressure (15-16 at engines). Trials (10.2.1903) 18,401.34ihp = 22.88kts at 175.97rpm and 17.148kg/cm² boiler pressure. 3 screws. 3 vertical triple expansion engines with 4 cylinders of 0.870m (1), 1.290m (1), and 1.360m (2) diameter and 0.700m stroke. 24 Guyot-du Temple boilers. 1,109t coal. Range 4787.81nm @ 10.4875kts.

**Armour:**

Decks: Armoured deck (extra mild steel): Amidships over engines and torpedo tubes flat 25mm, upper slope 45mm, lower slope 25mm. Fore and aft over boilers and magazines flat 15mm, upper slope 35mm, lower slope 15mm. At extreme bow 10mm. All deck armour on 20mm hull plating.

Guns: Shields for 164.7mm guns (steel) 72 mm.

Conning tower (special steel): 100 mm.

**Guns:**

(1903) 8 x 164.7mm/45 M1893 QF (1 forward, 1 aft, 6 in sponsons), 2 x 65mm/16 M1881 landing, 10 x 47mm/40 M1885 QF, 6 x 37mm/20 M1885 QF (for the boats). **Torpedoes:** 2 submerged tubes for 450mm M1892 torpedoes. **Searchlights:** 6 x 60cm.

*Jurien de la Gravière* (D2) Lorient Dyd/Indret.

On list 1.1897. Ord: 20.11.1896. K: 17.11.1897. L: 26.6.1899. Comm: 15.5.1901 (trials), 16.6.1903 (full).

Budget 1897 (some 1896 funds used). Machinery installed 7.5.1900 to 5.3.1902. Trial results approved 5.6.1903. Left Lorient 25.7.1903 to replace *D'Estrées* on the Atlantic station. In normal reserve at Lorient 9.3.1907 to 8.3.1911. To Toulon 4.1911, Morocco and Levant 1912.

---

Outboard profile and overhead view (*plan d'ensemble*) of the 1st class cruiser *Jurien de la Gravière*, built at Lorient on the plans of M. Bertin. The plans were signed in December 1908 at Lorient. The small calibre artillery carried at this time included 10 x 47mm M1885 (2 on the forecastle, 2 on the forward bridge directly above them, 2 on the bridge over amidships sponson, 2 on the upper deck aft of it, and 2 on the after bridge), and 6 x 37mm (for boats, with underway positions for 2 on the forward accommodation ladder platforms, 2 on the poop forward of the after bridge, and 2 on the deck at the extreme stern). There were also 2 x 65mm M1881 landing guns.

Assigned 5.1913 as *répétiteur* (signal relay ship) for the *1re Armée navale*. War service followed by a tour as station ship at Beirut, relieved by *Cassard* 10.1920. Struck 27.7.1921, disposal delayed by sale to Romania proposed 3.1921, to the Domaines for sale 5.10.1921, sold 28.12.1922 to M. Bertorello and BU at Villefranche sur Mer.

---

## (C) 2nd class cruisers (*Croiseurs de 2e classe*)

Were small *Croiseurs à barbette* and large *Éclaireurs d'escadre* before the 1.1885 fleet list.

*MILAN.* On list as *Éclaireur d'escadre* 1882. Unprotected cruiser with light guns, a steel hull, and a ram bow. Two funnels, three masts, schooner rig (later plain poles). Designed by Bertin. To *Croiseur de 2e classe* 1.1885, *Croiseur d'escadre de 3e classe* 1.1891, *Croiseur de 3e classe* 1.1892, *Contre-torpilleur d'escadre* 1.1897, and *Contre-torpilleur* 1.1901.

On 3 February 1880 the *Conseil des travaux* examined a preliminary proposal submitted by Émile Bertin on his own initiative for a fast aviso with a main armament of a revolving tube that launched torpedoes and with a light weight propulsion plant which Bertin claimed was capable of developing 3,800ihp with forced draught. Bertin later wrote on 31 March 1884 that the objective of the ship was to obtain, with the least displacement, a very high speed and a very great range of action. He sought the solution above all in the special dispositions of a very light hull structure in which all of the parts contributed to the solidity of the whole and in the use of a propulsion plant of four engines in two engine rooms, of which the forward ones could be disconnected for economical steaming. The Council reviewed additional details of this project on 8 June 1880 and asked for studies of both the machinery and the *tube-revolver lance-torpilles*. On 6 May 1881 the *Conseil d'Amirauté* while discussing the Programme of 1881 noted that *éclaireurs d'escadre* were a special type with high speed and excellent seagoing qualities that were to avoid combat, but that currently there were few of them so the Council did not create a separate category for them. On 24 May 1881 the *Conseil des travaux* reviewed a fully developed version of the design, now for an *éclaireur d'escadre* rather than an *aviso rapide*, and approved its construction mainly as a way of getting a small and inexpensive trials vessel for experimenting with new technology but also one that might render significant services as a fleet scout. It had reservations

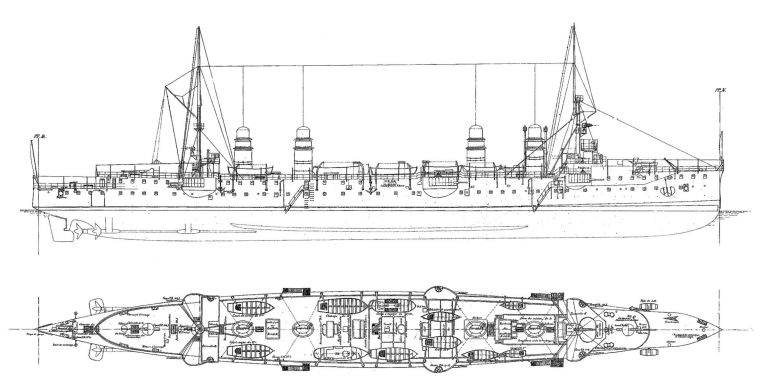

about the propulsion plant which included cylindrical boilers operating at the very high pressure of 10kg/cm². Similar boilers in the aviso *Chasseur* had been more prone to failures than the Belleville boilers in her sister *Voltigeur*, and the Council wanted Bertin to substitute Bellevilles in the new aviso so that further experiments could be conducted with them. As for the revolving tube for torpedoes, separate trials with it had not gone well and the Council recommended renouncing it. On 16 July 1881, the ship was formally reclassed as an *éclaireur d'escadre*.

The armament was changed several times before completion. In Bertin's original 1879 design it was two 138.6mm/21.3 M1870 guns, two 100mm guns (fore and aft), six 37mm revolving cannon, and two torpedo tubes. In 1880 it became three 100mm guns (one added amidships), six revolving cannon, and one torpedo tube forward. In May 1881 the Council recommended two 90mm guns (on forecastle and poop), eight revolving cannon, and two torpedo tubes, the latter possibly just above the waterline as in *Torpilleur nº 41* which had just run promising trials. On 19 June 1882 Minister of Marine Jauréguiberry approved a recommendation from Brest to fit five 100mm/26.2 M1881 guns (on forecastle and poop on central pivots, three on the centreline amidships movable to either side), eight 37mm revolving cannon, and two torpedo tubes. The torpedo tubes were suppressed on 19 September 1883.

In service the ship suffered from vibrations above 13 knots that became violent above 16.5 knots. She was decommissioned on 11 December 1890 for a refit at the Forges et Chantiers de la Méditerranée in which the boilers were removed and overhauled and the armament updated. She was recommissioned on 1 July 1892 for trials and definitively on 5 April 1893 after the boilers were fitted for experimental mixed coal and oil firing between December 1892 and February 1893. She was decommissioned again on 1 January 1900, the boilers were replaced with 8 new Bellevilles with economisers, she was then recommissioned on 15 December 1901 but saw no further active service before decommissioning for the last time on 1 June

1907. In 1889 her commander assessed that in war she would be valuable as either a fleet scout or as a cruiser, but that because of her large draught and her huge turning circle she would make a poor *contre-torpilleur*, a designation that she was to get eight years later.

**Dimensions & tons:** 92.440m wl & pp (tip fwd to rudder) x 10.040m ext, 10.00m wl. 1,672.285t disp. Draught: 4.007m mean, 4.776m aft. Men: 150 (191 in 1891).

**Machinery:** 765nhp and 3,880ihp (4 x 970ihp) designed at 150rpm and 14kg/cm² boiler pressure (10kg/cm² at the engines). Trials (18.4.1885) 3916.0ihp = 18.47kts at 152.80 rpm and 11.441kg/cm² boiler pressure. 2 screws. 4 horizontal compound engines (two on each shaft) with direct connecting rods and 2 cylinders of 0.532m and 1.050mm diameter and 0.60m stroke. 12 Belleville boilers. 308.7t coal. Range 5,000nm @ 10kts (could carry enough excess coal to reach 6,600 miles).

**Guns:.**

(1885) 5 x 100mm/26.2 M1881 (forecastle and poop on full circular tracks, 2 to starboard, 1 to port amidships on semi-circular tracks), 1 x 65mm/16 M1881 landing, 8 x 37mm revolving cannon. The 100mm at the ends and the 37mm had shields, the 100mm amidships had none.

(1888) 4 x 100mm (of which 1 on the forecastle), 1 x 65mm landing, 2 x 47mm/40 M1885 QF, 8 x 37mm revolving cannon. On 7.2.1888 one of the starboard 100mm was ordered removed in favour of equipment to lay blockade mines (*torpilles automatiques de blocus*), and on 18.12.1888 2 x 47mm QF were ordered added on the poop.

(1892) 2 x 100/26.2 M1881mm QF (converted, fore and aft), 1 x 65mm landing, 10 x 47mm QF, 2 x 37mm. All gun shields removed.

*Milan* A.C. Loire, Saint Nazaire/ACL, Nantes (engines designed by Jaÿ).
On list 1.1882. Ord: 1881. K: 21.3.1882. L: 25.5.1884. Comm: 2.1885 (trials), 8.8.1885 (full).
Budget 1882. From Saint Nazaire to Brest 26-30.1.1885. Trials 12.3.1885 to 6.8.1885, trial results approved 7.8.1885, from Brest to Toulon 11-17.8.1885, joined the *Escadre d'évolutions* 19.1.1886. Struck a rock leaving Brest 17.7.1890 and nearly lost to uncontrollable flooding, refitted by FCM La Seyne 1890-93. Struck 8.4.1908. School

The 2nd class cruiser (ex scout cruiser) *Milan* at Algiers probably in 1889 after the addition of two 47mm guns on the poop and before the removal of the gun shields. The bow of the torpedo cruiser *Condor* is on the left. *(NHHC from ONI album of French warships, NH-74961)*

for engineers at Toulon replacing *Vautour* 1908-1910, replaced by *Chasseloup-Laubat* 12.1910, for sale 1910-1911. Offered for sale 1.8.1911 by the Domaines with *Amiral Baudin, Magenta, Pascal,* and smaller vessels including torpedo boats and submarines. Sold on that date to M. Bénédic and BU at La Seyne 1912.

*N* (Unnamed) Toulon Dyd
Budget 1882. The 1883 budget showed this vessel as to be 10% built by the beginning of 1883 with another 10% to be done during 1883, but she was not in the 1884 budget.

*N* (Unnamed) Contract
Budget 1883. Not in the 1884 budget.

---

*DAVOUT* Class. *Croiseur de 2ᵉ classe.* Protected cruiser with main guns on the sides and ends and with a ram-shaped bow. Two funnels, two military masts. Designed by de Bussy. To *croiseurs d'escadre de 2ᵉ classe* 1.1891 and back to *croiseurs de 2ᵉ classe* 1.1892, to *Croiseur de 3e cl.* 1897.

On 2 December 1885 specifications prepared by the Direction of Material to serve as the basis for designing a 2ⁿᵈ class open-battery cruiser were referred by Minister of Marine Galiber to the *Conseil des travaux,* which examined them on 22 December 1885. They were essentially the specifications of 21 July 1885 for a 1ˢᵗ class open-battery cruiser scaled down: 2,600 tons vice 4,100 tons, 16 vice 17 knots at natural draught, 18 vice 19 knots at forced draught, 95m vice 105m length, and two 164.7mm guns in one pair of sponsons forward instead of four in two pairs forward and aft. The eleven designs produced in response to these specifications were not examined by the Council until 24 May 1887, and long before then the Minister (probably Aube) decided that a 20 knot speed was needed for commerce raiding. A design was prepared by *Inspecteur général du génie maritime* Louis de Bussy and construction of *Davout* and *Suchet* was ordered on 1 March 1887. The ships had de Bussy's characteristic rounded sides.

In mid-March 1887 the extraordinary budget for 1887 was promulgated and the ships that were to be built under it were announced. They included three first, three second, and three 3ʳᵈ class cruisers along with eight *contre-torpilleurs* of the *Ouragan* type and 24 *torpilleurs de 1ʳᵉ classe.* The 2ⁿᵈ class cruisers were *Davout* and *Suchet* at Toulon (which had previously been in the regular budget for 1887 and whose plans by de Bussy had not yet been approved) and a third named *Chanzy* at the Chantiers de la Loire that was to be similar to these two. No design by this firm for such a ship was on hand and she was probably to be built to de Bussy's plans for the other two. The ship was probably assigned to A.C. Loire by a ministerial order of 1 March 1887, and the Machinery Commission proceeded to negotiate a contract. Like that for the 1ˢᵗ class *Mogador,* this contract had not yet been concluded when a new Minister of Marine, Barbey, took office on 30 May 1887, and it was adjourned after he found that the navy was overextended financially and lacked the funds to carry out in full Aube's cruiser program.

The armament specified by Minister Krantz for the class on 16 April 1888 was four 164.7mm/30 M1884 guns (1 forward, 1 aft, and 2 in a pair of sponsons on the sides forward), four 47mm M1885 QF, and six 37mm M1885 QF. An order of 4 September 1889 added another two 164.7mm guns in a second pair of sponsons aft and four 65mm M1888, although there was no room for additional ammunition for these guns. In the meantime an order of 27 April 1888 directed the replacement of the original three masts with two military masts with 37mm guns in the lower tops. The ram-shaped (inverted) bow was not strengthened for ramming.

The boilers of *Davout* gave much trouble during trials, and because it was not possible to clean (*ramoner*) their furnaces or uptakes while the ship was underway speed fell off after a few days at sea and the ship could not be relied on for long-duration cruising. During a 1895-96 refit she received a conning tower and tube, both with 40mm armour, exchanged the 4mm shields on the 164.7mm guns with 54mm shields, and underwent boiler work. To save weight the military masts were ordered on 18 October 1895

to be replaced by simple pole masts and the 37mm in the tops were deleted. Between August and December 1900 *Davout* was reboiled with ten Niclausse boilers operating at 14kg/cm² boiler pressure. These were served by three funnels, one per boiler room, of which the smaller forward one served two boilers and the others four each. She ran trials three times between 1901 and 1903, reaching 19 knots in 1902, but on 22 November 1903 she was put in special reserve at Rochefort without re-entering service.

**Dimensions & tons:** 91.25m oa x 11.62m ext. 3,330t disp. Draught: 4.65m fwd, 6.00m aft. Men: 323 (1900).
**Machinery:** 1,580nhp and 8,950ihp (9,000ihp with auxiliaries) designed at 11.2kg/cm² boiler pressure. Speed 20kts. Trials (10.6.1892) 9,039.45ihp = 20.075kts. 2 screws. 2 horizontal triple expansion engines with 3 cylinders of 0.820m, 1.200m, and 1.920m diameter and 1.00m stroke. 8 cylindrical direct-flame boilers. 477t coal (534t maximum). Range 7,130nm @ 10kts.
**Armour:**
Decks: Armoured deck (extra mild steel) flat 82mm above the machinery, 30mm elsewhere, slopes 80mm, all on 20mm hull plating.
Guns: shields for 164.7mm guns 4mm, upgraded to 54mm 1895-96
Conning tower: 40mm (added 1895-96)
**Guns:**
(1892) 6 x 164.7mm/30 M1884 (1 forward, 1 aft, and 2 on each side on the upper deck in sponsons), 4 x 65mm/50 M1888 QF (on the forecastle under the bridge and on the poop), 4 x 47mm/40 M1885 QF, 8 x 37mm/20 M1885 QF. **Torpedoes:** 6 tubes for 356mm torpedoes (2 forward, 2 side, 2 aft, all above water).
(1894) All 164.7mm modified to 164.7mm/30 M1884 QF (DM 20.3.1894, done 21.7.1894 to 20.2.1895).
(1896-97) 4 x 37mm in the tops deleted when rig reduced leaving 4 x 37mm. After torpedo tubes removed, leaving 4.
(1900) Forward torpedo tubes removed, leaving 2 on the sides, remaining 4 x 37mm removed.

*Davout* Toulon Dyd/Indret (engines designed by Garnier).
On list 1.1888. Ord: 1.3.1887. K: 12.9.1887. L: 31.10.1889. Comm: 20.10.1890 (trials), 20.9.1892 (full).
Budget 1887 (delayed to the extraordinary 1887 budget, then moved to the ordinary 1888 budget). Joined the *Escadre de la Méditerranée* 9.1892. Decomm. 1.5.1909, assigned on 27.5.1909 to replace *Fulton* as school for stoking at Brest. Towed into Brest 16.8.1909 and moored at Landévennec. Struck 9.3.1910. Sold 23.10.1913 at Brest.

*Chanzy* (i) A.C. Loire.
Budget 1887 (extraordinary). Contract not concluded, adjourned in mid-1887 with that for *Mogador* (see above) in a cutback of the cruiser programme and never in the fleet lists although named in the budget.

---

*SUCHET. Croiseur de 2ᵉ classe.* Protected cruiser with main guns on the sides and ends and with a ram-shaped bow. Two funnels, two military masts. Designed by de Bussy and modified by Lhomme. To *croiseurs d'escadre de 2ᵉ classe* 1.1891 and back to *croiseurs de 2ᵉ classe* 1.1892, to *Croiseur de 3e cl.* 1897.

Construction was ordered on 1 March 1887 as a sister to *Davout* on plans by de Bussy. On 28 March 1887 a single submerged torpedo tube was ordered placed in the bow of *Suchet* in response to a request of the *Conseil des travaux* to study the idea, and she ended up with seven 356mm tubes instead of six. Minister Krantz's orders of 16 April 1888 and 4 September 1889 for the armament of *Davout* also applied to *Suchet.* However, naval constructor Delphin Albert Lhomme, the new director of naval construction at Toulon, felt that the engine room of *Suchet* was too cramped, making maintenance of the machinery and proper ventilation of the ship below the armoured deck very difficult, and that the boilers were of insufficient power. The construction of *Suchet* was therefore suspended on

20 March 1888. On 16 August 1890 Lhomme offered a project for lengthening and modifying *Suchet* by inserting a 7-metre section between the after boiler room and the forward engine room behind it, of which 2.16m was used to augment the volume of the engine rooms and the rest to add two return-flame cylindrical boilers back to back in a new fourth boiler room just forward of them. Minister Barbey approved the plans on 13 September 1890 and construction resumed 17 September 1890. Lengthening the ship also allowed moving the foremast and bridge 1.20m aft and lengthening the forecastle by the same amount, while the poop was lengthened 2.40m. The military masts were built nearly 3m shorter than those in *Davout* to improve stability. Lhomme substituted 100mm guns for the four 65mm guns in *Davout* and added four 47mm on the forward bridge. The ventilation problems, however, were not solved. On 28 January 1893 Minister Rieunier directed the conversion of the 164.7mm and 100mm/26.2 M1881 guns to QF.

*Suchet* had the same problem as *Davout* in that her cylindrical boilers could not be cleaned while they were in use. This reduced her speed on long transits to 13 or 14 knots, which she maintained by rotating the use of the boilers and allowing those not in use to cool down for cleaning. She could not use her bow for ramming in part because of the presence of the bow torpedo tube.

She underwent her only major repair period at Rochefort from September 1897 to June 1899. In 1898 her military masts were replaced by simple poles as ordered on 4 June 1897. She was placed in special reserve at Rochefort upon returning from the Caribbean in November 1902. By a contract of 6 May 1902 the Navy had ordered new Belleville boilers for her, the last of which was delivered in 1904, but work on the ship was abandoned according to a note of 19 September 1905 and the boilers remained in storage in the dockyard.

**Dimensions & tons:** 98.950m oa, 97.700m wl, 95.000m pp (tip fwd to rudder) x 12.124m ext and wl. 3,440.016t disp (designed). Draught: (designed) 5.350m mean, 5.900m aft (real). Men: 335 (1900).

**Machinery:** 1,580nhp and 9,500ihp designed at 11.2kg/cm² boiler pressure. Trials (20.3.1894) 9,504.35ihp at 135rpm = 20.413kts. 2 screws. Engines and boilers identical to those of *Davout* except that *Suchet* had

an additional pair of single-furnace cylindrical return flame boilers in a fourth boiler room, primarily to power auxiliary machinery in port. 529t coal (663t max).

**Armour:**

Decks: Armoured deck (extra mild steel) flat 82mm above the machinery, 30mm elsewhere, slopes 80mm, all on 20mm hull plating.

Guns: shields for 164.7mm guns 54mm.

Conning tower (special steel): 40mm

**Guns:**

(1894) 6 x 164.7mm/30 M1884 QF (1 forward, 1 aft, and 2 on each side on the upper deck in sponsons), 4 x 100mm/26.2 M1881 QF (on the forecastle under the bridge and on the poop), 2 x 65mm/16 M1881 landing, 8 x 47mm/40 M1885 QF, 8 x 37mm/20 M1885 QF.

**Torpedoes:** 7 tubes for 356mm torpedoes (1 submerged in the extreme bow, 2 forward, 2 side, and 2 aft above water).

(1896) After pair of torpedo tubes removed to provide accommodations for cadets.

(1898) Forward pair of torpedo tubes removed, leaving the bow tube and the amidships pair. The 4 x 37mm in the military tops were deleted.

*Suchet* Toulon Dyd/Indret (engines designed by Garnier).

On list 1.1888. Ord: 1.3.1887. K: 1.10.1887. L: 10.8.1893. Comm: 1.1.1894 (trials), 13.6.1894 (full).

Budget 1887 (delayed to the extraordinary 1887 budget, then moved to the ordinary 1888 budget). Construction reassigned from Brest to Toulon c1886. Suspended from 10.3.1888 to 17.10.1890. Machinery installed 26.9.1892 to 20.11.1893. Trials 20.3.1894 to 24.4.1894. Trial results approved 15.9.1894, admitted to active service in the *Escadre de la Méditerranée* 1.10.1894 replacing *Davout*. To reserve at Rochefort 20.11.1902 for reboilering, decomm. 11.11.1905 after reboilering cancelled and assigned that date as central ship for the 3rd flotilla of torpedo vessels of the Atlantic. Struck 24.4.1906, continued on central service for the same flotilla as annex to *Embuscade* 1906-1914. Hull put at the disposition of the merchant marine 28.8.1917, remained hulk (probably mooring hulk) at Rochefort to 1927. After recovery of non-ferrous metals sold 11.1927 to the Société Goldenberg.

---

*FRIANT* **Class.** *Croiseurs de 2ᵉ classe.* Protected cruisers with main guns on the sides and ends and with a ram-shaped bow. Three evenly-spaced funnels, two pole masts as completed. Designed by Lhomme. To *croiseurs d'escadre de 2ᵉ classe* 1.1891 and back to *croiseurs de 2ᵉ classe* 1.1892.

On 28 March 1890 Minister Barbey ordered naval constructor Lhomme at Toulon to prepare a design for a 2nd class cruiser of an enlarged *Davout* type. (Lhomme was also engaged in revising the design of *Davout's* sister *Suchet*.) Barbey wanted to augment the military strength of 2nd class cruisers and give them a range appropriate for their roles as cruisers. He specified a range of 6,000nm at 10 knots with a normal load coal but with bunker space to raise this to 8,000nm at 10 knots. The armament was to be as in the order of 4 September 1889 which had added two 164.7mm guns to *Davout* for a total of six. The curved armoured deck in *Davout* was to be replaced by the polygonal or mansard type with a flat top and sloping sides in *Cécille* and *Jean Bart*, which was to have the same strength as the deck in *Davout*. The new ship was to have multitubular instead of cylindrical boilers. The maximum speed was to be 18 knots at natural draught as in *Chanzy* with a probable speed with forced draught of 18.5 to 19 knots. The expected displacement was around 3,600 tons. Lhomme submitted his design on 21 August 1890 and on 27 August 1890 Minister Barbey referred it to the *Conseil des travaux* which examined it on 28 October 1890. The Council noted that Lhomme had made some useful additions not in the specifications, including four 100mm guns (also planned for *Suchet*) and approved the design subject to some changes. It noted that the hull lines were very similar to those of *Davout*.

---

The 2nd class cruiser *Suchet* probably on trials off Toulon in 1894, in a view from the technical characteristics document for the ship. Begun as a sister of *Davout*, this ship was lengthened during construction and her military masts were shortened by nearly three metres. The main battery is probably in place but the smaller guns appear to be missing. *(Feuille signalétique for the ship)*

The ships were initially designed with 164.7mm/30 M1881/84 BL guns, but three orders from Minister Barbey on 17 November 1890, 6 December 1890, and 10 January 1891 substituted 164.7mm/45 M1891 QF guns with a different breech mechanism and with shields. The higher weight of these led to a complete redesign of the upper portion of the ship. During fitting out the ships initially received short but heavy military masts as in *Suchet* with two enclosed tops. The initial design also included a light armament of eight 47mm QF (four in the lower tops) and twelve 37mm QF (four in the upper tops), and six 356mm M1887 torpedo tubes (2 forward, 2 amidships, 2 aft). On 12 March 1894 Minister of Marine Vice Admiral Auguste Alfred Lefèvre ordered the masts modified, the central part of each being cut off above the floor of the lower top (which was opened) and replaced with poles. At least two of the ships ran trials in this configuration. To increase stability the Minister, now Besnard, on 16 February 1895 ordered the removal of the lower tops and replaced the military masts with two metal pole masts with wooden topmasts. The same directive ordered the removal of the side and stern torpedo tubes and the embarkation of 66 tons of ballast. Minister Besnard on 6 June 1896 author-ized shortening the funnels by 1.25m. The ships were fitted with three different types of boilers to experiment with and compare them. Despite greater horsepower all three were slower than their model, *Davout*, because of incomplete combustion of coal in the boilers (especially in the Niclausse boilers) and a poor longitudinal distribution of weights and bad hull lines forward, which at speeds over 18 knots caused the bow to trim down by about 30cm. The ram-shaped (inverted) bow lacked any reinforcement except from the armoured deck and was unsuitable for ramming.

**Dimensions & tons:** (*Friant*) 97.500m oa, 97.050m wl, 94.000m pp (tip fwd to rudder) x 13.240m ext and wl. 3,771.227t disp (designed). Draught: (designed) 5.835m mean, 6.4125m aft (real). Men: 331.

**Machinery:** 9,000ihp designed at 15kg/cm² boiler pressure (17kg/cm² in *Bugeaud*). Speed 18.5kts. Trials (*C.L.*) 9,811ihp = 18.77kts, (*Friant*) 9,623ihp = 18.863kts, (*Bugeaud*) 9,913ihp at 134rpm = 18.95kts. 2 screws. 2 vertical triple expansion engines designed by Drory with 3 cylinders of 0.900m, 1.360m, and 1.960m diameter and 0.800m stroke for the HP and MP cylinders and 0.850m for the LP cylinders. Boilers: (*Friant*) 20 on the system of A. Collet & Cie. built by Niclausse, (*C.L.*) 20 Lagrafel et d'Allest built by Fraissinet at Marseille, (*Bugeaud*) 24 Belleville built at that firm's plant at Saint Denis. 600t coal (740t max). Range 3,550 nm @ 10kts (5,818nm @ 11kts in *Friant*, possibly with max coal).

**Armour:**

Decks: Armoured deck (extra mild steel) flat 30mm, upper and lower

The 2nd class cruiser *Chasseloup-Laubat* photographed by the Detroit Publishing Co. in the Hudson River in 1907 before or after participating in the Jamestown (Virginia) 300th Anniversary Exposition Naval Review in Hampton Roads. On the right of this spectacular view is Elevator A of the New York Central & Hudson River Railroad. (*Library of Congress, LC-D4-22443*)

slopes 80mm, all on 20mm hull plating. Splinter deck over the machinery and magazines 5mm.

Guns: shields for 164.7mm and 100mm guns 54mm.

Conning tower 55mm.

**Guns:**

(1894, as completed) 6 x 164.7mm/45 M1891 QF (1 forward, 1 aft, 4 in side sponsons), 4 x 100mm/45 M1891(2) QF (under the forward and after bridges), 1 x 65mm/16 M1881 landing, 4 x 47mm/40 M1885 QF, 11 x 37mm/20 M1885 QF. **Torpedoes:** 2 tubes for 356mm torpedoes (forward, above water).

(1897, *Friant*) light armament changed to 8 x 47mm and 3 x 37mm (soon removed)

(1900-02, others) light armament changed to 6 x 47mm and 3 x 37mm

(1907, *Friant* and *C.L.*) torpedo tubes removed.

(1915, *Friant*) light armament changed to 6 x 47mm and 2 x 37mm

*Chasseloup-Laubat* Cherbourg Dyd/F.C. Méditerranée, Marseille.

On list 1.1891. Ord: 17.11.1890 and 1.12.1890. K: 29.10.1891. L: 17.4.1893. Comm: 15.9.1894 (trials), 25.6.1895 (full).

Budget 1891. Engine contract 7.10.1891. Joined the *Escadre du Nord* 5.7.1895. Hull found badly fatigued when docked in early 1908. To reserve 1.1.1909, decomm. 22.2.1910. Struck 20.2.1911, hulk for the school for engineers and stokers and school for divers at Toulon with the centre funnel removed from 2.1912 to 1914 (replaced *Milan*, some of whose boilers she received). Converted to fresh water distilling ship for the Dardanelles operation, recomm. 16.6.1915 and towed into Mudros 29.7.1915 by *Vinh-Long*. Station ship at Corfu 1.1917 to 1.1919. Towed 5.1919 to Port Étienne (now Nouadhibou) in Mauritania for use as distilling ship. Sold 25.11.1920 to the Société Industrielle de la Grande Pêche and served as base ship for its trawlers at Port Étienne to 1925.

*Friant* Brest Dyd/F.C. Méditerranée, Marseille.

On list 1.1891. Ord: 15.12.1890 and 11.3.1891. K: 8.12.1891. L: 17.4.1893. Comm: 25.6.1894 (trials), 15.5.1895 (full).

Budget 1891. Engine contract 7.10.1891. Joined the *Escadre du Nord* 15.6.1895. Reboiled 1907 with new boilers of same type, then in constant service until ordered decomm. 29.7.1917 at Lorient. Ordered on 6.12.1917 to be converted to a base ship for submarines (fitted with repair facilities, retained only the centre funnel and armed only with two 75mm guns at the ends), left Lorient 20.6.1918 for Mudros where she joined the former transport *Shamrock*, then moved to Corfu as base ship and water distillation plant for the 3rd flotilla of submarines. Decomm. 7.1919. Struck 21.6.1920. Handed over in part payment to the firm salvaging *Liberté* and towed to Italy for BU in 1922.

*Bugeaud* Cherbourg Dyd/F.C. Méditerranée, Le Havre.

On list 1.1891. Ord: 29.1.1891 and 18.4.1891. K: 5.4.1892. L: 29.8.1893. Comm: 25.3.1895 (trials), 24.6.1896 (full).

Budget 1891. Construction reassigned from Toulon to Cherbourg c1890. Engine contract 7.10.1891. Admitted to active service in the *Escadre de la Méditerranée* 8.7.1896. Worn out on long Far East cruise 1900-1905 and decomm. 26.10.1905 at Rochefort. Struck 9.4.1906. Sold 9.2.1907 at Rochefort to Frank Rijsdijk' Scheepssloperij, Dordrecht, Holland and towed to Hendrik Ido Ambacht in the Netherlands to BU.

––––––––––

**DESCARTES Class.** *Croiseurs de 2e classe.* Protected cruisers with main guns in two double sponsons on the sides amidships, a steel hull sheathed with two layers of teak covered with copper, and a ram-shaped bow. Two wide funnels, two pole masts. Designed by de Bussy (A.C. Loire).

On 4 November 1890 Minister of Marine Barbey asked the *Conseil des travaux* to review specifications for open battery 1st class station cruisers (reclassed as 2nd class station cruisers on 2 March 1892) of the *Lapérouse*

and *Villars* types to replace existing 1st and 2nd class station cruisers. This was part of a mini-programme for station combatants that also included a 1st class station aviso that became *Kersaint* and a station gunboat that became *Surprise*. Barbey forwarded his own specifications based on a report from the Chief of the Naval General Staff and the Director of Materiel dated 28 October 1890, which the Council examined on 16 December 1890. The Minister's specifications included a maximum displacement of 2,500 tons, a speed of 16 knots at natural draught, ranges of 4,500nm at 10 knots with a normal coal supply and 6,000nm with a coal surcharge, an armament of four 164.7mm guns in sponsons and ten 100mm QF, a complete protective deck of two 10mm steel plates augmented over the engines and boilers by 20mm armour plating and a 4mm splinter deck, a cofferdam on top of the deck along the sides, and a three-masted barque rig with substantial sail area. The Council in its review stated that, without examining the utility of this kind of ship, it could accept the specifications with the addition of a modest forced draught capability, an increase in the range from 4,500nm to 5,500nm, and increased ammunition for the QF guns. It estimated the displacement with these changes as 2,900 tons. Barbey sent the specifications to the ports on 3 February 1891 with the speed raised to 18 knots with natural draught and 19 knots with moderately forced draught.

The draft budget for 1892 (submitted in February 1891) contained one station 1st class cruiser, *Descartes*, to be built by contract and another, *Pascal*, to be built in a dockyard. On 31 July 1891 the Council examined five designs for these ships received in response to Barbey's February 1891 directive and recommended those of the Ateliers et Chantiers de la Loire (de Bussy) and naval constructor Joseph Louis Léon Tissier for further development, although it admitted to a preference for the A.C. Loire design because of its unusually creative disposition of the armament. Tissier's design was used for the *Catinat* class, below. The A.C. Loire design was derived from *Davout*, all the dimensions being multiplied at about the same ratio. The hull lines were identical to those of *Davout*, suggesting that she would have no trouble making 19 knots as the smaller *Davout* was designed for twenty. The four large calibre guns were placed in pairs of sponsons close together amidships where two could fire forward and two aft without burdening the ends of the ship with their weight. Six of the ten 100mm guns were placed in embrasures on the sides and the other four on deck in a way that allowed six to fire forward and four aft. The Council replaced the uniform thickness of the deck armour in the specifications with 35mm on the flat portions, 50mm on the upper slopes, and 30mm on the lower slopes, all including plating. It also increased the splinter deck to 7mm and added a cellular layer filled with coal on top of the machinery. It reduced the horsepower for 19 knots from 9,000 to 8,500. Any weight savings were to be used to add to the deck armour over the machinery in preference to reducing displacement. The Council reviewed the modified design on 16 February 1892 and insisted on substituting Belleville boilers for the Lagrafel et d'Allest boilers in the design to get better internal arrangements amidships.

The hull was covered up to 1m above the waterline with two layers of teak topped by a 1mm layer of copper (2.5mm near the anchors). The ram-shaped (inverted) bow had a bronze stempost and, although somewhat reinforced, was not suitable for ramming in normal circumstances. Minister Rieunier on 14 June 1893 ordered the two 450mm torpedo tubes in the original design replaced with 356mm tubes. The design called for military masts, but these were ordered suppressed by Minister Faure on 9 June 1894 and they received pole masts. The ships were well regarded on foreign stations, particularly for the size and excellent disposition of their batteries of 164.7mm and 100mm guns and for their seagoing qualities. *Descartes* received many modifications during construction including the raising of her conning tower and the extension of her forecastle to abreast the after funnel to accommodate an increase from 320 to 386 men in the crew. At the end of 1896 her funnels were shortened by 1 metre and their low casings were raised. These changes resulted in her rolling badly, and both ships were crowded and poorly ventilated. The maximum operating pressure of the forward boilers in *Descartes* was reduced to 10kg/cm² after a fatal casualty in 1908 and that of her after boilers was reduced to 8.9kg/cm² after another casualty a year later.

**Dimensions & tons:** (*Descartes*) 100.700m oa, 99.400m wl, 96.300m pp (tip fwd to rudder) x 12.948m ext (above wl), 12.942m wl. 4,005.659t disp (designed). Draught: (designed) 6.010m mean, 6.860m aft. Men: 400.

**Machinery:** 8,300ihp designed at 17kg/cm² boiler pressure. Speed 19kts. Trials (*Descartes*) 8,828ihp at 134rpm = 19.588kts, (*Pascal*) 8,943ihp at 133rpm = 19.7kts. 2 screws. 2 vertical triple expansion engines with 4 cylinders of 0.890m (1), 1.320m (1), and 1.540m (2) diameter and 0.720 stroke. 16 Belleville boilers. 724t coal. Range 5,000nm @ 10kts.

**Armour:**

Decks: Armoured deck (extra mild steel) flat 25mm, upper slope 40mm, lower slope 20mm, all on 10mm hull plating. In *Descartes* a separate splinter layer of 10mm hull plating was located immediately under the flat deck armour over the machinery between frames 23 and 65.

Guns: shields for 164.7mm and 100mm guns 54mm.

Conning tower: 80mm. The conning tower of *Pascal* was located under the pilot house and that of *Descartes* was located a deck higher behind the pilot house. In *Descartes* there was an additional layer of 10mm hull plating on the conning tower.

The armour weights were 171.787 tons in *Descartes* and 113.818 tons in *Pascal*.

**Guns:**

(1896, as completed) 4 x 164.7mm/45 (in sponsons amidships, M1893 in *Pascal*, three M1887 and one M1891 in *Descartes*), 10 x 100mm/45 M1891(2) QF (4 in sponsons under the forecastle, 2 on the after end of the forecastle, 2 in sponsons forward of the poop and 2 on the poop), 8 x 47mm/40 M1885 QF, 4 x 37mm/20 M1885 QF.

**Torpedoes:** 2 tubes for 356mm torpedoes (sides, above water).

(1908) Torpedo tubes ordered removed 3.9.1908.

(1916-17) In 1916 *Descartes* landed 2 x 47mm and 2 x 37mm at Fort de France. In early 1917 she landed 2 x 100mm at Lorient for transfer to *Cosmao*, then in March she landed all but the two forward 164.7mm and two 37mm to arm other ships or send to the front.

*Descartes* (E1) A.C. Loire, Nantes/ACL, Nantes.

On list 1.1893. Ord: 17.8.1892 (contract). K: 1893. L: 27.9.1894. Comm: 12.2.1896 (trials), 1.1.1897 (full).

Budget 1892 (designated F). To Brest for trials 3-12.2.1896 (commissioned for transit 23.1.1896). To Cherbourg 28-29.9.1896 for the visit there of the Russian Tsar, then decomm. at Brest for work including modification of her funnels. Left for the Far East 25.1.1897, in reserve at Toulon 2.1902 to 8.1904, then back to the Far East escorting destroyers *Francisque* and *Sabre* and ten torpedo boats. Seagoing annex to the gunnery school in *Couronne*, then in *Tourville* (ex *Gironde*), at Toulon with *Latouche-Tréville* late 1908, replaced by *Requin* 1.1910. In Antilles 1912-1916, returned to Lorient 2.1917 and to reserve 2.1917, administratively decomm. 15.6.1917, replaced *Dupuy de Lôme* as mooring hulk 28.8.1918. Struck 10.5.1920. Sold 10.5.1921 at Lorient to M. Jacquart to BU.

*Pascal* (E2) Toulon Dyd/ ACL, Nantes.

On list 1.1893. Ord: 5.8.1892. K: 4.12.1893. L: 26.9.1895. Comm: 20.5.1896 (trials), 1.6.1897 (full).

Budget 1892 (designated E). Admitted to active service in the *Escadre de la Méditerranée* 6.7.1897, then in the Far East 1898-1905 (witnessed the destruction by the Japanese of the Russian cruiser *Varyag* and gunboat *Koreyets* at Chemulpo, Korea 9.2.1904 and took some survivors to Saigon). To special reserve at Toulon 15.2.1905 pending reconditioning but a naval staff note of 12.7.1905 reported that the repairs would not be completed until the end of 1906 and would only result in a ship of mediocre military value. Repairs were suspended and the ship

The 2nd class cruiser *Descartes*, designed for use on overseas stations, underway near Toulon after being attached to the gunnery school in around August 1908. During training outings to the Hyéres roadstead in 1909 she suffered a fire in a coal bunker in January and a boiler casualty in September, following which she was replaced as a training ship by *Requin* and placed in reserve in January 1910. She served in the Antilles from 1912 to 1917. Her main armament of four 164.7mm guns was concentrated in sponsons amidships, an arrangement that the *Conseil des travaux* found to be unusually creative and had replicated in *Protet* and *Catinat*. (Postcard by ELD)

was decomm. 10.6.1909. Struck 24.3.1910. Offered for sale 1.8.1911 at Toulon by the Domaines with *Amiral Baudin*, *Magenta*, *Milan*, and smaller vessels including torpedo boats and submarines, sold on that date to M. Bénédic and BU at La Seyne 1912.

*D'ASSAS* Class. *Croiseurs de 2e classe.* Protected cruisers with main guns on the sides and ends and with a ram-shaped bow. Three unevenly-spaced funnels, two pole masts. Designed by Lhomme. *Croiseurs légers* in 1.3.1920.

The design for these ships was described as a 'widened *Bugeaud*' with an extra 0.44m of beam to provide satisfactory stability with the newly-ordered rapid fire QF artillery. It was also lengthened 2.20m amidships to provide room for improved ammunition supply to the guns in the sponsons, leading to wider spacing between the second and third funnels. With hull lines at the bow slightly modified and the hull slightly lengthened, speeds improved over those of the *Friant* class but still remained under the trial speed of *Davout*. The designed armament was six 164.7mm, four 100mm, twelve 47mm QF, and sixteen 37mm guns; the small artillery was ordered on 21 August 1896 to be reduced to that shown below. As in the *Friant* class, use of the inverted bow for ramming was to be avoided.

**Dimensions & tons:**

(*Cassard, Du Chayla*) 99.650m oa, m wl, 99.250m pp x 13.680m ext and wl (14.300m outside sponsons). 3,957.072t disp (designed). Draught: (designed) 5.800m mean, 6.250m aft. Men: 385.

(*D'Assas*): 99.640m oa, 99.250m wl and pp x 13.680m ext and wl. 3,944.564t disp (designed). Draught: (designed) 5.800m mean, 6.250m aft (real). Men: .

**Machinery:** 10,000ihp designed at 15kg/cm² boiler pressure. Speed 19.8kts. Trials (*D'Assas*) 9,500ihp at 145rpm = 19.80kts; (*Du Chayla*) 10,005ihp at 147rpm = 19.86kts; (*Cassard*, 26.10.1897) 10,143ihp = 19.801kts. 2 screws. (*D'Assas*) 2 vertical triple expansion engines with 4 cylinders of 0.890m (1), 1.320m (1), and 1.540m (2) diameter and 0.760m stroke; (*Du Chayla*) 2 vertical triple expansion engines with 3 cylinders of 0.900m, 1.360m, and 2.080m and 0.840m stroke;

(*Cassard*) 2 vertical triple expansion engines with 4 cylinders of
0.920m (1), 1.360m (1), and 1.420m (2) diameter and 0.780m stroke.
20 Lagrafel et d'Allest boilers (built by the engine builders). 800t coal.
Range 6,350nm @ 10kts.

**Armour:**

Decks: Armoured deck (extra mild steel) flat 30mm, slopes 80mm, all on
20mm hull plating. Splinter deck over the machinery and magazines
6mm.

Guns: shields for 164.7mm and 100mm guns 54mm max.

Conning tower: 60mm (80mm in *D'Assas*).

**Guns:**

(1896, all as completed) 6 x 164.7mm/45 M1893 QF (M1887 QF in
*Du Chayla*) (1 forward, 1 aft, 4 in side sponsons), 4 x 100mm/45
M1891(2) or M1893 QF (under the forward and after bridges),
10 x 47mm/40 M1885 QF, 2 x 37mm/20 M1885 QF, and 3 x 37mm
revolving cannon. **Torpedoes:** 2 tubes for 356mm torpedoes (forward,
above water). **Searchlights:** 6 (1 on each mast, 2 in hull forward, 2 on
stern gallery)

(1898, *Cassard/Du Chayla*) 6 x 164.7mm, 4 x 100mm, 6 x 47mm,
3 x 37mm QF, 3 x 37mm revolving cannon (removed 1902), 2 torpedo tubes (removed 1906/1908).

(1901, *D'Assas*) 6 x 164.7mm, 4 x 100mm, 6 x 47mm, 6 x 37mm (3 in
1903), 3 x 37mm revolving cannon (removed 1906), 2 torpedo tubes

---

The 2nd class cruiser *D'Assas* in official mourning, with flags at half mast and yards
on the two masts tilted in opposite directions ('a-cockbill'). She is probably at
Villefranche at the end of the 1890s. (*NHHC from ONI, NH-64389*)

(1917-18, *Cassard*) By 1917 she had only 2 x 164.7mm and no small.
In 1918 she had 2 x 164.7mm, 4 x 90mm M1877. 2 x 47mm from
*Du Chayla* were added 1919

(1918, *Du Chayla*) 2 x 164.7mm, 4 x 75mm M1897 (in sponsons),
4 x 47mm

(1921, *Cassard* as gunnery school) 1 x 164.7mm (aft), 1 x 138.6mm
(fwd), 2 x 90mm (fwd sponsons), 2 x 75mm (after sponsons),
2 x 47mm

*D'Assas* (G1) A.C. Loire, Nantes/A.C. Loire, Saint Denis.

On list 1.1894. Ord: 15.11.1893. K: 1.4.1894. L: 28.3.1896.
Comm: 24.3.1897 (trials), 23.4.1898 (full).

Budget 1893 (designated Q). Arrived at Brest from Nantes 21.3.1897.
Trials completed 27.4.1898, to Toulon from Brest 29.4-5.5.1898. After
voyage repairs sailed 17.7.1898 to join the reserve squadron of the
*Escadre de la Méditerranée*. Left Toulon 3.4.1899 to bring the
Marchand mission home from Djibouti following the Fashoda incident. Left Brest for Saigon 9.3.1904 to replace *Bugeaud* but headed
home from Saigon 30.1.1906 because of repeated materiel problems
and placed in special reserve at Lorient 30.5.1906. Minister Thomson
on 24.9.1907 proposed refitting her at A.C. Loire as a minelayer but
the cost was prohibitive and she was decomm. 1.1.1908. Struck
9.3.1910, hulk for waste oil at Lorient 1910-1913, for sale 1913-1914,
sold 11.4.1914 to MM. Willer Peterson and Albrech of Copenhagen.

*Du Chayla* (G2) Cherbourg Dyd/Indret (engines designed by Félix
Edmond Théodore Godard).

On list 1.1894. Ord: 18.3.1893. K: 23.3.1894. L: 10.11.1895.
Comm: 15.7.1897 (trials), 19.2.1898 (full).

Budget 1893 (designated K). From Cherbourg to Toulon 20-27.2.1898 and joined the *Escadre de la Méditerranée*. Active in the Mediterranean during World War I until sent to the Indian Ocean 5.1917, landed her four 100mm guns at Port Said 8.1917. Returned to Bizerte 4.1918 and landed the four 164.7mm guns from her sponsons, which were soon replaced by four 75mm guns. Towed the Russian cruiser-yacht *Almaz* out of Sevastopol 28.4.1919, leaving her at Constantinople two days later. Decomm. 28.7.1921 at Cherbourg. Struck 27.10.1921, towed to Brest 1922 and used at the school for engineer officers there. Replaced by the World War I aviso *Vauquois*, she was towed to Lorient 12.1925 and was used as a landing hulk at the oil depot there. To the Domaines 29.3.1933 for sale at Lorient. Offered for sale and sold 15.11.1933 to M. Marret et Goltz and towed to Saint Nazaire 12.1933 to BU.

*G3* (Unnamed) Contract
Budget 1894 (not funded). This contract-built ship was included in the 1894 budget (submitted 5.1893) with the stipulation that no funds were to be spent on her during 1894. She were not contracted for and the 1895 budget (3.1894) deferred her indefinitely.

*Cassard* (G4) Cherbourg Dyd/FCM, Le Havre (engines designed by Sigaudy).

On list 1.1894. Ord: 17.10.1893. K: 22.10.1894. L: 27.5.1896. Comm: 21.6.1897 (trials), 7.2.1898 (full).
Budget 1894. From Cherbourg to Toulon 9-15.2.1898 and attached to the *Escadre de la Méditerranée*. Trial results approved 24.5.1898. Patrolled off North Africa during World War I until arriving at Bordeaux 7.5.1917 for changes to her armament. Resumed patrolling in the Red Sea and Mediterranean 3.1918. Ordered fitted at Toulon as gunnery school 4.11.1923. Replaced by *Tourville* (formerly the transport *Gironde*) 2.1924 which received all of her guns after a proposed transfer to Poland fell through. Intentionally grounded in mid-1924 in the mouth of the Rhône River as a target. Struck 27.7.1924. Sold 26.11.1925 at Toulon to the Société du Matériel Naval du Midi.

---

*CATINAT* Class. *Croiseurs de 2e classe.* Protected cruisers with main guns in two double sponsons on the sides amidships, a steel hull sheatherd with one layer of teak covered with copper, and a ram-shaped bow. Two funnels, two pole masts. Designed by Tissier.

On 31 July 1891 the Council examined five designs for open battery 1st class station cruisers (reclassed as 2nd class station cruisers on 2 March 1892) that it had received in response to specifications sent to the ports by

---

Outboard profile from the lines plan and plan of the shelter deck (*spardeck*) of the 2nd class cruiser *Protet* built on the plans of M. Tissier. The plans were signed by M. Baron, chief engineer at C.A. Gironde, on 1 December 1898 and were certified to represent the ship as fitted by naval constructor Bonvalet, the Navy's control officer at Bordeaux. The small calibre artillery carried at this time included 10 x

100mm M1893 QF guns (4 in sponsons on the upper deck forward, 2 in sponsons on the upper deck aft, 2 on the forecastle, and 2 on the poop), 10 x 47mm (4 on the 164.7mm sponsons, 4 on the 4 after 100mm sponsons, 1 on the forecastle at the tip of the bow, and 1 on the poop at the tip of the stern), and 4 x 37mm (2 on the pilot house and 2 on the stern gallery). There were also 2 x 65mm landing guns.

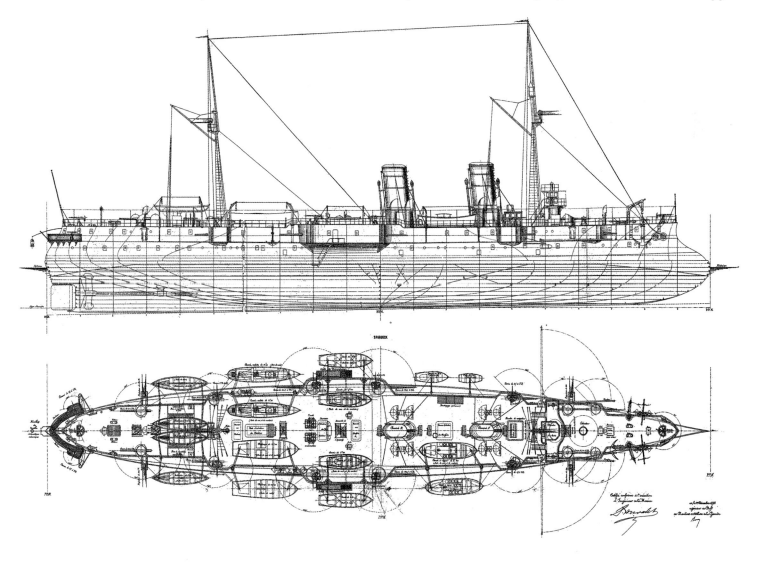

The 2<sup>nd</sup> class cruiser *Catinat* with much of the crew on deck in tropical helmets. She differed from her near sister in having rectangular ventilation trunks rather than cowl ventilators. The photo was probably taken during her long cruise on the Pacific Station from May 1905 to July 1909 which included ports from Central and South America to Australia. *(Private collection)*

Minister Barbey in February 1891. It selected a design by A.C. Loire for the two ships in the budget for 1892, but it also found the design by naval constructor Tissier satisfactory and it was used for the next two ships built, *Catinat* in the 1893 budget (deferred to 1894) and *Protet* in the 1894 budget (deferred to 1895).

Tissier saw a close similarity between the specifications for the new cruiser and the characteristics of *Bugeaud* and used as much of the design of *Bugeaud* as possible for the new ship to save both time and cost in building the new ships. The main dimensions were nearly identical, an increase of 0.26m in the beam being for carrying sail, and the increase in the depth of the hull was due to the addition of wooden hull sheathing. Tissier borrowed intact the hull lines and the machinery of *Bugeaud*. Because both the *Bugeaud* and *Descartes* designs derived from *Davout*, the A.C. Loire and Tissier designs were very similar, except the rounding of the hull above the waterline was absent in Tissier's. The Council recommended the same change in the protective deck as in *Descartes*, and savings elsewhere in weight allowed the deck to be further strengthened. As in *Descartes* the Council asked for the Lagrafel et d'Allest boilers in the design to be replaced with Belleville boilers to improve internal arrangements.

On 24 January 1893 Minister Rieunier forwarded to the Council Tissier's final revision of his design. In July 1891 he had placed his pairs of 164.7mm gun sponsons far apart as in *Bugeaud*, one pair being 16m forward of amidships, the other being 24m aft of it, with six of the ten 100mm guns being located between them. In his new design he imitated the arrangement in the A.C. Loire design with the 164.7mm guns being close together amidships that the Council had preferred in 1891. The Council approved his new plans on 7 March 1893 with a few small changes and they received final approval on 21 July 1893.

The designed light artillery of fourteen 47mm and five 37mm was later reduced to save weight. The ram-shaped (inverted) bow included a bronze stempost and was not designed for ramming. The two ships were built by two different contractors and differed in many small details. *Protet* for instance had cowl ventilators around the funnels while *Catinat* had rectangular ventilation trunks. Like the *Descartes* class they were poorly ventilated, even after *Protet* received four additional electric ventilators at San Francisco in 4-5.1900. *Catinat* suffered from excessive vibrations above 15 knots while *Protet* rolled and pitched more than her near-sister.

*The characteristics are based on a devis for* Protet *dated 1899.*

**Dimensions & tons:**

(*Protet*) 101.520m oa, 101.200m wl and pp x 13.604m ext & wl
(15.520m outside sponsons, 15.280m designed). 4,183.553t disp.
Draught: 6.070m mean, 7.011m aft (probably keel line projected*)*.
Men: 399.

(*Catinat*) 101.565m oa, 101.200m wl and pp x 13.600m ext and wl

(15.230m outside sponsons). 4,113.655t disp (designed). Draught: (designed) 6.000m mean, 6.800m aft (keel line projected).

**Machinery:** 9,000ihp designed at 140rpm and 17kg/cm² boiler pressure (12kg/cm² at the engines). Trials (*Protet* 1.12.1898) 9,425.6ihp = 20.284kts at 133.875rpm and 14.629kg/cm² boiler pressure; (*Catinat*) 9,933ihp = 19.61kts. 2 screws. 2 vertical triple expansion engines, those of *Protet* with 3 cylinders of 0.820m, 1,240m and 1.930m and 0.850m stroke and those of *Catinat* with 3 cylinders of 0.900m, 1.360m, and 1.960m diameter and 0.800m stroke except 0.850m for the LP cylinder. 16 Belleville boilers. 570.180t coal (normal), 743.780t (actual), 861.414t (capacity), all plus 47.211t oil. Range 6,000nm @ 10kts.

**Armour:**

Decks: Armoured deck (extra mild steel) flat 25mm, upper slope 40mm, lower slope 25mm, all on 20mm hull plating. Splinter deck over the machinery 7mm.

Guns: shields for 164.7mm and 100mm guns 54mm.

Conning tower 72mm of special steel in *Protet* and 80mm in *Catinat*

**Guns** 4 x 164.7mm/45 M1893 QF (in sponsons amidships), 10 x 100mm/45 M1891(2) QF (M1893 in *Protet*) (4 in sponsons under the forecastle, 2 on the after end of the forecastle, 2 in sponsons forward of the poop and 2 on the poop), 2 x 65mm/16 M1881 landing, 10 x 47mm/40 M1885, 4 x 37mm/20 M1885. **Torpedoes:** 2 tubes for 356mm torpedoes (sides, above water). **Searchlights:** 4.

*Catinat* (E3) F.C. Méditerranée, Le Havre-Graville/FCM, Le Havre (engines designed by Sigaudy).

On list 1.1895. Ord: 14.2.1894 (contract). K: 1894. L: 8.10.1896. Comm: 12.5.1897 (trials), 27.5.1898 (full).

Budget 1893 (designated P, delayed to 1894). To Cherbourg from Le Havre for trials 6.5.1897. To Brest 1.6.1898 and replaced *Friant* in the *Escadre du Nord*. She cruised in the Pacific between 5.1905 and 7.1909 but had constant materiel problems there, partly because she had been left 'completely abandoned' during 27 months in reserve at Lorient between 1903 and 1905. Her funnels were replaced at Sydney in 7.1907 after the rear one came close to falling over. To special reserve at Rochefort 29.7.1909. Repairs were prohibitively expensive and she was decomm. 16.2.1910. Struck 3.8.1910. Sold 17.7.1911 at Rochefort to BU.

*Protet* (E4) C.A. Gironde, Bordeaux-Lormont/Schneider, Creusot.

On list 1.1896. Ord: 14.8.1895 (contract). K: 5.11.1895. L: 6.7.1898. Comm: 6.8.1898 (trials), 20.4.1899 (full).

Budget 1894 (delayed to 1895). Construction authorized 9.5.1895. Machinery installed 7.9.1897 to 13.7.1898. Virtually complete when launched. Arrived at Rochefort from Bordeaux 3.8.1898, trial results approved 20.4.1899. Left 27.5.1899 to replace *Duguesclin* on the Pacific station. Relieved by *Catinat* at Dakar end 5.1905, returned to Rochefort 7.6.1905, to special reserve there 17.6.1905. Boilers in bad condition, repairs considered prohibitively expensive 'for a ship without military uses'. Decomm. there 1.3.1909. Struck 9.3.1910. Offered for sale 15.9.1910 at Rochefort. Sold 25.10.1910 to M. Barman representing a German firm. Left under tow 12.11.1910 but had to take refuge at the Ile d'Aix because of bad weather before proceeding to Hamburg in early December to BU.

*Jurien de la Gravière* (E5) Contract

Budget 1894 (not funded). This contract-built ship was included in the 1894 budget (submitted 5.1893) as E5 (unnamed) with the stipulation that no funds were to be spent on her during 1894. She were not contracted for and the 1895 budget (3.1894) deferred her indefinitely. The 1896 budget submission (5.1895) included a 2nd class station cruiser designated E5, named *Jurien de la Gravière*, and to be built at Cherbourg, but the Budget Commission on 13.7.1895 deleted all station cruisers including this one from the budget and cancelled credits for them on 24.10.1895.

*E6* (Unnamed) Contract

Budget 1894 (not funded). This contract-built ship was included in the 1894 budget (submitted 5.1893) with the stipulation that no funds were to be spent on her during 1894. She was not contracted for and the 1895 budget (3.1894) deferred her indefinitely.

---

## (D) 3rd class cruisers (*Croiseurs de 3e classe*). Were *Éclaireurs d'escadre* before the 1.1885 fleet list.

*FORBIN* Class. *Croiseurs de 3e classe.* Protected cruisers with main guns in widely spaced sponsons on the sides and with a ram-shaped bow. Two widely spaced funnels, three masts, schooner rig (later two pole masts). Designed by de Bussy. To *Croiseurs d'escadre de 3e classe* 1.1891 and back to *croiseurs de 3e classe* 1.1892.

In his book *La réforme de la Marine,* published at the very beginning of 1886, the leading publicist of the *Jeune École*, Gabriel Charmes, described that group's ideal commerce raiding cruiser as a relatively small vessel with an armament of only two 138.6mm guns and a speed of 20 knots, able to fall upon weak merchant vessels and fast enough to flee from anything stronger. On 1 February 1886 the new Minister of Marine, Rear Admiral Aube, asked *Inspecteur général du génie maritime* de Bussy for a cruiser whose specific wartime mission was to pursue and destroy fast merchant ships. On 2 February 1886 de Bussy completed specifications for the ship, which he called later in 1886 a *navire de proie* (prey) rather than a *navire de combat*. These included a speed of 18 knots for 12 hours and 19.5 knots for 2 hours, a steaming range of 2400nm at 10 knots (3,000nm with coal surcharge), a sizeable fore and aft rig with one square sail for winds from aft, a main armament of two 138.6mm guns in sponsons near the middle of the ship able to fire both forward and aft, a complete 40mm protective deck with a cofferdam around the sides, and the smallest displacement possible. The use of boilers with a small internal volume of water like Bellevilles was excluded.

Three of these small cruisers were included among the eight cruisers that Aube added in early 1886 to the 1887 budget. De Bussy used his specifications to prepare a detailed design, approved on 20 March 1886, for the two that were to be built in dockyards, *Forbin* and *Surcouf*. He also sent his specifications to private yards with a request for designs for the third ship. On 30 April 1886 five designs by commercial firms were referred to the *Conseil des travaux* which found that only the one by C. A. Gironde satisfied the specifications. This firm got the contract for *Troude*. The extraordinary 1887 budget added three more small cruisers, of which one, *Coëtlogon*, was built by a contractor to de Bussy's design and the other two, *Lalande* and *Cosmao*, were built by C. A. Gironde to their design.

The construction of *Coëtlogon* was initially assigned to Normand on 1 March 1887 but Normand was unable to undertake it and the contract for the hull and engines was reassigned on 12 April 1887 to a yard recently built by the *Compagnie Générale Transatlantique* at Penhoët, Saint Nazaire, to build ships for its passenger fleet. The engines of *Coëtlogon* were rejected on 28 May 1891 after laborious trials, and after Minister Barbey confirmed this decision on 18 January 1892 new ones were built and finally accepted 31 August 1894. The C.G.T. yard became the Chantiers et Ateliers de Saint Nazaire (Penhoët) in 1900. The engines of *Forbin* and *Surcouf* were ordered from the former Claparède plant at Saint Denis, which had been owned since 1886 by the Ateliers et Chantiers de la Loire of Saint Nazaire. Their plans were drawn by Claparède.

*Forbin* was completed for trials with the original armament, which had a main battery of only two 138.6mm guns in sponsons forward, but this was found to be weak compared to foreign ships (even the French *Chasseur* class avisos had four 138.6mm guns) and on 20 September 1889 two more 138.6mm guns in new sponsons aft were ordered added. The protection scheme was also enhanced by the addition of a full cellular layer. *Coëtlogon* received the artillery enhancements between September 1889 and February

1890 and the rest of the upgrade between October 1892 and July 1893. *Forbin* was upgraded between September 1891 and February 1893 and *Surcouf* between September 1892 and March 1893. Five torpedo tubes were planned but the one in the stern was quickly ordered suppressed on 23 June 1887. The two forward torpedo tubes were ordered deleted on 14 November 1895 and the two side ones on 24 January 1905. All of the guns originally had shields, but on 3 July 1896 the shields on the 47mm and 37mm guns were ordered deleted. The 138.6mm sponsons were found to be vulnerable to damage in heavy seas, though less so in *Coëtlogon* than in the other two. The ram-shaped bow was supported by four transverse bulkheads and by the armoured deck but was not intended for ramming.

*Forbin* was completed with the designed rig of four schooner-rigged masts and 674.53 sq.m. of sail) with one mast forward, one behind each funnel, and one aft, but the sails did little good and on 31 August 1889 a new rig was approved of three schooner masts with one between the funnels and 412.27 sq.m. of sail. During refits in 1892 *Forbin* and *Coëtlogon* had the mast between the funnels and the pole bowsprit removed, while the foremast was moved further aft and the after mast further forward. *Surcouf* lost her middle mast but kept her pole bowsprit. They retained 214.75 sq.m. of sail until sails were finally ordered abolished on 19 March 1906.

Although totally obsolete, *Surcouf* was retained in service in 1914 because of the critical shortage of small cruising ships, all cruiser construction since the late 1890s having been of armoured cruisers. She landed one 47mm and two 37mm guns in Cameroon while station ship there in 1916-17, and all of her guns (by then worn out) were removed at Gibraltar in August 1917 when she became a base ship there.

---

The 3rd class cruiser *Surcouf* with three masts, which she retained long after her two sisters lost their mainmasts in 1892. She probably lost hers at Rochefort in around 1906. This view probably dates from around the turn of the century. *(Postcard by ND)*

**Dimensions & tons:** 96.10m oa x 9.30m to 9.33m ext. 1,857t disp. (Full load after refitting: 1,966t for *Forbin*, 2,047t for *Surcouf*, 1,932t for *Coëtlogon*.) Draught: 4.50m mean, 5.40m aft. Men: 209.

**Machinery:** 1,050nhp and 6,200ihp designed at 7kg/cm$^2$ boiler pressure. Speed 20kts. Trials (*Forbin*, 1888-89) 6,022.51ihp = 20.638kts; (*Surcouf*, 9.9.1890) 6,208ihp at 133rpm = 20.515kts; (*Coëtlogon*, late 1893) 5,918.3ihp = 20.333kts. 2 screws. 2 horizontal compound engines with 2 cylinders of 0.935m and 1.870m diameter and 0.915m stroke. 6 two-furnace cylindrical Admiralty boilers. 200t coal (298t max). Range 2,395nm @ 10kts.

**Armour:** .

Decks: Armoured deck (iron) 40mm flat and slopes. Splinter deck below the armoured deck and above the engines 7mm.

Guns: unprotected.

Conning tower: A 40mm conning tower was added in 1889-90 (54mm in *Forbin*).

**Guns:**

(1888, *Forbin*) 2 x 138.6mm/30 M1881 BLR (in sponsons by the forward funnel), 3 x 47mm/40 M1885 QF, 4 x 37mm. **Torpedoes:** 4 tubes for 356mm torpedoes (2 forward and 2 side, all above water).

(1889) Main battery increased to 4 x 138.6mm/30 M1881 BLR by adding a pair of sponsons aft forward of the poop

(1893) 4 x 138.6mm/30 QF (converted, M1881 in *Forbin* and M1881/84 in *Surcouf*) 5 x 47mm QF, 3 x 37mm QF, 4 x 37mm revolving cannon, 4 torpedo tubes (2 tubes forward removed 1896)

(1905, *Forbin*) 4 x 138.6mm/30 M1881 QF, 9 x 47mm QF, 2 x 37mm QF for the boats, torpedo tubes removed after 1900.

(1905, *Surcouf*) As *Forbin* but had M1881/84 main guns and 7 x 47mm.

(1916, *Surcouf*) Add 2 x 47mm AA on deck forward.

*Forbin* Rochefort Dyd/A.C. Loire, Saint Denis.
On list 1.1886. Ord: 7.4.1886. K: 1886. L: 14.1.1888.
    Comm: 15.11.1888 (trials), 1.2.1889 (full).

Budget 1887. Engine contract 2.8.1886. Left Rochefort for Toulon 22.12.1889 and joined the *Escadre de la Méditerranée*. Re-boilered 1.1903. Decomm. 1.11.1911, condemned 20.3.1912 but ordered on 9.4.1913 to be retained as a hulk at Rochefort. Struck 27.11.1913, mooring hulk at Rochefort 1913-1914. Ordered on 28.4.1917 converted at Bordeaux to a replenishment hulk (*ponton-ravitailleur*) carrying 1,250 tons of coal (machinery removed and 8 cargo masts installed). Towed out of Bordeaux 1.2.1918 by the tug *Utrech* to the base at Corfu. After the war, towed out of Corfu 14.7.1919 by the tug *Byzantion* to Piraeus and sold there to BU.

*Surcouf* Cherbourg Dyd/A.C. Loire, Saint Denis.
On list 1.1886. Ord: 7.4.1886. K: 4.10.1886. L: 9.10.1889.
   Comm: 27.11.1889 (trials), 10.10.1890 (full).
Budget 1887. Named 7.4.1886. Engine contract 2.8.1886. Assigned 23.10.1890 to the *Escadre du Nord*, replacing *Épervier*. Re-boilered 11-12.1904 (first lit off 4.1905). Patrol service from Brest 1914-16, in West Africa 1916-1917, base ship at Gibraltar for the submarines on the Morocco squadron 1917-1919. Off main list by 3.1920, hulk at Rochefort. Struck 4.4.1921. Sold 10.5.1921 at Rochefort to M. Jacquart to BU.

*Coëtlogon* Compagnie Générale Transatlantique, Penhoët, Saint Nazaire/ same
On list 1.1888. Ord: 23.5.1887 (contract). K: 27.5.1887. L: 3.12.1888.
   Comm: 20.3.1890 (trials), 17.8.1893 (new trials), 20.9.1894 (full).
Budget 1887 (extraordinary). Construction reassigned from Normand to Penhoët c1887. Contract included engines. Hull accepted 25.8.1889, to Brest 15.9.1889 and decomm. 21.9.1889 for completion of armament and sponsons. After rejection of engines on 18.1.1892 placed in 3rd category reserve 5.3.1892, then towed to Saint Nazaire 25-26. 8.1892 by the tug *Haleur* to receive new engines. Returned to Brest 25.8.1893, final acceptance 31.8.1894. In full commission with the *Escadre du Nord* from 20.9.1894 to 20.8.1896, then to reserve at Lorient. The Maritime Prefect there wrote to the Minister on 15.1.1905 that 'This cruiser has always given rise to problems and it would be absolutely imprudent to rely on her now.' Decomm. 1.6.1905. Struck 26.8.1905, munitions depot hulk at Lorient 1905-1906. To the Domaines 9.4.1906 for sale, sold 11.8.1906 to M. Guilhaumon.

---

**TROUDE Class.** *Croiseurs de 3ᵉ classe.* Protected cruisers with main guns in closely spaced sponsons on the sides amidships and with a ram-shaped bow. Two closely spaced funnels, three masts, schooner rig (later three plain poles). Designed by Baron (C.A. Gironde). To *Croiseurs d'escadre de 3ᵉ classe* 1.1891 and back to *croiseurs de 3ᵉ classe* 1.1892.

In February or March 1886 de Bussy sent to private shipbuilders the specifications dated 2 February 1886 that he had used to design the cruisers of the *Forbin* class, whose mission in wartime was to pursue and destroy fast merchant ships. He asked them to submit designs for a third ship that was to be built by contract. Five private shipbuilders responded, and in its session of 25 May 1886 the *Conseil des travaux* accepted the design presented by Jean Baron, the chief engineer of the Chantiers et Ateliers de la Gironde at Bordeaux who as a naval constructor at Rochefort had previously designed *Torpilleur nº 2*. *Troude* was ordered to this design under the regular 1887 budget while two more ships, *Lalande* and *Cosmao*, were later added under the extraordinary 1887 budget.

The boilers of *Troude* came from a different supplier than the others and her machinery trials were laborious; she was only ready for acceptance trials two years after arriving at Rochefort from Bordeaux in April 1889. Like the *Forbin* class, these ships suffered from vibrations aft at high speeds. The ram-shaped (inverted) bow was not designed for ramming.

The *Troude* and *Forbin* classes went through the same changes during

and after construction. They began with a main armament of two 138.6mm guns, some 47mm and some 37mm guns, and five torpedo tubes. The torpedo tube in the stern was ordered on 23 June 1887 to be suppressed, a second pair of 138.6mm was ordered on 20 September 1889 to be added in new sponsons aft of the original pair (both pairs were close together amidships in the *Troude* class, further apart in the *Forbin* class). Pursuant to an order of 25 May 1893 a full cellular layer was added above the armoured deck, the main battery was converted to QF guns, the light artillery was reinforced, the rig was altered, and the sponsons were strengthened. These modifications were carried out in *Troude* and *Lalande* between October 1893 and May 1894 and in *Cosmao* between June 1894 and February 1895. The two forward torpedo tubes were ordered on 14 November 1895 to be deleted. *Troude* and *Cosmao* received a 40mm conning tower but by an order of 6 June 1896 *Lalande* remained without one. The two side torpedo tubes were ordered on 24 January 1905 to be deleted. The rig of the *Troude* class consisted of three schooner masts with 615.245 sq.m. (reduced to 281.100m in 1902) and otherwise remained essentially unchanged except that the mainmast of *Cosmao* was removed in January 1913.

*Cosmao* was still active in 1914 for the same reasons as *Surcouf* (a lack of small cruising ships after the purges of the previous decades and the policy of building only armoured cruisers) and even after a 1910 inspection report concluded that 'from a military point of view … she no longer exists'. She lost all her artillery at Gibraltar in December 1916 but was ordered on 29 March 1917 to be rearmed at Bordeaux with two 100mm guns from *Descartes* in the forward sponsons and four 90mm M1877 guns on the tops of all four sponsons. All the 47mm guns were removed. In 1918 half of these guns were removed, probably for use on other vessels.

**Dimensions & tons:** (*Cosmao*) 95.890m oa, 95.000m wl, 93.000m pp (tip fwd to rudder) x 9.500m ext and wl. 1,877.524t disp (designed). Draught: (designed) 4.270m mean, 5.170m aft. Men: 200. (Full load after refitting: 2,025t for *Troude*, 1,990t for *Lalande*, 2,070t for *Cosmao*.)
**Machinery:** 1,050nhp and 6,300ihp designed at 7kg/cm² boiler pressure. Speed 20.5kts. Trials (*Troude*, c1890) 6433.5ihp = 20.913kts; (*Lalande*, 21.2.1891) 6,560ihp at 133rpm = 20.887kts; (*Cosmao*, c1891) 6,384ihp = 20.603kts. 2 screws. 2 horizontal compound engines with 2 cylinders of 0.940m and 1.880m diameter and 0.915m stroke. 5 cylindrical Admiralty boilers. 270t coal (300t max). Range 2,110nm @ 10kts.
**Armour:** As *Forbin* class except *Troude* and *Cosmao* got a 40mm conning tower while *Lalande* got none.
**Guns:**
(1891) 4 x 138.6mm/30 M1881/84 BLR (in sponsons by the forward and after funnels, the after pair having been added c1889), 4 x 47mm/40 M1885 QF, 4 x 37mm/20 M1885 QF. **Torpedoes:** 4 tubes for 356mm torpedoes (two forward and 2 side, all above water).
(1894) 138.6mm/30 M1881/84 QF (converted, M1881/84 in *Lalande*, M1884 in *Cosmao*).
(1904) 4 x 138.6mm/30 M1881/84 QF, 9 x 47mm QF, 2 x 37mm QF for the boats, no landing, remaining two tubes for 356mm M1887 torpedoes (on sides) removed after 1900.
(1917, *Cosmao*) 2 x 100mm (from *Descartes*), 4 x 90mm, (1918) 1 x 100mm, 2 x 90mm.

*Troude* C.A. Gironde, Bordeaux-Lormont/Schneider, Creusot (boilers by Fraissinet of Marseille).
On list 1.1887. Ord: 16.8.1886 (contract). K: 27.8.1886. L: 22.10.1888.
   Comm: 6.12.1888 (trials), 5.2.1891 (full).
Budget 1887. Contract included engines. Comm for transit 15.11.1888, to Rochefort 24-25.11.1888 for completion and trials. Left Rochefort for Toulon 15.2.1891 and joined the *Escadre de la Méditerranée*. Reboilered 1900-02 at Rochefort. To special reserve 1.7.1906 at Rochefort. Struck 3.7.1907, for sale at Rochefort 1907-1908.

*Lalande* C.A. Gironde, Bordeaux-Lormont/Schneider, Creusot (including boilers).

On list 1.1888. Ord: 21.3.1887 (contract). K: 6.5.1887. L: 22.3.1889. Comm: 1.11.1889 (trials), 25.4.1891 (full).

Budget 1887 (extraordinary). Contract included engines. To Rochefort 13.4.1889 for completion and trials. Trial results approved 6.5.1891. Left Rochefort for Toulon 22.5.1891 and joined the *Escadre de la Méditerranée*. Reboilered 1902-05 at Rochefort. To special reserve at Bizerte 18.2.1909 for another reboilering, this postponed 3.11.1909 and refit cancelled 17.6.1910. Decomm. 15.4.1911. Struck 15.4.1911, for sale in Tunisia 1911-1912, to the Domaines 14.8.1912 for sale, sold 13.10.1912 to M. Boccara.

*Cosmao* C.A. Gironde, Bordeaux-Lormont/Schneider, Creusot (including boilers).

On list 1.1888. Ord: 25.4.1887 (contract). K: 1887. L: 29.8.1889.

The 3rd class cruiser *Troude* at Villefranche early in her career. The battleship *Hoche* is behind her in her original configuration (to 1894) with two military masts. In the left background is a torpedo cruiser. *(NHHC from ONI album of foreign warships dated about 1900, NH-88803)*

Comm: 13.9.1889 (trials), 8.8.1891 (full).

Budget 1887 (extraordinary). Construction reassigned from Normand to C.A. Gironde c1887. Contract included engines. Arrived at Rochefort 13.9.1889 for completion and trials. Trials completed 8.8.1891, left Rochefort for Toulon 14.8.1891 and joined the *Escadre de la Méditerranée*. Reboilered 1904-05 at Rochefort. On coastal patrol duty off Morocco in World War I, during which she landed her 138.6mm guns at Gibraltar 13-20.12.1916 and embarked a new armament at Bordeaux. Sent to the Levant station 10.1918, sent back to Rochefort 3.1919 when boilers found to be worn out. To normal reserve 25.4.1919. Struck 30.10.1919, hulk at Rochefort 1920-1927. Sold 1928 to Société Goldenberg to BU at Rochefort.

_____

**LINOIS.** *Croiseur de 3e classe.* Protected cruiser with main guns in sponsons on the sides and with a ram-shaped bow. Two funnels, two masts. Designed by Lagane (FCM La Seyne).

On 29 November 1890 Minister Barbey forwarded to the Forges et Chantiers de la Méditerranée (FCM) at La Seyne, specifications drafted by the Navy's Director of Materiel, Bienaymé, for a modified *Surcouf* type 3rd class cruiser for use in European waters that he planned to include in the

1892 budget. These specifications called for a displacement of around 2,100 tons, a speed of 19 knots with natural draught and 20 knots with moderately forced draught, multitubular boilers, and a range of 2,800nm at 10 knots with a normal coal supply and 3,200nm at 10 knots with a coal surcharge. The armament consisted of four 138.6mm QF guns in sponsons, two 100mm QF guns on the forecastle and poop, four 47mm QF guns above the 138.6mm gun sponsons, four 37mm revolving cannon in two military masts with armed tops as in *Davout*, and four tubes for 356mm torpedoes.

On 8 December 1890 Lagane, the director at FCM, reported that there was not enough room under the protective deck for multitubular boilers and asked to use Admiralty type cylindrical boilers instead. With these the ship could make 20 knots on forced draught with closed stokeholds but reasonable firing rates and 18.5 knots with open stokeholds. Lagane forwarded a preliminary design on 15 December 1890. The Admiralty boilers were heavier than the multitubular boilers and on 7 January 1891 the navy agreed to increase the displacement to 2,200 tons to accommodate them. Lagane forwarded a modified design on 9 February 1891 and Minister Barbey referred it to the *Conseil des travaux* on 17 February 1891.

The Council examined Lagane's design on 17 March 1891 and concluded that on the whole he had executed the Navy's specifications well. However, it lengthened the ship by one metre to 98m, increased the beam by the same proportion, and increased the displacement by 80 tons to 2,284 tons to provide the space needed for the boilers, to add some more coal to propel the larger hull, and to provide displacement to offset the weight of the water in the boilers. It reshaped the hull above the waterline to resemble that of *Cécille*. It decided against military masts as in *Davout* and felt that pole masts with external ladders and single tops containing only one revolving cannon each were sufficient. Masthead searchlights were also not needed, the four lower down sufficed. It moved the conning tower forward of the foremast and gave it 40mm armour (subsequently increased). Lagane was later asked to consider substituting vertical engines for the two horizontal triple expansion engines in his design and he offered two four-cylinder triple expansion engines which were adopted. Minister Barbey accepted Lagane's design on 10 April 1891 but more modifications followed. Minister Cavaignac on 8 March 1892 ordered the Machinery Commission to negotiate a contract with FCM for the ship which was to be named *Linois*. The contract was to include the use in the ship of some materials still on hand from the cancelled *Charles Martel*. The signed contract was forwarded to the Ministry on 4 August 1892 and approved on 12 August 1892.

This ship was widely rumoured in the press to have been designed and even built for Turkey, but the records on her origins contain no reference to Turkey and make it clear that she was designed to French navy specifications and built for that navy.

The 54mm shields for the 138.6mm guns were not installed until the end of 1896 after the ship had been in commission for 18 months. These guns were on mountings of a type unique to the ship. Their sponsons were a little too small, impeding training the guns to the forward and after extremes and slowing the rate of fire somewhat. The 100mm guns were too close to the ends of the ship, making them difficult to load for firing on the beam. In 1903 the two forward torpedo tubes were reported to be unusable in even moderate seas at slightly elevated speeds, and they were subsequently removed. The ram-shaped (inverted) bow was not intended for ramming. According to one of her commanders her length to beam ratio and the small area of her rudder were notably inferior to all of the navy's other ships, her speed was a step backwards (about one knot less), her boilers were too weak, and the labour needed to steam them at full speed could not be sustained. Cruisers of her size should also be able to carry twice as much coal.

*The characteristics are based on a devis dated 12.1895.*
**Dimensions & tons:** 102.200m oa, 100.000m wl, 98.003m pp (tip fwd to rudder) x 10.500m ext & wl. 2,344.652t disp. Draught: 4.508m mean, 5.525m aft. Men: 249.
**Machinery:** 6,600ihp designed at 164rpm and 11.250kg/cm² boiler pres-

The 3rd class cruiser *Linois* at Villefranche. The bow of a *D'Assas* class cruiser is on the right and the bow of the battleship *Bouvet* is on the left. *(Postcard by LL)*

sure (10.75kg/cm² at the engines). Trials (12.7.1895) 6,726.91ihp = 19.643kts at 165.525rpm and 11.050kg/cm² boiler pressure. 2 screws. 2 vertical triple expansion engines with 4 cylinders of 0.840m (1), 1.250m (1), and 1.330m (2) diameter and 0.600m stroke. 6 cylindrical direct flame Admiralty boilers (4 of 3.250m diameter and 2 of 2.864m diameter. 240t coal. Range 4,510.7nm @ 10.62kts.
**Armour:**
Decks: Armoured deck (extra mild steel) flat and slopes 40mm
Guns: Shields for 138.6mm and 100mm guns 54mm.
Conning tower (ordinary steel): 72mm.
**Guns:**
(1895) 4 x 138.6mm/45 M1891(2) QF (sponsons), 2 x 100mm/45 M1891(2) QF (forecastle and poop), 1 x 65mm/16 M1881 landing (used as a line throwing gun, *porte-amarres*), 4 x 47mm/40 M1885 QF, 2 x 37mm/20 M1885 QF, 4 x 37mm revolving cannon. **Torpedoes:** 4 tubes for 356mm M1887 torpedoes (2 forward and 2 sides, all above water). **Searchlights:** 4 x 60cm.
(1903-04) 4 x 138.6mm, 2 x 100mm, 6 x 47mm QF, 1 x 37mm QF for the boats, 4 torpedo tubes (the two forward ones soon removed)

*Linois* (H1) F.C. Méditerranée, La Seyne/FCM, Marseille.
On list 1.1893. Ord: 3.8.1892. K: 1892. L: 30.1.1894.
    Comm: 13.3.1895 (trials), 26.10.1895 (full).
Budget 1892 (designated D). Machinery installed 5.1894 to 29.1.1895. Trial results approved 15.7.1895. Full commission 26.10.1895 to replace *Lalande* in the reserve division of the *Escadre de la Méditerranée*. Refitted 1-4.1898, then served seven years in Morocco. Reserve at Toulon 1905-09. Spare boilers were built in 1906, conversion to an annex to the Naval Academy in *Borda* to replace *Bougainville* was considered in 1907, but Minister Thomson wrote on 2 April 1908 that credits were insufficient to refit the ship, partly because of exaggerated prices being asked to install the new boilers and partly because the Navy was spending too much on unproductive ships in reserve and needed to condemn some of them. Struck 9.3.1910. Sold 30.12.1910 to M. Martin.

----

***GALILÉE* Class.** *Croiseurs de 3e classe.* Protected cruisers with main guns in sponsons on the sides and with a ram-shaped bow. Two funnels, two masts. Designed by Albaret.

Naval constructor Jean Rosier Albaret, then Deputy director of materiel under Bienaymé, based his design on the specifications sent by Minister

Barbey on 23 November 1890 to FCM for *Linois* but he also included in it some improvements he felt to be advisable. He increased to 19 knots the speed at natural draught by using Belleville boilers, he increased to 72mm the thickness of the shields for the 138.6mm and 100mm guns and the conning tower, he gave the 138.6mm and 100mm guns the reglementary ammunition supply, he augmented the range with a normal coal supply to 3,000nm instead of 2,800nm and with bunkers full to 4400nm instead of 3200nm, and he restored the tonnage margin in the design to 4% from 3%. Based on a note from the Naval General Staff dated 19 February 1892 he placed the bow 100mm gun on a 70cm high platform (a change also made in *Linois*) and doubled the 47mm gun battery. The resulting design displaced 46 tons more than did *Linois*. The hull lines were derived from *Troude*.

On 21 May 1892 Minister Cavaignac forwarded Albaret's design to the *Conseil des travaux* for use, if it was acceptable, in building the 3rd class cruiser in the 1893 budget (*Galilée*). He wanted the plans and contracts for the ship to be prepared before the end of the year and asked the Council to examine the design on an urgent basis. The Council examined it on 21 June 1892. Albaret adopted two horizontal triple expansion engines in his design as Lagane had in *Linois* but proposed an alternative with two vertical four-cylinder triple expansion engines on each shaft. The Council was opposed to two engines on one shaft when a simpler solution was available, and the ship ended up with one three-cylinder vertical triple expansion engine on each shaft. Albaret adopted in his design the mansard type of protective deck, a polygonal type with a flat top and upper and lower sides sloping at increasing angles instead of the continuously curved type in *Surcouf*, but the Council felt that the upper sloping part had less protective value than the equivalent curved portions of the deck in *Surcouf* and, given the already weak 40mm thickness of the deck, opted for a curved connection between the flat top and the lower sloping side below the waterline. Finally it also moved the after 100mm gun aft to improve its depressed fire against torpedo boats attacking from astern. Like *Linois*, the ship also had two 37mm QF guns on the stern gallery for this purpose. Minister Burdeau approved Albaret's modified plans on 31 July 1892.

The two nearly-identical ships could be distinguished by the location of their after searchlights (on a platform on the poop in *Galilée* and on the after mast facing aft in *Lavoisier*). Their inverted bows were not designed for ramming. The two port 138.6mm guns in *Galilée* were rendered unserviceable by defective powder charges in 1909 ending her career.

*11. — "Le Galilée." — Croiseur éclaireur d'Escadre partant en mission à la recherche de "La Vienne".*
*A. Bougault*

The 3rd class cruiser *Galilée* stated to be departing to search for the missing transport *Vienne,* although here she is securely moored to a buoy, probably off Mourillon. The postcard caption calls her a *croiseur éclaireur d'escadre* (squadron scout cruiser), reflecting the fact that this class and *Linois* were built for action with a fleet in European waters and not duty on foreign stations. (*Postcard by A. Bougault*)

*The characteristics are based on a devis for* Galilée *dated 26.10.1897 and a devis for* Lavoisier *dated 23.4.1898.*

**Dimensions & tons:** 100.650m oa, 100.650m wl and pp (tip fwd to sternpost) x 10.700m ext & wl (10.900m outside sponsons). 2,355.599t disp. Draught: 4.5058m mean, 5.5193m aft. Men: 248. (*Lavoisier*) 2,353.022t disp. Draught: 4.5025m mean, 5.5160m aft.

**Machinery:** 6,400ihp designed at 165rpm and 17kg/cm² boiler pressure (12-13kg/cm² at engines). Trials (*Galilée* 25.8.1897) 7,047.6ihp = 19.796kts at 164.75rpm and 15.750kg/cm² boiler pressure; (*Lavoisier* 19.3.1898) 7,514.7ihp = 21.571kts at 173.81rpm and 16.687kg/cm² boiler pressure. 2 screws. 2 vertical triple expansion engines with 3 cylinders of 0.800m, 1,200m, and 1,860m diameter and 0.600m stroke. 16 Belleville boilers. 346t coal. Range (*Galilée*) 2,677.533nm @ 13.089kts; (*Lavoisier*) 2,296.673nm @ 15.817kts.

**Armour:**

Decks: Armoured deck (extra mild steel) flat and slopes 40mm.
Guns: Shields for 138.6mm and 100mm guns (special steel) 54mm.
Conning tower (cast steel): 52mm (on the bridge behind the pilot house)

**Guns:**

(1897-98) 4 x 138.6mm/45 M1887 (*Galilée*) or 138.6mm/45 M1893 (*Lavoisier*) QF (in sponsons), 2 x 100mm/45 M1891(2) QF (on forecastle and poop), 1 x 65mm/16 M1881 landing, 8 x 47mm/40 M1885 QF, 2 x 37mm/20 M1885 QF, 4 x 37mm revolving cannon.
**Torpedoes:** 2 tubes for 356mm M1887 torpedoes (sides, above water).
**Searchlights:** 4 x 60cm.

(1902) 4 x 138.6mm, 2 x 100mm, 1 x 65mm landing, 10 x 47mm QF, 1 x 37mm QF for the duty boat, 2 torpedo tubes for 356mm torpedoes. The torpedo tubes were removed from *Lavoisier* in 1906 and from *Galilée* in 1908 (having been reported useless in 1906).

(1915-17, *Lavoisier*) 4 x 138.6mm, 2 x 100mm, 2 x 47mmAA. Two other 47mm were landed in 10.1915 and 6 others were landed 8.1917, the ship having being instructed to retain only 2 x 47mm. Carried 8 Guiraud anti-submarine grenades on the poop while at sea, 4 from the trawler *Suzanne Céline* and 2 from the *Marrakchi*.

*Galilée* (H2) Rochefort Dyd/Indret (engines designed by Godard).
On list 1.1893. Ord: 20.8.1892. K: 11.4.1894. L: 28.4.1896. Comm: 1.3.1897 (trials), 28.10.1897 (full).
Budget 1893 (designated L). Machinery installed 31.1.1896 to 21.5.1897. Assigned to the *Escadre de la Méditerranée* 16.10.1897, trial results approved 26.10.1897, arrived at Toulon 8.11.1897 and joined the fleet there 10.11.1897. Operated primarily in the Mediterranean and specifically in Morocco and Tangier from 1903. Arrived at Rochefort 24.11.1909 and decomm. there 6.2.1910. Struck 3.8.1910, sold at Rochefort 17.11.1911.

*Lavoisier* (H3) Rochefort Dyd/Indret (engines designed by Godard).
On list 1.1894. Ord: 20.12.1893. K: 7.1.1895. L: 17.4.1897. Comm: 1.12.1897 (trials), 22.4.1898 (full).
Budget 1894. Machinery installed 6.3.1897 to 17.1.1898. Trial results approved 4.4.1898, placed in full commission 22.4.1898. Arrived at Toulon from Rochefort 3.5.1898 and joined the *Escadre de la Méditerranée*. To reserve 3.8.1901. Recomm. 16.3.1903 for the Newfoundland and Iceland station, made annual summer cruises there from Lorient and Rochefort thru 7.1914. War service in the Mediterranean to 4.1919. Arrived 8.1919 at Rochefort for repairs, ordered on 30.1.1920 to be decommissioned as soon as possible. Struck 7.6.1920. Sold 10.5.1921 at Rochefort to Jean Jules Louis Jacquart to BU.

———

*D'ESTRÉES* **Class.** *Croiseurs de 3e classe.* Protected cruisers with main guns on the forecastle and poop, secondary guns in sponsons, and with steel hulls sheathed with wood and copper. Two widely separated funnels, three masts, schooner rig. Designed by Tissier. *Croiseur léger* in 1.3.1920.

On 24 October 1889, a year before requesting the specifications for replacements for old 1st and 2nd class station cruisers that led to the *Descartes* and *Catinat* classes, Minister Krantz requested from the *Conseil des travaux* specifications for replacements for the small 230nhp and 250nhp station cruisers or avisos of the *Segond* and *Duchaffaut* types that were disappearing rapidly from the fleet. Krantz forwarded his own draft specifications which the Council examined on 12 November 1889, just after Barbey became Minister.

The result was a combination of old and new technologies in which the old dominated. Although the ship was to carry coal for 6,000nm at 10 knots the Council expected she would be spending much of her time under sail, and she was therefore to have a full barque rig and anything that might interfere with her sailing, notably twin screws, was excluded. She was to have a steel hull sheathed with wood and copper, one screw, a triple expansion engine, cylindrical or multitubular boilers, and a speed of 15 knots (considered enough since the ships being replaced could not make 13 knots) and provisions for modest forced draught. Her displacement was estimated at 1,600 tons. Her main battery was to be four 138.6mm BL guns in sponsons and five 65mm QF guns. The Council added to the Minister's specifications a protective deck over the machinery, but only against 65mm and smaller QF guns. Minister Barbey forwarded the final specifications to the ports on 17 December 1889, changing the 138.6mm guns to QF.

What followed was one of the slowest French ship procurements during this period. It took about seven years to get the first two replacements on order and eleven to get them into service. The main problem was the low priority of 3rd class station cruisers. On 15 July 1890 the Council reviewed five designs and selected two, by naval constructors Joseph Louis Léon Tissier and Albert Wahl, for further work. On 20 January 1891 the Council reviewed the designs from the two naval constructors and recommended the one by Tissier, although the sail plan seemed unbalanced and the stability after fuel consumption was questionable. By this time the thin protective deck consisted of 10mm hull plating end to end with another 10mm layer over the machinery. Minister Barbey approved the Council's recommendation on 6 February 1891. However, through late 1894 no 3rd class station cruisers appeared in the budgets, although the Programme of 1890 stated that twelve of these (which it then called 2nd class station cruisers) needed to be built.

On 20 October 1894 Minister of Marine Faure told Parliament that he planned to modify the 1895 budget with increased spending on new construction, and on 4 November 1894 he distributed a new list of ships to be built under that budget. In it the 1st class station cruiser *Jeanne d'Arc* was replaced by two *croiseurs grande vitesse* (*Guichen* and *Châteaurenault*) and two 3rd class station cruisers (K1 and K2). In December 1894 Tissier's 1891 design was sent back to the *Conseil des travaux*, but in the meantime the *Conseil supérieur* had decided that the speed of cruisers of this type should be increased by a knot to 16 knots with natural draught and 17 knots with moderately forced draught. The project was therefore removed from the agenda of the *Conseil des travaux* on 24 January 1895 and on the same date the ministry invited Tissier to rework his design accordingly. On 30 July 1895 the Council accepted Tissier's latest solution, which included a significant increase in displacement from 1,697 to 1,955 tons, a shift to twin screws with vertical triple expansion engines, and a modest reduction in the rig. The 1896 budget submission (5.1895) included another 3rd class station cruiser (K3, to be built at Rochefort), but the Budget Commission on 13 July 1895 deleted all 1896 station cruisers including K3 from the budget and cancelled credits for them on 24 October 1895. K1 and K2, the ships of the 1895 budget to have been built to Tissier's plans, were named on 23 August 1895 and negotiations were begun with FCM Le Havre for their construction, but on 4 December 1895 Minister Lockroy adjourned their construction until the budgetary situation permitted.

At this point Tissier evidently felt that the 1889 concept had been taken as far as it could go. In a note dated 26.11.1895, just after Lockroy became Minister and Bertin became Director of Material, Tissier proposed new specifications for 3rd class station cruisers, and a marginal note on the copy that made its way informally to the *Conseil des travaux* indicated that Bertin approved his proposal on 27 November 1895. Tissier's specifications made his ship more like *Surcouf*, *Linois*, *Galilée*, and HMS *Pelorus*, all four designed for operations in Europe rather than overseas. He noted that his design resembled *Pelorus* in speed and offensive strength but differed in having greater range and in using sheathing. His ship now had trivial sail area (three schooner-rigged masts with a square sail on the foremast). The displacement had grown to 2,452 tons from the 1,955 tons in the 1895 design and 1,697 tons in 1891. The length had similarly grown to 95m from 80m in 1895 and 75m in 1891. The ship still had a steel hull sheathed with wood and copper but had two screws and two vertical triple expansion engines as in the 1895 design, multitubular boilers, a speed of 20.5 knots with forced draught compared to 17 knots in 1895, and coal for 5,000nm at 10 knots or 7,500nm with coal surcharge. Her main battery was seven 100mm QF guns of which four were in sponsons, two on the forecastle and one aft. Protection consisted of a deck over the machinery of 20mm on the flat portion and 40mm on the slopes, 20mm plating over the magazines, and 10mm plating at the ends.

This design was discussed by the *Conseil des travaux* on 16 June 1896. The Council complained that the specifications on which it was based had not been submitted to it and stated that they did not respond to the conditions that the Council felt necessary for a station cruiser of this displacement. The Council insisted specially on the inadequacy of 100mm guns and on the necessary to include 138.6mm guns. It was willing to reduce the speed from 20.5 to 20 knots to make this possible. The final design included two 138.6mm guns instead of three 100mm on the forecastle and poop.

K1 (*D'Estrées*) was included in Lockroy's 1897 budget submitted in February 1896 and was then then started early with some leftover 1896 funds. Besnard's revision of the 1897 budget submitted in June 1897 included K2 (*Infernet*) to follow her. The first proposal in April 1897 for a supplemental 1897 budget contained two more 2,500-ton station protected cruisers at Rochefort (K3 and K4) but these were deleted in the revised programme of July 1897 in favour of the armoured cruisers C5 and C6.

In February 1900 after trials the commander of *D'Estrées*, while complaining about her weak armament, gave her unusual praise for her habitability (which was bad or worse in most ships of the period), her ample coal supply, and the very good arrangement of the engines and boilers which were placed in vast well ventilated compartments that permitted steaming at 17 to 18 knots for several days without fatiguing the personnel. The coal bunkers were also within easy reach of the boilers.

*Infernet* received a general inspection in 1903 while deployed in the Indian Ocean and the inspector stated that while the ship overall was in excellent condition, her eight Normand boilers were 'the most detestable boilers in service in large ships'. (They were, however, very successful in torpedo boats and also in *Châteaurenault*.) According to him, each boiler contained 1,014 tubes of 30mm diameter in a staggered arrangement that formed a truly inextricable network into which it was impossible to introduce a tool to clean out the scale in the tubes. As a result, after a period of operation, they became so clogged that their efficiency became insignificant and their pressure became very difficult to maintain. The boilers also burned an enormous amount of coal which made refuelling more and more complicated. The crew inspected the boilers at Diego Suarez and on 18 July 1905 her commander cabled Paris: 'All the boilers are in bad condition, the ship can no longer navigate in full security.' He requested that the ship be relieved, which she was at the end of the year. Her total length of service was a bit over five years.

*D'Estrées* had the same model boilers as *Infernet* but was more fortunate in their employment. During her Atlantic cruises *D'Estrées* had several opportunities to receive boiler maintenance, while *Infernet* had none in the Indian Ocean. By 1908 both *D'Estrées* and the older *Surcouf* needed boiler retubing, but the estimated cost of returning the ships to service was

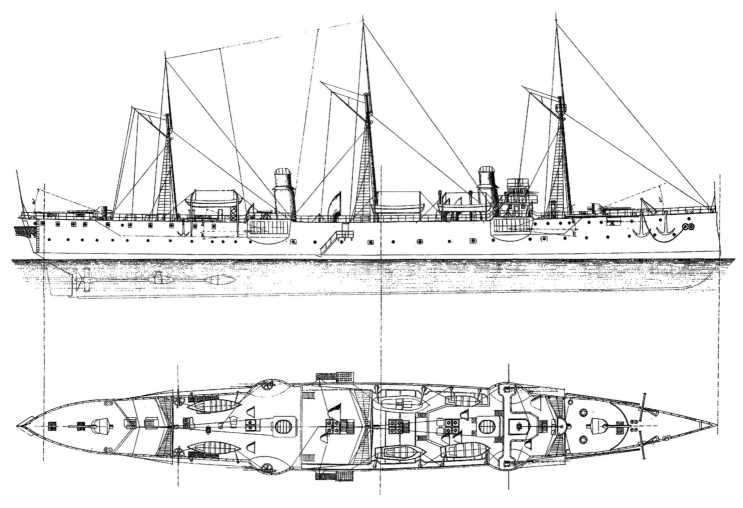

Outboard profile and overhead view (*plan d'ensemble*) of the 3rd class station cruiser *D'Estrées*, being built to the plans of M. Tissier. The plans were signed at Rochefort on 4 August 1899 by naval constructor Ch. Wall. The small calibre artillery carried at this time included 4 x 100mm/45 M1893 guns (on the upper deck in large sponsons), 8 x 47mm M1885 QF guns (4 on top of the 100mm sponsons, 2 on the poop abreast the after mast, and 2 on the upper deck in the hull forward of the bow 138.6mm gun), and 2 x 37mm M1885 QF guns for the boats. There was also 1 x 65mm M1881 landing gun.

201,940 and 84,717 francs respectively compared to over 530,000 francs for *Infernet*. The Deputy Central Director of Naval Construction recommended to Minister Picard on 21 January 1909 that, in view of the navy's shortage of ships of this type, the repairs should be authorized immediately. Both survived to help offset a severe shortage in small cruising ships during World War I.

*The characteristics are based on a devis for* D'Estrées *dated 5.2.1900 with data for* Infernet *from a devis dated 11.3.1901.*

**Dimensions & tons:** 98.540m oa, 95.000m wl and pp (tip fwd to stern) x 12.000m ext & wl (13.060m outside sponsons). 2,588.836t disp. Draught: 4.915m mean, 5.614m aft. Men: 247.

**Machinery:** 8,500ihp designed at 175rpm and 15kg/cm² boiler pressure (same at the engines). Trials (*D'Estrées* 29.11.1899) 8,772.4ihp = 20.222kts at 181.45rpm and 14.526kg/cm² boiler pressure; (*Infernet* 10.4.1900) 8,701.3ihp = 20.994kts at 180.55rpm and 14.543kg/cm² boiler pressure. 2 screws. 2 vertical triple expansion engines with 3 cylinders of 0.730m, 1.080m. and 1.700m diameter and 0.760m stroke. 8 Normand boilers. 534t coal. Range (*Infernet*) 6,485.148nm @ 9.672kts, 3,367.766nm @ 14.045kts.

**Armour:**

Decks: Armoured deck (extra mild steel) flat 20mm hull plating end to end, slopes 40mm hull plating over engines and boilers.

Guns: Shields for 138.6mm and 100mm guns (special steel) 54mm.

Conning tower: none.

**Guns:**

(1900-01) 2 x 138.6mm/45 M1893 QF (on forecastle and poop), 4 x 100mm/45 M1893 QF (on upper deck in sponsons), 1 x 65mm/16 M1881 landing, 8 x 47mm/40 M1885 QF, 2 x 37mm/20 M1885 QF for the boats. **Torpedoes:** none. **Searchlights:** 2 x 60cm.

*D'Estrées* (K1) Rochefort Dyd/Schneider, Creusot.

On list 1.1897. Ord: 29.7.1896. K: 3.3.1897. L: 27.10.1897. Comm: 20.2.1899 (trials), 16.2.1900 (full).

Budget 1895 (delayed, added to 1896). Machinery installation begun 25.7.1898, boilers first fired and first static trial 9.5.1899. Trial results approved 6.2.1900. Atlantic station 1900-03, 1906-08 and 1911. On 15.6.1912 replaced *Bougainville* as seagoing annex to the Naval Academy in *Borda* and then in *Duguay-Trouin* at Brest. Served in the Mediterranean and Indian Ocean during World War I. Struck 27.10.1922. Reserved 1922-1923 for conversion to a *patache* (police and customs hulk in a military port) at Toulon instead of *Inconstant* but instead sold 26.3.1924 to Bertorello Sanpierdarena of Italy.

*Infernet* (K2) C.A. Gironde, Bordeaux-Lormont/Schneider, Creusot.

On list 1.1897. Ord: 9.12.1896. K: 1896. L: 7.9.1899. Comm: 15.10.1899 (trials), 15.9.1900 (full).

Budget 1895 (delayed to 1897). Machinery installation begun 1.4.1899, boilers first fired and first static trial 11.9.1899. Transited to Rochefort 8.10.1899. Trial results approved 27.4.1900. Arrived at Brest

30.9.1900 and joined the *Escadre du Nord*. Detached from the *Escadre du Nord* 1.3.1901 (ordered 28.12.1900 and 9.2.1901) and designated to replace *Nielly* in the Indian Ocean. Left Brest 12.3.1901 for the Indian Ocean (DM 7.2.1901). Returned to Rochefort 1.1906 with serious boiler problems. Minister Thomson notified Rochefort on 8.10.1907 that he had decided to refit her, but a closer look by Indret in 4.1908 showed that the boilers would need at least a total retubing along with other work. On 5.5.1909 Minister Picard directed Rochefort to begin the process to condemn the ship. Struck 9.3.1910. Offered for sale 15.9.1910 at Rochefort, offered again 25.10.1910 and sold to German breakers. She was towed out of Rochefort by the tug *Hercule* but encountered bad weather and ran onto the Sauveterre beach 16.11.1910 at the Sables d'Olonne, could not be refloated and was BU in place. (*Protet*, also then under tow to German breakers, survived the same storm and arrived at Hamburg in December.)

---

## (E) Cruiser Torpedo Boat Carriers (*Croiseurs porte-torpilleurs*).

### Precursors

The idea of a torpedo boat mother ship was first advanced by the torpedo school at Boyardville in the 1870s. The function of this mother ship was to carry torpedo boats to the scene of action. This idea, along with that of carrying specially-built small torpedo boats on the decks of battleships, became quite common, and the French navy's torpedo school ship, the converted merchantman *Japon*, was equipped to carry five. The British also implemented the idea in HMS *Hecla*, a merchantman acquired and converted during the Russian war scare of 1878.

While developing the Programme of 1881, the *Conseil d'Amirauté* on 6 May 1881 concluded that it was indispensable to create special transports able to embark torpedo boats or craft and launch them for operations. It noted that *Japon* had been fitted out for this purpose but that this ship was already old and could not suffice. The navy needed a very fast ship able to get past cruisers and strike enemy fleets in their anchorages, then recover the boats' crews and return. It added two such ships to the programme, raising the total of transports from 34 to 36. On 18 October 1881 the *Conseil des travaux*, while examining a design to fit the transports *Mytho* and *Annamite* for transporting torpedo boats, called for a study of a special ship with a speed of 15 knots and a range equal to that of battleships that was fitted to carry the largest possible number of torpedo boats of the largest size that could be embarked and disembarked in moderate weather. In 1883 *Mytho* and *Annamite* carried to China some torpedo boats which carried out successful attacks under Courbet. In 1887 the British began construction of a fast cruiser also equipped as a torpedo depot ship and torpedo-boat carrier, HMS *Vulcan*. She was to accompany a fleet and support attacks by the torpedo boats carried by the battleships along with nine of her own against an enemy fleet in its harbour and also provide support to all of the fleet's torpedo boats and their torpedoes. *Vulcan* was commissioned in 1891.

---

**FOUDRE.** *Croiseurs porte-torpilleurs.* Cruiser-type hull dominated by two long gantries to handle small torpedo boats and with three small funnels clustered amidships between the gantries, two pole masts, and main guns in sponsons on the sides. Designed by Duplaà-Lahitte. To *Croiseur de 2ᵉ classe* 1.1908, *Croiseur de 2ᵉ classe* with the explanation *Aviation* 1.1914.

On 25 March 1890 the *Conseil des travaux* examined a proposal to convert the large transport *Gironde* to a *transport d'escadre* which would carry torpedo boats and supplies, but the Navy decided to build a new ship instead and on 9 April 1890 asked the Council for specifications for a *transport spécial d'escadre* (special squadron transport). The Council produced the specifications on 13 May 1890. The ship was to embark ten torpedo boats of 12 tons and 18 metres in length and the lifting gear was to be able to launch four of them simultaneously, two on each side. The boat handling gantry system developed at La Seyne for the Spanish battleship *Pelayo* and also used in the French *Marceau*, was suggested as a suitable model. The ship was to provide operational support for its boats and was to have a torpedo repair shop. The ship itself was to have two screws, a speed of 18.5 knots with natural draught, an armament of eight 100mm guns, a protective deck like that in *Jean Bart* with 60mm of steel on the flat portions and more on the slopes, a crew of 350 men including 80 for the torpedo boats, and two military masts.

On 18 November 1890 the Council examined three designs submitted in response to its specifications of 13 May 1890 and selected two of them, by naval constructors Jean Casimir Duplaà-Lahitte and Just Lucien Maurice, for further development. The design of Lahitte was 107.90m long, displaced 5,557 tons, and had machinery of 9,700ihp for 18.5 knots. It used the boat handling gantry system developed by FCM for *Pelayo* and *Marceau* and had two large gantries to handle the ten torpedo boats, one forward and one aft of the funnels, and smaller gantries each side of the funnels for her own boats. One of the few criticisms was that the form of the stern above water had a 'disgraceful look'. However, the Council also found that the displacement would need to be increased as the weights of some items had been underestimated. On 2 June 1891 it examined modified plans from the two constructors and selected those of Lahitte. The shape of the stern had been remedied and the ship was now 113.0 feet long and displaced 5,970 tons. The boat handling gear was for 12-ton boats as specified but on 12 May 1891 the Council had increased this to 15 tons in its specifications for the torpedo boats to be carried by this ship (see *Torpilleurs A-B* in Chapter 11) and added that it would be well to calculate for 16 tons in case it was decided to order from Yarrow as a trial some of the boats of the type adopted by the Admiralty for *Hecla* and *Vulcan* (see *Torpilleur C*). The ship's hull lines would have to be filled out somewhat to carry the heavier torpedo boats. Lahitte estimated that the time that a boat afloat alongside could be attached, raised, put into its position aboard, and the gear lowered for another boat was 1.5 minutes, the Council felt the real number was 9 to 10 minutes. On 20 October 1891 Minister Barbey approved Lahitte's final design, directed the Machinery Commission to negotiate for her construction, and named the ship *Seine* (traditionally transports were named after French rivers). She was reclassified as a cruiser and renamed *Foudre* one month later in recognition of her combat role. The number of torpedo boats to be carried was reduced from ten to eight on 27 February 1892. The signed contract for her construction was forwarded by the Machinery Commission on 9 June 1892 and approved on 6 July 1892.

*Foudre* was designed with military masts but during construction they were cut off at the level of the boat handling gantries and simple poles were substituted above this level. The ship had no shipboard torpedo installation but carried many torpedoes and 232 moored contact blockade mines to support the fleet that she accompanied. She had a large machine shop and foundry that could perform a wide range of repairs and she carried a great variety of supplies for ships in company. She could also support torpedo boats with coal, water, provisions, and even compressed air. She received *Torpilleur A* on 13 May 1896 and *Torpilleur B* on 24 September 1896 and also carried old vedettes like *Torpilleur 30* and *Torpilleurs 56-59*.

On 19 February 1896 a new Minister of Marine, Lockroy, wrote to the Maritime Prefect at Toulon stating that the lengthy experiments conducted with the transport *Japon* as a torpedo boat carrier gave rise to doubts on the military value of *croiseurs porte-torpilleurs* and on their ability to disembark their torpedo boats in the open ocean. In its most recent meeting the *Conseil supérieur* had advised postponing until after the trials of *Foudre* the other ships of this type in the Programme of 1890. Lockroy suggested going further, renouncing the torpedo boat role for *Foudre* too, and converting her into a cruiser. He asked Toulon to draw up a design for such a conversion as soon as possible. He also suspended the order for *Torpilleurs D* through *I* which she was to carry. The *Conseil des travaux* examined the resulting conversion design by Lahitte on 21 July 1896, found technical

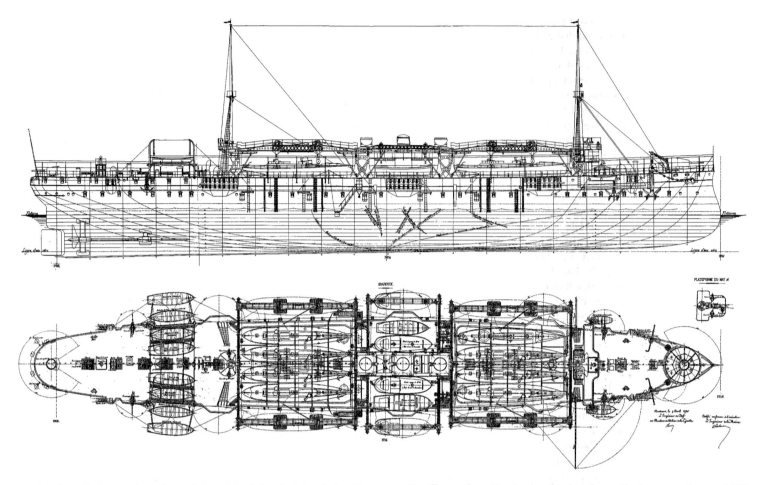

Outboard profile from the lines plan and plan of the shelter deck (*spardeck*) of the torpedo boat carrying cruiser *Foudre* built on the plans of M. Lahitte. Plans by the Chantiers et Ateliers de la Gironde were signed at Bordeaux on 9 April 1896 by the chief engineer of the company and certified to represent the ship as fitted by naval constructor Edelman, the Navy's control officer at Bordeaux. The small calibre artillery carried at this time included 8 x 100mm M1891 guns (her main gun armament: 1 on the forecastle, 1 on the poop, and 6 on the upper deck in large sponsons), 4 x 65mm M1891 QF guns (2 on the forecastle and 2 on the poop), and 5 x 37mm M1887 QF guns (3 in 4 positions on the sides of the shelter deck and 2 on the bridge above the commander's sea cabin). There were also 2 x 65mm M1881 landing guns stowed on the upper deck.

issues with it, and advised conducting full trials with *Foudre* as designed and completed before undertaking a conversion. By this time Besnard had replaced Lockroy as Minister. In August the Director of Materiel drafted a note to Toulon directing it to follow up on the recommendations of the Council, but the Director of Artillery intervened saying that the eight 164.7mm guns in Lahitte's design would not be available for two years. The conversion idea then appears to have been dropped.

On 14 April 1897 Minister Besnard accepted the torpedo boat handling system in *Foudre* following successful completion of the trials called for in the contract, which were with the ship immobile in an anchorage. But this was not sufficient to prove that it would work at sea, and Besnard directed two more trials, the first with the ship immobile in an anchorage but with an induced 10-degree list, then trials at sea in weather suitable for navigation by *Foudre*'s torpedo boats. The stationary trials with the 10-degree list were successfully conducted on 23 and 24 August 1897 and the first trials underway were conducted on 6 and 7 December 1897 to the full satisfaction of the ship's commander, but operations during summer exercises in 1898 through 1901 indicated that her torpedo boats were too small to operate at sea and could only be embarked and disembarked in a flat calm or in a harbour.

*Torpilleur-vedette C* arrived at Toulon from Cherbourg in August 1898 and was delivered to the naval construction directorate there for inspection on 5 October 1898. As of 1 November 1898 *Foudre* could embark within the next ten days six torpedo boats, *A, B, C*, and *Nos 30, 56*, and *57. Nos 58* and *59* seemed a bit too long to be hoisted on board without further study.

On 8 June 1899 Minister Lockroy informed Toulon that he had decided to replace the wooden-hulled cruiser *Iphigénie* with *Foudre* as school ship for midshipmen effective 1 October 1899, and he asked for the necessary design work. Vice Admiral Fournier, then Commander in Chief of the *Escadre de la Méditerranée*, wrote an impassioned response on 11 June 1899 stating that any naval force conducting a strategic operation needed an accompanying resupply force, and that *Foudre* was invaluable in this role, above all because of her repair facilities. Fournier had full information on the U.S. Navy's use of its converted repair ship USS *Vulcan* during the Spanish-American War, and for the past seven months he had been working to develop *Foudre*'s repair facilities including its personnel. This progress would be lost and *Foudre* would be wasted if she became a school ship. Lockroy left office one day after Fournier wrote his letter, and *Iphigénie* was instead replaced a year later by the transport *Tonquin*, which was renamed *Duguay Trouin*.

On 10 December 1900 *Foudre* was ordered fitted with a winch on the stern for handling a captive balloon. While she was in reserve between 1902 and 1904 it was decided to send her eight torpedo boats with four small submarines to join the *Défense mobile* at Saigon, and she carried them out in two voyages in 1904 and 1905, the after gantries being removed to accommodate the submarines. The removal of the after gantries was made permanent on 31 March 1905 and the forward gantries were ordered removed on 26 June 1907.

A confidential dispatch dated 9 June 1906 stated that *Foudre* should be considered primarily as a *transport ravitailleur d'escadres* (squadron replenishment ship), specifically carrying moored contact blockade mines (*torpilles automatiques mécaniques* or *mines de blocus*) and demolition ordnance (*torpilles de déblaiement*) for use by a fleet. On 27 November 1906 the Naval General Staff stated that with this in mind it made sense to fit her to lay the contact mines herself. On 3 June 1907 Minister of Marine Gaston Thomson ordered her fitted to carry permanently 300 to 400 Model 1906 contact mines while retaining the existing repair facilities, and on 11 April 1908 Thomson ordered Toulon to proceed with this plan, the number of mines to be 350. On 19 October 1908 the design for the conversion submitted by Toulon on 29 August 1908 received final approval. The mines would be laid by means of overhead rails leading to the stern, each mine being pushed by two men. Conversion work began in earnest in June 1909 and between April and July 1910 she participated in the summer exercises of the *Escadre de la Méditerranée* as a minelayer. The former torpedo aviso *Casabianca* was converted to a minelayer in 1911 and trials in December 1911 showed that using overhead mine rails like those in *Foudre* was impractical and 0.50m gauge deck rails like those in the Decauville railroad were adopted instead for both her, her sister *Cassini*, and *Foudre*. On 9 February and 22 March 1912 Minister of Marine Théophile Delcassé informed Toulon that *Foudre* was no longer to lay mines but was to be used as a mine transport accompanying the fleet and was to transfer mines to 450-ton and 800-ton destroyers which were to lay them. She would be fitted with double Decauville tracks on her 1st deck to take the mines from their storage holds to the point where they would be transferred to a minelayer, either through three loading ports on each side amidships and two in the stern or by davits. The overhead rail and arched mine ports would be retained. By 11 May 1912 the conversion had been cut back to a minimum but Toulon still did not know what kinds of mines and how many were to be carried.

In the meantime *Foudre* became involved with the navy's first experiments with aircraft. In January 1911 Minister of Marine Vice Admiral Boué de Lapeyrère indicated a desire to install on *Foudre* a 'platform for the departure and return of aeroplanes'. As of 31 October 1911 René Daveluy, the *Capitaine de vaisseau chargé de l'organisation de l'Aviation Maritime*, reported that the platform would be over 45m long, that it would be costly and require the removal of the after mast and a hoist, and that it was not to be proceed with until after numerous experiments ashore. However, it was possible to use *Foudre* in the role of housing aircraft by making only slight changes, the main ones being providing a light deck in the area formerly occupied by the after torpedo boats, putting a cargo boom on the after mast to hoist aircraft onto and off of the deck, and providing a light wood and cloth hangar to protect the aircraft when on board. Installation of the hangar was completed in early January 1912.

On 14 October 1912 a new commander of *Foudre*, Capitaine de frégate Fatou, who was also the *Commandant supérieur de l'Aviation Maritime*, wrote to the Chief of the Naval General Staff, which had an aviation section, with a plan to fit *Foudre* so that aircraft could take off from the ship rather than from the water using floats. The ship would assist by stopping or steaming into the wind. His proposal included a clear deck forward about 30m or 35m long, the space being cleared by moving the bridge, conning tower and the foremast aft into the space occupied by the forward group of torpedo boats. The foremast would get a boom like the one on the mainmast, the bow 100mm gun would be removed, and the funnels would be raised 4m. Between 1 February and 28 August 1913 Fatou cleared the forward part of the ship by moving the bridge and foremast back and made some of the other changes, while the platform was fitted by a contractor between February and April 1914. On 8 May 1914 a Caudron G3 piloted by René Caudron took off from this platform. *Foudre* entered World War I in this configuration. The 100mm gun that was removed in June 1913 was re-embarked at Malta by ship's company on 18 February 1915.

*The characteristics are based on a devis dated 28.1.1898.*

**Dimensions & tons:** 118.701m oa, 116.030m wl, 114.200m pp (tip fwd to rudder) x 15.648m ext (below wl, 17.200m outside sponsons), 15.608m wl. 6,076.314t disp. Draught: 6.240m mean, 7.372m aft. Men: 409.

**Machinery:** 11,500ihp designed at 109rpm and 15kg/cm$^2$ boiler pressure (12kg/cm$^2$ at the engines). Trials (27.10.1896) 11,807.7ihp = 19.578kts at 106.8875rpm and 13.462kg/cm$^2$ boiler pressure. 2 screws. 2 vertical triple expansion engines with 3 cylinders of 1.010m, 1.500m, and 2.320m diameter and 0.900m stroke. 24 Lagrafel et d'Allest boilers (built by Fraissinet, Marseille). 845.500t coal (capacity 915.842t). Range 7,507.10nm @ 9.9775kts.

**Armour:**

Decks: Armoured deck (extra mild steel) flat 44mm, upper and lower slopes 104mm, cellular layer with cofferdam above it.

Guns: Shields for 100mm guns 54mm.

Conning tower: 120mm (removed c1908)

**Guns:**

(1898) 8 x 100mm/45 M1891(2) Canet QF (1 on forecastle, 1 on poop, 6 in sponsons), 4 x 65mm/50 M1891 QF, 2 x 65mm/16 M1881 landing, 5 x 37mm/20 M1885 QF. **Torpedoes:** none for the ship. **Searchlights:** 6 x 60cm.

(1905) 8 x 100mm, 4 x 65mm QF, 2 x 65mm landing, 2 x 47mm/40 M1885 QF (called automatic, ordered added September 1901), 2 x 37mm QF for the boats. No torpedo tubes. By 1916 the 2 x 47mm were fitted for anti-aircraft fire.

*Foudre* (L1) C.A. Gironde, Bordeaux-Lormont/Schneider, Creusot. On list 1.1893. Ord: 8.6.1892 (contract). K: 1892. L: 20.10.1895. Comm: 1.2.1896 (trials), 23.10.1897 (full).

Budget 1892 (designated G). Named *Seine* 20.10.1891, renamed 30.11.1891. First static machinery trial 26.10.1895. Crew roster opened 1.2.1896, left Bordeaux 16.2.1896, arrived Toulon 6.3.1896. Accepted for service (*clôture d'armement*) 26.10.1897. Joined the *Escadre de la Méditerranée* 1.11.1897. To normal reserve 1.1.1902 and special reserve 9.2.1903. Recommissioned 1.3.1904, transported eight of her torpedo boats and four small submarines (*Protée, Lynx, Perle* and *Esturgeon*) to Saigon in two voyages 1904-1905. To special reserve at Toulon 12.1.1906. Designated for use as a repair ship 1907, boilers retubed 1909-10, recomm. as a minelayer 15.4.1910, returned to special reserve 1.7.1910 after manoeuvres with the *Escadre de la Méditerranée*. Recommissioned as an aviation transport 1.9.1911, helped create the naval air base at Saint Raphaël 1912, fuller aviation conversion at Toulon 1913 and early 1914. In World War I transported aircraft to Bonifacio 8.1914 and Port Said 11-12.1914, served as a depot and repair ship for armed trawlers at Mudros 3-5.1915 during the Dardanelles operation, then operated in the Eastern Mediterranean for the rest of the war. Rated *bâtiment atelier* (repair ship) 1.3.1920. Struck 27.7.1921. Sold 27.5.1922 to M. Saglia to BU.

## (F) Torpedo Cruisers (*Croiseurs torpilleurs*).

Added in the 1.1883 fleet list as *Torpilleurs éclaireurs* under *Bâtiments torpilleurs* but reclassed and moved to cruiser category as *croiseurs torpilleurs* 1.1885. To *Contre-torpilleurs d'escadre* 1.1896, to *Contre-torpilleurs* 1.1901, and to *torpilleurs d'escadre* 1.1914.

*CONDOR* Class. *Croiseurs torpilleurs.* Miniature protected cruisers with main guns under the forecastle, in sponsons amidships, and on the poop, and with a ram-shaped bow. One large funnel, three pole masts (later two) capable of spreading triangular sails. Designed by de Bussy.

In a five-day discussion ending on 16 August 1879 of a new Programme of 1879, the Conseil d'Amirauté added to the eight 2nd class coast defence ships in the Programme of 1872 four fast torpedo ships protected in the bow against small arms fire. They were to defend ports and harbours or accompany a battle squadron, but only in the waters in which they were stationed. They were to be fitted with torpedo tubes and spars, were not to exceed 1,000 tons, and were to be more habitable but somewhat slower than the smaller torpedo boats, being able to make 14 or 15 knots. They were to be called *gardes-côtes torpilleurs*. On 6 May 1881 when drafting the Programme of 1881, the Council decided that these ships, which did not yet exist, could not be considered coast defence ships and it moved them to the torpedo boat category. It explained that these were of larger dimensions and somewhat greater range than other torpedo boats, making them capable of reaching anchorages where the enemy would feel safe from cruisers or a blockading squadron. It felt that this type should be studied although only a few should be built.

On 29 July 1882 Minister of Marine Jauréguiberry forwarded to the *Conseil des travaux* a design for a 1,240-ton *torpilleur-aviso* produced by de Bussy as director of the *Service technique des constructions navales* to specifications supplied by the Minister, no doubt with de Bussy's help. These included a speed of 17 knots, a range of 1,800nm at 10 knots, an armoured deck 40mm to 60mm thick, an armament of five 10cm guns and five above-water torpedo tubes, and a displacement preferably not over 1,200 tons. The Minister and de Bussy felt this would be possible based on the example of the small cruiser *Arturo Prat* then building in Britain for Chile and two similar vessels built for China before her. (Chile sold *Arturo Prat* to Japan before completion and she was renamed *Tsukushi*.) De Bussy was inspired by the ability of Armstrong at Elswick to get a high speed and powerful artillery (two ten-inch guns) on a relatively small displacement. He felt that since the French ship would not carry the big guns she could be given instead the protection that the Chilean ship lacked.

De Bussy's design measured 68.0m in length and displaced 1,240 tons. The lines were based on *Arturo Prat* but with slightly more length and slightly less beam giving her even finer lines. The engines were those of the *Prat* with the diameter of the cylinders being augmented by 1/15$^{th}$ to obtain 3,200ihp and 17 knots. The machinery was very light but no lighter than that in *Milan*. The ship had four cylindrical direct-flame boilers as in *Prat*. The protective deck, absent from *Prat*, curved down amidships from near the waterline to 0.80m below it at the sides and it also curved down forward and aft of the machinery to the ends. It was made up of three plates, two of 10mm and one of 20mm. There was also a flat splinter deck below it over the machinery. The Council noted that the 40mm deck should be proof against the 64pdr guns in the British cruisers *Iris* and *Comus*, and while it was almost entirely below the waterline leaving the deck level above it vulnerable it was probably the most that could be done on the displacement and was better than the protection in the larger HMS *Comus*. The designed armament was five 100mm, four 37mm revolving cannon (the specifications were for eight), and five above-water torpedo tubes. The *Conseil des travaux* examined de Bussy's design on 1 August 1882 and accepted it with reservations only on the coal supply, the height of the amidships guns above the waterline, and the placement of the torpedo tubes. On 2 August 1882 Minister of Marine Jauréguiberry published his decision to begin construction of four *avisos-torpilleurs* and on 5 August 1882 he allocated them to two dockyards and ordered them to prepare to begin their construction. He issued similar orders for the eight armoured gunboats in the Programme of 1881 at the same time.

At this time the French were having difficulty settling on nomenclature for their larger torpedo craft. By the time their designs were discussed by the *Conseil des travaux* on 1 August 1882 the *Condor* class had become *torpilleur-avisos* and the smaller *Bombe* class *torpilleurs de haute mer*. The *Condor* class appeared in the *Liste de la Flotte* at the beginning of 1883 in the torpedo vessel category as *torpilleurs éclaireurs*, the *Bombe* class now being *torpilleurs avisos* and the largest torpedo boats being *torpilleurs gardes-côtes de 1re classe*. In the January 1885 fleet list the *Condor* class was moved to the cruiser category as *croiseurs torpilleurs* while the *Bombe* class moved to the aviso category as *avisos torpilleurs* and the torpedo vessel category gained the new *Balny* class *torpilleurs de haute mer* along with the *torpilleurs de 1re classe* and the smaller torpedo boat types.

The engines for three of the ships were built at Marseille, but those for *Condor* were built by R. & W. Hawthorn under a contract approved on

26 February 1883. The *Condor* class originally had three masts, but the middle one was suppressed by a ministerial order to Toulon on 10 March 1891. The replacement of the original 100mm guns with guns converted to QF was directed by Minister Barbey on 3 March 1891 and 27 May 1891. To accommodate them the ports in the forecastle had to be enlarged and the sponsons amidships lengthened 50cm at the front. The torpedo tubes were ordered removed by Minister Besnard on 22 March 1895. The inverted bow was unsuitable for ramming.

*The characteristics are based on a design plan dated 9.9.1882 and a devis for* Condor *dated 4.1.1887.*

**Dimensions & tons:** (Plan) c68.70m oa, 68.00 wl (wl fwd to wl aft), 66.00m pp (wl fwd to rudder) x 8.90m ext and wl. 1,242.891t disp. Draught: 4.169m mean, 4.775m aft. Men: 134. (Devis) 65.883m pp (wl fwd to rudder) x 8.904m ext and wl. 1,269.611t disp. Draught 4.24m mean, 4.70m aft.

**Machinery:**
(*Condor*) 500nhp (800nhp forced) and 3,200ihp designed at 139rpm and 7kg/cm$^2$ boiler pressure. Trials (2.11.1886) 3,334.46ihp = 17.512kts at 136.09rpm. 2 screws. 2 horizontal compound engines with return connecting rods and 2 cylinders of 0.762m and 1.524m diameter and 0.9144m stroke. 4 cylindrical direct flame boilers. 135t coal.
(*Faucon*, design) 500nhp (800nhp forced) and 3,300ihp forced designed at 130rpm and 7kg/cm$^2$ boiler pressure. Speed 17kts. 2 screws. 2 compound engines with direct connecting rods and two horizontal (slightly inclined at 6°) cylinders of 0.762m and 1.524m diameter and 0.914m stroke. 4 cylindrical direct-flame Admiralty boilers. 145.3t coal. Range 2,100nm @ 10kts.

**Armour:**
Decks: Armoured deck flat and slopes 40mm, with cofferdam. A separate 10mm splinter layer was located 0.25m below the armoured deck over the machinery.

**Guns:**
(1887) 5 x 100mm/26.2 M1881 (2 under the forecastle, 2 amidships in sponsons, 1 on the poop), 1 x 65mm/16 M1881 (landing), 6 x 37mm revolving cannon. **Torpedoes:** 5 above-water torpedo tubes for 356mm M1880 (4.42m) torpedoes (2 forward, 2 side, 1 stern). **Searchlights:** 2 x 40cm.
(1892) 5 x 100mm/26.2 M1881 QF, 4 x 47mm/40 M1885 QF, 4 x 37mm revolving cannon, 4 or 5 torpedo tubes (the stern tube may have been removed), 3 x 60cm searchlights.
(1895) 5 x 100mm, 6 x 47mm, 4 x 37mm QF, 2 x 37mm revolving cannon. All torpedo tubes removed.
(1901) 5 x 100mm, 8 x 47mm, 1 x 37mm QF for the boat.

*Condor* Rochefort Dyd/Hawthorn, Newcastle on Tyne.
On list 1.1883. Ord: c9.1882. K: 4.1883. L: 16.5.1885. Comm: 1.7.1886 (trials), 1.1.1887 (full).
Budget 1884. Engines installed by Mr. Brown 2.1885 to 8.1886. Boilers first lit off 23.2.1886. Arrived at Toulon 26.1.1887, joined the *Escadre d'évolutions* 26.2.1887. To 2$^{nd}$ category reserve 5.2.1890. Rejoined the *Escadre* fully manned 17.7.1891, artillery modified 1893, continued to serve in the *Escadre* and its reserve division until placed in 2$^{nd}$ category reserve 23.5.1895 for new boilers. Recommissioned 1.2.1896 to replace *Hirondelle* as station ship at Bizerte. Replaced *Milan* 1.8.1898 in the reserve division of the *Escadre*. Station ship in Crete 1898-1906. Replaced in Crete by *Faucon*, proposed for condemnation 25.7.1906 and decommissioned 20.8.1906. Struck 19.4.1907. Sold 27.11.1907 to M. Martin of Marseille.

*Épervier* Rochefort Dyd/F.C. Méditerranée, Marseille.
On list 1.1883. Ord: c9.1882. K: 13.3.1883. L: 15.10.1886. Comm: 20.10.1887 (trials), 13.4.1888 (full).
Budget 1884. Assigned to the *Escadre d'évolutions* 2.1888, joined the *Division navale cuirassée du Nord* later that year, but placed in 2$^{nd}$

category reserve 1890. In commission with the *Escadre du Nord* 1892-99 but only operated actively for a few months in 1892 and again in 1898. To 2nd category reserve 1899. Struck 5.11.1909, for sale at Cherbourg 1909-1911.

*Faucon* Toulon Dyd/F.C. Méditerranée, Marseille.
On list 1.1883. Ord: c2.8.1882. K: 6.11.1882. L: 14.7.1887.
   Comm: 17.10.1887 (trials). C: 5.1888.
Budget 1884. Trial results approved 8.5.1888. In 2nd category reserve 1888-91. In commission in the *Escadre de la Méditerranée* and its reserve division 1891-98, then in 2nd category reserve 1898-1906. Recommissioned in the *Escadre de la Méditerranée* to serve as station ship in Crete 1906-1909 in place of *Condor*. In the process of being condemned 1.1914. Off main list by 3.1920 and for sale at Toulon. Struck 1.10.1920. Sold 1921 to BU in Italy.

*Vautour* Toulon Dyd/F.C. Méditerranée, Marseille.
On list 1.1883. Ord: 2.8.1882. K: 10.11.1882. L: 25.4.1889.
   Comm: 5.6.1889 (trials), 25.1.1890 (full).
Budget 1884. Engine contract 3.4.1883. In commission in the *Escadre de la Méditerranée* and its reserve division 1890-1898, then to 2nd category reserve. Station ship at Constantinople 1900-1906. School for engineers at Toulon 1907-08, replaced there by *Milan*. Struck 3.2.1908, BU 1909.

---

**WATTIGNIES Class.** *Croiseurs torpilleurs.* Miniature protected cruisers with main guns under the forecastle, in sponsons amidships, and on the poop, and with a ram-shaped bow. One large funnel, three pole masts (later two). Designed by de Bussy.

In 1884 Gambetta's Minister of Marine Gougeard (from November 1881 to January 1882) published in his pamphlet *La marine de guerre, son passé et son avenir, cuirassés et torpilleurs,* his concept of the warship of the future, given that battleships were now doomed by torpedoes. It was a ship with the highest possible speed, armed primarily with the torpedo, and with a strong protective deck. The design that he published was essentially a *Condor* enlarged to 1,780 tons and 95m and with a speed between 20.5 and 21 knots. The Navy's objectives for a modified *Condor*, however, were as modest as Gougeard's were ambitious. In 1888 Minister Krantz asked de Bussy to modify the *Condor* design to reach 18 knots on trials and to carry two 65mm guns in place of two 37mm revolving cannon. De Bussy considered that with *Condor* already making 17.78 knots on 3,582ihp it would be sufficient to raise the power to 4,000ihp. and give the hull slightly finer lines. He retained the boilers of *Condor* but increased their operating pressure from 7kg/cm², to 11.26kg/cm², and he replaced compound with triple expanson engines. He uniformly stretched the frames of *Condor* slightly further apart to get another 2m of length to accommodate the triple expansion engines and slightly widened stokeholds. When the *Conseil des travaux* examined this design on 10 July 1888 its only change was to extend the forecastle back to the back of the bridge as in *Forbin* to improve seakeeping. *Fleurus* was introduced in the 1890 budget simply as a *bâtiment* (ship) at Cherbourg with no details.

*The characteristics are based on a devis for* Wattignies *dated 1892.*
**Dimensions & tons:** 70.985m oa, 70.009m wl, 68.012m pp (bow to rudder) x 8.908m ext & wl. 1,297.082t disp. Draught: 4.211m mean, 4.698m aft. Men: 185.
**Machinery:** 1,000nhp (forced) and 4,000ihp designed at 140rpm and 11.260kg/cm² boiler pressure. 2 screws. 2 triple expansion engines

The torpedo cruiser *Vautour*. The card's caption calls her a *contre-torpilleur d'escadre* (squadron torpedo boat destroyer), nomenclature that was in use from 1896 to 1900. *(Postcard by A. Bougault)*

with 3 cylinders of 0.600m, 0.900m, and 1.440m diameter and 0.900m stroke. 4 cylindrical direct flame Admiralty boilers. 130t coal. Range (designed) 1,800nm @ 12.5kts.
**Armour:** Probably as *Condor*.
**Guns:**
(1892) 5 x 100mm/26.2 M1881 QF (2 under the forecastle, 2 amidships in sponsons, 1 on the poop), 6 x 47mm/40 M1885 QF, 4 x 37mm revolving cannon. **Torpedoes:** 4 tubes for 356mm M1887 torpedoes (2 forward, 2 sides). **Searchlights:** 3
(1896) 5 x 100mm, 6 x 47mm, 2 x 37mm QF, 2 x 37mm revolving cannon. No torpedo tubes.

*Wattignies* Rochefort Dyd/Schneider, Creusot.
On list 1.1889. Ord: 26.7.1888. K: 8.10.1889. L: 9.4.1891.
   Comm: 15.2.1892 (trials).
Budget 1889. Construction begun 30.8.1888. Machinery contract 14.11.1888, installed 1.2.1891 to 17.9.1891. Arrived at Toulon 24.7.1892 after trials, in commission in the *Escadre de la Méditerranée* and its reserve division 1892 to 1898. Designated 9.1896 to replace *Marceau* as station ship in Crete. Relived by *Condor* in 1898 at Port Said, in 2nd category reserve at Rochefort 1899-1907. Struck 8.4.1908.

*Fleurus* Cherbourg Dyd/Schneider, Creusot.
On list 1.1891. Ord: 20.4.1890. K: 11.3.1891. L: 18.3.1893.
   Comm: 16.8.1893 (trials).
Budget 1890 (as an unnamed *bâtiment* at Cherbourg). Engine contract 18.2.1891. Began laborious trials in 1893, then to 2nd category reserve 1894 to replace her cylindrical boilers twice. Trials resumed 1896, then to 2nd category reserve 1897 to replace her boilers with torpedo boat Niclausse boilers. Trials resumed again in 1898, joined the *Escadre du Nord* in 1899, trials ended 3.1901 and ship immediately placed in 2nd category reserve at Brest. She was decomm. in 1903 after being in commission for a total of only 30 months. Struck 8.3.1910, school for engineers at Lorient 1910-1911, for sale at Lorient 1911-1912, mooring hulk at Rochefort 1912-1927. Sold 1928 to BU.

# Chapter Ten

# Avisos and Gunboats, 1882-1897

## I. AVISOS

### (A) 1st Class Avisos (*Avisos de 1re classe*).

Were *Avisos de stations* before the 1.1885 fleet list. To *Avisos de station de 1re classe* 1.1891, to *Avisos de 1re classe* 1.1892, to *Avisos* (classes omitted) 1.1909.

*INCONSTANT* Class. *Avisos de 1re classe.* 220nhp screw avisos with wooden hulls including three layers of crossed wooden planking on wooden frames with steel deck beams (possibly iron in *Fulton*) but no beam shelves, and ram-shaped (inverted) bows. One funnel, three masts, barque rig (later schooner rig with armed tops). Designed by Sabattier.

The avisos of the *Bisson* (1873) type were judged so successful that in 1880 it was decided to order two more from the dockyards. These were delayed a year, and in 1882 a third was added. On 24 March 1882 naval constructor de Bussy, Chief of the Service Technique, wrote a note on the hull system to be adopted for the two station avisos to be begun during 1882 at Toulon. He concluded that the diagonal system of Normand as used in the *Bisson* type (three layers of crossed diagonal and longitudinal planking) was superior to the conventional system (one layer of longitudinal planking) used in the otherwise similar *Chasseur* type because it was somewhat lighter and also needed fewer curved oak frames, which were becoming scarce. He recommended that the diagonal system be used for the aviso that was to be begun immediately at Toulon.

On 17 January 1887 Minister of Marine Aube authorized installing positions in the tops for the Hotckhiss revolving cannon. Two posts were created in the fore top in February 1887 and one was established on the top of the lower part of the mizzen mast. As of 1887 the crews of the guns and the revolving cannon in *Inconstant* were protected against musketry by chrome steel shields mounted on the guns. This protection was completed for the

The 1st class aviso *Inconstant* in the Far East. Her active service consisted of three years at Toulon followed by one long cruise in the Far East from 1890 to 1896. The 138.6mm gun on her forecastle is visible behind a shield. *(NHHC from Farenholt collection, previously ONI, NH-66081)*

revolving cannon by fixed or mobile plates in the tops and on the bridge wings. On 24 March 1887 the Minister ordered studying and implementing improvements to the ventilation in the stokehold in *Inconstant*, possible measures included raising the funnel by 2.50m. During the 1890-92 campaign of *Inconstant* it was noted that the revolving cannon in the tops were impeded by the small size of the tops and that shields had never been received for the revolving cannon although the tops and bridge wings had protective plating. On 13 July 1893 the ship was under fire from both sides at Paknam near Bangkok but the gun crews were protected on one side only.

*The characteristics are based on a devis for* Inconstant *dated 14.12.1886.*

**Dimensions & tons:** 63.650m oa, 61.521m pp (wl fwd to rudder), 61.550m pp (tip fwd to rudder) x 8.700m ext, 8.694m wl. 871.667t disp. Draught: 3.683m mean, 4.231m aft. Men: 116.

**Machinery:** 220nhp and 1,194ihp designed at 115rpm and $6.200kg/cm^2$ boiler pressure. Trials (17.5.1887) 1,182.97ihp = 12.89kts at 114.400rpm. 1 screw. 1 horizontal compound engine with return connecting rods and 2 cylinders of 0.860m and 1.440m diameter and 0.600m stroke. 2 reglementary cylindrical tubular return flame boilers. 114t coal. The contract for the engine for *Fulton* called for three cylinders but a contract amendment of 7.4.1884 changed it to two.

**Guns:** (1886) 3 x 138.6mm/30 M1881 (1 on forecastle, 2 on centreline on the upper deck), 1 x 100mm/26.2 M1881 (on poop), 1 x 65mm/16 M1881 landing, 4 x 37mm revolving cannon (5 from 1890 with 3 in the tops). **Torpedoes:** none.

*Inconstant* Toulon Dyd/Indret (engines designed by Garnier).

On list 1.1883. Ord: 28.3.1882. K: 2.5.1882. L: 14.7.1886.
    Comm: 14.12.1886 (trials), 12.6.1888 (full)

Budget 1881 (delayed to 1882). Construction reassigned from contract to Toulon 1880. Machinery installed 27.4.1886 to 23.10.1886. In commission for trials from 14.12.1886 to 7.6.1887, then to reserve. In full commission 12.6.1888 for the first of three short periods of fleet service in the Mediterranean, then conducted one cruise to the Far East in 1890-1896. Struck 4.9.1900 (published 11.9.1900), designated 13.6.1900 and 11.9.1900 to replace the sailing transport *Perdrix* as a *patache* (police and customs hulk in a military port) at Toulon, and served as such to 1926. Offered for sale and sold 26.10.1927 to M. Saglia.

*Papin* Toulon Dyd/Indret (engines designed by Garnier).

On list 1.1883. Ord: 28.3.1882. K: 2.5.1882. L: 11.11.1886.
    Comm: 24.6.1887 (trials). C: 8.1887.

Budget 1881 (delayed to 1882). Construction reassigned from contract to Toulon 1880. Machinery installed 11.1886 to 11.6.1887. Trials 8.1887, then to reserve. To full commission 15.5.1893 to replace *La Bourdonnais* at Madagascar. Returned to Lorient from the the Pacific 11.1.1900 with severe engineering problems. Struck 4.9.1900 (published 11.9.1900). On 4.10.1900 the Ministry of Foreign Affairs reported that the government of Ecuador had asked about the possibility of buying an aviso like *Papin* but later discussions were inconclusive. For sale at Lorient 1900-1902, sold 16.9.1902 to M. Trécanton.

*Fulton* Lorient Dyd/Claparède, Saint Denis (contract 23.7.1883).

On list 1.1883. K: 27.7.1882. L: 8.1.1887. Comm: 28.10.1887 (trials), 8.2.1889 (trials after repairs). C: 3.1889.

Budget 1883. Machinery installed 1.5.1887 to 20.9.1887. Initial trials in late 1887 revealed problems with the engine that needed nearly two years to resolve. Successful trials 3.1889, then to reserve. To full commission 25 9.1895 for a cruise to the Caribbean and North America, back to reserve 2.5.1899. Sales to Ecuador in 1900 and Colombia in 1901 considered without results, then laid up at Landévennec. Converted 9.1909 to coal hulk for Lézardrieux. Struck 1.7.1910, coal hulk at Brest 1910-1911, replenishment post for torpedo boats at Lézardrieux 1911-1914. Renamed *Trieux* 13.1.1914, her name having

just been given to a submarine to be laid down in 1914. Coal hulk at Lézardrieux 1920-1923 and at Cherbourg 1923-1926, off list 1926. BU at Brest 4.1933.

*N* (Unnamed) Lorient Dyd

Budget 1885 (delayed to 1887). One unnamed aviso de station (aviso de 1re classe) at Rochefort was added in the 1885 and 1886 budgets. It was not in the original 1887 budget (3.1886) but was shown in the revised 1887 budget (7.1886) at Lorient. It was not in the 1888 budget (3.1887). Its budgeted building costs were the same as for *Fulton*.

---

*KERSAINT. Aviso de 1re classe.* Large screw aviso with a steel hull, wood and copper sheathing, and a ram-shaped bow. Two funnels, three masts, barquentine rig. Designed by Raymond.

On 4 November 1890 Minister of Marine Barbey asked the *Conseil des travaux* to review specifications for a 1st class aviso for service on distant stations to replace the *Boursaint* and *Chasseur* types. This was part of a mini-programme for station combatants that also included a 1st (later 2nd) class station cruiser that became *Descartes* and a station gunboat that became *Surprise*. Barbey forwarded his own specifications based on a report from the Chief of the Naval General Staff and the Director of Materiel dated 28 October 1890, which the Council examined on 23 December 1890. The Minister's specifications included a maximum displacement of 1,000 tons and a maximum draught aft of 4.40m. The ship was to have a triple expansion engine, boilers operating at a pressure not under $10kg/cm^2$, a speed of 13 knots with natural draught, a range of 3,500nm at 10 knots, and bunkers able to carry a coal surcharge for a total of 4,500nm. The armament was to be one 138.6mm QF gun (on the forecastle), five 100mm guns (one aft and four on the sides with near axial fire, two forward and two aft), and seven light-model 37mm QF guns. The protection was to consist of 40mm hard steel shields on the 138.6mm and 100mm guns and on the conning tower. The ship was to have a fully developed barque rig on three masts, a steel hull with wood sheathing, and a 100-man crew. The Council raised the speed at natural draught to 14 knots (15 knots with forced draught) and the range to 4,000nm at 10 knots and enlarged the surcharge, resulting in a displacement it estimated at 1,340 tons. It also specified that the tops on the masts should be fitted to carry 37mm revolving cannon. The Minister forwarded the resulting specifications to the ports and to industry on 3 February 1891.

Seven designs were received, which the Council examined on 9 February 1892. It invited naval constructor Eugène Hippolyte Raymond, A.C. Loire, and C.A. Gironde to revise their designs but only Raymond did so. His first revision was submitted on 27 January 1893 and reviewed by the Council on 21 March 1893, and his second revision was forwarded to the Council by the ministry on 31 July 1893 and reviewed on 17 October 1893. Raymond tried to fit in a curved 20mm deck over the machinery but this caused unacceptable problems in hull structure and the Council had him reduce it to a regular 10mm deck and delete the 6mm splinter deck that he had inserted below it. At the Council's request he enlarged the armoured conning tower to one for four men that was nearly identical except for slightly reduced dimensions to the type with five men approved on 21 March 1893 for certain battleships in the *Escadre de la Méditerranée*.

The 1895 budget (submitted in March 1894) included an *aviso de station* (S2) designed by Raymond and to be built in a dockyard. On 14 May 1895 Minister of Marine Besnard ordered Rochefort to begin construction of an *aviso de station* and named her *Kersaint*. The 1896 budget submission (May 1895) included an *aviso de station* (S1) to be built at Toulon, but the Budget Commission on 13 July 1895 deleted all station ships including this one from the budget and cancelled credits for them on 24 October 1895. *Kersaint* is shown in the 1897 budget (February 1896) without designator and with money spent at Rochefort in both 1895 and 1896.

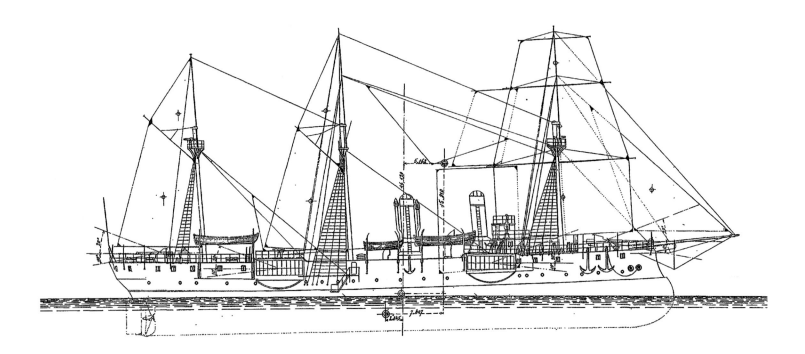

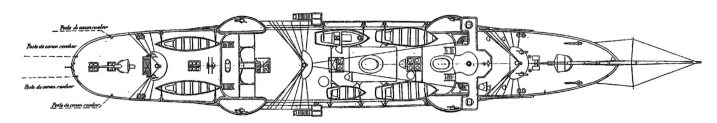

Mast and sail plan (longitudinal and horizontal views) of the 1st class aviso *Kersaint* built on the plans of naval constructor Raymond. The plans were signed by naval constructor Bruneau at Rochefort on 3 November 1898. Four positions for revolving cannon are labelled on the stern.

*The characteristics are based on a devis dated 9.11.1898.*

**Dimensions & tons:** 71.550m oa, 68.650m wl and pp (tip fwd to sternpost) x 10.500m ext & wl (11.400m outside sponsons). 1,296.419t disp. Draught: 4.248m mean, 4.831m aft. Men: 120.

**Machinery:** 2,200ihp designed at 120rpm and 15kg/cm² boiler pressure (12kg/cm² at the engines). Trials (17.9.1898) 2,399.5ihp = 16.114kts at 120.4rpm and 14.249kg/cm² boiler pressure. 1 screw. 1 vertical triple expansion engine with 4 cylinders of 0.810m (1), 1,200m (1), and 1.370m (2) diameter and 0.550m stroke. 8 Lagrafel et d'Allest boilers built by Fraissinet. 247t coal plus 17t oil. Range 2,033nm @ 15.326kts.

**Armour:**
Guns: shields (hardened steel) 54mm.
Conning tower (hardened steel): 40mm.

**Guns:**
(1898) 1 x 138.6mm/45 M1893 (on forecastle), 5 x 100mm/45 M1891(2) (4 in sponsons on upper deck, 1 on the poop), 1 x 65mm/16 M1881 landing, 7 x 37mm revolving cannon.
   **Torpedoes:** none. **Searchlights:** 2 x 40cm on the bridge.
(1915) The 138.6mm, the stern 100mm, and the port after 100mm were landed during mobilisation, they were re-embarked in Jan-Feb 1915. 2 mitrailleuses (machine guns) were added.
(1917) 1 x 138.6mm, 5 x 100mm, 1 x 65mm landing, 2 x 37mm revolving cannon, 2 mitrailleuses M1907. 5 x 37mm revolving cannon were ashore in unusable condition.

*Kersaint* (S2) Rochefort Dyd/Schneider, Creusot.
On list 1.1896. Ord: 14.5.1895. K: 19.8.1896. L: 28.8.1897.
   Comm: 10.6.1898 (trials), 11.11.1898 (full).
Budget 1895. Machinery contract 4.12.1895, approved 8.2.1896, machinery installed 10.8.1897 to 4.5.1898. Assigned to the *Escadre du Nord* 5.10.1898. Arrived at Rochefort and began to go into full commission 3.11.1898. Trial results approved 7.11.1898. In full commission 11.11.1898. From Rochefort to Brest 13-14.11.1898. Left Brest 15.1.1899 for Haiphong to replace *Bengali* in the Annam and Tonkin naval division. Left Saigon 15.9.1907 to replace *Vaucluse* at Noumea in the of the Eastern Pacific naval division, arrived 14.10.1907. Reboilered at Saigon 11.1917 to 6.1918 with boilers built for Greek destroyers but seized by France 12.1916. Wrecked 5.3.1919 on a coral reef while mooring in Papetoaï Bay on the island of Moorea near Tahiti, condemned as lost 18.7.1919, sold 27.2.1920 to M. Paquier of Moorea. Local lore claimed that her pilot was distracted by marital difficulties.

---

### (B) 2nd Class Avisos (*Avisos de 2e classe*).

Were *Avisos de flottille à hélice* and *à roues* before the 1.1885 fleet list. To *Avisos de station de 2e classe* 1.1891, to *Avisos de 2e classe* 1.1892, to *Avisos* (classes omitted) 1.1909.

*IBIS. Aviso de 2e classe.* 105nhp screw aviso with a galvanised iron hull and a clipper bow. One funnel, two masts, schooner-brig rig. Designed by Du Buit.

This small screw aviso was a further development by Paul Du Buit, the senior engineer at Graville, of his *Mouette* of 1879, which was a lengthened

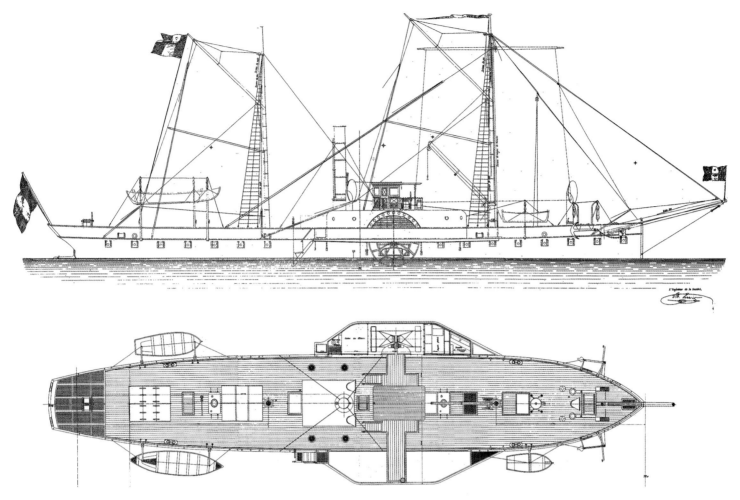

Sail plan and deck view of the avisos *Pingouin* and *Salamandre* including an interior view of the port paddle box. The undated plans by the Chantiers et Ateliers de Bacalan were signed by the engineer of the company, Ch. Verrier.

copy of his *Élan* of 1877 and of Normand's *Faon* of 1847. This type of vessel was generally used for fishery protection and pilot training. *Élan* and *Mouette* are described in Chapter 4.

*The characteristics are based on a devis dated 25.4.1885.*
**Dimensions & tons:** 42.60m wl, 42.60m pp x 6.23m ext (above wl), 6.16m wl. 279.1t disp. Draught: 2.235m mean, 2.345m aft. Men: 72.
**Machinery:** 105nhp and 425ihp designed at 154rpm and 6.2kg/cm$^2$ boiler pressure. Trials (21.4.1885) 341ihp = 11.27kts at 147 rpm and 5.86kg/cm$^2$ boiler pressure. 1 screw. 1 vertical compound engine with 2 cylinders of 0.48m and 0.93m diameter and 0.45m stroke. 2 tubular cylindrical boilers. 32.2t coal. Range 1,340nm @ 10kts.
**Guns:** (1885) 2 x 65mm/16 M1881 landing, 2 x 37mm Hotchkiss.

*Ibis* Rochefort Dyd.
On list 1.1883. K: 2.1882. L: 4.7.1883. C: 4.1885.
Budget 1884. Sail plan signed at Rochefort 6 April 1883 and approved by Minister Senator Charles Marie Brun on 10 May 1883. In 2$^{nd}$ category reserve at Cherbourg 1887-89. Channel and North Sea station (primarily fishery protection) 1895-1913, replaced by the destroyer *Yatagan* pending completion of *Flamant* and in reserve at Cherbourg 1913-14. Struck 10.5.1920 (as *aviso garde-pêche*). Sold at Cherbourg to BU.

---

**ALCYON Class.** *Avisos de 2$^e$ classe.* 55nhp paddle avisos with a composite hull with three layers of wooden planking on steel frames and with steel deck beams and beam shelves, and with a straight bow. One funnel, two

masts, schooner-brig rig (later schooner). Designed by Chaudoye for de Bussy's *Service technique*.

On 23 May 1882 the Maritime Prefect at Lorient asked his Director of Naval Construction, Perroy, if the port could build before the end of the year four vessels of the *Cigale* type without holding up other work. Perroy responded that it could, and that two each could be built on the slips where *Alouette* and *Turenne* had been built. Lorient received an order for two such vessels on 26 May 1882. Plans prepared by Lorient for two vessels for use in Senegal, based on those for *Cygne*, were approved on 22 August 1882 and at the same time the names *Alcyon* and *Jouffroy* were approved for the ships and inscribed on the *Liste de la Flotte*. Mean draught rose to 1.430m and displacement to 320.518 after addition in 1886 of a kiosk and changes to the paddle boxes to accommodate the revolving cannon. *Jouffroy* lay idle for nine years and *Alcyon* for eleven before finding employment. On 28 July 1896 the Colonial Ministry informed the Navy that the Governor General of Indochina had informed him that he could not use any of the five avisos made available by the navy because vessels specially built for Senegal were much less appropriate for river navigation in Indochina and the Navy's charges for them against the colony's budget were too high.

*The characteristics are based on a devis for* Alcyon *dated 21.9.1886.*
**Dimensions & tons:** 46.950m oa, 45.050m wl (bow to rudder), 45.000m pp (wl fwd to sternpost) x 7.350m ext & wl (12.264m outside the paddle boxes). 311.996t disp. Draught: 1.400m mean, 1.500m aft. Men: 25 (43 in 1898).
**Machinery:** 55 nhp and 225ihp designed at 120rpm (engines) and 4.132kg/cm$^2$ boiler pressure. Trials (17.9.1886) 231.8ihp = 7.6085kts at 105.5rpm. Paddles 3.880m diameter. 1 vertical compound geared engine with 2 cylinders of 0.430m and 0.770m diameter and 0.499m

stroke. Gear ratio 3 to 1 (engine to paddles). 1 cylindrical tubular return flame boiler. 60t coal.

**Guns:**
(1886, *Alcyon*) 2 x 4pdr (86mm) bronze mountain rifles (landing), 4 x 37mm revolving cannon.
(1895, *Alcyon*) 2 x 65mm/16 M1881 landing (2 positions on the upper deck forward and 2 aft), 4 x 37mm revolving cannon (2 positions on the paddle boxes, 2 on the extreme bow, and 2 on the extreme stern).

*Alcyon* Lorient Dyd/Indret (engines designed by Daniel Édouard Widmann)
On list 1.1883. Ord: 26.5.1882. K: 12.1882. L: 4.9.1884. Comm: 1.8.1886 (trials), 5.1898 (full).
Budget 1884. Named 22.8.1882. Machinery installed 21.4.1885 to 7.12.1885. Commissioned 8.1886 for trials, to reserve 24.9.1886 after trials, decomm. 1.1.1892. Full commission 15.4.1898 to replace *Cigogne* in the Congo with a few minor changes including the addition of bulwarks on the paddle boxes. Left Lorient for the Congo 24.5.1898. Decomm. at Libreville 11.4.1905 without replacement. Struck 19.4.1905, sold 8.8.1905 to the Chargeurs Réunis.

*Jouffroy* Lorient Dyd-Caudan.
On list 1.1883. Ord: 26.5.1882. K: 12.1882. L: 21.4.1887. C: 1887.
Budget 1884. Named 22.8.1882 for the Marquis de Jouffroy d'Abbans. In reserve 1887-1891, out of commission 1891-1896. To French Guiana 1896. Struck 9.3.1910, for sale at Fort de France 1910-1913.

---

*PINGOUIN* **Class.** *Avisos de 2ᵉ classe.* 55nhp paddle avisos with an iron hull and a straight bow. One funnel, two masts, schooner-brig rig (later schooner). Designed by Sabattier and Daymard.

These vessels were a further development of Daymard's *Cygne* of 1873 and *Cigale* of 1878, a type intended for Senegal, with the larger engine of the latter.

*The characteristics are based on a devis for* Pingouin *dated 16.4.1885.*
**Dimensions & tons:** 42.89m wl, 43.23m pp x 7.226m ext and wl. 294.9t disp. Draught: 1.171m mean and aft. Men: 37.
**Machinery:** 55nhp (later 60nhp) and 225ihp designed at 120rpm (engine) and 4.25kg/cm² boiler pressure. Trials (*Pingouin*, 30.1.1885) 250.6ihp = 7.031kts at 122.1rpm (engine). Paddles 3.94m diameter. 1 geared vertical compound engine with 2 cylinders of 0.45m and 0.80m diameter and 0.50m stroke. 1 tubular cylindrical boiler. 28.2t coal. Range 860nm @ 8.5kts.
**Guns:** (1885) 2 x 65mm/16 M1881 landing, 2 x 37mm Hotchkiss.

*Pingouin* Dyle et Bacalan, Bordeaux-Bacalan.
On list 1.1884. K: 13.9.1883. L: 7.10.1884. C: 9.2.1885.
Budget 1884. To Obock 1886 commanded by a premier maître. Transferred 10.6.1890 to the colony of Obock, off list 1890. Used as a quarantine station 1891-1912, then sank at Djibouti. The wreck, awash in the roadstead, still existed in 2015.

*Salamandre* Dyle et Bacalan, Bordeaux-Bacalan.
On list 1.1884. K: 13.9.1883. L: 5.12.1884. C: 1885.
Budget 1884. To Senegal 1886. Decomm. 1898 at Saint-Louis du Sénégal. Struck 11.8.1898.

---

*LAPRADE.* *Aviso de 2ᵉ classe.* 100nhp paddle aviso with an iron hull and a clipper bow. One funnel, two masts, schooner-brig rig.

This vessel was designed and built by Claparède at Saint Denis for the Colonial Administration. Her shallow draft was intended to permit her to ascend high up the rivers in Senegal to serve and protect the French trading posts there. After her launch at Saint Denis she was taken to

Cherbourg for completion and the fitting of a schooner-brig rig. She later moved from Senegal to Gabon at which time she was transferred to the Navy.

**Dimensions & tons:** 50m x 7m. 440t disp. Draught: 2m. Men: 60.
**Machinery:** 100nhp and 400ihp. Speed 10kts.
**Guns:** 2 x 65mm/16 M1881 landing.

*Laprade* Anc. Éts. Claparède, Saint Denis.
On list 1.1885. K: 15.2.1879. L: 15.1.1880. C: 5.1880.
Commissioned at Cherbourg 5.1880 on the account of the colony of Senegal. Acquired by the Navy 7.1884 from the Colonial Administration. In Gabon 1884 to 1887. Struck 31.7.1888.

---

*GOGAH.* *Aviso de 2ᵉ classe.* 100nhp paddle aviso with an iron hull.

Two iron-hulled paddle steamers, *Gogah* and *Nagotna* (below), belonging to the Bombay Steam Navigation Co. were purchased by the French at Bombay in 1884. They had been destined at one time for a passenger service on the Hoogly, and the French wanted them for use on the rivers in Tonkin. *Gogah* was built at Port Glasgow, Scotland, in 1870 for Joseph A. Shepherd and Hajee Joosub (Bombay Steam Navigation Co.) of Bombay.

**Dimensions & tons:** 56.39m x 6.40m. 335t disp. Depth: 2.26m. Men: 54 including 2 officers.
**Machinery:** 100nhp and 400ihp. Paddles. 2 cylinders.
**Guns:** none listed.

*Gogah* William Hamilton & Co., Port Glasgow, Bay Yard hull 7 (engines by David Rowan & Co, Glasgow)
On list 1.1885. L: 10.1870.
Purchased 1884 at Bombay and sent to Tonkin. Lay aground for six months in an arroyo in 1887. Decomm. 9.1887 and used as a depôt at Kwangchow Wan (Guangzhouwan, French Kouang Tchéou Wan). Struck 29.12.1891, for sale 1891-1892, hulk 1892-1893, dépôt 1893-1906, probably at Kwangchow Wan, for sale there 1906-1907.

---

*NAGOTNA.* *Aviso de 2ᵉ classe.* 80nhp paddle aviso with an iron hull.

The light draft iron river passenger and cargo paddle steamer *Nagotna* was built at Port Glasgow, Scotland in 1865 for the Bombay Coast and River Steam Navigation Co. That firm, founded in 1863, was liquidated 1868 and *Nagotna* passed in 1870 to Hajee Hassum Joosoob of Bombay and then to J. A. Shepherd of Shepherd & Co. and the Bombay Steam Navigation Co. She was reboiled in 1882 and had her deck repaired in 1883. When the French bought her she was being used to transport native passengers between Bombay and a neighbouring port in a large deckhouse.

On 1 January 1884 the Government of Bombay reported that French agents had contracted a purchase of two small steamers to be delivered at Goa and sent to Saigon. The purchase of *Nagotna* was concluded at Bombay in February 1884 for 5,000 pounds with M. Shapher, Director of the Bombay Steam Navigation Co. She arrived at Saigon on 23 March 1884, after which she received repairs to her hull, engine, and boilers, and was refitted for a European crew instead of a native Indian one. Platforms were fitted for 37mm revolving cannon. Hull measurements were taken off in May 1884. Machinery trials on 14 May 1884 were satisfactory but the Saigon arsenal had to calculate the indicated horsepower of the vessel as it did not have an indicator to measure it directly. She had two masts and a short cargo loading mast.

*The characteristics are based on a devis dated 21.5.1884.*
**Dimensions & tons:** 48.80m deck, 48.60m wl x 6.82m ext (11.20m outside paddle boxes), 6.80m wl. 335.392t disp. Draught: 1.80m mean, 2.00m aft. Men:45.
**Machinery:** 94nhp (nominally 80nhp) and 376ihp at 30rpm and 2.8kg/cm² boiler pressure. Paddles 4.86m diameter. 1 vertical

*Nagotna* was one of the two small paddle steamers purchased by France at Bombay in early 1884 for service in Tonkin, the other being the slightly larger *Gogah*. This small sketch appeared as an ornament at the end of an article on French paddle steamers by Commandant de Balincourt, and Pierre Le Conte (*Révue maritime*, no. 157 (1933), p. 54) and may have been drawn by one of the authors. It shows the deckhouse added for passenger service in India.

oscillating engine with 2 cylinders of 0.910m diameter and 0.910m stroke. 1 cylindrical boiler. 34.659t coal.

**Guns:** 2 x 37mm revolving cannon. 6 more were added 12.1885. All were in protected positions, two in the tops.

*Nagotna* Robert Duncan & Co., Port Glasgow (East Yard hull 11, engines by Blackwood & Gordon, Port Glasgow, in British sources or John Elder, Glasgow, in French sources).
On list 1.1885. L: 30.12.1864 C: 1865.
Purchased 1884 at Bombay and sent to Tonkin. arrived at Tourane (Da Nang) 26.5.1884 and left 29.6 for Ha Long Bay (*Baie d'Along*). Tonkin reported on 1.4.1885 that despite her great length and weak armament she had rendered important services. Having been built in 1864, however, she was showing her age. Decomm 24.11.1886 because of materiel failures and replaced by the service craft *Thuan Tiep* (see *Thuan An*, below). Struck 27.4.1887, hulk in Tonkin 1887-1890 (replaced *Kep*, ex *Surprise*, as station hulk and annex to *Adour* in Ha Long Bay). Worn out by 1890, sale authorised 19.9.1890, and sale reported 14.12.1890.

---

**THUAN AN.** *Aviso de 2ᵉ classe.* Small screw aviso. Captured.

Following the death in May 1883 of Henri Rivière at the hands of Chinese Black Flag pirates just west of Hanoi and after the death in July 1883 of the Emperor of Vietnam in his capital of Hue, French naval forces under Admiral Courbet moved south to tighten French control of the capital. After a two-day bombardment the French attacked and took the forts around Hue including those at Thuan An on 20 August 1883. Five days later France imposed its control over central Vietnam in a treaty while leaving a certain autonomy to its monarchy. In July 1885 the court at Hue revolted against the French, a regent taking the 12-year old Emperor into the mountains with his elephants, treasury, and three empresses. During this uprising an Annamite (Vietnamese) steamer built of wood at Hong Kong in 1882 was seized. She was named *Thuan An* and immediately placed in service with an ensign in command and a local crew, performing valuable service against the insurgency. Many tugs were leased at the beginning of 1885 and were manned in the same manner as *Thuan An*, and some 30 of them appeared as service craft in Tonkin in the 1887 fleet list. One of them, *Thuan Tiep*, was used as a transport with *Thuan An* from early 1887 in place of *Nagotna*.

A commission met on 12 May 1890 to consider the condemnation of *Thuan An* and reported that her engine was too weak for a ship of her size and her boiler could not be fired because of multiple leaks. She had very

poor qualities at sea and could not sail without danger in the Gulf of Tonkin even in the summer. She could operate for only a few months each year and because of her weak engine her speed was unacceptable. The commission recommended her condemnation and proposed that she be sold locally. *Thuan Tiep* was also condemned with *Thuan An* on 1 July 1890 for nearly identical reasons. She again replaced *Nagotna*, this time as station hulk in in Ha Long Bay. Her hull deteriorated there and on 16 June 1896 she was ordered turned over to the Domaines for sale.

**Dimensions & tons:** 45m x 6.60m. c400t disp. Draught (with 180 tons of cargo on board) 2.05m fwd, 3.20m aft.
**Machinery:** 1 screw. 1 vertical compound engine with 2 cylinders. 40t coal.
**Guns:** unknown

*Thuan An* Hong Kong.
On list 1.1886. In service 1885.
Rated as an aviso in 1885-1886. To service craft list 1.1887 as a tug in Tonkin, although used as a transport. Placed in reserve in Tonkin 16.10.1888, then served as a transport attached to to the station hulk *Adour* before being placed in reserve at Haiphong 22.10.1889. Condemned 1.7.1890.

---

***BENGALI.*** *Aviso de 2ᵉ classe.* 100nhp paddle aviso with crossed layers of wooden planking on wooden frames with iron deck beams and without beam shelves, and with a clipper bow. One funnel, two masts, schooner-brig rig. Designed by Normand.

On 19 March 1886 the Directorate of Material proposed to Minister of Marine Aube that the navy order from Normand an aviso with crossed layers of wooden planking like the *Ardent* of 1882. Normand was notified of the intended order and the vessel was named on 6 April 1886, and the contract was approved on 6 July 1886. The contract for the engines was approved on 2 September 1886.

*Bengali* lay idle until 1892 and was assigned to hydrographic duty at Saigon by late 1901. Her last commander lamented in 1904 that *Bengali* was the perfect hydrographic vessel for the areas in which her mission lay, and that it was 'with great regret that we had to renounce using such a precious tool', and that it was 'most regrettable that the *Bengali* type is disappearing without being replaced'.

*The characteristics are based on a devis dated 15.2.1889.*
**Dimensions & tons:** 58.030m oa, 54.505m wl, 54.560m pp (wl fwd to rudder) x 7.630m ext (above wl, 13.000m outside the paddle boxes), 7.550m wl. 567.266t disp. Draught: 2.207m mean, 2.164m aft. Men: 69
**Machinery:** 100 nhp and 400ihp designed (404.5ihp with auxiliaries) at 25rpm and 5kg/cm² boiler pressure. Trials (15.11.1888) 447.34ihp = 10.282kts at 27.137rpm. Paddles 5.5m diameter. 1 inclined compound engine with direct connecting rods and 2 cylinders of 0.840m and 1.290m diameter and 1.200m stroke. 1 cylindrical return flame boiler. 70t coal (81.770t in 1897).
**Guns:** 2 x 90mm/22 M1881 (1 on forecastle, 1 aft) with shields, 4 x 37mm revolving cannon (positions on the upper deck, foretop, and paddle boxes), 1 x 4pdr (86mm) bronze mountain rifle for use as a line throwing gun. Add 1 x 37mm/20 M1885 QF in the after top 1900 for use in a boat. 90mm guns landed 1901 for surveying duty.

*Bengali* Augustin Normand, Le Havre/A.C. Loire, Nantes (engines designed by Claparède).
On list 1.1887. Ord: 21.6.1886 (contract). K: 12.7.1886. L: 1.10.1887. C: 10.1888.
Budget 1888 (building). Machinery contract 16.8.1886, installed 12.1887 to 16.2.1888. Arrived at Cherbourg from builder 31.3.1888. Began commissioning for trials 17.9.1888, trial results approved

12.1888, then placed in 3rd category reserve 23.12.1888 and decomm. 1.1.1892. To full commission 15.6.1892 to replace *Oyapock* in French Guiana. Returned to Lorient 11.5.1896 and decomm. 24.5.1896. To full commission. 22.6.1897 to go to Saigon where she was to be placed in reserve. On hydrographic duty 1901-1904. Decomm. 19.6.1904. Struck 5.8.1904, sold 4.5.1905 at Saigon.

---

*UNKNOWN TYPE. Aviso de 2e classe.*
Only one 2nd class aviso was proposed between the paddle *Bengali* of 1887 and the screw *Chamois* of 1904, the former being a colonial paddle steamer and the latter being a screw school ship for pilots.

*U1* (Unnamed) Contract
Budget 1894 (not funded). This contract-built *aviso de 2e classe* was included in the 1894 budget (submitted 5.1893) with the stipulation that no funds were to be spent on her during 1894. She was not contracted for and the 1895 budget (3.1894) deferred her indefinitely.

---

## (C) 3rd Class Avisos (*Avisos de 3e classe*).

Were *Avisos de flottille à hélice* and *à roues* before the 1.1885 fleet list. To *Avisos de station de 3e classe* 1.1891 and *Avisos de 3e classe* 1.1892.

*DJOUÉ. Aviso de 3e classe.* 25nhp screw river launch with two funnels. Designed by builder to the requirements of Lieutenant de vaisseau Savorgnan de Brazza. Rated *Aviso de flottille* 24.4.1883, *Aviso de 3e classe* 1.1885, *Chaloupe à vapeur* 1.1888.

A law of 10 January 1883 allocated funds to a *Mission de l'Ouest africain* to continue and develop the work of Savorgnan de Brazza, who between 1876 and 1882 had conducted two major discovery expeditions along the Congo and Ogowe rivers. Brazza was designated leader of the new expedition by a decree of 5 February 1883 (just before he was promoted from Enseigne de vaisseau) and left France on 21 March 1883 to begin it. The mission itself ran from 21 April 1883 to 26 May 1885.

Brazza had Claparède at Saint Denis design two steam launches for his new expedition to the Congo, one paddle and one screw. The screw-propelled *Djoué* (the only colonial steam launch initially classed as an aviso) was to explore the Congo while the paddle *Licona* (see Steam Launches, *Chaloupes à vapeur,* below) was to provide communications between the Alima River (a Congo tributary) and Brazzaville. On 5 March 1883 the Navy accepted in principle Claparède's designs and on 15 March Claparède forwarded plans for use in drafting a contract. On 10 April 1883 the Machinery Commission (the *Commission permanente des machines et du grand outillage*) was directed to negotiate the contract, and it was approved on 10 May 1883. On 10 December 1883 Claparède was instructed to send the two dismantled craft to Le Havre for shipping to Gabon on a chartered packet. Both vessels arrived in Gabon in sections on 15 February 1884.

*Djoué* had a narrow hull, with a deck at the ends and around the edges with the centre uncovered except by a large awning. She had two boilers on the centreline, each with its own funnel and with a common stokehold between them. Her two small engines were aft of the boilers, and the gun was mounted near the bow.

The first *Djoué* only served for a short time. During a difficult portage for which she was disassembled and cases containing the parts were embarked on local pirogues, many of the pirogues capsized and the parts they carried were lost in the river. An order was therefore placed with the builder for another *Djoué*, identical in all respects to the first. This one was successfully tried in around September 1886.

Claparède on 21 July 1883 produced a plan for an apparently identical *chaloupe-canonnière démontable pour le Haut Niger* which became *Niger* (listed under Steam Launches below), and the later *Mage* was also similar. *Djoué* has been identified in error as the converted *Torpilleur no 4*.

The *Djoué*, a sectional and transportable vessel built for Savorgnan de Brazza that the navy classed as a 3rd class aviso. Brazza needed a small river steamer with very shallow draught and considerable speed to get through the rapids in the Congo River and able to be dismantled into pieces small enough to be transported in a caravan. She had two wood-burning tubular boilers that could also be dismantled. After the loss of many parts in a portage, a second *Djoué* was ordered entirely similar to the first, and as of September 1886 she had just been tried 'with remarkable success'. This drawing shows three stokers labouring in the stokehold between the two boilers and their funnels, two engineers tending to the engines near the stern, and the officer in charge, perhaps Savorgnan de Brazza, taking notes at the rail. The entire crew is European except for one African, perhaps a guide. For the overall appearance of this type vessel see the *chaloupe à vapeur Niger* below. (*Le monde illustré, 25 September 1886, page 196*)

---

**Dimensions & tons:** 18.6m x 2.6m excluding rudder. 28t disp. Draught 0.7m. Men: 15.
**Machinery:** 25nhp, 100ihp. Trials: 9kts. 2 screws. 2 single-cylinder engines. 2 tubular boilers.
**Guns:** 1 x 37mm revolving cannon.

*Djoué* Anc. Éts. Claparède, Saint Denis.
On list 1.1884. Ord: 10.5.1883 (contract approved). K: 1883. L: 1883. Comm: 2.1884
Accepted 12 December 1883. Replaced 1886 with an identical copy (see above). Offered to the Colonial Ministry at no charge 26.1.1892, finally accepted 9.7.1895 effective 1.1.1896. Struck 23.7.1895.

---

*OLUMO. Aviso de 3e classe.* 25nhp screw harbour passenger transport with an iron hull and a straight bow. One funnel aft, two masts, schooner-rigged mainmast and lugger rigged mizzen. Purchased.

In mid-January 1883 the navy agreed to support the expedition of de Brazza to the west coast of Africa (the Congo), and on 1 February 1883 it asked representatives in London to find and buy a screw steamer of 200 to 300 tons. On 17 March 1883 the navy directed London to negotiate for the purchase of the steamer *Two Roses*. The purchase was completed at the end of March, and on 4 April 1883 Paris informed Cherbourg that she would soon arrive there and assigned her the name *Olumo*. She arrived at Cherbourg from Hull on 10 April 1883 with her previous owner on board.

At Hull *Two Roses* had been used to carry travellers and their baggage for very short distances. She thus had no facilities for a crew or cargo and never went to sea. She had been authorized by the Board of Trade to carry 264 passengers in river service. At Cherbourg in April and May 1883 quarters for the crew and officers and a cargo hold were fitted. The machinery took up most of the after portion of the ship with the officers' spaces in the stern, the cargo hold amidships and the crew's quarters and storerooms forward. By the time the French refit was completed all that was left of the English ship was the iron hull, engine, boilers, and flat bottom.

The yard that built her, C. Norfolk & Co., was owned by John Norfolk and Christopher Norfolk, iron ship builders, located at the Baltic Iron Works, South Bridge Road, Borough of Kingston-upon-Hull (the full name of Hull). C. Norfolk & Co. was in liquidation in 1883.

*Olumo* was shown in the January 1884 *Annuaire de la Marine* as a *transport à vapeur* on a mission in West Africa commanded by Lieutenant de vaisseau De Brazza-Savorgnan (sic), who was appointed to command her on 18 July 1883.

*The characteristics are based on a devis dated 26.5.1883.*
**Dimensions & tons:** 24.40m wl (bow to rudder) x 5.50m wl. 171.850t disp. Draught: 2.15m maximum. Men: 26.
**Machinery:** 25nhp and 4.25kg/cm² boiler pressure. Trials (24.5.1883) 116.06ihp = 7.492kts at 135rpm. 1 screw. 1 vertical compound engine with 2 cylinders of 0.2935m and 0.559m diameter and 0.45m stroke. 1 cylindrical return flame boiler. 57.56t coal.
**Guns:** 1 x 4pdr (86mm) bronze mountain rifle

*Olumo* C. Norfolk & Co, Hull/Vulcan Ironworks Co., Hull.
On list 1.1884. Built: 1882. Comm: 26.5.1883.
Arrived at Cherbourg 10.4.1883, measurements taken off 8.5.1883 and first static machinery trial at Cherbourg 18.5.1883 following extensive modifications. Left Cherbourg for Dakar and Gabon 28.5.1883. Replaced at the end of December 1885 in the Gulf of Guinea by *Mésange*, returned to Lorient 11.6.1886 and decommissioned 25.6.1886. Found to be in bad condition, but even if not she had been chosen for a special purpose (the Brazza mission) and was unsuitable for any other use by the navy. Struck 13.12.1886. Sold 17.12.1887 at Lorient.

———————

**CIGOGNE Class.** *Aviso de 3ᵉ classe.* 40nhp paddle aviso with a galvanised steel hull and a straight bow. One funnel, two masts, schooner-brig rig (later schooner). Designed by Huet.

On 15 January 1884 the *Conseil des travaux* examined draft specifications for an *aviso de flottille à roues* of the *Basilic* type referred to it by Minister of Marine Peyron on 13 December 1883. These included a waterline length of 30.00m, a waterline beam of 5.50m, and a uniform 1.20 metre minimum draught, all these figures being very close to those of *Basilic*, whose comparable displacement was 112.913 tons. The new ship would have an armament of two 65mm QF and one revolving cannon, a speed of 9 knots, a steel hull, and masts and sails as in *Basilic*. The engines of *Basilic*, however, was not considered very suitable for the kind of service involved and new ones would need to be designed. The Council endorsed the specifications except for the 30m length which it though would need to be increased to 32m. On 23 December 1884 the Council examined the seven designs received in response to these specifications. It selected the one of naval constructor Victor Marie Pierre Auguste Huet as satisfying the specifications well, but then noted that a thorough study of service in the colonies had shown a need to lodge the white Europeans in the bow (a more healthy location for them) and the black Africans aft. Huet's revised plans were dated 28 February 1885. The ships were first shown belatedly in the 1888 budget as being built by Cail under an 1885 contract, both lay idle for years before being used.

*The characteristics are based on the design for* Lézard.
**Dimensions & tons:** 34.06m wl, 34.09m pp (wl fwd to rudder) x 5.504m ext and wl. 129.5t disp. Draught: 1.203m mean, 1.203m aft. Men: 28.
**Machinery:** 40nhp and 160ihp designed, 9.0kts at 33.65rpm and

4.25kg/cm² boiler pressure. Paddles 3.60m diameter. 1 compound engine with direct action and two inclined cylinders of 0.58m and 0.94m diameter and 0.69m stroke. 1 special tubular cylindrical boiler. 16.00t coal. Range 900nm @ 9kts.
**Guns:** 2 x 65mm/16 M1881 landing, 2 x 37mm Hotchkiss.

*Cigogne* Anc. Ets. Cail, Paris-Grenelle.
On list 1.1886. Ord: 24.8.1885 (contract). K: 12.10.1885. L: 2.9.1886. C: 3.1887.
Budget 1884. Contract included engines. In reserve 1888-91, out of commission 1891-93, replaced *Basilic* in Gabon 1893. Struck 23.4.1898. BU 1899.

*Lézard* Anc. Ets. Cail, Paris-Grenelle.
On list 1.1886. Ord: 24.8.1885 (contract). K: 12.10.1885. L: 23.2.1887. C: 1888.
Budget 1884. Contract included engines. In reserve 1888-91, out of commission 1891-98, replaced *Salamandre* in Senegal 1898-1904. Struck 5.8.1904, to the Domaines at Dakar 1.1906 to be sold.

———————

## (D) Aviso Transports (*Avisos-transports*).

Previously classed as *Transports avisos* and listed in the transport category but moved to the aviso category as *Avisos-transports* in the 1.1884 fleet list. To *Avisos* 1.1909.

**MEURTHE Class.** *Avisos-transports.* Aviso transports with wooden hulls, iron deck beams and beam shelves, and ram-shaped bows. One funnel just aft of the mainmast, three masts, barque rig.

These ships were ordered in 1882 to to Sabattier's design for the *Allier* class *transports avisos* modified with a ram-shaped (inverted) bow by de Bussy's *Service technique des constructions navales*.

*The characteristics are based on the design for* Durance *and* Meurthe.
**Dimensions & tons:** 63.54m wl (+0.24m ram), 65.04m (wl fwd to rudder) x 10.50m ext and wl. 1597.0t disp. Draught: 4.49m mean, 4.89m aft.
**Machinery:** 190nhp and 820ihp designed, 11kts at 85 rpm and 6.0 kg/cm² boiler pressure. 1 screw. 1 vertical compound engine with 2 cylinders of 0.70m stroke. 2 boilers.
**Guns:** 4 x 138.6mm, 2 x 90mm, 4 x 37mm.

*Meurthe* Rochefort Dyd.
On list 1.1883. K: 1.3.1882. L: 11.7.1885. Comm: late 1885 (trials), 1886 (full).
Budget 1883. Construction reassigned from Brest to Rochefort c1882. At Réunion and in the Indian Ocean 1886-90, then out of commission until sent to the Pacific 1900-01. Replaced by *Vaucluse* at Noumea and out of service there 3.1906. Struck 6.9.1906, for sale in New Caledonia 1906-1907.

*Durance* Rochefort Dyd.
On list 1.1883. K: 11.3.1882. L: 10.1.1887. Comm: 8.1887 (trials). C: late 1887.
Budget 1884. In reserve 1887-91, then in Tahiti 1891-95, Senegal 1897-99, and the Pacific 1900-05. Struck 4.12.1905, central ship of the 1ˢᵗ flotilla of submarines at Toulon 1905-1910. Sold 30.12.1910 at Toulon to BU.

———————

**AUBE Class.** *Avisos-transports.* Aviso transports with wooden hulls, iron deck beams and beam shelves, and clipper bows. One funnel just aft of the mainmast, three masts, barque rig. Design of Sabattier.

In the aviso transports ordered in 1883 and 1885 the Navy reverted to Sabattier's design for the *Allier* class with the original clipper bow.

The aviso-transport (ex transport aviso) *Meurthe* photographed at Algiers on 1 September (7$^{bre}$) 1886. She was one of two transport avisos ordered in 1882 with a ram-shaped (inverted) bow; those that followed in 1883 and 1885 had standard clipper bows. These small armed transports were moved in 1884 to the aviso part of the fleet list and redesignated *avisos-transports*, suggesting that they had become more important to the navy as cruising gunboats than as cargo carriers. *(NHHC from ONI album of French warships, NH-74880)*

**Dimensions & tons:** 63.70m wl x 10.50m ext. 1580t disp. Draught: 4.59m mean, 4.99m aft. Men: 118.
**Machinery:** 190nhp (220nhp in *Aube*, 200nhp in *Eure*, *Manche*, and *Vaucluse*) and 820ihp designed. Trials (*Aube*) 895ihp = 12.45kts at 90 rpm. 1 screw. 1 horizontal compound engine with direct connecting rods. 2 boilers.
**Guns:** 4 x 138.6mm, 2 x 90mm, 4 x 37mm. (*Vaucluse*) 2 x 138.6mm, 4 x 37mm.

*Aube* Augustin Normand, Le Havre.
On list 1.1884. K: 1884. L: 23.11.1885. Comm: 1886 (trials). C: 1887.
Budget 1885. In the Indian Ocean 1886-87, Indochina 1891-92, Tahiti 1894-99, and the Pacific 1899-1900. Struck 30.6.1904, for sale in New Caledonia 1904-1911.

*Eure* Augustin Normand, Le Havre.
On list 1.1884. K: 11.3.1884. L: 5.4.1886. C: 1889.
Budget 1885. Completed and to reserve 1889, full commission in the

Indian Ocean 1890-93 and the Pacific 1896-00. Struck 8.8.1901, hulk for the fixed defences at New Caledonia 1901-1906, for sale 1906-1911.

*Rance* Lorient Dyd/Indret.
On list 1.1884. Ord: 7.5.1883. K: 1883. L: 27.3.1888. C: 1890.
Budget 1885. Construction reassigned from Rochefort to Lorient c1884. Completed and to reserve 1890, full commission 20.1.1894 to 1896 for a hydrographic mission in the Indian Ocean followed by war service in Madagascar. Returned to the Indian Ocean 1899-1902 and back there again for a hydrographic mission 1905-08. Struck 3.8.1910, for sale at Toulon 1910-1911. Offered for sale 1.8.1911 at Toulon by the Domaines with *Amiral Baudin, Magenta, Pascal, Milan,* and smaller vessels including torpedo boats and submarines.

*Manche* Cherbourg Dyd/Indret.
On list 1.1886. Ord: 27.1.1885. K: 2.1886. L: 16.10.1890. C: 1891.
Budget 1886. Completed and to reserve 1891. In 2$^{nd}$ category reserve 1891-1902 except for cruises to Iceland and Newfoundland in 1891-92, 1897-98, 1900-01, and 1902-03. In the Indian Ocean 1904-05, then on hydrographic missions in Indochina 1905-06, the Far East 06-08, and Indochina 1908-14. Struck 4.3.1920, for sale at Saigon 1920-1922.

*Vaucluse* Rochefort Dyd/Indret.
On list 1.1886. Ord: 18.9.1885. K: 1.5.1886. L: 17.4.1901. Comm: 1901 (trials). C: 1902.

Budget 1887. Construction suspended from 1895 or before to 1901. Trials at Rochefort 1901-1902, then loaned to the PTT (Post Office) 1902-1905. In the Pacific 1905-07 and Indian Ocean 1907-08, then on a hydrographic mission hydrographique in Madagascar 1908-14. Listed as a *navire hydrographique* (hydrographic ship) 1920. Off main list 1920/1921 and for sale at Lorient 1921/1922. Hulk at Lorient 1922-1929, landing hulk 1929-1939. Sunk 19.6.1940 by aerial bombardment at Lorient. Refloated 12.1940, sunk again by aerial bombardment 2.1943. BU 1948 in place.

––––––––––

## (E) Torpedo Avisos (*Avisos-torpilleurs*).

Added in the 1.1883 fleet list as *Torpilleurs avisos* under *Bâtiments torpilleurs*, but moved to the aviso category as *Avisos-torpilleurs* 1.1885.

**BOMBE Class.** *Avisos-torpilleurs.* Oversized torpedo boats with a ram bow, low hull, single slightly raked funnel, and three similarly raked masts with light schooner rig and no bowsprit. Remained *Avisos-torpilleurs* 1.1896, to *Contre-torpilleurs* 1.1909.

On 15 July 1882 Minister of Marine Jauréguiberry forwarded to the *Conseil des travaux* a design for a 280-ton *torpilleur de haute mer* (called a *Torpilleur aviso* by January 1883) produced by naval constructor Théodore Jean Maurice Marchal for de Bussy's *Service technique des constructions navales* to specifications supplied by the Minister, no doubt with de Bussy's

–––––––––––––––––––––––––––––––––––––––

Sail and fittings (*armement*) plan by the Forges et Chantiers de la Méditerranée of the *Bombe* class torpedo aviso. The plans were signed on 19 June 1886 by the chief engineer at Graville, A. Marmiesse, and certified to represent the ship as fitted on 21 June 1886 by naval constructor A. Rabourdin. Note the original arrangement of two torpedo tubes side by side in the bow which proved unsatisfactory and the absence of the two after sponsons where the torpedo tubes were subsequently placed.

help. These included a speed of 18 knots for 5-6 hours, a range of 1,000nm at 12 knots, an armament of two light guns, two revolving cannon, and two fixed torpedo tubes above the waterline, and a crew of 45 men including 4 officers.

Marchal's design measured 55.60m in length, 6.80m beam on the waterline, 1.80m depth of hull, and displaced 280.589 tons. The three main hull dimensions were those of Normand's 27-metre torpedo boats multiplied by a factor of 2.06. The lines were the same forward and amidships but a little finer aft. The machinery consisted of four engines identical to those of the Normand 27-metre boats driving two screws, two screws being necessary for a vessel without sails. The boats could run on two engines only and could make 10 knots on a single engine. They had four boilers like the one in Normand's *Torpilleur nº 60* in two boiler rooms. Steaming on two engines and two boilers would allow maintenance on the others. The normal load of 53 tons of coal would give a range of 1,262nm at 12 knots and the bunkers could carry another 125 tons giving 4,238nm at 12 knots, although this would bring the boat too low in the water and was to be avoided. The design had two fixed tubes for 4.40-metre 356mm torpedoes above water in the bow as in *Torpilleur nº 60*. The armament was two 100mm guns amidships in sponsons and eight revolving cannon. The ample coal supply in its subdivided bunkers provided protection to the vitals. The Council approved the design with the single reservation that the size of the torpedo room should be increased to allow for the use of 5.75-metre 381mm torpedoes, a change that was not made.

The closely paired bow torpedo tubes proved unsatisfactory in trials and were moved to sponsons on the sides aft before entry into service. The design called for two propulsion groups on two shafts, each group with two 450ihp vertical compound engines of the type in Normand's torpedo boats with 2 cylinders of 0.32m and 0.58m diameter and 0.38m stroke operating at 335rpm and 8.1kg/cm$^2$ boiler pressure. Larger engines, one per shaft, were substituted during construction. The original torpedo boat boilers were unsatisfactory and were replaced in 1886-1890. The boats were built in part to accompany the fleet but their ends were low and they were overweight, making them poor sea boats, and they were too light to maintain

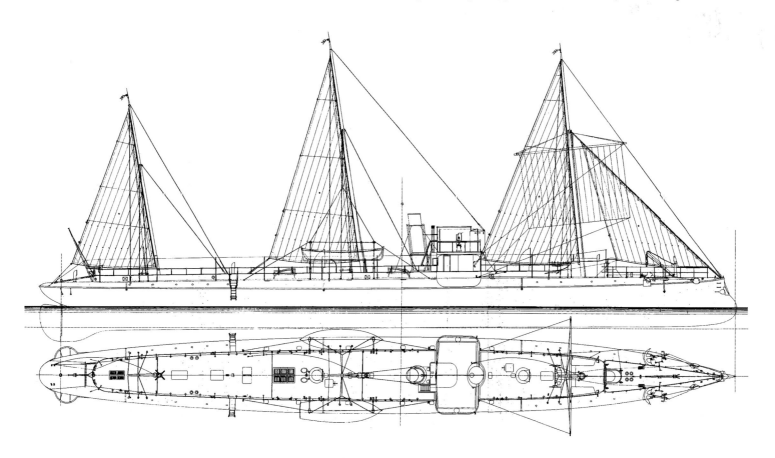

their speed in heavy seas. All ended up in the *Défenses mobiles* as leaders (*divisionnaires*) for torpedo boats, although their speed was 6-7 knots less than that of their torpedo boats.

The names *Achéron, Cocyte, Phlégéton,* and *Styx* were proposed for four of this class, but names of weapons, *Dragonne, Flèche, Couleuvrine,* and *Lance,* were finally assigned and the names of the infernal rivers were given to armoured gunboats. The *Bombe* class was moved in the January 1885 fleet list out of the torpedo boat category to the aviso category, leaving the *Balny* class *torpilleurs de haute mer* as the largest vessels in the torpedo boat listing.

On 9 December 1892 the *Conseil des travaux* rejected a design by naval constructor Aurous for an aviso carrying a mortar, stating that the principle of installing mortars on vessels of small displacement with little stability as a gun platform and no or practically no protection should be rejected, especially in a case like this one in which they constituted nearly exclusively the armament of the vessel. In 1895-96 during his first ministry Lockroy took up this idea on the proposition of Lieutenant de vaisseau Louël, an ordnance officer on his staff, and decided to convert *Dragonne* into an aviso-mortier. A mortar borrowed from the Army was mounted forward and trials were called successful, but as Lockroy was no longer Minister the matter was quickly dropped and the gun removed. When Lockroy returned to the Ministry in 1898 he ordered arming with short Army model guns all of the *Bombe/Dragonne* type and also asked an eminent commercial engineer to design a fast aviso-mortier. Work was in progress on mountings for and installation of the guns on the *Bombes* when he again left office in 1899 and once again the project was abandoned.

**Dimensions & tons:** 61.20m oa, 59.200m pp x 6.740m ext, 6.540m wl. 319.848t disp (designed), 321t (normal), 395-418t (full load). Draught: 1.60m forward, 1.80m mean, 2.00m aft, 2.90m aft under propeller guard (1.95m forward and 3.16m under guard at full load). Men: 53, including 4 officers.
**Machinery:** 1,800ihp designed at 8.5kg/cm² boiler pressure. Trials 18 to 18.5kts. 2 screws. 2 compound engines with 3 cylinders of 0.48m (1) and 0.56m (2) diameter and 0.40m stroke. 4 cylindrical boilers. 97t coal (normal), 110t (max). Range 1,700nm @ 10kts (designed).
**Guns:** 4 x 47mm QF (1 fore, 1 aft, 2 on the sides in sponsons under the bridge) 3 x 37mm revolving cannon. **Torpedoes:** 2 tubes for 356mm (4.42m) torpedoes (initially in the bow, soon moved to sponsons on the sides aft).

*Bombe* F.C. Méditerranée, Le Havre-Graville.
On list 1.1883. Ord: 29.11.1883 (contract). K: 1883. L: 16.4.1885. C: 1887.
Budget 1885. Left builder for Cherbourg 8.6.1885. Returned to builder for boiler repairs 7.5.1886. To reserve at Cherbourg 1887, to the Mediterranean soon afterwards. Reboiled 1886/90 with Du Temple boilers and 1901 with Lagrafel et d'Allest boilers. Struck 24.8.1909, for sale at Cherbourg 1909-1911.

*Couleuvrine* F.C. Méditerranée, Le Havre-Graville.
On list 1.1883. Ord: 29.11.1883 (contract). K: 1883. L: 30.6.1885. Comm: 4.1887 (trials), 1887 (full).
Budget 1885. Left builder for Cherbourg 21.8.1885. At Toulon 1887-1900. With *Dragonne,* tested early in her career with a Army 155mm mortar as a bateau canon like *Gabriel Charmes.* Struck 24.3.1910, offered for sale at Rochefort 17.11.1911.

*Dague* F.C. Méditerranée, Le Havre-Graville.
On list 1.1883. Ord: 29.11.1883 (contract). K: 1883. L: 30.7.1885. Comm: 7.11.1885 (trials), Comm: 29.1.1888 (full).
Budget 1885. From builder to Cherbourg 6.11.1885, boilers rejected for leaks, after initial trials and returned to builder and decomm. 30.4.1886. Towed to Le Havre 7.5.1886 for new boilers, back to Cherbourg and recomm. for trials 11.12.1887, manned for trials 19.12.1887. In naval review at Cherbourg 11.9.1888, to Toulon and

to reserve for repairs, comm. in the *Escadre d'évolutions* 17.6.1889, spent entire career in the Mediterranean. Received Du Temple boilers in 1892 which gave much trouble. Struck 18.10.1904. Sold 11.2.1905 at Toulon to Goutte of Marseille.

*Dragonne* F.C. Méditerranée, Le Havre-Graville.
On list 1.1883. Ord: 29.11.1883 (contract). K: 1883. L: 28.8.1885. C: 1888.
Budget 1885. Left builder for Cherbourg 6.11.1885. Returned to builder for boiler repairs 7.5.1886. To the Mediterranean soon after completion. Conducted trials 3.2.1897 with an Army 155mm mortar as a bateau canon like *Gabriel Charmes* and sank the hulk of the old paddle frigate *Panama* in the Rade des Vignettes just outside Toulon. Struck 9.3.1910, for sale at Toulon 1910-1911. Offered for sale 1.8.1911 at Toulon by the Domaines with *Amiral Baudin, Magenta, Pascal, Milan,* and smaller vessels including torpedo boats and submarines.

*Flèche* F.C. Méditerranée, Le Havre-Graville.
On list 1.1883. Ord: 29.11.1883 (contract). K: 1883. L: 8.11.1885. C: 1888.
Budget 1885. Completed and to reserve at Cherbourg 1888, to the Mediterranean soon afterwards. Received Lagrafel et d'Allest boilers 1898. Struck 24.3.1910, for sale in Tunisia (Bizerte) 1910-1912.

*Lance* F.C. Méditerranée, Le Havre-Graville.
On list 1.1883. Ord: 29.11.1883 (contract). K: 1883. L: 20.4.1886. Comm: 1888 (trials), 1890 (full).
Budget 1885. Reboiled by builder 1889-1890 with Normand boilers, in commission 1890. Entire career in the north. In reserve for modifications 1897-98, received Normand boilers, trials 8.1898. Struck 22.11.1913, for sale at Cherbourg 1913-1914.

*Sainte Barbe* Anc. Éts. Claparède, Saint Denis.
On list 1.1883. Ord: 27.8.1883 (contract). K: 1883. L: 10.10.1885. C: 1889.
Budget 1885. Contract included engines. Probably fitted out by Claparède at Rouen-Petit Quévilly. Reboiled 1886-89 with Lagrafel et d'Allest boilers. In reserve at Cherbourg 1889. Entire career in the north. Struck 3.11.1910. Offered for sale 20.7.1911 at Brest by the Domaines with *Formidable, Valmy,* and others.

*Salve* Anc. Éts. Claparède, Saint Denis.
On list 1.1883. Ord: 27.8.1883 (contract). K: 1884. L: 6.2.1886. C: 1889.
Budget 1885. Contract included engines. Fitted out by Claparède at Rouen-Petit Quévilly. Reboiled 1886-89 with Godart et Petit boilers and in 1893 with Oriolle boilers. In reserve at Cherbourg 1889. Entire career in the north. Refitted 1898 with modified Oriolle-type tubular boilers. Struck 28.7.1906. Sold at Lorient to BU.

---

*LÉGER* **Class.** *Avisos-torpilleurs.* Torpedo avisos with a low hull, a vertical bow, two vertical masts, and one large and tall vertical funnel. Designed by Marchal. Remained *Avisos-torpilleurs* with the *Bombe* class 1.1896, to *Contre-torpilleurs* 1.1909.

On 8 May 1888 Minister Krantz informed Lorient that he planned to start construction soon of two torpedo avisos like *Bombe* and added that before doing so he wanted to know if Marchal, the designer of *Bombe,* had any improvements to propose. On 19 June 1888 he invited Marchal to include in the new design boilers more powerful than those in *Bombe,* and a study of Belleville boilers was also soon directed. On 31 July 1888 the *Conseil des travaux* examined Marchal's proposal for the modifications. The Council noted that the hull would need to be enlarged to accommodate changes made to *Bombe* during construction and others proposed for the new ships, but it agreed with Marchal that increasing the length was to be ruled out because of its negative effect on manoeuvrability. *Bombe* also had hull lines

The torpedo aviso *Léger*. She and her sister *Lévrier* were initially to have been improvements on the *Bombe* class but after a lengthy design process little remained of *Bombe* except the low hull and the overall dimensions. All three torpedo tubes are visible here, with one in the bow, one between the foremast and the massive strictly vertical funnel, and one between the funnel and the after mast. Both of the deck tubes were stowed to port as seen here, but they could be pivoted to fire to either side of the ship. *(Postcard by A. Bougault)*

based on single screw torpedo boats which didn't fit well with twin screws. The depth of hull was increased without increasing the maximum draught to improve the vessel's seakeeping, and the lines of *Condor* and the form of her stern were applied amidships and aft to position the two engines and propeller shafts in the best possible way and minimize vibrations aft. The Council recommended triple expansion engines with two large diameter boilers like those in *Condor* but without increasing the power of the machinery. Toulon had requested three torpedo tubes instead of two, and the Council put one tube fixed in the bow as high up as possible and the other two, imitating the English practice, either paired or singly on a rotating platform amidships with fairly large arcs of fire both forward and aft of the beam. They could be pivoted on the two air shafts for the boilers and protected by 4mm chrome steel plating.

The Council examined the design for this class four more times, on 17 August, 9 November, 28 December 1888, and 22 March 1889. Marchal's first design had included a gigantic ram-shaped bow as in the contemporary armoured cruiser *Dupuy de Lôme* which the Council quickly changed, ultimately to a vertical bow. Marchal's second and third efforts included two 15-metre high funnels on which topmasts with observation posts were stepped, the Council preferred to add two small masts and return to the use of a single oval funnel with the condition that it would have to be tall enough to ensure adequate natural draught. The deckhouses would be concentrated amidships and the air shafts at the ends of the boiler rooms would be restored, one offset to starboard and the other to port,

where they would facilitate the aiming of torpedoes on that side. Marchal's fourth design redistributed the armament in a way that invited the Council to replace a 47mm gun forward with a 65mm gun. The Council also wanted to increase the power of the engines to 2,200ihp at natural draught as the boilers seemed able to provide the steam. The fifth revision resolved most outstanding issues except that the details of the torpedo tube installation amidships still needed further study. The Council wanted each tube to be able to fire to either side. The ships were delivered with one tube forward of the funnel and one aft of it, both normally stowed to port. The many changes from the *Bombe* design did not include an increase in torpedo size.

Despite their awkward appearance they turned out to be good sea boats. They were the first small ships to have Belleville boilers after the experiments with them in 1877 on *Torpilleur nº 7*. Their intended displacement of 414 tons was substantially exceeded. The machinery contract with Creusot was dated 7 August 1889. As in the *Bombe* class, their relatively large coal supply provided some protection to the hulls. Service speeds rarely reached 15 knots, their armaments were weak, and some critics saw them as inferior to the *Bombe* type, but both saw continuous active service.

**Dimensions & tons:** 62.80m oa, 60.92m pp x 6.80m. 517t disp.
   Draught: 2.72m forward, 3.20m aft.
**Machinery:** 2,200ihp designed at 17kg/cm² boiler pressure. Trials (*Léger*) 18.58kts, (*Lévrier*) 18.38kts. 2 screws. 2 triple expansion engines with 3 cylinders of 0.385m, 0.610m, and 0.920m diameter and 0.440m stroke. 2 Belleville boilers. 104t coal.
**Guns:** 1 x 65mm/50 QF (fwd), 3 x 47mm/40 M1885 QF (2 on sides in sponsons abreast the funnel, 1 aft), 2 x 37mm revolving cannon (above the bridge). **Torpedoes:** 3 tubes for 356mm (4.42m) torpedoes (1 bow, 2 on deck amidships forward and aft of the funnel).

*Léger* Lorient Dyd/Schneider, Creusot.
On list 1.1889. Ord: 4.1.1889. K: 1889. L: 4.8.1891. Trials: 1892.
   C: 7.1892.

Budget 1889. Engine contract 7.8.1889. *Escadre de la Méditerranée* 1893-1896, replaced *Lévrier* as station ship at Constantinople 1896-99, then to Crete. *Défense mobile* at Algiers as torpedo boat division leader 1902-08. Struck 24.8.1909, for sale at Toulon 1909-1910.

*Lévrier* Lorient Dyd/Schneider, Creusot.
On list 1.1889. Ord: 4/5.1.1889. K: 1889. L: 26.3.1891. Trials: 1892. C: 1.1893.
Budget 1889. Engine contract 7.8.1889. *Escadre de la Méditerranée* 1893-1896, briefly at Constantinople, then station ship at Crete 1896-99. *Défense mobile* at Ajaccio as division leader 1901-07. Struck 6.3.1908, retained at Toulon as gunnery target 1908-1910.

———

*D'IBERVILLE. Aviso-torpilleur.* Large torpedo aviso with a forecastle and poop, a ram-shaped bow, two pole masts, and two nearly vertical funnels with the navigating bridge between them. Designed by A.C. Loire. To *Contre-torpilleur d'escadre* 1.1896, to *Contre-torpilleur* 1.1901, and to *Torpilleur d'escadre* 1.1914 (directed 14.3.1913).

The extraordinary 1890 budget (law of 22 November 1889) included four *avisos-torpilleurs* of 420 tons and 18 knots similar to *Léger*. However, Minister Barbey and the *Conseil supérieur* soon substituted for these a larger type of 925 tons and 21.5knots, probably influenced by the Italian *Partenope*. On 3 June 1890 the Conseil drew up specifications for the ship that included a displacement not over 850 tons, a draught aft of about 3.50m, triple expansion engines, multitubular boilers, twin screws, a speed of 22 knots at forced draught and a normal range of 4,500nm at 10 knots with bunkers for 6,000nm at 10 knots. The armament was to be one 100mm QF gun forward, three 65mm QF guns (two in sponsons amidships and one aft), and four 37mm guns. The ship was to have six above-water tubes for the new 5-metre 450mm torpedo of which one in the bow was trainable to 5 degrees to either side, 4 on the sides had as wide training arcs as possible, and one in the stern was trainable to 20 degrees to each side. For protection the ship would have 40mm hard steel shields for the 100mm and 65mm guns and on the conning tower. Outboard of the engines and boilers would be side plating of 25mm hard steel from 50cm below the waterline to the upper deck, whose thickness would be increased to 15mm of hard steel. Additional protection within this area would be provided by coal bunkers on the sides and forward of the boiler room. The

crew would be 100 men. The rig was to be two military masts carrying only steadying sails and having armed tops, each with one of the 37mm QF guns at the top with a searchlight under it. There would be two smaller searchlights on the bridge wings over the side 65mm sponsons.

On 23 December 1890 the *Conseil des travaux* examined three designs received in response to these specifications and concluded that two (by FCM La Seyne and C.A. Gironde) had failed to meet the specifications while one (A.C. Loire) had met them only by taking advantage of a provision that the Council could no longer accept. The Council then changed the specified speed to 21.5 knots with the associated engine power and the range to 3,500 nm at 10 knots while reducing the thickness of the coal bunkers on the sides, although overall bunker capacity was to be increased. On 16 July 1890 Minister Barbey had directed that the side torpedo tubes were to be in twin mountings. The three firms were then invited to resubmit their proposals. On 21 April 1891 the Council examined resubmitted designs from A.C. Loire and C.A. Gironde (FCM La Seyne did not resubmit). The Council accepted the proposal of A.C. Loire subject to the replacement of the military masts with light masts, repositioning the two 37mm guns from the masthead tops to the after end of the forecastle and moving the masthead searchlights to the ends of the hull.

The press reported during 1890 that *Léger* and *Lévrier* were to be completed during the year and that three new vessels of that type named *D'Iberville, Catinat,* and *Lavoisier* along with a fourth unnamed vessel were to be commenced under the 1890 extraordinary budget. Ultimately only *D'Iberville* was charged to the extraordinary 1890 budget, *Cassini* being moved to the regular budget when her design was changed in 1891-2 and *Casabianca* following later (the names *Catinat* and *Lavoisier* having in the meantime been taken by cruisers).

**Dimensions & tons:** 82.015m oa, 81.900m wl, 80.00m pp x 8.200m ext (above wl), 8.080m wl. 924.585t disp (designed). Draught: (designed) 3.130m mean, 3.610m aft. Men: 144 including 8 officers (1900).

**Machinery:** 5,000ihp designed at 18kg/cm$^2$ boiler pressure. Speed 21.5kts. Trials (27.7.1894) 5060ihp = 21.61kts at 292.3rpm. 2 screws. 2 triple expansion engines with 4 cylinders of 0.56m (1), 0.86m (1), and 0.92m (2) diameter and 0.484m stroke. 8 Lagrafel et d'Allest boilers.

**Armour:**

Side: The regular 6mm sides over the machinery were reinforced with an extra internal layer of 7mm hard steel plating and an extra external layer of 12mm (7mm at the very top) hull plating for a total of 25mm.

Decks: The regular 6mm deck in the same area was reinforced with an extra 9mm layer of hull plating for a total of 15mm.

Conning tower (special steel): 40mm.

**Guns:**

(Design) 1 x 100mm QF forecastle, 3 x 65mm QF side sponsons and

———

Outboard profile from the lines plan and overhead view of the torpedo aviso *D'Iberville,* built on the plans of the Société des Ateliers et Chantiers de la Loire. The unsigned and undated plans by A.C. Loire show the torpedo tubes as designed and fitted, they were soon removed.

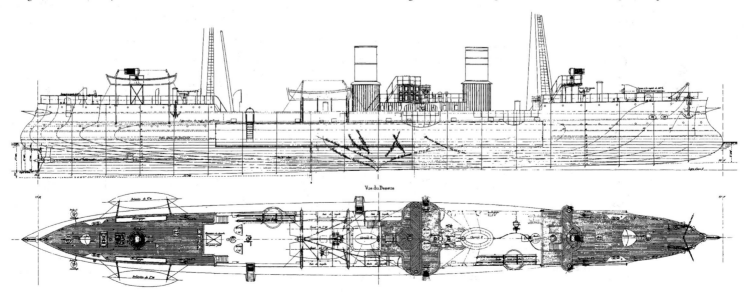

The bridge, located between the funnels, of the torpedo aviso *D'Iberville* at Toulon in 1898. Several sailors are demonstrating their specialties, including two lookouts and one signalman on the bridge and some gunners in the gun sponson, all in dress uniforms, and several engineers in work uniforms including one leaning on the after funnel. *(NHHC, NH-64455)*

poop, 4 x 37mm QF. **Torpedoes:** 6 tubes for 450mm torpedoes (1 in the bow, 1 in the stern, 1 deck mount with twin tubes forward to starboard and one aft to port, all above water). **Searchlights:** 4 x 60cm.
(1900) 1 x 100mm/45 M1891(2) Canet QF (forward), 3 x 65mm/50 M1891 Canet QF (1 aft, 2 sides), 6 x 47mm/40 M1885 QF, no torpedo tubes. 4 searchlights (later 2).

*D'Iberville* A.C. Loire, Nantes/A.C. Loire, Saint Denis.
On list 1.1892. Ord: 26.8.1891. K: 1891. L: 11.9.1893. Trials: 6.1894.
Budget 1890 (extraordinary). Service with the *Escadre de la Méditerranée* ending with station duty at Suda Bay, Crete, in 1898. Then in reserve

until assigned to the Governor General of French Indochina on 12.9.1908, causing significant enhancements in her accommodations. (She was previously considered in 1907 for use by to the Governor General of French West Africa replacing *Jeanne Blanche*.) Remained in the Far East into 1915, then patrolled off Algeria before being placed in pre-condemnation reserve at Toulon in 1917. For sale at Toulon 1920-1922. Struck 7.6.1920. Sold 1922 at Toulon to BU.

———————

*CASSINI* **Class.** *Avisos-torpilleurs.* Large torpedo aviso with a forecastle and poop, a ram-shaped bow, two raked masts, and two raked funnels with the navigating bridge between them. To *Contre-torpilleurs d'escadre* 1.1896, to *Contre-torpilleurs* 1.1901, and to *Torpilleurs d'escadre* 1.1914 (directed 14.3.1913).

Working plans prepared by the chief engineers at the builder's yards (Marmiesse at Graville, Baron at Bordeaux) from plans of *D'Iberville*. On 26 April 1892 the *Conseil des travaux* examined a design for a torpedo aviso from F.C. Méditerranée at Le Havre (Graville) based on the 22-knot coastal passenger vessel *Seine* that the yard had built in 1891 for the Dieppe-Newhaven service of the Cie. des Chemins de fer de l'Ouest. The displacement and length were identical to those of *D'Iberville* although the beam was greater (8.64m instead of 8.08m on the waterline and 8.70m instead of 8.20m maximum) and the depth of hull was less. The speed advantage over *D'Iberville* (22.0 knots vice 21.5 knots) was due almost entirely to the use of Thornycroft boilers which the Council opposed, and if these were abandoned the displacement would grow unacceptably. The Council therefore rejected the design and saw no need to ask the firm to revise it. In case the Minister (then Godefroy Cavaignac) wanted to proceed with it, however, the Council listed numerous additional objections including the placement of the two twin torpedo tube mountings opposite each other amidships where they could be disabled by a single projectile, the need for more 47mm and 37mm guns, the internal arrangements, the coal supply, the protection (some thicknesses being less than in *D'Iberville*), the nautical qualities, the scantlings, the inadequate depressed fire of the 100mm guns, the installation of the searchlights, and the external appearance of the vessel (with a high forecastle and three funnels).

On 16 November 1892 a torpedo aviso named *Cassini* was ordered from F.C. Méditerranée at Le Havre. The index to the proceedings of the *Conseil des travaux* states that *Cassini* was built to the April 1892 design, but if so the design was first transformed to resemble almost completely that of *D'Iberville*. Plans of *Cassini* dated 30 October 1894 call her an *aviso-torpilleur type D'Iberville*, and her characteristics as built were essentially identical to those of *D'Iberville* except for a 12cm increase in beam. One significant change was the reduction of the torpedo armament from six tubes to two single rotating tubes in the positions occupied by the twin mountings in *D'Iberville*, providing an opportunity to add seven 47mm QF

guns. Even these two tubes were not fitted because of a subsequent decision to remove from ships all above-water torpedo tubes that could not be properly protected. (*D'Iberville* eventually lost her tubes as well and plans dated 2 March 1896 of *Casabianca*, now called a *contre-torpilleur d'escadre,* do not show any.)

On 9 August 1893 another torpedo aviso named *Casabianca* was ordered from C.A. Gironde. Her characteristics were identical to those of *Cassini*, indicating that they were built to the same plans. The appearance of all three ships differed primarily in the funnels. Those of *D'Iberville* were nearly vertical with high casings, those of *Cassini* were raked with high casings and taller because of extensions added soon after completion, and those of *Casabianca* were raked with low casings. These three were the last French warships with their bridges between their funnels, their conning towers were forward of the foremast with a second bridge on all but *Cassini*. All three had good hull lines forward but bad lines aft (described as detestable in *Cassini*). They all were considered to be good sea boats and could still easily maintain a speed of 20 knots ten years after they entered service.

*Casabianca* was converted for minelaying in 1911 after being inactive since 1904 and *Cassini* followed a year later. Trials in *Cassini* in December 1911 showed that using overhead mine rails like those in *Foudre* was impractical and deck rails with the half-metre gauge used in the Decauville railroad were adopted instead for both her and *Cassini*. In their definitive configuration as minelayers the after 47mm gun and the mainmast were removed, the end of the poop was opened up, and two parallel sets of mine rails were fitted leading to a turntable on the stern. Each ship could carry 97 Harlé defensive mines, 120 Harlé blockade mines, or 140 Model 1906 mines.

**Dimensions & tons:** 82.000m oa, 80.000m wl & pp x 8.320m ext (above wl), 8.208m wl. 958.417t (*Cassini*), 959.996t (*Casabianca*) disp (designed). Draught (designed): 3.130m mean, 3.500m aft. Men: 143 (including 8 officers).

**Machinery:** 5,000ihp designed at 18kg/cm² boiler pressure. Speed 21.5kts. Trials (*Cassini*) 21.17kts, (*Casabianca*) 22kts. 2 screws. 2 triple expansion engines with 4 cylinders of 0.58m (1), 0.86m (1), and

Sail and fittings plan (*plan de voilure et pitonnage*) of the torpedo aviso *Cassini*, a vessel of the *D'Iberville* type modified by the Société des Forges et Chantiers de la Méditerranée. The plans were signed on 30 October 1894 by the chief engineer at Graville, A. Marmiesse. They show the two torpedo tubes that were deleted before completion and lack the extensions that were fitted to the funnels before delivery.

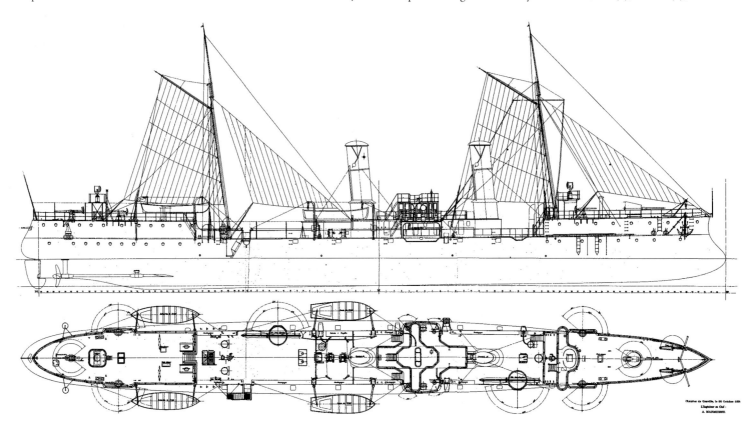

AVISOS AND GUNBOATS, 1882-1897

275

0.92m (2) diameter and 0.50m stroke. 8 Lagrafel et d'Allest boilers. 116t coal. Range 4,500mi @ 10kts.

**Armour:**

Side: The regular 6mm sides over the machinery were reinforced with an extra internal layer of 7mm hard steel plating and an extra external layer of 12mm (7mm at the very top) hull plating for a total of 25mm.

Decks: The regular 7.5mm deck in the same area was reinforced with an extra 7.5mm layer of hull plating for a total of 15mm.

Conning tower (special steel): 40mm.

**Guns:**

(Design) 1 x 100mm (forecastle), 3 x 65mm (side sponsons and poop), 7 x 47mm QF (including one in stern), 4 x 37mm QF (on amidships bridge). **Torpedoes:** 2 tubes for 450mm torpedoes (single deck mounts, one forward to starboard and one aft to port). **Searchlights:** 4 x 60cm.

(1895) 1 x 100mm/45 M1891 Canet QF (forecastle), 3 x 65mm/50 M1891 QF (side sponsons and poop), 7 x 47mm/40 M1885 QF (including one in stern), 4 x 37mm/20 M1885 QF. No torpedo tubes. 4 searchlights. The 37mm were removed by 1900.

(c1911, *Cassini* as minelayer) 1 x 100mm, 3 x 65mm, no 47mm. Fitted to lay 140 M1906 mines from overhead rails or 120 Harlé blockade mines from deck rails. Mainmast removed.

*Cassini* F.C. Méditerranée, Le Havre-Graville/FCM, Le Havre.
On list 1.1893. Ord: 16.11.1892. K: 1.1893. L: 5.6.1894. Trials: 1.1895.
Budget 1890 (extraordinary budget, delayed to 1892 and moved to the regular budget). At Cherbourg 1895-1900, exercises with the *Escadre du Nord* 1.1898. Later activity included patrols off Morocco in 1908. Converted to minelayer 1912. Listed 1.1913 and 1.1914 as a *contre-torpilleur mouilleur de mines* (destroyer minelayer). Mined or torpedoed by *UC-35* 28.2.1917 in the Strait of Bonifacio.

*Casabianca* C.A. Gironde, Bordeaux-Lormont/Schneider, Creusot.
On list 1.1894. Ord: 9.8.1893. K: 8.1893. L: 21.9.1895. C: 1895.
Budget 1893 (designated R). Out of commission 1904-1911. Converted to minelayer 1911. Listed 1.1913 and 1.1914 as a *contre-torpilleur mouilleur de mines*. One of her mines blew up prematurely in the night of 3-4.6.1915 while being laid off Smyrna, detonating the rest, destroying the stern and sinking the ship.

---

*DUNOIS* **Class.** *Contre-torpilleurs d'escadre.* Large torpedo aviso, later torpedo boat destroyer, with a turtleback bow, low stern, straight bow, two masts, and two funnels. Designed by Trogneux. To *Contre-torpilleurs* 1.1901, to *Torpilleurs d'escadre* 1.1914 (directed 14.3.1913).

On 13 February 1894 the *Conseil des Travaux* examined a design for a 640-ton, 21.5-knot torpedo aviso by naval constructor Georges Victor Trogneux, then charged with overseeing commercial work at Le Havre. Its main new feature was the use of four Normand boilers in a ship larger than a torpedo boat but still of small tonnage and high speed. The Council recommended that Trogneux revise his design and also that Normand examine under what conditions boilers of his system could be put in a ship like *D'Iberville* or *Cassini* to get superior speed and military strength. The Council also proposed that the Minister, then Vice Admiral Lefèvre, denominate such a ship an *aviso contre-torpilleur*, probably because it carried no torpedoes and French squadrons needed defences against not only torpedo boats but the new British destroyers.

On 21 June 1894 the Minister, now Félix Faure, asked for a design with six Normand boilers to increase the speed of the proposed ship to 22.5 knots. Other features of this design were a maximum displacement of 900 tons, an armament of five 65mm guns with at least six and if possible eight 47mm guns, no torpedoes, and a range of 4,000nm at 10 knots. On 18 December 1894 the Council examined two designs, the original one of Trogneux with four boilers revised as requested by the Council in February

1894 and the one with six boilers, now of 885 tons, requested by the Minister in June and also assigned by him to Trogneux. Both looked capable of execution with changes but the Council preferred the 885-ton design which had greater speed and range. Normand's study led him to propose a design with four large boilers of his system of a type not yet tried in place of six smaller ones of a known type which might be usable in *Cassini* but not in Trogneux's design because of the lesser length and height of that ship. The Council concluded by saying that it would be interesting to begin construction of a ship of any of these types both to show the potential of Normand boilers installed on a larger scale and on the value of the new hull lines which were one of the characteristic traits of these designs.

On 28 May 1895 Minister of Marine Besnard referred to the Council the revised and completed version of Trogneux's 885-ton, 22.5-knot design that had been examined by the Council in December 1894. It used Normand boilers, which weighed less than Belleville or d'Allest boilers of the same power. Its hull lines were derived from the seagoing torpedo boat *Dragon* and had the screws aft of the rudder as in some Normand boats. The hull above the waterline was lowered at the ends over about an eighth of the ship's length, especially aft, with a turtleback forward and with a low deck aft that at times would be awash. Protection was limited to the area over the engines and boilers and consisted of side plating reinforced with 25mm of hard steel from 0.6m below the waterline to 1.65m above it and a 14mm deck, half of hard steel, rising to 2m above the waterline in the middle. The speed remained 22.5 knots, the range 4,000nm at 10 knots, and the armament six 65mm and six 47mm guns. The Council accepted the design with its displacement increased to 900 tons and considered it superior to *Cassini* in artillery, speed, and range.

The 1896 budget submission (5.1895) included a *grand aviso torpilleur* (M3) to be built by contract. The Budget Commission on 13 July 1895 deleted many ships including this one from the budget, but Director of Materiel Bertin got it reinstated along with a second one. They appeared in the January 1896 fleet list as *Contre-torpilleurs d'escadre*. They were named for Jean de Dunois (Jean d'Orléans, count of Dunois) and 'La Hire' (the nickname for Étienne de Vignolles), both French military leaders during the Hundred Years War who campaigned alongside Joan of Arc.

Bilge keels were added in 1900 to control their heavy rolling, these offset a speed increase gained after trials by changing the screws. Although they failed to make either their designed speed or endurance, they were well regarded for being excellent sea boats, having good stability, and retaining their speed in service. They did, however, steer badly and their turning radius was too large. Proposals to convert *Dunois* to a Presidential yacht (1910), both ships to minelayers like *Cassini* (1911), and both ships to fast minesweepers (proposed by the Minister on 4 May 1912 and again considered in 1914 and 1916) were not proceeded with.

**Dimensions & tons:** 78.00m oa, 77.60m wl, 77.60m pp x 8.500m ext (above wl), 8.225m wl. 904.113t disp (designed). Draught (designed): 3.11m mean, 3.88m aft. Men: 128 (including 8 officers).

**Machinery:** 6,400ihp designed at 210rpm and 15kg/cm$^2$ boiler pressure. Speed 22.5kts. Trials (*Dunois*) 21.7kts at 7,997ihp and 221.65rpm, (*La Hire*) 22.118kts at 7,100ihp. 2 screws. 2 triple expansion engines with 4 cylinders of 0.62m (1), 0.88m (1), and 1.27m (2) diameter and 0.70mm stroke. 8 Normand-Sigaudy boilers (4 double-ended). 137t coal. Range 5,000nm @ 10kts (designed).

**Armour:**

Side: The regular 6mm sides over the machinery were reinforced with an extra internal layer of 7mm hard steel plating and an extra external layer of 12mm hull plating for a total of 25mm.

Decks: The regular 7mm deck in the same area was reinforced with an extra 7mm layer of hull plating for a total of 14mm.

Conning tower forward of bridge (hardened steel) 40mm.

**Guns:**

(1898) 6 x 65mm/50 M1891 QF (1 at each end, 2 on each side outboard

of the masts), 6 x 47mm/40 M1885 QF. **Torpedoes:** none.
**Searchlights:** 2 x 60cm.
(c1920, *La Hire* as school ship) 2 x 100mm M1917 (fore and aft),
6 x 47mm (3 on each side), launchers for 8 anti-submarine grenades.

*Dunois* Cherbourg Dyd/F.C. Méditerranée, Le Havre.
On list 1.1896. Ord: 28.12.1895. K: 15.9.1896. L: 6.10.1897. Comm:
25.5.1898 (trials). C: 7.1899.
Budget 1896. Trial results approved 5.7.1899. Briefly in the fleet, then
*Défense mobile* (division leader at Bizerte 1904-09). In 1914 was flagship for the flotillas of destroyers and submarines in the Channel.
From 10.1914 to 2.1915 belonged to the destroyer squadron at
Dunkirk, which carried out numerous bombardments of the Flemish
coast. Then served as escort ship 1915-18. Was part of the French division sent in 1919 to counter the Bolsheviks and Germans in the Baltic
states. Crew protests 21-23.6.1919 led to her replacement by the
destroyer *Mécanicien Principal Lestin* at end of July, arriving at
Cherbourg 3.8.1919. Struck 12.1.1920. Offered for sale 2.6.1920 at
Cherbourg.

*La Hire* Cherbourg Dyd/F.C. Méditerranée, Le Havre.
On list 1.1896. Ord: 28.12.1895. K: 2.12.1896. L: 3.11.1898. C:
10.1899.
Budget 1896. First trials 1.7.1899. Trial results approved 20.10.1899. At
Cherbourg 1899-1911. Seagoing annex to the school for gunnery at

Toulon in *Tourville* (ex *Gironde*) 1911-1914 to provide training on
small quick firing guns. Served as escort ship 1914-18. After the war
returned to the school for gunnery and the Mediterranean training
division at Toulon, this time as an annex to train pointers (1920-22).
Condemned 31.10.1922 and for sale at Toulon. Struck 12.2.1923.

---

# II. GUNBOATS

## (A) Gunboats (*Canonnières*).

### *1885 TYPE. Canonnières.*

Three new unnamed gunboats were included in the 1886 budget (submitted by Minister of Marine Peyron in March 1885). On 1 April 1885 the
Director of Materiel, expecting that new gunboats would soon be begun,
asked the advice of the *Conseil des travaux* on what type to build. The
Council recommended using *Gabès* and *Comète* as models except for less
draught and a single thick layer of hull planking on a composite or wood
hull instead of the double or triple layer in *Comète* and *Sagittaire*. (The
multiple layers were hard to repair.) The engine should be similar to the
Indret model in *Gabès*, which was lighter than the Claparède model in the
others, and the ships should be limited to two masts with a special rig. In
addition to the usual two 138.6mm and two 100mm guns, they would
have four 37mm revolving cannon, two in the tops and two on the bridge.
Since the navy had enough relatively new single-screw gunboats but no new
twin screw ones except for *Étoile,* the new vessels should have two screws,
which would also allow further reducing their draught.

These gunboats were not in the final 1887 budget submitted by Minister
of Marine Aube in mid-1886.

*N* (Unnamed) Rochefort
Budget 1886. Deleted c7.1886.

The *contre-torpilleur d'escadre* (squadron torpedo boat destroyer) *Dunois* or *Lahire*
in a photo that was originally attached to the technical characteristics documents
for both ships. These unusual vessels with their low ends turned out to be very
seaworthy and were in demand as small unit flagships. *(Feuille signalétique for the
ships)*

*N* (Unnamed) Contract
Budget 1886. Deleted c7.1886.

*N* (Unnamed) Contract
Budget 1886. Deleted c7.1886.

---

*SURPRISE. Canonnière.* Gunboat with a composite hull with two crossed layers of planking below the waterline and steel hull plating above it and a clipper bow. Three masts, barquentine rig. Designed by Normand.

On 4 November 1890 Minister of Marine Barbey asked the *Conseil des travaux* to review specifications for a gunboat comparable to *Météore* for service on distant stations. This was part of a mini-programme for station combatants that also included a 1st (later 2nd) class open-battery station cruiser that became *Descartes* and a 1st class station aviso that became *Kersaint*. Barbey forwarded his own specifications dated 28 October 1890 based on a report from the Chief of the Naval General Staff and the Director of Materiel, and the Council examined these on 23 December 1890. The Minister's specifications called for a maximum displacement of 500 tons, maximum draught aft of 3.30m, a boiler pressure not under 10kg/cm², a speed of 12 knots with natural draught and 13 knots with forced draught, a range of 2,000nm at 10 knots, and bunkers with room for one quarter more coal. The armament was to be two 100mm QF (one forward on the forecastle and one aft on the poop), four 65mm QF (on the sides with near axial arcs, 2 forward and 2 aft), and four 37mm revolving cannon in the superstructure. Protection was limited to 40mm shields of hard steel for the 100mm and 65mm guns. (On 9 June 1891 the Council recommended stronger shields for such guns.) The ship was to have a steel hull sheathed in wood and copper and a three-masted schooner rig with a square sail on the foremast. The crew was to be 85 men and the boats were to be as in *Météore*. The Council substituted a composite hull for the steel one with sheathing and increased the range with normal coal to 2,500nm at 10 knots with the expectation that the displacement would rise to 660 tons.

On 23 June 1891 the Council examined a design for a *canonnière de station* submitted by Normand in response to the specifications of 23 December 1890. Normand followed his earlier *Lion* type as closely as possible, although he had to lengthen the new ship by 7.80m and deepen it slightly to get the additional displacement needed to meet the specifications. (His design displaced 579.600 tons against 468.545 tons for *Lion*.) He deleted the small poop in *Lion*, making the new vessel flush decked aft of the forecastle. His composite hull used two crossed layers of wood hull planking at and below the waterline and steel plating above it. The width of the steel side plating was 2.10m, up from 1.15m in *Lion*. Normand used a single layer of wood planking in the lower part of his composite hull but the Council wanted the two crossed layers (in this case 75mm and 45mm) that the Navy was normally using in composite ships. The boilers were a special lengthened type of cylindrical boiler used in previous gunboats but operating at a higher pressure. The bowsprit was lowered to prevent interference with axial fire from the 100mm gun on the forecastle. This gun was moved back at least a metre because of the excessive weight it put on the bow of the ship. On 31 July 1891 Minister Barbey transmitted these and other changes to Normand.

On 11 June 1892 Minister Barbey presented his 1893 budget which included one station gunboat to be named *Surprise*. Normand's revised design was examined by the Council in January 1893. A 'contract in principle' was signed on 29 March 1893 but the Council wanted some more changes and it approved the new plans only on 27 November 1893. Normand objected for structural reasons to the cutouts for the 65mm gun sponsons that the Council wanted and it was only after the Artillery Directorate approved Normand's new design for the mountings for these guns in December 1894 that the plans were finally approved.

The 1896 budget submission (5.1895) included a second gunboat (T2) to be built by contract, but the Budget Commission on 13 July 1895 deleted all station ships including this one from the budget and cancelled credits for them on 24 October 1895.

*Surprise* had a series of problems beginning during trials with her trim (she was heavier than intended in the bow due to a miscalculation by her builder), her obsolete cylindrical boilers (which could not supply all the steam that her engine could use), her stability, and her heavy rolling. Her bowsprit was also mounted too low in the bow. These issues were largely corrected in two near sisters ordered in 1897 and 1898, *Décidée* (T'1) and *Zélée* (T'2), both of which are described in Chapter 18.

**Dimensions & tons:** 64.000m oa, 56.00m wl, 56.00m pp x 7.500m ext (above wl), 7.486m wl. 636.256t disp (designed). Draught (designed): 3.120m mean, 3.680m aft.
**Machinery:** 900ihp designed. Speed 13kts. Trials (12.6.1896) 897.36ihp = 13.341kts. 1 screw. 1 horizontal triple expansion engine with 4 cylinders (two LP). 2 special cylindrical direct flame boilers.
**Guns:**
(1895) 2 x 100mm/45 M1893 QF (fore and aft in 54mm shields), 4 x 65mm/50 M1891 QF (sponsons on the sides), 4 x 37mm revolving cannon (6 by 1900).

*Surprise* (T1) Augustin Normand, Le Havre/FCM, Le Havre (engines designed by Sigaudy).
On list 1.1894. Ord: 29.3.1893. K: 1893. L: 24.4.1895.
    Comm: 19.10.1895 (trials), 10.7.1896 (full).
Budget 1893 (designated S). Engine contract 29.3.1893, installation began 1.3.1895, first static machinery trial 18.6.1895. Arrived at Cherbourg for trials 15.10.1895. Resumed trials 1.6.1896 after corrections to trim. Trial report dated 4.7.1896. Assigned 15.11.1896 to the Far East naval division and left Cherbourg for the Far East 1.12.1896. Reboilered 1905 at Saigon with Belleville boilers. Returned to Toulon 16.5.1910. Stationed in Morocco 1911-13 and West Africa 1913-14. In late 1914 participated in operations against the Germans in Equatorial Guinea and Cameroon. In July 1916 assigned to escort the British cable ship *Dacia* and the requisitioned submarine transport *Kanguroo*, which were to cut and retrieve the German cable to South America, but on 3.12.1916 all three ships were torpedoed in the Funchal anchorage by the German submarine *U-38*, the gunboat being destroyed by a probable magazine explosion.

---

## (B) River Gunboats (*Chaloupes-canonnières*).

First two classes were *Avisos de flottille à roues* before the 1.1884 fleet list. To *Canonnières* 1.1909. See also River Gunboats (*Chaloupes à vapeur*) and Shallow-Draught Gunboats (*Canonnières à faible tirant d'eau*).

*ÉCLAIR* Class. *Avisos de flottille à roues.* River gunboats with one stern paddle wheel and an iron and steel hull. Designed by the Navy's *Direction du Matériel*. To *chaloupes canonnières à une roue* 1.1884.

In 1879 the first civilian governor of Cochinchina, Charles Marie Le Myre de Vilers, was instructed to keep an eye on affairs in Tonkin where France wanted to open the Red River (Hong River, Vietnamese Song Hong) for trade with Yunnan in China. He concluded that the main impediment to river traffic was the Black Flag pirates and that it would be possible to deal with them without involving either Hue or Peking and without risking troops on the ground by sending gunboats up the river to shell their encampments. Back in Paris the government of Jules Ferry, a strong advocate of colonial expansion, asked the Chambers for funds for an expedition to act against brigandage in the Red River valley and, after much opposition, succeeded on 21 July 1881 in getting 2.5 million francs. The Navy designed these two vessels for river service in Tonkin and Claparède began building them in October 1881. The stern paddle wheel was placed in a

The Claparède-designed river gunboat (*aviso de flottille à roues*, later *chaloupe canonnière à une roue*) *Éclair*, one of the first gunboats built for what became the extension of French control into Tonkin. The boat has a single well-protected stern paddle wheel and what appears to be a rotating platform with two guns behind vertical protection forward of the bridge. The image is a heliogravure of a photograph probably taken in 1884 or 1885 by Dr. Édouard Hocquard. (*Hocquard, 'Trente mois au Tonkin', in Le Tour du Monde, nouveau Journal des voyages, 1st semester 1889, p.41*)

trough in the hull with only a small part of it exposed, and a magazine reproduction of a photo seems to show the two 90mm guns on a rotating platform on the upper deck just forward of a conning position, both enclosed in vertical plating.

*The characteristics are based on an undated devis for* Éclair.
**Dimensions & tons:** 33.05m wl, 33.20m pp (wl fwd to rudder) x 12.0m ext and wl. 197.4t disp. Draught: 0.70m mean and max. 190t disp (195 from 1889). Men: 49.
**Machinery:** 75 nhp and 300ihp designed at 40rpm and 8.43kg/cm² boiler pressure. Trials (21.10.1882 in the river at Saigon) 300hp = 8.04kts at 46.4rpm and 9.00kg/cm² boiler pressure. Single paddle wheel aft, 3.70m diameter. 1 horizontal compound engine with 2 cylinders of 0.45m and 0.73m diameter and 1.20m stroke. 1 direct flame locomotive boiler with 2 cubical furnaces.
**Guns:**
(1882) 2 x 90mm, 4 x 37mm revolving cannon
(1894-95, *Trombe*) 2 x 90mm plus 5 (then 3) smaller

*Éclair* Anc. Éts. Claparède, Saint Denis.
On list 1.1882. K: 10.1881. L: 8.1882. C: 9.1882.
Transported to Saigon 1882 and re-launched there 8.1882. Escorted by *Drac* to Haiphong 28.5.1883. Struck 4.11.1889, for sale in Tonkin 1889-1890.

*Trombe* Anc. Éts. Claparède, Saint Denis.
On list 1.1882. K: 1881. L: 1882. C: 1882.
Transported to Saigon 1882 and re-launched there 11.8.1882. Convoyed by *Parseval* 28.4.1883 to Haiphong. Struck 18.3.1895. Sold in Tonkin for BU.

---

**BICHE Class.** Both *avisos de flottille à roues* 1.1882, *chaloupes canonnières à une roue* 1.1884. River gunboats with one stern paddle wheel, an iron and steel hull with a single long cabin on top, one thin funnel, and a ram bow. Designed by Farcy.

The designer of these vessels, Jérome Eugène Farcy, was known as the inventor of the screw *chaloupes-canonnières Mitrailleuse* and *Révolver* that distinguished themselves during the 1870-1871 war. Farcy, probably responding to the same circumstances that prompted the construction of the *Éclair* class, developed this new design to apply to a paddle vessel the hull form featuring the longitudinal troughs that he had used in the screw *chaloupes-canonnières*. The design seems to have had one feathering stern paddle wheel in two parts, each of which ran submerged in its own trough like the screws in the earlier vessels. On 6 August 1881 Minister of Marine Cloué approved a design by Farcy without consulting the *Conseil des travaux* and ordered two vessels from Claparède. However, in September Claparède, apparently alarmed by the complexity and experimental nature of the hull configuration, demanded 100,000 francs per vessel without guaranteeing the speed of 8 knots. The Minister rejected these terms and on 22 October 1881 annulled his approval of the plans. In November Claparède proposed a vessel for 80,000 francs with the same characteristics but with a classic hull and the 8 knot speed guaranteed, but this was also rejected. On 10 December 1881 Gambetta's new Minister of Marine, Gougeard, prompted by Farcy, referred the plans to naval constructor Godron, then secretary of the Machinery Commission, who concluded that the draught would be notably more and the speed less than predicted. The Minister, now Vice Admiral Jauréguiberry, referred Farcy's design to the *Conseil des travaux* which examined it on 7 March 1882. The Council recommended building the vessel as an experiment despite doubts about it, but to complete the experiment it also recommended building at the same time a second gunboat with a conventional hull form and the same displacement, draft, and engine power as Farcy's vessel. On 23 March 1882 Minister Jauréguiberry decided instead to order two vessels, *Biche* and *Chamois*, on Farcy's original plans from the Nouvelle Société du Rhône at Lyon. The builder refused to guarantee either the draught or the speed of the vessels, promising only that the engines would develop 54ihp. Nonetheless the two vessels were laid down at Lyon at the end of the year. In 1883 the firm went bankrupt and after the usual delays the yard was bought by M. Claudius Jouffray and construction resumed. In October 1884 the vessels were launched and completed. On trials in November the engines reached 59ihp but *Biche* only approached 3.42 knots and *Chamois* just reached 3.35 knots. Both were accepted in accordance with the contract on 29.12.1884 and towed to Toulon.

For new trials at Toulon in February-April 1885 weights were removed to restore the boats to their designed draught and the floats on the paddle wheels were modified. On 5 May 1885 Toulon reported that despite a notably higher power developed by the engine each boat had been unable to exceed 4 knots (and that only once) and they recorded a 3.75 knot average. The boats had been lightened to a point that excluded practical use and no military use could be found for them. But since the engines could furnish the designed 8 knots experiments continued. Possible modifications to the hulls were considered, then the paddle wheels were moved further forward, and in *Biche* the engine and boiler were moved forward 2m and the draught was increased to 62.5cm. New trials gave speeds of 7.25 knots at 54ihp and 8.36 knots at 84ihp, although the after deck was way too low. The naval constructors at Toulon then proposed substituting a flat bottom for the troughs in the hull to obtain better nautical qualities, and that project was accepted on 2 December 1885. In new trials in 1886 the desired speed was essentially reached but stability was unsatisfactory and manoeuvrability poor. At this point efforts to make the boats usable seem to have ceased. *Chamois* was briefly used for fishery protection near Rochefort but they were both gone by 1892. (See Jean Meirat in *Revue maritime*, January-February 1975, pages 197-199.)

*The characteristics are based on an undated devis for* Biche.
**Dimensions & tons:** 26.30m wl (+0.06m ram), 26.10m (wl fwd to rudder) x 4.0m ext and wl. 31.6t disp. Draught: 0.60m mean, 0.60m aft. 30t disp. (34t actual.) Men: 10.
**Machinery:** 25 nhp and 54ihp designed at 60-70 rpm and 5.0kg/cm²

boiler pressure. Speed (designed) 8kts. 1 paddle wheel in two parts aft. 1 horizontal compound engine with 2 cylinders of 0.28m and 0.46m diameter and 0.50m stroke. 1 direct flame boiler with 1 cubical furnace.

**Guns:** 1 x 65mm/16 M1881 landing on the forward end of the deck (removed 7.1888 in *Chamois*). Originally designed with 1 x 70mm, then 1 x 90mm.

*Biche* Ateliers et Chantiers du Rhone, Lyon.
On list 1.1882. K: 5.1882. L: 11.11.1884. C: 1885.
Towed to Toulon 25.1.1885 by tug *Utile*, trials 7.5.1885, out of commission 1886-90 (never used). Struck 31.12.1890. Sold 7.7.1891 at Toulon, sunk 1897.

*Chamois* Ateliers et Chantiers du Rhone, Lyon.
On list 1.1882. K: 1882. L: 1884. C: 1885.
Trials at Lyon 5.12.1884, towed to Toulon 25.1.1885 by tug *Utile*. Surveillance of the oyster beds at Arcachon 1889-91. Struck 28.11.1891. Sold 15.10.1892 at Rochefort to BU.

---

**HENRY RIVIÈRE Class.** *Chaloupes canonnières à une roue (démontable).* River gunboats with one stern paddle wheel and a galvanised steel hull. Designed and built (hull and engines) by Claparède.

In April 1883 the Chamber of Deputies approved by a large majority the first reading of a bill granting the sum of 5.5 million francs for a military expedition to secure a French protectorate in Tonkin. On 19 May 1883, Capitaine de vaisseau Henri Laurent Rivière, commander of the Cochinchina naval division, was ambushed and killed by Black Flag pirates while leading a column out of Hanoi. When the news of the disaster was received in Paris, the credits were voted unanimously on 26 May 1883. A 4,000-man expeditionary force was sent out and in 1884 the Far East naval division was upgraded to an *Escadre*. Primarily using funds for the expedition, Minister of Marine Peyron on 18 September 1883 directed the Machinery Commission to order five stern-wheel gunboats, explaining the next day that four were to be delivered to Haiphong and the fifth to Libreville in Gabon. A contract with Claparède was approved on 29 October 1883. The number of gunboats was still five in mid-December, the other two probably followed later in a contract amendment. The Tonkin gunboats were not in the regular budgets and were paid for with funds allocated specially to the expedition.

Claparède enlarged the cylinder dimensions during construction from the 0.320m and 0.500m diameter and 1.000m stroke in the contract to those of *Éclair* although the cylinders were lightened. The rotational speed of the engines was reduced to 32rpm by changes in the paddle wheel. One rotation of the engine produced one rotation of the paddle wheel. The horizontal shaft of the paddle wheel was 2.400m aft of the after bulkhead of the hull. The gunboats were transported to Tonkin in sections except for *Pionnier* which was sent to Gabon. An inspection report dated 4 August 1885 reported that the hull of *Garnier* was very fatigued, having been stove in and broken in a grounding, revealing the weak hull structure in this type 'happily since replaced by another type'. The bulkheads could not be counted on to be watertight and the present boilers were of 'vicious' construction and their model should be abandoned.

*The characteristics are based on a devis for a typical unit of the* Henri Rivière *type dated 1.12.1884 and drafted at Haiphong.*

**Dimensions & tons:** 37.375m pp (wl fwd to rudder) x 7.405m ext & wl x 1.30m depth of hull (*creux*, of which 0.600m below wl). Axis of paddle wheel 2.400m aft of the back end of the hull. 191.996t disp. (in fresh water) Draught: 0.890m mean, 0.900m aft. Men: 36 (later 50 including 1 officer).

**Machinery:** 65nhp and 250ihp designed at 55rpm (later 32rpm) and 8.43kg/cm² boiler pressure. Trials 290hp = 8.83kts. Stern paddle wheel (diameter 3.750m). 1 horizontal compound engine with direct connecting rods and 2 cylinders of 0.45m and 0.73m diameter and 1.20m

A paddle river sectional gunboat (*chaloupe canonnière à une roue, démontable*) built of steel for service in the rivers of Tonkin. The name on the side of the stern is *Pionnier*, the only one of the class that did not go to Tonkin. The big gun forward was a 90mm M1881 steel weapon, and there was another aft. The other guns were 37mm revolving cannon. Drawing by Henri Meyer. (*Le Journal illustré, 24 May 1885, page 173*)

stroke. 2 direct flame locomotive boilers side by side, each with a funnel. 42t coal (increased from the designed 17.500t.)

**Guns:** 2 x 90mm (1 forward and 1 aft), 4 x 37mm revolving cannon (3 on the platform deck and 1 in the top on the mast). There were six ports for revolving cannon on the platform deck. Some units later got a fifth 37mm revolving cannon.

*Henry Rivière* (*Henri Rivière*) Anc. Éts. Claparède, Saint Denis.
On list 1.1884. Ord: 22.10.1883. K: 1884. L: 1884 in France, 1885 in Tonkin. C: 1885.
Commissioned 10.7.1884 for trials in France, then to Tonkin in sections. Delivered and accepted 9.12.1884. In action 2-4.1885. Fitted 1886 for the use of the Chief of the Protectorate of Annam and Tonkin (90mm guns and kiosk removed, upper deck altered). Out of service 1889-97. In very good condition 1895. Struck 31.12.1897. Ceded to the Protectorate of Indochina 1.1.1898. Named *Henri Rivière* on plans

*Berthe de Villers* Anc. Éts. Claparède, Saint Denis.
On list 1.1884. K: 1884. L: 1885 in Tonkin. C: 21.1.1885.
To Tonkin in sections. Replaced 1901 as second reserve gunboat by *Arquebuse* and condemned. Struck 28.11.1901, for sale in Tonkin 1901-1902.

*Carreau* Anc. Éts. Claparède, Saint Denis.
On list 1.1884. K: 1884. L: 1885 in Tonkin. C: 9.4.1885.
To Tonkin in sections. Grounded on a sand bank and sank 22.5.1885. Efforts to refloat failed, replaced by *Bossant*. Struck 18.6.1886.

*Garnier* (*Francis Garnier*) Anc. Éts. Claparède, Saint Denis.
On list 1.1884. Ord: 22.10.1883. K: 1884. L: 1885 in Tonkin. C: 1885.
Completed in France 2.1884, arrived in Tonkin in sections by 12.1884. Tonkin reported on 18 December 1884 that they had changed her name to *Moulun*, but the ministry responded on 17 February 1885 that ship names must not be changed and directed restoration of the

original name. Active by 30.6.1885 (*Division du Tonkin*). Decomm. 1.10.1886, to be replaced by *Jacquin*. Hull reported on 23 May 1892 as stove in by unknown rock in the Black River (Song Bo) near Cho Bo and ship sunk. *Doucet* commissioned to help in salvage efforts for two months, then to be replaced by *Moulun*. Reported definitively lost 2.1.1893. Struck 26.2.1894 as *Francis Garnier*, wreck for sale in Tonkin 1894-1897. Named *Garnier* on plans.

**Jacquin** Anc. Éts. Claparède, Saint Denis.
On list 1.1884. K: 1884. L: 1885 in Tonkin. C: 8.4.1885.
To Tonkin in sections. Off main list 1909 and for sale at Saigon 1909-1910. Struck 3.8.1910.

**Moulun**  Anc. Éts. Claparède, Saint Denis.
On list 1.1884. K: 1884. L: 1885 in Tonkin. C: 1885.
To Tonkin in sections. In service on the Red River 1892-96. Decomm. 1.1.1897. Strike proposed 26.4.1897 as an economy measure. Struck 19.5.1897.

**Pionnier** Anc. Éts. Claparède, Saint Denis.
On list 1.1884. K: 1884. L: 16.4.1885 at Libreville. C: 1885.
Acceptance trials at Saint Denis before March 1885. To Libreville in sections 1885. Snagged a tree trunk and wrecked 6.6.1886 on the Ogowe River. Struck 9.9.1886.

———————

The screw sectional river gunboat (*chaloupe canonnière à hélice, démontable*) *Avalanche*, one of an eight-boat class of which six went to Tonkin and two to Madagascar. She is probably shown here in service at Haiphong or possibly Hanoi in the late 1890s. This photo was received by ONI in 1901. *(NHHC from ONI, NH-64398)*

**AVALANCHE Class.** *Chaloupes canonnières à hélice (démontables).* Sectional river gunboats with twin screws and a galvanised steel hull. Designed by A.C. Loire (Jaÿ).

Using funds for the Tonkin expedition, the Machinery Commission was ordered to contract for six sectional twin screw river gunboats and the vessels were named on 16 August 1883 and the contract was approved on 30 September 1883. Two more boats were added for Nossi-Bé on 15 September 1883. Hulls and engines were designed by former naval inspector Jaÿ, now with A.C. Loire. The hull was composed of 20 sections, and the craft had rudders at each end. The plan for *Arquebuse* (signed at Nantes by naval constructor Auguste Louis Henri Picart on 9 April 1884) shows just the stern, a note says 'The forward and after parts being similar, only the after part was drawn.' Such double-enders able to steam in either direction were called *amphidrome*.

Six of the boats were sent to Tonkin and *Redoute* and *Tirailleuse* went to Madagascar. Modifications to this and the *Estoc* types after arrival in Tonkin included removal of the bow rudder, which was quickly damaged making the boat unmanageable, enlarging the after rudder in compensation, replacing the material forming the upper deck (*paillotte*) with regular planking, moving the crew's berthing up under the upper deck, and add two circular emplacements (turrets) for 37mm guns with 6mm vertical plating on the upper deck.

Many river gunboats in Indochina including *Alerte* and *Bourrasque* were found in 1895 to be in bad condition, a situation attributed by the local naval station commander at Haiphong to the funding shortages experienced from the middle of 1890 to 1893 by the *Ateliers maritimes* (the local dockyard) at Haiphong, during which time urgent repairs piled up and the entire fleet was compromised. It was also due to massive reductions in reserve crews that made the remaining personnel unable to carry out maintenance.

In February 1897 the Tonkin gunboat flotilla consisted of six twin screw gunboats of the *Arquebuse* type of which one, *Avalanche*, was in commission, four stern wheel gunboats of the *Moulin* type of which one, *Jacquin*, was in commission, and one stern wheel gunboat of the *Bossant* type. These were still in quite good condition but of these *Arquebuse*, *Moulun*, and *Doucet* were proposed for disposal as an economy move. On 3 November 1897 Minister of Marine Besnard informed the station commander in Tonkin that, following the reorganization of maritime services in Annam and Tonkin on 1 January 1898, the local station was to be reduced to the station hulk *Adour*, two gunboats in commission, two gunboats in reserve (the four being *Avalanche*, *Jacquin*, *Casse-tête*, and *Berthe de Villers*), the *canots porte-torpilleurs* (small spar torpedo boats), and some service craft. The rest, including the gunboats *Arquebuse*, *Estoc*, *Mutine*, *Rafale*, and *Henry-Riviere*, were to be transferred to the military or civil administration of the colony.

*The characteristics are based on a devis for* Arquebuse *(canonnière en acier et démontable) dated 10.2.1884 and drafted at Nantes.*

**Dimensions & tons:** 30.44m pp (wl fwd to rudders) x 5.816m ext & wl x 2.27m creux (1.00m depth of hull). 114.520t disp (later 141t). Draught: 1.10m mean, 1.15m aft. Men: 26 (designed), 48 including 1 officer (service).

**Machinery:** 35nhp and 150.4ihp designed at 210rpm and 6kg/cm² boiler pressure. Trials (4.1.1884 in the Loire) 191.6ihp = 9.145kts (forced) at 248.5rpm and 6kg/cm² boiler pressure. 2 screws. 2 vertical compound engines with 2 cylinders of 0.230m and 0.420m diameter and 0.280m stroke. 1 cylindrical boiler. 10t coal (capacity for 25.6t). Range 400nm @ 8.5kts.

**Guns:** 2 x 90mm/22 M1878 bronze (1 near bow, 1 near stern, 2m high), 3 x 37mm revolving cannon (2 on the platform deck in sheet metal tubs, 5m high, and 1 in the masthead top, 9m high).

*Alerte* A.C. Loire, Nantes.
On list 1.1884. K: 10.1883. L: 12.1883 at Nantes. C: 1.1884.
Transported to Tonkin in sections 15.2.1884 by *Oise*. Taken out of commission 15-30.4.1888 and handed over 1.5.1888 to the *Service des bâtiments au réserve*. Struck 20.3.1896, attempts to sell 22 and 27.6.1896 failed, BU after one more sale attempt authorized 21.8.1896, reported BU 7.4.1897.

*Arquebuse* A.C. Loire, Nantes.
On list 1.1884. K: 1.10.1883. L: 22.12.1883 at Nantes. C: 1884.
Machinery installed 12.12.1883 to 29.12.1883. Transported to Haiphong in sections 5.2.1884 by *Isère*. Crew transferred to *Avalanche* and decomm. 1.10.1896. Strike proposed 26.4.1897 as an economy measure, continuation of maintenance ordered 19.5.1897. Struck 31.12.1897. Ceded to the Protectorate of Indochina 1.1.1898. Designated 1901 to replace as second reserve gunboat *Berthe de Villers*. Retroceded to the Navy by the Protectorate 25.12.1901 (back on list 1.1903) and, there now being another *Arquebuse*, the navy renamed her *Berthe de Villers*. Struck 15.2.1907, hulk in Indochina 1907-1909.

*Avalanche* A.C. Loire, Nantes.
On list 1.1884. K: 1883. L: 1884. C: 1884.
Transported to Tonkin in sections by merchantman *Ville de St. Nazaire*. Struck 15.2.1907, hulk at Haiphong 1907-1909.

*Bourrasque* A.C. Loire, Nantes.
On list 1.1884. K: 1883. L: 1884. C: 1884.
Transported to Tonkin in sections by merchantman *Ville de St. Nazaire*. Grounded in Tonkin 20.11.1884, refloated 1.4.1885. Struck 20.3.1896, for disposal in Tonkin 1896-1897. Attempts to sell 22 and 27.6.1896 failed, BU after one more sale attempt authorized 21.8.1896, reported BU 7.4.1897.

*Mutine* A.C. Loire, Nantes.
On list 1.1884. K: 1883. L: 1884. C: 30.6.1885.

Transported to Tonkin in sections by merchantman *Nantes*. Struck 31.12.1897. Ceded to the Protectorate of Indochina 1.1.1898. Renamed *Estoc* by the Protectorate in 1901 as she was going to replace *Estoc* at Kwangchow Wan. Retroceded to the Navy by the Protectorate as *Estoc* 25.12.1901 (back on list 1.1903). Administrative hulk at Kwangchow 1901-04. Commissioned 1.7.1906 to replace *Jacquin*, towed by *Vauban* 1908 from Port Courbet to Haiphong. Off main list 1909 and for sale in Indochina 1909-1910. Sold 1911 in Tonkin to BU.

*Rafale* A.C. Loire, Nantes.
On list 1.1884. K: 1883. L: 1884. C: 1884.
Transported to Tonkin in sections by merchantman *Bordeaux*. Decomm. 5.1890 in Tonkin. Replacement boiler taken from *Bourrasque* and completely refurbished 1891. Struck 31.12.1897. Ceded to the Protectorate of Indochina 1.1.1898. Renamed *Henry Rivière* by the Protectorate c1900. Retroceded to the Navy by the Protectorate as *Henry Rivière* 25.12.1901 (back on list 1.1903). Hydrographic mission 1902, decomm. at Haiphong 16.1.1908. Off main list 1909. Ordered sold 12.10.1909, sold 4.10.1910.

*Redoute* A.C. Loire, Nantes.
On list 1.1884. K: 1883. L: 1884. C: 1884.
Transported to Madagascar in sections by transport *Yonne*. In service with the Division of the Indian Ocean 28.9.1884. Struck 9.8.1889. Sold or BU 1890 at Nossi-Bé.

*Tirailleuse* A.C. Loire, Nantes.
On list 1.1884. K: 1883. L: 1884. C: 1884.
Transported to Madagascar in sections by transport *Yonne*. Struck 9.8.1889. Sold 1890 at Nossi-Bé to BU.

---

**BAÏONNETTE Class.** *Chaloupes canonnières à hélice (démontables).* Sectional river gunboats with twin screws and a galvanised steel hull. Designed by A.C. Loire (Jaÿ).

Probably again using funds for the Tonkin expedition, the Machinery Commission was ordered to contract for six more vessels like *Arquebuse*. They were named on 17 January 1884 and the contract was approved by 2 February 1884. On 23 February 1884 the office overseeing contract work forwarded a proposition to install a second mast aft and a contract amendment including this and other changes was approved on 31 March 1884. *Casse-tête*, *Cimeterre* and others were ordered held at Toulon on 14 May 1884 as they were not immediately needed in Tonkin. The bow rudder was ordered removed and the after rudder enlarged on 9 January 1885. On 26 January 1885 Toulon was informed that *Casse-tête* would be embarked for Tonkin on the *Shamrock*, which was to leave Toulon on 20 February 1885. All were in Tonkin or Saigon by early 1886.

*Estoc* was sent from France with space for 24 crew but soon had 48. In April 1887 the departing commander of *Estoc* reported that, with the experience of 19 months of operations including 14 within range of the rebels, he thought that the revolving cannon in the turrets on the upper deck should be suppressed, the two revolving cannon in the tops having always sufficed. The turrets themselves should be retained as shelters for musketeers and also for the ship's commander. This action was not taken. However, the ministry advised Cochinchina on 5 September 1887 that the after 90mm gun in *Cimeterre* would be replaced by a 37mm revolving cannon to be supplied by Toulon. She still had two 90mm guns and three 37mm revolving cannon (two in the masthead tops and one on deck that could be shifted from one side to the other) when she ran trials in April 1887. According to her trial report *Caronade* differed from others of the same type, *Bouclier* and *Baïonnette*, in changes to the internal arrangements. The captain's cabin was moved forward so he (the only officer on board) could observe the bridge watch, and the crew was moved aft.

**Dimensions & tons:** as *Avalanche*. Both classes as designed: 30.000m wl and pp x 5.800m ext, 5.780m wl x 2.270m depth of hull (*creux*, of which 1.000m below wl). 113.122t disp. Draught 1.090m fore and aft.

**Machinery:** as *Avalanche*. Designed: 160ihp.

**Guns:**

(1887 and 1892, *Estoc*) 2 x 90mm/22 M1881 steel (1 near bow, 1 near stern, 2m high), 4 x 37mm revolving cannon (2 on the platform deck in sheet metal tubs, 5m high, and 2 in the masthead tops, 9m high).

(1891, *Cimeterre*) 1 x 90mm/22 M1881 (near bow), 4 x 37mm revolving cannon (1 on the platform deck aft, 1 on the platform deck transportable from one side to the other, 2 in the masthead tops).

*Casse-tête* A.C. Loire, Nantes.

On list 1.1884. K: 1884. L: 1885 in Tonkin. C: 30.6.1885.

Transported to Tonkin in sections by *Shamrock*, left 20.2.1885. Comm. 21.5.1885. In reserve at Tonkin 1.1.1888. Full commission 5.8.1891, decomm. 16.4.1892, repaired 1893. Recomm. 1.10.1896 with the crew of *Estoc*. Struck 27.8.1907, mooring hulk at Haiphong for the torpedo boats there 1907-1909. Sold 1909 in Tonkin to BU.

*Baïonnette* A.C. Loire, Nantes.

On list 1.1884. K: 1884. L: 26.5.1885 at Saigon. C: 1885.

To Cochinchina in sections 1884. Struck 4.2.1908, assigned as replacement for hulk *Vaïco* or *Soïrap* (ex *Bouclier* or *Cimeterre*), hulk in Indochina 1908-1909, for sale in Indochina 1909-1910.

*Estoc* A.C. Loire, Nantes.

On list 1.1884. K: 1884. L: 15.7.1885 in Tonkin. C: 1885.

To Tonkin in sections. Struck 31.12.1897. Ceded to the Protectorate of Indochina 1.1.1898. Administrative hulk at Kwangchow Wan (Guangzhouwan) 1899. Renamed *Mutine* by the Protectorate. Retroceded to the Navy by the Protectorate as *Mutine* 25.12.1901 (back on list 1.1903). By 1903 was a near wreck hauled out in front of the administrative building at Kwangchow Wan. Struck 31.10.1903 and ordered sold in place. Sold 6.1905 to Amédée Merle, a local businessman.

*Bouclier* A.C. Loire, Nantes.

On list 1.1884. K: 1884. L: 1885 in Cochinchina. C: 1885.

Transported to Cochinchina in sections 1884 by *Bien-Hoa*. Replaced *Caronade* 9.1894, replaced by her 8.1898. Struck 9.4.1906, renamed *Soïrap* 1906 (replacing a tug acquired in Indochina in 1886 and hulked in 1895), hulk at Saigon 1906-1908, replaced by *Baïonnette* or *Caronade*, for sale at Saigon 1908-1910.

*Cimeterre* A.C. Loire, Nantes.

On list 1.1884. K: 1884. L: 1884. C: 1886 in Indochina.

Left for Indochina in sections 7.1.1886 on merchantman *Comorin* as a spare. Comm. for trials at Saigon 12.4.1887, in reserve there 15.6.1887 after trials. Full commission 12.6.1889 at Saigon to replace *Bouclier*. Administratively decomm. at Saigon 1.1.1895. To reserve at Saigon 1.1.1896. Used without modifications in 1897 as central ship for the *Défense mobile* at Saigon replacing *Sagaïe*. Struck 9.4.1906, renamed *Vaïco* 6.8.1906 (replacing a tug acquired in Indochina in 1886 and hulked in 1897), hulk in Indochina 1906-1908, replaced by *Baïonnette* or *Caronade*, ordered sold at Saigon 4.2.1908, sold 4.6.1909.

*Caronade* A.C. Loire, Nantes.

On list 1.1884. K: 1884. L: 1885. C: 1886 in Indochina.

Left for Indochina in sections 9.2.1886 on merchantman *Bordeaux*. Assembled at Saigon 4.1886, launched 3.5.1886, commissioned to replace *Escopette* 1.6.1886, ran trials 22.9.1886. Replaced by *Bouclier* and decomm. 20.9.1894, to reserve 29.4.1895 after trials. Comm. 1.8.1898 to replace *Bouclier*. Struck 4.2.1908, assigned as replacement for hulk *Vaïco* or *Soïrap* in Indochina (ex *Bouclier* or *Cimeterre*), hulk in

The screw sectional river gunboat *Caronade* at Saigon during a visit there by a Russian squadron between 15 and 19 March 1891. Behind her is the Russian cruiser *Pamyat Azova*. *Caronade* is full-dressed with large national ensigns and signal flags to celebrate an exchange of diplomatic notes between France and Russia that soon became the Franco-Russian alliance. She has an unusually elaborate canvas canopy. The six *Baïonnette* class gunboats including *Caronade* were virtually identical to the *Avalanche* class except that they had a slightly taller mainmast added that gave them a second armed top.

Indochina 1908-1909, conversion to workshop barge (*gabare-atelier*) at Saigon authorized 1.12.1909 but not carried out for lack of personnel and funds, sale recommended 17.8.1912, for sale at Saigon 1912-1913.

---

*BOBILLOT* **Class.** *Chaloupes canonnières à une roue (démontables).* Sectional shallow draft river gunboats with one stern paddle wheel, two funnels side by side, and a galvanised steel hull. Designed by Claparède.

In June 1884 the French established a remote outpost at Tuyen Quang in the interior of Tonkin far up the Clear River (a tributary of the Red River). Between 24 November 1884 and 3 March 1885 that post underwent an epic siege by the Chinese Yunnan Army and Black Flag irregulars, being relieved barely in time.

The *Société anonyme des anciens établissements Claparède* learned from its agent in Haiphong that none of the French gunboats in Tonkin including Claparède's own *Éclair* and *Henry Rivière* types could then ascend to Tuyen Quang and that only boats with less than half a metre of draught could do so for half of the year. On 18 March 1885 Claparède forwarded to Minister of Marine Besnard two designs for gunboats of very shallow draught for Tonkin. One measured 40m and the other 30m, both had a draught of 0.450m and a speed of 8 to 9 knots. The 30m design carried one 90mm gun forward and three revolving cannon and had side paddle wheels, each with its own two-cylinder simple-expansion engine and boiler and geared drive with a ratio of three to one. Claparède's agent pointed out that the engines could be without condensation because the boats would only operate in fresh water, and he also advised that the cantilever-supported stern wheel used by the English should be avoided at all costs. Claparède's two designs had side wheels with a hull beam of 7.40m and a beam over the paddle wheels of 10.80m. Otherwise in general arrangements they were reduced versions of *Henry Rivière*. On 3 April 1885 Tonkin sent a request for six gunboats with a draught of 50 to 60cm, a length of 30m, and a single paddle wheel to be available during November 1885. (On 29 May 1885 Tonkin stated that the new gunboats should be more like the *Éclair* type than the *Henry Rivière* type.)

On 14 April 1885 the *Conseil des travaux* examined Claparède's two designs. The Council noted that Claparède's studies showed the difficulty of designing gunboats with a draught not over 50cm with the relatively high speed and moderate dimensions needed for river navigation. It concluded that the 40 metre design was far from resolving the problem but that the 30 metre design with a reduced armament could be satisfactory with a modest increase in length and beam. It also needed more powerful machinery and needed to have the accommodations modified to put the officers and the white Europeans in general in the bow where the ventilation was better, a point of importance in the colonies. The combat deck, the masthead top for the revolving cannon, and the waterline needed protection against rifle bullets. The Council's latest information from Tonkin indicated that the draught must not exceed 50cm and the length 35m. The Council adopted in principle paddle wheels on the sides because of advantages in manoeuvring, in speed, and the ability to go in both directions (*amphidrome*), but it advised consulting with authorities in Tonkin to see if local conditions made stern wheels preferable. The ministry forwarded the question to Tonkin on 28 March 1885 and the boats were built with two paddle wheels in the stern coupled together and operated through gearing by a single engine without a condenser. The hull beam was increased to 11.00m, the former beam over the paddles.

Claparède signed a contract on 11 May 1885 (approved on 25 May 1885) for seven steel-hulled gunboats with very shallow draught and fourteen *chalands allèges* (lighter barges) of 35 tons (each gunboat was to tow two of the barges). The contract specified a maximum draught of half a metre, a minimum speed of 8.5 knots, and machinery of 300ihp. One boat (*Bossant*) was to be delivered to Toulon for trials, the other six were to be delivered directly to Haiphong. On 25 April 1885 Minister Besnard invited to the Minister of War to name three of the gunboats after men fallen in the latest campaign and on 20 May 1885 he replied with the names *Cuvellier*, *Rollandes*, and *Raynaud*, which were formerly assigned on 28 May 1885. The six boats that were not tried were accepted on 24 February 1886 on the basis of the trials of *Bossant*. The commander's shelter had 4mm protection and the masthead top was 4.50m above the upper deck. The commander of *Cuvellier* asked in 1887 for an artillery piece in addition to the revolving cannon, but the naval constructors did not think the structure of the boat was strong enough to support it.

On 8 May 1890 a commission met to inspect *Bossant* and recommend her condemnation. They found her hull in very bad condition, partly because of damage forward from a grounding and partly because some of the already very thin hull plating had significantly corroded. The engines and boilers needed major repairs and the supports for the paddle shaft had gone out of alignment. Having been assembled twice (at Toulon and in Tonkin), *Bossant* was the most fatigued of her class. She also did not have the wood covering on her lower deck which had been found indispensable in the sisters to prevent the crew slipping on the deck. More generally, the lack of a condenser in the class been reported by commanders as a major disadvantage and the shallow draught of half a metre for which so much had been sacrificed was now significantly exceeded, leaving only the disadvantages of the lightly built hull. An appreciation of *Raynaud*, *Bobillot*, and *Cuvellier* added the complaints that their beam, which was too large, exposed them to frequent groundings and that they steered badly and consumed large amounts of coal. Reports supporting the condemnation of *Rollandes* and *Doucet* in 1897 stated that the gunboats of this type had numerous design defects and had never given more than mediocre results except as troop transports. Their defects included poor manoeuvrability, excessive coal consumption, and costly maintenance of their wide bottoms in salt water. Their main advantage, the ability to carry a large number of passengers, had lost much of its importance in current conditions in Tonkin.

*The dimensions are from the contract.*
**Dimensions & tons:** 29.60m wl (30.06m trials) x 11.00m ext & wl x 1.20m depth of hull (*creux*). 120t disp (118t trials, 103t in contract). Draught: 0.50m mean (0.486m trials). Men: 49 including 1 officer.
**Machinery:** 75 nhp, 250ihp designed. Boiler pressure 10kg/cm². Speed

8.5kts (contract). Trials (*Bossant*, 18.9.1885, best run) 8.88kts at 136rpm and 10kg/cm² boiler pressure. 1 stern paddle wheel, geared drive. 1 high pressure engine with 2 cylinders. 2 locomotive boilers.
**Guns:**
(Design) 1 x 47mm/40 M1885 QF (forward upper deck), 4 x 37mm revolving cannon (1 aft and 2 sides on the upper deck, 1 in masthead top).
(Actual) 5 x 37mm revolving cannon. The 47mm were not delivered from France and the forward upper deck position was filled with a fifth 37mm revolving cannon. Positions were fitted on the upper deck for 1 x 37mm aft and 2 x 37mm on each side, the two extra positions allowing both of the side guns to be positioned on the same side.

*Bossant* Anc. Éts. Claparède, Saint Denis.
On list 1.1886. K: 1885. L: 1885 at Toulon. Comm: 24.8.1885 (Toulon, trials). C: 1.6.1886 (Tonkin).
Completed 1.7.1885. Assembled at Toulon 24.8.1885 for trials, trials at Toulon 18.9.1885, transported to Tonkin in sections c1.1886 by merchantman *Cormorin*. Her commissioning was authorized on 2 April 1886 to replace *Carreau* which could not be refloated. Re-launched in Tonkin 10.5.1886. To reserve 21.7.1887 with burned out boiler tubes and replaced by *Levrard*. Draught in service recorded as 0.68m aft, 0.72m forward, and 0.70m mean. Struck 30.7.1890, for sale in Tonkin 1890-1893.

*Bobillot* Anc. Éts. Claparède, Saint Denis.
On list 1.1886. K: 1885. L: 1885 at Haiphong. C: 25.2.1886.
Completed 19.7.1885, left Toulon 22.8.1885 for Haiphong in sections. Comm. at Haiphong in the Division of Tonkin 25.2.1886. Damaged in grounding 1.1890 and then used as floating guard post. To reserve 16.8.1894. Struck 2.6.1896. Ordered on 21.8.1896 to be BU if she couldn't be sold, reported on 7.4.1897 as having been BU.

*Cuvellier* Anc. Éts. Claparède, Saint Denis.
On list 1.1886. K: 1885. L: 1885 in Tonkin. C: 26.2.1886.
Left for Tonkin 22.8.1885 in sections. Comm. at Haiphong 26.2.1886. Draught in service 1887 recorded as 0.62m aft, 0.630m forward, and 0.625m mean. Floating guard post in Tonkin from 1892. Struck 2.6.1896 as *Cuvelier*. Ordered on 21.8.1896 to be BU if she couldn't be sold, reported on 7.4.1897 as having been BU.

*Doucet* Anc. Éts. Claparède, Saint Denis.
On list 1.1886. K: 1885. L: 1885 in Tonkin. C: 17.4.1886.
To Tonkin in sections. Strike proposed 26.4.1897 as an economy measure. Struck 19.5.1897.

*Levrard* Anc. Éts. Claparède, Saint Denis.
On list 1.1886. K: 1885. L: 1885 in Tonkin. Comm: 16.4.1886.

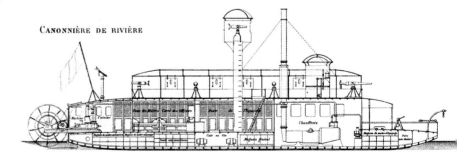

CANONNIÈRE DE RIVIÈRE

Inboard profile of a river gunboat of the *Bobillot* class. The drawing shows the designed armament of one 47mm and four 37mm guns, the port 37mm having been moved to a spare position on the starboard side. An additional 37mm gun was actually carried in place of the 47mm gun. It also shows a typical locomotive boiler. (*Léon Charles Callou, Cours de construction du navire, 1902*)

To Tonkin in sections. delivered 8.4.1886. Decomm. 26.10.1886 to facilitate repairs. Recomm. 21.7.1887 to patrol the upper part of the Red River. Reported 16.12.1887 as thrown onto rocks, to be repaired when drydock built. Struck 30.7.1890 and ordered sold. For sale in Tonkin 1890-1893.

*Raynaud* Anc. Éts. Claparède, Saint Denis.
On list 1.1886. K: 1885. L: 1885 in Tonkin. C: 22.5.1886.
Left for Tonkin 8.10.1885 in sections. Comm. in Tonkin 22.5.1886. Draught in service 1888-1890 0.67m aft, 0.72m fwd, and 0.70m mean (saw much combat action during this period). Floating guard post 1895-96. Struck 2.6.1896. Ordered on 21.8.1896 to be BU if she couldn't be sold, reported on 7.4.1897 as having been BU.

*Rollandes* Anc. Éts. Claparède, Saint Denis.
On list 1.1886. K: 1885. L: 1885 in Tonkin. C: 22.5.1886.
To Tonkin in sections. Draught in service 1886-1888 reported at 78cm aft, 79cm forward. In reserve at Haïphong 1.5.1888. The boilers saw no use after being repaired in 1888 but otherwise she was in as bad condition in 1896 as were *Bobillot*, *Raynard*, and *Cuvellier*. Struck 26.4.1897. Sold 1898 in Tonkin to BU.

———

*NIGER* and *MAGE*. *Chaloupes canonnières* (1891) on the Niger River. See *chaloupes à vapeur* (1886).

The sectional shallow draft sternwheel river gunboats of the *Opale, Onyx, Précieuse,* and *Brave* classes built for Benin and Madagascar in 1892-1895 were classed as steam launches (*chaloupes à vapeur*) instead of gun launches (*chaloupes canonnières*) and are listed after the earlier *chaloupes à vapeur* below.

———

# (C) Steam Launches (*Chaloupes à vapeur*).
This category was introduced in the January 1884 fleet list.

*MIRMIDON* Class. *Chaloupes à vapeur.* 8nhp screw steam launches with wooden hulls for colonial service. No masts or sails.

This group of small craft was obtained in six separate orders, probably with some minor differences in configurations between them. The contract for *Mirmidon* and *Pygmée* was approved on 19 January 1883. Their designer was named either Salvert or de Salvert, probably an engineer with Dyle et Bacalan. On 18 September 1883 the Machinery Commission was directed to contract for two *chaloupes à vapeur pontées* (decked launches), *Rubis* and *Turquoise*. On 31 January 1884 the Minister's cabinet asked for a replacement for the sailing fishery protection vessel *Bergeronnette* at Marseille. The Machinery Commission was directed 9 February 1884 to contract for a *chaloupe à vapeur* of the *Mirmidon* type, *Abeille*. Her contract was approved on 15 March 1884 as a supplement to the contract of 19 October 1883 for *Rubis* and *Turquoise*. On 31 July 1885 the Machinery Commission was directed to order a *chaloupe à vapeur* of the *Rubis* type, *Saphir*, for Gabon, and on 12 December 1885 the Machinery Commission was directed to order a *chaloupe à vapeur* of the *Rubis* type, *Émeraude*, also for Gabon. *Diamant* was built at the same time, and she and *Émeraude* transited the French canal system to Brest together, *Diamant* coming from Bordeaux and *Émeraude* from Toulon.
    A description of *Mirmidon* and *Pygmée* and a photo of a *Saphir*-type unit indicate that these vessels were essentially large ship's boats with four compartments, one in the bow decked over, one from there to amidships with a box-shaped deckhouse on top, an open area aft of amidships without any covering except a canvas awning for the engine, stokehold, and boiler, and a small covered compartment in the extreme stern. The two 37mm revolving cannon with their shields dominated the roof of the deckhouse. The freeboard amidships was 70cm. The open machinery compartment became a problem in *Abeille* when she was assigned to fishery protection

duty, because she had to stay at sea in rough weather to monitor several hundred fishing vessels and a single wave could put out the boiler fires. Their engines were vertical engines of the usual type for the navy's standard 10-metre *canots à vapeur* (steam pinnaces). The boiler was a steel boiler on the Bigot system of the type adopted on the latest 10-metre steam pinnaces. *Rubis* and *Turquoise* were referred to as *chaloupes à vapeur pontées* (decked steam launches), although the deck was probably limited to the forward part of the vessels as in the others. The wooden hulls were coppered below the waterline. The Colonial Department wrote on 31 July 1890 that gunboats of the *Rubis* type were not in the least bit suitable for service in Gabon.

*The characteristics are based on devis for* Mirmidon *and* Pygmée *(chaloupes à vapeur), both dated 4.1.1884.*
**Dimensions & tons:** 15.400m wl (bow to rudder) x 3.265m wl. 16.568t disp. Draught: 0.689m mean, 0.739m aft. Men: 15. *Abeille* measured 15.00m x 3.60m.
**Machinery:** 7.5nhp (notionally 8nhp) and 30ihp designed at 320rpm and 7kg/cm$^2$ boiler pressure. Trials (17.11.1883 at Toulon) 30.00ihp = 7.44kts at 296.5rpm. 1 screw. 1 vertical engine with 1 cylinder of 0.205m diameter and 0.180m stroke. 1 Bigot boiler. 0.5t coal.
**Guns:** 2 x 37mm revolving cannon. These were mounted on top of the small deckhouse on these vessels, one on each side.

*Mirmidon* Dyle et Bacalan, Bordeaux-Bacalan/Dyle et Bacalan.
On list 1.1884. Ord: 19.1.1883 (contract approved). K: 1.1.1883. L: 4.10.1883. C: 1884.
Named 19.1.1883. Boiler installed 4.10.1883. Engine installed 15.9.1883 to 4.10.1883. Accepted at Toulon 25.11.1883. Stability trials at Toulon 29.11.1883. To Senegal (Dakar) in *Finistère* 12.1883. Supported personnel of the colonial service in the Casamance river. Struck 23.7.1895 and ceded to the colonial service who rejected her, sold by the Domaines 9.4.1896.

*Pygmée* Dyle et Bacalan, Bordeaux-Bacalan/Dyle et Bacalan.
On list 1.1884. Ord: 19.1.1883 (contract approved). K: 1.1.1883. L: 24.9.1883. C: 1884.
Named 19.1.1883. Engine installed from 6.9.1883 to 24.9.1883. Boiler installed 24.9.1883. Accepted at Toulon 25.11.1883. Stability trials at Toulon 29.11.1883. To Senegal (Dakar) in *Finistère* 12.1883. Arrived in Gabon 12.5.1884, annexe to *Marabout*. Commander of *Cygne* reported 20.5.1897 that *Pygmée* had been condemned and sold by the colony. Struck 8.7.1897. Colony promised 28.7.1897 to reimburse the navy for selling its ship.

*Rubis* Dyle et Bacalan, Bordeaux-Bacalan.
On list 1.1884. Ord: 10.11.1883 (contract approved). K: 1883. L: 1884. C: 1885.
Named 18.9.1883. Accepted at Bordeaux 7.1894, machinery then dismantled for shipping. Arrived at Libreville 6.1.1885 on the transport *Ariège*. In Gabon and Congo 1887-97. Sank 17.2.1897 at her moorings, impossible to refloat. Struck 26.4.1897.

*Turquoise* Dyle et Bacalan, Bordeaux-Bacalan.
On list 1.1884. Ord: 10.11.1883 (contract approved). K: 1883. L: 1884. C: 1885.
Named 18.9.1883. Arrived at Brest 25.10.1884 under tow by *Laborieux*, then transported to Gabon by *Européen* with machinery removed. Boiler reinstalled 18.2.1885 and machinery reinstalled 18.3.1885. Stationed in Gabon, watched Spanish activities in adjacent Rio Muni. Sold by the Domaines 17.11.1896. Struck 26.4.1897.

*Abeille* Dyle et Bacalan, Bordeaux-Bacalan.
On list 1.1886. Ord: 15.3.1884 (contract approved). K: 1883. L: 1885. C: 1885.
Named 9.2.1884. Reported on 27 December 1884 to have replaced *Bergeronnette* as a fishery protection vessel in the Gulf of Marseille and

annexe to *Diligente* at Marseille. After repairs *Bergeronnette* was to be escorted to Bastia, Corsica, by *Albatros*. Launches of her type were designed for river service in Senegal and could not keep the sea with fishing vessels, causing her commander in February 1885 to request various improvements. By August 1891 she needed repairs and Toulon was directed to have Marseilles send her there and to repair her when they could. The Minister on 8.3.1892 asked for designs converting her to a *bateau omnibus* for the port of Toulon replacing or in addition to *Rapide*, the current *bateau omnibus* with similar characteristics, and a design was approved on 22.7.1892. On 6 December 1892 Toulon forwarded a contract it had made with Messrs. Seyre & Berthe for the conversion. Struck 10.1.1893 from the 1st part of the *Liste de la Flotte* and assigned to serve as a harbour transport for the Naval Construction Division at Toulon 1893-1904, sold 1904 at Toulon to BU.

*Saphir* T. H. Dubigeon & Fils, Nantes.
On list 1.1886. Ord: 15.10.1885 (contract approved). K: 1885. L: 1886. C: 1887 in Gabon.
Named 31.7.1885. Completed 2.6.1886. Acceptance trials 8.1886 (8 knots). To Gabon 1887 and Benin (Dahomey) 1892. Sank 10.5.1897 after striking a tree trunk in the Temboni River near Rio Muni which she was exploring in company with the aviso *Cigogne*. Struck 8.7.1897.

*Diamant* Dyle et Bacalan, Bordeaux-Bacalan.
On list 1.1886. K: 1885. L: 1886. C: 1887.
Arrived at Rochefort 9.11.1886, Nantes 5.1.1887, and Brest 25.1.1887 via the Canal de Bretagne. Embarked on *Ariège* 1.3.1887 for Libreville, arrived on the coast of Guinea 3.1887. On the Senegal station 1888-93. Ceded 16.11.1893 to the governor of the colony of Côte d'Ivoire for 16,000 francs, off list 1893.

*Émeraude* Mourraille & Cie., Toulon.
On list 1.1886. Ord: 23.2.1886 (contract approved). K: 1885. L: 1886. C: 1887.
Named 12.12.1885. Through canal system from Toulon to Bordeaux with *Diamant* 1886, to Rochefort 2.11.1886, to Nantes 4.1.1887, then to Brest 25.1.1887. Embarked on *Ariège* 1.3.1887 for Libreville, arrived 11.10.1887, assembly and trials completed by 18.11.1887. Initially served the settlements at Grand Bassam in Côte d'Ivoire and Porto-Novo, near Cotonou in Benin. Struck 30.4.1894, machinery sent back to France and hull sold at Cotonou 23.3.1895.

---

*LICONA*. *Chaloupe à vapeur*. 12nhp paddle steam launch with a catamaran hull and a single paddle wheel for colonial service. Designed by the builder to the requirements of Savorgnan de Brazza.

A law of 10 January 1883 allocated funds to a *Mission de l'Ouest africain* to continue and develop the work of Savorgnan de Brazza, who between 1876 and 1882 had conducted two major discovery expeditions along the Congo and Ogowe rivers. Brazza was designated leader of the new expedition by a decree of 5 February 1883 and left France on 21 March 1883 to begin it. The mission itself ran from 21 April 1883 to 26 May 1885.

Brazza had Claparède at Saint Denis design two steam launches for his new expedition to the Congo, one paddle and one screw. The screw-propelled *Djoué* (see 3rd Class Avisos) was to explore the Congo while the paddle *Licona* was to provide communications between the Alima River (a Congo tributary) and Brazzaville. On 5 March 1883 the Navy accepted in principle Claparède's designs and on 15 March Claparède forwarded plans for use in drafting a contract. On 10 April 1883 the Machinery Commission was directed to negotiate the contract, and it was approved on 10 May 1883. On 10 December 1883 Claparède was instructed to send the two dismantled craft to Le Havre for shipping to Gabon on a chartered packet, the order was repeated for *Licona* on 26 December 1883. Both vessels arrived in Gabon in sections on 15 February 1884.

*Licona*, described as an *embarcation à roue à très faible tirant d'eau*, was a

catamaran raft with a deck of light planking on two floats running the length of the vessel and with a paddle wheel between the floats aft. A single-cylinder engine to starboard drove the paddle wheel. The only other structures were two small boilers side by side forward, each with its own funnel, and awnings on frames running the length of the vessel. Brazza designed her to maximize deck space and facilitate maintenance while minimizing draught and weight. The contract required her to carry a load of two tons at a maximum draught of 0.4m.

*Licona* was assembled first but like the first *Djoué* her service was short. A commission on 6 September 1886 found that her boilers were in bad condition and proposed using her as a barge to transport men and material to the posts on the Ogowe River. The machinery and paddle wheels had already been taken on board the station ship *Mésange* and were sent back to France on the transport *Ariège*.

**Dimensions & tons:** 17.8m x 3.6m excluding rudder (estimated). 10t disp. Draught 0.4m (contract).
**Machinery:** 12 nhp, 1 centre paddle wheel, 1 engine with 1 cylinder.
**Guns:** 1 (1884), none (1885).

*Licona* Anc. Éts. Claparède, Saint Denis.
On list 1.1884. Ord: 10.5.1883 (contract approved). K: 1883. L: 1883. Comm: 2.1884.
Assembled in Gabon in early 1884. Out of service by 9.1886. Replaced as stationnaire in Guinea in 1887 by *Brazza*, a *chaloupe canonnière* built for the Ministry of Public Instruction (Education) that later became the Navy's *Ogowé*. Struck 10.5.1887.

---

*CARPE*. *Chaloupe à vapeur*. 7nhp triple screw steam launch for experimental use.

This craft was built to the design of a standard 10-metre steam launch modified at Lorient by naval constructor Marchal to test configurations using triple screws. Construction of the craft was proposed by de Bussy's *Service technique des Constructions navales* on 8 February 1883 on the grounds that *Brennus* and *Charles Martel* were to be the first armoured ships to receive triple screws and it would be well to conduct experiments first on a reduced scale to learn how to get the best advantages out of this configuration. The hull form was to replicate that of de Bussy's *Brennus* of 1882 on a scale of 1 to 10, while the three screws were to be installed in a way that allowed varying their relative positions. Questions to be examined included whether the wing screws should be placed next to the centre screw or ahead of it and how many blades the propellers should have. The dimensions and displacement of the launch would be very close to those of the navy's standard 10-metre steam launch with the exception that her draught would be much less, making her particularly useful for service in ports and roadsteads after her experimental role was completed. She was ordered and named on 8 June 1883.

On 27 May 1884 the call went out for a steam launch for the surveillance of the oyster beds at Morbihan, and on 7 June 1884 Lorient was asked if *Carpe* could perform this service during the winter. On 27 November 1884 Lorient reported on her nautical qualities and the operation of her machinery, and on 10 December it was decided that she was not suitable for the proposed duty.

On 15 July 1884 Lorient reported that *Carpe* had made her first sortie on 9 June to try out her machinery and made 622 rpm with no difficulty. She then conducted three experiments, two with all three screws and one with the two screws on the wing shafts. On 30 October 1884 Huin stated that the next step was to convert her hull lines aft to resemble those of his 1884 *Brennus* rather than de Bussy's 1882 design. The two wing shafts and their engines would be retained. Minister Peyron on 1 December 1884 approved the new trials and the modifications in principle but wanted more information first on how the measurements were being taken. The stern lines were finally modified at the beginning of 1886 and the reports on the new trials were delivered in September 1887. The trials were referred to in the discussions on the design of *Brennus* by the *Conseil des travaux* on 24 December 1887. No further use was found for *Carpe* and she was ordered in August 1891 to be sold, although her boiler was to be retained.

**Dimensions & tons:** 10.50m x 1.966m. 9.837t disp. Draught 0.77m.
**Machinery:** 7 nhp, 30ihp. 3 screws and 3 engines, later 2 screws and 2 engines. One standard steam launch boiler lengthened by about a half.
**Guns:** none.

*Carpe* Lorient Dyd.
On list 1.1884. Ord: 8.6.1883. K: 5.6.1883. L: 13.9.1884. C: 12.1884.
Propulsion trials with 3 screws at Lorient 1885-86. Out of service after trials concluded in 1887. Condemned 10.8.1891, sold at Lorient 29.4.1892. Lorient was authorized on 4.9.1891 to use two of her engines to power ventilators in *Brennus*.

---

**SENTINELLE Class.** *Chaloupes à vapeur.* 10nhp screw steam launches for fishery protection service.

These two steam fishery protection vessels were built at the Lorient Dockyard. They were somewhat larger than previous *chaloupes à vapeur* on the fleet list.

**Dimensions & tons:** 20.50m x 4.10m. 45t disp. Draught: 1.07m mean. Men: 9 to 13.
**Machinery:** 10 nhp, 35hp at 208rpm = 7.45kts (*Nautile*).
**Guns:** 1 x 37mm revolving cannon.

*Sentinelle* Lorient Dyd.
On list 1.1884. Ord: 15.11.1883. K: 15.9.1884. L: 28.3.1885. Comm: 29.3.1885 (trials), 18.4.1885 (full).
To Algeria 1886 as station ship and fishery protection vessel. Blown ashore and wrecked 14.2.1889 on the Algerian coast in the bay of Grand Canier near Cape Rosa. Struck 13.3.1889.

*Nautile* Lorient Dyd.
On list 1.1885. K: 1884. L: 1885. C: 1886.
Annex to *Javelot* in the Bidasoa River at Hendaye 1887-1901. Struck 8.8.1901.

---

**SURVEILLANT.** *Chaloupe à vapeur.* 8nhp screw steam launch for fishery protection service.

On 7 June 1882 the Maritime Prefect at Lorient decided on specifications for a fishery protection launch for the oyster beds in the Morbihan. It was to have a speed of at least 8 knots, a wood hull with if possible a flat bottom to allow intentional grounding, and a crew of 6-8 men. Naval constructor Trogneux at Lorient offered a design on 7 March 1883 and the *Inspecteur générale du Génie maritime* (de Bussy) approved it on 21 June 1883 with changes. The project was interrupted by hopes to use *Carpe* for this purpose, and when that idea was abandoned the ministry on 10 December 1884 asked Lorient for a design. The Machinery Commission was ordered on 19 January 1885 to contract for the ship which was named. A contract for a fishery protection vessel with the characteristics of Trogneux's design was signed on 18 May 1885 and notified on 3 June 1885. She was to be built in the facilities of M. A. Dubigeon, residing at Chantenay-sur-Loire and in those of M. Voruz at Nantes and then delivered to Lorient. She was under commercial operation by January 1897 when she was moved *pour ordre* (for the record) to the service craft list.

*The characteristics are based on the contract for the vessel.*
**Dimensions & tons:** 14.50m x 2.90m. 16.860t disp. Draught: 0.88m mean. Men: 5.
**Machinery:** 15 nhp and 55ihp designed at 260rpm and 6kg/cm² boiler pressure. 1 screw. 1 compound engine with 2 cylinders of 0.210m and 0.380m diameter and 0.240m stroke. 1 cylindrical tubular return flame boiler.
**Guns:** none.

*Surveillant* A. Dubigeon, Nantes.
On list 1.1885. Ord: 18.5.1885 (contract). K: 1885. L: 1886. C: 1886.
Named 19.1.1885. At Nantes 1.1886, fishery protection in the Morbihan as an annex to *Albatros* at Lorient 1887-90, annex to *Caudan* (a 650hp tug at Lorient) 1891-1896. Off main list 1896 and listed *pour ordre* with service craft at Rochefort 1.1897 for fishery protection duty in the bassin d'Arcachon. Assigned 11.4.1896 to replace *Crabe* in the bassin d'Arcachon. Left Brest 30.8.1896 under tow by *Drôme* for Rochefort, arrived 20.11.1896. Under commercial operation 1.1898, ran steam trials 6.5.1901, condemned 23.1.1904, for sale at Rochefort 1904-1906.

---

**NIGER Class.** *Chaloupe à vapeur* (*Niger*, 1.1887), *Chaloupe-canonnière* (both, 1.1892). 30ihp (8nhp) sectional twin screw steam launches for colonial service. Acquired. The similar *Djoué* was reclassed from an *aviso de 3ᵉ classe* to a *chaloupe à vapeur* in 1.1888.

In July and August 1883 Claparède produced a design for a *chaloupe-canonnière démontable pour le Haut Niger* which was very similar to that of *Djoué* (see *Avisos de 3ᵉ classe*, above). The craft was to carry 15 men, 10 days of provisions, 24 hours of fuel, and one Hotchkiss revolving cannon with its ammunition, and was to be shipped in 126 crates. The builder, the Société générale des Forges & Ateliers de Saint Denis, was a small firm adjacent to Claparède's Saint Denis yard. The craft was taken to Dakar and the crates were transported from there to Bamako on the upper Niger river on the backs of African porters. She was assembled and launched there in mid-1884 by Enseigne de vaisseau Froger. It took four months to transport her and three months to assemble her. She ran her trials between Bamako and Koulikoro in September 1884. She was commanded by Lieutenant de vaisseau Davoust from 1 January 1885 to 6 September 1886. In 1885 Davoust and Capitaine Delanneau headed for Timbuktu in *Niger* but only

The river gunboat (*chaloupe à vapeur*) *Niger*, with the barge *Manambougou* and a small sailing sharpie in tow, after leaving the French post at Manambougou (across the river from Bamako) on the upper Niger River on 1 July 1887 to try to reach and establish commercial relations with Timbuktu down the river. *Niger*, with her narrow hull and two funnels, was very similar to Savorgnan de Brazza's *Djoué* in the Congo (see 3ʳᵈ class avisos). The drawing was by the expedition's artist, Riou. *(Lt. Col. Galliéni, Deux campagnes au Soudan français, 1886-1888, Paris, 1891, page 199)*

got as far as Diafarabé. In 1886 *Niger* remained idle at Manambougou, Lieutenant de vaisseau Caron relieving Davoust and commanding the vessel from 6 September 1886 to 1 February 1888. *Niger* was transferred from the Colonial Administration to the Navy at some time in 1886, perhaps when Caron took command, but reverted to the Colonial Administration during 1887.

According to Galliéni, *Niger* was not in the least suited for navigation on the Niger River. She was elegant in form, but there were no accommodations for the crew and there was no stowage for the three months of provisions needed for the voyage. Finally and most important, her maximum speed was only 5 miles per hour while the currents of the Niger were often almost as fast. A construction yard was organized at Bamako and Caron remedied in part the lack of accommodations and stowage by building with resources at hand a barge, named *Manambougou* (12t, 10m x 2.80m) to be towed by *Niger*. In addition a small sailboat called a sharpie was built to go ashore every day and cut wood for fuel. (Galliéni had 8 tons of coal brought in on mules for use in extremely urgent situations.) Caron left Manambougou with *Niger*, the barge, and the sharpie on 1 July 1887 and on 18 August moored at Korioumé, the port of Timbuktu. Efforts to establish relations with the inhabitants of the city failed and after a difficult return voyage in which the barge was burned for fuel and a storm almost capsized the gunboat the expedition returned to Manambougou on 6 October 1887.

At Bamako Galliéni also began construction of a new gunboat with a wood hull. During a visit to Bamako in April 1887 Galliéni named her *Mage* after the naval officer who in 1857 first penetrated into Sudan. Her hull was ready in November 1887 to receive its engine but she proved unsatisfactory and when another *Mage* arrived from France she was renamed *Faidherbe*. She was never on the navy's fleet list.

Because the voyage of Caron had showed the risks of having only one gunboat sailing alone without any possible support, a second vessel was ordered in France. The plans for the new *chaloupe canonnière démontable pour le Haut Niger*, *Mage*, produced by the Société générale des Forges & Ateliers de Saint Denis, dated 31 October 1887 look like a copy of *Niger*. Upon his return to the Sudan in November 1887 Galliéni had to concern himself with the transport of the new gunboat, which arrived at Kayes in a large number of crates that had to be transported to the Niger. There she was assembled to sail in company with *Niger* on the next (1888) campaign under Davoust, who had returned to relieve Caron.

From 16 September to 24 October 1889 *Mage* under Lieutenant de vaisseau Jayme (who had relieved Davoust) and *Niger* under Ensign Hourst made another effort to reach Timbuktu, each towing a barge with provisions and firewood. *Niger* broke down en route but *Mage* reached Korioumé where she stayed for two days while Sub-Lieutenant Marchand (later of Fashoda fame) conducted discussions and collected information despite local hostility. The two vessels were transferred definitively from the Colonial Administration to the Navy during 1891. For more on these activities see E. Caron, *De Saint Louis au Port de Tomboukuou: voyage d'une canonnière française* (Paris 1891) and Galliéni, *Deux campagnes au Soudan français, 1886-1888* (Paris, 1891).

*The characteristics are for* Niger, Mage *being similar.*
**Dimensions & tons:** 18.750m wl x 2.60m moulded x 1.100m depth (*creux*). c28t disp. Draught 0.80m aft maximum. Men: 11 including 1 officer (21 including 2 officers in *Mage*).
**Machinery:** 30ihp (about 8nhp). 2 screws. 2 single-cylinder engines. 2 boilers.
**Guns:** 1 x 37mm revolving cannon.

*Niger* Forges & Ateliers de Saint Denis, Saint Denis.
On list 1.1887. K: 1884. L: 1884. C: 9.1884.
On the fleet list 1.1887 as a *chaloupe à vapeur* in commission as an annex to *Africaine*, transferred to the Colonial Administration 1887 and not on the 1.1888 fleet list. Returned by the Colonial Administration to

the Navy 1891 and restored to the list 1.1892 as a *chaloupe-canonnière*. Struck 1.6.1895, used as barge (*chaland*).

*Mage* Forges & Ateliers de Saint Denis, Saint Denis.
On list 1.1892. K: 1887. L: . C: 1887.
Ceded by the Colonial Administration to the Navy 1891, on the fleet list 1.1892 as a *chaloupe-canonnière*. Explored the Niger and the region of Timbuktu 1894 under LV Hourst. Active in Sudan 1895. Struck 1.6.1895, used as a barge.

--------

*OGOWÉ.* *Chaloupe à vapeur* (1887). 8nhp sectional twin screw steam launch for colonial service. Acquired.

In 1880 Dr Noël Ballay was charged by the Minister of Public Instruction (Education) to mount an expedition in Central Africa associated with the second Brazza expedition, which had started in 1879. With funds provided by the ministry Ballay purchased a *chaloupe à vapeur* from the Forges et Chantiers de la Méditerranée which could be transported in sections to the Alima River in Gabon, a tributary of the Congo River. Dr. Ballay set out for Africa without the launch in November 1880. He visited France briefly in late 1881 but the launch had not yet been successfully tried. In August 1882 he was able to start for the interior, carrying with him the steam launch which was named *Ballay* after himself. The party reached a tributary of the Alima, where they assembled the boat and launched her in June 1883. By this time the third Brazza expedition was in progress, and the launch was used in a transport service between the upper Ogowe and the Alima and for local explorations. On 15 February 1884 Brazza embarked in *Ballay*, descended the Alima and then the Congo, and arrived at Brazzaville at the end of April.

On 23 May 1885 the Minister of Public Instruction wrote to Minister of Marine Galiber that the decisions of the Council of Berlin had ended the work of the Ministry of Public Instruction in West Africa and that subsequent measures were up to the Minister of Marine. He therefore transferred to the Navy all of his personnel, facilities, and equipment to the Navy. In mid-December 1885 Capt. Rouvier of the Navy and Dr. Ballay, designated as boundary commissioners for the new French colony, embarked in *Ballay* at Brazzaville and started for the upper river. They concluded boundary negotiations with Belgian Congo commissioners at Nkunja, a French post 40 miles above the mouth of the Ubangi river, on 22 January 1886 and then proceeded to the Congo, arriving in France two months later. The launch, now named *Brazza*, was disassembled and transported to Cap Lopez, one section being lost during the transit.

In September 1886 the naval administration in Paris was advised that local naval authorities had taken the abandoned *chaloupe Ballay* to Libreville, rebuilt the missing section, repaired her at a cost of 14,000 francs, and were now using her as a *chaloupe canonnière* on the rivers in Gabon along with *Pygmée*. At this time the Navy had lost the new *Pionnier* in Gabon and was expecting to strike *Licona*. Paris renamed her for the Ogowe river in Gabon on 30 September 1886 and on 30 December 1886 asked the Colonial Administration to transfer her to the navy without cost. She appeared on the fleet list in January 1887 as a *chaloupe à vapeur* in commission. The Colonial Administration duly transferred her on 9 February 1887.

**Dimensions & tons:** .18m (keel) x 3.20m. c30t disp. Draught 0.50m fwd, 0.90m aft
**Machinery:** 8hp. 2 screws. 2 independent single-cylinder engines with cylinders of 0.159m diameter. 1 cylindrical tubular return-flame boiler.
**Guns:** 2 x 37mm revolving cannon

*Ogowé* (*Ogoue*) F.C. Méditerranée.
On list 1.1887. K: . L: . C: 1886.
Transferred by the Colonial Administration 9.2.1887 and commissioned as an annex to the hospital hulk *Alceste*, which was then the station ship for Gabon and the Congo. On 15.2.1887 Gabon informed Paris

that the hull of the launch was in poor condition, an inspection on 10.3.1887 confirmed its bad condition, and the navy initiated the process of striking her from the fleet list on 23.5.1887. Struck 5.7.1887, for disposal 1887-1889. The engines and boiler were left in Gabon to power tools in workshops ashore there.

---

*COURLIS* **Class.** *Chaloupes à vapeur.* 9nhp screw sail and steam launches with iron or steel hulls for fishery protection. Designed by A.C. Loire (ex Claparède), Saint Denis.

On 16 April 1888 the Machinery Commission was ordered to contact for a decked steam launch for fishery protection in the bay of (Mont) St. Michel. The contract was reported on 15 May 1888 as signed and was approved on 22 May 1888. The 13-metre vessel was named *Courlis* on 11 July 1888. On 14 May 1888 the Machinery Commission was ordered to contract for a 13-metre steam launch. The contract was reported on 21 June 1888 as signed and was approved on 27 June 1888. The vessel was named *Aigrette* on 11 July 1888. By August 1888 *Aigrette* was also intended for fishery protection in the bay of Mont Saint Michel with *Alcyone* as a base hulk. *Aigrette* and *Courlis* were inspected together at Cherbourg January 1889 for acceptance and criticised for sloppy construction. Each vessel was covered by a large canopy and had two masts with sails that could be lowered on deck (a maneuver that proved impossible when inspected) and a bowsprit. The screw propeller of *Courlis* was broken during trials on 14 January 1889 causing a dispute with the builder, and on 12 March 1889 *Courlis* was ordered to be kept in storage at Cherbourg until new orders were sent. In the meantime on 2 March 1889 Cherbourg and the commander of *Cuvier* who was also chief of the Granville fishery protection station reported on the inadequacy of *Aigrette* as a fishery protection vessel. The requirements had been for a vessel capable of making 12 knots, using salt water in her boiler, and capable of beaching instead of mooring at her base at Chausey. Instead *Aigrette* and *Courlis* steamed on fresh water at low boiler pressures, made only 7 knots (now reduced to 5 knots), could not beach because their water injection was near the keel, and had coal for only 5.5 hours of steaming, not enough for a normal patrol. The assignment to fishery protection was renounced on 12 March 1889 and *Aigrette* was ordered placed in storage.

**Dimensions & tons:** 13m x 3.60m. 20t disp. Draught: 1.12m mean.
**Machinery:** 9nhp, 40ihp designed. 1 cylindrical return-flame boiler.
**Guns:** probably none.

*Courlis* A.C. Loire (ex Claparède), Saint Denis.
On list 1.1889. Ord: 14.5.1888 (contract). K: 1888. L: 1888. C: 1.1889 (acceptance trials and delivery).
To storage at Cherbourg 3.1889. Cherbourg reported on 8.11.1889 the poor conditions of some of its small steam service craft and recommended that *Courlis* be assigned to the port movements directorate (*Direction des mouvements du port*) there. The assignment was approved 15 November 1889. Struck 16.5.1892 and inscribed on the list of service craft as a *chaloupe à vapeur* for the port movements directorate at Cherbourg and/or annex to *Buffle*. By 1920 was called *Chaloupe n° 114*. Condemned 19.9.1920, sold 23.5.1921 at Cherbourg to M. Leborgni.

*Aigrette* A.C. Loire (ex Claparède), Saint Denis.
On list 1.1889. Ord: 14.5.1888. K: 1888. L: 1888. C: 1.1889 (acceptance trials).
To storage at Cherbourg 3.1889. On 5.9.1889 the bureau of hydraulic works requested her assignment to the hydraulic works service at Brest for surveillance of the establishment of a sheltered anchorage at Lanninon in the Brest roadstead. Struck 13.6.1892 and inscribed on the list of service craft as a *chaloupe à vapeur* at Brest. Renamed *Lanninon* 3.3.1903, condemned 1914 and BU.

---

*CHÉLIFF* **Class.** *Chaloupes à vapeur.* 65nhp/260ihp small screw steamers with steel hulls for fishery protection. Designed by naval constructor Frédéric Alfred Schwartz.

On 13 May 1889 the Machinery Commission was directed to contract for a *chaloupe vedette* named *Seybouse* destined for fishery protection service on the coast of Algeria, a similar order was issued for *Chéliff*. The contract was approved on 20 August 1889. The design included a mobile torpedo tube forward but in early 1890 the contract was modified to excuse the builder from having to provide it. On 3 May 1892 the ministry directed Toulon that in wartime one tube for M1878 torpedoes was to be installed on the upper deck forward. This would have required the removal of the main mast. Both vessels served as intended on fishery protection duty.

*The characteristics are based on a devis for* Seybouse *(chaloupe-vedette) dated 26.3.1892.*
**Dimensions & tons:** 25.510m oa, 22.540m wl, 23.550m pp (wl fwd to rudder) x 4.540m ext (above wl), 4.240m wl. 54.109t disp. Draught: 1.431m mean, 2.097m aft (under propeller guard). Men: 14.
**Machinery:** 65nhp, 260ihp designed at 320rpm and 9kg/cm² boiler pressure. Trials (18.3.1892 at Toulon) 273ihp = 12.52kts at 302rpm. 1 screw. 1 vertical compound engine with 2 cylinders of 0.320m and 0.500m diameter and 0.330m stroke. 1 direct flame locomotive boiler. 5.5t coal.
**Guns:** 2 x 37mm/20 M1885 QF (bridge). **Torpedoes:** 1 tube planned, not installed.

*Chéliff* (*Chélif*) Dyle et Bacalan, Bordeaux-Bacalan/Dyle et Bacalan.
On list 1.1890. Ord: 7.8.1889. K: 1889. L: 2.1891. Comm: 23.6.1892.
Budget 1891. Machinery installed 1.10.1890 to 1.4.1891. Boiler installed 4.1891. To Toulon 1892, fishery protection duty to 1914. Rated *garde-pêche à vapeur* 1.1904. Decomm. 1914. Off main list by 3.1920 and for sale at Bizerte 1920. Struck 19.9.1920. Sold 1924 at Bizerte.

*Seybouse* Dyle et Bacalan, Bordeaux-Bacalan/Dyle et Bacalan.
On list 1.1890. Ord: 7.8.1889. K: 8.1889. L: 24.2.1891. Comm: 23.6.1892.
Budget 1891. Machinery installed 1.10.1890 to 1.4.1891. To Toulon and then to Algeria 1892. Rated *garde-pêche à vapeur* 1.1904. Returned from Algeria 1908 in bad condition, condemnation proposed 30.1.1911 but the Minister decided on 20.2.1911 to retain her although she was worn out. Struck 22.11.1913, sold 5.3.1914 to Maille de Marseille.

---

*TOPAZE.* *Chaloupe à vapeur.* 45ihp (10nhp) screw steam launch with a steel hull for colonial service.

On 29 and 31 May 1890 Minister Barbey ordered that a contract be negotiated for a steel *chaloupe à vapeur* of 16.50m (modified *Émeraude* type) for Gabon. The name was assigned on 5 June 1890. The contract was signed on 4 June 1890 and approved and notified on 9 June 1890. A contract modification of 6 August 1890 specified that she was to run trials at Saint Denis and then be delivered at Le Havre by 2 September 1890, where she would be dismantled to be carried to Gabon on the *Ville de Maccio* of the Cie. des Chargeurs-Réunis.

A report associated with the arrival in the colony of *Opale* in 1892 stated that *Topaze* and the other 15-metre *chaloupe* in Gabon, *Émeraude*, were becoming worn by hard service, their draught of 0.95m was considerable for their armament which consisted only of 2 revolving cannon placed on the upper deck (*paillotte*). Accommodations for the European crew were also poor.

*Characteristics are from the contract for the ship.*
**Dimensions & tons:** 16.50m pp x 3.58m wl. 27t disp. Draught: 0.85m mean, 0.90m aft. Men: 14.
**Machinery:** 45ihp designed (about 10nhp) at 280rpm and 7kg/cm²

boiler pressure. 1 screw. 1 engine with 1 cylinder of 0.230m diameter and 0.200m stroke. 1 return-flame boiler. 10kts.
**Guns:** 4 x 37mm revolving cannon.

*Topaze* A.C. Loire (ex Claparède), Saint Denis.
On list 1.1891. Ord: 4.6.1890 (contract). K: 1890. L: 1890. C: 1891.
In Cotonou (Benin) 1891-95. Dahomey (Benin) flotilla suppressed late 1895. Ceded to Colonial Ministry without charge 18.11.1895 and convoyed by the Navy to Grand Lahou, Ivory Coast, where the colony planned to use her in the Brandama River. Struck 18.11.1895.

---

**CORAIL.** *Chaloupe à vapeur.* 320ihp small screw steamer, iron or steel hull. Purchased.

This small steamer was built in 1888 as the mercantile *Éclaireur No 2*, a support craft for the West African operations of the Chargeurs Réunis. She had been used in postal service between Libreville and Saō Thomé under charter to the French since 1890. She was purchased on 25 April 1892 in Gabon from the Chargeurs Réunis for use in Benin. The name *Corail* (one in a series of names of ornamental stones then attributed to small gunboats or steam launches assigned to local stations in the colonies) was proposed 21 May 1892 either for the second gunboat foreseen in the contract for *Opale*, below, or for the steamer *Éclaireur* if she was found in good condition and her purchase was approved. Minister Cavaignac approved the purchase contract for *Éclaireur* and named her *Corail* on 3 June 1892. She

---

The shallow-draught river gunboat (*chaloupe à vapeur*) *Opale*, built for the French government by MM. Yarrow & Co. at Poplar. She was completed on 23 May 1892 and is shown here during trials on the Thames (with the Royal Naval College in the background) during which she made a speed of 10 miles per hour (English) at a draught of 18 inches. She became far more cluttered once she entered service in the colony, and also acquired a cloth canopy over much of the top deck. The photo was received by ONI on 14 June, probably in 1893. *(NHHC from Farenholt collection, previously ONI, NH-66027)*

was inscribed on the fleet list among the *chaloupes canonnières* and was to enter into full commission as soon as she was delivered to the Navy at Porto Novo from Libreville.

**Dimensions & tons:** 30m x 5.40m. Draught 1.20m aft (1.0m in 3.1893). Men: 35 including 2 officers.
**Machinery:** 320ihp. 2 screws. 2 vertical engines. Made 5.5kts at 240rpm in 3.1893.
**Guns:** 6 x 37mm revolving cannon (some on the bridge, some on an extension forward of the bridge).

*Corail* (builder unknown).
On list 1.1893. Built 1888.
Delivered by the Colonial Administration to the Navy 24.5.1892. A Navy commission docked the vessel at Ningué-Ningué and reported on 31.5.1892 that there was thin plating and numerous small holes in the bottom from corroded or missing rivets that had been temporarily plugged with cement but could not be reliably repaired. Later, in May 1893, her commander after experiencing two groundings and two engine casualties in this relatively deep draught ship during a two-day outing reported that neither the ship nor the engine could be relied upon, that they would never justify the expense of repairs, and that the ship would soon be unserviceable. After reporting several design defects he recommended operating *Corail* until the second *Opale* (*Onyx*) arrived, then transferring the crew to the new ship, and selling *Corail*. On 13.7.1893 the administration in Paris ordered that she should not be repaired. Decomm. 16.8.1893. Struck 31.10.1893 and given to the local service 24.2.1894 for use as a customs hulk at Adjara.

---

**FOURMI.** *Chaloupe à vapeur.* 80ihp screw steam launch for hydrographic service.

This small vessel was designed and built by Dyle et Bacalan at Bordeaux for hydrographic service on the French coast.

**Dimensions & tons:** 16.20m length. 22.8t disp. Draught: 1.60m.

**Machinery:** 80ihp = 8.9kts. 1 screw.
**Guns:** probably none.

*Fourmi* Dyle et Bacalan, Bordeaux-Bacalan/Dyle et Bacalan.
On list 1.1897. Ord: 21.10.1896. K: 1896. L: 1897. C: 1898.
Budget 1897 (late addition). In the acceptance process 1897-1898, briefly
    out of commission, then on hydrographic service on the French coast
    1898-1904, in reserve 1904-1909, probably for seasonal operations
    (annex to *Utile* 1908-1909). Off main list 1909. Tug at Lorient 1909-
    1922. Struck 29.12.1922. For sale at Rochefort 1922-1923, sailed
    commercially 1923-34.

---

## (D) River Gunboats (*Chaloupes à vapeur*).

River gunboats built between 1892 and 1895 for Benin and
Madagascar were classed as *Chaloupes à vapeur* instead of
*Chaloupes canonnières*.

*OPALE*. *Chaloupe à vapeur*. Sectional shallow draft river gunboat with a
stern paddle wheel.

On 27 April 1892 Minister Cavaignac decided to build one or two
gunboats of the *Bobillot* type for use in the Gulf of Benin, and on the same
day he approved a contract with Yarrow through Mr. Henry Chapman for
one or two river gunboats with one stern paddle wheel. The first vessel was
named *Opale* on 21 May 1892, the option to build the second was not
exercised. Yarrow based the design on that of the *Mosquito* and the *Herald*
of the British navy serving on the Zambesi. *Opale* was built in 23 working
days from start of construction to start of trials, 17 days less than promised.
Trials on the Thames were declared successful on 27 May 1892.

*Opale* was transported from London to Benin (Porto Novo) by the
British merchantman *Engineer* which left London on 4 June 1892, stopped
at Cherbourg to pick up her crew, and arrived at Lagos on 12 July 1892
where the craft was assembled. She transited from Lagos to Porto Novo and
commissioned in the Benin Flotilla on 6 August 1892. Gunnery trials
consisted of a bombardment of two Dahomian villages on 9 August 1892.

**Dimensions & tons:** 30.48m x 5.49m. 60t disp. Draught: 0.55m (0.60m
    max, 0.45m trials). Men: 34 including 2 officers.
**Machinery:** 100ihp. Trials 8.743kts average (fastest run 10.778kts at
    36rpm). Stern paddle wheel driven by two independent cylinders, one
    per side. 1 boiler.
**Guns:** 6 or 7 x 37mm revolving cannon (9 positions on the hull and on
    the flying deck).

*Opale* Yarrow, Poplar, UK.
On list 1.1893. K: 28.4.1892. L: 25.5.1892. Trials: 25.5.1892.
    Comm: 6.8.1892.
Reported on 25.4.1895 as converted and then operating as a tug.
    Dahomey (Benin) flotilla suppressed late 1895. Ceded to Colonial
    Ministry without charge 21.12.1895 effective 1.1.1896. Struck
    21.12.1895.

---

*ONYX*. *Chaloupe à vapeur*. Sectional shallow draft river gunboat with a
stern paddle wheel and a galvanised steel hull. Designed by A.C. Loire (ex
Claparède), Saint Denis.

On 30 December 1892 Minister of Marine Burdeau asked the French military commander in Benin, Brigadier General Alfred Dodds, for information
on the value of the vessels currently in the Benin flotilla and on the advisa-
bility of augmenting this force or changing its composition. On
9 February 1893 Dodds reported that the flotilla then included one aviso
(*Corail*), three gunboats (*Opale*, *Topaze*, and *Émeraude*), and one screw
steam launch (*Ambre*, ex *Jeannette*). He felt that this number would be sufficient if all of the vessels were usable, but *Corail* was all but completely

immobilized by the condition of her hull and the draught of the others was
such that between December and May only *Opale* was capable of providing
services between Porto Novo and Cotonou. None of them could ascend the
Oueme river higher than Danou before the high water season, but the
general wanted to take forces further upriver against Dahomey's King
Béhanzin, who had taken refuge there and was trying to reorganize the
debris of his army. Dodds's first priority was to give the flotilla as quickly as
possible a new gunboat of the modified *Opale* type to replace *Corail* and
then to follow with vessels of the same type to replace *Topaze* and *Émeraude*
when they became unserviceable. (Dodds executed the manoeuvre up the
Oueme river in 1894, capturing Béhanzin and ending the Dahomey war.)

Dodds also provided a report on recommended modifications to the
*Opale* type. Protection was to be increased by replacing the pilot house
forward with a small conning tower with protective plating, removable
plating would also be added around the *paillotte* (elevated deck) and on the
lower deck to protect the machinery. (The contract specified that the
plating would be at least 3mm thick.) The three revolving cannon on the
lower level were to be replaced with two quick fire guns, one on each side,
and two positions for quick fire guns were to be added amidships on the
*paillotte* to which the guns on the lower level could be moved. The four
revolving cannon on the corners of the *paillotte* would also be replaced with
quick fire guns.

On 13 April 1893 the Machinery Commission was directed to contract
for a stern-wheel river gunboat (*chaloupe à vapeur*) of the modified *Opale*
type which was named *Onyx*. The 1894 budget (submitted on 16 May
1893) included three *chaloupes à vapeur* designated X1 to X3 to be built by
contract. The first, *Onyx*, was to be ordered in advance in 1893. Instead of
exercising the option for a second vessel in the contract with Yarrow for
*Opale* the Navy contracted on 21 June 1893 with A.C. Loire, Saint Denis
for *Onyx*. The contract was approved and notified on 3 July 1893.

*The characteristics are based on the contract and plans for the vessel.*
**Dimensions & tons:** 32.440m (total including stern wheel and guards),
    26.890m wl (hull only at wl) x 5.500m wl. 60.572t disp. Draught:
    0.460m mean without fuel but with water in boiler (0.610m with 15t
    fuel, 0.660m max designed). Men: 33 including 1 officer.
**Machinery:** 100ihp designed at 36-39rpm and 10kg/cm$^2$ boiler pressure.
    Contract speed 8.5kts. Stern paddle wheel (3.1m diameter). 2 horizon-
    tal engines, each with 1 cylinder of 0.265m diameter and 0.760m
    stroke. (1 engine was on each side at the extreme stern directly driving
    the stern wheel.) 1 locomotive boiler. Could carry up to 50t coal or
    wood on an exceptional basis (draught 0.920m).
**Guns:** 6 x 37mm/20 M1885 QF (8 positions of which 6 on the elevated
    deck and two low on the bow).

*Onyx* (X1) A.C. Loire (ex Claparède), Saint Denis.
On list 1.1894. Ord: 7.1893. K: 1893. L: 29.9.1893. C: 13.1.1894.
Budget 1894 (ordered in advance), to replace *Corail*. Delivered to Lagos
    18.12.1883 by merchantman *Buccaneer*, successful trials 13.1.1894 and
    commissioned in Benin. Dahomey (Benin) flotilla suppressed late
    1895. Ceded to Colonial Ministry without charge 21.12.1895 effective
    1.1.1896. Struck 21.12.1895.

*X2, X3* (Unnamed) Contract
Budget 1894 (not funded). The 1894 budget (submitted 5.1893) includ-
    ed two more *chaloupes à vapeur* like *Onyx* to replace *Topaze* and *Émer-
    aude* with the stipulation that no funds were to be spent on them dur-
    ing 1894. They was not contracted for and the 1895 budget (3.1894)
    deferred them indefinitely. The end of the Dahomey War in 1894
    ended the need for the craft.

---

*PRÉCIEUSE* Class. *Chaloupes à vapeur*. Sectional shallow draft river
gunboats with a stern paddle wheel for the Madagascar campaign.
Designed by F.C. Méditerranée, Le Havre-Graville

The design of these vessels was based on *Opale* but they were smaller and had half her rated horsepower. On 27 October 1894 the French evacuated their nationals from Tananarive, Madagascar, following the refusal of the Hova government there to accept a treaty that would have made Madagascar a French protectorate. The French parliament quickly voted funds for a 15,000-man military expedition to Madagascar. This included twelve shallow-draught river gunboats, which were ordered and named in late 1894. Their design was inspired by Yarrow's *Opale*. They were built in six watertight sections to facilitate transport. There were two types from two builders, one with more powerful engines than the other. Protection was limited to the pilot house and the gun shields. They were built more slowly than hoped, but all had been launched by mid-1895 and by then several including *Précieuse* and *Espiègle* had successfully run their steam trials. All were probably in Madagascar by late 1895. They were used on the Betziboka River and its tributary the Ikopa River (at Ampapamena), which flowed from the vicinity of Tananarive to the northwest coast of the island. The gunboats were able to reach Ambato on the Betziboka but unable to go further upriver to Marololo where the Ikopa joined it. Their main function proved to be to tow barges to resupply French forces in Ankabouka. The eight small gunboats could each tow one barge alongside.

The battle of Tananarive on 30 September 1895 resulted in the surrender of the Hova queen and government, but the French then had to contend with insurgencies. General Gallieni arrived in early October 1896 to pacify the island. In December 1896 the gunboats were turned over to the Colonial Ministry for use in Gallieni's campaigns.

**Dimensions & tons:** 25m x 5.50m. 41t disp. Draught: 0.40m mean. Men: 20.
**Machinery:** 50ihp. Designed speed 6.5kts. 2 simple expansion engines. Stern paddle wheel.
**Guns:** 2 x 37mm/20 M1885 QF, one on each side of the pilot house.

*Espiègle* F.C. Méditerranée, Le Havre-Graville.
On list 1.1895. K: . L: 1895. C: 1895.
Struck 14.12.1896 and to Colonial Ministry.

*Éclatante* F.C. Méditerranée, Le Havre-Graville.
On list 1.1895. K: . L: 1895. C: 1895.
Struck 14.12.1896 and to Colonial Ministry.

*Impétueuse* F.C. Méditerranée, Le Havre-Graville.
On list 1.1895. K: . L: 1895. C: 1895.
Struck 14.12.1896 and to Colonial Ministry.

*Insolente* F.C. Méditerranée, Le Havre-Graville.
On list 1.1895. K: . L: 1895. C: 1895.
Struck 14.12.1896 and to Colonial Ministry.

*Précieuse* F.C. Méditerranée, La Seyne.
On list 1.1895. K: . L: 1895. Trials: 1.1895. C: 1895.
Trials at Toulon 1.1895. Struck 14.12.1896 and to Colonial Ministry.

*Poursuivante* F.C. Méditerranée, La Seyne.
On list 1.1895. K: . L: 1895. C: .
Struck 14.12.1896 and to Colonial Ministry.

*Rusée* F.C. Méditerranée, La Seyne.
On list 1.1895. K: . L: 1895. C: 1895.
Struck 14.12.1896 and to Colonial Ministry.

*Zélée* F.C. Méditerranée, La Seyne.
On list 1.1895. K: . L: 1895. C: 1895.
Struck 14.12.1896 and to Colonial Ministry.

---

**BRAVE Class.** *Chaloupes à vapeur.* Sectional shallow draft river gunboats with a stern paddle wheel for the Madagascar campaign. Designed by A.C. Loire (ex Claparède), Saint Denis

The river gunboat (*chaloupe à vapeur*) *Espiègle*, one of eight 50ihp craft built for the 1895 Madagascar expedition to a design based on *Opale*. The boiler is in the open under the protected pilot house between the two 37mm QF guns. Four 100ihp craft built to essentially the same design by the Chantiers de la Loire in their large plant at Saint Denis were all launched ahead of the contract schedule. (*Le monde illustré, 2 February 1895, p. 69*)

---

The design of these vessels was based on *Opale*, they were smaller than *Opale* as was the *Précieuse* type but had engine power twice that of *Précieuse* and equal to that of *Opale* and also had a slightly deeper draught. *Brave* used her 37mm guns in combat in mid-1895, otherwise the chief function of these boats was towing resupply barges. These four 100ihp gunboats could each tow two barges alongside.

**Dimensions & tons:** As *Précieuse* but 51t disp. and draught 0.50m mean.
**Machinery:** As *Précieuse* but 100ihp.
**Guns:** As *Précieuse*.

*Brave* A.C. Loire (ex Claparède), Saint Denis.
On list 1.1895. K: . L: 1895. C: 1895.
In service by mid-1895 in Madagascar. Struck 14.12.1896 and to Colonial Ministry.

*Infernale* A.C. Loire (ex Claparède), Saint Denis.
On list 1.1895. K: . L: 1895. C: 1895.
Struck 14.12.1896 and to Colonial Ministry.

*Invincible* A.C. Loire (ex Claparède), Saint Denis.
On list 1.1895. K: . L: 1895. C: 1895.
Struck 14.12.1896 and to Colonial Ministry.

*Vigilante* A.C. Loire (ex Claparède), Saint Denis.
On list 1.1895. K: . L: 1895. C: 1895.
Struck 14.12.1896 and to Colonial Ministry.

---

### (E) Fast Gunboats (*Bateaux canons*).

**GABRIEL CHARMES.** *Bateau canon.* Large torpedo boat hull by FCM La Seyne with a single 138.6mm gun on deck. Designed by Lagane and Canet (artillery).

Rear Admiral Théophile Aube took office as Minister of Marine on 7 January 1886. He was the leading spokesman within the Navy of the *Jeune École*, a movement within and outside the Navy that claimed that the torpedo boat had made the battleship obsolete. The civilian publicist Gabriel Charmes joined Aube in vigorously promoting the *Jeune École*, and he also offered the theory that vessels the size of torpedo boats could also take on other functions of large surface ships, include bombarding shore positions with artillery. Aube lost no time in experimenting with Charmes' theory, and on 19 April 1886 he ordered an experimental *bateau canon* from the Forges et Chantiers de la Méditerranée at La Seyne. On the same day Charmes died in Paris at age 35 of tuberculosis, and on 7 October 1886 Aube named the boat for him.

The *Gabriel Charmes* was similar to the *Balny* class of seagoing torpedo boats (see below) with the same length, about half a metre wider, and somewhat heavier. Instead of a torpedo armament she carried a single 138.6mm gun on deck forward of the conning position behind an oval breastwork with a handling room and magazine below it. Canet developed a mounting for the gun in which hydraulic brakes absorbed the force of recoil and then used it to return the gun to firing position. (He used some of this technology in developing the quick fire gun.) The gun recoiled only 55cm and the impact on the boat was slight. The gun mounting was capable of elevation but not training – the gun was trained by turning the boat. The calibre of the gun was relatively small but with the new high energy melinite explosives it was expected to cause considerable destruction ashore. The rate of fire was expected to be one round per minute or better. The minimal sail plan of the boat included a jib and a lug sail.

Machinery trials were successful but gunnery trials were not, because of the unpredictable motion of the small vessel and the difficulty of estimating range from such a small elevation above the water. The rate of fire was also very slow. At 1,000 metres, let alone at the desired 7,000 metres, the boat failed to put a single shell into an area representing a target 150m long and 20m wide. The trials commission and the Maritime Prefect at Toulon, Vice Admiral Dupetit-Thouars, agreed that the boat could not be used in the defense of or attack against a port except in a flat calm and only if the range to the target was known exactly for every round fired.

On 26 July 1887 the *Conseil des travaux* recommended converting the vessel to a torpedo boat. She was decommissioned on 2 August 1887 and on 4 August 1887 lost her name and was inscribed on the fleet list as *Torpilleur no 151*. The plans for conversion to a torpedo boat, approved on 1 October 1887, called for fitting a long torpedo spar and two 37mm guns forward and one twin torpedo tube mount for 381mm torpedoes amidships above the boiler. This design was approved by the *Conseil des travaux* on 20 December 1887, with the additon of a 40cm searchlight on the conning tower her displacement would have been 79.17 tons.

Minister Krantz, however, on 9 February 1888 superseded these plans by ordering her provisional fitting as a *contre-torpilleur* (defensive torpedo boat) armed with eight 37mm Hotchkiss guns, four forward of the conning tower in the position vacated by the 138.6mm gun, two above the boiler and two further aft in sponsons. Firing trials were conducted on 22 March 1888 with satisfactory results. Subsequently one of the guns forward of the conning tower was removed.

On 9 September 1889 it was proposed to complete this armament by adding a torpedo spar, a change that was also to be made in the smaller *Torpilleur no 68* which had also been converted into a *contre-torpilleur*. The *Conseil des travaux* approved this plan on 24 December 1889. The torpedo spar was intended to protect the *contre-torpilleurs* against enemy torpedo avisos and torpedo boats during a mêlée. In May 1890 *Torpilleur no 151* completed the installation of the torpedo spar salvaged from the seagoing torpedo boat *Avant-Garde*, recently wrecked on the Portuguese coast. The satisfactory trials of this spar were reported on 26 February 1891.

By 1891, however, the *contre-torpilleur* concept had been abandoned,

The *bateau-canon Gabriel Charmes*. The 138.6mm gun, which could elevate but not train, is in a large oval enclosure forward of the kiosk with its handling room and magazine in the hull below it. (*L'Illustration, Journal Universel, 18 December 1886, page 416*)

and a note of 3 March 1891 stipulated that *No 151* would be maintained in service as a *torpilleur porte-torpille* (spar torpedo boat). She never left the Toulon area. A note of 19 June 1896 indicated that she was considered to be without value. To give her a little more capability Minister Besnard on 25 August 1896 proposed removing two of her seven 37mm guns, the torpedo spar, and one of her two masts, and installing a deck-mounted 381mm torpedo tube above the boiler room and adding to her coal supply. These modifications were not carried out. A dispatch of 27 November 1900 removed her from the list of combatant vessels.

**Dimensions & tons:** 41.85m oa, 40.00m pp x 3.80m wl (2.40m on deck). 76.544t disp. Draught: 0.86m amidships, 2.00m aft under propeller guard. Men: 16.

**Machinery:** 580ihp designed at 9kg/cm² boiler pressure. Speed 19kts. Trials (23.2.1887) 19.85kts. 1 screw. 1 compound engine with 2 cylinders of 0.39m and 0.67m diameter and 0.38m stroke. 1 locomotive boiler. 9t coal. Range 700nm @ 12kts.

**Guns:**

(1887, as *bâteau canon*) 1 x 138.6mm/30 M1881.

(1888, as *contre-torpilleur no 151*) 8 x 37mm guns (later 7 x 37mm). One torpedo spar added 1890

***Gabriel Charmes***, later ***Torpilleur no 151***. F.C. Méditerranée, La Seyne. On list 1.1887. Ord: 19.4.1886. K: 1886. L: 23.9.1886. C: 26.7.1887. Not in budgets. Designated *bateau canon* 9.1886. First trials 23.9.1886 (19.4kts). Named 7.10.1886 for the publicist whom Admiral Aube admired, who had avocated this type of vessel, and who had just died prematurely. Failed official trials as *bâteau canon* 2.3.1887. To *Torpilleur de 1re classe* as *Torpilleur no 151* on 2.8.1887 (being converted 1.1888), to *Contre-torpilleur* 1.1889 (in reserve), back to *Torpilleur de 1re classe* as *Torpilleur no 151*, 1.1890 (in reserve). Struck 27.11.1900, renamed *Ringard* 27.11.1900, annex to the school for engineers at Toulon 1900-1907 as a school for stoking. Sold by the Domaines 3.4.1907 at Toulon to BU.

# Chapter Eleven

# Torpedo Boats and Submarines, 1882-1897

## I. TORPEDO BOATS

**(A) Seagoing Torpedo Boats (*Torpilleurs de haute mer*).**
Category added in the 1.1885 fleet list, to *Torpilleurs
d'escadre* 1.1899, back to *Torpilleurs de haute mer* 1.1901.

*BALNY* **Class.** *Torpilleurs de haute mer.* Normand type seagoing torpedo
boats with two torpedo tubes in the bow, one screw, one funnel, and three
masts (later one). To *torpilleurs de 1re classe* 1.1890.

On 20 May 1884 the Navy asked Normand for plans for a *torpilleur de
haute mer*, a torpedo boat that would be large enough to accompany the

fleet at sea. Normand submitted the design on 5 July 1884 and the *Conseil
des travaux* accepted it on 29 July 1884. The Machinery Commission was
directed on 9 August 1884 to order three of the vessels from Normand, the
others were built by two other builders to plans supplied by Normand.
Normand told the Council that the design was based on the torpedo boat
*Poti* which he had just delivered to Russia. It had the same propulsion plant
but the hull lines were closer to those of his *Torpilleurs nos 65-74* with an
additional section inserted amidships, a slightly deeper hull, and a vertical
bow as in *Torpilleurs nos 60-64*.

The nine boats were 7m longer than the torpedo boats built up to then
but were soon found to be much too small for the missions for which they
were intended and were reclassed as *torpilleurs de 1re classe* (*torpilleurs de
Défense mobile*) with the new *Nos 126-129* and *Nº 151* (ex *Gabriel Charmes*)
in January 1890. All nine underwent trials at Cherbourg. Only the
Normand trio were fully successful on trials, with the Claparède boats
remaining in trials for two to three years and *Edmond Fontaine* initially
being rejected. They were named for officers of the Navy and the *Troupes
de la Marine* (naval infantry and artillery) killed during the conquest of
Indochina, then in progress. These nine vessels first appeared belatedly in

The seagoing torpedo boat, later 1st class torpedo boat, *Doudart de Lagrée*
photographed at Algiers by Geiser during the time that the boat was based at
Toulon in 1887-89. She has two torpedo tubes side by side in the bow and a
37mm revolving cannon on each side outboard of the kiosk. (*NHHC from ONI
album of foreign warships dated about 1900, NH-88787*)

the 1886 budget (submitted in March 1885) along with two more that were not proceeded with.

**Dimensions & tons:** 40.75m wl (wl fwd to wl aft), 40.75m pp (wl fwd to rudder) x 3.33m ext (above wl), 3.27m wl. 58.5t disp (normal), 66t (full load). Draught: 0.50m fwd, 1.15m amidships, 2.55m aft under propeller guard (*sous crosse*). Men: 22.
**Machinery:** 580ihp designed at 310 rpm and 9.25kg/cm² boiler pressure. Speed 19kts. Trials (*Balny*, 21.6.1886) 20.471kts at 310.46rpm and 9.14kg/cm² boiler pressure, (*B. Willaumez*) 18.99kts. 1 screw. 1 vertical compound engine with 2 cylinders of 0.36m and 0.58m diameter and 0.38m stroke. 1 locomotive boiler. 12t coal. Range 2,000nm @ 11kts.
**Torpedoes:** 2 tubes in the bow for 356mm (4.42m) torpedoes. **Guns:** 2 x 37mm revolving cannon.

*Balny* Augustin Normand, Le Havre.
On list 1.1885. Ord: 9.8.1884. K: 1884. L: 6.2.1886. Trials: 6.1886.
Budget 1886. Named 19.8.1884, contract approved 3.10.1884. Left builder for Cherbourg 9.6.1886. Commissioned for trials 1.7.1886 after trials begun. From Cherbourg to Toulon 20-27.10.1886, then *Défense mobile* at Toulon, Algiers (1893), Toulon (1895, in reserve), and Corsica (1897). In 1905 became annex to the school for torpedo boat engineers in *Algésiras*. Renamed *Paillon* 5.1.1911. Annex to the school for torpedomen in *Cécille* at Toulon 1910-12. Struck 6.2.1912. Sold 25.11.1912 at Toulon to BU.

*Déroulède* Augustin Normand, Le Havre.
On list 1.1885. Ord: 9.8.1884. K: 1884. L: 19.4.1886. Trials: 7-10.1886.
Budget 1886. Named 19.8.1884, contract approved 3.10.1884. Left builder for Cherbourg 28.6.1886. Commissioned for trials 9.7.1886. *Escadre d'évolutions* at Toulon 1886-87. *Défense mobile* at Toulon 1887-91, Algeria 1892-96, Bizerte 1896-99 (repairs), Oran 1900-01, and Corsica 1901-05. 1st Mediterranean torpedo boat flotilla 1905. Struck 9.4.1906, sold 5.1.1907 to M. Goutte of Marseille.

*Doudart de Lagrée* Augustin Normand, Le Havre.
On list 1.1885. Ord: 9.8.1884. K: 1884. L: 5.7.1886. Trials: 10.1886.
Budget 1886. Named *Lagrée* 19.8.1886, renamed *Doudart de Lagrée* 29.10.1886. *Défense mobile* at Cherbourg 1886-87. *Escadre d'évolutions* at Toulon 1887. *Défense mobile* at Toulon 1887-89, reserve 1889-93. Reboilered 1893-95 with 2 Oriolle boilers. *Défense mobile* at Algiers 1895-1902, Tunisia 1902-03, Corsica 1903, Toulon 1903-05. Struck 4.12.1905, sold 5.1.1907 to M. Goutte of Marseille.

*Edmond Fontaine* Anc. Éts. Claparède, Saint Denis.
On list 1.1885. Ord: 23.2.1885. K: 1885. L: 23.1.1886. Trials: 8.1886-3.1889.
Budget 1886. Probably fitted out by Claparède at Rouen-Petit Quévilly. Division du Nord, then *Défense mobile* at Cherbourg. Rammed and nearly cut in half just outside Cherbourg 6-7.5.1891, docked and repaired. *Défense mobile* at Dunkirk 1893-98, then at Cherbourg. Struck 10.7.1903. Sold 1903 at Cherbourg.

*Bouët-Willaumez* Anc. Éts. Claparède, Saint Denis.
On list 1.1885. Ord: 23.2.1885. K: 1885. L: 12.2.1886. Trials: 7.1886-6.1889.
Budget 1886. Fitted out by Claparède at Rouen-Petit Quévilly. Following the delivery of this vessel and *Salve* at Rouen in 10.1886 that yard was dismantled and the equipment taken to Saint Nazaire. *Défense mobile* at Cherbourg. Tested a Petit et Godard tubular boiler c1890, this ordered modified for oil firing on 24.7.1893 and tested in 1895. Grounded and sunk 31.8 to 1.9.1900 on the Gautier rock at Bréhat (crew saved). Struck 25.10.1900, wreck for sale at Cherbourg 1900-1901.

*Capitaine Cuny* A.C. Loire, Nantes.
On list 1.1885. Ord: 23.2.1885. K: 1885. L: 3.6.1886. Trials: 7.1886-4.1887.

Budget 1886. *Défense mobile* at Cherbourg 1886-88 (trials and reserve), Toulon 1888-92, Algeria 1892-95, Toulon 1895-96 (reserve), Corsica 1896-1903, Toulon 1903-10. Struck 15.4.1911. Sold 25.11.1912 at Toulon.

*Capitaine Mehl* A.C. Loire, Nantes.
On list 1.1885. Ord: 23.2.1885. K: 1885. L: 3.6.1886. Trials: 8.1886-10.1887.
Budget 1886. *Défense mobile* at Cherbourg 1886-88 (trials and reserve), Toulon 1888-1892 (reserve), Algeria 1892-95 (reserve), Toulon 1895-97 (reserve), Corsica (1898-1905). 1st Mediterranean torpedo boat flotilla at Toulon (1904-08), fishery protection at Port Vendres (1908). Struck 15.10.1909. Sold 30.10.1910 at Toulon.

*Challier* A.C. Loire, Nantes.
On list 1.1886. Ord: 23.2.1885. K: 1885. L: 3.7.1886. Trials: 8.1886-5.1887.
Budget 1886. *Escadre d'évolutions* at Toulon 1888 to 1889. *Défense mobile* at Toulon 1889-92 (repairs and reserve), Algiers 1892-95, Toulon 1895-98 (out of commission), Corsica 1898-1901. Struck 24.10.1902 and machinery transferred to the school for torpedo boat engineers in *Algésiras*. For sale at Toulon 1904-1905, retained as gunnery target 1905-1906. Hull sold 8.6.1906 at Toulon to BU.

*Dehorter* Anc. Éts. Claparède, Saint Denis.
On list 1.1886. Ord: 23.2.1885. K: 1885. L: 9.3.1886. Trials: 8.1886-10.1888.
Budget 1886. Probably fitted out by Claparède at Rouen-Petit Quévilly. Arrived at Cherbourg 12.3.1886. *Défense mobile* at Cherbourg 1886 to 1904. Struck 2.3.1904 after repeated boiler failures. Sold 25.5.1904 for conversion into pleasure yacht *Nina d'Asty III*.

---

*OURAGAN. Torpilleur de haute mer.* A.C. Loire (Nantes) seagoing torpedo boat with four torpedo tubes on deck (two on each side), one screw, two funnels abreast, three masts, and a ram bow. To *éclaireur-torpilleur* (torpedo scout) 1.1888, *torpilleur de haute mer* 1.1890.

This boat was begun on speculation by A.C. Loire, Nantes, at the beginning of 1886 and was offered to the Navy on 7 July 1886 with a promised speed of 25 knots. She was delivered with three masts with light sails, but the middle mast was removed after sails for torpedo boats were suppressed in June 1890. The four-cylinder engine functioned as a quadruple expansion engine at lower speeds and as a triple expansion engine at high speeds, steam then being introduced simultaneously into the first two cylinders. It had two cylinders inclined 90 degrees relative to each other and two vertical. The boat never made more than 19.21 knots, and that with difficulty. In normal service *Ouragan* and her four later copies (below) rarely exceeded 1,400ihp and their practical speed was at best 16 knots and more often only 13 knots or 14 knots. However, they had a heavy armament, a long steaming range, excellent manoeuvring capabilities (while having trouble maintaining a set course) and comfortable accommodations, so they saw considerable use. The 356mm torpedoes in *Ouragan* and the repeat *Ouragan*s below were a shortened variant of the Model 1887 torpedo (4.70m long instead of 4.99m) that was not repeated. The original locomotive boilers had to be replaced soon after entering service.

**Dimensions & tons:** 47.25m oa, 46.72m wl, 46.00m pp x 4.82m ext, 4.73m wl. 106-114t disp (on plans), 140t (average, trials), 175-180t (full load). Draught: 1.20m fwd, 1.79m amidships, 2.90m aft under propeller guard. Men: 29-32.
**Machinery:** 1,700ihp designed at 10kg/cm² boiler pressure. Speed 25 kts (advertised). Trials (4.1888) 19.21kts at 303rpm. 1 screw. 1 composite quadruple expansion engine with 4 cylinders of 0.27m, 0.46m, 0.68m, and 1.00m diameter and 0.46m stroke. 2 locomotive boilers. Range 2,000nm @ 10kts.

**Torpedoes:** 6 tubes for 356mm M1887 short (4.70m) torpedoes (two bow tubes that were soon removed, 2 on the sides abreast the conning tower, 2 on the sides aft). **Guns:** 2 x 47mm revolving cannon (soon replaced with 2 x 47mm/40 M1885 QF).

*Ouragan* A.C. Loire, Nantes.
On list 1.1887. Ord: 23.8.1886. K: 8.1886. L: 12.3.1887.
  Trials: 4.1888-9.1889.
Budget 1887. Built by A.C. Loire without having been ordered, purchased 23.8.1886 (contract signed 6.9.1886). From Saint Nazaire to Toulon 20-26.6.1887. Decomm. at Toulon 1.10.1887 for modifications to her propulsion machinery. Trials resumed 1888, in service 1890 with the *Escadre de la Méditerranée*. Became school for stoking 26.10.1898. Struck 2.5.1901. Sold 25.10.1903 at Toulon to BU.

---

*COUREUR. Éclaireur-torpilleur.* Thornycroft seagoing torpedo boat with two torpedo tubes in the bow, two screws, two funnels (the forward one offset to starboard and the after one to port), one mast between the funnels, and a low clipper bow with a turtleback. To *torpilleur de haute mer* 1.1890.

---

The seagoing torpedo boat *Coureur* probably at Cherbourg during trials. Her two torpedo tubes were side by side in the bow. This photo was received by ONI on 7 December 1892. ONI noted on the photo that the vessel carried 47mm guns rather than the 37mm revolving cannon seen here, evidently reflecting an early change by the French. *(NHHC from ONI, NH-88789)*

Designed by Thornycroft for France as a copy of *Ariete* and *El Rayo*, built by them for Spain. She had two rudders, one forward and one aft of the screw, and Thornycroft's vaulted stern which resembled a double tunnel above the two screws. She was delivered with three masts but kept only the middle one between the funnels. She steered well but her hull scantlings were too weak.

**Dimensions & tons:** 45.32m oa, 44.94m wl x 4.45m ext, 4.34m wl. 97t (designed), 102.89t disp (normal), 127.16t (full load). Draught: 1.346m mean, 1.65m aft.
**Machinery:** 1,500ihp designed at 400rpm and 10kg/cm² boiler pressure. Speed 23.5kts. Trials (24.9.1888) 1,528ihp = 23.55kts at 380rpm with 23.62kts on her best measured mile. 2 screws. 2 vertical compound engines with 2 cylinders of 0.318m and 0.616m diameter and 0.381m stroke. 2 Thornycroft boilers. 8t coal. Range 2,700nm (designed), 900nm (actual) @ 10kts.
**Torpedoes:** 2 bow tubes for 356mm M1885 torpedoes. **Guns:** 2 x 47mm/40 M1885 QF.

*Coureur* Thornycroft, Chiswick, UK/Thornycroft.
On list 1.1888. Ord: 16.8.1887. K: 5.9.1887. L: 13.6.1888.
  Trials: 9-10.1888.
Budget 1887 (extraordinary). *Escadre d'évolutions* and *Escadre de la Méditerranée* 1889-95, then reserve at Toulon. School for apprentice pilots for Mediterranean torpedo boats 1899-1900. *Défense mobile* in Algeria and Tunisia 1902, then back to reserve at Toulon. Reboilered with Du Temple boilers 1903. To fishery protection duty 1910-1911

and rated *garde-pêche à vapeur* at Philippeville (Algeria), replaced by *Forban* 1911. Struck 23.11.1911, for sale in Tunisia 1911-1912.

*AVANT-GARDE. Éclaireur-torpilleur.* Normand seagoing torpedo boat with two torpedo tubes on deck (amidships and aft), one torpedo spar forward, two screws, and two funnels abreast. To *torpilleur de haute mer* 1.1890.

On 14 October 1886 Minister of Marine Aube issued specifications for a single screw *torpilleur de haute mer* based on the *Balny* type. Normand produced a series of three designs from which the Conseil des Travaux on 21 June 1887 selected one of 35m in length that ultimately became the 36-metre 1st class torpedo boat *Torpilleur nº 126*. On 23 June 1887 Normand submitted a design for an enlarged torpedo boat with two screws armed with two rotating torpedo tubes on deck. It was referred on 7 July 1887 to the Council which examined it on 19 July 1887. Normand enlarged its dimensions to improve seakeeping and habitability and gave it twin screws to reduce its likelihood of being disabled. The Council felt that twin screws did not offer sufficient advantages and preferred the *Torpilleur nº 126* design as a *torpilleur de haute mer*. On 29 July 1887 the Council was asked if, considering that another twin screw boat (*Coureur*) was being ordered from Thornycroft, Normand's boat should be ordered on a trial basis. Minister Barbey decided on 19 September 1887 to order the boat and on 22 September 1887 directed the Machinery Commission to negotiate a contract. The contract was approved on 15 November 1887 and the boat was named on 9 January 1888. She was a good sea boat and had two rudders (one forward and one aft of the screws) and three masts with light sails. She became Normand's prototype seagoing torpedo boat and inspired the designs of nearly all France's subsequent *torpilleurs de haute mer*, but her own career was brief as she was lost on a Portuguese sandbank on her way to entering service at Toulon.

**Dimensions & tons:** 45.45m oa, 42.02m pp x 4.51m ext, 4.42m wl. 117.98t disp (normal), 130.2t (full load). Draught: 1.30m mean, 2.40m aft under propeller guard. Men: 27.
**Machinery:** 1,250ihp designed at 10kg/cm$^2$ boiler pressure. Speed 20.5kts. Trials 1,450ihp = 20.97kts. 2 screws. 2 compound engines (type *Torpilleur nº 126*) with 2 cylinders of 0.44m and 0.692m diameter and 0.44m stroke. 2 locomotive boilers. 15t coal. Range 2,000nm @ 10kts.
**Torpedoes:** 2 single deck tubes for 356mm torpedoes (1 amidships and 1 aft), 1 torpedo spar forward. **Guns:** 2 x 47mm/40 M1885 QF.

*Avant-Garde* Augustin Normand, Le Havre.
On list 1.1888. Ord: 7.11.1887. K: 11.1887. L: 11.10.1889.
    Trials: 12.1889
Budget 1887 (extraordinary). Assigned to Toulon after trials at Cherbourg. En route ran onto a sandbank 25.2.1890 at Mira near Aveiro, Portugal and could not be refloated. BU in place, propulsion plant and some fittings recovered and used in *Archer*, below. Struck 28.4.1890.

*AGILE* **Class.** *Torpilleurs de haute mer.* FCM La Seyne seagoing torpedo boats with three torpedo tubes on deck (forward, amidships, and aft), one screw, one funnel, and two masts (later none). Designed by Lagane. Never rated *Éclaireurs-torpilleurs* in the fleet list, though they were so listed in the 1889 budget (mid-1888).

On 14 October 1886 Minister Aube communicated to commercial firms specifications for a single-screw *torpilleur de haute mer* based on *Balny*. Designs from F.C. Méditerranée, C.A. Gironde, Normand, Creusot, and A.C. Loire were firmly rejected by the *Conseil des travaux* on 29 March 1887 as not meeting the specifications and lacking in longitudinal stability. That FCM design was 41m long. Another 96-ton design by F.C.

Méditerranée was turned down on 5 July 1887. The Council wanted the 4.40-metre torpedoes replaced with 5.75-metre torpedoes and wanted two torpedo tubes, one forward of the kiosk as far back from the bow as possible and one aft. It also wanted the two 37mm revolving cannon replaced with two 37mm QF, or if possible two 47mm QF. On 18 May 1888 Minister Krantz asked Lagane to increase to three the number of trainable tubes without a fixed tube in the bow. Lagane had to increase the displacement to 103 tons, 6.5 tons over the limit in the specs. On 14 June 1888 the Minister referred to the Council Lagane's design for a 42.50-metre boat. On 22 June 1888 the Council stated that it was inferior to Normand's *Nº 126* and could not approve it unless F.C. Méditerranée made more changes and agreed to the same terms for trials that Normand had accepted. It recommended that if the firm did not agree Normand should be asked for a design for a *torpilleur de haute mer* derived from *Balny* and *Nº 126*. However, two boats were ordered from FCM on 25 July 1888. They had a single funnel and a relatively unobstructed deck. They were robust with perfect stability and economical machinery. They had excellent seakeeping qualities, although their bow lines were too fine and the vessels were overloaded forward giving them a tendency to be wet underway.

**Dimensions & tons:** 44.18m oa, 43.55m wl & pp x 4.55m ext, 4.50m wl. 103.28t disp, 121.30t (full load). Draught: 1.10m mean, 2.50m aft under propeller guard. Men: 29 including 2 officers.
**Machinery:** 1,100ihp designed at 310rpm and 12kg/cm$^2$ boiler pressure. Speed 20kts. Trials (*Agile*) 20.97kts. 1 screw. 1 vertical triple expansion engine with 3 cylinders of 0.44m, 0.64m, and 1.00m diameter and 0.42m stroke. 2 locomotive direct flame boilers. 14.5t coal (normal), 35t (max). Range 3,000nm @ 10.5kts.
**Torpedoes:** 3 tubes for 356mm M1887 torpedoes (1 on the forecastle, 1 amidships, and 1 aft). **Guns:** 3 x 37mm/20 M1885 QF.

*Agile* F.C. Méditerranée, La Seyne/FCM, Marseille.
On list 1.1889. Ord: 25.7.1888. K: 3q.1888. L: 4.7.1889.
    Trials: 9-11.1889.
Budget 1889. *Escadre de la Méditerranée* followed by reserve and repairs at Toulon 1894-1902. Reboilered 1902 with Niclausse boilers. *Défense mobile* at Oran, Algiers, and Bizerte 1902-09. Struck 24.3.1910, for sale in Tunisia (Bizerte) 1910-1912.

*Audacieux* F.C. Méditerranée, La Seyne.
On list 1.1889. Ord: 25.7.1888. K: 3q.1888. L: 8.5.1889.
    Trials: 2-5.1890.
Budget 1889. *Escadre de la Méditerranée* 1890. Sunk 1894 in collision with seagoing torpedo boat *Mousquetaire*, refloated. Sunk 10.7.1896 by seagoing torpedo boat *Chevalier* which rammed her off Corsica while she was being towed by the cruiser *Sfax*. Struck 25.9.1896.

**Later *OURAGAN* Class.** *Éclaireurs-torpilleurs* 1.1889, *torpilleurs de haute mer* 1.1890. A.C. Loire (Nantes) seagoing torpedo boats with four torpedo tubes on deck (two on each side), one screw, two funnels abreast (later on centreline in *Aventurier* and *Téméraire*), three masts (later two), and a ram bow.

On 24 July 1888 Minister Krantz referred to the *Conseil des travaux* specifications for a *torpilleur de haute mer* for use in inviting designs from industry. The draft 1889 budget (submitted mid-1888) included funds for ordering five such boats and the Minister wanted to be able to begin construction at the start of the budget year. The *torpilleurs de haute mer* then in the fleet or building were the *Balny* class, Normand's *Nºs 126* to *129*, and *Audacieux* and *Agile* from FCM La Seyne. (*Éclaireurs-torpilleurs* like *Avant-Garde* were not mentioned.) Of these the Minister felt the best were the Normand boats because their speed and range both exceeded those of the FCM boats, and he based his specifications on them. The Minister's specifications essentially replicated those of *Nº 126*, and he resisted raising the calibre of the two guns to 47mm because this would add

25 tons to the displacement. The Council reviewed these specifications on 31 July 1888 and stated that the 37mm gun did not have enough penetration capability to combat foreign torpedo boats of similar types now planned that would have guns up to 65mm, and it recommended adopting the 47mm guns and accepting the increased displacement. It also recommended that the torpedo tubes should be either be paired amidships or arranged as in *Nº 126* with a single tube amidships and the other on the stern, as other arrangements were likely to be unsuccessful.

On 4 December 1888 the Council reviewed five designs received in response to these specifications and found one by FCM acceptable with three changes and one by Normand capable of use with more significant changes, but neither would be ready to begin construction in early 1889 as the Minister wished. On 27 November 1888 A.C. Loire proposed building these four repeat *Ouragan*s at 500,000 francs each, and the 1889 funds were probably used to build them. The main difference between these and the prototype was that the contract speed was wisely reduced to 20.5 knots, which one slightly exceeded and the others approached within half a knot. They were delivered with three masts with light sails, but the middle mast was removed after sails for torpedo boats were suppressed in June 1890. The original locomotive boilers had to be replaced soon after entering service.

---

The seagoing torpedo boat *Téméraire* at Toulon after joining the *Escadre de la Méditerranée* in October 1891. A sister is in left background. The two port side torpedo tubes are covered with canvas as is the 47mm gun mounting between them. This photo was received by ONI on 7 December 1892. *(NHHC from ONI album of foreign warships dated about 1900, NH-88781)*

**Dimensions & tons:** As *Ouragan*.
**Machinery:** 1,600ihp designed at 10kg/cm$^2$ boiler pressure. Speed 20.5kts. Trials (*Aventurier*) 20.58kts, (*Téméraire*) 20.02kts at 296.9rpm. 1 screw. Machinery as *Ouragan*.
**Torpedoes:** 4 tubes for 356mm M1887 short (4.70m) torpedoes (2 on the sides abreast the conning tower, 2 on the sides aft).
**Guns:** 2 x 47mm/40 M1885 QF (heavy).

*Aventurier* A.C. Loire, Nantes/ACL, Nantes.
On list 1.1889. Ord: 19.12.1888. K: 1.1889. L: 13.4.1889. Trials: 6.1889-8.1891.
Budget 1889. *Escadre de la Méditerranée* c1891. Reboilered at Toulon 1898-99 (2 Du Temple boilers, 12kg/cm$^2$, two funnels on centreline). Tunisia and Algiers 1899-1905. 1$^{st}$ Mediterranean torpedo boat flotilla at Toulon 1905-09. Decomm. 1.5.1909. Struck 24.3.1910. Sold 1910 at Toulon.

*Téméraire* A.C. Loire, Nantes/ACL, Nantes.
On list 1.1889. Ord: 19.12.1888. K: 12.1888. L: 1.5.1889. Trials: 8.1889-8.1891.
Budget 1889. *Escadre de la Méditerranée* 1891-96, reserve squadron at Toulon 1897-98. Reboilered at Toulon 1898-99 (2 Niclausse boilers by contract 17.11.1897, 2,500ihp, 12.5kg/cm$^2$, two funnels on centreline). *Défense mobile* at Algiers 1899-1904. Reboilered again at Toulon 1905. Algeria 1906-07, in reserve at Bizerte 1907-08, then to Toulon. Struck 24.3.1910. Offered for sale 1.8.1911 at Toulon by the Domaines with *Amiral Baudin, Magenta, Pascal, Milan*, and smaller vessels, sold 2.8.1911 to BU.

*Défi* A.C. Loire, Nantes/ACL, Nantes.
On list 1.1889. Ord: 19.12.1888. K: 1.1889. L: 29.6.1889.
  Trials: 8.1891-1.1892. Comm: 19.1.1892 (full)
Budget 1889. *Escadre du Nord* 1892-93, reserve at Brest 1893-1901.
  Reboilered 1898-99 with two new locomotive boilers. *Défense mobile* at
  Saint Servan 1901-04, Lorient 1904-07. Reserve at Lorient (1908) and
  Brest (1909). Struck 20.2.1911, offered for sale 20.7.1911 at Brest by
  the Domaines with *Valmy* and others. Sold 20.7.1911 at Brest to BU.

*Alarme* A.C. Loire, Nantes/ACL, Nantes.
On list 1.1889. Ord: 19.12.1888. K: 10.1888. L: 1.6.1889.
  Trials: 10.1891-1.1892.
Budget 1889. *Escadre du Nord* 1892, reserve at Brest 1893-97, Granville
  1897-1900, Cherbourg 1900-05. Struck 5.6.1906. Sold 9.1906.

---

**DRAGON Class.** *Torpilleurs de haute mer.* Normand seagoing torpedo
boats of a a modified *Avant-Garde* type with two torpedo tubes (in the bow
and on the stern), two screws, two funnels, and one mast (none on trials).

When Normand's design for a *torpilleur de haute mer* based on *Nº 126* was
reviewed by the *Conseil des travaux* on 4 December 1888, Normand was
advised to lengthen it to increase the displacement for strengthening the
hull and place the two 47mm guns on the sides between the funnel and the
kiosk. The extraordinary 1890 budget (submitted 15 July 1889) included
ten *torpilleurs de haute mer* of 79.5 tons, but Minister Krantz decided that

The seagoing torpedo boat *Dragon* on trials off Cherbourg June-August 1892. Her
torpedo tubes included one in the bow and one on the extreme stern. This photo
was received by ONI on 7 December 1892. This successful vessel joined the
*Escadre de la Méditerranée* in 1893. *(NHHC from ONI album of foreign warships
dated about 1900, NH-88782)*

he wanted these to have water tube boilers and consulted Normand in June
1889 for a new design. The Minister and the *Conseil Supérieur* soon
increased the size of these boats to between 104 tons and 120 tons. They
ultimately included in the programme five of La Seyne's *Agile* type and five
of Normand's *Avant-Garde* type. Normand's contract for the three *Dragon*
class boats authorized him to put the rudder ahead of the screws in *Lancier*.
These three were successful boats in all respects.

**Dimensions & tons:** 44.21m oa, 42.01m wl, 41.93m pp x 4.50m ext,
  4.39m wl. 129t disp (full load). Draught: 1.30m mean, 2.40m aft
  under propeller guard. Draught (1893-94): 1.41m mean, 1.32m forward, 1.49m aft (low point of the keel), 2.10m aft (under the screws)
**Machinery:** 1,750ihp designed at 320rpm and 12kg/cm² boiler pressure.
  Speed 21kts. Trials (*Lancier*) 25.79kts. 2 screws. 2 vertical triple expansion engines with 3 cylinders of 0.37m, 0.52m, and 0.75m diameter
  and 0.414 stroke. 2 Du Temple boilers (3 folds). 22.31t coal.
**Torpedoes:** 2 tubes for 381mm M1887 torpedoes (1 bow, 1 deck aft).
  **Guns:** 2 x 47mm/40 M1885 QF.

*Dragon* Augustin Normand, Le Havre/Normand, Le Havre.
On list 1.1891. Ord: 9.4.1890. K: 20.12.1890. L: 29.4.1892.
  Trials: 6-8.1892. C: 15 or 20.9.1892.
Budget 1890 (extraordinary). Named *Condom* 28.1.1890, *Dragon*
  16.6.1890. Machinery installed 6.1.1892 to 17.3.1892. *Escadre de la
  Méditerranée*, then *Défense mobile* at Toulon 1893-1901. Tunisia naval
  division and 3rd Mediterranean torpedo boat flotilla at Bizerte 1902-
  10, also school for piloting for Algeria and Tunisia. Struck 3.8.1910,
  for sale in Tunisia (Bizerte) 1910-1912.

*Grenadier* Augustin Normand, Le Havre/Normand, Le Havre.
On list 1.1891. Ord: 9.4.1890. K: 1890. L: 20.8.1892. Trials: 11.1892-
  1.1893.
Budget 1890 (extraordinary). Named *Cépèt* 28.1.1890, *Grenadier*

16.6.1890. *Escadre du Nord* 1893-94, then *Défense mobile* at Brest. Reboilered 1902. *Défense mobile* at Cherbourg 1903, Dunkirk and 2nd Channel torpedo boat flotilla 1904-09. Annex to the school for local pilots (*école des patrons pilotes*) at Cherbourg 1910-11, rated *garde-pêche à vapeur* at Saint-Servan 1911-1912. Struck 21.5.1914, retained as target. Engines removed and reused in anti-submarine gunboat *Ardent* (ordered 12.1915). For sale at Brest 1920-1922.

*Lancier* Augustin Normand, Le Havre/Normand, Le Havre.
On list 1.1891. Ord: 9.4.1890. K: 1890. L: 19.12.1892. Trials: 4-5.1893.
Budget 1890 (extraordinary). Named *Esterel* 28.1.1890, *Lancier* 16.6.1890. *Escadre du Nord* 1893-99. By 1902 had two Normand boilers. *Défense mobile* at Brest and Saint Servan 1901-09. School for stoking of the 1st Atlantic torpedo boat flotilla 1909-10. Struck 3.11.1910. Hull sold at Cherbourg 1.1911.

––––––––––

*TURCO* **Class.** *Torpilleurs de haute mer.* A.C. Loire seagoing torpedo boats with two torpedo tubes (in the bow and on the stern), two screws, two funnels, and one mast (none on trials).

A.C. Loire at Nantes built these boats to Normand's plans for a modified *Avant-Garde* type but with engines and boilers of its own design. The engines were the same as those in *Torpilleurs nos 136-138* but with the HP cylinder enlarged to 0.34m in diameter from 0.315m.

**Dimensions & tons:** 42.06m oa, 42.00m wl, 41.94m pp x 4.51m ext,

The seagoing torpedo boat *Orage* at Toulon. Her two torpedo tubes were in the bow and on deck near the stern. The vessel may have been photographed during trials (Nov. 1891 to Feb. 1892), note the lack of paint on the hull and what may be contractor (civilian) personnel on deck. This photo was received by ONI in Washington on 7 December 1892. (*NHHC from ONI album of French warships, NH-88790*)

4.42m wl. 120.47t disp (normal), 124.47t (full load). Draught: 1.30m mean, 1.72m aft (hull), 2.10m aft under propeller guard. Men: 28.
**Machinery:** 1,800ihp designed at 320rpm and 14kg/cm² boiler pressure. Speed 21kts. Trials (*Turco*) 20.99kts, (*Zouave*) 1,356ihp = 20.12kts. 2 screws. 2 vertical triple expansion engines with 3 cylinders of 0.34m, 0.465m, and 0.65m diameter and 0.38m stroke. 2 Oriolle boilers. Range 2,000nm @ 10kts.
**Torpedoes:** 2 tubes for 381mm M1887 torpedoes (1 bow, 1 deck aft).
**Guns:** 2 x 47mm/40 M1885 QF.

*Turco* A.C. Loire, Nantes/ACL, Nantes.
On list 1.1891. Ord: 16.4.1890. K: 1890. L: 20.11.1891.
Trials: 4-6.1892.
Budget 1890 (extraordinary). Named *Faron* 28.1.1890, *Turco* 16.6.1890. *Escadre du Nord* 1892-94. Out of commission at Cherbourg 1895-98. Reboilered at Brest 1899-1900 with Du Temple boilers. *Défense mobile* in Tunisia 1900-04, at Toulon and 1st Mediterranean torpedo boat flotilla 1904-09 (from 10.1906 was school for stoking). Struck 3.8.1910. Offered for sale 1.8.1911 at Toulon by the Domaines with *Amiral Baudin*, *Magenta*, *Pascal*, *Milan*, and smaller vessels, sold 2.8.1911 to BU.

*Zouave* A.C. Loire, Nantes/ACL, Nantes.
On list 1.1891. Ord: 16.4.1890. K: 1890. L: 1.1892. Trials: 4-6.1892.
Budget 1890 (extraordinary). Named *Sicié* 28.1.1890, *Zouave* 16.6.1890. *Défense mobile* at Cherbourg 1892-94, reserve there 1894-98. Reboilered at Cherbourg 1899-1900 with Normand boilers. School for stoking at Cherbourg 1900-01. *Défense mobile* at Cherbourg and 1st Channel torpedo boat flotilla 1901-08. Struck 10.8.1908. Sold 2.12.1908 at Cherbourg to BU.

––––––––––

*ÉCLAIR* **Class.** *Torpilleurs de haute mer.* FCM La Seyne seagoing torpedo boats, copies of *Agile* with two torpedo tubes (in the bow and on the

stern), one screw, two funnels, and two masts (none on trials, later one).

The *Conseil des travaux* reviewed a FCM design for a *torpilleur de haute mer* based on *Agile* on 4 December 1888 and indicated that only three changes were necessary, but the project was then deferred to the 1890 budget and in mid-1889 Minister Krantz decided that these boats should have water tube boilers. The hull dimensions of the resulting design were the same as those of *Agile* but the hull scantlings were stronger and they had two tall, thin, slightly inclined funnels in place of the single short and wide one in the earlier boats. The Thornycroft boilers in this trio were considered 'without equal', but the bow torpedo tube was heavily criticised.

**Dimensions & tons:** As *Agile*. Trial displacements were around 106.335t for a mean draught of 1.192m, full load displacement reached 128.40t.
**Machinery:** Trials (*Orage*) 21.60kts. 1 screw. Engines as *Agile*.
  2 Thornycroft boilers built at La Seyne rated at 13.5kg/cm² boiler pressure.
**Torpedoes:** 2 tubes for 381mm M1887 torpedoes (1 bow, 1 deck aft).
  **Guns:** 2 x 37mm/20 M1885 QF (*Orage* had a third gun on top of the engine room ventilator forward of the mainmast.)

*Éclair* F.C. Méditerranée, La Seyne/FCM, Marseille.
On list 1.1891. Ord: 21.5.1890. K: 6.1890. L: 29.8.1891.
  Trials: 10.1891-5.1892.
Budget 1890 (extraordinary). Named *Lérins* 28.1.1890, *Éclair* 16.6.1890.
  *Escadre de la Méditerranée* 1892-98, Tunisia naval division and piloting duty in Algeria 1899-1902, *Défense mobile* at Toulon 1902-11 including service as school for the local pilots of Provence and Corsica 1905. For sale at Toulon 1910-1911. Struck 20.2.1911. Offered for sale 1.8.1911 at Toulon by the Domaines with *Amiral Baudin, Magenta, Pascal, Milan*, and smaller vessels. Sold 20.8.1911 at Toulon to BU.

*Kabyle* F.C. Méditerranée, La Seyne/FCM, Marseille.
On list 1.1891. Ord: 21.5.1890. K: 6.1890. L: 9.1891. Trials: 10.1891-2.1892.
Budget 1890 (extraordinary). Named *Molène* 28.1.1890, *Kabyle* 16.6.1890. *Escadre de la Méditerranée*, then *Défense mobile* at Toulon. Tunisia naval division 1902, then 1st Mediterranean torpedo boat flotilla at Toulon and school for stoking at Toulon. Reboilered 1908 with Solignac-Grille boilers which led to three serious accidents. Struck 13.7.1911, hull sold at Toulon 1911.

*Orage* F.C. Méditerranée, La Seyne/FCM, Marseille.
On list 1.1891. Ord: 21.5.1890. K: 6.1890. L: 15.10.1891.
  Trials: 11.1891-2.1892.
Budget 1890 (extraordinary). Named *Porquerolles* 28.1.1890, *Orage* 16.6.1890. *Escadre de la Méditerranée* 1892, then *Défense mobile* at Toulon. Tunisia naval division 1902, then *Défense mobile* at Toulon and the division of schools there. Annex to the school for engineers and stokers at Toulon 1910-14. Active war service in the Mediterranean 1914-18. Struck 21.6.1920. Sold 8.1.1921 at Toulon to BU.

---

**SARRAZIN Class.** *Torpilleurs de haute mer.* C.A. Gironde seagoing torpedo boats with two torpedo tubes (in the bow and on the stern), one screw, one funnel (later two), and two masts.

These two boats were built by C.A. Gironde, Bordeaux-Lormont to plans of FCM La Seyne's *Agile* type adapted for construction at Bordeaux by its chief engineer, Jean Baron. They had single short and wide funnels as in *Agile*. The engines were built by the Anciens Établissements Cail at Saint Denis. The boats steered well and had very good stability and only moderate rolling and pitching. They were presented for trials with Charles et Babillot boilers, which were precipitously removed following a severe accident in *Sarrazin* on 13 January 1894 that killed seven men including naval constructor Louis Léon Lazare André Mangini. Their engines, installed by

Cail, had poorly balanced propeller shafts that caused frequent failures and by October 1896 they could only sustain a speed of 18 knots. Their single Du Temple boiler made them unsuitable for use as division leaders or fishery protection vessels, duties that were felt to require two boilers.

**Dimensions & tons:** 44.30m oa, 44.15m wl, 40.265m pp x 4.55m ext, 4.50m wl. 104.13t disp (normal), 131.33m (full load). Draught: 2.70m aft under propeller guard.
**Machinery:** Trials (*Tourbillon*) 20.85kts. 1 screw. Engines as *Agile*. 1 Du Temple boiler (large model) rated at 15kg/cm² boiler pressure (as reboilered 1894).
**Torpedoes:** 2 tubes for 381mm M1887 torpedoes (1 bow, 1 deck aft).
  **Guns:** 2 x 37mm/20 M1885 QF.

*Sarrazin* C.A. Gironde, Bordeaux-Lormont/Cail, Saint Denis.
On list 1.1891. Ord: 9.4.1890. K: 3.1892. L: 25.6.1892. Trials: 10.1894.
Budget 1890 (extraordinary). Named *Noirmoutier* 28.1.1890, *Sarrazin* 16.6.1890. Trials at Rochefort 1892-95 (severe boiler accident 13.1.1894). To Toulon 1896, to *Escadre de la Méditerranée* 1898, then to *Défense mobile* at Toulon and pilot training for the coasts of Provence and Corsica. Reboilered 1904 with Guyot-du Temple boilers, single funnel replaced with two funnels. In reserve category B at Toulon from 11.1904. Struck 13.3.1908. Sold at Toulon 1908 to BU.

*Tourbillon* C.A. Gironde, Bordeaux-Lormont/Cail, Saint Denis.
On list 1.1891. Ord: 9.4.1890. K: 3.1892. L: 10.10.1892. Trials: 10.1894.
Budget 1890 (extraordinary). Named *Ouessant* 28.1.1890, *Tourbillon* 16.6.1890. Long trials at Rochefort, returned to the builder 1894 for modifications after accident to *Sarrazin*. *Escadre du Nord* 1896-1900, then *Défense mobile* at Saint Servan. Reboilered 1904, single funnel replaced with two funnels. Pilot training at Brest 1904-06, then reserve at Brest and *Défense mobile* at Cherbourg 1910. Struck 15.4.1911. Sold at Cherbourg to BU.

---

*VÉLOCE* **Class.** *Torpilleurs de haute mer.* FCM Le Havre *Coureur*-type seagoing torpedo boats with two torpedo tubes (2 in the bow in *Véloce*, 1 bow and 1 on deck amidships in *Grondeur*), two screws, two funnels, and one mast.

These two boats were designed and built by F.C. Méditerranée, Le Havre-Graville based on Thornycroft's *Coureur* but with more powerful propulsion machinery and greatly reinforced scantlings, the latter adding over 3 tons to their hull weight. The shape of their bows reflect their derivation from *Coureur* but their funnels were on the centreline. They retained Thornycroft's vaulted stern lines. They were heavy rollers and generated significant vibrations at high speeds. In a report of 5 November 1892 the *Inspection générale du Génie maritime* found these two vessels inferior to the *Dragon* (modified *Avant-Garde*) type.

**Dimensions & tons:** 45.50m oa, 45.07m wl & pp x 4.42m ext, 4.35m wl. 112.64t (designed), 119.26t disp (normal), 133.25t (with surcharge). Draught: 1.39m mean, 1.45m aft.
**Machinery:** 1,750ihp designed at 500rpm and 14kg/cm² boiler pressure. Speed 23.5kts. Trials (*Grondeur*) 23.85kts at 491.53rpm. 2 screws. 2 vertical triple expansion engines with 3 cylinders of 0.292m, 0.406m, and 0.648m diameter and 0.330mm stroke. 2 Thornycroft boilers built at Le Havre. 14t coal.
**Torpedoes:** 2 tubes (2 bow for 356mm torpedoes in *Véloce*, 1 bow and 1 deck for 381mm M1887 torpedoes in *Grondeur*).
  **Guns:** 2 x 47mm/40 M1885 QF.

*Véloce* F.C. Méditerranée, Le Havre-Graville/FCM, Le Havre.
On list 1.1891. Ord: 16.4.1890. K: 10.12.1890. L: 4.11.1891. Trials: 3.1892.
Budget 1891. *Escadre du Nord* 1893-95, then reserve at Brest. School for

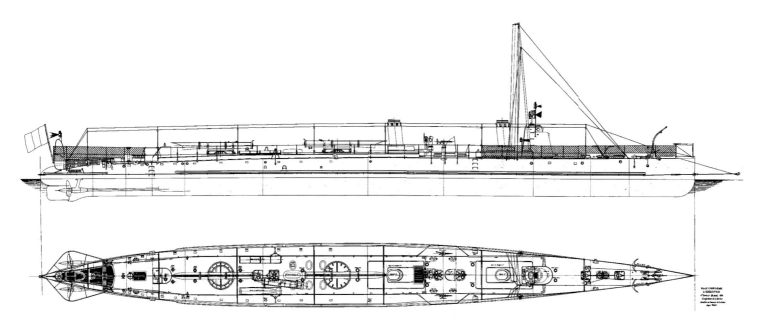

Outboard profile and overhead view (*plan d'ensemble*) of the high speed twin screw torpedo boat *Corsaire*. The plans were certified on 29 April 1893 to represent the ship as fitted by Wahl, the Navy's control officer for contract work in the Seine basin. Her two torpedo tubes were both on deck aft of the funnels.

stoking at Cherbourg, then back to reserve at Brest. Annex to the Naval Academy in *Borda* 1901. Struck 25.10.1909, for sale at Brest 1909-1910.

*Grondeur* F.C. Méditerranée, Le Havre-Graville/FCM, Le Havre.
On list 1.1891. Ord: 16.4.1890. K: 10.12.1890. L: 13.2.1892. Trials: 4.1892.
Budget 1891. *Escadre du Nord* 1893-95. Later *Défense mobile* at Dunkirk, same at Rochefort from 1902. To fishery protection duty 1910-11 and rated *garde-pêche à vapeur* in the Bidassoa. Served during World War I in the Brest sea frontier (saved the survivors of the torpedoed armoured cruiser *Kléber*). *Torpilleur* 1.3.1920, *Torpilleur d'escadre* 1.1922 and 1.1923 while station ship at Saint-Jean-de-Luz near the Bidassoa 1920-1923. Off main list 1923 (condemnation pending) and station vessel in the Bidassoa 1923-1924. Struck 10.11.1925. Sold 9.1.1926 at Rochefort to BU.

---

*ARCHER. Torpilleur de haute mer.* Normand seagoing torpedo boat with two torpedo tubes (in the bow and on the stern), two screws, one funnel, and one mast.

This boat consisted of the machinery of *Avant-Garde* salvaged from her wreck and put into a replacement hull ordered to the plans of *Avant-Garde* to carry it. The new boat had one funnel instead of the two abreast of the prototype and was armed differently. Like the prototype she was a good sea boat and manoeuvred well. The torpedo spar of *Avant-Garde* was not needed in *Archer* and was installed in 1890 in *Torpilleur nº 151* (ex *Gabriel Charmes*).

**Dimensions & tons:** As *Avant-Garde*.
**Machinery:** From *Avant-Garde*. Trials 20.52kts.
**Torpedoes:** 2 tubes for 381mm M1887 torpedoes (1 bow and 1 deck).
   **Guns:** 2 x 47mm.

*Archer* Augustin Normand, Le Havre.
On list 1.1891. Ord: 10.11.1890. K: 15.4.1891. L: 30.5.1893. Trials: 11.1893-1.1894. Comm: 6.2.1894 (full).
Budget 1891 (late addition). *Escadre du Nord* 1894-95. *Défense mobile* at

Brest to 1900 and at Dunkirk 1901-04. 1ˢᵗ Channel torpedo boat flotilla 1904-07. Struck 9.10.1907. Sold 4.3.1908 at Cherbourg to BU.

---

*CORSAIRE. Torpilleur de haute mer.* A.C. Loire seagoing torpedo boat with two torpedo tubes (on deck amidships and toward the stern), two screws, two funnels, and one mast (none on trials).

One of three extra fast boats called the *très rapides*, this boat was designed by A.C. Loire (formerly Claparède), Saint Denis. During 1890 Minister of Marine Barbey let it be known to a few leading firms that he would be receptive if they thought they could produce designs of seagoing torpedo boats with a speed approaching 27 knots. He left all latitude to the designers regarding the details except that he limited the displacement to that of France's largest current torpedo boat (about 120 tons). At their request he specified some of the items that would be carried during trials, including two torpedo tubes, four 450mm 5-metre torpedoes, and two 37mm QF guns. Three designs were presented and Minister Barbey referred them to the *Conseil des Travaux* on 21 January 1891.

The Council examined them on 14 April 1891. It felt that of the three designs the one by A.C. Loire came closest to what the Minister had asked for because of its 26-knot speed. Normand and FCM had guaranteed only 24.5 knots, but the Council felt that there was reason to hope that they would exceed this. The Council concluded that it would be interesting to order one of each for comparison.

A.C. Loire promised a speed of 26 knots with 2500ihp at 350rpm, the contract guaranteed 25.5 knots. Its hull lines aft imitated those of Thornycroft's *Coureur*. The design had three du Temple boilers with the after two sharing a funnel and stokehold and with all three boilers serving both engines. The two torpedo tubes were placed on the after half of the deck, one above the engine room, the other above the crew's berthing. They were manoeuvred and controlled from the after kiosk. The two 37mm guns were on the sides aft of the fore funnel. The designed displacements were 150.419 tons on trials and 164.189 tons full load. The Council objected strongly to the arrangement of the machinery and demanded that it be redesigned with two boilers, one serving each engine in an independent ensemble.

*Corsaire* was the last vessel other than colonial gun launches that was built at the former Claparède yard at Saint Denis, which A. C. Loire had bought in 1886. Her plans were countersigned at Saint Denis on 13 March and 29 April 1893 by Albert Wahl, the naval constructor overseeing commercial construction in the Seine basin. She was also the least successful of the *très rapides*, with an inadequate coal supply, excessively sharp stern lines, and poor steering and manoeuvrability. The British, however, were alarmed by these fast seagoing boats, and in 1891 Rear Admiral John Fisher, advocated responding with an enlarged torpedo boat that entered service in 1894 as the torpedo boat destroyer.

**Dimensions & tons:** 50.500m oa, 50.500m wl, 48.340m pp (tip fwd to rudder) x 4.460m ext, 4.400m wl. 150.774t disp (designed, trials), 171t (full load). Draught: (designed) 1.300m fwd (keel line projected), 1.300m amidships, 1.660m aft (keel line projected).
**Machinery:** 2,500ihp designed at 350rpm and 15kg/cm² boiler pressure. Speed 25.5kts. Trials 2,288ihp = 23.82kts at 355.46rpm, with 24.23kts on her best measured mile. 2 screws. 2 vertical triple expansion engines with 3 cylinders of 0.40m, 0.61m, and 0.92m diameter and 0.40m stroke. 2 Du Temple boilers (2 folds). 16t (normal), 21t (max) coal. Range 1,000nm @ 10kts.
**Torpedoes:** 2 tubes for 450mm torpedoes. **Guns:** 2 x 37mm revolving cannon (1893).

*Corsaire* A.C. Loire (ex Claparède), Saint Denis.
On list 1.1892. Ord: 8.7.1891 (contract). K: 12.1891. L: 5.10.1892. Trials: 4-8.1893. Comm: 29.9.1893 (full).
Budget 1891 (late addition). Machinery installed 15.8.1892 to 30.12.1892. *Escadre de la Méditerranée* 1893-97. Reclassed *Torpilleur*

---

The seagoing torpedo boat *Mousquetaire*, one of the three *très rapides* of 1891, off Cherbourg on 10 August 1893 during sea trials which ran from March to September 1893. The photo caption notes her speed as 24.77 knots, apparently being made at this time. The vessel's maximum speed on trials was 25.44 knots, somewhat higher than the 24.5 knot designed speed. Her two torpedo tubes were on deck between the funnels and near the stern. *(NHHC from ONI album of foreign warships dated about 1900, NH-88801)*

*de 1ʳᵉ classe* (*torpilleur de Défense mobile*) 8.1897, annex to *Borda* 10.1898, school for stoking at Brest 1900, same as annex to the school for engineers and stokers 1910-12. Struck 6.12.1912, for sale at Brest 1912-1913.

---

*MOUSQUETAIRE. Torpilleur de haute mer.* FCM Le Havre seagoing torpedo boat with two torpedo tubes (on deck between the funnels and near the stern), two screws, two funnels, and one mast (none on trials).

One of the three *très rapides*, this boat was designed by F.C. Méditerranée, Le Havre-Graville (chief engineer Marmiesse). In its design which the Council examined on 14 April 1891 the Le Havre firm promised a speed of 24.5 knots with 2,100ihp at 380-390 rpm. It gave its boat a ram bow and two Thornycroft boilers. Each engine formed with one boiler an independent unit. The two torpedo tubes were on the centreline, one amidships between the funnels and the other aft. The designed displacements were 125.000 tons on trials and 135.660 tons full load. The Council asked FCM to replace the ram with a straight bow and reduce the engine RPM at maximum speed which was excessive.

Shortly before the discussion of their original design for *Cassini* on 26 April 1892 FCM asked to change the boilers of *Mousquetaire* from Thornycroft to Du Temple models, to which the navy readily agreed. On preliminary trials the boat made only 22.27 knots and 23.85 knots with excessive coal consumption. The builder fitted feed water heaters and made other changes that produced better results in the final trials. The boat was successful in service, having good seakeeping qualities and accommodations but manoeuvring poorly and having an insufficient coal supply.

**Dimensions & tons:** 48.70m oa, 48.00m wl, 47.00m pp x 4.70m ext, 4.62m wl. 124.7t disp (at 1.26m mean draft). Draught: 1.15m fwd, 1.26m amidships, 1.68m aft.

**Machinery:** 2,100ihp designed at 14kg/cm² boiler pressure. Speed 24.5kts. Trials (10.8.1893) 24.77kts at 345.27rpm with 25.44kts on the best measured mile. 2 screws. 2 triple expansion engines with 3 cylinders of 0.40m, 0.60m, and 0.90m diameter and 0.40m stroke. 2 Du Temple boilers (3 folds). 22t coal. Range 800nm @ 15kts.

**Torpedoes:** 2 tubes for 450mm torpedoes. **Guns:** 2 x 37mm.

*Mousquetaire* F.C. Méditerranée, Le Havre-Graville.
On list 1.1892. Ord: 8.7.1891. K: 14.8.1891. L: 8.8.1892.
    Trials: 3-9.1893.
Budget 1891 (late addition). *Escadre de la Méditerranée* 1893-95. Repair and reserve at Toulon 1895-1902. Tunisia naval division and fishery protection duty in Algeria 1902-08. Annex to the Naval Academy at Brest 1908-10. For sale at Brest 1910-11. Struck 20.2.1911 offered for sale 20.7.1911 at Brest by the Domaines with *Valmy* and others. Sold 20.7.1911 at Brest to BU.

————————

*CHEVALIER. Torpilleur de haute mer.* Normand seagoing torpedo boat with two torpedo tubes (on deck between the funnels and near the stern), two screws, two funnels, and one mast (none on trials).

One of the three *très rapides*, this boat was designed by Normand who derived it from his *Avant-Garde*. In the design that the Council examined on 14 April 1891, Normand guaranteed a maximum speed on trials of 24.5 knots with 2,200ihp. He used his usual hull lines. The screws seen from aft overlapped by 0.40m, one being slightly forward of the other, an arrangement (also used in *Avant-Garde*) chosen to protect them by keeping them close to the hull. They were also placed as far aft as possible to reduce vibrations. The rudder was 2 metres forward of the screws, Normand claiming that this distance would limit adverse effects on steering while steaming ahead while providing other advantages. A second retractable rudder was also provided forward. The boilers were of a pattern patented by Normand based on du Temple and Thornycroft boilers. Each engine formed with one boiler an independent unit. The two torpedo tubes were placed on the sides near amidships. The designed displacements were 120.000 tons on trials and 130.870 tons full load. The Council asked Normand to renounce his efforts to mount torpedo tubes on the sides and to put them on the centre-line with the widest arcs possible, with special attention to targets forward of the beam. *Chevalier* was a resounding success making over 27 knots on trials and without vibrations in her machinery. The elimination of engine vibrations in *Chevalier* was the result of a long search by Normand for a reliable way of balancing the moving parts of reciprocating steam engines, a discovery made at about the same time by Yarrow in England. *Chevalier* was still able to make 25 knots on trials in 1910 and was the only one of the *très rapides* to serve in the 1914 war.

**Dimensions & tons:** 45.30m oa (including the *tampon de choc,* or shock buffer, extending from the top of the bow in most French torpedo boats), 43.78m wl, 44.00m pp x 4.50m ext, 4.37m wl. 120t disp (designed), 123t (trials), 136.76t (full load). Draught: 1.45m mean, 2.16m aft under screws.
**Machinery:** 2,200ihp designed at 340rpm and 15kg/cm² boiler pressure. Speed 24.5kts. Trials 3,000ihp = 27.22kts at 360.66rpm. 2 screws. 2 vertical triple expansion engines with 3 cylinders of 0.37m, 0.52m, and 0.756m diameter and 0.414m stroke. 2 Du Temple boilers (3 folds). 16.82t coal.
**Torpedoes:** 2 tubes for 450mm M1891 torpedoes. **Guns:** 2 x 37mm/20 M1885 QF.

*Chevalier* Augustin Normand, Le Havre/Normand, Le Havre.
On list 1.1892. Ord: 8.7.1891. K: 31.7.1891. L: 15.6.1893.
    Trials: 8-9.1893.
Budget 1891 (late addition). *Escadre de la Méditerranée* 1894, then reserve at Toulon 1894-97 (during which time she rammed and sank *Audacieux* 9-10.7.1896 during a night exercise). Reserve division 1897-

98, *Escadre de la Méditerranée* 1898-1900. Reboilered 1902-04 with Guyot-du Temple boilers while in reserve at Toulon. Station ship at Suda Bay, Crete, 1905, 1st Mediterranean torpedo boat flotilla 1905-10, in reserve at Toulon 1911-14. Toulon sea frontier and Provence patrol boat division 1914-18. Decomm. 6.1919. Off main list by 3.1920 and for sale at Toulon. Hull sold at Toulon 6.5.1920. Struck (retroactively) 1.10.1920.

————————

*LANSQUENET. Torpilleur de haute mer.* Experimental seagoing torpedo boat with two torpedo tubes (on deck on the bow and amidships), two screws, three raked funnels, and a ram bow.

This experimental torpedo boat was added to the 1893 budget using funding from the extraordinary budget for 1890. Ordered some months after the *très rapides,* this vessel was built by Paul Oriolle, a boiler manufacturer who had no experience with torpedo boat construction. Oriolle designed the boilers and engines, while the hull and screws were designed by Capitaine de frégate du Rocher du Quengo, who had been studying screw propellers in fast ships since 1872. The unusual vessel had a very fine ram bow, a curved deck shaped like an animal's shell, three sharply raked funnels, a prominent deck-mounted torpedo tube on the extreme bow, and a wide tunnel or vaulted stern intended to maximise the efficiency of the screws. Deck plating was 3mm thick amidships and 2mm at the ends. She had two conning towers, one forward and one aft, both of 4mm steel. She looked like a long narrow ram with a big bow gun (her bow torpedo tube).

**Dimensions & tons:** 52.63m oa, 52.22m wl & pp x 5.33m ext, 5.29m wl. 200.61t disp (actual), 138t (designed). Draught: 1.58m fwd, 1.70m aft (hull), 2.47m aft under propeller guard.
**Machinery:** 4,250ihp (for 25kts) designed at 17kg/cm² boiler pressure. Speed 26kts (contract). Trials barely 24kts. 2 screws. 2 triple expansion engines with 3 cylinders of 0.44m, 0.66m, and 1.01m diameter and 0.43m stroke. 4 Oriolle boilers.
**Torpedoes:** 2 deck tubes for 450mm torpedoes (1 on bow and 1 deck). **Guns:** 2 x 37mm.

*Lansquenet* (N1) Oriolle, Nantes.
On list 1.1893. Ord: 23.3.1892. K: 1892. L: 18.5.1893. Trials: 2.1894-1899. Comm: 8.8.1898 (full).
Budget 1893 (charged to the extraordinary budget for 1890). First trials 2.1894 interrupted by a broken piston rod (made of aluminium). Trials resumed 10.1894, but the original boilers were so disappointing that they had to be replaced after a few months. Finally accepted in 1898 for 22 knots against 26 promised, she was to join the *Escadre de la Méditerranée,* but after additional trials she had to have her propellers changed and to be lightened (she was seriously overweight). She was admitted to service in 1900 as a station ship at Dunkirk but only lasted a few weeks before striking the jetty, breaking her starboard propeller shaft and damaging her hull. She was then sent to Cherbourg for disposal. Struck 27.11.1900 and for sale at Cherbourg (hull and machinery). Sold 1901 to De la Brosse et Fouché who had bought the Oriolle yard after it failed in 1895. In 1905 Brosse asked permission to sell her after modifications to a second-rank naval power, but that sale never materialised.

————————

*ARIEL* **Class.** *Torpilleurs de haute mer.* Normand seagoing torpedo boats with two torpedo tubes (in the bow and forward of the after tower), two screws, two funnels, and one mast.

These two boats represented yet another Normand improvement on his *Avant-Garde. Aquilon,* below, would have been identical if she had not been given different boilers.

**Dimensions & tons:** 43.25m oa, 41.96m wl, 42.02m pp x 4.50m ext, 4.39m wl. 125t disp. Draught: 1.30m fwd, 2.05m aft under screws.

**Machinery:** 2,000ihp designed at 350rpm and 14kg/cm² boiler pressure. Speed 23.5kts. Trials (*Ariel*) 2,200ihp = 25.87kts. 2 screws. 2 vertical triple expansion engines with 3 cylinders of 0.37m, 0.52m, and 0.756m diameter and 0.414m stroke. 2 Du Temple boilers. 15t coal (at 125 tons displacement).

**Torpedoes:** 2 tubes for 381mm M1887 torpedoes (1 bow and 1 deck). **Guns:** 2 x 47mm/40 M1885 QF.

*Ariel* (N2) Augustin Normand, Le Havre/Normand, Le Havre.
On list 1.1893. Ord: 31.8.1892. K: 1893. L: 9.5.1895. Trials: 6.1895.
Budget 1892 (designated I). Assigned 14.4.1895 to the *Escadre du Nord*. Sunk 28-29.3.1898 in collision with cruiser *Friant* during a night exercise off Roscoff ten miles northeast of l'Aber-Wrac'h, the ships remaining attached long enough for the torpedo boat's entire crew to escape to the cruiser. Struck 5.1.1899. Hull (90 metres deep) sold to BU.

*Flibustier* (N3) Augustin Normand, Le Havre/Normand, Le Havre.
On list 1.1893. Ord: 31.8.1892. K: 2.1893. L: 27.12.1894. Trials: 3.1895.
Budget 1892 (designated H). *Escadre de la Méditerranée* 1895-1902. Reserve at Toulon 1902-08. Reboilered 1906-07. Fishery protection duty in Algeria 7.1908, rated *garde-pêche à vapeur* at Algiers from 1.1911, replaced there by *Cyclone* 1913. Struck 21.5.1914, retained as target. Engine removed 1.1916 at Bizerte and reused in anti-submarine gunboat *Alerte* (ordered 1.1916). Hulk sold 29.12.1923 at Bizerte to BU.

---

**TOURMENTE** Class. *Torpilleurs de haute mer.* A.C. Loire seagoing torpedo boats with two torpedo tubes (in the bow and aft of the funnels), two screws, two funnels, and one mast.

The design for these two boats was derived by A.C. Loire from plans of Normand's *Avant-Garde* supplied by the Navy. They had two rudders and steered well, kept the sea well, but their movements underway were brutal, with random rolling and with pitching that soon became fatiguing. The wide lines of the stern produced severe vibrations when struck by the sea. The original boilers were of a type with multiple folds (changes in direction) in the water tubes that quickly accumulated scale, could not be cleaned out, and had to be replaced after only a few years of use.

**Dimensions & tons:** 46.20m oa, 42.94m wl, 43.00m pp x 4.51m ext, 4.35m wl. 115t disp (131.5t full load). Draught: 0.80m fwd, 1.72m aft. Men: 27.
**Machinery:** 2,000ihp designed at 340rpm and 14kg/cm² boiler pressure. Speed 23.5kts. Trials (*Tourmente*) 24.28kts. 2 screws. 2 vertical triple expansion engines with 3 cylinders of 0.35m, 0.495m, and 0.71 diameter and 0.40m stroke. 2 Du Temple boilers (4 folds). Range 950nm @ 9.5kts.
**Torpedoes:** 2 tubes for 381mm M1887 torpedoes (1 bow and 1 deck). **Guns:** 2 x 47mm/40 M1885 QF.

*Tourmente* (N4) A.C. Loire, Nantes/ACL, Nantes.
On list 1.1893. Ord: 31.8.1892. K: 9.1892. L: 12.9.1893. Trials: 7.1894.
Budget 1892 (designated J). *Escadre de la Méditerranée* 1894-96, then reserve at Toulon. Reboilered 1898 with Normand boilers. Recommissioned for service at Suda Bay, Crete, 1905, then 1st (at Brest) and 3rd Atlantic torpedo boat flotillas 1907-09 and fishery protection duty at Granville and Saint Servan. Condemned 11.1910 and for sale at Brest. Struck 20.2.1911. Offered for sale 20.7.1911 at Brest by the Domaines with *Valmy* and others.

*Argonaute* (N5) A.C. Loire, Nantes/ACL, Nantes.
On list 1.1893. Ord: 31.8.1892. K: 1892. L: 11.10.1893. Trials: 2-6.1894.
Budget 1893 (designated T). *Escadre de la Méditerranée* 1894-96, then reserve at Toulon. Reboilered 1896 with Normand boilers. *Défense*

*mobile* at Bizerte 1903-06, 1st Atlantic torpedo boat flotilla at Brest 1906-08, 1st Channel torpedo boat flotilla at Cherbourg 1908-10. Struck 9.3.1910, for sale at Cherbourg 1910-1911.

---

**AVERNE** Class. *Torpilleurs de haute mer.* FCM Le Havre seagoing torpedo boats with two torpedo tubes (in the bow and aft of the funnels), two screws, two funnels, and one mast.

These two boats were designed and built by F.C. Méditerranée Graville to a design strongly influenced by Normand's *Dragon* (*Avant-Garde*). The hull plans were by Marmiesse and the boilers and engines were designed by Sigaudy (both engineers at Le Havre). The bow had very fine lines, passed smoothly through the water, and rose out of it completely at maximum speed. The stern lines formed a vault or tunnel. The original Du Temple boilers were of a type (with 4 folds, or nearly 180-degree bends in the tubes) that as in the *Tourmente* class quickly accumulated scale in the tubes that blocked the flow of water, produced tube failures, and could not be cleaned out.

**Dimensions & tons:** 43.83m wl, 42.50m pp x 4.60m ext, 4.54m wl. 114.56t disp (design), 121.80t (trials), 132.76t (full load). Draught: 1.28m mean, 2.01m aft under screws.
**Machinery:** 1,750ihp designed at 14kg/cm² boiler pressure. Speed 23.5kts. Trials (*Dauphin*) 24.64kts. 2 screws. 2 triple expansion engines with 3 cylinders of 0.35m, 0.50m, and 0.75m diameter and 0.41m stroke (Marshall type as in *Torpilleurs nos 177-179*). 2 Du Temple boilers (4 folds).
**Torpedoes:** 2 tubes for 381mm M1887 torpedoes (1 bow and 1 deck). **Guns:** 2 x 47mm/40 M1885 QF.

*Averne* (N6) F.C. Méditerranée, Le Havre-Graville.
On list 1.1893. Ord: 31.8.1892. K: 12.1892. L: 23.12.1893. Trials: 3-5.1894. Comm: 6.6.1894 (full).
Budget 1893 (designated U). *Escadre du Nord* 1894. *Défense mobile* at Brest and reserve and repairs there 1895-1900. Reboilered 1900 with two Normand return flame boilers. Tunisia naval division 1900-1904, school for the local pilots of Provence and Corsica and 2nd Mediterranean torpedo boat flotilla 1904-08. New boilers 1910. Annex to the school for torpedomen and the school for electricians at Toulon 1910-14, still at Toulon 1919. Struck 30.10.1919. Sold 2.3.1920 at Toulon to BU.

*Dauphin* (N7) F.C. Méditerranée, Le Havre-Graville.
On list 1.1893. Ord: 31.8.1892. K: 10.1892. L: 23.2.1894. Trials: 5-7.1894.
Budget 1893 (designated V). *Escadre du Nord* 1894-1896. *Défenses mobiles* at Brest and Lorient, then (1902) reserve group at Brest. *Défense mobile* at Toulon from 1904. Struck 9.3.1909, floating guard post at Rochefort 1909-1913. Renamed *Carpe* 26.5.1911. Hull sold at Rochefort 1913.

---

**AQUILON.** *Torpilleur de haute mer.* Normand seagoing torpedo boat with two torpedo tubes (in the bow and forward of the after tower), two screws, two funnels, and one mast.

This boat would have been identical to Normand's *Ariel* and *Flibustier* if not fitted with Normand's first return flame boilers instead of Du Temple boilers. She easily made 26.23 knots in April 1905.

**Dimensions & tons:** 43.24m oa, 42.02m pp x 4.39m wl. 120.13t disp. Draught: 1.45m fwd, 1.96m amidships, 2.47m aft under propeller guard.
**Machinery:** 2,000ihp designed at 360rpm and 14kg/cm² boiler pressure. Speed 23.5kts. Trials 26.16kts. 2 screws. 2 vertical triple expansion engines with 3 cylinders of 0.37m, 0.52m, and 0.756m diameter and

0.414m stroke. 2 Normand return flame boilers. 20t coal. Range 1,190nm @ 10kts.

**Torpedoes:** 2 tubes for 381mm M1887 torpedoes (1 bow and 1 deck).
  **Guns:** 2 x 47mm/40 M1885 QF.

*Aquilon* (N8) Augustin Normand, Le Havre/Normand, Le Havre.
On list 1.1894. Ord: 12.7.1893. K: 12.1893. L: 2.12.1895.
  Trials: 1-2.1896.
Budget 1893 (designated W, delayed to 1894). *Escadre du Nord* 1896-99. *Défense mobile* in Tunisia 1904-06. 2nd Atlantic torpedo boat flotilla at Lorient 1909. Seagoing annex to *Chamois* at the school for piloting at Saint Servan with armament removed 1910-13. Replaced by *Tramontane* 1913, decomm. at Brest 18.2.1914. Boilers tested 18.7.1915 and 18.9.1915. Engines removed and reused in anti-sub-marine gunboat *Inconstant* (ordered 12.1915). Struck 29.8.1916. Sold 4.11.1919 at Brest to BU.

---

*FORBAN. Torpilleur de haute mer.* Normand experimental seagoing torpedo boat with two torpedo tubes (between the funnels and forward of the after tower), two screws, two funnels, and one mast (none on trials).

On 28 November 1892 the Navy began discussions with Normand on building a 30-knot torpedo boat. He submitted his design for an experi-mental boat developed from the *Ariel* type on 26 January 1893. The hull lines were slightly slimmed and engines were as in *Torpilleurs nos 185-187* but were fitted with reinforced components. She received a new type of boiler patented by Normand on 10 October 1894 based on one in *Torpilleur no 149* patented on 7 January 1890, and extreme weight saving was applied to the design, including the use of 356mm instead of 381mm torpedoes. *Forban* made history on trials as the first ship to exceed 31 knots (on 23 August 1895 Yarrow's Russian destroyer *Sokol* broke the 30-knot barrier).

**Dimensions & tons:** 44.00m wl & pp x 4.64m wl. 126.519t disp (at 1.35m mean draught), 123.40t (normal), 152.10t (full load). Draught: 1.30m fwd, 1.40m aft.
**Machinery:** 3,260ihp designed at 345rpm and 15kg/cm² boiler pressure. Speed 29kts. Trials 3,775ihp = 31.025kts at 365rpm. 2 screws. 2 vert-ical triple expansion engines with 3 cylinders of 0.41m, 0.58m, and 0.84m diameter and 0.46m stroke. 2 Normand direct flame boilers. 18t coal. Range 1,000nm @ 10kts.

**Torpedoes:** 2 tubes for 356mm M1887 and M1892 torpedoes (both on deck). These were replaced with 450mm tubes in 1907.
  **Guns:** 2 x 37mm/20 M1885 QF.

*Forban* (N11) Augustin Normand, Le Havre/Normand, Le Havre.
On list 1.1894. Ord: 15.2.1893. K: 26.4.1893. L: 25.7.1895.
  Trials: 9-10.1895.
Budget 1893 (designated Z). *Escadre de la Méditerranée* 1896-1901, then reserve at Toulon. Tunisia naval division 1904-06. Reserve and repairs at Toulon 1907-08. Briefly on fishery protection duty at Algiers 1908, then 3rd Mediterranean torpedo boat flotilla at Bizerte 1908-11. To fishery protection duty 5.1911 and rated *garde-pêche à vapeur*, at Philippeville (Algeria). *Fronts de mer* at Algiers, Oran, and Bizerte 1914-18. Off main list by 3.1920 and for sale at Bizerte 1920. Sold 20.12.1920 at Bizerte to BU.

---

*MANGINI. Torpilleur de haute mer.* A.C. Loire seagoing torpedo boat with two torpedo tubes (in the bow and forward of the after tower), two screws, two funnels, and one mast.

This boat was designed by A.C. Loire, Nantes as an improved *Tourmente* type. The hull lines were similar to *Tourmente* except for a small modifica-tion in the stern. She had two rudders, and although overloaded forward was considered one of the best torpedo boats in the fleet, capable of giving 24 knots when needed, and saw very active service because of her qualities.

**Dimensions & tons:** 48.10m oa, 45.00m pp x 4.65m ext, 4.40m wl. 129.36t disp (normal), 142.74t (full load). Draught: 1.45m mean. Men: 27.
**Machinery:** 24kts designed. Trials 26.62kts. 2 screws. 2 vertical triple expansion engines with 3 cylinders of 0.38m, 0.54m, and 0.78m diam-eter and 0.82m stroke. 2 Du Temple boilers (3 folds) rated at 14kg/cm² boiler pressure. 25t coal.
**Torpedoes:** 2 tubes for 381mm M1887 torpedoes (1 bow and 1 deck).
  **Guns:** 2 x 47mm/40 M1885 QF.

*Mangini* (N10) A.C. Loire, Nantes/ACL, Nantes.
On list 1.1896. Ord: 31.1.1895. K: 1895. L: 13.6.1896. Trials: 9.1896-1.1897.
Budget 1893 (designated Y, delayed to 1895). Originally named *Cerbère*, renamed 26.1.1894 for the naval constructor killed in a boiler accident

---

Inboard profile of the seagoing torpedo boat (*torpilleur de haute mer*) *Forban*, published to celebrate the new record speed of 31.03 knots that she achieved on trials on 17 September 1895. Hull sections fore to aft are listed as: forward, forward rudder, crew, boilers and coal bunkers, engines, officers, petty officers, and after. Activities, also forward to aft, include two crew members in the tiny crew's quarters, the helmsman and the commander in the kiosk (C), stokers feeding the

two Normand water tube boilers, the cook in the galley (B), an engineer oiling the triple expansion engine, and an officer and several petty officers in their quarters aft (accessed through the hatch at A). Her two tubes for the smaller 356mm torpedo are between the funnels and on the after deck. The boat has the bow rudder and the single stern rudder forward of the screws favoured at the time by her builder, Normand. (*L'Illustration, 2 November 1895, page 358*)

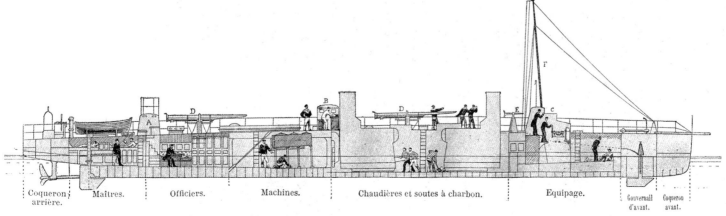

Coqueron arrière.   Maîtres.   Officiers.   Machines.   Chaudières et soutes à charbon.   Equipage.   Gouvernail d'avant.   Coqueron avant.

Coupe longitudinale du « Forban ».

105. BREST — Défense Mobile. Torpilleurs de haute mer

The seagoing torpedo boat *Mangini* in the *Défense Mobile* at the Ninon moorings at Brest. Her two torpedo tubes are in the bow and on deck aft. The boat behind her may be *Aquilon*. The F.M. overprint on the postage stamp means *franchise militaire*, a discounted rate for servicemen. *(Postcard)*

on *Sarrazin. Escadre du Nord* 1898, *Défense mobile* at Lorient (1901), Brest (1903), and Cherbourg (1905). Struck 1.7.1910. Sold 10.1911 at Cherbourg to BU.

---

*CYCLONE. Torpilleur de haute mer.* Normand seagoing torpedo boat with two torpedo tubes (head to tail on twin mount aft), two screws, two funnels 2.80m apart, and one mast.

Normand submitted a design for this improved *Forban* on 23 February 1896. On 1 July 1897 he summarized in a note to the Navy the key differences between this vessel and earlier twin screw torpedo boats derived from his *Avant-Garde* type. The displacement had increased to 148 tons from 125 tons, motive power had increased from 2,500ihp to 4,200ihp, and speed had increased from 26 knots to 29 knots, with the armament and operating range remaining the same.

**Dimensions & tons:** 46.35m oa, 45.00m wl & pp x 4.90m ext, 4.648m wl. 114.59t disp (normal), 152.39t (full load). Draught: 1.40m fwd, 1.50m aft (hull), 2.51m aft under propeller guard.
**Machinery:** 4,200ihp designed at 360rpm and 16kg/cm² boiler pressure. Speed 29kts. Trials 30.38kts at 347rpm. 2 screws. 2 triple expansion engines with 3 cylinders of 0.41m, 0.59m, and 0.89m diameter and 0.50m stroke. 2 Normand return flame boilers. 17.43t coal. Range 2,000nm @ 10kts.
**Torpedoes:** 2 tubes for 381mm M1887 torpedoes (on twin mounting aft, originally parallel, then head to tail). **Guns:** 2 x 47mm/40 M1885 QF.

*Cyclone* (N9) Augustin Normand, Le Havre/Normand, Le Havre.
On list 1.1897. Ord: 5.8.1896. K: 15.11.1896. L: 21.5.1898. Trials: 8-12.1898.
Budget 1893 (designated X, delayed to 1896). Originally named *Ténare*, renamed late 1895. Delivered from Le Havre to Cherbourg 27.7.1898. *Escadre de la Méditerranée* at Toulon 1899-1901. *Défense mobile* in Corsica 1901-03, Tunisia 1904-05, Toulon 1905-10, Bizerte 1910-14. To fishery protection duty 1913 and rated *garde-pêche à vapeur* at Algiers replacing *Flibustier*. Algiers sea frontier 1914-18, Bizerte patrol squadron 1919-20. Struck 1.10.1920.

---

*NEW TYPE. Torpilleur de haute mer.*

The design for this boat was still under study and only a few details (below) had been settled before she was cancelled for the second time in mid-1895. She would have been of a new type and not a repeat of an earlier design.

**Dimensions & tons:** 240t disp. **Men:** 39.
**Machinery:** 24.00kts. 2 screws. Normand boilers. Range 2,800nm @ 10kts.
**Torpedoes:** 2 tubes above water. **Guns:** 2 x 37mm QF.

*N12* (Unnamed) Contract
Budget 1894 (not funded). This contract-built *torpilleur de haute mer* was included in the 1894 budget (submitted 5.1893) with the stipulation that no funds were to be spent on her during 1894. She was not contracted for and the 1895 budget (3.1894) deferred her indefinitely. The 1896 budget submission (5.1895) reinstated her, but the Budget Commission on 13.7.1895 deleted many ships including this one from the budget and cancelled credits for them on 24.10.1895. N12 was not in the 1897 budget but reappeared in the 1898 budget as the lead ship of the *Siroco* class (see Chapter 16).

**Alternative designs by Normand**

Despite his success with high speed torpedo boats culminating in *Forban*, *Aquilon*, and *Cyclone*, Normand himself had a strong preference for seagoing torpedo boats with less speed (24 knots on trials, 22 knots in service) and greater tonnage (244 tons) for better seakeeping. In 1895 he submitted a proposal for such a boat along with his proposal for an aviso torpilleur that became France's first destroyer, *Durandal*. On 1 July 1897 he wrote that ideally the operating range of torpedo boats operating with the fleet should equal if not exceed that of the larger fleet units because of difficulties refuelling them and noted that a *Cyclone* with only 2,000ihp would have an operating range of 5,000 miles at 10 knots. He was also an advocate of armour for torpedo boats. France ordered ten more Normand-designed seagoing torpedo boats in 1898 and 1899, including six with side armour, but the type was then displaced by the destroyer which had many of the characteristics for fleet operations that Normand sought.

————————

# (B) 1ˢᵗ Class Torpedo Boats (*Torpilleurs de 1ʳᵉ classe*)

Were *Torpilleurs Garde-Côtes de 1ʳᵉ classe* before the 1.1885 fleet list.

**33-METRE TYPE, 2ND SERIES, 1883 ORDERS. *TORPILLEURS Nᵒˢ 65–74*. *Torpilleurs de 1ʳᵉ classe*.** Normand 33-metre torpedo boats with two torpedo tubes inside the bow, two funnels abreast, and a ram bow. To *Torpilleurs de 2ᵉ classe* 1.1890.

A second series of improved repeats of *No 27*, the most successful of the *trois grands* of November 1877, the first series having been *Nos 60-64* (see Chapter 5). The last six were added to the contract for the first four in a supplement dated 14 April 1883. Unlike *Nᵒˢ 60-64* they had ram bows, a feature later advocated by the leading publicist of the *Jeune École*, Gabriel Charmes, to protect the boats' torpedo tubes in case of collision with a ship or a harbour buoy and in an extreme situation for use against an interfering enemy torpedo boat. The ram bows proved to be a mistake as they raised a large bow wave and forced the boats to carry shorter tubes with the 356mm torpedo instead of the 381mm in *Nᵒˢ 60-64*. The boilers were of the same type as in the earlier group but a bit larger. Originally *Nᵒˢ 65-68* were to have had engines with cylinder dimensions as in *Nᵒˢ 60-64* and *Nᵒˢ 69-74* were to have had cylinders as in the larger *Balny* class, instead an intermediate model was adopted. *Nᵒ 74* had experimental hull lines by Normand, with a rounded bow that gave her a draft forward of 0.42m instead of 0.75m and a tunnel stern. *Nᵒ 65* had her funnels tilted outboard like rabbit ears. *Nᵒ 71* was the first French torpedo boat to reach 21 knots on the measured mile. They were good sea boats despite violent pitching. *Nᵒ 65* and *Nᵒ 69* transited to Toulon by sea for service in 1884-85 (*Nᵒ 69* stopping for brief service at Lorient) while *Nᵒ 68* made the same trip in 1885 via the inland waterway system (Paris 6 May, Lyon 27 May, Toulon 30 May). Of the boats that remained at Cherbourg, *Nos 66, 67, 70, 71,* and *72* made the round trip to Toulon for exercises in 1886-87 while *Nᵒ 74* did the same from Rochefort. *Nᵒ 71* returned from Toulon to Cherbourg July 1887 by the rail system to test that strategic capability. The masts in the 33-metre and 35-metre types were single light spars amidships that could be raised if needed. It was proposed to convert this group into *contre-torpilleurs* but only *Nᵒ 68* was so modified. They all became *Torpilleurs de 2ᵉ classe* in the 1890 fleet list.

**Dimensions & tons:** 33.75m wl (wl fwd to wl aft), 33.00m pp (wl fwd to rudder) x 3.28m ext (below wl), 3.26m wl. 49.280t disp. Draught: 0.75m fwd, 1.10m amidships, 1.945m aft under propeller guard. Men: 11.

**Machinery:** 500ihp designed at 320rpm and 8.43kg/cm² boiler pressure. Speed 20kts. Trials (*Nᵒ 66*) 521ihp = 20.306kts at 315.04rpm. The others made between 20.046kts and 20.948kts on trials. 1 screw. 1 compound engine with 2 cylinders of 0.36m and 0.48m diameter and 0.38m stroke. 1 locomotive boiler. 8.38t coal. Range 67 hours @ 12kts.

The 33-metre 1ˢᵗ class torpedo boat *Torpilleur nᵒ 65* at Cherbourg in the summer of 1884. She ran trials from here between May and July 1884. Aside from her ram-shaped bow with two smaller torpedo tubes she is very similar to *Torpilleur no 64* in the previous section. On the right are the coast defence ship *Fulminant* in reserve after completion and behind her the station cruiser *Vauban* fitting out. On the left are some cruisers in reserve. *(NHHC, NH-88796)*

**Torpedoes:** 2 bow tubes for 356mm (4.42m) torpedoes

*Torpilleur nº 65* Augustin Normand, Le Havre.
On list 1.1883. Ord: 29.1.1883. K: 1882. L: 29.4.1884. Trials: 5-8.1884.
*Défense mobile* at Toulon 1884-1903. Struck 7.3.1904. Sold 1904 at
Toulon to BU.

*Torpilleur nº 66* Augustin Normand, Le Havre.
On list 1.1883. Ord: 29.1.1883. K: 1882. L: 24.6.1884.
Trials: 8-10.1884.
*Défense mobile* at Cherbourg 1885-1907. Tested an experimental oil-fired
boiler developed by naval constructor Georges Guyot. Struck
6.12.1907, retained at Cherbourg as gunnery target 1907-1908.

The 33-metre 1st class (later 2nd class) torpedo boat *Torpilleur nº 74* photographed
at Villefranche in about 1890 showing her experimental stern. Her Berthon
collapsible canvas boat, standard on most torpedo boats, is prominent here.
*(NHHC from ONI album of foreign warships dated about 1900, NH-88785)*

Sold 2.12.1908 at Cherbourg to BU.

*Torpilleur nº 67* Augustin Normand, Le Havre.
On list 1.1883. Ord: 29.1.1883. K: 1882. L: 10.9.1884. Trials: 1.1885.
*Défense mobile* at Cherbourg 1885-87. Sunk 1.3.1887 in collision with
*Torpilleur nº 71* in the entrance to Sao Martinho do Porto, Portugal,
while both were en route to exercises at Toulon. Hulk destroyed by
torpedoes 17.3.1887. Struck 6.4.1887.

*Torpilleur nº 68* Augustin Normand, Le Havre.
On list 1.1883. Ord: 29.1.1883. K: 1882. L: 21.10.1884.
Trials: 10.1884-1.1885.
*Défense mobile* at Toulon 1885-1904. To *Contre-torpilleur* 1.1888, to
*Torpilleur de 2e classe* 1.1890. Struck 9.11.1904, for sale at Toulon
1904-1905.

*Torpilleur nº 69* Augustin Normand, Le Havre.
On list 1.1884. Ord: 14.4.1883. K: 1883. L: 20.1.1885. Trials: 1-5.1885.
*Défense mobile* at Lorient 1885, Toulon 1885-87, Lorient 1888-1901,

Brest 1901. Tested two Trépardoux tubular boilers (contract of 18.7.1891 with De Dion, Bouton & Trépardoux). Sank at Lorient 31.7.1895 after running onto the stern of the coast defence ship *Bouledogue* which was towing the unmanned torpedo boat, raised. Struck 7.11.1902, retained at Brest as gunnery target 1902-1908, for sale 1908-1909.

*Torpilleur nº 70* Augustin Normand, Le Havre.
On list 1.1884. Ord: 14.4.1883. K: 1883. L: 17.3.1885. Trials: 4-6.1885.
*Défense mobile* at Cherbourg 1885-95, Dunkirk 1896-1902. Struck 5.5.1905. Sold 1905 at Cherbourg to BU.

*Torpilleur nº 71* Augustin Normand, Le Havre.
On list 1.1884. Ord: 14.4.1883. K: 1883. L: 13.5.1885. Trials: 6.1885.
*Défense mobile* at Cherbourg 1885-94, Dunkirk 1895-1903. Collided with and sank *Torpilleur nº 67* 1.3.1887 near Lisbon while both were en route to exercises at Toulon. Reboiled 1897 with a Du Temple boiler. Struck 19.6.1903, retained at Cherbourg as gunnery target 1903-1906, for sale 1906-1907.

*Torpilleur nº 72* Augustin Normand, Le Havre.
On list 1.1884. Ord: 14.4.1883. K: 1883. L: 13.6.1885. Trials: 8.1885.
*Défense mobile* at Cherbourg 1885-94, Dunkirk 1895-1902. Reboiled 1897 with a Du Temple boiler. Collided with service craft *Becquet* 3.1903. Struck 25.7.1903, for sale at Cherbourg 1903-1904.

*Torpilleur nº 73* Augustin Normand, Le Havre.
On list 1.1884. Ord: 14.4.1883. K: 1883. L: 11.7.1885. Trials: 8.1885.
*Défense mobile* at Brest 1885-1903. Tested a Petit et Godard tubular boiler c1890. School for stoking from 6.1901. Retired 25.7.1903 and 10.1903. Retained as gunnery target at Brest 1903-1905 and at Lorient1905-1906.

*Torpilleur nº 74* Augustin Normand, Le Havre.
On list 1.1884. Ord: 14.4.1883. K: 1883. L: 14.4.1885. Trials: 6.1885.
*Défense mobile* at Rochefort 1885-98. Struck 22.11.1898, hull for sale at Rochefort 1898-1899.

---

**35-METRE TYPE, 1ST SERIES, 1885 ORDERS.** *TORPILLEURS Nos 75–104. Torpilleurs de 1re classe.* 35-metre torpedo boats with two torpedo tubes inside a long forecastle sloping down to the bow, two funnels abreast. Designed by the Forges et Chantiers de la Méditerranée at La Seyne (Lagane), Normand not participating in the project. Soon modified with one tube inside a shortened sloping forecastle and one tube on deck amidships. To *Torpilleurs de 2e classe* 1.1890.

When Minister of Marine Peyron and his staff planned the series of torpedo boats to follow *Nos 65-74* they had in mind only six boats. But political and press pressure caused his successor, Minister Galiber, to increase the number from 6 to 30 on 10 June 1885. Rather than approach Normand for a design (which he was already preparing) the Machinery Commission followed the Minister's instructions and ordered them to a design prepared by the Navy. Five firms offered to build six boats each (*Nos 75-104*) while Normand stood aside. (Schneider built his yard at Chalon-sur-Saône for this order.) Many objections were raised to the navy's design and on 7 August 1885 Minister Galiber suspended work already underway on a few boats and had the Machinery Commission approach Lagane at F.C. Méditerranée (France's leading torpedo boat designer after Normand). He submitted his proposal on 11 November 1885 and it was approved and the revised contracts issued on 23 November 1885. In the meantime Rear Admiral Aube became Minister of Marine and on 23 January 1886 he added ten more boats to the programme followed by another eleven on 6 February 1886. Aube also approved increasing the calibre of the torpedo tubes from 356mm to 381mm and their height above the water from the 68cm preferred by Normand to 1.20m.

Internal arrangements were much as Normand's *Nos 65-74* but they had

a high vertical bow and a forecastle covering the torpedo tubes and extending back to the conning tower. The second rudder was not in the bow but was aft, forward of the main rudder between the hull and the propeller shaft. The original contract of 22 June 1885 with Claparède for *Nos 81-86* was transferred on 31 May 1886 to A.C. Loire after it bought the Claparède firm; the first four boats were built at the former Claparède yard at Saint Denis and the last two were built at Nantes.

When the first 16 boats were presented for acceptance trials beginning in January 1887 only two (*Nos 99* and *100*) were accepted. The boilers of the others were totally inadequate, burning large amounts of coal and failing to come close to their contract speed. Of the 14 boats rejected in early 1887, *Nos 101-104* were sent back to La Seyne for new boilers and *Nos 105-114* were either sent to Cherbourg to be made usable or outright rejected. Builders other than La Seyne (which had provided the design) initially balked at replacing the boilers which had been specified by the Navy. However, A.C. Loire tried an Oriolle boiler in *Nº 75*, C.A. Gironde tried a Du Temple boiler in *Nº 115*, and Cail tried enlarging its locomotive boilers with more grate area.

The tophamper forward consisting of two torpedo tubes and the structure over them also raised grave concerns over stability, soon confirmed by *Nos 99* and *100* during exercises on 30 May 1887. On 27 March 1888 the *Conseil des travaux* declined to recommend the necessary changes to the entire class because of the need to get the 51 boats into service, although it did approve applying a design by naval constructor Charles Pierre Octave Joseph Ferrand to one of them. Then, while entering the Bay of Sanary just west of Toulon on 1 March 1889, *Nº 99* again experienced disturbing rolls a few minutes before *Nº 102* in company with her capsized. On 21 March 1889 *Nº 110* disappeared in a storm in the Channel, probably broken in half, *Nº 111* with her barely survived severe hull damage, while the older *Nos 55 and 71* in company handled the storm without unusual difficulty.

This time the *Conseil des travaux* accepted the need for drastic changes, which were tried out first on *Nº 99*. In March 1890 the process of modifying the rest of the class began. The bow was reduced 50cm in height and the number of bow tubes was reduced from two to one, the second one being moved to a rotating deck mount amidships. The hull lines were also changed, particularly above the waterline, and the hulls strengthened. The additional weight of these changes reduced the maximum speed of the boats to 17 knots and their normal speed to 13.5 knots. They became known as the *dos de chameau* (camel-back) type because of the hump that many got amidships when larger boilers were fitted, particularly larger locomotive boilers in some and taller Oriolle boilers in others. Some got special configurations. The fixed bow tube of *Nº 100* and probably *Nº 99* was left exposed on top of the bow rather than encased in a short forecastle as in the other boats. The refloated *Nº 101* received a rotating deck tube forward of the conning tower instead of the fixed bow tube, thus having two rotating tubes. The salvaged *Nº 102* was rebuilt at La Seyne from March 1891 to June 1892 with two small funnels, one well aft of the other, and the original two bow tubes. *Nº 93* had experimental funnels exhausting under the waterline. Many also got two 37mm guns. The last of these reconfigured boats ran trials and entered service in 1891. *Nos 77, 102, 108, 109,* and *115* later got one or two Du Temple boilers which increased their speed to 16.5 knots. All of the 35-metre boats became *Torpilleurs de 2e classe* in the 1890 fleet list.

**Dimensions & tons:** 33.75m wl, 35.00m pp x 3.35m ext, 3.33m wl. 53.750t disp with 3t of coal, 58.258t with 8.38t of coal. Draught: 0.52m fwd, 0.89m amidships, 2.05m aft under propeller guard.

**Machinery:** 525ihp designed at 335rpm and 9kg/cm² boiler pressure (increased to 9.5kg/cm² on 18.7.1885 at the request of FCM). Speed 20kts. Trials (*Nº 87*) 632ihp = 19.44kts at 335.06rpm. The others made between 18.25kts and 20.51kts on trials with their new boilers. 1 screw. 1 compound engine with 2 cylinders of 0.37m and 0.64m diameter and 0.36m stroke. 1 locomotive boiler. 8.38t coal. Range 430-590nm @ 12kts.

**Torpedoes:** 2 bow tubes for 381mm (5.85m) torpedoes, later one bow tube and one rotating tube amidships. **Guns:** 2 x 37mm revolving cannon added, later changed in some to 2 x 37mm/20 M1885 QF.

*Torpilleur n° 75* A.C. Loire, Nantes.
On list 1.1886. Ord: 22.6.1885. K: 1886. L: 31.1.1887. Accepted: 1891.
Budget 1887. Trials at Brest began 4.1887 with a breakdown. *Défense mobile* at Brest 1890-98, Saint Servan 1899-1902. Struck 2.6.1903, retained as gunnery target at Brest 1903-1905 and at Lorient 1905-1906.

*Torpilleur n° 76* A.C. Loire, Nantes.
On list 1.1886. Ord: 22.6.1885. K: 1886. L: 24.2.1887. Accepted: 1891.
Budget 1887. *Défense mobile* at Brest 1887-92. During manoeuvres in the Brest roadstead on 20.7.1892 collided with the ram of the coast defence ship *Tempête* and sank. Raised and condemned. Struck 22.10.1892, for disposal at Brest 1892-1894.

*Torpilleur n° 77* A.C. Loire, Nantes.
On list 1.1886. Ord: 22.6.1885. K: 1886. L: 6.4.1887. Accepted: 1891.
Budget 1887. Trials at Brest 10.1887 (original boiler, 17.749kts) and 6.1891 (Oriolle boiler, 18.86kts with 20.17kts on her best measured mile). Capsized 18.12.1891 in dock at Lorient during an inclining experiment, refloated 20.12.1891. *Défense mobile* at Lorient 1892-1908. Struck 11.6.1908, retained at Lorient as gunnery target 1908-1909 and as torpedo target 1909-1910. Sold 1913 at Lorient to BU.

*Torpilleur n° 78* A.C. Loire, Nantes.
On list 1.1886. Ord: 22.6.1885. K: 1886. L: 7.4.1887. Accepted: 1891.
Budget 1887. Trials at Brest 2.1888 (original boiler, 18.127kts) and 11.1891 (Oriolle boiler, 19.99kts). *Défense mobile* at Brest 1892, Lorient 1893-1908. Oriolle boiler replaced with a Guyot-du Temple boiler. Damaged 1.1906 in collision with the destroyer *Sagaïe*. Struck 11.6.1908, retained at Lorient as gunnery target 1908-1909, for sale 1909-1911.

*Torpilleur n° 79* A.C. Loire, Nantes.
On list 1.1886. Ord: 22.6.1885. K: 1886. L: 22.7.1887. Accepted: 1891.
Budget 1887. Final trials at Brest 7.1891. *Défense mobile* at Brest 1891-92, Lorient 1893-1907. Struck 11.5.1907. Sold 1908 at Lorient to BU.

*Torpilleur n° 80* A.C. Loire, Nantes.
On list 1.1886. Ord: 22.6.1885. K: 1886. L: 5.8.1887. Accepted: 1891.
Budget 1887. Final trials at Brest 9.1891. *Défense mobile* at Brest 1891-1901. Struck 14.6.1901. Sold 1902 at Brest to BU.

*Torpilleur n° 81* Anc. Éts. Claparède/A.C. Loire, Saint Denis.
On list 1.1886. Ord: 22.6.1885. K: 1886. L: 31.1.1887. Accepted: 1891.
Budget 1887. *Défense mobile* at Brest 1888-1904 (including time in reserve). Original boiler replaced with Oriolle boiler 1891. Struck 9.6.1904. BU 1905 at Brest.

*Torpilleur n° 82* Anc. Éts. Claparède/A.C. Loire, Saint Denis.
On list 1.1886. Ord: 22.6.1885. K: 1886. L: 26.3.1887. Accepted: 1889.
Budget 1887. Trials with Oriolle boiler 2.1889 (19.10kts). *Défense mobile* at Brest 1888-92. Hull modified at Bordeaux 1891-92. *Défense mobile* at Lorient 1893-1907. Struck 11.5.1907. Sold 1907 at Lorient to BU.

*Torpilleur n° 83* Anc. Éts. Claparède/A.C. Loire, Saint Denis.
On list 1.1886. Ord: 22.6.1885. K: 1886. L: 6.7.1887. Accepted: 1891.
Budget 1887. *Défense mobile* at Brest 1888-96. Sunk 9.11.1896 in collision with *Torpilleur n° 61*. Struck 26.4.1897.

*Torpilleur n° 84* Anc. Éts. Claparède/A.C. Loire, Saint Denis.
On list 1.1886. Ord: 22.6.1885. K: 1886. L: 6.8.1887. Accepted: 1891.
Budget 1887. Trials in 1888 with original boiler (17.27kts) and with Oriolle boiler (20.51kts). *Défense mobile* at Brest 1888-98, Saint Servan

1898-1902, Brest 1903. Struck 9.2.1904, retained at Brest as gunnery target 1904-1908, for sale 1908-1909.

*Torpilleur n° 85* A.C. Loire, Nantes (ex Anc. Éts. Claparède, Saint Denis).
On list 1.1886. Ord: 22.6.1885. K: 1886. L: 22.7.1887. Accepted: 1891.
Budget 1887. *Défense mobile* at Brest 1888-92, Toulon 1893-95, Algiers 1896-97, Oran 1898-1900. Struck 25.8.1900, for sale at Toulon 1900-1903.

*Torpilleur n° 86* A.C. Loire, Nantes (ex Anc. Éts. Claparède, Saint Denis).
On list 1.1886. Ord: 22.6.1885. K: 1886. L: 5.8.1887. Accepted: 1891.
Budget 1887. *Défense mobile* at Brest 1888-92, Lorient 1893-1908. Made 16.05kts with a new locomotive boiler in 1902. Struck 11.6.1908, annex to the school for engineers at Lorient 1908-1911, for sale at Lorient 1911-1912.

*Torpilleur n° 87* Anc. Ets. Cail, Paris-Grenelle.
On list 1.1886. Ord: 22.6.1885. K: 1886. L: 9.3.1887. Accepted: 1891.
Budget 1887. *Défense mobile* at Cherbourg 1888-99, Saint Servan 1899-1904. Struck 15.11.1904, for sale at Brest 1904-1905.

*Torpilleur n° 88* Anc. Ets. Cail, Paris-Grenelle.
On list 1.1886. Ord: 22.6.1885. K: 1886. L: 14.4.1887. Accepted: 1891.
Budget 1887. *Défense mobile* at Cherbourg 1888-1902. Struck 17.2.1903, retained at Cherbourg as gunnery target 1903-1906.

*Torpilleur n° 89* Anc. Ets. Cail, Paris-Grenelle.
On list 1.1886. Ord: 22.6.1885. K: 1886. L: 28.5.1887. Accepted: 1891.
Budget 1887. *Défense mobile* at Cherbourg 1888-1903, at Brest 1903-1907. Struck 19.8.1907, renamed *Enclume* 1907 and annex to the school for engineers at Brest 1907-1909, for sale 1909-1910, torpedo target 1910-1911, replaced by *Torpilleur n° 235* and reverted to *Torpilleur n° 89* 1912. Offered for sale at Brest 16.12.1913.

*Torpilleur v 90* Anc. Ets. Cail, Paris-Grenelle.
On list 1.1886. Ord: 22.6.1885. K: 1886. L: 11.1887. Accepted: 1891.
Budget 1887. *Défense mobile* at Cherbourg 1888 and, after rebuilding, 1891-97, then *Défense mobile* at Dunkirk 1897-98 and Cherbourg 1898-1907. While so assigned designated during 1904-07 as escort for

The rebuilt 35-metre 2nd class (formerly 1st class) torpedo boat *Torpilleur n° 82* passing the citadel at Port Louis near Lorient. Tophamper has been reduced and one of the two bow torpedo tubes has been moved to a deck mounting aft of the two funnels. *(Postcard by Laurent-Nel, Rennes)*

the 1st Flotilla of Submarines of the Channel. Struck 6.12.1907, retained at Cherbourg as gunnery target 1907-1909, for sale 1909-1912.

*Torpilleur n° 91* Anc. Ets. Cail, Paris-Grenelle.
On list 1.1886. Ord: 22.6.1885. K: 1886. L: 5.11.1887. Accepted: 1891.
Budget 1887. *Défense mobile* at Cherbourg 1888-98, Saint Servan 1898-1901. Struck a rock 12.3.1901 near the Héaux de Bréhat in northern Brittany, towed to nearby Lézardrieux where she sank. Refloated. Struck 23.4.1901.

*Torpilleur n° 92* Anc. Ets. Cail, Paris-Grenelle.
On list 1.1886. Ord: 22.6.1885. K: 1886. L: 18.1.1888. Accepted: 1888.
Budget 1887. *Défense mobile* at Cherbourg 1888-97, Brest 1898-1903 (school for stoking from 1901). Struck 8.5.1903, retained at Brest as gunnery target 1903-1909, for sale 1909-1910.

*Torpilleur n° 93* Schneider, Chalon-sur-Saône.
On list 1.1886. Ord: 22.6.1885. K: 1886. L: 7.2.1887. Accepted: 1889.
Budget 1887. *Défense mobile* at Toulon 1888-93, Algiers 1894-96, Toulon 1896-1902, Corsica 1902-1904, Toulon 1904-1910. Renamed *Gapeau* 11.1910. Annex to the school for torpedomen at Toulon 1910-13. Struck 22.11.1913, target vessel at Toulon 1913-1914, for sale 1920. Sold 1921 at Toulon to BU.

*Torpilleur n° 94* Schneider, Chalon-sur-Saône.
On list 1.1886. Ord: 22.6.1885. K: 1886. L: 19.2.1887. Accepted: 1890.
Budget 1887. *Défense mobile* at Toulon 1888-1909. Struck 13.8.1909.

*Torpilleur n° 95* Schneider, Chalon-sur-Saône.
On list 1.1886. Ord: 22.6.1885. K: 1886. L: 5.4.1887. Accepted: 1890.
Budget 1887. *Défense mobile* at Toulon 1888-1909. Struck 15.10.1909, for sale at Toulon 1909-1910.

*Torpilleur n° 96* Schneider, Chalon-sur-Saône.
On list 1.1886. Ord: 22.6.1885. K: 1886. L: 16.6.1887. Accepted: 1890.
Budget 1887. *Défense mobile* at Toulon 1888-1905. Struck 4.12.1905. For sale at Toulon, then retained as gunnery target. Sunk by battleship *Iéna* during the 1906 target practice.

*Torpilleur n° 97* Schneider, Chalon-sur-Saône.
On list 1.1886. Ord: 22.6.1885. K: 1886. L: 3q.1887. Accepted: 1889.
Budget 1887. Trials at Toulon 7.1889. *Défense mobile* at Toulon 1889-95, Corsica 1896-1902. Struck 7.3.1904, used as target, for sale at Toulon 1904-1905. Sold 11.1905 at Toulon to BU.

*Torpilleur n° 98* Schneider, Chalon-sur-Saône.
On list 1.1886. Ord: 22.6.1885. K: 1886. L: 3q.1887. Accepted: 1890.
Budget 1887. Tested variants of boilers for 35-metre boats ordered for Japan before conducting French trials. *Défense mobile* at Toulon 1888-1907. Struck 12.8.1907, retained at Toulon as gunnery target 1907-1908. Sold 1908 at Toulon to BU.

*Torpilleur n° 99* F.C. Méditerranée, La Seyne.
On list 1.1886. Ord: 22.6.1885. K: 1886. L: 20.1.1887. Accepted: 1887.
Budget 1887. Trials 2.1887 (19.87kts). This and *N° 100* were the first 35-metre boats to be commissioned for trials. *Défense mobile* at Toulon 1887-97, Corsica 1898-1902, Toulon 1902. Struck 11.4.1902, used as demonstration engine for the torpedo boat officers at the torpedo boat school at Toulon 1902-1904, retained as gunnery target 1904-1906, sold 1906 at Toulon to BU.

*Torpilleur n° 100* F.C. Méditerranée, La Seyne.
On list 1.1886. Ord: 22.6.1885. K: 1886. L: 18.2.1887. Accepted: 1887.
Budget 1887. *Défense mobile* at Toulon 1887-95, Algiers 1896-98. Struck 3.2.1899. Sold 1899 to BU.

*Torpilleur n° 101* F.C. Méditerranée, La Seyne.
On list 1.1886. Ord: 22.6.1885. K: 1886. L: 18.3.1887. Accepted: 1888.
Budget 1887. Her first trials, between 5.1887 and 11.1888, included a

The 35-metre 1st class torpedo boat *Torpilleur n° 99*, built at Graville for the French Navy. This drawing shows the original design for the 35-metre boats, with short wide funnels and both torpedo tubes side by side in the bow. The boats were designed by the Forges et Chantiers de la Méditerranée at La Seyne, Normand not participating in the programme. *(E.Monod, L'Exposition universelle de 1889, Paris 1890, Vol. 3, p. 257)*

serious boiler accident on 4.8.1887 and ended with the rejection of the boat. After modifications she was assigned to the *Défense mobile* at Toulon until 1903, and from 1899 was also annex to the school for torpedo boat officers. Struck 16.4.1903, for sale at Toulon 1903-1904.

*Torpilleur n° 102* F.C. Méditerranée, La Seyne.
On list 1.1886. Ord: 22.6.1885. K: 1886. L: 6.4.1887. Accepted: 1888.
Budget 1887. *Défense mobile* at Toulon from 1887. Capsized in a following sea and sank 1.3.1889 in the Passe des Embiez near Le Brusq west of Toulon, 6 dead and 10 survivors. Restored to service, *Défense mobile* at Toulon to 1905 and in 1898-99 was annex to the school for torpedo boat engineers in *Algésiras*. Struck 4.12.1905. Sold 5.1.1907 to M. Goutte of Marseille.

*Torpilleur n° 103* F.C. Méditerranée, La Seyne.
On list 1.1886. Ord: 22.6.1885. K: 1886. L: 29.4.1887. Accepted: 1888.
Budget 1887. *Défense mobile* at Toulon 1887-98, Bizerte 1898-1901, Toulon 1901-1908. Struck 10.8.1908, retained at Toulon as gunnery target 1908-1909, for sale 1909-1910. Sold c8.1910 at Toulon to BU.

*Torpilleur n° 104* F.C. Méditerranée, La Seyne.
On list 1.1886. Ord: 22.6.1885. K: 1886. L: 10.6.1887. Accepted: 1888.
Budget 1887. Trials at Toulon 27.7.1887 with original boiler (19.20kts) and 11.1888 with new boiler (19.04kts). *Défense mobile* at Toulon 1887-96, Corsica 1896-98, Toulon 1898-1900. Struck 8.3.1900, for sale at Toulon 1900-1904.

---

**35-METRE TYPE, 2ND SERIES, 1886 ORDERS. *TORPILLEURS Nos 105–125*.** *Torpilleurs de 1re classe.* To *Torpilleurs de 2e classe* 1.1890.

See the 1st series of 35-metre boats ordered in 1885 for the characteristics and history of this second series, which was ordered in 1886.

*Torpilleur n° 105* F.C. Méditerranée, Le Havre-Graville.
On list 1.1886. Ord: 15.2.1886. K: 1886. L: 26.1.1887. Accepted: 1889.
Budget 1887. Trials at Cherbourg c1887 and 1891. *Défense mobile* at

Cherbourg 1887-1900, Dunkirk 1901-1902. Struck 6.9.1906, for sale at Cherbourg 1906-1907.

*Torpilleur n° 106* F.C. Méditerranée, Le Havre-Graville.
On list 1.1886. Ord: 15.2.1886. K: 1886. L: 26.2.1887. Accepted: 1889. Budget 1887. *Défense mobile* at Cherbourg 1888-1904. Struck 3.5.1904. Sold 1.9.1904 at Cherbourg to BU.

*Torpilleur n° 107* F.C. Méditerranée, Le Havre-Graville.
On list 1.1886. Ord: 15.2.1886. K: 1886. L: 25.3.1887. Accepted: 1889. Budget 1887. *Défense mobile* at Cherbourg to 1900, Dunkirk 1901-1902, Brest 1903-1906. Sent back to the builders in 1889 for new boiler and in 1891 to modify the hull. Struck 24.4.1906. Sold 26.7.1906 at Brest to BU.

---

The 35-metre 1st class torpedo boats *Torpilleurs n° 101* and *n° 102* in the water alongside the battleship *Marceau* on the ways behind them at the Forges et Chantiers de la Méditerranée at La Seyne. The photo was probably taken soon before the launch of the battleship on 24 May 1887. On the other side of the battleship another image shows *No 103* essentially complete but still on the ways. The funnels and other details have been modified since the original design in the drawing of *No 99*, above. *(NHHC from ONI album of French warships, NH-74856)*

*Torpilleur n° 108* F.C. Méditerranée, Le Havre-Graville.
On list 1.1886. Ord: 15.2.1886. K: 1886. L: 23.4.1887. Accepted: 1889. Budget 1887. *Défense mobile* at Cherbourg 1887-1902. Struck 7.11.1902, retained at Cherbourg as gunnery target 1902. Left Cherbourg under tow for Brest by *Cassini*, tow line broke and the unmanned torpedo boat went aground 16.12.1902 near Plymouth. Towed into Brest by *Buffle* 2.1.1903. Condemned 20.2.1903 and sunk in the 1903 gunnery exercises.

*Torpilleur n° 109* F.C. Méditerranée, Le Havre-Graville.
On list 1.1886. Ord: 15.2.1886. K: 1886. L: 10.5.1887. Accepted: 1890. Budget 1887. *Défense mobile* at Cherbourg 1887-1904. Tested oil firing of boiler 1892. Tested the Leblond-Caville multitubular boiler 1900. Struck 8.8.1904, retained at Cherbourg as gunnery target 1904-1906.

*Torpilleur n° 110* F.C. Méditerranée, Le Havre-Graville.
On list 1.1886. Ord: 15.2.1886. K: 1886. L: 23.7.1887. Accepted: 1889. Budget 1887. Trials at Cherbourg, accepted 12.1887 with trial speed of 18.60kts. Left Le Havre with *N° 111* escorted by *N°s 71* and *55* to return to Cherbourg but encountered a storm and disappeared 21.3.1889 with all hands off Barfleur. Off list 1890. *N°s 110* and *111* had just been reboiled at Graville and, since they were of the same type as *N° 102*, just lost at Toulon, it was felt prudent to escort them

with older boats. The structural damage found in *Nº 111* suggested that *Nº 110* broke up in the heavy seas.

*Torpilleur nº 111* F.C. Méditerranée, Le Havre-Graville.
On list 1.1886. Ord: 15.2.1886. K: 1886. L: 4.7.1887. Accepted: 1889.
Budget 1887. Badly damaged 21.3.1889 by the storm that sank *Nº 110*. *Défense mobile* at Cherbourg 1889-1901, Rochefort 1901-1904. Struck 28.12.1904, for sale at Rochefort 1904-1905.

*Torpilleur nº 112* F.C. Méditerranée, Le Havre-Graville.
On list 1.1886. Ord: 15.2.1886. K: 1886. L: 5.10.1887. Accepted: 1889.
Budget 1887. Initial trials at Cherbourg 5.1888 (only 17.01kts). *Défense mobile* at Cherbourg 1888-1900, Dunkirk 1901-1902, Cherbourg 1903-1905. Sent back to the builders in 1889 for new boiler and in 1891 to modify the hull. Tested Renard boiler (like the one in *Libellule*) 1905. Struck 28.12.1906. Sold 20.3.1907 at Cherbourg to BU.

*Torpilleur nº 113* F.C. Méditerranée, Le Havre-Graville.
On list 1.1886. Ord: 15.2.1886. K: 1886. L: 20.12.1887. Accepted: 1889.
Budget 1887. *Défense mobile* at Cherbourg 1888-1900 except 1898 at Dunkirk. Grounded 8.1900. Struck 27.11.1900, hull for sale at Cherbourg 1900-1901.

*Torpilleur nº 114* F.C. Méditerranée, Le Havre-Graville.
On list 1.1886. Ord: 15.2.1886. K: 1886. L: 30.11.1887. Accepted: 1889.
Budget 1887. Trials at Cherbourg (originally 19.20kts, on 22.5.1891 after modifications and at full load could not exceed 15.83kts). *Défense mobile* at Cherbourg 1889-1901, Rochefort 1902-1903. Struck 27.6.1903, retained at Rochefort as gunnery target 1903-1906, for sale 1906-1907.

*Torpilleur nº 115* C.A. Gironde, Bordeaux-Lormont.
On list 1.1886. Ord: 15.2.1886. K: 1886. L: 9.4.1887. Accepted: 1889.
Budget 1887. *Défense mobile* at Rochefort 1889-1908. Reboilered 1889, hauled out and hull modified 1891. Struck 10.3.1909, offered for sale at Rochefort 17.11.1911.

*Torpilleur nº 116* C.A. Gironde, Bordeaux-Lormont.
On list 1.1886. Ord: 15.2.1886. K: 1886. L: 10.5.1887. Accepted: 1889.
Budget 1887. *Défense mobile* at Rochefort 1889-1902. Reboilered 1889, hauled out and hull modified 1891. Struck 17.11.1903, retained at Rochefort as gunnery target 1903-1906, for sale 1906-1907. Sold 5.9.1907 at Rochefort to BU.

*Torpilleur nº 117* C.A. Gironde, Bordeaux-Lormont.
On list 1.1886. Ord: 15.2.1886. K: 1886. L: 17.6.1887. Accepted: 1889.
Budget 1887. *Défense mobile* at Rochefort 1889-1904. Reboilered 1889, hauled out and hull modified 1891. Struck 23.9.1904, retained at Rochefort as gunnery target 1904-1906, for sale 1906-1907. Sold 5.9.1907 at Rochefort to BU.

*Torpilleur nº 118* C.A. Gironde, Bordeaux-Lormont.
On list 1.1886. Ord: 15.2.1886. K: 1886. L: 23.7.1887. Accepted: 1889.
Budget 1887. *Défense mobile* at Rochefort 1889-1902. Reboilered 1889, hauled out and hull modified 1891. Struck 30.5.1902, retained provisionally at Rochefort 1902-1906, for sale 1906-1907. Sold 5.9.1907 at Rochefort to BU.

*Torpilleur nº 119* C.A. Gironde, Bordeaux-Lormont.
On list 1.1886. Ord: 15.2.1886. K: 1886. L: 20.8.1887. Accepted: 1889.
Budget 1887. *Défense mobile* at Rochefort 1887-1902. Reboilered 1889, hauled out and hull modified 1891. Struck 30.5.1902, retained provisionally at Rochefort 1902-1906, for sale 1906-1907. Sold 5.9.1907 at Rochefort to BU.

*Torpilleur nº 120* C.A. Gironde, Bordeaux-Lormont.
On list 1.1886. Ord: 15.2.1886. K: 1886. L: 15.5.1889. Accepted: 1889.
Budget 1887. *Défense mobile* at Rochefort 1889-91, Toulon 1892-1901. Reboilered 1889, hauled out and hull modified 1891. Struck 2.5.1901, for sale at Toulon 1901-1902.

*Torpilleur nº 121* Schneider, Chalon-sur-Saône.
On list 1.1886. Ord: 15.2.1886. K: 1886. L: 1q.1889. Accepted: 1889.
Budget 1887. Trials at Toulon 7.1889. Reboilered 1889, hull modified 1891. *Défense mobile* at Toulon to 1893, Algiers 1893-97, Bizerte 1898-1900. Struck 25.8.1900, for sale at Toulon 1900-1904.

*Torpilleur nº 122* Schneider, Chalon-sur-Saône.
On list 1.1886. Ord: 15.2.1886. K: 1886. L: 2q.1889. Accepted: 1889.
Budget 1887. *Défense mobile* at Toulon to 1894, Bizerte 1895-97, Algiers 1898. Reboilered 1889, hull modified 1891. Towed back to Toulon 6.1898 by *Condor*. Struck 22.11.1898, hull for sale at Toulon 1898-1899.

*Torpilleur nº 123* Schneider, Chalon-sur-Saône.
On list 1.1886. Ord: 15.2.1886. K: 1886. L: 3q.1889. Accepted: 1889.
Budget 1887. *Défense mobile* at Toulon 1889-98, Corsica 1898-1901, and Toulon 1901. Struck 25.7.1903, for sale at Toulon 1903-1905. Target 1904, Sold 16.6.1905 at Toulon to BU.

*Torpilleur nº 124* Schneider, Chalon-sur-Saône.
On list 1.1886. Ord: 15.2.1886. K: 1886. L: 3q.1889. Accepted: 1890.
Budget 1887. *Défense mobile* at Toulon 1890-97, Corsica 1897-1901. Collided 17.9.1901 with *Torpilleur no 139* during a night exercise south of the Îles Sanguinaires near Ajaccio, Corsica, and sank under tow in 80 metres of water. Struck 23.10.1901.

*Torpilleur nº 125* Schneider, Chalon-sur-Saône.
On list 1.1886. Ord: 15.2.1886. K: 1886. L: 11.8.1889. Accepted: 1890.
Budget 1887. *Défense mobile* at Toulon c1890-1903. Struck 16.4.1903, for sale at Toulon 1903-1904.

---

**EXPERIMENTAL 35-METRE TYPE, 1886 ORDER. *TORPILLEUR Nº 150* (ex *Nº 126*).** *Torpilleur de 1re classe.* Special 35-metre torpedo boat with one torpedo tube in a narrow bow with a torpedo spar on top, two funnels abreast, and a wide stern. Designed by Terré. To *Torpilleur de 2e classe* 1.1890.

On 31 July 1885 the *Conseil des Travaux* rejected a design for a cruiser by Laurent-François-Maurice Terré, a naval constructor at Toulon who had developed his own theories on hull lines. The Council suggested he try his lines instead on a single screw vessel with dimensions like *Torpilleur nº 56* or *Torpilleur nº 58* (both torpedo launches). On 3 November 1885 the Council examined a lines plan from Terré for a 34-metre torpedo boat and asked him for a new design having the length, displacement, and armament of the 35-metre type torpedo boats recently ordered. By now the plans for the 35-metre type were being heavily criticised by naval constructors in several dockyards, particularly Toulon, and Minister Galiber on 14 November 1885 ordered Terré to proceed with the study. On 11 March 1886 the Council examined Terré's design for a 35-metre boat with his experimental lines and recommended that the vessel should be built to try the new hull lines. On 13 April 1886 Minister Aube approved Terré's latest design and ordered Toulon to build her. A drawing of this ship in the *Aide-Mémoire d'Artillerie navale* of 1890 shows a very narrow bow with two tubes above water and a torpedo spar, broadening to a very wide stern, the maximum beam being about 7m from the stern. The hull was laid down on 1 August 1886 as *Nº 126* but the designation was changed to *Nº 150* during 1887. The propulsion machinery was ordered by contract of 5 July 1886 from the builder of *Torpilleurs nos 99-104*.

The boat ran its first series of trials in July and August 1887 but made only 16.74 knots instead of the designed 19 knots. The shortfall was ascribed to the boiler not being powerful enough and to the fact that Terré's hull lines prevented the generation of bow and stern waves underway, even at high speeds. These waves wasted power but were necessary for the effective operation of a screw propeller located just below the waterline as in torpedo boats. A later assessment argued that her lines forward were too narrow while those aft were too expansive. On 17 October 1888 Louis de Bussy, the Inspecteur général du Génie maritime, recommended accepting *N° 150* despite its failure to make its contract speed because it had provided some useful lessons about the effects on seakeeping of the longitudinal distribution of weights that would be useful in designing all future long and narrow vessels. The commander of the *Défenses sous-marines* at Toulon, however, was less charitable, noting that because her lines resembled those of the other 35-metre boats, she had always been considered dangerous at sea despite her relatively satisfactory stability trials. After the accident to *N° 102*, a 35-metre boat, *N° 150* was decommissioned and returned to sea only very occasionally to train stokers and test special types of coal.

**Dimensions & tons:** 35.00m pp x 3.92m or 4.05m ext (vice 3.35m in the regular 35-metre type). 54.254t disp, 54.63t on trials. Draught: 2.00m aft under propeller guard.
**Machinery:** 525ihp and 19kts designed. Trials (24.8.1887) 16.74kts at 312rpm. 1 screw. Engine and boiler probably as in *Torpilleurs n°s 99-104*. 8.4t coal. Range 660nm @ 12kts.
**Torpedoes:** 2 bow tubes for 381mm torpedoes, one torpedo spar, 2 x 37mm guns (not mounted).

*Torpilleur n° 150* Toulon Dyd/F.C. Méditerranée, La Seyne.
On list 1.1887. Ord: *circa* 3.1886. K: 1.8.1886. L: 9.6.1887. Trials: 17.10.1888.
Not in budgets. Originally designated *N° 126* in 1886, re-designated *N° 150* during 1887. Struck 19.11.1895 at Toulon, annex to the school for engineers at Toulon 1895-1900. Toulon reported her in bad condition 3.7.1900, ordered 25.7.1900 to be sold by the Domaines. Sold 30.3.1901 to M. Bedotti for 410 francs.

---

**The *Défenses mobiles* expanded**
With the advent in the Ministry of Marine of Admiral Aube and the ideas of the *Jeune École*, the concept of *défenses mobiles* which dated back to the late 1870s was greatly expanded. By an order dated 26 March 1886 Aube set up a system of *centres de Défense mobile* and *points d'appui* that allowed extending torpedo boat defences along much of the coasts of France and French North Africa. In 1893 the *Centres de Défense mobile* were at Dunkerque, Cherbourg, Brest, Lorient and Rochefort in the Channel and Atlantic and at Toulon, Ajaccio and Algiers in the Mediterranean. By then 98 torpedo boats were in the North and 75 in the Mediterranean, many dispersed in small ports and inlets between the centres. The system continued to grow and only began to shrink after the departure of Camille Pelletan from the Ministry in 1905.

---

**36-METRE TYPE, 1887 & 1888 ORDERS (PROTOTYPES). *TORPILLEURS N°s 126–129*.** *Torpilleurs de 1re classe.* Normand 36-metre type torpedo boats with two torpedo tubes (on deck aft of the funnel and on the stern), one funnel, and two masts.

On 14 October 1886 Minister of Marine Aube issued specifications for a *torpilleur de haute mer* based on the *Balny* type. Normand submitted two designs, of which the first had dimensions of 40m by 3.70m and the second, which replaced the first, measured 39m by 3.90m and had a displacement of 75.8 tons and a guaranteed speed of 21 knots. On 29 March 1887 the *Conseil des travaux* rejected the designs from Normand and four other firms as not meeting the specifications and lacking in longitudinal stability. On 24 May 1887 Normand, sent to the Navy a third torpedo boat design which had dimensions of 35m by 4.05m, a displacement of 77.3 tons, and a guaranteed speed of 21 knots. In both the revised

second and the new third designs Normand placed two rotating single deck tubes for 5.75-metre torpedoes aft of the kiosk, one on top of the boiler and the other on top of the accommodations aft. He also raised the kiosk to improve vision from it, put a bridge deck on top, and replaced the two revolver cannon whose fire was impeded by the tubes with a single gun on top of the ventilation shaft at the after end of the engine. Normand explained the third design by saying he expected that the qualities at sea of the shorter and wider type would be better than the those of the longer narrower one. He expected the speeds to be the same. The Minister, now Barbey, forwarded Normand's designs to the *Conseil des Travaux* on 4 June 1887 and it examined them again on 21 June 1887. The Council selected the 35-metre design guided largely by Normand's preference for the new proportions but stated that one 37mm gun was not enough, the kiosk was too far forward, the habitability was bad, and the pointed shape of the stern did not provide enough protection against the sea. It felt Normand had shortened the design too much and recommended increasing the displacement particularly to improve the habitability. It recommended that, if the Minister intended to build such a boat, that Normand present a more complete design. On 27 July 1887 the *Conseil des travaux* recommended ordering two boats, now 36m in length, which became *N°s 126* and *127*. Into 1888 they were sometimes called *torpilleurs de haute mer* like *Balny* but they were given numbers instead of names and were always considered to be 1st class torpedo boats.

Normand reported on 6 May 1888 that he could undertake the construction of two more boats like *N°s 126* and *127*. On the next day the Machinery Commission was directed to contract with Normand for a third boat identical to *N°s 126* and *127* and on 17 May it was directed to contract for a fourth boat. The first one was to be *N° 128* and the second one *N° 129*. The contract for both was approved on 31 May 1888 as a supplement to the contract for *N°s 126* and *127*.

Normand's new boats and all later numbered boats (*numérotés*) had two rudders including one in the bow that could be retracted into the hull. Typical turning circles were 729m in diameter with the after rudder only and 253m with both rudders. *N°s 126-129* had two masts capable of carrying a few emergency sails, but sails on torpedo boats were suppressed on 17 June 1890 and later boats had a single mast. While the propulsion plants of *N°s 126-129* were of a traditional type, with compound engines and locomotive boilers, they contained many small innovations by Normand that improved their performance and reliability. Compared with the 35-metre type, their trials in mid 1889 made a sensation. However, trial results did not represent speeds in service, as French boats lost an average of three knots from their acceptance speed very soon after entering service due to scale accumulating in the boiler tubes and general wear and tear in the engines and hulls.

The only significant flaw reported in *N°s 126-129* was the use of a deck-mounted torpedo tube on the stern in place of a fixed tube in the bow. Normand had wanted to avoid overloading the bow – a key reason for the problems with the 35-metre type – but the torpedoes in the stern deck tube were rapidly thrown out of alignment and rendered unreliable by the vibrations aft from the unbalanced reciprocating engines and by the violent pitching of the boat in head seas. (A few years later both Normand, in *Chevalier*, and Yarrow figured out how to balance the moving parts of reciprocating engines, greatly reducing their vibrations.)

**Dimensions & tons:** 36.85m oa, 35.95m wl & pp x 3.92m ext/wl. 79.53t disp max. (on trials 71.99t, 73.16t, 71.0t, and 70.5t respectively). Draught: 0.80m fwd, 1.15m amidships, 2.65m aft under propeller guard. Men: 21.
**Machinery:** 900ihp designed at 320rpm and 10kg/cm² boiler pressure. Speed 21kts. Trials (*N° 129*) 21.28kts at 318.4rpm. 1 screw. 1 compound engine with 2 cylinders of 0.44m and 0.692m diameter and 0.44m stroke. 1 locomotive boiler. 12t coal. Range 1,800nm @ 10kts.
**Torpedoes:** 2 deck tubes for 381mm torpedoes (one aft of the funnel and one on the stern). **Guns:** 2 x 37mm revolving cannon (1 forward and 1 aft).

*Torpilleur nº 126* (ii) Augustin Normand, Le Havre.
On list 1.1888. Ord: 12.9.1887. K: 1887. L: 1.4.1889. Trials: 4-8.1889.
Budget 1887 (extraordinary). To the *Escadre d'évolutions* in the
    Mediterranean and the *Escadre de la Méditerranée* 11.1889-1893 for
    experimental operations, then to *Défense mobile* in Corsica 1893-94,
    Toulon for boiler overhaul, Tunisia 1900-1901, Toulon 1901-1902 to
    receive new Normand boiler, Corsica 1902-1907. Decomm. 6.1907.
    Struck 18.6.1908. Sold 10.1908 at Toulon to BU.

*Torpilleur nº 127* Augustin Normand, Le Havre.
On list 1.1888. Ord: 12.9.1887. K: 1887. L: 26.7.1889.
    Trials: 9-11.1889.
Budget 1887 (extraordinary). To the *Escadre d'évolutions* in the
    Mediterranean and the *Escadre de la Méditerranée* 11.1889-1893 for
    experimental operations, then to *Défense mobile* in Corsica 1893-99,
    Tunisia 1899-1902, Corsica 1903. Reboilered 1905 with a new
    Normand boiler, then to the 2nd Mediterranean torpedo boat flotilla
    1905-1909. Struck 15.10.1909. Offered for sale 1.8.1911 at Toulon by
    the Domaines with *Amiral Baudin, Magenta, Pascal, Milan,* and smaller
    vessels, sold to BU.

*Torpilleur nº 128* Augustin Normand, Le Havre.
On list 1.1889. Ord: 23.5.1888. K: 1888. L: 7.1.1890. Trials: 3-6.1890.
Budget 1889. To the *Division cuirassé du Nord* (later the *Escadre du Nord*)
    6.1890 for experimental operations. New boiler 10.1897, then to the
    *Défense mobile* at Saint Servan. Reboilered 1905-06 at Brest with a
    Guyot-du Temple boiler, then to the *Défense mobile* at Brest. Renamed
    *Brûlot* 5.1.1911. Annex to the school for seamen in *Calédonien* at Brest
    11.1910 to 1912. Struck 4.4.1913. Offered for sale at Brest
    16.12.1913, sold 26.1.1914.

*Torpilleur nº 129* Augustin Normand, Le Havre.
On list 1.1889. Ord: 23.5.1888. K: 1888. L: 22.3.1890.
    Trials: 11-12.1890.
Budget 1889. To the *Division cuirassé du Nord* (later the *Escadre du Nord*)
    1.1891 for experimental operations. To *Défense mobile* at Cherbourg
    1893 for trials of oil fuel in a locomotive boiler. New locomotive boiler
    3.1897, to *Défense mobile* at Saint Servan 1897-1904, then out of
    service. Struck 15.2.1909. Offered for sale 20.7.1911 at Brest by the
    Domaines with *Valmy* and others.

---

**34-METRE TYPE, 1889 ORDERS.** *TORPILLEURS Nᵒˢ 130–144.*
*Torpilleurs de 2ᵉ classe.* Normand 34-metre torpedo boats with one torpedo
tube on the stern, one torpedo spar forward, one funnel, and one mast.
This type was called *ventre-à-terre* (literally belly on the ground) because
they were so low on the water.

In 1888 the Forges et Chantiers de la Méditerranée at Le Havre built three
copies of the French 35-metre torpedo boats for Romania which became
their *Naluca, Smeul,* and *Sborul.* The company provided information on
these boats to the Ministry and Minister Krantz gave it an oral invitation
to prepare a proposal for a *torpilleur garde-côtes* for the French navy. The
Minister wanted to introduce two major new technologies – triple expansion engines and water tube boilers. The locomotive boiler was well suited
to torpedo boats because it was long and low and easy to handle, but it
reached its limit at 10kg/cm² boiler pressure and higher pressures were
needed to operate triple expansion engines and retain a speed advantage
over larger warships. On 30 October 1888 the Minister sent written specifications similar to those it had given to FCM Le Havre to four other
firms, Normand, Creusot, A.C. Loire, and C.A. Gironde. He specified a
galvanized steel hull, a triple expansion engine, two rotating torpedo tubes
on deck for 5.75-metre torpedoes plus a torpedo spar forward, two 37mm
QF guns with shields, a crew of 18 men, a normal coal supply for 35 hours
at 12 knots and one hour at 20 knots, one searchlight, and one signal mast
without sails.

On 23 November 1888 the *Conseil des Travaux* examined the FCM Le
Havre proposal for a *torpilleur garde-côtes*. (The term *torpilleur garde-côtes*
used consistently by the *Conseil des Travaux* for these boats suggests they
were seen as different from the *torpilleurs* including *Nᵒ 126* examined by
the Council in June 1887 and the *torpilleurs de haute mer* examined in
March 1887.) The Council did not comment on the specifications because
Minister Krantz had not asked it to and simply concluded that the design
generally met them. On 18 December 1888 the Council examined designs
from Normand, A.C. Loire and C.A. Gironde responding to the same specifications. The four firms all offered triple expansion engines, a maximum
of 20 knots, and two 37mm guns on the sides amidships, with the following additional characteristics:

FCM Le Havre. 41.25m pp x 3.45m max beam, displ. 62.738t full load.,
    2 tubes on a twin mount amidships, one modified torpedo boat boiler.

C.A. Gironde. 41.00m pp x 3.90m max beam, displ. 65.948t full load,
    2 single tubes amidships and aft, one torpedo boat boiler.

A.C. Loire. 40.90m pp x 3.50m max beam, displ. 61.575t full load,
    2 single tubes amidships and aft., one Oriolle boiler.

Normand: 33.00m pp x 3.50m max beam, displ. 50.700t full load, 2 tubes
    on a twin mount aft, one Du Temple boiler.

The Council noted that all four designs fulfilled the programme but that
Normand's did so with the smallest and thus least expensive design. The
Council lost little time in selecting it. The difference in size owed a lot to
the Du Temple boiler, which was 4 tons lighter and saved overall 17 tons
of displacement. However, its top and the roof over it rose above the deck,
preventing the placement of the twin mount for 5.75-metre torpedoes
amidships. (It would have been possible with the 5-metre torpedoes then
in development.) The Council also recommended lengthening the hull to
34m and adding two tons to give a stronger hull. Normand changed the
armament to a single deck tube on the stern and a torpedo spar on the bow.

They were ordered as *Torpilleurs de 1ʳᵉ classe* but were shown as
*Torpilleurs de 2ᵉ classe* when they first appeared in the fleet list in January
1890. The orders for the 15 torpedo boats in the 1890 budget were distributed among four builders, all using Normand's plans for the hulls. The
extraordinary 1890 budget (law of 22 November 1889) was to have
included another thirty of this 34-metre type, but money ran out after 21
of the larger 36m type were charged to it instead (*Nᵒˢ 147-49* and *152-69*).

**Dimensions & tons:** 34.00m pp x 3.50m ext. 53.09t disp. Draught:
    0.60m fwd, 0.90m amidships, 2.14m aft under propeller guard.
    Men: 18.
**Machinery:** 720ihp designed at 13kg/cm² boiler pressure. Speed 20kts.
    1 screw.
**Engines:** 1 triple expansion with 3 cylinders as follows
    Normand boats. 0.33m, 0.47m, and 0.64m diameter and 0.3/m
        stroke.
    A.C. Loire boats: 0.315m, 0.465m, and 0.65m diameter and 0.38m
        stroke.
    Schneider & Gironde boats: 0.33m, 0.47m, and 0.64m diameter and
        0.37m stroke.
**Boilers:** 1 Du Temple water tube boiler (5 folds)
**Trials** (best): (*Nᵒ 135*) 21.39kts at 328rpm.
**Torpedoes:** 1 deck tube for 381mm torpedoes aft, 1 torpedo spar for-
    ward. In 1900 the torpedo spar was removed and a second tube was
    added to the deck mount aft. **Guns:** 2 x 37m/20 M1885 QF (light).

*Torpilleur nº 130* Augustin Normand, Le Havre.
On list 1.1890. Ord: 23.1.1889. K: 1889. L: 9.6.1890. Trials: 8.1890.
Budget 1890. *Défense mobile* at Toulon 1891, to Brest for new boiler
    1903. Renamed *Grille* 1910. Annex to the school for engineers and
    stokers at Brest 1910-12. Reserved as torpedo boat target 1913. Struck
    29.8.1916. Sold at Brest 23.9.1920.

*Torpilleur n⁰ 131* Augustin Normand, Le Havre.
On list 1.1890. Ord: 23.1.1889. K: 1889. L: 21.8.1890. Trials: 9.1890.
Budget 1890. *Défense mobile* at Toulon 1891, Brest 12.1909. Renamed
    *Sifflet* 12.1909. Annex to the school for engineers and stokers at Brest
    1910-12. Reserved as torpedo boat target 1913. Struck 29.8.1916.
    Sold at Brest 23.9.1920.

*Torpilleur n⁰ 132* Augustin Normand, Le Havre.
On list 1.1890. Ord: 23.1.1889. K: 1889. L: 30.8.1890. Trials: 2.1891.
Budget 1890. *Défense mobile* at Toulon 1891, Algiers 1892-95, then to
    *Défense mobile* and in reserve at Toulon. Struck 20.2.1911. Offered for
    sale 1.8.1911 at Toulon by the Domaines with *Amiral Baudin*,
    *Magenta*, *Pascal*, *Milan*, and smaller vessels including torpedo boats

*Torpilleur n⁰ 133* Augustin Normand, Le Havre.
On list 1.1890. Ord: 23.1.1889. K: 1889. L: 28.12.1890. Trials: 1.1891.
Budget 1890. *Défense mobile* at Toulon 1891, Bizerte 1893, then Algeria.
    Sunk 11.1897 in collision with *Doudart de Lagree* off Cap Matifou in
    Algeria. Struck 1.1.1898.

*Torpilleur n⁰ 134* Augustin Normand, Le Havre.
On list 1.1890. Ord: 23.1.1889. K: 1889. L: 12.2.1891. Trials: 3.1891.
Budget 1890. *Défense mobile* at Toulon 1891, then various Mediterranean

---

Crewmen posing on the 34-metre 2nd class torpedo boat *Torpilleur n⁰ 143* during
the 1890s. A man is in the commander's position in the kiosk above and behind
the helmsman's position. In the left foreground is the after end of the torpedo spar
and its track on the deck. *(NHHC from ONI, NH-64376)*

assignments. Struck 12.8.1907. Sunk 1907 as target by the seagoing
school for gunnery practice in *Pothuau*.

*Torpilleur n⁰ 135* Augustin Normand, Le Havre.
On list 1.1890. Ord: 23.1.1889. K: 1889. L: 31.3.1891. Trials: 4.1891.
Budget 1890. *Défense mobile* at Toulon 1891, Corsica 1893, grounded
    and sunk near Calvi 1895, raised and repaired at Toulon. Renamed
    *Grenade* 1910. Annex to the school for gunnery at Toulon 1910-12.
    Struck 26.3.1912, for sale 1912-1913, target vessel at Toulon 1913-
    1914, back in service as annex to the school for torpedoes at Toulon
    1914-1920, for sale at Toulon 1920, sold 1921 at Toulon to BU.

*Torpilleur n⁰ 136* A.C. Loire (ex Claparède), Saint Denis.
On list 1.1890. Ord: 13.2.1889. K: 1889. L: 22.4.1890. Trials: 8.1890-
    2.1891.
Budget 1890. *Défense mobile* or in reserve at Brest (1891), Dunkirk
    (1899), and Brest (1903). Struck 10.8.1908, for sale at Brest 1908-
    1909.

*Torpilleur n⁰ 137* A.C. Loire (ex Claparède), Saint Denis.
On list 1.1890. Ord: 13.2.1889. K: 1889. L: 17.5.1890. Trials: 12.1890-
    2.1891.
Budget 1890. *Défense mobile* or in reserve at Brest. Reboilered 1900-01.
    Struck 24.4.1906.

*Torpilleur n⁰ 138* A.C. Loire (ex Claparède), Saint Denis.
On list 1.1890. Ord: 13.2.1889. K: 1889. L: 1890. Trials: 9.1890-
    1.1891.
Budget 1890. *Défense mobile* or in reserve at Brest. Reboilered three

times, in 1897 (Du Temple with 4 folds), 1898 (Du Temple with 2 folds), and 1905. Struck 11.6.1908, retained at Brest as gunnery target 1908-1909, for sale 1909-1910.

*Torpilleur n° 139* Schneider, Chalon-sur-Saône.
On list 1.1890. Ord: 13.2.1889. K: 1889. L: 1890. Trials: 1891-92.
Budget 1890. *Défense mobile* in Algeria 1893-95, then in *Défense mobile* or in reserve at Toulon. Condemned 10.1906 and for sale at Toulon. Struck 27.4.1907, probably after being expended as a target by the seagoing school for gunnery practice in *Pothuau*.

*Torpilleur n° 140* Schneider, Chalon-sur-Saône.
On list 1.1890. Ord: 13.2.1889. K: 1889. L: 1890. Trials: 7.1891.
Budget 1890. *Défense mobile* in Algeria 1893-95, then in *Défense mobile* or in reserve at Toulon. Back to *Défense mobile* in Algeria and Tunisia and in 3.1907 replaced *N° 62* as escort for submarines in the 1st Flotilla of Submarines in the Mediterranean. Renamed *Périscope* 11.1910. Annex to the submarine station at Toulon 1910-12. Struck 27.12.1912 (as *Périscope*). Sold 1915 at Toulon to BU.

*Torpilleur n° 141* Schneider, Chalon-sur-Saône.
On list 1.1890. Ord: 13.2.1889. K: 1889. L: 1890. Trials: 1891-92.
Budget 1890. *Défense mobile* in Algeria 1893-95, reserve at Toulon, and *Défense mobile* at Toulon 1903. Replaced *Torpilleur n° 103* in 10.1907 at the school for torpedo boat engineers. Struck 1.3.1909, for sale at Toulon 1909-1912, target vessel 1912-1913, for sale 1913-1914. Sold 3.1914 at Toulon to BU.

*Torpilleur n° 142* C.A. Gironde, Bordeaux-Lormont/Schneider, Creusot.
On list 1.1890. Ord: 13.2.1889. K: 1889. L: 6.9.1890. Trials: 6.1891.
Budget 1890. *Défense mobile* in Tunisia to 1897. Reboilered 1898-99 at Toulon with a Du Temple boiler with 2 folds and remained stationed there. Struck 20.5.1911. Offered for sale 1.8.1911 at Toulon by the Domaines with *Amiral Baudin, Magenta, Pascal, Milan,* and smaller vessels.

*Torpilleur n° 143* C.A. Gironde, Bordeaux-Lormont/Schneider, Creusot.
On list 1.1890. Ord: 13.2.1889. K: 1889. L: 16.10.1890. Trials: 1891.
Budget 1890. *Défense mobile* at Algiers 1892, Corsica 1893, and then Toulon. Renamed *Siagne* 11.1910. Annex to the school for torpedomen at Toulon 1910-12. Struck 4.7.1912, retained as target 1912-1914.

*Torpilleur n° 144* C.A. Gironde, Bordeaux-Lormont/Schneider, Creusot.
On list 1.1890. Ord: 13.2.1889. K: 1889. L: 28.11.1890. Trials: 11.1891.
Budget 1890. *Défense mobile* at Toulon 1892. Used in 8.1892 for trials of oil firing. *Défense mobile* in Algeria 1895-98, then at Toulon. Renamed *Argens* 11.1910. Annex to the school for torpedomen at Toulon 1910-12, on aviation service 1912-1913. Off main list 1913 and target vessel at Toulon 1913 1914. Struck 21.5.1914. For sale 1920.

---

## 36-METRE TYPE, 1890 TRANCHE (TYPE 126 MODIFIÉ).
*TORPILLEURS Nos 145–149* and *152–171. Torpilleurs de 1re classe.* Normand 36-metre type torpedo boats with two torpedo tubes (in the bow and on the stern), one funnel, and one mast.

The extraordinary 1890 budget (law of 22 November 1889) included 30 *torpilleurs garde-côtes* of 53 tons like *N° 130*. However, Minister Krantz and the Conseil Supérieur almost immediately increased their size to 79.5 tons after the trial results of *Nos 126* and *127* showed the excellence of the 36-metre design. The Navy decided to repeat that design for the 1890 boats except for adopting triple expansion engines and water tube boilers and restoring the bow torpedo tube. It notified Normand of this decision on 19 October 1889 and Normand's design was examined by the *Conseil des travaux* on 21 January 1890 with minor changes suggested. On the same

date the Machinery Commission was directed to prepare contracts for 22 boats of this type designated '126 lightly modified'. The extraordinary portion of the 1890 budget was used to fund 21 of the boats (the budget could not fund all 30 of the planned boats after the size increase) and the budget for 1891 included two unnumbered units (type *N° 126*) that became *Nos 145-146*. (Normand built these between *N° 154* and *N° 170*.) These were all contracted for in April 1890, and two more, *Nos 170-171*, were added as late additions to the 1891 budget. The single deck torpedo tube that was retained was the one at the extreme stern, producing an arrangement only encountered elsewhere among the *Défense mobile* boats in the *N° 126* and *N° 130* types. During stationary trials of *N° 153* the phenomenon of cavitation was observed for the first time.

The orders were distributed among five builders, all using Normand's hull plans but each responsible for selecting and supplying engines and boilers that would produce trial results of 1,000ihp and 21 knots with coal consumption that would permit steaming 1,800 nautical miles at 10 knots with a maximum of 10.5 tons of coal. This led to a lot of variety in the machinery of the group. *Nos 155-157* were ordered from the Chantiers et Ateliers de la Gironde at Bordeaux and *Nos 158-160* were ordered from the Anciens Établissements Cail at Paris, but Minister Barbey approved an arrangement under which all six hulls would be built at Bordeaux and all of the engines by Cail. These were to have had Charles et Babillot boilers, but after the accident involving this type of boiler in the seagoing torpedo boat *Sarrazin* this was changed to a Du Temple boiler, considerably delaying delivery of these six boats. (Trials of the Charles et Babillot boilers already installed in *N° 158* also produced serious problems.) All six ran acceptance trials at Rochefort. The first three then went to Toulon while the last three went to Brest. *Nos 161-163*, built at Saint Denis, were initially rejected because of very high fuel consumption and the jets of flame ejected from their funnels at high speed, both indicative of inefficient combustion in the boilers; their trials ultimately lasted around 20 months each. *Nos 167-169*, built by Schneider, also experienced lengthy trials. These and *Nos 164-166* had two boilers and two funnels as built.

**Dimensions & tons:** 37.80m oa, 35.94m pp x 4.00m ext, 3.90m wl. 75-79.5t disp (82.15t full load). Draught: 0.88m fwd, 1.15m amidships, 2.58m aft under propeller guard. Men: 22-23.
**Machinery:** 1,000ihp designed at 12kg/cm² boiler pressure. Speed 21kts. 1 screw. 10.5t coal. Range 1,800nm @ 10kts (only about 1,200nm @ 10kts in *Nos 155-160* because of high fuel consumption).
*Engines*: 1 triple expansion with 3 cylinders as follows
    Normand boats: 0.41m, 0.58m, and 0.84m diameter and 0.46m stroke.
    Gironde/Cail boats: 0.41m, 0.59m, and 0.82m diameter and 0.44m stroke.
    A.C. Loire boats: 0.385m, 0.55m, and 0.80m diameter and 0.44m stroke.
    FCM Le Havre boats: 0.38m, 0.56m, and 0.82m diameter and 0.44m stroke.
    Schneider boats: 0.42m, 0.61m, and 0.85m diameter and 0.44m stroke.
*Boilers* (all tubular):
    Normand boats: 1 Du Temple (4 folds) in *Nos 145-146*, 1 Du Temple (2 folds) in *Nos 147, 154,* and *170-171*, 1 Normand direct flame in *Nos 148-149, 152-153*.
    Gironde/Cail boats: Originally 1 Charles et Babillot, changed to 1 Du Temple (3 folds) during construction.
    A.C. Loire boats: 2 Oriolle (2 funnels)
    FCM Le Havre boats: 2 Thornycroft (2 funnels)
    Schneider boats: 2 De Dion-Bouton-Trépardoux (2 funnels)
*Trials* (best):
    Normand boats: (*N° 149*) 24.51kts at 339.20rpm.
    Gironde/Cail boats: (*N° 160*) 22.20kts at 307.38rpm.
    A.C. Loire boats: (*N° 162*) 21.81kts at 315.9rpm.

FCM Le Havre boats: (*N⁰ 164*) 21.77kts at 338.25rpm.
Schneider boats: (*N⁰ 167*) 21.04kts at 327.79rpm.
**Torpedoes:** 2 tubes for 381mm M1887 torpedoes (1 in the bow, 1 on deck aft). **Guns:** 2 x 37mm/20 M1885 QF (on sides amidships).

*Torpilleur n⁰ 145* Augustin Normand, Le Havre.
On list 1.1891. Ord: 2.4.1890. K: 1890. L: 14.3.1893. Trials: 6-7.1893.
Budget 1891. *Défense mobile* at Cherbourg 1893, Brest 1893-98, Saint Servan 1898-1900, then Cherbourg. Reboilered 1897 and 1905. Struck 5.11.1909, for sale at Cherbourg 1909-1910, torpedo target at Dunkirk 1910-1914. Sunk during practice firing 1914.

*Torpilleur n⁰ 146* Augustin Normand, Le Havre.
On list 1.1891. Ord: 2.4.1890. K: 1890. L: 15.5.1893. Trials: 6-7.1893.
Budget 1891. To Cherbourg c1893, also at Dunkirk. Struck 19.10.1908, retained at Cherbourg as gunnery target 1908-1909, for sale 1909-1911.

*Torpilleur n⁰ 147* Augustin Normand, Le Havre.
On list 1.1891. Ord: 2.4.1890. K: 1890. L: 3.10.1891. Trials: 9-12.1891.
Budget 1890 (extraordinary). To Cherbourg c1891. Original boiler replaced with 2 Guyot-du Temple boilers 1904. *Défense mobile* at Cherbourg and 1st and 2nd Channel torpedo boat flotillas 1905-06. Struck 19.10.1908, retained at Cherbourg as gunnery target 1908-1909, for sale 1909-1911.

*Torpilleur n⁰ 148* Augustin Normand, Le Havre.

Two 1st class torpedo boats, probably the 36-metre *Torpilleur n⁰ 148* in the foreground and the 37-metre *Torpilleur n⁰ 223* behind her, at the torpedo boat station at Tréguier near Brest. *Torpilleur n⁰ 148* was refitted with two boilers and two funnels in 1906. *(Postcard by Villard, Quimper)*

On list 1.1891. Ord: 2.4.1890. K: 1890. L: 17.12.1891. Trials: 2-3.1892.
Budget 1890 (extraordinary). To Cherbourg c1892, also at Dunkirk. 2nd Channel torpedo boat flotilla 1905-06. Original Normand boiler replaced with 2 Guyot-du Temple boilers in 1906. Struck 3.11.1910. Sold 1911 at Cherbourg to BU.

*Torpilleur n⁰ 149* Augustin Normand, Le Havre.
On list 1.1891. Ord: 2.4.1890. K: 1890. L: 15.3.1892. Trials: 5.1892.
Budget 1890 (extraordinary). To Cherbourg c1892. *Défense mobile* at Cherbourg and Dunkirk, 1st and 2nd Channel torpedo boat flotillas 1905-06. New boilers 1905 and 1909. Struck 23.11.1911, for sale at Cherbourg 1911-1912, target vessel at Dunkirk 1912-1914, for sale at Cherbourg 1920-1922. Sold 1922 at Cherbourg to BU.

(*Torpilleur n⁰ 150.* Originally designated *Torpilleur n⁰ 126*, listed after *Torpilleur n⁰ 125*.)
(*Torpilleur n⁰ 151.* See fast gunboat *Gabriel Charmes*.)

*Torpilleur n⁰ 152* Augustin Normand, Le Havre.
On list 1.1891. Ord: 2.4.1890. K: 1890. L: 24.6.1892. Trials: 4-9.1892.
Budget 1890 (extraordinary). To Cherbourg c1892, *Défense mobile* at Brest, then Dunkirk. 2nd Channel torpedo boat flotilla 1906. Original boiler replaced with 2 Normand boilers 1905. Struck 23.11.1911, for sale at Brest 1911-1912, retained at Brest for conversion to torpedo target 1912-1914, for sale 1920-1922, BU 1922 at Brest.

*Torpilleur n⁰ 153* Augustin Normand, Le Havre.
On list 1.1891. Ord: 2.4.1890. K: 1890. L: 3.2.1893. Trials: 3-4.1893.
Budget 1890 (extraordinary). To Cherbourg c1893 also at Dunkirk. Original boiler replaced with 2 Guyot-du Temple boilers 1906. School for stoking at Cherbourg 1909-10. Struck 23.11.1911, for sale at Cherbourg 1911-1912.

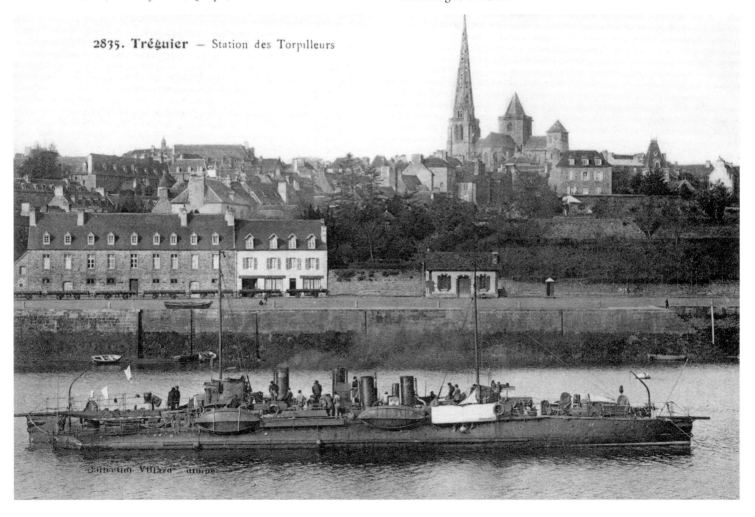

2835. Tréguier — Station des Torpilleurs

*Torpilleur nº 154* Augustin Normand, Le Havre.

On list 1.1891. Ord: 2.4.1890. K: 1890. L: 4.11.1892. Trials: 11.1892-4.1893.

Budget 1890 (extraordinary). *Défense mobile* at Cherbourg twice, also at Dunkirk twice, and finally laid up at Brest. Original boiler replaced with two 1904-06. Struck 6.12.1912, hulk at Brest 1912-1913, BU 1913 at Brest.

*Torpilleur nº 155* C.A. Gironde, Bordeaux-Lormont/Anc. Ets. Cail, Paris-Grenelle.

On list 1.1891. Ord: 9.4.1890. K: 1890. L: 1.2.1892. Trials: 7.1895-1.1896.

Budget 1890 (extraordinary). *Défense mobile* at Toulon c1896, then Bizerte 1897-1904. New boiler at Toulon 1902. 5th Mediterranean torpedo boat flotilla at Oran 1906-08. Struck 9.3.1910, torpedo target at Oran 1910-1914, sold 1914 to BU.

*Torpilleur nº 156* C.A. Gironde, Bordeaux-Lormont/Anc. Ets. Cail, Paris-Grenelle.

On list 1.1891. Ord: 9.4.1890. K: 1890. L: 1.1892. Trials: 11.1895-1.1896.

Budget 1890 (extraordinary). *Défense mobile* at Toulon 1896-98, Bizerte 1898-1909. Struck 24.3.1910, for sale in Tunisia 1910-1911.

*Torpilleur nº 157* C.A. Gironde, Bordeaux-Lormont/Anc. Ets. Cail, Paris-Grenelle.

On list 1.1891. Ord: 9.4.1890. K: 1890. L: 1.1892. Trials: 2.1896.

Budget 1890 (extraordinary). *Défense mobile* at Toulon 1896-98, Bizerte 1898-1904, then 4th Mediterranean torpedo boat flotilla at Bizerte. Struck 9.3.1910, for sale at Toulon 1910-1911. Offered for sale 1.8.1911 at Toulon by the Domaines with *Amiral Baudin, Magenta, Pascal, Milan*, and smaller vessels.

*Torpilleur nº 158* C.A. Gironde, Bordeaux-Lormont/Anc. Ets. Cail, Paris-Grenelle.

On list 1.1891. Ord: 9.4.1890. K: 1890. L: 14.4.1892. Trials: 8.1895-1.1896.

Budget 1890 (extraordinary). To Brest, in reserve there 1901, to Cherbourg 1907. School for stoking 1908. Struck 3.8.1910, torpedo target at Cherbourg 1910-1914, for sale 1920-1922. Sold 1922 at Cherbourg to BU.

*Torpilleur nº 159* C.A. Gironde, Bordeaux-Lormont/Anc. Ets. Cail, Paris-Grenelle.

On list 1.1891. Ord: 9.4.1890. K: 1890. L: 2q.1892. Trials: 1.1896.

Budget 1890 (extraordinary). *Défense mobile* at Brest, from 1905 1st Atlantic (*Océan*) torpedo boat flotilla. Struck 5.12.1908. Sold 8.1910 at Brest to BU.

*Torpilleur nº 160* C.A. Gironde, Bordeaux-Lormont/Anc. Ets. Cail, Paris-Grenelle.

On list 1.1891. Ord: 9.4.1890. K: 1890. L: 1892. Trials: 3-4.1896.

Budget 1890 (extraordinary). *Défense mobile* at Rochefort and Brest. Struck 10.8.1908. Sold 1909 at Cherbourg to BU.

*Torpilleur nº 161* A.C. Loire (ex Claparède), Saint Denis.

On list 1.1891. Ord: 16.4.1890. K: 1890. L: 1q.1891. Trials: 11.1891-5.1893.

Budget 1890 (extraordinary). *Défense mobile* at Dunkirk 1894-96, Cherbourg 1896-99, Brest from 1899, then Cherbourg. Original boilers replaced with two Guyot-du Temple boilers. School for stoking 4.1910 for the 1st Atlantic torpedo boat flotilla. Struck 23.11.1911, for sale at Brest 1911-1912.

*Torpilleur nº 162* A.C. Loire (ex Claparède), Saint Denis.

On list 1.1891. Ord: 16.4.1890. K: 1890. L: 13.6.1891. Trials: 7.1892-5.1893.

The 36-metre 1st class torpedo boat *Torpilleur nº 158* returning into the basins at Dunkirk. Her two torpedo tubes are in the bow and on the extreme stern. *(Postcard by C.A.R.)*

Budget 1890 (extraordinary). *Défense mobile* at Cherbourg and Brest to 1904. Original boilers replaced with two Guyot-du Temple boilers 1904. 2nd Atlantic torpedo boat flotilla 1906-10. Struck 23.11.1911, for sale at Lorient 1911-1912.

*Torpilleur nº 163* A.C. Loire (ex Claparède), Saint Denis.

On list 1.1891. Ord: 16.4.1890. K: 1890. L: 10.7.1891. Trials: 7.1892-5.1893.

Budget 1890 (extraordinary). *Défense mobile* at Cherbourg, Dunkirk and Lorient to 1902. Original boilers replaced with Guyot-du Temple boilers 1902. 3rd Atlantic torpedo boat flotilla at Rochefort 1903-07, then in reserve at Rochefort. Struck 4.4.1913. Sold 1913 at Rochefort to BU.

*Torpilleur nº 164* F.C. Méditerranée, Le Havre-Graville.

On list 1.1891. Ord: 9.4.1890. K: 1890. L: 8.9.1891. Trials: 4-5.1892.

Budget 1890 (extraordinary). Career at Cherbourg. Original boilers replaced 1901 with Du Temple boilers. School ship for local pilots at Cherbourg, then school for stoking for the 1st Channel torpedo boat flotilla at Cherbourg. Struck 15.2.1909. Sold 1909 at Cherbourg to BU.

*Torpilleur nº 165* F.C. Méditerranée, Le Havre-Graville.

On list 1.1891. Ord: 9.4.1890. K: 1890. L: 30.11.1891. Trials: 4-6.1892.

Budget 1890 (extraordinary). *Défense mobile* at Lorient. Original boilers replaced with Normand boilers 1902. School for piloting at Lorient 1904, 3rd Atlantic torpedo boat flotilla at Rochefort 1905-07, then in reserve at Rochefort. Struck 24.3.1910. Offered for sale 15.9.1910 at Rochefort to BU.

*Torpilleur nº 166* F.C. Méditerranée, Le Havre-Graville.

On list 1.1891. Ord: 9.4.1890. K: 1890. L: 5.2.1892. Trials: 4-7.1892.

Budget 1890 (extraordinary). 1st Channel torpedo boat flotilla at Cherbourg to 1902, then the 2nd at Dunkirk. Original boilers replaced 1901 with Guyot-du Temple boilers. 1st Atlantic torpedo boat flotilla at Brest. Struck 9.3.1910. Sold 2.1911 at Cherbourg to BU.

*Torpilleur nº 167* Schneider, Chalon-sur-Saône.

On list 1.1891. Ord: 22.4.1890. K: 1890. L: 8.12.1891. Trials: 7.1892-3.1893.

Budget 1890 (extraordinary). *Défense mobile* in Tunisia, then Toulon. Original boilers replaced 1901-02 by a direct flame Du Temple boiler (3 folds) rated at 14kg/cm² boiler pressure. 5th Mediterranean torpedo boat flotilla at Oran, then annex to the fishery protection torpedo boat *Flibustier* at Bizerte 1902-08. Struck 15.10.1909, for sale in in Algeria 1909-1910. Sold 10.1910 at Oran to BU.

*Torpilleur nº 168* Schneider, Chalon-sur-Saône.
On list 1.1891. Ord: 22.4.1890. K: 1890. L: 1q.1892. Trials: 7.1892-5.1894.
Budget 1890 (extraordinary). *Défense mobile* at Toulon 1894-1901. Hard aground at Le Brusq 3.1897, salvaged. Original boilers replaced 1901-03 by a direct flame Du Temple boiler (3 folds) rated at 14kg/cm$^2$ boiler pressure. 3$^{rd}$ Mediterranean torpedo boat flotilla 1903-07, then briefly to the 1$^{st}$ flotilla at Toulon. Retired 3.10.1908, retained as gunnery target at Toulon 1908-1909, for sale 1909-1910, sold 1911 at Toulon to BU.

*Torpilleur nº 169* Schneider, Chalon-sur-Saône.
On list 1.1891. Ord: 22.4.1890. K: 1890. L: 1892. Trials: 7.1892-1894.
Budget 1890 (extraordinary). *Défense mobile* in Corsica 1894-99. Original boilers replaced 1900-01 by a direct flame Du Temple boiler (3 folds) rated at 14kg/cm$^2$ boiler pressure. *Défense mobile* in Tunisia 1901, then 3$^{rd}$ Mediterranean torpedo boat flotilla. Struck 18.6.1908, retained at Toulon as gunnery target 1908-1909, for sale 1909-1911. Offered for

The 36-metre 1$^{st}$ class torpedo boat *Torpilleur nº 169* and other torpedo boats at the torpedo boat station in Ponty Bay at Bizerte. The many differences in details between boats of the same or similar classes built by different builders are evident in this view. *(Postcard by ND)*

sale 1.8.1911 at Toulon by the Domaines with *Amiral Baudin, Magenta, Pascal, Milan*, and smaller vessels, sold 1911 to BU.

*Torpilleur nº 170* Augustin Normand, Le Havre.
On list 1.1891. Ord: 26.11.1890. K: 1890. L: 28.8.1893. Trials: 12.1893-1.1894.
Budget 1891 (late addition). *Défense mobile* at Brest and in reserve there to 1903. Boiler replaced with one return-flame Du Temple boiler. 2$^{nd}$ Channel torpedo boat flotilla 1904-07, then 1$^{st}$ Atlantic torpedo boat flotilla 1907-11. Struck 4.4.1913, retained at Brest for conversion to torpedo target 1913-1914. Engine removed and reused with that of *Nº 197* in anti-submarine gunboat *Agile* (ordered 2.1916). For sale 1920-1922, BU 1922 at Brest.

*Torpilleur nº 171* Augustin Normand, Le Havre.
On list 1.1891. Ord: 26.11.1890. K: 1890. L: 26.9.1893. Trials: 12.1893-2.1894.
Budget 1891 (late addition). Shifted between the 1$^{st}$ Channel torpedo boat flotilla at Cherbourg and the 2$^{nd}$ flotilla at Dunkirk 1894-1911. Struck 26.3.1912, target vessel at Cherbourg 1912-1914. Sunk 3.1914 during firing practice.

———————

**36-METRE TYPE, 1891 TRANCHE. *TORPILLEURS Nos 172–181*.** *Torpilleurs de 1re classe.* Normand 36-metre type torpedo boats with two torpedo tubes (in the bow and on deck amidships), one funnel, and one mast.

The 1891 boats were as *Nº 145* except that they had their deck torpedo tube amidships instead of on the stern. The Director of Naval Construction proposed this change to Minister Barbey on 20 September 1891 to minimise the effects of vibration on torpedo alignment based on a recommendation of 14 September 1891 from the *Service des Défenses sous-marines*. In the 1891 group the designed power was also increased from 1,000ihp to 1,350ihp.

**Dimensions & tons:** as *Nº 145*. Men: 23.
**Machinery:** 1,350ihp designed at 14kg/cm² boiler pressure. Speed 22kts. 1 screw.
*Engines*: 1 triple expansion with 3 cylinders as follows
    A.C. Loire boats: 0.40m, 0.55m, and 0.80m diameter and 0.44m stroke.
    FCM Le Havre boats: 0.38m, 0.56m, and 0.82m diameter and 0.44m stroke (Marshall type).
    Schneider boats: 0.425m, 0.61m, and 0.87m diameter and 0.45m stroke.
*Boilers*: 1 Du Temple (2 folds)
*Trials* (best):
    A.C. Loire boats: (*Nº 173*) 23.13kts at 337.90rpm.
    FCM Le Havre boats: (*Nº 179*) 23.78kts at 320.87rpm.
    Schneider boats: (*Nº 180*) 22.08kts.
**Torpedoes:** 2 tubes for 381mm M1887 torpedoes (1 in the bow, 1 on deck amidships). **Guns:** 2 x 37mm/20 M1885 QF (on sides amidships).

*Torpilleur nº 172* A.C. Loire, Nantes.
On list 1.1892. Ord: 4.11.1891. K: 1891. L: 22.10.1892. Trials: 2-4.1893.
Budget 1892. *Défense mobile* at Toulon 1893-1901, Tunisia 1902-04, 3rd Mediterranean torpedo boat flotilla at Bizerte 1905-08. Struck 5.11.1909, for sale in Tunisia 1909-1910, torpedo target at Bizerte 1910-1914. Sold 7.1919 at Bizerte to BU.

*Torpilleur nº 173* A.C. Loire, Nantes.
On list 1.1892. Ord: 4.11.1891. K: 1891. L: 5.11.1892. Trials: 3-5.1893.
Budget 1892. *Défense mobile* at Toulon 1894, Corsica 1894-95, reserve at Toulon 1895-99, *Défense mobile* at Toulon 1900, Bizerte 1901-02, reserve at Toulon 1902-03, *Défense mobile* at Corsica 1903-07, Toulon 1907-10. Renamed *Huveaune* 11.1910, annex to the school for torpedomen and the school for electricians at Toulon 1910-14. Engine and that of *Nº 183* removed and reused in anti-submarine gunboat *Sans Souci* (ordered 12.1915). Struck 30.10.1919. Sold 2.3.1920 at Toulon to BU.

*Torpilleur nº 174* A.C. Loire, Nantes.
On list 1.1892. Ord: 4.11.1891. K: 1891. L: 19.11.1892. Trials: 4-6.1893
Budget 1892. *Défense mobile* at Lorient 1893-95, Algeria and 4th Mediterranean torpedo boat flotilla 1895-1903. Reboilered 1904 with a Guyot-du Temple boiler. *Défense mobile* at Toulon 1904-05, 2nd Mediterranean torpedo boat flotilla at Corsica 1905-1910. Struck 23.11.1911, for sale at Toulon 1911-1912, retained as gunnery target 1912-1914. Removed from list of condemned vessels c7.1914. Sold 1919 at Toulon to BU.

*Torpilleur nº 175* A.C. Loire, Nantes.
On list 1.1892. Ord: 4.11.1891. K: 1891. L: 15.2.1893. Trials: 6.1893.
Budget 1892. *Défense mobile* at Toulon 1893-95, Algeria 1895-1903, Toulon 1903-05, 3rd Mediterranean torpedo boat flotilla at Bizerte 1905-10. Struck 15.4.1911, for sale in Tunisia 1911-1912. Sold 8.1912 at Bizerte to BU.

*Torpilleur nº 176* A.C. Loire, Nantes.
On list 1.1892. Ord: 4.11.1891. K: 1891. L: 17.2.1893. Trials: 6-8.1893.

Budget 1892. *Défense mobile* at Toulon 1893-94, Corsica 1894-95, Toulon 1896-1903. Reboilered with a Guyot-du Temple boiler. 3rd Mediterranean torpedo boat flotilla at Bizerte 1903-09. Struck 24.3.1910, for sale in Tunisia 1910-1911. Sold 8.1911 at Bizerte to BU.

*Torpilleur nº 177* F.C. Méditerranée, Le Havre-Graville.
On list 1.1892. Ord: 11.11.1891. K: 1891. L: 18.2.1893. Trials: 5-7.1893.
Budget 1892. *Défense mobile* at Toulon 1893-95, Corsica 1895-96, Tunisia 1897-1902. Reboilered 1902-03 at Toulon with an experimental Brillé boiler which proved unsuccessful in trials in 1903. Exercise division of the 2nd Mediterranean torpedo boat flotilla at Ajaccio 1904-08. Struck 15.10.1909, for sale at Toulon 1909-1910.

*Torpilleur nº 178* F.C. Méditerranée, Le Havre-Graville.
On list 1.1892. Ord: 11.11.1891. K: 1891. L: 18.4.1893. Trials: 6-7.1893.
Budget 1892. *Défense mobile* at Toulon 1893-1897, Tunisia 1898-1901. Reboilered 1902-04 at Toulon with a Guyot-du Temple boiler. 2nd Mediterranean torpedo boat flotilla at Ajaccio 1905-07, 1st flotilla at Toulon 1908-10. Renamed *Las* 11.1910. Annex to the school for torpedomen and the school for electricians at Toulon 1910-14. Engine and that of *Nº 187* removed and reused in anti-submarine gunboat *Étourdi* (ordered 12.1915). Struck 30.10.1919, target vessel at Toulon 1920. Sunk 27.11.1921 in firing practice.

*Torpilleur nº 179* F.C. Méditerranée, Le Havre-Graville.
On list 1.1892. Ord: 11.11.1891. K: 1891. L: 31.5.1893. Trials: 8.1893.
Budget 1892. Trials at Cherbourg, to Toulon 1893. Reboilered 1903 at Toulon. *Défense mobile* at Toulon 1893-1895, Algeria (Oran group) 1895-1902. Reboilered 1903 at Toulon with a Guyot-du Temple boiler. 2nd Mediterranean torpedo boat flotilla at Ajaccio 1904-08. Struck 15.10.1909, for sale at Toulon 1909-1910.

*Torpilleur nº 180* Schneider, Chalon-sur-Saône.
On list 1.1892. Ord: 25.11.1891. K: 1891. L: 14.9.1892. Trials: 2-7.1893.
Budget 1892. Penalized on trials for poor stability. *Défense mobile* at Toulon 1893-95, Algeria (Oran) 1895-1901. Reboilered 1901 at Toulon with a Du Temple boiler. 5th Mediterranean torpedo boat flotilla at Oran 1902-08, *Défense mobile* at Toulon 1908-09. Struck 4.2.1909, for sale at Toulon 1909-1911, target vessel 1911-1913, for sale 1913-1914.

*Torpilleur nº 181* Schneider, Chalon-sur-Saône.
On list 1.1892. Ord: 25.11.1891. K: 1892. L: 1893. Trials: 3.1893-2.1894.
Budget 1892. *Défense mobile* at Toulon 1894-95, Algiers 1895-98, Toulon 1898-1902. Reboilered with a Normand boiler. *Défense mobile* in Tunisia 1902-04, 4th Mediterranean torpedo boat flotilla 1904-06, *Défense mobile* at Toulon 1907. Struck 6.3.1908, for sale at Toulon 1908-1909, retained for trials 1909-1913, for sale 1913-1914.

---

**36-METRE TYPE, 1892 TRANCHE.** *TORPILLEURS Nᵒˢ 182–191* (P1-10). *Torpilleurs de 1ʳᵉ classe.*

The 36-metre boats for 1892 began as repeats of *Nº 172*. On 11 June 1892 the Machinery Commission was directed to contract for ten 1st class torpedo boats, *Nᵒˢ 182-191*, of the modified *Nº 145* type. On 16 June 1892 Normand asked for an order for some of the new torpedo boats, and on 10-11 July the commission was told to contract directly with Normand for six of them. A signed contract with Normand for *Nᵒˢ 182-187* was forwarded by the commission on 12 August 1892 and approved on 24 August 1892. On 13 October 1892 a signed contract with FCM Le Havre for *Nᵒˢ 188-191* was forwarded, it was approved on 22 October

1892. On 14 December 1892 Normand proposed to modify the bow and stern lines of *Nos 186-187*. The new lines were fuller underwater and finer at the waterline with a slightly fuller stern to keep it from dipping below the waterline. On 24 December 1892 Normand asked permission to use in *Nos 182-185* boilers identical to those that had been tried with success in *Nos 148, 149* and *152*. *Nos 186-187* were to have a new type of Du Temple boiler modified by Normand. The six Normand boats produced 1,700 to 1,710ihp on trials, while those from other builders were less successful.

**Dimensions & tons:** as *No 145*. Men: 23.
**Machinery:** 1,350ihp designed at 14kg/cm² boiler pressure. Speed 22kts. 1 screw.
*Engines*: 1 triple expansion with 3 cylinders
  Normand boats: 0.41m, 0.58m, and 0.84m diameter and 0.46m stroke.
  FCM Le Havre boats: 0.38m, 0.56m, and 0.82m diameter and 0.44m stroke (Marshall type).
*Boilers*: One Normand direct flame except *Nos 186-187*, one Du Temple-Normand.
*Trials* (best):
  Normand boats: (*No 187*) 24.67kts at 337.16rpm.
  FCM Le Havre boats: (*No 191*) 25.38kts at 354.07rpm.
**Torpedoes:** 2 tubes for 381mm M1887 torpedoes (1 in the bow, 1 on deck amidships). **Guns:** 2 x 37mm/20 M1885 QF (on sides amidships).

*Torpilleur n° 182* (P1) Augustin Normand, Le Havre.
On list 1.1893. Ord: 27.7.1892. K: 1892. L: 15.9.1894. Trials: 10-11.1894.
Budget 1893. *Défense mobile* at Brest 1894-1901, Rochefort 1901-02, 3rd Atlantic torpedo boat flotilla at Rochefort 1902-09. Struck 24.3.1910. Offered for sale 15.9.1910 at Rochefort to BU.

*Torpilleur n° 183* (P2) Augustin Normand, Le Havre.
On list 1.1893. Ord: 27.7.1892. K: 1892. L: 16.10.1893. Trials: 11.1894.
Budget 1893. *Défense mobile* at Brest 1894-1901, Rochefort and 3rd Atlantic torpedo boat flotilla there 1901-13. Reboilered 1906 with a Normand boiler. Annex to *Foudre* for aviation support duty (no new name) 7.1913 to 1914 with *Torpilleur n° 187*. Damaged 4.1914 in

collision with *No 187*, not repaired. Engine and that of *No 173* removed and reused in anti-submarine gunboat *Sans Souci* (ordered 12.1915). Struck 30.10.1919, sold at Toulon 2.3.1920.

*Torpilleur n° 184* (P3) Augustin Normand, Le Havre.
On list 1.1893. Ord: 27.7.1892. K: 1892. L: 14.12.1894. Trials: 3.1895.
Budget 1893. *Défense mobile* at Lorient 1895-1900, Rochefort and 3rd Atlantic torpedo boat flotilla there 1900-1910, *Défense mobile* at Cherbourg 1911-14. Reboilered 1907 with a Normand boiler. Struck 22.11.1913, for sale at Cherbourg 1913-1914. Converted to target 5.1914. For sale at Cherbourg 1920-1922.

*Torpilleur n° 185* (P4) Augustin Normand, Le Havre.
On list 1.1893. Ord: 27.7.1892. K: 1892. L: 1.1895. Trials: 5.1895.
Budget 1893. Trials and initial service at Cherbourg. Reboilered 1.1902 with a Normand boiler. Renamed *Gravonne* 12.4.1911. Annex to the school for torpedomen at Toulon 1911-14. Struck 30.10.1919, target vessel at Toulon 1920-1922. Struck 12.2.1923. Sold 1923 at Toulon to BU.

*Torpilleur n° 186* (P5) Augustin Normand, Le Havre.
On list 1.1893. Ord: 27.7.1892. K: 1892. L: 7.6.1895. Trials: 7.1895.
Budget 1893. *Défense mobile* at Toulon 1895-96, Tunisia 1896-99, Corsica 1900-01, Algeria 1901-04, 5th Mediterranean torpedo boat flotilla at Oran 1905-07, *Défense mobile* at Toulon 1908-09, 3rd Mediterranean torpedo boat flotilla at Bizerte 1909-11. Struck 23.11.1911, for sale in Tunisia 1911-1912.

*Torpilleur n° 187* (P6) Augustin Normand, Le Havre.
On list 1.1893. Ord: 27.7.1892. K: 1892. L: 25.8.1895. Trials: 11.1895.
Budget 1893. *Défense mobile* at Brest 1895-1900, Rochefort and 3rd Atlantic torpedo boat flotilla there 1901-1913. Reboilered 4.1910 with a Guyot-du Temple boiler. Annex to *Foudre* for aviation support duty (no new name) 7.1913 to 1914 with *Torpilleur n° 183*. Collided 4.1914 with *No 183*, repaired 1914. Engine and that of *No 178* removed and reused in anti-submarine gunboat *Étourdi* (ordered 12.1915). Struck 30.10.1919, sold at Toulon 2.3.1920.

*Torpilleur n° 188* (P7) F.C. Méditerranée, Le Havre-Graville.
On list 1.1893. Ord: 12.10.1892. K: 1892. L: 19.5.1894. Trials: 10.1894-5.1895.
Budget 1893. *Défense mobile* at Lorient 1895-1900, Rochefort and 3rd Atlantic torpedo boat flotilla there 1901-12. Reboilered with a Normand boiler 1906-07. Struck 22.11.1913, for sale at Rochefort 1913-1914.

*Torpilleur n° 189* (P8) F.C. Méditerranée, Le Havre-Graville.
On list 1.1893. Ord: 12.10.1892. K: 1892. L: 16.10.1894. Trials: 11.1894-6.1895.
Budget 1893. *Défense mobile* at Lorient 1895-1901, Rochefort and 3rd Atlantic torpedo boat flotilla there 1901-09. Reboilered 1907-08 with a Normand boiler. *Défense mobile* at Cherbourg 1901-11. Struck 20.2.1911, for sale at Cherbourg 1911-1912.

*Torpilleur n° 190* (P9) F.C. Méditerranée, Le Havre-Graville.
On list 1.1893. Ord: 12.10.1892. K: 1892. L: 19.11.1894. Trials: 12.1894-5.1895.
Budget 1893. *Défense mobile* at Toulon 1895-1897, Tunisia 1897-1900, Algeria (Oran) 1900-02, Toulon 1903 for boiler repairs and reserve. 4th Mediterranean torpedo boat flotilla at Algiers 1905-07, *Défense mobile* at Toulon 1907-09. Renamed *Cendrier* 1910. Annex to the school for engineers and stokers at Toulon 1910-14. Struck 30.10.1919, for sale at Toulon 1920-1924.

*Torpilleur n° 191* (P10) F.C. Méditerranée, Le Havre-Graville.
On list 1.1893. Ord: 12.10.1892. K: 1892. L: 2.12.1894. Trials: 4-6.1895.

The 36-metre 1st class torpedo boat *Torpilleur n° 187*. The after torpedo tube in the later 36-metre boats including this one was amidships just aft of the funnel instead of on the stern. The funnel is smaller than usual for this type, possibly because of her experimental Du Temple-Normand boiler. She and *n° 186* also had experimental hull lines in the bow and stern. *(Postcard by M.D.)*

Budget 1893. *Défense mobile* at Toulon 1895, Corsica 1896-1900, Toulon 1900 for boiler repairs, Algeria 1901, Toulon 1905-06 for boiler work, 4th Mediterranean torpedo boat flotilla at Algiers 1906-08. Grounded 6.1908 at Ras Acrata near Algiers, refloated but not repaired. Struck 24.2.1909. Sold 22.5.1909 and BU at Algiers.

---

### '36-METRE' TYPE, 1893 TRANCHE. *TORPILLEURS Nos 192–200* (P11-19). *Torpilleurs de 1re classe.*

The 1893 boats were initially repeats of *No 172* except that they were one metre longer because of the greater size of their boilers. On 13 October 1892 the Machinery Commission forwarded a signed contract with C.A. Gironde for *Nos 192-194*; it was approved on 22 October 1892. On 10 November 1892 the Machinery Commission forwarded a signed contract with Cail for *Nos 195-197*, on 17 November 1892 the commission was directed to increase from three to four (including *No 198*) the number of boats to order from Cail. The revised contract was forwarded on 24 November 1892 and approved on 1 December 1892. On 22 December 1892 C.A. Gironde asked permission to increase some dimensions of the engine and boiler in *Nos 192-194*. On 3 February 1893 Cail asked to substitute for the Du Temple boilers with a grate area of 177 sq.m. in *Nos 195-198* larger ones with a grate area of 200 sq.m. On 3 March 1893 the Machinery Commission was directed to contract for two more 1st class torpedo boats, *Nos 199-200*, a contract with Cail was approved on 22 July 1893,

Unlike the later boats of the 37-metre type which had two boilers and two funnels, these nine like most of the earlier torpedo boats had only one of each. The trials of these boats were particularly long and difficult. The six boats built by Cail at Saint Denis, at a site on the Seine across the Canal Saint Denis from the former Claparède yard, were the last built in the Paris region. Cail also built the engines, while Schneider built the boilers. The furnaces in their enlarged Du Temple boilers were too long for efficient firing by the stokers and the boats were accepted at reduced speeds with penalties. They were known in service for the thick smoke and big flares of flames from their funnels.

**Dimensions & tons:** 37.00m pp x 4.00m ext. 80.5t-82.0t disp. Draught: 1.15m fwd, 1.25m amidships, 2.60m aft under propeller guard. Men: 23.
**Machinery:** 1,350ihp designed at 15kg/cm² boiler pressure. Speed 22kts (23kts in the Cail boats). 1 screw.
*Engines:* 1 triple expansion with 3 cylinders as follows
   C.A. Gironde boats: 0.425m, 0.61m, and 0.87m diameter and 0.45m stroke (Schneider type).
   Cail boats: 0.42m, 0.62m, and 0.92m diameter and 0.45m stroke.
*Boilers:* 1 Du Temple boiler with smaller diameter tubes and long furnaces.
*Trials* (best):
   C.A. Gironde boats: (*No 192*) 23.54kts at 321.85rpm.
   Cail boats: (*No 199*) 22.60kts at 304rpm.
**Torpedoes:** 2 tubes for 381mm M1887 torpedoes (1 in bow, 1 on deck amidships). **Guns:** 2 x 37mm/20 M1885 QF (on sides amidships).

*Torpilleur no 192* (P11) C.A. Gironde, Bordeaux-Lormont/Schneider, Creusot.
On list 1.1893. Ord: 12.10.1892. K: 1892. L: 21.4.1894. Trials: 5.1894-3.1895.
Budget 1893. From Bordeaux to Rochefort 4-7.5.1894. *Défense mobile* in Algeria 1896-1908, Toulon 1909-10. Grounded 28.1.1910 on the rocks of the Île Sainte Marguerite near Cannes, not refloated. Struck 27.5.1911. Wreck sold 7.1911 to BU.

*Torpilleur no 193* (P12) C.A. Gironde, Bordeaux-Lormont/Schneider, Creusot.
On list 1.1893. Ord: 12.10.1892. K: 1892. L: 25.5.1894. Trials: 7.1894-9.1895.
Budget 1893. *Défense mobile* in Algeria (Oran) 1895-1907, Toulon 1907-

08. Original boiler replaced 1908 with two Du Temple boilers. 4th Mediterranean torpedo boat flotilla at Algiers 1909-12. To fishery protection duty 4.1912, renamed *Moulouya* and rated *garde-pêche à vapeur* at Oran. Her relief by *No 289* was planned for 6.1914 but she continued in this role during the war. Condemned 6.1919. Sold 12.1923 at Oran to BU.

*Torpilleur no 194* (P13) C.A. Gironde, Bordeaux-Lormont/Schneider, Creusot.
On list 1.1893. Ord: 12.10.1892. K: 1892. L: 18.7.1894. Trials: 3-4.1895.
Budget 1893. *Défense mobile* at Rochefort and 3rd Atlantic torpedo boat flotilla there for her entire career. School for piloting 1895-96. Reboilered 1905. Struck 28.5.1909, torpedo target at Rochefort 1909-1913, for sale 1913-1914.

*Torpilleur no 195* (P14) Anc. Ets. Cail, Saint Denis.
On list 1.1893. Ord: 23.11.1892. K: 1892. L: 24.1.1894. Accepted: 6.1898.
Budget 1893. Rejected 1894, to be replaced. *Défense mobile* at Brest 1898-1905, 2nd Atlantic torpedo boat flotilla at Lorient 1906-11. Boiler retubing started 1908 at Lorient but went badly and boat condemned. Struck 6.2.1912. Sold 11.11.1912.

*Torpilleur no 196* (P15) Anc. Ets. Cail, Saint Denis.
On list 1.1893. Ord: 23.11.1892. K: 1892. L: 11.3.1894. Accepted: 11.1897.
Budget 1893. *Défense mobile* at Lorient 1898-1900, Brest 1900-1903, Dunkirk 1903-05, Cherbourg 1905-06 for replacement of original boiler with two Guyot-du Temple boilers. 5th Mediterranean torpedo boat flotilla at Oran 1906-1911. To fishery protection duty, renamed *Chiffa* 1910 and rated *garde-pêche à vapeur* at Oran. Struck 27.12.1912 (as *Chiffa*). Sold 11.1913 at Bizerte to BU.

*Torpilleur no 197* (P16) Anc. Ets. Cail, Saint Denis.
On list 1.1893. Ord: 23.11.1892. K: 1892. L: 29.4.1894. Accepted: 2.1898.
Budget 1893. *Défense mobile* at Lorient 1898-1901, Brest 1901-03, 2nd Atlantic torpedo boat flotilla at Lorient 1903-10, Brest torpedo boats 1910-12. Original boiler replaced in 1907-08 with two Du Temple boilers. Condemned 17.7.1913, for disposal (restricted sale) 1913-1914. Engine and that of *No 170* removed and reused in anti-submarine gunboat *Agile* (ordered 2.1916). Sold at Brest 23.9.1920.

*Torpilleur no 198* (P17) Anc. Ets. Cail, Saint Denis.
On list 1.1893. Ord: 23.11.1892. K: 1892. L: 7.9.1894. Accepted: 4.1897.
Budget 1893. *Défense mobile* at Toulon and 1st Mediterranean torpedo boat flotilla 1897-1905, 3rd Mediterranean torpedo boat flotilla in Algeria 1906-08. Struck 10.8.1908. Sold at Toulon 2.12.1908.

*Torpilleur no 199* (P18) Anc. Ets. Cail, Saint Denis.
On list 1.1894. Ord: 14.6.1893. K: 1893. L: 1.12.1894. Accepted: 26.6.1898.
Budget 1893. *Défense mobile* at Cherbourg 1898, Dunkirk 1898-1900, Cherbourg 1900-04, 2nd Channel torpedo boat flotilla at Dunkirk 1905-06. Struck 6.12.1907, for sale at Cherbourg 1907-1908, retained at Cherbourg as gunnery target 1908-1909, ordered sold 24.12.1909, sold 7.2.1911.

*Torpilleur no 200* (P19) Anc. Ets. Cail, Saint Denis.
On list 1.1894. Ord: 14.6.1893. K: 1893. L: 19.3.1895. Accepted: 10.1897.
Budget 1893. *Défense mobile* at Rochefort and 3rd Atlantic torpedo boat flotilla there 1897-1912. Reboilered with one Guyot-du Temple boiler 7.1905. Struck 4.4.1913. Sold 27.10.1913 at Rochefort.

---

## 37-METRE TYPE, 1895 PROTOTYPES. *TORPILLEURS Nos 201– 205* (P20-24). *Torpilleurs de 1re classe.* Normand 37-metre type torpedo boats with two torpedo tubes (in the bow and on deck amidships), two funnels, and one mast.

The 1894 budget included five new 1st class torpedo boats of the 36-metre type, P20 to P24 and four 2nd class torpedo boats of an unspecified type, Q1 to Q4, all to be built by contract. These were all then deferred to 1895, with the result that the January 1895 fleet list contained no new torpedo boats. The original 1895 budget submission of 24 July 1894 included only P20 and P21 but a revision of 11 November 1894 restored P22 through P24. The four 2nd class boats remained deferred and were never numbered or built.

The 1st class boats in the 1895 budget were built to a new 37-metre design with two boilers and two funnels. In early 1896 the Navy asked Normand to design a torpedo boat with two boilers. The design was immediately adopted and applied to *Nos 201-205* (ex P20-24), which had been ordered in May 1895. They were completely successful, reaching 26 knots on trials. The change to two boilers was opposed by some but the navy put two boilers in all subsequent torpedo boats. In addition, when it became necessary to replace the single boilers in torpedo boats prior to *No 201*, they were often given two boilers. The funnels of these five boats were larger and more widely spaced than in *No 206* and later boats.

**Dimensions & tons:** 39.16m oa, 37.00m wl & pp x 4.13m ext, 3.92m wl. 83.7-84.25t disp. Draught: 1.15m fwd, 1.20m amidships, 2.60m aft under propeller guard. Men: 23.
**Machinery:** 1,500ihp designed at 15kg/cm² boiler pressure. Speed 24kts. Trials (*No 204*) 25.79kts at 356.75rpm (25.94kts on her best measured mile). 1 triple expansion engine with 3 cylinders of 0.39m, 0.55m, and 0.84m diameter and 0.50m stroke. 2 Normand direct flame boilers. 10.5t coal.
**Torpedoes:** 2 tubes for 381mm M1887 torpedoes (1 in bow, 1 on deck amidships). **Guns:** 2 x 37mm/20 M1885 QF (on sides amidships).

*Torpilleur no 201* (P20) Augustin Normand, Le Havre.
On list 1.1896. Ord: 22.5.1895. K: 1895. L: 4.1.1897. Trials: 3-4.1897.
Budget 1894 (delayed to 1895). *Défense mobile* at Toulon 1897-1900, the Corsica and the 2nd Mediterranean torpedo boat flotilla 1900-10. Renamed *Manomètre* 1910. Annex to the school for engineers and stokers at Toulon 1910-14. Struck 30.10.1919, target vessel at Toulon 1920-1922. Sold 1922 at Toulon to BU.

*Torpilleur no 202* (P21) Augustin Normand, Le Havre.
On list 1.1896. Ord: 22.5.1895. K: 1895. L: 20.3.1897. Trials: 4-5.1897.
Budget 1894 (delayed to 1895). *Défense mobile* in Tunisia 1897-1900, Corsica 1900-02, Toulon 1902-06, 4th Mediterranean torpedo boat flotilla at Algiers 1906-10. Struck 16.10.1912, for sale in Tunisia 1912-1913, torpedo target at Bizerte 1913-1914.

*Torpilleur no 203* (P22) Augustin Normand, Le Havre.
On list 1.1896. Ord: 22.5.1895. K: 1895. L: 2q.1897. Trials: 6.1897.
Budget 1894 (delayed, then late addition in 1895). *Défense mobile* at Rochefort 1897-1898, Toulon 1898-1900, Corsica 1901-05, 1st Mediterranean torpedo boat flotilla at Toulon 1905-10, Bizerte 1911. Struck 23.11.1911, for sale at Toulon 1911-1912, retained as gunnery target 1912-1913, for sale 1913-1914.

*Torpilleur no 204* (P23) Augustin Normand, Le Havre.
On list 1.1896. Ord: 22.5.1895. K: 1895. L: 2q.1897. Trials: 8-9.1897.
Budget 1894 (delayed, then late addition in 1895). *Défense mobile* at Brest 1897-1902, Cherbourg and 1st Channel torpedo boat flotilla from 1902. Struck 3.11.1910. Sold 7.1911 at Cherbourg to BU.

*Torpilleur no 205* (P24) Augustin Normand, Le Havre.
On list 1.1896. Ord: 22.5.1895. K: 1895. L: 2q.1897. Trials: 9-11.1897.
Budget 1894 (delayed, then late addition in 1895). *Défense mobile* at

Cherbourg 1897-98, Dunkirk 1898-1903, boilers retubed at Cherbourg, then to 1st Channel torpedo boat flotilla there 1905-09. Collided with destroyer *Catapulte* and damaged 8.1909. Struck 24.3.1910, for sale at Cherbourg 1910-1911.

---

## 37-METRE TYPE, 1896 TRANCHE. *TORPILLEURS Nos 206–211* (P25-30). *Torpilleurs de 1re classe.* Normand 37-metre type torpedo boats with two torpedo tubes (in the bow and on deck amidships), two funnels (smaller and closer together than in *No 205*), and one mast.

The 1896 budget as submitted in May 1895 included two torpedo boats for coast defence (P25 and P26, later *Nos 206-07*) to be built by contract, which were among the few ships not later deleted by the Budget Commission from that budget. *Nos 208-11* were added to the 1896 budget after it was passed.

**Dimensions & tons:** 39.16m oa, 37.00m wl & pp x 4.06m ext, 3.92m wl. 86-91t disp. Draught: 1.15m fwd, 1.20m amidships, 2.60m aft under propeller guard. Men: 23.
**Machinery:** 1,500ihp designed at 15kg/cm² boiler pressure. Speed 24kts. Trials (*No 210*) 24.12kts at 354.10rpm (24.57kts on her best measured mile). 1 screw. 1 triple expansion engine with 3 cylinders of 0.39m, 0.55m, and 0.84m diameter and 0.50m stroke. 2 Guyot-du Temple boilers. 10.5t coal.
**Torpedoes:** 2 tubes for 381mm M1887 torpedoes (1 in bow, 1 on deck amidships). **Guns:** 2 x 37mm/20 M1885 QF (on sides amidships).

*Torpilleur no 206* (P25) C.A. Gironde, Bordeaux-Lormont.
On list 1.1897. Ord: 29.7.1896. K: 1896. L: 16.8.1897. Trials: 10.1897-1.1899.
Budget 1896. *Défense mobile* at Brest 1899 and 1st Atlantic torpedo boat flotilla 1899-1906, 1st Channel torpedo boat flotilla then torpedo boats at Cherbourg 1908-1915. Retired 8.1915, torpedo target. For sale at Cherbourg 1920-1922.

*Torpilleur no 207* (P26) C.A. Gironde, Bordeaux-Lormont.
On list 1.1897. Ord: 29.7.1896. K: 1896. L: 30.9.1897. Trials: 7-8.1898.
Budget 1896. *Défense mobile* at Toulon and 1st Mediterranean torpedo boat flotilla 1900-11. Renamed *Étoile* 1911. Annex to the school for gunnery at Toulon 1911-12. Struck 16.10.1912, for sale 1912-1913, sunk 1913 during gunnery practice while under tow by *Samson* off the Pointe de Carqueiranne east of Toulon.

*Torpilleur no 208* (P27) C.A. Gironde, Bordeaux-Lormont.
On list 1.1897. Ord: 29.7.1896. K: 1896. L: 28.10.1897. Trials: 1897-9.1898.
Budget 1896 (late addition). Initially rejected for insufficient speed (22.8kts). *Défense mobile* in Algeria (Oran) and 5th Mediterranean torpedo boat flotilla 1900-10. Renamed *Marteau* 1910. Annex to the school for engineers and stokers at Toulon 1910-14. Struck 25.2.1919. Reported sold 3.1920 at Toulon to BU although still carried in the 1.1924 fleet list as for sale.

*Torpilleur no 209* (P28) C.A. Gironde, Bordeaux-Lormont.
On list 1.1897. Ord: 29.7.1896. K: 1896. L: 29.11.1897. Trials: 12.1897-9.1898.
Budget 1896 (late addition). *Défense mobile* at Brest and 1st Atlantic torpedo boat flotilla 1899-1911. Struck 23.11.1911, for sale at Brest 1911-1912.

*Torpilleur no 210* (P29) C.A. Gironde, Bordeaux-Lormont.
On list 1.1897. Ord: 29.7.1896. K: 1896. L: 12.1.1898. Trials: 11.1898-9.1899.
Budget 1896 (late addition). *Défense mobile* at Brest and 1st Atlantic torpedo boat flotilla 1899-1911. Struck 23.11.1911, for sale at Brest 1911-1912.

*Torpilleur no 211* (P30) C.A. Gironde, Bordeaux-Lormont.
On list 1.1897. Ord: 29.7.1896. K: 1896. L: 12.2.1898. Trials: 8.1898-
1.1899.
Budget 1896 (late addition). *Défense mobile* at Brest and 1st Atlantic
torpedo boat flotilla 1899-1911 (Saint Servan station 1910),
Cherbourg 1912. Damaged in collision with destroyer *Catapulte* 1911.
Struck 30.7.1912. BU 1913 at Brest.

*Further tranches of the 37-metre type torpedo boats are in Chapter 16.*

---

## (C) 2nd Class Torpedo Boats (*Torpilleurs de 2e classe*)

The categories of *torpilleur de 2e classe* and *torpilleur-vedette*
(torpedo launch) were added in the 1.1883 fleet list and
*torpilleur de 3e classe* in 1.1890, all by reclassifications except
for the single group below.

*2ND CLASS TORPEDO BOATS.* Four second-class torpedo boats designated Q1 to Q4 were in the 1894 budget to be built by contract. They may
have been intended as successors to the 34-metre type, by then 2nd class.
They were not given *Torpilleur* numbers and were not built. By October
1898 (the 1899 budget) the designator Q had been shifted to submarines.

### Q1 to Q4 (Unnamed) Contract

Budget 1894 (not funded). These contract-built *torpilleurs de 2e classe*
were included in the 1894 budget (submitted 5.1893) with the
stipulation that no funds were to be spent on them during 1894. They
were not contracted for and the 1895 budget (3.1894) deferred them
indef-initely.

---

## (D) Portable Torpedo Boats (*Torpilleurs à embarquer*).

Added in the 1.1894 fleet list. To *Torpilleurs vedettes* 1.1909.

*TORPILLEURS A–B* (R1-2). *Torpilleurs à embarquer*. Steel hulls. One
torpedo tube in a downward-sloping enclosure on the bow, one funnel at
the front of a long machinery casing amidships, a cylindrical conning
position on the casing aft.

When specifications for the *croiseur porte-torpilleurs Foudre* were drafted in
May 1890 the navy had six *torpilleurs vedettes* that such a ship could
embark, *Nos* 29-30 and *Nos* 56-59. These, however, were already old and
were armed only with torpedo spars, and on 3 March 1891 Minister Barbey
asked the *Conseil des Travaux* to develop specification for new portable
boats. The Council examined the matter on 12 May 1891. It began by
compiling data on *Torpilleurs nos* 29-30, *Torpilleurs nos* 58-59, two designs
for 2nd class torpedo boats drafted by Thibaudier and Normand in 1882
similar to *Nos* 58-59 but not built, and the Royal Navy's 2nd class torpedo
boat designed by Yarrow. It then defined the mission of the boats. It
excluded the idea of them participating in a fleet battle at sea, a task of
which it felt only *torpilleurs de haute mer* were capable. Instead their
mission was surprising at night an enemy fleet in a roadstead, the transport
bringing them to about 15 miles of their target and the boats escaping at
high speed after firing. (Unlike most other vessels most of their activity
would be at high speed with high coal consumption.) The final characteristics were a displacement fully equipped of 14.5 tons, a total length including the rudder of not over 19m, one tube for M1887 356mm 5-metre
torpedoes (320kg weight) in the bow with a protective covering, a seven-
man crew, coal for four hours at 15.5 knots with bunker capacity for
10 hours at 15 knots, machinery to sustain the highest possible speed with
Du Temple or similar boilers, and special provisions for raising steam
quickly. Trials were to last two hours with a half hour at maximum speed
(ultimately set at 16⅓ knots) and the rest at 0.75 knots less. The boats
needed to be strong and their manoeuvrability exceptional. Minister
Barbey promulgated the specifications on 2 June 1891.

Two portable torpedo boats (*Torpilleurs à embarquer* or *torpilleurs-vedettes*) of the
*Torpilleur A* type embarked in *Foudre* under the after gantry during tethered
balloon experiments in 1901. In the boat visible here the conning tower is aft on
the right, the funnel with its top folded back is forward to the left behind the
single bow torpedo tube which slopes down to the bow under protective plating.
The folded portion of the funnel of the boat on the starboard side of the ship is
also visible. *(NHHC, NH-64202)*

On 15 December 1891 the Council examined three designs submitted
in response to the specifications by C.A. Gironde, F.C. Méditerranée, and
Scheider at Creusot, plus a note from Normand objecting in principle to
the specifications. (He recommended shorter and wider craft capable of
only 13.5 knots but able not only to attack but also to serve as defensive
picket boats.) The main differences between the three designs were in beam
and stability, in coal consumption at 15.5 knots, and in the system of
construction and the weight reserved for the hull. In all three areas
Creusot's solution was the most satisfactory. Creusot expected to reach (but
did not guarantee) 16.5 knots at 210ihp. The Council wanted Creusot to
add protection around the torpedo tube consisting of 4 to 5mm of steel on
top and 3mm on the sides and to try out some alternative topside arrangements. On 3 May 1892 the Council examined Creusot's revised design.
The final topside arrangement had the funnel offset to starboard to allow
loading the torpedo tube, the kiosk (conning tower) for the commander
and helmsman located aft of the engine and offset to port to see past the
funnel, the engine room vent moved to starboard out of the line of sight
from the kiosk, and the funnel fitted with an extension at the top to prevent
smoke from obscuring the view from the kiosk but hinged to prevent interference with launching and recovering the boats. The kiosk had 4mm hard
steel protection.

The 1894 budget included nine contract-built *torpilleurs embarqués*
designated R1 to R9, of which the first two were to be ordered in advance
(*par anticipation*) in 1893 with some 1893 funds. R3 was also ordered in
advance in 1893 to a different design with an experimental aluminium
hull, while R4 to R9 ended up being deferred to 1899.

**Dimensions & tons:** 18.50m oa, 18.20m pp x 3m. 14.625t disp.
    Draught: 0.52m fwd, 1.425m aft under propeller guard.
**Machinery:** 250ihp designed at 14kg/cm² boiler pressure. Speed 17kts.
    Trials 17.5kts in rough seas. 1 screw. 1 compound engine. 1 Du
    Temple boiler. Endurance 100nm.
**Torpedoes:** 1 tube in bow for 356mm (4.99m) torpedoes.

*Torpilleur A* (R1) Schneider, Chalon-sur-Saône.
On list 1.1894. Ord: 2.8.1893. K: 1893. L: 1894. C: 1894.

Budget 1894 (ordered in advance). To Toulon c1894. Received by *Foudre* 13.5.1896. In service at Saigon 1906. Struck 15.4.1911.

*Torpilleur B* (R2) Schneider, Chalon-sur-Saône.
On list 1.1894. Ord: 2.8.1893. K: 1893. L: 1894. C: 1895.
Budget 1894 (ordered in advance). To Toulon c1895. Received by *Foudre* 24.9.1896. In service at Saigon 1906. Struck 3.11.1910.

————

***TORPILLEUR C*** (R3). *Torpilleur à embarquer.* Aluminium hull. Flush decked launch with funnel and machinery casing amidships.

*Torpilleur à embarquer* R3 was included in the 1894 budget (submitted 5.1893) with the stipulation that no funds were to be spent on her during 1894. The French, however, wanted to experiment with the Royal Navy's 2nd class torpedo boat designed by Yarrow, and they ordered an example in August 1893, although unlike the two Schneider boats without using 1893 funds. Construction of this experimental boat was supervised by the French naval attaché at London, the contract delivery date being 31 July 1894 at London. The ordering of this boat abroad provoked violent protests in France, where the aluminium yacht *Vandenesse* had just been built at Saint Denis. The hull of *Torpilleur C* was changed in 1896 at Cherbourg because of corrosion. The boat arrived at Toulon from Cherbourg in August 1898 and was delivered to the naval construction directorate there for inspection on 5 October 1898. As of 1 November 1898 she was to be available within the next ten days to embark on *Foudre*.

**Dimensions & tons:** 19m x 2.85m. 14t disp (aluminium hull only 2.5t). Draught: 1.45m
**Machinery:** Trials 20.5kts average on six measured mile runs at 591rpm. 1 screw. 1 engine with 3 cylinders. 1 Yarrow tubular boiler.
**Torpedoes:** 1 torpedo tube or 1 torpedo spar on the bow.

*Torpilleur C* (R3) Yarrow, Poplar, UK.
On list 1.1894. Ord: 16.8.1893. K: 1893. L: 1894. C: 1894.
Budget 1894. In reserve 1900-10. Renamed *Têt* 1910. Annex to the school for torpedomen at Toulon. Not listed 3.1920. Struck 29.6.1921.

————

***TORPILLEURS D–I*** (R4-9). *Torpilleurs à embarquer.* Steel hulls.

These boats, the remainder of the loadout for *Foudre*, were included in the 1894 budget (submitted May 1893) with the stipulation that no funds were to be spent on them during 1894. They were not contracted for then and the first 1895 budget (3.1894) deferred them indefinitely. They were restored in the second 1895 budget (11.1894) and in the 1896 budget (5.1895). Minister of Marine Lockroy, sceptical of the torpedo transport idea, initiated a study of converting *Foudre* to a regular cruiser on 19 February 1896 and around the same time he suspended the order for *Torpilleurs D* through *I*, which were omitted from the 1897-98 budgets (2.1896 and 4.1897). On 17 December 1897, with Lockroy gone and *Foudre* about to begin trials at sea with *Torpilleurs A & B*, the Chief of the Naval General Staff suggested it was time to proceed with the order for her other six boats. They were finally built under the 1899 budget (10.1898), with the contract being issued in April 1898.

Characteristics as *Torpilleurs A & B*.

*Torpilleur D* (R4) Schneider, Chalon-sur-Saône.
On list 1.1896. Ord: 25.4.1898. K: 1897. L: 1899. C: 1899.
Budget 1894 (delayed to 1899). To Toulon c1899. In service at Saigon 1906-1909. Ceded to king of Luang-Prabang 1909, off list 1909.

*Torpilleur E* (R5) Schneider, Chalon-sur-Saône.
On list 1.1896. Ord: 25.4.1898. K: 1897. L: 1899. C: 1899.
Budget 1894 (delayed to 1899). To Toulon c1899. In service at Saigon 1906. Struck 15.4.1911.

*Torpilleur F* (R6) Schneider, Chalon-sur-Saône.
On list 1.1896. Ord: 25.4.1898. K: 1897. L: 1899. C: 1899.
Budget 1894 (delayed to 1899). To Toulon c1899. In service at Saigon 1906. Struck 3.11.1910.

*Torpilleur G* (R7) Schneider, Chalon-sur-Saône.
On list 1.1896. Ord: 25.4.1898 and 7.9.1898. K: 1898. L: 1899. C: 1899.
Budget 1894 (delayed to 1899). To Toulon c1899. In service at Saigon 1906. At Saigon 1911-14. Off main list 1914-1920. Service craft in Indochina 1920, off list 1920-1921.

*Torpilleur H* (R8) Schneider, Chalon-sur-Saône.
On list 1.1896. Ord: 25.4.1898 and 7.9.1898. K: 1898. L: 1899. C: 1899.
Budget 1894 (delayed to 1899). To Toulon c1899. In service at Saigon 1906. Struck 15.4.1911.

*Torpilleur I* (R9) Schneider, Chalon-sur-Saône.
On list 1.1896. Ord: 25.4.1898 and 7.9.1898. K: 1898. L: 1899. C: 1899.
Budget 1894 (delayed to 1899). To Toulon c1899. In service at Saigon 1906. Struck 15.4.1911.

————

**Transfers to Saigon**

Experience with *Foudre* during fleet operations between 1898 and 1901 showed that her torpedo boats were too small to keep the sea and could only be embarked and disembarked in calm water in a roadstead or port. Laid up in 1902, *Foudre* was recommissioned on 1 March 1904, embarked four of her torpedo boats under her forward gantry at Toulon, added the submarines *Protée* and *Lynx* aft at Cherbourg after removal of her after gantry, and delivered them all to Saigon in June 1904. *Foudre* made another voyage to Saigon between August and October 1905 carrying the submarines *Perle* and *Esturgeon* and four more of her torpedo boats and escorting the destroyer *Rapière* and six 1st class torpedo boats (*Nos 255, 284-86,* and *291-92*). All of the *torpilleurs à embarquer* except for the aluminium-hulled *Torpilleur C* were at Saigon by October 1905. By then their speed had fallen to 14 knots.

————

## (E) Torpedo Launches (*Torpilleurs vedettes*).

Added in the 1.1883 fleet list, all by reclassifications except one experimental unit (*Libellule*) in Chapter 16.

————

## (F) Defensive Torpedo Boats (*Contre-torpilleurs*) (all by reclassification).

In his *La réforme de la Marine*, published at the very beginning of 1886, the leading publicist of the Jeune École, Gabriel Charmes, added to the fleet of the future a third type of small ship to the two that he had advocated in 1884, the torpedo boat (now *torpilleur d'attaque*) and the *bateau canon*. The third type was the *torpilleur de défense*, whose task was to sweep away enemy torpedo boats trying to interfere with the attack boats. The defensive boats would have three or four large Hotchkiss guns and a spar torpedo to be used as a ram, primarily to break through harbour defences but also to sink ships. True to their missions, the attack boats would have no guns and the defensive boats would have no Whitehead torpedoes. They would always move in pairs, one attack and one defensive.

Three months later the term *contre-torpilleur* first appeared in the official nomenclature of the Navy when Minister of Marine Aube on 17 March 1886 directed converting into *contre-torpilleurs* the torpedo boats of the *No 65* type, whose ram-shaped bows raised bow waves that were too visible but would be useful in ship-to-ship combat. The design was prepared by naval constructor Joseph Louis Léon Tissier at Toulon. After conversion they were to have an armament of four 37mm revolving cannon arranged with one forward on the conning tower, one on each side, and one aft. Armaments with more 37mm guns were considered but rejected because of the excessive crew size and weight required. Ultimately only *Torpilleur no 68* was converted, being reclassified from a *torpilleur de 1re classe* during 1887. In 1890 this boat also received a torpedo spar for self-defence in a mêlée against enemy torpedo avisos.

In February 1888 *Torpilleur no 151* (ex *Gabriel Charmes*) was provisionally reclassified from a *torpilleur de 1re classe* and fitted as a *contre-torpilleur* armed with eight 37mm Hotchkiss guns, four forward of the conning tower in the position vacated by the 138.6mm gun (soon reduced to three), two above the boiler and two further aft in sponsons. Like *No 68* and for the same reason she also received a torpedo spar in 1890, hers coming from the wrecked *Avant-Garde*.

In the January 1890 fleet list *No 151* reverted to a *torpilleur de 1re classe* and *No 68* to a *torpilleur de 2e classe*. By 1891 the *contre-torpilleur* concept had been abandoned, and a note of 3 March 1891 stipulated that *No 151* would be maintained in service as a *torpilleur porte-torpille* (spar torpedo boat). To give them a little more capability Minister Besnard on 25 August 1895 proposed replacing two 37mm guns and the spar on each boat with a deck tube over the boilers (356mm in *No 68* and 381mm in *No 155*) but the modification was not carried out.

Six torpedo cruisers and five torpedo avisos were reclassified as *Contre-torpilleurs d'escadre* during 1895. *Durandal* and *Hallebarde* (see Chapter 15) were added during 1896 beginning the long series of French destroyers.

---

# II. SUBMARINES

## (A) Submarine Boats (*Bateaux sous-marins*).

To *Sous-marins* in the 1.1909 fleet list. See *Bâtiments spéciaux à hélice* in Chapter 4 for *Plongeur* (1861).

### The Goubets. Not acquired.

In 1885 and 1895 the civilian engineer Claude Désiré Goubet built two small submarines in hopes that the Navy would accept them, but neither was acquired and neither appeared on the Navy's *Liste de la flotte*. Goubet took out a patent for his first boat on 26 October 1885 and after the Commission for Inventions of the *Conseil des travaux* examined this *bateau torpilleur sous-marin* on 15 February 1886 and invited the inventor to conduct trials in the presence of a special commission, Minister of Marine Aube signed a contract with Goubet on 12 September 1886, construction started on 26 September 1886, and the vessel was launched in March 1887. Called *Goubet I*, she was 5m long, 1m wide, weighed 1.8 tons submerged and 1.6 tons surfaced, and was manned by the captain and a crewman sitting back to back under a cupola amidships. The ends were pointed and the single screw was driven by a one-horsepower electric motor powered by non-rechargeable batteries. The screw was pivoted horizontally to steer, a technology developed by Goubet. The boat would have used towing torpedoes in combat. She dived for the first time in 1888 at Paris. She was delivered on 2 November 1888 and ran trials at Cherbourg in 1890-92 that revealed her main defect – she could not be steered reliably submerged with the pivoting screw. The navy rejected her definitively in 1892 but made a 20,000 franc payment in 1894.

In 1895 Goubet at his own expense launched a second submarine under the 1886 contract. *Goubet II* was 8m long, 1.75m wide, weighed 6.7 metric tons, was shaped much like *Goubet I* and had the same kind of pivoting screw. This boat had a four-horsepower electric motor for propulsion (turning at 250rpm for 6 knots), this time powered as in all subsequent electric submarines by rechargeable batteries (accumulators). She also had a crew of three and two torpedo launch devices on the sides. *Goubet II* ran trials between November 1899 and spring 1901 but had the same problem steering submerged as did *Goubet I* and the contract was cancelled in 1901.

Ironically, along with most of the *Jeune École*, another Aube disciple, the politician and journalist Camille Pelletan, expressed great interest in Goubet and his submarines. In early 1901 he spent two and a half hours underway at Toulon in *Goubet II* and found her much superior to either of the 'official' submarines, *Gymnote* and *Gustave Zédé*, which he also visited. This fascination with very small submarines for defensive use continued after he became Minister of Marine in 1902. The journal *Le Figaro* reported on 3 November 1902 that Pelletan had ordered a third Goubet to be built in the Toulon dockyard by naval constructor Tissier, but the public announcement of the project came on the same day as the announcement that Pelletan had suspended the construction of thirteen Laubeuf submersibles at Toulon, and it became politically impossible to proceed with the third Goubet. His *Guêpes* and the *Vedette immersible Q61*, however, were strongly influenced by the Goubets.

*Goubet I* was sold on 7 May 1906 at Noyon for scrap. *Goubet II* was sold at a bankruptcy auction on 12 September 1902 at Saint Ouen just outside Paris. She was later bought by the Russians at Toulon, embarked on the battleship *Tsesarevich* on 19 November 1903, and taken to Port Arthur where she was given a 20hp engine. The Japanese captured her there and sold her to the Chinese, at which point she disappears from the historical record.

---

***GYMNOTE.*** *Bateau sous-marin.* Single steel hull, electric propulsion. Designed by Gustave Zédé

Gustave Alexandre Zédé was the son in law of Charles Henri Dupuy de Lôme, who participated in the project until his death in 1885. Zédé had left his naval post as Director of Naval Construction in 1880 to join his father in law as a director at the Forges et Chantiers de la Méditerranée at La Seyne. Zédé first offered a design for a submarine boat in 1883 but two successive Ministers of Marine, Peyron and Galiber, were not interested, the latter just having placed a big order for 30 coastal torpedo boats. Théophile Aube, however, who became minister on 7 January 1886, was interested in innovations and first examined a new project by Zédé on 5 February 1886 as one of his experiments with small craft as alternatives to battleships. The order to build the 'bateau sous-marin' was given on 22 November 1886, the electrical propulsion machinery was ordered on 3 March 1887, and the plans received Ministerial approval on 9 April 1887. Naval constructor Gaston Romazzotti, a nephew of Zédé, was assigned to produce the detailed plans and oversee the construction. The Army officer Arthur Constantin Krebs, who on 9 August 1884 had piloted the world's first fully-controlled free flight in the dirigible *France* at the Parc d'Aérostation militaire de Chalais-Meudon, was charged with the electrical installations including the motor, which was his invention and which was essentially a scaled-up version of his electric dirigible motor. Minister Krantz named the vessel *Gymnote* on 30 January 1888 and she appeared as such on the fleet list. The initial crew consisted of Zédé, Krebs, Romazzotti, Lieutenant de vaisseau Baudry de Lacantinerie (the only sailor in the group) and chief foreman Picon, who had directed the construction of the boat. A military crew of six led by Lieutenant de vaisseau Darrieus was assigned in early 1890 to conduct military as well as technical trials. Her endurance with her original battery operating at 133 amperes out of the 400 ampere maximum was around four hours. She was dependent on shore facilities or a support ship to recharge her battery. Submerged trials were run with half a metre of water over the top of the conning tower.

She underwent frequent modifications during the 1890s as an experimental platform. She originally had only one set of horizontal planes aft whose main purpose was to keep the boat from diving too steeply. However, if the water was at all choppy she would not dive at all, staying surfaced with her bow down. Adding a second pair of horizontal planes amidships in 1893-94 and then a new type of horizontal planes aft in 1895 resolved this problem. The variable pitch propeller blades invented by naval constructor Maugas could be rotated to go from ahead to stop, allowing changes in speed without stopping the motor. They were immobilized in 1901 when equipment to reverse the motor electrically was added.

On 6 January 1897 Minister Besnard ordered her to be hauled out for a major refit in 1897-1898 in which she was lengthened 0.60m by the insertion of a section amidships. She also received a new 90hp Sautter-Harlé electric motor designed to operate at 200 volts and 500rpm, although it was normally used at 100 volts and 250 to 300rpm to get better range. She also received a new battery (her third). Horizontal planes were added forward, the amidships planes were removed, and fixed horizontal fins were added before the after planes, giving her excellent control while diving and submerged. A small superstructure was added in the form of a narrow platform for the crew to stand on while the boat was on the surface. Finally she received her first armament, two 356mm torpedoes, one on each side in launchers with claws and a sliding lock developed by Tissier. These devices used articulated parallelograms to drop the torpedo as far as possible from the hull and parallel to the submarine's heading. The torpedoes were half submerged when the boat was on the surface.

### As built (1888)

**Dimensions & tons:** 17.200m oa & pp x 1.800m ext. 28.218t disp (surfaced), 29.350t (submerged). Draught: 1.670m mean. Men: 5.

**Machinery:**
(surfaced): 51hp at 250rpm. Speed 8kts (designed). Trials 33.4hp measured at the shaft. 1 screw (variable pitch to 1901). 1 Krebs electric motor built by the Forges et Chantiers de la Méditerranée at Le Havre.
(submerged): Trials 24.9hp at the shaft.

**Torpedoes:** None

### Rebuilt (1898-1900)

*The characteristics are based on a devis dated 1900.*

**Dimensions & tons:** 17.80m oa & pp x 1.80m ext. 29.71t disp (surfaced), 30.9t (submerged). Draught: 1,720m mean. Men: 6 including 1 officer. Reserve buoyancy: 3.9%

**Machinery:**
(surfaced): 91hp (82hp at the shaft) at 500rpm. Trials (1898-99) hp = 7.31kts at 415rpm. 1 screw. 1 electric motor by Sautter-Harlé (contract 9.10.1897). Range (trials) 85nm @ 4.85kts.
(submerged): Trials (1898-99) hp = 4.27kts at 401rpm. Range (trials) 48nm @ 3.21kts.

**Torpedoes:** 2 Tissier side launch devices for 356mm Model 1887 torpedoes.

*Gymnote* (Q1) Toulon Dyd/F.C. Méditerranée, Le Havre (electric motor). On list 1.1888. Ord: 22.11.1886. K: 20.4.1887. L: 24.9.1888. Comm: 11.1888 (trials), 1.5.1900 (full).
Named 31.1.1888. Launched 24.9.1888 in the presence of Vice Admiral Bergasse duPetit-Thouars, launched again on 10.11.1888. First under-

way trials 17.11.1888 in Toulon roadstead. Passed under the keel of a blockading battleship in 1890 without being seen. Hauled out for modifications 6.1.1897, completed 4.1.1900. Trial results approved and first full commissioning 1.5.1900. In drydock 19.6.1907 when it flooded accidentally, repairs were uneconomical, condemned 10.9.1907 and decommissioned 3.10.1907. Struck 22.5.1908, retained at Toulon for trials 1908-1911. Hulk used as pontoon to raise wrecks. Offered for sale 1.8.1911 at Toulon by the Domaines with *Amiral Baudin, Magenta, Pascal, Milan*, and smaller vessels including torpedo boats, sold 2.8.1911 to M. Bénédic to BU.

———

*GUSTAVE ZÉDÉ. Bateau sous-marin.* Single hull of unpainted *bronze Roma,* electric propulsion. Designed by Romazzotti.

Romazzotti based his design on a sketch design by Gustave Alexandre Zédé. In his June 1890 report on the early trials of *Gymnote* Romazzotti analysed the possible military uses for a submarine and focused on two types, a '*bateau d'attaque*' acting as a coast defence torpedo boat and having a speed of at least 15 knots and displacing 250 to 300 tons, and a '*canot sous-marin*' for short range missions with little need for speed and a displacement of only around 15 tons. The navy preferred the first option and asked Romazzotti to design such a boat. His project was presented on 19 August 1890 and construction was ordered on 4 October 1890. On the same date the boat was named *Sirène* and ordered built. She was renamed *Gustave Zédé* in 1891 after that naval constructor died in Paris on 27 April 1891 after being injured in a laboratory experiment with explosive torpedo fuel. Romazzotti called her an 'enlarged *Gymnote*', but at a displacement of 266 tons vice 30 tons she was almost nine times larger. Her design called for a 750hp electric motor producing a speed of 13 knots on the surface (the Navy wanted 15 knots). Sautter-Harlé was chosen as supplier of the motor on 18 July 1891 and the contract was dated 12 September 1891.

The most difficult part of the design proved to be the battery, which filled most of the boat, and trials with the first one, after half the cells had to be removed, produced a speed of only 8 knots. A new battery was ordered on 29 April 1896 and first used 2 September 1898, and the boat finally ran her official acceptance speed trials in October 1899, producing a speed of 9.22 knots on the after motor at high power with a range at that speed of 65 nautical miles. On both motors in series but at less power she made 8.13 knots for a range of 88 miles, and on the after motor alone at lower power she made 5.84 knots for a range of 176 miles. Submerged speeds were about three quarters of the surface figures. On 6 June 1905, after receiving another new battery, she made her best ever speed of 12.7 knots with a corresponding range of only 28 nautical miles. Submerged she nearly reached 10 knots but the practical limit was 6 knots because of vibrations in the periscope.

The depth limit was considered to be 15 metres, but keeping such a long submarine submerged at that depth proved practically impossible in bad weather. Like *Gymnote* and the other early all-electric submarines she was dependent on shore facilities or a supporting surface ship to recharge her battery. At depths under two metres she had to operate with all hatches closed making air replenishment for the crew impossible, and she would soon have to run for sheltered water to reopen her hatches. In practice she was normally limited to a distance of 20 miles from her base.

Inboard profile of the submarine boat (*bateau sous-marin*) *Gymnote*, probably from a study of submarines produced in the school for torpedoes on *Algésiras* in 1894-95. This drawing shows her in her original configuration with practically no superstructure. The three items labelled on top of the boat are the *casque* (literally helmet, a primitive conning tower), a compass, and a periscope, with on the bottom a screw for raising the *casque*.

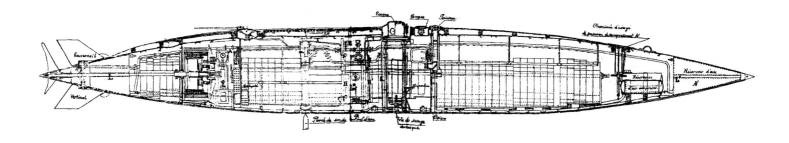

As originally built with horizontal planes aft only she was unable to dive reliably, but this was remedied as in *Gymnote* by adding a second set of horizontal planes amidships and fixed horizontal fins aft in 1896, then a third set forward in 1899. In 1897 she was considered fit for military use and fitted with a bow tube for 450mm torpedoes and a small conning tower for the commander. In 1899 she received ministerial permission to transit on the surface from Toulon to Marseille, a distance of some 55 miles. In 1901 she was fitted with a removable navigation platform on top of the conning tower and she made two more 'long' voyages, one from Toulon to Ajaccio and one from Nice to Marseille. In 1904 a trunk was built around the main access hatch and an enlarged platform was placed over both this and the conning tower.

*The characteristics are based on a devis dated 9.12.1899.*

**Dimensions & tons:** 48.500m oa & pp x 3.200m ext (4.35m over amidships horizontal planes). 261.392t disp (surfaced), 269.650t (submerged). Draught: 3.222m mean. Men: 10 including 2 officers. Reserve buoyancy: 3.1%

**Machinery:**
(surfaced): 720hp at 250rpm. Trials (8.10.1899) 9.22kts. 1 screw. 2 electric motors on the same shaft. Range (trials) 176nm @ 5.84kts.
(submerged): Speed 6.5kts. Range 105nm @ 4.47kts.

**Torpedoes:** 1 internal bow tube for 450mm Model 1891 torpedoes (a short model without the Obry gyroscope).

*Gustave Zédé* (Q2) Toulon Dyd/Sautter-Harlé, Paris (electric motors)
On list 1.1892. Ord: 4.10.1890. K: 1891. L: 1.6.1893. Comm: 1.5.1900 (full).
Budget 1892. Named *Sirène* 4.10.1890, renamed *Gustave Zédé* 1.5.1891. Installation of motor by Sautter-Harlé begun 1.2.1893, first static machinery trials 12.11.1894. Conducted an exercise attack on the battleship *Magenta* off the Salins d'Hyères 12.1898. Trials ended (*clôture des essais*) 12.1899. President of the Republic Loubet submerged in her at Cherbourg in 1901, after which she conducted a successful simulated attack (with the assistance of the tug *Utile*) on the battleship *Charles Martel* at Ajaccio. Struck 9.8.1909, for disposal at Toulon by scrapping 1909-1910, for sale 1910-1911. Offered for sale 1.8.1911 at Toulon by the Domaines with *Amiral Baudin, Magenta, Pascal, Milan*, and smaller vessels including torpedo boats, sold 2.8.1911 to M. Bénédic to BU.

---

*MORSE. Bateau sous-marin.* Single hull of *bronze Roma*, electric propulsion. Designed by Romazzotti.

Romazzotti felt that the jump in size from *Gymnote* to *Gustave Zédé* had been too large and proposed this intermediate design. The *Conseil des travaux* on 27 October 1891 examined an initial design by Romazzotti dated 23 April 1891 and approved it in principle, although the Council wanted numerous changes and a complete review of the calculations before approving it. On 11 November 1891 Minister Barbey directed the use of a steel hull instead of Romazzotti's bronze one. The Council examined Romazzotti's modified design on 17 May 1892. The original electric motor of 350hp and 275 rpm was replaced with one of 360hp (exactly half of the motor in *Gustave Zédé*) and 250rpm, allowing the use of a larger propeller. In both submarines the motors consisted of two separate sections on the same shaft and connected electrically. *Morse* was designed to maintain a speed of 13 knots for nearly three hours. Romazzotti wanted to retain the bronze hull and the Council successfully supported him.

The Chief of the *Service des Défenses sous-marins* questioned the use of the new short 450mm torpedoes (nominal length 4m, actually 4.17m) in this boat. Sixteen of these had just been received from Fiume for the *torpilleurs ultra-rapides* (*Corsaire, Mousquetaire*, and *Chevalier*) that had just been ordered. He told the Council that initial experience with this model had led the torpedo experts to feel that its use should not become general

because, compared to the new 5-metre 450mm torpedoes, their short length degraded their ability to maintain a course and they were also very difficult to regulate. Romazzotti's April 1891 design had used the 5-metre torpedoes but the Council recommended changing to the shorter ones because they were also being used in *Gustave Zédé*.

Minister Cavaignac decided on 13 June 1892 to build this submarine at Cherbourg. Cherbourg was notified of this decision on 9 July 1892 and was also informed that she would be named *Morse* and that her construction would be overseen by naval constructor Jean Ernest Simonot. During the ministry of Félix Faure (May 1894-January 1895) it was proposed to alter this purely electric submarine into a *sous-marin autonome à grand rayon d'action* as proposed by Fernand Forest, who had invented an internal combustion engine. He proposed a boat propelled on the surface by two of his oil engines and submerged by an electric motor powered by a battery that could be recharged by a dynamo coupled to either engine. A design for a 360hp oil engine was prepared, but Romazzotti opposed the modification due to the volatility of the fuel and it was set aside. (Romazzotti, however, later incorporated a similar system in his *Naïade* and *Sous-marin X* designs.) On 30 May 1896 Minister Besnard asked for a new study of the design for the boat, construction was effectively ordered on 19 June 1897, and the two electric motors were contracted for with Sautter-Harlé on 22 November 1897. Trials began in 1899 and the boat was accepted on 17 April 1900.

One feature of this boat was the *évolueurs*, two small auxiliary propellers mounted on the sides just forward of the after horizontal planes that were geared to the main shaft and functioned essentially as side thrusters. They were intended primarily to help aim the boat when firing torpedoes from their fixed launchers and to manoeuvre in restricted spaces. The pitch of the blades of the main propeller could be varied as in *Gymnote* before 1901, the decision having been taken not to use in *Morse* the electrical reversing equipment used in *Gymnote* after 1901. This feature also helped control the load on the electric motor, although it probably caused some loss of speed. *Morse* had horizontal planes fore and aft but not amidships and fixed horizontal fins forward of the after planes. She dived in a creditable two minutes. For two copies with steel hulls see *Français* (Q11) and *Algérien* (Q12) in Chapter 17.

*The characteristics are based on a devis dated 8.5.1901.*

**Dimensions & tons:** 36.500m oa & pp x 2.750m ext, m wl. 142.926t disp (surfaced), 149.312t (submerged). Draught: 2.870m mean. Men: 9 including 1 officer, increased 1900 to 12 including 2 officers. Reserve buoyancy: 4.3%

**Machinery:**
(surfaced): 300hp at 450rpm. Speed 12kts (designed), 7.25kts (actual). Trials 284hp = kts. 1 screw (variable pitch) with two auxiliary side-thrusting screws. 2 electric motors by Sautter and Harlé (two motors on one shaft). Batteries 52.5 tons. Range 130-140nm (designed), 90nm (actual) @ 4.3kts.
(submerged): Speed 5.5kts (designed and actual).

**Torpedoes:** 1 internal bow tube for short 450mm Model 1891 torpedoes. (Two Tissier side launch devices for longer 450mm Model 1892 torpedoes were added in 1900 but were removed in 1901 because the steel torpedoes caused a severe electrolytic reaction with the unpainted bronze hull).

*Morse* (Q3) Cherbourg Dyd/Sautter-Harlé, Paris (electric motors).
On list 1.1893. Ord: 9.7.1892 and 19.6.1897. K: 22.2.1898. L: 4.7.1899. Comm: 3.3.1900 (full).
Budget 1894. Installation of machinery began 5.1.1899, first static machinery trials 11.7.1899, full speed trials 3.3.1900. At Cherbourg for nearly her entire career. Severe acid corrosion of her bronze hull found 10.1908. Condemnation proposed 14.9.1909. Struck 9.3.1910. Sold 8.7.1911 at Cherbourg.

# Chapter Twelve

# Transports and Sailing Vessels, 1882-1897

## I. TRANSPORTS

### (A) 2nd Class Transports (*Transports de 2e classe*).
Were *Grands Transports* before the 1.1885 fleet list.
To *Transports* (classes omitted) 1.1909.

*MAGELLAN* **Class.** *Transports de 2e classe.* Large convict transports (*transports de forçats*) with an iron and steel hull and imitation knee bow. One funnel, three masts, ship rig. Designed by Saglio.

Two sail transports were included in the 1882 budget (submitted in January 1881) to be built by contract to replace the old two-decker ships of the line including *Navarin*, *Loire* and *Tage* that were transporting convicts to New Caledonia. They were shown as *transports mixtes* (sailing transports with auxiliary steam propulsion) in the 1883 budget (submitted in March 1882). On 31 January 1882 the *Conseil des travaux* approved a

design for a *transport mixte* for New Caledonia by naval constructor Clauzel with numerous modifications and thanked Saglio for his conscientious study, but the ships ended up being built to a design by Saglio that essentially replicated the old ships in iron and steel.

Two more unnamed ships of this type, now called *grands transports,* were included in the 1885 budget (February 1884), one was named *Pacifique* (at Brest) and the other was to be built by contract. They were suspended by Minister Aube on 27.1.1886. *Pacifique* was restored to the building programme during 1888 but was cancelled in early 1892.

*The characteristics are based on the ships' design.*

**Dimensions & tons:** 69.06m wl, 71.000m pp (wl fwd to rudder) x 16.60m ext, 16.50m wl. 3,991.457t disp (designed). Draught (designed): 6.600m mean, 7.10m aft. Men: 430.

**Machinery:** 200nhp and 820ihp designed including auxiliary machinery, 8.50kts at 48 rpm and 4.133kg/cm$^2$ boiler pressure. 1 screw. 1 vertical compound engine with 2 cylinders of 0.96m and 1.66m diameter and 1.12m stroke. 2 high cylindrical boilers. 380t coal. Range 2,000nm @ 7kts.

**Guns:** 2 x 138.6mm (upper deck).

*Magellan* A.C. Loire, Saint Nazaire.
On list 1.1883. K: 25.9.1882. L: 8.8.1884. C: 1.1886.
Budget 1882 (sail), 1883 (mixte). First launch attempt failed 24.7.1884 (stuck in the mud after entering the water). Completed and to reserve

Undated longitudinal and horizontal views (*plan de pitonnage*) of the transports *Magellan* and *Calédonien* with machinery of 820ihp produced by the Ateliers et Chantiers de la Loire. These ships were designed to replace the old converted two-decker ships of the line that had been transporting convicts to New Caledonia and their design largely imitated those ships. Pitons are literally eye bolts through which a rope could be passed, *plans de pitonnage* like these show many details of the exterior appearance of the ships.

**MAGELLAN - CALÉDONIEN.**
APPAREIL A HÉLICE DE **820** CHEVAUX INDIQUÉS.

PLAN DE PITONNAGE

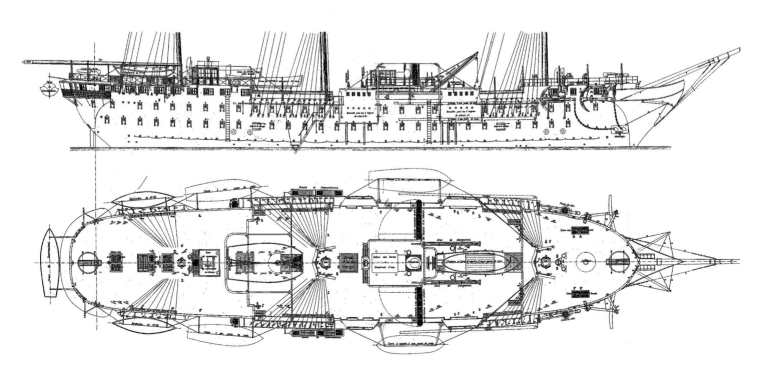

1886, in commission 1887. Out of service 1892 as a convict transport and by 1.1898 was in reserve at Landévennec. Assigned to the school for boys in at Brest 14.12.1898. Struck 14.12.1908, annex to the school for boys at Brest in *Bretagne* (ex *Fontenoy*) 1908-1910, *Bretagne* (ex *Mytho*) 1910-1912, and *Armorique* (ex *Bretagne* ex *Mytho*) 1912-1914. After the war continued to serve with *Armorique* as school for apprentice seamen 1920-c1932, then as centre hulk for submarines c1932-1936. Struck again as hulk 7.3.1936 (decision promulgated 3.4.1936). BU at Brest.

*Calédonien* A.C. Loire, Saint Nazaire.
On list 1.1883. K: 8.1882. L: 5.10.1884. Comm: 1885 (trials), 1886 (full).
Budget 1882 (sail), 1883 (mixte). Seagoing annex to the school for gunnery in *Couronne* at Toulon 1895-1907 (replaced *Saint Louis/Cacique*, replaced by *Latouche-Tréville*). School for seamen at Lorient with guns removed 1907-1911, school for boatswains 1911-1912. Off main list 1912 but retained as barracks hulk for the school for naval infantry at Lorient 1912-1914. Auxiliary services at Lorient 1920-1924, for sale at Lorient 1924-1925. Struck 14.3.1925.

*Pacifique* Brest Dyd/Indret.
On list 1.1885. Ord: 5.1884. K: 8.1885. Cancelled.
Budget 1885 (2.1884). Named *Pacifique* and had a 200nhp engine as in *Calédonnien* and *Magellan* by 1.1885. Construction suspended 27.1.1886. Back on fleet list 1.1889-1.1892. As resumed was to have had an engine built by contract, but this engine was still not in the 1891 budget (2.1890). The 1892 budget (2.1891) stated that the construction of *Pacifique* had been suspended. Last shown in fleet list 1.1892 with an engine of 1000ihp maximum and 700ihp normal as in *Calédonnien* and *Magellan*. Not in the 1893 budget (3.1892). Cancelled 1-3.1892, hull dismantled on the ways.

*N* (Unnamed) Contract.
Budgets 1885 (2.1884) and 1886 (3.1885). To be contract built. Not in the 1887 budget (3.1886), construction probably suspended with *Pacifique* 27.1.1886.

---

# (B) 3rd Class Transports (*Transports de 3e classe*).

Were *Transports pour le matériel et le service des stations* before the 1.1885 fleet list. To *Transports* 1.1909.

*DRÔME. Transport de 3e classe.* Cargo ship with a steel hull, a flush deck except for a forecastle, and a straight bow. One funnel between the main and mizzen masts, three masts, light barquentine rig.

On 31 March 1885 the ministry asked if there was a steamer available with approximately the same dimensions as the *Oise*, which had been lost in February. The ministry soon renounced the idea of buying a steamer and on 25 April 1885 the Machinery Commission was directed to contract for a transport of the *Caravane* type for littoral service, which was named *Drôme*. A contract was signed with the *Société des anciens établissements Claparède* on 7 December 1885 and approved on 26 December 1885. Claparède prepared the design and planned to build the ship at its yard at Rouen-Petit Quévilly, which had previously built several small cargo ships, but at the beginning of 1886 the Ateliers et Chantiers de la Loire at Saint Nazaire purchased the Claparède yards at Rouen and Saint Denis and transferred the construction of the hull of *Drôme*, still on Claparède's plans, from Rouen to Saint Nazaire. The machinery was built at Saint Denis. After the delivery at Rouen of the torpedo avisos *Salve* and *Bouet-Willaumez* in October 1886 the Petit Quévilly yard was dismantled and its equipment moved to Saint Nazaire.

The shields for the 90mm guns were landed at Brest in February 1895. The forward one blocked the view of the officer of the deck. In 1900 her commander recommended landing the bow gun. When recommissioned in

The 3rd class transport *Drôme*. This cargo ship, which had her machinery well aft, was built for logistics service along the French coast to replace the transport *Oise*, which had just been lost. She was in reserve from completion in 1888 to 1892 and then was in constant use until lost in 1918. *(Postcard by HL)*

---

October 1914 after one of her rare repair periods the ship had no guns, the 90mm having been landed many years previously. A request made on 12 October 1914 and approved by Minister Augagneur on 22 October 1914 led to the delivery of some 47mm/40 M1885 QF guns that then existed at Lorient. These remained on board until January 1916. Submarines had larger guns and on 25 January 1916 a request was made for one 65mm forward and one 75mm aft. It was approved on 28 January 1916 and work was completed on 2 February 1916. Paris wanted to replace the Navy 75mm guns with an Army 75 but the C.O. objected that the navy gun was much more appropriate for the ship and Paris relented on 15 March 1916. The funnel was raised in early 1917.

*The characteristics are based on a devis dated 1.1893.*
**Dimensions & tons:** 71.670m oa, 69.530m wl, 69.530m pp (wl fwd to rudder) x 9.648m ext, 9.582m wl. 1,674.192t disp (2,172.780t with 900t cargo). Draught: 4.108m mean, 5.168m aft (5.008m and 5.559m with 900t cargo). Men: 80.
**Machinery:** 275nhp and 1,075ihp designed at 80rpm and 6kg/cm² boiler pressure. Trials (30.1.1893) 1,323.37ihp = 12.173kts at 88.5rpm and 6.197kg/cm² boiler pressure. 1 screw. 1 vertical compound engine with 2 cylinders of 0.890m and 1.550m diameter and 0.900m stroke. 2 cylindrical return flame boilers built by Claparède. 215t coal.
**Guns:**
(1893) 2 x 90mm/22 M1881 (1 on forecastle, 1 on poop), 1 x 4pdr (86mm) bronze rifle on the forecastle used as a line-throwing gun (*porte-amarres*) for mooring the ship.
(1907) No guns. (1913) One line-throwing gun.
(1916-17) 1 x 65mm/50 QF (forecastle), 1 x 75mm S.A. M1908 Schneider (poop).

*Drôme* A.C. Loire, Saint Nazaire/A.C. Loire (ex Claparède), Saint Denis.
On list 1.1886. Ord: 7.12.1885 (contract). K: 10.6.1886. L: 10.3.1887. Comm: 1.12.1887 (trials). C: 1888.
Budget 1887. Machinery installed 1.4.1887 to 23.6.1887. Arrived at Brest from Saint Nazaire 4.8.1887. Commissioned for trials 1.12.1887. Trial results approved 7.1888. Placed in 3rd category reserve 21.8.1888 and out of commission 21.12.1891. Ordered commissioned 27.12.1892 and entered into full commission for the first time on 2.1.1893 for coastal service replacing *Caravane* (which soon returned to service).

Mined off Marseille 28.1.1918, having strayed from the swept channel, and sank in 30 seconds with her cargo of 1,500 barrels of fuel oil, which ruptured and caught fire. The mine was laid by *UC-67*.

## II. SAILING VESSELS

### (A) Sail Training Frigates (*Frégates à voiles*).

**MELPOMÈNE Class.** *Frégates à voiles.* Sail training frigate with iron deck beams and beam shelves. Three masts, ship rig. Designed by Guichard, then Saglio.

On 6 March 1883 the *Conseil des travaux* examined a design for a sailing frigate for training seamen (*gabiers*) and helmsmen (*timoniers*) by naval constructor Maurice Jules Guichard (then on leave without pay to work in industry) and sent it back to Brest for numerous changes including the suppression of artificial ventilation (which did not seem to be needed for a ship of this type) and to adopt traditional forms for the bow and stern like those in old frigates like *Thémis*, *Flore*, and *Vénus*. On 31 July the Council approved a design for the same ship by naval constructor Victor Saglio with a few changes in details.

*The characteristics are based on the ships' design.*
**Dimensions & tons:** 52.25m wl, 52.45m pp (wl fwd to rudder) x 13.84 m ext and wl. 1999.9t disp. Draught: 6.00m mean, 6.50m aft. Men: 500.
**Guns:** (1891) 8, (1893) 6 medium (164mm to 90mm) and 5 small, (1896) 6 medium and 15 small.

---

The sail training frigate *Melpomène* in the military port at the Lorient dockyard, probably during a training visit from Brest. Note the longboats hanging off the starboard side and the rectangular nets spread under all three masts. The moorings of the *Défense mobile* extended downriver from here, ships under construction and hulks were upriver. The light-coloured destroyer with the "S" on the bow, not part of the *Défense mobile*, is *Sagaïe*. (Postcard by H. Laurent, Port-Louis)

*Melpomène* Rochefort Dyd.
On list 1.1884. Ord: 8.8.1882. K: 19.10.1883. L: 20.8.1887.
   Comm: 15.9.1890.
Budget 1884. Named 9.8.1883. Construction reassigned from Toulon to Lorient c1883 and to Rochefort c1884. Replaced *Résolue* as seagoing school for seamen at Brest 1890, trials under sail 22.10.1890, left the next day on first training cruise. School closed 1904, to reserve at Landévennec 16.1.1904. Struck 16.6.1904, provisionally retained at Brest 1904-1908, post for torpedo boats at l'Aber-Wrac'h 1908-1911 (replacing *Obligado* from 1905), replenishment post for torpedo boats at l'Aber-Wrac'h 1911-1914. For sale at Brest 1920-1922, condemned 18.5.1921, to Lorient as hulk 1922-1929, landing hulk 1930-1939. Renamed *Ponton Nº 2* in 1932. Sunk 19.6.1940, BU 1943.

*Andromède* Lorient Dyd.
On list 1.1884. Ord: 8.8.1882. K: 7.1884. Cancelled 1892.
Budget 1884. Named 9.8.1883. Started at Toulon 27.10.1883 but construction reassigned to Lorient c1884. Construction stopped 1887 in favour of more urgent work. Last shown in the fleet list in 1.1892. The 1892 budget stated construction of *Andromède* (and *Pacifique*) was suspended, the ships were not in the 1893 budget. Construction abandoned 1892, hull sold at auction.

---

### (B) Sail Training Corvettes (*Corvettes à voiles*).

**SYLPHE Class.** *Corvettes à voiles.* Sail training corvette with iron deck beams and beam shelves. Three masts, ship rig (514 sq.m. of sail). Designed by Guichard, then Saglio.

The navy in the 1880s maintained two former sailing brigs to support its schools at Brest by conducting training evolutions under sail in the roadstead there. The brigs then in use were *Janus*, launched in 1848, completed in 1860, struck in 1884, used as an annex to the Naval Academy in the hulk *Borda* until 1897, and offered for sale at Brest 16.12.1913; and *Nisus*,

launched in 1850, refitted 1864 for training use, struck in 1866, and used until 1914 as an annex to the school for boys in the hulk *Bretagne*. *Janus* was refitted in 1881-82 with a three-masted square rig and called a 'brig with 3 masts', and *Nisus* also had three masts as a training vessel. On 20 March 1883 the *Conseil des travaux* examined a design by naval constructor Guichard for a sailing brig to replace the brigs that supported the school hulks at Brest. It approved Guichard's design subject to modifications that included increasing the beam a little to increase stability under sail, shortening and raising the lines of the stern, and basing the form of the bow on that of another old brig, *Obligado*. On 31 July 1883 the Council examined a design by Saglio of a vessel now called simply a sailing ship for the same purpose and approved it with minor modifications. Saglio's final design, dated 9 August 1883, replicated the hull dimensions of *Janus* and also the three-masted rig she had been given as a school ship. They were shown as sailing brigs in the 1884 and 1885 budgets but as sailing corvettes in the fleet lists.

*The characteristics are based on the ships' design.*
**Dimensions & tons:** 33.94m wl, 34.38m pp (wl fwd to rudder) x 9.80m ext (above wl), 9.60m wl. 486.6t disp. Draught: 4.10m mean, 4.60m aft.
**Guns:** none.

*Sylphe* Brest Dyd.
On list 1.1884. K: 10.9.1883. L: 30.8.1886. Comm: 10.7.1887.
Budget 1884. Named 8.1883. Annex to the school for boys (*Austerlitz*, then *Bretagne*) 1887-1912, then to the flagships of the Atlantic training division (*Châteaurenault*, then *Gloire*) 1912-1914. Off main list by 3.1920 (condemned 18.5.1921), hulk at Lorient 1920-1929, landing hulk 1929-1939, renamed *Ponton No 3* c1932. Struck 3.4.1936 as *Sylphe* and to the Domaines 1936 for sale, still afloat as a hulk in the inner harbour at Lorient until sunk there by air bombardment 1943.

*Bayonnais* Brest Dyd.
On list 1.1884. K: 10.9.1883. L: 28.9.1886. C: 18.9.1888.
Budget 1884. Annex to the school for boys (*Austerlitz*, then *Bretagne*) 1887-1903. Annex to *Saône* 1908-11 as depot for training apprentice seamen and at the same time as annex to the school for seamen in *Calédonien*. Decomm. 12.4.1912. For sale at Brest 3.1920. Struck 19.9.1920 as a brig. Sold 7.12.1920 to M. L'Hermitte.

## (C) Sail Schooners and Cutters (*Goélettes et Cutters*).

*ÉPERLAN. Garde-pêche* 1.1885, *Cutter* 1.1886. Cutter with a wooden hull.
On 18 May 1883 the Navy asked Normand to present a design for a fishery protection cutter like *Hareng* (see Chapter 7), a very satisfactory vessel that he had previously delivered to the navy, but larger (17m length instead of 16.50m). Normand enlarged the vessel even more than requested to accommodate the 22-man crew and 15 days of provisions carried by the cutters *Capelan* and *Lévrier*, whose data had been communicated to him. These two vessels displaced 71 tons compared to the 57 tons of *Hareng*. The upper works in Normand's design were elegant and resembled pleasure yachts. The *Conseil des travaux* approved the design on 15 January 1884.

*The characteristics are based on Normand's design as reviewed and approved by the Conseil des travaux on 15.1.1884.*
**Dimensions & tons:** 19m x 5.20m. 71.009t disp. Men: 22 including 1 officer.
**Guns:** 2.

*Éperlan* Augustin Normand, Le Havre.
On list 1.1885. K: 15.3.1884. L: 1.12.1884. C: 3.1885.
Joined *Mouette* on the North Sea fishery station, later the Channel and North Sea station, at Cherbourg 1885. Struck 19.10.1908, for sale at Cherbourg 1908-1909.

*PAPEETE. Goëlette.* Schooner with a wooden hull.
This schooner was built for service on the French local station for the Society Islands by Matthew Turner of Benicia, California, for 106,846 francs. Turner built several hundred sailing ships during his career including the French *Nu-Hiva* and *Taravao* for the same station in 1881, and he also had extensive business interests in Tahiti. He built *Papeete* to a design for schooners for the packet trade that he also used for several other schooners. *Papeete* was known for a quick passage from San Francisco to Tahiti of 17 days, presumably her delivery voyage in 1892. She was sold in 1921 but then had a second life in the French navy as *Zélée* from 1931 to 1940.

**Dimensions & tons:** 110t disp. Men: 25 including 1 officer.
**Guns:** none.

*Papeete* Matthew Turner, Benicia, Calif.
On list 1.1893. K: c1891. L: 1892. C: 1892.
From San Francisco to Papeete under French flag with an American crew 2-19.3.1892. Struck 25.10.1900. Sold 1901 at Tahiti to Emile Martin. Requisitioned 27.2.1906 to carry aid to the Tuamotu Islands after they were devastated by a typhoon but not put on the fleet list. Sold 28.12.1921 to Charles Morton Palmer of Maxwell & Cie. Repurchased 18.7.1931 by the Navy, renamed *Zélée*, restored to the fleet list, and reconditioned by Walker at Fare Ute, Papeete. Decomm. 5.9.1940 and BU at Taunoa, Papeete.

## (D) Sail Fishery Protection Vessels (*Garde-pêche à voiles*).

*Mutin* (on list January 1883) and *Railleur* (on list January 1884), both in the 1883 budget, are described in Chapter 7 with the *Hareng* class of 1881, to which they belonged. The five below joined the earlier fishery protection vessels except for the *Hareng* class in being relisted *pour ordre* (for the record) in 1897-98 with service craft because they were under commercial operation and then being moved to a special fisheries list on January 1908. Fishery protection vessels added to that non-naval list after 1908 are not recorded here.

*Passe-Partout.* 11 tons, 9 men. On list 1.1884. Built at Martigue for Toulon (K: 1883, L: 1884). Off main list 1896 and listed *pour ordre* with service craft at Toulon 1.1897 and as a *garde-pêche* under commercial operation 1.1898. On special fisheries list 1908 to 1911 at Port Vendres.

*Brochet.* 10 tons, 10 men. On list 1.1886. Built at Martigues for Toulon (K: 1885, L: 1886). Off main list 1896 and listed *pour ordre* with service craft at Toulon 1.1897 and as a *garde-pêche* under commercial operation 1.1898-1.1899. Decomm. 26.5.1899 at Sète, condemned 4.8.1900. Replaced by steam *Brochet* (see Chapter 18).

*Cormoran.* 26 tons, 8 men. On list 1.1891. Built by Augustin Normand at Le Havre for Cherbourg (ord: 29.10.1890. K: 3.1.1891. L: 23.6.1891. C: 1892). Off main list 1897 and listed *pour ordre* with service craft at Brest and as a *garde-pêche* under commercial operation 1.1898. On special fisheries list 1908 to 1914 at Cancale.

*Active.* First appeared on the service craft list as a *chaloupe pontée* (decked launch) at Rochefort 1.1873, placed in service as *chaloupe pontée* 1.1895 and converted. On service craft list with *Turbot* 1.1896 as a *garde-pêche*, with the similar *Barbue* and *Fauvette* remaining *chaloupes pontées*. Listed *pour ordre* with service craft at Rochefort 1.1897 and as a *garde-pêche* under commercial operation 1.1898. Not listed 1.1899.

*Sarcelle.* On list 1.1900 *pour ordre* with service craft (sail) at Rochefort and under commercial operation as a *garde-pêche*. On special fisheries list 1908 to 1914 at Marennes.

# Part Three

# Towards a Modern Battle Fleet, 1897-1914

The Fashoda Incident, an intense colonial confrontation with Britain over the upper Nile that came to a head in September and October 1898, forced the French to admit their naval impotence against Britain and back down in November. The shock of this admission helped end the political divisions over naval issues of the 1890s and refocus attention both inside and outside the Navy on the main battle fleet, initially against England. The Programme of 1898 added some armoured cruisers for commerce raiding against England to the earlier programmes directed against the Triple Alliance, and the Programme of 1900 focused on the battle fleet at the expense of coast defence and station fleets with the size of battleships increased from 12,000 to over 14,000 tons and with the combat fleet reduced to three main ship types (battleships, armoured cruisers, and destroyers) and the coast defence fleet reduced to two (torpedo boats and submarines). Overseas stations were to use cast-offs from the combat fleet, obsolete ships, and a few specialised types like gunboats that were to be built outside the programme. Between 1898 and 1905 the diplomacy of Foreign Minister Delcassé led to the Anglo-French Entente in 1904, and in 1907 the Anglo-Russian Entente completed the Triple Entente as a counterweight to the Triple Alliance.

Successive governments and Ministers of Marine had a significant effect on naval progress during this period. A Ministry of Republican Defence under the moderate Republican Waldeck-Rousseau responded to the Dreyfus Affair by purging the Army and limiting the influence of the church in France. It also gave the Navy the very productive ministry of Jean-Louis de Lanessan from 1899 to 1902 which produced the Programme of 1900. In contrast with all previous naval programmes since 1857, it was formally signed into law on 9 December 1900. De Lanessan, like Édouard Lockroy before him, was for many years an adherent to the *Jeune École* but changed his views when faced with the practical problems of running the navy. The Radical party won the 1902 election resulting in the Combes ministry of 1902-5 which enacted the full separation of church and state and also gave the Navy the disastrous ministry of Camille Pelletan. Pelletan, nicknamed the 'wrecker' or 'demolisher' of the navy, was an old-school *Jeune École* advocate who revived the torpedo boat versus battleship controversy, did his best to delay the construction of the battleships of the 1900 programme, and cancelled a group of Laubeuf submersibles which were larger than the tiny single-hulled submarines that he preferred.

The Combes ministry was followed in 1905 by the even more radical ministry of Georges Clemenceau, whose Minister of Marine, Gaston Thomson (1905-08), returned the navy to equilibrium after the disruptions of Pelletan without doing anything innovative. Three naval programmes were drafted by the *Conseil supérieur* during the Thomson ministry, in 1905, 1906, and 1907, but these and a fourth in 1909 were drafted without reference to fiscal realities and had little legislative impact. Clemenceau's successor as premier, Aristide Briand, selected as Minister of Marine Vice Admiral Boué de Lapeyrère (1909-11) who impelled an increase in readiness of the navy that was matched by Briand's Minister of War, General Jean Brun. Boué de Lapeyrère also ordered France's first true *Dreadnought*-type battleships and developed what became the Programme of 1912 that defined the navy with which France entered World War I. Like

the Programmes of 1857 and 1900 it was formally passed into law by Parliament, ensuring serious efforts to carry it out. However, the outbreak in August 1914 of a war that was expected to last six months ended nearly all naval construction as workers in both the naval dockyards and the commercial shipyards were mobilised and sent to the front.

The creation in 1895 of a *Section technique* and the appointment of Émile Bertin to head it in 1896 brought standardisation to French ship design at the same time that political and economic developments made possible larger tonnages. Between 1896 and his retirement in 1905 Bertin dominated the design of large French naval ships to the same extent that Dupuy de Lôme did in the 1850s and 1860s. He obtained the adoption in the *Patrie* class of 1901 of an armour protection scheme that he had advocated since 1890 in which the vulnerable narrow but thick waterline armour belt with a single protective deck in previous French battleships was replaced by armour covering much more of the ship's side plus two armour decks with a cellular layer in between. Two important technological advances occurred in 1897, one being the introduction of Normand's *Durandal* type destroyer to defend battle fleets against torpedo boats and to respond to the destroyers introduced by the British in the early 1890s and the other being the acceptance in a design competition of Laubeuf's double-hulled submersible *Narval* as an alternative to the single-hulled submarines based on *Gymnote*. In competitive trials in 1904 the double-hulled submersible *Aigrette* proved her operational superiority over the single-hulled submarine *Sous-Marin X*, clearing the way for a large submarine building effort that continued to 1914.

Technological change in the battle fleet resumed on a large scale in 1905 with the design in Britain of HMS *Dreadnought* with a uniform calibre main armament of ten 305mm guns and with turbine propulsion. At the same time the French were designing their *Danton* class battleships and chose a mixed-calibre main armament of four 305mm and twelve 240mm guns, again with turbine propulsion. History has shown that the choice of a mixed calibre armament for the *Dantons* was a huge missed opportunity, but at the time French naval leaders uniformly favoured it for its substantially higher rate of fire at the combat ranges then expected. The advantages of a uniform calibre main battery for centralised gun fire control were also not yet fully appreciated. Another major technological advance of this period was diesel engines, particularly in submarines, but the only nation to build reliable diesels before 1914 was Germany. France, faced with the inability to build diesels in quantity, built eighteen more steam submarines (the *Pluviôse* class and *Thermidor*) before changing in 1906 to domestically-produced diesels for the *Brumaire* and *Bernoulli* classes. The larger diesel engines in later French submarines were notoriously unreliable and the French were still designing their largest cruising submarines with steam surface propulsion in 1914.

The only naval combat operations between 1897 and 1914 were the multi-national response to the Boxer Rebellion in China (1900) and the conquest of Morocco (beginning in 1907 after the Algesiras Conference cleared the way). As before, these overseas operations had no effect on building programmes, though like the conflict with China in 1884-1885 the Boxer Rebellion resulted in the second temporary expansion of the Far East Division into a full *Escadre*.

## Chapter Thirteen

# Battleships, 1897-1914

### (A) Battleships (*Cuirassés d'escadre*).

*IÉNA. Cuirassé d'escadre.* Battleship with two twin centreline main battery turrets. Two funnels, two military masts. Designed by Thibaudier.

At the beginning of 1897 France was building towards the fleet of 28 squadron battleships that the *Conseil supérieur* had called for in December 1896 in its Programme of 1896. With the three *Charlemagnes* and *Henri IV* under construction the Navy needed eight more battleships (A3 and A8 to A14) to reach the objective. The previously deferred A3 was included by Minister of Marine Édouard Lockroy in the original 1897 budget (submitted in February 1896) as a ship to be built at Brest to Bertin's 14,000-ton design, but on 13 May 1896 Minister of Marine Vice

Admiral Besnard changed it to a 9,000-ton *cuirassé d'escadre* analogous to *Henri IV*. This idea was dropped and Besnard then had Director of Materiel Thibaudier design an 'enlarged *Charlemagne*'. On 1 April 1897 Besnard included two 12,000-ton enlarged *Charlemagnes*, A3 and A8, in a draft supplemental budget for 1897. In July A3 was moved to the regular 1897 budget as *Iéna* replacing the 9,000-ton ship and A8 was deferred.

On 23 December 1896 Thibaudier, responding to instructions from Besnard, examined prospective modifications to the 12,000-ton *Charlemagne* type battleship which he had designed in 1893. He included some changes previously agreed to, including raising the upper edge of the main belt from 50cm to 90cm above the waterline while reducing its thickness (without plating) from 400mm to 320mm, a change made possible by using Harvey cemented armour. The thickness of the side above the belt and the central redoubt with the casemates was increased from 75mm to 110mm (including plating). The power of the engines and the steaming range were also increased to handle the increased displacement, and the hull was lengthened slightly. The Minister forwarded Thibaudier's study to the *Section technique* with instructions to determine the impact of removing one 305mm gun (making the after turret a single mounting), changing the secondary guns from 138.6mm to 164.7mm, and deleting the two underwater stern torpedo tubes. Thibaudier delivered a second study on 9 February 1897 and felt that deleting the fourth 305mm gun offered some

Outboard profile and overhead view (*plan d'ensemble*) of the battleship *Iéna*, built on the plans of M. Thibaudier and signed by naval constructor Lyasse at Brest probably on 31 October 1900. The small calibre artillery carried at this time included 8 x 100mm/45 M1893 guns (2 on the lower bridge forward, 4 on top of the amidships casemates, and 2 on the after bridge), 20 x 47mm/40 M1885 guns (8 on the lower platforms of the military masts, 4 on the shelter deck in the forward and after superstructures, 6 in the hull sides on the battery deck, and 2 on the same level in the admiral's gallery), and 2 x 37mm for the boats. There were also 2 x 65mm M1881 guns for the landing party.

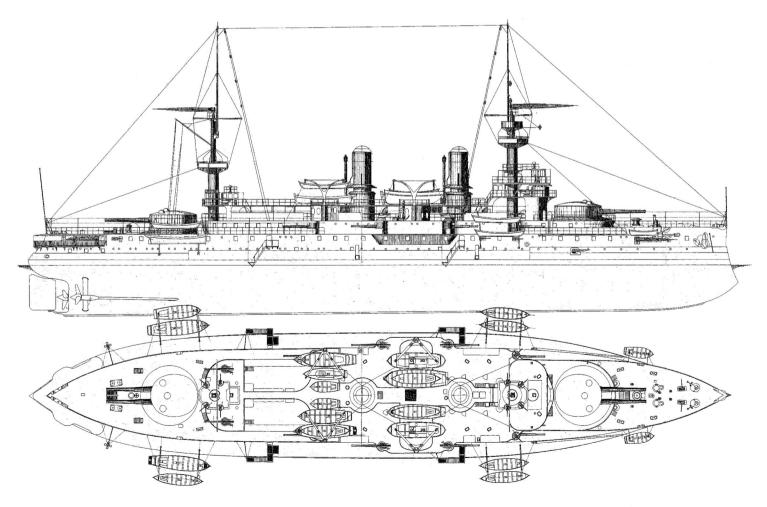

technical advantages but would reduce the military value of the ship compared to foreign equivalents, all of which had four guns, and opted instead to delete the two medium guns in shields on deck, making the secondary battery eight 164.7mm in casemates. This design was submitted to the *Conseil des travaux* on 11 February 1897 and approved by it on 4 March 1897 with relatively minor changes and an acknowledgment that displacement could be allowed to reach 12,200 tons. On 27 November 1897 Minister Besnard directed that *Iéna* retain Model 1893 164.7mm guns rather than upgrade to the new Model 1893-96.

**Dimensions & tons:** 122.31m oa, 120.82m wl (+1.300m ram), 122.150m pp (tip fwd to stern) x 20.84m ext (above wl), 20.81m wl. 12,104.634t disp (designed and normal). Draught: (designed) 7.950m mean, 8.450m aft. Men: 701 including 33 officers without flag, add 15 officers and 63 men with flag.

**Machinery:** 15,300ihp designed (natural draught) at 125rpm and 18kg/cm² boiler pressure. Designed speed 17kts. Trials (16.7.1901) 16,589ihp = 18.11kts (forced). 3 screws. 3 vertical triple expansion engines with 4 cylinders of 1.040m (1), 1.520m (1) and 1.580m (2) diameter and 0.760m stroke. 20 Belleville boilers. 770t coal (normal), 1,165t (surcharge) + 50t oil. Range 4,400nm @ 10.3kts.

**Armour:**
Side: Belt at waterline (cemented steel except special steel at the extreme ends) 320mm amidships, 272mm fwd, 224mm aft. Total height amidships 2.4m of which 0.9m above wl. Side above belt (special steel) 120mm lower and 80mm upper strakes, total height 1.5m, except 60mm forward where it was taller. Transverse bulkhead forward 150mm.
Guns: 305mm turrets (cemented steel) 290mm with 250 fixed bases. Casemates (special steel) 90mm sides with 72mm mobile gun shields.
Decks: Armoured (extra mild steel) 65mm on 18mm hull plating. Splinter deck 34mm hull plating.
Conning tower: 298mm max.

**Guns:** 4 x 305mm/40 M1893-96 (twin turrets), 8 x 164.7mm/45 M1893 QF (casemates), 8 x 100mm/45 M1893, 2 x 65mm/16 M1881 landing, 20 x 47mm/40 M1885, 2 x 37mm/20 M1885 QF for the boats. **Torpedoes:** 4 tubes for 450mm M1892 torpedoes (2 above water, 2 submerged). **Searchlights:** 6 x 60cm.

*Iéna* (A3) Brest Dyd/F.C. Méditerranée, Marseille.
On list 1.1898. Ord: 3.4.1897. K: 15.1.1898. L: 1.9.1898.
    Comm: 1.11.1899 (trials), 14.4.1902 (full).
Budget 1897. Installation of machinery completed 31.3.1900. Underway trials 11.1.1901 to 1.7.1901. Replaced *Charles Martel* 1.5.1902 as a division flagship in the *Escadre de la Méditerranée*. Drydocked 2.3.1907 at Toulon for minor maintenance work, devastated there 12.3.1907 by seven internal explosions and subsequent fires. The disaster was initially blamed on unstable *poudre B* propellent, later investigations could not identify the precise cause. 118 men out of 630 assigned were lost and the ship was a constructive total loss. Decomm. 3.7.1907. Refloated 8.10.1908, condemned 1908 and retained as a gunnery target. Struck 6.3.1909. Towed 27.7.1909 to Mèdes Point on the island of Porquerolles and subjected to fire from multiple types of guns, foundered there 2.12.1909. Wreck for sale 1909-1911, sold 21.12.1912 by the Administration des Domaines with the wreck of the coast defence ship *Tempête* to Lazare Nicolini of Toulon. Salvage operations interrupted 1.8.1914, resumed 18.9.1915 and continued through the late 1920s, the wreck being resold several times. Some more metal was recovered following another sale in 1957 but some remains in place.

---

*SUFFREN. Cuirassé d'escadre.* Battleship with two twin centreline main battery turrets and six single secondary battery turrets on the sides. Two funnels, two military masts. Designed by Thibaudier.

The 1898 budget submission (May 1897) included two 12,000-ton battleships, A9 and A10, but A10 was omitted before July 1897. In early 1898 the Chief of the Naval General Staff forwarded to Director of Material Thibaudier parameters for a modified *Iéna* design that would increase combat stability and offensive and defensive strength without exceeding by much the displacement on which the cost estimates in the new Programme of 1898 had been based. Following Minister Besnard's instructions he asked Thibaudier to submit the design as soon as possible to the *Conseil des travaux*, an action that followed on 16 February 1898. The displacement rose from 12,081 tons for *Iéna* to 12,278 tons. The hull was again slightly enlarged. For the secondary battery Thibaudier offered two options: twelve 164.7mm guns in six twin turrets or ten of them, six in single turrets and four in a casemate redoubt on the deck level below the turrets, the secondary turret guns being behind 130mm armour. The Council tended to prefer the single turret option. The top edge of the main belt was again raised, to 1.10m, the thickness of the belt was again reduced, to 300mm.

The Council examined the design on 5 April 1898. While noting that it was a notable improvement over its predecessors, the Council stated that it no longer met the standards for protection, buoyancy and stability just established by the Council after extensive study, and it withheld its approval. For example, the new standards called for the top of the belt to be 2.15 metres above the waterline instead of Thibaudier's 1.10 metres. This change alone would require a total reworking of the design above the waterline and the addition of at least 300 tons. Minister Besnard was unwilling to start over on the design and on 21 April 1898 he ordered from Brest the version of Thibaudier's design with the single secondary battery turrets.

Deck terminology above the main deck was changed in 1900 while *Suffren* was building. The battery deck (*pont de la batterie* or *pont intermédiaire*) became the 1st deck (*1er pont*) and the upper deck (*pont des gaillards*) became the 2nd deck (*2e pont*). The original terminology is used here for *Suffren* to facilitate comparison with the similar *Iéna* and *Charlemagne* types and the new is used for later classes.

**Dimensions & tons:** 125.900m oa, 124.250m wl (+1.250m ram), 125.500m pp (tip fwd to stern) x 21.420m ext, 21.360m wl. 12,795.437t disp (designed), 12,892.43t (normal). Draught: (designed) 7.950m mean, 8.450m aft. Men: 668 including 31 officers. Add 11 officers and 63 men with flag.

**Machinery:** 15,900ihp designed (natural draught) at 130rpm and 18kg/cm² boiler pressure. Designed speed 17kts. Trials (12.11.1903) 16,809.9ihp = 17.910kts (forced) at 133.56rpm. 3 screws. 3 vertical triple expansion engines with 3 cylinders of 0.950m, 1.460m, and 2.250m diameter and 0.800m stroke. 24 Niclausse boilers. 770t coal (normal), 1,223t (surcharge) + 52t oil. Range 4,170nm @ 8.4kts.

**Armour:**
Side: Belt at waterline (cemented steel except special steel at the extreme ends) 300mm amidships, 250mm fwd, 230mm aft. Total height amidships 2.5m of which 1.1m above wl. Side above belt (special steel) 110mm amidships (height 2.12m), 70mm bow. This belt, taller than in *Iéna* and fully protecting the side between the belt and the casemates, ended abreast the after 305mm turret where there was a 110mm transverse bulkhead and the deck was thickened. There was no transverse bulkhead forward.
Guns: 305mm turrets (cemented steel) 290mm front with 250mm fixed bases. 164.7mm turrets (special steel) 102mm front with 110mm max fixed bases. Casemates (special steel) 110mm max.
Decks: Armoured (extra mild steel) 55mm (60 mm aft of the after turret) on 20mm hull plating. Splinter deck 38mm hull plating.
Conning tower (cemented steel): 274mm front max.

**Guns:**
(1902) 4 x 305mm/40 M1893-96 (twin turrets), 10 x 164.7mm/45 M1893-96 (6 in single turrets and 4 in casemates), 8 x 100mm/45 M1893, 2 x 65mm/16 M1881 landing, 22 x 47mm/40 M1885,

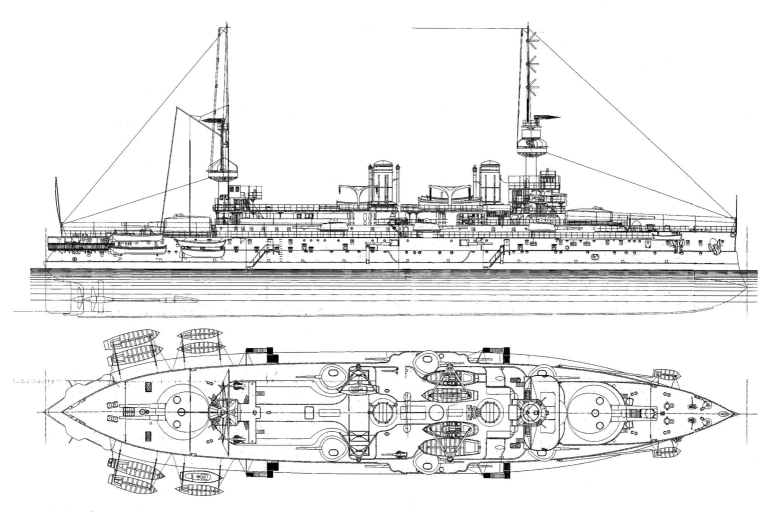

Outboard profile and overhead view (*plan d'ensemble*) of the battleship *Suffren*, built on the plans of M. Thibaudier and signed by naval constructor Deparis at Brest on 14 January 1904. The vertical lines at the ends of the ship show the fore and aft perpendiculars, in this case at the tip of the ram forward and the intersection of the stern with the waterline aft. The small calibre artillery carried at this time included 8 x 100mm/45 M1893 guns (2 on the lower bridge forward, 4 on the shelter/3rd deck between the funnels, and 2 on the after bridge), 22 x 47mm/40 M1885 guns (8 on the lower platforms of the military masts, 4 on the shelter deck in the forward and after superstructures, 8 in the hull sides on the battery/1st deck, and 2 on the same level in the admiral's gallery), and 2 x 37mm QF guns (on the upper bridge, also for the boats). There were also 2 x 65mm M1881 guns for the landing party.

2 x 37mm/20 M1885 QF. **Torpedoes:** 4 tubes for 450mm M1892 torpedoes (2 above water and 2 submerged). **Searchlights:** 6 x 60cm.
(1.1917) 4 x 100mm and 16 x 47mm were removed to arm requisitioned vessels, leaving only 4 x 47mm in the foretop and 2 x 47mm on HA (high angle) mounts on the after deck.

*Suffren* (A9) Brest Dyd/Indret.
On list 1.1899. Ord: 21.4.1898. K: 5.1.1899. L: 25.7.1899.
Comm: 10.10.1901 (trials), 3.2.1904 (full).
Budget 1898. Machinery installed 22.1.1900 to 15.7.1902. Machinery trials 9.1902 to 11.1903, gunnery trials 1.1902 to 1.1904.
Unprecedented firing trials against an armour plate mounted on the fore turret were conducted on 18.8.1903, in part to persuade Minister of Marine Pelletan of the effectiveness of modern armour. (*Masséna* fired 305mm shells from a range of 100 metres.) Left Brest 10.2.1904 and became flagship of the *Escadre de la Méditerranée* at Toulon. Flagship of the Mediterranean school division 11.11.1913 to 1.4.1914, then became flagship of the *Division de complément* of the *1re Armée navale*. Torpedoed 26.11.1916 by the German submarine *U-52* off Lisbon while en route to Lorient for repairs. The single torpedo apparently detonated a magazine and the ship sank instantly with all 648 men on board, her debris scraping the submarine on the way down.

**The Programme of 1900**
Diplomatic developments including the Fashoda crisis and rapid naval construction activity abroad after the French adopted the Programme of 1898 revealed the need for a new review of the constitution of the French fleet. In late 1899 Minister de Lanessan and some of his colleagues in the Waldeck-Rousseau ministry decided to address not only the composition of the fleet but also other aspects of France's maritime security by presenting Parliament with five bills, one to increase the number of ships in the fleet (the Programme of 1900), one to improve the arsenals and port facilities in France and overseas, one to improve French coast defences, one to improve colonial defences including for the navy's overseas bases, and one to extend France's network of overseas submarine cables. By including his fleet programme in legislation Lanessan got formal Parliamentary acceptance of the programme and commitment to fund it, both of which had been lacking for all previous French naval programmes since Minister Hamelin's and Dupuy de Lôme's Programme of 1857.

The intellectual basis of the 1900 programme was Admiral Fournier's concept of a single fleet in European waters made up of both battleships and large cruisers that could be used against either England or Germany. Against England, commerce raiders would inflict direct damage and force the British fleet to blockade French ports within the reach of French torpedo boats, while the battle fleet would maintain an active defensive posture that would wear down the English and perhaps provide an opportunity for a decisive blow. The transfer of coast and colonial defence to the Army allowed the Navy to concentrate all its modern assets on Europe. After much initial work including a preparatory memo to the Minister from the Naval General Staff, Minister de Lanessan on 29 November 1899 presided at the meeting in which the *Conseil supérieur* laid down the programme. It recommended that:

1. The fleet was to consist of two *Armées navales* (fleets), one centred on Toulon and one on Brest, each with two *escadres* (squadrons). The fleets were to be strong enough to ensure the defence of French military ports and take the offensive if needed in the Channel and the western Mediterranean, where it was impossible for France to accept the preponderance of any other navy.

2. The number of 28 battleships set by the *Conseil supérieur* on 17 December 1896 (four squadrons of six and four replacements) was to be retained. Of these six needed to be built, and their displacement was to be increased from the 12,000 tons adopted for battleships by the Council on 17 December 1896 to 14,865 tons (specifically Bertin's design for the *Patrie* class as approved by the *Conseil des travaux*).

3. The number of 25 armoured cruisers set by the Council on 17 January 1898 was to be retained. Six of these needed to be built and their displacement was to be increased to 12,400 tons provided the speed of the design then under consideration by the *Conseil des travaux* could be increased from 21 to 22 knots. (The Council was also aware of Bertin's larger 23-knot design.) Before the programme was sent to Parliament the number of armoured cruisers was changed to 24 (eight divisions of three) and the number to be built fell to five.

4. The Council could not reach a consensus on small cruisers of a displacement intermediate between 12,400-ton armoured cruisers and 300-ton *contre-torpilleurs*, and de Lanessan finally got it to decide to build five of the *estafettes* (dispatch cruisers) of 4,000 tons, 23 knots, and with eight 100mm guns being studied by the *Conseil des travaux* (one per squadron and one replacement) but specifying that these were not to be included in the programme legislation but were to be built under the annual budgets.

5. Normand's *Durandal* and *Hallebarde* were adopted as prototypes for a single category of *contre-torpilleurs* (torpedo boat destroyers) that would henceforth operate with the fleet. De Lanessan stated that funds would be available in the programme law to build 25.

6. The Council decided to maintain the category of *torpilleurs de haute mer* (seagoing torpedo boats) in addition to the larger *Durandal* type that would also support the fleet, although none were to be built. The current 1st class torpedo boats were to continue to be the backbone of the *défenses mobiles*.

7. Construction of the submarines and submersibles now building was to continue, experiments were to be conducted to determine the best types, and more were to be built as promptly as possible for both defence and attack.

In its background paper to Minister de Lanessan, the Naval General Staff stated that the construction of a special coast defence fleet no longer seemed necessarily as obsolete ships could be used. Likewise new foreign ships had made the specialized types formerly built for the overseas stations obsolete and it now made sense to replace them with units with the same military value as those built for European waters. All force planning and new construction would thus be concentrated on a single fleet for use in European waters.

The Government's five bills were presented on 30 January 1900 and all but the coast defence and cable bills eventually became law. De Lanessan's bill on the composition of the fleet asked to build 6 new battleships, 5 armoured cruisers, 28 *contre-torpilleurs*, 112 1st class torpedo boats, and 26 submarines or submersibles in a period of eight years for about 476.8 million francs. The Chamber not only accepted the programme but reduced the time limit to seven years and (on an amendment by Pelletan)

added more funds for submarines and torpedo boats. The programme language was then changed to apply the 476.8 millions to the battleships, armoured cruisers and *contre-torpilleurs* and to apply another 68.3 million francs to torpedo boats, submarines and submersibles whose number would be determined later. The programme was adopted by the Chamber of Deputies on 30 June 1900 and became law on 9 December 1900 after approval by the Senate. The full programme is in Appendix F.

---

*PATRIE* **Class.** *Cuirassés d'escadre.* Battleships with two twin centreline main battery turrets and six twin secondary battery turrets on the sides. Three funnels in groups of two and one, one military mast and one pole mast. Designed by Bertin.

The French first considered battleships in the 14,000-ton range in 1889 in response to the British Naval Defence Act but pressure from *Jeune École* politicians and navy traditionalists forced a reduction to 12,000 tons. Bertin produced his first large (13,631-ton) battleship design in 1891 as a way of presenting his radically different protection scheme for large ships, involving a much taller main armoured belt and two armoured decks. The Council on 8 December 1891 acknowledged that Bertin's armour scheme provided better protection for the vitals of the ship than the scheme in ships then building but rejected out of hand the twin main battery turrets in the design and feared that the displacement would be unacceptable. Bertin returned to the charge after Minister of Marine Lockroy made him Director of Materiel in late 1895. Lockroy planned to build the battleship A3 that was in the 1897 budget to Bertin's 14,000-ton design but Besnard replaced Lockroy in the Ministry at the end of April and changed A3 to a 9,000-ton ship analogous to *Henri IV*. (She ultimately became the 12,000-ton *Iéna*.)

Bertin, now chief of the *Section technique des constructions navales*, was so insistent that a large displacement was indispensable for a battleship that on 18 October 1897 Besnard asked him to explain as clearly and completely as possible his ideas on protection. Bertin responded on 16 November 1897 with a preliminary design for a 13,600-ton battleship and three explanatory notes. The *Conseil des travaux* examined these between 11 and 19 February 1898. As Bertin related it in 1906, the change of opinion in favour of an effective system of protection for battleships dated to the beginning of 1898. The conversion had come as the result of trials of sectional models of *Charles Martel* that were resumed at Brest by an engineer from Toulon after being begun by Bertin in 1891. The exhaustive report on these trials converted the naval constructors who had previously designed to *Conseil des travaux* specifications some of the worst *chavirables* (Bertin's term for ships that were inherently unstable) but who had now become Council members. (Bertin specifically had in mind Huin, who joined the Council on 1 December 1897.) The larger picture was also changing – Germany was about to pass Tirpitz's First Naval Law which called for a fleet of 17 modern battleships by 1903, the colonial confrontation with Britain that became the Fashoda crisis was brewing, and France was beginning to recover from the long economic recession that had begun in the 1870s, potentially making more funding available. In the February 1898 meetings the Council essentially endorsed Bertin's ideas and established new standards for protection of the stability and buoyancy of large warships. Specifically, it stated that all armoured ships would have an armoured caisson or box over the entire length of the ship except possibly the extreme stern to preserve the stability and buoyancy of the ship during combat. (This implied a rejection of the soft ends in the British *Majestic* type.) The bottom of the caisson and the belt would be far enough below the waterline that it would not emerge at angles of heel of about eight degrees or less. The caisson would have two armoured decks, one on its top and one at the bottom. In between would be the ship's cellular layer (*entre-pont cellulaire*) with minute subdivision including a row of cofferdams (watertight cells) along the sides. The upper armoured deck on the main deck level would be horizontal and lie at the top of the belt. The lower

The battleship *Patrie*, then in the 2nd *Escadre*. She and the five other battleships of the *Patrie* and *Démocratie* classes passed from the 1st to the 2nd *Escadre* on 1 August 1911, the new *Danton* class becoming the 1st *Escadre*. *(Postcard by M.D.)*

armoured deck on the 1st platform level would have a flat central part slightly above the waterline over the ship's vitals and on the sides angle down to meet the lower edge of the belt. Its resistance combined with that of the vertical belt armour that formed the sides of the caisson would prevent any projectiles from penetrating into the vitals of the ship. The side belt would have uniform thickness from its upper edge to 0.50 metres below the waterline. The Council also stated that there should be no hesitation in adopting the necessary displacements and asked for a complete study of a first-class battleship that met the new standards. On 5 April 1898, instead of endorsing the traditional protection battleship scheme as it had for *Iéna* on 4 March 1897, the Council refused to accept the design for *Suffren* with its traditional hull protection, citing a need for a main belt 2.15 metres high instead of the 1.10 metres in the design plus a complete restructuring of the remainder of the hull protection.

On 20 May 1898 the *Section technique* delivered to Besnard preliminary characteristics for a 15,000-ton battleship which on 5 May 1898 Minister Besnard used to create formal requirements. Besnard specified an armament of four 305mm guns in twin turrets with 320mm armour (including plating), fourteen 164.7mm guns in single turrets and casemates with 140mm armour, eight 100mm guns in shields, twenty 47mm guns, and two submerged and two above water torpedo tubes. Hull protection was to follow the Council's new February 1898 guidance, speed was set at 18 knots and the range at 5,000nm at 10 knots. Plans were prepared quickly. The design had a displacement of 15,000 tons, length of 133 metres, and engine power of 18,250ihp. The secondary battery was in four single turrets and ten casemates. Protection consisted of a 300mm belt (including plating, the thickness that the British had adopted the previous year) rising to 2.20m above the waterline, a 50mm flat upper armoured

deck (including plating), and a 60mm curved lower armoured deck that rose to the level of the waterline in the centre and sloped down to meet the belt at its lower edge 0.50m below the waterline. The caisson rose to 2.20m above the waterline amidships (2.60m in the bow) and descended to 1.50m below the waterline amidships, which would prevent the lower edge from being exposed at a heel of under seven and a half degrees.

Minster Lockroy referred the design on 30 June 1898 to the *Conseil des travaux*, which examined it on 22 July 1898. The Council noted that it appeared to have a straight bow as in Bertin's big cruisers and insisted on a robust ram. It recalled its long-standing preference for twin turrets for the secondary battery and felt some of the 164.7mm guns should be in twin turrets, perhaps permitting an increase to 16 barrels. Recent deliberations of the Council had concluded that a range of 4,000nm at 10 knots was sufficient, saving 215 tons of coal and possibly making it possible to keep the displacement under 15,000 tons. The Council asked for these and other modifications and for the portions of the design it had not yet seen. On 2 August 1898 Minister Lockroy asked the *Section technique* to prepare a full design with the expectation of laying down the ship during 1899. A8 was included in the 1899 budget (submitted in October 1898) with her design 'under study' and with A10 in the 1900 budget (July 1899) as 14,865-ton ships. While the Council and Bertin's *Section technique* now felt that 14,000 tons were needed for a balanced battleship, the *Conseil supérieur* persisted in wanting no more than 12,000 tons, reiterating this point twice on 17 December 1898 and 17 January 1899.

The *Conseil des travaux* examined Bertin's completed design on 28 February 1899. The displacement was now down to 14,865 tons, engine power was 17,475ihp, and normal range was 4,195nm at 10 knots. The secondary battery consisted of four twin turrets, two single turrets, and four guns in casemates, although Bertin proposed doubling the single turrets at the cost of 110 tons, an option that the Council quickly embraced. Bertin also offered with drawings an option with a secondary battery of twelve 194mm guns in twin turrets, that gun performing better in twin turrets than did the 164.7mm, at the expense of some reductions in the armour. (The Naval General Staff opposed this prescient change on the grounds that the 164.7mm gun was already larger than foreign secondary batteries and that rapidity and volume of fire should not be sacrificed to an unneeded increase in calibre.) There were still eight 100mm guns, now in a single battery. The height of the belt was increased to 2.30m above the waterline and the upper armoured deck was now 60mm of hard steel and the lower one 50mm on the flat parts and 70mm on the slopes. The Council enthusiastically approved Bertin's design with the sixteen 164.7mm guns and with a few additional changes, including replacing the after military mast with a simple signal mast, deleting the 100mm guns from the design, and adding instead two more 164.7mm casemates and some more 47mm guns. Minister Lockroy then on 29 May 1899 directed the *Section technique* to rework the design as suggested by the Council and also to increase the speed to 19 knots, if necessary with a slight reduction in the upper armoured deck.

Bertin's new plans were completed and presented to the new Minister (de Lanessan) on 8 August 1899. The need for the new minister to become informed and then inform Parliament, combined with the desire to combine the reform of battleship design with a new general fleet programme, caused more delays. Construction was deferred to the 1901 budget (May 1900), Minister de Lanessan approved the plans on 10 July 1900, six ships were authorized on 9 December 1900 by Parliamentary approval of the *Statut Naval* of 1900, and the order for the first ship (*Patrie*) was placed on 28 January 1901. Then, between 1902 and 1905, a new minister, Deputy Camille Pelletan, an old school extreme *Jeune École* advocate who disliked battleships on principle, interposed new delays. A contract for 305mm guns, signed on 16 May 1902, was not notified to the contractors until 4 August 1903. The first of the new ships only started trials in 1906.

The main battery guns elevated to 12 degrees for a maximum range of 12,500 metres. The design as of 1905 called for an anti-torpedo boat battery of twenty-six 47mm/50 M1902 guns (an improved version of the M1885) including 16 behind ports in the hull, 6 in the superstructures, and 4 in the foretop, plus two 37mm M1902 on the conning tower bridge However, it became clear that the 47mm gun was too small to be effective against modern destroyers, and after the commanding officer of *République* pointed out that the British were using 76mm and the Germans 88mm guns Minister of Marine Thomson on 22 August 1905 ordered the replacement of the sixteen 47mm in the hull and the above water torpedo tube in the stern with thirteen 65mm/50 M1902 guns (10 behind ports on the 1st deck, 2 on the main deck aft, and 1 in place of the after above-water torpedo tube). The ships retained ten 47mm guns in the military top and on the forward and after superstructures. The remaining two above water torpedo tubes were removed shortly after the August 1905 directive and reallocated to torpedo boats, leaving only two submerged tubes. Initially there were to have been six 60cm searchlights, but on 23 February 1904 the two on the mastheads were changed to 75mm. (*République* was completed with 60cm searchlights on the mastheads.) The four remaining 60cm searchlights were to illuminate targets for the 65mm guns. *Patrie* was originally to have received Normand small tube boilers derived from those in *Jeanne d'Arc* but this was changed on 20 December 1902. The ships carried no oil fuel because mixed firing with oil was abandoned on 1 December 1904. The design of the conning tower was as in *Suffren*, it proved too small for the 9 occupants. The view from it was obstructed by the bridge wings, which were removed in 1912-13.

**Dimensions & tons:** 135.250m oa, 131.000m wl (+2.800m ram), 133.800m pp (tip fwd to stern) x 24.250m ext and wl. 14,870.220t disp (designed, *Patrie*). Draught: (designed) 8.200m mean, 8.375m aft (real). Men: 742 including 32 officers without flag, 809 including 44 officers with flag.

**Machinery:** 17,500ihp designed (contract) at 110rpm and 18kg/cm² boiler pressure (15.5 kg/cm² at the engines). Designed speed 18kts.

Trials (*République*, 20.9.1906) 18,832ihp = 19.148kts at 120.83rpm and 17.005kg/cm² boiler pressure. 3 screws. 3 vertical triple expansion engines, those in *République* with 4 cylinders of 0.860m (1), 1,250m (1), and 1.400m (2) diameter and 1.150m stroke and those in *Patrie* with 3 cylinders of 0.880m, 1.310m, and 1.960m diameter and 1.150m stroke. 24 Niclausse boilers. 900t coal (normal), 1,800t (surcharge). Range 8,400nm @ 10kts.

**Armour:**

Side: Belt at waterline (cemented steel except special steel in extreme bow) 280mm amidships, 180mm fwd, 180mm aft. Total height amidships 2.2m of which 0.7m above wl. Upper strake 280mm amidships (height 1.6m), 180mm fwd, 180mm aft. Side above belt forward (special steel) 64mm.

Guns: 305mm turrets (cemented steel) 360mm max with 246mm max fixed bases. 164.7mm turrets 138mm front and sides (cemented steel) with 140mm max fixed bases (special steel). Casemates 140mm faces (cemented steel) and gun shields (special steel).

Lower armoured deck: flat (construction steel) 17mm, slopes (special steel) 36mm, all on 34mm hull plating.

Upper armoured deck: flat (construction steel) 18mm on 36mm hull plating.

Conning tower: 266mm max.

**Guns:**

(1906) 4 x 305mm/40 M1893-96M (turrets fore and aft), 18 x 164.7mm/45 M1893-96M (6 twin turrets and 6 casemates), 13 x 65mm/50 M1902, 10 x 47mm/50 M1902, 2 x 37mm/20 M1885 QF.

**Torpedoes:** 2 submerged tubes for 450mm M1904 torpedoes.

**Searchlights:** 6 x 60mm in *République*, 2 x 75mm and 4 x 60cm in *Patrie* in which the upper searchlights were ordered on 23.2.1904 to be changed from 60cm.

(1915-17) On 8.12.1915 the light armament for these two ships was fixed at 8 x 65mm and 4 x 47mm. The remaining guns were removed for use on patrol craft. In 1916, 4 x 47mm guns were given HA mounts. Three anti-aircraft machine guns were ordered added on 30.5.1916 and this number was doubled on 18.6.1917. In 11-12.1917 the 164.7mm guns from the after and amidships casemates in both ships were removed to help defend the Army base at Salonika, Greece.

*République* (A8) Brest Dyd/A.C. Loire, Saint Denis.

On list 1.1902. Ord: 28.6.1901. K: 2.12.1901. L: 4.9.1902. Comm: 20.5.1906 (trials), 12.1.1907 (full).

Budget 1899 (delayed to 1901). Named 23.3.1901. Engines installed 18.4.1904 to 23.3.1905, boilers first lit off 12.6.1906. Trials 7.1906 to 1.1907. Assigned 1.1.1907 to the *Escadre de la Méditerranée*. In 1914 was in the *2e Escadre de ligne* of the *1re Armée navale*. Blown ashore at Mudros 17-18.11.1917, to Toulon 1.1918. One gun in each 305mm turret was worn out and was replaced 1-2.1918, but on 14.2.1918 the replacements were ordered removed and sent to the front. With only two 305mm guns on board she was placed in training reserve (*réserve d'instruction*) 15.2.1918 and normal reserve 28.3.1918. She housed Greek sailors until placed in squadron reserve (*réserve d'escadre*) 21.10.1918 and normal reserve 1.7.1919. The school squadron at Toulon on 15.9.1919 was *République*, *Patrie*, and *Démocratie*, with *Justice* in the same role at Brest. Underway early 9.1919 to try newly installed 100mm guns. Entered dockyard 2.10.1919 to have her two 305mm turrets removed. School for gunnery as of 3.1920. Ordered replaced in the schools 9.12.1920 by *Diderot* (then in reserve). Decomm. 21.5.1921. Struck 29.6.1921. Sold to Vincenzo Rizzo and left Toulon 11.1922 to BU at Savona.

*Patrie* (A10) F.C. Méditerranée, La Seyne/FCM, Marseille.

On list 1.1902. Ord: 7.8.1901 (contract). K: 1.4.1902. L: 17.12.1903. Comm: 10.8.1906 (trials), 1.7.1907 (full).

Budget 1900 (delayed to 1901). Construction reassigned from Toulon to contract c1900. Named 23.3.1901. Contract notified 4.9.1901. Engines installed 5.9.1903 to 17.8.1904, boilers first lit off 19.4.1906. Trials 7.1906 to 10.1907, then joined the *Escadre de la Méditerranée*. In 1914 was in the *2ᵉ Escadre de ligne* of the *1ʳᵉ Armée navale*. Returned to Toulon 15.6.1919 from Constantinople. Assigned to the Training Division (*Division d'instruction*) 1.8.1919 replacing *Victor Hugo*, in service 1.9.1919. Her 305mm turrets were removed in late 1919 or early 1920. School for torpedoes as of 1920. Ordered replaced in the schools 9.12.1920 by *Voltaire* (then in reserve) but retained as school for torpedoes and electricity 19.2.1921. Decomm. 20.6.1927 and replaced by *Condorcet*. Condemned 9.1.1928. Retained as a stationary school for engineers at Saint Mandrier 1927-1936, then condemned again 7.11.1936 and handed over to the Domaines for sale. Sold 25.9.1937 to M. Van Acker to BU.

---

**DÉMOCRATIE** Class. *Cuirassés d'escadre*. Battleships with two twin centreline main battery turrets and six single secondary battery turrets on the sides. Three funnels in groups of two and one, one military mast and one pole mast. Designed by Bertin.

The announcement in 1902 that the British *King Edward VII* class would have a secondary battery of four 9.2-inch (234mm) guns caused the French to conclude that its 164.7mm M1893-95 gun was no longer competitive, and Minister of Marine Pelletan on 3 December 1902 suspended construction of 164.7mm turrets and casemates. Faced with a choice between twin turrets with a more powerful 164.7mm M1902 gun and single turrets with a 194mm M1902 gun, a ministerial commission appointed on 20 February 1903 chose the 194mm option, five votes to four (the majority including Bertin and Pelletan). (Twin 194mm turrets were not seriously considered because of weight and difficulties with ammunition supply.) The modified plans were approved by Minister Pelletan on 14 October 1903 and the new secondary armament was fixed on 14 December 1903 as ten 194mm/50 M1902 guns in six single turrets and four casemates. *République* and *Patrie* were too far advanced to be changed. The decision was subsequently heavily criticised for reducing the number of barrels on the ships and because the heavier ammunition was harder to handle.

The bridge wings were removed in 1912-13 to clear sight lines from the conning tower. Tethered balloons were fitted to *Démocratie* in 1918, requiring the removal of all but the lowest portion of the mainmast. The balloons proved to be hard to use in heavy weather and the experiment was soon abandoned.

**Dimensions & tons:** 135.250m oa, 131.000m wl (+2.800m ram), 133.800m pp (tip fwd to stern) x 24.250m ext and wl. 14,919.253t disp (designed, *Démocratie*). Draught: (designed) 8.200m mean, 8.375m aft (real). Men: 742 including 32 officers without flag, 809 including 44 officers with flag.

**Machinery:** 18,000ihp designed (contract) at 110rpm and 18kg/cm² boiler pressure (*Justice*) or 21kg/cm² boiler pressure (others). Designed speed 18kts. Trials (*Liberté*, 14.9.1907) 20,434ihp = 19.31kts at 120.4rpm and 20.54kg/cm² boiler pressure. 3 screws. 3 vertical triple expansion engines. Engines of *Liberté* (4 cylinders) as *République*, those of *Démocratie* and *Justice* (3 cylinders) as *Patrie*, those of *Vérité* with 3 cylinders of 0.860m, 1.240m, and 1.920m diameter and 1.150m stroke. 22 Belleville boilers (24 Niclausse boilers in *Justice*). 900t coal (normal), 1,800t (surcharge). Range 8,400nm @ 10kts.

**Armour:**
Side: Belt at waterline (cemented steel except special steel in extreme bow) 280mm amidships, 180mm fwd, 180mm aft. Total height amidships 2.2m of which 0.7m above wl. Upper strake 280mm amidships (height 1.6m), 180mm fwd, 180mm aft. Side above belt forward (special steel) 64mm.
Guns: 305mm turrets (cemented steel) 360mm max with 246mm max fixed bases. 194mm turrets 156mm front and sides (cemented steel)

with 143mm max fixed bases (special steel) except 130mm max fixed bases (cemented steel) in *Justice*. Casemates 174mm faces (cemented steel), 160mm gun shields except 170mm gun shields in *Vérité*.
Lower armoured deck: flat (construction steel) 17mm, slopes (special steel) 36mm, all on 34mm hull plating.
Upper armoured deck: flat (construction steel) 18mm on 36mm hull plating.
Conning tower: 266mm max.

**Guns:**
(1907) 4 x 305mm/40 M1893-96M (twin turrets), 10 x 194mm/50 M1902 (6 single turrets and 4 casemates), 13 x 65mm/50 M1902, 10 x 47mm/50 M1902, 2 x 37mm/20 M1885 QF. **Torpedoes:** 2 submerged tubes for 450mm M1904 torpedoes. **Searchlights:** 2 x 75mm (foremast and after bridge) and 4 x 60cm (hull sides).
(1915-17) The light armament for these three ships was fixed on 8.12.1915 at 10 x 65mm and 8 x 47mm. The remaining guns were removed for use on patrol craft. In 1916, 4 x 47mm guns were given HA mounts. Three anti-aircraft machine guns were ordered added on 30.5.1916 and this number was doubled on 18.6.1917.

*Liberté* (A11) A.C. Loire, Saint Nazaire/ACL, Saint Denis.
On list 1.1903. Ord: 21.5.1902 (contract). K: 11.1902. L: 19.4.1905. Comm: 5.9.1907 (trials), 13.4.1908 (full).
Budget 1902. Engines installed 1.11.1905 to 18.4.1906, boilers first lit off 2.5.1907. Sailed from her builder at Saint Nazaire 5.9.1907 to Brest where her main armament was fitted and she conducted trials. Trials 7.1907 to 4.1908. Left Brest for Toulon 18.3.1908 and joined the *Escadre de la Méditerranée*. On 25.9.1911 in the roadstead at Toulon a fire broke out in her forward magazines leading to the detonation of around 50 tons of explosives. The forward 55 metres of the ship essentially disintegrated and the remaining decks were peeled back over the stern. 210 men died including 67 on nearby ships and craft that were struck by debris. Unstable *Poudre B* was blamed, compounded by excessive heat in the magazines and constant handling of ammunition during refits. The incident followed previous ammunition-related fires in *Amiral Duperré* (13.5.1896), *Vauban* (2.9.1900), *Descartes* 25.10.1900), *Forbin* (14.4.1901), *Charlemagne* (30.12.1904), and *Iéna* (12.3.1907). Ordered struck 20.10.1911. Struck 25.10.1911. Salvage suspended during the war. Contract signed 28.7.1921 with Boursier, Borrely and Sidensner, Sidensner being a former Russian navy engineer who had raised the dreadnought *Imperatritsa Mariya* at Sevastopol in 1917-19 after a magazine explosion and assisted in refloating the grounded French *Mirabeau* there in 1919, in both cases using compressed air. The firm was to receive in payment 23,000 tons of condemned ships (the navy chose *Vérité*, *Démocratie* and *République*, and the firm also got *Mirabeau*, *Charlemagne*, *Brennus*, and others). Air compressors were put on the old cruiser *Latouche Tréville* and two discarded submarines were used as pontoons. The remains of *Liberté* were refloated and docked 21.2.1925 in a graving dock at Toulon to BU.

*Démocratie* (A12) Brest Dyd/F.C. Méditerranée, Le Havre.
On list 1.1903. Ord: 5.4.1902. K: 1.5.1903. L: 30.4.1904. Comm: 5.7.1907 (trials), 9.1.1908 (full).
Budget 1902. Allocation to Brest announced 3.1902. Engines installed 1.5.1905 to 15.5.1905, boilers first lit off 26.12.1906. Trials 5.1907 to 1.1908, then joined the *Escadre de la Méditerranée*. In 1914 was in the *2ᵉ Escadre de ligne* of the *1ʳᵉ Armée navale*. Returned to Toulon from Constantinople 11.6.1919. To schools 10.7.1919, to special reserve 1.4.1920. Decomm. 31.12.1920. Struck 18.5.1921. Sold to Vincenzo Rizzo and left Toulon 9.1922 to BU at Savona.

*Justice* (A13) F.C. Méditerranée, La Seyne/FCM, Marseille.
On list 1.1903. Ord: 21.5.1902 (contract). K: 1.4.1903. L: 27.10.1904. Comm: 17.7.1907 (trials), 15.4.1908 (full).
Budget 1902. Trials 6.1907 to 4.1908, then joined the *Escadre de la*

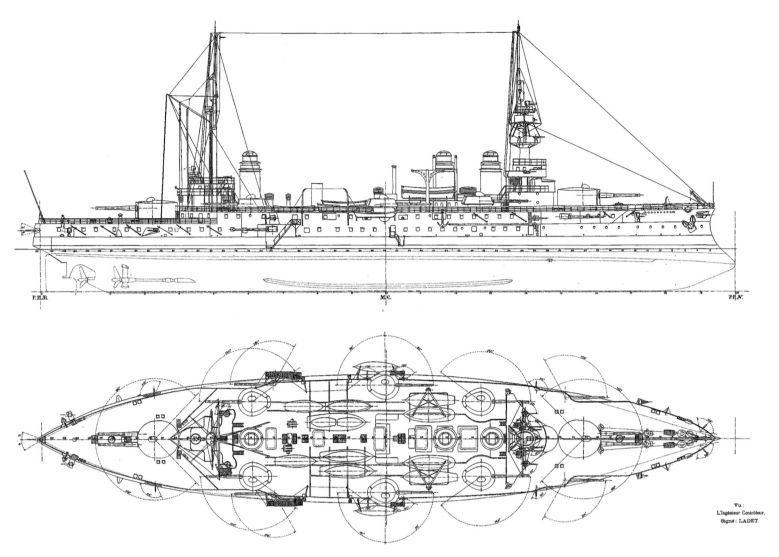

Undated outboard profile and overhead view (*plan d'ensemble*) of the 14,870-ton battleship *Justice*, built by the Forges et Chantiers de la Méditerranée at La Seyne on the plans of M. Bertin, and bearing the names of the director of the yard, Rimbaud, and the Navy's control officer, Ladet. The small calibre artillery carried at this time included 13 x 65mm/50 M1902 guns (10 behind ports on the 1st deck, 2 on the main deck aft, and 1 in the stern on the main deck in place of the deleted above-water stern torpedo tube), 10 x 47mm/50 M1902 guns (4 in the fighting top 2 on the forward superstructure, and 4 on the aft superstructure), and 2 x 37mm guns for the boats.

---

*Méditerranée*. In 1914 was in the *2ᵉ Escadre de ligne* of the *1ʳᵉ Armée navale*. Assigned to the division of schools of the Atlantic at Brest 15.5.1919, to reserve 1.7.1919, conversion lasted to 12.1919. School ship as of 3.1920. To special reserve 1.4.1920, replaced by *D'Entrecasteaux* and towed to Landévennec 27.7.1920. Decomm. 1.3.1921. Struck 29.11.1921. Sold 30.12.1921 at Brest to M. Jacquart and towed to Hamburg 5.1922 to BU.

*Vérité* (A14) C.A. Gironde, Bordeaux-Lormont/Schneider, Creusot.
On list 1.1903. Ord: 21.5.1902 (contract). K: 4.1903. L: 28.5.1907. Comm: 5.1.1908 (trials), 11.9.1908 (full).
Budget 1902. Engines installed 3.1905 to 4.1906, boilers first lit off 14.5.1907, all before launching. Embarked her main armament at Brest from 14.10.1907. Trials 10.1907 to 9.1908. Before entering service she took the President of the Republic to the Baltic between 5 July and 6 August 1908, she then ran her long distance (four day endurance) trial before joining the *Escadre de la Méditerranée*. In 1914

was flagship of the *2ᵉ Escadre de ligne* of the *1ʳᵉ Armée navale*. To reserve 1.8.1919 after machinery repairs abandoned, to special reserve effective 1.10.1919. Struck 18.5.1921. Sold to Vincenzo Rizzo and left Toulon 6.1922 to BU at Savona.

---

## The Programme of 1905

Soon after Deputy Gaston Thomson replaced Camille Pelletan as Minister of Marine on 24 January 1905, Parliament on 23 February 1905 during its discussion of Pelletan's 1905 budget invited the government to present as soon as possible a new shipbuilding programme. The *Conseil supérieur* met between 10 and 15 May 1905 and produced it as part of a new programme for the constitution of the fleet.

For battleships, the May 1905 fleet programme added a fifth squadron of six battleships to replace the nine now obsolete coast defence ships that had existed in 1900, which with the 28 battleships in the 1898 and 1900 programmes produced a planned fleet of 34 battleships. Of the existing 37 battleships, 23 would remain at the end of the programme period leaving eleven to be built. In 1905 the Council felt that the speed of 18 knots, main armament, and protection of the *Patrie* class were generally suitable for new battleships, but the medium battery needed to be increased from 164.7mm to at least 194mm guns, the calibre of the light artillery needed to be increased to 65mm, and the hull needed to receive anti-torpedo protection.

For armoured cruisers, the 1905 programme adopted two types, a 1ˢᵗ class in the 13,600- to 14,000-ton range for European waters and a 2ⁿᵈ class of about 9,000 tons based on the *Dupleix* type for overseas. Two types were needed because ships of over 9,000 tons could not enter many overseas ports. Of the eighteen units of each type in the programme, ten of the 1st class and six of the 2nd class needed to be built. For European waters each of the five battleship *escadres* needed a scouting division of three 1st class armoured cruisers with three replacement units, while the four main overseas stations needed a total of 12 of the 2nd class armoured cruisers, including an *escadre* of six on the China station, plus two replacements and a reserve force of four more to be sent where needed in time of crisis.

The Council included scouts (*éclaireurs d' escadre*) in the programme. (They had also discussed them in 1900 but had not included them in that programme.) These 3,600-ton light cruisers were to link the armoured cruiser scouting groups to the main body of battleships and also carry orders and information like *estafettes*. It provided one scout for each of five *escadres* with a sixth as a spare.

The Council as before wanted each battleship to be accompanied by a *contre-torpilleur*, and in 1905 it extended this to the six armoured cruisers on the China station. With these 36 and seven replacements, 43 *contre-torpilleur*s were needed for fleet use. In addition 38 were needed as leaders for the *Défenses mobile* and 28 were needed for independent defensive service in French ports, producing a total of 109 *contre-torpilleurs* of which 66 needed to be built. In 1905 new units were to be of the 336-ton type now building but enlarged with bows strengthened for ramming.

The Council's approach to torpedo boats and submarines was that to some degree their functions overlapped and that it was important for economy reasons not to build duplicative capabilities. Because the submarine was potentially a more complete instrument than the torpedo boat (which could not attack in the daytime except under unusual circumstances), the Council cut back significantly on the number of torpedo boats needed, retaining 170. About 50 replacements would be needed by 1919, but the Council saw no use in inscribing them in the current programme. It endorsed Normand's 98-ton type for these vessels. It also retained a category of torpedo vessels for fleet use smaller than *contre torpilleurs* (the former *torpilleurs de haute mer*) as it had done in 1900, but it again omitted them from the building programme. On the other hand, it included 82 offensive submarines in the fleet programme with 72 to be built, because it had great hopes for this type of ship which could act offensively at considerable distances for several days, and it also included 49 defensive submarines with 18 to be built, in part because of the apparent success of the *Naïade* type.

## The Programme of 1906

Subsequently the results of the Russo-Japanese War became clear and Germany presented a new naval law (the *Novelle*) to the Reichstag. On 2 February 1906 Thomson had the *Conseil supérieur* take another look at the naval programme which it did in March 1906.

For battleships, the Naval General Staff argued that in light of the rapid growth of foreign navies (primarily the German) a larger effort was needed and raised its recommended number of battleships to be built from 11 to 24. The Council accordingly set the planned force size at 38 battleships at the end of 1917, when 14 of the existing 32 battleships would still remain in the fleet. (With continued retirements and no follow-on programme the fleet size would fall to 33 battleships in 1921.) The Council gave first priority for construction to six battleships (the *Danton* class) in an initial *tranche* that also included ten enlarged *contre-torpilleurs* and 20 submersibles, with another six battleships to follow before construction of cruisers resumed. In 1906, reflecting the work done to date on the *Danton* design, it called for a displacement of 18,000 tons, length of 145 metres, speed of 19 knots, an armament of four 305mm M1902 guns, twelve 240mm M1902 guns, sixteen 75mm guns, eight 47mm guns, and two submerged torpedo tubes (more if possible), and a protection scheme built around a 270mm main belt. It recommended against fitting the six ships with turbines but wanted an experiment conducted on a smaller ship.

The Council made big changes in armoured cruisers in the 1906 programme. It renounced the 2nd class armoured cruisers, their place to be filled by existing ships, and reduced the total number of armoured cruisers

in the programme from 36 to 20. Of these, fourteen from the three *Montcalm*s to the two *Edgar Quinet*s would still exist at the end of the programme period, leaving six to be built. These were to be three to four knots faster than the fastest battleships, have a large calibre armament, and a displacement of not over 16,000 tons if possible. These six, however, would only be built starting in 1910 at a rate of one per year and only after the first twelve new battleships were in hand.

The Council retained the six scouts (*éclaireurs d'escadre*) in the 1905 programme, but it decided that the six to be built, like the six armoured cruisers, would not be begun until the first twelve battleships had been laid down, delaying them to at least 1910.

The Council also retained the 109 *contre-torpilleurs* (with 66 to be built) in the 1905 programme despite the reductions in the armoured cruiser force that some were to support. The ten *contre-torpilleurs* that were included in the priority programme with the six *Danton*s were to be of the type with the reinforced bows mentioned in 1905 but now up to 520 tons. (They became the 450-tonners.) The earlier types of *contre-torpilleurs* back to *Durandal* were to be handed down to coastal use as the newer ones became available.

Plans for torpedo boats and submarines were unchanged from 1905. The 20 submersibles in the priority programme with the six *Danton*s were to include 17 of Laubeuf's *Pluviôse* type, two of a larger long-range type (probably *Archimède* and *Mariotte*) and Maurice's *Charles Brun*.

The Minister included in the 1906 budget the 6 battleships along with 6 *contre-torpilleurs* and 20 offensive submarines, and followed in the 1907 budget with 5 more *contre-torpilleurs* and 10 more offensive submarines and in the 1908 budget with 10 more *contre-torpilleurs* and 5 more offensive submarines. The full programmes of 1905 and 1906 are in Appendix F.

----

*DANTON* Class. *Cuirassés d'escadre*. Battleships with two twin centreline main battery turrets and six large twin secondary battery turrets on the sides. Five funnels in groups of three and two, one heavy pole mast forward and one regular pole mast aft. Designed by Lhomme.

The design was produced by the *Section technique* under Delphin Albert Lhomme, with much of the work being done by naval constructor Numa Émile Prosper Gayde. Following the adoption of the Programme of 1905 by the *Conseil supérieur* in May 1905 Minister of Marine Thomson proposed a first tranche of the programme to consist of three 16,500-ton battleships with four 305mm M1893-96 guns, twelve 194mm guns or preferably larger, reciprocating engines producing 18 knots, and most other characteristics as *Patrie*. In early June 1905 Thomson had *Directeur central des constructions navales* Auguste René Dudebout prepare specifications for the three 1906 battleships to be sent to the ports and to the *Section technique* with a request for designs. On 26 June 1905 Chief of the Naval General Staff Touchard convened a conference with Dudebout, Lhomme, and Director of Artillery Brigadier General Gossot, and the group decided that to get the long-range fire at 5,000 to 7,000 metres that was needed under modern conditions a 240mm secondary battery was necessary. It also decided to replace the anti-torpedo boat armament of twenty-four 65mm guns proposed by the *Section technique* with sixteen 75mm and eight 47mm guns. Dudebout on 30 June 1905 offered Minister of Marine Thomson three options based on these discussions and the Minister chose the largest and most expensive one, an 18,000-ton ship with four 305mm and twelve 240mm guns, though he set 18,000 tons as a maximum. Knowledge of the Japanese *Satsuma* with her four 305mm and twelve 254mm guns may have contributed to this decision.

On 27 July 1905 this option was sent to the ports with a request for new designs. On 26 August 1905 Thomson, on the urging of the Budget Commission, asked the ports and the *Section technique* to try to get a speed above 18 knots. The *Section technique* on 12 December 1905 was able to raise the speed to 19 knots and engine power to 22,500ihp but at the cost of some armour protection. This and one other design received in response to the July 1905 invitation were referred to the *Comité technique* on 15 January 1906 and the design of Lhomme and the *Section technique* was selected. However, the Committee felt that it was necessary either to increase the displacement, reduce the speed back to 18 knots, or make further reductions in protection that would make it hard to call the resulting ship a battleship. At this point the Naval General Staff looked at two more radical options, one with ten 305mm guns in which single 305mm turrets replaced the twin 240mm turrets and one with six 305mm and twelve 194mm guns. The first had to be rejected because its displacement was too high while the third was also rejected, leaving the design with four 305mm and twelve 240mm guns as still the best choice. The rate of broadside and the frequency of hitting would also be greater with the mixed battery than with the all-305mm battery.

Between 26 and 31 March 1906 the *Conseil supérieur*, based on major developments abroad during 1905, revisited the naval programme. It felt that any major changes in the 18,000-ton design would be impossible without causing enormous delays in construction of the ships, and in view of world conditions asked that this not be done and that any further improvements be left to later ships. On 6 March 1906, in view of the rapid growth of the German, American, and Japanese fleets and other factors, Minister Thomson and the Budget Commission agreed to double the first tranche of the 1906 programme from three to six battleships. (The new ones all got 'A' designators like those of the first three followed by 'bis'.) The first three ships were funded in the 1906 budget while the other three were added in the 1907 budget to be begun with 1906 funds. The 1906 naval programme was written into the 1906 budget bill and was discussed by Parliament between 6 and 23 March 1906. The budget was passed on 17 April 1906. On 26 April 1906 Lhomme submitted final plans for ministerial approval, the displacement now being 18,234 tons, and on 8 May 1906 battleship A15 was assigned to Brest, A15bis to Lorient, and the Machinery Commission (the *Commission permanente des machines et du grand outillage*) was ordered to contract for the other four. The non-traditional names of the ships, assigned at this time, reflected the personal admiration of Minister Thomson for the Encyclopedists (Diderot), enlightenment philosophers (Voltaire), and the leaders of the early stages of the French Revolution.

However, two more major changes were made to the design. During the Parliamentary discussions of the 1906 budget in March 1906 the issue of giving the ships turbines was raised for the first time. The British had been able to get significantly more speed with the new technology than with reciprocating machinery. During its discussions of the 1906 programme at the end of March the *Conseil supérieur* was consulted on this issue and responded with a unanimous 'no' out of concern over the construction delays and the other risks of introducing the new technology on such a large scale. It did ask for an experiment in a smaller ship, and also asked for a mission to be sent to Britain to learn more about activity there. The question came up again when the Senate debated the budget on 12 April 1906. The mission to Britain returned on 1 June 1906 and on 11 July 1906 the *Section technique* completed specifications for the installation of Parsons turbines in the ships. On 26 July 1906 the Machinery Commission was ordered to get bids based on these specifications. Four offers for reciprocating machinery and two for turbines were received and Dudebout suggested building three ships with reciprocating engines and three with turbines. However, the Chamber on 12 December 1906 and the Senate on 25 December 1906 insisted on turbines in all six ships and Minister Thomson on 26 December 1906 ordered their adoption. The contracts for the hulls, engines, and turrets of the remaining four ships, delayed by Parliamentary interpellations, were also signed on the same day.

The final major change was in the model of the large guns. On 3 August 1906 Thomson ordered a study of using larger and heavier 305mm M1906 guns (requiring redesigned turrets) in place of the 305mm M1893-96 guns that had been in the design since May 1905. Thomson adopted the newer model 305mm guns and also newer model 240mm guns on 27 November 1906. Tests had shown that the best hull form for getting the designed

20-knot speed included a straight bow, and when deciding on turbines on 26 December 1906 Minister Thomson also ordered this change, making these the first French battleships since the 1860s except for *Brennus* without a ram bow. (Bertin had proposed a straight bow for the *Patrie* class but was overruled by conservatives on the *Conseil des travaux*.). The lines of the stern also had to be altered for four screws. New plans with these last major changes were again presented to Minister Thomson for approval on 28 March 1907.

This class had an *entrepont cellulaire* (cellular layer) with 186 watertight compartments similar in concept to that in *Patrie* behind the belt. It was also the only class of French battleships before the 1920s other than *Henri IV* to have anti-torpedo protection. In this class it consisted of an internal bulge (*caisson de protection sous-marine*) inside the hull below the lower armoured deck extending between the two 305mm turrets. Its inner bulkhead was 2m from the hull side, and was constructed of 3 layers of 15mm special steel with 3% nickel, and the caisson was subdivided into 23 compartments on each side of the ship. Between the caisson and the ship's vitals were 16 watertight compartments on each side of the ship, of which 12 were void and four were coal bunkers.

The turbines were in 3 engine rooms. Each wing shaft had its own engine room with one HP ahead turbine and one HP astern turbine. The inboard shafts shared an engine room on the centreline and each shaft had one cruising ahead turbine (HP to starboard and MP to port) and one LP ahead turbine whose casing also housed an astern turbine.

In addressing this design during its discussions in March 1906 of the Programme of 1906 the *Conseil supérieur* made a special point of stipulating that the ships should have no bridge or navigation shelter (pilot house) above the conning tower. In addition, nothing was to be placed against the outer sides of the conning tower. The Council was concerned about debris falling on the conning tower during action and disabling it. This produced a very austere forward superstructure in both this class and the *Edgar Quinet* class armoured cruisers with practically no location protected against the weather outside the conning tower for the underway watch.

The boilers were not ordered until 3 June 1908. Much time was lost considering Babcock & Wilcox and d'Allest boilers, which were eventually found to be too large to fit into the ships whose compartments had been designed for the Belleville and Niclausse boilers that ultimately were fitted. The performance of the Belleville boilers was generally satisfactory, but the Niclausse boilers lacked the flexibility and power to work well with turbines and also burned coal inefficiently, causing them to generate vast amounts of smoke and even to eject showers of sparks and flames from their funnels. The main problem with the propulsion plants in these ships, however, was that their early-model direct drive turbines had a voracious appetite for steam and therefore coal. During fleet operations in 1914 *Mirabeau* had to keep at least 20 of her 26 Belleville boilers on line at all times. Actual experience varied widely between the six ships because they had four different combinations of turbine manufacturers and boiler types, but overall the steaming range of this class with full bunkers was rated at 3,500nm at 10 knots, less than half of the rated 8,400nm at 10 knots of the preceding type with its reciprocating engines.

Tethered balloons were fitted to *Mirabeau* at Toulon between April and July 1917, to *Vergniaud* in late 1917, to *Condorcet* in 1918, and to *Voltaire* in July 1918, requiring the removal of all but the lowest portion of the mainmast. The balloons proved to be hard to use in heavy weather and the experiment was soon abandoned. *Diderot* was the only member of the class to retain both masts after the war.

**Dimensions & tons:** 146.600m oa, 145.000m wl and pp x 25.800m ext (below wl), 25.660m wl. 18,358.983t (designed, *Danton*). Draught: (designed) 8.262m mean, 8.438m aft (real). Men: 856 including 25 officers without flag, add 14 officers and 55 men with flag.

**Machinery:** 22,500shp designed at 300rpm and 18kg/cm$^2$ boiler pressure. Designed speed 19.25kts. Trials (*Voltaire*, 9.5.1911) 28,850shp = 20.663kts at 332.42rpm and 18.52kg/cm$^2$ boiler pressure. 4 screws.

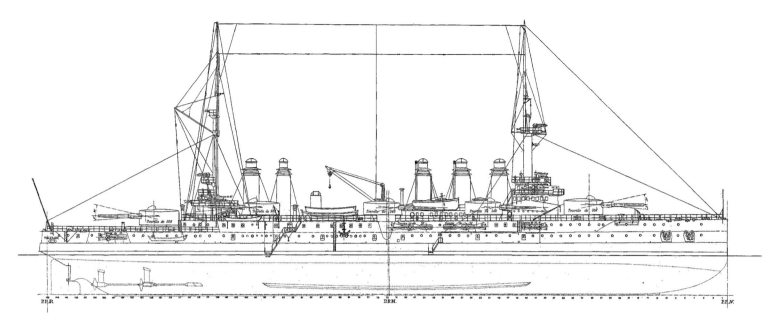

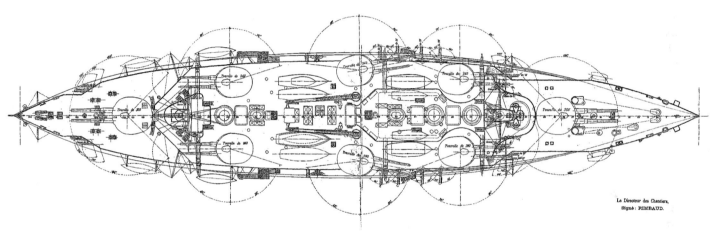

Undated outboard profile and overhead view (*plan d'ensemble*) of the 18,235-ton battleship *Voltaire*, built by the Forges et Chantiers de la Méditerranée at La Seyne on the plans of M. Lhomme, and bearing the names of the director of the yard, Rimbaud, and the Navy's control officer, Ladet. The small calibre artillery carried at this time included 16 x 75mm/62.5 M1908 guns (12 behind ports on the 1st deck and 4 aft on the main deck), 8 x 47mm/50 M1902 Hotchkiss guns (4 on the forward and 4 on the after superstructure), and 2 x 37mm/20 M1885 guns for the boats. There were also 2 x 65mm/16 M1881 landing guns.

8 Parsons turbines (direct drive). 26 boilers (Belleville in the two dockyard ships and *Voltaire*, Niclausse in the other three). 965t coal (normal), 2,027t (surcharge). Range 3,500nm @ 10kts.

**Armour:**

Side: Belt at waterline (cemented steel except in the extreme bow) 250mm amidships, 180mm fwd, 180mm aft. Height of combined belt (two strakes) about 4m amidships with 1.6m below the wl to 2.4m above. Side above belt forward (special steel) 64mm.

Guns: 305mm turrets (cemented steel) 340mm max with 246mm max fixed bases. 240mm turrets 225mm max (cemented steel) with 154 mm max fixed bases (special steel).

Lower armoured deck: flat (construction steel) 15mm, slopes (special steel) 40mm, all on 30mm hull plating.

Upper armoured deck: flat (construction steel) 16mm on 32mm hull plating.

Underwater protection: Internal bulge consisting of 45mm of hull plating (60kg construction steel) from frame 20 to frame 125 with inner wall 2m from the side of the ship and watertight compartments on both sides.

Conning tower: 266mm max.

**Guns:**

(1911) 4 x 305mm/45 M1906 (2 twin turrets), 12 x 240mm/50 M1902-06 (6 twin turrets), 16 x 75mm/62.5 M1908 (12 behind ports on the 1st deck, 4 aft on the main deck), 2 x 65mm/16 M1881 landing, 8 x 47mm/50 M1902, 2 x 37mm/20 M1885 QF for the boats. **Torpedoes:** 2 submerged tubes for 450mm M1909R torpedoes. **Searchlights:** 8 x 75mm.

(1915-17) The after four 75mm guns on the main deck were removed and their ports plated over because they proved impossible to work in a seaway, reducing the number of these guns to 12. The 4 x 47mm on the after superstructure were landed for use in patrol craft and the 4 x 47mm on the forward superstructure were given HA mountings and moved to locations more favourable for AA fire.

(1918-23) 2 x 75mm M1897G (Guerre) Army guns were added on the tops of the forward 240mm turrets (*Voltaire* in 9.1918, *Condorcet* in 1919, and *Diderot* in 3.1923). *Diderot* in the early 1920s added 3 x 47mm on the after superstructure.

*Danton* (A15) Brest Dyd/F.C. Méditerranée, La Seyne (turbines).

On list 1.1907. Ord: 8.5.1906 and 29.12.1906. K: 9.1.1908. L: 4.7.1909. Comm: 22.2.1911 (trials), 24.7.1911 (full).

Budget 1906. Launch attempt 22.5.1909 failed. Boiler installation begun 9.8.1909, boilers first lit off and first static trials 7.1.1911. Trials 3-6.1911 at Brest, results approved 24.7.1911. Represented France at

The battleship *Diderot*, probably in the 1920s. During World War I the paint was scraped from the turrets and replaced with a dark mix of soot and grease informally known as *bouchon gras*. This material was retained in many ships through the 1920s. *Diderot* was the only member of the class to retain both masts after the war. (*Éditions Gaby, Postcard by Artand, Editeur, Nantes*)

the Spithead review of 24.6.1911. To Toulon from Brest 10-15.8.1911. In 1914 was in the *1ʳᵉ Escadre de ligne* of the *1ʳᵉ Armée navale*. Torpedoed 19.3.1917 by the German submarine *U-64* southwest of Sardinia. Hit on the port side by two torpedoes, one under the bridge and one in boiler room Nº 2, capsized and sank in 36 minutes. 296 men lost, 806 saved. Wreck located 18.1.2008.

**Mirabeau** (A15bis) Lorient Dyd/Ch. Penhoët, Saint Nazaire (turbines).
On list 1.1907. Ord: 8.5.1906 and 29.12.1906. K: 4.5.1908.
  L: 28.10.1909. Comm: 12.5.1911 (trials), 1.8.1911 (full).
Budget 1906 (late addition). Boilers first lit off 9.9.1910. Trials 5-6.1911 at Lorient and 6-8.1911 at Toulon, results approved 10.8.1911. In 1914 was in the *1ʳᵉ Escadre de ligne* of the *1ʳᵉ Armée navale*. Driven ashore in a violent snowstorm at Sevastopol 8.2.1919 while seeking a safer mooring. To refloat her 6,000 tons had to be removed, including the turret armour, guns, eighteen boilers, coal, ammunition, and the upper strake of the armour belt. Refloated 6.4.1919 and docked at Sevastopol, but hurredly undocked 15.4.1919 in the face of the advancing Red Army. After re-embarking the guns, ammunition, and lower strake of the armour belt, *Mirabeau* was towed out of Sevastopol 5.5.1919 by *Justice* and five tugs and taken to Toulon. There she was found not worth refitting and was decomm. and condemned 22.8.1919. Struck 30.10.1919. Handed over to the company salvaging *Liberté* and towed out of Toulon 28.4.1922 to Savona to BU.

**Voltaire** (A16) F.C. Méditerranée, La Seyne/FCM, La Seyne (turbines).
On list 1.1907. Ord: 26.12.1906 (contract). K: 8.6.1907. L: 16.1.1909.
  Comm: 10.3.1911 (trials), 5.8.1911 (full) .
Budget 1906. Boilers first lit off 1.1.1910. Trials 10.1910 to 6.1911 at Toulon, results approved 31.7.1911. In 1914 was in the *1ʳᵉ Escadre de ligne* of the *1ʳᵉ Armée navale*. Torpedoed 10.10.1918 in the passage north of Kythira Island, Greece, by *UB-48*, two torpedoes hit together in the bow but the ship survived. To postwar special reserve 30.11.1919. Ordered recomm. 25.5.1921 and left Toulon 11.8.1921 for training and exercise duty at Brest. Left Brest with *Diderot* 13.1.1927 and assigned to training duty at Toulon 1.2.1927. Joined *Diderot* at Brest 27.11.1929 as school ship for reserve midshipmen (*aspirants de réserve*). To special reserve 15.4.1930 and moved to

Landévennec. Condemned 17.3.1937. Run aground and scuttled 31.5.1938 on the plateau of La Recherche in Quiberon Bay as a gunnery target. Wreck sold 12.1949 to the Société Mario Sella which formed the Société Voltaire to break up the wreck in place. The first load of scrap was landed at Lorient in 3.1950.

**Diderot** (A16bis) Ch. Penhoët, Saint Nazaire/Ch. Penhoët, Saint Nazaire (turbines).
On list 1.1907. Ord: 26.12.1906 (contract). K: 20.10.1907.
  L: 20.4.1909. Comm: 10.3.1911 (trials), 25.7.1911 (full).
Budget 1906 (late addition). Boilers first lit off 22.9.1910. To Brest from Saint Nazaire 3.1911. Trials 3-6.1911, results approved 31.8.1911. To Toulon from Brest 23-27.8.1911. In 1914 was flagship of the *1ʳᵉ Escadre de ligne* of the *1ʳᵉ Armée navale*. To postwar special reserve 11.11.1919. Ordered recomm. 25.5.1921, recomm. 15.9.1921 and left Toulon 19.9.1921 for training and exercise duty at Brest. The three-ship naval division of the Channel and the North Sea having been dissolved, left Brest with *Voltaire* 13.1.1927 to form a new two ship training squadron at Toulon, becoming school for apprentice stokers and gunners on 1.2.1927. Left Toulon 22.10.1929 to become school for the officer cadets of the reserve at Brest. To special reserve 12.1930 and moved to Landévennec. Used there as a barracks hulk by 1.1937. Condemned 17.3.1937. Sold 30.7.1937 to M. Gosselin-Duriez and towed to Dunkirk 31.8.1937 to BU.

**Condorcet** (A17) A.C. Loire, Saint Nazaire/Ch. Penhoët, Saint Nazaire (turbines).
On list 1.1907. Ord: 26.12.1906 (contract). K: 23.8.1907. L: 19.4.1909.
  Comm: 5.1.1911 (trials), 25.7.1911 (full).
Budget 1906. Boilers first lit off 1.10.1910. To Brest from Saint Nazaire 11.1910. Trials 11.1910 to 6.1911, results approved 29.7.1911. To Toulon from Brest 10-15.8.1911. In 1914 was in the *1ʳᵉ Escadre de ligne* of the *1ʳᵉ Armée navale*. To postwar special reserve 25.10.1919. Left Toulon 1.12.1921 after completion of dockyard work for training and exercise duty at Brest in a three-ship naval division with *Voltaire* and *Diderot*. To Toulon 1927 as school for electricians and torpedomen (embarking the school from *Patrie* 19.9.1927) and moved between Toulon and Salins d'Hyères until 1934 (primarily under tow from 1931). Declared by the Minister on 20.3.1935 to be no longer mobilizable. Off main list 1936. School ship (hulk) at Toulon 1936-1939. Not scuttled 27.11.1942, used by the Germans as an accommodation hulk, then fitted as an anti-aircraft platform in early 1944 and some superstructures removed. Sunk by air bombardment 7.3.1944, raised 9.1945. Condemned 14.12.1945, to the Domaines for disposal, BU completed 1949.

**Vergniaud** (A17bis) C.A. Gironde, Bordeaux-Lormont/F.C. Méditerranée, La Seyne (turbines).
On list 1.1907. Ord: 26.12.1906 (contract). K: 7.1908. L: 12.4.1910.
  Comm: 10.5.1911 (trials), 18.12.1911 (full).
Budget 1906 (late addition). Boilers first lit off 15.5.1911. To Toulon from Bordeaux 6.1911 with a crew of only 73 men to embark guns and run trials. Trials 10-11.1911, results approved 30.12.1911. In 1914 was in the *1ʳᵉ Escadre de ligne* of the *1ʳᵉ Armée navale*. To postwar special reserve 19.11.1919. France could retain only three of the four surviving *Danton*s under the Washington naval arms limitation treaty. *Vergniaud* was judged to be in the worst condition and was decomm. 6.6.1921. Struck 27.10.1921, retained at Toulon for trials 1921-1927. Trials included bombs and toxic gases. Beached on Notre Dame beach at Porquerolles after damaged by bombs from an airship on 17.6.1924, trials continued into August. To the Domaines for sale 5.1928. Sold 27.11.1928 to the Société Métallurgique du Littoral Méditerranéen to BU.

## The Programme of 1907

In October 1907 Minister Thomson convened the *Conseil supérieur* to take its third look at the fleet programme since 1905. The Council reviewed the 1906 programme and, after considering a proposal by the Naval General Staff to begun in 1909-1910 six battleships (three in 1909 and three in 1910), two armoured cruisers, 14 *contre-torpilleurs*, and 12 submersibles, decided to retain intact the entire 1906 programme including its emphasis on battleships and postponement of all armoured cruiser construction. It then directed its attention to the main battery distribution for the battleships. It once again rejected the principle of a uniform calibre for the main battery and accepted a mixed armament of 305mm and 240mm guns with only two of the thirteen flag officer members dissenting and one abstaining. The Council preferred an armament of six 305mm (in three axial turrets) and twelve 240mm but would accept eight 305mm (two axial turrets and two on the sides amidships) and eight 240mm guns if a reduction was needed to keep within the 21,000-ton limit imposed by available graving docks and by the budget.

## The Programme of 1909

On 25 November 1908 the Chamber of Deputies asked the Government to present as soon as possible a bill for an Organic Law for the Navy to cover the constitution of the fleet, recruiting of manpower, and the administrative organisation of the navy's forces and arsenals. (It had made a similar request on 29 November 1907.) On 28 January 1909 the Naval General Staff presented to Minister of Marine Alfred Picard, a *conseilleur d'état*, a note on the proposed law. In February 1909 Minister Picard moved to consult the *Conseil supérior* on both this organic law and on the characteristics of the ships to be laid down in 1910. In preparation for the meetings the Naval General Staff produced a recommendation for a fleet of 28 battleships and 14 armoured cruisers, the former being the number specified in 1896 but never attained (leaving aside coast defence ships) while the latter reflected the ratio between battleships and large cruisers adopted by Admiral von Tirpitz. In March 1909 the *Section permanent* of the *Conseil supérieur* objected strongly to this recommendation, stating that it was inferior to the programme adopted back in 1890 although today's needs were far greater and accusing the Naval General staff of being unable to ignore fiscal considerations. It said that the role of the *Conseil supérieur* was to make exclusively military recommendations and leave all considerations of resource limits to the Minister and Parliament. It recommended that the Council retain the Programme of 1906 or one as close to it as possible.

Minister Picard opened the meetings, which lasted into June, by having the Council on 17 and 18 May 1909 define a new programme for the composition of the fleet. His first question was whether two different types of large combatant ships, battleships and armoured cruisers, should continue to be maintained in the programme or if they should be combined into a single type. The Council stated that in view of the development of foreign navies and the need for France to make a serious effort to retain her rank among them it was important above all to increase its number of battleships, and it decided to provide henceforth only for a single kind of large combat ship. The Council had already considered such an action in 1906 as it was becoming clear that the advent of the battle-cruiser in Britain and Germany meant that armoured cruisers would be as large as battleships. The Council set the quantity of large combat ships at 45 battleships (*cuirassés*) including five replacements. For torpedo boats the Council decided to retain two types, one of not under 600 tons to accompany the fleets and one of not over 300 tons for the coastal flotillas. Sixty of the larger type including replacements were to be maintained as were 84 of the smaller (including 12 replacements). The Council retained only one category of submarines (there being doubts that the other category, defensive submarines, was still viable) and decided to maintain 64 including 16 replacements. Mine warfare made its appearance in this programme with three minelayers and eight minesweepers, although most of the mine force was to come from the merchant marine. In later discussions 12 *éclaireurs*

*d'escadre* including two replacements were added for the squadrons. These were to have the highest speed possible and be lightly armed and armoured. Other units were provided for the stations and miscellaneous functions including 10 'station ships' to be like *Infernet* and not over 3,000 tons, 12 avisos and gunboats, 3 surveying ships (which were also to be equipped to raise underwater cables), 3 coastal transports, two repair ships for the fleets, and one school ship (the seagoing school for midshipmen). In the near term, service on the overseas stations would be provided by the existing armoured cruisers. The full programme is in Appendix F.

---

*COURBET* **Class.** *Cuirassés d'escadre.* Dreadnought battleships with six twin main battery turrets, four on the centreline and two on the sides. Three funnels in groups of two and one, a pole foremast between the funnel groups and a pole mainmast. Designed by Lhomme and Lyasse.

Léon Alphonse Lyasse replaced Lhomme as Chief of the *Section technique* on 15 November 1909 and Achille François Charles Louis replaced Dudebout as *Directeur central des constructions navales* in a major administrative reform by the new Minister, Boué de Lapeyrère, following a series of fifteen serious accidents in the previous three years including the explosion of the battleship *Iéna*. Lhomme had directed most of the preliminary work on the class while Lyasse had been deputy director of the *Section technique*, Lyasse finished up the design of France's first dreadnoughts.

During its discussion of the Programme of 1906 the *Conseil supérieur* gave preliminary thought to the characteristics of the battleships that were to follow the six *Dantons*. Displacement was limited to 19,000 tons by the dimensions of existing ports and drydocks. All members agreed that the ships should have at least four 305mm guns and a majority wanted six along with as many 240mm guns as were possible within the 19,000-ton limit. The medium battery was to be eighteen 100mm guns instead of the 75mm guns in *Danton*, the anti-torpedo boat battery would be at a minimum twelve 47mm guns, and there would be more submerged torpedo tubes if possible. Torpedo protection of the hull would be omitted if it would help get an armament as strong as those in foreign battleships, the British having obtained comparable torpedo protection using coal in side compartments. A speed of 19 knots was needed, and should be augmented by any speed bonus gained by using turbines with the same power as that needed for 19 knots with reciprocating engines.

In October 1907 the *Conseil supérieur* returned to battleship characteristics. It again rejected the principle of a single calibre main battery and adopted a ship with four 305mm and twelve 240mm guns, all in twin turrets plus eighteen 100mm and twelve 47mm guns and four torpedo tubes. On 15 November 1907 Minister Thomson ordered the *Section technique* to develop a design to these specifications and it produced a ship like the *Danton*s but enlarged to include some features like the 100mm medium battery left out of them due to the need to rush them into production. The underwater protection was also omitted. By this time, however, the use of single calibre armaments was becoming more and more generalised in foreign navies and on 15 November 1907 Minister Thomson also ordered the *Section technique* to produce studies with uniform batteries of 305mm, 274.4mm and 240mm guns. Uniform batteries of 274.4mm and 240mm guns were not considered further, the former because the Germans had begun replacing their 280mm guns with 305mm in their latest designs. The mixed calibre design was completed on 25 January 1908 and was to be circulated to the ports, but on 1 February 1908 Thomson suspended this communication and then on 15 February 1908 ordered the Section technique to develop further the several possible solutions.

On 10 July 1908 Lhomme, the head of the *Section technique*, put forward two alternative studies. One was a much modified 21,600-ton version of the enlarged *Danton* proposed by the *Conseil supérieur* in 1907, while the other was a 23,200-ton variant of that design with a uniform armament of twelve 305mm in six twin turrets including two superfiring with twelve 138.6mm guns in casemates. Minister Thomson ordered further developments of these designs which were completed on 24 December 1908. He then referred these for comment to the commanders of the *Escadre de la Méditerranée* (Vice Admiral Germinet) and the *Escadre du Nord* (Vice Admiral Jauréguiberry). Both preferred the design with the uniform 305mm battery to the mixed calibre design but objected to the towering structure forward formed by the superfiring turret and the tall conning tower which Jauréguiberry called a huge 'target' and which also weighted down the bow. Both wanted to increase the secondary artillery to sixteen or eighteen 138.6mm guns and Germinet proposed suppressing the 47mm guns as ineffective.

In a note prepared for the October 1907 meeting of the *Conseil supérieur* the Naval General Staff had recommended studying turrets with three and four guns, and in particular an arrangement with triple turrets at the ends and twin turrets on the sides. To respond to the comments from the fleet commanders the *Section technique* without specific orders prepared a third design of 22,200 tons with twelve 305mm guns in two triple turrets at the ends and three twins, one superfiring aft and two on the sides, plus eighteen 138.6mm guns. Lhomme issued a full report on this design on 26 February 1909. On 25 March 1909 the Naval General Staff, asked to review the three designs, embraced the single calibre principle, based both on foreign practice and on considerations of simplicity of battery alignment and fire control, and also stated that no calibre under 305mm should be considered for the uniform battery. It had the same concerns as the fleet commanders over the towering 'target' forward in the twin turret design and recommended the design with triple turrets, noting that it felt the risks associated with the triple turrets were manageable. Minister Picard decided to consult the *Conseil supérieur* on the designs during its May-June 1909 deliberations on the Organic Law so that he could ask Parliament for the funds to lay the first two down at the beginning of 1910, and that Council also selected the triple turret design.

On 24 July 1909 Vice Admiral Boué de Lapeyrère became minister and moved decisively to end the delays over the design. In September 1909 he ordered preparation of a final design with the six twin turrets of the second design and the secondary battery and protection of the third design but with only four of the twelve 47mm anti-torpedo boat guns retained. Subsequently he ordered the adoption of much roomier British pattern turrets (the British having shared the technology under the Entente Cordiale), on 25 November 1909 the abandonment of Bullivant anti-torpedo nets, and on 17 December 1909 a further increase in the secondary battery from eighteen to twenty-two 138.6mm guns. This definitive design was soon approved by the *Conseil supérieur*. The first two ships were added to the 1910 budget by special legislation of March 1910 and ordered from the Lorient and Brest dockyards on 1 August 1910, with the orders confirmed and ships named on 11 August 1910. Two contract ships were added to the 1911 budget by special legislation of February 1911. Their contracts, signed on 30 June 1911, were for hulls, engines, and turrets. On 1 August 1911 the contractors were notified of the acceptance of the contracts and the assignment of the ships' names.

This class had an *entrepont cellulaire* similar to that in *Patrie* except that the narrow side longitudinal passageways inboard of the cofferdams were replaced with a broad central passageway, also subdivided by watertight doors, through which passed the funnel uptakes and ventilation trunking. Nearly all of the space between this passageway and the cofferdams at the side of the ship was occupied by coal bunkers. The anti-torpedo caisson of the *Danton* class was not replicated in this or following classes. Eighteen of the 138.6mm guns were in a large armoured redoubt on the 1st deck that extended from abreast the fore turret to ten frames aft of the wing turrets, their protection was two decks high and covered the side down to the main belt. The other four 138.6mm guns were in a smaller single-deck redoubt on the main deck between the two after turrets.

The turbines were in 3 engine rooms aft of the boiler rooms. Each wing shaft had its own engine room with one HP ahead turbine and one HP astern turbine. The inboard shafts shared an engine room on the centreline and each had one cruising turbine (HP to starboard and MP to port)

and one LP ahead turbine whose casing also housed an astern turbine.

A weakness in this otherwise successful class was the inadequate 12-degree elevation of its main battery guns, which gave a range of only 13,500 metres, less than that in foreign counterparts. Between 1922 and 1925 the elevation was increased to 23 degrees, giving a range of 26,000 metres without any change in ammunition.

Tethered balloons were fitted to *Courbet* in 1918, requiring the removal of all but the lowest portion of the mainmast. The balloons proved to be hard to use in heavy weather and the experiment was soon abandoned.

The Washington Treaty allowed France radically to reconstruct its existing dreadnoughts but the French saw no strategic need to do so, particularly since the cost would have been prohibitive. Instead they carried out modest reconstructions to improve seaworthiness (the ships were heavy in the bow because of the location of the forward turrets), extend gun range (the main guns in Italian battleships had nearly twice the theoretical range of their French equivalents because they elevated to 20 degrees instead of 12 degrees), improve fire control, and enhance anti-aircraft defences. The French undertook only limited refurbishment of the propulsion machinery and made no attempt to remedy the ship's severe weaknesses in horizontal (deck) and underwater protection.

The *Courbet* class ships (excluding *France*, lost on an uncharted rock in 1922) underwent two major refits before 1931. The first refit included increasing the main gun elevation from 12 to 23 degrees (increasing their range from 13,500m to 26,000m), adding a tripod foremast with a control top, removing the bow armour to improve seakeeping and offset the weight of the tripod, enlarging the bridge structure, trunking the first and second funnels together into a single taller funnel (except in *Paris*, the first ship to be done, in which the first funnel was simply moved aft 2.5 metres and the first two raised two metres), installing new oil-fired Du Temple boilers in N° 1 stokehold, and fitting a new AA armament of four 75mm M1918 guns (replacing two 75mm M1897G and four 47mm/50 M1902 guns). Two 47mm M1885 guns were also provided for saluting. The work was done to *Paris* at Brest from 25 October 1922 to 25 November 1923, to *Courbet* at La Seyne (F.C. Méditerranée) from 9 July 1923 to 16 April 1924 (her AA and saluting armament had already been upgraded in 1920-21), and to *Jean Bart* at Toulon from 12 October 1923 to 29 January 1925. The second refit added a Saint Chamond-Granat director control system for the 305mm and 138.6mm guns with a director control tower atop the tripod mast and other fire control upgrades throughout the ship. The mainmast was also replaced by a stronger one placed 2 metres forward of the old one and the port boat crane was lengthened to permit handling a 6-ton seaplane. In *Courbet* and *Jean Bart* all of the boilers were replaced with boilers procured for the *Normandie* class, those on two of the five stokeholds (N°s 1 and 3) being oil-fired, the old cruising turbines were replaced with geared cruising turbines, and the four 75mm M1918 AA guns were replaced with seven 75mm M1922-24 guns. In *Paris* the forward funnel were moved back touching the second funnel and both were raised another two metres. The work was done to *Paris* at Toulon between 16 August 1927 and 15 January 1929, to *Courbet* at La Seyne between 15 January 1927 and 12 January 1931, and to *Jean Bart* at Toulon between 7 August 1929 and 28 September 1931. *Paris* received the AA gun upgrade in a third refit at Toulon between 1 July 1934 and 21 May 1935 and also had her existing boilers refurbished. Torpedo tubes were removed from *Jean Bart* in 1933 and from *Courbet* in 1937-38.

**Dimensions & tons:** 166.000m oa, 165.000m wl and pp x 27.000m ext and wl. 23,474.950t disp (designed and normal, *Courbet*), 25,579t (with surcharge). Draught: (designed) 8.852m mean, 9.012m aft (real). Men: 1,115 (1,187 with flag). Men: 1,115 without flag, 1,187 with.

**Machinery:** 28,000shp designed at 21kg/cm² boiler pressure (18kg/cm² in *Courbet*). Designed speed 21kts. Trials (*Courbet*, 23.5.1913) 28,991shp = 20.809kts at 296.5rpm. 4 screws. 8 Parsons turbines (direct drive). 24 Belleville boilers (24 Niclausse in *Courbet*). 906t coal (normal), 2,700t (surcharge) + 250t oil. Range 4,200nm @ 10kts.

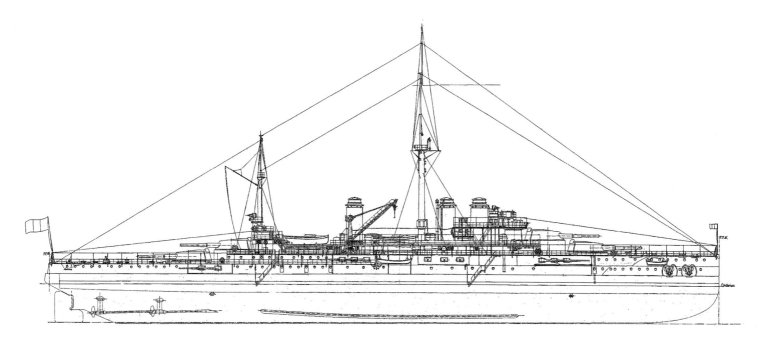

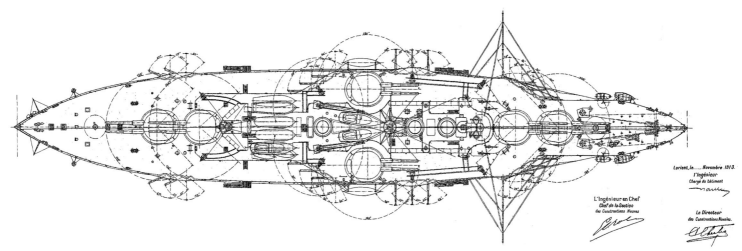

Outboard profile and overhead view (*plan d'ensemble*) as fitted of the battleship *Courbet*, built at Lorient on the plans of M. Lyasse. The plans were signed in November 1913 by the naval constructor in charge of the ship. The small calibre artillery on these plans is limited to 4 x 47mm/50 M1902 guns (on the first superstructure/lower bridge deck forward outboard of the conning tower except two in *France* on the after bridge, all primarily for saluting), and 2 x 37mm M1907 guns for the boats. There were also 2 x 65mm/16 M1881 landing guns.

**Armour:**

Side: Belt at waterline (cemented steel) 250mm amidships, 160mm fwd, 160mm aft. Height amidships from 1.700m below the wl to 2.350m above. Side above belt: see casemate redoubts, below.

Guns: 305mm turrets (cemented steel) 250mm faces and sides with 236mm max fixed bases.

Casemate redoubts: Central redoubt (forward and amidships casemates with deck below, 4.50m high) 160mm (cemented steel) except 160mm (special steel) over the 138.6mm gun positions, 142mm (cemented steel) near the wing 305mm barbettes, and 232mm (cemented steel) plates on the outboard sides of each wing barbette. Transverse bulkheads at forward and after ends 160mm. After redoubt (after casemates) 160mm (cemented and special steel) sides and transverse bulkheads.

Lower armoured deck: Flat (construction steel) 12mm, slopes (special steel) 42mm, all on 28mm hull plating.

Upper armoured deck (flat, located at the bottom of the central redoubt):

12mm hull plating within the central redoubt, 48mm hull plating from there to frame 146 near the bow, from the after end of the central redoubt to the forward end of the after redoubt, and from its after end to frame 18 near the stern, 30mm hull plating from there aft to the stern and from frame 146 forward to the bow.

Decks in casemate redoubts: 1st deck (halfway up the central redoubt) 8mm hull plating, increased to 10mm and 12mm near the sides. 2nd deck (at the top of the central redoubt) 30mm hull plating, increased to 40mm over the amidships casemates. (Top of after redoubt) 30mm hull plating.

Conning tower (cemented steel): 266mm max.

**Guns:**

(1913) 12 x 305mm/45 M1906-10 (6 twin turrets), 22 x 138.6mm/55 M1910 (18 in six sections of three guns in a casemate redoubt on 1st deck, 4 in two sections of two in a casemate redoubt aft on the main deck), 2 x 65mm/16 M1881 landing, 4 x 47mm/50 M1902 (primarily for saluting), 2 x 37mm M1885 QF boats. **Torpedoes:** 4 submerged tubes for 450mm M1909R torpedoes. **Searchlights:** 2 x 75cm, 8 x 90cm mobile.

(1915) HA mountings provided for the 4 x 47mm on the lower bridge platform.

(c1918) 2 x 75mm M1897G (Guerre) Army guns on HA mountings added to the AA armament.

(1921-25) New AA armament of 4 x 75mm M1918 AA replaced the earlier six guns.

(1927-38) New AA armament of 7 x 75mm M1922-24 fitted in *Jean Bart* and *Courbet* in 1927-31. *Paris* received this AA upgrade in 1934-35, the guns being in shields. In 1937-38 *Courbet* and *Paris* received a few of the new 13.2mm Hotchkiss AA machine guns. Torpedo tubes were removed from *Jean Bart* in 1933 and from *Courbet* in 1937-38.

*Jean Bart* (A1) Brest Dyd/F.C. Méditerranée, La Seyne (turbines).
On list 1.1911. Ord: 1.8.1910. K: 10.11.1910. L: 22.9.1911.
  Comm: 20.3.1913 (trials), 2.9.1913 (full).
Budget 1910 (late addition). Yard notified of order and ship's name 11.8.1910. Official machinery trials 4-5.1913. In fleet service at Toulon 19.11.1913. In 1914 was in a division *hors rang* (outside the regular fleet structure) for the new dreadnoughts in the *1ʳᵉ Armée navale*. Escorted French President Poincaré in *France* on a state visit to Kronshtadt in July 1914. Torpedoed 21.9.1914 by the Austrian submarine *U-12* in the Strait of Otranto, a single torpedo causing the flooding of the three foremost compartments in the bow and partly flooding the fourth before the crew controlled the damage. Assigned 1.7.1935 to the training division replacing *Condorcet*. Off main list 1936. School ship at Toulon 1936-1939. Hulked 1.8.1936, embarked the school for radiomen 1.10.1936. and renamed *Océan* 1.1.1937. Out of service 1.12.1937 because she was worn out, retained as accommodation hulk for the schools. Seized intact by the Germans at Toulon 27.11.1942 and used for tests. Damaged by Allied bombers 7.3.1944 and sunk by the Germans 15.3.1944 to keep her from capsizing. Refloated 10.1945 after superstructures and armour removed. Condemned 14.12.1945, BU 1946 at Brégaillon.

*Courbet* (A2) Lorient Dyd/Ch. Penhoët, Saint Nazaire (turbines).
On list 1.1911. Ord: 1.8.1910. K: 10.1910. L: 23.9.1911.
  Comm: 3.5.1913 (trials), 8.10.1913 (full).

The battleship *Paris* photographed in 1925-26 after her first major reconstruction in 1922-23. Her first funnel was moved back close against the second one to accommodate the new tripod mast and enhanced fire control systems. Sisters *Courbet* and *Jean Bart*, refitted later in 1923-25, had their first two funnels merged into a single broad fore funnel. The base of the old mast has become a ventilation shaft. The turrets and the casemate guns are covered with dark *bouchon gras*. *(NHHC, NH-88983b)*

Budget 1910 (late addition). Yard notified of order and ship's name 11.8.1910. Official machinery trials 5-7.1913. In fleet service at Toulon 19.11.1913. In 1914 was flagship of the division *hors rang* of the *1ʳᵉ Armée navale*. To the training division 1931. Participated in the defence of Cherbourg until sailing for Portsmouth 20.6.1940. Seized there 3.7.1940 by the British, handed over 10.7.1940 to the FNFL (Free French Naval Forces). Served as anti-aircraft battery 8.1940 to 1.1941, decomm. 31.3.1941 and became supply depot. Commissioned in the RN 22.3.1943 as target ship in Loch Striven for weapons development (Operation 'Substance'), reduced to care and maintenance in the Clyde 28.1.1944. Scuttled 9.6.1944 off Hermanville in Normandy near Ouistreham to form an artificial port. Broken up in place beginning in 1946 by the La Sirène company, re-sold in 1952 and 1970 when demolition completed.

*France* (A3) A.C. Loire, Saint Nazaire/ACL, Saint Nazaire (turbines).
On list 1.1912. Ord: 30.6.1911 (contract). K: 30.11.1911. L: 7.11.1912.
  Comm: 1.4.1914 (trials), 1.7.1914 (full).
Budget 1911 (late addition). Yard notified of order and ship's name 1.8.1911. Before completing trials or loading ammunition carried French President Poincaré on a state visit to Kronshtadt between 16 and 29.7.1914, returning early as war became imminent. Departed Brest for Toulon 2.8.1914, trials completed and in fleet service 10.10.1914, joining the division *hors rang* of the *1ʳᵉ Armée navale*. Struck an uncharted rock while entering Quiberon Bay 26.8.1922, of the five stokeholds all but Nº 3 (which was not steaming) flooded through a long gash on the port side of the hull leaving the ship without power. She capsized to port about three hours later with only three of her crew lost. Struck 24.2.1923. Wreck sold to the Cie. Neptune 5.1935, demolition carried out in 1938-39, resumed in 1952, and after resale to the Société Atlantique ended in late April 1958.

*Paris* (A4) F.C. Méditerranée, La Seyne/FCM, La Seyne (turbines).
On list 1.1912. Ord: 30.6.1911 (contract). K: 10.11.1911. L: 28.9.1912.
  Comm: 15.3.1914 (trials), 22.8.1914 (full).
Budget 1911 (late addition). Yard notified of order and ship's name 1.8.1911. Official machinery trials 21-30.7.1914, in fleet service 1.8.1914 and joined the division *hors rang* of the *1ʳᵉ Armée navale*. To the training division 1932. Bombed by German aircraft at Le Havre 11.6.1940, repaired at Brest, then on 18 June carried 1,600 *mousses*

(boys) from the *Armorique* from Brest to Plymouth. Seized by the British there 3.7.1940 and used as base ship for trawlers and small ships during the war. Returned 7.1945, towed into Brest 21.8.1945, and continued to serve as base ship. Removed from the *Liste de la Flotte* between 1.1950 and 3.1951. Condemned 21.12.1955, designated Q64. Towed from Brest to Toulon 5-6.1956 to BU at La Seyne.

---

### The Programme of 1912 or *Loi naval sur la Constitution de la Flotte*

On 2 February 1910 Minister of Marine Boué de Lapeyrère convened a most unusual meeting of the *Conseil supérieur*. He began by informing the members (six Vice Admirals on active service) that the President of the Republic had asked them to join him the next day at the Élysée Palace, his official residence, for a meeting of the *Conseil supérieur* over which President Fallières would preside. Also in attendance would be Prime Minister Briand, the Minister of Marine, and the Minister of War. The purpose of the meeting was for the Minister of Marine to present before the *Conseil supérieur* and the other attendees the main features of a naval programme that he had elaborated beginning with the decisions of the *Conseil supérieur* of June 1909 (the Programme of 1909) and subsequently modified. The Minister then explained that he had convened the current meeting, not for another vote, but to explain the programme that he was going to present the next day and for which he was taking full responsibility in the full knowledge that the Council members would object to it. (He predicted accurately, the opposition at the end of the meeting to the large resource-based reduction in battleships was intense.)

The Vice Admiral and Minister then stated that as a member of the Council in June 1909 he had voted as a sailor for the programme, but that upon becoming a member of the government he had become aware of other key factors that needed to be considered, specifically the current state of the foreign and domestic policies of France. He had taken the Programme of 1909 to the Minister of Finances (the able Georges Cochery) who told him very directly that it could never be realized. Then, taking into account a declaration by the Government that it would be satisfied if France had a navy capable of becoming master of the Mediterranean but not in the north, he refocused the Programme on the combined navies of Austria and Italy. After determining that in 1920 these two would have 27 battleships he chose the figure of 28 for France – the same figure that had been recommended by the Naval General Staff in May 1909. Considering that the size of battleships had grown to 23,000 tons, to want 45 battleships was to attempt the impossible but it might be possible to get 28.

Minister Boué de Lapeyrère added that there were still problems with the Minister of Finances who, when told that the programme would include not only the ships but also the infrastructure needed to support them and the supplies and personnel needed to operate them, said that of the 416 million franc expenditure planned for 1911 alone he would be unable to provide 50 millions. Without agreement from the Minister of Finances, it was decided that the Council of Ministers needed to get Parliamentary approval of the programme in the form of a Law on the Constitution of the Fleet.

Turning to the programme itself Minister Boué de Lapeyrère explained that compared to the May 1909 decisions of the Council it included 28 battleships instead of 45, 10 *éclaireurs* instead of 12, 52 torpedo craft (*bâtiments torpilleurs de haute mer*) instead of 60, and 94 submarines instead of 64. The changes in the *éclaireurs* and torpedo craft were driven by the reduction in the number of battleship squadrons which they were to support, the ratios of 2 *éclaireurs* and 12 torpedo craft per squadron set by the Council having been retained. The change in submarines was caused by the intention of the Minister to return to two types, one of coast defense submarines of 400 tons and one of larger offensive submarines with a large range of action, of which there were to be three *escadrilles* (squadrons) each of 12 submarines based at Cherbourg, Oran, and Bizerte.

A bill containing this programme and the *Loi navale sur la Constitution*

*de la Flotte* of which it was part was duly presented to the Chamber of Deputies on 9 February 1910. The Chamber's *Commission de la Marine* first reported on it on 14 March 1910. It then underwent a series of changes by successive *Commissions de la Marine*, one following the advent of Deputy Théophile Delcassé as Minister of Marine changing the financial provisions but none changing the programme itself. It was finally passed into law on 30 March 1912. The programme went further than earlier French programmes in specifying the budget under which each ship was to be begun, setting a rigid schedule for the entire programme. As of 1912 fifteen battleships in the programme already existed and three were to be begun in 1912 (the *Bretagne* class), two in 1913, two in 1914, four in 1915, and two in 1917 for a total of 28. With the worsening international situation, the programme was accelerated in the 1913 and 1914 budgets resulting in four ships in 1913 (the *Normandie* class), one in 1914 (*Béarn*), and four in 1915 (the *Lyon* class). The full programme is in Appendix F.

---

**BRETAGNE Class.** *Cuirassés d'escadre.* Super-dreadnought battleships with five twin centreline main battery turrets including one between the funnels. Two funnels, two pole masts. Designed by Lyasse and Doyère.

The design was begun by Lyasse and continued by Charles Doyère when he became Chief of the *Section technique* after Lyasse retired in November 1911. In November 1909 the British laid down their first capital ships with 13.5-inch (343mm) guns, HMS *Orion* and *Lion*. This came after the *Courbet* class was designed but before any of the ships were authorized. In a meeting on 10 January 1910 the *Conseil supérieur* decided to give 340mm guns to the second pair, which was to be begun in 1911. The design and construction of the new gun would have delayed those ships, however, and the idea was dropped, and instead work began on a 340mm 45-calibre gun for the next class of French dreadnoughts. Unlike the British the French did not have the option of increasing the length or displacement of their 305mm-gunned ships to support the larger 340mm turrets and guns because they were constrained by the size of existing graving docks. The *Conseil supérieur* initially asked the *Section technique* to prepare a design with a displacement of 23,500 tons and with six 340mm turrets arranged as in *Courbet*, but the designers reported that the structure of the ship would have to be lightened to the point where it could neither sustain the weight of the turrets nor withstand the recoil forces of the guns. It was suggested, however, that a five-turret design could be produced on the same dimensions as *Courbet* with a centreline turret amidships in place of the two wing turrets. This solution was accepted by the *Conseil supérieur* and subsequently approved by the new Minister of Marine, Théophile Delcassé, after he took office on 2 March 1911.

On 10 November 1911 de Lanessan, now back in the Chamber of Deputies, submitted a bill authorizing the government to lay down immediately a battleship to replace *Liberté*, lost to an internal explosion on 25 September 1911, in addition to the ships already in the 1912 budget. On 3 February 1912 the Minister of Finances informed the commission that the government would fix at 17 instead of 16 the number of battleships to be included in the bill for the new *Statut naval* (Programme of 1912, below). On 6 February 1912 the *Commission de la Marine* reported that Article 2 of the *Statut naval*, which was passed soon afterwards, required that if a ship were lost its replacement would be laid down in the following year at the latest. The three new ships were then added to the 1912 budget by special legislation of early 1912. The two dockyard ships were ordered and their names assigned on 1 May 1912 as late additions to the 1912 budget, and the contract for the replacement of *Liberté*, named *Lorraine*, was signed on 26 June 1912 and probably notified on 15 July 1912.

In order to simplify design and construction, the hull dimensions of the *Bretagne* class were kept identical to those of *Courbet*. However, the turrets were larger, and the *Section technique* worked them in by leaving the superfiring turrets where they were and moving the bow turret half a metre closer to the bow and the after turret one metre closer to the stern. The axis of the centre turret was 1.5 metre aft of the axis of the wing turrets in *Courbet*, allowing the turret to fit trained forward into the space between the funnels. To make this possible the uptakes for the forward boiler rooms were trunked into a single wide funnel and the pole foremast was relocated to the after end of the bridge. This resulted in a more cramped arrangement of the bridge, mast, and fore funnel than in *Courbet* and more importantly added even more weight to the already overloaded bow.

*Bretagne* and *Lorraine* had the now-traditional Niclausse and Belleville large water tube boilers, while *Provence* had newer Guyot-Du Temple small water tube boilers built at Indret. This boiler, previously fitted in some armoured cruisers, was triangular in cross-section with two water drums at its base and a larger cylindrical steam drum at its apex. Small-tube boilers were more efficient because of their greater heating area but were more difficult to maintain and also took up more space in the boiler rooms.

Bullivant anti-torpedo nets had been fitted to French battleships in the 1880s but were then abandoned. The ships of the *Bretagne* class were fitted with them, however, probably out of concern that they might have to operate from unprotected anchorages in the eastern Mediterranean. During the Dardanelles campaign three battleships were sunk by torpedoes despite having their nets deployed, and the nets were removed from the *Bretagne* class in 1917-18.

The turbines were in three engine rooms aft of the boiler rooms. Each wing shaft had its own engine room with one HP ahead turbine. The inboard shafts shared an engine room on the centreline and each shaft had one LP ahead turbine. There were no cruising turbines, and the astern turbines were housed in the casings for the ahead turbines.

This class shared the weakness of the *Courbet* class in the inadequate 12-degree elevation of its main battery guns, which in this class gave a range of only 14,500 metres. *Lorraine* was completed in 1917 with the elevation of the after turret experimentally increased to 18 degrees, increasing the range to 21,000 metres without any change in ammunition. The elevation of the other turrets of the class was similarly raised in 1919-23, and it was again increased in 1924-1927 to 23 degrees with a 23,700 metre range.

In 1914-15 fourteen 138.6mm guns intended for *Bretagne* were sent to Verdun where they were captured during a German attack in February 1916. Tethered balloons were fitted to *Bretagne* in 1919, requiring the removal of all but the lowest portion of the mainmast. The balloons proved to be hard to use in heavy weather and the experiment was soon abandoned.

The *Bretagne* class ships underwent two major refits before 1931, with *Bretagne* having the work done in three phases. All of these refits were done at the Toulon dockyard. The first refit included increasing the elevation of the main battery guns from 12 to 18 degrees (increasing their range from 14,500m to 21,000m), adding a tripod foremast with a director fire control top (Vickers system in *Bretagne*, Laurant Paquelier in the others), raising the forward funnel four metres (initially only one metre in *Provence* and *Lorraine*), removing the forward four 138.6mm guns (which were unusable in heavy seas, this had been done in *Provence* in 1919), and replacing the AA armament (two 75mm M1897G and two 47mm HA guns) with four 75mm M1918 guns on high angle (HA) mountings. The work was done to *Bretagne* between 12 June 1919 and 18 October 1920, to *Lorraine* between 10 November 1921 and 4 December 1922, and to *Provence* between 1 February 1922 and 4 July 1923. The second refit included increasing the elevation of the main battery guns again, from 18 to 23 degrees (for 23,700m), removing the bow armour to improve seakeeping, installing new oil-fired boilers in Nº 6 stokehold (the aftermost one), and lengthening the port crane to handle a seaplane. In *Provence* and *Lorraine* the mainmast was replaced by a stronger one placed 2 metres forward of the old one. The work was done to *Bretagne* between 1 May 1924 and 28 September 1925, to *Lorraine* between 15 November 1924 and 4 August 1926, and to *Provence* between 12 December 1925 and 11 July 1927. Between 15 November 1927 and 12 May 1928 *Bretagne* received a Saint Chamond-Granat director fire control system in place of her Vickers system and received the new mainmast already fitted to the others. *Lorraine*

received oil fired boilers in a second stokehold, number 5, during a third refit at Brest between 17 December 1929 and 6 March 1931 and between August and October 1932 she had her four old 75mm AA guns replaced with six 75mm M1922 guns. (A seventh on the stern was not mounted.)

It had originally been expected that these three ships would be replaced by new construction in 1934-36, but the extension of the 'battleship holiday' in the London Treaty of 1930 meant that they would remain in service into the 1940s. In 1931-34 *Bretagne* and *Provence* received a third refit intended to extend their service lives to 1944-45, including complete conversion to oil fired boilers, new turbines on all four shafts in *Bretagne* (only the inboard shafts in *Provence*), installing a Saint Chamond-Granat director fire control system on the fire control top (replacing an earlier version in *Bretagne*) and installation of a new anti-aircraft battery of eight 75mm M1922 guns (vice four 75mm). The four 138.6mm guns in the hull aft were also removed, leaving fourteen 138.6mm guns, and the torpedo tubes were removed. During these refits the after funnel was raised to the same height as the fore funnel. The work was done to *Bretagne* at Toulon and La Seyne between 1 July 1932 and 12 November 1934 and to *Provence* at Brest between 30 September 1931 and 20 August 1934.

Between 18 September 1934 and 20 November 1935 *Lorraine* received a fourth refit at Brest during which her amidships 340mm turret was removed to make room for aviation facilities. A hangar was installed with room for three seaplanes and an elevator to raise the aircraft to the trainable catapult on the hangar roof. The boat cranes were lengthened and strengthened to handle aircraft. The funnels were moved further apart and made thinner to accommodate the aircraft installations and the after one was raised. The relocation of the forward funnel required rebuilding the forward bridge structure. Her 75mm AA guns were replaced with eight 100mm guns in four twin mountings and she received her first two 13.2mm Hotchkiss AA machine gun mounts on the after mast. She also received the same complete conversion to new oil fired boilers and most of the other upgrades given her two sisters in 1931-34 including the removal of the four after 138.6mm guns and torpedo tubes. She added a quadruple 13.2mm mount on the foremast in late 1937. In February and March 1940 her four twin 100mm AA mounts were removed to equip the new *Richelieu* and replaced with eight 75mm M1922 guns. When reactivated at Oran between March and May 1944 her aviation equipment was landed and with the help of a U.S. repair ship (probably *Vulcan*, AR-5) she received fourteen 40mm guns in single mounts and twenty-five 20mm guns in single mounts.

**Dimensions & tons:** 166.000m oa, 165.000m wl and pp x 27.000m ext and wl. 23,597.457t disp (designed, *Bretagne*), 23,960t (normal load as completed), 26,600t (with surcharge). Draught: (designed) 8.712m mean, 8.872m aft (real). Men: 1,193 including 34 officers without flag, add 8 officers and 49 men with.

**Machinery:** 28,000shp designed at 18kg/cm² boiler pressure (21kg/cm² in *Lorraine*). Designed speed 21kts. Trials (*Provence*, 13.10.1915) 21.505kts at 297.51rpm. 4 screws. 4 Parsons turbines 24 Niclausse (18 kg/cm²) boilers in *Bretagne*, 18 Guyot-Du Temple (18 kg/cm²) in *Provence*, 24 Belleville (21 kg/cm²) in *Lorraine*. 906t coal (normal), 2,700t (surcharge) + 300t oil. Range 4,700nm @ 10kts.

**Armour:**
Side: Belt at waterline (cemented steel) 250mm amidships, 160mm fwd, 160mm aft. Height amidships from 1.700m below the wl to 2.350m above. Side above belt: see casemate redoubts, below.

Guns: 340mm turrets (cemented steel) 300mm faces and sides with 236mm max fixed bases.

Casemate redoubts: Central redoubt (forward and amidships casemates with deck below, 4.50m high) 160mm (cemented steel) except 160mm (special steel) over the 138.6mm gun positions and 142mm (cemented steel) outboard of the midships 340mm turret. Transverse bulkheads at forward and after ends 160mm. After redoubt (after casemates) 160mm (cemented and special steel) sides and transverse bulkheads.

Lower armoured deck: flat (construction steel) 12mm, slopes (special steel) 42mm, all on 28mm hull plating.

Upper armoured deck (located at the bottom of the central redoubt): flat 10mm hull plating within the central redoubt, 48mm hull plating from there to frame 146 near the bow, from the after end of the central redoubt to the forward end of the after redoubt, and from its after end to frame 18 near the stern, 30mm hull plating from there aft to the stern and from frame 146 forward to the bow.

Decks in casemate redoubts: 1st deck (halfway up the central redoubt) 12mm hull plating near the centreline, 20mm towards the sides. 2nd deck (at the top of the central redoubt) 30mm hull plating. Top of after redoubt probably protected as in *Courbet*.

Conning tower (cemented steel): 266mm max.

**Guns:**

(1915) 10 x 340mm/45 M1912 (5 twin turrets), 22 x 138.6mm/55 M1910 (18 in six sections of two guns and two of three guns in a casemate redoubt on the 1st deck, 4 in two sections of two in a casemate redoubt aft on the main deck), 2 x 65mm/16 M1881 landing, 2 x 47mm/50 M1902 (primarily for saluting). **Torpedoes:** 4 submerged

Outboard profile and overhead view of the battleship *Provence*, built at Lorient on the plans of M. Doyère. The plans were signed on 18 June 1915 by the naval constructor in charge of the ship, L. É. Poiget. The small calibre artillery on these plans is limited to 2 x 47mm/50 M1902 guns (on the first superstructure deck/lower bridge deck outboard of the conning tower, primarily for saluting, instead of 4 originally planned). There were also 2 x 65mm/16 M1881 landing guns.

tubes for 450mm M1909R torpedoes. **Searchlights:** 12 x 90cm (14 in *Provence*).

(1915) 5 x 47mm/40 M1885 added, one on each of the main turrets, for sub-calibre (exercise) firing and use in the boats. HA mountings provided for the 2 x 47mm/50 M1902.

(1918) 2 x 75mm/50 M1897G (Guerre) Army guns on HA mountings added to the AA armament.

(1919-23) The forward 4 x 138.6mm guns were removed, leaving 18. New AA armament of 4 x 75mm M1918 on high angle (HA) mountings replaced the earlier six guns.

(1932, *Lorraine*) New AA armament of 6 x 75mm M1922 fitted. (A seventh on the stern was not mounted.).

(1931-34, *Bretagne* and *Provence*) New AA armament of 8 x 75mm M1922 in single mounts fitted. These guns had fully protective shields in *Provence*, the shields were retrofitted to *Bretagne* in 1935. The four 138.6mm guns in the stern were also removed, leaving 14, and the torpedo tubes were removed.

(1934-35, *Lorraine*) New AA armament of 8 x 100mm in four twin shielded twin mountings fitted. The four 138.6mm guns in the stern were also removed, leaving 14, and the torpedo tubes were removed.

(1940, *Lorraine*) The four twin 100mm AA mounts were removed to equip the new *Richelieu* and replaced with 8 x 75mm M1922 in shielded single mounts.

(1944, *Lorraine*) Added (at Oran) 14 x 40mm guns and 25 x 20mm guns, all on single AA mounts.

*Bretagne* (A5) Brest Dyd/F.C. Méditerranée, La Seyne (turbines). On list 1.1913. Ord: 1.5.1912. K: 22.7.1912. L: 21.4.1913.

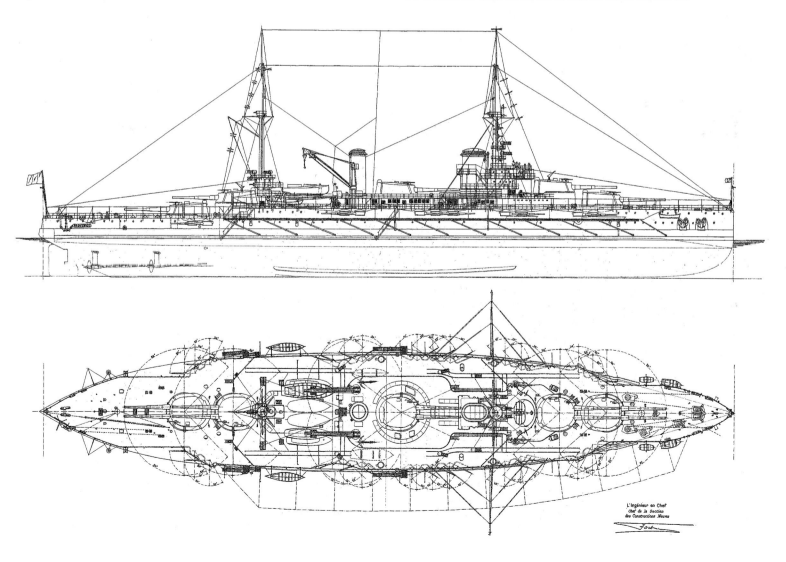

Comm: 1.3.1915 (trials), 29.11.1915 (full).

Budget 1912 (late addition). Yard notified of order and ship's name 1.5.1912. Left Brest for Toulon 6.6.1915. Official machinery trials 7-8.1915. Admitted to active service 10.2.1916. Left Toulon 4.5.1916 to join the fleet. Hit by four British 15in shells 3.7.1940 at Mers el-Kebir, blew up and capsized with the loss of 1,012 men. Wreck BU there between 1952 and 21.12.1954.

*Provence* (A6) Lorient Dyd/A.C. Loire, Saint Nazaire (turbines).
On list 1.1913. Ord: 1.5.1912. K: 21.5.1912. L: 20.4.1913.
Comm: 10.3.1915 (trials), 20.1.1916 (full).

Budget 1912 (late addition). Yard notified of order and ship's name 1.5.1912. Left Lorient for Toulon 12.8.1915. Official machinery trials 8-13.10.1915. Entered active service 1.3.1916. Completed trials and working up 9.5.1916. Hit aft by a British 15in shell 3.7.1940 at Mers el-Kebir and beached. Refloated 26.7.1940, repaired at Oran and left for Toulon 6.11.1940. Assigned to the training division 1.1942. Scuttled at Toulon 27.11.1942. Refloated 11.7.1943 by the Italian Fortunato Serra company. Her 75mm AA battery and two 340mm guns were refurbished and used ashore. Ship towed to Balaguier where cut down to the main deck. Sunk again 9.1944. Remains refloated 1949 and towed to Brégaillon to BU.

*Lorraine* (A6bis) Ch. Penhoët, Saint Nazaire/Ch. Penhoët, Saint Nazaire (turbines).
On list 1.1913. Ord: 26.6.1912 (contract). K: 7.11.1912. L: 30.9.1913.
Comm: 1.9.1915 (trials), 1.7.1916 (full).

Budget 1912 (late addition). Left Saint Nazaire 4.2.1916, arrived Toulon via Brest and entered active service 10.3.1916 before completing trials. Completed trials 24.7.1916 without the 340mm guns for the after turret. (This turret was being modified to increase the maximum elevation from 12 to 18 degrees, and the guns were only fitted in 7.1917.). Left Toulon 6.8.1916 to join the fleet. Interned at Alexandria, Egypt, 3.7.1940. Rallied to the Free French 31.5.1943 and sailed around Africa for Oran 22.6.1943. Refitted 3.1944 at Oran with additional anti-aircraft armament and active for the rest of the war. To Toulon as school ship 6.1945, immobilised 2.1947 due personnel shortage, to Special Reserve B as accommodation ship and removed from the *Liste de la Flotte* 7.7.1950, decomm. 29.11.1952, and condemned 17.2.1953 at Toulon. Sold at auction 27.11.1953 and towed to Brégaillon (La Seyne) 1.1954 to BU.

---

*NORMANDIE* Class. *Cuirassés d'escadre.* Super-dreadnought battleships with three quadruple centreline main battery turrets (one forward, one amidships aft of the funnels and mast, and one aft). Two funnels, a single pole mast aft of the after funnel. Designed by Doyère.

Work on the design for the two ships then planned for the 1913 budget began on 6 December 1911 when the *Comité technique* of the *Conseil supérieur* examined the design of *Bretagne* and, recalling the bad experience with *Amiral Baudin* and *Formidable*, strongly objected to the amidships turret of *Bretagne* because of its restricted arcs of fire. The *Directeur central des constructions navales*, Gaston Romazzotti, realized that if the *Conseil supérieur* and Minister Delcassé shared this view a new design would be needed for the 1913 ships. He asked Delcassé for guidance on the speed of the ships and the calibre and distribution of their main battery and the Minister referred the matter to the *Conseil supérieur* on 5 January 1912. In the meantime Doyère and the *Section technique* developed three alternatives (all avoiding amidships turrets) which they presented on 1 February 1912: a *Bretagne* with increased speed (over 21 knots), a 20-knot ship with twelve 340mm guns in one quadruple turret and one superfiring twin turret at each end, and a ship with sixteen 305mm guns with two quadruple turrets of which one was superfiring at each end. Doyère also attached a study of quadruple turrets by Saint-Chamond. The French were still limited by the

dimensions of their graving docks, although the *Section technique* felt that dimensions could grow to 170 to 172 metres length, 27.5 metres beam, and 8.8 metres draught for a 25,000-ton displacement.

The *Conseil supérieur* on 3-4 April 1912 recommended and Minister Delcassé confirmed that the 1913 ships be developments of the ten-gun *Bretagne* unless a quadruple turret could be developed in time. On 6 April 1912 Delcassé authorized Doyère to negotiate a contract with Saint Chamond for the preparation of a design for a quadruple turret. On 26 June 1912 Doyère reported that this work was far enough along that it was clear the turret was feasible. Doyère's *Section technique* had therefore begun work on two new designs, a Project A7 with ten 340mm guns in five twin turrets as in *Bretagne* and a Project A7bis with twelve 340mm guns in three quadruple turrets of which one was amidships. This arrangement had been proposed by Vice Admiral Bellue, commander of the 2nd *escadre* and also a member of the *Conseil supérieur*, when the fleet had been asked to comment on designs, and it was attractive enough for the *Section technique* to draw it up on 30 March 1912. In its June version the middle turret was placed in a partially obstructed position between the funnels as in *Bretagne*, but the design offered a way to get both a twelve 340mm gun armament and a speed increase to 21 knots instead of one or the other. The *Conseil supérieur* wanted a mixed secondary battery of eighteen 138.6mm and twelve 100mm but Doyère was unable to supply it and instead worked in a total of twenty-four 138.6mm guns on three levels. Doyère stated that he was unable to sustain a full effort on both designs much longer and asked that a choice be made by 15 July 1912. He recommended Project A7bis for the 1913 ships, on 5 July 1912 the Naval General Staff also recommended it, and the *Conseil supérieur* approved it on 8 July 1912. The vote was eight for and six against, those in favour being seven vice admirals and Doyère and those opposed being three vice admirals, two Inspectors General, and the Director of Artillery. Project A7bis was later rearranged with wide arcs of fire cleared for the amidships turret over the stern. The plans were approved by the *Comité technique* on 26 October 1912 and by Minister Delcassé on 31 October 1912.

The Law of Finances for the 1913 budget, passed on 30 July 1913, authorized moving battleships A9 and A10 up from 1914 to 1913. Contracts for *Normandie* (I7 ex A7) and *Languedoc* (I8 ex A8) had already been signed on 18 April 1913 and orders for *Flandre* (A9) and *Gascogne* (A10) were notified to the dockyards on 30 July 1913. (In 1913 the budget designator for contract-built battleships was changed from A to I, for *industrie*). On 20 August 1913 Minister of Marine Senator Pierre Baudin made it known that the government, when presenting to Parliament the 1914 budget, would ask for another modification to the construction schedule in the law of 30 March 1912. Instead of two battleships to be laid down on 1 October 1914, the 1914 budget would contain only one battleship (*Béarn*, I11), but it was to be moved forward to 1 January 1914. It would be of the *Normandie* type and would give the navy three four-ship divisions armed with 340mm guns. As the new ship was intended to form a division with the three turbine-propelled *Bretagne*s, she would be entirely turbine propelled. The second 1914 ship (I12) would be deferred to 1915 and would be of a new type.

A key feature in the first four ships of this class was the reversion to reciprocating engines for the wing shafts. The initial trials of the *Danton* class had revealed the voracious appetite of direct drive turbines for coal. Turbines were most efficient at high rotational rates while screw propellers were more efficient at moderate rates. The loss in turbine efficiency was particularly great at cruising speeds. With large geared turbines still some years away, a composite plant with reciprocating engines optimized for cruising speeds on the outboard shafts and turbines for high speeds on the inboard shafts was the most satisfactory option. The engines in the *Normandie* class (except *Béarn*) were in three engine rooms side by side aft of the amidships turret. The large centreline engine room contained one HP ahead turbine on the starboard inboard shaft exhausting into one LP ahead turbine on the port inboard shaft. The smaller side engine rooms contained the reciprocating engines, which also provided the cruising and

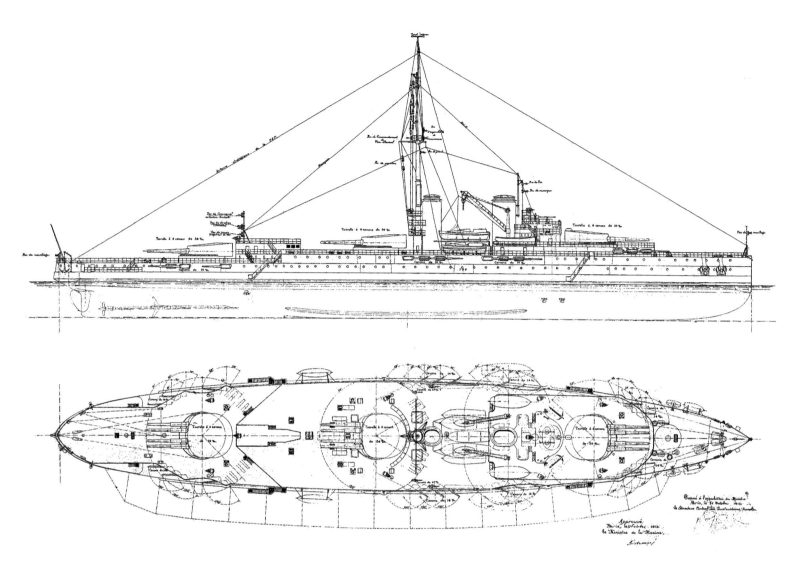

Outboard profile and overhead view (*plan d'ensemble*) of an unnamed 25,200-ton Type 1913 battleship as of 1 March 1913. The plans were signed on 31 October 1912 by the Chief of the Section Technique and approved by the Minister on the same date. They were approved on 18 April 1913 to be attached to the contract with the Société de la Gironde (who built *Languedoc*), and copies were made at Bordeaux on 25 June 1913. Although sent to Bordeaux, this set of plans shows the 21 Guyot-Du Temple boilers in *Normandie* and *Gascogne* instead of the 28 Bellevilles in *Flandre* and *Languedoc*. In July 1913 a conning tower of new design featuring an armoured rangefinder hood was substituted for the original one shown here. The small calibre artillery planned at this time was limited to 4 x 47mm/50 M1902 guns (on the 2nd deck amidships abeam the 2nd funnel, primarily for saluting).

astern functions. In *Béarn* the turbines occupied all three engine rooms, the two HP turbines in the side engine rooms exhausting into the two LP turbines in the centre engine room. Forward of each LP turbine was a pair of cruising turbines, one HP and one IP, that exhausted into the LP turbines. The HP and IP cruising turbines rotated at 2,600rpm and 1,200rpm respectively and were geared to their shafts, making this a partially geared turbine plant.

The single mast was positioned just aft of the funnels on the advice of the wireless telegraphy expert on the design committee that it had to be sited amidships to provide the correct lengths and disposition of the wireless antennas for transmission and reception; its location just aft of the funnels caused considerable concern during the design process. The design re-introduced anti-torpedo side protection in the form of a 1.6m highly subdivided offset between the hull and the inner bottom plating and a 30mm internal longitudinal bulkhead with three layers, one of them flexible, that extended nearly the entire length of the ship, 3m from the side of the ship amidships and 2m at the ends. The compartments between the inner bottom and this bulkhead were to be filled with coal.

Work on these ships effectively ended with the mobilization in late July 1914. The only work then done was to clear the slips, which occurred for *Normandie*, *Flandre*, and *Gascogne* between September and October 1914

and for *Languedoc* in May 1915, the ships being between 49 and 65 percent complete. A ministerial circular of 9 July 1915 stated that the completion of these ships was not considered urgent and that new contracts for materials should not be given. This was followed on 23 July 1915 by a circular stopping all work relating to the artillery. Subsequently much material procured for these ships was diverted to other uses. On 16 January 1918 (renewed 26 June 1919) a firm decision was made to suspend all work on the first 4 ships, only proceeding with the work necessary to launch *Béarn* (although orders were also given to stop diversion of their materials).

On 12 January 1920 Minister of Marine Georges Leygues submitted to Parliament a bill providing for the definitive stop of construction of the five battleships and the laying down of 6 *éclaireurs d'escadre* and 12 *torpilleurs éclaireurs*. On 19 June 1921 a new minister submitted another bill that called for the stop of construction on the battleships, the laying down in 1921 of three light cruisers, six *contre-torpilleurs*, 12 *torpilleurs*, and 12 submarines, and finally the conversion of *Béarn* to an aircraft carrier. This programme became law on 18 April 1922. In the meantime the Washington Naval Treaty, which excluded these ships, was signed on 6 February 1922 and the incomplete hulls were subsequently sold for scrapping.

**Dimensions & tons:** 176.400m oa, 175.000m wl and pp x 27.000m ext and wl. 25,168.262t disp (designed), 25,250t (normal load), 28,270 (with surcharge). Draught: (designed) 8.662m mean, 8.835m aft (real). Men: 1,204 including 44 officers with flag.

**Machinery:**

(first 4): 32,000ihp/shp designed with natural draught at 280rpm for the inboard shafts (turbines) and 115rpm for the wing shafts (reciprocating) and 20kg/cm² boiler pressure for 21kts (45,000ihp/shp for 22.5kts was considered possible with forced draught). 4 screws. 2 turbines and 2 reciprocating engines, the latter with 4 cylinders of 1.16-1.18m (1), 1.66-1.73m (1) and 1.98m (2) diameter and 1.15m stroke, the cylinder diameters varying slightly by manufacturer. 21 Guyot-Du Temple boilers in *Normandie* and *Gascogne,* 28 Belleville boilers in *Flandre* and *Languedoc.* 900t coal (normal), 2,700t (surcharge) + 300t oil. Range 6,600nm @ 12kts (using reciprocating engines only).

(*Béarn*): 32,000shp designed at 260rpm and 20kg/cm² boiler pressure for 21kts. 4 screws. 4 direct drive Parsons main ahead/astern turbines and 4 geared cruising turbines. 28 Niclausse boilers. When completed as an aircraft carrier in 1923-27 *Béarn* received the composite turbine/reciprocating plant ordered for *Normandie* and built by A.C. Loire, Saint Denis, and 12 Normand small-tube boilers of a postwar type.

**Armour:**

Side: Belt at waterline (cemented steel) 300mm amidships, 160mm fwd, 140mm aft. Height amidships from 1.7m below the wl to 2.35m above. Side above belt: see casemate redoubts, below.

Guns: 340mm turrets (cemented steel) 300mm max with 250mm max fixed bases.

Casemate redoubt: A three-deck high structure above the belt rising to the 3rd deck forward, 2nd deck amidships, and 1st deck aft and extending from ten frames forward of the forward 340mm turret to five frames aft of the after 340mm turret on the 1st deck, from the same position forward to abreast the amidships turret on the 2nd deck, and from the same position forward to abreast the forward turret on the 3rd deck. The height amidships was two deck levels or 4.50m on top of

The incomplete battleship *Languedoc* at the pointe de Pen Forn at Landévennec after World War I. The forefunnel is up and the after one is lying on deck amidships as is the mast. The forward barbette has a flat cover while the other two barbettes have much larger covers that may also protect partially-completed turrets. Discarded torpedo boats and service craft lie alongside. *(Postcard by R. de Chalus, Landévennec)*

the belt. The sides were uniformly 160mm cemented steel armour except for 160mm special steel over the 138.6mm gun positions. Transverse bulkheads at its ends were160mm, including a forward bulkhead three decks high before the fore turret and three after bulkheads each one deck high.

Lower armoured deck: flat (construction steel) 14mm for 7m on each side of centreline, 28mm outboard of this to the slopes, slopes (special steel) 42mm on 28mm hull plating.

Upper armoured deck (located at the bottom of the casemate redoubt): flat 26mm hull plating within the casemate redoubt and 30mm fore and aft of the casemate redoubt.

Decks in casemate redoubt. The top deck of the casemate redoubt (the 2nd deck except aft where it was the 1st deck and forward where it was the 3rd deck) had 40mm of plating. Inside the casemate amidships and forward the 1st deck had 12mm of plating.

Conning tower: 266mm max (300mm including the 34 mm of regular plating to which the armour was attached).

Guns: 12 x 340mm/45 M1912M (3 quadruple turrets), 24 x 138.6mm/55 M1910 (casemates in 8 sections of 3 guns of which 2 were forward on the 2nd deck, 4 amidships on the 1st deck, and 2 aft on the main deck), 4 x 47mm/50 M1902 (primarily for saluting). **Torpedoes:** 6 submerged tubes for 450mm M1909R torpedoes. **Searchlights:** 11 x 90cm.

*Normandie* (A7/I7) A.C. Loire, Saint Nazaire/ACL, Saint Nazaire (Parsons turbines).

On list 1.1914. Ord: 18.4.1913 (contract). K: 18.4.1913. L: 19.10.1914. C: no. (Delivery planned for 3.1916).

Budget 1913. Work halted 7.1914 except to clear the slipway, hull 65% and engines 70% complete in 12.1917. Parts of three turrets were in place. Towed from Saint Nazaire to Lorient 1915, back at Saint Nazaire by 8.1918. Towed to Quiberon Bay under a contract of 14.9.1918, taken to Lorient 9.1919. Construction stopped (*arrêté*) 12.9.1919 and abandoned 18.4.1922. Off main list 1922 and contract being cancelled 1922-1923. Offered for sale 26.11.1924 and sold to Ettore Fratelli Serra at La Spezia, to be BU in France. Hull towed from Lorient to Toulon to BU.

*Languedoc* (A8/I8) C.A. Gironde, Bordeaux-Lormont/Schneider, Creusot (Schneider-Zoelly turbines).

On list 1.1914. Ord: 18.4.1913 (contract). K: 1.5.1913. L: 1.5.1915. C: no. (Delivery planned for 4.1916).

Budget 1913. Work halted 7.1914 except to clear the slipway, hull 49% and engines 73% complete in 12.1917. Undocked at Bordeaux 14.2.1918 to clear the basin. Construction stopped 12.9.1919 and abandoned 18.4.1922. Off main list 1922 and contract being cancelled 1922-1923. Towed 4.1925 to Port de Bouc, sold by builder 24.6.1925 to the Société Fratelli Serra (the Italian firm that had bought *Normandie* in 1924). Attempts to break her up in concert with the Chantiers de Provence led to lawsuits between the partners in 3.1927.

*Flandre* (A9) Brest Dyd/Ch. Penhoët, Saint Nazaire (Parsons turbines).

On list 1.1914. Ord: effective 1.10.1913 (yard notified 30.7.1913). K: 6.10.1913. L: 20.10.1914. C: no. (Commissioning for trials planned for 8.1916).

Budget 1913. Work halted 7.1914 except to clear the slipway. Moored at Landévennec with one funnel up. Hull 65% and engines 60% complete in 12.1917. Construction stopped 12.9.1919 and abandoned 18.4.1922. Off main list 1922 and reserved at Brest 1922-1923. Sold 14.6.1923 to Adelcini Luigeri, an Italian residing at Toulon, and BU in France.

*Gascogne* (A10) Lorient Dyd/A.C. Bretagne, Nantes (Rateau-Bretagne turbines) and Indret (reciprocating).

On list 1.1914. Ord: effective 1.10.1913 (yard notified 30.7.1913).

K: 10.10.1913. L: 20.9.1914. C: no. (Commissioning for trials planned for 8.1916).

Budget 1913. Work halted 7.1914 except to clear the slipway. Hull 60%, turbines 44%, and reciprocating engines 75% complete in 12.1917. Towed from Lorient to Brest 1915, back at Lorient by 8.1919. Construction stopped 12.9.1919 and abandoned 18.4.1922. Off main list 1922 and reserved at Lorient 1922-1923. Sold 14.9.1923 at Lorient to the Société d'Entreprise et de Produits de l'Ouest. The incomplete reciprocating engines were BU at Indret.

*Béarn* (I11) F.C. Méditerranée, La Seyne/FCM, La Seyne (turbines). On list 3.1920. Ord: 30.12.1913 (contract). K: 5 (or 10).1.1914. L: 15.4.1920. C: not as battleship. (Delivery planned for 11.1916).

Budget 1914. Work halted 23.7.1914, hull 25% and turbines 17% complete in 12.1917. Early proposal for conversion to an aircraft carrier dated 13.1.1920, *Conseil supérieur* endorsed the concept 13.3.1920. When launched to clear the slip 15.4.1920 the lower armoured deck was the top deck, and successful aircraft trials 20-24.10.1920 using a wooden platform built on this led to a firm decision to convert her to an aircraft carrier. Work on conversion plans began 8.1.1921, conversion authorized 18.4.1922, conversion contract with FCM approved 4.8.1923, ship first underway 10.5.1927, to full commission 16.4.1928, and joined the fleet 1.5.1928. Immobilized in the Antilles 1940-43, used as aircraft transport 1945-46, to special reserve 1.10.1946. Barracks hulk for submarines at Toulon 12.1948. Condemned 31.3.1967. Sold 4.9.1967 to BU at La Spezia.

---

**LYON Class.** *Cuirassés d'escadre.* Super-dreadnought battleships with four quadruple centreline main battery turrets (one forward, one between the funnels, and two aft including one superfiring). Two funnels, a single pole mast forward of the after funnel. Designed by Doyère.

Work on a new design for the four ships planned for 1915 began with a memorandum from the *Section technique* to the Minister, now Pierre Baudin, dated 19 September 1913 asking for basic guidelines for the ships and suggesting options. Doyère explained that the limits on hull size that had restricted the *Jean Bart*, *Bretagne*, and *Normandie* classes no longer existed because of the anticipated completion during 1915-16 of larger graving docks at Brest, Toulon, and Lorient. Doyère provided four proposed designs, two of which reflected French knowledge of the ships of the British 1912 and 1913 programmes which had 381mm 15-inch guns. Doyère's list included one of 27,500 tons with fourteen 340mm guns in three quadruple and one twin turrets, one of 28,500 to 29,000 tons with sixteen 340mm guns in four quadruple turrets, one of 27,500 tons with eight 381mm guns in four twin turrets, and one of 29,500 to 30,000 tons with ten 381mm guns. The designs that added a fourth turret to the three in *Normandie* put it between the two forward and the single after boiler rooms and moved the original amidships turret to a superfiring position aft.

Doyère preferred to use the existing 340mm M1912 gun instead of a 381mm gun which had yet to be designed and which could not begin prototype trials for another two years, noting that the expected battle ranges in the Mediterranean were expected to be at 12,000 metres or less which was well within the capabilities of the 340mm gun. Its maximum range for opening fire was 15,000 metres but ranges were expected to close rapidly.

A second memorandum from the *Section technique* on 19 September 1913, while assuming that a mixed reciprocating and turbine installation as in *Normandie* or an all-turbine arrangement as in *Béarn* was most likely, noted that considerable progress had been made by Parsons in developing large geared turbines and recommended against ruling out such a plant, which would offer major advantages. The machinery installation were never selected because of the war.

On 24 November 1913 the *Conseil supérieur*, considering the views of the just reestablished *Conseil d'Amirauté*, chose the 29,000-ton design with four quadruple 340mm turrets. Although a more powerful 340mm 50-calibre gun had been proposed, the Council chose to retain the existing 340mm 45-calibre gun but with a longer projectile with a detachable ballistic cap that would give it an underwater trajectory of up to 100 metres at 6,000 metres after it struck the water. The Council also wanted to adopt a new semi-automatic model of 138.6mm gun that would soon be available. It would fire at 12 to 15 rounds per minute instead of 5 to 6 for the model in *Bretagne* and would be mounted in sections of two vice three. Twenty of the semi-automatic guns could be substituted for 24 regular guns at a cost of only 15 tons. Existing records do not confirm the adoption of this gun.

Outgoing Minister Baudin preferred the heavier 340mm 50 calibre gun and got the *Conseil d'Amirauté* to support it, but the *Conseil supérieur* was not persuaded and on 2 February 1914 made a final decision in favour of the 340mm M1912 45-calibre gun. It also decided that the ships must have protection against large calibre projectiles traveling underwater.

The *Section technique* presented an initial memorandum on a protection scheme for the ships on 17 June 1914, including a proposal to reduce the casemate armour from 160mm to 100mm (without plating) and increase the internal anti-torpedo bulkhead from the 30mm in the *Normandie* class to 80mm (35mm at the bottom) to protect against both torpedoes and shells with an underwater trajectory. Before this could be discussed the war intervened and brought all design work to a halt. By this time the displacement of the ships was 29,600 tons.

Programme designations were assigned on 3 December 1913 for the four 1915 ships and the single 1914 ship, *Béarn* (I11), and the names followed. The two 1915 ships assigned to be built by contract (I12-I13) were to be begun on 1 January 1915 and the two assigned to arsenals (A14-A15) were to be begun on 1 April 1915, all under the 1915 budget. However, that budget was never passed because of the war and the orders were never placed. (The tables in the draft 1915 budget mis-numbered these ships as *Duquesne* (A13), *Tourville* (A14), *Lyon* (I15) and *Lille* (I16).)

*The following figures represent the design at the time that work stopped in August 1914*

**Dimensions & tons:** 194.5m oa, 190.00m pp x 29.00m wl. 29,600t disp.

**Machinery:** 38,000 to 40,000shp. Speed 21kts. 4 screws. Probably composite machinery as in the *Normandie* class with vertical triple expansion engines and turbines, although geared turbines were also under discussion.

**Armour:**

Side: Belt at waterline 300mm maximum,

Guns: 340mm turrets 300mm faces. Casemates 160mm on 20mm plating (a reduction to 100mm on 20mm was proposed).

Lower armoured deck: flat 42mm, slopes 70mm.

Upper armoured deck: flat 40mm.

**Guns:** 16 x 340mm/45 M1912M (four quadruple turrets), 24 x 138.6mm/55 M1910 (single casemates arranged in redoubts on three levels as in *Normandie*), 2 x 47mm/50 M1902.

**Torpedoes:** 6 submerged 450mm tubes as in *Normandie*.

*Lyon* (I12) Ch. Penhoët, Saint Nazaire.
Budget 1915. To have been ordered begun 1.1.1915. Stopped 8.1914.

*Lille* (I13) F.C. Méditerranée, La Seyne.
Budget 1915. To have been ordered begun 1.1.1915. Stopped 8.1914.

*Duquesne* (A14) Brest Dyd..
Budget 1915. To have been ordered begun 1.4.1915. Stopped 8.1914.

*Tourville* (A15) Lorient Dyd..
Budget 1915. To have been ordered begun 1.4.1915. Stopped 8.1914.

# Chapter Fourteen

# Cruisers, 1897-1914

## (A) Armoured Cruisers (*Croiseurs cuirassés*).
### From *Croiseurs de 1re classe* in the 1.1897 fleet list

*DUPLEIX* Class. *Croiseurs cuirassés.* Armoured cruiser with four twin main battery turrets (two at the ends and two on the sides). Four funnels in two pairs, two pole masts. Steel hull, copper sheathing deleted in the 1898 redesign. Designed by Bertin.

On 31 December 1896 the *Conseil des travaux* examined preliminary characteristics for a 'cruiser sheathed in copper and fitted to carry a division flag' prepared by the *Section technique*. The Council noted that the specifications originally adopted by Minister Besnard required a displacement of 7,900 tons, well above the original 6,800-ton limit. The specifications were changed to bring the displacement down to 7,300 tons, but the Council rejected them, preferring a station variant of its enlarged *Dupuy de Lôme* of December 1896.

The 1897 budget submitted by Lockroy in February 1896 and modified by Besnard in June 1896 included two 1st class stations cruisers designated by Lockroy C3 and C'1 and by Besnard D2 and D3. D2 became the 5,500-ton protected cruiser *Jurien de la Gravière* and D3 was originally a similar ship to be built by contract. In late 1896 Minister Besnard had Director of Materiel Thibaudier prepare preliminary characteristics for an armoured cruiser on the plans of *Pothuau* but enlarged to 6,300 tons, sheathed and coppered and with accommodations for a division flag. On a first look Thibaudier had to increase the displacement to 6,800 tons, and the *Section technique* (Bertin), charged with the detailed calculations, found that around 7,900 tons were needed. Minister Besnard agreed to increase the displacement but only to 7,300 tons and the *Section technique* then developed firm characteristics which were examined by the *Conseil des travaux* on 31 December 1896. The Council criticised in particular the inadequate range and protection of the ship. The council felt it should be a combat ship with armour effective against medium artillery. Its range was also insufficient for overseas where France lacked coaling stations. The Council felt there was no need to make a special class of armoured cruisers and that the new ship should have the same characteristics as the *croiseur cuirassé d'escadre* that on 8 May 1896 it had called a *Dupuy de Lome agrandi*.

On the orders of Besnard the *Section technique* established a new design whose displacement was raised to 7,600 tons to take into account the criticisms of the Council to the extent possible but whose armament had to be reduced by two of the side 164.7mm guns. This was forwarded by Besnard on 22 April 1897 and examined by the Council on 4 May 1897. According to the Council the new design differed from the December one only in a slightly thicker belt (100mm instead of 86mm), a fairly notable increase in range, the reduction in the armament, and an augmentation of 300 tons in the displacement. On 4 May 1897 the Council judged it a little preferable to the December design for protection and range but deplored the reduction in offensive strength, which was now inadequate, and again rejected the design. It maintained its opinion that there was no need for a special class of station armoured cruisers and added that this was also the opinion of the *Conseil supérieur*. It did concede that the details in Bertin's design were well thought out, although it did not like the great length of the ship or the use of Du Temple boilers.

Besnard wanted to slim down the design and wrote to Bertin on 5 August 1897 asking for preliminary characteristics for a cruiser for overseas stations of 4,500 to 4,700 tons and 110 metres length to be built at

Rochefort. Characteristics for a 4,650-ton ship were examined on 1 September 1897 by the Council's summer committee, which limited itself to suggesting changes. Minister Besnard then referred a modified 4,984-ton, 120-metre design to the full Council on 17 November 1897. The Council felt that it differed little from *Jurien de la Gravière* and bluntly stated that, given the displacement, the type of protection of the vitals below the waterline (a protective deck) and the absence of all protection for the gun battery, this ship did not fulfil the conditions necessary for a combat ship. If intended instead as a simple scout its speed was insufficient and its displacement and cost were too high. This criticism applied by extension to all protected cruisers and that issue was referred to the *Conseil supérieur de la marine*, which largely confirmed this view on 17 January 1898.

In the meantime Rochefort needed work, and Besnard returned to the 7,600-ton design of April 1897. He had the plans revised to restore the two 164.7mm guns, adding another 100 tons. On 8 September 1897 he ordered the Machinery Commission to contract for two armoured cruisers of 7,700 tons, and on 18 December 1897 he ordered Rochefort to begin construction of a third ship to be named *Dupleix* to replace the 5,500-ton D3 in the 1897 budget. The contracts for two ships were concluded on 28 December 1897 and notified on 2 February 1898.

The design showed its origins in *Pothuau* in its protection system, which differed from that in Bertin's other cruisers. It had a belt of uniform thickness and a single armoured deck that sloped down to meet the belt at its lower edge. There was a cellular layer above it but no upper armoured deck to form its roof (this deck had only the usual 6mm hull plating), and there was no light upper belt forward.

The ships as begun had a main armament of ten 164mm guns (2 in single turrets at the ends, 8 in casemates on the sides. In the summer of 1898 the *Conseil des travaux* proposed replacing these with four twin turrets, two at the ends and two on the sides, along with the addition of four 100mm QF guns. Minister de Lanessan supported the idea and on 3 August 1898 asked Bertin to prepare the new plans which were also to include deletion of the copper sheathing. Bertin in a memo dated 13 August 1898 reiterated his dislike of the ships in general and of twin turrets with QF guns in particular, the latter because he felt the discharge of the first gun in a turret would disrupt loading and aiming the second gun. Bertin finished the plans in March 1899 and Minister de Lanessan approved the revisions on 6 April 1899. The contracts for *Desaix* and *Kléber* were modified on 5 September 1900 and 22 August 1900 respectively.

*The characteristics are based on a devis for* Kléber *dated 28.9.1905.*

**Dimensions & tons:** 132.100m oa, 130.000m wl, 130.000m pp (tip fwd to stern) x 17.880m ext (above wl), 17.800m wl (18.500m outside amidships sponsons). 7,724.401t disp. Draught: 7.050m mean, 7.420m aft (real). Men: 569 including 19 officers without flag, another 5 officers and 33 men with flag.

**Machinery:**

(*Dupleix*): 17,100ihp designed at 20kg/cm² boiler pressure. Designed speed 21kts. Trials (13.9.1902) 17.870ihp = 20.89kts at 142.83rpm. 3 screws. 3 vertical triple expansion engines with 4 cylinders. 24 Belleville boilers. 815t coal (normal), 1,270t (surcharge). Range 3,548nm @ 10kts with normal coal, 5,545nm @ 10kts with surcharge.

(*Desaix*): 17,100ihp designed at 20kg/cm² boiler pressure. Designed speed 21kts. Trials (17.11.1903) 17.861ihp = 20.61kts at 148.75rpm.

The 7,700-ton armoured cruiser *Kléber* in Hampton Roads flying a Rear Admiral's flag on 12 June 1907 during the Jamestown (Virginia) 300th Anniversary Exposition Naval Review. The numerous horizontal slots at the top of the turret sides were to ventilate combustion gases during rapid firing of the guns, a problem revealed in trials of *Dupleix* in March 1902. *(NHHC, 19-N-11-21-35)*

3 screws. 3 vertical triple expansion engines with 4 cylinders. 24 Belleville boilers. 831t coal (normal), 1,266t (surcharge). Range 4,468nm @ 11kts with normal coal, 6,806nm with surcharge. (*Kléber*): 17,100ihp designed at 150rpm and 18kg/cm² boiler pressure (15kg/cm² at the engines). Designed speed 21kts. Trials (14.10.1903) 16,531.2ihp = 21.255kts at 144.83rpm and 17.031kg/cm² boiler pressure. 3 screws. 3 vertical triple expansion engines with 3 cylinders of 0.860m, 1.255m, and 1.950m diameter and 0.800m stroke. 20 Niclausse boilers.), 815t coal (normal), 1,220t (surcharge) + 65t oil. Range 5,236nm @ 10kts with coal surcharge.

**Armour:**
Side: Belt at waterline (special steel) 102mm amidships, 84mm fwd. Height amidships 3.20m, from 1.20m below the waterline to 2.00m above.
Guns: 164.7mm turrets 110mm front (cemented steel) with 120mm max fixed bases (special steel).
Armoured deck (meeting bottom of belt): flat (construction steel) 22mm, upper slope (extra mild steel/*métail St Jacques*) 50mm, lower slope (construction steel) 22mm, all on 20mm hull plating.
Conning tower (special steel): 120mm max.

**Guns:**
(1902) 8 x 164.7mm/45 M1893-96 (twin turrets), 4 x 100mm/45 M1893 QF (casemates), 2 x 65mm/16 M1881 landing, 10 x 47mm/40 M1885 QF, 4 x 37mm/20 M1885 QF. **Torpedoes:** 2 above-water tubes for 450mm M1892 torpedoes. **Searchlights:** 6 x 60cm.
(1908) Torpedo tubes removed from *Kléber*.

*Dupleix* (D3) Rochefort Dyd/F.C. Méditerranée, Le Havre.
On list 1.1898. Ord: 18.12.1897. K: 18.1.1899. L: 28.4.1900. Comm: 15.3.1902 (trials), 15.9.1903 (full).
Budget 1897. Machinery installed 17.4.1900 to 4.3.1902. Full power trials 9.1902, trial results approved 15.9.1903. Left Rochefort 22.9.1903 for a cruise to West Africa and South America. In 1914 was in the Far East naval division. War service in the Far East 1914-15, Eastern Mediterranean 1915, and West Africa (Dakar) 1917. Struck 27.9.1919, central ship for the reserve at Landévennec 1920-1922.

*Desaix* (D4) A.C. Loire, Saint Nazaire/ACL, Saint Denis.
On list 1.1898. Ord: 28.12.1897 (contract). K: 18.1.1899. L: 21.3.1901. Comm: 6.8.1902 (trials), 5.4.1904 (full).
Budget 1897 (supplemental). Contract modified 5.9.1900. Full power trials 11.1903, trial results approved 22.1.1904. Left Cherbourg 25.4.1904 for Toulon and the *Escadre de la Méditerranée*. In 1914 was in reserve in the *2ᵉ Escadre légère* at Brest. War service in the Channel 1914, Eastern Mediterranean 1915, and West Africa 1916-17. Struck 27.7.1921, sale to Belgium under consideration 1921, for sale at Toulon 1921-1927 and sold 1927 to BU. A transfer to Poland was under consideration in 1924-1926 but in the end *D'Entrecasteaux* became available and was transferred instead.

*Kléber* (D5) C.A. Gironde, Bordeaux-Lormont/Schneider, Creusot.
On list 1.1898. Ord: 28.12.1897 (contract). K: early 1899. L: 20.9.1902. Comm: 26.9.1902 (trials), 4.7.1904 (full).
Budget 1897 (supplemental). Contract modified 22.8.1900. Was complete when launched. Boilers first lit off 20.9.1902, first static machinery trial 24.9.1902. Damage incurred during launch repaired in drydock 10.10.1902 to 11.11.1902, left Bordeaux for trials at Cherbourg 15.12.1902. Official machinery trials 10.1903 to 5.1904. Left Cherbourg 11.7.1904 for Toulon and the *Escadre de la Méditerranée*. In 1914 was in reserve in the *2ᵉ Escadre légère* at Brest.

War service in the Channel 1914-15, Eastern Mediterranean 1915, and West Africa 1916-17. Mined and sunk 27.6.1917 off the Île de Molène near Brest while returning from Dakar.

---

**GUEYDON Class.** *Croiseurs cuirassés.* Armoured cruiser with two single main battery turrets at the ends and secondary guns on the sides. Four funnels in two pairs, one military and one pole mast. Designed by Bertin.

Besnard's 1897 budget included a 1st class *croiseur d'escadre* designated C3, essentially a sister to *Jeanne d'Arc* with a secondary battery of 164.7mm instead of 138.6mm guns. This 11,456-ton ship was rejected by the *Conseil des travaux* on 17 March 1897. To replace it Besnard on 18 March 1897 selected one of two preliminary sets of characteristics for 9,500-ton station armoured cruisers already developed by the *Section technique*, deleting the wood and copper sheathing. He picked the 21-knot ship over the 20.5-knot ship. In early April 1897 he instructed Bertin to prepare a design which Bertin submitted to Besnard on 30 June 1897. The *Conseil des travaux* examined it on 27 July 1897 and, while noting that it was generally similar to the *Dupuy de Lôme agrandi* of 30 December 1896 that the

Council had been recommending for some time, it contained some flaws, mainly in speed (20 knots was enough) and protection. With these and some lesser issues corrected the Council found the design acceptable but also asked that a new design be prepared for future armoured cruisers. On 13 August 1897 one ship of this type named *Gueydon* was ordered at Lorient and one named *Dupetit-Thouars* was ordered at Toulon. A third, *Montcalm*, was ordered from FCM La Seyne. *Dupetit-Thouars* compared to *Gueydon* had a much longer bridge on the after superstructure extending around the after funnel.

*The characteristics are based on a devis for* Dupetit-Thouars *dated 15.5.1905.*

**Dimensions & tons:** 139.997m oa, 138.000m wl, 138.000m pp (tip fwd to stern) x 19.500m ext (above wl, also beam at amidships sponsons), 19.400m wl. 9,859.798t disp. Draught: 7.190m mean, 7.671m aft. Men: 580 including 25 officers (*D-T*, 1905), 620 including 23 officers without flag and another 12 officers and 64 men with flag (*Montcalm* 1906)

**Machinery:**
(*D-T*) 19,600ihp designed at 135rpm and 20kg/cm² boiler pressure

---

Outboard profile and overhead view (*plan d'ensemble*) of the 1st class armoured cruiser *Gueydon* built at Lorient on the plans of M. Bertin. The plans were signed at Lorient on 23 December 1902 by the naval constructor in charge of the ship, Ch. Lepeltier. The vertical lines at the ends of the ship show the fore and aft perpendiculars, in this case and for all later armoured cruisers the intersection of the bow and stern with the waterline at the designed draught. The small calibre artillery carried at this time included 4 x 100mm/45 M1893 QF guns (on the 2nd deck abreast the fore and after funnels), 16 x 47mm QF guns (4 on the lower

platform of the military foremast, 2 on the forward lower bridge, 2 on the 2nd deck over the 2nd pair of casemates, 2 on the after bridge, and 6 behind ports in the hull of which the forward pair was on the 1st deck and the others on the main deck amidships and aft; alternatively these six could be placed on 2 empty mountings on the fore bridge, 2 on the after bridge, and 2 on the 2nd deck), and 4 x 37mm QF guns (2 on the bridge wings and 2 on the quarterdeck/2nd deck aft, in *Dupetit-Thouars* this pair was on the forward extension of the after bridge deck). There were also 2 x 65mm M1881 landing guns stowed on the main deck.

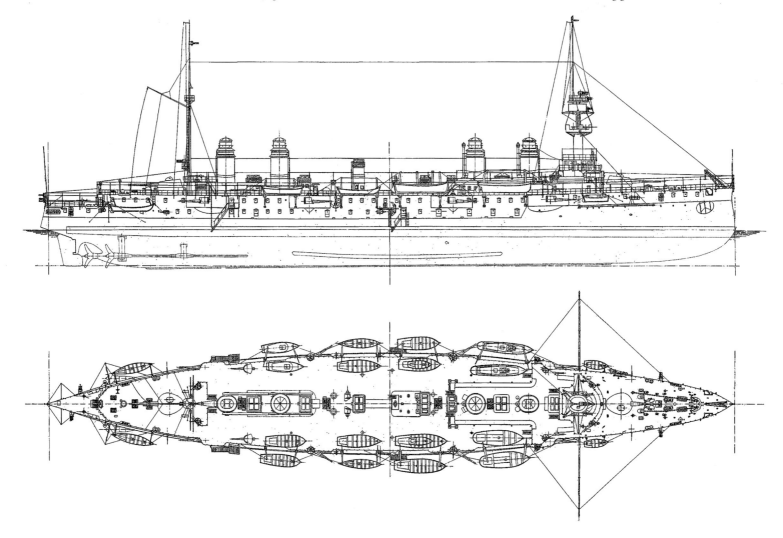

The 1st class armoured cruiser *Dupetit-Thouars* between 1905 and 1908. She was built more slowly than the other ships of the *Gueydon* and *Gloire* classes and only completed trials in 1905. Compared to her sisters, she had a much longer bridge on the after superstructure extending around the after funnel. An armoured cruiser of the *Gloire* class is beyond her bow and one of the *Léon Gambetta* class is in the background astern. *(Postcard by Ewile, 2 rue Amsterdam, Paris)*

(15kg/cm² at the engines). Designed speed 21kts. Trials (14.2.1905) 21.944.0ihp = 22.021kts at 139.346rpm and 19.275kg/cm² boiler pressure. 3 screws. 3 vertical triple expansion engines with 3 cylinders of 0.940m, 1.380m, and 2.150m diameter and 0.850m stroke. 28 Belleville boilers built by Delaunay Belleville. 950t coal (normal), 1,748.052t (surcharge) + 80t oil. Range on 1 engine 6,188nm @ 10kts with normal coal, 11,322nm @ 10kts with surcharge. (Two engines would be used for cruising at 12 and 14kts and all three at 15kts and above.)

(*Gueydon*): 19,600ihp designed at 18kg/cm² boiler pressure. Designed speed 21kts. Trials (23.12.1902) 19.668ihp = 20.30kts at 135.23rpm. 3 screws. 3 vertical triple expansion engines with 4 cylinders. 28 Niclausse boilers. 940t coal (normal), 1,727t (surcharge). Range 3,825nm @ 10kts with normal coal, 7,028nm @ 10kts with surcharge.

(*Montcalm*): 19,500ihp designed at 17kg/cm² boiler pressure. Designed speed 21kts. Trials (13.11.1901) 19,735ihp = 21.14kts at 135.97rpm.

3 screws. 3 vertical triple expansion engines with 4 cylinders. 20 Normand-Sigaudy boilers (8 double-ended and 4 single-ended). 1,020t coal (normal), 1,670t (surcharge). Range 3,700nm @ 10kts with normal coal, 6,090nm @ 10kts with surcharge.

**Armour:**

Side: Belt at waterline (special steel) 150mm amidships, 90mm fwd, 80mm aft. Total height amidships 1.950m of which 0.60m above wl. Upper strake 95mm amidships (height 1.550m), 75mm fwd, 75mm aft. Side above belt forward (special steel) 57mm.

Guns: 194mm turrets 161mm fronts (cemented steel) with 176mm max fixed bases (special steel). 164.7mm casemates (special steel) 102mm max. 100mm gun shields 72mm.

Lower armoured deck (extra mild steel): flat 30mm, upper slope 55mm, lower slope 30mm, all on 20mm hull plating.

Upper armoured deck: flat (mild/construction steel) 6mm on 10mm hull plating.

Conning tower (cemented steel): 174mm max.

**Guns:**

(1901) 2 x 194mm/40 M1893-96 (turrets), 8 x 164.7mm/45 M1893-96 QF (casemates), 4 x 100mm/45 M1893 QF, 2 x 65mm/16 M1881 landing, 16 x 47mm/40 M1885 QF, 4 x 37mm/20 M1885 QF.

**Torpedoes:** 2 submerged tubes for 450mm M1892 torpedoes.

**Searchlights:** 6 x 60cm.

*Dupetit-Thouars* (C3) Toulon Dyd/Schneider, Creusot.
On list 1.1898. Ord: 13.8.1897. K: 17.4.1899. L: 5.7.1901.
  Comm: 1.12.1904 (trials), 15.5.1905 (full).
Budget 1897. Machinery installed 19.9.1901 to 16.1.1904. Official machinery trials 12.1904 to 2.1905, results approved 21.5.1905. To *disponibilité armée* (ready but manned only by a nucleus crew) 17.6.1905 while awaiting orders to depart for the Far East, to full commission 28.8.1905 and sailed for Saigon 17.9.1905. In 1913-14 was assigned to the Atlantic training division at Brest. War service in the Channel 1914-15, Mediterranean 1915, West Africa 1916, Caribbean 1916-17, and Atlantic 1918. Torpedoed and sunk 7.8.1918 by the German submarine *U-62* 400nm off Brest while escorting a convoy from New York.

*Gueydon* (C5) Lorient Dyd/A.C. Loire, Saint Denis.
On list 1.1898. Ord: 13.8.1897. K: 2.8.1898. L: 20.9.1899.
  Comm: 15.10.1901 (trials), 1.9.1903 (full).
Budget 1897 (supplemental). Full power trials 12.1902, final official trials 5.1903. Departed Lorient for Saigon 3.10.1903. At Brest 1913-14 with the school for carpenters and sail makers embarked. War service in the Channel 1914-15, West Africa 1916, Caribbean 1916-17, Atlantic 1918, and the Arctic (Murmansk) 10.1918-6.1919. Ordered 21.8.1925 to replace *Pothuau* as seagoing school for gunnery practice, equipment transhipped at Toulon 1926. Condemned 24.7.1935 as seagoing vessel, barracks hulk at Brest for the naval preparatory school 1935-1939. In 1943 the Germans in Brest made the hulls of *Gueydon* and the World War I avisos *Aisne* and *Oise* into a dummy *Prinz Eugen* to decoy British bomber pilots. Destroyed during the occupation of Brest.

*Montcalm* (C6) F.C. Méditerranée, La Seyne/FCM, Marseille.
On list 1.1898. Ord: 22.12.1897 (contract). K: 27.9.1898. L: 27.3.1900.
  Comm: 22.7.1901 (trials), 24.3.1902 (full).
Budget 1897 (supplemental). Named 8.9.1897. Full power trials 11.1901. Left Toulon for Brest 26.3.1902 to embark President Loubet for a voyage to Kronshtadt, then sent to the Far East 3.1903. In 1914 was flagship of the Far East naval division. War service in the Far East 1914-15, Eastern Mediterranean 1915, Caribbean 1916-17, and Atlantic 1918. Off main list 1925, barracks hulk at Brest 1925-1939. Condemned 28.10.1926. Barracks for the school for apprentice seamen at Brest 1931. Renamed *Montcalm II* 12.1932 and *Trémintin* 1.10.1934. Barracks for the school for boys 25.9.1934 to 16.6.1940. Destroyed 1942-43.

---

**GLOIRE Class.** *Croiseurs cuirassés.* Armoured cruiser with two single main battery turrets at the ends and four single secondary battery turrets on the sides. Four funnels in two pairs, one military and one pole mast. Designed by Bertin.

On 24 February 1898 Minister Besnard forwarded to the *Conseil des Travaux* the plans of *Montcalm* as they had been approved for execution after receiving the modifications requested by the Council on 27 July 1897. The 1898 budget contained three armoured cruisers of the *Montcalm* type and Besnard decided that these ships would receive wood hull sheathing freeing them from the need for drydocking. He also agreed to raise their displacement to 10,000 tons and asked the Council what improvements should be made to increase their military value over the *Montcalm* type. The *Section technique*, having been asked the same question, recommended only one change, adding two more 164.7mm guns with shields amidships.

    The Council considered specifications for the new ships between 26 April and 3 May 1898. It concluded that relatively little could be done within the limits set by Minister Besnard, its chief recommendations being to add more ammunition for the 194mm guns, increase the designed tonnage margin, and redistribute some thicknesses in the armour to improve protection. It did not recommend adding the two unprotected 164.7mm guns suggested by the *Section technique*. More could be done in a 10,000-ton ship if the Minister were willing to reduce the speed to 20 knots and delete some of the coal in order to release weight to improve protection, particularly in the belt and the two armoured decks. Distribution of the secondary battery would be improved by mounting either all eight of the 164.7mm guns in twin turrets or four of them in single turrets The Council also recommended deleting the wood hull sheathing, in part because attaching it to Harvey armour was not technically possible without losing the extra properties of the armour. The Council also listed further improvements in armament and protection that could be achieved if the Minister allowed an increase to 11,500 tons (12,000 with sheathing).

    On 10 May 1898 Minister Besnard ordered the *Section technique* to design an armoured cruiser of 10,000 tons following the ideas of the Council and without wood sheathing. On 17 August 1898 the Minister, now Édouard Lockroy, referred the resulting design to the Council whose temporary summer committee examined it on 20 August 1898. The committee dismissed Bertin's attempt to use the extra displacement in a 11,500-ton ship to increase speed and range rather than protection and offensive strength, as the Council had repeatedly insisted, and turned to the 10,000-ton design that had been referred to it. The committee made very few changes, one of note being a recommendation to add some above-water torpedo tubes to the two submerged tubes in the design as had just been done for battleships earlier in the year. The committee concluded that the design represented great progress over *Montcalm* and would produce a combat ship of serious military value.

    On 17 September 1898 Minister Lockroy ordered three cruisers to this design, C4 (*Condé*) at Cherbourg C7 (*Gloire*) at Lorient, and C8 (*Sully*) by contract. On 8 April 1899 Lockroy ordered C4 to be moved to Lorient, where she was built after C7 and the class was soon filled out by orders for C9 (*Marseillaise*) at Brest and C10 (*Amiral Aube*) by contract. Only *Sully* was originally given flag facilities, including an enlarged conning tower.

    In 1906 Bertin wrote concerning this class that *Montcalm*, *Sully*, and *Marseillaise* all met the conditions of their programme and received careful work. But he continued to feel that the necessity of building cruisers inferior to their rivals, both in power and in speed, never was demonstrated. For such ships to operate alone was risky, while to tie them to a battleship squadron was a waste of 21 knots. The best results for fleet operations would be obtained by a squadron of *Patrie* type battleships with *Jurien de la Gravière* type cruisers as scouts linked by simple dispatch vessels of 3,000 tons. He felt that armoured cruisers were best in the role of isolated runners on the trade routes, master of the sea lanes wherever there was no battleship squadron. Ships able to capture passenger ships and escape enemy cruisers with their speed would get full respect from commercial powers, and if they were also able to destroy cruisers that tried to counter their operations they would become both a menace to enemy commerce and effective protection to French commerce. Their main quality was speed for individual operations, followed by extended range.

    The machinery of both this and the preceding class was prematurely worn by constant steaming during the war. At the end of the war the two surviving ships of the *Gueydon* class were found to be in somewhat better condition than the four of the *Gloire* class, so they were the ones retained for postwar service.

*The characteristics are based on a devis for* Amiral Aube *dated 30.8.1905 with additional information from a devis for* Marseillaise *dated 16.1.1904 and a devis for* Sully *dated 28.1.1904.*

**Dimensions & tons:** 139.790m oa, 137.860m wl & pp (tip fwd to stern) x 20.200m ext & wl. 10,020.754t disp (normal). Draught: 7.000m mean, 7.690m aft (keel line projected), 7.550m (real). Men: 615 including 25 officers without flag.

**Machinery:**
(*Am. Aube* & *Marseillaise*) 20,500ihp designed at 138rpm and 20kg/cm$^2$

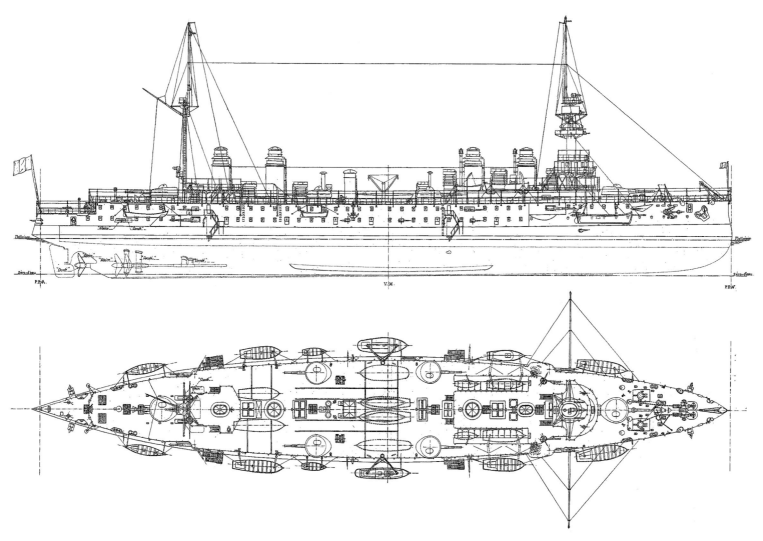

Outboard profile and overhead view (*plan d'ensemble*) of the 1st class armoured cruisers *Gloire* and *Condé* built at Lorient on the plans of M. Bertin. The plans were signed at Lorient on 1 August 1904 by the naval constructor in charge of the ship, P. V. Lejeune. The small calibre artillery carried at this time included 6 x 100mm/45 M1893 QF guns (2 on the 2nd deck over the forward 164.7mm casemates, 2 on the 1st deck amidships, and 2 on the 1st deck above the after 164.7mm casemates), 19 x 47mm/40 M1885 QF guns (4 on the lower platform of the military foremast, 2 on the lower forward bridge, 2 on the after bridge, 1 in the bow on the 1st deck, 2 on the 1st deck forward of the forward 194mm turret, and 8 on the main deck including 2 outboard of the second funnel, 4 between the 164.7mm turrets, and 2 in the stern), and 4 x 37mm M1885 QF guns (2 on the after bridge by the fourth funnel and 2 on the 1st deck (quarterdeck) at the extreme stern, these two being on the lower forward bridge in *Sully*). There were also 2 x 65mm M1881 landing guns stowed on the 1st deck amidships.

---

boiler pressure (14.5 to 15.5kg/cm² at engines). Designed speed 21kts. Trials (*Am. Aube* 17.12.1903) 22,015.83ihp = 21.877kts at 141.36rpm and 19.440kg/cm² boiler pressure; (*Marseillaise* 5.8.1903) 21,578.0ihp = 21.641kts at 139.82rpm and 19.749kg/cm² boiler pressure. 3 screws. 3 vertical triple expansion engines with 4 cylinders of 0.970m (1), 1.400m (1), and 1.560m (2) diameter and 0.850m stroke. 28 Belleville boilers built by Delaunay Belleville. (*Am. Aube*) 970t coal (normal), 1,650t (surcharge) + 80t oil. Range 5,108.09nm @ 11.243kts. (*Marseillaise*) 1,046t coal (normal), 1,689.990t (surcharge) + 84.507t oil. Range 6,031.5nm @ 10.327kts.

(*Sully*) 20,500ihp designed at 138rpm and 20kg/cm² boiler pressure (15.5kg/cm² at engines). Designed speed 21kts. Trials (23.4.1903) 20,514.54ihp = 21.4065kts at 139.542rpm and 19.125kg/cm² boiler pressure. 3 screws. 3 vertical triple expansion engines with 3 cylinders of 0.970m, 1.440m, and 2.150m diameter and 0.850m stroke. 28 Belleville boilers. 970t coal (normal), 1,898t (surcharge) + 65t oil. Range 8,615.7125nm @ 9.8925kts with normal coal.

(*Condé*): 20,500ihp designed. Designed speed 21kts. Trials (11.5.1904) 22,331ihp = 21.31kts at 142.22rpm. 3 screws. 3 vertical triple expan-sion engines with 3 cylinders. 28 Niclausse boilers. 970t coal (normal), 1,602t (surcharge). Range 5,575nm @ 10kts with normal coal, 9,207nm @ 10kts with surcharge.

(*Gloire*): 20,500ihp designed. Designed speed 21kts. Trials (19.1.1904) 21,334ihp = 21.27kts at 139.56rpm. 3 screws. 3 vertical triple expan-sion engines with 3 cylinders. 28 Niclausse boilers. 970t coal (normal), 1,572t (surcharge). Range 4,850nm @ 10kts with normal coal, 7,860nm @ 10kts with surcharge.

**Armour:**

Side: Belt at waterline 150mm amidships (cemented steel), 90mm fwd, 80mm aft (both special steel). Total height amidships 2.000m of which 0.650m above wl. Upper strake 130mm amidships (cemented steel) (height 1.626m), 90mm fwd, 80mm aft (both special steel). Side above belt forward (special steel) 40mm.

Guns: 194mm turrets (cemented steel) 160mm front with 174mm max fixed bases. 164.7mm turrets (special steel) 96mm front with 104mm max fixed bases. 164.7mm casemates (special steel) 102mm max.

Lower armoured deck (construction steel): flat 25mm, upper slope 25mm, lower slope 20mm, all on 20mm hull plating.

Upper armoured deck (construction steel): flat 24mm except 10mm in
the bow forward of frame 30, all on 10mm hull plating.
Conning tower (cemented steel): 174mm max, (elliptical except larger
flagship model extended at the rear in *Sully*)
**Guns:** 2 x 194mm/40 M1893-96 (centreline turrets), 8 x 164.7mm/45
M1893-96 QF (4 in side turrets, 4 in casemates), 6 x 100mm/45
M1893 QF, 2 x 65mm/16 M1881, 19 x 47mm/40 M1885 QF, 4 x
37mm/20 M1885 QF. **Torpedoes:** 5 tubes for 450mm M1892 torpedoes (1 above water in the stern 2 above water on the sides, and 2 submerged on the sides). **Searchlights:** 6 x 60cm.

*Condé* (C4) Lorient Dyd/F.C. Méditerranée, Le Havre.
On list 1.1899. Ord: 17.9.1898 at Cherbourg, 8.4.1899 at Lorient. K:
20.3.1901. L: 12.3.1902. Comm: 15.9.1903 (trials), 12.8.1904 (full).
Budget 1898. Construction reassigned from Cherbourg to Lorient 1899.
Full power trials 5.1904. Joined *Gloire* and *Amiral Aube* in the
*Escadre du Nord* 10.1904. In 1914 was in the *1re Division légère* of the
*2e Escadre légère* at Brest. War service in the Caribbean 1914-1917,
Atlantic 8.1918, and the Arctic (Murmansk) 6-10.1919. Replaced by
*Gueydon* and to special reserve at Brest 15.3.1920. Barracks for the
school for naval infantry at Lorient 1922. Condemned 15.2.1933 as a
mobilizable ship, refitted 11.1933 for continued use at the school in
Lorient. Used by the Germans at Lorient as a depot for submarines,
then towed to the mouth of the Gironde estuary for use as a target
for aircraft. Sunk 1944 by Allied aircraft, BU ten years later.

*Gloire* (C7) Lorient Dyd/Schneider, Creusot.
On list 1.1899. Ord: 17.9.1898. K: 5.9.1899. L: 27.6.1900.
Comm: 2.1.1903 (trials), 28.4.1904 (full).
Budget 1898. Full power trials 1.1904. Joined the *Escadre du Nord* 1904.
Flagship 1913-14 for the Atlantic training division with the school for
boatswains embarked. War service in the Channel 1914-15, West
Africa and Caribbean 1916-17, and Atlantic 1918. Off main list c1921
and for sale at Brest 1921-1922. Struck 7.7.1922. Sold c1923.

*Sully* (C8) F.C. Méditerranée, La Seyne/FCM, Marseille.
On list 1.1899. Ord: 24.5.1899 (contract). K: 1899. L: 4.6.1901.
Comm: 26.1.1903 (trials), 8.1.1904 (full).
Budget 1898. Machinery installed 26.5.1902 to 22.12.1902. Official
machinery trials 5-6.1903. Departed for service in the Far East
Squadron (*Escadre*) soon after commissioning. Wrecked 30.9.1905 in
Ha Long Bay (*Baie d'Along*) near Haiphong, total loss (guns recovered
1.1906). Struck 31.10.1905, wreck for sale in Tonkin 1905-1907, then
abandoned.

*Marseillaise* (C9) Brest Dyd/A.C. Loire, Saint Denis.
On list 1.1900. Ord: 19.6.1899. K: 10.1.1900. L: 14.7.1900.
Comm: 10.2.1902 (trials), 16.1.1904 (full)
Budget 1899. Machinery installed 20.6.1901 to 18.4.1902. Official
machinery trials 4-10.1903. Assigned to the *Escadre du Nord*
13.11.1903. In 1914 was in the *1re Division légère* of the *2e Escadre
légère*, the cruiser force at Brest. War service in the Channel 1914-15,
Caribbean 1916-17, and Atlantic 1918. In reserve 1922-23. School for
gunnery in the Mediterranean training division 1923-28. Off main list
1928 (condemnation pending). For sale by the Domaines 1929-1933.
Struck 13.2.1932. To *Marseillaise II* 12.1932. BU 12.1933-4.1934 at
Brégaillon near Toulon.

*Amiral Aube* (C10) A.C. Loire, Saint Nazaire/ACL, Saint Denis.
On list 1.1900. Ord: 9.8.1899 (contract). K: 2.1901. L: 9.5.1902.
Comm: 15.4.1903 (trials), 11.4.1904 (full).
Budget 1899. Machinery installed 15.4.1902 to 18.3.1903. Official
machinery trials 10.1903 to 5.1904, results approved 5.5.1904, ship
accepted for service 7.5.1904 and joined the *Escadre du Nord*. In 1914
was in the *1re Division légère* of the *2e Escadre légère* at Brest. War service in the Channel 1914-15, Eastern Mediterranean 12.1915-3.1916,

Caribbean 1916-17, and the Arctic (Murmansk) 3-10.1918. To special
reserve at Lorient 1.10.1919. Off main list c1921 and for sale at
Lorient 1921-1922. Struck 7.7.1922. Sold c1924.

---

*LÉON GAMBETTA* **Class.** *Croiseurs cuirassés.* Armoured cruiser with two
twin main battery turrets at the ends and six twin secondary battery turrets
on the sides. Four funnels in two pairs, one military and one pole mast.
Designed by Bertin.

The year 1898 administered two shocks to French naval planning. In
March 1898 the Reichstag passed German Admiral Tirpitz's First Naval
Law, which called for a fleet of 16 modern battleships plus a flagship of
which seven were to be built by 1903. The Fashoda crisis, an intense colonial confrontation with Britain, followed in September and October 1898,
forcing the French to admit their naval impotence against Britain and back
down in November. In compensation, the French economy which had
been in recession since the Franco-Prussian War and a stock market crash
in 1882 had largely recovered by 1896.

Armoured cruisers were needed both as fleet units against the new
German fleet and as commerce raiders against Britain. On 12 August 1898
the Naval General Staff (EMG), which had already examined battleships
and small *croiseurs-estafettes*, turned to armoured cruisers. It felt that the
*Dupleix*, *Gueydon*, and *Gloire* types lacked the offensive power of the ships
currently building abroad and called for a ship derived from *Gloire* with the
same protection and speed but a greatly enhanced armament of two
194mm and sixteen 164.7mm guns. With these and the same protection,
21-knot speed and 10,000nm range as *Gloire*, the new 11,700-ton ships
could stand up to the British *Cressy* and German *Fürst Bismarck*. (The 23-
knot British *Drake* class, a response to *Jeanne d'Arc*, was considered an
outlier.) The Naval General Staff presented its specifications for the new
ship in a note dated 1 February 1899 and Minister Lockroy asked the
*Section technique* for a preliminary design. The General Staff considered
this design on 20 June 1899, by which time the number of 194mm guns
had been doubled to four and the displacement had risen again to 12,416
tons. The *Conseil des travaux* in turn examined the design on 28 July 1899
and suggested few changes, in part because most of the characteristics had
already been approved in the Ministry. On 14 November 1899 the Council
examined an alternative design by Bertin for a 13,160-ton ship with a
uniform armament of eight 194mm and ten 100mm guns along with the
speed of 23 knots and range of 12,000nm at 10 knots of *Jeanne d'Arc*. It
rejected that design but stated that if the Minister, now de Lanessan,
wanted to proceed with such a ship it should be given an armament identical to that of the 12,416-ton design. On 15 November 1899 de Lanessan
ordered the *Section technique* to draw up a detailed design for the 12,416-
ton ship, and on 4 January 1900 he ordered its speed increased to 22 knots
On 5 June 1900 the Council examined new versions of both designs, one
now of 12,551 tons, 148.35m length, 27,500ihp, and 22 knots and the
other of 13,179 tons 156.8m length, 32,000ihp, and 23 knots. The smaller
design had four boiler rooms and four funnels, the larger one had a larger
forward boiler room and five funnels. The Council regarded both designs
as very well done but concluded that in the current condition of various
European navies a speed of 23 knots instead of 22 knots was not worth the
extra cost. It recommended the 22-knot design for the ships about to be
begun under the 1900 budget. and *Jules Ferry* was ordered at Cherbourg on
28 June 1900 and *Léon Gambetta* at Brest on 2 July 1900. *Victor Hugo*
followed under the 1901 budget at Toulon but was later moved to Brest.
Two more ships of this class were planned under the 1902 budget to
provide the five required by the Programme of 1900, but they were built to
two revised designs.

The actual steaming range of these three ships fell well below that in
their design. All had flag facilities including an enlarged conning tower
identical to the one in *Sully*. A useful recognition feature was the boat
cranes amidships. *Léon Gambetta* had 'Y' frames as in the *Dupleix* and

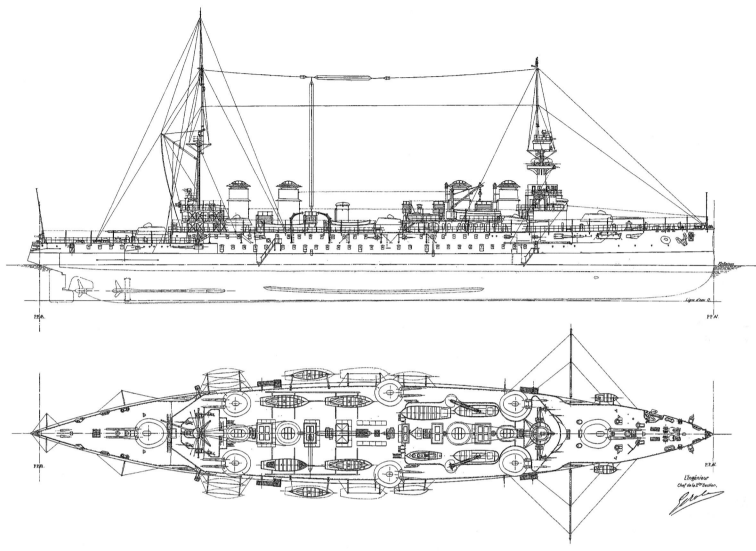

Outboard profile and overhead view (*plan d'ensemble*) as fitted of the 1st class armoured cruiser *Victor Hugo* built at Lorient on the plans of M. Bertin. The plans were signed at Lorient on 1 April 1907 by the naval constructor in charge of the ship, P. V. Lejeune. The small calibre artillery carried in this ship at this time included 24 x 47mm/50 M1902 Schneider QF guns (4 in the lower platform of the military foremast, 2 on the upper forward bridge, 2 on the lower forward bridge, 4 on the upper after bridge, 2 on the lower after bridge, and 10 behind ports in the hull on the 1st deck near the four 2nd deck turrets), and 2 x 37mm M1885 QF guns for the boats. There were also 2 x 65mm M1881 landing guns. Her sisters carried the earlier 47mm/40 M1885 Hotchkiss QF gun.

---

*Gloire* classes, *Victor Hugo* had cranes with an elevating boom, and *Jules Ferry* had 'goose neck' cranes (as did the four final armoured cruisers).

*The characteristics are based on a devis for* Léon Gambetta *dated 21.7.1905.*

**Dimensions & tons:** 148.350m oa (*V.H.* 149.07m), 146.510m wl & pp x 21.400m ext and wl (22.605m outside wing turrets). 12,849.593t disp (with coal surcharge). Draught: 7.791m mean, 8.4215m aft. Men: 734 including 26 officers without flag, add 4 officers and 41 men with flag.

**Machinery:**

(*L.G.*): 27,500ihp designed at 125rpm and 19.5kg/cm² boiler pressure (17kg/cm² at the engines). Designed speed 22kts. Trials (22.4.1905) 28,715ihp = 23.006kts at 126.43rpm and 18.042kg/cm² boiler pressure. 3 screws. 3 vertical triple expansion engines with 4 cylinders of 1.060m (1), 1.606m (1), and 1.760m (2) diameter and 1.000m stroke. 28 Niclausse boilers. 1,223t coal (normal), 1,911.243t (surcharge) + 100t oil. Range 7,373nm @ 10.380kts with surcharge.

(*J.F.*): 29,000ihp designed (the increased power being expected from the small-tube boilers). Designed speed 22kts. Trials (7.12.1906)

28.743ihp = 22.56kts at 124.51rpm. 3 screws. 3 vertical triple expansion engines with 4 cylinders. 20 Guyot-Du Temple boilers. 1,320t coal (normal), 2,100t (surcharge). Range 7,500nm @ 10kts.

(*V.H.*): 27,500ihp designed at 21.5kg/cm² boiler pressure (16.5kg/cm² at the engines). Designed speed 22kts. Trials (2.3.1907) 28.344ihp = 22.26kts at 127.00rpm. 3 screws. 3 vertical triple expansion engines with 4 cylinders. 28 Belleville boilers. 1,322t coal (normal), 2,000t coal (surcharge). Range 5,020nm @ 10kts with normal coal, 7,567nm @ 10kts with surcharge.

**Armour:**

Side: Belt at waterline 150mm amidships (cemented steel), 90mm fwd, 80mm aft (both special steel). Total height amidships 2.050m of which 0.650m above wl. Upper strake 130mm amidships (cemented steel, height 1.650m), 90mm fwd, 80mm aft (both special steel). Side above belt forward (special steel) 40mm.

Guns: 194mm turrets 138mm front (cemented steel) with 140mm max fixed bases (special steel). 164.7mm turrets (special steel) 102mm front with 102mm max fixed bases. 164.7mm casemates (special steel) 102mm max.

Lower armoured deck: flat (construction steel) 15mm, upper slope (special steel) 35mm, lower slope (construction steel) 10mm, all on 30mm hull plating.

Upper armoured deck (construction steel): flat 22mm except 9mm in the bow forward of frame 25 (the conning tower), all on 11m hull plating.

Conning tower (cemented steel): 174mm max (enlarged flagship model as in *Sully*).

**Guns:** 4 x 194mm/40 M1893-96 (twin turrets), 16 x 164.7mm/45 M1893-96 QF (6 twin turrets and 4 casemates), 2 x 65mm/16 M1881 landing, 24 x 47mm/40 M1885 Hotchkiss QF (47mm/50 M1902 Schneider QF in *V.H.*), 2 x 37mm/20 M1885 QF (boats). **Torpedoes:** 2 tubes for 450mm M1892 torpedoes (M1904 in *V.H.*). The design also included 3 above water tubes, two near the forward 194mm turret and one in the stern, which were removed from *L.G.* in 3.1906 and suppressed during construction in the others. **Searchlights:** 6 x 60cm.

*Jules Ferry* (C11) Cherbourg Dyd/Indret.
On list 1.1901. Ord: 28.6.1900. K: 19.8.1901. L: 23.8.1903.
    Comm: 23.6.1905 (trials), c1.1907 (full).
Budget 1900. Trials 7.1905 to 12.1906, results approved 10.1.1907. Left Cherbourg 4.2.1907 for Toulon, trials continued to 5.1907. Active

1.6.1907 as cruiser flagship in the *Escadre de la Méditerranée*. In 1914 was in the *1re Escadre légère* of the *1re Armée navale*. War service in the Mediterranean 1914-18. In the Far East 1923-1925. Struck 19.1.1927. Sold 1928 at Toulon to BU.

*Léon Gambetta* (C12) Brest Dyd/Ch. Penhoët, Saint Nazaire.
On list 1.1901. Ord: 2.7.1900. K: 15.1.1901. L: 26.10.1901.
    Comm: 1.12.1903 (trials), 25.7.1905 (full).
Budget 1900 (late addition). Machinery installed 1.5.1902 to 31.8.1903. Trials 2.1904 to 7.1905, results approved 7.7.1905. Left Brest for Cherbourg 3.8.1905 to become flagship of the cruiser force in the *Escadre du Nord*. In 1914 was in the *1re Escadre légère* of the *1re Armée navale*. War service in the Mediterranean 1914-15. Torpedoed and sunk 27.4.1915 by the Austrian submarine *U-5* in the entrance to the Strait of Otranto.

*Victor Hugo* (C13) Lorient Dyd-Caudan/Indret.
On list 1.1902. Ord: 11.3.1901 at Toulon, 3.6.1902 at Lorient. K: 2.3.1903. L: 30.3.1904. Comm: 15.3.1906 (trials), 16.4.1907 (full).
Budget 1901. Construction reassigned from Toulon to Lorient 3.6.1902, much material had to be transported to Lorient and Lorient's workload delayed the keel laying to 3.1903. Machinery installed 7.1904 to 26.6.1906. Manned for trials 15.1.1907. Trials 2-4.1907. Left Lorient 8.5.1907 for New York and the Jamestown Exposition, then joined the cruiser force of the *Escadre de la Méditerranée*. In 1914 was in the *1re Escadre légère* of the *1re Armée navale*. War service in the Mediterranean 1914-18. In the Far East 1922-1923, then to reserve at Toulon 11.8.1923. Struck 20.1.1928. Sold 26.11.1930 at Toulon to BU.

The 1st class armoured cruiser *Victor Hugo*, probably during the 1920s. The turrets are covered with the dark mix of soot and grease informally known as *bouchon gras* that was adopted during World War I and retained in the 1920s. The after casemate 164.7mm gun has been removed, an action also taken in *Jules Ferry* but not in the similar *Jules Michelet*. Some of the positions for 47mm guns in the hull have also been plated over. In 1920 *Victor Hugo* retained sixteen 47mm guns while *Jules Ferry* retained eleven. *(Private collection)*

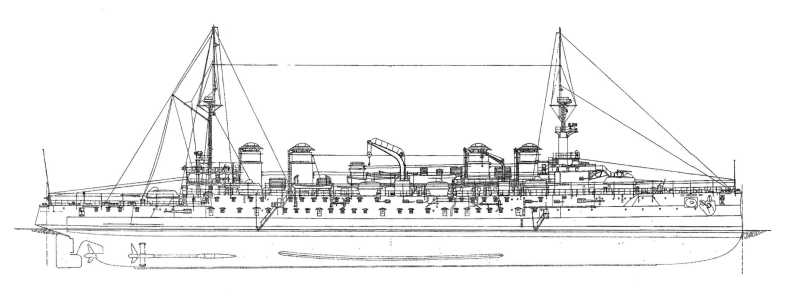

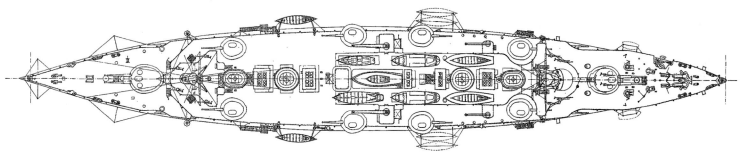

Outboard profile and overhead view (*plan d'ensemble*) as fitted of the 1st class armoured cruiser *Jules Michelet* built at Lorient on the plans of M. Bertin. The plans were signed at Lorient on 26 October 1908 by the naval constructor in charge of the ship, Rolland Boris. The small calibre artillery carried at this time included 24 x 47mm/50 M1902 QF guns (2 on the forward turret, 4 on the upper forward bridge, 2 on the lower bridge deck firing through ports, 6 on the upper after bridge, and 10 in the hull on the 1st deck with 4 around the base of the forward 164.7m turret and 6 clustered between the amidships 164.7mm turrets), and 2 x 37mm M1885 QF guns for the boats. There were also 2 x 65mm M1881 landing guns.

*JULES MICHELET*. *Croiseur cuirassé*. Armoured cruiser with two twin main battery turrets at the ends and eight single secondary battery turrets on the sides. Four funnels in two pairs, one heavy pole mast forward and one regular pole mast aft. Designed by Bertin.

*Jules Michelet* was to be ordered under the 1902 budget (submitted in March 1901) as the fourth unit of the *Léon Gambetta* class, and as built she had had a hull identical to that of the *Gambetta* class except for modifications to the shaft brackets. However, in March 1902 trials of *Dupleix* revealed a critical problem with the twin 164.7mm turret that was also in the later ships. Noxious gases given off by ignition of the powder in the two quick fire guns built up so quickly in the turret that the effective rate of fire of each gun was reduced to two rounds per minute while otherwise it was capable of three. Higher rates of fire risked asphyxiating the gun crews. The gases were supposed to be evacuated through three slots at the top of the turret walls on each side but these proved unable to clear a small cramped twin turret. This issue, added to Bertin's long-standing opposition to twin turrets on grounds of degraded accuracy of fire, resulted to a change from twin to single turrets in *Jules Michelet* and also in *Ernest Renan*. A fourth single turret was worked in on each side in *Jules Michelet*, and four guns in single turrets each with a rate of fire of three rounds per minute were considered equivalent in practice to six guns in twin turrets each capable of two rounds per minute. Bertin also hoped to get more speed out of the ship by giving her Guyot-du Temple small tube boilers (also used in *Jules Ferry*) but these hopes were disappointed.

When the construction of *Victor Hugo* was moved from Toulon to Lorient on 3 June 1902, the construction of *Jules Michelet*, which had been ordered about two months previously (5 April 1902) was given lower prior-ity. Assembly on the slipway at Caudan began only after the launch of *Victor Hugo* on 30 March 1904. External differences in addition to the wing turrets were a major reconfiguration of the forward superstructure, including the replacement of the lower platform on the military foremast with its 47mm guns by a searchlight platform, the replacement of the forward navigating bridge by a bridge on the enlarged conning tower, and the replacement of the pilot house by the conning tower itself. Two of the guns displaced from the military top were mounted atop the forward turret. Internal changes involved mainly the rearrangement of the magazines, shell rooms, and hoists for the single 164.7mm turrets. She was initially to have been armed with the new Model 1902 194mm and 164.7mm 50-calibre guns and she duly received the new model 194mm guns, but the need to develop the 164.7mm/50 M1902 gun disappeared when the secondary armament of the *Démocratie* class battleships was changed from 164.7mm to 194mm and *Jules Michelet* instead received surplus 164.7mm/45 M1893-96M guns. Like the *Gambetta* class she was fitted to receive a flag.

**Dimensions & tons:** 149.070m oa, 146.500m wl and pp x 21.400m ext and wl. 12,608.501t disp (designed). Draught: (designed) 7.690m mean and 8.1758m aft. Actual measurements on 26.10.1908 were 13,489.923t disp. at a draught of 8.091m mean and 8.577m aft. Men: 773 including 26 officers without flag, add 4 officers and 34 men with a rear admiral.

**Machinery:** 29,000ihp designed at 18kg/cm² boiler pressure (17kg/cm² at the engines). Designed speed 22.5kts. Trials (17.9.1908) 30,253ihp = 22.86kts at 128.4rpm. 3 screws. 3 vertical triple expansion engines with 4 cylinders. 20 Guyot-Du Temple boilers. 1,330t coal (normal),

1,900t (surcharge). Range 4,689nm @ 10kts with normal coal, 6,877nm @ 10kts with surcharge.

**Armour:**

Side: Belt at waterline (thickest plates cemented, others special steel) 150mm amidships, 90mm fwd, 80mm aft. Total height amidships 2.050m of which 0.650m above wl. Upper strake 130mm amidships (probably cemented steel, height 1.650m), 90mm fwd, 80mm aft. Side above belt forward (special steel) 40mm.

Guns: 194mm turrets (special steel) 156mm front & sides with 147mm max fixed bases. 164.7mm turrets (special steel) 122mm front with 103mm max fixed bases. 164.7mm casemates (special steel) 138mm faces.

Lower armoured deck: flat (construction steel) 15mm, upper slope (special steel) 35 mm, lower slope (construction steel) 10mm, all on 30mm hull plating.

Upper armoured deck (construction steel): flat 22mm except 9mm in the bow, all on 11m hull plating.

Conning tower: 174mm max (enlarged flagship model as in *Sully*).

Guns: 4 x 194mm/50 M1902 (twin turrets), 12 x 164.7mm/45 M1893-96M QF (8 single turrets and 4 casemates), 2 x 65mm/16 M1881 landing, 24 x 47mm/50 M1902 QF, 2 x 37mm/20 M1885 QF for the

boats. **Torpedoes:** 2 submerged tubes for 450mm M1904 torpedoes. **Searchlights:** 2 x 75cm and 4 x 60cm.

*Jules Michelet* (C14) Lorient Dyd-Caudan/Indret.
On list 1.1903. Ord: 5.4.1902. K: 1.6.1904. L: 31.8.1905.
   Comm: 1.4.1908 (trials), 10.12.1908 (full).
Budget 1902. Boilers installed 1-6.1906. Official trials 8-9.1908. Trial results approved 9.12.1908. Admitted to active service 1.1909 and attached to the *Escadre de la Méditerranée* and its successor, the *1re Escadre*. During 1910 she was placed in the reserve division of the *1re Escadre*, during 1911 she joined the *2e Escadre* of the *1re Armée navale*. Seagoing annex to the school for gunnery in *Tourville* (ex *Gironde*) at Toulon with *Requin* 15.1.1912 to 1913 (replaced *Latouche-Tréville*, replaced by *Charlemagne*). In 1.1914 was the only ship in the reserve of the *1re Armée navale*. She soon rejoined the *1re Escadre légère* of the *1re Armée navale*. War service in the Mediterranean 1914-18 and in the Black Sea 3-4.1919. In the Far East 1922-1923 and 1925-1929, decomm. 1929 at Toulon and used as a target for aircraft and submarines. Condemned 3.5.1936, for sale by the Domaines 1936-1937. Sunk as a target by submarine *Thétis* during manoeuvres 8.5.1937.

———————

*ERNEST RENAN. Croiseur cuirassé.* Armoured cruiser with two twin main battery turrets at the ends and eight single secondary battery turrets on the sides. Six funnels in two groups of three, one heavy pole mast forward and one regular pole mast aft. Designed by Bertin (his last armoured cruiser before retirement in March 1905).

*Ernest Renan* was initially to have been ordered under the 1902 budget

The armoured cruiser *Ernest Renan* between early 1912 and the outbreak of World War I. She is displaying a white band on the second funnel to identify her as the second ship in the first division of the first light squadron (*escadre légère*) of the fleet (*Armée navale*) in the Mediterranean. She retained this marking into 1917. The photo is from a glass negative in the Bain News Service photograph collection at the Library of Congress. *(LOC ggbain-11005)*

(submitted in March 1901) as the fifth and last unit of the *Léon Gambetta* class but was deferred to the 1903 budget. She had the same main and secondary armaments as *Jules Michelet,* but more speed was needed to match the new British armoured cruisers of the *Black Prince* and *Warrior* classes and to get at least 23 knots it was necessary to return to the long, slim hull form and six groups of boilers of Bertin's *Jeanne d'Arc*. Bertin had hoped to get even more speed – 25 knots with 42,000ihp, by using Guyot-du Temple small tube boilers – but the Navy's choice of Niclausse large-tube boilers instead rendered this impossible. (Bertin bitterly claimed that this choice had been based on 'other than military' considerations.) The hull design and propulsion plant were largely repeated in the following *Edgar Quinet* class. Unlike the previous four ships *Ernest Renan* was not fitted as flagship.

**Dimensions & tons:** 159.00m oa, 157.00m wl and pp x 21.36m ext and wl. 13,653.678t disp (designed). Draught: (designed) 7.840m mean, 8.180m aft (real). Actual measurements on 22.5.1909 were 13,776.466t disp. at a draught of 7.880m mean and 8.310m aft (real). Men: 823 including 22 officers.

**Machinery:** 36,000ihp designed at rpm and 21kg/cm² boiler pressure (17kg/cm² at the engines). Designed speed 23kts. Trials (12.3.1909) 37,023ihp = 24.44kts at 136.25rpm and 15kg/cm² boiler pressure. 3 screws. 3 vertical triple expansion engines with 4 cylinders of 1.18m (1), 1.73m (1), and 1.98m (2) diameter. 42 Niclausse boilers. 1,300t coal (normal), 2,000t (surcharge). Range 3,359nm @ 10kts with normal coal, 5,168nm @ 10kts with surcharge.

**Armour:**
Side: Belt at waterline (thickest plates cemented steel, others special steel) 150mm amidships, 90mm fwd, 80mm aft. Total height amidships 2.050m of which 0.650m above wl. Upper strake 130mm amidships (probably cemented steel, height 1.650m), 90mm fwd, 80mm aft. Side above belt forward (special steel) 40mm.
Guns: 194mm turrets (special steel) 156mm front with 147mm max fixed bases. 164.7mm turrets (special steel) 122mm front with 103mm max fixed bases. 164.7mm casemates 138mm facade (special steel) with 138mm mobile shields (*acier qualité artillerie*).
Lower armoured deck: flat (construction steel) 15mm, upper slope (special steel) 35 mm, lower slope (construction steel) 10mm, all on 30mm hull plating.
Upper armoured deck (construction steel): flat 22mm except 9mm in the bow, all on 11m hull plating.
Conning tower (cemented steel): 174mm max (non-flag elliptical model as in *Gloire*).
**Guns:** 4 x 194mm/50 M1902 (twin turrets), 12 x 164.7mm/45 M1893-96M QF (8 in single turrets, 4 in casemates), 16 x 65mm/50 M1902 Schneider QF, 2 x 65mm/16 M1881 landing, 8 x 47mm/50 M1902 QF, 2 x 37mm/20 M1885 QF for the boats. Two M1907 machine guns (*mitrailleuses*) added later. **Torpedoes:** 2 submerged tubes for 450mm M1906M torpedoes. **Searchlights:** 2 x 75cm, 4 x 60cm.

*Ernest Renan* (C15) Ch. Penhoët, Saint Nazaire/Ch. Penhoët, Saint Nazaire.
On list 1.1903. Ord: 26.8.1903 (contract). K: 1.10.1904. L: 9.4.1906. Comm: 15.4.1908 (trials), 1.2.1909 (full).
Budget 1902 (delayed to 1903). Preliminary trials began 21.5.1908, official trials began 21.8.1908. To Toulon from Lorient 13-17.12.1908. Full power trials 3.1909. Fully active 21.6.1909, entered service in the cruiser force of the *1re Escadre* (formerly the *Escadre de la Méditerranée*) in the Mediterranean 10.1909. In 1914 was in the *1re Escadre légère* of the *1re Armée navale*. War service in the Mediterranean 1914-18 and in the Black Sea 3-4.1919. School for gunnery 1927-28, target ship 1931. Condemned 3.5.1936, for sale by the Domaines 1936 but remained target ship at Toulon 1937-1939.

---

**EDGAR QUINET Class.** *Croiseurs cuirassés.* Armoured cruiser with eight main battery turrets, two twin turrets at the ends and six single turrets on the sides. Six funnels in two groups of three, one heavy pole mast forward and one regular pole mast aft. Designed by Lhomme.

Armoured Cruiser C16 (later *Edgar Quinet*) appeared in the 1904 budget (submitted in June 1903) as an exact sister of *Ernest Renan*. C17 (later *Waldeck-Rousseau*) joined her in the 1905 budget (March 1904) but by that time the design of the ships were 'under study' and no characteristics were published. Soon after he took office on 24 January 1905 Minister of Marine Thomson set up a commission under Vice Admiral Touchard of the Naval General Staff with two Vice Admirals from the *Conseil supérieur* and the President of the *Conseil des travaux* to review the characteristics of C17. Thomson wanted C17 to be a copy of an existing type as a new design would delay her construction beyond 1905. The Commission reported on 15 February 1905 that none of the members recommended repeating the existing design for *Edgar Quinet* (C16), in which the search for excessive speed had led to a length that would reduce the ship's manoeuvrability and a displacement over 14,000 tons but with an armament barely equivalent to that of the *Jules Ferry* type and less well protected. *Ernest Renan* had a speed of 23 knots which most members considered desirable for armoured cruisers, but at the cost of an additional 10 metres length and 1000 tons displacement, entirely due to the increase in speed as her armament was inferior to that of *Jules Ferry*. The commission acknowledged that the rate of fire of the twelve twin turret guns in *Jules Ferry* was equivalent to that of the eight single turret guns in *Ernest Renan*, but then stated that this would no longer be the case with the simultaneous fire possible with a new firing apparatus. (The problems in the turrets of the *Dupleix* type had also largely been remedied and could be completely overcome if the internal diameter of the turrets were slightly enlarged.) The Commission first decided that C17 should have the characteristics of the *Jules Ferry* type, but after Minister Thomson noted that several members seemed willing to accept the larger displacement and speed of *Ernest Renan* it concluded that C17 should have the characteristics of *Ernest Renan* but with the armament of the *Jules Ferry* type. A new design was requested from the *Section technique* and on 22 April 1905 the dockyards were given new characteristics of 14,100 tons with four 194mm guns and sixteen 164.7mm guns (probably all M1902). C17 was ordered from Lorient on 31 July 1905 to be identical to C16 (which had been ordered from Brest on 27 August 1904) and Brest was to act as lead yard for the two ships.

Another design change came soon after *Edgar Quinet* was laid down when it was decided on 29 January 1906 to replace the 164.7mm medium guns with 194mm guns in six single wing turrets and four casemates, giving the ships a single-calibre armament of fourteen 194mm guns. The reason was essentially the same as that which caused in 1903 the replacement of the 164.7mm medium guns with 194mm guns in the last four battleships of the *Patrie* class. At the extended battle ranges now expected the 164.7mm gun could no longer be expected to penetrate 150mm of Krupp face-hardened armour while the 194mm gun still could. The reduced number of barrels and reduced rate of fire had to be accepted to ensure that the French cruisers were not outgunned by their latest foreign counterparts. A final change to the armament occurred on 17 June 1907 with the replacement of all smaller calibre guns with twenty 65mm QF guns. The ships differed in appearance from Bertin's cruisers due to the replacement of Bertin's cramped *tourelles-barbettes* (barbette turrets) with more traditional enclosed *tourelles-fermées* (enclosed turrets) with vertical sides that extended down almost to the weather deck and because of the replacement of Bertin's half-cased funnels with funnels in which the outer casings extended to the top. The ships shared the bare but large diameter foremasts of *Jules Michelet* and *Ernest Renan* but with their forward superstructures even more severely stripped down. Both ships were fitted with extensive flag accommodations.

The Niclausse boilers of *Waldeck-Rousseau* incurred a penalty for excessive coal consumption during the ship's trials, leading to much lower figures

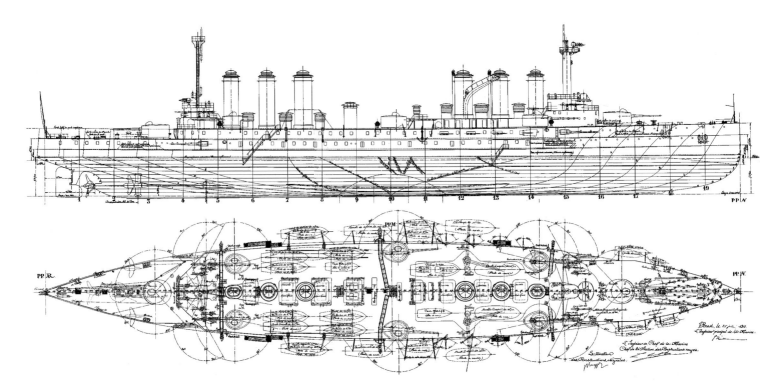

Outboard profile from the lines plan and overhead view of the armoured cruiser *Edgar Quinet* built on the plans of M. Lhomme. The plans were signed at Brest on 25 June 1910. The small calibre artillery carried at this time included 20 x 65mm/50 M1902 QF guns (2 on the forward single turrets, 4 on the forward upper bridge, 6 on the lower after bridge, and 8 in the hull on the 1st deck), 2 x 47mm M1902 guns (in the gunroom on the 1st deck), and 2 x 37mm M1885 QF guns (in the master gunner's magazine on the 1st platform deck). There were also 2 x 65mm M1881 landing guns stowed in the gunroom on the 1st deck.

(probably cemented steel, height 1.650m), 90mm fwd, 80mm aft. Side above belt forward (special steel) 40mm (90mm below forward casemates).

Guns: Twin 194mm turrets (special steel) 174mm front with 151mm max fixed bases. Single 194mm turrets (special steel) 174mm front with 148mm max fixed bases. 194mm casemates (special steel) 164mm faces, expanded into two redoubts spanning the width of the ship.

Lower armoured deck: flat (construction steel) 15mm, upper slope (special steel) 35 mm, lower slope (construction steel) 10mm, all on 30mm hull plating.

Upper armoured deck (construction steel): flat 20mm except 10mm in the bow forward of frame 30 (the conning tower), all on 10mm hull plating.

Conning tower (cemented steel): 174mm (new elliptical flagship type).

**Guns:** 14 x 194mm/50 M1902 (4 in twin turrets, 6 in single turrets, 4 in casemates), 20 x 65mm/50 M1902 QF. 2 x 65mm/16 M1881 landing, 2 x 47mm/50 M1902, 2 x 37mm/20 M1885 QF. **Torpedoes:** 2 submerged tubes for 450mm M1906M torpedoes. **Searchlights:** 8 x 75cm.

(below) for steaming range for *Waldeck-Rousseau* than for *Edgar Quinet* with her Bellevilles.

**Dimensions & tons:** 158.900m oa, 157.000m wl and pp x 21.500m ext and wl. 14,043.776t disp (designed, *E.Q.*). Draught: (designed) 7.890m mean, 8.233m aft (real). Actual measurements for *E.Q.* on 19.5.1910 were 14,068.644t normal disp. and 15,204.775t with coal surcharge at a draught of 7.4025m fwd, 8.3975m aft. Actual measurements for *W.R.* on 18.10.1910 were 14,041.869t normal disp. with 1,202.032t coal and 15,321.844t with 2,341.140t coal at a draught of 7.440m fwd, 7.89m mean, and 8.34m aft. Men: (*E.Q.*) 861 including 25 officers without flag, 907 including 30 officers with flag. (*W.R.*) 841 men including 21 officers without flag, 889 including 29 officers with flag.

**Machinery:** 36,000ihp designed at rpm and 21kg/cm² boiler pressure (17kg/cm² at engines). Designed speed 23kts. 3 screws. 3 vertical triple expansion engines with 4 cylinders. 40 boilers (Belleville in *E.Q.*, Niclausse in *W.R.*).

(*E.Q.*): Trials (6.8.1910) 37,189ihp = 23.49kts at 135.24rpm. 1,242t coal (normal), 2,150t (surcharge). Range 5,100nm @ 10kts with normal coal, 8,820nm @ 10kts with surcharge.

(*W.R.*): Cylinders measured 1.18m (1), 1.73m (1), and 1.98m (2) diameter. Trials (8.12.1911) 36.110ihp = 23.10kts at 129.23rpm. 1,242t coal (normal), 2,100t (surcharge). Range 3,030nm @ 10kts with normal coal, 5,110nm @ 10kts with surcharge.

**Armour:**

Side: Belt at waterline (thickest plates cemented steel, others special steel) 150mm amidships, 90mm fwd, 80mm aft. Total height amidships 2.050m of which 0.650m above wl. Upper strake 130mm amidships

*Edgar Quinet* (C16) Brest Dyd/Schneider, Creusot.

On list 1.1905. Ord: 27.8.1904. K: 6.11.1905. L: 21.9.1907.
Comm: 4.1909 (trials), 15.12.1910 (full).

Budget 1904. Engine contract 31.1.1906. Boilers installed 7.1908. Machinery trials 6-8.1910, results approved 2.9.1910. Entered service 4.1911 in the *1re Division légère* of the *1re Escadre* in the Mediterranean. In 1914 was in the *1re Escadre légère* of the *1re Armée navale*. War service in the Mediterranean 1914-18. Assigned as seagoing school for midshipmen 1928 to replace *Jeanne d'Arc* until the new *Jeanne d'Arc* was ready. Two boiler rooms and their funnels removed, the four casemate guns removed, training spaces and seaplane facilities added. Began first world training cruise 10.1928 and second 10.1929. Ran onto an unknown rock 4.1.1930 off Cap Blanc, Algeria, wreck broke in half in a storm and lost 9.1.1930. Struck 16.2.1930.

*Waldeck-Rousseau* (C17) Lorient Dyd/Indret.

On list 1.1906. Ord: 31.7.1905. K: 16.6.1906. L: 4.3.1908.
Comm: 1.12.1910 (trials), 8.8.1911 (full).

Budget 1905. Engines ordered 15.5.1906. Boilers installed 1.6.1908.

Manned for trials 13.1.1911. Machinery trials began at Lorient 18.1.1911, delayed when port screw and propeller shaft damaged by striking wreck or unknown rock 2.2.1911, resumed 7.1911 but interrupted by problems with feed pumps. To Toulon 8.1911, placed in full commission there 15.8.1911, and assigned to the *1re Division légère* of the *1re Escadre* in the Mediterranean while awaiting parts. Full power trials 12.1911. Fully active 18.1.1912, machinery accepted 24.1.1912, and ship reassigned 10.2.1912 as flagship of her division. In 1914 was flagship of the *1re Escadre légère* of the *1re Armée navale*. War service in the Mediterranean 1914-18 and in the Black Sea 3-4.1919 (mutiny subdued). In the Far East 4.1929-1932, in reserve 1932-36 at Brest. Condemned 14.6.1936 (decision promulgated 15.7.1936), hulk at Brest (Landévennec) 1937, to the Domaines 1938 for sale, destroyed 1944 during the occupation.

----

## (B) Smaller Cruisers.

*DISPATCH CRUISERS. Éclaireurs d'escadre*, then *Croiseurs estafettes*.

The idea for small, fast, lightly armed cruisers first received serious attention in 1894 in the form of fleet scouts (*Éclaireurs d'escadre*). In response to an order from Minister of Marine Félix Faure, the *Conseil des travaux* on 27 July 1894 drew up specifications for an *éclaireur d'escadre*. The ship was to have a displacement of at least 1,400 tons, two screws and eight Normand boilers, a designed speed of 23 knots with forced draught and at least 20 knots (changed in November to 19 knots) at natural draught for 24 hours, a range of 5,000nm at 10 knots with normal coal, an armament of five 100mm QF and seven 47mm QF guns and no torpedoes, and protection (either deck or side) for the machinery of at least 15mm horizontal and 60mm vertical. Minister Faure forwarded these specifications to the ports on 16 August 1894 but his successor, Minister Besnard, withdrew them on 2 February 1895 because the type was not included in the Programme of 1894 as just decided by the *Conseil supérieur* in December 1894. For the same reason the Council rejected a design by naval constructor Maurice for a 25-knot *éclaireur d'escadre* on 12 March 1895 and another by naval constructor Trogneux on 13 November 1896.

On 10 December 1897, the *Conseil des travaux*, asked to examine a design referred to it by Minister of Marine Besnard for a 5,000-ton protected cruiser for overseas service, stated that, given the sizeable displacement, the type of protection of the vitals below the waterline (a protective deck), and the absence of all protection for the gun battery, this ship did not fulfil the conditions necessary for a combat ship. If intended instead as a simple scout its speed was insufficient and its displacement and cost were too high. This criticism applied by extension to all protected cruisers and the issue of whether protected cruisers should be removed from the fleet programme was referred to the *Conseil supérieur* which addressed it on 17 January 1898. A note to the Council summarized as follows the argument by many officers against protected cruisers. A protected cruiser, when given the relatively powerful armament that it was then the rule to give them, became illogical because to give it a barely sufficient speed and range of action one had to give it a considerable displacement. The resulting expense was out of all proportion to the military value of a ship that, because of its vulnerability, could not be seen as intended for combat. The report continued that recent exercises had shown the dangers to cruisers assigned to maintain contact with an enemy force at night. If because of large dimensions they could not escape by a quick turn an enemy turning back to attack them, they would need to be able to withstand sustained enemy fire. It did not appear therefore that protected cruisers should be employed in this manner. Light cruisers if weather permitted and armoured cruisers in all circumstances were the only types suitable for maintaining contact with the enemy, though protected cruisers could be used to relay information from this cruiser back to the main force. But for this role of carrying orders or information, it would suffice to have ships of high speed and satisfactory endurance at sea but armed

only with light guns, not only to reduce displacement but to prevent them from being distracted from their mission in order to fight. It might not be necessary or appropriate, however, to substitute light cruisers for protected cruisers in the stations. The Programme of 1896 showed a need to build two protected cruisers for the European fleets (after *Lavoisier*/H3) and three for the stations (after *Infernet*/K2) The Council decided by a vote of 5 to 4 that the two protected cruisers to be built under the programme of 1896 for the fleet and the three for the stations should be of the *estafette* (dispatch) type.

On 1 August 1898 the *Section technique* was given specifications for a *croiseur estafette* (dispatch cruiser) and in October 1898 two of the vessels were included in the draft 1899 budget under the programme designators H4 and H5. (H1 to H3 were the designators for *Linois*, *Galilée*, and *Lavoisier*.) On 6 January 1899 the *Conseil des travaux* examined the preliminary design produced by the *Section technique*, whose characteristics are below. The Council noted that it had consistently affirmed that it regarded as combat ships only battleships and cruisers of 10,000 tons or more – it had even rejected 2nd class armoured cruisers. There was thus nothing in the combatant fleet between 10,000-ton cruisers and 300-ton destroyers. It was this gap that the new type was meant to fill. Its essential role was that of bearer of orders and information for the admiral, and for this reason it needed high speed, a serious steaming range, and good seakeeping qualities allowing it to fulfil any mission in either good or bad weather. It was not a combat ship and its armament and offensive power were secondary considerations. The design had two widely separated funnels, two signal masts, a bridge that the Council felt was too close to the bow, and a freeboard of 5.84m amidships and 6.70m at the bow. To this design the Council wanted to add a 40mm conning tower, two torpedo tubes above the waterline, and two more 47mm guns near the after bridge. Minister of Marine Lockroy on 4 May 1899 directed the *Section technique* to prepare a complete design taking into account the conclusions of the *Conseil des travaux*.

During its deliberations on the Programme of 1900 on 29 November 1899 the *Conseil supérieur* considered the *croiseur estafette* and could not come to a consensus on either its employment or its characteristics. Minister de Lanessan, presiding over the session, finally drew the Council's attention back to the 4,000-ton design just developed by the *Conseil des travaux* and got a majority to agree to building five of them (one for each of the four battle squadrons in the programme plus a spare), but the Minister and the Council then agreed that they should not be included in the extraordinary 1900 building programme but instead be built under annual budgets. They were never included in an annual budget and never appeared in the fleet list. The *Conseil supérieur* again considered this type, now called *éclaireurs*, when drawing up the 1905 and 1906 fleet programmes. This time the Council specified for them a 3,600-ton displacement, a 24-knot speed, a 6,000nm range, a protective deck over the machinery, and an armament of 65mm or at most 100mm guns. It included in the programme one *éclaireur* or light cruiser for each of the five *escadres* in the programme with a sixth as a spare. However, in 1906 the Council decided that these would not be begun until the first twelve battleships had been laid down, delaying their start of construction to at least 1910.

**Dimensions & tons:** 120.00m pp x 13.60m wl. 4,050t disp.
    Draught: 5.10m mean, 5.50m aft (real). Men: 411.
**Machinery:** Speed 23kts (20kts for extended periods at moderately forced draught). 3 screws. 3 engines in 3 engine rooms. 4 centreline boiler rooms located fore and aft of the engine rooms. 600t coal (normal), 800t (surcharge). Range 6,000nm with normal coal, 8,000nm with surcharge.
**Armour:**
Deck (hard steel): 30mm flat, 40mm slopes.
Conning tower: 40mm (addition requested by *Conseil des travaux*)
**Guns:** 8 x 100mm (1 bow, 1 stern and 6 sides), 1 x 65mm (landing),
    12 x 47mm (addition of 2 more on after bridge requested by *Conseil*

*des travaux*), 4 x 37mm (boat). **Torpedoes:** 2 tubes above water (addition requested by *Conseil des travaux*). **Searchlights:** 4 x 60cm.

*H4* (Unnamed) Rochefort Dyd.
Budget 1899. Not in the 1900 budget.

*H5* (Unnamed) Contract.
Budget 1899. Not in the 1900 budget.

———————

***FLOTILLA LEADERS.*** *Éclaireurs d'escadre*, then *Convoyeurs d'escadrille*. Light cruisers with eight 138.6mm guns (four on the centreline in shields and four in unprotected casemates amidships), three funnels, and two pole masts.

The *Statut naval* of 1912 called for the construction of ten fast *éclaireurs d'escadre* or fleet scouts to be in service by 1920. These would have been the first small cruisers laid down by France since the *D'Estrées* class third class station cruisers of 1896, all later cruising ships having been large armoured cruisers. On 17 March 1913 the *Conseil supérieur* opted for a 6,000-ton ship and three of these were included in the draft budget for 1914 designated C1, C2, and C3, all to be built by contract. The design approved by Minister Baudin on 30 November 1913 had the following characteristics.

*1913 Éclaireurs d'escadre.*
**Dimensions & tons:** 145m pp x 15.20m. 6,000t disp. Draught: 6.30m aft. Men: 516.
**Machinery:** 34,000ihp. Speed 27kts. 2 screws, 2 geared turbines, 10 boilers, mixed coal and oil firing. 700t coal and 500t oil. Range 5,400nm @ 12kts.
**Armour:**
Sides: 50mm (100mm over machinery) from 1.12m below the waterline to 4.8m above.
Guns: Shields 100mm.
Deck: 40mm.
Conning tower: 170mm.
**Guns:** 10 x 138.6mm (1 at each end and 4 on each side), 3 x 47mm saluting. **Torpedoes:** 2 submerged tubes for 450mm torpedoes. **Searchlights:** 6 x 90cm.

When made public this design provoked heavy criticism, notably in the Budget Commission in the Chamber of Deputies, where its cost was considered too high for its questionable military utility. In the north, however, France needed smaller ships comparable to the new British 3,500-ton *Arethusa*-class 'light armoured cruisers' to lead flotillas of destroyers, and in December 1913 a new minister of marine (Ernest Monis) got the

*Convoyeur d'escadrilles de 5000tx Lamotte-Picquet with modifications proposed in 1915. (Henri Le Masson from a plan dated 11 May 1915 in SHD 8DD1-150)*

Chamber to pass a modification to the 1912 *Statut naval* adding six *convoyeurs d'escadrille* (squadron escorts), of which the first were to be laid down no later than 1 November 1914. (An *escadrille* was normally a squadron of six destroyers, a *flotille* being several *escadrilles*.) On 2 February 1914 the *Conseil supérieur* recommended building four *convoyeurs d'escadrille* as soon as possible using the funds authorized for the three *éclaireurs d'escadre*. Minister of Marine Senator Armand Gauthier de l'Aude approved the new design for the ships on 16 June 1914. A law of 15 July 1914 authorized ordering three *convoyeurs d'escadrille* in late 1914 under the 1914 budget. On 17 July 1914 Minister Gauthier ordered one ship from Toulon and named her *Lamotte-Picquet*, the process for selecting contractors to build the other two having already been initiated on 2 June 1914. They were to have been ordered during the fourth trimester of 1914 and the keel laying of *Lamotte-Picquet* was planned for late October or early November, but the war intervened before this or the selection of builders for the other two ships could occur. On 30 October 1914 Minister of Marine Deputy Jean Victor Augagneur authorized Toulon to resume preparatory measures for laying down *Lamotte-Picquet*, but Paris then began considering revisions to the design, and on 13 March 1915 the ministry cancelled its instructions to Toulon of 17 July and 30 October 1914, stating that the design would be reworked according to new specifications. A new 5,026-ton, 143.80 metre design that added anti-aircraft guns and more main battery ammunition and changed to two screws was discussed in July 1915 but rejected, and no further action was taken on new cruisers until the postwar cruiser design process began in 1919.

*1914 Convoyeurs d'escadrille.*
**Dimensions & tons:** 138.00m pp x 13.80m. 4,500t disp. Draught: 4.80m. Men: 357.
**Machinery:** 40,000ihp. Speed 29kts. 4 screws. 4 turbines, 12 Guyot-Du Temple boilers forward of the engines, 4 with mixed oil and coal firing and 8 oil fired. 300t coal and 500t oil. Range 3,300nm @ 16kts.
**Armour:** Sides 28mm over the machinery amidships with end bulkheads of 16mm forward and 14mm aft.
**Guns:** 8 x 138.6mm/55 M1910 (in single shielded mounts, two superfiring pairs fore and aft and two casemate mounts on each side amidships), 2 x 47mm/50 M1902 (for saluting). **Torpedoes:** 4 tubes for 450mm torpedoes above water in the hull amidships on the main deck directly above the engine rooms.

***Lamotte-Picquet*** (ex C1) Toulon Dyd.
Budget 1914. Construction reassigned from contract to Toulon 1914. Projected to lay down 10-11.1914, deferred.

*N* (Unnamed) (ex C2) Contract.
Budget 1914. Contractor not selected, deferred.

*N* (Unnamed) (ex C3) Contract.
Budget 1914. Contractor not selected, deferred.

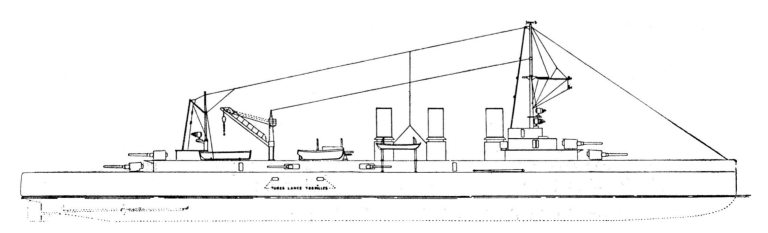

# Chapter Fifteen

# Torpedo Boat Destroyers, 1897-1914

**(A) Torpedo Boat Destroyers (*Contre-torpilleurs d'escadre*).** Four *contre-torpilleurs d'escadre* were building in the 1.1897 fleet list: *Dunois, La Hire, Durandal,* and *Hallebarde*. To *Contre-torpilleurs* 1.1901 (not changed until 1910 in budgets), all to *torpilleurs d'escadre* by a Ministerial order of 14.3.1913.

## Origins of the French Destroyer

The appearance of French *torpilleurs de haute mer* beginning with *Ouragan* in 1888 and particularly the three *très rapides* begun in 1891 prompted the British to look for a response. In 1891 Rear Admiral John Fisher, who later created the Dreadnought battleship and the battle cruiser, advocated using an enlarged torpedo boat with weights such as coal minimised to solve the problem. He became Controller (Third Sea Lord) in February 1892 and asked the Director of Naval Construction for specifications for a 27-knot ship with a powerful armament. The first two British destroyers (which the French called *contre-torpilleurs*) to enter service were Yarrow's *Havock* in January 1894 and Thornycroft's *Decoy* in February 1894.

The French developed their *contre-torpilleurs* for different reasons, though like the British they ended up with enlarged torpedo boats. They had been aware of the need to defend a fleet against torpedo boats since at least 1886, when Minister of Marine Aube on 17 March 1886 directed converting into *contre-torpilleurs* the torpedo boats of the *N° 65* type (see Chapter 11). By the time the *Conseil supérieur*'s Programme of 1891 was completed in July 1891 the French planned to use their torpedo cruisers (*Condor* etc.) as *contre-torpilleurs d'escadre* in the fleet supplemented as such by five enlarged *avisos-torpilleurs* yet to be built (*D'Iberville* and later). In early 1895 these five *avisos torpilleurs* were reclassified as *contre-torpilleurs d'escadre* and torpedo tubes were deleted from their armaments. In the meantime in December 1894 the Programme of 1894 introduced two new types of ships, a 220-ton *torpilleur de haute mer* in the European fleet and a 300-ton torpedo boat leader (*chef de groupe de torpilleurs des défenses mobiles*) in the coast defence fleet. All sixteen of the seagoing torpedo boats needed to be built (the existing ones no longer being counted) and 20 of the 30 *chefs de groupes* (*avisos torpilleurs*) needed to be built (the small *avisos torpilleurs* of the *Bombe* and *Léger* classes temporarily filling in the other ten). On 20 April 1895 Minister Besnard asked the Council to establish new specifications for the 220-ton *torpilleur de haute mer* and 300-ton *aviso torpilleur*. On 28 May 1895 the Council specified for the *aviso torpilleur* a displacement of 320 to 375 tons and 26 knots while expecting the *torpilleur de haute mer* to come in at 225 to 245 tons and 24 knots.

On 7 June 1895 Augustin Normand entered the picture by submitting a design for a *grand torpilleur* of 285 tons that could also serve as a *contre torpilleur*. He was asked to redo his design taking into consideration the specifications just adopted by the Council. On 7 September 1895 Normand reported that to meet the Council's specifications the *aviso torpilleur* would need to displace 403 tons instead of 375 while the torpedo boat at 244 tons could be within the Council's range. Normand, however, continued to prefer a single ship type able to serve in both roles and on 14 October 1895 he submitted a design for a ship of 285 to 300 tons, modifying his *grand torpilleur* to meet the speed, armament, and operational range in the Navy's programme. He proposed one design with two armament options, one for use as a *torpilleur de haute mer* in the fleet and one as an *aviso torpilleur* (*torpilleur divisionnaire* or *conducteur de flottille*) for coast defence. The navy asked for numerous changes, and on 18 February

1896 Normand submitted a new design again including two options for armaments. Minister Lockroy referred this design to the *Conseil des travaux* on 6 March 1896 and it examined Normand's '*Projet de petit bâtiment de 300t pouvant servir suivant le cas de torpilleur d'escadre ou d'aviso-torpilleur*' on 14 April 1896. As a *torpilleur* the vessel would carry three single 381mm torpedo tubes and two 47mm guns, as a *divisionnaire* it would have one 65mm and seven 47mm guns and one torpedo tube. The council accepted the design, its only major reservation being that it felt the ship should have a single armament instead of two alternatives. It felt that the gun armament should be one 65mm and six 47mm, the remainder to be decided after trials. In addressing the Council Normand said that he too preferred a single armament as in his design of 7 June 1895, the use of alternatives being a response to Navy specifications.

---

## 300-Ton Type

The French 300-ton destroyers are normally listed in two sub-groups, 32 of the *Durandal* group with 381mm torpedoes and 23 boats of the later *Claymore* group with 450mm torpedoes. There were, however, other smaller changes based on experience that produced additional sub-groups, generally with small increases in displacement. The main changes were in hull form, particularly the configuration of the hull above the waterline and the superstructures.

***DURANDAL* Class.** *Contre-torpilleurs d'escadre.* Normand 300-ton type destroyers with a single 65mm gun forward and six 47mm guns on the sides, two torpedo tubes on deck between the funnels and on the stern, a flush deck, two widely spaced funnels, and two masts (later one). Designed by Normand.

The two original Normand prototypes were designed to be fitted as either an *aviso-torpilleur* or a *torpilleur d'escadre* as needed. The 1896 budget submission (May 1895) included an *aviso torpilleur* for coast defence (m1) to be built by contract, which was one of the few ships not later deleted by the Budget Commission from that budget. On 20 May 1896 Minister Besnard directed that Normand be given a contract for an *aviso-torpilleur* to be named *Durandal*. On 30 July 1896 Director of Material Bertin advised Besnard that a *torpilleur d'escadre* M'1 was in a supplement to the 1896 budget just voted by Parliament on 13 July 1896 with the provision that the contract be awarded in September using 1896 money. Bertin advised that the most recent plans approved for such a ship were those of *Durandal*, and that M'1 could be ordered immediately with a price reduction by adding her as a second vessel to the contract then in preparation with Normand for *Durandal*. He added that the *Durandal* type was slower than British *contre-torpilleurs* then under construction or in trials but that Normand, consulted in the spring, did not think he could take on the construction of a 30-knot *contre-torpilleur*. On 1 August 1896 Minister Besnard told the Machinery Commission that he had decided that the *torpilleur d'escadre* M'1 would be of the *Durandal* type, would be ordered from Normand, and would be named *Hallebarde*. He was eager to take advantage of Normand's offer of a 70,000 franc discount if two vessels were ordered together. The 1897 budget showed *Durandal* as an *aviso-torpilleur* (M1) and *Hallebarde* as a *torpilleur d'escadre* (M'1). By 1898 *Durandal* and *Hallebarde* had both become *contre-torpilleurs d'escadre*. The M-prime programme designator (M') was used for new *contre-torpilleurs* until 1905-06 when it briefly became MM and then M.

The hull lines of Normand's design were based on the seagoing torpedo boat *Flibustier* but with a fuller stern and much more robust scantlings. The propellers and rudder were submerged as deeply as possible, both having their tops almost a metre below the waterline and with the bottom support of the rudder doing double duty as a propeller guard. This location increased their efficiency especially when the ship was pitching. Unusually, however, the single rudder was located well forward of the twin screws, where it could not benefit from their wash. As a result, the ship's turning diameter at 17 knots was a very wide 450 metres, about twice the desired amount. All of the 300-ton destroyers had this stern configuration, inherited from *Flibustier* and other later Normand seagoing torpedo boats, but in later destroyers the rudder returned to its normal position at the very stern where it had always been on the smaller torpedo boats. Above the waterline Normand limited the height of the hull by adding an elevated manoeuvring or walking deck consisting of wooden grating 0.80m above the hull from the stern to near the bow. Waves striking the ship from the sides or quarters would pass between the low hull and the walking deck instead of breaking on the hull sides and crashing on board.

The two boilers were based on those of the seagoing torpedo boat *Aquilon* but were much larger, given the larger size of the destroyer. They had good fuel efficiency despite the long furnaces that made it difficult for the stokers to maintain an even layer of burning coal. The engines were an extrapolation of those in *Torpilleur n° 201* and the seagoing *Cyclone*, all measurements scaled up by a ratio of 1.15. These engines retained the robust structure of their predecessors, complete with the steam jackets on the cylinders and feed water heaters that the British had omitted from their early destroyer engines to lighten the machinery and achieve extreme trial speeds. The French engines were designed for 4,800ihp at natural draught and 5,200ihp maximum at forced draught for a relatively modest 26 knots, but it was found possible in later ships to expand their basic design to 6,800ihp and even 7,200ihp, the cylinder diameters in the latter case being 0.51m, 0.79m, and 1.23m with a stroke of 0.59m. (The engines of *Hallebarde* were re-rated at 5,600ihp at forced draught by Minister de Lanessan on 5 September 1899.) The engines were installed in two individual engine rooms between the two boiler rooms, an arrangement that reduced the vibrations at high speed common in light craft, made it easier to maintain the trim of the boats, and gave them the characteristic wide spacing between the funnels (one per boiler room).

*The characteristics are based on a devis for* Hallebarde *dated 25.11.1899.*
**Dimensions & tons:** 56.80m oa, 55.000m wl & pp (tip fwd to stern) x 6.300m ext (above wl), 5.96m wl. 278.04t disp (trials, *Durandal*), 308.500t (normal), 364.593t (full). Draught: 2.1975m mean, 2.617m aft, 3.00-3.20m aft under rudder guard. Men: 62 including 4 officers.

France's first destroyer (*contre-torpilleur*), *Durandal*. Note the rounded shape of the hull as in a torpedo boat with a wooden walking deck almost a metre above it, in this case supporting much of the boat's crew. (*NHHC from Farenholt collection, previously ONI, NH-64459*)

**Machinery:** 5,200ihp designed at 300rpm and 16kg/cm$^2$ boiler pressure. Speed 26kts. Trials (*Durandal*, 9.5.1899) 5,300ihp = 27.42kts, (*Hallebarde* 21.8.1899) 5,199ihp = 26.9kts at 297.67rpm and 15.450kg/cm$^2$ boiler pressure. 2 screws. 2 vertical triple expansion engines with 3 cylinders of 0.472m, 0.678m, and 1.024m diameter and 0.574m stroke. 2 Normand return flame boilers. 37.6t coal (normal), 100t coal (max, of which 78t in the bunkers, 15t on deck and 7t in the stokeholds).

**Guns:** 1 x 65mm/50 M1891 (on platform forward), 6 x 47mm M1885 (3 per side). **Torpedoes:** 2 single deck tubes for 381mm M1887 torpedoes (1 amidships and 1 on the stern). **Searchlights:** 1 x 40cm.

*Durandal* (M1) Augustin Normand, Le Havre/Normand, Le Havre.
On list 1.1897. Ord: 5.8.1896. K: 25.8.1896. L: 11.2.1899. Trials: 4-7.1899. Comm: 10.1899 (full).
Budget 1896. *Escadre du Nord* 1899, *Défense mobile* at Dunkirk 1903 as flotilla leader. In 1914 was leader for the 2nd submarine squadron (*escadrille*) of the *2e Escadre légère* at Calais. Attached to several patrol units 1914-18 including the Normandy patrol boat division. Struck 7.4.1919. Offered for sale 2.6.1920 at Cherbourg. Sold 22.2.1921 at Cherbourg to BU.

*Hallebarde* (M'1) Augustin Normand, Le Havre/Normand, Le Havre.
On list 1.1897. Ord: 12.8.1896. K: 25.8.1896. L: 8.6.1899. Trials: 7-8.1899. Comm: 12.9.1899 (full).
Budget 1896 (late addition). Added to the contract of 5.8.1896 for *Durandal*. Machinery installed 22.12.1898 to 1.7.1899. Left Le Havre for Cherbourg 13.7.1899, entered into commission for trials 17.7.1899, in full commission 28.8.1899, then left for Toulon 13.9.1899 to replace *Éclair* in the *Escadre de la Méditerranée*. Became leader (*divisionnaire*) for the 1st submarine squadron of the *1re Armée navale* at Toulon 12.1912. War service in the Mediterranean. Struck 4.3.1920. Sold 20.4.1921 at Rochefort to BU.

---

**FAUCONNEAU Class.** *Contre-torpilleurs d'escadre.* Normand 300-ton type destroyers with general configuration as *Durandal.*

Two slightly modified Normand prototype *contre-torpilleurs* were included in the initial 1897 budget. Compared to the first two prototypes they had reinforced hull scantlings, and they had a higher bow (30cm) and stern (10-15cm) as proposed by Normand in July 1897.

**Dimensions & tons:** 57.64m oa, 56.000m wl & pp x 6.300m ext (above wl), 5,950m wl. 277.56t to 280.48t disp (trials), 311.10t (normal), 343t-344t (full load). Draught: 2.250m mean, 3.000m aft under rudder guard. Men: 52, including 4 officers.

**Machinery:** 5,200ihp designed at 300rpm and 16kg/cm$^2$ boiler pressure. Speed 26kts. Trials (*Espingole*) 27.25kts. 2 screws. 2 triple expansion engines with 3 cylinders of 0.472m, 0.678m, and 1.024m diameter and 0.574m stroke. 2 Normand return-flame boilers. 37.6t coal (normal). Range 2,300nm @ 10kts.

**Guns:** 1 x 65mm/50 M1891 (on platform forward), 6 x 47mm M1885 (3 per side). **Torpedoes:** 2 single deck tubes for 381mm M1887 torpedoes.

*Fauconneau* (M'2) Augustin Normand, Le Havre/Normand, Le Havre.
On list 1.1898. Ord: 14.4.1897. K: 29.4.1897. L: 2.4.1900. Trials: 5-7.1900. Comm: 7.1899 (full).
Budget 1897. *Escadre du Nord* 1900, *Défense mobile* at Brest 1903. Reboilered 1911-12. In 1914 was leader for the 1st submarine squadron of the *2e Escadre légère* at Cherbourg. War duty in the Channel and from 1915 in the Mediterranean. Struck 15.1.1921. Sold 1.6.1921 at Rochefort to BU.

*Espingole* (M'3) Augustin Normand, Le Havre/Normand, Le Havre.
On list 1.1898. Ord: 14.4.1897. K: 29.4.1897. L: 28.6.1900. Trials: 8-9.1900.

Budget 1897 (late addition). *Escadre de la Méditerranée* 12.1900. Struck a rock at Cape Lardier and sank 4.2.1903 in the Hyères roadstead in 29 metres of water. Salvage efforts failed. Struck 16.9.1903.

---

**PIQUE Class.** *Contre-torpilleurs d'escadre.* Normand 300-ton type destroyers with general configuration as *Durandal* except for four funnels in two widely spaced pairs. Hull of steel with 3% nickel. Designed by builders using Normand's hull design

Four more *contre-torpilleurs* were added in a supplement to the 1897 budget. Their builders used Normand's hull design but gave the boats four boilers and four funnels instead of the two of each in Normand's design. The smaller furnaces were easier for the stokers to handle but the additional boilers increased the complexity of the propulsion plant. The two boiler rooms together were 2.5 metres longer than those of *Durandal*. Of this 1.5 metres were recovered by shortening the engine rooms and accommodations, leaving an increase of 1 metre in waterline length and 11 tons in the four-boiler design. The four-boiler ships also had a different distribution of weights with a higher centre of gravity. Their trials were more laborious than those of most of the two-boiler ships, and *Pique* was the only one of the 75 300-ton destroyers (including those built for export) that failed to make her contract speed. *Épee* and *Yatagan* were somewhat more successful in this regard than were *Pique* and *Framée* (*Yatagan* made 27.07 knots on trials). The engines of *Pique* were rated at 5,700ihp in 1901 and were re-rated to 5,600ihp maximum by Minister Pelletan on 23 July 1902. The boilers were Normand type, not Normand-Guyot.

The four *Pique* class boats along with *Fauconneau* and *Espingole*, above, were to have had ram bows, which were actually fabricated, but on 20 September 1898 the Navy decided to remain with the vertical bows of *Durandal* and *Hallebarde*. At the time the Russians were in the process of ordering five four-funnelled 300-ton destroyers like *Pique* (*Forel* and *Sterlyad* from Normand and *Osetr*, *Kefal*, and *Losos* from the FCM yard at Graville) and they bought the ram bows for use in these ships. The French Navy did not repeat the four-boiler type but the Russians ordered eleven more on 10 December 1904 during the Russo-Japanese war. These also had ram bows.

*The characteristics are based on a devis for* Pique *(contre-torpilleur d'escadre) dated 23.5.1901.*

**Dimensions & tons:** 58.205m oa, 56.620m wl, 56.620m pp x 6.312m ext (above wl, 6.548m outside the rubbing strakes), 5.960m wl. 319.102t disp (normal), 347.821t (with a surcharge of 34.230t coal). Draught: 2.406m mean, 2.788m aft, 3.02m aft under rudder guard. Men: 61 including 4 officers.

**Machinery:** 5,200ihp designed at 310rpm and 16kg/cm$^2$ boiler pressure (16kg/cm$^2$ at the engines). Speed 26kts. Trials (*Pique* 1.2.1901) 5,441ihp = 25.887kts at 300.97rpm and 16.235kg/cm$^2$ boiler pressure. 2 screws. 2 triple expansion engines with 3 cylinders of 0.460m, 0.660m, and 1.000m diameter and 0.590m stroke. 4 Normand type boilers built by FCM. 33.630t coal (normal), 67.860t (with surcharge). Range with normal coal 1,541.30nm @ 14.05kts.

**Guns:** 1 x 65mm/50 M1891 QF (on platform forward), 6 x 47mm M1885 QF (3 per side). **Torpedoes:** 2 single deck tubes for 381mm M1887 torpedoes (1 amidships and 1 on the stern). **Searchlights:** 1 x 40cm.

*Pique* (M'4) F.C. Méditerranée, Le Havre-Graville/FCM, Le Havre (engines designed by Pierre Sigaudy).
On list 1.1898. Ord: 27.10.1897. K: 10.1897. L: 31.3.1900. Trials: 7.1900-5.1901. Comm: 5.1901 (full).
Budget 1897 (supplemental). Machinery installed 15.11.1899 to 17.6.1900. *Escadre de la Méditerranée* 1901, *Défense mobile* in Algeria 1903. In special reserve 1914. War service in the Mediterranean including the Dardanelles. Struck 28.1.1921. Sold 28.7.1921 at Toulon to BU.

*Épée* (M'5) F.C. Méditerranée, Le Havre-Graville/FCM, Le Havre.
On list 1.1898. Ord: 27.10.1897. K: 16.5.1898. L: 27.7.1900.
   Comm: 2.1.1901 (trials), trials: 1-7.1901.
Budget 1897 (supplemental). *Escadre de la Méditerranée* 8.1901, *Défense mobile* in Corsica (including pilot training) 1903. In special reserve 1914, then leader for the 3rd squadron of submarines of the *2ᵉ Escadre légère* at Cherbourg 1914-15. At Bizerte 1916 and Toulon 1917-18. Off main list by 3.1920 and for sale at Toulon. Struck 1.10.1920. Sold 8.1.1921 at Toulon to BU.

*Framée* (M'6) A.C. Loire, Nantes/ACL, Nantes.
On list 1.1898. Ord: 27.10.1897. K: 1897. L: 29.6.1899.
   Trials: 2-6.1900.
Budget 1897 (supplemental). Arrived at Lorient from Nantes 25.1.1900. Assigned to the *Escadre de la Méditerranée* 29.6.1900 but detailed to the *Escadre du Nord* while awaiting transit orders. Sunk in the night of 10-11.8.1900 in collision with the battleship *Brennus* off Cape St. Vincent. Struck 26.10.1900.

*Yatagan* (M'7) A.C. Loire, Nantes/ACL, Nantes.
On list 1.1898. Ord: 27.10.1897. K: 1897. L: 20.3.1900.
   Trials: 5-10.1900.
Budget 1897 (supplemental). Arrived at Lorient from Nantes for trials

The destroyer *Yatagan* at Le Havre, one of four 300-tonners built with four funnels for four boilers instead of two of each. She became the station ship for the Channel and the North Sea in December 1913, temporarily replacing the screw aviso *Ibis* in this fishery protection role. She is wearing the old two-tone black and 'wet canvas' paint scheme that was also worn by some destroyers assigned as leaders for the torpedo boats of the *Défense mobile*. (Postcard)

27.5.1900. *Escadre du Nord* 1900, *Défense mobile* at Cherbourg 1904. Temporarily replaced the fishery protection ship *Ibis* in 1913 pending completion of *Flamant*. War service on fishery protection duty in the Channel. Sunk in the night of 3.11.1916 in collision with the British cargo ship *Teviot* off Dieppe.

_____

**PERTUISANE** Class. *Contre-torpilleurs d'escadre.* Normand 300-ton type destroyers with general configuration as *Durandal*.

Four copies of Normand's *Fauconneau* and *Espingole* were built under the 1899 budget at the Rochefort dockyard, which until 1905 was the only dockyard building destroyers and which remained the principal French destroyer-building dockyard to 1914. The budgets indicate that construction of M'8 and M'9 was reassigned from contract to Rochefort while the two added later were assigned directly to the dockyard. The only difference between these four vessels and the Normand boats was that the Rochefort units had their funnels raked slightly aft. Four 300-tonners were ordered fitted as light minelayers by ministerial dispatches of 27 April 1909 (*Flamberge* in this class and the later *Baliste*) and November 1911 (the later *Hache*, and *Massue*) in response to lessons from the Russo-Japanese war. A few others got light minesweeping gear in 1910.

**Dimensions & tons:** Generally as *Fauconneau*. Designed: 56.120m oa, 56.000m wl, 56.000m pp x 6.300m ext (above wl), 5.940m wl. 305.770t disp. Draught: 2.250m mean, 2.650m aft (keel line projected). *Flamberge*: 306.844t, *Rapière*: 306.769t, both with modified keel (DM 25.8.1900) at 2.450m mean and 2.850m aft (keel line projected).
**Machinery:** as *Fauconneau*. Trials (*Pertuisane*) 26.96kts.
**Guns and torpedoes:** as *Fauconneau*.

*Pertuisane* (M'8) Rochefort Dyd/Schneider, Creusot.
On list 1.1900. Ord: 8.6.1899. K: 9.4.1900. L: 5.12.1900.
  Trials: 2-9.1902. Comm: 25.9.1902 (full).
Budget 1899. *Escadre de la Méditerranée* 1902 (replaced *Flibustier*). In
  reserve at Cherbourg 1914. War service in the Channel. Off main list
  1922. Struck 16.3.1923, reserved for firefighting trials at Brest 1923-
  1928. Sold 20.4.1928 at Brest to BU.

*Escopette* (M'9) Rochefort Dyd/Schneider, Creusot.
On list 1.1900. Ord: 8.6.1899. K: 9.4.1900. L: 20.12.1900.
  Trials: 6.1902-1.1903. Comm: 26.1.1903 (full).
Budget 1899. 1st trials 5.1.1903. *Escadre du Nord* 1903, *Défense mobile* at
  Brest 1903. In 1914 was leader for the 2nd submarine squadron of the
  *2e Escadre légère* at Calais. War service at Cherbourg and Dunkirk.
  Struck 4.4.1921. Sold 10.7.1922 at Cherbourg.

*Flamberge* (M'10) Rochefort Dyd/Schneider, Creusot.
On list 1.1900. Ord: 8.6.1899. K: 2.1.1901. L: 28.10.1901.
  Trials: 1-7.1903. Comm: 15.8.1903 (full)
Budget 1899 (late addition). *Escadre du Nord* 1903. Fitted as light
  minelayer 4.1910 at Brest. Reboilered at Brest 1914. To the
  Mediterranean 1915, at Salonica 1918. Off main list by 3.1920 and
  for sale at Toulon. Struck 1.10.1920. Sold 8.1.1921 at Toulon to BU.

*Rapière* (M'11) Rochefort Dyd/Schneider, Creusot.
On list 1.1900. Ord: 8.6.1899. K: 2.1.1901. L: 16.7.1901.
  Trials: 10.1902-5.1903. Comm: 13.3.1903 (full).
Budget 1899 (late addition). *Escadre de la Méditerranée* 1903, Far East
  Squadron (*Escadre*) 8.1905 to 5.1907, at Cherbourg 1907. In 1914
  was in the 3rd destroyer squadron (*escadrille*) of the *2e Escadre légère* at
  Cherbourg. To the Mediterranean 9.1915 with five other Channel
  300-tonners to form the new Mixed Anti-Submarine Flotilla of the
  *Armée navale* which quickly grew to counter the submarine threat. At
  Bizerte 1916-19. Struck 27.10.1921. Sold 25.3.1923 at Bizerte to BU.

---

*TAKOU* (captured). *Contre-torpilleur d'escadre.* Schichau (German)
280-ton destroyer with a ram bow, two torpedo tubes, two funnels, and one
mast.

*Takou*, formerly the Chinese *Hai Ching*, was one of a class of four destroyers launched in Germany for China in 1898. All four were boarded and
captured by the destroyers HMS *Whiting* and HMS *Fame* at a dock at the
Taku forts in northeastern China on 17 June 1900 and divided among the
four Powers participating in the Western response to the Boxer Rebellion.
*Hai Lung* became the British *Taku*, *Hai Hse* became the German *Taku*, and
*Hai Hua* became the Russian *Leytenant Burakov*. This lightly built vessel
had very fine lines forward and a very light stern, had an exaggerated and
rapid roll, and even slight pitching lifted her screws out of the water. She
never approached her designed speed in French service. When her boilers
were replaced after wearing out prematurely the French considered rearming her with four 47mm (heavy) and two 37mm guns and two tubes for
French 381mm torpedoes but evidently did not do so before she ran
aground.

**Dimensions & tons:** 60.00m oa, 59.00m pp x 6.40m ext, 6.30m wl.
  280t disp. Draught: 1.40m (2.00m max). Men: 32.
**Machinery:** 6,000ihp designed at 16kg/cm$^2$ boiler pressure. Speed 32kts.
  2 screws. 2 triple expansion engines. 4 Thornycroft direct-flame boilers. 66.8t coal. Range 2,000nm at cruising speed.
**Guns:** 6 x 47mm (light). **Torpedoes:** 2 single tubes for 356mm torpedoes.

*Takou* Schichau, Elbing.
On list 1.1901. Captured 17.6.1900. Comm: 20.6.1900.
Named, inscribed on the list, and commissioned 20.6.1900 in northeast
  China. Arrived at Saigon 13.5.1901. Explored the Yangtse 1901, then

attached as leader to the Saigon torpedo boat flotilla. Grounded on
rocks at Poulo Condor 22.2.1911, decomm. 3.1911. Refloated
27.4.1911 and towed to Saigon 2.5.1911 by the armoured gunboat
*Styx*. Condemned as not worth repairing 30.9.1911. Struck
23.11.1911. Sold 1912 at Saigon.

---

*ARQUEBUSE* **Class.** *Contre-torpilleurs d'escadre.* Normand 300-ton type
destroyers with general configuration as *Durandal* but two knots faster.

These were the first two tranches of destroyers (ten in the 1900 budget and
ten in 1901) built under the Programme of 1900, which also provided for
the six battleships of the *Patrie* and *Démocratie* classes and other ships. On
24 April 1900 the *Conseil des travaux* selected a modified *Durandal* design
by Normand with higher pressure boilers for an additional two knots of
contract speed over a design by the *Section technique* for a destroyer of 400
tons, 66 metres length, 8,000ihp, and 30 knots. A design by Normand for
a destroyer with 50mm of armour over the machinery was also turned
down. On 4 May 1900 Minister de Lanessan ordered the Machinery
Commission to contract with Normand for *Arquebuse* and *Arbalète*
(M'14-15) and ordered *Carabine* and *Sarbacane* (M'12-13) built at the
Rochefort dockyard to Normand's design. The superstructures in this class
were larger than in the previous 300-tonners, and an incident with
*Mousquet* during her trials in April 1903 caused the mainmasts in this class
to be removed to save topweight.

*The characteristics are based on a devis for* Pistolet *dated 21.9.1903.*
**Dimensions & tons:** 56.581m oa, 56.300m wl & pp (tip fwd to stern) x
  6.380m ext (6.420m, probably outside the rubbing strakes) 5.987m
  wl. 307.206t disp (normal), 357.158t (full). Draught: 2.457m mean,
  2.851m aft (keel line projected), 3.20m aft under rudder guard.
  Men: 62 including 4 officers.
**Machinery:** 6,300ihp designed at 310rpm and 18kg/cm$^2$ boiler pressure
  (also at the engines). Speed 28kts. Trials (*Pistolet* 23.7.1903)
  6,573.99ihp = 29.0375kts at 301.32rpm and 17.868kg/cm$^2$ boiler
  pressure, (*Arbalète*) 7,136ihp = 31.374kts at 311.13rpm (the fastest trials of all the 300-tonners), (*Mousqueton*) 28.78kts (the slowest of her
  class). 2 screws. 2 vertical triple expansion engines with 3 cylinders of
  0.480m, 0.740m, and 1.140m diameter and 0.580m stroke. *Pistolet*
  had 2 Du Temple Guyot boilers built by A.C. Loire (some had
  Normand boilers). 26.8t coal (normal), 76t coal (with surcharge).
  Range (with normal coal and 1 boiler) 1,198.57nm @ 9.779kts,
  640.38nm @ 14.426kts.
**Guns:** 1 x 65mm/50 M1891 QF (on platform forward), 6 x 47mm
  M1885 QF (3 per side). **Torpedoes:** 2 single deck tubes for 381mm
  M1887 torpedoes (1 amidships and 1 on the stern). **Searchlights:** 1 x
  40cm.

*Carabine* (M'12) Rochefort Dyd/Le Havre.
On list 1.1901. Ord: 4.5.1900. K: 15.7.1901. L: 21.7.1902.
  Trials: 5-9.1903. Comm: 9.1903 (full).
Budget 1900. *Escadre de la Méditerranée* 1903 (replaced *Hallebarde*). In
  reserve and under repair at Bizerte 1913-15, Mediterranean service
  1915-18. Lost bow back to the bridge in collision with British merchantman *Mentor* 1.10.1918, reached Bizerte 12.1918. Struck
  8.1.1919. Sold 26.7.1919 at Bizerte to BU.

*Sarbacane* (M'13) Rochefort Dyd/Le Havre.
On list 1.1901. Ord: 4.5.1900. K: 1.10.1901. L: 12.3.1903.
  Trials: 10-12.1903. Comm: 12.1903 (full).
Budget 1900. *Escadre de la Méditerranée* 1903. 1914 was leader for the
  2nd submarine squadron of the *1re Armée navale* at Bizerte.
  Mediterranean service including Dardanelles 1914-18. Off main list by
  3.1920 and for sale at Toulon. Struck 1.10.1920. Still for sale at
  Toulon 1.1922.

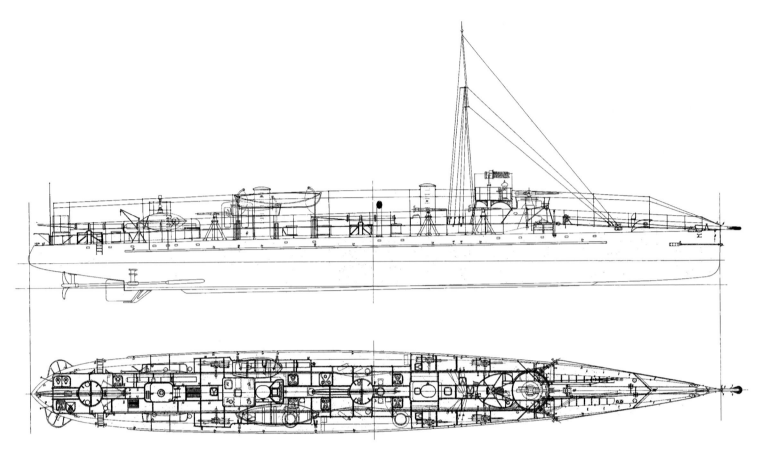

Longitudinal and plan views (*plan de pitonnage*) as fitted of the destroyers *Carabine* and *Sarbacane*. The plans were signed at Rochefort on 18 August 1904 by naval constructor Hendlé. *Plans de pitonnage* show small fittings including *pitons* (eye bolts through which ropes could be passed) along with many details of the exterior appearance and structure of the ships.

*Arquebuse* (M'14) Augustin Normand, Le Havre/Normand, Le Havre.
On list 1.1901. Ord: 1.8.1900. K: 1901. L: 15.11.1902. Trials: 1-5.1903.
  Comm: 5.1903 (full).
Budget 1900. *Escadre du Nord* 1903. New boilers at Lorient 1911. In
  1914 was in the 3rd destroyer squadron of the *2e Escadre légère* at
  Cherbourg. To the Mediterranean 9.1915 to form the new Mixed
  Anti-Submarine Flotilla of the *Armée navale*, there through 1918.
  Struck 10.5.1920. Sold 2.3.1921 at Bizerte to M. Kalfon Vita.

*Arbalète* (M'15) Augustin Normand, Le Havre/Normand, Le Havre.
On list 1.1901. Ord: 1.8.1900. K: 23.11.1900. L: 28.4.1903.
  Trials: 5-8.1903. Comm: 8.1903 (full).
Budget 1900. *Escadre de la Méditerranée* 1903. In 1914 was leader for the
  1st submarine squadron of the *1re Armée navale* at Toulon.
  Mediterranean service including Dardanelles 1914-18. Struck
  21.6.1920. Sold 10.5.1921 at Toulon to BU.

*Mousquet* (M'16) A.C. Loire, Nantes/ACL, Nantes.
On list 1.1901. Ord: 14.11.1900. K: 11.1900. L: 7.8.1902.
  Trials: 2-5.1903. Comm: 6.1903 (full).
Budget 1900. *Escadre de la Méditerranée* 1903. Arrived in the Far East
  4.1904 escorted by cruiser *D'Assas*. Reserve at Saigon 1911-14,
  recommissioned 5.3.1914 to replace *Fronde*. Sunk 28.10.1914 off
  Penang, Malaya, while pursuing the German raiding cruiser *Emden*.

*Javeline* (M'17) A.C. Loire, Nantes/ACL, Nantes.
On list 1.1901. Ord: 14.11.1900. K: 11.1900. L: 15.10.1902.
  Trials: 3-6.1903. Comm: 30.6.1903 (full).

Budget 1900. Contract notified to builder 27.11.1900. Machinery
  installed 3.11.1902 to 12-13.2.1903. *Escadre du Nord* 1903. Arrived in
  the Far East 4.1904 escorted by cruiser *D'Assas*. Returned to Rochefort
  30.5.1907. In 1914-15 was leader for the Cherbourg submarines
  (*Sous-marins de Cherbourg*, a defensive force) and later the 3rd submarine squadron there, and in 1915-18 was leader for the 3rd Channel
  torpedo boat squadron. Struck 12.1.1920. Offered for sale 2.6.1920 at
  Cherbourg. Sold 8.1920 at Cherbourg to BU.

*Sagaïe* (M'18) F.C. Méditerranée, Le Havre-Graville/FCM, Le Havre.
On list 1.1901. Ord: 7.11.1900. K: 1901. L: 15.11.1902.
  Trials: 10.1902-4.1903. Comm: 4.1903 (full).
Budget 1900. *Escadre du Nord* 1903, *Défense mobile* at Lorient 1903.
  Reboilered at Lorient 1911-12. Activated from special reserve at
  Cherbourg 1.8.1914. To the Mediterranean 9.1915 (vice *Bombarde*) to
  form the new Mixed Anti-Submarine Flotilla of the *Armée navale*, at
  Bizerte from 1917. Off main list by 3.1920 and for sale at Lorient.
  Struck 1.10.1920. Sold 12.4.1921 at Lorient to BU.

*Épieu* (M'19) F.C. Méditerranée, Le Havre-Graville/FCM, Le Havre.
On list 1.1901. Ord: 7.11.1900. K: 1901. L: 17.1.1903. Trials: 3-6.1903.
  Comm: 7.1903 (full).
Budget 1900. *Escadre de la Méditerranée* 1903, *Défense mobile* at
  Rochefort 1904. In 1914 was in the 3rd destroyer squadron of the
  *2e Escadre légère* at Cherbourg. Reboilered at Cherbourg 11-12.1914.
  To the Mediterranean 9.1915 to form the new Mixed Anti-Submarine
  Flotilla of the *Armée navale*, later to Bizerte. Struck 28.1.1921. Sold
  20.5.1922 at Bizerte to BU.

*Harpon* (M'20) C.A. Gironde, Bordeaux-Lormont/Nantes.
On list 1.1901. Ord: 14.11.1900. K: 11.1900. L: 20.10.1902.
  Trials: 11.1902-3.1903.
Budget 1900. *Escadre du Nord* 1903, *Défense mobile* at Cherbourg 1903.
  Out of reserve at Cherbourg late 1914, Dunkirk flotilla (Flemish
  Banks) 1915, then reboilered at Cherbourg. Normandy patrol boat

division and Cherbourg patrol boat squadron 1915-18. Struck 5.3.1921. Sold 10.7.1922 at Cherbourg to BU.

*Fronde* (M'21) C.A. Gironde, Bordeaux-Lormont/Nantes.
On list 1.1901. Ord: 14.11.1900. K: 1.1901. L: 17.12.1902. Trials: 1-3.1903. Comm: 4.1903 (full).
Budget 1900. *Escadre de la Méditerranée* 1903. Arrived in the Far East 4.1904 escorted by cruiser *D'Assas*. To reserve at Saigon 1914. Recomm. 3.1915 to return to France, Mediterranean 1915-18. Struck 30.10.1919. Sold 6.5.1920 at Toulon to BU.

*Francisque* (M'22) Rochefort Dyd/Nantes.
On list 1.1902. Ord: 5.3.1901. K: 5.2.1903. L: 2.3.1904. Trials: 3-4.1904. Comm: 4.1904 (full).
Budget 1901. *Escadre de la Méditerranée* 1903. From Toulon to Saigon escorted by cruiser *Descartes* 10.9.1904 to 25.12.1904. Returned to Brest 1907, fitted as light minesweeper there 8.1910. In 1914 was leader for the 1st submarine squadron of the *2e Escadre légère* at Cherbourg. Channel service including Normandy patrol boat division 1915-18. Struck 4.4.1921. Sold 10.7.1922 at Cherbourg to BU.

*Sabre* (M'23) Rochefort Dyd/Nantes.
On list 1.1902. Ord: 5.3.1901. K: 1903. L: 15.4.1904. Trials: 5-6.1904. Comm: 6.1904 (full).
Budget 1901. From Toulon to Saigon escorted by cruiser *Descartes* 10.9.1904 to 25.12.1904. *Escadre du Nord* 1907, *Défense mobile* at Brest 1911. In 1914 was leader for the 1st submarine squadron of the *2e Escadre légère* at Cherbourg. Mediterranean 1915-18. Patrol boat squadron at Rochefort 1918-19. Struck 15.1.1921. Sold 1.6.1921 at Rochefort to BU.

*Dard* (M'24) Ch. Penhoët, Rouen-Grand Quévilly/Ch. Penhoët, Saint Nazaire
On list 1.1902. Ord: 29.5.1901. K: 15.10.1902. L: 10.9.1903. Trials: 12.1903-4.1904. Comm: 5.1904 (full).
Budget 1901. Left the yard 8.10.1903. *Escadre de la Méditerranée* 1904. 1914 was leader for the 2nd submarine squadron of the *1re Armée navale*. Mediterranean service 1915-18 (at Port Said from 1917). Decomm. 5.12.1918 at Bizerte. Retired 3.4.1919. Sold 20.12.1920 at Bizerte to BU.

*Baliste* (M'25) Ch. Penhoët, Rouen-Grand Quévilly/Ch. Penhoët, Saint Nazaire
On list 1.1902. Ord: 29.5.1901. K: 20.11.1902. L: 22.10.1903. Trials: 12.1903-6.1904. Comm: 6.1904 (full).
Budget 1901. Left the yard 8.12.1903. *Escadre du Nord* 1904. Fitted as light minelayer 3.1910 at Cherbourg (rails removed 7.1914). At Cherbourg 1914-15, to the Mediterranean 9.1915. Struck 30.10.1919. Sold 6.5.1920 at Toulon to BU.

*Mousqueton* (M'26) Schneider, Chalon-sur-Saône/Schneider, Creusot.
On list 1.1902. Ord: 29.5.1901. K: 1901. L: 4.11.1902. Trials: 9.1903-8.1904. Comm: 9.1904 (full).
Budget 1901. *Escadre de la Méditerranée* 1905. In 1914 was leader for the 2nd submarine squadron of the *1re Armée navale* at Bizerte. Mediterranean 1914-18. Struck 10.5.1920. Sold 15.4.1921 at Bizerte to M. Kalfon Vita.

*Arc* (M'27) Schneider, Chalon-sur-Saône/Schneider, Creusot.
On list 1.1902. Ord: 29.5.1901. K: 1901. L: 24.12.1902. Trials: 7.1903-7.1904. Comm: 7.1904 (full).
Budget 1901. *Escadre de la Méditerranée* 1905, *Défense mobile* at Oran 1907. In special reserve 1.1914, leader for the 2nd submarine squadron of the *1re Armée navale* at Bizerte from 7.1914. Mediterranean including Dardanelles 1914-18. Off main list by 3.1920 and for sale at Toulon. Struck 1.10.1920. Sold 9.1.1921 at Toulon to BU.

*Pistolet* (M'28) A.C. Loire, Nantes/ACL, Nantes.
On list 1.1902. Ord: 22.5.1901. K: 9.1901. L: 29.5.1903. Trials: 6-8.1903. Comm: 21.9.1903 (full)
Budget 1901. Machinery installed 22.4.1903 to 4.6.1903. Assigned 9.9.1903 to replace *Escopette* in the *Escadre du Nord*. Arrived in the Far East 4.1904 escorted by cruiser *D'Assas*. Reboilered at Saigon 1915, returned to Toulon 19.1.1916. Western Mediterranean patrol division 1916-18. Struck 30.10.1919. Sold 6.5.1920 at Toulon to BU.

*Bélier* (M'29) A.C. Loire, Nantes/ACL, Nantes.
On list 1.1902. Ord: 22.5.1901. K: 9.1901. L: 29.5.1903. Trials: 1.1904-3.1904. Comm: 4.1904 (full).
Budget 1901. *Escadre du Nord* 1904. In 1914 was in the 3rd destroyer squadron of the *2e Escadre légère* at Cherbourg. Reboilered 1915, to the Mediterranean 9.1915 to form the new Mixed Anti-Submarine Flotilla of the *Armée navale*, Mediterranean to 1919. Struck 28.1.1921. Sold 20.5.1922 at Bizerte to BU.

*Catapulte* (M'30) F.C. Méditerranée, Le Havre-Graville/FCM, Le Havre.
On list 1.1902. Ord: 29.5.1901. K: 1901. L: 1.4.1903. Trials: 5-9.1903. Comm: 10.1903 (full).
Budget 1901. *Escadre du Nord* 1904. In 1914 was in the 3rd destroyer squadron of the *2e Escadre légère* at Cherbourg. Reboilered at Cherbourg 1914-15. To the Mediterranean 9.1915 to form the new Mixed Anti-Submarine Flotilla of the *Armée navale*. Sunk 18.5.1918 in collision near Bizerte southwest of La Galite, Tunisia, with the British merchantman *Warrimoo*, the destroyer's depth charges detonating and sinking both ships.

*Bombarde* (M'31) F.C. Méditerranée, Le Havre-Graville/FCM, Le Havre.
On list 1.1902. Ord: 29.5.1901. K: 6.12.1901. L: 26.6.1903. Trials: 8-11.1903. Comm: 26.11.1903 (full).
Budget 1901. *Escadre du Nord* 1903. Fitted as light minesweeper 8.1910 at Brest. In 1914 was in the 3rd destroyer squadron of the *2e Escadre légère* at Brest. In the north to 1916, Mediterranean 1917-18. Struck 10.5.1920. Sold 20.4.1921 at Rochefort to BU.

---

***CLAYMORE* Class.** *Contre-torpilleurs d'escadre.* Normand 300-ton type destroyers with general configuration as *Durandal* except for larger torpedoes and many changes in details.

On 20 November 1901 Normand presented a new destroyer design with numerous changes to the *Arquebuse* design. It consolidated all the ship control and navigation equipment in one bridge structure, modified the hull form to reduce rolling, and modified the stern to improve turning qualities. This design was discussed by the *Conseil des travaux* on 7 January 1902 and accepted. The Council again reviewed the design along with revisions suggested by Normand following an incident in December 1901 in which *Pique* nearly capsized in good weather raising concerns about stability. The Council asked for the hull to be widened amidships but narrowed aft and several measures to improve turning qualities, all while keeping the centre of gravity as low as possible and keeping the metacentric height at the level designed for *Arquebuse*. *Claymore* (M'37), the Normand prototype, was ordered on 2 September 1903, her construction having been reassigned from Rochefort during 1903, and because five *Arquebuse*-class ships previously ordered at Rochefort (M'32-36) had not yet been begun they were changed to the new type. The M' programme designator was used in the budgets for new destroyers into 1905, but the only function of the prime symbol or apostrophe had been to distinguish the *aviso-torpilleur Durandal* (M1) from the *torpilleur d'escadre Hallebarde* (M'1). In the 1906 budget (submitted on 6 July 1905) the designator for all destroyers became MM and in the 1907 budget it was simplified to M.

The ships of the *Claymore* class were about 20 tons heavier than their predecessors and, by an order of Minister Pelletan of 2 March 1904, they became the first French destroyers with 450mm torpedo tubes. Following

Collection H. Laurent, Port-Louis

3396. - BREST. - Le poste de mouillage des torpilleurs à la Ninon

The destroyers *Stylet*, *Fleuret*, and *Bombarde* (left to right) at the Ninon moorings for torpedo craft behind a breakwater in the Brest roadstead. Torpedo boats are moored closer to the shore. *Stylet* and *Fleuret* (left and centre) are of the *Claymore* class of 300-tonners which introduced a major change in hull form as well as larger torpedoes and taller funnels, while *Bombarde* (right) is of the preceding *Arquebuse* class and is typical of the earlier 300-tonners. *(Postcard by H. Laurent, Port Louis)*

experiments directed by the *Conseil des travaux* they were given new hull lines with reconfigured hull sides above the waterline. The crew's galley was moved forward of the foremast from abaft the after funnel, the bridge was raised and put on top of it, all of the navigating equipment was consolidated in a new enclosed pilot house placed on the bridge, and the searchlight formerly on a platform in this location was put on top of the bridge. The funnels were also heightened. On entry into service the ships were found to have excessive topweight, and it was decided to remove the bridge wings and move some of the navigation equipment to lower locations. Except for *Claymore* all of the units of this class were built by dockyards, and their trials were less satisfactory than those of the preceding *Arquebuse* class. Those of *Stylet* and *Tromblon* took over a year and the ships were finally accepted for only 6,000ihp.

*Pierrier* became an experimental ship when in 1903 the Delaunay-Belleville firm proposed to put engines of its design with forced lubrication into a 300-ton destroyer. These were triple expansion engines with four cylinders and rated like the conventional engines in the class at 6,800ihp. They were delivered 25 months late, then had problems with lubricants being carried over into the boilers, and were only accepted in November 1910. The problems with boiler contamination recurred during the guaranty period and the engines had to be completely overhauled a second time. Ultimately they were judged to be much too fragile for destroyer use

and in 1911 after only 800 hours of operation the ship reverted to classic lubrication. Forced lubrication, however, was an idea with much merit, and it soon succeeded in the 450-ton *Lansquenet* and *Mameluck*.

**Dimensions & tons:** 58.280m oa, 58.000m wl, 58.000m pp x 6.530m ext (above wl), 6.200m wl. 337.362t disp (designed). Draught: (designed) 2.450m mean, 3.393m aft (real, under the propeller guard).
**Machinery:** 6,800ihp designed. Speed 28kts. Trials (*Claymore*) 7,200ihp = 30.35kts at 311rpm. 2 screws. 2 engines (experimental type in *Pierrier*). 2 Normand boilers (Du Temple in the Toulon boats). 30t coal. Range 2,300nm @ 10kts.
**Guns:** 1 x 65mm/50 M1902 (on platform forward), 6 x 47mm/50 M1902 (3 per side). **Torpedoes:** 2 single deck tubes for 450mm torpedoes (1 amidships and 1 on the stern). Torpedoes were M1892 in M'32-37 and M1906 in the others.

*Stylet* (M'32) Rochefort Dyd/Schneider, Creusot.
On list 1.1903. Ord: 12.5.1902. K: 21.3.1904. L: 18.5.1905. Trials: 1-4.1907. Comm: 25.3.1907 (accepted).
Budget 1902. *Escadre du Nord* 1907. In 1914-15 was in the 2nd destroyer squadron of the *2e Escadre légère* at Brest. Atlantic patrol squadron 1916, Bretagne patrol boat divisions 1917-18. Off main list by 3.1920 and for sale at Brest. Struck 14.5.1921. Sold 12.8.1921 at Brest to BU.

*Tromblon* (M'33) Rochefort Dyd/Schneider, Creusot.
On list 1.1903. Ord: 12.5.1902. K: 8.7.1904. L: 17.6.1905. Trials: 12.1906-4.1907. Comm: 25.3.1907 (accepted).
Budget 1902. *Escadre du Nord* 1908. In 1914 was in the 1st destroyer squadron of the *2e Escadre légère* at Brest. Channel 1914-18. Off main list by 3.1920 and for sale at Brest. Struck 14.5.1921. Sold 12.8.1921 at Brest to BU.

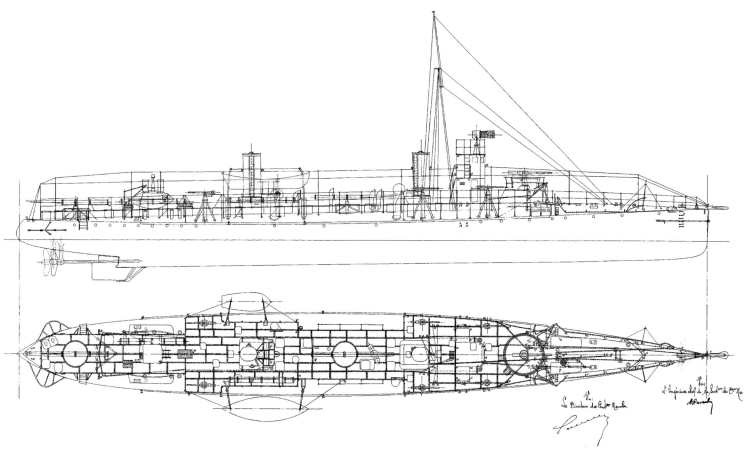

Longitudinal and plan views (*plan de pitonnage*) as fitted of the destroyers *Fleuret* and *Coutelas*. The plans were signed at Rochefort on 10 April 1908 by naval constructor Ch. François. The heavy lines on the plan view are the walking deck.

*Pierrier* (M'34) Rochefort Dyd/Delaunay-Belleville, Saint Denis.
On list 1.1904. Ord: 5.8.1903. K: 6.10.1904. L: 28.2.1907.
  Trials: 7-11.1908. Comm: 11.1908 (full).
Budget 1903. *Escadre du Nord* 1908-09 (trials of machinery with forced lubrication), reserve at Rochefort 1909-11 (machinery modified to standard lubrication), *Défense mobile* at Oran 1912. In 1914 was in the 4th destroyer squadron of the *1re Armée navale*. War service in the Mediterranean. Struck 27.7.1921. Sold 1.3.1922 at Toulon to BU.

*Obusier* (M'35) Rochefort Dyd/Indret.
On list 1.1904. Ord: 5.8.1903. K: 10.5.1904. L: 9.3.1906.
  Trials: 6-9.1907.
Budget 1903. *Escadre du Nord* 1907, *Défense mobile* at Brest 1912. In 1914 was in the 1st destroyer squadron of the *2e Escadre légère* at Brest. Dunkirk 1915-18. Struck 27.5.1921. Sold 6.3.1922 at Cherbourg to BU.

*Mortier* (M'36) Rochefort Dyd/Indret.
On list 1.1904. Ord: 5.8.1903. K: 12.9.1904. L: 23.3.1906.
  Trials: 10.1907-1.1908. Comm: 1.1908 (full).
Budget 1903. *Escadre du Nord* 1908-09, then to the Mediterranean. In 1914 was in the 4th destroyer squadron of the *1re Armée navale*. War service in the Mediterranean including the Dardanelles. Provence patrol boat division 1917-19. Annex to the school for torpedomen in *Patrie* 6.1919 to 10.1923. Struck 30.3.1927. Offered for sale and sold 26.10.1927 at Toulon to BU.

*Claymore* (M'37) Augustin Normand, Le Havre/Normand, Le Havre.
On list 1.1904. Ord: 2.9.1903. K: 1904. L: 14.3.1906. Trials: 4-5.1906.
  Comm: 8.1906 (full).

Budget 1903. *Escadre de la Méditerranée* 1906. To Brest 1910 and fitted as light minesweeper 9.1910 there to test the Ronar'ch sweep gear. In 1914-15 was in the 2nd destroyer squadron of the *2e Escadre légère* at Brest. Bretagne patrol boat division 1916-18. Baltic 1920, Atlantic Flotilla at Brest 1922-24. Off main list 1924 at Brest (condemnation pending). Decomm 4.6.1925. Struck (condemned) 19.3.1926 and attached to the school for engineer cadets (*école des élèves ingénieurs mécaniciens*). Engines and boilers removed and taken to Laninon for training 1927, hull sold 24.4.1928.

*Carquois* (M'38) Rochefort Dyd/Indret.
On list 1.1905. Ord: 5.7.1904. K: 10.7.1905. L: 26.6.1907.
  Trials: 4-8.1908.
Budget 1904. *Escadre de la Méditerranée* 1908. In 1914-15 was in the 1st destroyer squadron of the *2e Escadre légère* at Brest. North Sea flotilla at Dunkirk 1916-18. Flotilla of the 3rd maritime region (3rd aviso squadron) 1919-26, decomm. at Brest 1926. Off main list 1926 and for sale at Brest as a patrol craft 1926-1929. Condemned 1.12.1930. Sold 9.7.1931 at Brest to BU.

*Trident* (M'39) Rochefort Dyd/Indret.
On list 1.1905. Ord: 5.7.1904. K: 10.7.1905. L: 5.12.1907.
  Trials: 10.1908-1.1909. Comm: 11.1.1909 (full).
Budget 1904. *Escadre du Nord* 1909. In early 1914 was in the 5th destroyer squadron of the *1re Armée navale*. War service in the Mediterranean including the Dardanelles. School for stoking at Toulon during the 1920s. Struck 13.11.1931. Sold 29.11.1932 at Toulon to BU.

*Fleuret* (M'40) Rochefort Dyd/Le Havre.
On list 1.1906. Ord: 5.5.1905. K: 1906. L: 14.12.1906. Trials: 8.1907-3.1908.
Budget 1905. *Escadre du Nord* 1908. In 1914-15 was in the 2nd destroyer squadron of the *2e Escadre légère* at Brest. North Sea Flotilla at Dunkirk 1916-17, Normandy patrol boat division at Cherbourg 1918. Struck

12.1.1920. Target at Cherbourg 1922-1923. Sunk as towed target 1923.

*Coutelas* (M'41) Rochefort Dyd/Le Havre.
On list 1.1906. Ord: 5.5.1905. K: 3.2.1906. L: 12.1.1907.
  Trials: 9.1907-3.1908.
Budget 1905. *Escadre de la Méditerranée* 1908. In early 1914 was in the
  5th destroyer squadron of the *1re Armée navale*. War service in the
  Mediterranean including the Dardanelles. Bizerte patrol squadron
  1919. Struck 28.1.1921. Sold 20.5.1922 at Bizerte to BU.

*Cognée* (M44) Toulon Dyd/F.C. Méditerranée, Marseille.
On list 1.1906. Ord: 5.5.1905. K: 1.5.1906. L: 26.11.1907.
  Trials: 8-12.1908.
Budget 1905 (late addition). *Escadre de la Méditerranée* 1908. In early
  1914 was in the 5th destroyer squadron of the *1re Armée navale*.
  War service in the Mediterranean including the Dardanelles. Struck
  27.7.1921. Sold 1.3.1922 at Toulon to BU.

*Hache* (M45) Toulon Dyd/F.C. Méditerranée, Marseille.
On list 1.1906. Ord: 5.5.1905. K: 1.8.1906. L: 15.2.1908.
  Trials: 12.1908-6.1909.
Budget 1905 (late addition). *Escadre de la Méditerranée* 1909. Fitted as
  light minelayer 6.1912 (ordered 11.1911). During 1914 joined the 4th
  destroyer squadron of the *1re Armée navale*. War service in the
  Mediterranean including at Port Said. Annex to the school for torpedo-
  men in *Patrie* as of 3.1920. Struck 27.7.1921. Sold 12.12.1921 at
  Toulon to BU.

*Massue* (M46) Toulon Dyd/F.C. Méditerranée, Le Havre.
On list 1.1906. Ord: 5.5.1905. K: 1.11.1906. L: 19.9.1908.
  Trials: 2.1909-6.1909.
Budget 1905 (late addition). *Escadre de la Méditerranée* 1909-11. Fitted as
  light minelayer 6.1912 (ordered 11.1911). During 1914 joined the 4th
  destroyer squadron of the *1re Armée navale*. War service in the
  Mediterranean including the Dardanelles. Mediterranean training div-
  ision at Toulon 1919-26. Off main list 1926 and for sale at Toulon.
  Struck 30.3.1927. Offered for sale and sold 26.10.1927 at Toulon to
  BU.

---

**BRANLEBAS Class.** *Contre-torpilleurs d'escadre.* Normand 300-ton type
destroyers with general configuration as *Claymore.*

This type was very similar to the *Claymore* type but was a bit heavier (340
to 344 tons) and had a higher freeboard (2.90m vice 2.60m). The hull sides
above the waterline were again reconfigured to increase stability. The bow
was 30cm higher than in previous destroyers. Like the *Claymore* class, the
*Branlebas* class had a sizeable bridge supporting a sturdy pilot house with a
searchlight on top. Finally, light protection of 20mm plating was fitted
around engine and boiler compartments as in the *Siroco* class seagoing
torpedo boats at a cost of 12 tons. The additional weight of these ships
caused Minister Thomson to decide on 8 October 1907 to reduce their trial
speed from 28 knots to 27.5 knots and also caused them to roll in beam
seas. The orders were allocated to Normand for *Branlebas* and *Fanfare*
(M53-54) on 4 November 1905 and to three other builders on
8 November 1905, and two ships that had been ordered previously at
Rochefort but not begun (M'42-43) were changed to the new type. M47
and M49-52 were named on 15 July 1905, an alternative name of *Flamme*
also being suggested for M47. M47 to M54 replaced twenty torpedo boats
(P190-P209) in the original 1905 budget.

**Dimensions & tons:** 60.120m oa (*Glaive/Poignard*), 59.950m oa
  (*Sape/Gabion*), 58.000m wl & pp x 6.280m ext and wl (6.790m outside the rubbing strakes). 345.606t disp (designed). Draught: 2.460m
  mean, 3.393m aft (real, under rudder guard).
**Machinery:** 6,800ihp designed at 18kg/cm² boiler pressure.

Speed 27.5kts (originally 28kts). Trials (*Sape*) 29.82kts at 299.92rpm,
  (*Branlebas*) 6,700ihp = 28.76kts at 303rpm. 2 screws. 2 triple expan-
  sion engines with 3 cylinders of 0.51m, 0.79m, and 1.23m diameter
  and 0.59m stroke. 2 Normand or Du Temple boilers (the latter in the
  Penhoët pair and perhaps others). 30t coal (normal), 80t coal (max).
  Range with normal coal 2,300nm @ 10kts.
**Guns:** 1 x 65mm/50 M1902 (on platform forward), 6 x 47mm/50
  M1902 (3 per side). **Torpedoes:** 2 single deck tubes for 450mm
  M1906 torpedoes (1 amidships and 1 on the stern).

*Glaive* (M'42) Rochefort Dyd/Indret.
On list 1.1906. Ord: 5.5.1905. K: 3.2.1908. L: 10.9.1908.
  Trials: 4-9.1910.
Budget 1905. Left Rochefort 1.10.1910 to join the *Escadre du Nord.*
  Fitted 2.1911 as light minesweeper. In 1914-15 was in the 2nd destroy-
  er squadron of the *2e Escadre légère* at Brest. Brest patrol squadron
  1916-18. Assigned 7.1921 to the division of schools of the Atlantic at
  Brest for instruction of engineer officer cadets. Out of service
  2.12.1930. Struck 13.2.1932. Sold 4.10.1932 at Brest to BU.

*Poignard* (M'43) Rochefort Dyd/Indret.
On list 1.1906. Ord: 5.5.1905. K: 1908. L: 3.7.1909. Trials: 4-11.1910.
Budget 1905. *2e Escadre* (formerly the *Escadre du Nord*) at Brest 1911,
  then to Oran. In early 1914 was in the 5th destroyer squadron of the
  *1re Armée navale*. War service in the Mediterranean including the
  Dardanelles and Salonica. Minesweeping squadron at Port Said 1919-
  20. Off main list 1925 and for sale at Toulon. Struck 3.5.1926. Sold
  25.5.1927 at Toulon to BU.

*Sabretache* (M47) De la Brosse et Fouché, Nantes/De la Brosse, Nantes.
On list 1.1906. Ord: 8.11.1905. K: 6.1906. L: 5.2.1908.
  Trials: 4-9.1908. Comm: 10.1908 (full).
Budget 1905 (late addition). *Escadre de la Méditerranée* 1908. In early
  1914 was in the 5th destroyer squadron of the *1re Armée navale*. War
  service in the Mediterranean including the Dardanelles and the Eastern
  Mediterranean. Off main list by 3.1920, sold 2.3.1920 at Bizerte to
  M. Kalfon Vita. Struck 10.5.1920.

*Oriflamme* (M48) De la Brosse et Fouché, Nantes/De la Brosse, Nantes.
On list 1.1906. Ord: 8.11.1905. K: 6.1906. L: 4.4.1908.
  Trials: 5-9.1908. Comm: 10.1908 (full).
Budget 1905 (late addition). *Escadre de la Méditerranée* 1908. In 1914
  was in the 1st destroyer squadron of the *2e Escadre légère* at Brest.
  North Sea flotilla at Dunkirk 1914-18. In reserve at Cherbourg from
  6.1919. Struck 27.5.1921. Sold 6.2.1922 at Cherbourg to BU.

*Étendard* (M49) Dyle et Bacalan, Bordeaux-Bacalan/Dyle et Bacalan.
On list 1.1906. Ord: 8.11.1905. K: 4.12.1905. L: 20.3.1908.
  Trials: 5.1908-2.1909. Comm: 15.2.1909 (full).
Budget 1905 (late addition). Contract notified to builder 4.12.1905. Left
  Bordeaux for Rochefort 25.4.1908, began commissioning for trials
  9.5.1908, completed 1.7.1908. *Escadre du Nord* 1909. In 1914 was in
  the 1st destroyer squadron of the *2e Escadre légère* at Brest. North Sea
  flotilla at Dunkirk 1914-17. Sunk in the night of 24-25.4.1917 by
  gunfire from raiding German destroyers off Dunkirk which blew up
  her magazine, no survivors.

*Fanion* (M50) Dyle et Bacalan, Bordeaux-Bacalan/Dyle et Bacalan.
On list 1.1906. Ord: 8.11.1905. K: 12.1905. L: 4.5.1908. Trials: 7.1908-
  2.1909. Comm: 2.1909 (full).
Budget 1905 (late addition). *Escadre du Nord* 1909. In 1914-15 was in
  the 2nd destroyer squadron of the *2e Escadre légère* at Brest. Atlantic
  destroyer squadron 1916-18. Run into 23-24.11.1917 by American
  merchantman *Wyandotte*, able to make port. Struck 27.5.1921. Sold
  6.2.1922 at Cherbourg to BU.

The destroyer *Gabion*, a unit of the final batch of 300-tonners, the *Branlebas* class. The hull sides are now nearly vertical, although the vessel retains the elevated walking deck of the earlier 300-tonners. *(NHHC from ONI, NH-64468)*

*Sape* (M51) Ch. Penhoët, Rouen-Grand Quévilly/Ch. Penhoët, Saint Nazaire

On list 1.1906. Ord: 8.11.1905. K: 25.5.1906. L: 23.9.1907.
  Trials: 3-11.1908. Comm: 11.1908 (full).
Budget 1905 (late addition). Left the yard 19.12.1907. *Escadre du Nord* 1908. In 1914 was in the 4th destroyer squadron of the *1re Armée navale*. War service in the Mediterranean including the Dardanelles and eastern Mediterranean. 5th patrol squadron of the South coast flotilla (Toulon) 1919-24. Off main list 1925 and for sale at Toulon. Struck 3.5.1926. Sold 24.5.1927 at Toulon to BU.

*Gabion* (M52) Ch. Penhoët, Rouen-Grand Quévilly/Ch. Penhoët, Saint Nazaire

On list 1.1906. Ord: 8.11.1905. K: 2.7.1906. L: 21.12.1907.
  Trials: 2-11.1908.
Budget 1905 (late addition). Left the yard 21.1.1908. *Escadre du Nord* 1908. In 1914-15 was in the 2nd destroyer squadron of the *2e Escadre légère* at Brest. Channel and Atlantic 1916-18. Off main list by 3.1920 and for sale at Brest. Struck 14.5.1921. Sold 12.8.1921 at Brest to BU.

*Branlebas* (M53) Augustin Normand, Le Havre/Normand, Le Havre.
On list 1.1906. Ord: 8.11.1905. K: 11.1905. L: 8.10.1907.
  Trials: 11.1907-7.1908.
Budget 1905 (late addition). *Escadre du Nord* 1908. In 1914 was in the 1st destroyer squadron of the *2e Escadre légère* at Brest. North Sea flotilla 1915. Mined and sunk in the night of 30.9.1915 two miles north of the Nieuport sea buoy on the Flemish Banks. Struck 6.11.1915.

*Fanfare* (M54) Augustin Normand, Le Havre/Normand, Le Havre.
On list 1.1906. Ord: 8.11.1905. K: 11.1905. L: 19.12.1907.
  Trials: 1-9.1908.
Budget 1905 (late addition). *Escadre de la Méditerranée* 1908. In 1914 was in the 5th destroyer squadron of the *1re Armée navale*. War service in the Mediterranean including the Dardanelles. Flotilla of the Algeria-Tunisia maritime district 1919-24. Off main list 1924 (condemnation pending). Struck 28.4.1925. Sold 8.8.1925 at Bizerte.

---

**300-tonners in World War I**
During World War I the armament of the 300-ton destroyers underwent several changes. Those based at Dunkirk faced an increasingly dangerous air threat on the Flemish Banks, and in 1915 the mountings of their two after 47mm guns were modified for high-angle fire. In 1917 many 300-tonners had an 8mm machine gun mounted on the after torpedo tube, the gun being moved to the after conning tower when that tube was removed. By the end of the war many 300-tonners had two anti-aircraft machine guns and four positions where they could be mounted. The need to combat submarines also led to numerous armament changes. On many 300-tonners the 65mm gun was replaced with a more satisfactory 75mm gun (war model). At the end of 1917 the after torpedo tube was replaced on some ships with a Thornycroft anti-submarine mortar, the amidships torpedo mounting being increased to two tubes. Rails were also fitted for launching six or twelve depth charges. The after tube was restored when the Thornycroft mortar was removed in 1918.

**450-Ton Type**
In January 1906 Augustin Normand submitted two designs for a destroyer more advanced than his *Claymore*. These were among his last designs, as he died on 11 December 1906. They were extrapolations of *Claymore* with a single-calibre armament of six 65mm guns and three tubes instead of two

for 450mm torpedoes. (The Navy decided to put the third tube in the bow.) They had reciprocating engines and four boilers in two boiler rooms. The rudder, which had been forward of the screws in the 300-tonners was returned to its normal position in the extreme stern aft of the screws. Design B had an elevated walking deck as in the 300-tonners which required a bit more beam and displacement to maintain stability, while Design A, which Normand recommended, dispensed with it. The *Comité technique* approved Design A in its meeting on 3 February 1906, and in a note of 3 May 1906 *Directeur centrale des constructions navales* Dudebout proposed to Minister Thomson that the new destroyers planned in the Programme of 1906 have general characteristics nearly identical to those of Normand's design. However, in contrast to the 300-tonners, all of which followed Normand's designs closely, each builder was left free to produce their own detailed design based on the general specifications for the type, which included a maximum displacement, a speed of 28 knots and an armament of six 65mm guns and three 450mm torpedo tubes, two on deck and one in the bow. Minister Thomson on 3 April 1906 had already directed the adoption of turbines and reciprocating engines with forced lubrication. It took another six months to decide how many of the ships would have turbines and to order the first six boats (three reciprocating and three with turbines on 24 October 1906). Five more orders followed a year later (four of them deferred from 1906). The 1908 budget (submitted on 11 May 1907) contained ten more 450-tonners, all of which were named but not ordered. These were reprogrammed as the first seven 800-tonners and the remaining three of the ten names, *Fougasse*, *Latte*, and *Revolver*, were dropped. Two more 450-tonners were belatedly ordered in early 1910 from the Rochefort Dockyard at the same time as the second batch of 800-tonners.

The programme as executed was:

6 x 450-tonners: M55-60, 1906 budget, 1907 fleet list.
5 x 450-tonners: M61-65, 1907 budget, 1908 fleet list, of which M61-64 had been deferred from the 1906 budget.
2 x 450-tonners: M84-85, 1910 budget, 1910 fleet list.

### (a) Five 450-tonners with reciprocating engines

These ships, plus two more late units listed below, were variants of Normand's Design A, with their engines in two engine rooms amidships between two boiler rooms, each of which had two boilers and two funnels. All seven ships thus had the same general appearance with four tall thin funnels in two widely spaced pairs with two deck-mounted torpedo tubes between them, although the funnels of *Spahi* and *Lansquenet* were slightly taller than those of the others. They all had two propeller shafts. Differences in the machinery of the seven ships were largely responsible for them falling into five classes, which also had slight differences in hull dimensions and compartment lengths. When *Spahi* ran preliminary trials at the beginning of the summer of 1908 it was found that the choice of forced lubrication for the reciprocating engines in the 450-tonners had been premature – as in the prototype installation in the 300-ton *Pierrier* lubricants were carried over by the feed water into the boilers where they burned, causing small explosions. Forced lubrication was soon abandoned in *Spahi*, *Hussard*, and *Carabinier*, but the problems with it were solved in *Lansquenet* and *Mameluck* and because of its great operational benefits it became standard in future reciprocating machinery. Trial results for the seven reciprocating-engined 450-tonners varied from 7,500ihp to 7,750ihp (9,000ihp in *Spahi*) for speeds between 27.05 knots and 29.80 knots. Overall *Lansquenet* had by far the most successful trials in this group, particularly for endurance. In service these 450-tonners displaced around 100 tons more than their trial displacements (530 to 550 tons instead of 410 to 430 tons), easily maintained 24.5 knots in formation, and could reach 26 knots in service when new. Heavy seas, however, soon slowed them and the other 450-tonners to 14 knots. They formed a destroyer flotilla in the *1re Armée navale* in the Mediterranean from 1912 (six ships with one spare) and served in the Mediterranean for the entire war, from 1916 as anti-submarine escorts and patrol vessels,

particulary in the Aegean. By the mid-1920s the five survivors were serving in the *Défense mobile* in Tunisia.

———————

**SPAHI.** *Contre-torpilleur d'escadre.* FCM Le Havre 450-ton type (reciprocating) with six 65mm guns (two on the centreline and four on the sides), three torpedo tubes (one in the bow and two on deck between the funnels), a flush deck, four funnels in two widely spaced pairs (the engines being in between), and one tall mast forward and one short radio mast aft. Normand design adapted by builder. Coal-fired.

*Spahi* was commissioned for trials on 25 September 1908 but so much trouble was encountered with the forced lubrication in the engines that it was decided on 5 January 1909 to replace it with the Calouin lubrication system. The ship's trials resumed in September 1909.

**Dimensions & tons:** 68.150m oa, 64.600m wl, 64.600m pp x 6.582m ext and wl (6.890m outside the rubbing strakes). 432.018t disp (designed), 455t (normal), 490t (full load). Draught: (designed) 2.537m mean, 3.040m aft (under the screws). Men: 76 including 3 officers.
**Machinery:** 9,000ihp designed at 18kg/cm² boiler pressure. Speed 28kts. Trials 29.43kts. 2 screws. 2 engines with 4 cylinders of 0.51m (1), 0.79m (1), and 0.87m (2) diameter. 4 Normand boilers. 38t coal (normal), 100t (surcharge).
**Guns:** 6 x 65mm/50 M1902 (3 singles forward, 3 aft).
  **Torpedoes:** 3 tubes for 450mm M1906 torpedoes (2 single deck tubes amidships, 1 bow tube).

*Spahi* (M55) F.C. Méditerranée, Le Havre-Graville/FCM, Le Havre.
On list 1.1907. Ord: 24.10.1906. K: 1906. L: 30.5.1908. Trials: 10.1908. In service: 7.1910. Comm: 15.8.1910 (full).
Budget 1906. Construction reassigned from Rochefort to contract 1906. To the *1re Escadre* (formerly the *Escadre de la Méditerranée*) in the Mediterranean 15.8.1910. In 1914 was in the 2nd destroyer squadron of the *1re Armée navale*. War service in the Adriatic from 5.1915 and in the Black Sea 1919. Struck 28.12.1927. Sold 1928 to M. Risso of Toulon to BU.

———————

**CARABINIER.** *Contre-torpilleur d'escadre.* Ch. Penhoët 450-ton type (reciprocating) with general configuration as *Spahi*. Normand design adapted by builder. Coal-fired.

*Carabinier* was the slowest of the 450-tonners, failing to make her designed speed of 28 knots by almost a knot.

**Dimensions & tons:** 64.81m oa, 64.20m wl & pp x 6.58m ext, 6.48m wl. 446t disp (520t full load). Draught: 2.98m aft. Men: 76 including 3 officers.
**Machinery:** 8,200ihp designed at 18kg/cm² boiler pressure. Speed 28kts. Trials 27.05kts . 2 screws. 2 engines with 4 cylinders of 0.51m (1), 0.79m (1), and 0.87m (2) diameter. 4 Guyot-Du Temple boilers. 30t coal (normal), 100t (surcharge).
**Guns:** 6 x 65mm/50 M1902 (3 singles forward, 3 aft).
  **Torpedoes:** 3 tubes for 450mm M1906 torpedoes (2 single deck tubes amidships, 1 bow tube).

*Carabinier* (M60) Ch. Penhoët, Rouen-Grand Quévilly/Ch. Penhoët, Saint Nazaire
On list 1.1907. Ord: 24.10.1906. K: 30.5.1907. L: 10.10.1908. Trials: 12.1908. In service: 10.1909.
Budget 1906. Left the yard 11.11.1908. Assigned to the *1re Escadre* in the Mediterranean 1.4.1910. In 1914 was flagship of the 2nd destroyer squadron of the *1re Armée navale*. War service in he Adriatic from 5.1915. Wrecked 13.11.1918 off Latakia in Syria, wreck destroyed by explosives 15.11.1918.

———————

*HUSSARD* **Class.** *Contre-torpilleurs d'escadre.* A.C. Loire 450-ton type (reciprocating) with general configuration as *Spahi.* Normand design adapted by builder. Coal-fired.

*Hussard* had a difficult time initially because of her forced lubrication but eventually became the fastest of the 450-tonners fitted exclusively with reciprocating engines. She did, however, continue to experience many mechanical problems.

**Dimensions & tons:** 65.80m wl & pp x 6.90m ext, 6.60m wl. 407t disp. Draught: 3.00m aft (3.02m in *Mameluck*). Men: 76 including 3 officers.
**Machinery:** 7,750ihp designed at 18.5kg/cm² boiler pressure. Speed 28kts. Trials (*Hussard*) 29.80kts, (*Mameluck*) 29.75kts. 2 screws. 2 engines with 3 cylinders of 0.55m, 0.78m, and 1.23m diameter and 0.59m stroke. 4 Du Temple boilers. 37t coal (normal), 100t (surcharge).
**Guns:** 6 x 65mm/50 M1902 (3 singles forward, 3 aft).
  **Torpedoes:** 3 tubes for 450mm M1906 torpedoes (2 single deck tubes amidships, 1 bow tube).

*Hussard* (M59) A.C. Loire, Nantes/ACL, Nantes.
On list 1.1907. Ord: 24.10.1906. K: 1906. L: 12.9.1908. Trials: 9.1910. Comm: 27.6.1911 (full). In service: 9.1911.
Budget 1906. To the 1st destroyer squadron of the *1re Armée navale* 27.6.1911. In 1914 was flagship of the 4th destroyer squadron of the *1re Armée navale* then consisting of some 300-tonners. War service in the Aegean 1916 with the 4th destroyer squadron and in the Black Sea 1919 with the 2nd destroyer squadron. Off main list c1921 and for sale at Bizerte 1921-1924. Struck 29.3.1922. Sold to M. Boccara of Tunis.

The destroyer *Hussard*, one of seven 450-ton destroyers with reciprocating engines. They could be recognized by the widely spaced pairs of funnels, the two engines being between two pairs of boilers. She wore the Roman numeral IV on her bow between June and October 1911. *(Postcard by ELD)*

*Mameluck* (M62) A.C. Loire, Nantes/ACL, Nantes.
On list 1.1908. Ord: 30.10.1907. K: 1907. L: 10.3.1909. Trials: 7.1909. In service: 6.1911. Comm: 27.6.1911.
Budget 1906 (delayed to 1907). To the 1st destroyer squadron of the *1re Armée navale* 27.6.1911. In 1914 was in the 2nd destroyer squadron of the *1re Armée navale*. War service in the Adriatic from 5.1915 and in the Black Sea 1919. Struck 28.12.1927.

---

*LANSQUENET.* *Contre-torpilleur d'escadre.* Dyle et Bacalan 450-ton type (reciprocating) with general configuration as *Spahi.* Normand design adapted by builder. Coal-fired.

*Lansquenet* had the largest coal bunker capacity of the reciprocating 450-tonners, with 118 tons instead of the typical 95 tons of the others. She was regarded by some as the most successful of the 450-tonners with reciprocating engines. The hulls of *Enseigne Henry* and *Aspirant Herber* below were copies of *Lansquenet* but they had different boilers.

**Dimensions & tons:** 67.41m oa, 64.00m wl & pp x 6.61m ext, m wl. 542t disp (550t full load). Draught: 2.96m aft. Men: 77 including 4 officers.
**Machinery:** 8,120ihp designed at 18kg/cm² boiler pressure. Speed 28kts. Trials 28.84kts. 2 screws. 2 engines with 3 cylinders of 0.55m, 0.78m, and 1.23m diameter and 0.59m stroke. 4 Normand boilers. 35t coal (normal), 100/118t (surcharge). Range with normal coal 2,260nm @ 14kts and 2,880nm @ 10kts.
**Guns:** 6 x 65mm/50 M1902 (3 singles forward, 3 aft).
  **Torpedoes:** 3 tubes for 450mm M1906 torpedoes (2 single deck tubes amidships, 1 bow tube).

*Lansquenet* (M61) Dyle et Bacalan, Bordeaux-Bacalan/Dyle et Bacalan.
On list 1.1908. Ord: 30.10.1907. K: 1907. L: 20.11.1909. Trials: 1.1910. In service: 10.1910.
Budget 1906 (delayed to 1907). To the *1re Escadre* in the Mediterranean

15.8.1910. In 1914 was in the 2$^{nd}$ destroyer squadron of the *1$^{re}$ Armée navale*. War service in the Adriatic from 5.1915 and in the Black Sea 1919. Struck 28.2.1928, barracks hulk at Bizerte 1928. Sold 2.5.1929 at Bizerte to MM. Boccara, Scalabrino & Cie of Tunis to BU.

---

### (b) Two 450-tonners with both turbines and reciprocating engines

The final trial report on *Torpilleur n° 243*, an experimental torpedo boat with Rateau turbines, recommended trying a mixed propulsion system that Rateau and Yarrow were experimenting with in 1904 that combined reciprocating and turbine engines to get around the problem of the high fuel consumption of turbine plants at low and medium speeds. (Turbines became very inefficient when rotating below their rated maximum speed while propellers became inefficient at high rotational speeds.) The *Section technique* decided to try this formula in two of the 450-tonners. These ships each had one reciprocating engine and two main turbines on three propeller shafts. Steam from the boilers first entered the forced-lubrication reciprocating engine, which was on the centre propeller shaft, and then exhausted into both of the turbines, which were on the wing shafts. The reciprocating engine would provide economical steaming at low and medium speeds while the turbines would take over at high speeds. In addition to their main propulsion turbines the port shaft had an astern turbine and the starboard shaft had a cruising turbine.

The experiment had mixed results. Of the six 450-tonners that had turbines only, *Voltigeur* succeeded in transiting from Brest to Toulon without refuelling – although she did it exclusively on her reciprocating engines. Drawbacks of the mixed propulsion scheme included the 30 metres of hull length occupied by the machinery at the expense of crew accommodations and the complexity of the mixed propulsion system, less suited for rapid manoeuvres than either the all-reciprocating or all-turbine plants. Any advantage in fuel consumption was not felt to compensate for these disadvantages and the system was not repeated in the 800-ton destroyers that followed. (Mixed propulsion did not become widespread until the gas turbine and diesel era.) In addition to coping with problems with their brand new turbine technology (Rateau impulse in one and Bréguet reaction in the other), the two mixed propulsion 450-tonners also had to contend with numerous problems during trials with their forced lubrication reciprocating engines.

---

*VOLTIGEUR. Contre-torpilleur d'escadre,* 450-ton type (turbine and reciprocating) with general configuration as *Spahi* except that the four funnels were evenly spaced forward, the engines being aft of the boilers. Normand design adapted by builder. Coal-fired.

*Voltigeur* had Rateau turbines, which were impulse turbines, instead of the reaction turbines in the other turbine 450-tonners (Bréguet in *Tirailleur* and Parsons in the other four). They were modified by her builder's chief engineer, the former naval constructor Alfred Maxime Laubeuf who had designed the submersible *Narval*. Laubeuf also modified the stern lines of the design, giving them a vaulted form to get better water flow to the propellers and higher trial speeds. *Voltigeur* was the fastest of the 450-tonners on trials, but in service the hollow lines aft made the ship hard to steer, generated shocks and vibrations in the hull structure and weakened the hull in bad weather and in drydock. Her turbines also fouled extraordinarily quickly, and in December 1915 all of the low pressure blades of the starboard turbine had to be simply removed. Her builder, De la Brosse et Fouché, became the Ateliers and Chantiers de Bretagne in 1909.

**Dimensions & tons:** 65.60m wl & pp x 6.95m ext, 6.82m wl. 594t disp (600t full load). Draught: 2.97m aft. Men: 79 including 4 officers.
**Machinery:** 8,500hp designed at 18kg/cm$^2$ boiler pressure. Speed 28kts. Trials 31.30kts. 3 screws. 2 Rateau turbines, 1 reciprocating engine. 4 Normand boilers. 45t coal (normal), 109t coal (surcharge). Range with normal coal 1,590nm @ 14kts and 2,160nm @ 10kts.

**Guns:** 6 x 65mm/50 M1902 (3 singles forward, 3 aft). **Torpedoes:** 3 tubes for 450mm M1906 torpedoes (2 single deck tubes amidships, 1 bow tube).

*Voltigeur* (M56) De la Brosse et Fouché, Nantes/De la Brosse, Nantes (Rateau turbines).
On list 1.1907. Ord: 24.10.1906. K: 1906. L: 25.3.1909. Trials: 10.1909. In service: 4.1910.
Budget 1906. Construction reassigned from Rochefort to contract 1906. To the *1$^{re}$ Escadre* in the Mediterranean 15.8.1910. Equipped with two tracks aft for a total of 20 mines 9.1913. In 1914 was in the 3$^{rd}$ destroyer squadron of the *1$^{re}$ Armée Navale*. War service in the Aegean and eastern Mediterranean from 1915. Struck 10.5.1920, sold 16.11.1920 to M. Kalfon Vita of Tunis.

---

*TIRAILLEUR. Contre-torpilleur d'escadre,* 450-ton type (turbine and reciprocating) with general configuration as *Voltigeur*. Normand design adapted by builder. Coal-fired.

*Tirailleur* had Bréguet reaction turbines in contrast to *Voltigeur's* Rateau impulse turbines. She was slightly smaller than *Voltigeur* and her trial speed was over two knots less, but her more normal hull lines spared her from some of the problems experienced by the other mixed propulsion ship. Her freeboard was as high as that of the 450-tonners with reciprocating engines, making her a better seaboat than most of the turbine boats.

In 1909 Schneider, who had very close relations with C.A. Gironde, launched on speculation at Chalon sur Saône another 450-tonner named *Acté* with the characteristics and appearance of *Tirailleur* less the reciprocating engines. She had Schneider-Zoelly turbines and was coal fired. She became the Peruvian *Teniente Rodriguez* in 1911 and lasted to 1944.

**Dimensions & tons:** 63.10m oa, 63.00m wl & pp x 6.90m ext, 6.40m wl. 479t disp (549t full load). Draught: 2.89m aft. Men: 78 including 3 officers.
**Machinery:** 7,800hp designed at 18kg/cm$^2$ boiler pressure. Speed 28kts. Trials 28.82kts. 3 screws. 2 Bréguet turbines, 1 reciprocating engine. 4 Du Temple boilers. 45t coal, 100t (surcharge).
**Guns:** 6 x 65mm/50 M1902 (3 singles forward, 3 aft).
**Torpedoes:** 3 tubes for 450mm M1906 torpedoes (2 single deck tubes amidships, 1 bow tube).

*Tirailleur* (M57) C.A. Gironde, Bordeaux-Lormont/Maison Bréguet, Paris (Bréguet turbines).
On list 1.1907. Ord: 24.10.1906. K: 1906. L: 27.11.1908. Trials: 3.1909. In service: 7.1910.
Budget 1906. Construction reassigned from Toulon to contract 1906. To the *1$^{re}$ Escadre* in the Mediterranean 15.8.1910. In 1914 was in the 3$^{rd}$ destroyer squadron of the *1$^{re}$ Armée Navale*. War service in the Aegean and eastern Mediterranean from 1915. Struck 29.6.1921, for sale at Toulon 1921-1922.

---

### (c) Four 450-tonners with turbines

These all-turbine ships had four Parsons turbines on three propeller shafts. The centre shaft had a high pressure turbine while the port and starboard shafts each had a low pressure turbine with both ahead and astern elements. The starboard shaft also had a high pressure cruising turbine. The three shafts did not have their own independent supplies of steam but all ran off of a single supply, steam being routed only to the engines that were appropriate to the ship's operational activities. At 14 knots (cruising speed) or less, the steam from all boilers entered the high pressure cruising turbine on the starboard shaft, then exhausted into the high pressure turbine on the centre shaft which in this configuration functioned as a medium pressure turbine, and finally exhausted into the low pressure turbine on the port shaft, in what could be called a triple-expansion mode. At higher speeds the steam entered the high pressure turbine on the centre shaft and exhausted into the two low pressure turbines on the wing shafts, essentially a double expansion mode. As in the mixed propulsion ships it was hoped that this system would improve efficiency and reduce fuel consumption at low speeds, but its complexity and its inflexibility (the inability to control the shafts separately) led to its not being repeated in the 800-ton destroyers.

In both the mixed propulsion and all-turbine ships the engines had to be placed aft of the boiler rooms instead of between them because the propeller shafts had to be higher in the hulls to be connected to the direct-drive turbines. This produced an arrangement with four boilers and four evenly spaced funnels and two deck-mounted torpedo tubes aft of them. The exceptions were *Janissaire*, which had three White Forster boilers and three funnels, and *Fantassin*, whose four funnels were grouped in pairs. The six turbine 450-tonners, like six of the seven with reciprocating engines, formed a single squadron in the *Armée navale* at the outbreak of the war. They spent the entire war in the Adriatic and the Mediterranean. Unlike the reciprocating engined ships, however, only one of the turbine ships (*Cavalier*) remained in service beyond July 1921. The 450-tonners were the last French light craft with the horizontal *tampon de choc* (shock buffer) that had been carried at the top of the bow by nearly all French torpedo boats and destroyers since 1877 as a protection against collisions.

---

*CHASSEUR. Contre-torpilleur d'escadre,* 450-ton type (turbine) with general configuration as *Voltigeur.* Designed by Normand. Coal-fired.

The turbines for *Chasseur* were built by the *Cie. Electro-Mécanique* at Le Bourget under license from Parsons and were successful in trials. However, they corroded badly in service, partly from lack of experience operating them and partly because the techniques for building them had not been perfected. The corrosion was already severe in January 1913, and when the

Inboard profile and deck view of the destroyer *Janissaire* built by the Chantiers de Normandie at Grand Quevilly near Rouen. The plans were dated there on 1 June 1910 and certified to represent the ship as fitted on 2 October 1911 by the navy's control officer at Le Havre, J. A. Laffargue.

turbines were opened in August 1917 after heavy wartime use their condition was found to be disastrous. She also lost speed quickly in a seaway because her freeboard was lower than that of most 450-tonners.

**Dimensions & tons:** 67.650m oa, 64.200m wl, 64.200m pp x 6.584m ext and wl (6.856m outside the rubbing strakes). 447.179t disp (designed), 492t (normal), 514t (full load). Draught: (designed) 2.697m mean, 2.818m aft. Men: 76 including 3 officers.
**Machinery:** 7,200shp designed (accepted at 9,000ihp) at 15kg/cm² boiler pressure. Speed 28kts. Trials (31.7.1909) 8,000shp = 30.393kts at 938.43rpm. 3 screws. 4 Parsons turbines. 4 Normand boilers. 30t coal (normal), 99t coal (surcharge). Range with normal coal 1,160nm @ 14kts and 1,400nm @ 10kts.
**Guns:** 6 x 65mm/50 M1902 (3 singles forward, 3 aft).
  **Torpedoes:** 3 tubes for 450mm M1906 torpedoes (2 single deck tubes amidships, 1 bow tube).

*Chasseur* (M58) Augustin Normand, Le Havre/C.E.M. Le Bourget (Parsons turbines).
On list 1.1907. Ord: 24.10.1906. K: 1906. L: 20.2.1909. Trials: 5.1909. In service: 11.1909.
Budget 1906. Construction reassigned from Toulon to contract 1906. To the *1re Escadre* in the Mediterranean 1909. In 1914 was in the 3rd destroyer squadron of the *1re Armée Navale*. War service in the Aegean 1915 and the Adriatic 1916. Struck 30.10.1919. Sold 6.5.1920 at Toulon to BU.

---

*JANISSAIRE. Contre-torpilleur d'escadre,* 450-ton type (turbine) with general configuration as *Voltigeur* except that the third funnel was omitted. Normand design adapted by builder. Oil-fired.

*Janissaire* had three White-Forster boilers, the first in the French Navy, which were blamed for her relatively low trial speed. They also accounted for her silhouette with only three unevenly spaced funnels. Her builder was identified on her plans as the Chantiers de Normandie, Grand Quévilly, near Rouen. The Chantiers de Normandie began operations in 1894 and

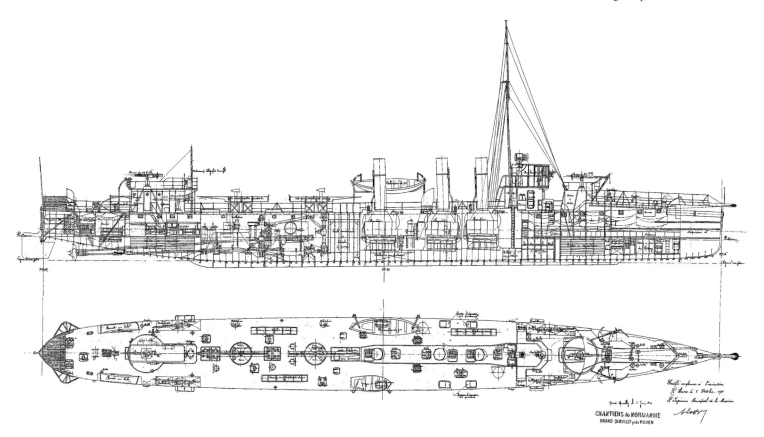

were sold to the Chantiers et Ateliers de Saint Nazaire – Penhoët in 1901, but the original name remained in common use for many years afterwards.

**Dimensions & tons:** 68.100m oa, 64.500m wl, 64.500m pp x 6.600m ext and wl (7.062m outside the rubbing strakes). 457.281t disp (designed), 514t normal. Draught: (designed) 2.65345m mean, 2.872m aft (real, under the keel). Men: 69 including 5 officers.

**Machinery:** 7,650shp designed at 15kg/cm$^2$ boiler pressure. Speed 28kts. Trials 28.57kts. 3 screws. 4 Parsons turbines. 3 White Forster boilers (oil fired). 50t oil (normal), 100t (max).

**Guns:** 6 x 65mm/50 M1902 (3 singles forward, 3 aft). **Torpedoes:** 3 tubes for 450mm M1906 torpedoes (2 single deck tubes amidships, 1 bow tube).

*Janissaire* (M63) Ch. Penhoët, Rouen-Grand Quévilly/Ch. Penhoët, Saint Nazaire (Parsons turbines).

On list 1.1908. Ord: 30.10.1907. K: 27.1.1909. L: 12.4.1910. Trials: 9.1910. In service: 6.1911.

Budget 1906 (delayed to 1907). Left the yard 7.6.1910. To the 2$^{nd}$ destroyer squadron of the *1$^{re}$ Armée navale* 5.8.1911. Equipped with two tracks aft for a total of 20 mines 9.1913. In 1914 was in the 3$^{rd}$ destroyer squadron of the *1$^{re}$ Armée Navale*. War service in the Aegean and eastern Mediterranean from 1915. Struck 7.6.1920. For sale at Toulon 1920, target there 1921-1922.

---

*FANTASSIN. Contre-torpilleur d'escadre,* 450-ton type (turbine) with general configuration as *Voltigeur* except that the four funnels were in two adjacent pairs. Normand design adapted by builder. Oil-fired.

*Fantassin* was considered to be a good seaboat and a 'good ship' even though, like *Cavalier* and *Chasseur* which were constantly wet, her freeboard forward was less than that of the reciprocating 450-tonners. *Janissaire* had a somewhat higher forecastle and wider stern than did the other turbine boats and also earned a reputation as a good seaboat.

**Dimensions & tons:** 68.950m oa, 65.400m wl, 65.400m pp x 6.550m ext and wl (6.875m outside the rubbing strakes). 460.454t disp (designed), 494t (normal), 560t (full load). Draught: (designed)

---

The destroyer *Fantassin*. Like the other turbine-propelled 450-tonners she had all four of her boilers ahead of the engines, but she was the only one to have her four funnels grouped in pairs. She wore the letters FN on her bow from June 1912 to her loss in 1916. *(Postcard by LL, Levy fils et Cie, Paris)*

2.545m mean, 2.665m aft. Men: 68 including 3 officers.

**Machinery:** 8,600shp designed at 15kg/cm$^2$ boiler pressure. Speed 28kts. Trials 30.04kts. 3 screws. 4 Parsons turbines. 4 Normand boilers (oil fired). 64t oil (normal), 110t (max). Range with normal oil 1,470nm @ 14kts and 1,520nm @ 10kts.

**Guns:** 6 x 65mm/50 M1902 (3 singles forward, 3 aft). **Torpedoes:** 3 tubes for 450mm M1906 torpedoes (2 single deck tubes amidships, 1 bow tube).

*Fantassin* (M64) F.C. Méditerranée, Le Havre-Graville/FCM, Le Havre (Parsons turbines).

On list 1.1908. Ord: 30.10.1907. K: 1907. L: 17.6.1909. Trials: 4.1910. In service: 6.1911.

Budget 1906 (delayed to 1907). To the *1$^{re}$ Escadre* in the Mediterranean 9.9.1910. In 1914 was flagship of the 3$^{rd}$ destroyer squadron of the *1$^{re}$ Armée Navale*. War service in the Aegean from 1915. Sunk 5.6.1916 in collision with *Mameluck* off Fano in the Ionian Sea.

---

*CAVALIER. Contre-torpilleur d'escadre,* 450-ton type (turbine) with general configuration as *Voltigeur*. Designed by Normand. Oil-fired.

*Cavalier* was a replica of *Chasseur* except that she was oil-fired. Her turbines did not suffer the same problems as those of *Chasseur* and she was regarded by some as the most successful of the 450-tonners with turbines. The freeboard forward of *Cavalier* and *Chasseur* was less (2.5m to 2.6m) than that of the reciprocating 450-tonners (3.1m) and they were the wettest of the 450-tonners and lost speed quickly in a seaway. *Cavalier* lost her bow torpedo tube in a collision with *Fantassin* on 17 August 1914 and it was never replaced. It was on *Cavalier* that the phenomenon of hull cavitation was first observed (cavitation had previously been observed only with pumps and screw propellers).

**Dimensions & tons:** 67.65m oa, 64.20m wl & pp x 6.61m ext, 6.60m wl. 527t disp. Draught: 3.18m aft. Men: 69 including 4 officers.

**Machinery:** 8,600shp designed at 16kg/cm$^2$ boiler pressure. Speed 28kts. Trials 31.02kts. 3 screws. 4 Parsons turbines. 4 Normand boilers (oil fired). 65t oil (normal), 110t (max).

**Guns:** 6 x 65mm/50 M1902 (3 singles forward, 3 aft). **Torpedoes:** 3 tubes for 450mm M1906 torpedoes (2 single deck tubes amidships, 1 bow tube).

*Cavalier* (M65) Augustin Normand, Le Havre/F.C. Méditerranée, Le Havre (Parsons turbines).

On list 1.1908. Ord: 30.10.1907. K: 1907. L: 9.5.1910. Trials: 6.1910. In service: 1.1911.

Budget 1907. To the 2$^{nd}$ destroyer squadron of the *1$^{re}$ Armée Navale* 29.3.1911. In 1914 was in the 3$^{rd}$ destroyer squadron of the *1$^{re}$ Armée Navale*. War service in the Aegean and eastern Mediterranean from 1915. School for stoking, Toulon, 1920-1927. Condemned 28.10.1927. For sale at Toulon 1927-1929, sold by the Domaines 1930-1932.

---

**(d) Two late 450-tonners with reciprocating engines**

The 1910 budget included five 800-tonners and two 450-tonners. (It also included two seagoing torpedo boats that were not proceeded with.) The safest type of 450-tonner was chosen, one with reciprocating engines without forced lubrication. They were also the only 450-tonners to be built in a Navy dockyard.

*ENSEIGNE HENRY* **Class.** *Contre-torpilleurs d'escadre.* Rochefort Dyd. 450-ton type (reciprocating) with general configuration as *Spahi*. Normand design adapted by builders. Coal-fired.

These, the only dockyard-built 450-tonners, were ordered after the first batch of 800-tonners. Their hulls were copies of *Lansquenet* but they had different boilers. Their reciprocating engines had ordinary instead of forced lubrication, sparing them the extended trials of other 450-tonners. They were a bit heavier than the other 450-tonners, 475.76 tons on trials instead of 408.85 tons to 427.57 tons.

**Dimensions & tons:** 67.390m oa, 64.000m wl & pp x 6.612m ext and wl (7.040m outside the rubbing strakes). 430.010t disp (designed), 475t (normal). Draught: (designed) 2.567m mean, 3.000m aft (under the screws). Men: 76 including 3 officers.
**Machinery:** 7,500ihp designed at 18kg/cm² boiler pressure. Speed 28kts. Trials (*Henry*) 28.46kts, (*Herber*) 28.25kts. 2 screws. 2 engines with 3 cylinders of 0.55m, 0.78m, and 1.23m diameter and 0.59m stroke. 4 Guyot-Du Temple boilers. 35t coal (normal), 100t (surcharge).
**Guns:** 6 x 65mm/50 M1902 (3 singles forward, 3 aft).
  **Torpedoes:** 3 tubes for 450mm M1909R torpedoes (2 single deck tubes amidships, 1 bow tube).

*Enseigne Henry* (M84) Rochefort Dyd/Indret
On list 1.1910. Ord: 2.1910. K: 11.1910. L: 12.5.1911. Trials: 2.1912. In service: 4.1912. Comm: 1.5.1912 (full).
Budget 1910. To the 2nd destroyer squadron of the *1re Armée Navale* 5.1912. War service in the Adriatic from 5.1915 and in the Black Sea 1919. To the *Défense mobile* at Tunisia 1919. Struck 9.6.1928. Sold 2.5.1929 at Bizerte to MM. Boccara, Scalabrino & Cie of Tunis to BU.

*Aspirant Herber* (M85) Rochefort Dyd/Indret
On list 1.1910. Ord: 2.1910. K: 12.1910. L: 30.4.1912. Trials: 5.1912. In service: 8.1912.
Budget 1910. To the 2nd destroyer squadron of the *1re Armée Navale* 1912. War service in the Adriatic from 5.1915 and in the Black Sea 1919. Grounded near Sfax 17.10.1920 but refloated and became the

Longitudinal and plan views (*plan de pitonnage*) as fitted of the squadron destroyers (*contre-torpilleurs d'escadre*) *Enseigne Henry* and *Aspirant Herber*. The plans were signed at Rochefort on 4 June 1912 by naval constructor Martin.

longest-lived of the 450-tonners. Condemned 1.12.1930 and for sale by the Domaines. BU 1931 at Bizerte. (Name often rendered *Herbert* in error.)

**800-Ton Type**
In October 1907, when considering the Programme of 1907, the *Conseil Supérieur de la Marine* discussed the Navy's future requirements for destroyers in light of two decisions recently taken, to renounce the types of submarines classified as 'defensive' and to lay down no more seagoing (*haute mer*) or *Défense mobile* torpedo boats. The anticipated service life of a destroyer was set at 16 years from launch, and with 30 of the older destroyers thus scheduled to leave the fleet between 1913 and 1919 the Council determined that the navy needed to build 63 more destroyers between 1909 and 1919, or six to seven per year.

The Council also asked for destroyers with better seakeeping, to be secured by increasing their size and giving them raised forecastles. *Directeur Central des Constructions Navales* Dudebout referenced this requirement in a note to the Naval General Staff dated 28 April 1908 and also reported that gunnery trials just carried out in March against the discarded torpedo aviso *Lévrier* had shown that at ranges over 1,000 a 65mm gun could not inflict critical damage on light vessels, although it could damage machinery at shorter ranges. The ensuing design process resulted in a new 800-ton destroyer type with two 100mm and four 65mm guns and two twin 450mm deck torpedo mounts. (The 65mm was retained in the armament because it was easy to handle and had a high rate of fire.) Propulsion was to be exclusively by turbines, but great freedom was left to the builders to choose the type and disposition of the turbines and the number of screws. All of the ships were to have oil fired boilers and the contract speed was set at 31 knots. This programme was sent to prospective bidders on 31 May 1908 by the *Section technique*. The design specifications underwent some modifications in July, including the deletion of a bow torpedo tube. The ten 450-tonners in the 1908 budget (submitted on 11 May 1907) were reprogrammed as the first seven 800-tonners.

Although built to different designs, most of these ships had a similar silhouette because they all had four boilers located forward of the engine

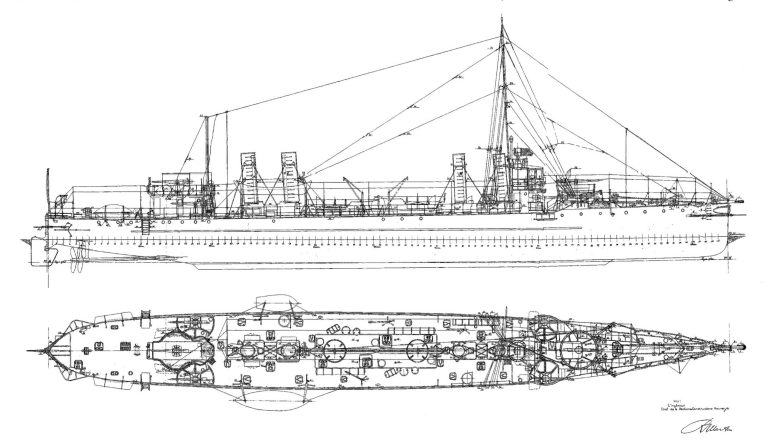

room. Each boiler had its own funnel except in *Casque*, in which all four boilers were installed facing in opposite directions from those in the otherwise similar *Bouclier*, putting boilers two and three back to back and able to exhaust into a single large funnel instead of two. All of the ships had two shafts except for *Casque* and *Bouclier* which had three. Another feature common to the 800-tonners was the raised forecastle, often with flat sides and a vertical bow. *Casque* was again an exception in that her forecastle had rounded turtleback edges, and some of the later ships had some outward flare to the sides of the bow and a slightly raked stem. They may be considered to fall into three groupings: an initial batch of twelve (1908 and 1909 budgets), a batch of six (1910 budget) that was able to take advantage of lessons learned from the first units of the first batch, and a final batch of three (1913 budget) including one experimental boat that again incorporated lessons from earlier boats.

All of the early 800-tonners were too lightly built – as, in the French view, were the contemporary British 760-ton, 75-metre *Acorn* type destroyers. All had to be reinforced in the stern to resist the vibrations from the screws and from pitching. The vertical slab sides in some of the early ships (particularly *Fourche*, *Faulx*, and *Bouclier*) were found to be something to avoid in future designs, and the rounded or V-shaped underwater stern lines of *Casque*, *Bouclier*, and *Boutefeu* were preferred to the concave lines aft of *Cimeterre*, *Dague*, *Fourche*, and *Faulx*. Overall the lines of *Boutefeu*, with some outward flare to hull sides in the bow, relatively high freeboard amidships and aft, and V-shaped stern lines, were considered particularly worth reproducing. The masts were found to be too flimsy as soon as the first ships, *Casque* and *Bouclier*, began trials. In 1914 Toulon tried a tripod mast on *Dague*, repeated it on *Commandant Lucas*, and then on the three last 800-tonners. The navigating bridges were also found to be too low, their deck being only 75cm above the forecastle and visibility being

---

Inboard profile and deck view of the squadron destroyers *Cimeterre* and *Dague*. The plans were signed at Bordeaux on 9 January 1913 by the director of the Chantiers et Ateliers de la Gironde and certified to represent the ships as fitted by the navy's control officer, V. Bricart.

impaired by the forward 100mm gun. During the war some were enlarged by the addition of a sea cabin, an upper bridge for the gunnery officer and lookouts and longer bridge wings. Wartime modifications increased the displacement of these ships to between 900 and 950 tons and reduced their maximum speed to around 26 knots.

While their 100mm and 65mm gun armament was considered satisfactory their torpedo armament was inadequate for combat use. Their twin tubes were originally to have been placed on the centreline but they would have had to be raised very high over the deck for the rear of the torpedo to clear the deck edge after firing and the tubes were instead placed on the sides. There, however, only two torpedoes could be launched per side, which was not enough for a torpedo action. This problem was addressed in the design of the last 800-tonner, *Enseigne Gabolde*, in which two triple tube mounts were placed on the centreline. During the war one 75mm or 47mm gun on a high angle mounting was added to some of the ships in response to the growing air and submarine threat along with two 8mm Model 1907 St-Étienne machine guns on high-angle mountings and 8 or 10 depth bombs.

The programme as executed was as follows:

7 x 800-tonners: M66-72, 1908 budget, 1909 fleet list (originally 450-tonners)

8 x 800-tonners: M73-80, 1909 budget, 1911 fleet list (M73-75 also in the 1908 budget as 450-tonners)

3 x 800-tonners: M81-83, 1910 budget, 1911 fleet list

3 x 800-tonners: M86-88, 1913 budget, 1914 fleet list

---

**CIMETERRE Class.** *Contre-torpilleurs d'escadre.* C.A. Gironde 800-ton type with two 100mm guns on the centreline and four 65mm guns on the sides, four torpedo tubes in pairs on the sides aft of the funnels, a forecastle, four funnels in two adjacent pairs, and one tall mast forward and one short radio mast aft. Designed by builder to Navy specifications.

*Cimeterre* and *Dague* had Bréguet turbines on two propeller shafts. Each shaft had a pair of turbines, one HP and one LP, with the HP exhausting

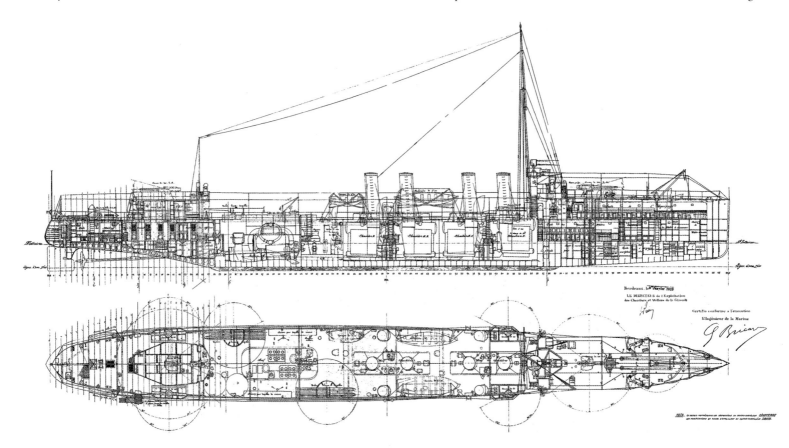

into the LP. The Bréguet turbines had one clear advantage over the other types in that they did not need to be warmed up before use, allowing these two ships to get underway with one hour notice while *Bouclier* with her Parsons turbines needed three hours between lighting off and leaving the pier. The initial trials of *Cimeterre* in June-August 1911 were unsatisfactory and the turbines were modified to reduce rotational speed. New trials in March 1912 were also disappointing, causing the screws to be changed. Lessons learned from these trials made the trials of *Dague* much easier. The underwater hull lines aft were concave over the screws, improving water flow and increasing trial speeds but also causing heavy pounding when the ship pitched and overall weakness in the stern structure.

**Dimensions & tons:** 77.200m oa, 76.000m wl and pp x 7.804m wl (8.040m outside the rubbing strakes). 733.830t disp (designed), 747.007t & 733.830t (trials, *Cimeterre* & *Dague*), and 894t & 876t (normal, same). Draught: (designed) 2.940m mean and aft (real, under the rudder). Men: 81/88 including 4 officers.

**Machinery:** 13,500shp designed at 16kg/cm² boiler pressure. Trials (*Dague*, 4.4.1912) 32.84kts, (*Cimeterre*, 26.7.1912) 31.15kts. 2 screws. 4 Bréguet turbines. 4 Du Temple boilers. 120t oil (normal), 140t oil (max).

**Guns:** 2 x 100mm/45 M1893 guns (fore and aft), 4 x 65mm/50 M1902 (on sides near the 100mm). Later added 1 x 47mm AA in *Cimeterre*. **Torpedoes:** 4 tubes for 450mm M1906 torpedoes in two twin deck mounts (one on each side aft of the funnels, en echelon).

*Cimeterre* (M66) C.A. Gironde, Bordeaux-Lormont/Maison Bréguet, Paris (Bréguet turbines).
On list 1.1909. Ord: 26.8.1908. K: 1909. L: 13.4.1911. Comm: 6.1911 (trials), 10.9.1912 (full).
Budget 1908. Arrived Lorient 20.6.1911 for trials. Arrived at Toulon 27.10.1912 and joined the 1st destroyer squadron of the *1re Armée navale*. Joined the new 6th destroyer squadron of the *1re Armée navale*

when it was formed 1.1.1914. War service in the Adriatic from early 1916. Struck 10.7.1926.

*Dague* (M67) C.A. Gironde, Bordeaux-Lormont/Maison Bréguet, Paris (Bréguet turbines).
On list 1.1909. Ord: 26.8.1908. K: 1910. L: 27.6.1911. Comm: 20.2.1912 (trials), 20.5.1912 (full).
Budget 1908. Completion delayed to incorporate lessons from early trials of *Cimeterre*. Arrived Lorient 14.1.1912 for trials. Arrived at Toulon 3.8.1912 and joined the 1st destroyer squadron of the *1re Armée navale*. Sunk 24.2.1915 by a floating mine off Durazzo while attached to the *1re Armée navale*. Struck 25.2.1915.

--------

**FOURCHE Class.** *Contre-torpilleurs d'escadre.* De la Brosse et Fouché 800-ton type with general configuration as *Cimeterre*. Designed by builder to Navy specifications,

The plans for *Fourche* and *Faulx* were signed by Laubeuf (hull) and Rateau (machinery). Each of the two propeller shafts in these ships had one Rateau main propulsion turbine. There was also a cruising turbine on the port shaft and an astern turbine on the starboard shaft. The hull sides of these ships at the bow were completely vertical. This and the fact that the bows with their forecastles were heavy made them poor sea boats. The underwater hull lines aft were concave over the screws, producing heavy pounding during pitching and other problems similar to those encountered in the 450-ton *Voltigeur*. De la Brosse et Fouché became the Ateliers and Chantiers de Bretagne in 1909.

The squadron destroyer *Fourche*, one of the first batch of 800-ton destroyers. The sides of her bow were flat and nearly vertical. She was assigned the bow letter F in June 1912; by March 1914 it was FR. *(NHHC from ONI, NH-64467)*

**Dimensions & tons:** 75.152m oa, 74.95m pp x 7.65m wl (7.93m outside the rubbing strakes). 727.383t & 733.822t disp (trials, *Fourche* & *Faulx,*) 859t & 867t (normal, same). Draught: 2.89m aft. Men: 81 including 4 officers.
**Machinery:** 12,500shp designed at 16kg/cm² boiler pressure. Trials (*Fourche*, 11.9.1911) 32.11kts, (*Faulx*, 12.9.1912) 32.01kts. 2 screws. Rateau turbines. 4 Du Temple boilers. 120t oil (normal), 140t oil (max).
**Guns:** 2 x 100mm/45 M1893 guns (fore and aft), 4 x 65mm/50 M1902 (on sides near the 100mm). **Torpedoes:** 4 tubes for 450mm M1906 torpedoes in two twin deck mounts (one on each side aft of the funnels, en echelon).

*Fourche* (M68) De la Brosse et Fouché, Nantes/De la Brosse, Nantes (Rateau turbines).
On list 1.1909. Ord: 26.8.1908. K: 1909. L: 21.10.1910. Comm: 20.7.1911 (trials), 4.12.1911 (full).
Budget 1908. Left Nantes for trials at Lorient 13.5.1911. Arrived at Toulon 24.3.1912 and joined the 1st destroyer squadron of the *1re Armée navale* 1.4.1912. War service in the Adriatic from 12.1915. Torpedoed 23.6.1916 by the Austrian submarine *U-15* in the Strait of Otranto.

*Faulx* (M69) De la Brosse et Fouché, Nantes/De la Brosse, Nantes (Rateau turbines).
On list 1.1909. Ord: 26.8.1908. K: 1909. L: 2.2.1911. Comm: 15.2.1912 (trials), 1.11.1912 (full).
Budget 1908. Arrived at Lorient from Nantes for trials 28.12.1911. Major problems with the screws delayed trials. Arrived at Toulon 29.12.1912 and joined the 1st destroyer squadron of the *1re Armée navale*. War service in the Adriatic from early 1916. Sank 10.4.1918 after colliding with *Mangini* in the Strait of Otranto.

---

**BOUTEFEU.** *Contre-torpilleur d'escadre.* Dyle et Bacalan 800-ton type with general configuration as *Cimeterre* except that the funnels were equally spaced. Designed by builder to Navy specifications.

*Boutefeu* had two propeller shafts, each driven by one Zoelly main propulsion turbine. During trials in October 1911 the rotational speed of the turbines was judged excessive and it was reduced by removing several rotors in the LP turbine and reducing the diameter of the screws. Problems continued to be encountered with the turbines through the summer of 1912 and continued after full commissioning. The least successful of the 800-tonners, *Boutefeu* was in special reserve for most of 1915 and only reported to her squadron at Brindisi on 18 January 1916.

**Dimensions & tons:** 77.260m oa, 76.485m pp x 7.880m wl (8.164m outside the rubbing strakes). 735.339t disp (trials), 862t (normal). Draught: 2.942m aft. Men: 81 including 4 officers.
**Machinery:** 14,000shp designed at 16kg/cm² boiler pressure. Trials (11.1912) 31.42kts. 2 screws. Zoelly turbines. 4 Dyle et Bacalan boilers. 120t oil (normal), 140t oil (max).
**Guns:** 2 x 100mm/45 M1893 guns (fore and aft), 4 x 65mm/50 M1902 (on sides near the 100mm). **Torpedoes:** 4 tubes for 450mm M1906 torpedoes in two twin deck mounts (one on each side aft of the funnels, en echelon).

*Boutefeu* (M70) Dyle et Bacalan, Bordeaux-Bacalan/Schneider, Creusot (Zoelly turbines).
On list 1.1909. Ord: 26.8.1908. K: 1909. L: 2.5.1911. Comm: 1.9.1911 (trials), 25.11.1912 (full).
Budget 1908. Arrived at Lorient from Bordeaux 28.8.1911. Arrived at Toulon 16.1.1913 and joined the 1st destroyer squadron of the *1re Armée navale*. War service in the Adriatic from early 1916. Mined off Brindisi 15.5.1917 in a field laid by *UC-25*.

---

**BOUCLIER.** *Contre-torpilleur d'escadre.* Normand 800-ton type with general configuration as *Cimeterre* except that the funnels were nearly equally spaced. Designed by builder to Navy specifications.

The hull plans for *Bouclier* were produced by Émile Galodée of the Normand firm, who also started those of *Francis Garnier*. The ship's Parsons turbines were built by the *Cie. Électro-Mécanique* at Le Bourget. The turbine installation consisted of a HP turbine on the centre shaft that exhausted into two LP turbines, one on each wing shaft. For low speeds there was a cruising turbine on the starboard shaft that exhausted into the HP turbine on the centre shaft. In this mode all four turbines were running and the starboard shaft was thus more heavily loaded than the port shaft because it had two turbines. This ship and the other with the same plant, *Casque*, produced excellent trial speeds and fuel efficiency but the three-screw plant with interdependent engines made manoeuvring the ship difficult. To get independent operation of the wing shafts the high speed turbine on the centre shaft had to be isolated and a large number of valves had to be operated to get one wing shaft going ahead and the other astern or to get them going at different speeds. No such problems existed in the other 800-tonners, which had two shafts each with its own independent turbine installation. The Normand-Sigaudy boilers in *Bouclier* and *Casque* were considered far better than the Du Temple, Guyot-Du Temple, and Dyle and Bacalan boilers in other 800-tonners because they were the only ones designed specifically for oil firing. In the others the furnaces were not large enough to fully burn the oil introduced through the nozzles. In contrast with the other early 800-tonners *Bouclier* had a slight outward flare in the hull sides at the bow which aided in seakeeping, although her low stern made her wet aft.

**Dimensions & tons:** 72.32m oa, 71.20m wl & pp x 7.57m wl (7.814m outside the rubbing strakes). 660.44t disp (trials), 709.285t (designed), 790t (normal). Draught: (designed) 2.8196m mean, 2.980m aft (real). Men: 81/88 including 4 officers.
**Machinery:** 13,000shp designed at 16kg/cm² boiler pressure. Trials (18.9.1911) 35.339kts at 1034.2rpm. 3 screws. Parsons turbines. 4 Normand-Sigaudy boilers. 120t oil (normal), 140t oil (max). Range with normal oil 1,170nm @ 14kts (designed).
**Guns:** 2 x 100mm/45 M1893 guns (fore and aft), 4 x 65mm/50 M1902 (on sides near the 100mm). Later added 1 x 75mm AA.
**Torpedoes:** 4 tubes for 450mm M1909R torpedoes in two twin deck mounts (one on each side aft of the funnels, en echelon).

*Bouclier* (M71) Augustin Normand, Le Havre/C.E.M. Le Bourget (Parsons turbines).
On list 1.1909. Ord: 25.11.1908. K: 1909. L: 29.6.1911. Comm: 23.8.1911 (trials), 10.1.1912 (full).
Budget 1908. Arrived at Toulon 26.2.1912 from Cherbourg, joined the 1st destroyer squadron of the *1re Armée navale* 1.4.1912 but then became *hors rang* (outside the regular structure) as the flagship of the Destroyer and Submarine Flotillas of the *1re Armée navale*. War service in the Adriatic from 5.1915. Renamed *Bouclier II* 1932 to free name for new ship. Condemned 15.2.1933 at Toulon, for sale by the Domaines 1933-1935.

---

**CASQUE.** *Contre-torpilleur d'escadre.* FCM Le Havre 800-ton type with general configuration as *Cimeterre* except that the second and third funnels were merged into a single large funnel. Designed by builder to Navy specifications.

The hull of *Casque* was designed by MM. Bernard and Bonnet of the Graville yard and the machinery was designed by M. Sigaudy of the former Mazeline plant at Le Havre, both establishments now owned by the Forges et Chantiers de la Méditerranée. The Parsons turbine installation was built by the *Cie. Électro-Mécanique* at Le Bourget as in *Bouclier*. The boilers were the same model as in *Bouclier* but installed differently. The form of her bow

differed from that of the other 800-tonners in that it was shaped like a turtleback as in the 300-tonners and 450-tonners (although it was a deck higher), with curved edges and a slight downward slope towards the bow. Like the earlier destroyers her bow was designed to pierce waves and shed water off the rounded deck easily, while the high bows in the other 800-tonners were designed to cut through the waves, throwing the water to either side and keeping the flat deck dry. Comparative trials of *Casque* and *Bouclier* favoured the high slightly flared bow of the latter. *Casque* was the first 800-tonner to be launched and the first to run trials.

**Dimensions & tons:** 75.15m oa, 75.00m pp x 7.53m wl (7.84m outside the rubbing strakes). 667.671t disp (trials), 820t (normal). Draught: 2.99 m aft. Men: 81/88 including 4 officers.
**Machinery:** 14,400shp designed at 16kg/cm² boiler pressure. Trials (28.6.1911) 34.897kts. 3 screws. Parsons turbines. 4 Normand-Sigaudy boilers. 120t oil (normal), 140t oil (max).
**Guns:** 2 x 100mm/45 M1893 guns (fore and aft), 4 x 65mm/50 M1902 (on sides near the 100mm). **Torpedoes:** 4 tubes for 450mm M1909R torpedoes in two twin deck mounts (one on each side aft of the funnels, en echelon).

*Casque* (M72) F.C. Méditerranée, Le Havre-Graville/C.E.M. Le Bourget (Parsons turbines).
On list 1.1909. Ord: 2.12.1908. K: 1909. L: 25.8.1910. Comm: 20.5.1911 (trials), 16.10.1911 (full).
Budget 1908. Left Le Havre for Cherbourg 12.5.1911. Preliminary underway trials 8-9.5.1911. Arrived at Toulon 12.11.1911 from Cherbourg and joined the 1st destroyer squadron of the *1re Armée navale*. War service in the Adriatic from 12.1915. Off main list 1925 and for sale at Toulon 1925-1926. Condemned 26.3.1926. Struck 14.9.1926. Sold 25.5.1927 to the Société du Matériel Naval du Midi.

---

**CAPITAINE MEHL.** *Contre-torpilleur d'escadre, Torpilleur d'escadre* (1913). A.C. Loire 800-ton type with general configuration as *Cimeterre*. Designed by builder to Navy specifications.

The Parsons turbines for *Capitaine Mehl* were built by the *Cie. Électro-Mécanique* at Le Bourget. For this and the next two ships Parsons replaced the complex three-shaft design in *Bouclier* and *Casque* with a simpler two shaft design without a cruising turbine. In order to improve the efficiency of the turbines, Parsons installed upstream of the reaction stages, three impulse rotors receiving the high-pressure steam coming from the boilers. Problems were encountered with the dummy rings in the reaction stages and all three ships produced disappointing initial trial results. However, when recommissioned for trials 23 September 1913 after three months of turbine modifications *Capitaine Mehl* made a relatively satisfactory 31.772 knots.

**Dimensions & tons:** 78.10m oa, 78.10m pp x 7.778m wl (8.214m outside the rubbing strakes). 768.625t disp (trials), 836t (normal). Draught: 2.57m aft. Men: 81/88 including 4 officers.
**Machinery:** 15,000shp designed at 16kg/cm² boiler pressure. Speed 31kts. Trials (3.10.1913) 31.772kts. 2 screws. Parsons turbines. 4 Du Temple boilers. 120t oil (normal), 140t oil (max).
**Guns:** 2 x 100mm/45 M1893 guns (fore and aft), 4 x 65mm/50 M1902 (on sides near the 100mm). Later added 1 x 75mm AA.
**Torpedoes:** 4 tubes for 450mm M1909R torpedoes in two twin deck mounts (one on each side aft of the funnels, en echelon).

*Capitaine Mehl* (M73) A.C. Loire, Nantes/C.E.M. Le Bourget (Parsons turbines).
On list 1.1911. Ord: 16.2.1910 (contract 9.6.1910). K: 1910. L: 20.4.1912. Comm: 14.6.1913 (trials), 5.11.1913 (full).
Budget 1908 (delayed to 1909). To Lorient 22.12.1912 for lengthy trials, initially by builder. Assigned *hors rang* as a flagship of the Destroyer

and Submarine Flottillas of the *2e Escadre légère* 11.1913 (the others in this status being *Dunois* and *Francis Garnier*, see also *Bouclier*). War service in the Channel. Struck 10.7.1926.

---

**DEHORTER.** *Contre-torpilleur d'escadre, Torpilleur d'escadre* (1913), Ch. Penhoët 800-ton type with general configuration as *Cimeterre*. Designed by builder to Navy specifications.

*Dehorter* had hybrid Parsons turbines with both reaction and impulse stages like those in *Capitaine Mehl*. Trial results were disappointing, in part because of the turbines and in part because she ran her trials with a heavy displacement of 829 tons instead of 750 to 772 tons for most of the others. The height of her bow and the slight outward flare of its sides were both improvements over the strictly vertical bows in some of the earlier 800-tonners.

**Dimensions & tons:** 76.32m oa, 75.50m pp x 7.73m wl (7.814m outside the rubbing strakes). 772.485t disp (trials), 870t (normal). Draught: 2.925m aft. Men: 81/88 including 4 officers.
**Machinery:** 16,000shp designed at 16kg/cm² boiler pressure. Speed 31kts. Trials (26.2.1913) 29.314kts. 2 screws. Parsons turbines. 4 Du Temple boilers. 120t oil (normal), 140t oil (max).
**Guns:** 2 x 100mm/45 M1893 guns (fore and aft), 4 x 65mm/50 M1902 (on sides near the 100mm). **Torpedoes:** 4 tubes for 450mm M1909R torpedoes in two twin deck mounts (one on each side aft of the funnels, en echelon).

*Dehorter* (M74) Ch. Penhoët, Rouen-Grand Quévilly/Ch. Penhoët, Saint Nazaire (Parsons turbines).
On list 1.1911. Ord: 16.2.1910. K: 28.11.1910. L: 18.4.1912. Comm: 20.9.1912 (trials), c3.1913 (full).
Budget 1908 (delayed to 1909). Left the yard 18.9.1912. By 1.10.1913 had joined the 1st destroyer squadron of the *1re Armée navale*. Joined the new 6th destroyer squadron of the *1re Armée navale* when it was formed 1.1.1914, reassigned 10.6.1914 as leader of the Mediterranean submarine flotilla. War service as submarine flotilla flagship in the *1re Armée navale*, participated in the landings at Athens 1.12.1916, in action in the Adriatic 22.12.1916. Off main list 1926 and for sale at Brest as a patrol craft 1926-1928. Struck 15.2.1933. Sunk 11.1933 when the merchantman *Jamaique* collided with her in the approaches to the Loire River while the merchant tug *Doctor Roux* was towing her from Brest to Nantes for demolition.

---

**FRANCIS GARNIER.** *Contre-torpilleur d'escadre, Torpilleur d'escadre* (1913), Normand 800-ton type with general configuration as *Cimeterre* except that the funnels were nearly equally spaced. Designed by builder to Navy specifications

The design for *Francis Garnier* was based on Normand's *Bouclier* with slightly increased dimensions. She had hybrid Parsons turbines like those in *Capitaine Mehl* and *Dehorter* with similarly disappointing trial results. After reaching a maximum of 29.84 knots in trials between December 1912 and July 1913 she underwent turbine modifications but these failed to produce any improvement in maximum speed. This was the first ship in which exhaust steam from the auxiliary machinery was used to heat the feed water before it entered the boiler, an efficiency enhancement that was soon universally adopted. This ship shared a design defect with *Bouclier* in that her deck sloped down towards the stern, making her unusually wet aft.

**Dimensions & tons:** 75.36m oa, 74.00m pp x 7.644m wl (7.834m outside the rubbing strakes). 746.127t disp (trials), 780t (designed), 832t (normal). Draught: 3.26m aft. Men: 81/88 including 4 officers.
**Machinery:** 18,000shp designed at 16kg/cm² boiler pressure. Speed 31kts. Trials 29.84kts. 2 screws. Parsons turbines. 4 Normand-Sigaudy boilers. 120t oil (normal), 140t oil (max).

**Guns:** 2 x 100mm/45 M1893 guns (fore and aft), 4 x 65mm/50 M1902 (on sides near the 100mm). **Torpedoes:** 4 tubes for 450mm M1909R torpedoes in two twin deck mounts (one on each side aft of the funnels, en echelon).

*Francis Garnier* (M75) Augustin Normand, Le Havre/C.E.M. Le Bourget (Parsons turbines).
On list 1.1911. Ord: 19.1.1910. K: 1910. L: 1.10.1912.
  Comm: 3.4.1913 (trials), 9.2.1914 (full).
Budget 1908 (delayed to 1909). Assigned *hors rang* as a flagship of the Destroyer and Submarine Flottillas of the *2e Escadre légère* 20.2.1914. War service in the Channel. Off main list 1925 and for sale at Toulon 1925-1926. Struck 10.2.1926.

-------

**COMMANDANT BORY.** *Contre-torpilleur d'escadre, Torpilleur d'escadre* (1913). Dyle et Bacalan 800-ton type with general configuration as *Cimeterre* except that the funnels were equally spaced. Designed by builder to Navy specifications.

Initial trials of *Commandant Bory* at Lorient in late 1912 revealed serious problems with her Zoelly turbines. The turbines were removed in January 1913 and sent back to Schneider for work and she was only again presented for trials on 11 December 1913, when problems with the propellers were revealed. The ship finally met the conditions on 23 June 1914 for starting official trials and her turbines performed well, but she failed to make her contract speed, because her boilers could not maintain effective combustion of oil fuel at speeds over 24 knots. She remained limited to around 24 knots in service, while most of the other 800-tonners could push to 26 or 27 knots and *Casque* could reach 29.

**Dimensions & tons:** 77,260m oa, 76.525m pp x 7.776m wl (8.164m outside the rubbing strakes). 741t disp (trials), 780t (designed), 805t (normal). Draught: 2.985m aft. Men: 81/88 including 4 officers.
**Machinery:** 14,115shp designed at 16 or 18kg/cm² boiler pressure. Speed

Inboard profile and deck view of the squadron destroyer (*torpilleur d'escadre*) *Comandant Lucas*. The plans were signed at Toulon on 29 May 1915 by naval constructor Wisdorff.

31kts. Trials (16.7.1914) 30.68kts at 667rpm. 2 screws. Zoelly turbines. 4 Dyle et Bacalan boilers. 120t oil (normal), 140t oil (max).
**Guns:** 2 x 100mm/45 M1893 guns (fore and aft), 4 x 65mm/50 M1902 (on sides near the 100mm). **Torpedoes:** 4 tubes for 450mm M1909R torpedoes in two twin deck mounts (one on each side aft of the funnels, en echelon).

*Commandant Bory* (M76) Dyle et Bacalan, Bordeaux-Bacalan/Schneider, Creusot (Zoelly turbines).
On list 1.1911. Ord: 12.1.1910 (contract). K: 6.1910. L: 14.9.1912.
  Comm: 1.11.1912 (trials), 2.8.1914 (full).
  Budget 1909. Joined the 6th destroyer squadron of the *1re Armée navale* 8.1914. War service in the Adriatic from 5.1915. Struck 29.7.1926.

-------

**COMMANDANT RIVIERE.** *Contre-torpilleur d'escadre, Torpilleur d'escadre* (1913). C.A. Gironde 800-ton type with general configuration as *Cimeterre*. Designed by builder to Navy specifications.

The design for *Commandant Rivière* was based on that of *Cimeterre* and *Dague* with practically the same dimensions. The concave lines in the stern of *Cimeterre* were somewhat attenuated in the new design although the large overhang at the stern was retained. As was their custom, C. A. Gironde launched the ship virtually complete with the machinery installed on the ways. She was fitted with turbines built by Bréguet.

**Dimensions & tons:** 77.35m oa, 76.40m pp x 7.820m wl (8.090m outside the rubbing strakes). 764.755t disp (designed), 800t (normal). Draught: (designed) 2.730m mean, 2.730m aft (keel line projected), 3.000m aft (real, under the rudder). Men: 81/88 including 4 officers.
**Machinery:** 14,500shp designed at 16kg/cm² boiler pressure.
  Speed 31kts. Trials (22.5.1913) 32.35kts. 2 screws. Bréguet turbines. 4 Du Temple boilers. 120t oil (normal), 140t oil (max).
**Guns:** 2 x 100mm/45 M1893 guns (fore and aft), 4 x 65mm/50 M1902 (on sides near the 100mm). **Torpedoes:** 4 tubes for 450mm M1909R torpedoes in two twin deck mounts (one on each side aft of the funnels, en echelon).

*Commandant Rivière* (M77) C.A. Gironde, Bordeaux-Lormont/Maison Bréguet, Paris (Bréguet turbines).

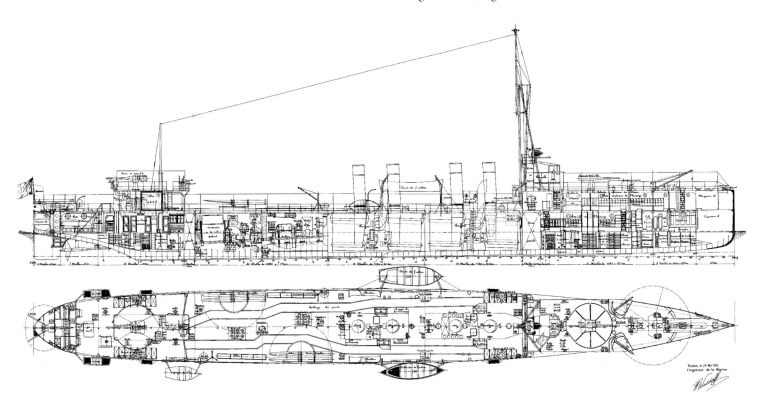

On list 1.1911. Ord: 16.2.1910. K: 1910. L: 2.10.1912.
   Comm: 20.11.1912 (trials), 15.6.1913 (full).
Budget 1909. To Lorient 20.11.1912 for trials. Arrived at Toulon
   9.8.1913, by 1.10.1913 had joined the 1st destroyer squadron of the *1re
   Armée navale*. Joined the new 6th destroyer squadron of the *1re Armée
   navale* when it was formed 1.1.1914. War service in the Adriatic from
   5.1915. Condemned 15.2.1933, for sale by the Domaines 1933-35.

---

***COMMANDANT LUCAS.*** *Contre-torpilleur d'escadre, Torpilleur d'escadre*
(1913). Toulon Dyd. 800-ton type with general configuration as *Cimeterre*.
Designed by the *Section technique.*

The design for *Commandant Lucas* was based on that of *Commandant Mehl*
and the ship was given Bréguet turbines built at Indret. In its designs for
this ship, the *Bisson* class, and *Protet*, the *Section technique* made the hull
more robust than in the earlier 800-tonners at a cost of about 50 tons.
Because of this weight increase their contract speed was reduced from
31 knots to 30 knots. However, these four *Section technique* ships and their
contract-built contemporary *Mangini* retained the vertical bow side plating
with lack of flare of most of the earlier 800-tonners with the corresponding
penalties in seakeeping.

**Dimensions & tons:** 78.100m oa, 78.100m wl & pp x 7.752m wl
   (7.964m outside the rubbing strakes 1.050m above wl). 772.354t disp
   (designed), 862t (normal). Draught: (designed) 2.690m mean, 3.050m
   aft (keel line projected), 2.942m aft (real). Men: 81/88 including 4
   officers.
**Machinery:** 16,000shp designed at 16kg/cm² boiler pressure. Speed
   30kts. Trials 30.02kts. 2 screws. Bréguet turbines. 4 Guyot-Du Temple
   boilers built at Indret. 120t oil (normal), 140t oil (max).
**Guns:** 2 x 100mm/45 M1893 guns (fore and aft), 4 x 65mm/50 M1902
   (on sides near the 100mm). **Torpedoes:** 4 tubes for 450mm M1909R
   torpedoes in two twin deck mounts (one on each side aft of the
   funnels, en echelon).

*Commandant Lucas* (M78) Toulon Dyd/Indret (Bréguet turbines).
On list 1.1911. Ord: 1.10.1911. K: 2.1912. L: 11.7.1914.
   Comm: 11.3.1915 (trials), 5.1915 (full).
Budget 1909 (delayed to 1910). Construction reassigned from contract to
   Toulon 1911. Joined the destroyer flotilla of the *1re Armée navale*
   4.7.1915, to the Adriatic 12.1915. Condemned 15.2.1933, for sale by
   the Domaines 1933-1934.

---

***MAGON.*** *Contre-torpilleur d'escadre, Torpilleur d'escadre* (1913). A.C.
Bretagne 800-ton type with general configuration as *Cimeterre* except for a
slight clipper shape to the bow. Designed by builder to Navy specifications.

*Magon* had not only some outward flare to the sides of the bow but a slight
clipper profile to the stem, which was destroyed in a collision and replaced
with a straight bow. A.C. Bretagne was the new name for De la Brosse et
Fouché at Nantes.

**Dimensions & tons:** 83.00m oa, 78.10m pp x 7.80m wl (8.063m outside the rubbing strakes). 851t disp (designed), 912t (normal).
   Draught: 3.10m aft. Men: 81/88 including 4 officers.
**Machinery:** 18,000shp designed at 16 or 18kg/cm² boiler pressure. Speed
   30kts. Trials 32.02kts. 2 screws. Rateau turbines. 4 Du Temple boilers.
   140t oil (normal), 160t oil (max).
**Guns:** 2 x 100mm/45 M1893 guns (fore and aft), 4 x 65mm/50 M1902
   (on sides near the 100mm) . Later added 1 x 75mm AA.
   **Torpedoes:** 4 tubes for 450mm M1909R torpedoes in two twin deck
   mounts (one on each side aft of the funnels, en echelon).

*Magon* (M79) A.C. Bretagne, Nantes/ACB, Nantes (Rateau turbines).
On list 1.1911. Ord: 24.10.1910 (contract) and 29.5.1911. K: 1.1911.

L: 19.4.1913. Comm: 19.1.1914 (trials), 10.6.1914 (full).
Budget 1909 (delayed to 1910). Left Nantes for Lorient 17.8.1913, trials
   delayed by turbine damage. Briefly joined the 6th destroyer squadron
   of the *1re Armée navale* at Toulon in mid-1914. War service in the
   Adriatic from 5.1915, to the Channel late 1915. Off main list 1925
   and for sale at Brest 1925-1926. Struck 3.5.1926.

---

***MANGINI.*** *Contre-torpilleur d'escadre, Torpilleur d'escadre* (1913).
Schneider 800-ton type with general configuration as *Cimeterre*. Designed
by builder to Navy specifications.

The delay between laying down and launching *Mangini* was probably due
to the need to modify the Zoelly turbines as was being done in
*Commandant Bory*. The hull was built at Schneider's yard at Chalon-sur-
Saône and floated down the Saône and Rhône rivers in a specially built
transporter dock to Saint Louis de Rhône where her superstructure, funnels
and mast were installed. This work was completed January 1914 but her
trials were delayed by a serious boiler room fire.

**Dimensions & tons:** 78.50m oa, 78.10m pp x 7.800m wl (8.063m outside the rubbing strakes). 805t disp (designed), 850t (normal).
   Draught: 3.05m aft. Men: 81/88 including 4 officers.
**Machinery:** 15,800shp designed at 16 or 18kg/cm² boiler pressure. Speed
   30kts. Trials 30.93kts. 2 screws. Zoelly turbines. 4 Du Temple boilers.
   140t oil (normal), 150t oil (max).
**Guns:** 2 x 100mm/45 M1893 guns (fore and aft), 4 x 65mm/50 M1902
   (on sides near the 100mm). Later added 1 x 75mm AA.
   **Torpedoes:** 4 tubes for 450mm M1909R torpedoes in two twin deck
   mounts (one on each side aft of the funnels, en echelon).

*Mangini* (M80) Schneider, Chalon-sur-Saône/Schneider, Creusot (Zoelly
   turbines).
On list 1.1911. Ord: 22.2.1911 (contract) and 29.5.1911. K: 6.1911.
   L: 31.3.1913. Comm: 10.4.1914 (trials), 8.8.1914 (full).
Budget 1909 (delayed to 1910). Joined the destroyer flotilla of the *1re
   Armée navale* at Toulon upon completion of trials in 1914. War service
   in the Adriatic from 12.1915. Condemned 15.2.1933, for sale by the
   Domaines 1933-1934.

---

***BISSON*** Class. *Contre-torpilleur d'escadre, Torpilleur d'escadre* (1913),
Toulon Dyd. 800-ton type with general configuration as *Cimeterre*.
Designed by the *Section technique*

The design for *Bisson* and *Renaudin* was based on that of *Commandant
Mehl* except for a reduction of the overhang of the stern obtained by lengthening the straight portion of the keel aft by about four metres. They were
given Bréguet turbines instead of the Parsons turbines in *Commandant
Mehl*.

**Dimensions & tons:** 78.100m oa, 78.100m wl & pp x 7.78m wl (7.964
   outside the rubbing strakes, 1.05m above wl). 772.354t disp (designed),
   800t (normal). Draught: (designed) 2.690m mean, 3.050m aft (keel
   line projected), 2.942m aft (real). Men: 81/88 including 4 officers.
**Machinery:** 15,000shp designed at 16kg/cm² boiler pressure. Speed
   30kts. Trials (*Bisson*) 31.05kts, (*Renaudin*) 30.55kts. 2 screws. Bréguet
   turbines. 4 Guyot-Du Temple boilers by Indret. 120t oil (normal),
   140t oil (max).
**Guns:** 2 x 100mm/45 M1893 guns (fore and aft), 4 x 65mm/50 M1902
   (on sides near the 100mm). **Torpedoes:** 4 tubes for 450mm M1909R
   torpedoes in two twin deck mounts (one on each side aft of the funnels, en echelon).

*Bisson* (M81) Toulon Dyd/Maison Bréguet, Paris (Bréguet turbines).
On list 1.1911. Ord: 23.11.1910. K: 1.1.1911. L: 12.9.1912.
   Comm: 10.2.1913 (trials), 8.9.1913 (full).

Budget 1909 (delayed to 1910). By 1.10.1913 had joined the 1st destroyer squadron of the *1re Armée navale*. Joined the new 6th destroyer squadron of the *1re Armée navale* when it was formed 1.1.1914. War service in the Adriatic from 5.1915. Condemned 15.2.1933, for sale by the Domaines 1933-1935.

*Renaudin* (M82) Toulon Dyd/Maison Bréguet, Paris (Bréguet turbines).
On list 1.1911. Ord: 23.11.1910. K: 1.2.1911. L: 20.3.1913.
    Comm: 10.7.1913 (trials), 1.1.1914 (full).
Budget 1909 (delayed to 1910). Joined the new 6th destroyer squadron of the *1re Armée navale* when it was formed 1.1.1914. War service in the Adriatic from 12.1915. Torpedoed and broken in half 18.3.1916 off Durazzo by the Austrian submarine *U-6*.

––––––––––

**PROTET.** *Contre-torpilleur d'escadre, Torpilleur d'escadre* (1913). Rochefort Dyd. 800-ton type with general configuration as *Cimeterre*. Designed by the *Section technique*.

The design for the hull of *Protet* was probably based on the design of *Commandant Mehl* and the ship received Parsons turbines. Each turbine casing contained, from forward to aft, a cruising turbine, a HP turbine, a medium pressure turbine, a low pressure turbine, and an astern turbine. The cruising and HP turbine shared a common steam injection line, and the cruising turbine when in use exhausted into the HP turbine. Speed trials were not run because of the outbreak of the war but on preliminary trials she made about 30 knots.

––––––––––

The squadron destroyer *Protet* at Cette after World War I. *Protet* joined the fleet a month after the start of the war in 1914. *(Postcard by Collection Artistique Pinède, Cette)*

**Dimensions & tons:** 78.100m oa, 78.100m wl & pp x 7.752m wl (8.216m outside the rubbing strakes). 772.805t disp (designed), 869.214t (normal). Draught: (designed) 2.690m mean, 3.050m aft (keel line projected), 2.942m aft (real). Men: 81/88 including 4 officers.
**Machinery:** 16,000shp designed at 16kg/cm² boiler pressure. Speed 30kts. 2 screws. Parsons turbines. 4 Guyot-Du Temple boilers. 120t oil (normal), 140t oil (max).
**Guns:** 2 x 100mm/45 M1893 guns (fore and aft), 4 x 65mm/50 M1902 (on sides near the 100mm). **Torpedoes:** 4 tubes for 450mm M1909R torpedoes in two twin deck mounts (one on each side aft of the funnels, en echelon).

*Protet* (M83) Rochefort Dyd/Indret (Parsons turbines).
On list 1.1911. Ord: 12.4.1911. K: end 1911. L: 15.10.1913.
    Comm: 1.4.1914 (trials), 3.9.1914 (full).
Budget 1910. Joined the new 6th destroyer squadron of the *1re Armée navale* on completion of trials soon after the start of the war. Part of the 1st destroyer squadron of the *1re Armée navale* in the Adriatic 10.1914. War service in the Adriatic from 5.1915 to late 1915, in action there 22.12.1916. Mutinous activities of engineering officer André Marty discovered 16.4.1919 at Galatz, Romania, three days before mutiny broke out in French battleships at Sevastopol. Annex to the school for communications (*école des transmissions*) 1931. Condemned 15.2.1933, for sale by the Domaines 1933-1935, barracks hulk for the school for communications at Toulon 1935-1936.

––––––––––

***MECANICIEN-PRINCIPAL LESTIN* Class.** *Torpilleurs d'escadre*. Rochefort Dyd. 800-ton type with general configuration as *Cimeterre*. Designed by the *Section technique*.

The naval programme voted by Parliament in 1912 reduced the number of

destroyers in the fleet to 52, thereby reducing the number to be ordered in the 1913 budget to three (*M.P. Lestin, Enseigne Roux,* and *Enseigne Gabolde*) and the number for 1914 to zero. The planners counted on the 300-tonners to be able to function as fleet destroyers, but war experience showed that larger destroyers were needed.

The three ships in the 1913 budget were named for officers who died heroically in the explosions of the battleships *Iéna* and *Liberté.* The first two, *Mécanicien-Principal Lestin* and *Enseigne Roux,* were designed by the *Section technique* as extrapolations of the *Bisson* design except for the propulsion machinery and more flare in the bow. Their hybrid Parsons turbines were as those in *Francis Garnier* and *Dehorter.* Although *Lestin* and *Roux* were well advanced when the war began they were suspended in August 1914, to be resumed at the beginning of 1915. The turbines and boilers of *Roux* (and probably *Lestin*) were only ordered on 6 February 1915. The ships were fitted from the outset to be able to operate as either minelayers or fast minesweepers. Their bow lines were not much better than in the earlier 800-tonners but they were both regarded by their commanders as excellent ships, handling and keeping the sea well.

**Dimensions & tons:** 82.60m oa, 82.00m wl & pp x 8.200m wl (8.614m outside the rubbing strakes). 896.062t disp (designed). 943 & 939t (normal, *Lestin* & *Roux*). Draught: (designed) 2.720m mean, 3.100m aft (keel line projected), 3.000m aft (real). Men: 81/97 including 4 officers.
**Machinery:** 17,000shp designed at 16kg/cm² boiler pressure. Speed 30kts. Trials (*Lestin*) 31.21kts, (*Roux*) 30.41kts. 2 screws. Parsons turbines. 4 Du Temple boilers. 140t oil (normal), 200t oil (max).
**Guns:** 2 x 100mm/45 M1893 guns (fore and aft), 4 x 65mm/50 M1902 (on sides near the 100mm). Later added 1 x 75mm AA.
   **Torpedoes:** 4 tubes for 450mm M1909R torpedoes in two twin deck mounts (one on each side aft of the funnels, en echelon).

*Mécanicien-Principal Lestin* (M86) Rochefort Dyd/A.C. Loire, Saint Denis (Parsons turbines).

Longitudinal and horizontal views (*plan de pitonnage*) of the squadron destroyers *Mécanicien Principal Lestin* and *Enseigne Roux.* The plans were signed at Rochefort on 23 March 1916.

On list 1.1914. Ord: 28.2.1913. K: 12.11.1913. L: 15.5.1915.
   Comm: c4.1916 (trials), accepted 9.6.1916.
Budget 1913. Began her career with the *1re Armée navale* in the Mediterranean, participated in the landings at Athens 1.12.1916, transferred to the Flanders Flotilla at Dunkirk at the beginning of 1918. Replaced *Dunois* as flagship of a squadron in the Baltic 7.1919. Struck 30.5.1936 (decision promulgated 15.7.1936).

*Enseigne Roux* (M87) Rochefort Dyd/A.C. Loire, Saint Denis (Parsons turbines).
On list 1.1914. Ord: 28.2.1913. K: 1.12.1913. L: 13.7.1915.
   Comm: 19.11.1915 (trials), 2.2.1916 (full).
Budget 1913. Joined the Flanders Flotilla at Dunkirk. upon completion. Struck 10.8.1937 (decision promulgated 18.10.1937). BU 1938 at Bizerte.

————

*ENSEIGNE GABOLDE. Torpilleur d'escadre.* Completed postwar with three 100mm guns on the centreline including one superfiring forward, four torpedo tubes in pairs on the centreline aft of the funnels, a forecastle, four funnels in two adjacent pairs (the first pair taller), and one tall mast forward and one short mast aft. Experimental ship designed by Normand.

A note from the Naval General Staff (EMG) to the *Section technique* dated 12 September 1912 took note of the problems with the trials of the first 800-tonners and suggested that new destroyers should be in the 800- to 1,000-ton range with a speed of 33 knots. It also recommended trying geared turbines as a remedy for the excessive fuel consumption of existing turbines. The 800-ton M88 in the 1913 budget became an experimental ship for geared turbines and her construction was assigned to France's most reliable destroyer builder, Normand, whose Chief Engineer, Fernand Fenaux, was to produce the detailed design after doing the necessary studies. The ship was named *Enseigne Gabolde* for an officer who died heroically in the explosion of the battleship *Liberté.* The Parsons turbines were built by the *Cie. Électro-Mécanique* at Le Bourget but the gearing was ordered directly from Parsons in England. The specifications below are for the prewar design by Fenaux. The turbine plant consisted of two independent groups of Parsons turbines each with a HP turbine (2,500rpm), a LP turbine (1,500rpm) and a cruising turbine (3,700rpm), all connected by reduction

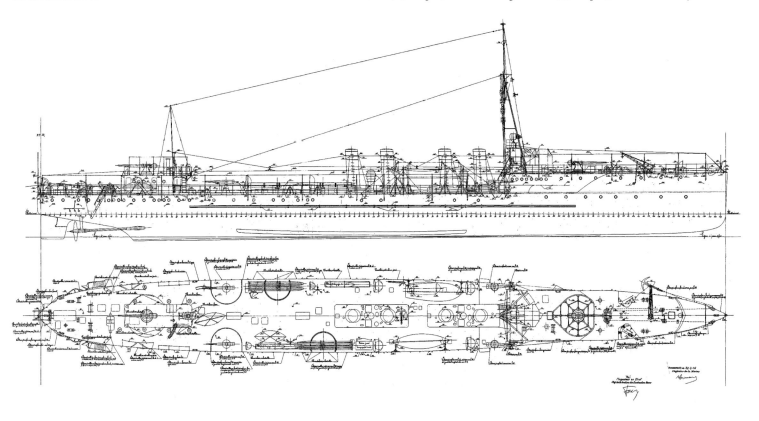

gearing to a shaft that turned at 440rpm at full power. Her triple torpedo tubes were a change from the earlier 800-tonners intended to overcome the fact that the earlier ships with two twin mounts, one to port and one to starboard, could only fire two torpedoes at the same time on either beam. *Gabolde* could fire six on one beam or three simultaneously on each beam.

*Enseigne Gabolde* had just been laid down when the war started and was immediately stopped because of mobilisation of shipyard workers. An order was given on 9 July 1915 to resume work but the turbine builder stated they were incapable of building the turbines. The builder finally agreed on 30 May 1916 but demanded a 17-months delay and the Navy gave up hope of finishing the ship during the war. Completed components were then used in repairs of other ships. The four boilers replaced the single oil-fired boiler in each of four destroyers, the ex-Argentine *Opiniâtre* and *Téméraire* and the ex-Greek *Panther* and *Ætos*. Her ventilators replaced those in *Bouclier* which had proven to be very inadequate and which were also worn out.

On 21 August 1918 the Naval General Staff asked the *Directeur Central des Constructions Navales* to resume work on *Enseigne Gabolde* without delay and listed changes to be made to the armament. The two triple 450mm torpedo tube mounts were to be replaced with two twin 550mm mounts, the two forward 65mm guns were to be replaced with a 100mm gun, and the 100mm guns were to be arranged as in the British W class with two forward including one superfiring and one on the stern, all on the centreline. The remaining two 65mm were to be fitted for antiaircraft fire, but the ship actually received a 75mm antiaircraft gun. Work resumed in September 1918. *Enseigne Gabolde* was also completed with a new type of bridge larger than in her predecessors. Her forward funnels were raised during trials.

**Dimensions & tons:** 82.600m oa, 82.076m wl, 82.076m pp x 8.210m wl (8.597 outside the rubbing strakes). 907.931t disp (designed). Draught: 2.740m mean, 3.120m aft (keel line projected), 3.245m aft (real, under the screws). Men: 86 including 6 officers.

**Machinery:** 20,000shp designed at 17kg/cm² boiler pressure. Speed 31kts. Trials (spring 1923) 26,000shp = 33.45kts. 2 screws. 6 Parsons

geared turbines. 4 Normand-Sigaudy boilers. 120t oil (normal), 200t (max). Range with normal oil 1,300nm @ 14kts.

**Guns:**
(1914, designed) 2 x 100mm/45 M1893 guns (fore and aft), 4 x 65mm/50 M1902 (sides). **Torpedoes:** 6 tubes for 450mm torpedoes in two triple deck mounts on the centreline.

(1918, redesigned) 3 x 100mm (including one superfiring forward), 2 x 65mm AA (completed with 1 x 75mm AA instead), 4 tubes for 550mm torpedoes in two twin deck mounts on the centreline.

*Enseigne Gabolde* (M88) Augustin Normand, Le Havre/C.E.M. Le Bourget (turbines), Parsons (gearing).
On list 1.1914. Ord: 22.10.1913. K: 29.6.1914. L: 23.4.1921. Comm: mid-1923 (trials), 1.1924 (full).
Budget 1913. Construction suspended late 1914, resumed 8.1918, and completed 7.1923. Struck 21.6.1938 (decision promulgated 5.7.1938). Sold 1940 at Toulon to BU.

---

**Observations on the 800-tonners**

On 6 March 1913, after assessing the technical strengths and weaknesses of each of the early 800-tonners for the *Comité Technique*, the Navy's permanent trials commission presented a more general observation. Noting that by leaving multiple shipbuilders free to produce their own designs, even if following a general specification established by the navy, the Navy ended up with ships designed more to produce brilliant trial results and large contract bonuses rather than to perform the hard duty that would be expected of them in actual service. Specifically, destroyers would need to be able to operate at high speed in all types of weather, and robust hulls were needed to ensure the necessary endurance. It would thus be better, for destroyers as well as for other ships, to have the *Section technique* design the hulls and limit the individual contractors to submitting proposals for the engines and boilers that they wanted to provide. World War I intervened before this recommendation could be further considered, but it was applied in the major destroyer building programs of the 1920s which consisted of large classes built to single designs. These designs, with their clipper bows with flaring sides and high freeboard amidships and aft, also showed that the lessons from the prewar and wartime comparisons of the different designs of the 800-ton destroyers had been taken into account.

---

Inboard profile and deck view of the squadron destroyer *Enseigne Gabolde*, built on the plans of the Société Anonyme des Chantiers et Ateliers Augustin Normand under a contract of 22 October 1913. The plans were certified on 23 February 1924 to represent the ship as fitted by the navy's control officer at Le Havre.

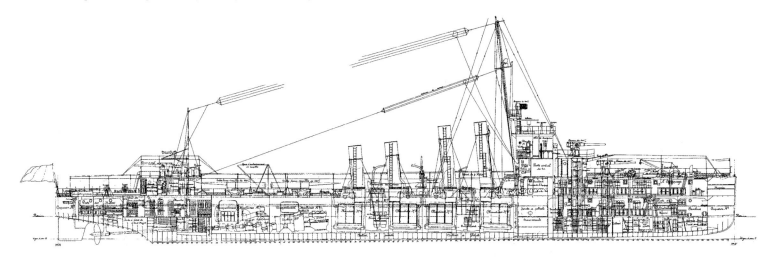

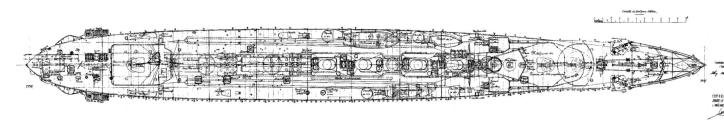

# Chapter Sixteen

# Torpedo Boats, 1897-1914

**(A) Seagoing Torpedo Boats (*Torpilleurs de haute mer*).**
To *Torpilleurs d'escadre* in the 1.1899 fleet list, back to *Torpilleurs de haute mer* 1.1901. *Torpilleurs* 1.3.1920, *Torpilleurs d'escadre* 1.1922.

*SIROCO* **Class.** *Torpilleurs de haute mer.* Normand seagoing torpedo boat with three torpedo tubes aft of the funnels (one twin head-to-tail and one single mount), two funnels, one mast, and light side armour. Designed by Normand.

In the 1898 budget (submitted on 18 May 1897) the French resumed building *torpilleurs de haute mer* in quantity by including five boats to Normand's latest design, the *Cyclone* (ex *Ténare*) of 1896. A sixth boat was soon added. These six boats were called the 'armoured *Cyclone* type' because they included the light armour over the machinery that Normand was then advocating for both torpedo boats and destroyers at the expense of a few knots' speed. Normand believed that the 17-18 tons of armour in this class was sufficient to protect the engines and boilers against the 57mm and

76mm guns of British destroyers. The armour limited the designed trial speed to 26 knots instead of the 29 knots in *Cyclone* and the later similar but unarmoured *Bourrasque* class, below.

In 1913-14 these boats were still regarded as excellent vessels, keeping the sea perfectly, handling swells well, and still capable of 23-24 knots at full load without straining.

**Dimensions & tons:** 46.50m oa, 45.00m wl & pp x 5.15m ext, 5.04m wl. 114.92t disp (normal), 185.80t (full load). Draught: 1.60m amidships. Men: 30 including 2 officers.

**Machinery:** 4,200ihp designed at 360rpm and 16kg/cm$^2$ boiler pressure. Speed 26kts. Trials (*Siroco*) 28.72kts at 355rpm, (*Audacieux*) 26.19kts. 2 screws. 2 triple expansion engines with 3 cylinders of 0.41m, 0.59m, and 0.89m diameter and 0.50m stroke. 2 Normand return flame boilers. 25t coal. Range 2,500nm @ 10kts.

**Armour:** (High resistance construction steel) Sides 24mm over boilers and engines from deck to 20cm below waterline, end bulkheads 24mm to 40cm below wl, deck 9mm, weight 17-18 tons.

**Torpedoes:** 3 tubes for 381mm M1887 torpedoes (originally 1 on deck forward and two aft of the funnels on single centreline mounts, the bow tube being almost immediately removed as unusable, then a twin mount (two tubes head to tail) and a single mount aft of the funnels).

The seagoing torpedo boat (*torpilleur de haute mer*) *Audacieux* before 1906 with a torpedo tube on the bow. (*Postcard by H. Laurent, Port-Louis*)

875. - Le Contre-Torpilleur *Audacieux*

Collection H. Laurent, Port-Louis

**Guns:** 2 x 47mm/40 M1885 QF (on sides aft of the conning tower).

*Siroco* (*Sirocco*) (N12) Augustin Normand, Le Havre/Normand,
  Le Havre.
On list 1.1899. Ord: 10.8.1898. K: 22.8.1898. L: 20.2.1901.
  Trials: 6-7.1901.
Budget 1898. *Défense mobile* at Brest 1902-05, 1st Atlantic torpedo boat
  flotilla 1905-10, fishery protection at Granville 1910, Brest torpedo
  boats 1910-1914, Cherbourg torpedo boats 1914-1915, Algeria 1916-
  17, Oran 1918, and Bizerte 1919-24, including fishery protection at
  Algiers 1921-23. Off main list 1924 at Bizerte (condemnation
  pending). Struck 5.5.1925. Sold 10.8.1925 at Bizerte to BU.

*Mistral* (N13) Augustin Normand, Le Havre/Normand, Le Havre.
On list 1.1899. Ord: 10.8.1898. K: 8.1898. L: 4.5.1901.
  Trials: 7-8.1901.
Budget 1898. *Défense mobile* at Brest, 1st Atlantic torpedo boat flotilla,
  and Brest sea frontier 1902-18. In the flotilla of the 2nd Maritime
  District after the war performing oceanographic work in the Gléanans
  Islands off southern Brittany 1921 and in a minesweeping squadron
  1922-27. Renamed *Borée* 1.1925 to free the name *Mistral* for a new
  destroyer. Off main list 1926 and for sale at Brest as a patrol craft.
  Struck 17.5.1927. Sold 18.4.1928 at Brest to BU.

*Simoun* (N14) F.C. Méditerranée, Le Havre-Graville/FCM, Le Havre.
On list 1.1899. Ord: 14.9.1898. K: 2.11.1899. L: 23.3.1901.
  Trials: 7-9.1901.
Budget 1898. *Défense mobile* at Brest and 1st Atlantic torpedo boat flotilla
  1902-11, Cherbourg torpedo boats 1912, and Dunkirk torpedo boats
  1912-18. In caretaker status at Cherbourg 1919-23. Off main list
  1923 and for sale at Rochefort. Struck 20.4.1924. Sold 27.11.1924 at
  Rochefort to BU.

*Typhon* (N15) F.C. Méditerranée, Le Havre-Graville/FCM, Le Havre.
On list 1.1899. Ord: 14.9.1898. K: 15.12.1899. L: 15.6.1901.
  Trials: 10.1902-1.1903.
Budget 1898. *Défense mobile* at Brest and 1st Atlantic torpedo boat flotilla
  1903-10, Cherbourg torpedo boats and 1st squadron of Normandy
  patrol boat division 1911-18. Off main list c1921 and for sale at Brest
  1921-1922. Struck 9.6.1922. Target at Brest 1922-1927. Sold
  3.3.1928 at Rochefort.

*Trombe* (N16) A.C. Loire, Nantes/ACL, Nantes.
On list 1.1899. Ord: 21.9.1898. K: 1.8.1898. L: 30.7.1900.
  Trials: 7-9.1901.
Budget 1898. Commissioned for trials in early 9.1900, ran aground
  29.9.1900 at 23 knots near Groix. The whole bow back to the conning
  tower had to be rebuilt. *Défense mobile* at Brest and 1st Atlantic torpedo
  boat flotilla 1902-06, then reserve at Brest 1907-09. Reboilered at
  Brest 1910. Cherbourg torpedo boats and submarine flotilla at Calais
  1911-13, then Cherbourg torpedo boats and Le Havre sea frontier
  1914-18. Struck 4.4.1921, for sale at Cherbourg 1921-1922. Sold
  6.1.1928 at Cherbourg to BU.

*Audacieux* (N17) A.C. Loire, Nantes/ACL, Nantes.
On list 1.1899. Ord: 21.9.1898. K: 1.8.1898. L: 29.8.1900.
  Trials: 10-11.1900.
Budget 1898 (late addition). *Défense mobile* at Brest (in reserve) 8.1901-
  1905, 1st Channel torpedo boat flotilla 1905-09, seagoing annex to the
  Naval Academy in *Borda*, then in *Duguay-Trouin*, at Brest 1909-14.
  Brest sea frontier 1914-18. Seagoing annex to *Chamois* at the school
  for piloting at Saint Servan 1919, replaced there by *Alerte* (built 1916)
  in 1920. Off main list 1920-1921 and for sale at Brest 1921-1922.
  Target at Brest 1922-1926. Struck 12.2.1923. Sold 10.3.1926 to BU.

---

**BOURRASQUE** Class. *Torpilleurs de haute mer.* Normand seagoing

torpedo boat with two torpedo tubes aft of the funnels (one twin mount),
two funnels, and one mast. Designed by Normand.

By the time the 1899 budget was submitted in October 1898 the navy had
drawn back from the idea of armoured torpedo boats, and the four boats
in the 1899 budget were called the '*Cyclone* type without armour'. Speeds
generally returned to the higher level of the unarmoured *Cyclone*. The two
Normand boats exceeded 31 knots on trials, although the two Bordeaux
boats failed to make their 30-knot contract speed.

**Dimensions & tons:** 46.57m oa, 45.00m wl & pp x 5.06m ext, 4.78m
  wl. 120.885t disp (normal), 167.5t (full load). Draught: 2.50m aft
  under rudder guard.
**Machinery:** 3,800ihp designed at 18kg/cm² boiler pressure. Speed 29kts.
  Trials (*Bourrasque*) 4,434ihp = 31.54kts, (*Borée*) 29.01kts. 2 screws.
  2 triple expansion engines with 3 cylinders of 0.41m,0.59m, and
  0.89m diameter and 0.50m stroke. 2 Normand return flame boilers.
  18.25t coal (normal), 34.30t (surcharge). Range with normal coal
  2,000nm @ 10kts.
**Torpedoes:** 2 tubes for 381mm M1887 torpedoes (on one deck mount
  aft mounted head to tail). **Guns:** 2 x 47mm/40 M1885 QF (on sides
  aft of the conning tower).

*Bourrasque* (N18) Augustin Normand, Le Havre/Normand, Le Havre.
On list 1.1900. Ord: 21.6.1899. K: 6.1899. L: 31.8.1901. Trials: 1.1902.
  Comm: 6.5.1902 (full).
Budget 1899. Preliminary trials 21.9.1901. *Défense mobile* at Toulon
  1903-04. *Défense mobile* at Bizerte, 3rd Mediterranean torpedo boat
  flotilla, Bizerte torpedo boats, and Bizerte minesweeping squadron
  1905-20. Struck 27.10.1921, for sale at Bizerte 1921-1923. Sold
  25.3.1923 at Bizerte to BU.

*Rafale* (N19) Augustin Normand, Le Havre/Normand, Le Havre.
On list 1.1900. Ord: 21.6.1899. K: 15.7.1900. L: 27.11.1901.
  Trials: 1-2.1902.
Budget 1899. *Défense mobile* at Toulon 1903, Bizerte 1904-5, 3rd
  Mediterranean torpedo boat flotilla there 1906-12, Cherbourg torpedo
  boats 1912-14, and Dunkirk torpedo boats 1915-18. Sunk 1.2.1917 at
  Boulogne by accidental explosion of 30 anti-submarine grenades,
  raised and returned to service. Struck 4.4.1921, for sale at Cherbourg
  1921-1922. Sold 6.1.1922 at Cherbourg to BU.

*Borée* (N20) C.A. Gironde, Bordeaux-Lormont/A.C. Loire, Saint Denis.
On list 1.1900. Ord: 26.7.1899. K: 1900. L: 23.3.1901. Trials: 3-12.1901.
Budget 1899. *Défense mobile* at Toulon (in reserve) 1901-04, Tunisia
  naval division 1904-09, 3rd Mediterranean torpedo boat flotilla at
  Bizerte 1909-12, Toulon torpedo boats 1913-18. Off main list by
  3.1920 and for sale at Toulon 1920. Struck 1.10.1920. Sold 1921 at
  Toulon to BU.

*Tramontane* (N21) C.A. Gironde, Bordeaux-Lormont/A.C. Loire,
  Saint Denis.
On list 1.1900. Ord: 26.7.1899. K: 1900. L: 21.5.1901.
  Trials: 6-11.1901.
Budget 1899. *Défense mobile* at Toulon 1902-04 and Bizerte 1905-11.
  Reboilered 1911 at Bizerte. Reserve at Brest 1912-13. Replaced
  *Aquilon* as seagoing annex to *Chamois* at the school for piloting at
  Saint Servan 1913-14. War service with the Brest torpedo boats and at
  Dunkirk 8.1914-1915, then to Algeria 1915-18. Reserve at Bizerte
  1919-21. Struck 27.10.1921, for sale at Bizerte 1921-1922. Sold
  25.3.1923 at Bizerte to BU.

---

**Seagoing torpedo boats after 1900.**
By 1900 operating experience with the latest seagoing torpedo boats in the
*Escadre de la Méditerranée* and the *Escadre du Nord* showed that to give such
small boats trial speeds approaching 30 knots too much had to be given up

26. - BIZERTE. - La Baie Ponty - La Station des Torpilleurs

Collection Régence

The seagoing torpedo boat *Borée* (BO) at the torpedo boat station in Ponty Bay at Bizerte after 1912. *(Postcard by Régence)*

in robustness of the hull, engines and boilers for them to be capable of sustained operations with a fleet in anything more than a flat calm. Waves of any height would soon reduce them to around 20 knots. In the meantime the success of the first destroyers offered a more satisfactory type of small vessel to operate with the fleet. On 17 March 1900 Minister de Lanessan reassigned all the seagoing torpedo boats to the Défenses mobiles. Two groups of seven of the most recent seagoing boats were formed at Brest and Toulon for potential use with the fleets in case of mobilisation until enough destroyers were available. The admirals on the *Conseil supérieur* were loath to give up on this well-liked type, however, and included it in the structure of the fleet in 1900, 1905, and 1906, although they did not ask for any more to be built. In 1907 the navy confirmed that it would lay down no more *torpilleurs de haute mer*, although this type made a final appearance in the 1910 budget.

### 1910 TYPE. *Torpilleurs de haute mer.*

The 1910 budget (submitted on 18 June 1909 by Minister of Marine Picard) included 2 *torpilleurs de haute mer* 'of 200 tons' to be ordered by contract in 1910. This budget also contained two 450-ton destroyers (another superseded type) and five of the then-standard 800-ton destroyers. The characteristics published in the budget (below) are similar to those of the *Siroco* class (above).

**Dimensions & tons:** 45.0m x 4.9m. 180.92t disp. Draught: 2.60m aft max. Men: 25 including 2 officers.

**Machinery:** 4,200ihp. Speed 26kts. 2 screws. 2 vertical triple expansion engines. Normand boilers. 20t coal. Range 2,000nm @ 10kts.
**Torpedoes:** 3 torpedo tubes. **Guns:** 2 x 47mm QF.

*N22* (Unnamed) Contract
Budget 1910. Not shown in the fleet lists or in the 1911 budget.

*N23* (Unnamed) Contract
Budget 1910. Not shown in the fleet lists or in the 1911 budget.

### (B) 1st Class Torpedo Boats (*Torpilleurs de 1re classe*).
To *Torpilleurs* 1.3.1920, *Torpilleurs d'escadre* 1.1922.

**37-METRE TYPE, 1897 TRANCHE.** *TORPILLEURS Nos 212–235* (P35-45, 31-34, 46-54). *Torpilleurs de 1re classe.* Normand 37-metre type torpedo boats with two torpedo tubes (in the bow and on deck amidships), two funnels, and one mast.

*Nos 212-213* (P35-36) were the only new torpedo boats in the original 1897 budget. Contracts for *Nos 212-218* (P35-41) were in preparation as of January 1897. *Nos 214-222* (P37-44) were added after the budget was passed in March 1897. *Nos 223-226* (P31-34), all dockyard boats, completed late. All were built to Normand's plans for *Nos 201-205*, although some builders including A.C. Loire, Nantes, produced their own detailed drawings for the hulls and engines. The machinery plans for *No 227* and probably the other boats built by Normand were attributed to Pierre Sigaudy, the chief engineer of the Forges et Chantiers de la Méditerranée at Le Havre, who also collaborated with Normand in the development of the Normand-Sigaudy boiler. The Normand and Du

Temple boilers used in the 37-metre type from *No 212* were very similar, both being return-flame boilers, and together they became standards for these and later French torpedo boats.

**Dimensions & tons:** 39.16m oa, 37.00m wl/pp x 4.20m ext, 4.04m wl. 90.6t disp. Draught: 1.17m fwd, 1.22m amidships, 2.60m aft under propeller guard. Men: 23. *Torpilleurs nos 223-226*: As *Nos 201-205* (q.v.)
**Machinery:** 1,800ihp designed (1,500ihp in *Nos 222, 223-226* and *230-232*) at 345rpm and 15kg/cm² boiler pressure. Speed 24kts. Trials (*No 215*) 27.07kts at 352.48rpm, (*No 222*, 16.7.1898) 1,925.1ihp = 24.871kts at 363.27rpm and 14.750kg/cm² boiler pressure, (*No 232*) 24.32kts at 346.49rpm. 1 screw. 1 triple expansion engine with 3 cylinders of 0.39m, 0.56m, and 0.84m diameter and 0.50m stroke in 1,800ihp boats and 3 cylinders of 0.41m, 0.59m, and 0.88m diameter and 0.44m stroke in 1,500ihp boats. 2 Guyot-Du Temple boilers except 2 Normand return flame boilers in *Nos 212-215, 223, 225* and *227-229*. 10.5t coal. Range (*No 227*) 989.352nm @ 14.252kts.
**Torpedoes:** 2 tubes for 381mm M1887 torpedoes (1 trainable on deck amidships, 1 fixed in the bow). **Guns:** 2 x 37mm/20 M1885 guns (on sides by the forward funnel, although in some including *Torpilleurs nos 230-232* they were on the sides aft of the second funnel).

*Torpilleur no 212* (P35) Augustin Normand, Le Havre.
On list 1.1897. Ord: 3.2.1897. K: 1897. L: 5.10.1899. Trials: 10-11.1899.
Budget 1897. *Défense mobile* at Cherbourg 1900, Dunkirk and 2nd Channel torpedo boat flotilla 1901-07, training division of the 1st Channel torpedo boat flotilla at Cherbourg 1908-12. Struck 22.11.1913, target at Calais 1913-1914, for sale at Cherbourg 1920-1922.

*Torpilleur no 213* (P36) Augustin Normand, Le Havre.
On list 1.1897. Ord: 3.2.1897.K: 1897. L: 3.11.1899. Trials: 11.1899-1.1900.
Budget 1897. *Défense mobile* at Cherbourg 1900, Dunkirk, then 2nd Channel torpedo boat flotilla and Dunkirk torpedo boats 1900 11. Struck 22.11.1913, for sale at Brest 1913-1914, torpedo target at Lorient, engine reused in anti-submarine gunboat *Railleuse* (ordered 12.1915), for sale at Lorient 1920, sold 10.1920 at Lorient to BU.

*Torpilleur no 214* (P37) Augustin Normand, Le Havre.
On list 1.1897. Ord: 3.2.1897.K: 1897. L: 16.12.1899. Trials: 1-3.1900.
Budget 1897 (late addition). *Défense mobile* at Dunkirk, then 2nd Channel torpedo boat flotilla and Dunkirk torpedo boats 1900 12. Struck 22.11.1913, for sale at Brest 1913-1914, torpedo target at Lorient, engine reused in anti-submarine gunboat *Malicieuse* (ordered 12.1915), for sale at Lorient 1920, sold 10.1920 at Lorient to BU.

*Torpilleur no 215* (P38) Augustin Normand, Le Havre.
On list 1.1897. Ord: 3.2.1897. K: 1897. L: 13.2.1900. Trials: 3-4.1900.
Budget 1897 (late addition). *Défense mobile* at Dunkirk, then 2nd Channel torpedo boat flotilla 1900-06. Badly damaged 8.11.1906 in night collision with another torpedo boat of her flotilla, sent to Cherbourg for repairs and boiler retubing 1907-09. Renamed *Foyer* 1910. Annex to the school for engineers and stokers at Brest 1910-14. Struck 4.4.1920. BU 1920 at Brest.

*Torpilleur no 216* (P39) Schneider, Chalon-sur-Saône.
On list 1.1897. Ord: 17.2. and 10.3.1897. K: 1896. L: 4.1898. Trials: 9.1898-4.1899.
Budget 1897 (late addition). *Défense mobile* at Corsica 1899-1901, Toulon 1901-06, 3rd Mediterranean torpedo boat flotilla at Bizerte 1907-11. Struck 6.2.1912. Sold 1912 at Toulon to BU.

*Torpilleur no 217* (P40) Schneider, Chalon-sur-Saône.
On list 1.1897. Ord: 17.2. and 10.3.1897. K: 1896. L: 5.1898. Trials: 11.1898-7.1899.

Budget 1897 (late addition). *Défense mobile* at Toulon 1900-01, Corsica and 2nd Mediterranean torpedo boat flotilla 1901-11 1901. Renamed *Ragas* 25.10.1911. Assigned 25.11.1911 as annex to the school for torpedomen and the school for electricians in *Marceau* at Toulon 1911-13. Retired 1914 (condemnation pending). Engine reused in anti-submarine gunboat *Boudeuse* (ordered 3.1916). Struck 27.2.1920. Sold 1920 at Toulon to BU.

*Torpilleur no 218* (P41) Schneider, Chalon-sur-Saône.
On list 1.1897. Ord: 17.2. and 10.3.1897. K: 1896. L: 6.1898. Trials: 12.1898-8.1899.
Budget 1897 (late addition). *Défense mobile* at Toulon 1899-1904, Corsica and 2nd Mediterranean torpedo boat flotilla 1904-12. Struck 22.11.1913, target at Toulon 1913-1914, for sale 1920. Sold 9.1920 at Toulon to BU.

*Torpilleur no 219* (P42) Schneider, Chalon-sur-Saône.
On list 1.1898. Ord: 10.3.1897. K: 1897. L: 7.1898. Trials: 1-3.1899.
Budget 1897 (late addition). *Défense mobile* at Toulon, then Corsica, then 1st Mediterranean torpedo boat flotilla at Toulon 1900-12. Struck 22.11.1913, target at Toulon 1913-1914, for sale 1920. Sold 9.1920 at Toulon to BU.

*Torpilleur no 220* (P43) Schneider, Chalon-sur-Saône.
On list 1.1898. Ord: 10.3. 1897. K: 1897. L: 8.1898. Trials: 5-6.1899.
Budget 1897 (late addition). *Défense mobile* at Toulon and 1st Mediterranean torpedo boat flotilla at Toulon 1900-07, 3rd Mediterranean torpedo boat flotilla at Bizerte 1908-11. Struck 6.2.1912. Sold 1913 at Toulon to BU.

*Torpilleur no 221* (P44) A.C. Loire, Nantes.
On list 1.1898. Ord: 18.3.1897. K: 1896. L: 4.1898. Trials: 4-7.1898.
Budget 1897 (late addition). *Défense mobile* in Algeria (Oran) 1900-06, 1st Mediterranean torpedo boat flotilla at Toulon 1907-11. Renamed *Ringard* 1911. Annex to the school for engineers and stokers at Toulon 1911-13. Retired 1914 (condemnation pending). Engine reused in anti-submarine gunboat *Dédaigneuse* (ordered 3.1916). Struck 27.2.1920. Sold 1920 at Toulon to BU.

*Torpilleur no 222* (P45) A.C. Loire, Nantes.
On list 1.1898. Ord: 18.3.1897. K: 1896. L: 21.4.1898. Trials: 6-7.1898.
Budget 1897 (late addition). Machinery installed 25.5.1898 to 14.6.1898. *Défense mobile* in Algeria and 5th Mediterranean torpedo boat flotilla at Oran 1900-07, 1st Mediterranean torpedo boat flotilla at Toulon 1907-11. Renamed *Rouable* 11.1911. Annex to the school for engineers and stokers at Toulon 1911-12 and to the submarine station there 1912-14. Off main list by 3.1920 and for sale at Toulon 1920. Struck 1.10.1920.

*Torpilleur no 223* (P31) Cherbourg Dyd.
On list 1.1898. Ord: 28.4.1897. K: 3.9.1900. L: 12.3.1902. Trials: 7-9.1902.
Budget 1897. *Défense mobile* at Cherbourg and 1st Channel torpedo boat flotilla 1903-08, 2nd Channel torpedo boat flotilla at Dunkirk 1908-10. Decomm. 1910 with boiler in bad condition. Struck 15.4.1911. Sold 1912 at Cherbourg to BU.

*Torpilleur no 224* (P32) Cherbourg Dyd.
On list 1.1898. Ord: 28.4.1897. K: 3.9.1900. L: 8.3.1904. Trials: 5-8.1904.
Budget 1897. *Défense mobile* at Cherbourg and 1st Channel torpedo boat flotilla1904-07, 2nd Channel torpedo boat flotilla and Dunkirk torpedo boats 1908-1918. Struck 8.1.1919. Sold 12.1920 at Cherbourg to BU.

*Torpilleur no 225* (P33) Toulon Dyd.
On list 1.1898. Ord: 28.4.1897. K: 1.6.1898. L: 20.3.1902.

Trials: 1-5.1903.

Budget 1897. Construction reassigned from Cherbourg to Toulon c1898. *Défense mobile* at Toulon and 1st Mediterranean torpedo boat flotilla 1903-06, 5th Mediterranean torpedo boat flotilla 1907-11. Decomm. 11.1912 at Sidi Abdallah. Struck 22.11.1913, torpedo target at Bizerte 1913-1914. Sold 7.1919 at Bizerte to BU.

*Torpilleur no 226* (P34) Toulon Dyd.
On list 1.1898. Ord: 28.4.1897. K: 1.6.1898. L: 10.7.1902.
Trials: 6-9.1903.

Budget 1897. Construction reassigned from Cherbourg to Toulon c1898. *Défense mobile* at Toulon, then 1st Mediterranean torpedo boat flotilla and Toulon torpedo boats 1903-12. Renamed *Étau* 1912. Annex to the school for engineers and stokers at Toulon 1912-13, to the aviation ship *Foudre* at Saint Raphaël 1913-14, then to the submarine station at Toulon. Struck 30.10.1919, target at Toulon 1920-1922. Sold 1922 at Toulon to BU.

*Torpilleur no 227* (P46) F.C. Méditerranée, Le Havre-Graville.
On list 1.1898. Ord: 1.9.1897. K: 2.3.1898. L: 22.7.1899.
Trials: 11-12.1899. Comm: 25.5.1900.

Budget 1897 (supplemental). Engine installation begun 14.3.1899, 1st static trial 9.9.1899. *Défense mobile* at Cherbourg 1899-1900, Dunkirk 1900-1903, Cherbourg 1903-1908, 2nd Channel torpedo boat flotilla at Dunkirk 1909-12. Struck 30.7.1912, torpedo target at Cherbourg 1912-1913. Sold 1913 at Cherbourg to BU.

*Torpilleur no 228* (P47) F.C. Méditerranée, Le Havre-Graville.
On list 1.1898. Ord: 1.9.1897. K: 7.3.1898. L: 21.8.1899.
Trials: 12.1899-4.1900.

Budget 1897 (supplemental). Engine installation begun 27.4.1899, 1st static trial 30.10.1899. *Défense mobile* at Cherbourg, then 1st Channel torpedo boat flotilla and Cherbourg torpedo boats 1900-1912. Struck 21.5.1914. For sale at Cherbourg 1920. Sold 6.1920 at Cherbourg to BU.

*Torpilleur no 229* (P48) F.C. Méditerranée, Le Havre-Graville.
On list 1.1898. Ord: 1.9.1897. K: 4.3.1898. L: 9.1.1900.
Trials: 2-5.1900.

Budget 1897 (supplemental). Engine installation begun 15.7.1899, 1st static trial 15.1.1900. *Défense mobile* at Cherbourg, then 1st Channel torpedo boat flotilla and Cherbourg torpedo boats 1900-1912. Struck 22.11.1913, for sale at Cherbourg 1913-1914.

*Torpilleur no 230* (P49) C.A. Gironde, Bordeaux-Lormont.
On list 1.1898. Ord: 1.9.1897. K: 1897. L: 6.5.1899. Trials: 6-11.1899.

Budget 1897 (supplemental). *Défense mobile* at Lorient and 2nd Atlantic torpedo boat flotilla 1900-09. 1st Channel torpedo boat flotilla and Cherbourg torpedo boats 1909-12. Struck 22.11.1913, for sale at Cherbourg 1913-1914.

*Torpilleur no 231* (P50) C.A. Gironde, Bordeaux-Lormont.
On list 1.1898. Ord: 1.9.1897. K: 1897. L: 6.1899. Trials: 7.1899.

Budget 1897 (supplemental). *Défense mobile* at Lorient and 2nd Atlantic torpedo boat flotilla 1900-10, Dunkirk torpedo boats 1910-1918 (in the Boulogne sub-group in 1915). Struck 12.1.1920. Sold 1920 at Cherbourg to BU.

*Torpilleur no 232* (P51) C.A. Gironde, Bordeaux-Lormont.
On list 1.1898. Ord: 1.9.1897. K: 1897. L: 6.1899. Trials: 7-8.1899.

Budget 1897 (supplemental). *Défense mobile* at Lorient and 2nd Atlantic torpedo boat flotilla 1900-12. Struck 16.10.1912, for sale at Lorient 1912-1913.

*Torpilleur no 233* (P52) Schneider, Chalon-sur-Saône.
On list 1.1898. Ord: 25.8.1897. K: 1897. L: 2.1899. Trials: 9-11.1899.
Budget 1897 (supplemental). *Défense mobile* at Toulon 1899-1900,

*A 37-metre 1st class torpedo boat, probably* Torpilleur no 228, *leaving Le Havre. She is captioned in error as a seagoing torpedo boat. (Postcard by LL)*

Corsica and 2nd Mediterranean torpedo boat flotilla 1900-05, 1st Mediterranean torpedo boat flotilla at Toulon 1905-09, 4th Mediterranean torpedo boat flotilla and Algiers torpedo boats 1909-11, Tunisia torpedo boats 1911-13. Struck 22.11.1913, torpedo target at Bizerte 1913-1914.

*Torpilleur no 234* (P53) Schneider, Chalon-sur-Saône.
On list 1.1898. Ord: 25.8.1897. K: 1897. L: 2.1899. Trials: 8-11.1899.

Budget 1897 (supplemental). *Défense mobile* at Toulon 1899-1900, Corsica and 2nd Mediterranean torpedo boat flotilla 1900-06, 1st Mediterranean torpedo boat flotilla at Toulon 1906-07. Sunk accidentally 5.10.1907 northwest of Cap Bénat east of Hyères, refloated. Struck 5.12.1908. Sold 8.1909 at Toulon to BU.

*Torpilleur no 235* (P54) Schneider, Chalon-sur-Saône.
On list 1.1898. Ord: 25.8.1897. K: 1897. L: 5.1899. Trials: 10.1899-1.1900.

Budget 1897 (supplemental). *Défense mobile* at Toulon 1900, Corsica and 2nd Mediterranean torpedo boat flotilla 12.1900-1909, Corsica torpedo boats 1910-12. Renamed *Enclume* (replacing *Torpilleur no 89*) 1912. Annex to the school for engineers and stokers at Toulon 1912-13, to the aviation ship *Foudre* at Saint Raphaël 1913-14, then to the school for engineers at Toulon. Struck 30.10.1919, for sale at Toulon 1920-1923. Sold 1923 at Toulon to BU.

---

**37-METRE TYPE, 1898 TRANCHE.** *TORPILLEURS Nos 236–242* (P55-61). *Torpilleurs de 1re classe.* Normand 37-metre type torpedo boats as *Torpilleur no 212*.

The 1898 budget contained six more regular 37-metre boats. The colonial boat *No 242* (P61) and the experimental boat *No 243* (P62) were added to the 1898 budget after it was passed.

**Dimensions & tons:** As *Torpilleur no 212*.
**Machinery:** 1,500ihp designed at 15kg/cm² boiler pressure. Speed 24kts. Trials (*No 238*) 25.26kts at 368.2rpm, (*No 241*) 24.29kts at 351.05rpm. 1 screw. 1 triple expansion engine with 3 cylinders of 0.39m, 0.55m, and 0.84m diameter and 0.50m stroke (0.425m, 0.61m, and 0.87m diameter and 0.45m stroke in *Nos 236-238*). 2 Guyot-Du Temple boilers. 10.5t coal.
**Torpedoes and guns:** As *Torpilleur no 212*.

The 37-metre 1st class torpedo boat *Torpilleur no 238* with other torpedo boats and a service barge at Cherbourg during World War I. The boat on the right has had her bow torpedo tube removed and is probably in subsidiary service. *(NHHC, NH-55730)*

**Torpilleur nº 236** (P55) A.C. Loire, Nantes.
On list 1.1899. Ord: 27.4.1898. K: 1898. L: 12.5.1899. Trials: 6-7.1899.
Budget 1898. *Défense mobile* at Lorient and 2nd Atlantic torpedo boat flotilla 1900-13, Cherbourg torpedo boats 1913-14. Retired 1914. Target 10.1914. Engine reused in anti-submarine gunboat *Tapageuse* (ordered 12.1915). Struck 7.6.1920. For sale at Cherbourg 1920-1922. Sold 1922.

**Torpilleur nº 237** (P56) A.C. Loire, Nantes.
On list 1.1899. Ord: 27.4.1898. K: 1898. L: 1899. Trials: 8-11.1899.
Budget 1898. *Défense mobile* at Lorient and 2nd Atlantic torpedo boat flotilla 1900-11. Decomm. 1910 to change boiler. Struck 6.2.1912, for sale at Lorient 1912-1913.

**Torpilleur nº 238** (P57) A.C. Loire, Nantes.
On list 1.1899. Ord: 27.4.1898. K: 1898. L: 1899. Trials: 10.1899.
Budget 1898. *Défense mobile* at Lorient, then 2nd Atlantic torpedo boat flotilla 1900-08, 2nd Channel torpedo boat flotilla at Dunkirk 1909-11, Cherbourg torpedo boats and Normandy patrol boat division 1912-18. Struck 12.1.1920. Sold 5.1921 at Cherbourg to BU.

**Torpilleur nº 239** (P58) C.A. Gironde, Bordeaux-Lormont.

On list 1.1899. Ord: 27.4.1898. K: 1898. L: 11.1899. Trials: 12.1899-1.1900.
Budget 1898. *Défense mobile* at Brest 1900-1903, Rochefort and 2nd Atlantic torpedo boat flotilla 1903-13, Cherbourg torpedo boats and Normandy patrol boat division 1912-18. Struck 12.1.1920. Sold 12.1920 at Cherbourg to BU.

**Torpilleur nº 240** (P59) C.A. Gironde, Bordeaux-Lormont.
On list 1.1899. Ord: 27.4.1898. K: 1898. L: 12.1899. Trials: 1-3.1900.
Budget 1898. *Défense mobile* in Algeria and 5th Mediterranean torpedo boat flotilla at Oran 1900-07, Bizerte torpedo boats 1909-1912. Struck 22.11.1913, for sale at Bizerte 1913-1914, recomm. at Bizerte for war, struck again 30.10.1919, BU 1919 at Bizerte.

**Torpilleur nº 241** (P60) C.A. Gironde, Bordeaux-Lormont.
On list 1.1899. Ord: 27.4.1898. K: 1898. L: 1.1900. Trials: 2-4.1900.
Budget 1898. *Défense mobile* in Algeria and 5th Mediterranean torpedo boat flotilla at Oran 1900-07, Oran torpedo boats 1909-1910, then decomm. at Bizerte. Struck 22.11.1913, for sale at Bizerte 1913-1914, recomm. at Bizerte for war, struck again 30.10.1919. Sold 1919 at Bizerte to BU.

**Torpilleur nº 242** (P61) (Colonial) Schneider, Chalon-sur-Saône.
On list 1.1899. Ord: 26.3.1898. K: 1898. L: 20.4.1901.
  Trials: to 10.1901.
Budget 1898 (late addition). Transported to Saigon in sections, assembled and trials conducted there. In reserve 1.12.1901, trials conducted

annually thereafter along with service as needed including during 1914-18. To *Torpilleur colonial Nº 6-S* (Saigon) 1.1902. To *Torpilleur de 1re classe* 1.1909. Struck 21.6.1920. Sold 11.1920 at Saigon to BU.

---

## 37-METRE EXPERIMENTAL TURBINE TYPE, 1899. *TORPILLEUR Nº 243* (P 62). *Torpilleur de 1re classe.* Experimental turbine torpedo boat with hull based on Normand's 37-metre type.

The turbine-propelled *Nº 243* was added to the 1898 budget after it was passed. Her hull and boilers were identical to *Nos 253-257* but she had Rateau turbines instead of reciprocating machinery. The contract called for the replacement of the turbines with a reciprocating engine as in *Nos 227-229* if the speed did not exceed 20 knots. She had two propeller shafts, each with three propellers (which were changed often during trials). She was accepted on 16 May 1904 with a disappointing speed of only 21 knots. Her trials also demonstrated the outstanding weakness of early turbine installations, exceptionally high coal consumption, particularly at cruising speeds. *Nº 243* burned twice as much coal at 20 knots as *Nº 229* did and around three times as much at 14 knots.

**Dimensions & tons:** As *Torpilleur nº 253.*
**Machinery:** Designed for 24kts. Trials 21 kts. Rateau turbines. 2 Normand return flame boilers.
**Torpedoes and guns:** As *Torpilleur nº 212.* Rearmed in 1916 after re-acquired as patrol vessel *Patrouilleur 243* with 2 x 47mm, guns and two 58mm mortars for launching 11.5kg anti-submarine bombs.

*Torpilleur nº 243* (P62) F.C. Méditerranée, Le Havre-Graville.
On list 1.1899. Ord: 7.9.1898. K: 21.2.1899. L: 16.7.1901.
   Trials: 22.8.1902 to 16.5.1904.
Budget 1898 (late addition). Trials of her Rateau turbines at Le Havre and Cherbourg concluded 1904, only 21 knots achieved. The recommendation of the trial commission on 13.7.1904 to replace the turbines with a reciprocating engine and several later similar schemes were not carried out. No operational service. Struck 15.4.1911, hull (still in good condition) sold 7.1911 to Normand. Re-purchased from Normand by contract of 10.11.1915 as *Patrouilleur 243* but listed as torpedo boat through 1920. Assigned to Cherbourg for operations 6.1916. To caretaker status 3.1921. Struck 4.8.1922. Sale 12.1922 failed, target at Brest 1922-1923. Sunk as target 19.5.1923.

---

## 37-METRE TYPE, 1899 TRANCHE. *TORPILLEURS Nos 244–255* (P63-74). *Torpilleurs de 1re classe.* Normand 37-metre type torpedo boats as *Torpilleur nº 212.*

The 1899 colonial boat for Saigon (*Nº 244*) was built by Schneider to its plans for *Nos 245-250.* She was begun in advance with a small amount of 1898 funding. She and the 1898 colonial boat (*Nº 242*) were prefabricated in sections by Schneider for assembly at Saigon, officially they were built by the Saigon dockyard. *Nos 277* and *9-S* were built in the same way and *Nos 368* and *369* were to have been as well.

**Dimensions & tons:** As *Torpilleur nº 212* except *Nos 245-250*: 38.86m oa, 37.00m wl/pp x 4.22m ext. 87t-90.8t disp. Draught: 1.35m amidships. Men: 23.
**Machinery:** 1,800ihp designed (1,500ihp in *Nos 244* and *251-252*) at 15kg/cm² boiler pressure. Speed 24kts. Trials (*Nº 255*) 25.60kts at 345.25rpm, (*Nº 245*) 24.44kts at 365.55rpm. 1 screw. 1 triple expansion engine with 3 cylinders of 0.39m, 0.55m, and 0.84m diameter and 0.50m stroke. 2 Guyot-Du Temple boilers except 2 Normand return flame boilers in *Nos 253-255.* 10.5t coal.
**Torpedoes and guns:** As *Torpilleur nº 212.*

*Torpilleur nº 244* (P63) (Colonial) Schneider, Chalon-sur-Saône.
On list 1.1899. Ord: 30.12.1898. K: 1898. L: 22.7.1902.

Trials: to 3.1903 (accepted).
Budget 1899. Transported to Saigon in sections, assembled and trials conducted there. To *Torpilleur colonial Nº 7-S* (Saigon) 1.1902. To 1st China seas torpedo boat flotilla 1906. To *Torpilleur de 1re classe* 1.1909. Her hull, built partially of non-galvanized metal, corroded rapidly, decomm. 6.8.1909. Struck 3.11.1910. Sold 1921 at Saigon to BU.

*Torpilleur nº 245* (P64) Schneider, Chalon-sur-Saône.
On list 1.1900. Ord: 29.3.1899. K: 1899. L: 8.1900. Trials: 10-11.1900.
Budget 1899. *Défense mobile* at Toulon 1901-04. To Saigon, to *Torpilleur colonial Nº 10-S* (Saigon) 1904. *Défense mobile* at Saigon 1904, then 2nd China seas torpedo boat flotilla 1905. To *Torpilleur de 1re classe* 1.1909. Decomm. 15.3.1910. Struck 3.11.1910. Sold 7.1921 at Saigon to BU.

*Torpilleur nº 246* (P65) Schneider, Chalon-sur-Saône.
On list 1.1900. Ord: 29.3.1899. K: 1899. L: 10.1900. Trials: 12.1900-1.1901.
Budget 1899. *Défense mobile* at Toulon 1901-04. To Saigon, to *Torpilleur colonial Nº 11-S* (Saigon) 1904. *Défense mobile* at Saigon 1904, then 2nd China seas torpedo boat flotilla 1905. To *Torpilleur de 1re classe* 1.1909. Decomm. 15.3.1910. Struck 3.11.1910. Sold 8.1921 at Saigon to BU.

*Torpilleur nº 247* (P66) Schneider, Chalon-sur-Saône.
On list 1.1900. Ord: 29.3.1899. K: 1899. L: 12.1900. Trials: 1-4.1901.
Budget 1899. *Défense mobile* at Toulon 1901-04. To *Torpilleur colonial Nº 12-S* (Saigon) 14.11.1904. *Défense mobile* at Saigon 1904-05, 1st, then 2nd China seas torpedo boat flotillas 1906-11. To *Torpilleur de 1re classe* 1.1909. Struck 15.4.1911. Sold 8.1921 at Saigon to BU.

*Torpilleur nº 248* (P67) Schneider, Chalon-sur-Saône.
On list 1.1900. Ord: 29.3.1899. K: 1899. L: 1.1901. Trials: 3-6.1901.
Budget 1899. *Défense mobile* at Toulon 1901-04. To *Torpilleur colonial Nº 13-S* (Saigon) 14.11.1904. *Défense mobile* at Saigon, then 1st and 2nd China seas torpedo boat flotillas 1904-11. To *Torpilleurs de 1re classe* 1.1909. Struck 15.4.1911. Sold 8.1921 at Saigon to BU.

*Torpilleur nº 249* (P68) Schneider, Chalon-sur-Saône.
On list 1.1900. Ord: 29.3.1899. K: 1899. L: 3.1901. Trials: 4-8.1901.
Budget 1899. *Défense mobile* in Corsica 1901-04. To *Torpilleur colonial Nº 14-S* (Saigon) 14.11.1904. *Défense mobile* at Saigon, then 1st and 2nd China seas torpedo boat flotillas 1904-10, Saigon torpedo boats 1910-14. To *Torpilleurs de 1re classe* 1.1909. Struck 21.5.1914. Engine sent back to France and reused with that of *Nº 254* in gunboat *Coquette* (ordered 11.1917). Hull BU at the Saigon dockyard in 1917.

*Torpilleur nº 250* (P69) Schneider, Chalon-sur-Saône.
On list 1.1900. Ord: 29.3.1899. K: 1899. L: 4.1901. Trials: 7-8.1901.
Budget 1899. *Défense mobile* in Corsica 1901-04, then Toulon and the 1st Mediterranean torpedo boat flotilla 1904-18. Grounded and sank 26.3.1905 at the Pointe de Marégau near La Seyne, refloated. Replaced *Ringard* (ex *Torpilleur nº 221*) as annex to the school for engineers and stokers at Toulon (not renamed) 10.1913 to 1914. In the Suez Canal 1915 and in Syria 1916-17 (captured a Turkish schooner carrying arms 30.12.1916). After torpedo tube replaced with a 47mm QF 2.1916. Struck 4.3.1920. Sold 6.1921, BU 1922 at Bizerte.

*Torpilleur nº 251* (P70) A.C. Loire, Nantes.
On list 1.1900. Ord: 29.3.1899. K: 1899. L: 4.1900. Trials: 6-7.1900.
Budget 1899. *Défense mobile* at Lorient 1900-12, Dunkirk torpedo boats 1913-14. Sunk 26.10.1914 in collision with the destroyer *Oriflamme*. Struck 25.1.1915.

*Torpilleur nº 252* (P71) A.C. Loire, Nantes.
On list 1.1900. Ord: 29.3.1899. K: 1899. L: 31.5.1900. Trials: 1900.
Budget 1899. Trials at Lorient. Used 1918-19 as light minesweeper.

Struck 12.1.1920, target at Cherbourg 1922-1923, struck again 28.1.1923. Sunk off Cherbourg c1923.

**Torpilleur nº 253** (P72) F.C. Méditerranée, Le Havre-Graville.
On list 1.1900. Ord: 2.8.1899. K: 1899. L: 16.8.1901. Trials: 9-11.1901.
Budget 1899. *Défense mobile* at Cherbourg 1901-04, Toulon and 1st Mediterranean torpedo boat flotilla 1904-07, 2nd Mediterranean torpedo boat flotilla at Ajaccio 1907-09, 3rd Mediterranean torpedo boat flotilla at Bizerte and Bizerte torpedo boats 1909-14. Retired c1914. Engine reused in anti-submarine gunboat *Courageuse* (ordered 3.1916). Last listed at Bizerte 1919.

**Torpilleur nº 254** (P73) F.C. Méditerranée, Le Havre-Graville.
On list 1.1900. Ord: 2.8.1899. K: 1899. L: 28.9.1901.
  Trials: 10-11.1901.
Budget 1899. *Défense mobile* at Cherbourg 1901-04, Toulon 1904. To *Torpilleur colonial Nº 15-S* (Saigon) 14.11.1904. Arrived at Saigon 25.12.1904, 2nd China seas torpedo boat flotilla to 1913. To *Torpilleur de 1re classe* 1.1909. Retired 3.1914 following decision not to repair her. Engine sent back to France and reused with that of *Nº 249* in gunboat *Coquette* (ordered 11.1917). Hull probably BU at the Saigon dockyard in 1917.

**Torpilleur nº 255** (P74) F.C. Méditerranée, Le Havre-Graville.
On list 1.1900. Ord: 2.8.1899. K: 1899. L: 31.10.1901. Trials: 12.1901-3.1902.
Budget 1899. *Défense mobile* at Cherbourg 1902-04, Toulon 1904-05. Escorted to Saigon by *Foudre* 8-10.1905. To *Torpilleur colonial Nº 16-S* (Saigon) 1.1906. 1st China seas torpedo boat flotilla 1906-09, Saigon torpedo boats 1910-19. To *Torpilleur de 1re classe* 1.1909. Struck 21.6.1920. Sold 11.1920 at Saigon to BU.

---

**37-METRE TYPE, 1900 TRANCHE. *TORPILLEURS Nos 256–265*** (P75-84). *Torpilleurs de 1re classe.* Normand 37-metre type torpedo boats as *Torpilleur nº 212.*

The 1900 batch introduced one new yard, Dyle et Bacalan, to the programme. Dyle built its boats (Nos 264-265 and later Nos 273-274) to Normand's plans for Nos 212-215.

**Dimensions & tons:** As *Torpilleur nº 212.* Men: 23.
**Machinery:** 1,800ihp designed (1,500ihp in *Nos 258-260*) at 15kg/cm² boiler pressure (16kg/cm² in *Nos 264-265*). Speed 24kts designed. Trials (*Nº 260*) 26.24kts at 347.53rpm, (*Nº 261*) 24.66kts at 345.67rpm. 1 screw. 1 triple expansion engine with 3 cylinders of 0.39m, 0.55m, and 0.84m diameter and 0.50m stroke. 2 Guyot-Du Temple boilers except 2 Normand return flame boilers in *Nos 256-257* and *Nos 264-265*. 10.5t coal.
**Torpedoes and guns:** As *Torpilleur nº 212.*

**Torpilleur nº 256** (P75) F.C. Méditerranée, Le Havre-Graville.
On list 1.1901. Ord: 20.6.1900. K: 1899. L: 29.11.1901.
  Trials: 1-6.1902.
Budget 1900. *Défense mobile* at Dunkirk, then 2nd Channel torpedo boat flotilla and Dunkirk torpedo boats 1902-13. Struck 22.11.1913, target at Cherbourg 1913-1914. Engine reused in anti-submarine gunboat *Capricieuse* (ordered 3.1916). For sale at Cherbourg 1920. Sold 6.1920 at Cherbourg to BU.

**Torpilleur nº 257** (P76) F.C. Méditerranée, Le Havre-Graville.
On list 1.1901. Ord: 20.6.1900. K: 1900. L: 11.2.1902. Trials: 3-5.1902.
Budget 1900. *Défense mobile* at Dunkirk and 2nd Channel torpedo boat flotilla 1902-10. Damaged 9.12.1910 in collision with destroyer *Escopette*, not repaired. Struck 23.11.1911, for sale at Cherbourg 1911-1912.

**Torpilleur nº 258** (P77) C.A. Gironde, Bordeaux-Lormont.
On list 1.1901. Ord: 20.6.1900. K: 1900. L: 12.8.1901.
  Trials: 8-11.1901.
Budget 1900. *Défense mobile* at Brest 1902-05, 1st Channel torpedo boat flotilla at Cherbourg 1906, 2nd Channel torpedo boat flotilla at Dunkirk and Dunkirk torpedo boats 1907-18, Boulogne torpedo boat group 1918. Struck 12.1.1920. Sold at Cherbourg to BU.

**Torpilleur nº 259** (P78) C.A. Gironde, Bordeaux-Lormont.
On list 1.1901. Ord: 20.6.1900. K: 1900. L: 2.10.1901.
  Trials: 10-11.1901.
Budget 1900. *Défense mobile* at Brest 1901-05, 1st Channel torpedo boat flotilla at Cherbourg 1905-10, Dunkirk torpedo boats 1911-18, Boulogne torpedo boat group 1918. Struck 12.1.1920. Sold 7.1922 at Cherbourg to BU.

**Torpilleur nº 260** (P79) C.A. Gironde, Bordeaux-Lormont.
On list 1.1901. Ord: 20.6.1900. K: 1900. L: 31.10.1901.
  Trials: 11-12.1901.
Budget 1900. *Défense mobile* at Brest and 1st Atlantic torpedo boat flotilla 1902-09, seagoing annex to the Naval Academy in *Borda*, then in *Duguay-Trouin*, at Brest 1910-14. Off main list by 3.1920 and for sale at Brest. Struck 7.6.1920. Sold 11.1920 at Brest to BU.

**Torpilleur nº 261** (P80) Schneider, Chalon-sur-Saône.
On list 1.1901. Ord: 20.6.1900. K: 1900. L: 28.3.1902. Trials: 6-7.1902.
Budget 1900. *Défense mobile* in Corsica 1902-04. Designated 14.11.1904 for the Indian Ocean torpedo boat flotilla at Diégo Suarez (later Diégo Suarez torpedo boats) and became *Torpilleur colonial Nº 1-M* (Madagascar). To *Torpilleur de 1re classe* 1.1909. Blown ashore by a cyclone 24.11.1912 in Madagascar, raised but not repaired, condemnation proposed 15.2.1913. For sale at Diégo Suarez 1913-1914. Off list c1914. Sold 1915 at Diégo Suarez to BU.

**Torpilleur nº 262** (P81) Schneider, Chalon-sur-Saône.
On list 1.1901. Ord: 20.6.1900. K: 1900. L: 17.5.1902. Trials: 5-8.1902.
Budget 1900. *Défense mobile* in Corsica 1902-04. Designated 14.11.1904 for the Indian Ocean torpedo boat flotilla at Diégo Suarez (later Diégo Suarez torpedo boats) and became *Torpilleur colonial Nº 2-M* (Madagascar). To *Torpilleur de 1re classe* 1.1909. Blown ashore by a cyclone 24.11.1912 in Madagascar, hull broke up and sank. For sale at Diégo Suarez 1913-1914. Off list c1914.

**Torpilleur nº 263** (P82) Schneider, Chalon-sur-Saône.
On list 1.1901. Ord: 20.6.1900. K: 1900. L: 24.6.1902.
  Trials: 8-12.1902.
Budget 1900. *Défense mobile* in Corsica 1903, badly damaged when mooring at Ajaccio 27.10.1903, sent back to Toulon in a floating dock, damaged again when the slipway where she under repair caught fire and its roof fell on her, repairs completed 9.1905. 2nd Mediterranean torpedo boat flotilla at Ajaccio 1905-10, 4th Mediterranean torpedo boat flotilla at Algiers 1910-12, Bizerte torpedo boats 1912-18. Off main list by 3.1920 and for sale. Struck 7.6.1920. Sold 15.4.1921 at Bizerte to M. Kalfon Vita.

**Torpilleur nº 264** (P83) Dyle et Bacalan, Bordeaux-Bacalan.
On list 1.1901. Ord: 20.6.1900. K: 1900. L: 11.12.1901.
  Trials: 1-4.1902.
Budget 1900. *Défense mobile* at Rochefort 1902-04. *Défense mobile* in Algeria (Oran), then 5th Mediterranean torpedo boat flotilla at Oran and Oran torpedo boats 1904-11. Bizerte torpedo boats 1912-14. Retired c1914. Engine reused in anti-submarine gunboat *Curieuse* (ordered 2.1916). Last listed 1919 at Bizerte. BU 1920 at Bizerte.

**Torpilleur nº 265** (P84) Dyle et Bacalan, Bordeaux-Bacalan.
On list 1.1901. Ord: 20.6.1900. K: 1900. L: 24.2.1902. Trials: 3-5.1902.
Budget 1900. *Défense mobile* at Rochefort 1902-04. *Défense mobile* in

Algeria (Oran), then 5th Mediterranean torpedo boat flotilla at Oran and Oran torpedo boats 1904-11. Bizerte torpedo boats 1912-15. Retired 3.1915. Engine reused in anti-submarine gunboat *Gracieuse* (ordered 2.1916). Sold 12.1923 at Bizerte.

---

**37-METRE TYPE, 1901 TRANCHE.** *TORPILLEURS N⁰ˢ 266–277* (P85-96). *Torpilleurs de 1ʳᵉ classe.* Normand 37-metre type torpedo boats as *Torpilleur n⁰ 212.*

The 1901 batch included the only two boats built by the Forges et Chantiers de la Méditerranée at La Seyne since the 35-metre type of 1885. Like *N⁰ˢ 242* and *244, N⁰ 277* was built in sections for assembly at the arsenal at Saigon.

**Dimensions & tons:** As *Torpilleur n⁰ 212.* Men: 23.
**Machinery:** 1,800ihp designed at 15kg/cm² boiler pressure (16kg/cm² in *N⁰ˢ 273-274*). Speed 24kts designed. Trials (*N⁰ 274*) 26.62kts at 327.94rpm, (*N⁰ 272*) 24.67kts at 349.45rpm. 1 screw. 1 triple expansion engine with 3 cylinders of 0.39m, 0.55m, and 0.84m diameter and 0.50m stroke. 2 Guyot-Du Temple boilers except 2 Normand return flame boilers in *N⁰ˢ 269-270* and *N⁰ˢ 273-274*. 10.5t coal.
**Torpedoes and guns:** As *Torpilleur n⁰ 212.*

*Torpilleur n⁰ 266* (P85) A.C. Loire, Nantes.
On list 1.1902. Ord: 15.5.1901. K: 1901. L: 1902. Trials: 8-10.1902.
Budget 1901. *Défense mobile* at Brest, 1ˢᵗ Atlantic torpedo boat flotilla and Brest torpedo boats 1903-19. Used 1918-19 as light minesweeper. Off main list 1921 and for sale at Brest 1921-1922. Struck 27.10.1922. Target at Brest 1922-1923, target at Lorient 1923-1930. Sold 1931 at Lorient to BU.

*Torpilleur n⁰ 267* (P86) A.C. Loire, Nantes.
On list 1.1902. Ord: 15.5.1901. K: 1901. L: 9.1902. Trials: 10.1902.
Budget 1901. *Défense mobile* at Brest, 1ˢᵗ Atlantic torpedo boat flotilla and Brest torpedo boats 1903-19. Off main list by 3.1920 and for sale at Brest. Struck 7.6.1920. Sold 11.1920 at Brest to BU.

*Torpilleur n⁰ 268* (P87) A.C. Loire, Nantes.
On list 1.1902. Ord: 15.5.1901. K: 1901. L: 1902. Trials: 11.1902.
Budget 1901. *Défense mobile* at Brest, 1ˢᵗ Atlantic torpedo boat flotilla and Brest torpedo boats 1903-19. Struck 4.4.1920. BU at Brest.

*Torpilleur n⁰ 269* (P88) F.C. Méditerranée, La Seyne.
On list 1.1902. Ord: 15.5.1901. K: 1901. L: 20.8.1902. Trials: 10-12.1902.
Budget 1901. *Défense mobile* at Cherbourg and 1ˢᵗ Channel torpedo boat flotilla 1903-11, Toulon torpedo boats 1912-19. Retired 1919. Sold 5.1920 at Toulon to BU. Struck (retroactively) 26.11.1920.

*Torpilleur n⁰ 270* (P89) F.C. Méditerranée, La Seyne.
On list 1.1902. Ord: 15.5.1901. K: 1901. L: 4.10.1902. Trials: 11.1902 1.1903.
Budget 1901. *Défense mobile* at Cherbourg and 1ˢᵗ Channel torpedo boat flotilla 1903-11, Toulon torpedo boats 1912-13. Annex for the Mediterranean school division (not renamed) 1913-14. Retired 1919, for sale at Toulon 1920. Sold 5.1920 at Toulon to BU.

*Torpilleur n⁰ 271* (P90) Schneider, Chalon-sur-Saône.
On list 1.1902. Ord: 15.5.1901. K: 1901. L: 19.8.1902. Trials:10.1902-5.1903.
Budget 1901. *Défense mobile* at Toulon 1903-1904. Designated 14.11.1904 for the Indian Ocean torpedo boat flotilla at Diégo Suarez and became *Torpilleur colonial N⁰ 3-M* (Madagascar). To *Torpilleur de 1ʳᵉ classe* 1.1909. Prematurely worn out and ordered on 12.10.1909 to be decomm. Struck 20.2.1911, for sale at Diégo Suarez 1911-1914. Sold 1920 at Diégo Suarez to BU. Struck again (retroactively) as *N⁰ 271* 1.10.1920.

37-metre and 38-metre 1st class torpedo boats of the *Défense mobile* at Lorient at their moorings in the Scorff river. *Torpilleurs no 252* and *no 352* behind her are clearly identified. In the background is one of the large covered slipways at Caudan across the river from the main Lorient dockyard. *(Colorized postcard by Laurent-Nel, Rennes)*

*Torpilleur n⁰ 272* (P91) Schneider, Chalon-sur-Saône.
On list 1.1902. Ord: 15.5.1901. K: 1901. L: 27.10.1902. Trials: 3-5.1903.
Budget 1901. *Défense mobile* at Toulon 1903-1904. Designated 14.11.1904 for the Indian Ocean torpedo boat flotilla at Diégo Suarez and became *Torpilleur colonial N⁰ 4-M* (Madagascar). To *Torpilleur de 1ʳᵉ classe* 1.1909. Prematurely worn out and decomm. 8.10.1910 for condemnation. Struck 20.2.1911, for sale at Diégo Suarez 1911-1914.

*Torpilleur n⁰ 273* (P92) Dyle et Bacalan, Bordeaux-Bacalan.
On list 1.1902. Ord: 15.5.1901. K: 1901. L: 3.12.1902. Trials: 1-3.1903.
Budget 1901. *Défense mobile* at Dunkirk and 2ⁿᵈ Channel torpedo boat flotilla 1903-06, 5ᵗʰ Mediterranean torpedo boat flotilla at Oran 1906-09, Bizerte torpedo boats 1910-1914. Retired c1914. Engine reused in anti-submarine gunboat *Moqueuse* (ordered 3.1916). In 1.1918 was command vessel (*bâtiment de commandement*) for the 2ⁿᵈ submarine squadron at Bizerte. Sold 7.1919 at Bizerte to BU.

*Torpilleur n⁰ 274* (P93) Dyle et Bacalan, Bordeaux-Bacalan.
On list 1.1902. Ord: 15.5.1901. K: 1901. L: 30.1.1903. Trials: 3.1903.
Budget 1901. *Défense mobile* at Dunkirk and 2ⁿᵈ Channel torpedo boat flotilla 1903-06, 5ᵗʰ Mediterranean torpedo boat flotilla at Oran 1906-10, Bizerte torpedo boats 1911-1919. Struck 4.3.1920. Sold 1.8.1921 at Bizerte with the submarines *Ventôse* and *Berthelot* to M. Kalfon-Vita of Tunis.

*Torpilleur n⁰ 275* (P94) C.A. Gironde, Bordeaux-Lormont.
On list 1.1902. Ord: 15.5.1901. K: 1901. L: 22.8.1902. Trials: 9.1902.
Budget 1901. *Défense mobile* at Rochefort and 3ʳᵈ Atlantic torpedo boat flotilla 1903-09, Cherbourg torpedo boats 1909-11, Brest torpedo boats and the Brittany torpedo boat division 1911-1920. Off main list by 3.1920 and for sale at Brest. Struck 7.6.1920. Sold 12.1920 at Brest to BU.

*Torpilleur n⁰ 276* (P95) C.A. Gironde, Bordeaux-Lormont.
On list 1.1902. Ord: 15.5.1901. K: 1901. L: 16.9.1902. Trials: 10.1902.
Budget 1901. *Défense mobile* at Rochefort and 3ʳᵈ Atlantic torpedo boat flotilla 1903-12, Cherbourg torpedo boats 1913-19. Struck 12.1.1920,

target at Cherbourg 1922-1923. Sunk at sea 1.1923. Struck again 28.1.1923.

***Torpilleur nº 277*** (P96) (Colonial) Schneider, Chalon-sur-Saône.
On list 1.1902. Ord: 25.2.1901. K: 1901. L: 12.9.1903.
   Trials: 11-12.1903.
Budget 1901. To *Torpilleur colonial Nº 8-S* (Saigon) 1901. Transported in
   sections to Saigon and assembled there. Trials in the river at Saigon
   produced 24.05 knots at 331.5rpm. *Défense mobile* at Saigon, then
   (1907) 1st China seas torpedo boat flotilla. To *Torpilleur de 1re classe*
   1.1909. Struck 3.11.1910. Sold 1915 at Saigon to BU.

---------

### 37-METRE TYPE, 1902 TRANCHE. *TORPILLEURS Nos 278–292* and *TORPILLEUR COLONIAL Nº 9-S* (P97-112). *Torpilleurs de 1re classe.* Normand 37-metre type torpedo boats as *Torpilleur nº 212.*

In the 1902 batch the builders were asked to meet higher standards for the
machinery. The designed horsepower was raised from 1,800ihp to
1,900ihp, designed speed was raised from 24 knots to 26 knots, designed
boiler pressure went from 15 to 16.5kg/cm², and the cruising range (which
depended on fuel efficiency) was calculated for 14 knots instead of 10
knots, a change also made for all other new ships. The designed horsepower
was again officially raised to 2,000ihp after all the 1,900ihp boats exceeded
this in trials. The designed power of the single colonial boat, *Nº 9-S*, was
only 1,500ihp for a speed of 24 knots vice 26 knots in the others. This
batch brought the Chantiers de Normandie yard at Rouen (Grand
Quévilly), owned by the Chantiers et Ateliers de Saint Nazaire (Penhoët)
since 1901, into the programme. They subcontracted the engines of their
three boats to Schneider, who used the plans of Normand's engines for
*Nos 278-280* in *Nos 287-292*. Normand boilers were fitted in *Nos 278-80*
and Guyot-du Temple boilers in the others.

**Dimensions & tons:** As *Torpilleur nº 212.* Men: 23.
**Machinery:** 1,900ihp designed (officially raised to 2,000ihp after all
   1,900ihp boats exceeded this in trials, except 1,500ihp designed in
   *Nº 9-S*) at 345rpm and 16.5kg/cm² boiler pressure. Speed 26kts (24kts
   in *9-S*). Trials (*Nº 290*) 27.43kts at 333.42rpm, (*Nº 281*) 25.90kts at
   359.9rpm. 1 screw. 1 triple expansion engine with 3 cylinders of
   0.39m, 0.55m, and 0.84m diameter and 0.50m stroke (3 cylinders of
   0.48m, 0.59m, and 0.89m diameter and 0.50m stroke in *Nos 278-
   280*). 2 Guyot-Du Temple boilers except 2 Normand return flame
   boilers (built by Normand) in *Nos 278-280*. 10.5t coal (normal) =
   929.779nm @ 13.91kts (*Nº 278*).
**Torpedoes and guns:** As *Torpilleur nº 212.* The 381mm torpedoes were a
   long 6.03-metre model vice the usual 5.75-metre type.

***Torpilleur nº 278*** (P97) Augustin Normand, Le Havre.
On list 1.1902. Ord: 16.10.1901. K: 1901. L: 8.10.1903.
   Trials: 12.1903-1.1904. Comm: 6.2.1904 (full)
Budget 1902. Machinery installed 9.7.1903 to 15.10.1903. *Défense
   mobile* at Cherbourg and 1st Channel torpedo boat flotilla 1904-06,
   2nd Channel torpedo boat flotilla at Dunkirk 1906-11, Cherbourg torpedo boats 1911-20. Used as light minesweeper 1918-20. Struck
   29.6.1921. Sold 2.1922 at Cherbourg to BU.

***Torpilleur nº 279*** (P98) Augustin Normand, Le Havre.
On list 1.1902. Ord: 16.10.1901. K: 1901. L: 18.1.1904.
   Trials: 3-4.1904.
Budget 1902. *Défense mobile* at Cherbourg 1904-05, 2nd Channel torpedo
   boat flotilla at Dunkirk and Dunkirk torpedo boats 1905-18 (based at
   Boulogne 1917-18). Struck 12.1.1920 Sold 9.1920 at Cherbourg to
   BU.

***Torpilleur nº 280*** (P99) Augustin Normand, Le Havre.
On list 1.1902. Ord: 16.10.1901. K: 1901. L: 2.3.1904. Trials: 3-5.1904.
Budget 1902. *Défense mobile* at Cherbourg 1904-06, 2nd Channel torpedo

boat flotilla at Dunkirk and Dunkirk torpedo boats 1906-19 (based at
   Boulogne 1917-18). Struck 12.1.1920. Sold 9.20 at Cherbourg to BU.

***Torpilleur nº 281*** (P100) A.C. Loire, Nantes.
On list 1.1903. Ord: 14.1.1903. K: 1902. L: 1q.1904. Trials: 5-6.1904.
Budget 1902. *Défense mobile* at Brest and 1st Atlantic torpedo boat flotilla
   1904-11, Toulon torpedo boats 1911-18 (at Brindisi 1915 and at
   Corfu 1917-18). Off main list by 3.1920 and for sale at Toulon. Sold
   5.1920 at Toulon to BU. Struck (retroactively) 1.10.1920.

***Torpilleur nº 282*** (P101) A.C. Loire, Nantes.
On list 1.1903. Ord: 14.1.1903. K: 1903. L: 1q.1904. Trials: 5-7.1904.
Budget 1902. *Défense mobile* at Brest, then 1st Atlantic torpedo boat
   flotilla and Brest torpedo boats 1904-19. Struck 4.4.1920. Sold
   12.1920 at Brest to BU.

***Torpilleur nº 283*** (P102) A.C. Loire, Nantes.
On list 1.1903. Ord: 14.1.1903. K: 1903. L: 2q.1904. Trials: 7-9.1904.
Budget 1902. *Défense mobile* at Brest, then 1st Atlantic torpedo boat
   flotilla and Brest torpedo boats 1904-19. Struck 4.4.1920. Sold
   12.1920 at Brest to BU.

***Torpilleur nº 284*** (P103) F.C. Méditerranée, Le Havre-Graville.
On list 1.1903. Ord: 7.1.1903. K: 1903. L: 16.4.1904. Trials: 5-7.1904.
Budget 1902. *Défense mobile* at Cherbourg 1904-05. Designated for
   Saigon 5.1905 and became *Torpilleur colonial Nº 17-S* (Saigon).
   Escorted to Saigon by *Foudre* 8-10.1905. 1st China seas torpedo boat
   flotilla and Saigon torpedo boats 1906-14, Indochina naval division
   1914-18. To *Torpilleur de 1re classe* 1.1909. Struck 21.6.1920. Sold
   11.1920 at Saigon to BU.

***Torpilleur nº 285*** (P104) F.C. Méditerranée, Le Havre-Graville.
On list 1.1903. Ord: 7.1.1903. K: 1903. L: 28.5.1904. Trials: 7-8.1904.
Budget 1902. *Défense mobile* at Cherbourg 1904-05. Designated for
   Saigon 5.1905 and became *Torpilleur colonial Nº 18-S* (Saigon).
   Escorted to Saigon by *Foudre* 8-10.1905. 1st China seas torpedo boat
   flotilla and Saigon torpedo boats 1906-14, Indochina naval division
   1914-18. To *Torpilleur de 1re classe* 1.1909. Off main list by 3.1920.
   Struck 14.5.1921. Reported sold 8.1921 at Saigon to BU although still
   carried in the 1.1924 fleet list as for sale.

***Torpilleur nº 286*** (P105) F.C. Méditerranée, Le Havre-Graville.
On list 1.1903. Ord: 7.1.1903. K: 1903. L: 29.7.1904. Trials: 8.1904.
Budget 1902. *Défense mobile* at Cherbourg 1904-05. Designated for
   Saigon 5.1905 and became *Torpilleur colonial Nº 19-S* (Saigon).
   Escorted to Saigon by *Foudre* 8-10.1905. 1st China seas torpedo boat
   flotilla and Saigon torpedo boats 1906-14, Indochina naval division
   1915-18. To *Torpilleur de 1re classe* 1.1909. Struck 21.6.1920. Sold
   11.1920 at Saigon to BU.

***Torpilleur nº 287*** (P106) Schneider, Chalon-sur-Saône.
On list 1.1903. Ord: 7.1.1903. K: 1903. L: 14.5.1904. Trials: 5-9.1904.
Budget 1902. Designated 4.7.1904 for the Indian Ocean torpedo boat
   flotilla at Diégo Suarez and became *Torpilleur colonial Nº 5-M*
   (Madagascar). To *Torpilleur de 1re classe* 1.1909. Decomm. 10.1909,
   condemnation decided 12.1910. Struck 20.2.1911, for sale at Diégo
   Suarez 1911-1914. Sold 1917 at Diego Suarez to BU.

***Torpilleur nº 288*** (P107) Schneider, Chalon-sur-Saône.
On list 1.1903. Ord: 7.1.1903. K: 1903. L: 17.7.1904. Trials: 6-11.1904.
Budget 1902. 2nd Mediterranean torpedo boat flotilla in Corsica 1905-
   13, Toulon torpedo boats 1913-20 (at Corfu 1915-17). Struck
   29.6.1921, torpedo target at Toulon 1921-1923. Sold 5.1925 at
   Toulon to BU.

***Torpilleur nº 289*** (P108) Schneider, Chalon-sur-Saône.
On list 1.1903. Ord: 7.1.1903. K: 1903. L: 26.7.1904. Trials: 8-11.1904.
Budget 1902. 2nd Mediterranean torpedo boat flotilla in Corsica 1905-

The 37-metre *Torpilleur no 282* leaving the locks at Morlaix, a town near Brest. The boat spent her entire career assigned to Brest. *(Postcard by ND)*

09, 3rd Mediterranean torpedo boat flotilla at Bizerte, then Bizerte torpedo boats and Tunisia division of patrol boats 1909-18. Designated to replace the fishery protection vessel *Moulouya* (ex *Torpilleur no 193*) but grounded 1919 on the beach at Nabeul in Tunisia, refloated, decomm. 1.5.1919. Off main list by 3.1920 and for sale at Bizerte. Struck 26.11.1920. Sold 1.1921 at Bizerte to BU.

*Torpilleur no 290* (P109) Ch. Penhoët, Rouen-Grand Quévilly/Schneider, Creusot.

On list 1.1903. Ord: 7.1.1903. K: 20.8.1903. L: 2.5.1904. Trials: 6-7.1904.

Budget 1902. Left the yard 13.7.1904. Designated 1904 for the Indian Ocean torpedo boat flotilla at Diégo Suarez and became *Torpilleur colonial No 6-M* (Madagascar). To *Torpilleur de 1re classe* 1.1909. Condemnation proposed 4.1910. Struck 20.2.1911, for sale at Diégo Suarez 1911-1914. Sold 1915 at Diego Suarez to BU.

*Torpilleur no 291* (P110) Ch. Penhoët, Rouen-Grand Quévilly/Schneider, Creusot.

On list 1.1903. Ord: 7.1.1903. K: 15.9.1903. L: 30.5.1904. Trials: 8-9.1904.

Budget 1902. Left the yard 31.7.1904. *Défense mobile* in Corsica 1904-05. Designated for Saigon 1905 and became *Torpilleur colonial No 20-S* (Saigon). Escorted to Saigon by *Foudre* 8-10.1905. 1st China seas torpedo boat flotilla and Saigon torpedo boats 1906-21. To *Torpilleur de 1re classe* 1.1909. Off main list by 3.1920. Struck 28.11.1922. Engine removed 1922 to replace that of *Torpilleur no 273* in anti-submarine

gunboat *Moqueuse*. Target at Saigon 1922-1923. Sold 11.1923 at Saigon to BU.

*Torpilleur no 292* (P111) Ch. Penhoët, Rouen-Grand Quévilly/Schneider, Creusot.

On list 1.1903. Ord: 7.1.1903. K: 24.10.1903. L: 30.6.1904. Trials: 8-10.1904.

Budget 1902. Left the yard 11.8.1904. *Défense mobile* in Corsica 1904-05. Designated for Saigon 1905 and became *Torpilleur colonial No 21-S* (Saigon). Escorted to Saigon by *Foudre* 8-10.1905. 1st China seas torpedo boat flotilla and Saigon torpedo boats 1906-21. To *Torpilleur de 1re classe* 1.1909. Off main list by 3.1920. Struck 28.11.1922. Engine removed 1922 to replace that of *Torpilleur no 214* in anti-submarine gunboat *Malicieuse*. Target at Saigon 1922-1923. Sold 11.1923 at Saigon to BU.

*Torpilleur colonial no 9-S* (P112) Schneider, Chalon-sur-Saône.

On list 1.1903. Ord: 14.8.1902. K: 1902. L: 29.2.1904. Trials: 4-7.1904.

Budget 1902. Transported in sections to Indochina and assembled at Saigon. Trials in the river at Saigon produced 24.40 knots at 341.5rpm. *Défense mobile* at Saigon, then 1st China seas torpedo boat flotilla. To *Torpilleur de 1re classe* 1.1909. Struck 3.11.1910. Sold 1912 at Saigon to BU.

### 37-METRE EXPERIMENTAL TURBINE TYPE, 1903. *TORPILLEUR No 293* (P113). *Torpilleur de 1re classe.* Experimental turbine torpedo boat with hull based on Normand's 37-metre type.

Two experimental turbine boats were funded by the 1903 budget, one with Parsons turbines and one with Bréguet-Laval turbines. In the first of these,

*N° 293*, the hull of Normand's *Torpilleur n° 278* was reproduced but lengthened 2.50m and given finer lines aft and flatter longitudinal sections. The turbine installation was ordered from Parsons in England. It included 5 reaction turbines on 3 shafts, each shaft with 1 screw. The steam entered a HP turbine and exhausted to a MP and then to an LP turbine, each on its own propeller shaft. There was also an astern turbine and a cruising turbine for speeds up to 14 knots for a total of five turbines on three shafts. *N° 293* was accepted in July 1904 after trials that were without incident. At 10 knots and 14 knots her coal consumption was about twice that of *N°ˢ 278-280*, and it was clear that with her very limited radius of action it would be hard to integrate her into a standard torpedo boat flotilla.

**Dimensions & tons:** 39.5m wl x 4.12m wl. 95.47t disp. Draught: 1.18m fwd, 1.25m amidships, 2.60m aft under the propeller guard.

**Machinery:** 2,000ihp designed at 15kg/cm² boiler pressure. Speed 26kts. Trials 26.20kts (27.30kts max on the measured mile). 5 Parsons turbines on 3 shafts, each shaft with 1 screw. 2 Normand boilers. 15t coal.

**Torpedoes and guns:** As *Torpilleur n° 212*.

*Torpilleur n° 293* (P113) Augustin Normand, Le Havre/Parsons, England.
On list 1.1903. Ord: 29.10.1902. K: 3.1903. L: 17.3.1904. Trials: 5-9.1904.
Budget 1903. Renamed *Bouilleur* 1910. Annex to the school for engineers and stokers at Brest 1910-12 and to the Division of schools of the Atlantic at Brest 1912-14. Struck 29.8.1916, for sale at Brest 1920-1922.

---

**37-METRE EXPERIMENTAL TURBINE TYPE, 1903.** *TORPILLEUR N° 294* (P114). *Torpilleurs de 1ʳᵉ classe.* Experimental turbine torpedo boat with hull based on Normand's 37-metre type.

The second experimental turbine boat in the 1903 budget was built under a contract of 11 March 1903 with Maison Bréguet, who built only engines and therefore subcontracted the hull to C.A. Gironde, Bordeaux-Lormont. At this time Bréguet and Rateau were the only French turbine builders, and Rateau turbines were already running trials in *N° 243*. The turbine plant in *N° 294* included five Bréguet-Laval reaction turbines on three propeller shafts, although each shaft had two screws instead of one screw as in *N° 293*. The boat had no cruising turbine but instead had two astern turbines on the central shaft. The lack of a cruising turbine made her even less economical of fuel than *N° 293* at 14 knots and the astern turbines were slow to take effect.

**Dimensions & tons:** 38.45m wl x 4.09m ext, 3.95m wl. 97.47t disp designed, 101t to 102t actual. Draught: 1.08m fwd, 1.40m amidships, 2.24m aft.

**Machinery:** 1,800ihp designed at 16.5kg/cm² boiler pressure. Speed 24kts. Trials 25.14kts. 5 Bréguet-Laval turbines on 3 shafts, each shaft with 2 screws. 2 Guyot-Du Temple boilers.

**Torpedoes and guns:** As *Torpilleur n° 212*.

*Torpilleur n° 294* (P114) C.A. Gironde, Bordeaux-Lormont/Maison Bréguet, Paris (Bréguet turbines).
On list 1.1904. Ord: 11.3.1903. K: 1903. L: 2.8.1904. Trials: 8.1904-5.1905.
Budget 1903. Renamed *Réchauffeur* 1910. Annex to the school for engineers and stokers at Brest 1910-14. Struck 29.8.1916, for sale at Brest 1920-1922.

---

**38-METRE TYPE, 1903 TRANCHE.** *TORPILLEURS N°ˢ 295–317 and 368* (P115-138). *Torpilleurs de 1ʳᵉ classe.* Normand 38-metre type torpedo boats with three torpedo tubes (one in the bow and two in a twin mount on deck amidships), two funnels, and one mast.

The regular boats built under the 1903 budget introduced a new 38-metre design, whose main purpose was to add a third torpedo tube. The single pivoting tube amidships was replaced with two tubes mounted side by side on a rotating platform pointed in opposite directions. This allowed the boat's commander, once the mounting was trained on the beam, to fire to either side as the tactical situation dictated without having to move the tube or expose his crew on deck. Initially it was intended to mount tubes for the long (6.03m) 381mm torpedoes that had already been adopted for the previous series but by a contract modification of 23 November 1904 the calibre of the tubes was increased to 450mm for 5.05m (5.25m with the firing mechanism) Model 1892 torpedoes. These torpedoes were soon fitted with Obry regulators which brought the torpedoes back to the intended course after the impact of launch. Their warheads were also 90kg instead of 42kg in the 381mm torpedoes. Consideration was given to fitting the boats with 47mm rather than 37mm guns, but it was decided that the difference was meaningless against the 76mm and 57mm guns carried by destroyers and the two old 37mm/20 M1885 QF guns were retained. However, the propulsion plant was not augmented to offset the increased weight of the boat, and speeds in service were generally less than for the previous 37-metre type. They still generally could reach a speed of 22.5 or 23 knots in service and maintain it for several hours without risking damage to the machinery.

Once again Normand was asked for a design, which he submitted during the summer of 1903. Normand received the orders for the first two boats in the 1903 batch, and the rest (except for one colonial boat not built as such) were distributed three each to seven builders through competitive bidding. This batch brought the Chantiers Dubigeon of Nantes into the torpedo boat programme. Curiously the length and displacement of this type were almost exactly as those of *Torpilleur n° 1*, built some 28 years previously.

In November 1912 the Navy decided to exchange the 450mm torpedo tubes in some of the 38-metre torpedo boats, for which the large tubes had proven to be too heavy, with the 381mm tubes of the first 32 destroyers of the *Durandal* type, whose 23 later near sisters already carried the larger tubes. However, as of August 1914 this change had not been implemented.

**Dimensions & tons:** 40.17m oa, 38.00m wl/pp x 4.40m ext, 4.24m wl. 97.5t disp (designed), 101t to 103t (actual). Draught: (designed) 1.88m amidships, 2.64m aft under the propeller guard. Men: 23.

**Machinery:** 2,000ihp designed at 17kg/cm² boiler pressure. Speed 26kts. Trials (*N° 299*) 27.65kts at 344.9rpm, (*N° 303*) 25.65kts at 331.72rpm. 1 screw. 1 triple expansion engine with 3 cylinders of 0.42m, 0.60m, and 0.90m diameter and 0.50m stroke except in *N°ˢ* 295-296 with cylinders of 0.41m, 0.59m, and 0.89m and 0.50m stroke. 2 Normand boilers in the Normand, Dyle, FCM, and Dubigeon boats and 2 Guyot-Du Temple boilers in the others. 11.8t coal (normal), 18t coal (surcharge). Range 1,000nm @ 14kts with normal coal, 2,000nm @ 10kts with coal surcharge.

**Torpedoes:** 3 tubes for 450mm M1892 torpedoes (1 fixed in the bow, 2 on one deck mount amidships mounted head to tail). M1904 torpedoes in *No 368*. **Guns:** 2 x 37mm/20 M1885 QF guns (on sides amidships).

*Torpilleur n° 295* (P115) Augustin Normand, Le Havre.
On list 1.1904. Ord: 11.11.1903. K: 1903. L: 1.1906. Trials: 4-8.1906.
Budget 1903. 1ˢᵗ Channel torpedo boat flotilla and Cherbourg torpedo boats 1906-19. Struck 12.1.1920. Sold 9.1920 at Cherbourg to BU.

*Torpilleur n° 296* (P116) Augustin Normand, Le Havre.
On list 1.1904. Ord: 11.11.1903. K: 1903. L: 24.4.1906. Trials: 5-7.1906.
Budget 1903. 1ˢᵗ Channel torpedo boat flotilla and Cherbourg torpedo boats 1906. One of the two deck tubes removed 1913. Struck 18.5.1921. Sold 1.1922 at Cherbourg to BU.

A working party on a 38-metre 1st class torpedo boat torpedo boat handling stores at Cherbourg during World War I. The fore funnel is on the left, and the shack on the right behind the after funnel was set up in port for the galley. *(NHHC, NH-55865)*

*Torpilleur n⁰ 297* (P117) C.A. Gironde, Bordeaux-Lormont.
On list 1.1904. Ord: 23.12.1903. K: 1903. L: 26.7.1905.
  Trials: 10.1905-1.1906.
Budget 1903. 1ˢᵗ Channel torpedo boat flotilla and Cherbourg torpedo
  boats 1906-20. Used as light minesweeper 1919-20. Struck 27.7.1921.
  Sold 5.1922 at Cherbourg to BU.

*Torpilleur n⁰ 298* (P118) C.A. Gironde, Bordeaux-Lormont.
On list 1.1904. Ord: 23.12.1903. K: 1903. L: 9.10.1905.
  Trials: 11.1905-2.1906.
Budget 1903. Intended for service at Brest but suffered major boiler
  casualty en route and remained at Lorient 1906-07. At Cherbourg by
  1914, at Ajaccio 1916-18. Boiler repairs at Toulon stopped after the
  Armistice. Off main list by 3.1920 and for sale at Toulon. Sold 5.1920
  at Toulon to BU. Struck (retroactively) 1.10.1920.

*Torpilleur n⁰ 299* (P119) C.A. Gironde, Bordeaux-Lormont.
On list 1.1904. Ord: 23.12.1903. K: 1903. L: 28.10.1905.
  Trials: 12.1905-3.1906.
Budget 1903. 1ˢᵗ Atlantic torpedo boat flotilla and Brest torpedo boats
  1906-18. Struck 15.1.1921. Sold 12.1921 to BU.

*Torpilleur n⁰ 300* (P120) Dyle et Bacalan, Bordeaux-Bacalan.

On list 1.1904. Ord: 23.12.1903. K: 1903. L: 27.10.1905.
  Trials: 11.1905-2.1906.
Budget 1903. 3ʳᵈ Atlantic torpedo boat flotilla at Rochefort, then
  1ˢᵗ Channel torpedo boat flotilla and Cherbourg torpedo boats 1906-
  16. Sunk 1.11.1916 by a mine in the roadstead at Le Havre.

*Torpilleur n⁰ 301* (P121) Dyle et Bacalan, Bordeaux-Bacalan.
On list 1.1904. Ord: 23.12.1903. K: 1903. L: 10.1905. Trials: 12.1905-
  5.1906.
Budget 1903. 1ˢᵗ Channel torpedo boat flotilla, then Cherbourg torpedo
  boats and Normandy patrol boat division 1906-17, Brest patrol boats
  and Brittany patrol boat division 1917-18. Used as light minesweeper
  1918-20. Struck 29.11.1921. Sold 3.1922 at Brest to BU.

*Torpilleur n⁰ 302* (P122) Dyle et Bacalan, Bordeaux-Bacalan.
On list 1.1904. Ord: 23.12.1903. K: 1903. L: 14.12.1905.
  Trials: 1-3.1906.
Budget 1903. 1ˢᵗ Channel torpedo boat flotilla and Cherbourg torpedo
  boats 1906-16, Normandy patrol boat division 1916-19. Struck
  4.4.1921. Sold 7.1922 at Cherbourg to BU.

*Torpilleur n⁰ 303* (P123) A.C. Loire, Nantes.
On list 1.1904. Ord: 23.12.1903. K: 1903. L: 27.12.1904.
  Trials: 9-12.1905.
Budget 1903. 1ˢᵗ Atlantic torpedo boat flotilla and Brest torpedo boats
  1906-14, then Rochefort torpedo boats and Gascony patrol boat divi-
  sion. Struck 10.5.1920. Sold 1920 at Rochefort.

2204. - Torpilleur en Essais

A 38-metre 1st class torpedo boat, probably *Torpilleur no 303*, running trials. Masts were normally lowered during trials to achieve the best possible speed. This group of boats introduced the twin torpedo tube mounting in which the tubes pointed in opposite directions, giving the boat's commander greater tactical flexibility. *(Postcard by H. Laurent, Port Louis)*

*Torpilleur no 304* (P124) A.C. Loire, Nantes.
On list 1.1904. Ord: 23.12.1903. K: 1903. L: 24.1.1905. Trials: 12.1905-2.1906.
Budget 1903. 1st Atlantic torpedo boat flotilla and Brest torpedo boats 1906-16. Loire patrol boat division 1917-18. Used as light minesweeper 1918-19. Retired 1919, for sale at Lorient 1920. Sold 10.1920 to BU.

*Torpilleur no 305* (P125) A.C. Loire, Nantes.
On list 1.1904. Ord: 23.12.1903. K: 1903. L: 23.2.1905. Trials: 2-5.1906.
Budget 1903. 1st Atlantic torpedo boat flotilla and Brest torpedo boats 1906-15, Dunkirk torpedo boats 1915-18. Off main list by 3.1920 and for sale at Cherbourg 1920. Struck 26.11.1920.

*Torpilleur no 306* (P126) F.C. Méditerranée, Le Havre-Graville.
On list 1.1904. Ord: 23.12.1903. K: 1903. L: 6.5.1905. Trials: 6-10.1905.
Budget 1903. 1st Channel torpedo boat flotilla at Cherbourg 1905-06, 2nd Channel torpedo boat flotilla and Dunkirk torpedo boats 1906-11, boilers retubed 1912-13, Cherbourg torpedo boats and Normandy patrol boat division 1914-20. Used as light minesweeper 1918-20. Sold 3.1921 at Cherbourg (or Brest) to BU. Struck (retroactively) 29.11.1921.

*Torpilleur no 307* (P127) F.C. Méditerranée, Le Havre-Graville.
On list 1.1904. Ord: 23.12.1903. K: 1903. L: 7.1905. Trials: 8-12.1905.
Budget 1903. 1st Channel torpedo boat flotilla at Cherbourg 1906-07, 2nd Channel torpedo boat flotilla and Dunkirk torpedo boats 1907-12, Cherbourg torpedo boats and Normandy patrol boat division 1913-19. Off main list by 3.1920 and for sale at Cherbourg. Struck 26.11.1920. Sold 5.1921 at Cherbourg to BU.

*Torpilleur no 308* (P128) F.C. Méditerranée, Le Havre-Graville.
On list 1.1904. Ord: 23.12.1903. K: 1903. L: 13.9.1905. Trials: 10.1905-1.1906.
Budget 1903. 1st Channel torpedo boat flotilla at Cherbourg 1906-07,

2nd Channel torpedo boat flotilla and Dunkirk torpedo boats 1907-12, Cherbourg torpedo boats and Normandy patrol boat division 1913-19. Used as light minesweeper 1917-19. Struck 27.5.1921. Sold 5.1921 at Cherbourg to BU.

*Torpilleur no 309* (P129) Schneider, Chalon-sur-Saône.
On list 1.1904. Ord: 23.12.1903. K: 1903. L: 6.1905. Trials: 11.1905-3.1906.
Budget 1903. 1st Mediterranean torpedo boat flotilla at Toulon 1906-14, Dardanelles 1915, Salonica trawler group 1916-18, Constantinople 1918-19, reserve at Bizerte 6.1919. Struck 4.3.1920. Sold 12.1920 at Bizerte to BU.

*Torpilleur no 310* (P130) Schneider, Chalon-sur-Saône.
On list 1.1904. Ord: 23.12.1903. K: 1903. L: 8.1905. Trials: 12.1905-5.1906.
Budget 1903. 1st Mediterranean torpedo boat flotilla at Toulon 1906-14. Salonica trawler group 1916-17, Provence torpedo boat division 1918. School for stoking, Toulon, 1920-1924. Off main list 1924 (condemnation pending). Struck 10.11.1925. Sold 5.1927 at Toulon to BU.

*Torpilleur no 311* (P131) Schneider, Chalon-sur-Saône.
On list 1.1904. Ord: 23.12.1903. K: 1903. L: 1905. Trials: 1-5.1906.
Budget 1903. 1st Mediterranean torpedo boat flotilla and Toulon torpedo boats 1906-16. Salonica trawler group 1916-18. In reserve 1918 at Bizerte. Struck 4.3.1920. Sold 1.1921 at Bizerte to BU.

*Torpilleur no 312* (P132) Ch. Penhoët, Rouen-Grand Quévilly.
On list 1.1904. Ord: 23.12.1903. K: 1903. L: 17.6.1905. Trials: 7-12.1905.
Budget 1903. Left the yard 13.7.1905. 1st Atlantic torpedo boat flotilla and Brest torpedo boats 1906-16, Oran flotillas 1916-18, then reserve at Bizerte. Struck 4.3.1920. For sale at Bizerte 1920-1922. Target at Bizerte 1922-1939.

*Torpilleur no 313* (P133) Ch. Penhoët, Rouen-Grand Quévilly.
On list 1.1904. Ord: 23.12.1903. K: 1.12.1904. L: 3.8.1905. Trials: 9-12.1905.
Budget 1903. Left the yard 21.8.1905. 1st Channel torpedo boat flotilla and Cherbourg torpedo boats, then Normandy patrol boat division 1906-19. Used as light minesweeper 1917-18. Retired 1920, for sale at Cherbourg 1920. Sold 5.1921 at Cherbourg to BU.

*Torpilleur no 314* (P134) Ch. Penhoët, Rouen-Grand Quévilly.
On list 1.1904. Ord: 23.12.1903. K: 1.12.1904. L: 3.8.1905. Trials: 11.1905-1.1906.
Budget 1903. Left the yard 21.8.1905. 1st Channel torpedo boat flotilla, then Dunkirk torpedo boats 1906-18, Calais torpedo boat group 1918. Off main list by 3.1920 and for sale at Cherbourg. Struck 26.11.1920. Sold 5.1921 at Cherbourg to BU.

*Torpilleur no 315* (P135) A. Dubigeon, Nantes.
On list 1.1904. Ord: 23.12.1903. K: 1903. L: 1905. Trials: 8-10.1905.
Budget 1903. 1st Channel torpedo boat flotilla and Cherbourg torpedo boats, then Normandy patrol boat division 1906-18. Used as light minesweeper 1918-19. In 1919 classed in the auxiliary fleet as escort for minesweeping units at Calais and Le Havre, belonged to the flotilla of the 1st Maritime Region 1919-32. Condemned 20.6.1933. For sale by the Domaines 1933-1934, BU at Cherbourg.

*Torpilleur no 316* (P136) A. Dubigeon, Nantes.
On list 1.1904. Ord: 23.12.1903. K: 1903. L: 1905. Trials: 10.1905-1.1906.
Budget 1903. 1st Channel torpedo boat flotilla and Cherbourg torpedo boats, then Normandy patrol boat division 1906-18. Used as light minesweeper 1917-18. Struck 27.7.1921. Sold 5.1922 at Cherbourg to BU.

The 38-metre 1st class torpedo boat *Torpilleur no 314* in a drydock designed specifically for torpedo boats at Cherbourg in 1915-17. She has the clutter on deck typical of dockyard overhauls. *No 314*'s single large propeller extended below the keel and was protected by a metal frame running under it from the keel to the bottom of the rudder. Here the rudder and parts of the frame appear to have been landed for repairs. Two 37-metre boats behind her, *No 206* and *No 236* have been dismantled pending use as storage hulks and two derelict submarines, possibly *Naiade* class, are just ahead of the dock with *No 314*. (*NHHC, NH-55869*)

*Torpilleur no 317* (P137) A. Dubigeon, Nantes.

On list 1.1904. Ord: 23.12.1903. K: 1903. L: 1905. Trials: 11.1905-2.1906.

Budget 1903. 1st Channel torpedo boat flotilla and Cherbourg torpedo boats 1906-16, Dunkirk torpedo boats 1916. Mined 27.12.1916 off Calais.

*Torpilleur no 368* (P138) Toulon Dyd.

On list 1.1905. Ord: 23.6.1904. K: 1904. L: 2.3.1907. Trials: 7-12.1907.

Budget 1903 (delayed to 1904). Planned as the 1903 colonial boat to be like *9-S* and to be shipped in sections to Saigon and assembled there, but this plan was abandoned and she was built instead at Toulon with experimental machinery with forced lubrication. Torpedo boat number assigned and vessel built with *No 369* below. 2nd Mediterranean torpedo boat flotilla at Ajaccio 1908-11, to 1st Mediterranean torpedo flotilla at Toulon 1912 for assignment to the Mediterranean school division. At Taranto 1915, Corfu 1916-17, and Bizerte 1918. *Garde-pêche T368* at Bizerte 1920 and at Algiers 1922-1924. Off main list 1924 at Bizerte (condemnation pending). Struck 28.4.1925. Sold 8.1925 at Bizerte to BU.

**38-METRE TYPE, 1904 TRANCHE. *TORPILLEURS Nos 318–367* and *369*** (P139-189). *Torpilleurs de 1re classe.* Normand 38-metre type

torpedo boats as *Torpilleur no 295*. Designed by Normand.

The 1904 batch of 38-metre boats brought De la Brosse et Fouché of Nantes into the programme. The Penhoët yard at Rouen proposed to build one of its nine boats, *Torpilleur no 366,* with an experimental reciprocating engine that used high pressure superheated steam introduced into the engine through valves controlled by Lentz's patent poppet valve gear. Although the speed requirement was set at only 25 knots this engine proved unsatisfactory in trials and was replaced at the builder's expense with a standard engine.

The 1903 budget included one colonial boat, P138, and the 1904 budget added P189. They were to be built in sections and assembled at Saigon. They followed *Torpilleurs S-8* and *S-9* in the listing and probably would have been named *S-10* and *S-11*. However, the plan to make them colonial boats was abandoned and instead they were assigned to Toulon to be built with experimental forced lubrication engines of the Delaunay-Belleville type. P138 became *Torpilleur no 368* and P189 became *Torpilleur no 369*, both now under the 1904 budget. Their engines had cylinders measuring 0.415m, 0.62m, and 0.93m in diameter and a 0.48m stroke. The trials of the two boats were long and difficult, and they were finally accepted at only 1,800ihp vice 2,000ihp with a best speed of 24.89 knots in *No 368* and 25.26 knots in *No 369*. They were, however, economical boats which performed long service. Forced lubrication (which allowed a reduction in engine room personnel) was then tried in the destroyer

*Pierrier* and some 450-ton destroyers, and because of its operational advantages it was generally adopted after the problems with it were worked out.

**Dimensions & tons:** as *Torpilleur n° 295*. Men: 23.
**Machinery:** 2,000ihp designed (1,800ihp in *N°s 368-369*) at 17kg/cm$^2$ boiler pressure. Speed 26kts. Trials (*N° 365*) 27.68kts at 340.56rpm, (*N° 352*) 25.65kts at 334rpm. 1 screw. 1 triple expansion engine with 3 cylinders of 0.42m, 0.60m, and 0.90m diameter and 0.50m stroke except in *N°s 366* and *368-369* (see above). 2 Normand boilers in the Normand, Dyle, FCM, Dubigeon, and Brosse et Fouché boats and 2 Guyot-Du Temple boilers in the others.
**Torpedoes and guns:** as *Torpilleur n° 295* but torpedoes are M1904.

*Torpilleur n° 318* (P139) Augustin Normand, Le Havre.
On list 1.1905. Ord: 20.7.1904. K: 1904. L: 6.8.1906. Trials: 9.1906-10.1907.
Budget 1904. 1st Channel torpedo boat flotilla and Cherbourg torpedo boats 1907-11, Dunkirk torpedo boats 1912-18. Off main list c1921 and for sale at Cherbourg 1921-1922. Struck 7.7.1922. Retained as a target towing vessel, target at Cherbourg 1926-1927.

*Torpilleur n° 319* (P140) Augustin Normand, Le Havre.
On list 1.1905. Ord: 20.7.1904. K: 1904. L: 4.8.1906. Trials: 10.1906-10.1907.
Budget 1904. 1st Channel torpedo boat flotilla and Cherbourg torpedo boats 1907-11. Mined 19.1.1915 off Nieuport. Struck 19.5.1915.

*Torpilleur n° 320* (P141) Augustin Normand, Le Havre.
On list 1.1905. Ord: 20.7.1904. K: 1904. L: 20.10.1906. Trials: 11.1906-5.1907.
Budget 1904. 1st Channel torpedo boat flotilla 1907-10, Dunkirk torpedo boats 1911-18. Used as light minesweeper 1918-20. Struck 12.1.1920 and BU.

*Torpilleur n° 321* (P142) Augustin Normand, Le Havre.
On list 1.1905. Ord: 20.7.1904. K: 1904. L: 22.11.1906. Trials: 12.1906-10.1907.
Budget 1904. 1st Channel torpedo boat flotilla 1908-11, Dunkirk torpedo boats 1912-18. Used as light minesweeper 1918-20. Flotilla of the 1st Maritime Region at Cherbourg 1920-28, then in the 1st aviso flotilla at Cherbourg 1928-35 with a wartime assignment as escort for minesweeping units at Calais and at Le Havre. Struck 14.6.1936 (decision promulgated 15.7.1936). Sold 8.1937 at Cherbourg to BU.

*Torpilleur n° 322* (P143) A. Dubigeon, Nantes.
On list 1.1905. Ord: 3.8.1904. K: 1904. L: c26.10.1905. Trials: 2-7.1906.
Budget 1904. 2nd Atlantic torpedo boat flotilla and Lorient torpedo boats 1906-13, Dunkirk torpedo boats 1913-19. Used as light minesweeper 1918-19. Struck 4.4.1921. Sold 1.1922 at Cherbourg to BU.

*Torpilleur n° 323* (P144) A. Dubigeon, Nantes.
On list 1.1905. Ord: 3.8.1904. K: 1904. L: 9.1.1906. Trials: 4-7.1906.
Budget 1904. 2nd Atlantic torpedo boat flotilla and Lorient torpedo boats 1906-13, Dunkirk torpedo boats 1913-18. Struck 12.1.1920. BU 1920.

*Torpilleur n° 324* (P145) A. Dubigeon, Nantes.
On list 1.1905. Ord: 3.8.1904. K: 1904. L: c9.4.1906. Trials: 6-12.1906.
Budget 1904. 2nd Atlantic torpedo boat flotilla at Lorient 1907-09, 1st Atlantic torpedo boat flotilla and Brest torpedo boats 1909-17, Gascony patrol boat division 1917-18 (used as light minesweeper). Off main list 1921 and for sale at Brest 1921-1922. Target at Brest 1922-c1930. Condemned 7.5.1924.

*Torpilleur n° 325* (P146) C.A. Gironde, Bordeaux-Lormont.
On list 1.1905. Ord: 3.8.1904. K: 1904. L: 16.3.1906. Trials: 4-6.1906.
Budget 1904. 3rd Atlantic torpedo boat flotilla at Rochefort 1906-08,

5th Mediterranean torpedo boat flotilla at Oran 1908-13, Bizerte torpedo boats and Tunisia patrol boat division 1914-19. Mined 22.1.1919 off Tunis.

*Torpilleur n° 326* (P147) C.A. Gironde, Bordeaux-Lormont.
On list 1.1905. Ord: 3.8.1904. K: 1904. L: 10.4.1906. Trials: 5.1906-10.1907.
Budget 1904. 3rd Atlantic torpedo boat flotilla and Rochefort torpedo boats 1907-14, Cherbourg torpedo boats and Normandy patrol boat division 1914-19. Retired 1920. Sold 10.1920 at Cherbourg to BU.

*Torpilleur n° 327* (P148) C.A. Gironde, Bordeaux-Lormont.
On list 1.1905. Ord: 3.8.1904. K: 1904. L: c3.7.1906. Trials: 7.1906-1.1907.
Budget 1904. 3rd Atlantic torpedo boat flotilla and Rochefort torpedo boats 1908-13, Cherbourg torpedo boats and Normandy patrol boat division 1914-17. Rochefort torpedo boats 1917-18 (used as light minesweeper). Refitted after the war, served at Brest in the Atlantic flotilla (2nd minesweeping squadron 1923-24) and then the flotilla of the 2nd Maritime District (minesweeping squadron 1925-26 and 2nd aviso squadron 1927-29). Condemned 1.12.1930. For sale by the Domaines 1929-1930. Sold 6.1931 at Brest to BU.

*Torpilleur n° 328* (P149) C.A. Gironde, Bordeaux-Lormont.
On list 1.1905. Ord: 3.8.1904. K: 1904. L: 9.6.1906. Trials: 6.1906-8.1907.
Budget 1904. 5th Mediterranean torpedo boat flotilla at Oran 1907-11, Bizerte torpedo boats 1912-17, Toulon from 1917. School for stoking at the school for apprentice engineers, Toulon, 1920-1924. Struck 9.12.1925. Sold 3.1927 at Toulon to BU.

*Torpilleur n° 329* (P150) C.A. Gironde, Bordeaux-Lormont.
On list 1.1905. Ord: 3.8.1904. K: 1904. L: 3.7.1906. Trials: 7.1906-1.1907.
Budget 1904. 3rd Atlantic torpedo boat flotilla at Rochefort 1907-08, 5th Mediterranean torpedo boat flotilla at Oran 1908-13, Bizerte torpedo boats 1913, Tunisia patrol boat division 1915-18. Struck 7.6.1920. Sold 10.1927 at Bizerte to BU.

*Torpilleur n° 330* (P151) C.A. Gironde, Bordeaux-Lormont.
On list 1.1905. Ord: 3.8.1904. K: 1904. L: c7.1906. Trials: 8.1906-1.1908.
Budget 1904. 3rd Atlantic torpedo boat flotilla at Rochefort 1907-08, 5th Mediterranean torpedo boat flotilla at Oran 1908-12, Bizerte torpedo boats and Tunisia patrol boat division 1913-19. Used as light

The 38-metre 1st class torpedo boat *Torpilleur no 332* underway near Toulon. Her twin torpedo tube mounting does not appear to be on board although a caisson for a reserve torpedo is present on the port rail. *(Postcard by Diaz, Toulon)*

A 38-metre 1st class torpedo boat exercising inside the breakwater at Cherbourg during World War I. The muzzle of the near tube and the breech of the far tube are to the right. The double mounting was on rollers on a circular base and was rotated to its combat position by a couple of crewmen pushing it. The galley shack has been left in position behind the after funnel, indicating that this was a training run and not a combat patrol. *(NHHC, NH-55735)*

minesweeper after the war in North Africa, then school for stoking at Bizerte, and then on fishery protection duty in Algeria 1923-1926. Off main list 1926 and for sale at Bizerte. Struck 18.2.1927. Sold 10.1927 at Bizerte to BU.

*Torpilleur nº 331* (P152) C.A. Gironde, Bordeaux-Lormont.
On list 1.1905. Ord: 3.8.1904. K: 1904. L: 9.1906. Trials: 11.1906-1.1908.
Budget 1904. 3rd Atlantic torpedo boat flotilla and Rochefort torpedo boats 1908-12, Cherbourg torpedo boats 1913-15. Sunk 13.6.1915 off Barfleur after collision with British merchantman *Arleia*.

*Torpilleur nº 332* (P153) Dyle et Bacalan, Bordeaux-Bacalan.
On list 1.1905. Ord: 17.8.1904. K: 1904. L: 23.5.1906. Trials: 7.1906-1.1907.
Budget 1904. 3rd Atlantic torpedo boat flotilla at Rochefort 1907, 4th Mediterranean torpedo boat flotilla at Algiers 1907-10, Oran torpedo boats 1910-12, Bizerte torpedo boats 1913-16, operations in Greece 1916-17. School for stoking at Toulon 1920-1925. Struck 9.12.1925. Sold 1927 at Toulon to BU.

*Torpilleur nº 333* (P154) Dyle et Bacalan, Bordeaux-Bacalan.
On list 1.1905. Ord: 17.8.1904. K: 1904. L: 9.6.1906. Trials: 8.1906-1.1907.
Budget 1904. 3rd Atlantic torpedo boat flotilla at Rochefort 1907, 4th Mediterranean torpedo boat flotilla at Algiers 1907-10, Oran torpedo boats 1910-12, Bizerte torpedo boats and Tunisia patrol boat division 1913-18. Sunk 12.3.1918 in collision off Kelibia (Calibia) near Tunis. Wreck for sale at Bizerte 1920-1922.

*Torpilleur nº 334* (P155) Dyle et Bacalan, Bordeaux-Bacalan.
On list 1.1905. Ord: 17.8.1904. K: 1904. L: 7.1906. Trials: 9.1906-8.1907.
Budget 1904. 3rd Atlantic torpedo boat flotilla at Rochefort 1907-10, Brest torpedo boats 1910-15, Gascony patrol boat division 1915-18. Struck 10.5.1920. Sold 6.1920 at Rochefort to BU.

*Torpilleur nº 335* (P156) Dyle et Bacalan, Bordeaux-Bacalan.
On list 1.1905. Ord: 17.8.1904. K: 1904. L: 9.1906. Trials: 10.1906-12.1907.
Budget 1904. 3rd Atlantic torpedo boat flotilla at Rochefort 1908-10, Brest torpedo boats 1910-14, Dunkirk torpedo boats 1914-15, Oran flotillas 1916-18, at Bizerte 1919. Off main list by 3.1920 and for sale at Bizerte 1920. Struck 26.11.1920. Sold 6.1921 to BU.

*Torpilleur nº 336* (P157) Dyle et Bacalan, Bordeaux-Bacalan.
On list 1.1905. Ord: 17.8.1904. K: 1904. L: c8.1906. Trials: 9.1906-12.1907.
Budget 1904. 3rd Atlantic torpedo boat flotilla at Rochefort 1908-10,

Brest torpedo boats 1910-15, Ajaccio torpedo boats 1916, Toulon torpedo boats 1917-19. Mediterranean school division, annex to the school for engineers and stokers 1920-25, new boilers 1925 and to the flotilla of the 3rd Maritime Region (3rd aviso squadron). Struck 29.9.1931. Sold 1932 at Toulon to BU.

*Torpilleur n° 337* (P158) Dyle et Bacalan, Bordeaux-Bacalan.
On list 1.1905. Ord: 17.8.1904. K: 1904. L: 11.1906. Trials: 10.1907-4.1908.
Budget 1904. 3rd Atlantic torpedo boat flotilla at Rochefort 1908-11, Cherbourg torpedo boats and Normandy patrol boat division 1914-18. Flotillas of the 2nd Maritime Region and the 2nd Maritime District 1923-30. Condemned 30.6.1931. Sold 11.1931 at Brest to BU.

*Torpilleur n° 338* (P159) De la Brosse et Fouché, Nantes.
On list 1.1905. Ord: 17.8.1904. K: 1904. L: 26.2.1906. Trials: 4-5.1906.
Budget 1904. 2nd Atlantic torpedo boat flotilla at Lorient 1906-10, Brest torpedo boats 1910-16, Gascony patrol boat division 1917-18. Struck 1.10.1920. Sold 6.1921 at Rochefort to BU.

*Torpilleur n° 339* (P160) De la Brosse et Fouché, Nantes.

Five 1st class torpedo boats and their leader, the seagoing torpedo boat *Typhon* (TY), at Cherbourg during World War I. The torpedo boats from left to right are probably *N°s 352, 306, Typhon, 295, 297,* and *239. Typhon* has a cap on her fore funnel to protect her enlarged wartime bridge. *(NHHC, NH-55732)*

On list 1.1905. Ord: 17.8.1904. K: 1904. L: 25.4.1906. Trials: 6-9.1906.
Budget 1904. 2nd Atlantic torpedo boat flotilla at Lorient 1907-10, Brest torpedo boats 1911-15, Ajaccio flotillas 1916-18, Bizerte flotilla 1919-24. Off main list 1924 (condemnation pending). Struck 28.4.1925. Sold at Bizerte 8.1925.

*Torpilleur n° 340* (P161) De la Brosse et Fouché, Nantes.
On list 1.1905. Ord: 17.8.1904. K: 1904. L: 21.9.1906. Trials: 7-9.1907.
Budget 1904. 3rd Atlantic torpedo boat flotilla and Rochefort torpedo boats 1908-13, Cherbourg torpedo boats 1914-17, Normandy patrol boat division 1917-19. Sank accidentally off Le Havre 8.4.1917, refloated. Off main list by 3.1920 and for sale at Cherbourg 1920. Struck 26.11.1920. Sold 5.1921 to BU.

*Torpilleur n° 341* (P162) F.C. Méditerranée, Le Havre-Graville.
On list 1.1905. Ord: 3.8.1904. K: 1904. L: 22.1.1906. Trials: 2-11.1906.
Budget 1904. 2nd Channel torpedo boat flotilla and Dunkirk torpedo boats 1912-18 (Calais group 1917-18). Used as light minesweeper in the Normandy flotilla 1918-20. Struck 27.7.1921. Sold 5.1922 at Cherbourg to BU.

*Torpilleur n° 342* (P163) F.C. Méditerranée, Le Havre-Graville.
On list 1.1905. Ord: 3.8.1904. K: 1904. L: 1.1906. Trials: 3-7.1906.
Budget 1904. 2nd Channel torpedo boat flotilla and Dunkirk torpedo boats 1906-18 (Calais group 1917-18). Off main list 1921 and for sale at Cherbourg 1921-1922. Struck 4.8.1922, converted 9.1922 at

Cherbourg to target for the Boulogne sea frontier 1922, sunk c1924, wreck sold at Boulogne 12.1924 although still carried in the 1.1926 fleet list as for sale.

*Torpilleur no 343* (P164) F.C. Méditerranée, Le Havre-Graville.
On list 1.1905. Ord: 3.8.1904. K: 1904. L: 24.3.1906. Trials: 6-8.1906.
Budget 1904. 2nd Channel torpedo boat flotilla and Dunkirk torpedo boats 1906-19 (Calais group 1917-18). Struck 12.1.1920. Sold 1920 to BU.

*Torpilleur no 344* (P165) F.C. Méditerranée, Le Havre-Graville.
On list 1.1905. Ord: 3.8.1904. K: 1904. L: 20.4.1906. Trials: 6-8.1906.
Budget 1904. 2nd Channel torpedo boat flotilla and Dunkirk torpedo boats 1906-18 (Calais group 1917-18). Struck 12.1.1920. Sold 1920 to BU.

*Torpilleur no 345* (P166) F.C. Méditerranée, Le Havre-Graville.
On list 1.1905. Ord: 3.8.1904. K: 1904. L: 11.5.1906. Trials: 6-9.1906.
Budget 1904. 2nd Channel torpedo boat flotilla and Dunkirk torpedo boats 1906-18. Struck 12.1.1920. Sold 1920 to BU.

*Torpilleur no 346* (P167) F.C. Méditerranée, Le Havre-Graville.
On list 1.1905. Ord: 3.8.1904. K: 1904. L: 7.6.1906. Trials: 8-10.1906.
Budget 1904. 2nd Channel torpedo boat flotilla and Dunkirk torpedo boats 1906-18 (Calais group 1917-18). Struck 12.1.1920. Sold 1920 to BU.

*Torpilleur no 347* (P168) A.C. Loire, Nantes.
On list 1.1905. Ord: 3.8.1904. K: 1904. L: 2q.1906. Trials: 6-9.1906.
Budget 1904. 1st Mediterranean torpedo boat flotilla and Toulon torpedo boats 1907-14. Collided 9.10.1914 with *Torpilleur no 348*. Struck 17.10.1914. Sold 1915 at Toulon to BU.

*Torpilleur no 348* (P169) A.C. Loire, Nantes.
On list 1.1905. Ord: 3.8.1904. K: 1904. L: 2q.1906. Trials: 6-9.1906.
Budget 1904. 1st Mediterranean torpedo boat flotilla and Toulon torpedo boats 1907-14. Collided 9.10.1914 with *Torpilleur no 347*. Struck 17.10.1914. Sold 1915 at Toulon to BU.

*Torpilleur no 349* (P170) A.C. Loire, Nantes.
On list 1.1905. Ord: 3.8.1904. K: 1904. L: 10.11.1905. Trials: 7-8.1906.
Budget 1904. 1st Mediterranean torpedo boat flotilla and (from 5.1907) Toulon torpedo boats. At Corfu 1916-17, Provence patrol boat division 1917-18, Bizerte flotilla 1919-37. Condemned and struck 25.11.1937 (decision promulgated 10.1.1938), for sale by the Domaines 1937-1938. Sold 1938 at Toulon to BU.

*Torpilleur no 350* (P171) A.C. Loire, Nantes.
On list 1.1905. Ord: 3.8.1904. K: 1904. L: 7.5.1906. Trials: 8.1906.
Budget 1904. 2nd Atlantic torpedo boat flotilla and Lorient torpedo boats 1906-13, Dunkirk torpedo boats 1913-18 (Calais group 1917-18). Struck 4.4.1921. Sold 7.1922 at Cherbourg to BU.

*Torpilleur no 351* (P172) A.C. Loire, Nantes.
On list 1.1905. Ord: 3.8.1904. K: 1904. L: 5.6.1906. Trials: 9-10.1906.
Budget 1904. 2nd Atlantic torpedo boat flotilla and Lorient torpedo boats 1907-13, Dunkirk torpedo boats 1913-19, then reserve at Cherbourg. Off main list 1921 and for sale at Cherbourg 1921-1922. Struck 4.8.1922, target at Cherbourg for coastal batteries 1922-1926. Wreck damaged 4.1926 and sold 1926 at Cherbourg to BU.

*Torpilleur no 352* (P173) A.C. Loire, Nantes.
On list 1.1905. Ord: 3.8.1904. K: 1904. L: 5.7.1906. Trials: 10.1906-1.1907.
Budget 1904. 2nd Atlantic torpedo boat flotilla and Lorient torpedo boats 1907-13, Cherbourg torpedo boats and Normandy patrol boat division 1913-20. Struck 27.7.1921. Sold 5.1922 at Cherbourg to BU.

*Torpilleur no 353* (P174) Schneider, Chalon-sur-Saône.
On list 1.1905. Ord: 3.8.1904. K: 1904. L: 2q.1906. Trials: 6.1906-3.1907.

Budget 1904. 1st Mediterranean torpedo boat flotilla and Toulon torpedo boats 1907-18, including Dardanelles 1915, Salonica 1916-17, and use as a light minesweeper 1917-18. Struck 4.3.1920. BU 1921 at Bizerte.

*Torpilleur no 354* (P175) Schneider, Chalon-sur-Saône.
On list 1.1905. Ord: 3.8.1904. K: 1904. L: 2q.1906. Trials: 6.1906-5.1907.
Budget 1904. 1st Mediterranean torpedo boat flotilla at Toulon 1907-09, 5th Mediterranean torpedo boat flotilla at Oran 1909-10, Bizerte torpedo boats 1911-18. Retired 4.1919. For sale at Bizerte 1920-1922, target at Bizerte 1922-1924, target at Toulon for coastal batteries in Corsica 1924 to 8.9.1926.

*Torpilleur no 355* (P176) Schneider, Chalon-sur-Saône.
On list 1.1905. Ord: 3.8.1904. K: 1904. L: 2q.1906. Trials: 7-11.1906.
Budget 1904. 1st Mediterranean torpedo boat flotilla at Toulon 1907-09, 5th Mediterranean torpedo boat flotilla at Oran 1909-12. Bizerte from 1913, Tunisia patrol boat division during war, at Corfu 1919. Off main list by 3.1920 and for sale at Bizerte 1920. Struck 26.11.1920. Sold 11.1920 at Bizerte to BU.

*Torpilleur no 356* (P177) Schneider, Chalon-sur-Saône.
On list 1.1905. Ord: 3.8.1904. K: 1904. L: 6.1906. Trials: 7.1906-1.1907.
Budget 1904. 1st Mediterranean torpedo boat flotilla at Toulon 1907-09, 5th Mediterranean torpedo boat flotilla at Oran 1909-14, Bizerte torpedo boats and Tunisia patrol boat division 1914-18. Retired 1920, for sale at Bizerte 1920-1922.

*Torpilleur no 357* (P178) Schneider, Chalon-sur-Saône.
On list 1.1905. Ord: 3.8.1904. K: 1904. L: 7.1906. Trials: 10.1906-7.1907.
Budget 1904. 2nd Mediterranean torpedo boat flotilla at Ajaccio 1907-11, Toulon torpedo boats 1912-16 (including the Dardanelles in 1915 and Corfu c1916), Tunisia patrol boat division 1917-18. School for stoking at Bizerte 5.1920. Struck 15.1.1921, sold at Bizerte 6.1921.

*Torpilleur no 358* (P179) Schneider, Chalon-sur-Saône.
On list 1.1905. Ord: 3.8.1904. K: 1904. L: 9.1906. Trials: 1-8.1907.
Budget 1904. 2nd Mediterranean torpedo boat flotilla at Ajaccio 1907-11, Toulon torpedo boats 1912-14. Wrecked 3.1914 on Cap Lardier near Hyères, hull refloated in three parts. Struck 3.1915.

*Torpilleur no 359* (P180) Ch. Penhoët, Rouen-Grand Quévilly.
On list 1.1905. Ord: 3.8.1904. K: 14.2.1905. L: 10.3.1906. Trials: 4-7.1906.
Budget 1904. Left the yard 23.3.1906. 1st Mediterranean torpedo boat flotilla and Toulon torpedo boats 1907-14. Dardanelles 1915, Salonica 1916, Tunisia patrol boat division at Bizerte 1917-19. Struck 1.10.1920. Sold 6.1921 to BU.

*Torpilleur no 360* (P181) Ch. Penhoët, Rouen-Grand Quévilly.
On list 1.1905. Ord: 3.8.1904. K: 3.4.1905. L: 11.4.1906. Trials: 4-7.1906.
Budget 1904. Left the yard 21.4.1906. 1st Mediterranean torpedo boat flotilla and Toulon torpedo boats 1907-14. Brindisi 1915, Corfu 1916-17, Provence patrol boat division 1918. School for stoking at Toulon, 1920-1922. Struck 4.8.1922. Torpedo target at Toulon 1922-1923. Grounded 2.1924 at Frioul near Marseille after being damaged by 240mm coastal batteries. Wreck sold 2.1925 to BU.

*Torpilleur no 361* (P182) Ch. Penhoët, Rouen-Grand Quévilly.
On list 1.1905. Ord: 3.8.1904. K: 8.4.1905. L: 27.1.1906. Trials: 5-8.1906.
Budget 1904. Left the yard 8.5.1906. 3rd Mediterranean torpedo boat flotilla, Bizerte torpedo boats, and Tunisia patrol boat division 1907-18. Struck 27.10.1921, for sale at Bizerte 1921-1922. Torpedo target at Toulon 1922-1930/2.

*Torpilleur n° 362* (P183) Ch. Penhoët, Rouen-Grand Quévilly.
On list 1.1905. Ord: 3.8.1904. K: 15.6.1905. L: 12.5.1906.
 Trials: 6-7.1906.
Budget 1904. Left the yard 27.5.1906. 3rd Mediterranean torpedo boat
 flotilla, Bizerte torpedo boats, and Tunisia patrol boat division 1907-
 18. Struck 27.10.1921, for sale at Bizerte 1921-1922. Torpedo target
 at Toulon 1922-1930/2.

*Torpilleur n° 363* (P184) Ch. Penhoët, Rouen-Grand Quévilly.
On list 1.1905. Ord: 3.8.1904. K: 30.8.1905. L: 9.6.1906.
 Trials: 6-10.1906.
Budget 1904. Left the yard 20.6.1906. 3rd Mediterranean torpedo boat
 flotilla and Bizerte torpedo boats 1907-15. Corfu 1916-17, Bizerte
 1917-18, mainly for repairs. Struck 10.5.1920. Sold 11.1920 at Bizerte
 to BU.

*Torpilleur n° 364* (P185) Ch. Penhoët, Rouen-Grand Quévilly.
On list 1.1905. Ord: 3.8.1904. K: 28.6.1905. L: 20.4.1906.
 Trials: 7-11.1906.
Budget 1904. Left the yard 12.7.1906. 3rd Mediterranean torpedo boat
 flotilla, Bizerte torpedo boats, and Tunisia patrol boat division 1907-
 19. Off main list by 3.1920 and for sale at Bizerte 1920. Struck
 26.11.1920. Torpedo target at Toulon 1922-1925. Grounded 2.1924
 at Frioul near Marseille after damaged by coastal batteries. For sale at
 Toulon 1925-1929, sold by the Domaines 1930-1932.

*Torpilleur n° 365* (P186) Ch. Penhoët, Rouen-Grand Quévilly.
On list 1.1905. Ord: 3.8.1904. K: 16.11.1905. L: 24.7.1906.
 Trials: 10-11.1906.
Budget 1904. Left the yard 2.8.1906. 1st Channel torpedo boat flotilla at
 Cherbourg 1907-11, Brest torpedo boats 1912-16, Dunkirk torpedo
 boats (Calais group) 1917-18. Struck 4.4.1921. Sold 1.1922 at
 Cherbourg to BU.

*Torpilleur n° 366* (P187) Ch. Penhoët, Rouen-Grand Quévilly.
On list 1.1905. Ord: 3.8.1904. K: 5.12.1905. L: 16.11.1906.
 Trials: 4-5.1909.
Budget 1904. Left the yard 19.12.1906. Built with an experimental Lentz
 engine which proved unsatisfactory on trials and was replaced with a
 standard engine (see above). Off main list 1921 and for sale at Bizerte
 1921-1922. Struck 9.6.1922. Target at Bizerte 1922-1939.

*Torpilleur n° 367* (P188) Ch. Penhoët, Rouen-Grand Quévilly.
On list 1.1905. Ord: 3.8.1904. K: 21.12.1905. L: 19.9.1906.
 Trials: 9.1906-2.1907.
Budget 1904. Left the yard 11.10.1906. 1st Channel torpedo boat flotilla
 1907-11, Brest torpedo boats 1911-16, Gascony patrol boat division
 1916-18. Struck 7.6.1920. Sold 8.1921 at Rochefort to BU.

(*Torpilleur n° 368* (P138): Listed after *Torpilleur n° 317* (P137) above.)

*Torpilleur n° 369* (P189) Toulon Dyd.
On list 1.1905. Ord: 23.6.1904. K: 1904. L: 3.1907. Trials: 10.1907-
 3.1908.
Budget 1904. Planned as the 1904 colonial boat to be like *9-S* and to be
 shipped in sections to Saigon and assembled there, but this plan was
 abandoned and she was built instead at Toulon with experimental
 forced lubrication machinery. 2nd Mediterranean torpedo boat flotilla,
 then 1st Mediterranean torpedo boat flotilla and Toulon torpedo boats.
 At Taranto spring 1915, Corfu 1916-17, Provence patrol boat division
 1918-19. Annex to *Patrie* at Toulon 1920 to at least 1924. One of
 three old torpedo boats (with *N°s 321* and *349*) still on the list 1.1936
 as treaty-exempt vessels. Active as patrol craft at Bizerte 1939-40.
 Retired 1941 at Bizerte, hoisted onto the quay by the dockyard crane
 at Sidi Abdallah mid-1942 and BU.

**1905 TRANCHE.**
The 1905 budget contained 20 more torpedo boats designated P190 to
P209. It did not contain a special boat for Saigon. All 20 boats were
cancelled after the fall of the ministry in which Camille Pelletan was
Minister of Marine and replaced with destroyers M47-54. No *Torpilleur*
numbers were assigned.

**Torpedo boats after 1905**
In its discussions of the Programme of 1905 in May 1905, the *Conseil
supérieur* cut back significantly on the number of *Défense mobile* torpedo
boats needed, retaining 170. The current inventory was well above that
number, indicating that no more needed to be built in the near term.
About 50 replacements would be needed by 1919, but the Council saw no
use in inscribing them in the current programme. In May 1909 the *Conseil
supérieur* decided that torpedo boats should no longer be assigned exclusively to the defence of ports but should instead be grouped in such a way
that if necessary they could be concentrated *en masse* for offensive operations. It therefore ended the system of dispersing the *Défense mobile*
torpedo boats among many points along the coast and instead concentrated
them in flotillas that by 1914 were at Dunkirk, Cherbourg, Brest, Toulon,
Bizerte, and Oran.

## (C) Torpedo Launches (*Torpilleurs vedettes*).

*LIBELLULE. Torpilleur vedette.* Experimental turbine torpedo launch.

This experimental *torpilleur vedette* was designed by Émile Bertin, then
Chief of the *Section technique*. She had a boiler designed by Colonel
Charles Renard, a naval constructor best known for his experiments with
dirigibles, driving a Rateau steam turbine. The very flat hull lines were
inspired by those of *N°s 130-144* (the *ventre-à-terre* type). The hull was
built of light galvanized plates of two to four millimetres thickness. The
boat had three rudders, one forward and two aft.
 The contract called for delivery for trials on 18 May 1900, but the boiler,
built by the *Établissement Central d'Aérostation Militaire* at Chalais-
Meudon, took nearly 6 years to complete (1898-1904). This boiler operated automatically, burning kerosene at a very intense level of combustion
to evaporate water into steam nearly instantly. The boiler weighed
2.38 kilograms per horsepower compared with 7.8kg in *Torpilleur n° 183*
(the best of the *numérotés*) and 6.6kg in *Forban* (the best of the seagoing
torpedo boats). It was very technologically advanced, but with 16 independent tube banks, each operating independently and many other unique
features it was far too complex to be practical for maritime use. It was also
very noisy in operation and had a small feed water supply which it totally
consumed in three hours. Some of the ideas of Colonel Renard, including
the small volume of water in the boiler (the main cause of its light weight)
and its rapid evaporation into steam, were revived in French boiler design
in 1930-1939.

**Dimensions & tons:** 36,40m pp x 3.40m ext, 3.32m wl. 40t disp.
 Draught: 1.90m aft under screws.
**Machinery:** 1,200ihp designed at 1,750rpm. Trials 15.2kts maximum at
 1,703rpm. 1 propeller shaft with 3 screws as in *N° 243*. Rateau steam
 turbine. 1 Renard boiler.
**Torpedoes:** (designed) 1 tube for 381mm M1887 torpedoes on deck
 amidships aft of the single funnel.

*Libellule* F.C. Méditerranée, La Seyne/Chalais-Meudon
On list 1.1900. Ord: 10.5.1899. K: 1900. L: 3.2.1905.
Budget 1899 (late addition). Transited from Le Havre to Cherbourg in
 five hours 25.7.1905. Decomm. 9.1905, never entered service. Struck
 15.4.1911.

# Chapter Seventeen

# Submarines, 1897-1914

## (A) Submarine Boats (*Bateaux sous-marins*) and Submersible Autonomous Torpedo Boats (*Torpilleurs autonomes submersibles*).

To *Sous-marins* in the 1.1909 fleet list.

### Competition of 1896.

After seven years of experience with *Gymnote* and with two more experimental submarines, *Gustave Zédé* and *Morse*, under construction, Minister of Marine Édouard Lockroy on 26 February 1896 promulgated in the *Journal Officiel* the rules for a competition, open to all, for a design for a *torpilleur sous-marin*. The requirements were a speed of 12 knots, a range of 100 miles at 8 knots, a range submerged of 10 miles at 8 knots, two torpedoes ready for launch, and a maximum displacement of 200 tons. Entries were to be submitted within a year. The requirement for operational range was later relaxed to allow consideration of pure submarines with electric motors like *Gymnote* which had produced promising results. 47 entries were received of which 26 were considered to have merit. The entries were examined by the *Conseil des travaux* on 4 June 1897. After noting with regret that no company (Normand, Forges et Chantiers de la Méditerranée, Chantiers de la Loire or Chantiers de la Gironde) had participated, the Conseil proceeded to evaluate the six complete submarine designs that it had received. Three were submitted by three naval constructors: Gaston Romazzotti (his electric *Morse*), Gabriel Émile Marie Maugas (a synthesis of his experience with the electric *Gymnote* and *Gustave Zédé*), and Alfred Maxime Laubeuf (a type with steam and electric propulsion that was autonomous in that it could charge its batteries without returning to port). Also participating were two civil engineers: Fernand Forest (an autonomous 136-ton vessel with a 500hp combination of a heavy oil engine of his invention and electric motors) and H. Philippeau (an autonomous 16-ton vessel with oil and electric motors), and a Pole now resident in Paris, Stefan Drzewiecki (another autonomous steam and electric design). Laubeuf, considering the speed requirement unrealistic, paid attention only to the specified tonnage in producing his submission. He submitted his design on 24 March 1897. The Council's staff reported that the one really new idea in the submissions was Laubeuf's proposal for annular water ballast tanks outside the pressure hull and inside a second regular hull. It concluded that, while the project of Maugas for a *bateau sous-marin non autonome* could be accepted in principle (and eventually was for the *Farfadet* class in 1899), the construction of Laubeuf's *torpilleur submersible autonome* was of more immediate interest. The Council also recommended trying Drzewiecki's torpedo dropping gear (trainable launchers) and Forest's heavy oil engine, the latter in torpedo boats. Laubeuf's double hull concept became the basis of nearly all submarine designs from the early 1900s to the advent of single-hulled nuclear submarines in the 1960s. Many years later (in 1935) Laubeuf noted that as of 1897 he had never even seen a submarine.

---

*NARVAL. Torpilleur autonome submersible.* Double hull, steam surface propulsion. Designed by Laubeuf.

While the designers of the early electric submarines focused on developing the ability to navigate underwater, Laubeuf sought to give submerged navigation an operational dimension. His military concept for his boat was that she would leave Cherbourg or Brest at nightfall, arrive before dawn off a British port, dive and torpedo ships entering the roadsteads of Portsmouth,

Plymouth, or the mouth of the Thames. She would light fires in her boiler after nightfall and return to base. On 9 August 1897 the Ministry informed the Maritime Prefect at Cherbourg, where Laubeuf was assigned, that the Council had selected Laubeuf's project and directed him to invite Laubeuf to prepare a definitive design. The *Conseil des travaux* examined that design on 3 May 1898. Laubeuf's double hull design consisted of an outer hull of regular plating based on Normand's *Torpilleurs nos 130-144* (the *ventres-à-terre*) enclosing an inner hull of heavier plating with circular cross sections (ellipsoidal at the ends). Laubeuf expected that diving would take about 20 minutes – the fires in the boiler would have to be extinguished, all the hull openings closed, the steam engine disengaged and the electric motor started before the ballast tanks could be opened and filled with 95 tons of water. Slow diving speed was initially an argument against the Laubeuf submersible, although with crew training and technical improvements times were eventually improved to twelve minutes in *Narval*, five minutes in *Sirène*, and four minutes in *Aigrette*. Minister Besnard ordered her construction and named her on 1 June 1898. The contract for the electric motors with Hillairet-Huguet of Paris was dated 30 September 1898. The electric motors could be used as generators to recharge the batteries when the vessel was steaming on the surface. The original 15kg/cm² boiler was provided by the Cie. des procédés Adolphe Seigle whose design was based on the Normand type, it was replaced in 1903 by a smaller and lighter Du Temple boiler rated at 16kg/cm². The battery was replaced in 1901. In comparative trials in 1904 the double-hulled *Aigrette* submerged half a minute faster than the single-hulled *Sous-marin X*. The Drzewiecki trainable launchers could be used only submerged. (The same was true of the later Simonot trainable launchers and the ubiquitous fixed launch cages.) *Narval* had fuel for full speed for 21 hours or 600nm at cruising speed. In service she could easily sustain 10 knots surfaced and 6.5 knots submerged and transit 500nm @ 6.5 knots on the surface (three days on patrol). Her autonomy submerged of 60nm @ 3.25 knots or 11nm @ 5 knots could be extended by recharging the battery.

*The characteristics are based on a devis dated 15.12.1900.*

**Dimensions & tons:** 34.000m oa, wl & pp x 3.800m ext, 3.765m wl. 117t disp (surfaced), 202.193t (submerged, trials). Draught: 1.865m mean (trials). Men: 13. Reserve buoyancy: 42.1%

**Machinery:**

(surfaced) 255ihp designed (220ihp effective) at 450rpm and 15kg/cm² boiler pressure (13.5kg/cm² at the engines). Speed 9.88kts. Trials (1.5.1900) 8.148kts. 1 screw. 1 vertical triple expansion engine with 3 cylinders of 0.195m, 0.310m, and 0.510m diameter and 0.230m stroke. 1 Seigle boiler. 3,130 litres (3 tons) oil. Range (trials) 345nm @ 8.83kts.

(submerged) 86hp at 360rpm. Speed 5.30kts. 2 electric motors on one shaft. Batteries 19 tons. Range (trials) 58nm @ 2.83kts.

**Torpedoes:** 4 Drzewiecki trainable launchers for 450mm M1892 torpedoes.

*Narval* (Q4) Cherbourg Dyd/H. Brûlé & Cie., Paris

On list 1.1899. Ord: 1.6.1898. K: 23.11.1898. L: 21.10.1899. Comm: 26.10.1899 (trials), 26.6.1900 (full).

Budget 1898 (late addition). Machinery installed 23.11.1898 to 11.12.1899. Preliminary trials completed 4.4.1900. Trial results approved 6.1900. Conducted a simulated raid on Brest from Cherbourg after remaining underway for 48 hours 23-24.5.1901,

*Le Submersible " Espadon "*

The submersible *Espadon* showing the overall configuration of the four boats of the *Sirène* class with a long and low casing or breakwater enclosing the kiosk and funnel. This configuration was repeated in most later submersibles. The kiosk has an extension behind it that is not on the next image. *(Postcard by P. B., Cherbourg, NHHC, NH-55770)*

The submersible *Narval* off Quai Surcouf in the centre of Saint-Malo. She is rigged for surface navigation with canvas stretched on her railings and a collapsible Berthon boat lashed between the two starboard Drzewiecki trainable torpedo launchers. The photo was taken after February 1903 when she received a new Du Temple boiler and the funnel was moved slightly aft. *(Postcard by ELD)*

stayed submerged for 12 hours 13.6.1901 and conducted a night attack on the battleship *Henri IV* anchored at Cherbourg. New Du Temple boiler first fired 26.2.1903. Condemnation proposed 11.1.1909, struck from 1st part of the fleet list 27.1.1909, struck from the fleet list and condemned 9.3.1909, retained for use as an oil tank (*citerne à pétrole*) 1909-1914, trials with oil firing of the boiler 25.10.1910, request for the Administration des Domaines to sell the vessel 27.4.1914, sold 2.6.1920 at Cherbourg to M. Lagrange to BU.

---

*SIRÈNE* **Class.** *Torpilleurs autonomes submersibles.* Double hull, steam surface propulsion. Designed by Laubeuf.

Following the success of *Narval* Minister Lockroy in 1899 wanted to order eight copies, but Laubeuf had already completed the plans for an improved *Narval* and the order to build two of these (Q5-6) was given in June 1899 followed by two more (Q13-14) in May 1900. These were designed for the same operational scenario as *Narval*, essentially a 36-hour raid in the Channel, for which a relatively small range on the surface (400 miles at 7.5 knots) and minimal habitability would be sufficient. Laubeuf noted that another 24 hours could be added to the mission if necessary but in no case should they be at sea for more than three days. The new boats were half sisters of *Narval*, with essentially the same dimensions and submerged displacement, but the outer hull was conceived differently. That of *Narval* was complete, enclosing all of the pressure hull including the ends. This led to narrow spaces between the two hulls at the top and the bottom that were hard to build and nearly impossible to clean and maintain. In *Sirène* Laubeuf suppressed the top and bottom parts of the outer hull, retaining only the side portions with a flat wooden deck over the pressure hull between them. The steam engines were built by Maison Brûlé and the electric motors by Hillairet-Huguet.

Repeating the exercise conducted by *Narval* the previous year, the four

Côte d'Emeraude    2014. SAINT-MALO — Le Sous-Marin " Le Narval "

submersibles of this class together conducted a raid from Cherbourg against Brest on 25-30 July 1902 escorted by *Torpilleur nº 60*, at the end of which they attacked the coast defence ship *Fulminant*. (They inadvertently surfaced alongside her.) In early autumn 1902 the four *Sirènes* and *Narval* conducted a blockade of the roadstead of Saint-Vaast-la-Hougue during which they remained submerged for 12 hours during the daytime. Although eventually judged a bit slow and of insufficient range, all remained in the inventory to 1919.

*Silure* is shown as Q13 and *Espadon* as Q14 in the budgets (our source for all the Q numbers) but the two numbers are reversed in other sources and *Espadon* was the first one of the two launched and commissioned for trials.

**Dimensions & tons:** 32.50m oa & pp x 3.904m ext, 3.892m wl. 157.008t disp (surfaced, trials), 213t (submerged, trials). Draught: 2.505m mean (trials). Men: 12 including 2 officers. Reserve buoyancy: 26.3%

**Machinery:**
(surfaced) 275ihp designed (250ihp effective) at 433rpm and 16kg/cm$^2$

boiler pressure (15kg/cm$^2$ at the engine). Speed 9.75kts. Trials (30.8.1901, *Sirène*) 287.81ihp = 9.81kts at 416rpm. 1 screw (fixed pitch). 1 vertical triple expansion engine with 3 cylinders of 0.200m, 0.320m, and 0.525m diameter and 0.40m to 0.68m stroke for the HP, MP, and LP cylinders. 1 Du Temple boiler. 4,500 litres oil. Range (trials) 534.705nm @ 6.868kts.

(submerged) 100hp at 340rpm. Speed 5.80kts. Trials (5.9.1901, *Sirène*) 121hp = 5.585kts. 1 electric motor with 2 armatures on one shaft. Battery 27 tons. Range (trials) 51.55nm @ 3.4kts.

**Torpedoes:** 2 Tissier side launchers (replaced in 1906 with fixed launch cages) and 2 Drzewiecki trainable launchers aft, all for 450mm M1892 torpedoes.

*Sirène* (Q5)  Cherbourg Dyd/H. Brûlé & Cie., Paris.
On list 1.1900. Ord: 20.6.1899 and 11.4.1900. K: 28.8.1900. L: 4.5.1901. Comm: 14.12.1901 (full).
Budget 1899. Named 7.1899. Steam machinery installed 28.8.1900 to 29.5.1901. In 1914 was assigned to the Cherbourg submarines (*Sous-marins de Cherbourg*, the defensive submarine force there). In the Brittany submarine squadron 1.1918 for the school for underwater detection at Brest. Struck 12.11.1919. Sold 12.11.1920 with her three sisters to M. Pissenem of Brest to BU.

*Triton* (Q6)  Cherbourg Dyd/H. Brûlé & Cie., Paris.
On list 1.1900. Ord: 20.6.1899 and 11.4.1900. K: 28.8.1900. L: 13.7.1901. Comm: 1.6.1902 (full).
Budget 1899. Construction reassigned from Brest to Cherbourg before

The submersible *Espadon* alongside a pier at Cherbourg. The nearest sailor is working on the watertight hatch that was closed over the retractable funnel when submerging. The hose lines leading into the kiosk (conning tower) beyond it may be for fresh water. The original sliding screw Tissier torpedo side launchers alongside the casing were replaced in 1906 with the fixed torpedo launch cages seen here. Here the port cage is loaded with a 450mm torpedo. *(NHHC, NH-55747)*

6.1899. Named 7.1899. Steam machinery installed 20.5.1901 to 6.8.1901. Trials 12.1901, trial results approved 1.3.1902. In 1914 was assigned to the Cherbourg submarines. Struck 12.11.1919. Sold 12.11.1920 with her three sisters to M. Pissenem of Brest to BU.

*Silure* (Q13) Cherbourg Dyd/H. Brûlé & Cie., Paris.
On list 1.1901. Ord: 1.5.1900. K: 1900. L: 29.10.1901.
  Comm: 21.7.1902 (full).
Budget 1900. Steam machinery installed 16.9.1901 to 30.11.1901. In trials at Cherbourg 1.1902. In 1914 was assigned to the Cherbourg submarines. In the Brittany submarine squadron 1.1918 for the school for underwater detection at Brest. Struck 12.11.1919. Sold 12.11.1920 with her three sisters to M. Pissenem of Brest to BU.

*Espadon* (Q14) Cherbourg Dyd/H. Brûlé & Cie., Paris.
On list 1.1901. Ord: 1.5.1900. K: 1900. L: 31.8.1901. Comm: 10.1901 (trials), 1.6.1902 (full).
Budget 1900. Steam machinery installed 19.7.1901 to 2.10.1901. In 1914 was assigned to the Cherbourg submarines. In the Normandy submarine squadron 1.1918. Struck 12.11.1919. Sold 12.11.1920 with her three sisters to M. Pissenem of Brest to BU.

---

**FARFADET Class.** *Bateaux sous-marins.* Single hull, electric propulsion. Designed by Maugas.

Maugas, like Romazzotti an advocate of single-hulled electric-drive submarines ever since he had participated in some of the trials of *Gymnote*, was concerned about the lack of watertight compartments in the earliest French submarines. *Gymnote* and *Zédé* had no interior watertight bulkheads at all and *Morse* and her two replicas (*Français* and *Algérien*, below) had only two transverse ones. The boats submerged by flooding a few small ballast tanks and surfaced by blowing these with compressed air or in an emergency by releasing solid ballast. Neither could save the sub in case of major internal flooding. In 1895 Maugas produced a design in which the central part of the hull was subdivided by horizontal and vertical watertight bulkheads. Some of the new compartments were water ballast tanks, and blowing these and releasing the solid ballast could surface the boat even if one compartment was flooded. Maugas submitted this design in the 1896 competition, and while Laubeuf's double-hulled design prevailed the Maugas design was well received and the *Conseil des travaux* stated that it would be used in the event of a decision to build purely electric submarines. Such a decision was taken three years later, resulting in the *Farfadet* class, which was a single hulled type intermediate in size between *Gustave Zédé* and *Morse*. Q7 to Q10 first appeared in the 1899 budget (submitted in October 1898) as sisters to *Narval* with Q5-Q6 but were soon changed. The numbers Q1-Q4 were assigned retroactively.

Maugas's system, however, created new dangers by putting large water ballast tanks inside the pressure hull. When diving the air expelled from the top of these tanks by water entering at the bottom could escape only through a small opening in the conning tower hatch or through the hatch itself. The crew being unaware of the purpose of the small opening would wait until the last moment to slam the main hatch closed during diving. On 5 July 1905 while *Farfadet* was submerging after exiting the basin at Sidi Abdallah the hatch jammed and the boat flooded through it and sank in the Bizerte roadstead, killing 14 of the 17 men on board. Another problem was that the internal bulkheads of the ballast tanks were made of relatively light sheet metal which could contain the water inside the pressure hull under normal operation but would rupture if exposed to the pressure of the sea outside the pressure hull. On 16 October 1906, while *Lutin* was submerging in Lake Bizerte, a pebble lodged in the ballast refill valve, jamming it open, exposing the ballast tank to external pressures and rupturing it, sinking the boat in 30 metres of water with the loss of all 16 men on board. Several weeks later Minister Thomson required that the internal bulkheads of water ballast tanks in single-hulled submarines be able to

resist the same pressures as the pressure hull. The remaining two *Farfadet* class units were taken out of service in 1906 and never recommissioned, although *Farfadet* was later repaired and recommissioned under the name *Follet*. Advocates of double hulled submarines like *Narval* were quick to point out that such accidents could not occur in them because the main ballast tanks were outside the pressure hull.

The first three boats had two electric motors on a single propeller shaft and *évolueurs* (auxiliary side-thrusting screws to help steer the boat) on the sides of the stern geared to the main shaft. *Lutin*, however, had two shafts with one motor on each and no *évolueurs*, which gave her about a knot speed advantage over the other three, but the two shafts did not give as much directional control over the stern as did the *évolueurs* in the others. The two propellers in *Lutin* were 1.22 metres in diameter while the single screws in the other three were larger, 1.50 metres in diameter. All four had variable pitch main propellers, which Maugas used to change speed without stopping the electric motor and thus maximize its efficiency. The contract with Sautter-Harlé for the main propulsion electric motors was dated 27 January 1900.

**Dimensions & tons:** 41.350m oa (41.496m *Lutin*), 40.900m pp x 2.900m ext, 2.045m wl (2.025m *Lutin*). 184.971t disp (surfaced, *Gnome*), 202.471t (submerged, *Gnome*). Draught: 2.696m mean, 2.7185m aft (both *Gnome*). Men: 14 including 2 officers. Reserve buoyancy: 8.6%
**Machinery:**
(surfaced) 300hp at 450rpm. Speed 6.10kts. Trials (*Gnome* 27.4.1905) 183.08hp = 6.8kts at 243.75rpm. 1 screw (variable pitch) with two auxiliary side-thrusting screws except 2 screws (variable pitch) and no auxiliary screws in *Lutin*. 2 electric motors on one shaft except in *Lutin*, in which they were on two shafts. Batteries 49 tons. Range 430nm @ 7.75kts.
(submerged) Speed 4.30kts. Trials (*Gnome* 11.4.1905) 89.4hp = 4.471kts at 200rpm. Range 28nm @ 4.32kts.
**Torpedoes:** 4 Tissier side launchers for 450mm M1892 torpedoes, two on each side. Replaced in *Lutin* by 4 fixed launch cages on platforms, two aimed forward and two aimed aft, all at 10.3 degrees off the boat's axis.

*Farfadet* (Q7) Rochefort Dyd/Sautter-Harlé, Paris (electric motors).
On list 1.1900. Ord: 27.9.1899. K: 2.4.1900. L: 17.5.1901. Comm: 29.8.1902 (full).
Budget 1899. Construction reassigned from Brest to Rochefort c1899. Machinery installed 24.12.1900 to 31.8.1901. Assigned 8.1903 with *Korrigan* to the defence of Tunisia and towed to Bizerte in company with *Korrigan*. Sank 5.7.1905 in diving accident at Bizerte (14 of 17 men lost). Refloated 15.7.1905 after much difficulty, hull towed to Toulon 11.10.1905. Renamed *Follet* 17.12.1908, put back into service 9.1909. Struck 22.11.1913, reportedly sold 4.6.1914 at Bizerte to BU but still listed as for sale there 1920-1924.

*Korrigan* (Q8) Rochefort Dyd/Sautter-Harlé, Paris (electric motors).
On list 1.1900. Ord: 27.9.1899. K: 23.4.1900. L: 24.1.1902.
  Comm: 29.8.1902 (full).
Budget 1899. Construction reassigned from Lorient to Rochefort c1899. Machinery installed 17.8.1901 to 4.4.1902. Assigned 8.1903 with *Farfadet* to the defence of Tunisia and towed from Rochefort to Bizerte 1903. Out of commission from 1906. Struck 3.8.1910, for sale in Tunisia 1910-1911. Sold 10.8.1911 at Bizerte to M. Boccara to BU.

*Gnôme* (Q9) Rochefort Dyd/Sautter-Harlé, Paris (electric motors).
On list 1.1900. Ord: 27.9.1899. K: c1901. L: 23.7.1902.
  Comm: 2.6.1905 (full).
Budget 1899. Machinery installed 30.6.1902 to 8.12.1902. Towed from Rochefort to Bizerte 7-20.6.1906. Out of commission from 1906. Struck 3.8.1910, for sale in Tunisia 1910-1912. Sold 24.3.1912 at Bizerte to M. Boccara to BU.

The submarine *Lutin*, moving from left to right. The frame over the front of the conning tower on this and other early submarines was intended to prevent objects from snagging on the submarine when submerged. Note that much of the stern is submerged – its end is near the vertical staff at the left of the photo. *(NHHC, NH-55999)*

*Lutin* (Q10) Rochefort Dyd/Sautter-Harlé, Paris (electric motors).
On list 1.1900. Ord: 27.9.1899. K: 27.2.1902. L: 12.2.1903.
    Comm: 17.9.1903 (trials), 1904 (full).
Budget 1899. Machinery installed 7.7.1902 to 16.3.1903. Completed
    trials during 1904. Towed from Rochefort to Bizerte 7-20.6.1906.
    Sank 16.10.1906 with all hands in a diving accident in Lake Bizerte.
    Refloated 24.10.1906 and docked 26.10.1906 to recover victims.
    Struck 6.9.1907, retained for trials at Toulon 1907-1911. Used as
    gunnery target at Toulon 1908, then for refloating experiments.
    Offered for sale 1 August 1911 at Toulon by the Administration des
    Domaines with *Amiral Baudin, Magenta, Pascal, Milan,* and smaller
    vessels and sold 2.8.1911 to M. Bénédic to BU.

---

**FRANÇAIS Class.** *Bateaux sous-marins.* Single hull, electric propulsion.
Designed by Romazzotti.

In 1899 after the humiliation of the Fashoda crisis with Great Britain and
the trials of *Gustave Zédé* the large daily newspaper *Le Matin* opened a
public subscription to offer a submarine as a gift of the Nation to the Navy.
Emotions were high and enough funds were raised to buy two submarines.
They were copies of Romazzotti's *Morse* except that they had steel instead
of bronze hulls and carried two torpedoes externally on the sides near the
conning tower. (*Morse* was unable to carry these steel weapons because of
their galvanic reaction with her bronze hull).

*The characteristics are based on a devis for* Français *dated 1.6.1902.*
**Dimensions & tons:** 36.780m oa, 36.500m pp x 2.750m ext. 147.112t
    disp (surfaced), 152.832t (submerged, trials). Draught: 2.875m mean.
    Men: 13. Reserve buoyancy: 3.8%
**Machinery:**
(surfaced) 300hp at 450rpm. Speed 10.10kts. Trials (*Français* 26.3.1901)
    307.3hp = 11.21kts at 233rpm. 1 screw (variable pitch). 2 electric
    motors on one shaft. Range (trials) 51.524nm @ 9.526kts.
(submerged) Speed 8.30kts. Trials (*Français* 5.7.1901) 55.05hp = 4.72kts
    at 181.5rpm on one motor only. Range (trials) 78.193nm @ 4.72kts.

**Torpedoes:** 1 internal bow tube and 2 Tissier side launchers, one on
    either side of the walking deck forward of the conning tower, for
    450mm M1892 torpedoes. The Tissier side launchers were later
    replaced with Drzewiecki trainable launchers that were moved back to
    alongside the conning tower

*Français* (Q11) Cherbourg Dyd/Sautter-Harlé, Paris (electric motors).
On list 1.1900. Ord: 8.4.1899. K: c1899. L: 29.1.1901.
    Comm: 1.6.1902 (full).
Budget 1899 (late addition). Machinery installed 28.8.1900 to
    29.1.1901. Trials completed during 1901. 'Torpedoed' the coast
    defence ship *Bouvines* twice during exercises in September 1902.
    Damaged by fire 31.10.1912. Condemned 26.3.1914. Struck
    21.5.1914 and handed over to the Domaines for sale. For sale at
    Cherbourg 1920. Sold 25.5.1921 to M. Paris of Cherbourg to BU.

*Algérien* (Q12) Cherbourg Dyd/Sautter-Harlé, Paris (electric motors).
On list 1.1900. Ord: 8.4.1899. K: 3.10.1899. L: 25.4.1901.
    Comm: c1902 (full).
Budget 1899 (late addition). Trials completed during 1901. Spent career
    at Cherbourg. Sunk 11.1.1907 by negligence in the basin at
    Cherbourg without personnel losses, refloated. Struck 21.5.1914. For
    sale at Cherbourg 1920-1922.

*For Q13 and Q14, ordered in 1900, see the Sirène (Q5) class above.*

---

**Submersibles vs. Sous-marins**
The successful completion of *Narval's* trials in June 1900 opened a period
of competition between what would soon be called *Torpilleurs autonomes
submersibles,* double-hulled vessels like *Narval,* and *Bateaux sous-marins* or
pure submarines, single-hulled craft like *Morse* and *Français.* Laubeuf's
success with *Narval* was no doubt a factor when the 1901 budget was
submitted on 31 May 1900 with eight new submersibles, Q15 to Q22,
with specifications identical to *Silure* and *Espadon* including steam engines
and boilers. Q15-16 were to be built at Cherbourg and Q17-22 at Toulon.
However, at this time the Navy's leadership wanted to continue to develop
underwater craft along multiple paths. In December 1900 the *Conseil
supérieur* recommended three courses of action: developing a unique type
of propulsion machinery that would work both surfaced and submerged
(an idea already under study by Maurice and others), in the meantime
laying down immediately more submersibles of the *Triton* type, and also

developing a new type of electrically propelled *Gymnote* (referring to a proposal from Zédé). In 1902, soon after leaving office, the Minister of Marine during this time, Jean-Marie de Lanessan, wrote in an anonymous volume entitled *Le Programme Maritime de 1900-1906* that he felt the Navy needed two types of submarines, one of small dimensions, limited range and a primarily defensive mission that could be built in large quantities, and one with as large a range as possible intended to carry the offensive to the enemy's coast. He also noted the importance of autonomy – the ability to recharge batteries without returning to base – to both types of submarines, because submarines would have serious military value only if they could remain submerged and out of sight of the enemy for long periods. He also referred to the desirability of developing a single type of submarine propulsion machinery but acknowledged the difficulties of this effort.

---

*NAÏADE* **Class.** *Bateaux sous-marins.* Single hull, electric propulsion with benzol-powered dynamos. Designed by Romazzotti.

While preparing the design for *Sous-marin X* (below) Romazzotti was also working on developing a new type of electrically propelled *Gymnote*. He disliked large submarines and worked to return to a type smaller than *Morse* and about the size of *Gymnote*. In late 1900 he addressed to Minister de Lanessan a preliminary design for a submarine with characteristics provided by the Naval General Staff. These were an endurance of 11 to 12 hours at 6.5 knots surfaced or 5 knots submerged, propulsion that for the moment was purely electric with batteries, and an armament of two 450mm torpedoes in Tissier side launchers. In a dispatch of 28 December 1900 Minister de Lanessan invited him to present a fully developed proposal.

Romazzotti met the Navy's conditions with a boat of 23.50m length, 2.26m diameter, and displacements of 68 tons on the surface and 70.8 tons submerged. The hull reproduced quite faithfully the overall arrangements of *Français* and *Algérien* (an enlargement of the *flotteur* or flotation tank to increase reserve buoyancy was later abandoned). The conning tower consisted of a kiosk for conning personnel and behind it a bronze tower or *massif central* that supported the periscope, air intakes and external electrical connections. On its platform personnel could enjoy fresh air in good weather. In addition to the rudders above and below the stern as in *Morse* the boat also had a rudder under the bow to allow her to steer as well going astern as going ahead.

Propulsion was provided by two electric motors, each of 35hp on the single propeller shaft driving a variable pitch propeller. Up to 6.5 knots one motor sufficed, beyond that two were needed and could produce 8 knots and even 9 knots for a few moments by adjusting the battery connections and the pitch of the propeller blades. The battery could provide on the surface 44nm at 8 knots, 78nm at 6.5 knots, 144nm at 4.8 knots and submerged 33nm at 6 knots, 60nm at 5 knots, and 105nm at 3.5 knots.

Romazzotti then argued that this vessel could be made autonomous by replacing 29 of the 128 elements of the battery with a 70hp oil dynamo. This dynamo would provide the current needed to propel the vessel on the surface, and would also permit recharging the batteries for submerged navigation. The provision of 850 to 900 litres of fuel would give a range on the surface of 200nm at 6.5 knots or 125nm at 8 knots (an augmentation of 120% over the purely electric design) at the cost of a reduction of only 21% in the submerged ranges.

The *Conseil des travaux* discussed this design on 19 March 1901, noted that the proposal for a oil dynamo was not sufficiently documented to be adopted, and found other problems with the design. On 30 March Minister de Lanessan referred to the Council a revised design from Romazzotti, which benefitted from a recalculation of the weight of the batteries, which became both lighter and more powerful than first expected. This boat could run submerged for 15 hours at 6.5 knots. The Council considered this design on 2 April 1901 and stated that Romazzotti

had resolved all of its concerns with the previous design, and it also advocated hastening as much as possible the experimental construction of one submarine fitted with a oil dynamo for propulsion on the surface as proposed by Romazzotti.

De Lanessan had evidently already been won over to Romazzotti's ideas, seeing in his design one of the two type of submarines that France needed, a small but autonomous defensive submarine that could be built in large quantities. In the 1902 budget (submitted 29 March 1901), he replaced the eight Laubeuf submersibles in the 1901 budget with the first eight units of the *Naïade* class as Q15-22 and then added 12 more *Naïade*s (Q23-34) along with three experimental submarines (X, Y, and Z, Q35-37, the experiments being twin screws, diesel engines, and the elusive unique engine). All 23 vessels were to be built using 1901 funds under authority contained in a clause in the 1901 budget to make such additions after passage of the budget. Within days of the advice of the *Conseil des travaux* Minister de Lanessan on 3 April 1901 ordered twenty *Naïade*s from three dockyards, names for all being assigned and Cherbourg being designated the lead yard. On 19 April 1901 Minister de Lanessan invited Cherbourg to study the adoption of an oil engine in a *Naïade* class submarine. On 8 July 1901 de Lanessan in a circular advised the ports that he intended to make the *Naïade* class submarine autonomous by adding an oil engine, and on 24 December 1901 the Machinery Commission (the *Commission permanente des machines et du grand outillage*) was asked to order 20 dynamos with benzol engines from Panhard and Lavassor. All twenty *Naïade*s were thus built with Romazzotti's autonomous propulsion system. In its final version this system used a single benzol engine driving two dynamos, making it possible to either power the electric motor with both dynamos or power it at reduced speed with one dynamo while recharging the battery with the other.

On 12 March 1903 Romazzotti recommended modifications to the above-water portions of the hull and on 21 March 1903 naval constructor Gaston Denis Alexandre Tréboul recommended changes to the above-water flotation tanks in response to a 19 February 1903 order from Minister Pelletan. The changes were approved on 17 August 1903. As a result, there were two basic groups of *Naïade*s by appearance, one with the walking deck on top of the flotation tanks amidships of uniform height and with a concave breakwater at the front end of the flotation tanks over the bow, and the other with the walking deck stepped down forward abreast the conning tower and with its front end tapered down to meet the top of the bow. The second group had the flotation tank (*flotteur*) under the walking deck forward of the conning tower omitted, lowering the deck there. The earlier boats at each dockyard were built with the first configuration, but starting with *Lynx* or *Ludion* at Cherbourg, *Phoque* at Rochefort, and *Anguille* at Toulon the second configuration was adopted.

Commonly nicknamed *fritures* (fried fish) because many had fish names, the little *Naïade*s were denigrated by Émile Bertin as *noyades* (drownings). With slight radius of action and no habitability, they were intended for short-duration missions in the Channel and the protection of the approaches to Dunkirk. The maximum diving depth was considered to be 30 metres, although *Bonite* was lowered to a depth of 90 metres by a floating crane without adverse effects. The boats had no watertight compartments.

The benzol engines were built by the Société des Anciens Établissements Panhard et Levassor, a major automobile manufacturer, to a design by their chief engineer, Arthur Constantin Krebs, who had designed the electric motor in *Gymnote* and who was now also the firm's director. They were four-cycle engines with four cylinders. Their fuel, benzol, was a volatile liquid derived from the distillation of coal or as a by-product of the fabrication of coke. They were essentially upscaled automobile engines. The dynamos were built by Sautter, Harlé & Cie. By using dynamos Romazzotti eliminated all physical connection between the thermal engine and the propeller shaft, as was done much later in modern diesel-electric submarines. The electric motors were built by the Société d'éclairage électrique to their plans. To take *Ludion* as an example, her electric motor was

The submarine *Alose*, one of the twenty *Naïade* class *fritures*. Untypically for this class, some of the bow is visible while underway. She has the revised, lower walking deck configuration forward of the conning tower. The torpedo launch cages normally outboard of her after casing are not installed. *(Postcard by M.D.)*

built by Maison Hillairet Huguet at Paris (contract 18 December 1901), installation begun 10 July 1903, and the 1st static machinery trial occurred on 27 February 1904. Her oil (benzol) motor with dynamo was built by the Anciens établissements Panhard et Levassor at Paris (contract 19 February 1902). Her batteries were embarked on 4-8 February 1904 and first discharged on 27 February 1904.

The use of the benzol engine for recharging the batteries significantly increased the capabilities of the boats, but its use for propulsion on the surface proved to be problematic. The commander of *Souffleur* noted in 1906 that the benzol engine was of an old model that gave constant trouble and that its fuel was dangerous, but he also said that removing it would deprive the vessel of 50% of its value and that it had given his boat an economical surface speed of 7 knots. However, the engine lacked an exhaust pipe for use underway, and crews attempted to use it at sea by having the exhaust go up through the conning tower hatch. Benzol, in addition to being almost as volatile as gasoline, is toxic in excess, and an overdose can produce a high followed by unconsciousness. Paul Chack, the commander of *Grondin* from 1906 to 1908, once found his entire crew passed out inside the boat while entering Toulon, and noted that even with two hatches open and a ventilator constantly running, ventilation inside the boat was insufficient when running on the benzol engine. The benzol engine and its dynamo in *Souffleur* were not used during the entire period from 1 March 1908 to 31 August 1909. By 1910 there was a firm ban on using the benzol engine for propulsion, its use being restricted to recharging the battery in port. However, on 11 January 1910 Toulon conducted trials with *Thon* equipped with external fuel tanks and a ventilator, improvised tanks having already been installed in *Truite* in early 1909. *Thon* was able to run on the benzol engine with only the conning tower hatch open and with remarkable results (no water leaks, no odour, almost double the operational range, and no need for a lengthy recharge of the battery afterwards).

The concept of small defensive submarines under 400 tons was aban-

doned in later fleet programme and all of the *Naïade*s were struck from the fleet list in 1912-1914. Paris hopefully wired Saigon on 1 July 1915 to ask on what date *Protée* and *Lynx* could be reactivated, but Saigon replied on 2 July 1915 that they could not as the material of the submarines had been dispersed and the periscopes destroyed. When Italy was developing its even smaller B class small submarines (40/46 tons, 15.12 metres) during World War I it asked on 21 September 1915 for the loan of a now-obsolete *Naïade* for examination.

Although small, these submarines were not as small as they appear on most photos. Normally only the midships portion, with its flotation tanks, walking deck, conning tower and fixed launch cages, was visible when the submarines were on the surface, but this accounted for only a little over half the length of the submarine. The bow was usually awash or submerged and the long stern was totally submerged.

*The characteristics are based on a devis for* Ludion (*Torpilleur sous-marin*) *dated 5.5.1905, along with some from a devis for* Bonite *dated 27.2.1905.*

**Dimensions & tons:** 23.949m oa, 23.750m pp (stempost to after end of propeller cone) x 2.260m ext & wl. 70.398t disp (surfaced), 73.567t (submerged). Draught: 2.540m mean. Men: 9 (13 in *Bonite*). Reserve buoyancy: 4.31%

**Machinery:**

(surfaced) (petrol engine with dynamo): 65hp designed at 700rpm. Speed 7.20kts. Trials (*Ludion*, 8.9.1904) 104.30hp = 8.217kts at 275rpm. 1 screw (variable pitch) plus 2 two auxiliary side-thrusting screws (*hélices auxiliaires évolueurs*). Current for the electric motor could be augmented on the surface by 2 electric dynamos driven by 1 vertical oil (benzol) four-cycle engine with 4 balanced cylinders of 0.170m diameter and 0.180m stroke. 0.775t benzol. Range 200nm @ 5.5kts.

(submerged) 70hp at 240-245rpm (290rpm with lighter load). Speed 5.98kts. Trials (*Naïade*, 11.7.1904) 91.78hp = 5.322kts at 252rpm. 1 electric motor with two armatures consisting of two partial motors of 35hp each linked to each other and on the same shaft. Batteries 20 tons. Range 30nm @ 4.10kts.

**Torpedoes:**

(1904) 2 fixed launch cages (*appareils à déclanchement sous-marins* or underwater release devices) for 450mm M1892 torpedoes, one on each side of the walking deck aft of the conning tower. The starboard cage faced forward and launched at an angle of 7 degrees off the boat's axis while the port cage faced aft and launched parallel to the boat's axis.

(1910) On 6.1.1910 the port cage was ordered to be re-rigged facing forward. (*Souffleur* and probably others already had this arrangement in 1909.) After 1910 some boats received Thélot launch devices for 356mm exercise torpedoes in place of or inside the 450mm cages.

*Naïade* (Q15) Cherbourg Dyd/Panhard et Levassor (benzol)
On list 1.1902. Ord: 3.4.1901. K: 16.1.1902. L: 22.9.1902.
  Comm: 17.4.1905 (full).
Budget 1901. Completion delayed by explosive trials which ended on 7 May 1903. Re-launched 20.2.1904. Condemned 27.3.1914, Struck 21.5.1914. Used in explosive experiments from 11.1916. For sale at Cherbourg 1920. Sold 17.3.1921 at Cherbourg to M. Burnouf to BU.

*Protée* (Q16)  Cherbourg Dyd/Panhard et Levassor (benzol).
On list 1.1902. Ord: 3.4.1901. K: 1.4.1902. L: 8.10.1903.
  Comm: 12.4.1904 (full at Cherbourg).
Budget 1901. At Cherbourg for trials 1.1904. Transported with *Lynx* by

---

The submarine *Ludion* in drydock at Cherbourg showing the entire boat including the portions normally submerged. The portion of the boat visible when surfaced extends from the after casing with its torpedo launch cages to the walking deck forward of the conning tower. The small slot forward of the after dive plane is for a side thrusting screw. Her sister *Méduse* is docked on the right. *(NHHC, NH-55742)*

*Foudre* to Saigon 22.4.1904 to 15.6.1904. Condemned 27.3.1914, Struck 21.5.1914. Sold 3.3.1920 at Saigon to M. Tran Song Fay.

*Perle* (Q17)  Toulon Dyd/Panhard et Levassor (benzol).
On list 1.1902. Ord: 3.4.1901. K: 23.4.1902. L: 1.12.1903.
  Comm: 8.12.1904 (full).
Budget 1901. Transported with *Esturgeon* by *Foudre* to Saigon 16.8.1905 to 29.10.1905. Struck 7.6.1912. Sold 1.2.1913 at Saigon to M. Tran Lan to BU.

*Esturgeon* (Q18)  Toulon Dyd/Panhard et Levassor (benzol).
On list 1.1902. Ord: 3.4.1901. K: 26.4.1902. L: 4.1.1904.
  Comm: 8.12.1904 (full).
Budget 1901. Transported with *Perle* by *Foudre* to Saigon 16.8.1905 to 29.10.1905. Struck 7.6.1912. Sold 1.2.1913 at Saigon to M. Truong Nong to BU.

*Bonite* (Q19)  Toulon Dyd/Panhard et Levassor (benzol).
On list 1.1902. Ord: 3.4.1901. K: 2.5.1902. L: 6.2.1904.
  Comm: 27.2.1905 (full).
Budget 1901. First static machinery trials 11.4.1904. Trial results approved 26.12.1904. Condemned 27.3.1914, Struck 21.5.1914. for sale at Rochefort 1920. Sold 14.4.1920 at Toulon to the Société de matériel naval du Midi with *Aigrette, Anguille, Cigogne* and *Turquoise.*

*Thon* (Q20)  Toulon Dyd/Panhard et Levassor (benzol).
On list 1.1902. Ord: 3.4.1901. K: 9.6.1902. L: 19.3.1904.
  Comm: 26.10.1905 (full).
Budget 1901. Dived to 30 metres during trials 23.5.1906. Condemned

27.3.1914, Struck 21.5.1914. Received 'modifications for military purposes' in 1916, sank 10.12.1916 off Cap Bon while being towed to Corfu for use as a decoy.

*Souffleur* (Q21) Toulon Dyd/Panhard et Levassor (benzol).
On list 1.1902. Ord: 3.4.1901. K: 21.6.1902. L: 21.4.1904.
  Comm: 26.10.1905 (full).
Budget 1901. Trials completed 21.8.1905. Out of commission at Bizerte from 1.4.1913. Condemned 27.3.1914, Struck 21.5.1914. Sold 10.10.1918 at Bizerte to M. Vernisse. Hull cut into section and used as floats in the construction of piers in the Bay of Ponty.

*Dorade* (Q22) Toulon Dyd/Panhard et Levassor (benzol).
On list 1.1902. Ord: 3.4.1901. K: 30.6.1902. L: 14.5.1904.
  Comm: 26.10.1905 (full).
Budget 1901. Condemned 27.3.1914, Struck 21.5.1914. for sale at Toulon 1920. Sold 12.11.1920 at Toulon to the Société de matériel naval du Midi after being offered unsuccessfully at auction on 13.9.1920.

*Lynx* (Q23) Cherbourg Dyd/Panhard et Levassor (benzol).
On list 1.1902. Ord: 3.4.1901. K: 12.5.1902. L: 24.11.1903.
  Comm: 12.4.1904 (full at Cherbourg).
Budget 1901 (late addition). At Cherbourg for trials 1.1904. Transported with *Protée* by *Foudre* to Saigon 22.4.1904 to 15.6.1904. In full commission 26.1.1905. Condemned 27.3.1914, Struck 21.5.1914. Sold 3.3.1920 at Saigon to M. Quac Thu.

*Ludion* (Q24) Cherbourg Dyd/Panhard et Levassor (benzol).
On list 1.1902. Ord: 3.4.1901. K: 2.6.1902. L: 7.1.1904.
  Comm: 25.1.1904 (trials), 9.1.1905 (full).
Budget 1901 (late addition). Condemned 27.3.1914, Struck 21.5.1914. Preparing for explosion trials with *Méduse* 14.5.1916, sunk 29.10.1916, raised and directed 9.11.1916 to be replaced by *Naïade*. For sale at Cherbourg 1920. Sold 17.3.1921 at Cherbourg to M. Burnouf to BU.

*Loutre* (Q25) Rochefort Dyd/Panhard et Levassor (benzol).
On list 1.1902. Ord: 3.4.1901. K: 8.12.1902. L: 22.8.1903.
  Comm: 6.8.1904 (full).
Budget 1901 (late addition). Condemned 27.3.1914, Struck 21.5.1914. For sale at Rochefort 1920.

*Castor* (Q26) Rochefort Dyd/Panhard et Levassor (benzol).
On list 1.1902. Ord: 3.4.1901. K: 9.2.1903. L: 5.11.1903.
  Comm: 5.11.1904 (full).
Budget 1901 (late addition). Condemned 27.3.1914, Struck 21.5.1914. Fate unknown.

*Phoque* (Q27) Rochefort Dyd/Panhard et Levassor (benzol).
On list 1.1902. Ord: 3.4.1901. K: 9.4.1903. L: 16.3.1904.
  Comm: 28.2.1905 (full).
Budget 1901 (late addition). Condemned 27.3.1914, Struck 21.5.1914. Probably sold at Rochefort.

*Otarie* (Q28) Rochefort Dyd/Panhard et Levassor (benzol).
On list 1.1902. Ord: 3.4.1901. K: 1903. L: 16.4.1904.
  Comm: 26.4.1905 (full).
Budget 1901 (late addition). Condemned 27.3.1914, Struck 21.5.1914. For sale at Rochefort 1920.

*Méduse* (Q29) Rochefort Dyd/Panhard et Levassor (benzol).
On list 1.1902. Ord: 3.4.1901. K: 3.4.1903. L: 15.6.1904.
  Comm: 4.10.1905 (full).
Budget 1901 (late addition). Condemned 27.3.1914, Struck 21.5.1914. Prepared for explosion tests at Cherbourg with *Ludion* at the end of 5.1916. For sale at Cherbourg 1920. Sold 17.3.1921 at Cherbourg to M. Burnouf.

*Oursin* (Q30) Rochefort Dyd/Panhard et Levassor (benzol).
On list 1.1902. Ord: 3.4.1901. K: 3.4.1904. L: 26.9.1904.
  Comm: 20.10.1905 (full).
Budget 1901 (late addition). Condemned 27.3.1914, Struck 21.5.1914, struck again 27.2.1920 when she was also condemned and ordered transferred to the Domaines for sale. Sold 1920 at Brest.

*Grondin* (Q31) Toulon Dyd/Panhard et Levassor (benzol).
On list 1.1902. Ord: 3.4.1901. K: 12.9.1902. L: 16.7.1904.
  Comm: 3.1.1906 (full).
Budget 1901 (late addition). Struck 4.4.1913. Sold 15.11.1913 at Bizerte to M. Boccara et Cie.

*Anguille* (Q32) Toulon Dyd/Panhard et Levassor (benzol).
On list 1.1902. Ord: 3.4.1901. K: 9.10.1902. L: 3.8.1904.
  Comm: 31.7.1907 (full).
Budget 1901 (late addition). Completed trials during 1906. Condemned 27.3.1914, Struck 21.5.1914. For sale at Toulon 1920. Sold 14.4.1920 at Toulon to the Société de matériel naval du Midi with *Aigrette*, *Bonite*, *Cigogne* and *Turquoise*.

*Alose* (Q33) Toulon Dyd/Panhard et Levassor (benzol).
On list 1.1902. Ord: 3.4.1901. K: 17.11.1902. L: 13.10.1904.
  Comm: 31.7.1907 (full).
Budget 1901 (late addition). Completed trials during 1906. Condemned 27.3.1914, Struck 21.5.1914. Towed from Toulon to Fréjus for use with *Cigogne* as target by aircraft (the instructions for the explosion tests were dated 17.5.1917). Sunk 28.3.1918 while under tow at 8 knots by two bombs dropped at 10 metres altitude by a seaplane. Wreck found 26.10.1975, raised by COMEX (a deep diving company) 27.5.1976, purchased by them from the Domaines 1977 and displayed at the COMEX headquarters at Marseille.

*Truite* (Q34) Toulon Dyd/Panhard et Levassor (benzol).
On list 1.1902. Ord: 3.4.1901. K: 28.11.1902. L: 14.4.1905.
  Comm: 26.7.1905 (trials), 1906 (full).
Budget 1901 (late addition). Completed trials during 1906. Condemned 27.3.1914, Struck 21.5.1914. Sold 10.10.1918 at Bizerte to M. Vernisse to BU. Hull cut into section and used as floats in the construction of piers in the Bay of Ponty.

---

*SOUS-MARIN X* (later *DAUPHIN*). *Bateau sous-marin*. Single hull with two screws, electric propulsion with benzol-powered dynamos. Designed by Romazzotti.

By a dispatch of 6 November 1900 Minister de Lanessan referred to the *Conseil des travaux* for examination two projects related to submarine navigation, one by the *Section technique* (see *Sous-marin Y*) and one by naval constructor Maugas (see *Sous-marin Z*). He said that a third project from naval constructor Romazzotti would follow, which it did later in November. The Council examined Romazzotti's project on 14 December 1900. Its essential feature was the use of an oil motor using air from the atmosphere for navigation on the surface and using compressed air from internal tanks for submarine navigation. It thus had much in common with the project of the *Section technique*, which also called for using a unique engine both on the surface and submerged. Romazzotti's boat was 25.60m long, 2.25m in diameter, 72.620 tons on the surface, 77.840 tons submerged, and had a 50hp engine (the largest that Panhard et Levassor could then make) to produce speeds of 7.5 knots on the surface and 5.6 knots submerged. The Council recommended its immediate approval and emphasized the urgency of proceeding with its construction and trials, although it felt it prudent to lay down only one such boat for the moment.

In his 1902 budget (submitted 29 March 1901), Minister of Marine de Lanessan not only included the 20 small pure submarines of the *Naïade* class (above) but added three experimental pure submarines (Q35-37).

The submarine *Sous-marin X* moving from left to right. Note the two flagstaffs in the water to the left, each marking the location of one of the boat's two sterns. The coast defence ship *Jemmapes* or *Valmy* is in the background. *(Postcard by P.B. Cherbourg)*

Although they first appeared in the 1902 budget all 23 vessels were to be built using 1901 funds, suggesting that de Lanessan as of March 1901 considered the programme urgent.

During 1901 Romazzotti abandoned the design for a submarine with a unique oil engine that the *Conseil des travaux* had examined on 14 December 1900 in favour of an offensive variant of the *Naïade* type that became *Sous-marin X*. The new project had many features in common with the *Naïade*s, including internal arrangements and the type of propulsion machinery, but the *Naïade*s, with their small size and relatively low speeds, were considered strictly defensive submarines. Romazzotti's *bateau sous-marin offensif* was much larger than the *Naïade*s (37.40 vice 23.75 metres long) and had two propeller shafts instead of one. There were two electric motors, one on each shaft, that were powered submerged by the battery and on the surface either by the battery or by two dynamos driven by two benzol engines. To accommodate the additional machinery Romazzotti adopted a complex shape for the hull, replacing the usual hull with circular cross sections for most of its length with one that started out in the bow with a normal circular section, took on a cross section resembling a figure 8 lying on its side amidships, and branched out into two separate submerged circular hulls, one for each shaft, toward the stern. The result was a Y-shaped hull with one bow and two sterns, each of which had a propeller. Because the boat was to remain at sea for extended periods habitability was increased by providing an elevated platform on top of the central tower to give the crew access to fresh air. The new boat had three sets of horizontal planes instead of the two in the *Naïade*s, adding a pair amidships, and had another plane aft between the screws. Romazzotti's design proposal included five torpedo tubes (one fixed in the bow, two

fixed launch cages forward and two Drzewiecki trainable launchers) but as built one of the fixed launch cages was repositioned aft of the tower and one was omitted.

On 10 December 1901 the *Conseil des travaux* discussed Romazzotti's proposal for a *bateau sous-marin offensif*. It noted that the main elements of the new design (displacement, range, speed, and mode of propulsion) had already received Ministerial approval, leaving it little to discuss. It was sceptical of the Y-shaped hull, which it felt might fall short of providing the intended 30 metre diving depth, but was willing to try the experiment. On 13 May 1902 the Council discussed additional modifications to the design including the extension of the elevated platform over the after hatchway which was raised to support it.

The two electric motors and the dynamos were built by Sautter, Harlé of Paris under a contract of 7 January 1903 and the benzol engines were built by Panhard-Levassor under a contract of the same date.

*Sous-marin X* was described in *La Vie Maritime* in 1907 as follows. 'The *X*, with a reserve buoyancy of 8%, was to cover 300 miles at 7 knots with the ability to recharge her batteries en route. Having two engines, it was to be a competitor to the *Sirène* type submersibles but with a substantially greater submerged range under electric power. Her totally superficial habitability consisted of a platform four metres long and two metres above the hull, and an ingenious kind of extendable conning tower allowed the commander to rise above his boat until the moment of submergence. The *X* made two main transits, Brest to Cherbourg and Cherbourg to Dunkirk, with her benzol engines of the *Naïade* type, the second in April 1906. The two benzol engines failed in succession during the second voyage, a crankshaft broke in one, a cylinder cracked in the other.' Since then the *X* was reduced to a pure electric submarine. 'The range of the *X*, which two years ago was 90 miles on the surface at 5 knots and 60 miles at 3.6 knots submerged, fell respectively to 55 miles and 40 miles. The *X* thus finds itself for the moment as a purely defensive submarine like *Français*, *Algérien* and *Morse*, able to be used only in a limited distance around Cherbourg.'

**Dimensions & tons:** 37.700m oa, 37.400m pp x 3.124m ext (4.340m outside the amidships horizontal planes). 165.379t (surfaced), 179.519t (submerged). Draught: 2.397m, 2.408m aft (keel lines projected). Men: 15 including 2 officers. Reserve buoyancy: 7.9%

**Machinery:**

(surfaced) 260hp designed at 500rpm. Speed 10.5kts. Trials (28.1.1905) 219.429hp = 8.373kts at 349.75rpm using the benzol engines. 2 screws (variable pitch). 2 petrol (benzol) engines with 4 cylinders of 0.250m diameter and 0.70m stroke driving 2 dynamos. Range 170nm @ 8kts

(submerged) 230hp at 360rpm. Speed 5.5kts. Trials (28.4.1905?) 162.5hp = 6.167kts at 211.625rpm. 2 electric motors, one on each shaft. Range 60nm @ 4.5kts.

**Torpedoes:** 1 internal bow tube, 2 Drzewiecki trainable launchers on each side of the after conning tower, and one launch cage on the centreline aft of the after tower (aimed aft and trainable up to 12 degrees each side of the axis), all for 450mm torpedoes.

*Sous-marin X* (Q35) Cherbourg Dyd/Panhard et Levassor (benzol).

On list 1.1902. Ord: 10.1.1902. K: 20.4.1903. L: 15.11.1904. Comm: 1904 (trials), 18.12.1905 (full).

Budget 1901 (late addition). Machinery installed 29.6.1904 to 21.1.1905. Trials at Cherbourg 1905-07. Renamed *Dauphin* 13.2.1911. Decomm. 1.6.1913. Struck 21.5.1914. For sale at Cherbourg 1920-1922.

---

*SOUS-MARIN Z. Bateau sous-marin.* Single hull, diesel surface propulsion. Designed by Maugas.

By a dispatch of 6 November 1900 Minister de Lanessan submitted to the *Conseil des travaux* for examination a project related to submarine navigation drafted by naval constructor Maugas. The Council examined it on 19 December 1900. Maugas added to his *Farfadet* type a diesel engine for use on the surface and for recharging the battery, making her a *bateau sous-marin autonome* to compete with *Narval*, Laubeuf's *submersible autonome*. He aimed for speeds of 12 knots on the surface as in *Narval* and 7 knots submerged as in *Morse*. Her size and hull lines resembled those of *Farfadet* (the hull was only 0.60m longer) but her appearance was totally different because she had had an elevated platform 2.30 metres above the hull between the conning tower and the exhaust funnel for the diesel engine and a walking deck forward over a free-flooding ballast tank. A second walking deck was added aft while she was inactive at Cherbourg after 1905. Her pressure hull aft contained two compartments for the diesel engine and its auxiliary machinery, and two smaller compartments for the electric motor, both the diesel and the motor being on the single propeller shaft. She first received a diesel by Sautter-Harlé of 120hp (80hp effective), contract of 8 May 1901, one of the first of its kind built in France, and when this gave mediocre results it was replaced with a more powerful one by Sautter of 190hp that gave only slightly better results. She was the only French submarine to have four pairs of horizontal planes (including one somewhat aft of amidships and one between it and the forward planes). She also had a pair of *évolueurs* on the sides of the stern like those in *Farfadet*.

*Sous-marin Z* arrived at Cherbourg 19 July 1904. Her moment in history ended when her comparative trials with *Aigrette* were completed 2 May 1905. She then ruptured her propeller shaft on 26 May 1905. Her diesel engine failed on 1 June 1906 and its removal was requested on 23 June 1906. A decision was taken on 26 April 1907 to give her an extensive refit. The propeller shaft along with the *évolueurs* and the variable pitch propeller would be repaired and the diesel would be removed and replaced with two kerosene motor-generators by Sautter converted from Petithomme's diesels for the two *Guêpes* (120hp each). *Sous-marin Z* had the same internal structure as the *Farfadet* class and it was therefore necessary to strengthen her internal ballast tanks to resist 5kg pressure following the loss of *Lutin*. This work would have cost half the value of the subma-

The submarine *Sous-marin Z* at the end of a tow line. Note the two flagstaffs, one for the national ensign and a smaller one to mark the stern. (*Postcard by P.B. Cherbourg*)

rine and she would also need a new battery costing more than the refit. Condemnation was first proposed 26 February 1908 and she was decommissioned effective 1 March 1909. Condemnation was definitively proposed on 23 June 1909, striking her from the fleet list was proposed by the *Conseil supérieur* on 7 November 1909, approved by the Naval General Staff (EMG) on 26 January 1910, and promulgated in the *Bulletin officiel de la Marine* on 9 March 1910.

**Dimensions & tons:** 42.027m oa, 41.35m pp x 2.98m ext (4.180 over the amidships horizontal planes). 202t disp (surfaced), 222t (submerged). Draught: 2.82m mean. Men: 16 including 2 officers. Reserve buoyancy: 9%

**Machinery:**

(surfaced) 190hp designed. Speed 9kts. Trials vs. *Aigrette* 181hp = 7.876kts. 1 screw. 1 diesel engine. Range 500nm @ 5kts.

(submerged) Speed 7.10kts. Trials vs. *Aigrette* 180.4hp = 5.846kts. 1 electric motor. Range 45nm @ 4kts.

**Torpedoes:** 2 internal tubes side by side in the bow for 450mm torpedoes (same arrangement as in *Émeraude*).

*Sous-marin Z* (Q36) Rochefort Dyd/Sautter-Harlé, Paris.

On list 1.1902. Ord: 10.6.1901. K: 16.8.1902. L: 28.3.1904. Comm: 3.6.1904 (trials), 1905 (full?)

Budget 1901 (late addition). Ordered on 4.6.1904 to prepare for comparative trials with *Aigrette* at Cherbourg, arrived at Cherbourg from Rochefort for trials 19.7.1904. Trials with *Aigrette* completed 2.5.1905. Major break in propeller shaft 26.5.1905 followed by other casualties, was probably never in full commission. Struck 9.3.1910. Sold 8.7.1911 at Cherbourg.

---

*SOUS-MARIN Y. Bateau sous-marin.* Single hull, unique diesel propulsion (surfaced and submerged). Designed by the *Section technique.*

By a dispatch of 6 November 1900 Minister de Lanessan submitted to the *Conseil des travaux* for examination a project for adapting an oil engine to submarines drafted by the *Section technique* and bearing the date 24 September 1900. The project was very complete, but in a note dated 23 November 1900 the *Section technique* proposed various modifications to it. The project consisted of adapting to a hull identical to that of *Sirène* and

*Triton* a diesel engine that would propel the boat both on the surface and submerged. The *Conseil des travaux* examined the project on 14 December 1900 with naval constructor Emmanuel Marie Victor Petithomme participating as the expert on the diesel. The Council concluded that the project was susceptible for immediate approval with a few reservations but felt it would be prudent to lay down only one boat for the moment.

This led eventually to *Sous-marin Y*, an experimental submarine ordered on 12 August 1901 to be built to plans of the *Section technique* developed by Émile Bertin and naval constructor Lucien Étienne Beausire with Petithomme's diesel. The diesel engine was ordered from the Compagnie française des moteurs à gaz et des constructions mécaniques (holder of the Otto patents in France) by a contract of 13 November 1901 (notified 20 November 1901). The engine was designed to propel the boat on the surface at 10 knots on 4 cylinders in the normal way and propel it dived in one of two modes. It could produce a submerged speed of 6 knots on 2 or 4 cylinders using compressed air previously stored in tanks at $150g/cm^2$ and exhausting combustion gases underwater, or it could move the boat more slowly on 1 cylinder with the exhaust gases being temporarily stored under pressure and then discharged intermittently. Trials of the engine at the factory between 18 July 1904 and 13 February 1905 showed the impossibility of running the diesel submerged with compressed air, and trials on board the submarine in March 1907 showed the impossibility of discharging exhaust from the engine underwater. Thus the boat could only move on the surface. On 31 October 1906 Minister of Marine Thomson ordered Toulon to study installing an electric motor and batteries for submerged navigation, and a design sent to Paris on 5 July 1907 was approved by Thomson on 12 December 1907. However, trials of the diesel on the surface were also interrupted frequently by mechanical failures. On 24 April 1908 Thomson suspended the refit ordered on 12 December 1907 and on 16 May 1908 plans to convert her were abandoned. On 24 June 1908 Thomson asked Toulon to propose condemnation of the submarine in view of the high cost that would be required for her conversion. She was cannibalized for parts (the periscope, the Drzewiecki trainable launchers, and some of the rudder control equipment) for *Oméga* (later *Argonaute*), which originally was to have had a similar propulsion plant.

**Dimensions & tons:** 44.90m oa x 3.00m ext. 213t disp (surfaced), 226t (submerged). Draught: 2.750m. Men: 15. Reserve buoyancy: 5.8%
**Machinery:**
(surfaced) 250hp designed at 320rpm. Speed 10kts (designed). 1 screw. 1 diesel engine with 4 cylinders.
(submerged) Speed 6kts (designed) from the unique diesel engine.
**Torpedoes:** 2 superimposed internal tubes in the bow, 2 Drzewiecki trainable launchers on the sides, and 1 fixed launch cage aft, all for 450mm torpedoes.

*Sous-marin Y* (Q37) Toulon Dyd/Cie. Française des Moteurs à Gaz, Paris.
On list 1.1902. Ord: 12.8.1901. K: 22.5.1902. L: 24.7.1905. Comm: 25.7.1905 (trials).
Budget 1901 (late addition). Commissioning for trials authorised 23.7.1905. Never completed trials because it was found that she could move only on the surface. Decomm. 1.3.1909. Struck 22.4.1909, retained for trials at Toulon 1909-1911. Offered for sale 1 August 1911 at Toulon by the Administration des Domaines with *Amiral Baudin, Magenta, Pascal, Milan*, and smaller vessels, sold 2.8.1911 to M. Bénédic to BU.

---

***AIGRETTE* Class.** *Torpilleurs autonomes submersibles*. Double hull, diesel surface propulsion. Designed by Laubeuf.

The 1902 budget (submitted 29 March 1901) contained no new submarines to be begun in 1902, probably because of the big orders then being placed for the 20 *fritures* and three experimental boats under the

1901 budget. It did contain 5 new *bateaux sous-marins* (Q38-42 at Toulon) to be begun in 1903 and 26 more (Q43-68 at three dockyards) in 1904. These were all listed as being powered by electric motors and batteries, and cost figures suggest that they would have been larger than the *Naïade*s and smaller than the *Sirène*s.

A year later the pendulum swung back towards the submersible when the *Conseil des travaux* on 15 April 1902 approved a new Laubeuf submersible design. Laubeuf wanted a submarine that could move from Toulon to Taranto, the southernmost of the large Italian naval bases, and cruise off that port. To achieve this in the new design he sought to improve the habitability and seakeeping of the *Sirène* type and also to reduce to a minimum the time needed for submerging. To accomplish the former, he had increased displacement and reserve buoyancy. (*Narval* performed far better in heavy seas than *Sirène*, suggesting he had reduced reserve buoyancy too much in *Sirène*.) Times for submerging had already decreased from the initial half hour in *Narval* to 7 minutes 18 seconds in *Triton*, and Laubeuf felt they were unlikely to go much lower unless a diesel engine replaced the steam machinery. He therefore offered two variants of the new design, one with a diesel and one with steam. He calculated the operating range with steam to be 215 miles at 10.5 knots or 448 miles at 8 knots while the range with a diesel would be much larger, 939 miles at 9.3 knots and 1,352 miles at 8 knots. Laubeuf noted that manoeuvres that were then difficult for diesels like going astern or manoeuvring in port, could be performed by the electric motors if necessary. The council recommended the steam variant as a safe choice but also recommended building a diesel boat as an experiment.

On 13 May 1902 de Lanessan signed an order to lay down 13 *Aigrette* class submersibles. The boats, Q43 to Q50 (Toulon) and Q38 to Q42 (Cherbourg), were to be inscribed on the Liste de la Flotte as *Aigrette, Cigogne, Cygne, Eider, Grèbe,. Héron, Macreuse,* and *Marabout* (at Toulon) and *Pingouin, Plongeon, Pluvier, Pélican,* and *Vanneau* (at Cherbourg). Toulon was the lead yard for the class and would supply plans to Cherbourg. On 3 June 1902 Minister de Lanessan moved the order for the armoured cruiser *Victor Hugo* from Toulon to Lorient and urged Toulon to accelerate its work on submarines and submersibles. At least *Aigrette* and *Cigogne* and perhaps all were to be diesel propelled.

This success of the submersible proved to be brief. De Lanessan left office on 7 June 1902 and on 19 July 1902 his successor, Camille Pelletan, replied to a report from Toulon on orders for engines for the 13 submersibles with a directive to place no such orders without his permission. This was followed by an order on 8 August 1902 not to place any orders of

The submersible *Aigrette*, in which a diesel engine was substituted for steam propulsion on the surface. She ran comparative trials with *Sous-marin Z* in 1905 with her electric motor before her diesel was installed. *(Postcard by P.B. Cherbourg, NHHC, NH-55759)*

any kind for these boats without permission. On 14 August 1902 Toulon sent a list of orders already placed (including all materials for the hulls, some of which had already been delivered). On 6 September 1902 Minister Pelletan decided to proceed with only one submersible at Toulon, increasing the number to two in his formal dispatch on 10 September. *Aigrette* and *Cigogne* at Toulon now became Q38-39. In the 1903 budget (submitted 14 October 1902) Q41-58 were unspecified *sous-marins* or submersibles for which no firm plans probably existed, and in fact of the many submarines Pelletan planned only six submarines and two submersibles (the latter requested by Toulon) actually joined the fleet.

The diesel engines of *Aigrette* were built by the Société des moteurs à gaz et de constructions mécaniques (Maison Otto). On 7 May 1902 the Director of Naval Construction had proposed ordering two MAN diesels from Diesel's plant at Augsburg for this class (then still of 13 boats), but the French holders of licences from Diesel claimed that this decreased the value of their French patents and that they could build the engines as well as Augsburg could. They were given the contract on 31 October 1902 but had great difficulty building these engines of 'an absolutely new type' and delivered them late with substantial penalties. The boats had three pairs of horizontal planes instead of the two in earlier submersibles, adding a pair amidships. Time to dive was reduced to 3 minutes in this class from 7 minutes in the *Sirène* class. The fuel in these and probably other early diesel boats was kerosene.

**Dimensions & tons:** 35.85m oa, 35.29m wl x 4.05m ext, 4.028m wl. 177.8t disp (surfaced), 253.3t (submerged). Draught: 2.63m mean and aft. Men: 14 including 2 officers. Reserve buoyancy: 29.7%

**Machinery:**

(surfaced) 140hp (effective) designed at 400rpm. Speed 9.25kts. *Aigrette* in trials vs. *Sous-marin Z* using her electric motor 180hp = 8.976kts. 1 screw. 1 four-cycle diesel engine with 4 cylinders of 0.280m diameter and 0.300m stroke. Fuel was kerosene (*pétrole lampant*, density 0.81). Range 1,300nm @ 8kts (vice 340nm @ 8kts in the steam *Sirène* type).

(submerged) 130hp at 360rpm. Speed 6.20kts. *Aigrette* in trials vs. *Sous-marin Z* 182hp = 8.46kts. 1 electric motor with 2 armatures on 1 shaft. Batteries 29 tons. Range 65nm @ 3.8kts.

**Torpedoes:** 2 fixed launch cages aimed forward at 5 degrees off the boat's axis and 2 Drzewiecki trainable launchers on deck aft, all for 450mm M1892 torpedoes. In *Cigogne* one of the fixed launch cages was turned around in 1910 to fire aft.

*Aigrette* (Q38) Toulon Dyd/Cie. Française des Moteurs à Gaz, Paris.
On list 1.1903. Ord: 13.5.1902. K: 3.11.1902. L: 23.2.1904.
  Comm: 1904 (trials), 29.5.1908 (full).
Budget 1902 (late addition). Preliminary underway trials 6.4.1904. Electric motor installed and tried 5.1904. Arrived at Cherbourg 18.7.1904 from Toulon with electric propulsion only to conduct experimental trials with *Sous-marin Z*. New preliminary underway trials at Cherbourg 5-12.9.1904. Comparative trials with *Z* during 2-5.1905. Delivery of diesels scheduled 1.12.1905. Definitive trials with diesels begun 11.6.1906, diesels and electric motor accepted 17.7.1906. Frame of diesel cracked 15.10.1906. Decision of 13.5.1908 sent her from Cherbourg to the school for underwater navigation (*École de navigation sous-marine*, ENSM) at Toulon. Trial results approved and *1er armement* 29.5.1908. In 1914 was assigned to the Brest submarines (*Sous-marins de Brest*, the defensive submarines there). In the Normandy submarine squadron 1.1918. Struck 12.11.1919. Sold 14.4.1920 at Toulon to the Société de matériel naval du Midi with *Anguille, Bonite, Cigogne* and *Turquoise*.

*Cigogne* (Q39) Toulon Dyd/Cie. Française des Moteurs à Gaz, Paris.
On list 1.1903. Ord: 13.5.1902. K: 23.1.1903. L: 8.11.1904.
  Comm: 18.7.1906 (full).
Budget 1902 (late addition). Underway trials of electric motors began 17.3.1905. Trials interrupted 1-3.1906 to install the diesel. Diesel

accepted 1.6.1906 after preliminary trials. Official underway trials 7.7.1906 to 2.8.1906. Served at the school for underwater navigation (ENSM) at Toulon. In 1914 was assigned to the Toulon submarines (the defensive submarines there). Arrived at Brindisi from Toulon 2.7.1915. At the aviation school at Saint Raphaël for anti-submarine work, 1.1918. Condemned and struck 12.11.1919. Sold 14.4.1920 at Toulon to the Société de matériel naval du Midi with *Aigrette, Anguille, Bonite,* and *Turquoise.*

---

*SUBMERSIBLE OMÉGA* (Ω) (later *ARGONAUTE*). *Torpilleur autonome submersible* (to *Sous-marins* 1.1909). Double hull, steam surface propulsion (originally unique diesel for both surfaced and submerged). Designed by the *Section technique* (Bertin and Petithomme) and modified by Beaumarchais.

This submersible was to have had the same type of unique diesel by Petithomme as *Sous-marin Y* (Q37) but of 334hp vice 250hp. Following the failure of *Y* this diesel was ordered on 28 May 1907 to be replaced with half of the propulsion system of a *Pluviôse* class steam submarine (350/230hp). The plans for the modification were produced by naval constructor Charles Louis Marie Delarue Caron baron de Beaumarchais, and she was completed in 1909 as a submersible with a single shaft similar to *Aigrette* and *Cigogne*. The portion of her walking deck forward of the conning tower was later removed, probably during the war. The contract for the electric motor with the Cie. Générale Électrique de Nancy was dated 16 May 1906.

On 18 August 1910 the commander of the 1st flotilla of submarines wrote to his superior that Minister of Marine Vice Admiral Boué de Lapeyrère had orally invited the commander of *Oméga* to propose another name for that submarine and he proposed the name *Argonaute*, then held by a *torpilleur de haute mer* that was in the process of being condemned on 1 January 1910. The EMG 2nd section picked up this suggestion on 2 September 1910 and it was made official in a letter to the Maritime Prefect of Toulon dated 27 September 1910. In March 1912 the commander of the boat wrote that she had qualities on the surface similar to *Pluviôse* except for a limited range due to her single shaft, but she had a poor submerged range and a slow dive time similar to the earlier *Sirène*.

**Dimensions & tons:** 48.9m oa, 47m pp (wl fwd to rudder) x 4.2m ext. 304.950t disp (surfaced), 400.955t (submerged). Draught: 2.901 fwd, 2.843m mean, 2.785m aft. Men: 22. Reserve buoyancy: 24.0%

**Machinery:**

(surfaced) 350ihp designed at 400rpm and 16.5kg/cm² boiler pressure (15.5kg/cm² at the engine). Speed 10.2kts. Trials (1911) 302ihp = 9.47kts at 389rpm. 1 screw (fixed pitch). 1 vertical triple expansion engine with 3 cylinders of 0.225m, 0.340m, and 0.550m diameter and 0.270m stroke. 1 Du Temple return-flame boiler. 14,100 litres oil. Range (trials) 1,200nm @ 7.7kts.

(submerged). 234hp at 360rpm. Speed 6.02kts. Trials (1911) 204hp = 5.18kts at 328rpm. 1 electric motor. Range (trials) 43.2nm @ 3.28kts.

**Torpedoes:** 2 internal bow tubes (probably superimposed), 2 Drzewiecki trainable launchers (from *Sous-marin Y*) underwater amidships, and two fixed launch cages under the walking deck at the very stern aimed aft 1°30' off the boat's axis, all for 450mm M1906 torpedoes.

*Oméga* (Ω) (Q40) Toulon Dyd/A.C. Loire, Saint Denis.
On list 1.1903. Ord: 26.1.1903. K: 15.2.1904. L: 28.11.1905.
  Comm: 21.1.1911 (full).
Budget 1902 (late addition). Machinery installed 1.4.1909 to 29.10.1909. Renamed *Argonaute* 27.9.1910. Trial results approved and in full commission 21.1.1911. In 1914 was assigned to the Toulon submarines (defensive submarines there). Arrived at Brindisi from Toulon 2.7.1915. At the school for underwater detection at Bandol near Toulon (part of the ENSM), 1.1918. Retired (struck) 20.5.1919,

ordered sold 17.10.1919. Sale at Toulon of 10.5.1921 to M. Jean Jacquart of Paris fell through and a new sale was ordered on 17.10.1929, outcome unknown.

———

*ÉMERAUDE* **Class.** *Bateaux sous-marins* (to *Sous-marins* 1.1909). Single hull with two screws, diesel surface propulsion. Designed by Maugas

The designer of this class, Maugas, was with Romazzotti one of the two main French advocates of the single-hulled pure submarine. He had previously designed the *Farfadet* class and *Sous-marin Z* and had secured the support of the *Conseil supérieur* for the pure submarine. The displacement of the new design was just under twice that of *Z* with the objective of increasing surfaced and submerged speed and range, moving the torpedo launchers inside the hull, and improving crew accommodations. Two other key differences were that the new boat had twin screws with fixed blades and had no internal watertight compartments, although it did have nine internal bulkheads that divided the interior into ten spaces and helped strengthen the hull. The reserve buoyancy, however, decreased slightly to 7.6%, reflecting the boat's low freeboard (0.39m amidships) and leaving a small margin of error in case of a leak. The crush depth was calculated at 120 metres, meaning the boat could dive safely to 40 metres. They were easily recognized by the single long tower amidships with an even longer platform on top 2.5 metres above the waterline. There were two ways to charge batteries while underway: one diesel propelling the boat while the other charged the batteries, or with one diesel propelling the boat and the other both propelling the boat and charging the batteries. The boats had the usual three pairs of horizontal planes including one amidships, although trial reports suggested that the amidships pair was of little use.

The diesels for the three Cherbourg boats were built by Sautter Harlé & Cie. These engines which ran at a slightly higher speed that the previous types were fragile and their trials were long and difficult. As with many early diesels, they could not go astern and the electric motors had to be used instead.

**Dimensions & tons:** 44.900m oa, 44.650m pp x 3.900m ext (5.916m over horizontal planes). 394.450t disp (surfaced), 426.707t (submerged). Draught: 3.710m mean, 3.766m aft. Men: 25 including 2 officers. Reserve buoyancy: 7.6%

**Machinery:**
(surfaced) 600hp designed at 340rpm. Speed 11.50kts. Trials (Cherbourg boats) 691hp = 11.259kts. 2 screws (fixed pitch). 2 four-cycle diesel engines with 4 cylinders of 0.375m diameter and 0.460m stroke. 13,800 litres oil. Range (trials) 1,875nm @ 7.5kts.
(submerged) 600hp at 340rpm. Speed 9.20kts. Trials (Cherbourg boats) 600hp = 8.5kts. 2 electric motors (1 on each shaft, each with two armatures). Batteries 82 tons. Range (trials) 235nm @ 2.5kts.

**Torpedoes:** 4 internal tubes (2 side by side in the bow, each with a reload torpedo behind it, and 2 side by side in the stern) for 450mm M1892 (later M1904) torpedoes. The stern tubes were intended for fire to the sides using torpedoes fitted with Obry gyroscopes. **Guns:** *Turquoise* and *Topaze* were the first French submarines to receive a gun, one 37mm each in August 1915.

*Émeraude* (Q41) Cherbourg Dyd/Sautter-Harlé, Paris.
On list 1.1904. Ord: 24.10.1903. K: 17.10.1904. L: 6.8.1906. Comm: 11.11.1908 (full).
Budget 1903. First underway machinery trials 16.6.1907, official trials of diesels 22.8.1907. Made 11.507 knots on the surface on 5.5.1908 and 9.205 knots submerged on 5.6.1908, both during official trials at Cherbourg. In 1914 was assigned to the Brest submarines (defensive submarines there). In the 3rd submarine squadron at Corfu 1.1918. Condemned 24.10.1919. Struck 1.12.1919, for sale at Toulon 1920-1922. Reserved for experiments 13.1.1921. Sold 27.1.1923 at Toulon to M. Salvator Bertorelli to BU.

The submarine *Opale*, here captioned a 'submarine cruiser', moving from left to right. This six-boat class added diesel propulsion on the surface to the pure submarine just as the *Aigrette* class did for the submersible. *(Postcard by P.B. Cherbourg)*

*Opale* (Q42) Cherbourg Dyd/Sautter-Harlé, Paris.
On list 1.1904. Ord: 24.10.1903. K: 20.10.1904. L: 20.11.1906. Comm: 19.12.1908 (full).
Budget 1903. First underway machinery trials 23.2.1907, official trials of diesels 27.4.1907. In 1914 was assigned to the Brest submarines. On detached duty at Mudros 1.1918. Struck 12.11.1919. To the Domaines for sale 15.9.1920. Sold 10.5.1921 at Toulon to M. Jean Jacquart to BU.

*Rubis* (Q43) Cherbourg Dyd/Sautter-Harlé, Paris.
On list 1.1904. Ord: 24.10.1903 K: 1.12.1904. L: 27.6.1907. Comm: 11.12.1909 (full).
Budget 1903. First underway machinery trials 28.7.1908, official trials of diesels 28.8.1908. In 1914 was assigned to the Brest submarines. In the 3rd submarine squadron at Corfu 1.1918. Struck 12.11.1919. Sold 10.5.1921 at Toulon to M. Jean Jacquart to BU.

*Saphir* (Q44) Toulon Dyd/Sautter-Harlé, Paris.
On list 1.1904. Ord: 24.10.1903. K: 11.3.1905. L: 6.2.1908. Comm: 10.12.1910 (full).
Budget 1903. First underway machinery trials 28.6.1908, official trials of diesels 10.5.1910. In 1914 was assigned to the Bizerte submarines. Grounded 15.1.1915 off Chanak while submerged attempting to penetrate the Dardanelles, released solid ballast to surface and destroyed by Turkish shore batteries.

*Topaze* (Q45) Toulon Dyd/Sautter-Harlé, Paris.
On list 1.1904. Ord: 24.10.1903. K: 30.3.1905. L: 2.7.1908. Comm: 10.12.1910 (full).
Budget 1903. First underway machinery trials 3.12.1909, official trials of diesels 10.5.1910. In 1914 was assigned to the Bizerte submarines. On detached duty at Mudros 1.1918. Struck 12.11.1919. To the Domaines for sale 15.9.1920. Sold 10.5.1921 at Toulon to M. Jean Jacquart to BU.

*Turquoise* (Q46) Toulon Dyd/Sautter-Harlé, Paris.
On list 1.1904. Ord: 24.10.1903. K: 27.4.1905. L: 3.8.1908. Comm: 10.12.1910 (full).
Budget 1903. First underway machinery trials 4.3.1910, official trials of diesels 18.7.1910. In 1914 was assigned to the Bizerte submarines. Caught in a net off Nagara in the Dardanelles 30.10.1915, forced by a Turkish shore battery to surface and surrender. Towed to Istanbul,

commissioned 10.11.1915, and named *Müstecip Onbaşi* after the artillery officer who captured her. Used from 12.1915 as a stationary battery charging vessel for German U-boats. Officially returned to France 1.7.1919 and towed to Toulon by sloop *Algol*. Struck 12.11.1919. Sold 14.4.1920 at Toulon to the Société de matériel naval du Midi with *Aigrette, Anguille, Bonite,* and *Cigogne.ç*

## Programme changes 1904-1905

The 1904 budget (submitted 16 June 1903) showed Q41-58 as *bateaux sous-marins* or submersibles to be begun in 1903 of which Q41-48 were 301-ton units at Cherbourg and Q49-58 were units of unspecified size at Toulon. By the time the 1905 budget was submitted on 30 March 1904 the Pelletan ministry had changed this programme to two *Circé* class submersibles (Q47-48 at Cherbourg), ten *Guêpe bateaux sous-marins* (Q49-52 at Toulon, Q53-55 at Cherbourg, and Q56-58 at Toulon), and two modified *Émeraude bateaux sous-marins* (Q59-60 at Rochefort). Q47-52 were originally planned to be begun in 1904 and Q53-60 in 1905. Q47-50 and Q59-60 were laid down but only the two submersibles, Q47-48, were completed.

## CIRCÉ Class.

*Torpilleurs autonomes submersibles* (to *Sous-marins* 1.1909). Double hull with two screws, diesel surface propulsion. Designed by Laubeuf.

Taking into account the lessons of the manoeuvres of 1902 and 1904 and many transits between Cherbourg and Brest between those years, Laubeuf designed a submersible twice the size of his *Aigrette*, with two screws instead of one, better speed and endurance on the surface, and especially better habitability. The new design could carry a large enough crew to operate on the surface with three watch sections instead of the two in *Aigrette* and to recharge batteries on the surface and operate submerged with two watch sections instead of the entire crew. All hands were still needed to dive, surface, and conduct torpedo attacks. The Navy staff succeeded in October 1904 in getting Minister Pelletan to order two units of this type at Toulon. On 12 April 1905 the new Minister of Marine, Thomson, informed the Senate of the forthcoming laying down of these two submersibles, which he called 'offensive' because they were diesel propelled. They were designed for two four-cycle diesels each of 280hp and 4 cylinders, but French industry was not yet able to produce the engines and they were ordered from Maschinenfabrik Augsburg Nürnberg AG (MAN) in Germany instead. The names *Albatros* and *Cygne* may have been proposed for these boats but mythological names were selected instead. Both boats dived to 25 metres during trials, which was then considered their safe diving limit. They had three sets of horizontal planes plus one rudder forward and three aft.

*The characteristics are based on a devis for* Calypso *(sous-marin) dated 17.9.1909.*

**Dimensions & tons:** 47.130m oa, 46.180m pp (extreme bow to 550mm from extreme stern) x 4.904m ext, 4.898m wl. 361.231t disp (surfaced, actual), 498t (submerged, trials). Draught: 3.083m mean, 3.236m aft. Men: 22 including 2 officers. Reserve buoyancy: 27.5%.

**Machinery:**
(surfaced) 630hp designed at 412rpm. Speed 11.90kts. Trials (*Circé* 19.9.1908) 901.1hp = 11.93kts; (*Calypso* 13.2.1909) 969.7hp = 11.916kts at 400rpm. 2 screws. 2 four-cycle diesel engines with 4 cylinders of 0.330m diameter and 0.360m stroke. 9.110t oil. Range 2,168nm @ 8kts.
(submerged) 360hp designed at 330rpm. Speed 7.70kts. Trials (*Circé* 25.6.1909) 394hp = 7.73kts at 340.5rpm; (*Calypso* 20.7.1909) 390hp = 7.291kts at 316rpm. 2 electric motors. Batteries 66.3 tons. Range (trials) 82.5nm @ 3.6kts.

**Torpedoes:**
(1909) 2 fixed launch cages amidships aimed forward at 5 degrees off the axis, 2 fixed launch cages behind these aimed aft at 5 degrees off the

The submersible *Calypso*, seen here, and her sister *Circé* were twice the size of *Aigrette* and her sister *Cigogne* and had two screws instead of one. Their diesels had to be ordered in Germany because French industry could not produce them. *(Postcard by ELD, imp. E. Le Deley, Paris)*

axis, and 2 Drzewiecki trainable launchers on deck at the stern each with an arc of fire on its beam from 20 to 170 degrees. All of these were for 450mm M1906 torpedoes although they could also carry M1892 torpedoes.
(1911) In 1911 the after pair of fixed launch cages was turned around to bear forward. An internal bow torpedo tube was also included in the design but was ordered removed by Minister Picard on 18.1.1909 following the accident in *Fresnel*. **Guns:** On 29.3.1911 a support for a 37mm gun was ordered installed.

*Circé* (Q47) Toulon Dyd/MAN Augsburg.
On list 1.1905. Ord: 8.10.1904. K: 3.4.1905. L: 13.9.1907. Comm: 1.8.1909 (full).
Budget 1904. Diesel engine installed 10.12.1907 to 3.4.1908. Trial results approved 16.7.1909. In 1914 was in the 2nd submarine squadron of the *1re Armée navale* at Bizerte. Dardanelles 11.1914 to 2.1915, Adriatic operations 1915-1918. In the 1st submarine squadron at Brindisi 1.1918. Torpedoed and sunk 20.9.1918 by *U-47* off Cattaro.

*Calypso* (Q48) Toulon Dyd/MAN Augsburg.
On list 1.1905. Ord: 8.10.1904. K: 11.4.1905. L: 24.10.1907. Comm: 5.8.1909 (full).
Budget 1904. Diesel engine installed 1.3.1908 to 10.10.1908. Trial results approved 5.8.1909. In 1914 was in the 2nd submarine squadron of the *1re Armée navale* at Bizerte. Rammed by *Circé* following a steering failure in that boat 7.7.1914 off Cap Lardier east of Toulon and sank in 15 metres of water (3 lost).

## GUÊPE Class.

*Bateaux sous-marins.* Single hull, unique diesel propulsion (surfaced and submerged). Designed by Petithomme

This type was called a *Sous-marin défensif* on Petithomme's plans. Camille Pelletan, who preferred defensive to offensive submarines, had been fascinated with *Goubet II* ever since he rode her as a deputy and then wrote about her in two articles in *Le Matin* on 18 April 1901 and 23 August 1901. In a modification to the 1904 budget in late 1903 or early 1904 he added to the building programme ten *Guêpes* (Q49-58) of 45 tons and 20.50m length that were even smaller than the *Naïades* and looked like enlarged Goubets. According to the 1905 budget (submitted 30 March 1904) Q49-52 were to be begun in 1904 at Toulon and Q53-55 were to follow in 1905 at Cherbourg along with Q56-58 at Toulon. After more programme changes Q49-50 were ordered at Cherbourg on 27 October 1904, but Pelletan left the ministry in January 1905 and their construction was soon suspended. They were shown in the 1907 budget (submitted 26 June 1906) as to be commissioned for trials in August 1908 and December 1908 respectively, but construction was definitively stopped in March 1908 and the boats were never launched. The diesels for the two boats were proposed for conversion by Sautter to kerosene motor-generators (120hp each) to replace the failed diesel engine in *Sous-marin Z*, but the project was abandoned.

Petithomme on 10 October 1904 reported the programme that he had been given for these boats as 30 to 60 tons, range of 150 miles at 9 to 10 knots, submerged speed to be as fast as possible for short periods with the ability to remain submerged at reduced speed for two to three hours, the ability to retract the air intakes and the conning tower, and a crew of 4 to 5 men at most 'with the least troublesome installation possible, especially from the point of view of air supply'. He was also to see if he could do without electricity. His design included a round hull tapering to points at the end and a small cupola on top as in the Goubets and other early submarines, a single screw, horizontal planes fore and aft and a rudder aft of the screw. To get the high speed required and minimize disturbances in the water that would reveal the boat's presence other projections from the hull were limited to docking keels, a conning tower based on that of *Gymnote* that had five view ports and was 0.45m high, and two torpedoes each side of the conning tower in Drzewiecki trainable launchers. Petithomme noted that as in his previous projects (*Sous-marin Y* and *Oméga*) he provided a unique diesel engine for propulsion on the surface and submerged, but instead of storing the air for combustion submerged in the form of compressed air (at 150kg in *Y* and 200kg in *Oméga*) he used oxygen stored in tubes at a pressure of 200 atmospheres. In addition, to remain invisible while submerged it was necessary to retain on board at least for a time the exhaust gases, which as in *Y* and *Oméga* were pumped by a compressor into a special tank for later discharge into the sea. The diesel engine occupied a quarter of the length of the boat and consisted of four cylinders for ahead movement, two cylinders behind them for both ahead and astern movement, and a clutch between the two groups. The hull structure was based on the larger *Naïade*, and the new boat could be expected to dive safely to 30 metres as several of the *Naïade*s had. Batteries were provided for eight incandescent lamps and for the horizontal plane mechanisms. Petithomme's diesel would have worked no better in these boats than it did in *Sous-marin Y*.

**Dimensions & tons:** 20.55m oa, 20m wl (tip of bow to tip of stern) x 2.10m ext. 44.329t disp (surfaced), 49.667t (submerged). Draught: 2.02m. Men: 7 including 1 officer. Reserve buoyancy: 10.8%.
**Machinery:**
(surfaced) 240hp designed (6 cylinders) at 450rpm. Speed 10.5kts. 1 screw. 1 diesel engine. 720kg oil. Range 378nm @ 8kts.
(submerged) 240hp (6 cylinders) at 450rpm. Speed 9kts. Designed to use the unique diesel with its pressurized oxygen tanks for submerged propulsion. Range 80nm @ 6kts.
**Torpedoes:** 2 Drzewiecki trainable launchers for 450mm M1904 torpedoes.

*Guêpe nᵒ 1* (Q49) Cherbourg Dyd.
On list 1.1905. Ord: 27.10.1904. Not built.
Budget 1904. Last shown in fleet list 1.1907. Cancelled 3.1908.

*Guêpe nᵒ 2* (Q50) Cherbourg Dyd.
On list 1.1905. Ord: 27.10.1904. Not built.
Budget 1904. Last shown in fleet list 1.1907. Cancelled 3.1908.

---

**IMPROVED ÉMERAUDE Class.** *Bateaux sous-marins.* Single hull, diesel surface propulsion. Designed by Petithomme.

The numbers Q59 and Q60 were reserved for new *bateaux sous-marins* at Rochefort in the 1905 budget (submitted 30 March 1904). The boats were probably ordered in October 1904 and they duly appeared in the January 1905 fleet list. The 1906 budget (submitted on 6 July 1905) showed Q59 and Q60 as Laubeuf submarines (submersibles) to be ordered in 1905 at Cherbourg, reflecting the shift to submersibles during 1905. A report that the two Petithomme submarines were laid down at Rochefort on 18 October 1905 and 21 December 1905 is not credible although they may have been laid down at the end of 1904.

**Dimensions & tons:** 54.98m x 3.90m. 426t disp.
**Machinery:**
(surfaced) 600hp (total). 2 screws. 2 diesel engines.
(submerged) 2 electric motors.
**Torpedoes:** unknown.

*Q59* (Unnamed) Rochefort Dyd.
On list 1.1905. Ord: 10.1904. Not built.
Budget 1905. Last fleet list 1.1905. Cancelled.

*Q60* (Unnamed) Rochefort Dyd.
On list 1.1905. Ord: 10.1904. Not built.
Budget 1905. Last fleet list 1.1905. Cancelled.

---

**Q61 (*VEDETTE DE DION*).** Single hull, electric propulsion with internal combustion generator. Designed by the Marquis de Dion.

Q61 (which never received a regular name) was not shown in the new construction budget, perhaps because it was a personal project of Minister Pelletan and was charged to his portion of the budget. She was described as a *vedette immersible* and informally called the *Vedette de Dion* after her builder. In mid-1904 the Marquis de Dion, a famous automobile manufacturer and proprietor of the Maison De Dion, Bouton & Cie. at Puteaux, presented Minister of Marine Pelletan with a design for a small submarine. Pelletan wanted defensive vice offensive submarines and was fascinated by the tiny *Goubet II* and its inventor, whose merits he had praised in two articles in *Le Matin* on 18 April 1901 and 23 August 1901. Dion's boat was a bit larger than *Goubet II* (whose length was 8 metres and diameter 1.75 metres), but had the same cylindrical hull that tapered to a point at each end with a small cupola on top. It used an electric propulsion system (battery, electric motor, and internal combustion generator) similar to one that Dion had designed for his automobiles. A drawing of this *Projet de sous-marin* in Navy records at Vincennes is dated Puteaux, 25 May 1904. Half the size of the *Guêpe*s, the craft was destined to be embarked on battleships. The contract for the hull was signed with the Cie. des Forges de Chatillon, Commentry et Neuves-Maisons on 18 October 1904 (it was approved by Pelletan and notified on 20 October 1904). The hull was to be delivered to Puteaux where the machinery was to be installed. The engine, battery, and other electrical components were ordered from the Maison de Dion on 3 November 1904.

On 3 March 1905 a new Minister of Marine, Thomson, decided to move the assembly and trials of the submarine to Toulon, in part because all work on submarines was considered secret and was to be restricted to dockyards. Paris had little information on Dion's design or calculations and realised that Toulon would have to redo most of the work as well as negotiate new arrangements with the two contractors. The Q number (Q61) of this boat became her name and was not reused when the submarine programme was reworked in 1905. The builders of the hull duly completed their contract and shipped the hull to Toulon. A supplement to Dion's contract was concluded on 26 July 1905, but on 31 August 1906 Minister of Marine Thomson informed Dion of his intention to cancel the contract because 'it did not seem that the Department could find in the execution of the contract new elements leading to progress in submarine navigation.' Thomson cancelled the Dion contract on 15 February 1907.

On 30 March 1907 Paris asked Toulon if the hull of *Q61* could be used in some manner in that port. Toulon replied on 2 May 1907 that they could find no use for her. On 12 June 1907 *Directeur centrale des constructions navales* Dudebout proposed condemnation of the hull, following which *Q61* would cease to appear on the *Liste de la flotte* as under construction. He also proposed using her as a hulk for experiments in submarine salvage. Minister Thomson approved these recommendations on 12 June 1907 and on 24 June 1907 advised Toulon of that decision and the proposed use for the hull. On 25 January 1910 Minister Boué de Lapeyrère advised Toulon that the hulks of *Narval* and *Lutin* were now also available for submarine salvage experiments and because of their size were more suitable, and that he had decided that *Q61* should be turned over to the Domaines for sale. In response to a ministerial order of 8 June 1910 Toulon produced a plan dated 5 August 1910 for her conversion into a floating oil tank, but the conversion was not carried out and the hull was instead placed on the sale list in late 1910.

**Dimensions & tons:** 11.120m oa, 10.880m pp x 1.980m diameter. 21.011t disp.

**Machinery:** 1 screw. 1 electric motor powered by one four-cylinder internal combustion engine.

**Torpedoes:** Unknown. None shown on the 1904 drawing.

*Q61* (Unnamed) Forges de Chatillon, Commentry/De Dion, Bouton & Cie.

On list 1.1905. Ord: 18.10.1904 (contract). Hull delivered 10.1905.

Begun 18.4.1904. Toulon received and took custody of the hull (without engines) in October 1905, probably putting it into storage at Mourillon. Off main list 1906. Retained for trials at Toulon 1907-1910, for sale 1910-1911. Offered for sale 1 August 1911 while stored ashore in the Mourillon docks at Toulon by the Administration des Domaines with *Amiral Baudin, Magenta, Pascal, Milan,* and smaller vessels.

---

### Submersibles vs. Sous-marins: The decision

It became apparent that the contest between submersibles and pure submarines needed to be resolved in order to simplify the building programme, and comparative trials between the newest submersible, *Aigrette*, and the newest pure submarine, *Sous-marin Z* (which had been designed with such a competition in mind), were ordered in June 1904. Gaston Thomson, who took over the Ministry of Marine from Camille Pelletan on 24 January 1905, accelerated this process and between 10 and 15 March 1905 four days of intensive trials were held to compare the two boats. Both boats were brand new and neither had completed its regular trials. (*Aigrette*'s diesels were not functional until 1906.) The results were unambiguous. *Aigrette* using electric propulsion had superior manoeuvrability, a higher speed both surfaced and submerged, and better performance in bad weather. Most surprisingly, the biggest traditional advantage of the pure submarine over the submersible, diving speed, had disappeared. *Aigrette* dived in 4 minutes 22 seconds while *Sous-marin Z* took 4 minutes 55 seconds. During 1905 the navy, as it accelerated constructions of submersibles, decided to stop construction of the single-hulled *Guêpes* (Q49-58) and modified *Émeraudes* (Q59-60) as well as the *vedette immersible* Q61. The comparative trials commission reportedly even talked of stopping work on the six single-hulled *Émeraudes* (Q41-46) and converting them into double-hulled submersibles, although this idea was quickly abandoned.

### The Programmes of 1905 and 1906

In May 1905, shortly after Pelletan left the ministry, the *Conseil supérieur* met at the direction of Minister of Marine Gaston Thomson for the first time in two years to discuss a programme for the constitution of the fleet. As part of this fleet it determined that the Navy needed 82 offensive submersibles (10 existing) and 49 defensive *sous-marins* (41 existing). It assigned high value to offensive submarines because they could project their

activities to a considerable distance and prolong them for many days without calling on external resources. The defensive submarines were needed for the protection of naval ports and bases in France and in the colonies. These 131 submarines along with 66 destroyers and 170 torpedo boats were distributed among some 30 ports and bases in France, North Africa, and the Colonies including the five main naval ports. Future offensive submarines were to have a displacement of 450 to 500 tons (type not determined) and, given the satisfactory results given by the *Naïade* type of defensive submarines, it was likely that this type would be continued with a few modifications. As a first installment on this programme Minister Thomson on 26 August 1905 ordered the first 18 submersibles of Laubeuf's *Pluviôse* type under a supplement to the 1905 budget.

Because of the Russo-Japanese war and the rapid growth of some foreign navies, particularly the German, Minister of Marine Thomson on 2 February 1906 summoned the *Conseil supérieur* to revisit the question of a fleet programme. which it did in March 1906. It reaffirmed its 1905 programme for submarines but for 1906 gave first priority for construction to six battleships (the *Danton* class), ten enlarged *contre-torpilleurs* (the 450-tonners), and 20 more submersibles. These 20 were to include 17 of the of 550-ton *Pluviôse* type (one of which later became Bourdelle's *Amiral Bourgois*), two of a larger type *à grand rayon d'action* (long range), and one of a type proposed by naval constructor Maurice with his *chaudière accumulatrice*. This led to the orders on 29 October 1906 for 16 more submersibles of the *Pluviôse* type followed by orders on 31 December 1906 for four experimental submarines (Q73-74, 82, and 89), all under the 1906 budget.

---

*PLUVIÔSE* Class. *Torpilleurs autonomes submersibles* (to *Sous-marins* 1.1909). Double hull, steam surface propulsion. Designed by Laubeuf. To *Sous-marins de 2e classe* 1.1923.

On 12 April 1905 Thomson informed the Senate of the forthcoming laying down of the two *Circé* class diesel submersibles and stated that they would be followed by 18 more similar submersibles. The navy would have preferred diesel engines in all but given the problems encountered with the few diesels delivered to date it decided to fit the first 18 new boats with steam as in the earlier submersibles. The 1906 budget (submitted on 6 July 1905) contained the promised 18 Laubeuf submersibles (Q51-60 and Q62-69, with Q59-60 having been changed to the Laubeuf design). They were ordered on 26 August 1905, and in June 1906 all were listed in the 1907 budget as steam propelled. The contracts for 18 steam propulsion plants were probably placed around this time, all in the Paris region where the Navy's only established steam engine builder at that time was A.C. Loire at Saint Denis. The 1906 budget also contained 20 more submersibles (Q70-89) to be begun in 1906 under the Programme of 1906 (see below) but provided no details about them except that they were *à l'étude* (under study). Q80-82 were originally at Toulon but had been moved to Rochefort by June 1906. 16 of the 1906 boats were ordered on 29 October 1906 to the Q51 design, the other four having become experimental craft. In May 1907 all 16 were listed in the 1908 budget as steam except Q62-63, whose propulsion was not specified but which were probably planned as diesel boats. The steam engines ordered in 1906 were probably assigned, not just to the 1905 batch as initially intended, but to submarines in both the 1905 and 1906 batches as they became ready to receive them. Q51-Q60 and Q62-Q69 were named at the same time, probably on 12 March 1908, while the others (probably including the four experimental boats) were named later, probably on 17 July 1909. The list in the 1909 budget (submitted 19 May 1908) showed the final allocations in this class, with 18 steam and 16 internal combustion engines distributed among both batches. Most of the diesels were probably ordered in 1908 – *Brumaire*'s diesels were built by Augustin Normand under a contract of 21 October 1908. An 18th unit of this class, *Thermidor* (Q57), became the prototype for the hull and armament configuration of the *Brumaire* class

The submarine (submersible before 1909) *Ventôse*, second unit of the 18-boat *Pluviôse* class (including the variant *Thermidor*), at Cherbourg. Steam surface propulsion was used for this class because of problems experienced with early diesels. The absence of the upper vertical rudder dates the photo to the later part of World War I, but her superstructure appears to have undergone few

modifications since construction. Her port side torpedo launch frames are loaded, and she was also one of the few boats of her class that retained her bow torpedo tube after the 1908 accident to *Fresnel*. The hulks of two 37-metre torpedo boats are to the left (perhaps *Nos 236* and *256,* which donated their engines to the anti-submarine gunboats *Tapageuse* and *Capricieuse* in 1916). *(NHHC, NH-55752)*

although she had steam propulsion and is listed separately below. The Toulon boats, *Monge, Ampère* and *Gay-Lussac,* had the larger openings under the raised deck of the *Brumaire* class but were otherwise *Pluviôse* class units.

Laubeuf explained his concept for the design as follows. To act at large distances and to have vessels capable of making true cruises it was necessary to increase again endurance at sea and habitability. It was also necessary to augment surfaced speed to travel in less time the distances separating the submarine's base from its target and submerged speed to increase the chances of an attack on ships that were underway. The *Circé* type provided the solution with diesel engines, the new project did the same with steam engines. Laubeuf noted that each solution had its advantages and draw-backs. In 1905 steam engines were more flexible to operate than diesels and they were also more readily available. On the other hand, they took up more space and had less endurance – steam engines consumed four times as much fuel as diesels for a given distance at a given speed. When diving there were more manoeuvres to be made and valves to be closed with steam than with diesels, and he estimated diving times at 5 minutes with steam and 4 minutes with diesels. (With practice the steam boats were able to dive

in 4 minutes.) He pointed out that, since the compartment for surface machinery was larger for steam than for diesel boats, diesels could easily be substituted in the same design when they became available.

To fit steam in the new boats the engine room of *Circé* was lengthened by 4 metres, increasing surfaced displacement by 52 tons and submerged displacement by 55 tons. The diving time and surfaced speed of *Circé* were retained, though endurance on the surface remained less (800 miles instead of 1,460). During trials several ballast tanks were converted to fuel surcharge tanks, increasing the fuel supply to 27 tons and the endurance to 1,250nm. The walking deck or *passerelle* above the outer hull in many of Laubeuf's designs resembled the walking deck above the hull in Normand's *Durandal* type 300-ton destroyers. In both the submarines and the destroy-ers the conning officer was exposed to the elements on an open platform above and behind the conning tower, which sheltered the helmsman.

The propulsion plant was essentially that of *Sirène* doubled, with two sets of machinery on two propeller shafts. The shafts were only 1.4m apart, the starboard one being slightly longer to allow the large diameter screws to overlap. It was possible to steam on one screw with only 5 or 6 degrees of rudder correction and disconnect the other shaft, making it available for recharging batteries or for maintenance. It was also possible if necessary to steam and recharge at the same time on the same shaft. The designed fuel capacity was 16,200 litres but the after pair of ballast tanks was converted to oil tanks, raising this to 27,700 litres. The range at 10 knots which as designed was 584 miles and which in practice was 800 miles because fuel consumption by the steam plant was less than expected became 1,250 miles with the surcharge in the after tanks.

While returning to La Pallice from sea trials on 5 October 1908 *Fresnel* struck a jetty and damaged her bow planes. This caused a leak because the mechanism for the planes passed through the pressure hull. The boat sank in shallow water but was quickly raised on 9 November and restored to service. This accident, however, revealed the vulnerability of the bow torpedo tube and caused the decision to remove it from boats of this class that were still under construction and from *Pluviôse, Prairial,* and *Messidor.* The orders to remove it from *Prairial* and *Ampère* were dated 18 January 1909 and 15 February 1909 respectively and the tube was removed from *Prairial* in September 1909. *Ventôse, Germinal,* and *Floréal* retained the bow tube and on 18 March 1910 it was ordered restored to *Vendémiaire.* These received a *bout-dehors* (bowsprit) extending from the top of the bow to protect it like the *tampon de choc* (shock buffer) in torpedo boats.

*The characteristics are based on a devis for* Germinal *dated 1908.*

**Dimensions & tons:** 50.75m oa (51.12 with the cover to the bow torpedo tube), 50.04m wl, 50.75m pp x 4.955m wl (7.01m over the amidships horizontal planes). 403.984t disp (surfaced, 417t with fuel surcharge), 552.945t (submerged). Draught: 3.045m mean, 3.153m aft. Men: 25 including 2 officers. Reserve buoyancy: 26.9% (24.6% with fuel surcharge)

**Machinery:**

(surfaced) 700ihp designed at 400rpm and 16.5kg/cm$^2$ boiler pressure (15.5kg/cm$^2$ at the engines). Speed 12kts. Trials (*Ampère* c1911) 11.63kts at 385rpm. 2 screws. 2 vertical triple expansion engines with 3 cylinders of 0.225m, 0.340m, and 0.550m diameter and 0.270m stroke. 2 Du Temple return-flame boilers. 24.939 tons (27,710 litres) of oil. Range (trials) 1,390nm @ 8.5kts.

(submerged) 460hp at 560rpm. Speed 8kts. Trials (*Monge* c1911) 7.4kts at 325rpm. 2 electric motors each with 1 armature. Batteries 64 tons. Range (trials) 56nm @ 3.5kts.

**Torpedoes:** 1 internal bow tube (removed from most 1909), 2 fixed launch cages on the ballast tanks outboard of the conning tower aimed forward at 7 degrees off the axis, 2 fixed launch cages on the ballast tanks behind these aimed aft at 5 degrees off the axis, 2 Drzewiecki trainable launchers side by side on the walking deck aft, all for 450mm M1906 torpedoes. The after pair of fixed launch cages was ordered on 22.2.1910 to be turned around to fire forward at 8 degrees off the axis.

**Guns:** Added to some during the war, including a 75mm aft on *Fructidor* by 1918 and a 37mm aft on *Watt* also by 1918.

*Pluviôse* (Q51)  Cherbourg Dyd/A.C. Loire, Saint Denis.
On list 1.1906. Ord: 26.8.1905. K: 25.5.1906. L: 27.6.1907.
    Comm: 5.10.1908 (full).
Budget 1905 (late addition). Rammed 26.5.1910 by the Calais-to-Dover packet *Pas de Calais* and sank in 17 metres of water 2,500 metres from the Calais jetty (crew lost). Refloated 12.6.1910, repaired and returned to service. In 1914 was in the the 1st Submarine Squadron of the *2e Escadre légère* at Cherbourg. In the Normandy submarine squadron 1.1918. Struck 12.11.1919. For sale at Cherbourg 1919-1920. Withdrawn from sale 7.10.1920 and reserved for trials of a tubular dock recovered in Germany for testing submarines by simulating the pressure experienced during immersion. Compression trials 30.6.1921 and 15.12.1924. For sale at Cherbourg 1924-1925. To the Domaines for sale 16.2.1925, sold 4.9.1925 at Cherbourg to MM. Paris and Alaterre.

*Ventôse* (Q52)  Cherbourg Dyd/A.C. Loire, Saint Denis.
On list 1.1906. Ord: 26.8.1905. K: 25.5.1906. L: 23.8.1907.

The *Pluviôse* class submarine *Papin* returning to base after attacking a group of Austrian torpedo boats in the Adriatic off the Dalmatian coast on 9 September 1915 and torpedoing one of them, *51 T.* (The forward half of the Austrian boat remained afloat and was towed to Pola and rebuilt.) *Papin* was commanded by Lieutenant de vaisseau Cochin, standing on the bridge at left, and his second in command, Enseigne de vaisseau Laboureur, is seated on the breakwater in the foreground. The two torpedo launch cages are empty, with their torpedoes probably expended during the attack. The photograph was evidently taken on 10 September 1915 in the approaches to the port of Bari as *Papin* entered at around 1800 hours. (*L'Illustration, 25 September 1915*)

    Comm: 11.9.1907 (trials), 5.10.1908 (full).
Budget 1905 (late addition). In 1914 was in the the 1st Submarine Squadron of the *2e Escadre légère* at Cherbourg. At Brest scheduled for Bizerte 1.1918. In bad condition at Bizerte 15.10.1918. Condemned 16.10.1919. Struck 1.12.1919. Sold 1.8.1921 at Bizerte with *Berthelot* and *Torpilleur no 274* to M. Kalfon-Vita of Tunis.

*Germinal* (Q53)  Cherbourg Dyd/A.C. Loire, Saint Denis.
On list 1.1906. Ord: 26.8.1905. K: 25.5.1906. L: 7.12.1907.
    Comm: 1.2.1908 (trials), 30.12.1908 (full).
Budget 1905 (late addition). In 1914 was in the the 1st Submarine Squadron of the *2e Escadre légère* at Cherbourg. At Brest scheduled for Bizerte 1.1918. Condemned 16.10.1919. Struck 1.12.1919. Sold 11.6.1921 at Bizerte to M. Crispin of Marseille.

*Floréal* (Q54)  Cherbourg Dyd/A.C. Loire, Saint Denis.
On list 1.1906. Ord: 26.8.1905. K: 1.3.1907. L: 18.4.1908.
    Comm: 16.6.1909 (full).
Budget 1905 (late addition). In 1914 was in the the 1st Submarine Squadron of the *2e Escadre légère* at Cherbourg. At Brest scheduled for

Bizerte 1.1918. Rammed accidentally 2.8.1918 by the British auxiliary cruiser *Hazel* at the Dardanelles, taken under tow by the destroyer *Baliste* but foundered en route to Salonica.

*Prairial* (Q55)  Cherbourg Dyd/A.C. Loire, Saint Denis.
On list 1.1906. Ord: 26.8.1905. K: 1.3.1907. L: 26.9.1908.
   Comm: 19.6.1909 (full).
Budget 1905 (late addition). In 1914 was in the the 1st Submarine Squadron of the *2ᵉ Escadre légère* at Cherbourg. In the Normandy submarine squadron 1.1918. Sunk 29.4.1918 in collision with British merchantman *Tropic* off the entrance to the channel at Le Havre in 29 metres of water.

*Messidor* (Q56)  Cherbourg Dyd/A.C. Loire, Saint Denis.
On list 1.1906. Ord: 26.8.1905. K: 1.3.1907. L: 24.12.1908.
   Comm: 30.11.1909 (full).
Budget 1905 (late addition). In 1914 was in the 1st submarine squadron of the *1ʳᵉ Armée navale* at Toulon. Adriatic operations 1914-1916. With the school for underwater navigation (ENSM) at Toulon 1.1918. Struck 12.11.1919, for sale at Toulon 1920. Reserved 9.4.1921 for experiments with underwater explosions. Sold 23.9.1922 at Toulon to M. Pitaluga to BU.

*Fructidor* (Q58)  Cherbourg Dyd/A.C. Loire, Saint Denis.
On list 1.1906. Ord: 26.8.1905. K: 2.3.1908. L: 13.11.1909.
   Comm: 29.6.1910 (full).
Budget 1905 (late addition). In 1914 was in the 1st Submarine Squadron of the *2ᵉ Escadre légère* at Cherbourg. In the Normandy submarine squadron 1.1918. Struck 12.11.1919. Sold 23.5.1921 at Cherbourg to the Société d'approvisionnement métallurgiques et de matériels d'industrie to BU.

*Vendémiaire* (Q59)  Cherbourg Dyd/A.C. Loire, Saint Denis.
On list 1.1906. Ord: 26.8.1905. K: 2.3.1908. L: 7.7.1910.
   Comm: 27.7.1910 (trials), 4.2.1911 (full).
Budget 1905 (late addition). Cut in half and sunk 8.6.1912 in collision with battleship *Saint Louis* during exercises between the northwest tip of the Cotentin Peninsula and the island of Alderney. The wreck was discovered in 2017 slightly to the north of its expected position.

*Papin* (Q64).  Rochefort Dyd/A.C. Loire, Saint Denis.
On list 1.1906. Ord: 26.8.1905. K: 5.5.1906. L: 4.1.1908.
   Comm: 1.9.1909 (full).
Budget 1905 (late addition). In 1914 was in the 1st submarine squadron of the *1ʳᵉ Armée navale* at Toulon. In the Morocco squadron 1.1918. Adriatic operations 1914-1916. Retired 1919. For sale at Brest 1920-1922.

*Fresnel* (Q65)  Rochefort Dyd/A.C. Loire, Saint Denis.
On list 1.1906. Ord: 26.8.1905. K: 1.10.1906. L: 16.6.1908.
   Comm: 22.2.1911 (full).
Budget 1905 (late addition). Rammed the jetty and sank 6.10.1908 at La Pallice during trials, refloated 9.11.1908 and repaired. In 1914 was in the 1st submarine squadron of the *1ʳᵉ Armée navale* at Toulon. Adriatic operations 1914-1915. While blockading Cattaro on 5.12.1915 was driven aground by pursuing Austrian warships at the mouth of the Bojana river and destroyed by gunfire from the Austrian destroyer *Warasdiner*.

*Berthelot* (Q66)  Rochefort Dyd/A.C. Loire, Saint Denis.
On list 1.1906. Ord: 26.8.1905. K: 8.4.1907. L: 18.5.1909.
   Comm: 1.2.1910 (full).
Budget 1905 (late addition). In 1914 was in the 1st Submarine Squadron of the *2ᵉ Escadre légère* at Cherbourg. In the 2nd submarine squadron at Bizerte 1.1918. Condemned 16.10.1919. Struck 1.12.1919. Sold 1.8.1921 at Bizerte with *Ventôse* and *Torpilleur nº 274* to M. Kalfon-Vita of Tunis to BU.

*Monge* (Q67)  Toulon Dyd/A.C. Loire, Saint Denis.
On list 1.1906. Ord: 26.8.1905. K: 17.5.1906. L: 31.12.1908.
   Comm: 2.8.1910 (full).
Budget 1905 (late addition). In 1914 was in the 1st submarine squadron of the *1ʳᵉ Armée navale* at Toulon. Adriatic operations 1914-1915. Rammed, then sunk 29.12.1915 by the Austrian cruiser *Helgoland* off Cattaro.

*Ampère* (Q68)  Toulon Dyd/A.C. Loire, Saint Denis.
On list 1.1906. Ord: 26.8.1905. K: 22.11.1906. L: 30.10.1909.
   Comm: 1.11.1910 (full).
Budget 1905 (late addition). In 1914 was in the 1st submarine squadron of the *1ʳᵉ Armée navale* at Toulon. Adriatic operations 1914-1916. In the Morocco squadron 1.1918. Struck 12.11.1919. Sold 23.9.1922 at Toulon to BU.

*Gay Lussac* (Q69)  Toulon Dyd/A.C. Loire, Saint Denis.
On list 1.1906. Ord: 26.8.1905. K: 11.10.1906. L: 17.3.1910.
   Comm: 14.1.1911 (full).
Budget 1905 (late addition). Named 12.3.1908. In 1914 was in the 1st submarine squadron of the *1ʳᵉ Armée navale* at Toulon. Adriatic operations 1914-1916. In the 2nd submarine squadron at Bizerte 1.1918. Condemned 16.10.1919. Struck 1.12.1919. Sold 11.6.1921 at Bizerte to M. Crispin of Marseille to BU.

*Watt* (Q75)  Rochefort Dyd/A.C. Loire, Saint Denis.
On list 1.1907. Ord: 29.10.1906. K: 19.8.1907. L: 18.6.1909.
   Comm: 15.3.1910 (full).
Budget 1906. Named 17.7.1909. In 1914 was in the 1st Submarine Squadron of the *2ᵉ Escadre légère* at Cherbourg. In the 2nd submarine squadron at Bizerte 1.1918. Condemned 16.10.1919, struck 1.12.1919. Sold 11.6.1921 at Bizerte to M. Crispin of Marseille to BU.

*Cugnot* (Q76)  Rochefort Dyd/A.C. Loire, Saint Denis.
On list 1.1907. Ord: 29.10.1906. K: 1.2.1908. L: 14.10.1909.
   Comm: 10.9.1910 (full).
Budget 1906. Named 17.7.1909. In 1914 was in the 1st submarine squadron of the *1ʳᵉ Armée navale* at Toulon. Adriatic operations 1914-1916. In the 2nd submarine squadron at Bizerte 1.1918. Condemned 16.10.1919, struck 1.12.1919. Sold 11.6.1921 at Bizerte to M. Crispin of Marseille to BU.

*Giffard* (Q77)  Rochefort Dyd/A.C. Loire, Saint Denis.
On list 1.1907. Ord: 29.10.1906. K: 3.9.1908. L: 10.2.1910.
   Comm: 13.10.1910 (full).
Budget 1906. Named 17.7.1909. In 1914 was in the 1st Submarine Squadron of the *2ᵉ Escadre légère* at Cherbourg. In the 2nd submarine squadron at Bizerte 1.1918. Condemned 16.10.1919. Struck 1.12.1919. Sold 11.6.1921 at Bizerte to M. Crispin of Marseille to BU.

––––––––––

**THERMIDOR.** *Torpilleur autonome submersible* (to *Sous-marin* 1.1909). Double hull, steam surface propulsion. Designed by Laubeuf and Simonot.

One *Pluviôse* class submarine under construction at Cherbourg was selected as a testbed for the hull configuration of the diesel-powered *Brumaire* class and became essentially a *Brumaire* class unit with steam propulsion. On 28 January 1909 Minister Picard ordered testing in *Thermidor* the changes in external lines (specifically of the ballast tanks) proposed by naval constructor Jean Ernest Simonot for the *Brumaire* class. (Simonot was chief of the new construction section at Cherbourg from December 1907 into 1914.) The boat also received most of the topside arrangements of the *Brumaires* including the bow torpedo tube and the arrangement of the torpedo launchers as taken from Hutter's *Archimède* and Q90 designs. The launchers were later rearranged in the *Brumaire* class but not in *Thermidor*.

The submarines *Thermidor* (centre) and *Fructidor* (left) alongside the surrendered German *U-151* (ex mercantile *Oldenburg*) photographed at Cherbourg in 1920 by the American visitor Robert W. Neeser. The differences between the original *Pluviôse* class (including *Fructidor*) and the unique *Thermidor* (with the topside arrangement originally planned for the diesel-powered *Brumaire* but with the steam propulsion of *Pluviôse*) are clearly shown. The topside changes in *Thermidor* included a lower breakwater around the kiosk, fewer but larger limber holes under the walking deck, four fixed launch cages under the walking deck amidships and forward instead of in the open on the ballast tanks, and two Drzewiecki launchers aft under the walking deck instead of two launch cages on it. Both received the same wartime modifications including a sheltered bridge (*baignoire*) above the original kiosk for the navigating personnel, a new fixed funnel with an air intake pipe for navigating partially submerged, and a 75mm gun on a fixed mounting aft of the funnel. *(NHHC, NH-43779)*

**Dimensions & tons:** 52.15m oa, 51.37m wl x 5.42m wl (7.32m over the amidships horizontal planes). 396t disp (surfaced, 407t with fuel surcharge), 551t (submerged). Reserve buoyancy: 28.1% (26.1% with fuel surcharge)

**Machinery:**
(surfaced) As the *Pluviôse* class except 23.362 tons (25,957 litres) oil.
(submerged) As the *Pluviôse* class

**Torpedoes:** 1 bow tube, 4 fixed launch cages under the walking deck probably arranged as in *Archimède* with one pair abreast the conning tower aimed forward angled slightly off the axis and the other pair behind it aimed forward with a greater angle off the axis, plus 2 Drzewiecki trainable launchers side by side under the walking deck aft, all for 450mm torpedoes. The forward pair of fixed launch cages was moved to a position well forward of the conning tower during the war.

**Guns:** A 75mm gun was fitted on the walking deck aft above the Drzewiecki trainable launchers in 1916.

*Thermidor* (Q57)  Cherbourg Dyd/A.C. Loire, Saint Denis.
On list 1.1906. Ord: 26.8.1905. K: 2.3.1908. L: 3.7.1909.
    Comm: 13.7.1910 (full).
Budget 1905 (late addition). In 1914 was in the 1st Submarine Squadron of the 2e *Escadre légère* at Cherbourg. In the Normandy submarine squadron 1.1918. Struck 12.11.1919. Sold 23.5.1921 at Cherbourg to the Société d'approvisionnement métallurgiques et de matériels d'industrie to BU.

**BERNOULLI Class.** *Torpilleurs autonomes submersibles* (to *Sous-marins* 1.1909). Double hull, diesel surface propulsion. Designed by Laubeuf and the Toulon dockyard.

The first three diesel-propelled units built at Toulon, *Bernoulli, Joule,* and *Coulomb*, did not receive the *Brumaire* class hull modifications (except for some larger openings under the raised deck) and essentially remained *Pluviôse* class submarines with diesel engines. On 29 October 1906 Minister Thomson ordered that the *Brumaire* type was to consist of *Pluviôse* (Q51) type submarines in which steam propulsion was replaced by diesel engines of 420 effective horsepower without any modifications in the interior or exterior hulls or to the superstructure. Preparations to build this type at Toulon began in March 1907 using drawings for the steam-propelled *Monge*, and the laying down of lines and fabrication of hull components began in June 1907 based on plans from Cherbourg that did not specify the type of engines. The type of diesels was only decided on 4 February 1908 and the type of electric motors on 30 May 1908. Preliminary assembly on the building ways began for *Bernoulli* and *Joule* in March 1908 and for *Coulomb* in December 1908. Plans for the diesels were finally received in November 1908. In the meantime work was largely suspended when the yard received a dispatch from Minister Thomson dated 29 August 1908 announcing the probable modifications in the exterior hull lines and the superstructure that had been under discussion in Paris since June. The dockyard argued that construction was too far along on these three ships to apply the directive to them and Minister Picard agreed on 22 January 1909. More delays followed when some plates for the external hull were found to be of poor quality and had to be replaced, when in early 1909 Toulon received orders to delete the bow torpedo tube, and when on 12 January 1910 the yard received the order to reinstall it. The six diesels for these three boats was received between 13 and 29 months late. Ultimately *Bernoulli* remained on the ways for 3 years and 3 months and the other two for three years and six months, over three times the expected figures, and all three then endured lengthy trials due to problems with the diesels and modifications ordered on 17 October 1910 to the Drzewiecki trainable launchers.

*The characteristics are based on a devis for* Joule *dated 10.5.1912.*
**Dimensions & tons:** 50.75m oa, 50.03m wl, 50.75m pp x 4.955m wl (7.012 outside the midships horizontal planes). 400.593t disp (surfaced), 548.000t (submerged). Draught: 3.043m mean, 3.149m aft. Reserve buoyancy: 26.9%
**Machinery:**
(surfaced) As the *Brumaire* class except 13,854 litres oil. Trials (*Joule* c1912) 12.1kts at 378rpm.
(submerged) As the *Brumaire* class. Trials (*Joule* c1912) 6.8kts at 290rpm.
**Torpedoes:** 1 internal bow tube, 6 torpedo launchers arranged as in the *Pluviôse* class on the ballast tanks and on top of the walking deck aft except that the two amidships launchers were Drzewiecki trainable launchers instead of fixed launch cages. **Guns:** Ordered 29.3.1911 fitted with a support for a 37mm gun. *Bernoulli* received a 47mm gun forward and a machine gun during the war.

*Bernoulli* (Q83) Toulon Dyd/Sautter-Harlé, Paris.
On list 1.1907. Ord: 29.10.1906. K: 5.3.1908. L: 1.6.1911. Comm: 12.6.1911 (trials), 29.10.1912 (full).
Budget 1906. Named 17.7.1909. In 1914 was in the 2nd submarine squadron of the *1re Armée navale* at Bizerte. Adriatic operations 1914-1918, also to Dardanelles 3.1915. In the 1st submarine squadron at Brindisi 1.1918. Left Brindisi 10.2.1918 and failed to return 13.2.1918, probably mined off Durazzo.

*Joule* (Q84) Toulon Dyd/Sautter-Harlé, Paris.
On list 1.1907. Ord: 29.10.1906. K: 20.3.1908. L: 7.9.1911. Comm: 10.5.1912 (full).
Budget 1906. Named 17.7.1909. In 1914 was in the 2nd submarine

squadron of the *1re Armée navale* at Bizerte. Adriatic operation 8.1914, Dardanelles 3-5.1915. Mined 1.5.1915 trying to enter the Dardanelles.

*Coulomb* (Q85) Toulon Dyd/Sautter-Harlé, Paris.
On list 1.1907. Ord: 29.10.1906. K: 17.10.1908. L: 13.6.1912. Comm: 28.10.1912 (full).
Budget 1906. Named 17.7.1909. In 1914 was in the 2nd submarine squadron of the *1re Armée navale* at Bizerte. Dardanelles 2.1915, Adriatic operations 1916-1918. In the 1st submarine squadron at Brindisi 1.1918. Decomm. 8.2.1919. Struck 12.11.1919, for sale at Toulon 1920-1926. Planned 26.6.1923 for use as a target for aviation. Sold 25.6.1927 at Toulon to M. Pons.

---

**BRUMAIRE Class.** *Torpilleurs autonomes submersibles* (to *Sous-marins* 1.1909). Double hull, diesel surface propulsion. Designed by Laubeuf and Simonot. To *Sous-marins de 2e classe* 1.1923.

On 29 October 1906 Minister Thomson ordered that the *Brumaire* type was to consist of *Pluviôse* (Q51) type submersibles in which steam propulsion was replaced by diesel engines of 420 effective horsepower without any modifications in the interior or exterior hulls or to the superstructure. However, on 13 July 1908 Minister Thomson referred to the *Comité technique* various proposals assembled by naval constructor Bourdelle for changes in the external lines, the superstructures, and the batteries of what were now called the Q70 type submersibles. The *Pluviôse* hull form did not seem able to make good use of the replacement of 350ihp steam engines with 420hp diesels, and Simonot proposed new exterior hull lines that would allow the boats to attain greater speeds without altering the inner hulls. His lines were judged superior to those of the original *Pluviose* and of Hutter's later Q90 type submersibles (see below) and would even allow use of engine power above 420hp if the engine builders could provide them without changing the size or rpm of the engines. Regarding the superstructures, a note of 29 June 1908 by naval constructor André Jacques Lévy recommended adopting for the Q70 type the disposition of superstructures adopted for the Q90 type (and also in *Archimède*) which allowed placing

---

The submarine (submersible before 1909) *Brumaire* at Dunkerque. She was the lead ship of a group of 18 submarines like *Pluviôse* but with diesel propulsion. All but the three variants of the *Bernoulli* type also received numerous refinements to the *Pluviôse* design including larger openings under the walking deck and placement of the torpedo launchers under it as seen in this relatively early view. The two solid beams seen here under the walking deck aft of the conning tower were manipulated from within the boat to train the two starboard Drzewiecki torpedo launchers. *(Postcard by LL)*

the torpedo launchers under the walking deck. (It was later decided to replace the two after fixed launch cages with Drzewiecki trainable launchers.) In the same note Lévy also recommended augmenting the power of the batteries and thereby the electric motors. Bourdelle recommended adopting Simonot's revised hull lines, testing them on an experimental hull if possible, and accepting both of Lévy's proposals, and the *Comité technique* concurred. *Thermidor* of the *Pluviôse* class became the testbed for Simonot's hull lines and also the revised superstructure layout. However, the first three diesel submarines at Toulon, *Bernoulli, Joule,* and *Coulomb,* were too far advanced when Toulon received word of the changes, and these were completed with the original *Pluviôse* class hull configuration (see the *Bernoulli* class, above). The diesels were built by A.C. Loire (Saint Denis), Sautter-Harlé (Paris), Augustin Normand, Indret, and Sabathé (Saint Étienne). *Brumaire's* diesels were built by Augustin Normand under a contract of 21 October 1908. On 23 May 1909 Minister Picard directed the addition of a second *enseigne de vaisseau* and another internal toilet because cruises with the diesels could be longer than those with steam.

*Curie* was caught in harbour nets while trying to enter Pola and scuttled on 20 December 1914. The Austrians raised her and put her in service as their *U-14*. In 1917-18 they rebuilt her. Exterior features included an 88mm deck gun and a large conning tower with a fully-equipped navigating bridge while internal features included two Austrian MAN diesels of 450hp, comfortable accommodations, and an excellent periscope. The French recovered her after the war and in general commented favourably on many of the Austrian changes. They replaced the 88mm deck gun with a French 75mm gun and had to replace some of the other Austrian equipment when spares ran out.

*The characteristics are based on a devis for* Brumaire *dated 6.3.1912.*
**Dimensions & tons:** 52.15m oa, 51.34m wl, 52.15m pp x 5.42m wl (7.202 outside the midships horizontal planes). 397.308t disp (surfaced), 551.267t (submerged). Draught: 3.046m mean, 3.194m aft. Men: 25 including 3 officers (the third officer to be embarked as needed). Reserve buoyancy: 27.9%
**Machinery:**
(surfaced) 725hp normal rated (840hp designed) at 400rpm. Speed 13kts. 2 screws. 2 four-cycle diesel engines with 6 cylinders. 15,054 litres oil. Range (trials) 2,000nm @ 9.6kts.
(submerged) 660hp at 350rpm. Speed 8.80kts. 2 electric motors. Batteries 69 tons. Range 84nm @ 5kts
**Torpedoes:** 1 internal bow tube, 2 fixed launch cages under the walking deck abreast of the conning tower aimed forward at 6 degrees off the axis, 2 Drzewiecki trainable launchers immediately behind these, 2 Drzewiecki trainable launchers side by side under the walking deck aft, all for 450mm M1909R or M1911V torpedoes. **Guns:** During the war some received a 37mm M1885 gun (*Montgolfier* c1914), a 47mm gun (*Le Verrier, Foucault, Faraday*), or a 75mm Army M1897 gun (*Frimaire, Montgolfier, Newton*).

*Brumaire* (Q60) Cherbourg Dyd/Augustin Normand
On list 1.1906. Ord: 26.8.1905. K: 20.7.1909. L: 29.4.1911.
　Comm: 20.3.1912 (full).
Budget 1905 (late addition). First static diesel trials 16.6.1911 and electric trials 1.6.1911. In 1914 was in the 2nd Submarine Squadron of the *2e Escadre légère* at Calais. In the Brittany submarine squadron 1.1918. Off main list 1928 (condemnation pending). Struck 16.7.1930. Sold 3.8.1931 at Cherbourg to M. Cousin to BU.

*Frimaire* (Q62) Cherbourg Dyd/Augustin Normand.
On list 1.1906. Ord: 26.8.1905. K: 20.7.1909. L: 26.8.1911.
　Comm: 9.10.1912 (trials), 9.10.1913 (full).
Budget 1905 (late addition). In 1914 was in the 2nd Submarine Squadron of the *2e Escadre légère* at Calais. In the Brittany submarine squadron 1.1918. Condemned 10.12.1923, struck 20.12.1923. Trials hulk at Cherbourg 1923-1929 (used as target 10.2.1924). Sold 2.9.1931 at

Cherbourg to M. Cousin to BU for the notional sum of 305 francs.

*Nivôse* (Q63) Cherbourg Dyd/Augustin Normand.
On list 1.1906. Ord: 26.8.1905. K: 20.7.1909. L: 6.1.1912.
　Comm: 19.10.1912 (full).
Budget 1905 (late addition). In 1914 was in the 2nd Submarine Squadron of the *2e Escadre légère* at Calais. In the Brittany submarine squadron 1.1918. Condemned 30.6.1921 and struck 27.7.1921. Sold 8.4.1922 at Cherbourg to M. Cousin to BU.

*Foucault* (Q70) Cherbourg Dyd/Indret.
On list 1.1907. Ord: 29.10.1906. K: 1910. L: 15.6.1912.
　Comm: 20.6.1914 (trials).
Budget 1906. Named 17.7.1909. Joined the 3rd Submarine Squadron of the *2e Escadre légère* at Cherbourg during 1914. To the Mediterranean late 1915, Adriatic operations 1916. Bombed and sunk 15.9.1916 off Cattaro by two Austrian seaplanes, crew saved. She was the first submarine sunk by air attack.

*Euler* (Q71) Cherbourg Dyd/Indret.
On list 1.1907. Ord: 29.10.1906. K: 1910. L: 12.10.1912.
　Comm: 5.9.1913 (full).
Budget 1906. Named 17.7.1909. In 1914 was in the 2nd Submarine Squadron of the *2e Escadre légère* at Calais. In the Brittany submarine squadron 1.1918. Struck 21.7.1927. Sold 3.5.1928 at Cherbourg to M. Cousin.

*Franklin* (Q72) Cherbourg Dyd/Indret.
On list 1.1907. Ord: 29.10.1906. K: 1910. L: 22.3.1913.
　Comm: 13.7.1914 (full).
Budget 1906. Named 17.7.1909. Joined the 3rd Submarine Squadron of the *2e Escadre légère* at Cherbourg during 1914. To the Mediterranean late 1915, Adriatic operations 1916-1918. In the 1st submarine squadron at Brindisi 1.1918. Condemned and struck 24.11.1922 (date of a circulaire promulgated in the *Bulletin officiel* on 28.11.1922). Sold 22.3.1923 at Bizerte to M. Boccara of Tunis.

*Faraday* (Q78) Rochefort Dyd/A.C. Loire, Saint Denis.
On list 1.1907. Ord: 29.10.1906. K: 21.7.1909. L: 27.6.1911.
　Comm: 28.6.1912 (full).
Budget 1906. Named 17.7.1909. In 1914 was in the 2nd submarine squadron of the *1re Armée navale* at Bizerte. Adriatic operations 1914-1918, also Dardanelles 11.1914 to 3.1915. In the 1st submarine squadron at Brindisi 1.1918. Condemned 29.9.1921, struck 27.10.1921. Sold 20.5.1922 at Bizerte to M. Boccara of Tunis to BU.

*Volta* (Q79) Rochefort Dyd/Augustin Normand.
On list 1.1907. Ord: 29.10.1906. K: 21.7.2909. L: 23.9.1911.
　Comm: 13.12.1912 (full).
Budget 1906. Named 17.7.1909. In 1914 was in the 2nd Submarine Squadron of the *2e Escadre légère* at Calais. In the Brittany submarine squadron 1.1918. To Adriatic 2.1918 to replace the lost *Bernoulli*. Condemned and struck 27.10.1922. Sold 22.3.1923 at Bizerte to M. Boccara of Tunis.

*Newton* (Q80) Rochefort Dyd/Augustin Normand.
On list 1.1907. Ord: 29.10.1906. K: 1.2.1910. L: 18.5.1912.
　Comm: 25.3.1914 (full).
Budget 1906. Named 17.7.1909. Assigned to the 1st or 3rd Submarine Squadron of the *2e Escadre légère* at Cherbourg 5.3.1914. In the Brittany submarine squadron 1.1918. Damaged by water getting into battery 10.1925. Condemned and struck 20.12.1926. Sold 15.4.1927 at Cherbourg to the Union des syndicats ouvriers de la Manche.

*Montgolfier* (Q81) Rochefort Dyd/Sabathé, Saint Étienne.
On list 1.1907. Ord: 29.10.1906. K: 7.3.1910. L: 18.4.1912.
　Comm: 8.8.1914 (full).

Budget 1906. Named 17.7.1909. Joined the 3rd Submarine Squadron of the *2e Escadre légère* at Cherbourg during 1914. In the Brittany submarine squadron 1.1918. Condemned 30.6.1921, struck 27.7.1921. Sold 8.4.1922 at Cherbourg to M. Cousin to BU.

*Arago* (Q86) Toulon Dyd/Sabathé, Saint Étienne.
On list 1.1907. Ord: 29.10.1906. K: 18.1.1909. L: 28.6.1912.
   Comm: 28.6.1912 (trials), 28.6.1913 (full).
Budget 1906. Named 17.7.1909. In 1914 was in the 2nd submarine squadron of the *1re Armée navale* at Bizerte. Adriatic operations 1915-1918. Struck 27.10.1921, for sale at Toulon 1921-1928, used as floating dock gate at Toulon 1928-1931 (first for the basin for tankers at Toulon, replaced there by *Astrée* 28.1.1930 and moved to the fuelling basin). Sold 25.6.1931 at Toulon to the Société de Matériel Naval du Midi.

*Curie* (Q87) Toulon Dyd/Augustin Normand.
On list 1.1907. Ord: 29.10.1906. K: 25.5.1909. L: 18.7.1912.
   Comm: 18.7.1912 (trials), 18.7.1913 (full).
Budget 1906. Named 17.7.1909. In 1914 was in the 2nd submarine squadron of the *1re Armée navale* at Bizerte. Caught in the defensive nets and sunk 20.12.1914 during an attempt to enter the Austrian port of Pola. Salvaged 21.12.1914 to 2.2.1915 by the Austrians, rebuilt and put into service 1.6.1915 as their *U-14*. Recovered at Cattaro 10.11.1918, manned at Corfu 18.11.1918, returned to Toulon 24.12.1918, back on French fleet list as *Curie* 17.7.1919. Condemned 8.3.1928, struck 29.3.1928. Sale at Toulon 25.7.1930 fell through, sold 26.11.1930 to M. Caselli.

*Le Verrier* (Q88) Toulon Dyd/Augustin Normand.
On list 1.1907. Ord: 29.10.1906. K: 4.8.1909. L: 31.10.1912.
   Comm: 30.10.1913 (full).
Budget 1906. Named 17.7.1909. First commissioned 30.10.1913. In 1914 was in the 2nd submarine squadron of the *1re Armée navale* at Bizerte. Adriatic operations 1914-1918, also Dardanelles 11.1914 to 3.1915. In the 1st submarine squadron at Brindisi 1.1918. Retained for trials at Bizerte 1923-1924 and at Toulon 1924-1926. Condemned 30.12.1924. Struck 3.2.1925. Used for trials with underwater explosions in connection with the design of the submarine minelayers of the *Saphir* class. Sold 25.6.1927 at Toulon to M. Saglia.

───────

### The competition of 1906
In March 1906 the *Conseil supérieur* decided that the 20 submersibles to be begun in 1906 should include two *à grand rayon d'action* (long range) larger than the *Pluviôse* type. These were to be of at least 500 tons, 12 to 15 knots speed on the surface and 10 or 11 knots submerged, and 2,500 to 3,000nm range. They were to carry six torpedoes and preferably have diesel propulsion. With the Russo-Japanese war in mind the Council specified that these submarines should be able to operate as far as Indochina. The Council also formally recommended that Laubeuf be asked to design them. The Council also included among the 20 submersibles for 1906 one with special boilers proposed by Maurice and one with Sabathé diesels proposed by Bourdelle.
   Without waiting for this formal action by the Council, Minister Thomson on 6 February 1906 opened a competition for designs for a faster and longer-range submarine with the following characteristics:

- Maximum speed on the surface: 15 knots (vice 12 knots in *Pluviôse*), fast enough to accompany a squadron of battleships.
- Range on the surface at 10 knots with normal fuel: 1,250 nautical miles (vice 584nm in *Pluviôse*),
- Same with fuel surcharge: 2,500nm
- Maximum speed submerged: 10 knots (vice 7.7 knots in *Pluviôse*)
- Range submerged at 5 knots: 100nm.

The military characteristics were provided in a later note dated 29 July

*161  BREST. — Le Sous-Marin " Archimède " et le fond de l'Arsenal. — LL.*

The submarine (submersible before 1909) *Archimède* in the upper reaches of the Brest arsenal at the beginning of her career. She was one of four experimental submarines (including *Mariotte*, below) designed in response to a competition of 1906 intended to get greater operating ranges and higher speeds for submarines. She was essentially a much-improved version of the steam-propelled *Pluviôse* class with an armament of seven torpedo launchers including two Drzewiecki trainable launchers under the walking deck aft. *(Postcard by LL)*

1906. They called for two internal torpedo tubes forward, two more aft, and four Drzewiecki trainable launchers on the sides for a total of 8 torpedoes ready to launch. Time for diving was to be 4 minutes, provisions for 12 days were to be carried, and the boat was to be able to dive safely to 40 metres. The requirements for operating range were also refined, becoming 1,640nm and 2,410nm on the surface at 10 knots and 40.3nm submerged at 5 knots.
   Four entirely different proposals were received and all four were accepted and built as experimental submarines. They followed the last *Brumaire* class boats in each of the three submarine-building dockyards. Q73 and Q74 at Cherbourg were the long range submarines asked for by the *Conseil supérieur*, Q82 at Rochefort was Bourdelle's boat, and Q89 at Toulon was Maurice's boat. Of these the two long range boats, Hutter's *Archimède* and Radiguer's *Mariotte*, were reasonably successful while Bourdelle's *Amiral Bourgois* and Maurice's *Charles Brun* were failures. *Amiral Bourgois* was called on her plans a *submersible à grand rayon d'action*.

───────

***ARCHIMÈDE.*** *Torpilleur autonome submersible (to Sous-marin 1.1909).* Double hull, steam surface propulsion. Designed by Hutter.

*Archimède* was one of the four experimental submarines built as a result of the competition of 6 February 1906. Naval constructor Julien Eugène Hutter offered a submersible with about 30% reserve buoyancy derived directly from the steam-propelled *Pluviôse* type. The designer increased the reserve buoyancy to reach the high maximum surfaced speed and to get the seakeeping qualities needed to attain the prescribed operational range. To keep the displacement from becoming excessive he gave his boat finer lines by eliminating the cylindrical portion amidships, a lighter hull structure by using cylindrical sections and closely-spaced frames, a more intense battery discharge rate, boilers with vertical tubes to give a higher steam generation rate, and faster engine piston speeds obtained by lengthening the stroke. A note of 29 June 1908 by naval constructor Lévy recommended adopting in the *Brumaire* class the disposition of superstructures adopted for the Q90 type and in *Archimède* which allowed placing the torpedo launchers under the walking deck. (It was later decided to replace the two after fixed launch cages in the *Brumaire* class with Drzewiecki trainable launchers.)

*The characteristics are based on a devis dated 19.9.1910.*

**Dimensions & tons:** 60.900m oa, 60.245m wl, 60.000m pp x 5.630m ext, 5.577m wl. 580.434t disp (surfaced), 808.744t (submerged). Draught: 3.838m mean, 4.415m aft. Men: 29 including 3 officers. Reserve buoyancy: 28.2%

**Machinery:**

(surfaced) 1,688ihp designed at 340rpm and $17kg/cm^2$ boiler pressure. Speed 14.92kts (max 15.2kts). 2 screws. 2 triple expansion engines with 3 cylinders of 0.330m, 0.480m, and 0.735m diameter and 0.375m stroke. 2 Guyot Du Temple boilers. 28,120 litres (normal) of oil, could increase fuel to 46,260 litres by using three exterior ballast tanks as surcharge. Range (trials) 1,100nm normal or 2,910nm with surcharge @ 10kts.

(submerged) 1,220hp. Speed 10.95kts (max 11.25kts). 2 electric motors. Batteries 115.3 tons. Range (trials) 160nm @ 3kts.

**Torpedoes:** 1 internal bow tube, 4 fixed launch cages under the walking deck all aimed forward, one pair just forward of the conning tower aimed at 6 degrees off the axis and the other pair behind it aimed at 10 degrees off the axis, plus 2 Drzewiecki trainable launchers under the walking deck aft, all for 450mm M1906 torpedoes. **Guns:** Received a 47mm gun aft c1915.

*Archimède* (Q73) Cherbourg Dyd/Indret.
On list 1.1907. Ord: 31.12.1906. K: 2.1.1908. L: 4.8.1909.
    Comm: 1.1910 (trials), 22.9.1910 (full).

---

The submarine *Mariotte*, designed to achieve the greater ranges and speeds called for in the 1906 competition using a pure submarine derived from the *Émeraude* type instead of a submersible. She is shown here during World War I with camouflage paint and false bow wave before entering the Dardanelles, where she was lost. Her high bow which contained the conning tower gave her the nickname the 'toothbrush'. *(NHHC, NH-55745)*

Budget 1906. Named 17.7.1909. First static machinery trials 20.10.1909. Underway trials 2-6.1910, entry into service delayed to 9.1911 by engineering problems. In 1914 was in the 1st Submarine Squadron of the *2e Escadre légère* at Cherbourg. To Harwich at British request 11.1914 to help blockade Helgoland, returned to Cherbourg late 12.1914 with storm damage to her funnel. To the Mediterranean from Cherbourg with *Gustave Zédé* 4.1915. Served in the Adriatic 12.1915 to 4.1917. To the Morocco squadron 1.1918 but was by then worn out. To the Domaines for sale 28.10.1919, struck 12.11.1919. Sold 4.10.1921 at Toulon.

---

***MARIOTTE.*** *Torpilleur autonome submersible* (to *Sous-marin* 1.1909). Single hull, diesel surface propulsion. Designed by Radiguer.

*Mariotte* was a single-hulled submarine but was called a *submersible de 530tx* on her plans instead of a *bateau sous-marin*. She was designed by naval constructor Charles Félix Adolphe Radiguer who had directed the construction of *Sous-marin X* and was one of the four experimental boats built as a result of the competition of 6 February 1906. The challenge for Radiguer was to meet the requirements of the competition with a single-hulled pure submarine derived from the *Émeraude* type. To accomplish this without excessive displacement Radiguer kept the reserve buoyancy of the boat as low as possible while moving most of it forward where it would ensure that the boat rose over waves properly and give the bow high free-board. The result was a low hull with a flat top and curved bottom and a freeboard of only about 0.6 metres from amidships to the stern surmounted from amidships to the bow with a high forecastle or casing up to 2.6 metres tall. Radiguer likened his approach to that taken in the battleship *Henri IV* in which the monitor type of warship was improved by the addition of a high forecastle. The forecastle concealed a conning tower whose top barely rose above the deck (a shelter for the conning officer was added temporarily on top of the bow during trials) and also contained the entire torpedo

armament. Overall the boat had a designed reserve buoyancy of 15%, but Radiguer calculated that the reserve buoyancy of the bow alone was 25.6%, a figure comparable to that for submersibles. She had two pairs of horizontal planes, one forward and one aft. Her maximum dive depth was 35 metres. Her diesels were built by Sautter-Harlé and her electric motors by Bréguet.

Her submerged speed of 11.5 knots was remarkable for its day and after the problems with her diesels were worked out in 1913 she became with *Archimède* the most successful of the four experiments. She dived to 25 metres on 21 November 1911. She was nicknamed the 'toothbrush' because of her appearance.

**Dimensions & tons:**
64.750m oa, 61.537m wl, m 64.750pp x 4.300m ext, 3.310m wl. 544.501t disp (surfaced), 633.648t (submerged). Draught: 3.818m mean, 3.820m aft. Men: 32 including 3 officers. Reserve buoyancy: 14.1%.

**Machinery:**
(surfaced) 1,400hp designed at 395rpm. Speed 14.26kts. 2 screws. 2 four-cycle diesel engines with 6 cylinders of 0.400m diameter. 16.58t oil. Range (trials) 1,658nm @ 10kts.
(submerged) 1,000hp at 400rpm. Speed 11.66kts. 2 electric motors. Batteries 118.5 tons. Range (trials) 143nm @ 5kts.
**Torpedoes:** 4 internal tubes in the bow in superimposed pairs, 2 Drzewiecki trainable launchers in the sides of the forecastle behind removable plating shaped like blisters, all for 450mm M1906M torpedoes.

*Mariotte* (Q74) Cherbourg Dyd/Sautter-Harlé, Paris.
On list 1.1907. Ord: 31.12.1906. K: 30.3.1908. L: 2.2.1911. Comm: 5.2.1913 (full).
Budget 1906. Named 17.7.1909. Official diving trials 8-22.8.1911. Diesels installed 1.3.1912 to 28.7.1912. Official diesel trials 23.10.1912 to 11.12.1912. Assigned 16.1.1913 to the 2nd Submarine Squadron of the *2e Escadre légère* at Calais and joined 11.2.1913. To the Mediterranean 6.1915. Starboard screw snagged a mine cable 26.7.1915 while trying to penetrate the Dardanelles, forced to surface, damaged by Turkish shore batteries, scuttled near Cape Nara, and crew captured.

————————

**AMIRAL BOURGOIS.** *Torpilleur autonome submersible* (to *Sous-marin* 1.1909). Double hull, Sabathé diesel surface propulsion. Designed by Bourdelle

*Amiral Bourgois* was an enlarged version of the diesel-propelled *Brumaire* type designed by naval constructor Pierre Marc Bourdelle with a special type of diesel engine. She was one of the four experimental submarines built as a result of the competition of 6 February 1906. The diesels operated on the Sabathé mixed combustion system and were fuelled by kerosene. The Sabathé cycle is one in which combustion takes place partly explosively and partly at constant pressure and which resembles partly the Otto cycle and partly the Diesel cycle. Schneider had major problems building these engines and they finally completed successful trials only in December 1916. The electric motors were ordered on 18 December 1907. *Amiral Bourgois* was designed without a walking deck but one was added during trials. She dived to 25 metres on 27 February 1914 but saw no active war service. Vice Admiral Siméon Bourgois experimented with the screw propeller, was the father of the submarine *Plongeur*, and supported the *Jeune École*.

**Dimensions & tons:** 56.200m oa, 56.560m wl, 56.000m pp x 5.520m ext, 5.412m wl. 579.769t disp (surfaced), 746.187t (submerged). Draught: 3.7095m mean and fwd, 3.7070m aft. Men: 29 including 3 officers. Reserve buoyancy: 22.3%
**Machinery:**
(surfaced) 1,400hp designed at 300rpm. Speed 13.85kts. Trials

(19.8.1913) 1,354hp = 13.85kts at 314.1rpm. 2 screws. 2 four-cycle diesel engines with 4 cylinders of 0.485m diameter and 0.480m stroke. 15,420 litres oil (kerosene). Range (designed) 2,500nm @ 10kts, (trials 1916) 1,500nm @ 10kts.
(submerged) 1,000hp at 270rpm. Speed 8.65kts (could push to 1,120hp and 280rpm for a half hour). 2 electric motors. Batteries 122.4 tons. Range (designed) 100nm @ 5kts, (trials 1916) 89nm @ 4.2kts.
**Torpedoes:** 2 superimposed internal bow tubes, 1 external watertight stern tube, 4 Drzewiecki trainable launchers in pairs under the walking deck, one pair forward of the conning tower and one aft, all for 450mm M1911V torpedoes. **Guns:** A mounting for a 37mm M1885 gun was fitted forward of the conning tower. One 65mm was installed 10.8.1917.

*Amiral Bourgois* (Q82) Rochefort Dyd/Schneider, Creusot.
On list 1.1907. Ord: 31.12.1906. K: 19.5.1908. L: 25.11.1912. Comm: 7.8.1914 (full).
Budget 1906. Named 17.7.1909. Diesels received 4.5.1912. First surface trials of electric motors 21.7.1913. Diesel trials begun 19.8.1913. Because of the war was put into full commission 7.8.1914 and assigned to the *2e Escadre légère* at Cherbourg, left Rochefort for Cherbourg 7.9.1914. At that time the diesels had been run for only 9 hours. Satisfactory diesel endurance trials 17.12.1916. In the Normandy submarine squadron 1.1918. Assigned 13.5.1918 to the school for underwater navigation (ENSM) at Toulon with orders to fix her motors. Work ordered stopped 25.11.1918. Struck 12.11.1919, for sale at Toulon 1920-1926 (reserved for torpedo tests). Sold 25.6.1927 at Toulon to M. Saglia.

————————

**CHARLES BRUN.** *Torpilleur autonome submersible* (to *Sous-marin* 1.1909). Single hull, unique steam propulsion (surfaced and submerged). Designed by Maurice.

*Charles Brun* was one of the four submarines built as a result of the competition of 6 February 1906. For more than ten years her designer, naval constructor Just Lucien Maurice, had been trying to develop a unique (closed cycle) engine for use both on the surface and submerged. On 14 June 1898 and 19 June 1900 the *Conseil des travaux* had examined designs by Maurice for small submersibles using a *chaudière accumulatrice* submerged and on the surface. On 11 March 1902 the Council considered four variants for a full-sized submersible proposed by Maurice, of which the basic one was for a 282-ton vessel (313 tons submerged) that used a unique steam engine supplied with steam by a regular Normand boiler and a Maurice *chaudière accumulatrice* to propel the boat on the surface with fires lit at a maximum speed of 18 knots and submerged with fires out with steam continuing to be generated by retained heat in both boilers but particularly the Maurice boiler. The Council concluded that none of the four variants could be approved for the double reason that many of their features had a serious risk of failure and that none of them would give sufficient range when submerged. Following this discussion Minister de Lanessan on 22 May 1902 asked the Machinery Commission to contract with Delaunay-Belleville for an experimental Maurice *chaudière-accumulatrice*, which was set up ashore at Cherbourg.

The Maurice boiler had double concentric tubes. The combustion gases passed inside the interior tube and transferred heat to a mixture of sodium acetate and potassium in the space between the tubes. This mixture, once it melted at 212 degrees centigrade, heated the water in the boiler outside the tubes. When the boat submerged and the burners of the boilers were extinguished the sodium acetate mix continued to generate steam in the water surrounding the tubes until it solidified. When the boat surfaced the burners would be lit off to melt the sodium acetate mix and resume navigation.

In *Charles Brun*, his submission for the 1906 competition, Maurice proposed to reach high speeds both surfaced and submerged with displacements considerably less than those called for in the specifications for the competition by using his unique propulsion system. His 1906 design omitted the Normand boiler in his 1902 design and instead included two Maurice boilers, each consisting of two parts. It also had a small battery and two 100hp electric motors. The shore-based prototype of the Maurice boiler at Cherbourg had functioned well but the plant on the submarine did not, initially producing little steam while ejecting large amounts of smoke and flames from the funnels. This combustion problem was later resolved but the amount of steam generated was still well under that generated by the prototype. The operation of the plant and the internal temperature on the boat both proved satisfactory but the submerged performance was totally inadequate: ten minutes at 7 knots and three and a half hours at 3 knots with a submerged range of 10.7nm at 2.8 knots against a designed range of 100nm. Unlike electric storage batteries the Maurice boiler performed better when used at high rates of discharge in a relatively short time, and extending a dive beyond about three hours was thus technically unfeasible.

A successful test dive to 25 metres was conducted on 10 October 1912 and new speed trials on the surface were run on 21 May 1913 producing good results, but in post-trial inspections extensive damage to the two boilers due to a manufacturing error was discovered. The after boiler could be repaired with spare tubes, but repairs to the forward boiler would prolong trials by 8 to 10 months. It was decided instead to close the series of trials with one more submerged run under steam using the after boiler alone. This trial was conducted on 7 August 1913 and was considered to have proven the possibility of navigating underwater by steam without impact on habitability. The critical shortfall in submerged performance remained, however, and even if the electric motors had also been used it would still have been very insufficient. In addition, diving the boat was a lengthy and complex operation, repairs that were easy on other submarines were difficult and time consuming on this one, and finally *Charles Brun* steered badly and had a huge turning circle. For these reasons the trials commission concluded that the military use of *Charles Brun* could not be envisaged and advised against putting her into full commission (*armement définitif*). It also turned down a proposal from the ship's commander to replace the forward boiler with a battery taken from a decommissioned *Naïade* type submarine. Condemnation proceedings were initiated on 20 October 1913.

Beginning in January 1914 the hull was lightened by the removal of much equipment and then ballast was added for use in testing floating drydocks at Toulon and Oran (the latter test being cancelled when the war began). Stability issues caused by this work prevented her conversion in August 1914 into a floating water tank for Bizerte, but by March 1916 Toulon had a shortage of water tanks and on 1 July 1916 the Chantiers et Ateliers de Provence at Port de Bouc received a contract for the conversion of the submarine. She was at Port de Bouc in September 1916 but was probably not converted, as she was called a 'submarine hull' when she was struck in 1920.

**Dimensions & tons:** 45.600m oa, 45.000m wl, 45.000m pp x 4.000m. 359.862t disp (surfaced), 452.544t (submerged). Draught: 3.521m mean, 3.612m aft. Men: 25 including officers. Reserve buoyancy: 20.5%

**Machinery:**
(surfaced) 1,300ihp designed at 425rpm and 30kg/cm² boiler pressure (18.5kg/cm² at the engine). Speed 13.54kts. Trials (21.5.1913) 1098.2ihp = 13.592kts at 352.5rpm. 2 screws. 2 triple expansion engines with 3 cylinders of 0.250m (HP), 0.390m (MP), and 0.600m (LP) diameter and 0.350m (HP) and 0.34m (MP & LP) stroke. 2 Maurice sodium acetate boilers (*chaudières accumulatrices*) each consisting of two independent units and each with its own funnel. 11,440 litres oil plus 2,000 litres surcharge in a ballast tank. Range (trials) 1,050nm @ 7.15kts.
(submerged) Supplementary electric system: 200hp. Speed 7.25kts. Trials (22.8.1912) 296ihp (192 effective) = 6kts at 215rpm for 41 minutes, (9.9.1912) 7.25kts at 259.7rpm for 10 minutes. 2 electric motors.

Batteries 23.8 tons. Range (designed) 100nm, (trials 1912) 4nm @ 6kts, 6.5nm @ 4kts, 10.7nm @ 2.8kts.
**Torpedoes:** 2 superimposed internal tubes in the bow, 2 Drzewiecki trainable launchers under the walking deck near the stern and two fixed launch cages in the stern aimed directly aft, all for 450mm torpedoes. A preliminary design had the two internal bow tubes plus 4 Drzewiecki trainable launchers amidships.

*Charles Brun* (Q89) Toulon Dyd/Indret.
On list 1.1907. Ord: 31.12.1906. K: 4.4.1908. L: 14.9.1910. Commissioning suspended 8.1913.
Budget 1906. Named 17.7.1909. Trials at Toulon from 10.1910 to 8.1913, never put into service because of severe performance shortfalls. Condemnation proposed 20.10.1913. Stripped hull used 1914 to test a floating drydock at Toulon. Engine reused in anti-submarine gunboat *Espiègle* (ordered 12.1915). Contract awarded 1.7.1916 for conversion to a floating water tank. Struck 7.6.1920 as a 'submarine hull'. Sold 30.12.1920 at Toulon to M. Saglia to BU.

---

*Q90 (HUTTER) TYPE. Torpilleurs autonomes submersibles* (to *Sous-marins* 1.1909). Double hull, diesel surface propulsion. Designed by Hutter.

The ambitious submarine building programme continued in the 1907 budget (submitted 26 June 1906) which added to the building programme ten *sous-marins*, Q90-91 at Cherbourg, Q92-94 at Rochefort, and Q95-99 at Toulon, to follow the large programme of Laubeuf submersibles (Q51-89 less Q61 and four experimental). No technical details were provided on Q90-99, which were listed as *à l'étude*. They were also listed as *sous-marins* in the 1908 budget (submitted 11 May 1907), along with five more (Q100-104, all at Rochefort). On 8 October 1907 Minister Thomson directed the laying down of ten submersibles called 'type 1907' on plans by Hutter including Q90-91 at Cherbourg, Q92-94 at Rochefort, and Q95-99 at Toulon. (Hutter had also designed the experimental *Archimède*.) Hutter's design was based on Labeuf's and Simonot's diesel-propelled variant of *Pluviôse* with the same dimensions and displacement. Q90-99 first appeared in the January 1908 *Liste de la Flotte*. A note from Admiral Philibert, inspecteur général des flotilles, calls these 'replicas of *Papin*' with the following characteristics: Displacement 398/555 tons, Dimensions 52m x 5.10m, Speed 13.5/10 knots, Range 1,400nm at 13 knots surfaced and 70nm at 5.3 knots submerged. The lines of Hutter's design were tested in a towing tank in around 1908 with those of the original *Pluviôse* and the proposed modified Q70 (the *Brumaire* type). The 1909 budget (submitted 19 May 1908) showed Q90 and all later boats (now up to Q110) as *submersibles* vice *sous-marins*. The specifications below are from the 1909 budget (submitted 19 May 1908) for Q90-Q99, which were ordered on 8 October 1907; they are close to but do not exactly match those of any other class in that budget.

**Dimensions & tons:** 50.745m x 5.10m wl. 398t disp. Draught: 3.276m aft.
**Machinery:** 860hp (equivalent) = 13.00kts. 2 screws. Internal combustion engines.

*Q90-Q91.* To be built at Cherbourg. Budget 1907. Reordered in 1910 budget.

*Q92-Q94.* To be built at Rochefort. Budget 1907. Not in 1910 budget.

*Q95-Q99.* To be built at Toulon. Budget 1907. Not in 1910 budget.

*Q100-104.* To be built at Rochefort. Budget 1908. Not in 1910 budget.

*Q105-106.* To be built at Cherbourg. Budget 1909. Not in 1910 budget.

*Q107-108.* To be built at Rochefort. Budget 1909. Not in 1910 budget.

*Q109-110.* To be built at Toulon. Budget 1909. Not in 1910 budget.

---

## (B) Submarines (*Sous-marins*).

### Restructuring the submarine programme, 1909-1910

The distinction between submarines (*bateaux sous-marins*) and submersibles (*torpilleurs autonomes submersibles*) was dropped in the January 1909 fleet list and in the 1910 budget (submitted 18 June 1909) and all were thereafter called submarines (*sous-marins*). On 18 May 1909 the *Conseil supérieur* specified a number of 64 submarines in the navy instead of the 82 offensive and 49 defensive submarines it had called for in 1905 and 1906. These included three groups of six in the north (at Dunkirk or Calais, Cherbourg and Brest), another three groups of six in the Mediterranean (at Toulon, Oran, and Bizerte), an additional group of six for long range operations in each area, and 16 replacement units. The submarine procurement programme was then restructured. In the 1910 budget (submitted 18 June 1909) and the January 1910 fleet list everything after Q89 was omitted (the Q numbers were then reused), except that Q90-91 were retained as *type à l'étude,* to begin construction at Rochefort in 1910. In November 1909 submarines were re-grouped in 'offensive' or 'defensive' divisions according to their tonnage.

On 2 February 1910 Minister Boué de Lapeyrère chaired a meeting of the *Conseil supérieur* in which he informed them of a new naval programme that he had developed. His starting point had been the decisions of the *Conseil supérieur* of June 1909, but he had learned from the Minister of Finances that that programme was unaffordable and, the government having stated that it would be satisfied if France maintained mastery of the Mediterranean, he had reduced the number of battleships from 45 to 28. His new programme, however, increased the number of submarines from 64 to 94 because he intended to separate them into two categories:

1. Coast defence submarines responsible for protecting and making free the entrances to our military ports, preventing the laying of mines, etc… They are submarines of 400 tons.
2. Three squadrons (*escadrilles*) of 12 offensive submarines with a long range of action distributed between the three strategic points of Cherbourg, Oran, and Bizerte. The fleet commander could and should use, depending on the circumstances, the offensive squadron located within his area of operations. Associated documents indicate these were to be of around 700 tons.

The number of 94 submarines was included in a bill on the constitution of the fleet first submitted on 9 February 1910 and ultimately approved as the Naval Law of 30 March 1912 (the Programme of 1912). Internal documents indicate that by then the 94 submarines included 73 defensive submarines (400 to 600 tons) and 21 seagoing submarines (*sous-marins de haute mer*); 55 of these 94 submarines already existed and 39 remained to be built. The 55 existing boats included in the defensive category 17 *Pluviôse,* 16 *Brumaire,* 10 *Clorinde* (all 400 tons), Q102 (520 tons), 3 experimental (530 tons), and Q107-108 (630 tons), and in the seagoing category 2 *Gustave Zédé* (800 tons) and Q105-106 (833 tons). In 1914 many of the seagoing positions were filled by *Pluviôse* and *Brumaire* class units.

---

*CLORINDE* Class. *Sous-marins (Sous-marins garde-côtes et de blocus).* Double hull, diesel surface propulsion. Designed by Hutter. To *Sous-marins de 2e classe* 1.1923.

These two submarines were built to plans from Cherbourg (where Hutter had served until June 1909, he served in the *Section technique* from December 1910 into 1914) that were referred to the *Section technique* by the Minister on 11 April 1910, submitted for ministerial approval on 1 July 1910, and approved on 7 July 1910. In the 1911 budget (submitted 28 June 1910) Q90 and Q91 were to be ordered at Rochefort at the end of 1910 for laying down in 1911. Their construction at Rochefort was ordered by Minister Delcassé on 17 November 1910 and both were laid

down on the same day about a year later. The MAN-Loire diesel engines were ordered on 23 November 1910.

Hutter's 1910 design was probably an update of his 1907 design for Q90, which in 1908 had inspired many of the changes made in the *Pluviôse* design to produce the *Brumaire* design. The new design was derived from *Brumaire* with the following modifications. The elliptical sections of the pressure hull were replaced with cylindrical sections for greater strength. Finer lines were provided at the ends of the outer hull. A stronger battery was provided which increased designed submerged speed from 9 knots to 9.5 knots while increasing submerged range at 5 knots from 84nm to 100nm. The internal bow torpedo tube of the *Brumaire*s was omitted and the boat was armed with two fixed launch cages angled out near the bow and six Drzewiecki trainable launchers, all under the walking deck. Other changes were not so successful. The 420hp four-cycle diesels of the *Brumaire*s were replaced with lighter and smaller 650hp two-cycle 400-rpm diesels that were expected to increase surface speed from 13 knots to 15 knots. These, however, experienced multiple incidents during trials at the factory and were accepted for only 400hp. They gave a speed of 11-12 knots, about equal to that of the *Brumaire*s. A slight reduction was accepted in the designed surface range at 10 knots (1,930nm instead of 2,000nm), but in reality it fell to 1,440nm, well under the 2,180nm of *Newton.* Thoughts of updating them after the war were abandoned.

**Dimensions & tons:** 53.950m oa, 52.750m wl, 53.950m pp x 5.100m wl (7.324m outside midships horizontal planes). 421.457t disp (surfaced), 574.145t (submerged). Draught: 3.454m mean, 3.5m aft. Men: 27 including 2 officers. Reserve buoyancy: 26.6%
**Machinery:**
(surfaced) 1,300hp at 400rpm (designed), 800hp at 340rpm (as accepted) Speed: 15kts (designed), 13kts (as accepted). Trials (*Cornélie*) 750hp = 13.361kts at 358.2rpm. 2 screws. 2 two-cycle single-acting diesel engines (MAN type) with 8 cylinders of 0.290m diameter and 0.310m stroke. 11,813 litres oil. Range (trials) up to 1,240nm @ 10.815kts.
(submerged) 700hp at 320rpm. Speed 9.5kts (designed), 9kts (as accepted). Trials (1916) 608hp = 9kts at 311.5rpm. 2 electric motors. Batteries 80 tons. Range (trials) 104nm @ 5.205kts.
**Torpedoes:** 2 fixed launch cages angled out at 4°30' off the axis near the bow and 6 Drzewiecki trainable launchers for 450mm M1906 torpedoes, all under the walking deck. On 2.11.1917 the fixed launch cages forward were ordered replaced by fixed torpedo tubes in the same location. The replacement of the after Drzewiecki trainable launchers with fixed launch cages was authorized for *Clorinde* on 18.4.1918 and for *Cornélie* on 16.11.1918. **Guns:** 1 x 47mm M1885 gun was ordered added on 17.9.1915 and on 31.5.1916. A M1907 machine gun was authorized on 29.6.1916. A 47mm gun entirely hidden behind the breakwater forward was installed in *Cornélie* at Rochefort in 8.1916. The replacement of the 47mm by a 75mm guns was directed on 8.12.1917 and on 31.3.1918. The installation of a 75mm gun in *Clorinde* was authorized on 18.4.1918.

*Clorinde* (Q90) Rochefort Dyd/A.C. Loire, Saint Denis.
On list 1.1911. Ord: 17.11.1910 effective 30.12.1910. K: 6.11.1911. L: 2.10.1913. Comm: 25.9.1916 (trials), 17.9.1917 (full).
Budget 1910. Named 28.9.1910. Stationary machinery trials begun 30.10.1916, underway trials 5-6.1917. Assigned to the Normandy submarine squadron 1.1918 (still running trials). Cracks in engine cylinders reported 29.11.1924, believed beyond repair. Decomm. 27.10.1925. For sale at Cherbourg 1925-1926. Struck 15.1.1926. Sold 15.4.1927 to the Union des syndicats ouvriers de la Manche.

*Cornélie* (Q91) Rochefort Dyd/A.C. Loire, Saint Denis.
On list 1.1911. Ord: 17.11.1910 effective 30.12.1910. K: 6.11.1911. L: 29.10.1913. Comm: 1.4.1916 (trials), 18.8.1916 (full).
Budget 1910. Named 28.9.1910. Diesel engines accepted at the factory 14.1.1915 and installation begun 1.1915. First static diesel trials

2.5.1916, first underway diesel trials 9.5.1916, and dive trials 9.6.1916. In the Normandy submarine squadron 1.1918. Refit with parts removed from *Clorinde* authorized 12.1923 and new diesels proposed late 1924. Pre-condemnation decommissioning decided 4.2.1926, to be completed 13.3.1926, some material to be landed for *Laplace*. Condemnation proposed 20.11.1926. Condemned and struck 20.12.1926. Sold 15.4.1927 to the Union des syndicats ouvriers de la Manche.

_____

## Competition of 1909

After taking office on 24 July 1909, Minister of Marine Boué de Lapeyrère opened a new competition to create a *sous-marin de haute mer*, specifically 'a type of submarine capable, with its practical speed, its range of action, its habitability, and its nautical qualities, of conducting operations on the high seas.' Specifications were on the surface a speed of 20 knots and a range of 1,200nm at 14 knots, submerged a speed of 11 knots and range of 100nm at 5 knots. The boat was also to have 8 torpedoes of which 6 were ready to

launch and 12 days of provisions. Six projects were submitted, including four designs by Beaumarchais, Fenaux, Hutter and Simonot derived more or less from Laubeuf's submersibles, a variant of *Charles Brun* by Maurice with closed cycle propulsion, and a single hulled design by Maugas with internal ballast tanks moved to the ends and reserve buoyancy increased to 19.3%. Only one project was proceeded with, that of Simonot for *Gustave Zédé*, although numerous ideas were borrowed from that of naval constructor Fernand Alphonse Fenaux. The defensive counterpart to the offensive *Sous-marin de haute mer* was the *Sous-marin garde-côtes et de blocus*.

_____

*GUSTAVE ZÉDÉ. Sous-marin (Sous-marin de haute mer)*. Double hull, steam surface propulsion (originally and later diesel). Designed by Simonot. To *Sous-marins de 1re classe* 1.1923.

The 1911 budget (submitted 28 June 1910) added Q92 and Q93 as 750-ton submarines at Cherbourg, one to be ordered in 1910 and one in 1911. The decision to order two submarines to Simonot's design was taken on 28 September 1910. Construction of the two subs at Cherbourg was ordered by Minister Boué de Lapeyrère on 14 February 1911 and by Minister Delcassé on 8 July 1911. Features of the new design included:

– The use of near-circular sections in the pressure hull for maximum strength
– The addition of a large superstructure above the pressure hull for most of the length of the boat to shelter personnel at anchorages and at sea

The forward part of the submarine *Cornélie* on the right with her radio mast raised in a view of submarines at Cherbourg taken by the American visitor Robert W. Neeser in 1920. Behind her and three surrendered U-boats are the wartime conning towers of *Nivôse* and the new *Joëssel* with its rounded after end. The U-boats were retained as *Jean Autric* (*U-105*), *Trinité Schillemans* (*UB-94*), and *Victor Réveille* (*U-79*). (NHHC, NH-43779)

outside war zones. The high structure was also intended to help the boat make its designed 20-knot surface speed. An elevating navigating bridge was also provided.

– A new distribution of torpedo tubes, with two watertight internal tubes in the bow and six non-watertight external Simonot trainable launchers.

– Omission of the amidships horizontal planes, leaving two pairs fore and aft. This arrangement was also applied to later submarines.

Two two-cycle MAN diesels were ordered on 26 January 1911 from A.C. Loire, Saint Denis, who built diesels on license from Augsburg. The choice of untested large two-cycle diesels was driven by a search for high surface speeds. On 23 October 1911, given the lack of progress on the engines, A.C. Loire offered to provide more robust engines at no extra cost. The Director of Naval Construction accepted this offer, but MAN ultimately declared itself incapable of providing plans for engines of 2,400hp and the contract with A.C. Loire was cancelled on 29 April 1912. Other sources of diesels were ruled out because they could not produce the desired surface speed, and a contract was signed on 31 July 1912 with Delaunay-Belleville for steam engines. This did not affect sister *Néréide*, whose large two-cycle diesels were being built domestically by Schneider.

Problems were encountered with elevating the navigating bridge and on 12 February 1915 the Maritime Prefect at Cherbourg authorized its replacement with a removable shelter aft of the conning tower. The high superstructure failed to help the boat reach 20 knots – not only was that speed never reached but the thin plating was unable to resist heavy seas and the structure increased the visibility of the boat. In April 1915 *Gustave Zédé* reported for duty in the Adriatic, where one mission in May 1915 in an intense anti-submarine environment showed that the hour needed to raise boiler pressure after surfacing and before recharging batteries was a critical tactical vulnerability. *Gustave Zédé* was detached from Mediterranean duty in December 1915 and on 13 December 1915 Cherbourg was advised that she would soon arrive for the reduction of her superstructures, which was also to be done in *Néréide*. Freeboard at the bow was to be reduced from 2.60m to around 2m. She was also to receive two 75mm guns at this time. On 15 March 1916 the Simonot trainable launchers were replaced with external watertight tubes.

In 1922-24 *Gustave Zédé* underwent major modifications at Cherbourg. Her steam engines and boilers were removed and she received two MAN four cycle 6-cylinder type Q6 diesels (1,200hp each for 15 knots). The *devis d'armement* for *Gustave Zédé* says that these diesels were removed from the former German *U-165*, which sank by accident in the Weser on 18 November 1918 and was raised before being struck on 21 February 1919. In this reconstruction *Gustave Zédé* also got new electric motors (ordered on 13 February 1923), new batteries, an enlarged conning tower with a navigating bridge, and a trainable twin torpedo tube mount replacing the single tubes under the after end of the walking deck.

*The original characteristics are based on a devis dated 30.4.1915.*

**Dimensions & tons:** 74.000m oa, 73.270m wl, 74.000m pp x 6.000m ext & wl (6.994m over bow planes). 849.562t disp (surfaced), 1,098.524t (submerged). Draught: 3.741m mean, 4.202m aft. Men: 43 including 3 officers. Reserve buoyancy: 22.7%

**Machinery:**

(surfaced, steam, 1915) 4,000ihp at 330rpm and 19kg/cm² boiler pressure (17kg/cm² at engines), 3,500ihp effective. Speed: 19kts designed, 20kts hoped for, 16kts effective. Trials 17.57kts. 2 screws. 2 Delaunay-Belleville vertical triple expansion engines with 3 cylinders. 2 Du Temple return-flame boilers. 68.791t oil (74,773 litres). Range (trials) 1,242.38nm @ 13.383kts.

(surfaced, diesel, 1925): 2,400hp at 450rpm. Trials (18.1.1925) 15.59kts at 459.51rpm. 2 screws. 2 MAN four-cycle diesel engines with 6 cylinders of 0.45m diameter and 0.420m stroke. Range 2,004nm @ 9.195kts.

(submerged) 1,640hp at 240rpm. Speed 11kts (designed). Trials

(21.8.1913) 1,874.7hp = 11.44kts at 241rpm, 2 electric motors. Batteries 158.2 tons. Range 135nm @ 5kts. (New motors, 7.4.1925) 1,554hp (effective) = 9.29kts at 353.5rpm. 2 electric motors. Range 56nm @ 4.46kts.

**Torpedoes:**

(1915) 2 internal bow tubes, 6 Simonot trainable launchers under the walking deck in the bow, forward of the deck gun, and under the after end of the walking deck, all for 450mm M1911V torpedoes. **Guns:** Originally none, 2 x 75mm guns assigned 16.12.1915 with *Gustave Zédé* given priority for them on 17.1.1916 over *Néréide*.

(1925): 2 internal bow tubes, 2 watertight fixed tubes under the walking deck in the bow, 2 Simonot trainable launchers under the walking deck forward of the deck gun, 2 watertight tubes in a trainable twin mount under the after end of the walking deck, all for 450mm M1911V torpedoes. **Guns:** (1925) 1 x 75mm forward on disappearing mount, 1 x 75mm aft on fixed mount.

*Gustave Zédé* (Q92) Cherbourg Dyd/Delaunay-Belleville, Saint Denis. On list 1.1911. Ord: 14.2.1911. K: 7.8.1911. L: 20.5.1913. Comm: 5.1913 (trials), 10.10.1914 (full).

Budget 1911. Named by 1.1911. Underway trials with electric motors 28.5-25.8.1913. Boilers installed 30.10.1912 and first lit off 6.4.1914. First static machinery trials 8.4.1914, underway steam trials 6-9.1914. Assigned to the *2e Escadre légère* at Cherbourg by an order of 30.9.1914 effective 1.10.1914. To the Mediterranean 1.4.1915, one Adriatic operation 5.1915 followed by patrol in Ionian Islands. Back to Cherbourg 12.1915 for modifications. In the Morocco squadron 1.1918. Decommissioned at Toulon 11.1918. Returned to Cherbourg 1922 to be updated and have steam plant replaced with diesels. Ran underway trials at Cherbourg 12.1924-4.1925. Put in conservation 30.7.1930 because of the bad condition of her battery. Pre-condemnation report issued 27.6.1936. Struck 27.1.1937 (decision promulgated 26.4.1937). Sold at Brest 21.4.1938 to L'Hermitte Frères.

---

***NÉRÉIDE.*** Sous-marin (*Sous-marin de haute mer*). Double hull, diesel surface propulsion. Designed by Simonot. To *Sous-marin de 1re classe* 1.1923.

*Néréide* was a sister of *Gustave Zédé*, ordered at the same time from the same dockyard, but she retained the orginally-intended diesel propulsion. Her Schneider-Carels diesels were ordered from Schneider on 25 January 1911. The reduction of the superstructure was first proposed 16 April 1915. On 13 December 1915 Cherbourg was advised that the superstructures of this submarine and *Gustave Zédé* were to be reduced, and *Néréide* entered service with the revised configuration.

In 1921-22 *Néréide* underwent major modifications at Toulon similar to those performed on *Gustave Zédé* in 1922-24 except that there was no steam machinery to remove. The cylinders of her diesel engine were replaced with eight new ones made by Schneider to increase their rated power from 1,200hp to 1,800hp (3,600hp for two engines). They gave much trouble during trials and were accepted limited to 900hp each. She also received new batteries, an enlarged conning tower with a navigating bridge, and a trainable twin torpedo tube mount replacing the single tubes under the after end of the walking deck.

*The characteristics are based on a devis dated 31.10.1916.*

**Dimensions & tons:** 74.000m oa, 73.270m wl, 74.000m pp x 6.000m ext & wl (6.994m over bow planes). 850.276t disp (surfaced) 1,087.879t (submerged). Draught: 3.753m mean, 4.1m aft. Men: 43 including 3 officers. Reserve buoyancy: 21.8%

**Machinery:**

(surfaced) 4,800hp (designed), 2,400hp at 350rpm (as downgraded). Speed 20kts (designed), 16kts (as downgraded). Trials 17.3kts, (2.6.1916) 18.323kts at 291.2rpm, (10.6.1916) 2,335hp = 16.885kts

The submarine *Néréide* entering Brest shortly after World War I (moving from right to left). The reason for displaying her name in oversized letters on the breakwater is unknown. *(NHHC, NH-55746)*

The submarines *Néréide* (left, bow out) and *Andromaque* (centre, bow in) at Cherbourg in 1916 or 1917. *(NHHC, NH-55857)*

at 285.87rpm. 2 screws. 2 two-cycle diesels engines with 8 cylinders of 0.450m diameter. 56.700t oil (70,000 litres). Range (trials) 1,125/2,700nm @ 14.17kts without/with fuel surcharge.
(submerged) 1,640hp at 240rpm. Speed 11kts (designed). Trials (24.6.1916) 1,414hp (effective) = 10.503kts at 217.5rpm. 2 electric motors. Batteries 158.2 tons. Range (trials) 359nm @ 2.762kts.

**Torpedoes:** 2 internal bow tubes, 2 watertight fixed tubes under the walking deck forward, 2 Simonot trainable launchers under the walking deck forward of the deck gun, and 2 Simonot trainable launchers under the walking deck aft of the conning tower, all for 450mm M1911V torpedoes. During the 1922 refit the after Simonot trainable launchers were replaced with a trainable twin tube mount. **Guns:** 1 x 75mm M1897 AA on deck forward and a M1907 machine gun.

*Néréide* (Q93)  Cherbourg Dyd/Schneider, Creusot
On list 1.1911. Ord: 14.2.1911. K: 11.1.1912. L: 9.5.1914.
   Comm: 24.5.1914 (trials), 31.10.1916 (full).
Budget 1911. Named by 1.1911. First underway trials of electric motors 28.5.1914. Assigned to the 2nd Mediterranean Squadron upon entry in service. In the Brittany submarine squadron 1.1918. Updated at Toulon after the war, including with new cylinders for the diesels. First diesel trials on 18.10.1922 after 1921-22 refit produced incidents and approval was given on 30.3.1923 to suspend official trials and place her in service with power limited to 900hp instead of 1,800hp per diesel. Ordered to reserve at Toulon 20.6.1931. Condemned 24.7.1935 (decision promulgated 27.8.1935). Sold 10.12.1936 at Toulon to M. Van Acker to BU. She had been sunk during experiments and the buyer was to raise her within 6 months.

**Expanded submarine construction 1912-1914**
The submarine programme expanded again in the 1912 budget (submitted 12 July 1911), which contained Q94-102. The 1913 budget (submitted 29 March 1912) contained three unnumbered 800-ton submarines, which became the two smaller Q103-4 in 1914, and the 1914 budget (submitted 4 November 1913 and 15 January 1914) added Q105-114.

**AMPHITRITE Class.** *Sous-marins (Sous-marins garde-côtes et de blocus).* Double hull, diesel surface propulsion. Designed by Hutter. To *Sous-marins de 2e classe* 1.1923.

The design for this unusually large class (for its time) was the first by Hutter to be accepted after he joined the *Section technique* in December

1910. The boats were called the modified *Clorinde* type, the only significant modifications being the widening of the hull lines in the stern to gain a higher speed on the surface and the reduction to two pairs of horizontal planes instead of three, the forward and midship pairs being replaced by a set called 'middle-forward' placed about a quarter of the ship's length aft of the bow. They offered no real progress over the *Brumaire* type, whose operational range on the surface was considerably greater. They encountered the same problems with their two-cycle 650hp diesels as did the *Clorinde*s. All eight submarines were ordered on 8 January 1912. The decision was made on 11 September 1915 to convert to minelayers the last boat at Rochefort (Q95) and the last one at Toulon (Q99), whose engines at Indret had been suspended for more important war work. These two boats were ordered on 15 March 1916 to be taken to Le Havre after launch for conversion to minelaying submarines and are listed here as a separate class.

The diesels in *Amphitrite* were built under a contract of 6 September 1911 by the Société des Moteurs Sabathé, a subsidiary of the Forges de la Chaléassière at Saint Étienne. They were 2-cycle engines with 6 cylinders of 0.310m diameter and 0.390m stroke. They were designed to deliver a total of 1,300hp at 400rpm. Trials on 16 November 1915 produced 615hp for 12.7 knots at 324rpm. Trials on 15 June 1917 after lengthy repairs produced the results shown below.

The diesels in *Andromaque* and *Ariane* were built by A.C. Loire at Saint Denis under a contract of 6 September 1911. They had 8 cylinders and were designed to deliver a total of 1,300hp at 400rpm. They were built under license from MAN which led to delays, engines for both were accepted at the factory 14 April 1915 without ever producing their designed power.

The diesels of *Artémis, Aréthuse,* and *Atalante* were built by Schneider, also under a contract of 6 September 1911. They were 2-cycle engines with 6 cylinders of 0.300m diameter and 0.360m stroke. They were designed to deliver a total of 1,300hp at 400rpm. They gave the best results of the three types. The fuel in all six boats was kerosene.

*The characteristics are based on a devis for* Amphitrite *dated 11.2.1918.*
**Dimensions & tons:** 52.980m wl, 53.950m pp (end to end) x 5.410m ext (6.840m outside forward horizontal planes). 418,316t disp (surfaced), 614.404t (submerged). Draught: 3.307m mean, 3.458m aft.

Men: 27 including 2 officers. Reserve buoyancy: 31.9%
**Machinery:**
(surfaced) 1,300hp at 400rpm (designed), 800hp (realised). Speed 15kts (designed), 12-13kts (realised). Trials (*Amphitrite*, 15.6.1917, 90% power) 1,170hp = 14.56kts at 400.8rpm. 2 screws. 2 diesel engines (Chaléassière two-cycle in Q94, Schneider two-cycle in Q96-98, and MAN-Loire two-cycle in Q100-101). 12.184t oil (kerosene) (14,769 litres). Range (trials, *Amphitrite*) 785.8kts @ 13.03kts
(submerged) 700hp at 320rpm. Speed 9.5kts. 2 electric motors. Batteries 77.5 tons. Range 100nm @ 5kts
**Torpedoes:** Two fixed watertight tubes under the walking deck near the bow aimed forward at 4°25' off the axis (ordered on 21.4.1916 to replace the fixed launch cages originally there), 6 Drzewiecki trainable launchers under the walking deck, 2 forward of the conning tower, 2 amidships and 2 aft. A circular of 20.6.1921 replaced the after pair of Drzewiecki trainable launchers with fixed launch cages. These were all for 450mm M1906 torpedoes except for M1911V in *Artemis*.
**Guns:** 1 x 47mm M1885 QF aft of the conning tower (replaced after the war at least in *Atalante* and *Amphitrite* by a 75mm) and a M1907 machine gun.

*Amphitrite* (Q94) Rochefort Dyd/Chaléassière, Saint Étienne.
On list 1.1913. Ord: 8.1.1912. K: 25.11.1912. L: 9.6.1914.
    Comm: 24.11.1915 and 9.3.1917 (trials), 6.2.1918 (full).
Budget 1912. Named 30.5.1913. Electric motors installed 22.9.1914 to 28.6.1915, installation of diesel engines begun 8.7.1915. Decomm. 31.8.1916 for repairs to the diesels and crew transferred to *Clorinde*. First static trials of diesels after repairs 26.5.1917. Assigned to the Brittany submarine squadron 1.1918 (still running trials), assigned to Cherbourg on commissioning 6.2.1918. Placed in reduced availability 1.11.1925 because of the condition of her diesels, post-repair trials 5.1927 satisfactory but to reserve 1.10.1927. Renamed *Amphitrite II* 20.4.1928. To special reserve 24.1.1931 because of condition of ballast tanks. *Conseil supérieur* rejected proposal to condemn 22.6.1932. Condemned 24.7.1935 (decision promulgated 27.8.1935). Sold 14.5.1936 at Brest to MM. L'Hermitte frères.

*Artémis* (Q96) Toulon Dyd/Schneider, Creusot
On list 1.1913. Ord: 8.1.1912. K: 1.4.1912. L: 14.10.1915.
    Comm: 15.10.1915 (trials), 8.5.1916 (full).
Budget 1912. Named 30.5.1913. Official underway trials 23.10.1915. Last trials 1.5.1916. Diesels accepted 18.11.1916. Adriatic operations 1916-1918. In the 1st submarine squadron at Brindisi 1.1918. Refitted at Bizerte in 1923 and 12.1924 to 7.1925 including machinery overhauls and replacement of after Drzewiecki trainable launchers with fixed launch cages. Diesels and compressors failed 19.11.1925. Decision 14.12.1926 to decommission and recommend condemnation. Struck 5.5.1927. Sold 6.10.1927 to MM. Boccara, Scalabrino & Cie of Tunis.

*Aréthuse* (Q97) Toulon Dyd/Schneider, Creusot.
On list 1.1913. Ord: 8.1.1912. K: 14.6.1912. L: 20.4.1916.
    Comm: 19.4.1916 (trials), 10.7.1916 (full).
Budget 1912. Named 30.5.1913. 1st trials of electric motors 24.4.1916. Underway trials 2.5.1916. Adriatic operations 1916-1918. In the 1st submarine squadron at Brindisi 1.1918. Refitted 1924-25 including replacement of after Drzewiecki trainable launchers with fixed launch cages but one diesel still unreliable. Condemnation proposed 22.12.1926, one diesel needing a total rebuild. Condemned 8.3.1927. Sold 2.5.1929 at Bizerte by the Domaines to MM. Boccara, Scalabrino & Cie of Tunis to BU.

*Atalante* (Q98) Toulon Dyd/Schneider, Creusot.
On list 1.1913. Ord: 8.1.1912. K: 23.9.1912. L: 15.4.1915.
    Comm: 14.4.1915 (trials), 22.12.1915 (full).

Budget 1912. Named 30.5.1913. Underway trials 4.6.1915. Adriatic operations 1916-1918. In the 1st submarine squadron at Brindisi 1.1918. Refit at FCM La Seyne 1922-23 included replacement of after Drzewiecki trainable launchers with fixed launch cages and her 47mm gun with a 75mm. Condemnation envisaged 23.3.1927. Renamed *Atalante II* 20.4.1928. Battery assigned to *Joëssel* 4.7.1928. Condemnation proposed 1.7.1932. Condemned 24.7.1935 (decision promulgated 27.8.1935). Sold 14.2.1936 at Bizerte to MM. Boccara, Scalabrino & Cie of Tunis to BU.

*Ariane* (Q100) Cherbourg Dyd/A.C. Loire, Saint Denis.
On list 1.1913. Ord: 8.1.1912. K: 12.8.1912. L: 5.9.1914.
    Comm: 6.9.1914 (trials), 20.4.1916 (full).
Budget 1912. Named 30.5.1913. 1st trials of electric motors 8.9.1914, diesel trials begun 14.7.1915, full power trial 8.12.1915. Adriatic operations 1916-1917. Sunk 19.6.1917 by two torpedoes from the Austrian *U-62*, ex German *UC-27*, east of Cape Bon, Tunisia. Eight survivors were rescued by the escorting torpedo boat *Bourrasque* which *Ariane* had been following in line ahead while searching for enemy submarines.

*Andromaque* (Q101) Cherbourg Dyd/A.C. Loire, Saint Denis.
On list 1.1913. Ord: 8.1.1912. K: 23.10.1912. L: 13.2.1915.
    Comm: 29.1.1915 (first), 22.6.1916 (full).
Budget 1912. Probably named 30.5.1913. 1st trials of diesels 4.1.1916. With the school for underwater navigation (ENSM) at Toulon 1.1918. Received an extension of operating range instead of a full overhaul 11.1922. Retained her 47mm gun and after Drzewiecki trainable launchers to the end. Condemned 25.10.1926. Hull used 23.12.1927 to protect the gates of the Vauban basins at Toulon. Sold 30.5.1928 to M. Bruneau at Toulon to BU, but still carried in the 1.1929 and 1.1930 fleet list as for sale at Toulon.

---

*ASTRÉE* **Class (Minelaying conversions).** *Sous-marins mouilleurs de mines* 1.3.1920. Double hull, diesel surface propulsion. Design by Hutter modified for minelaying by Normand.

The construction of the last *Amphitrite* class submarine at Rochefort (*Astrée*) and the last one at Toulon (*Amaranthe*) had been interrupted when construction of their two-cycle MAN diesels that had been ordered on 8 September 1911 at Indret to plans purchased from A.C. Loire at Saint Denis had been stopped because of more urgent war work. In 1915 the Naval General Staff indicated that minelaying submarines would be useful for certain special missions, and the decision was made on 11 September 1915 to convert these two boats to minelayers. On 15 March 1916 Augustin Normand received a contract to convert them with the Normand-Fenaux minelaying system and to complete and install their Indret diesels, and the incomplete boats were towed to Le Havre for conversion. However, reliable sources differ on the attributions of the diesels. The *devis d'armement* for both subs show the diesels as all completed by Augustin Normand. A postwar report on war lessons shows the engines of *Astrée* as completed by Normand and those of *Amaranthe* by A.C. Loire, Saint Denis. A third version, also from official documents, shows on each boat one Indret/Normand engine to port and one A.C. Loire St. Denis engine to starboard. The instructions from A.C. Loire, Saint Denis for operating the diesels supplied by them for *Clorinde, Cornélie, Andromaque,* and *Ariane* also applied to *Astrée* and *Amaranthe*. Cherbourg on 8 June 1918 supplied instructions for the alterations made by Indret and Normand.

    A circular of 31 March 1918 on the installation of 75mm guns on all the submarines of the *Clorinde* and modified *Clorinde* (*Amphitrite*) classes stated that this change would not be made on the two minelaying submarines. Their gun armament was limited to a M1907 machine gun (*mitrailleuse*). The six side torpedo tubes on the *Amphitrite* class were also suppressed in the minelayers, leaving them with two fixed tubes forward.

For minelaying these boats had ten vertical free-flooding mine launch tubes in enlarged side ballast tanks amidships outboard of the conning tower, five closely spaced per side. Each contained one spherical Sautter-Harlé mine 0.770m in diameter with a charge of 60kg of nitrocellulose. The larger tanks also allowed increasing the diesel fuel supply from 13 tons to 18 tons.

**Dimensions & tons:** 52.980m wl, 53.950m pp (end to end) x 5.834m wl (6.436m outside bow planes). 452.264t disp (surfaced, trials), 609.409t (submerged, trials). Draught: 3.460m mean (trials). Men: 29 including 2 officers. Reserve buoyancy: 25.8%. Beam of *Amarante* was 5.842m wl (6.600m outside bow planes)

**Machinery:**
(surfaced) 1,300hp (designed), 800hp (realised). Speed 15kts (designed), 12-13kts (realised). Trials (*Amaranthe*, 13.9.1917) 846.10hp = 12.164kts at 359.93rpm, (*Astrée*, 28.3.1918) 846hp = 11.967kts at 336.6rpm. 2 screws. 2 two-cycle MAN diesel engines with 8 cylinders. 19.440kg (normal) oil. Range (trials) 1,747nm @ 7,5kts.
(submerged) 700hp at 320rpm. Speed 9.5kts. Trials (*Astrée*, 5.4.1918) 623.74hp (effective, 672.86 indicated) = 7.852kts at 280.44rpm. 2 electric motors. Batteries 80 tons. Range (trials) 107.6nm @ 4.036kts.
**Torpedoes:** 2 fixed watertight torpedo tubes under the walking deck near the bow aimed forward at 6°34' off the axis in *Astrée* and 6°54' in *Amaranthe*. These were for 450mm torpedoes M1909 in *Astrée* and M1906 in *Amaranthe*. **Mines:** Ten vertical mine launch tubes with ten mines. **Guns:** One M1907 machine gun

*Astrée* (Q95) Rochefort Dyd/Indret
On list 1.1913. Ord: 8.1.1912. K: 25.11.1912. L: 6.12.1915.
    Comm: 10.8.1917 (trials), 11.6.1918 (full)
Budget 1912. Named 30.5.1913. Towed to Le Havre 1916 after launch. Converted to minelayer 1916-17. Diesels completed by Normand 5.10.1916. First static diesel trials 26.10.1917. Assigned to the Submarine Centre at Cherbourg 1.1918 (still running trials). Diesel trials 26.3.1918. Minelaying trials 4.1918. Sent from Cherbourg to Toulon a few months before the end of the war for use at Brindisi but no wartime operations there. The bad performance of her diesels condemned her to spend much of her time in reduced availability pierside, inactivity that caused premature corrosion of the ballast tanks. Decomm. 16.5.1928. Struck 9.11.1928. Replaced *Arago* 28.1.1930 as a floating dock gate for the basin for tankers at Toulon. Sale 25.7.1930 at Toulon to the Société de Matériel Naval du Midi fell through, sold 26.11.1930.

*Amaranthe* (*Amarante*) (Q99) Toulon Dyd/Indret
On list 1.1913. Ord: 8.1.1912. K: 3.12.1912. L: 11.11.1915. Comm: c3.1917 (trials), 14.1.1918 (full).
Budget 1912. Named 30.5.1913. Towed to Le Havre 1916 after launch. Converted to minelayer 1916-17. First static diesel trials 26.5.1917. Minelaying trials 11.8.1917. Underway diesel trials 13.9.1917 & 30.10.1917. Sub accepted 28.11.1917. Sent from Cherbourg to Toulon for use at Brindisi. Assigned to the 1st submarine squadron at Brindisi 1.1918 (still running trials). Adriatic operations 8-11.1918. Numerous problems with diesels noted 25.10.1918. Condemnation proposed 31.8.1919, suspended 16.10.1919. Diesels in very bad condition by 1925. Struck 3.2.1925. Battery to be transferred ashore, torpedo tubes to be reused in *Dupuy de Lome* and *Sané*, and diesels turned over to the Domaines for disposal. For sale at Toulon 1924-1928. Hull used 23.10.1927 to protect the gates of the Vauban basins. Sold 30.5.1928 to M. Bruneau of Toulon.

---

**BELLONE Class.** *Sous-marins* (*Sous-marins garde-côtes et de blocus agrandis*). Double hull, diesel surface propulsion. Designed by Hutter. To *Sous-marins de 2e classe* 1.1923.

Construction of all three boats of this new class was ordered on 26 June 1912. The order to begin construction of the two boats at Toulon was given on 3 October 1912 effective 1 January 1913. These were submarines derived from *Clorinde* with high reserve buoyancy and with their displacement increased to improve habitability. (The habitability improvements, however, were not achieved because of poorly designed internal arrangements.) The diameter of the pressure hull was increased enough to allow better placement of the batteries, longer periscopes, and more powerful diesels. The diesels were designed for 1,800hp and a speed of 17 knots instead of 1,300hp and 15 knots in predecessor classes, but as in those classes they failed to develop their designed power or speed and lengthy problems with the diesels prevented their participation in the war. Their designed range on the surface at 10 knots was 2,300nm. Like all of the smaller French submarines since the *Pluviôse* class they had a totally unprotected navigation platform above a small kiosk, although an enlarged conning tower with a navigating bridge was later fitted. They were not identical sisters – Rochefort's *Bellone* had more tapered lines aft than the two Toulon boats.

The diesels of *Bellone* and *Hermione* were supplied by the Société des moteurs Sabathé, which was a subsidiary of the Forges de la Chaléassière at Saint Étienne, under a contract of 18 September 1912, and those of *Gorgone* were Sulzer two-cycle diesels supplied by the Forges et Chantiers de la Méditerranée at Le Havre by a contract of the same date. The commander of *Hermione* noted on 5 December 1918 that his boat's diesels were pushed too hard at 900hp each and that they should not be pushed beyond 650hp. The diesels of *Gorgone* had three significant failures in 1917 alone.

**Dimensions & tons:** 60.600m oa, 59.950m wl x 5.404m ext & wl (6.850m outside bow planes). 539.771t disp (surfaced), 803.850t (submerged). Draught: 3.410m mean, 3.787m aft. Men: 28 including 3 officers. Reserve buoyancy: 32.9%
**Machinery:**
(surfaced) 1,800hp (designed), 1,640hp at 380rpm (realised). Speed 17kts (designed) 15kts (realised). Trials (*Bellone*, 12.9.1916) 1,600hp = 15.867kts at 360.6rpm. 2 screws. 2 two-cycle diesel engines (Sulzer in *Gorgone*, Sabathé in others) with 6 cylinders of 0.350m diameter and 0.390m stroke (0.370m and 0.380m in *Gorgone*). Range (trials) 1,858.5nm @ 11.999kts.
(submerged) 800hp (effective). Speed 9.5kts. Trials (5.1917) 449.4hp = 8.240kts at 221.45rpm. 2 electric motors. Batteries 97.3 tons. Range 100nm @ 5kts.
**Torpedoes:** 2 internal bow tubes at the waterline aimed at 5°45' off the axis, 4 Simonot trainable launchers (Drzewiecki trainable launchers in *Bellone* according to her 1917 devis), on the sides under the walking deck, one pair forward of the conning tower and one abreast of it, 2 fixed launch cages aft aimed aft at 5°10' off the axis. All launchers were for 450mm torpedoes (M1906M in *Bellone*, M1911V in the others). The fixed launch cages were later replaced with watertight tubes. **Guns:** 1 x 75mm gun M1897G on a disappearing mount (a fixed mount in *Gorgone*) was added in 1918 aft of the conning tower. *Hermione* had her 75mm gun moved forward of the conning tower c1925. They also carried a M1907 machine gun

*Bellone* (Q102) Rochefort Dyd/Chaléassière, Saint Étienne
On list 1.1913. Ord: 8.1912. K: 23.4.1913. L: 8.7.1914.
    Comm: 22.4.1915 (trials), 12.7.1917 (full).
Budget 1912. Named 30.5.1913. Trials 3.10.1916 to 12.7.1917. Assigned to the Brittany submarine squadron 1.1918 (still running trials). Refitted at Brest in 1924 and again in 1925-26. To Cherbourg 1928 for pre-inactivation overhaul, to reserve at Cherbourg 1929. Condemnation proposed 2.6.1933. Condemned 29.7.1935 (decision promulgated 27.8.1935). Sold 18.5.1936 at Brest to M. L'Hermitte to BU.

The submarine *Gorgone* (or possibly *Hermione* on trials) at Toulon during World War I. The battleship *France* is in the left background. *(NHHC, NH-55753)*

**Hermione** (Q103) Toulon Dyd/Chaléassière, Saint Étienne
On list 1.1913. Ord: 3.10.1912 effective 1.1.1913. K: 14.4.1913.
  L: 15.3.1917. Comm: 1917 (trials), 27.4.1918 (full)
Budget 1913. Named 30.5.1913. Construction suspended from late
  8.1914 to late 11.1915. Assigned to the Brittany submarine squadron
  1.1918 (still running trials). Official underway trial 15.1.1918.
  Summary trial and trial results accepted 24.4.1918. Major refit completed at Brest 26.3.1922, refitted again 1927. Sent to Cherbourg
  9.1930 to be placed in reserve after repairs. Condemnation proposed
  12.6.1933. Condemned 29.7.1935 (decision promulgated 27.8.1935).
  Sold 6.8.1936 to M. L'Hermitte frères at Brest.

**Gorgone** (Q104) Toulon Dyd/F.C. Méditerranée, Le Havre.
On list 1.1913. Ord: 3.10.1912 effective 1.1.1913. K: 2.6.1913.
  L: 23.11.1915. Comm: 22.10.1915 (trials), 12.10.1916 (full)
Budget 1913. Named 30.5.1913. Construction suspended from
  1.10.1914 to 15.2.1915. Trials 14.2.1916-6.11.1916. Adriatic operations 12.1916 to 11.1917. Under repair at Toulon 1.1918. Refitted
  1921-22 and 1923-24. To Cherbourg and ordered placed in reserve
  10.1.1929. To special reserve 1.7.1931. Condemnation proposed at
  Brest 4.6.1932. Condemned 24.7.1935 (decision promulgated
  27.8.1935). Sold 18.5.1936 at Brest to L'Hermitte Frères.

---

**DUPUY DE LÔME Class.** *Sous-marins (Sous-marins de haute mer)*.
Double hull, steam surface propulsion (later diesel). Designed by Hutter.
To *Sous-marins de 1re classe* 1.1923.

The urgent demand for high surface speeds led Hutter, now in the *Section technique*, to produce a design to specifications similar to those for Simonot's *Gustave Zédé*. It had identical steam propulsion on the surface, electric motors and batteries of the same power, and an identical torpedo armament. However, Hutter's design had more reserve buoyancy (34% vice 23%), different hull lines, circular sections for a stronger pressure hull, and low superstructures rather than the high ones soon cut back in *Gustave Zédé*. The steam engines were built by Delaunay-Belleville under a contract of 15 January 1913 while those of *Sané* were built by the same firm under a contract of 21 January 1913. A 47mm AA gun was added to the design aft of the superstructure on 24 August 1915 and was replaced by a 75mm gun on 19 November 1915. Both were assigned to the Morocco squadron when they entered active service in 1918.

After the war the steam plants in each were replaced with German

diesels, Germania Krupp in *Dupuy de Lôme* and Körting in *Sané*, increasing their operational range. *Dupuy de Lôme* also received 4 electric motors from the German submarine *U-91*. Their superstructure was rebuilt, including a new arrangement of torpedo tubes under a higher walking deck and a larger conning tower with a navigating bridge. *Sané* dived to 50 metres on 11 February 1926. Her steam engine was reused in the Yangtse gunboat *Francis Garnier* (1927).

**Dimensions & tons (original with steam):** 75.000m oa, 74.615m wl, 75.000m pp x 6.386m wl (7.900m outside bow horizontal planes). 852.924 tons disp (surfaced, *DdeL*), 853.7t (*Sané*), 1,291.003t (submerged) (*DdeL*), 1,291.779t (*Sané*). Draught: 3.609m mean, 4.046m aft. Men: 41 including 3 officers. Reserve buoyancy: 33.9%

**Machinery:**
(surfaced, steam, 1915) 4,000ihp designed at 340rpm and 18kg/cm$^2$ boiler pressure (17kg/cm$^2$ at the engines). Speed 19kts. Trials (*Sané*, 20.4.1916) 3,366.1ihp = 18.02kts at 322.1rpm and 18kg/cm$^2$ boiler pressure. 2 screws. 2 vertical triple expansion engines with 3 cylinders. 2 Du Temple return-flame boilers. Oil fired (*pétrole R*, density 0.92). Range (trials) 960nm @ 14.2kts.
(surfaced, diesel, 1925) 2,400hp at 420rpm. Trials (*Sané*) 13.7kts at 346rpm. 2 screws. 2 two-cycle Germania-Krupp diesel engines in *Dupuy de Lôme* with 6 cylinders of 0.390m diameter and 0.550m stroke and 2 MAN four-cycle diesel engines in *Sané* with 6 cylinders of 0.45m diameter and 0.420m stroke. Range (*Sané*) 2,340nm @ 13.7kts with normal fuel and 4,000nm with fuel surcharge.
(submerged) 1,640hp at 270rpm. Speed 11kts. Trials (*Sané*, 16.7.1916) 1,653.6hp = 10.936kts at 241.1rpm. 2 electric motors. Batteries 156.0 tons. Range (trials) 134.674nm @ 5.78kts.

**Torpedoes:**
(1915) 2 internal bow tubes aimed at 3 degrees off the axis, 2 Simonot trainable launchers forward on the sides under the walking deck, 2 Simonot trainable launchers on each side of the conning tower under the walking deck, 2 fixed launch cages (later replaced with watertight tubes) in the after end of the superstructure under the walking deck aimed aft at 7°30' off the axis. All tubes were for 450mm M1911V torpedoes. **Guns:** 1 x 47mm was ordered on 10/14.8.1915 to be fitted but was ordered on 19.11.1915 to be replaced with 1 x 75mm, 1 x 75mm (light submarine gun) was ordered on 21.4.1916 to be fitted on the walking deck aft of the amidships breastwork on a disappearing mount. On 13.9.1917 1 x 65mm/50 M1888-91 was ordered added to *Sané* forward of the breastwork; it was later replaced by a 75mm Army gun. A 7mm M1907 machine gun was also carried.
(1925) 2 internal bow tubes aimed at 2°30' off the axis, 2 fixed exterior watertight tubes under the walking deck forward aimed forward at 7°18' off the axis, 2 trainable exterior watertight tubes under each side of the walking deck aft of the conning tower, and 2 fixed exterior watertight tubes under the raised desk aft aimed aft at 6°29' off the axis. **Guns:** 1 x 75mm light submarine gun on the walking deck forward of the conning tower on a disappearing mount, 1 x 75mm M1897G aft of the trainable torpedo tubes on a fixed M1916 mount. A M1907 Hotchkiss machine gun was also carried.

**Dupuy de Lôme** (Q105) Toulon Dyd/Delaunay-Belleville, Saint Denis.
On list 1.1913. Ord: 28.2.1913. K: 1.9.1913. L: 9.9.1915.
  Comm: 8.9.1915 (trials), 22.7.1916 (full).
Budget 1913 (late addition). Probably named 30.5.1913. Underway trials
  of electric motors 7.10.1915. First boiler lit off 11.10.1915. Deep dive
  trials 22.6.1916. Assigned to the Morocco squadron 1.1.1918.
  Updated and re-engined at FCM La Seyne under a contract of
  9.8.1923 with completion due 10.2.1924. Received two Germania
  Krupp two-cycle 6-cylinder diesels from the German submarine *U-113*
  that were modified by A.C. Loire, Saint Denis. To Cherbourg for
  reconditioning 25.2.1930. Condemnation proposed 12.6.1933.

Condemned 29.7.1935 (decision promulgated 27.8.1935). Sold 6.8.1938 at Toulon to BU.

*Sané* (Q106)  Toulon Dyd/Delaunay-Belleville, Saint Denis.
On list 1.1913. Ord: 28.2.1913. K: 29.12.1913. L: 27.1.1916.
  Comm: 26.1.1916 (trials), 9.1916 (full)
Budget 1913 (late addition). Named 30.5.1913. First boiler lit off 5.2.1916, static trials of electric and steam motors 14.2.1916, underway trials of electric motors 18.2.1916, trials of motors after inspections 21.7.1916, final trial (*essai récapulatif*) 8.8.1916. Assigned to Morocco squadron 1.1.1918. Updated and re-engined at FCM La Seyne 1923-1925, receiving two Körting diesels from the German submarine *U-121* whose modification at Indret was reported completed 6.1.1923. Refit work by FCM La Seyne accepted 10.12.1925. Major overhaul of diesels at Brest 3.10.1929 to 20.6.1930. Assignment to Saigon 6.1930 abandoned because of numerous faults, proposal of 9.1930 to send from Brest to Toulon to replace *Néréïde* also abandoned. Work to place her in conservation status begun at Brest 19.3.1931 and completed at Cherbourg 31.7.1931. By this time her diesels were unusable because spare parts were unavailable. Condemned 24.7.1935 (decision promulgated 27.8.1935). Towed from Landévennec to Brest 15.6.1936 for sale. Sold 6.8.1938 at Brest to BU.

---

**DIANE Class.** *Sous-marins* (*Sous-marins garde-côtes et de blocus* agrandi). Double hull, diesel surface propulsion. Designed by Simonot. To *Sous-marins de 1ʳᵉ classe* 1.1923.

Upset by the decision to replace the diesels in his *Gustave Zédé* with steam machinery, Simonot presented a new design based on *Gustave Zédé* with dimensions scaled down by a factor of 0.92 and using 900hp Sulzer diesels adapted from those in *Gorgone*, which appeared reliable, instead of steam engines. Instead of the hull sections being rigorously circular as in the *Clorinde* and *Bellone* types, they were slightly pear shaped in the new design, being slightly wider at the bottom. Compared to the *Bellone* type the displacement was increased from 523 to 633 tons, primarily to increase the boat's submerged speed from 9.5 to 11.5 knots and the submerged range at 5 knots was increased from 100nm to 130nm. The designed reserve buoyancy was 29%. The torpedo armament was increased from 8 to 10 launchers including two bow tubes, two fixed launch cages firing forward, four Simonot trainable launchers on the sides, and two fixed launch cages aimed aft. (The fixed launch cages were replaced with watertight tubes during the war.) One 75mm M1897 gun with high angle capability and a machine gun were ordered on 19 November 1915 to be added. A decision to reduce the superstructures was dated 2 May 1915 and on 6 October 1915 it was decided to install a 75mm gun.

Simonot designed this class for the usual 900hp diesels but left room for a 1,100hp type then being built by Schneider for Japan. The diesels and electric motors of *Diane* were ordered on 12 February 1913 from the Société des moteurs Sabathé (a subsidiary of the Forges de la Chaléassière at Saint Étienne). These fell behind schedule and on 7 October 1915 the British Admiralty agreed to sell two 800hp Vickers diesels built by Harland & Wolff in Belfast for use in *Diane*. (The Chaléassière diesels originally ordered for *Diane* ran factory trials on 14 May 1918 and were used instead in the gunboat *Guerrière*, ordered in November 1917.) *Daphné* encountered the same problems as did the *Bellone*s with her Sulzer two-cycle 900hp diesels built by the Forges et Chantiers de la Méditerranée at Le Havre under a contract of 12 February 1913. In accordance with a Ministerial order of 22 December 1915 these diesels were not pushed above 820hp.

The surviving unit of the class, *Daphné*, received a thorough refit at Brest between December 1924 and March 1925. The main work was on the diesels, which were completely overhauled. Other work included adding a full navigating bridge to the conning tower and otherwise enlarging the

superstructure, doubling her fuel supply from 20,000 litres to 42,000 litres, doubling her stores of motor oil, compressed air, and water, and replacing the disappearing mounting of her 75mm gun with a fixed mounting.

**Dimensions & tons:** 68.00m oa, 67.750m wl, 68.00m pp x 5.530m ext & wl (7.038 over bow planes). 673.101t disp (surfaced), 900.722t (submerged). Draught: 3.558m mean. Men: 34 including 3 officers. Reserve buoyancy: 25.3%.
**Machinery:**
(surfaced, in *Daphné*): 1,800hp at 380rpm (designed), 1,640hp (realised). Speed 17kts (designed), 15kts (realised). Trials (c5.1916) 1,620hp = 15kts. 2 screws. 2 Sulzer two-cycle diesel engines with 6 cylinders. 27,350 litres/22.150t oil (normal), 45,240 litres/36.645t (surcharge). Range (trials 23.9.1916) 1,250nm @ 13.7kts (normal), 2,600nm or more (surcharge).
(surfaced, in *Diane*): 1,600hp. 2 Vickers four-cycle diesel engines with 8 cylinders using solid injection built by Harland & Wolff, Belfast, substituted for original Sabathé/Chaléassière diesels, ratings and trial results unknown.
(submerged) 1,400hp at 340rpm. Speed 11.5kts. Trials 10.952kts. 2 electric motors. Batteries 131 tons. Range (trials) 110nm @ 5kts.
**Torpedoes:** 2 internal bow tubes at the waterline aimed at 3°30' off the axis, 2 exterior bow tubes (originally fixed launch cages) under the forward end of the walking deck aimed at 9 degrees off the axis, 4 Simonot trainable launchers on the sides under the walking deck of which two were forward of the conning tower and two aft of it, 2 exterior tubes (originally fixed launch cages) in the stern under the after end of the walking deck aimed directly aft, all for 450mm M1911V torpedoes. **Guns:** 1 x 75mm M1897G Army field gun on a high-angle disappearing mount aft of the conning tower plus a M1907 Hotchkiss machine gun.

*Diane* (Q107)  Cherbourg Dyd/Harland & Wolff, Belfast.
On list 1.1913. Ord: 12.11.1912 effective 1.1.1913. K: 16.3.1913. L: 30.9.1916. Comm: c12.1916 (trials), 31.3.1917 (full).
Budget 1913 (late addition). Named 30.5.1913. Preliminary diesel trials 7.12.1916. Deep dive trials 17.1.1917 (to 35 metres for 5 minutes, leaks and cracks appeared at 20 metres). Official speed trials 27.3.1917 followed by nearly three months of unavailability. Assigned 31.8.1917 to the 3ʳᵈ submarine squadron of the Brittany patrol division at Brest. In the Brittany submarine squadron 1.1918. Used to escort large sailing ships to the Azores. Exploded and lost with all hands 11.2.1918 around 200 miles WSW of Ireland while escorting the 4-masted steel-hulled barque *Quevilly* to the Azores. Loss assessed to be a battery explosion because no German submarine claimed credit.

*Note:* The steel-hulled **Quevilly**, which carried oil cargo and had auxiliary diesel propulsion, duly arrived in the Azores on 21 February 1918 and was loaned to the U.S. Navy's Naval Overseas Transportation Service to serve as a station oil tanker there. She remained a French vessel operated by a French crew and was released to her owner by NOTS on 12 April 1919. Renamed **Deodata** in 1925, her rig was removed. She was mined by the German submarine U-19 on 21 October 1939.

*Daphné* (Q108)  Cherbourg Dyd/F.C. Méditerranée, Le Havre.
On list 1.1913. Ord: 12.11.1912 effective 1.1.1913. K: 3.9.1913. L: 25.10.1915. Comm: c11.1915 (trials), 7.1916 (full).
Budget 1913 (late addition). Named 30.5.1913. Construction interrupted 8.1914 to 4.1915. Launched without diesels on board. First trials with electric motors 11.11.1915. Diesels installation begun 15.1.1916, underway diesel trials 9.5.1916 to 1.6.1916. Acceptance of trial results delayed to 28.10.1916. Joined the 3ʳᵈ submarine squadron of the Brittany patrol division at Brest 6.1917. In the Brittany submarine squadron 1.1918. Refitted at Brest 1924-25. To Bizerte 10.1926. To normal reserve at Toulon 21.1.1931. Condemnation report 28.5.1934.

The submarine *Daphné*, which became operational in June 1917 and was based at Brest for the rest of the war. Her sister *Diane* was lost to a probable battery explosion at sea in February 1918. *(NHHC from Nimitz collection, NH-62461)*

Condemned 24.7.1935, (decision promulgated 27.8.1935). Sold 25.11.1936 at Toulon to MM Bonturi Frères to BU.

*JOËSSEL* **Class.** *Sous-marins* (*Sous-marins de haute mer*). Double hull, diesel surface propulsion (originally steam). Designed by Simonot. To *Sous-marins de 1ʳᵉ classe* 1.1923.

On 25 March 1913 Cherbourg submitted a design to Paris by its chief of new construction, Simonot, for a derivative of the steam-propelled submarines *Gustave Zédé* and *Néréide* that had 5,000shp 400rpm geared steam turbines instead of reciprocating engines. (They shared the innovation of geared turbines with the destroyer *Enseigne Gabolde*, ordered at about the same time.) These would allow them to make 21 knots on the surface and be true *sous-marins de haute mer* (called unofficially *sous-marins d'escadre*) capable of operating with the fleet. They were to have ten torpedo tubes as in the original design for the *Diane* class (two interior bow tubes, two fixed launch cages firing forward, two more firing aft, and four external Simonot trainable launchers) and were to have one 75mm M1914 gun on a disappearing mount at the after end of the superstructure.

In a descriptive notice on the original steam design dated 15 October 1913 and updated 20 June 1914, Simonot explained that he had repeated the general arrangements of *Gustave Zédé* (in her original configuration) with an expansion of the superstructures requested by the *Comité technique*, but had also incorporated modifications based on lessons from the construction and trials of *Gustave Zédé*, some of which had already been incorporated in the design of the 630-ton reduced versions of *Gustave Zédé* (*Diane* and *Daphné*) that he had proposed in 1912. Thus the highest portions of the superstructure were concentrated amidships, the freeboard aft was greatly increased as in the 630-ton design to increase the reserve buoyancy of the stern, and the overall reserve buoyancy of the boat was increased to 30% by the changes to the stern and also by increasing the volume of the outer hull at the bow. The underwater hull lines of *Gustave Zédé* were retained as they had proven satisfactory, the only modification being that the new boat floated 0.17m deeper. The external configuration of the ballast tanks with their flat tops imitated that in the *Pluviôse* type and their hull sections were slightly pear shaped as in Simonot's *Diane*. The machinery spaces were designed to receive 5,000shp 400rpm geared steam turbines built by the Cie. Électromécanique du Bourget or by the Maison Bréguet. With the normal load of 66 tons of fuel the operating range at 14 knots would be 1,200nm. Steam was to be supplied by two boilers of the size of those in the destroyer *Durandal*, each with its own funnel just aft of the conning tower, but oil-fired.

In its meeting on 30 April 1913 the *Conseil supérieur* asked for an

increased effort on *sous-marins de haute mer*, and six more large submarines were included in the draft 1915 budget (submitted 7 July 1914) as Q115 through Q120. Q115-Q118 were initially attributed to Cherbourg and Q119-Q120 to Rochefort, but on 9 August 1914 the first two were allotted to Cherbourg (estimated to be of the *Joëssel* type based on their builder and budget cost figures), the next two to Toulon, and the last two to Rochefort (all four estimated to be of the *Laplace* type). They were to have been formally ordered on 1 January 1915 but because of the war the orders were not placed. The contracts for components were cancelled by a circular of 18 February 1915 which added that construction was deferred to 1918 at the earliest.

Work on both submarines was suspended from September 1914 to 1 May 1916 due to the war, and during this period the *Joëssel* class and the concurrent *Laplace* class were fundamentally redesigned. Even when they were first designed in 1913 the overall superiority of diesel engines over steam for submarines was uncontested. However, at that time there were grave doubts as to whether diesel engines could be built that were robust enough to drive large submarines at high speeds. When confronted with operational requirements for speeds that only steam engines could produce, the prewar solution was to resort to steam with all its drawbacks instead of renouncing the requirements. War experience changed this view, and on 15 March 1915 Vice Admiral Charles-Eugéne Favereau, then commanding the *2ᵉ Escadre légère* of armoured cruisers and light craft in the Channel, wrote that 'New submarines must be diesel propelled. We'll get what speed we can, but we must have diesels.' The Naval General Staff reported to the Minister on 31 March 1915 that commanders were unanimous in favour of diesels which alone could assure minimum visibility during surface navigation, a quick transition from surfaced to submerged navigation, and simultaneous propulsion and recharging of batteries while operating semi-submerged. For these military reasons the staff stated that it renounced the use of steam engines 'for the 6 submarines of 1914 (type *Joëssel* and *Lagrange*)'. The staff noted, however, that changing from steam to diesel would cause a reduction of three or four knots in maximum surface speed which would affect the strategic role intended for these submarines. The *Conseil supérieur* was consulted on this strategic issue and agreed with the change.

Two Schneider-Carels diesels of 2,900hp and 330rpm were ordered for each submarine from Schneider, Creusot by a contract of 22 December 1915. On the next day a design was proposed for the replacement of steam machinery by diesels in the two boats of the *Joëssel* class, and a note of 23 March 1916 provided more details on the revised design, which also included improvements like those made to the *Diane* class. The turbines, which had already been built, were to be diverted to two anti-submarine avisos, probably *Oise* and *Marne*, which were ordered on 23 April 1916. The ten torpedo tubes in the original design were to be replaced with two internal tubes in the bow, two external watertight tubes under the walking deck near the bow, one trainable twin-tube mounting under the walking deck aft of the conning tower (later replaced with two single tubes), and two external watertight tubes under the walking deck in the stern. In addition, fuel capacity inside the boat was to be increased, and the height of the superstructures were to be reduced to a strict minimum. The Ministerial order of 7 May 1916 that approved this redesign also added a second 75mm gun. Displacement figures indicate that the reserve buoyancy of the original design was substantially reduced in the final one. In service these two submarines had chronic problems with their diesels, propeller shafts and screws. They were sent to Saigon in 1929-31 where they were perpetually in maintenance status until condemned in 1936.

**Dimensions & tons:** 74.00m oa, wl, & pp x 6.00m ext (7.126m outside forward planes). 915.4t disp (surfaced), 1,203.093t (submerged). Draught: 4.073m mean, 4.328m aft. Men: 46 in *Joëssel*, 55 in *Fulton*, both including 3 officers. Reserve buoyancy: 23.9%
**Machinery:**
(surfaced) 2,900hp designed at 330rpm. Speed 16.5kts. Trials (*Joëssel*)

2,700.58hp = 16.895kts at 320.53rpm, (*Fulton*) 3,000hp = 17.001kts at 322.65rpm. 2 screws. 2 two-cycle diesel engines with 8 cylinders. 120t oil (*Joëssel*). Range (trials) 2,930nm @ 16.895kts on two diesels or 8,147nm @ 10.302kts on one diesel.

(submerged) 1,640hp at 270rpm. Speed 11kts. Trials (*Joëssel*, 21.1.1918) 1,464.06hp = 10.466kts at 227.63rpm. 2 electric motors. Batteries 151.8 tons. Range (trials) 122.5nm @ 5.187kts.

**Torpedoes:** 8 tubes, all watertight, for 450mm M1911V torpedoes: 2 internal in the bow aimed 4°23'off the axis, 2 external under the walking deck near the bow aimed forward 6°15' off the axis, 2 on a mount trainable to either side under the walking deck aft of the conning tower, and 2 external under the walking deck in the stern aimed directly aft. **Guns:** 2 x 75mm guns (light submarine type) on disappearing mounts, one forward and one aft of the conning tower, and one M1907 machine gun.

*Joëssel* (Q109) Cherbourg Dyd/Schneider, Creusot.
On list 1.1914. Ord: 26.9.1913 effective 1.1.1914. K: 26.1.1914.
L: 21.7.1917. Comm: c8.1917 (trials), 1.2.1919 (full).
Budget 1914. Probably named by 7.1913. Work suspended from 9.1914 to 1.5.1916. Launched before diesels installed. First underway trials with electric motors 25.8.1917. First diesel embarked 7.5.1918. Underway diesel trials 26.9.1918 to 21.11.1918. Assigned to Brest squadron 27.12.1918. Trial results accepted 1.1.1919. Refitted at Toulon 1922-23. To Bizerte 10.1926. From Bizerte to Saigon 19.10.1931 to 27.2.1932. Spent most of her time at Saigon under repair, with the port propeller shaft falling out of alignment in 1933. Condemnation proposed 3.4.1935 with *Fulton* and others. Struck 14.5.1936 (decision promulgated 15.7.1936). Sold 16.10.1936 to M. Ngo-Duy and BU. Joseph Joëssel was an engineer of the *Génie Maritime* who served at Indret from 1869 to 1880 and who invented the balanced rudder.

*Fulton* (Q110) Cherbourg Dyd/Schneider, Creusot.
On list 1.1914. Ord: 26.9.1913 effective 1.1.1914. K: 6.1914.
L: 1.4.1919. Comm: c4.1919 (trials), 10.7.1920 (full).
Budget 1914. Probably named by 7.1913. Work suspended from 9.1914 to 1.5.1916. Launched 1919 with diesels on board. Underway diesel trials 30.4.1919 to 7.5.1919. Assigned 8.5.1920 to the submarine flotilla at Toulon. Trial results accepted and to full commission 10.7.1920. Refitted at Toulon 1922-23. To Bizerte 10.1926. To Indochina 1931. Condemnation proposed 3.4.1935 with *Joëssel*, the wartime avisos *Craonne* and *Vitry le François*, and the sloops *Algol* and *Regulus*. Struck 14.5.1936 (decision promulgated 15.7.1936). Sold 18.11.1936 at Saigon and BU.

*Q115* (Unnamed) Cherbourg Dyd.
Budget 1915. To have been ordered late 1914 to begin 1.1.1915. Not ordered because of war.

*Q116* (Unnamed) Cherbourg Dyd.
Budget 1915. To have been ordered late 1914 to begin 1.1.1915. Not ordered because of war.

---

*LAPLACE* **Class.** *Sous-marins* (*Sous-marins de haute mer*). Double hull, diesel surface propulsion (originally steam). Designed by Hutter. To *Sous-marins de 1ʳᵉ classe* 1.1923.

Just as Simonot based his design for the *Joëssel* class on his *Gustave Zédé*, Hutter based his design for the *Laplace* class on his *Dupuy de Lôme*. On 23 July 1913 Minister of Marine Baudin notified Toulon that he planned to begin construction at Toulon on 1 January 1914 of two seagoing submarine of 840 tons and with geared turbines, *Lagrange* (Q112) and *Regnault* (Q113). They differed from the two submarines *Dupuy de Lôme* (Q105) and *Sané* (Q106) building at Toulon only in the substitution of geared

turbines of 4,000shp providing a speed of 20 knots for the 4,000ihp 19-knot reciprocating engines in *Dupuy de Lôme*, in the addition of two fixed torpedo launch cages firing forward, in some changes to the bridge, and in an increase in the volume of the exterior ballast tanks amidships above the waterline which increased the designed reserve buoyancy from 33% to 35.88%. The inner (pressure) hull was not modified. The boats were designed for 50 metres depth. Toulon was told to start ordering components right away, and Du Temple boilers were ordered for *Lagrange* on 27 August 1913. Minister Baudin gave similar orders on 28 August 1913 for the unnamed Q114.

As noted above for the *Joëssel* class, the 1915 budget (submitted 7 July 1914) contained six more large submarines of which ultimately four (Q117-Q120) were to have been formally ordered on 1 January 1915 from the two dockyards that were building the *Laplace* class. Because of the war these boats were not ordered.

Also as noted above for the *Joëssel* class, in 1915 and early 1916 the decision was taken to replace the steam turbines in the six large submarines that had been begun in early 1914 with diesels. The contracts for the turbines and boilers for *Lagrange* were ordered cancelled on 13 June 1915. Two Sulzer diesels were ordered for each submarine from the Forges et Chantiers de la Méditerranée under a contract of 15 December 1915. The turbines that had been built for the four submarines of the *Laplace* class were probably used in the anti-submarine avisos *Somme*, *Aisne*, *Yser*, and *Meuse*, which were ordered on 7 May 1916. The revised design included an increase in fuel capacity from 52 tons to 56 tons. It also included ten torpedo tubes and launchers arranged as in the *Diane* class, which may have been carried over from the steam design as it was also in the steam design for the *Joëssel* class. This was changed later to eight tubes as in the *Joëssel* class. Maximum diving depth 50 metres.

*The characteristics are based on a devis for* Romazzotti *dated 10.9.1918.*
**Dimensions & tons:** 75.200m oa, 74.578m wl, 75m pp x 6.384m wl (7.9m outside forward planes). 866.805t disp (surfaced), 1,318.117t (submerged). Draught: 3.695m mean, 4.017m aft. Men: 45 including 4 officers. Reserve buoyancy: 34.2%
**Machinery:**
(surfaced) 2,600hp designed (2,900hp in *Regnault*) at 325rpm. Speed 16.5kts. Trials (*Regnault*) 2,800hp = 15.9kts at 295rpm. 2 screws. 2 two-cycle Sulzer diesel engines with 6 cylinders of 0.450m diameter and 0.440m stroke. Range (trials) 5,500nm @ 10.5kts (*Romazzotti*, 225rpm on one engine).
(submerged) 1,640hp. Speed 11kts. Trials (*Lagrange*, 6.5.1925) 9.26kts. 2 electric motors. Batteries 155.2 tons. Range 125nm @ 5kts.
**Torpedoes:** 8 tubes, all watertight, for 450mm M1911V torpedoes: 2 internal in the bow aimed 3° off the axis, 2 external under the walking deck near the bow aimed forward 7°19' off the axis, 2 on a mount trainable to either side aft of the conning tower, and 2 external under the walking deck in the stern aimed aft 6°26' off the axis.
**Guns:** 2 x 75mm guns, one light submarine model on a disappearing mount forward of the conning tower and one M1897G (Army) on a retractible mounting forward of the training torpedo tube mount.aft of the conning tower. One M1907 Hotchkiss machine gun (M1914 in *Lagrange* and *Laplace*).

*Laplace* (Q111) Rochefort Dyd/F.C. Méditerranée, Le Havre.
On list 1.1914. Ord: 27.11.1913 effective 1.1.1914. K: 11.1914.
L: 12.8.1919. Comm: c1921 (trials), 1.12.1923 (full).
Budget 1914. Probably named by 7.1913. Updated at Cherbourg after the war. To normal reserve 21.1.1935. In the process of being condemned 1936-1939. Struck 19.4.1939 (decision promulgated 16.7.1939). Sold 1940 at Toulon to BU.

*Lagrange* (Q112) Toulon Dyd/F.C. Méditerranée, Le Havre.
On list 1.1914. Ord: 27.11.1913 effective 1.1.1914. K: 1.4.1914.
L: 31.5.1917. Comm: 30.5.1917 (trials), c2.1918 (full)

The submarine *Lagrange* installing radio equipment (*appareil TSF sous-marine*) at the radio facility at Toulon with radio masts raised. The installation of an arc transmitter was ordered on 29 March 1917 and the installation of a spark transmitter transferred from *Hermione* was ordered on 15 September 1917. Note also the torpedo tube mount trained to port amidships and the large high-angle gun pointed straight up forward. The boat also ran regular underway trials from June to December 1917. (*Private collection*)

Budget 1914. Named by 7.1913. Trials of diesels 9.6.1917 to 19.1.1918. Assigned to the 3rd submarine squadron at Corfu 1.1918 (still running trials). Electric motors accepted 1.2.1918, accepted for service 2.2.1918. Updated at Toulon 1922-23. Refitted with new propeller shafts 1923, then found cracks in mountings for two diesel engines. More repairs 1926-27, to reserve 10.9.1930 effective 14.12.1930 and to special reserve 24.1.1931. Condemnation proposed 3.1.1933. Depth change trials conducted 8.1934. Condemned 24.7.1935 (decision promulgated 27.8.1935). Sold 25.11.1936 at Toulon to M. Bonturi to BU.

*Regnault* (Q113)  Toulon Dyd/F.C. Méditerranée, Le Havre.
On list 1.1914. Ord: 27.11.1913 effective 1.1.1914. K: 8.1914. L: 26.6.1924. Comm: 1.10.1924 (trials). C: 9.2.1926.
Budget 1914. Named by 7.1913. Assigned to 3rd submarine squadron at Toulon 1.2.1926. Final trial and trial results accepted 9.2.1926. Diesels broke down 10.9.1926, post repair trials 1.1928. Major refit completed 11.1930. Trials 27.1.1932, then put in conservation. Condemnation process begun 1935. Condemned 21.4.1938 (decision promulgated 5.7.1938). Sold 24.11.1938 at Toulon to the Société Navale du Midi of Marseille.

*Romazzotti* (Q114)  Toulon Dyd/F.C. Méditerranée, Le Havre.
On list 1.1914. Ord: 27.11.1913 effective 1.1.1914. K: 10.1914 (planned), 18.4.1916 (actual). L: 21.3.1918. Comm: 20.3.1918 (trials), 9.9.1918 (full).
Budget 1914. Still unnamed 1.1914. Still in commissioned status

1.7.1920 after completing trials but ceased to be considered as commissioned 12.12.1920. Refitted 1922-23 at Toulon. Series of failures reported to the Minister 2.6.1924 followed by major diesel failure 28.10.1924. More repairs at La Seyne 1925 and 1927-28. Ordered put in conservation without repairs 19.3.1931. Condemnation proposed 1.4.1933. Condemned 24.7.1935 (decision promulgated 27.8.1935), used in depth charge experiments 1935-36 by the *Centre d'Etudes Pratiques Sous-Marines* (CEPSM) at Toulon while for sale by the Domaines, condemned as hulk 16.2.1937, sold 26.5.1937 to M. Bonturi of Brégaillon (La Seyne) to BU.

*Q117* (Unnamed) Toulon Dyd. (ex Cherbourg)
Budget 1915. To have been ordered late 1914 to begin 1.1.1915. Not ordered because of war.

*Q118* (Unnamed) Toulon Dyd. (ex Cherbourg)
Budget 1915. To have been ordered late 1914 to begin 1.1.1915. Not ordered because of war.

*Q119* (Unnamed) Rochefort Dyd.
Budget 1915. To have been ordered late 1914 to begin 1.1.1915. Not ordered because of war.

*Q120* (Unnamed) Rochefort Dyd.
Budget 1915. To have been ordered late 1914 to begin 1.1.1915. Not ordered because of war.

_____

*Postwar submarine classifications.*
The division of the French submarine force into two sizes, large seagoing and smaller coastal, that effectively emerged following the 1906 and 1909 competitions was confirmed in the submarine classifications adopted on 30 March 1922: 1st class submarines were anything over 700t surface displacement, 2nd class submarines were anything under that level. Large numbers of both types were built between the wars. There was also a separate category for all minelaying submarines.

# Chapter Eighteen

# Minor Combatants and Auxiliaries, 1897-1914

## I. MINOR COMBATANTS

### (A) 2nd Class Avisos (*Avisos de 2e classe*).
To *Avisos* (classes omitted) in the 1.1909 fleet list.

*CHAMOIS. Aviso de 2e classe* (pilot school ship). Screw *aviso* with a flush deck and a straight bow. One funnel, two pole masts. To *Aviso* (1909), *Patrouilleur* 1.3.1920.

*Chamois*, ordered and begun in 1904, was built to replace *Élan*, which had been the seagoing school ship for pilots at Saint Servan from July 1878. She appeared in the 1905 budget (submitted on 30 March 1904) as an *aviso de 2e classe, école de pilotage* (school for piloting). Lieutenant de vaisseau Louis Fatou, who commended *Élan* from September 1901 to September 1903, was largely responsible for the plans of *Chamois*, of which he became the first commander.

**Dimensions & tons:** 50.08m oa x 7.70m ext. 431t disp. Draught: 2.40m max. Men: 87 including 8 officers.
**Machinery:** 600ihp = 12.61kts. 1 screw. 2 du Temple boilers. 75t coal.
**Guns:** none listed. 1 x 44cm searchlight. Later 2 x 65mm

*Chamois* C.A. Provence, Port de Bouc/C.A. Provence, Marseille.
On list 1.1906. Ord: 29.6.1904. K: 13.7.1904. L: 7.12.1905. C: 29.12.1905.
Budget 1904 (late addition). Was running trials 1.1906. Full commission 19.12.1906. Seagoing school for piloting at Saint Servan in place of *Élan* 1907-14. Designated after the general mobilisation as a boarding vessel based at Brest. From January 1916 was attached to the patrol division of the western Mediterranean. In the 9th patrol squadron in the Aegean 1917 and at the *Centre d'aérostation* (Centre for captive balloons) at Patras 1918-1919. Credited with commissioned war service between 31.12.1916 and 19.6.1919. Resumed pilot school service at Saint Servan 1919, replaced by *Ancre* there 1924. Off main list 1924 at Brest (condemnation pending). Struck 9.12.1925. Towed from Saint

The aviso *Chamois* near the school for pilots at Saint Servan where she replaced *Élan* as seagoing training ship in 1907. After war service she resumed pilot training duty there until 1924. *(Postcard by LL)*

Nazaire to Bordeaux, arriving 14.9.1925. Struck 9.12.1925. Offered for sale by the Domaines at Brest 25.8.1927, potentially for further use. Renamed *Sédentaire*, she served as a hulk at Verdon for the pilots of the Gironde until 1949 and then became a restaurant at Arcachon.

---

*JEANNE BLANCHE. Aviso de 2e classe.* Steam yacht with clipper bow. One funnel, two masts, schooner-brig rig. Acquired. To *Aviso* (1909)

*Jeanne Blanche* was built in 1894 at FCM La Seyne as a private yacht for Rodolphe Faulquier, a candle and soap tycoon from Montpellier, to a design by the shipyard's director, Aimable Lagane, and with M. Lego of the yard directing her construction. Faulquier died in early 1905 and it was announced on 18 February 1905 that he had willed the yacht to the French State for the exclusive use of the President of the Republic. Instead she was assigned to the Governor General of French West Africa for use on his inspection tours and in 1908 was reassigned for use by the French ambassador at Constantinople. The characteristics below are for the yacht as built.

**Dimensions & tons:** 60.80m on deck, 51.00m pp x 7.40m ext (moulded). 420t disp. Draught: 3.25m mean.
**Machinery:** 820ihp designed at 130rpm and 10kg/cm[2] boiler pressure. Trials 915ihp = 14.5kts. 1 screw. 1 vertical triple expansion engine with 3 cylinders of 0.460m, 0.730m, and 1.080m diameter and 0.700m stroke. 1 cylindrical tubular return-flame boiler.
**Guns:** Two small (for saluting) and one searchlight as yacht.

*Jeanne Blanche* F.C. Méditerranée, La Seyne.
On list 1.1908. K: 1893. L: 29.11.1894 (also reported as the completion date). C (navy): c1906.
Builder's hull 917. Initially assigned to the Governor General of French West Africa. Sent from Dakar 2.1907 to assist in salvage of cruiser *Jean Bart* on Sahara coast. In February 1907 the Ministry of Marine considered replacing her in West Africa with the torpedo-aviso *D'Iberville*. Replaced *Mouette* 1908 as yacht of the French ambassador at Constantinople. Fitted as a patrol vessel and armed 1913. Left Constantinople 10.1914 and took refuge in Sevastopol. Was on the Danube in 3.1918, Sevastopol being threatened by advancing German forces, and was sold 4.1918 at a low price to the Romanian Navy. Returned by Romania to France 1919. Struck 1.10.1920 as a yacht. Mercantile *Drief* 1920, *Saint-Hélier* 1922, *Roberto Ivens* 1927, *Terra Nova* 1929. Wrecked 18.2.1930 at Burgeo on the south coast of Newfoundland.

---

*UTILE. Aviso de 2e classe* (hydrographic ship). Screw aviso with a flush deck and a straight bow. One funnel, two masts, schooner rig. To *Aviso* (1909)

*Utile* first appeared on the fleet list in January 1894 as a service craft (specifically a large tug or *remorqueur des mouvements*) under construction for the harbour authorities at Toulon. She served in this capacity at Toulon from 1895 to 1907. The vessel was then converted to a surveying ship in 1907 to replace *Chimère* and moved to the main fleet list in January 1908 as an *aviso* (*navire hydrographique*) at Brest. Her builder, Satre, Fils Aîné & Cie., had yards at Arles and Lyon, after about 1896 the Lyon yard built only engines.

**Dimensions & tons:** 49.51m oa x 7.57m ext. 475t disp. Draught: 3.41m max. Men: 64 including 6 officers.

**Machinery:** 700ihp = 13.02kts. 1 screw. 1 cylindrical boiler. 61t coal.
**Guns:** (1936) 1 x 100mm.

*Utile* Satre, Fils Aîné & Cie., Lyon.
On list 1.1908. K: 1894. L: 20.7.1894. C: 1895.
Served as a tug (service craft) at Toulon 1895-1907. Assigned 2.1907 to
   the hydrographic mission on the west coast of France replacing
   *Chimère* and commissioned for the summer hydrographic campaigns
   either at Lorient or Cherbourg, being placed in special reserve in
   between. During the war was credited with commissioned war service
   between 13.11.1917 and 1.10.1919. *Navire hydrographique* 1920-
   1938. Reboilered with 2 Niclausse boilers 1922. Struck 13.6.1939
   (decision promulgated 16.7.1939). Still at Cherbourg 1941.

---------

## (B) Avisos (*Avisos*).

**FLAMANT (*QUENTIN ROOSEVELT*).** *Aviso* (fishery protection ship).
Screw aviso with a forecastle, long amidships island, straight bow and
counter stern. One tall funnel, two masts.

On 20 March 1912 the Naval General Staff listed the special ships planned
for the 1913 and later budgets including a replacement for the fishery
protection school ship *Ibis* of 1883 in the North Sea. A new aviso was duly
listed in the 1913 budget (submitted in March 1912) as to be ordered in
mid-1913 to replace *Ibis*. Plans dated 4 October 1913 by the *Section technique* were signed by its chief, Charles Doyère. The 1914 budget (submitted in November 1913) showed her as an *Aviso garde-pêche*, design incomplete, to be ordered in a dockyard in the 4th trimester of 1913 under the
1914 budget. Construction at Rochefort was ordered on 29 January 1914
and the name *Flamant* was assigned, but work soon stopped because of the
war. Three plans dated between May and December 1914 were signed by
naval constructor André Pierre Simon Lamouche at Rochefort, two of
which were corrected in June 1918 by naval constructor Albert Max Louis
Waldman at Rochefort under a ministerial order of 7 September 1917. The
aviso was renamed *Quentin Roosevelt* in late 1919 for the youngest son of
former American President Theodore Roosevelt who joined the French Air
Force and was killed in aerial combat over France on 14 July 1918. The
funnel was ordered shortened by 1.50m on 13 March 1919. She was listed
simply as a *garde-pêche* (fishery protection ship) by 1936.

**Dimensions & tons:** 50.00m oa, 47.00m wl/pp x 8.42m ext and wl
   (8.85m outside rubbing strake). 650t disp (585t Washington, 671.461t
   for stability trials). Draught: 3.966m max (at 2.9m forward of the aft
   pp). Men: 44 including 1 officer, later 58 including 5 officers.
**Machinery:** 1,200ihp designed at 13kg/cm² boiler pressure. Speed
   14.2kts. Trials 1,100ihp at 122rpm. 1 screw. 1 vertical triple expansion
   engine. 2 cylindrical return-flame boilers. 90t coal (normal), 100t (sur-
   charged). Range 1,500nm @ 10kts.
**Guns:**
(1918) 2 x 75mm M1897G (Guerre, forward and aft), one St. Étienne
   machine gun M1907 for AA fire (after bridge), two depth charge racks
   and minesweeping gear on the stern, 1 x 60cm searchlight
(1919) The after 75mm gun, its platform, and the depth charge racks
   were ordered on 13.3.1919 to be removed.

*Flamant/Quentin Roosevelt* Rochefort Dyd.
On list 1.3.1920. Ord: 29.1.1914. K: 7.1914. L: 27.10.1917.
   Comm: 17.4.1918 (1st time).
Budget 1913 (delayed to 1914). Construction reassigned from contract to
   the Rochefort Dockyard 1914. Her length was limited to 50 metres to
   allow her to use the Caledonian Canal between England and Scotland
   to move between the Irish and North Seas, but she was still 50cm too
   long for the shortest lock. In service 5.1918. Renamed *Quentin
   Roosevelt* 1.4.1919. Fishery patrols in the Channel and North Sea from
   1920. A ministerial circular dated 27.6.1939 called for her removal

from service in 8.1941 and replacement by the *aviso dragueur La
Furieuse*, which was ordered on 18.12.1939, but the war prevented
construction of the new aviso. *Quentin Roosevelt* was fitted as an auxiliary minesweeper late in 1939 and moved from Cherbourg to
Portsmouth, England on 18.6.1940. Seized by the Royal Navy
3.7.1940. As HMS *Quentin Roosevelt* (FT317) used to train Belgian
recruits to the Royal Navy Section Belge (RNSB) and then to transport
troops and equipment. From 1.1941 to 1.1942 was manned by a
Belgian crew under British command and integrated into the RNSB as
the Free French (FNFL) lacked personnel to man her. Became a Royal
Navy training ship 1.1942, then refitted as anti-submarine chaser and
based at Kirkwall in Scotland as part of the 24th Anti-Submarine
Group. Returned to the French Navy 6.1945 and again used for
fishery protection. Struck 14.2.1947 at Cherbourg. Offered for sale by
the Domaines 15.2.1950, BU 1955.

---------

*UNNAMED. 1 ship.* Aviso, *Kersaint* type.

On 20 March 1912 the Naval General Staff listed the special ships planned
for the 1913 and later budgets, including a station aviso that had not yet
been designed and probably would not be for some time. It appeared for
the first time in the budget for 1915 (submitted in July 1914) in the form
of a large aviso like *Kersaint* for service on the foreign stations. The project
became irrelevant with the outbreak of the war and the 1915 budget that
was to have funded it was never passed.

**Dimensions & tons:** 1,500t disp.

*N* (Unnamed) Rochefort Dyd
Budget 1915, to order mid-1915. Probably not designed. Cancelled.

---------

## (C) Gunboats (*Canonnières*).

**DÉCIDÉE Class.** *Canonnières.* Gunboats with a composite hull with two
crossed layers of planking below the waterline and steel plating above it and
a clipper bow. Three masts, barquentine rig. Designed by Normand.

A second gunboat (T2) like the *Surprise* (T1) of 1893 that had been included
in the 1896 budget submission of May 1895 and then cancelled was reinstated in the 1897 budget (submitted in February 1896) as T'1 (*Décidée*).
She was followed in 1898 by T'2 (*Zélée*). These two ships differed slightly
from their prototype, mostly to correct defects encountered in *Surprise*.
Weights were redistributed to correct the trim, the beam at the master frame
was increased from 7.484m to 7.930m to increase stability, bilge keels were
added to reduce rolling, the bowsprit was raised, and water tube boilers were
fitted that could supply all of the steam needed by the engine. These,
however, were Niclausse boilers whose tubes frequently failed and whose
imperfect fuel combustion sometimes made funnels glow red hot. (*Zélée* had
to replace her funnel in 1907 and again in 1912.) The endurance of *Zélée*
with 94 tons of coal was in practice 2,600 miles at 7 knots while the *devis
d'armement* (commissioning report) said it should be 4,700 miles at
10 knots, a defect attributed credibly by her commander to the Niclausse
boilers, although the poor quality of the coal available in the Pacific was
probably an additional factor. The engine design was as in *Surprise*.
   On 20 March 1912 the Naval General Staff listed the special ships
planned for the 1913 and later budgets, including an 800-ton *Décidée* type
gunboat. This vessel had originally been proposed by the staff on
15 September 1910 and was to have an armament of two 100mm and four
65mm guns. The ship was never included in a budget, however, in part
because the *Section technique* was overloaded with more urgent work.

**Dimensions & tons:** (*Décidée*) 60.365m oa, 56.190m wl & pp x 8.040m
   ext (above wl), 7.936m wl. 646.894t disp (designed), 680t (full).
   Draught (designed): 3.100m mean, 3.670m aft.
**Machinery:** 900ihp designed. Speed 13kts. Trials (20.5.1900, *Décidée*)

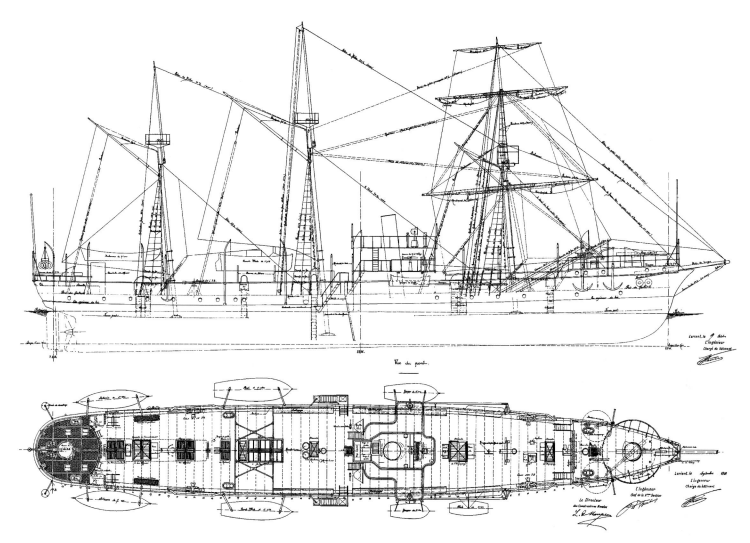

Sail plan and deck view of the station gunboat (*canonnière de stations*) *Décidée* built at Lorient on the plans of M. Augustin Normand. The plans were signed in September-October 1900 by the naval constructor in charge of the ship, J. Fraisse.

890.96ihp = 13.911kts, (1900, *Zélée*) 13.315kts. 1 screw. 1 horizontal triple expansion engine with 4 cylinders (two LP). 2 Niclausse boilers. Range: (*Décidée*) 1,889 nm with normal coal, 2,322 nm with max coal.

**Guns:** 2 x 100mm/45 M1893 QF (fore and aft in 54mm shields), 4 x 65mm/50 QF M1891 in sponsons on the sides, 4 x 37mm revolving cannon. In 1900, 6 x 37mm/20 M1885 QF replaced the four revolving cannon.

*Décidée* (T'1) Lorient Dyd/FCM, Le Havre.
On list 1.1898. Ord: 20.4.1897. K: 9.5.1898. L: 20.6.1899.
  Comm: 11.1899 (trials), 6.7.1900 (full).
Budget 1897. Engine contract 21.7.1897, installation began 20.3.1899, first static trial 17.8.1899. Left Lorient for the Far East 7.7.1900. Grounded off Chengling in the middle Yangtse 26.6.1914, refloated nearly two years later and left Saigon 16.2.1918 for Europe. Patrolled in the eastern Mediterranean until 3.1920. Listed as *Patrouilleur* 3.1920. Proposed for condemnation 20.1.1922. Struck 29.3.1922. School of wireless radio as a hulk at Toulon 1922-1929 (also annex to the school for engineers with *Moselle* in 1929), relieved by *Bouclier* 25.1.1929. For sale by the Domaines 1929-33. Condemned definitively 25.4.1931.

*Zélée* (T'2) Rochefort Dyd/FCM, Le Havre.
On list 1.1899. Ord: 21.4.1898. K: 21.2.1899. L: 18.10.1899.
  Comm: 1.5.1900 (trials), 16.7.1900 (full).

Budget 1898 (late addition). Boilers first fired 20.3.1900. Left Rochefort 1.8.1900 to replace the schooner *Papeete* on the Pacific station at Tahiti. Decomm. at Tahiti 8.8.1914 and all but the forward 100mm gun moved ashore for defence of Papeete. Re-manned by 35 men 11.8.1914 when the German cargo ship *Walküre* was reported in the area. *Walküre* was duly seized when she entered Papeete the next day, unaware of the war. *Zélée* again put out of service 13.8.1914 but machinery maintained in readiness to allow scuttling in the channel. Sunk 22.9.1914 by gunfire from German *Gneisenau* and *Scharnhorst* while tied up alongside *Walküre* at the mole at Papeete. Sunken hulk sold 5.12.1919 and mostly dismantled in place through 1925; the remains are a dive site today.

---

## (D) Shallow-Draught Gunboats (*Canonnières à faible tirant d'eau*).

To *Canonnières* in the 1.1909 fleet list.

### Western expansion into China.

On 1 March 1891 the Chinese established a customs post at Chungking on the upper Yangtse River, opening the area to the outside world. The lower Yangtse from Shanghai to Hankow was navigable by ocean-going ships and the middle Yangtse up to Ichang was passable for small steamers of up to 550 tons. Steam navigation in the upper Yangtse above Ichang was blocked by steep gorges and some 600 miles of rapids until in 1896 a steam launch owned by a British merchant succeeded in passing through them and reaching Chungking (Chongqing). The French had special interests in the upper Yangtse including French Catholic missions and commercial enterprises in

Szechwan (Sichuan) Province and at Chungking. In southern China, on 6 June 1897 Chinese authorities opened to foreign traffic the Si-Kiang (Si River or West River), which extends from Canton and Hong Kong westward into the mountains of Yunnan. It was navigable for 240 miles from Hong Kong to Wuchow, beyond which there were numerous rapids. This area was of strategic interest to the French because of its proximity to Indochina, although French commercial interests remained focused on the great entrepôt at Canton. Finally, in 1900 the Boxer Rebellion brought Western naval forces back to the region of the Peï-Ho (now Hai-Ho) River and Peking, where French *chaloupes-canonnières* had operated in 1860 as part of an earlier international intervention.

***

***ARGUS* Class.** *Canonnières à faible tirant d'eau.* Sectional river gunboats with two propeller shafts in tunnels and a steel hull. One funnel, one mast. *Chaloupes à faible tirant d'eau* 1.1901 only, to *Canonnières* 1.1909.

In 1896 or 1897 the British Royal Navy ordered five 145-foot long specialised river gunboats, three from Thornycroft and two from Yarrow. Thornycroft's *Woodcock* and *Woodlark* (their hulls 326 and 327) were sent in sections to Shanghai where they were assembled in late 1898 for service on the Yangtse River. Thornycroft's *Melik* (hull 328) and Yarrow's *Sultan* and *Sheikh* were given additional protective plating on the superstructure and sent to the Nile River in Egypt where in 1898 they participated in the occupation of Sudan by Lord Kitchener. The basic design for all six vessels met what became the basic requirements for a river gunboat, which were a very shallow draft, well-protected screw propellers, very good manoeuvrability, and an armament consisting of many small-calibre guns and machine guns able to engage multiple targets at short range.

On 6 July 1899 Minister of Marine de Lanessan decided to order two copies of *Woodcock* and *Woodlark* for French service in China. On 4 August 1899 a contract was awarded to Thornycroft for *Argus* (hull 342) and *Vigilante* (hull 343), specifying that they were to be shipped to Hong Kong in sections and assembled there. The two French ships thus did not follow their British near sisters to the Yangtse but were used near Hong Kong at Canton and on the Si-Kiang, which extended far to the west in southern China. There they explored all three western branches of the Si-Kiang river system, *Vigilante* in July 1905 reaching Lungchow (Longzhou) near the border with French Tonkin.

Unlike some Western gunboats in China these were true combatant vessels. The hulls and superstructure, including a conning tower on the bridge, were protected by 4mm plating proof against rifle bullets. The hatches in the decks could be closed and ports opened in them for use as firing positions. However, their habitability in hot climates was very poor and they had poor ventilation and internal lighting, the oil lamps simply making the interior hotter. The order for the gunboats included two 40-ton barges for carrying troops; these were moored at Canton and served as supply bases for the gunboats which had no base ashore.

Upon the outbreak of war in August 1914 both vessels were decommissioned at Hong Kong in accordance with standing mobilisation orders. A proposal in 1917 to exchange them for a 3,000-ton cargo ship belonging to the Chinese government was abandoned. At the end of the war they were judged to be in too poor condition to be reactivated. A proposal in 1919 to build new hulls for their machinery was dropped and the hulls were sold early that year, the engines and boilers being sent to Saigon. Two new river gunboats, also named *Argus* and *Vigilante*, were built at Toulon and assembled at Hong Kong in 1924.

**Dimensions & tons:** 44.20m x 7.32m. 130t disp. Draught: 0.60m.
**Machinery:** 1,150ihp designed at 10kg/cm² (14psi) boiler pressure. Speed 13kts. 2 shafts in tunnels with 2 screws on each shaft in the Thornycroft 'screw-turbine' arrangement. 2 compound engines. 2 'Speedy' type water tube boilers able to burn wood or coal.
**Guns:** 2 x 90mm/22 Army M1877 on Navy M1879 mountings at the ends of the superstructure, 4 x 37mm QF on the sides of the super-

The shallow-draft gunboat *Argus*, seen here, and her sister *Vigilante* operated in the vicinity of Canton and Hong Kong and to the west along the Si-Kiang river system well into southern China. *(NHHC, NH-64200)*

structure. One 50cm searchlight on the pilot house powered by a steam dynamo.

***Argus*** Thornycroft, Chiswick, UK.
On list 1.1900. Ord: 4.8.1899. K: 1899. L: 20.3.1900.
    Comm: 13.9.1900 at Hong Kong.
Budget 1899 (late addition). First trials on the Thames 6.4.1900 reached 10 knots. Then disassembled and the 11 sections embarked 10.5.1900 and shipped to Hong Kong 18.5-27.6.1900 on the P&O cargo ship *Banca*. After reassembly there by Thornycroft ran successful trials 17-25 July 1900. The guns were sent from France 1.8.1900 and installed in September behind 4mm shields. Reboilered 1907-08 with new Speedy Schedule B boilers which were larger than the old ones. Decommissioned at Hong Kong 1914, docked 1916 and 1917 by the French agent there to keep her afloat. Retired 1919. Sold 5.2.1919 at Hong Kong to M. Chang Ping.

***Vigilante*** Thornycroft, Chiswick, UK.
On list 1.1900. Ord: 4.8.1899. K: 1899. L: 20.3.1900.
    Comm: 13.9.1900 at Hong Kong.
Budget 1899 (late addition). Trials on the Thames 4.1900. 11 sections shipped to Hong Kong, partly on the P&O cargo ship *Banca* and partly on the merchantman *Sado Maru*. She arrived in poor condition on 17.7.1900 because of bad weather encountered en route and needed three weeks of repairs before assembly could start. Ran successful trials early 9.1900, accepted 17.9.1900. Reboilered 7-9.1907 at Hong Kong with new Speedy schedule B boilers. Decommissioned at Hong Kong 1914, docked 1917. Retired 1919. Sold 5.2.1919 at Hong Kong to M. Chang Ping.

***

***CERBÈRE* Class** (not built). *Canonnières à faible tirant d'eau.*

On 6 May 1900 HMS *Woodcock* and *Woodlark* arrived at Chungking, inaugurating the British gunboat presence on the upper Yangtse River. The Germans in turn tried to establish their presence there but their vessel was poorly suited to the mission and was lost in rapids only 30 miles upstream from Ichang. The French could not be indifferent to the activities of their European imperialistic competitors, and at the beginning of 1901 Minister de Lanessan decided to build in France two new gunboats for the upper Yangtse. He specified the speed of 16 knots that the commander in the Far East, Vice Admiral Édouard Pottier, felt was necessary to get through the rapids in the river. On 24 March 1901 he ordered the *Section technique* to develop a preliminary design with a maximum draft of 1.50 metres, a maximum speed of 16.5 knots, coal for 100 hours at 12 knots, an armament of two 90mm guns with shields and four 37mm QF guns, and a crew of 33 men including 2 officers. Ideally, he wanted vessels that could make the passage from France to the Far East on their own bottoms (a condition that the *Conseil des travaux* felt impossible to meet). Finally, he asked only for a preliminary design, leaving it to the contractors to produce the detailed design. On 2 April 1901 the *Conseil des travaux* examined a proposal from the *Section technique* with the following characteristics:

**Dimensions & tons:** 60m x 8m. 338t disp. Draught: 1.50m. Freeboard amidships 1.87m.

**Machinery:** 1,150ihp designed at 300rpm. Speed 16.5kts. 2 shafts each with 2 screws 1.6m apart and of different diameters in a tunnel. 2 engines. 2 boilers with vertical tubes. 32t coal (45 tons with surcharge).

**Guns:** 2 x 90mm (1 forward and 1 aft), 4 x 37mm (2 on the lower bridge forward, 2 on deck aft).

All accommodations were inside the hull, and the only superstructures were the galleys, the water closets and latrines, and the bridge with its shelters. A foremast forward of the bridge would carry a 40cm searchlight. The Council asked for numerous changes in this design to improve it for river service. Minister de Lanessan on 29 April 1901 sent back to the *Section technique* for more work, including raising the height of all the guns above the waterline to about 5 metres. The names *Cerbère* and *Guetteur* were assigned by a decision of 6 July 1901 but a telegram from Admiral Pottier dated 29 July 1901 in which he informed Paris of his decision to purchase *Olry* (below) interrupted the programme. It was reduced on 24 September 1901 to one gunboat and on 14 November 1901 the order was given to suspend awarding the contract, which had already been assigned to the Société de la Gironde at Bordeaux.

———

**OLRY.** *Canonnière à faible tirant d'eau.* River steamer with two screws in tunnels and a steel hull. One funnel, one mast. Purchased. To *Canonnière* 1.1909.

On 24 May 1901 the French ambassador in Peking wrote to Vice Admiral Pottier, commander of the French Far East Squadron, complaining that numerous appeals from the Embassy to the Ministry of Foreign Affairs to send a French gunboat to the Szechwan region on the upper Yangtse river above Chungking had produced no results. A previous Ambassador had asked for two gunboats, one of which he wanted to go above Chungking, only to see *Argus* and *Vigilante* built but assigned to the Si-Kiang instead. The Ambassador felt that the recent British success and ongoing German efforts meant that the French had no more time to lose, and he asked the Admiral to send one of the small vessels that he had on hand to Chungking to show the French flag alongside the British and eventually the German flags. A willing Admiral Pottier wrote to Minister de Lanessan on 10 June 1901 proposing to build or purchase a small gunboat at Shanghai to be sent to the upper Yangtse. As soon as experience was gained with this first vessel he proposed that a second be built in France or at Shanghai, as it was undesirable to leave a single vessel isolated so far from the nearest operating base.

In his letter to the Minister, Pottier laid out the characteristics he felt were necessary for a vessel on the upper Yangtse. They included a speed of 14 to 16 knots to force the rapids, excellent control of the ship's direction of movement, meaning a short hull and a large rudder, many watertight compartments, a double bottom, a boiler that could handle sudden large changes in demand from the engines, and two propeller shafts in tunnels. Not long afterwards, however, the admiral selected a ship that met practically none of these conditions but was available. Her speed was only 11 knots, she had no watertight compartments or double bottom, and her return-flame locomotive boilers could not handle rapid changes in engine speeds. Minister de Lanessan authorized the purchase on 29 July 1901 and

The shallow-draft gunboat *Olry* was purchased at Shanghai in 1901 to establish a French presence on the upper Yangtse River. She had a robust hull but her machinery wore out from intense use. She was relieved by the new *Doudart de Lagrée* at Chungking in December 1909. *(Private collection)*

named the ship *Olry*. The contract was dated 22 August 1901. The vessel was already practically complete at her builder's yard and was delivered on 10 September 1901 and commissioned on 18 September 1901.

*Olry* was placed under the command of Lieutenant de vaisseau Émile-Auguste-Léon Hourst on the recommendation of Colonel Marchand of Fashoda fame, who was then in China. Hourst was experienced in river exploration and led *Olry* and and her tender, the steam launch *Takiang*, on an ambitious voyage up the Yangtse. *Olry* left Shanghai for the upper Yangtse 2 October 1901, under tow by the cruiser *Descartes* to Hankow. She left Hankow 10 October 1901 and arrived at Ichang 17 October 1901. There she was lightened as much as possible before attempting the passage of the rapids to Szechwan. She departed Ichang 23 October 1901 and reached Chungking on 13 November 1901 after an arduous transit, inaugurating the presence of the French Navy on the upper Yangtse. Hourst built a base for her and *Takiang* at Wangkiato (now within Chungking), just below the junction of the Yangtse and the Kialing River, where the Société Française du Szechwan (a Catholic mission) had empty warehouses. (This is now open to tourists as the French Navy Barracks.) On 22 May 1902 *Olry* joined *Takiang* upriver from Chungking at Suifou (Suchow, now Yibin), the limit of navigation on the Yangtse, and on 23 July she reached her farthest point from Shanghai at Kiatin (Kiating, now Leshan) on the river Min.

*Olry* was strongly built, her steel hull with four compartments surviving many groundings and strong machinery vibrations at certain speeds, but her accommodations were cramped. The intense use during the 1901 expedition up the Yangtse wore her out prematurely. Her boilers continued to give constant trouble and her commander reported in January 1909 that the engines could not be pushed above 210rpm (the normal speed being 270rpm) because of excessive vibrations.

**Dimensions & tons:** 35.05m x 6.70m. 165t disp. Draught: 1.0m. Men: 24 including 4 officers.

**Machinery:** 530ihp at 9 kg/cm² boiler pressure. Speed 11kts. Trials: 10.45kts. 2 screws in tunnels. 2 compound engines. 2 locomotive boilers (coal-fired fire-tube).

**Guns:** 6 x 37mm QF (one pair forward of the bridge and two aft, all on the shelter deck).

*Olry* Farnham Boyd & Co., Shanghai.
On list 1.1902. L: 1901. Comm: 18.9.1901.
Accepted 20.10.1901 while at Ichang headed for the upper Yangtse although she had failed to make the desired speed of 11 knots.

Condemned while at Chungking 1.12.1909. Descended the Yangtse to Shanghai under her own power 7.5.1910 to 4.6.1910 and turned over to the French Consul there for sale. Struck 1.7.1910. Sold at Shanghai to a Chinese buyer.

---

**PEÏ-HO.** On service craft list at Saïgon as tug *Lieutenant Contal* 1.1902-1.1905. Renamed *Peï-Ho* and to the main list as a *Canonnière à faible tirant d'eau* 1.1906. Screw river tug with low flush deck. One funnel, two masts. Steel hull. Purchased. *Canonnière* 1.1909, *Canonnière de rivière* 1.3.1920.

During the Boxer rebellion, the French Navy created at Tangku (now Binhai) in a bend of the Peï-Ho (now Hai-Ho) river upriver from the Taku forts an administrative centre to support transport operations for the occupying force. In 1905, having lost its purpose, this base was suppressed, but to retain a presence in the Bohai Gulf, one of the tugs (rated as a service craft) sent to Tangku from Saïgon, *Lieutenant Contal*, was converted into a gunboat by the addition of three revolving cannon, renamed *Peï-Ho*, moved to the main fleet list, and stationed there. In contrast to the *Olry* and *Takiang* from the same shipbuilder she had few technical difficulties throughout her two-decade career, although unlike the two Yangtse gunboats she was not prematurely worn out by intensive service.

**Dimensions & tons:** 31.40m x 5.48m. 123t disp. Draught: 2m.
   Men: 24 including 2 officers plus 5 Chinese.
**Machinery:** 280ihp for 10kts. 2 screws. 2 vertical compound engines.
   1 cylindrical return-flame boiler.
**Guns:** 3 x 37mm Hotchkiss revolving cannon (2 forward of the pilot house and 1 on the stern). These replaced 1922 (just before her commander received orders to dispose of the ship) with two machine guns forward and a 47mm QF on the stern.

*Peï-Ho* ex *Lieutenant Contal* Farnham Boyd & Co., Shanghai.
On list 1.1906. L: 1901. In service: 1901. Comm: 1905.
On the Peï-Ho river 1905 as station ship at Tangku, then at Tientsin from 1911 to 1922. Laid up in drydock from 1914 until recommissioned 6.10.1919. The French withdrew from the region during 1922. Struck 4.8.1922. Sold 15.11.1922 at Tientsin to Trung-Ho & Co after a final sortie on 2 October to test her new 47mm gun.

---

**DOUDART DE LAGRÉE.** *Canonnière*, in 1909 budget (submitted 19.5.1908) as *canonnière à faible tirant d'eau pour le Haut-Yang-Tsé*. Sectional river gunboat with two screws in tunnels and a steel hull. One funnel, one mast. Name rendered *Doudard de Lagrée* through 1.1912. *Canonnière de rivière* 1.3.1920.

The design process for a new gunboat for the upper Yangtse, suspended in 1901 when *Olry* was purchased, resumed in 1905 when the repeated mechanical casualties to that ship made it clear that a new ship would soon be needed to replace her. Thanks to the delay the navy was now able to draw on the experience of two commanders of *Olry*, Lieutenants de vaisseau Hourst and Louis Théophile Audemard. Hourst had proposed a design in 1901 that was supported in 1903 by the commander of the Far East Squadron. By then two more designs had been proposed by naval constructor Doyère, then on detached duty in a Chinese yard, and by Lieutenant Audemard, produced in 1903 at Chungking during one of *Olry*'s many breakdowns. A technical commission (probably the *Comité technique*, which had replaced the *Conseil des travaux* on 21 April 1905) met on 13 December 1905 with Hourst and Audemard in attendance to decide on the specifications to propose to Minister Thomson. The resulting design was based primarily on Audemard's, though with many adjustments. The parameters adopted were a length of 45 to 50 metres, a draft of 1 metre, and a minimum speed of 14 knots. Propulsion was to be by semi-immerged screws in tunnels as in Thornycroft's *Argus*. A new feature was a spoon-shaped bow similar to that of Chinese junks, which gave additional buoy-

ancy to the bow as it entered rapids. (This was apparently proposed by Doyère and endorsed by both Hourst and Audemard). The commission did not specify an armament but did specify 10mm chrome steel plating on the pilot house and the machinery spaces and 5mm gun shields. A debate over habitability was resolved with a decision to accommodate all European crew members in deckhouses and all the Chinese below the main deck. On 2 April 1906 Minister Thomson asked the *Section technique* for a new gunboat design based on the specifications elaborated on 13 December 1905.

Almost two years later a contract for a new Yangtse gunboat was signed on 9 March 1908 with De la Brosse et Fouché at Nantes and was approved on 20 March 1908. Audemard supervised the construction for the Navy and insisted on the spoon bow when the contractor produced initial drawings with a conventional bow. The final design had four rudders and two propeller shafts in tunnels, each with only one propeller. The electric dynamo powered one 30cm searchlight and four electric lamps, two in the engine room and two in the boiler room. Her first commander was Audemard, now a Capitaine de frégate. The main shortcoming of the design proved to be in longitudinal strength, which had to be reinforced on several occasions. In 1918, 8mm armour was placed around the pilot house, 6mm armour was added over the machinery spaces, and the guns received 8mm shields, increasing displacement by 7 tons, deepening draught by 20cm, and decreasing speed by one knot.

In 1912 mobilization orders were promulgated to French gunboats on the Yangtse that, in the event of war with Germany, they were to proceed to Shanghai to be decommissioned at Shanghai Docks. The officers and crews were then to proceed to Hong Kong where they would be distributed among the ships of the seagoing China Naval Division and local naval forces in Indochina. *Doudart de Lagrée* duly reported to Shanghai after learning of the outbreak of war in August 1914. Similarly, *Peï-Ho* was decommissioned at the outbreak of the war at Tangku and *Argus* and *Vigilante* were decommissioned at Hong Kong. In December 1917 at the request of the Ministry of Foreign Affairs the Navy decided to reactivate *Doudart de Lagrée*, which left Shanghai Docks in August 1918 after her armament was modified and armour added.

**Dimensions & tons:** 52.30m oa, 51m pp x 7m ext (outside rubbing strakes), 6.70m wl. 243t disp (with normal coal). Draught: 1m.
   Men: 59 including 4 officers but excluding Chinese crew.
**Machinery:** 900ihp designed at 15kg/cm² boiler pressure. Trials (Nantes, 10 hours) 14kts. 2 screws. 2 reciprocating engines. 2 Fouché boilers. 27.50t coal (normal), 45t (surcharge). 4 rudders.
**Guns:**
(1909) 6 x 37mm M1885 QF at the ends of the upper deck and outboard of the funnel.
(1918) 1 x 75mm forward, 2 x 37mm M1885 and 4 M1907 machine guns on the upper deck.
(1933) The 37mm M1885 replaced by 37mm M1916 from *Balny*.

*Doudart de Lagrée* De la Brosse et Fouché, Nantes/De la Brosse, Nantes.
On list 1.1909. Ord: 11.3.1908. K: 3.1908. L: 4.2.1909. C: 16.8.1909.
Budget 1909. Trials completed 10.3.1909. Transported in 13 sections from Saint Nazaire to Shanghai by merchantman *Kouang-Si* between 5.5.1909 and 4.7.1909. Undocked at Shanghai 15.7.1909, began trials 1.8.1909, trials completed 25.9.1909, and accepted 3.10.1909. First arrived at Chungking 12.11.1909. Decomm. 1914 at Shanghai, recomm. 1918 with a revised armament and additional armour. Mainmast added 1926 to support radio antennas. Reboilered at Shanghai 1928. Decomm. 20.11.1939 at the Kiousin Docks at Shanghai and placed in caretaker status. Struck 25.7.1941 and turned over to the consular agent at Shanghai as representative of the Administration des Domaines.

---

**BALNY.** *Canonnière de rivière* 1.3.1920. Sectional river gunboat with two screws in tunnels and a steel hull. Two funnels, two masts.

The Chinese revolution of 1911 made it clear that France needed more than one gunboat on the Yangtse. France was unable to respond when Wu Chang rebelled in October 1911 and seized Hankow, putting the foreign concessions there at risk, because *Doudart de Lagrée* was already contending with unrest in Szechwan. The decision to build a second gunboat like *Doudart de Lagrée* was taken four months later, on 7 February 1912, but was then delayed for budgetary reasons. The ship was ordered from De la Brosse et Fouché (which became A.C. Bretagne) on 18 June 1913 under the 1913 budget for delivery January 1915. She was launched in June 1914 but the war prevented her shipment to China and she was left incomplete, her engines being removed for use on one of the river gunboats at the front. After the armistice these were recovered and the ship finally arrived in sections at Shanghai on 10 November 1921 in the cargo ship *Commandant Dorise*. She was reassembled at the Franco-Chinese works at Kiousin and additional longitudinal strengthening was added based on experience with *Doudart de Lagrée*. After trials on the Whangpoo (Huangpu) River she was placed in full commission in March 1922, left Shanghai for the upper Yangtse on 6 April 1922, and arrived at Chungking on 9 May 1922. Her specifications were practically identical to those of *Doudart de Lagrée* but her appearance differed as she had two funnels instead of one, two masts, and additional deckhouses. She was completed with a top on the foremast which was quickly removed in 1923 when armour was fitted as in *Doudart de Lagrée*.

**Dimensions & tons:** As *Doudart de Lagrée*.
**Machinery:** As *Doudart de Lagrée* but with 2 funnels and only 3 rudders.
**Guns:**
(1921) 1 x 75mm M1916 forward, 2 x 37mm M1916 at the after end of the superstructure, 4 machine guns.
(1932) The 2 x 37mm replaced with two Stokes Brandt 81mm mortars.

*Balny* De la Brosse et Fouché, Nantes/De la Brosse, Nantes.
On list 1.3.1920. Ord: 18.6.1913. K: 1913. L: 8.6.1914. Comm: 26.2.1921.
Budget 1913. Transported 1921 with *La Grandière* (ordered 1920) from Saint Nazaire to Shanghai by the merchantman *Commandant Dorise* and reassembled at the Franco-Chinese yard at Kiousin. Last refitted at Shanghai 12.1936-1.1937. Refitted afloat at Chungking 3-4.1940. Ordered decommissioned at her moorings at Wangkiato 18.9.1940, weapons removed and ship placed in conservation. Struck 25.7.1941. Ceded to the Chinese government 1944, still in service as *Fa Ku* 1962.

---

## (E) Steam Launches (*Chaloupes à vapeur*).

*TAKIANG. Chaloupe à vapeur.* River steam launch with a low flush deck and multiple deckhouses. One funnel, one mast. Purchased. Given a new junk-type hull 1905.

When it was decided in 1901 to purchase *Olry* for service on the upper Yangtse it was also decided to purchase a small steam launch to serve her as a tender. Purchased from the builder of *Olry* on 7 September 1901, she was delivered with that vessel three days later, on 10 September 1901. She was one of two twin screw steam launches built by that company as their hulls 660 and 661. Takiang (Great River) was another name for the Yangtse River.

*Takiang* left Shanghai for the upper Yangtse under tow by the paddle aviso *Alouette*. She was quickly found to be unstable, coming close to capsizing many times. Only later did the French learn that she had previoulsy been sold to a tea merchant in Hankow and that she had capsized in a light wind on smooth water, causing the buyer to refuse to pay for her. She left Hankow on 7 October for Ichang lashed alongside a Chinese steamer. She joined *Olry* at Ichang, where a caisson was lashed on each side to improve her stability and a junk was lashed outboard of one caisson. She left Ichang 23 November 1901 under the direction of the pilot who had just navigated *Olry* through the rapids. During the transit to Chungking, in December 1901, her engine failed, then her boiler failed, and she finished the transit being hauled through the rapids by coolies and then towed by her junk. She joined *Olry*

on 21 December 1901 at her base at Wangkiato just below Chungking. On 8 March 1902 she was sent to Suifou in Szechwan as a scout for *Olry*, arriving on 23 March 1902. She left there 24 June 1902 heading up the river Min and arrived at Kiatin 29 June 1902, again as a scout for the larger vessel. While there Lieutenant de vaisseau Hourst heard of massacres of Christians in the region and took steps to protect them, causing him to be criticised by the anti-clerical Minister of Marine, Pelletan, for his 'semi-episcopal' cruise.

In 1903 the wooden hull of *Takiang* was judged unusable because of damage from frequent groundings and from shipworms. The heavy use during the 1901 expedition up the river prematurely wore out a vessel that had been weak to begin with. In December 1903 Lieutenant de vaisseau Audemard, then commanding *Olry*, proposed building a new junk-type hull and putting the original ship's engines, boiler, screws, and guns into it. The new hull measured 23.30m x 3.53m with a draught of 0.45m and weighed twice as much as the original vessel. It was launched on 22 January 1905 at Chungking and ran trials on 21 February 1905, when it was found that she could not get over 5 knots, in part because the screws could not be put into tunnels and their tops emerged 0.23m from the water. The new *Takiang* was essentially unable to operate without coolies ashore pulling on lines, the normal way for moving junks upriver. Her boiler began to fail in 1906 and the commander of *Olry* recommended condemnation in 1907, a recommendation rejected then and when repeated in 1908 by the admiral commanding the Far East Squadron. Given the poor condition of the boilers of *Olry*, the admiral evidently wanted to keep the French flag flying at Wangkiato on *Takiang* until the arrival of *Doudart de Lagrée*, which ultimately relieved both vessels.

**Dimensions & tons:** (original vessel) 13,72m pp x 2.67m. 70t disp. Draught: 0.81m.
**Machinery:** 7kts. 2 screws. 2 compound engines with 2 cylinders of 0.10m and 0.15m diameter and 0.13m stroke. 1 locomotive boiler.
**Guns:** 2 x 37mm QF.

*Takiang* Farnham Boyd & Co., Shanghai.
On list 1.1902. Built: c1901. C: 9.1901.
Original *Takiang* unserviceable 1903. New junk-style hull built at Chungking 1904-05. This second *Takiang* and *Olry* were replaced by *Doudart de Lagrée*. Decomm. 1.12.1909 at Chungking. Struck 1.7.1910 with *Olry*, for sale 1910-1911. Engines and boiler sent to Saigon and (second) hull sold locally.

---

*MASCOTTE. Chaloupe à vapeur.*
This steam launch was built at Constantinople for the French government to replace *Étincelle* (purchased 1879) as annex to the station ship there. The contractual delivery date was 9 August 1902 and the cost was around 20,000 francs.

**Dimensions & tons:** 31t disp. Men: 6.
**Machinery:** 300ihp.
**Guns:** probably none.

*Mascotte* Établissements Georges-Bernard Jost, Constantinople.
On list 1.1903. In service 1902. Annex to *Mouette* and later to *Jeanne Blanche* at Constantinople. Seized by the Ottoman government 11.1914, commissioned 6.10.1915 for the Bosporus Fortification Command. Decommissioned 11.1918. While alongside the British tanker *Kwang Sang* on 19.12.1918 a barge loaded with petrol caught fire which spread to her. Wreck sold in 1919 by the French government, then repaired in 1919 by Établissements Georges-Bernard Jost and hired out for daily cruises at Istanbul.

---

*SONDE. Chaloupe à vapeur.* Steam launch with straight bow, cruiser stern, flush deck with bulwarks at ends, and small pilot house. One tall funnel, one pole mast. Designed by builder.

The 1911 budget (submitted in June 1910) contained one *chaloupe à vapeur* for the hydrographic service, to be laid down in March 1911. This tiny vessel was assigned as a tender to the hydrographic aviso *Utile* and was later described as a tug.

**Dimensions & tons:** 19.80m oa x 4.65m ext. 51t disp. Draught: 1.76m max. Men: 10.

**Machinery:** 165ihp. Speed 10kts. 1 screw. 1 vertical compound engine. 1 Oriolle boiler. 6t coal.

**Guns:** probably none.

*Sonde* Decout-Lacour, La Rochelle.

On list 1.1911. Ord: 23.3.1910. K: 3.1911. L: 1911. C: 1911.

Budget 1910 (late addition). Reported 28.7.1911 as entering service to join *Utile* at Dunkirk as her annex for hydrographic work on the northern coasts of France. *Utile* and *Sonde* recommissioned on 15.4.1914 and were to leave Cherbourg on 1.5.1914 for their annual summer mission. *Navire hydrographique* 1920, was a tug (service craft) at Brest by 1936. Struck 8.6.1937 (decision promulgated 18.10.1937). For sale 10.1937.

---

## (F) Minelayers (*Mouilleus de mines*).

### Early French naval minelaying

The maritime use of floating and submerged devices filled with gunpowder to destroy enemy targets goes back to the sixteenth century, but it was the Russo-Japanese War of 1904-1905 that fully revealed their potential in naval warfare. During that war the Japanese lost to mines two battleships, two cruisers, two destroyers, a torpedo boat, and a minelayer while the Russians lost one battleship (the flagship of the irreplaceable Admiral Makarov), one cruiser, two destroyers, a torpedo boat, a gunboat, and a minelayer. (Both minelayers were lost on their own mines.) The minefields continued to be dangerous after the war, sinking several merchant ships. This experience had two consequences, one being the inclusion in the 1907 Hague Convention of rules restricting the use of sea mines and the other being the development of mine warfare forces in most major navies including the French.

Minister of Marine Vice Admiral Boué de Lapeyrère stated that when he took over the Ministry in July 1909 he found no minelaying capability in place. In 1911 French naval depots held an inventory of 800 M1885 mines, 1,500 M1892 mines, and 1,500 M1906 mines, the first two types being totally outdated and the third having an inability to resist currents that effectively limited its use to the Mediterranean. Boué de Lapeyrère was able to cancel another 1,500 of the M1906 mines when he became Minister in July 1909 but had to accept the rest, which he intended the converted *Foudre* to carry. (The M1906 mines were withdrawn from service in 1916 following the accident that sank the minelayer *Casabianca*.) In 1909 two new types of mines were presented to the Navy by private firms, one by Sautter-Harlé and one by Vickers-Bréguet. Boué de Lapeyrère expedited trials of the Sautter-Harlé type at Cherbourg by Lieutenant de vaisseau Thomazi that showed they could be laid in heavy seas, that the explosion of one would not detonate another 25 metres away, that they could resist the heavy currents in the Rance river, and that they could also be used as command detonated mines for harbour defence. Most subsequent procurement, however, was of the Vickers-Bréguet type.

These mines were deployed by minelaying ships, which began to appear in navies around the turn of the century. The French adapted five small 3rd class cruisers of the *Cosmao* type to carry M1882 or 1892 moored mines, but these obsolete mines had inadequate charges (25kg maximum) and the new M1906 mines were too heavy. After the Russo-Japanese War the French considered adapting 2nd class cruisers of the *Friant* and *Du Chayla* types but this idea was not pursued. For larger minelayers the French briefly considered converting cruisers like *Jurien de la Gravière* but in 1906 they settled on *Foudre*, a 20-knot cruiser-type ship originally built to carry torpedo boats with the fleet. Conversions work began on *Foudre* in 1908 and between April and July 1910 she participated in the summer exercises

of the *Escadre de la Méditerranée* as a minelayer, but she was reassigned to aviation duty in 1912. A coherent French policy for laying sea mines appeared around 1909, guided in particular by Minister Boué de Lapeyrère. For offensive mining on the enemy's coasts or in the approaches to its ports, minelayers had to be of small dimensions to remain invisible to coastal defences, and they also needed to be fast and highly manoeuvrable. The Minister secured an offer from Normand for two such ships (see below). A larger minelayer projected in 1914 was also designed for high-speed offensive minelaying and not for operations with the fleet. For defensive minelaying in French waters, large numbers of heavy (over 250kg) mines would have to be laid, ruling out the use of small launches as in the past and requiring relatively large ships. Finally, minelayers accompanying the fleet would need the speed to keep up with the larger ships and would have to be large enough not to be slowed by bad weather.

The 300-ton destroyers of Normand's *Durandal* type responded perfectly to the requirements for fleet operations, and in March 1909 the Navy decided to adapt some of them for minelaying. Following trials with one ship, Boué de Lapeyrère had four 300-ton destroyers fitted with rails for Sautter-Harlé mines, *Flamberge* and *Baliste* in 1910 and (following a November 1911 decision) *Hache* and *Massue*. It was also proposed to convert some 450-ton destroyers including *Enseigne Henry* (conversion ordered October 1912) and perhaps *Janissaire* and *Voltigeur*, but no 450-tonners were in fact converted. The last six planned 800-ton destroyers were to have had both minelaying and minesweeping capabilities, but their number was reduced to three in the 1913 budget and only two of them, *Mécanicien-Principal Lestin* and *Enseigne Roux*, were completed during the war.

For defensive mining the Navy turned back to smaller ships without the speed of destroyers and selected the 925-ton *Casabianca* and *Cassini* for conversion. After trials in *Casabianca* in 1911 both were fully converted in 1912 to carry the M1906 mine in the Mediterranean. *Foudre* would have joined them if completed as a minelayer, although her speed and manoeuvrability were by then both deficient.

---

***PLUTON* Class.** *Mouilleurs de mines.* Steamer effectively flush decked and with a port in the stern for two mine launch rails. One funnel, two pole masts.

In 1909 the Navy asked Normand to design a dedicated minelayer and Normand offered to Minister Boué de Lapeyrère to provide immediately two of 800 tons and 21 knots and carrying 120 Sautter-Harlé mines. The design work was entrusted to the retired naval constructor Charles Pierre Octave Joseph Ferrand, now working for Normand. The two ships that were built to this design were much smaller than contemporary foreign purpose-built minelayers but they had a shallow draft that would allow them to venture into mined waters and their appearance was closer to that of a coastal steamer, or tug than it was to a warship, allowing them to operate discretely. Their mission was to proceed to enemy coasts and lay mines in the passages and exit channels from harbours occupied by enemy naval forces, a speed of about 13 knots with a range of 3,000nm being enough for a mission against coasts in the North undertaken at maximum speed by a ship leaving a Channel port or for a mission against Mediterranean coasts by a ship leaving Toulon. (The first commander of *Cerbère* wrote that she lacked the qualities needed for this mission because she was much too slow, carried too few mines to act alone, and despite not looking like a warship also did not resemble a merchant ship and would be quickly recognized.) They had a rudder in the bow as well as the usual one aft. They were designed to carry 120 Sautter-Harlé Nº1 mines on four parallel tracks on the main deck which served two mine ports in the stern, although *Cerbère* and probably *Pluton* carried the lighter model of Bréguet mine on initial commissioning. One searchlight was added after completion. The foremast in *Pluton* was strengthened in March 1917 to allow loading heavy Bréguet mines and on 18 June 1917 the Minister ordered adapting the rails on *Cerbère* for the heavy Bréguet mines. *Pluton* experi-

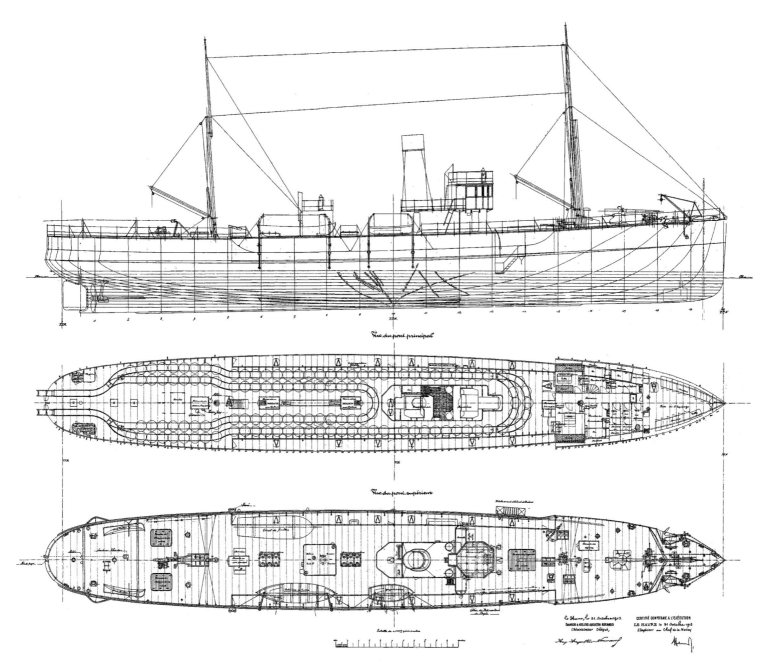

Outboard profile from the lines plan and plan of the main deck (*pont principal*) and upper deck (*pont supérieur*) of the minelayer (*navire poseur de mines*) *Pluton*, built on the plans of the Société Anonyme des Chantiers et Ateliers Augustin Normand under a contract of 23 March 1910. The plans were certified on 21 October 1913 to represent the ship as fitted by the navy's control officer at Le Havre. The main deck was the mine deck and the upper deck was the weather deck.

enced strong vibrations in her hull at 175-185rpm (15 knots) and 80-90rpm (7 knots), meaning that her maximum sustained speed for periods over 24 hours was 14 knots. Her maximum practical speed was 16 knots at 200rpm (and 650 tons displacement) for periods up to 10 hours. Rolling and pitching were both severe. *Pluton* lost her forward rudder in a collision with *Casque* at Mudros on 29 October 1918, it had proved to be virtually useless in service and was not replaced.

Although built to the same design, these two ships were built by different shipyards and were not identical. The upper deck was raised slightly at the extreme stern in *Cerbère* but not in *Pluton*. The funnel of *Cerbère* was also a bit greater in diameter than that of *Pluton* and her bridge was a little more developed. The comparable dimensions of *Cerbère* were recorded as 60.76m length x 8.30m beam.

*The characteristics are mostly from a descriptive register for* Pluton *dated 23 August 1913.*

**Dimensions & tons:** 60.750m oa (including rudder and *tampon de choc*, or shock buffer), 59.000m wl & pp x 8.092m ext & wl (8.546m outside hull fittings). 573.971t disp (designed), 641.026t (normal), 667.526t (with 26.5t fuel surcharge). Draught: (designed) 2.713m mean, 3.146m aft. Men: 69 including 3 officers.

**Machinery:** 4,000ihp (plus 40ihp for auxiliary machinery) designed at 270rpm and 18kg/cm$^2$ boiler pressure. Rated at 6,150ihp in 1915 and 5,400ihp in 1920. 20.01kts (*Pluton*), 19.80kts (*Cerbère*). 2 screws. 2 triple expansion engines with 3 cylinders of 0.480m, 0.740m, and 1.160m diameter and 0.584m stroke. 2 Normand boilers (Du Temple in *Cerbère*). 148t coal (normal, total bunker capacity 174.500t) = 4,301.8nm @ 10.27kts or 3,040.9nm @ 13.15kts.

**Guns:**

(1913) 1 x 75mm/62.5 Model S.A. M1908 (Schneider) on the bow.

(War, *Pluton*) Add 1 x 75mm M1908 on the stern, 1 x 47mm AA just forward of the after 75mm

(War, *Cerbère*) Add 1 x 47mm/50 M1902 aft (DM 9.5.1916). This was replaced by 1 x 75mm (Army) by a ministerial telegram of 4.7.1917. Two machine guns added on *Cerbère* 1.1919.

*Pluton* (a1) Augustin Normand, Le Havre/Normand, Le Havre.
On list 1.1911. Ord: 23.3.1910. K: 1911. L: 10.3.1913. Comm: 26.8.1913.
Budget 1910 (late addition). Assigned to the *2e Escadre légère* at Cherbourg on 9.8.1913. Laid mines off Zeebrugge and with *Cerbère* off the Flanders coast 10-11.1914, then moved to the Mediterranean c1915 where she laid several mine fields in 1915-17. In the Black Sea 1919 and off Syria 1920. Decomm. 11.1920 Struck 27.10.1921, for sale at Toulon 1921-1923.

*Cerbère* (a2) A.C. Bretagne, Nantes/ACB, Nantes.
On list 1.1911. Ord: 5.4.1911. K: 1911. L: 13.7.1912. Comm: 28.6.1913.
Budget 1911. In service with the *2e Escadre légère* at Cherbourg 6.1913. Served initially in the Channel mining areas that might be used by German submarines, to Morocco for patrol duty 9.1916 returning several times to the Atlantic including a minelaying mission on the Vergoyer Bank near Boulogne 7.1917, then to the eastern Mediterranean 3.1919 where she transported up to 440 Syrian refugees. Struck 27.10.1921, for sale at Toulon 1921-1923.

---

*UNNAMED MINELAYER. Mouilleur de mines.*

On 20 March 1912 the Naval General Staff listed the special ships planned for the 1913 and later budgets, including two 20-knot ships for minesweeping and minelaying to follow *Cerbère*. They were to have one 75mm gun each. The 1914 budget contained one ship to be ordered in the first trimester of 1914 and built by contract, while the 1915 budget, which was never passed, contained the same ship to be ordered in mid-1915 to replace *Cassini* and *Casabianca*. The characteristics of the ship, which had grown since 1912, were discussed in a memorandum dated 17 June 1914 and were based on those of the German *Albatros* and *Nautile* and three 3,500-ton minelayers reported building in Italy. Of key importance, she was to be able to steam 800 miles at her full speed of 25 knots (which would require a trial speed of 27 knots) plus 400 miles at 15 knots. This would allow her to raid the Elbe from Cherbourg (460 miles), Naples from Toulon (400 miles) or Taranto from Bizerte (550 miles). A loadout of 300 mines would be needed for the Jade and 265 mines for La Spezia. The following characteristics from a very preliminary design were reported in a memorandum of 26 June 1914.

**Dimensions & tons:** 85.0m x 9.5m. 1,420t disp. Draught: under 4.0m
**Machinery:** 17,500 to 18,000ihp. Speed 27kts at a displacement of 1,250 tons, 25kts at 1,420 tons.
**Guns:** 2 x 138.6mm (new model destroyer guns, one forward, one aft). 2 searchlights. 300 mines

*N* (Unnamed) Contract.
Budget 1914 (delayed to 1915). Not built.

---

## (G) Minesweepers.

### Early French naval minesweeping
In 1909 the *Conseil supérieur* included eight minesweepers in its 1909 fleet program. Impressed by a report on minesweeping by Capitaine de vaisseau Ronarc'h, Minister Boué de Lapeyrère charged him to buy two trawlers. He found one at Lorient and the other at Saint Nazaire and was given full authority to decide by experiment what was needed to outfit them and to buy the equipment. The Minister then decided to buy two trawlers for each port and to build four specially designed minesweepers with the intent of attaching one to each of the four battle squadrons in the naval programmes.

In 1910 the French Navy tested on the destroyer *Fourche* minesweeping gear developed by Admiral Ronarc'h that used a water kite or depressor to submerge the tow line close to the sweeper's stern, from which point two sweep lines were deployed that were spread apart by otter boards in the same way that trawlers spread the lines attached to the mouths of their nets and that were kept at the desired depth by floats that were deployed by small davits near the stern. In contrast to this single-ship sweep, the British used two ships to deploy a single sweep line. The *drague Ronarc'h* remained in service from 1912 to 1944 and strongly influenced later systems, notably the British Oropesa sweep, named after the World War I hired trawler that first tested it. To tow the *drague Ronarc'h* small shallow draft ships like trawlers sufficed, and many of these would be requisitioned in wartime to supplement the few in the peacetime navy.

---

*HERSE* Class. *Dragueurs de mines* 1.1914. Trawler-type minesweepers with one tall funnel amidships and one mast. *Dragueurs* 1.3.1920.

These vessels were funded under the 1913 budget (submitted March 1912) which allowed the navy to build up to 2,000 tons of ships not itemized in the budget. On 20 March 1912 the Naval General Staff listed the special ships planned for the 1913 and later budgets, including three minesweepers of 250 tons and 12 knots to a design already prepared by Brest to be ordered at the beginning of 1913 and delivered during that year. (Other ships in this list were the Yangtse gunboat *Balny*, an enlarged *Décidée* type gunboat, a replacement for the fishery protection school ship *Ibis* (*Flamant*), two 20-knot ships for minesweeping and minelaying to follow *Cerbère*, a station aviso, and the transport *Seine* which had just been ordered.) On 27 December 1912 the Machinery Commission (known from 1910 as the *Commission Centrale des Machines et du Grand Outillage*) was directed to order four minesweepers, two for Toulon and two for Bizerte. They were named on 12 June 1913 and their contract was signed on 21 May 1913, and approved by Minister Baudin and notified on 16 June 1913. Although they were listed in the 1st line in the fleet lists, the building standards in the contract were those for service craft (*bâtiments de servitude*).

When *Herse* transited from La Seyne to Toulon for delivery on 16 June 1914 she conducted preliminary machinery trials, and, while generating 735ihp, well above the contract, she made only 10.8 knots instead of the specified 12 knots. The initial trial speeds of the others also fell short. The builder felt the problem was due to the screw propeller being too small, but the war intervened and replacement of the screws was deferred due to operational requirements. The hulls of *Charrue* and *Herse* were also badly corroded by 1916, which was thought to have been due to their being sent to the Dardanelles without taking the time to paint their bottoms. *Pioche*

The minesweeper *Herse* at Mykonos, probably in 1917-18. One of a class of four built for the navy at La Seyne in 1913-14, *Herse* and her sister *Charrue* were assigned in February 1915 to the 2nd squadron (*escadrille*) of the Dardanelles minesweeper flotilla while the other two sisters, *Rateau* and *Pioche*, joined the 1st squadron. From 1 June 1917 to 1 July 1918 *Herse* belonged to the naval force based at Salonica, and from 5 June to 11 November 1918 she was integrated into the Aegean Squadron (*Escadre*). (*Forum.pages14-18.com*)

was then still in good condition. *Herse* was lost under tow on 5 February 1920 and on 3 April 1920 the Minister informed Toulon that he was renouncing the use of *Rateau*, *Charrue*, and *Pioche* which no longer suited the role for which they had been built and which should be immediately decommissioned.

*The characteristics are from the contract for the ships.*
**Dimensions & tons:** 36,80m oa, 34.00m pp x 6.80m ext. 255.570t disp. Draught: 1.98m mean, 2.396m aft. **Men:** 14.
**Machinery:** 600ihp designed at 150rpm and 10kg/cm² boiler pressure. Speed 12kts. 1 screw. 1 vertical compound engine with 2 cylinders of 0.540m and 0.970m diameter and 0.550m stroke. 1 cylindrical tubular return-flame boiler. 35t coal.
**Guns:** 2 x 47mm QF.

*Herse* F.C. Méditerranée, La Seyne.
On list 1.1914. Ord: 21.5.1913. K: 1913. L: 1914. C: 3.8.1914.
Budget 1913 (late addition). Builder's hull 1062. Named 12.6.1913. Accepted from the builder 3.8.1914, accepted for service (*clôture d' armement*) 7.8.1914. Dardanelles 1915. Sunk 5.2.1920, 31 miles from Bizerte, while under tow from there to Toulon, suspected causes included bad condition of the hull or more likely a sudden influx of water through the stern gland.

*Rateau* F.C. Méditerranée, La Seyne.
On list 1.1914. Ord: 21.5.1913. K: 1913. L: 1914. C: 3.8.1914.
Budget 1913 (late addition). Builder's hull 1063. Named 12.6.1913. Delivered to Toulon 1.8.1914. Accepted from the builder 3.8.1914, accepted for service 7.8.1914. Dardanelles 1915. Struck 5.3.1921, for sale at Toulon 1921-1922, bids too low and reinscribed 2.6.1922 as a ship in reserve, again for sale at Toulon 1922-1923, struck again 24.2.1923 and to the Domaines. Sold 26.4.1923 at Toulon to M. Saglia.

*Charrue* F.C. Méditerranée, La Seyne.
On list 1.1914. Ord: 21.5.1913. K: 1913. L: 1914. C: 7.8.1914.
Budget 1913 (late addition). Builder's hull 1064. Named 12.6.1913. Delivered at Toulon 18.7.1914. Accepted from builder and accepted for service 7.8.1914. Dardanelles 1915. Struck 5.3.1921, for sale at Toulon 1921-1922, bids too low and reinscribed 2.6.1922 as a ship in reserve, again for sale at Toulon 1922-1923, struck again 24.2.1923 and to the Domaines. Sold 26.4.1923 at Toulon to M. Vidal.

*Pioche* F.C. Méditerranée, La Seyne.
On list 1.1914. Ord: 21.5.1913. K: 1913. L: 1914. C: 10.8.1914.
Budget 1913 (late addition). Builder's hull 1065. Named 12.6.1913. Delivered at Toulon 18.7.1914. Accepted from builder and accepted for service 10.8.1914. Dardanelles 1915, later cited for her role in defending Marseille against offensive mining. Struck 5.3.1921, for sale at Toulon 1921-1922, bids too low and reinscribed 2.6.1922 as a ship in reserve, again for sale at Toulon 1922-1923, struck again 24.2.1923 and to the Domaines. Sold 26.4.1923 at Toulon to M. Ventad.

---

## PURCHASED MINESWEEPERS. *Bâtiments dragueurs de mines.*

Five trawlers were purchased in France in 1910 and 1911 for use as minesweepers. These purchased vessels were typed as *Bâtiments dragueurs de mines* and listed in the second part of the fleet list, in contrast with the purpose-built *Herse* class minesweepers which were classed as *Dragueurs de mines* and listed in the first part of the fleet list.

*Damier*. Originally British trawler *Vindex* launched 1896 by Cochrane & Cooper, Beverley, Humberside, UK (yard N° 163). Delivered to first owner, Atlas Steam Fishing Co. of Grimsby, 19.1.1897. Sold 7.1901 to Benoit & Co, Le Crusic (to St. Nazaire 1910) and renamed *Damier*. Purchased 1910, on list 1.1911.

**Dimensions & tons:** 28.53m x 6.19m, 147grt. **Men:** 15. **Machinery:** 340ihp. Speed 9.02kts. 1 screw. 1 triple expansion engine, 1 boiler. **Guns:** 1 x 47mm.

Credited with commissioned war service between 2.8.1914 and 1.9.1919. In the 1st patrol squadron 1916. Retired 11.1919. Sold 1921, became French *Artha*. Wrecked 8.1.1933 off the Île d'Yeu.

*Lorientais*. Originally British trawler *Maude* launched 1900 by Cochrane and Cooper, Selby, North Yorkshire, UK (yard N° 281, the builder moved from Beverley in 1898). Delivered to first owner, W.F. Harris of Hull and Peter Hancock of Milford Haven, 5.1901. Sold 15.8.1901 to Louis Bigot of Lorient, France, and renamed *Lorientais*. New boiler 1908. Purchased 1910, on list 1.1911.

**Dimensions & tons:** 33.74m x 6.40m. 433t disp. **Men:** 15. **Machinery:** 370ihp. Speed 9.68kts. 1 screw. 1 triple expansion engine. **Guns:** 1 x 47mm.

School ship at Boulogne on 2.4.1914. In 1918 was in the 6th patrol division at Dunkirk. Retired 1919. Sale offer 27.8.1919 failed. Sold 9.1919 to M. Noblanc of Lorient, renamed *Maurice et Jean* 17.8.1920, *Madeleine et Madeleine* 1.9.1925, and *Epagneul* 1929. Sold 4.1938, left Fécamp 6.4.1938 to BU in Germany.

*Alcyon*. Ex French trawler *Lizzie* launched by Earle's Co., Hull (UK), 1897, purchased 1911, in service 1911 as minesweeper, and on list 1.1912.

**Dimensions & tons:** 32.00m x 6.40m. 300t disp. **Men:** 15. **Machinery:** 320ihp. Speed 8.5kts. 1 triple expansion engine. 1 boiler. **Guns:** 1 x 47mm.

Surveyed at Saint Nazaire 6.1910. Credited with commissioned war service between 2.8.1914 and 24.6.1919. In Calais Flotilla 1914-18 as *Alcyon I*. Retired 1919. Was Italian *Lanciotto Piero* when requisitioned at Naples on 26.9.1940 as patrol boat *V.79* and then as subchaser *AS.80*. At Argostoli 9.1943, sunk, refloated by the Greeks.

*Iroise*. Ex French trawler *Marie-Marcelle*, built 1907 by Blasse at Nantes, purchased 1911, on list 1.1912.

**Dimensions & tons:** 36.99m x 6.43m. 223grt. **Men:** 15. **Machinery:** 432ihp. Speed 10kts. 1 triple expansion engine. 1 boiler. **Guns:** 1 x 47mm.

Surveyed at La Rochelle 12.1909. Credited with commissioned war service between 2.8.1914 and 24.10.1919. Retired 11.1919.

*Orient*. Ex French trawler *Orient*, built 1908 with sister *Occident* by De La Brosse et Fouché of Nantes, purchased 1911, on list 1.1912.

**Dimensions & tons:** 43.30m x 6.88m. 385t disp. **Men:** 15. **Machinery:** 500ihp. Speed 11kts. 1 triple expansion engine, 1 boiler. **Guns:** 1 x 47mm.

Surveyed at Bordeaux 11.1911. Credited with commissioned war service between 2.8.1914 and 26.5.1919. Retired 11.1919. Delivered 1.1920 to François Fourny & Cie at Boulogne for fishing. Requisitioned 1939 at Boulogne, seized by the Germans 1940 as *V.1802*, sunk 11.11.1944 at Memel by allied aircraft.

---

# II. AUXILIARIES

## (A) Transports (*Transports*).

**LOIRET.** *Transport*. Cargo ship with merged forecastle and bridge island and a straight bow. One funnel, two masts. Purchased. Originally rated as 3rd Class Transport (*Transport de 3ᵉ classe*), to *Transports* 1.1909.

*Loiret* was built in the UK as the cargo ship *Paris* for the London & Paris

SS Co Ltd (Strick) of Swansea. She was purchased by the French Navy in 1900 to replace the lost *Caravane*.

**Dimensions & tons:** 72.85m oa x 9.88m ext. 2,200t disp. Draught: 5.00m max. Men: 61 including 3 officers.
**Machinery:** 1,050ihp. Speed 11.50kts. 1 screw. 2 Belleville and 1 auxiliary boilers. 193t coal.
**Guns:** 1 x 65mm. (1924) none.

*Loiret* Wood Skinner, Bill Quay, UK.
On list 1.1902. K: 1899. L: 12.5.1900. C: 9.6.1900 (merchant). C: 7.1901 (French trials).
Named 1901. Listed as *Transport* 1920-1936. Struck 25.1.1937 (decision promulgated 26.4.1937). Sold 2.7.1937 at Brest to BU.

————————

*SEINE. Transport.* Cargo ship with three islands and a straight bow. One funnel, two masts.

On 29 September 1910 Director of the *Service technique* Lyasse signed a sketch design for a *transport du littoral* that became the coastal transport *Seine*. The completed design, which replicated the standard three-island freighters of the day, was signed on 8 July 1911 and approved on 25 July 1911. The contract to build the ship was concluded on 14 February 1912 with the Chantiers & Ateliers de Provence, Port de Bouc.

**Dimensions & tons:** 81.40m oa x 11.05m ext. 3,157t disp. Draught: 5.40m max. Men: 68 including 4 officers.
**Machinery:** 1,930ihp. Speed 12.60kts. 1 screw. 4 cylindrical boilers. 260t coal.
**Guns:** (1915) 1 x 65mm line throwing gun. (1917) 1 x 75mm (Guerre, on poop), 2 x 65mm (on forecastle, the line throwing gun also retained). (1921) none.

*Seine* (T) C.A. Provence, Port de Bouc/C.A. Provence, Marseille.
On list 1.1914. Ord: 14.12.1912. K: 1912. L: 1913. C: 18.8.1913.
Budget 1912. Construction reassigned from dockyard to contract 1912. Trials ended (*clôture des essais*) 31.7.1913. Listed as *Transport* 1920-1933. Collided 13.12.1932 with the British merchantman *Great End* in the Charente River while departing Rochefort, returned for a week of repairs. Departed again 20.12.1932, uncontrollable leaks developed and she sank in the evening of 21.12.1932 southwest of the Île d'Oléron while under tow. Struck 13.1.1933.

————————

## (B) Oilers (*Transports-pétroliers*).

*RHÔNE. Transport-pétrolier.* Oil tanker with three islands with the bridge amidships, the machinery aft, and a straight bow. One tall funnel, two masts. Purchased.

This commercial tanker was built under a contract of 7 May 1909 between the Société de Pétroles-Transports (a single-ship subsidiary of the Compagnie Mixte) and the Chantiers de Normandie at Rouen (Grand Quévilly), owned since 1901 by the Chantiers et Ateliers de Saint Nazaire (Penhoët). The ship was towed from Rouen to Saint Nazaire after launch for the installation of her propulsion machinery. She was named *Radioléine* on 22 May 1910 when delivered to her owners. The Navy purchased and renamed her on 23 October 1910.

**Dimensions & tons:** 112.50m oa, 106.70m pp x 13.75m ext. 7,779t disp. Draught: 7.06m aft. Men: 60 including 3 officers.
**Machinery:** 2,400ihp at 83rpm and 13kg/cm² boiler pressure. Speed 11.53kts. 1 screw. 1 triple expansion engine with 3 cylinders of 0.62m, 1.02m, and 1.69m diameter and 1.22m stroke. 2 cylindrical boilers. 570t coal.
**Guns:** (1915) 1 x 65mm, 2 x 47mm. (1924) none. (1938) 1 x 100mm.

*Rhône* Ch. Penhoët, Rouen-Grand Quévilly.
On list 1.1911. K: 15.7.1909. L: 26.3.1910. C: 1.3.1911.
In merchant service 22.5.1910, chartered by the Navy 1.1.1911, in naval service 1.3.1911. Listed as *Transport* 1.1913, *transport* with notation *pétrolier* 1.1914, and as *pétrolier* 1920-1939. Credited with commissioned war service between 2.8.1914 and 24.10.1919. Torpedoed and sunk 20.12.1940 by the German submarine *U-37* off Port Étienne while en route from Casablanca to Dakar and while saving the survivors of the escorting submarine *Sfax* which *U-37* had previously torpedoed.

————————

*GARONNE. Transport-pétrolier.* Oil tanker with three islands with the bridge amidships, the machinery aft, and a straight bow. One funnel, three masts. Purchased.

This commercial tanker was ordered on 3 October 1911 as *Lucellum* by the Lucellum Steamship Co. Ltd., a single-ship firm. She was delivered in December 1912. The Navy purchased her in January 1913 from Moss & Co. She was delivered to the navy at Amsterdam, inscribed on the fleet list, and renamed on 21 January 1913. Her commanding officer was assigned to the ship on 1 April 1913. A replacement *Lucellum* with the same dimensions was launched on 14 June 1913.

**Dimensions & tons:** 121.00m oa x 15.50m ext. 11,000t disp. Draught: 8.00m max. Men: 65.
**Machinery:** 2,400ihp at 73rpm and 12.65kg/cm² boiler pressure. Speed 11.33kts. 1 screw. 1 triple expansion engine with 3 cylinders of 0.66m, 1.12m, and 1.83m diameter and 1.22m stroke. 2 cylindrical boilers. 500t coal.
**Guns:** (1924) none.

*Garonne* James Laing & Sons, Sunderland, UK/George Clark, Sunderland.
On list 1.1914. K: 1912. L: 24.10.1912. C: 12.1912.
Listed as *Transport* with notation *pétrolier* 1.1914. Credited with commissioned war service between 2.8.1914 and 19.3.1916 and between 8.9.1919 and 24.9.1919. Chartered to the British 18.3.1916 at Malta and renamed *Fleur de Lys*. Returned 7.1919 at Cherbourg and listed as *pétrolier* 1920-1939. At Toulon 27.11.1942 but not scuttled. Sunk at Toulon 11.3.1944 by air bombardment, scuttled 20.6.1944 to block the northern pass at Toulon, raised 24.10.1945, condemned 9.2.1946, struck 19.4.1946.

————————

*MEUSE. Transport-pétrolier.* Oil tanker.

The Navy ordered construction of one tanker (*transport-pétrolier*) on 17 December 1913 under the 1914 budget for delivery in July 1915. She was built to Bureau Veritas (mercantile) standards by the Chantiers de Normandie yard at Rouen (Grand Quévilly), then owned by the Chantiers et Ateliers de Saint Nazaire (Penhoët). The Navy contract was one of many cancelled at the outbreak of World War I, more than half of the workers at this yard having been mobilised. She was delivered to the French merchant marine 2 October 1916.

**Dimensions & tons:** 117.5m x 15.6m. 11,233t disp. Men: 46.
**Machinery:** 2,400ihp. 11kts. 1 screw. 1 triple expansion engine, 3 boilers
**Guns:** 2 x 65mm (1917, one forward and one aft)

*Meuse* Ch. Penhoët, Rouen-Grand Quévilly.
On list 1.1914. Ord: 17.12.1913. K: 1914. L: 17.6.1916. C: 11.1916.
Budget 1913 (late addition). Navy acquisition cancelled late 1914, completed as mercantile *Meuse II* (renamed 16.6.1916). Delivered 2.10.1916. Sailed for Borneo 11.1916 under civilian operation to load petroleum residue for the navy's *Service des Poudres* (gunpowder service). Time chartered 23.5.1917 to the Société Lille-Bonnières et

Colombes. Torpedoed and sunk 17.8.1917 by *UC-72* 140nm south-west of Ushant while en route from Brest to New York in ballast.

## (C) Steam Fishery Protection Vessels (*Garde-pêche à vapeur*).

The fishery protection vessels added to the fleet list from 1899 included four ships in the regular fleet plus seven listed as service craft under commercial operation. Some were listed as *Chaloupes à vapeur garde-pêche* while building. *Chélif* and *Seybouse* were moved to this category in January 1904.

*SENTINELLE* **Class.** *Garde-pêche à vapeur.* Screw trawlers with raised fore-castle and straight bow. One funnel, two masts. Purchased.

On 16 December 1899 Minister de Lanessan approved buying a fishery protection vessel in Britain. On 28 December 1899 a contract was signed and approved for the purchase of the trawler *City of York*, renamed *Sentinelle*, from Hagerup Doughty & Co., Ltd., of Grimsby, UK. She was manned and commissioned on 14 May 1900 by transferring her crew from the fishery protection vessel *Hareng*. Her commander was a 1st class pilot (*Pilote de 1ère classe*).

*Estafette* was her sister *City of Glasgow* purchased three years later from the same owner.

*The characteristics are based on a devis for* Sentinelle *dated 3.7.1900.*
**Dimensions & tons:** 42.010m oa, 39.46m wl (tip fwd to stern) x 7.000m ext & wl. 471.253t disp. Draught: 3.195m mean, 3.839m aft. Men: 20.
**Machinery:** 450ihp designed at 110rpm and 12.65kg/cm² boiler pressure. Trials (23.6.1900) 574ihp = 10.885kts at 105.02rpm and 11.35kg/cm² boiler pressure. 1 screw. 1 triple expansion engine with 3 cylinders of 0.371m, 0.585m, and 0.913m diameter and 0.685m stroke. 1 cylindrical return flame boiler. 90t coal. Range 4,704nm @ 8.012kts, 2,145nm @ 10.885kts.
**Guns:** 1 x 47mm/40 M1885 QF.

*Sentinelle.* Mackie & Thomson, Govan, UK (yard Nº 148).
On list 1.1900. L: 17.12.1896. C: 1897. In service 1899.
Annex (tender) to *Ibis* in 1904 and *Yatagan* in 1914. Struck 1.10.1920. Sale offer of 23.5.1921 for further operation unsuccessful. Sold 11.1921 to M. Rodeiron of Cherbourg.

*Estafette.* Mackie & Thomson, Govan, UK (yard Nº 147)
On list 1.1903. L: 17.12.1896. C: 1897. In service 1902.
Annex to *Ibis*, later *Yatagan*, on the Channel and North Sea station (fishery protection). Mined and sunk 21.4.1916 near Dyck while operating out of Dunkirk as a boarding vessel. The mine was laid by the German submarine *UC-6*.

*QUI-VIVE.* *Garde-pêche à vapeur.* Small screw steamer, flush-decked. One funnel, one mast.

Listed while building as a *chaloupe à vapeur garde-pêche*, *Qui-Vive* was built to replace the even smaller *Nautile* (1887) as a fishery protection vessel in the Bidasoa river on the border with Spain. She spent her entire naval career there.

**Dimensions & tons:** 24.14m x 4.80m. 70t disp. Draught 1.80m. Men: 10.
**Machinery:** 180ihp. 11.4kts
**Guns:** 1 x 37mm.

*Qui-Vive* Decout-Lacour, La Rochelle
On list 1.1901. K: 1901. L: 1902. C: 1903.
Was running trials 1.1903. Initially assigned to Saint Jean de Luz in the Bidasoa, replacing *Nautile*. Remained there during the war. Struck 12.3.1920. Probably became the coastal packet *Qui Vive* of the Société de Navigation à Vapeur l'Ilaise, Ile d'Yeu, registered 31.12.1920. Sold

three times 1934-37, all to owners at La Rochelle, later fate unknown.

*GOLO.* *Garde-pêche à vapeur.* Small screw steamer, flush-decked. One funnel, two masts.

Also listed while building as a *chaloupe à vapeur garde-pêche*, *Golo*, barely larger than *Qui-Vive*, gave Toulon and Corsica a dedicated naval steam fishery protection vessel that they had recently lacked.

**Dimensions & tons:** 25m x 5.5m. 52t disp. Men: 12.
**Machinery:** 270ihp
**Guns:** 2 x 37mm.

*Golo* Dyle et Bacalan, Bordeaux-Bacalan.
On list 1.1902. Ord: 2.10.1901. K: 1901. L: 1903. C: 7.1903.
Stationed at Toulon and in Corsica. Credited with commissioned war service between 2.8.1914 and 3.8.1919. Served in the Mediterranean 1914-1919 under the name *Golo I* (*Golo II* being a Corsica mail steamer requisitioned in 1914 and wrecked in 1917). Retired 1919, to the Port Director at Toulon for operation 11.8.1919.

## COMMERCIALLY-OPERATED FISHERY PROTECTION VESSELS (STEAM).

The first steam-powered vessel to join the many small sailing fishery protection vessels on the French naval fleet list was the *chaloupe à vapeur Surveillant* of 1886 (see Chapter 10), which was assigned in the late 1880s or early 1890s to fishery protection duty. With the sailing craft she was listed *pour ordre* (for the record) from January 1897 with service craft because she was under commercial operation. Seven more steam-powered vessels (and no more sailing craft) joined this category *pour ordre* as service craft between 1899 and 1906. All of the commercially operated fishery protection vessels were moved to a separate list for *Surveillance des pêches* in January 1908 and vessels acquired after that date are not listed here.

*Trieux.* 150ihp. On list 1.1900. Built 1899, at Brest 1899-1904, at Rochefort 1904-1907. On special fisheries list 1908 to 1914 at Port de Bouc, renamed *Vanneau* 1908.

*Pétrel.* 275ihp. On list 1.1900. Built by F.C. Méditerranée, Le Havre-Graville (K: 1899, L: 1900) for commercial operation. In service at Rochefort 1.1903, to Lorient 1.1905. On special fisheries list 1908 to 1914 at Lorient. Designated *Pétrel I* during war service 2.8.1914 to 6.5.1919 to distinguish her from a trawler requisitioned at Le Havre.

*Pénerf.* Steam, 7ihp. On list 1.1900, launched and in service 1899. At Lorient 1.1900. On special fisheries list 1908 to 1913 at Auray, renamed *Berder* 1908.

*Brochet.* Steam, ex British yacht *Zeus* purchased 11.7.1898, commissioned 26.5.1899, on list 1.1900, and operated commercially at Toulon 1900-02. Replaced the sailing *Brochet* at Sète.

*Albatros.* 235ihp. On list 1.1902. Built by the Chantiers et Ateliers de Saint Nazaire (Penhoët) (K: 1903, L: 1904, in service 1.1905) for commercial operation. On special fisheries list 1908 to 1914 at Saint Servan. Commissioned 1915 as *Albatros I*, minesweeper and boarding vessel attached to the Channel trawler flotilla. Badly damaged 26-27.10.1916 in raid by 12 German destroyers of the Flanders flotilla at Cape Gris Nez.

*Girelle.* 150ihp, ex *Souvenir*. On list 1.1903. At Toulon under commercial operation 1903. On special fisheries list 1908 to 1914 at Cette.

*Suzy.* 35ihp. On list 1.1907 at Rochefort as a *garde-pêche automobile* or *canot automobile*. Renamed *Andernos* 1908. On special fisheries list 1908 to 1914 at Arcachon.

# Appendix A

# French Naval Artillery, 1858-1914

These data are mostly from a lengthy official French tabular document entitled *Renseignements sur les Bouches à Feu de l'Artillerie Navale de tous Calibres & Modèles* that is now in the U.S. National Archives (Record Group 38, Register 12008A). It was forwarded on 17 July 1919 by the *Directeur Central de l'Artillerie Navale* through channels to the U.S. Naval Attaché, Rear Admiral Andrew Theodore Long, who had requested it on 31 May 1919. The French asked that the Americans reciprocate by providing similar information on American naval artillery, but it

| Designation (M = Modèle) | Type | Cal., mm. | Cal., inch | Model | Length total, mm. | Length, Cals. | Weight Gun, kg | Projectile, kg. |
|---|---|---|---|---|---|---|---|---|
| **Smoothbores** | | | | | | | | |
| Obusier de 16cm | Smoothbore, shell | 163.0 | 6.4 | 1827, 1849 | 2176 | 13.0 | 1480 | 10.00 |
| 30pdr No.1 (long) | Smoothbore | 164.7 | 6.5 | 1849 | 2775 | 16.5 | 3035 | 15.34 |
| Canon de 50 [livres] (50pdr) | Smoothbore | 194 | 7.6 | 1849 | 3170 | 16.4 | 4624 | 25.15 |
| **Army 1858-59 (bronze)** | | | | | | | | |
| Canon-obusier de 4 [kg] de montagne | MLR | 86.5 | 3.4 | 1859 | 820 | 11 | 101 | 4 |
| Canon-obusier de 12 [livres] de campagne (12pdr) | MLR | 121.0 | 4.76 | 1858 | 1910 | 17 | 620 | 5.9 |
| **Modèle 1858-60** | | | | | | | | |
| 14cm M1858-60 No.1 | MLR | 140.0 | 5.5 | 1858-60 | 2875 | 17.45 | 2300 | 18.65 |
| 14cm M1858-60 No.2 | MLR | 138.7 | 5.5 | 1858-60 | 2678 | 16.5 | 1830 | 18.65 |
| 16cm M1858-60 bouche (muzzle) | MLR | 164.7 | 6.5 | 1858-60, ex 1858 | 3250 | 16.7 | 3640 | 31.49 |
| 16cm M1858-60 culasse (breech) | BLR | 164.7 | 6.5 | 1858-60 | 2950 | 15.97 | 3640 | 31.49 |
| Obusier de 22cm rayé fretté | MLR | 223.3 | 8.8 | 1858-60 | 2840 | 10.53 | 3700 | 82 |
| **Modèle 1864** | | | | | | | | |
| 14cm rayé M1864 | BLR | 138.6 | 5.5 | 1864 | 2060 | 13.5 | 1900 | 18.65 |
| 16cm rayé M1864 | BLR | 164.7 | 6.5 | 1864 | 3385 | 19.2 | 5000 | 31.49/45 |
| 19cm rayé M1864 | BLR | 194 | 7.6 | 1864 | 3800 | 18.1 | 8000 | 53.25/75 |
| 24cm rayé M1864 | BLR | 240 | 9.4 | 1864 | 4560 | 17.5 | 14,500 | 100/144 |
| 27cm rayé M1864 | BLR | 274.4 | 10.8 | 1864 | 4660 | 15.4 | 20,500 | 144/216 |
| **Modèle 1870 (iron)** | | | | | | | | |
| 14cm | BLR | 138.6 | 5.5 | 1870 | 3135 | 21.3 | 2690 | 23 |
| 16cm (added late) | BLR | 164.7 | 6.5 | 1870 | 3710 | 21 | 5000 | – |
| 19cm No.1 long | BLR | 194 | 7.6 | 1870 | 4150 | 19.77 | 7960 | 75 |
| 24cm | BLR | 240 | 9.4 | 1870 | 4940 | 18.97 | 15,660 | 144 |
| 27cm | BLR | 274.4 | 10.8 | 1870 | 5380 | 18 | 23,200 | 180/216 |
| 32cm No.1 long | BLR | 320 | 12.6 | 1870 | 6700 | 19.3 | 39,000 | 345 |
| **Modèle 1870 Modifié (1870M)** | | | | | | | | |
| 14cm | BLR | 138.6 | 5.5 | 1870M | 3135 | 21.3 | 2665 | 28 |
| 24cm | BLR | 240 | 9.4 | 1870M | 4940 | 18.97 | 15,500 | 144 |
| 27cm | BLR | 274.4 | 10.8 | 1870M | 5380 | 18 | 23,220 | 216 |
| 32cm | BLR | 320 | 12.6 | 1870M | 6700 | 19.3 | 38,985 | 345 |
| **Modèle 1870-81 (iron)** | | | | | | | | |
| 32cm | BLR | 320 | 12.6 | 1870-81 | 8512 | 25 | 42,800 | 345 |
| **Modèle 1875 (steel)** | | | | | | | | |
| 10cm | BLR | 100 | 3.9 | 1875 | 2821 | 26.49 | 1200 | 12 |
| 27cm No.1 | BLR | 274.4 | 10.8 | 1875 | 5872 | 19.75 | 27,800 | 180/216 |
| 27cm No.2 | BLR | 274.4 | 10.8 | 1875 | 5870.7 | 19.75 | 24,800 | 180/216 |
| 34cm de 18 cal à petite chambre. | BLR | 340 | 13.4 | 1875 | 6700 | 18.03 | 48,550 | 350/420 |
| 34cm de 21 cal à petite chambre. | BLR | 340 | 13.4 | 1875 | 7720 | 21.03 | 50,890 | 350/420 |
| 42cm de 22 cal. | BLR | 420 | 16.5 | 1875 | 9900 | 22 | 76,785 | 650/780 |
| 42cm de 19.35 cal. | BLR | 420 | 16.5 | 1875 | 8781 | 19.35 | 76,500 | 650/780 |

is not known if this occurred. Guns in the French list that are not known to have gone to sea are omitted here. A few models were added from the official *Aide-Mémoire d'Artillerie Navale*, 1873/1892.

**Notes. Some ships or classes known to have carried the weapons are shown, these are not in the 1919 document.**

30pdr shell gun in a few transports. For the converted 22cm obusier see M1858-60 below
30pdr smoothbore. *Vénus, Decrès*
50pdr smoothbore, used as heavy battery guns with 164.7mm rifles. *Normandie, Couronne, Magenta, Provence, Héroïne, Dévastation.*

Army smoothbore 4pdr mountain gun with Lahitte rifling. Design based on a longer (160cm) 4pdr field gun of 1858 that was not strong enough and was not used. Replaced in Navy as a landing gun by the 65mm BLR.
M1853 bronze army smoothbore field gun (the *Napoléon*) with Lahitte rifling. Originally in reserve, but used by the Army from 1863 because the 1858 4pdr field gun was not strong enough. Replaced in Navy for large boats and avisos by the 90mm BLR, also used as secondary battery in some ironclads.

Converted 18pdr long. Plans dated 9.7.1863. *Vénus, Infernet, Hamelin, Linois, Bourayne.*
Converted 18pdr short. 1st plans dated 25.4.1867. *Decrès, Hamelin, Ducouëdic.*
Shaped like the 36pdr smoothbore. First rifling instruction dated 15.3.1858 (M1858), *tables de construction* dated 30.11.1859, new rifling profile adopted 3.12.1860 (M1858-60) and all M1858 guns converted. *Gloire* (initially M1858), *Couronne, Vénus.*
1st plans dated 14.3.1861. *Gloire* after trials, *Invincible, Vénus.*
Converted (rifled and hooped) smoothbore shell guns (obusiers) M1827 including some modified in 1837 and 1841. Plans dated 16.8.1864. Used as upper deck pivot guns. *Couronne, Magenta, Provence, Héroïne.*

Adopted 20.4.1867 and often called M1867, 1st plans dated 4.7.1867. *Decrès, Linois,* planned for *Bourayne*
1st plans dated 25.10.1864. *Provence, Héroïne, Belliqueuse, Palestro, Implacable, Embuscade, Decrès, Châteaurenault, Infernet, Bourayne*
1st plans dated 25.10.1864. *Gloire, Couronne, Magenta, Provence, Héroïne, Belliqueuse, Alma, Implacable, Embuscade, Bourayne.*
1st plans dated 25.10.1864. *Gloire, Couronne, Magenta, Provence, Héroïne, Océan ,Taureau, Cerbère, Onondaga, Implacable, Imprenable*
1st plans dated 21.12.1864. *Océan, Suffren*

1st plans dated 2.9.1872. *Savoie, Héroïne, Océan, Friedland, Richelieu, Colbert, Redoutable, Al. Duperré, Belliqueuse, Victorieuse, Bayard, Duguesclin, Duquesne, Iphigénie, Naïade, Aréthuse, Châteaurenault, Infernet, Sané, Duguay-Trouin, Lapérouse, Talisman, Hamelin, Bourayne, Duchaffault, Rigault de Genouilly, Boursaint, Chacal, Aspic, Sagittaire, Gironde, Allier.*
1st plans 12.10.1877. *Iphigénie, Naïade,* planned for *Dubourdieu.*
Plans approved 11.1.1872. *Provence, Héroïne, Belliqueuse, Montcalm, Victorieuse, Bayard, Duguesclin, Duquesne, Duguay-Trouin.*
1st plans 5.5.1872, major changes 1875. *Provence, Héroïne, Suffren,Richelieu, Colbert, La Galissonnière, Victorieuse, Onondaga.*
1st plans 27.5.1872, major changes 1875. *Océan, Marengo, Suffren, Friedland, Richelieu, Colbert.*
Plans 16.4.1875 (long model). Proposed for *Redoutable* (2 guns above redoubt), *Dévastation* (2 ships, see 1870M), *Tempête* (3 ships), *Tonnerre* (3 ships) but none fitted. Probably coastal.
Rifling details of M1870 changed 1879, sometimes called M1879.
*Dévastation, Vauban, Naïade, Champlain, Villars*
*Bayard, Duguesclin.*
*Dévastation*
Proposed for *Dévastation* class (2 ships, 4 guns in redoubt). Not embarked, probably coastal.

1st plans 28.10.1881. A coastal gun retrofitted for the redoubt in *Dévastation* (1 ship) in 1889.

1st plans 17.11.1873.
1st plans 6.7.1876. *Redoutable, Courbet, Tempête, Tonnerre, Fulminant.*
1st plans 21.10.1873 modified 14.11.1876. *Redoutable* redoubt (only 4 guns built)
Small chamber. 1st plans 6.7.1876, new design 12.8.1879. 90cm of tube exposed at muzzle. *Dévastation, Duperré* (original), *Vengeur*
Small chamber. 1st plans 6.9.1881. 91.5cm of tube exposed at muzzle. *Tonnant, Furieux*
1st plans 10.1877 (20 cal), to 21 cal 15.1.1878, to 22 cal 15.9.1879. *Indomptable, Caïman, Requin* (6 guns built)
One 420mm gun built at 21 cal to use a tube whose end was defective, another like it built to arm one ship. After ruptures at the end of the tube during tests the length was reduced to 19.35 cal. *Terrible*

| Designation (M = Modèle) | Type | Cal., mm. | Cal., inch | Model | Length total, mm. | Length, Cals. | Weight Gun, kg | Projectile, kg. |
|---|---|---|---|---|---|---|---|---|
| **Modèle 1875-79 (steel)** | | | | | | | | |
| 37cm (*Formidable*) | BLR | 370 | 14.6 | 1875-79 | 11,185 | 28.52 | 76,280 | 455/560 |
| 37cm (*A. Baudin*) | BLR | 370 | 14.6 | 1875-79 | 11,185 | 28.52 | 72,580 | 455/560 |
| **Misc. 1877-79** | | | | | | | | |
| Canon revolver de 37mm | Can Rev | 37 | 1.5 | (1877) | 1180 | 20 | 210 | — |
| Canon revolver de 47mm | Can Rev | 47 | 1.9 | — | 1730 | 25 | 575 | — |
| 65mm (bronze) M1879 | BLR | 65 | 2.6 | 1879 | 1091 | 15 | 95 | 2.7 |
| 90mm (bronze) | BLR | 90 | 3.5 | (1879) | 2168 | 22 | 605 | — |
| **Modèle 1881** | | | | | | | | |
| 65mm steel | BLR | 65 | 2.6 | 1881 | 1154 | 16 | 95 | 3.49 |
| 90mm steel | BLR | 90 | 3.5 | 1881 | 2168 | 22.11 | 540 | 8 |
| 10cm | BLR | 100 | 3.9 | 1881 | 2821 | 26.19 | 1200 | 14 |
| 14cm | BLR | 138.6 | 5.5 | 1881 | 4372 | 30 | 3260 | 30 |
| 16cm No.1 lourd (heavy) | BLR | 164.7 | 6.5 | 1881 | 4867 | 28 | 5100 | 45 |
| 16cm No.2 léger (light) | BLR | 164.7 | 6.5 | 1881 | 4867 | 28 | 3970 | 45 |
| 24cm | BLR | 240 | 9.4 | 1881 | 7225 | 28.5 | 18,000 | 144 |
| 27cm | BLR | 274.4 | 10.8 | 1881 | 8266 | 28.5 | 27,850 | 216 |
| 34cm de 21 cal. | BLR | 340 | 13.4 | 1881 | 7715 | 21 | 47,750 | 350/420 |
| 34cm | BLR | 340 | 13.4 | 1881 | 7715 | 21 | 47,900 | 350/420 |
| 34cm de 28.5 cal. (long) | BLR | 340 | 13.4 | 1881 | 10,265 | 28.5 | 52,000 (est.) | 350/420 |
| **Modèle 1881 T.R. (QF)** | | | | | | | | |
| 10cm | QF | 100 | 3.9 | 1881 QF | 2821 | 26.04 | 1200 | 14 |
| 14cm | QF | 138.6 | 5.5 | 1881 QF | 4372 | 29.85 | 3250 | 30/35 |
| 16cm | QF | 164.7 | 6.5 | 1881 QF | 4857 | 29.87 | 5080 | 45/52 |
| **Modèle 1884** | | | | | | | | |
| 14cm (some converted to QF) | BLR | 138.6 | 5.5 | 1884 | 4372 | 30 | 3250 | 30 |
| 16cm (all converted to QF) | BLR | 164.7 | 6.5 | 1884 | 5194 | 30 | 5000 | 45 |
| 24cm | BLR | 240 | 9.4 | 1884 | 7585 | 30 | 18,210 | — |
| 27cm | BLR | 274.4 | 10.8 | 1884 | 8677 | 30 | 28,710 | 216 |
| 34cm de 28.5 cal | BLR | 340 | 13.4 | 1884 | 10,265 | 28.5 | 51,244 | 350/420 |
| **Modèle 1884 T.R. (QF)** | | | | | | | | |
| 14cm TR | QF | 138.6 | 5.5 | 1884 QF | 4372 | 29.85 | 3250 | 30/35 |
| 16cm TR | QF | 164.7 | 6.5 | 1884 QF | 5194 | 29.87 | 5000 | 45/52 |
| **Modèle 1885** | | | | | | | | |
| 37mm léger | QF | 37 | 1.5 | 1885 | 842 | 20 | 38 | 0.455/0.510 |
| 47mm léger (not adopted) | QF | 47 | 1.9 | 1885 | 1325 | 25 | 95 | 1.075/– |
| 47mm | QF | 47 | 1.9 | 1885 | 2048 | 40 | 237 | 1.5/1.5 |
| **Modèle 1887** | | | | | | | | |
| 14cm (all converted to QF) | QF | 138.6 | 5.5 | 1887 | 6450 | 45 | 3850 | 30/35 |
| 16cm (all converted to QF) | QF | 164.7 | 6.5 | 1887 | 7600 | 45 | 6500 | 45/54.9/52.6 |
| 19cm | BLR | 194 | 7.6 | 1887 | 9046 | 45 | 10,770 | 75/90.3/89.5 |
| 27cm de 45 cal | BLR | 274.4 | 10.8 | 1887 | 12,800 | 45 | 34,000 | 216/255 |
| 30cm de 45 cal | BLR | 305 | 12 | 1887 | 13,992 | 45 | 45,740 | 292/340 |
| 34cm de 42 cal (corps long) | BLR | 340 | 13.4 | 1887 | 14,700 | 42 | 61,660 | 420/490 |
| **Modèle 1888** | | | | | | | | |
| 65mm, fermeture à coins | QF | 65 | 2.6 | 1888 | 3450 | 50 | 540 | 4/4.17 |
| **Modèle 1891** | | | | | | | | |
| 65mm, fermeture à coins | QF | 65 | 2.6 | 1891 | 3450 | 50 | 540 | 4/4.17 |
| **Modèle 1891(2)** | | | | | | | | |
| 100, à tourillons | QF | 100 | 3.9 | 1891 (2) | 4646.5 | 45 | 1700 | 14/16 |
| 138.6, à tourillons | QF | 138.6 | 5.5 | 1891 (2) | 6465 | 45 | 4177 | 30/35 |
| 164.7, à tourillons | QF | 164.7 | 6.5 | 1891 (2) | 7672.5 | 45 | 7055 | 45/54.9/52.6 |

**Notes. Some ships or classes known to have carried the weapons are shown, these are not in the 1919 document.**

1st plans approved 30.8.1880. Three built by St-Chamond for *Formidable*.
1st plans approved 30.8.1880. Three built by Creusot for *Al. Baudin*.

1st plans 8.9.1877. Hotchkiss system revolving cannon (also called revolver cannon) with 5 rifled barrels (740mm bore), a breech mechanism, and a central shaft.
As 37mm revolving cannon but larger, too heavy for most shipboard uses. A few embarked from 1887. (1175mm bore)
First plans approved 7.10.1875. Replaced the canon de 4 de montagne MLR for landings.
First plans 7.2.1879, new plans 7.6.1880. 60 built from metal of old 12pdrs. Replaced the canon de 12 de campagne MLR for large boats and small avisos.

First plans approved 2.7.1881. For use on board ship and for landings. Same breech mechanism as the bronze 65mm.
First plans approved 2.7.1881. Same type breech mechanism as the 100mm M1881.
First plans approved 2.7.1881. Main battery of *Milan* and *Condor*.
Plans approved 25.1.1882. Same breech mechanism as the M1870 gun. *Courbet, Al. Baudin, Hoche, Brennus* (1883), *Dubourdieu, Sfax, Tage, Cécille, Jean Bart* (only the 3 after guns), *Isly, Alger, Forbin, Troude, Inconstant, Gabriel Charmes*
Plans approved 2.7.1881. *Aréthuse, Dubourdieu, Sfax, Tage, Cécille, Jean Bart, Isly, Alger*
Plans approved 25.1.1882. *Al. Duperré* (under forecastle), *Naïade*.
Plans approved 24.8.1882. *Fusée*
Without trunnions, plans approved 3.9.1881. *Hoche, Achéron, Phlégéton*. Also a model with trunnions (3.9.1881, 28,200kg) in *Redoutable* (1893, 7 guns in redoubt and on deck on old mountings)
With trunnions, tubed, plans approved 14.10.1881. 95cm of tube exposed at muzzle. A few built at Firth. *Courbet* (2 guns in redoubt), *Duperré* (3 guns in 1891, 1 in 1894).
With trunnions, not tubed, plans approved 30.6.1881. M1881 lighter and slimmer than M1875, entire tube covered. *Courbet* (2 guns in redoubt).
Without trunnions, not tubed, plans approved 30.6.1881 *Hoche, Marceau* (2 guns), *Magenta, Brennus* (1883). There was also a model with trunnions, not tubed (30.6.1881, 52,700kg) and one without trunnions and tubed (8.12.1885).

Converted M1881. Main battery of *Milan, Condor*, and *Wattignies*.
Converted M1881. *Courbet, Al. Baudin, Hoche, Duquesne, Sfax, Jean Bart* (after 3 guns), *Isly, Alger, Forbin & Troude* (some M1884?), *Phlégéton & Styx*.
Converted M1881. *Sfax, Alger, Isly* (M1884?)

Plans approved 4.8.1885. *Marceau, Jean Bart* (the 3 forward guns)
Plans approved 14.8.1886. *Davout*.
First plans approved 10.8.1886. *Redoutable* (in redoubt on M1896 mountings, rearmed 1898)
With trunnions, plans approved 3.2.1886. *Redoutable* (1893, 1 gun on stern on old mounting). There was also a model without trunnions (3.2.1886, 28,084kg)
Without trunnions, 1st plans 26.12.1884. *Neptune* (changed from M1881 while building), *Marceau* (2 guns).

Converted M1884. *Marceau, Neptune, Magenta, Tage, Cécille, Jean Bart* (the 3 forward guns)
Converted M1884. *Al. Baudin, Tage, Cécille, Jean Bart, Davout, Suchet*

*Canon à tir rapide léger système Hotchkiss*. (740mm bore)
*Canon à tir rapide léger système Hotchkiss*. Field gun, not adopted except for one reported on the steam pinnace of *Marceau* in 1897. (1175mm bore)
*Canon à tir rapide à grande puissance système Hotchkiss* (auto-recoil QF), sometimes called heavy (*lourd*). Plans for mounting approved 19.8.1887, shield 31.10.1889, a semi-automatic version (TSA) also made. (1878mm bore)

No trunnions. *Al. Charner, Galilée*. (4000kg with trunnions)
No trunnions. *Brennus, Dupuy de Lôme, Descartes* (3 guns), *Du Chayla*. (6720kg with trunnions)
No trunnions. *Dupuy de Lôme, Al. Charner*
No trunnions. *Charles Martel, Carnot, Jauréguiberry*. (Guns in *Jauréguiberry* 37,680kg)
No trunnions. *Charles Martel, Carnot, Jauréguiberry, Al. Tréhouart, Bouvines*. (Guns in *Jauréguiberry* 49,620kg)
No trunnions, long body. *Brennus, Jemmapes, Valmy*. All seven guns to plans dated 4.10.1890 except forward gun on *Jemmapes*, to plans dated 4.7.1888 (57,842kg). The two forward guns in *Brennus* were *à corps court* (short body), with a single-piece core shorter than the normal 7.850m but with the same overall length.

Wedge breech.

Wedge breech, a modified M1888.

With trunnions.
With trunnions (there were also special guns without trunnions) *Charles Martel, Carnot, Jauréguiberry, Bouvet, Masséna, Pothuau* (4 guns), *Linois*.
With trunnions (there were also special guns without trunnions). *Friant, Descartes* (1 gun).

| Designation (M = Modèle) | Type | Cal., mm. | Cal., inch | Model | Length total, mm. | Length, Cals. | Weight Gun, kg | Projectile, kg. |
|---|---|---|---|---|---|---|---|---|
| **Modèle 1892 long T.R. (QF)** | | | | | | | | |
| 100, système Canet sans tourillons | QF | 100 | 3.9 | 1892 long | 5500 | 53.31 | 2230 | 14/16 |
| **Modèle 1893** | | | | | | | | |
| 100 de 45 cal. | QF | 100 | 3.9 | 1893 | 4646.5 | 45 | 1700 | 14/16 |
| 138.6 de 45 cal sans tourillons | QF | 138.6 | 5.5 | 1893 | 6445 | 45 | 4080 | 30/35 |
| 164.7 sans tourillons de 45 cal | QF | 164.7 | 6.5 | 1893 | 7672.5 | 45 | 6625 | 45/54.2/52.6 |
| 194 de 40 cal sans tourillons | BLR | 194 | 7.6 | 1893 | 8076 | 40 | 10,840 | 75/90.3/89.5 |
| 240 de 40 cal sans tourillons | BLR | 240 | 9.4 | 1893 | 10,045 | 40 | 20,750 | 144/170 |
| 274.4 de 25 cal | BLR | 274.4 | 10.8 | 1893 | 7305 | 25 | 21,950 | 216/255 |
| 274.4 de 45 cal sans tourillons | BLR | 274.4 | 10.8 | 1893 | 12,812 | 45 | 35,490 | 216/255 |
| 305 de 45 cal sans tourillons | BLR | 305 | 12 | 1893 | 13,992 | 45 | 45,370 | 292/340 |
| 305 de 40 cal sans tourillons | BLR | 305 | 12 | 1893 | 12,685 | 40 | 44,050 | 292/340 |
| 340 de 35 cal | BLR | 340 | 13.4 | 1893 | 12,500 | 35 | 52,882 | 420/490 |
| **Modèle 1893-96** | | | | | | | | |
| 164.7 de 45 cal sans tourillons | QF | 164.7 | 6.5 | 1893-96 | 7742 | 45 | 8190 | 45/54.9/52.3 |
| 194 de 40 cal sans tourillons | BLR | 194 | 7.6 | 1893-96 | 8120 | 40 | 12,682 | 75/90.3/89.5 |
| 240 de 40 cal sans tourillons | BLR | 240 | 9.4 | 1893-96 | 10,052 | 40 | 23,987 | 144/170 |
| 274.4 de 40 cal sans tourillons | BLR | 274.4 | 10.8 | 1893-96 | 11,501 | 40 | 35,040 | 216/255 |
| 305 de 40 cal sans tourillons | BLR | 305 | 12 | 1893-96 | 12,775 | 40 | 48,075 | 292/349.4/348.4 |
| **Modèle 1893-96M** | | | | | | | | |
| 164.7 de 45 cal | QF | 164.7 | 6.5 | 1893-96M | 7742 | 45 | 8190 | 45/54.9/52.3 |
| 305 de 40 cal | BLR | 305 | 12 | 1893-96M | 12,775 | 40 | 48,075 | 292/349.4/348.4 |
| **Modèle 1902** | | | | | | | | |
| Tube-canon de 37mm de 40 cal. | QF | 37 | 1.5 | 1902 | 1600 | 40 | 77.1 | 0.5 |
| 47mm de 50 cal | QF | 47 | 1.9 | 1902 | 2530 | 50 | 338 | 2 |
| 65mm de 50 cal | QF | 65 | 2.6 | 1902 | 3450 | 50 | 594 | 4/4.17 |
| 100 de 50 cal (not deployed) | QF | 100 | 3.9 | 1902 | 5209 | 50 | 1976 | 16 |
| 164.7 de 50 cal (not deployed) | QF | 164.7 | 6.5 | 1902 | 8593.6 | 50 | 8900 | 52/54.9/52.3 |
| 194 de 50 cal | BLR | 194 | 7.6 | 1902 | 10,110 | 50 | 15,180 | 86 |
| **Modèle 1902 mod 1906** | | | | | | | | |
| 240 M1902 M$^{ion}$ 1906 | BLR | 240 | 9.4 | 1902-06 | 12,220 | 49.5 (50) | 29,550 | 221 |
| **Modèle 1906** | | | | | | | | |
| 305 M1906 | BLR | 305 | 12 | 1906 | 14,175 | 45 | 54,560 | 435.6 |
| **Modèle 1906-10** | | | | | | | | |
| 305 M1906-10 | BLR | 305 | 12 | 1906-10 | 14,176 | 44.67 | 54,560 | 418.35 |
| **Modèle 1908** | | | | | | | | |
| 75mm S.A. M1908 Schneider | QF | 75 | 3 | 1908 Schneider | 4856.5 | 62.5 (65) | 1450 | 6.4 |
| **Modèle 1910** | | | | | | | | |
| 138.6 M1910 | QF | 138.6 | 5.5 | 1910 | 7854 | 55 | 5250 | 36.5 |
| **Modèle 1912** | | | | | | | | |
| 340 M1912 | BLR | 340 | 13.4 | 1912 | 16,115 | 45 | 66,280 | 540 |

NOTES TO TABLE: Lengths are nominal (face of muzzle to back of base ring) for muzzleloaders, maximum for breechloaders. The designations in the list shift from centimetres to the exact calibre in millimetres with the Modèle 1891 guns reflecting a change ordered by the Minister on 6 December1893. Until 1862 the weight of the shell for the 16cm M1858 and 1860 rifles was 30.4kg. The M1881 and M1884 138.6mm and 164.7mm models were virtually identical except for the breech mechanism and were interchangeable on board ship. They are sometimes combined as M1881-84. The M1887, M1891, and M1893 138.6mm and 164.7mm were virtually identical except for slightly different weights. The M1891 164.7mm differed from the M1881/84 164.7mm only in the closing of the breech.

Primary sources:
U.S. National Archives, Record Group 38 (Office of Naval Intelligence), Register 12008A, 25 July 1919. Reference provided by Dr. Norman Friedman.
*Aide-Mémoire d'Artillerie Navale*, 1873/1892.

**Notes. Some ships or classes known to have carried the weapons are shown, these are not in the 1919 document.**

Canet system, no trunnions. 29 bought, 24 assigned to *Bouvines, Al. Tréhouart, Jemmapes* and *Valmy*, the last two couldn't take them and got the originally planned M1891(2), 6 Canet went to *Dévastation* instead of M1891(2).

No trunnions. In *Charlemagne, Henri IV, Pothuau* (6 guns), *D'Entrecasteaux, Jeanne d'Arc, Guichen, Châteaurenault, Lavoisier, D'Estrees, Kersaint.* (4320kg with trunnions)
No trunnions. In *Brennus* (special type), *Iéna, Pascal, D'Assas, Catinat, Guichen, Châteaurenault, Jurien de la Gravière.* (6950kg with trunnions)
No trunnions. *Pothuau, Jeanne. d'Arc*
No trunnions. *D'Entrecasteaux, Courbet* (1900, upper deck) (22,780kg with trunnions)
Previously M1870-93. *Courbet & Dévastation* (1900 and 1902, in redoubt)
No trunnions. In *Bouvet, Masséna* (replaced M1887 May 1893)
No trunnions. In *Bouvet, Masséna* (replaced M1887 May 1893)
No trunnions. In *Charlemagne* class (probably developed for it).
Built to replace the 42cm M1875 in *Requin*, reassigned to *Terrible*.

No trunnions. *Suffren, Dupleix, Gueydon, Gloire, Léon Gambetta.*
No trunnions. *Gueydon, Gloire, Léon Gambetta.*
No trunnions. *Dévastation* (1902, upper deck), *Furieux*
No trunnions. *Henri IV* and *Caïman, Indomptable, Requin* rebuilt
No trunnions. *Iéna, Suffren*

*République, Jules Michelet, Ernest Renan*
Plans dated 25.1.1902. *République, Justice*

Development stopped and gun not deployed. 37mm M1885 retained instead for use in boats.
*République, Justice, Danton, Courbet, Bretagne, Normandie, Victor Hugo, Jules Michelet, Ernest Renan, Edgar Quinet,* and destroyers from *Stylet* to *Fanfare.*
*République, Justice, Ernest Renan, Edgar Quinet,* 300t destroyers from *Stylet* to *Fanfare,* 500t and 800t destroyers.
Development stopped.
Proposed to replace the older 164.7 in the *République* type but the 194 was adopted instead. Also intended for *Jules Michelet* and *Ernest Renan* but the earlier model in *République* was used instead
Plans dated 27.2.03 & 11.9.03. *Justice, Jules Michelet, Ernest Renan, Edgar Quinet.*

*Danton.*

*Danton*

*Jean Bart*

*Danton*

*Jean Bart, Bretagne, Normandie, Lyon, Lamotte-Picquet*

*Bretagne.* (*Normandie* and *Lyon* classes to have had a M1912M)

The after port 194mm/50 Model 1902 turret on the battleship *Justice*, photographed in the Hudson River off New York City during the Hudson-Fulton celebration in September-October 1909. This is a mature example of the *tourelle-barbette* used for medium-calibre guns in Émile Bertin's ships. It had a compact turret cupola protected by steeply angled armour plates on top of a truncated inverse cone of barbette armour protruding above the weather deck. The floor of the gunhouse was about halfway between the ship's deck and the bottom of the cupola. *(NHHC, 19-N-60-12-8)*

# Appendix B

# French Torpedoes, 1880-1912

French torpedo development was heavily dependent on Robert Whitehead and his firm at Fiume (now Rijeka in Croatia) in the Austro-Hungarian Empire. From the signing of an initial agreement on 5 April 1873 nearly every French torpedo model through 1898 and most through 1914 were purchased from Fiume or built under licence at the Toulon dockyard. In about 1905 the French turned to Schneider's factory at Hyères as an alternate source for torpedoes. Whitehead as part of a British conglomerate opened a torpedo factory at St. Tropez (Gassin) east of Toulon in 1912, not to supply the French but to support other export customers.

| | Diameter (mm) | Diameter (in) | Length (m) | Weight (kg) | Charge (kg dry cotton) | Ranges and speeds | Orders to 1.1.1898 | Notes |
|---|---|---|---|---|---|---|---|---|
| Modèle 1873 | 356 | 14 | 4.26 | 175 | dynamite | 400m at 7kts | 2 Whitehead, 5 Ind., 8 Toulon | |
| Modèle 1876 | 381 | 15 | 5.85 | 360 | 18 & 21 | 400m at 20kts | 100 Whitehead, 2 Ind. | |
| Modèle 1877 | 356 | 14 | 4.41 | 240 | 12 | 400m at 21kts | 67 Whitehead | |
| Modèle 1878 | 356 | 14 | 4.41 | 260 | 18 | 400m at 21kts | 108 Ind. | |
| **Modèle 1880** | | | | | | | | |
| Small model | 356 | 14 | 4.42 | 272 | 18 | 400m at 23kts | 253 Whitehead | Used as exercise torpedoes by 1898 |
| Large model | 381 | 15 | 5.70 | 405 | 34 | 400m at 23kts | 92 Whitehead | |
| **Modèle 1885** | | | | | | | | |
| Small model | 356 | 14 | 4.49, later 4.99 | 282 | 20 | 400m at 27kts | 182 Whitehead | Lengthened to 4.99m to carry charges as in M1887. |
| Large model | 381 | 15 | 5.70 | 407 | 34 | 400m at 28kts | 192 Whitehead | |
| **Modèle 1887** | | | | | | | | |
| Small model | 356 | 14 | 4.99 | 318 | 45, later 42 | 400m at 27kts | 425 Whitehead, 240 Toulon | |
| Small model (shortened) | 356 | 14 | 4.70 | 310 | 40 | 400m at 27kts | 76 Toulon, not repeated | Short type in *Ouragan* type torpedo boats. |
| Large model | 381 | 15 | 5.68 | 423 | 42 | 400m at 28.5kts, 600m at 27kts | 501 Whitehead, 650 Toulon | |
| Modèle 1889 | 450 | 17.7 | 5.01 | 502 | 80 to 75 | 400m at 32kts, 800m at 28kts | 94 Whitehead, 6 Toulon | |
| Modèle 1891 | 450 | 17.7 | 4.17 | 439 | 75 to 67 | 400m at 29kts, 800m at 26kts | 23 Whitehead, not repeated | Short type in *Corsaire, Mousquetaire, Chevalier, Gustave Zédé*, and *Morse*. |
| Modèle 1892 | 450 | 17.7 | 5.05 | 530 | 75 | 400m at 31kts, 800m at 27.5kts | 132 Whitehead, 100 Toulon thru 1.1.1898 | |
| Modèle 1904 | 450 | 17.7 | 5.07 | 640 | 88 | 2000m at 24kts | — | Higher pressure air with nickel steel reservoir. |
| Modèles 1906 & 1906M | 450 | 17.7 | 5.07 | 640 | 108 | 2000m at 24kts, 600m at 36.5kts (M1906), 38.5kts (M1906M) | — | Larger charge. |
| Modèle 1909R (Rechauffeur) | 450 | 17.7 | 5.25 | 691.5 | 108 | 2000m at 34kts, 3000m at 30kts | — | France's first heated torpedo (a dry heater). For battleships and destroyers |
| Modèle 1911V (Vitesse) | 450 | 17.7 | 5.25 | 658 | 108 (148) | 1000m at 42kts. | — | Water injected into the combustion chamber, making it a wet heater. A fast, short-range torpedo for submarines. |
| Modèle 1911D (Distance) | 450 | 17.7 | 5.47 | 730 | 108 (148) | 6000m at 24kts | — | A slower, long-range wet heater torpedo for modern battleships. |
| Modèle 1912D (Distance) | 450 | 17.7 | 6.75 | 1000 | 108 (148) | 8000m at 28kts | Whitehead and Schneider both developing 1913 | As 1911D with water cooling of the piston rods added. For modern battleships. |

**Notes:**

Ind. indicates commercial purchases other than Whitehead. There were also 25 trial torpedoes of models not repeated: 10 x M1882 (356mm, 3.75m), 12 x M1877-83 and M1878-83 (356mm, 4.25m), 2 'babies' (305mm, 2.90m, 1883, a Whitehead model for small boat use with dropping gear), and 1 x M1887T (a further shortened M1887, 356mm, 4.60m, T = Toulon). Of the 3,282 torpedoes listed through 1.1.1898, about 2,650 were in service on that date. The torpedo boats of the 1902 tranche, which fell between the two sources for this table, had 381mm torpedoes of a long 6.03-metre model vice the usual 5.68 or 5.75-metre type. This model was abandoned for the 1903 tranche boats in late 1904.

**Primary sources:**

Ministère de la Marine, École Supérieure de Marine, *Sous-marins, Torpilles*. Conférences de M. Tissier, Ingénieur de la Marine. Paris, 1898-1899 (Confidential).

Ministère de la Marine, École Supérieure de la Marine, *Torpilles automobiles, Méthodes de tir*, Conférences de Mr. le Capitaine de Corvette Puech, 1920.

Norman Friedman, *Naval Weapons of World War I*, pp345-346.

Dr. Friedman also provided the above French sources.

# Appendix C

# French Ministers of Marine, 1851-1914

From 1791 the political head of the French Navy was called the Minister of Marine and the Colonies, a title which was maintained with some exceptions until 14 March 1889, when the colonies were transferred to the Ministry of Commerce and Industry. The holders of the post from 1855 to 1914 are listed below. 'Rep. Assemb. Nat.' indicates a representative in the Assemblée Nationale, the single house of the French legislature in 1871-76. Some Presidents of the Council led multiple cabinets which are distinguished by numbers.

| From | To | Minister of Marine | Titles | Cabinet(s) | Party (cabinet) |
|---|---|---|---|---|---|
| | | **Second Empire** | | | |
| 3 Dec 1851 | 19 Apr 1855 | Théodore Ducos | Senator | — | — |
| 19 Apr 1855 | 24 Nov 1860 | Ferdinand Alphonse Hamelin | Admiral, Senator | — | — |
| 24 Nov 1860 | 20 Jan 1867 | Comte Prosper de Chasseloup-Laubat | Senator | — | — |
| 20 Jan 1867 | 4 Sep 1870 | Charles Rigault de Genouilly | Admiral, Senator | — | — |
| | | **Third Republic** | | | |
| 4 Sep 1870 | 18 Feb 1871 | Martin Fourichon (Designated 4 Sep 1870, assumed functions at Paris 15 Sep 1870, evacuated to Bordeaux 16 Sep 1870. Dompierre d'Hornoy acted par intérim 5-17 Sep 1870.) | Vice Admiral | Trochu | Orléaniste |
| 19 Feb 1871 | 24 May 1873 | Louis Pierre Alexis Pothuau | Vice Admiral, Rep. Assemb. Nat. | Dufaure 1, 2 | Républicain modéré |
| 25 May 1873 | 16 May 1874 | Charles Marius Albert de Dompierre d'Hornoy | Vice Admiral, Rep. Assemb. Nat. | de Broglie 1, 2 | Républicain modéré |
| 22 May 1874 | 9 Mar 1876 | Marquis Louis Raymond de Montaignac de Chauvance | Rear Admiral, Rep. Assemb. Nat. | de Cissey, Buffet, Dufaure 3 | Conservateur, Monarchiste modéré, Républicain modéré |
| 9 Mar 1876 | 16 May 1877 | Martin Fourichon | Vice Admiral, Senator for life | Dufaure 4, Simon | Républicain modéré |
| 23 May 1877 | 19 Nov 1877 | Albert Auguste Gicquel des Touches | Vice Admiral | de Broglie 3 (formed 17 May 1877) | Orléaniste |
| 23 Nov 1877 | 13 Dec 1877 | Albert Edmond Louis baron Roussin | Vice Admiral | de Rochebouet | Monarchiste |
| 13 Dec 1877 | 30 Jan 1879 | Louis Pierre Alexis Pothuau | Vice Admiral, Senator for life | Dufaure 5 | Républicain modéré |
| 4 Feb 1879 | 19 Sep 1880 | Jean Bernard Jauréguiberry | Vice Admiral, Senator for life | Waddington, de Freycinet 1 | Républicain modéré |
| 23 Sep 1880 | 10 Nov 1881 | Georges Charles Cloué | Vice Admiral | Ferry 1 | Républicain modéré |
| 14 Nov 1881 | 26 Jan 1882 | Auguste Gougeard | Capitaine de vaisseau, Councillor of State | Gambetta | Union républicaine |
| 30 Jan 1882 | 28 Jan 1883 | Jean Bernard Jauréguiberry | Vice Admiral, Senator for life | de Freycinet 2, Duclerc | Républicain modéré |
| 31 Jan 1883 | 17 Feb 1883 | François Césaire de Mahy (par intérim) | Deputy, Minister of Agriculture | Fallières (formed 29 Jan 1883) | Républicain modéré |
| 21 Feb 1883 | 9 Aug 1883 | Charles Marie Brun | Senator | Ferry 2 | Républicain modéré |
| 9 Aug 1883 | 30 Mar 1885 | Alexandre Louis François Peyron | Vice Admiral, Senator for life | Ferry 2 | Républicain modéré |
| 6 Apr 1885 | 29 Dec 1885 | Charles Eugène Galiber | Rear Admiral | Brisson 1 | Union républicaine |
| 7 Jan 1886 | 17 May 1887 | Hyacinthe Laurent Théophile Aube | Rear Admiral, from 17 Mar 1886 Vice Admiral | de Freycinet 3, Goblet | Républicain modéré, Radical-socialiste |
| 30 May 1887 | 4 Dec 1887 | Édouard Barbey | Senator | Rouvier 1 | Union républicaine |
| 11 Dec 1887 | 5 Jan 1888 | François Césaire de Mahy | Deputy | Tirard 1 | Indépendent |
| 5 Jan 1888 | 14 Feb 1889 | Jules François Émile Krantz | Vice Admiral | Tirard 1, Floquet | Indépendent, Parti radical |
| 22 Feb 1889 | 13 Mar 1889 | Constant Louis Benjamin Jaurès (died 13 March 1889) | Vice Admiral, Senator for life | Tirard 2 | Indépendent |
| 19 Mar 1889 | 10 Nov 1889 | Jules François Émile Krantz | Vice Admiral | Tirard 2 | Indépendent |
| 10 Nov 1889 | 18 Feb 1892 | Édouard Barbey | Senator | Tirard 2, de Freycinet 4 | Indépendent, Républicain modéré |
| 27 Feb 1892 | 12 Jul 1892 | Godefroy Cavaignac | Deputy | Loubet | Républicain modéré |
| 12 Jul 1892 | 10 Jan 1893 | Auguste Laurent Burdeau | Deputy | Loubet, Ribot 1 | Républicain modéré |

| From | To | Minister of Marine | Titles | Cabinet(s) | Party (cabinet) |
|---|---|---|---|---|---|
| 12 Jan 1893 | 23 Nov 1893 | Adrien Barthélemy Louis Rieunier | Vice Admiral | Ribot 2 (formed 11 Jan 1893), Dupuy 1 | Républicain modéré |
| 3 Dec 1893 | 22 May 1894 | Auguste Alfred Lefèvre | Vice Admiral | Casimir-Périer | Républicain modéré |
| 30 May 1894 | 15 Jan 1895 | Félix Faure | Deputy | Dupuy 2, 3 (interim to 17 Jan 1895) | Républicain modéré |
| 28 Jan 1895 | 28 Oct 1895 | Armand Louis Charles Gustave Besnard | Vice Admiral | Ribot 3 (formed 26 Jan 1895) | Républicain modéré |
| 1 Nov 1895 | 23 Apr 1896 | Édouard Lockroy | Deputy | Bourgeois | Parti radical |
| 28 Apr 1896 | 28 Jun 1898 | Armand Louis Charles Gustave Besnard | Vice Admiral | Méline | Centre-droit |
| 28 Jun 1898 | 12 Jun 1899 | Édouard Lockroy | Deputy | Brisson 2, Dupuy 4, 5 | Union républicaine, Républicain modéré |
| 22 Jun 1899 | 3 Jun 1902 | Jean-Louis (Jean Marie Antoine) de Lanessan | Deputy | Waldeck-Rousseau | Républicain modéré |
| 7 Jun 1902 | 18 Jan 1905 | Camille Pelletan | Deputy | Combes | Parti radical |
| 24 Jan 1905 | 22 Oct 1908 | Gaston Thomson | Deputy | Rouvier 2, 3, Sarrien, Clemenceau 1 | Union républicaine (Rouvier), Parti radical |
| 22 Oct 1908 | 20 Jul 1909 | Alfred Picard | Councillor of State | Clemenceau 1 | Parti radical |
| 24 Jul 1909 | 27 Feb 1911 | Augustin Emmanuel Hubert Gaston Marie Boué de Lapeyrère | Vice Admiral | Briand 1, 2 | Parti républicain-socialiste |
| 2 Mar 1911 | 21 Jan 1913 | Théophile Delcassé | Deputy | Monis, Caillaux, Poincaré 1 | Parti radical, Alliance démocratique (Poincaré) |
| 21 Jan 1913 | 2 Dec 1913 | Pierre Baudin | Senator | Briand 3, 4, Barthou | Parti républicain-socialiste, Alliance démocratique |
| 9 Dec 1913 | 20 Mar 1914 | Ernest Monis | Senator | Doumergue 1 | Parti radical |
| 20 Mar 1914 | 2 Jun 1914 | Armand Gauthier de l'Aude | Senator | Doumergue 1 | Parti radical |
| 9 Jun 1914 | 12 Jun 1914 | Émile Chautemps | Deputy | Ribot 4 | Républicain modéré |
| 13 Jun 1914 | 3 Aug 1914 | Armand Gauthier de l'Aude | Senator | Viviani 1 | Parti républicain-socialiste |
| 3 Aug 1914 | 29 Oct 1915 | Jean Victor Augagneur | Deputy | Viviani 1, 2 | Parti républicain-socialiste |

**Source:** Jolly, Jean, *Dictionnaire des parlementaires français*, vol. 1, Paris, 1960.

*Appendix D*

# Naval Shipbuilding Directorates and Councils, 1859-1914

French naval ship design and construction was managed during the period of this book by a single directorate within the Ministry of Marine. It was renamed in 1901 without change in responsibilities. Within this directorate two services and sections (one temporary and one permanent) were established to handled ship design. Two successive high-level advisory councils provided the Minister guidance on naval programmes and shipbuilding policy, and a council followed by a committee provided recommendations on technical issues.

## 1. *Directorates*
**Direction du Matériel.**
1859-1869 Dupuy de Lôme, Stanislas Charles Henri Laur (or Laurent), Directeur des constructions navales, director. (Promoted to Inspecteur général du génie maritime 9 March 1867)

1869-1881 Sabattier, Victorin Gabriel Justin Épiphanès, Directeur des constructions navales, director
1881-1883 De Fauque de Jonquières, Jean Philippe Ernest, Vice Amiral, director
1883-1889 Peschart d'Ambly, Charles Frédéric, Directeur des constructions navales, director
1889-1893 Bienaymé, Arthur François Alphonse, Directeur des constructions navales, director
1893-1895 Lemaire, Jules Omer, Directeur des constructions navales, director
1895-1896 Bertin, Louis Émile, Directeur des constructions navales, director (from 13 November 1895)
1896-1901 Thibaudier, Jules César Claude, Directeur des constructions navales, director (from 22 July 1896). (His title changed to Directeur du Génie maritime 1901)

### Direction centrale des constructions navales
1901-1904 Thibaudier, Jules César Claude, Directeur du Génie maritime, director (from 22 July 1896)
1904-1909 Dudebout, Auguste René, Directeur du Génie maritime, director (from 30 July 1904)
1909-1912 Louis, Achille François Charles, Directeur du Génie maritime, director
1912-1914 Romazzotti, Gaston, Directeur du Génie maritime, director

## 2. Services and sections
### Service technique des constructions navales
1881-1882 De Bussy, Marie Anne Louis, Directeur des constructions navales, chief (from 9 December 1881)

Minister of Marine Gougeard created the *Service technique des constructions navales* on 9 December 1881 and immediately appointed de Bussy as its head. This service drew its designs from naval constructors assigned elsewhere within the Navy. De Bussy was still using the title *Chef du service technique des Constructions navales* in late October 1882 but the two *services techniques* of the *Direction du Matériel* (the other being for artillery) were no longer listed as of January 1883. De Bussy became a member of the *Conseil d'Amirauté* on 1 March 1883.

### Section technique des constructions navales
1895-1896 Hauser, Alphonse, Ingénieur de 1ère classe de la marine, chief (from 1 August 1895)
1896-1905 Bertin, Louis Émile, Directeur des constructions navales, chief (from 22 July 1896). (His title changed to Directeur du Génie maritime 1901)
1905-1909 Lhomme, Delphin Albert, Directeur du Génie maritime, chief.
1909-1911 Lyasse, Léon Alphonse, Directeur du Génie maritime, chief.
1911-1914 Doyère, Charles, Directeur du Génie maritime, chief.

Minister of Marine Besnard established the *Section technique des constructions navales* within the Directorate of Materiel by decrees of 9 July 1895, 7 November 1895, and 22 July 1896. Directed by an officer of the génie maritime designated by the Minister, it took over functions handled since 1883 by the the inspector general of the Génie maritime (initially de Bussy) using naval constructors assigned elsewhere. Émile Bertin was demoted by Minister Besnard in July 1896 from Director of Materiel to chief of the *Section technique* to his great resentment, but he then built it into an organisation more influential in matters of ship design than the *Direction centrale des constructions navales* of which it was part. During 1913 the *Section technique des constructions navales* was renamed the *Service technique des*

*constructions navales* without other changes. Later the acronym STCN came into common use.

**Note on titles:** *Directeur des constructions navales* and (from 1901) *Directeur du Génie maritime* were ranks within the *Génie maritime*, not administrative positions. In 1901 the *Directeur du matériel* became the *Directeur central des constructions navales*, (an administrative position). The *Inspecteur général du Génie maritime* was both the top officer in the *Génie maritime* (the only one to hold this rank) and one of the Navy's Inspectors General (an administrative position).

## 3. Councils and Committees
### Conseil d'Amirauté de la Marine
The main council of the pre-revolutionary navy, it was re-established in 1824 to advise the Minister on a wide range of issues from naval strategy and ship characteristics to arcane administrative matters. Its members were the navy's most senior and experienced admirals. It was abolished on 21 October 1890 after most of its functions had been reassigned.

A new *Conseil d'Amirauté* was established on 7 September 1913. Its members were the Minister of Marine, the Chief of the Navy General Staff, two other Vice Admirals from the central administration, and the head of the Minister's staff as secretary.

### Conseil des travaux de la Marine
Formed in 1831 to advise the Minister on technical issues relating to the construction of ships. The literal translation is Council of Works. Replaced by the *Comité technique* on 21 April 1905. Its members included the Chief of the Naval Staff, the Director of Materiel, the Director of Artillery, selected admirals, and technical experts, the latter organised into several sections.

### Conseil supérieur de la Marine
One of several councils formed on 5 December 1889 to take over some of the functions of the *Conseil d'Amirauté*. The *Conseil supérieur* advised the Minister on naval strategy, building programmes, and the military characteristics of ships among other things.

### Comité technique de la Marine
This committee replaced the *Conseil des travaux* on 21 April 1905. It operated as part of the *Conseil supérieur*, not as an independent Council, and had three sections, the first for seagoing ships, the second for defensive ships and installations including torpedo boats and submarines, and one for materiel and personnel.

**Source:** *Annuaire de la Marine.*

EXERCICE DE CANON A TIR RAPIDE A BORD DU " MARCEAU "

Sailors training on a 47mm/40 Model 1885 heavy Hotchkiss quick-fire gun on board *Marceau* next to a broadside 340mm/28.5 M1881 or M1884 barbette gun. The 47mm gun is set up in a position once occupied by one of the ship's four 65mm guns, suggesting that the photo was taken after the ship became a training ship for apprentice torpedo boat seamen in 1906. The ship's 340mm guns were probably not fired after 1900. *(Postcard by A. Bougault, Toulon-sur-mer)*

*Appendix E*

# Selected French Naval Constructors, 1859-1914

The following French naval constructors are mentioned in this book for work performed from 1859 onwards. A Royal Ordinance of 25 March 1765 created the title of ingénieurs constructeurs de la Marine, gave these formerly civilian naval constructors a military uniform, and defined the structure of the new corps. A law of 21 October 1795 decided that the constructors who built the Navy's ships would henceforth be recruited from graduates of the new École polytechnique, and a regulation of 27 April 1800 introduced the name Génie maritime for this corps. The English term 'naval constructor' is used in this book for what the French then called ingénieurs du Génie maritime. The dates in this list include officers while on leave without pay to work in industry but not while working in industry after leaving the service. The parts of this book in which these constructors appear are shown in the right column, some most commonly used first names are in brackets.

| Last name | First names | Entered Génie | Last active | Part(s) in this book |
|---|---|---|---|---|
| Albaret | Jean Rosier | 1862 | 1905 | 1, 2 |
| Audenet | Camille | 1843 | 1874 | 1 |
| Aurous | Jules | 1845 | 1890 | 1, 2 |
| Auvynet | Augustin | 1861 | 1869 | 1 |
| Auxcousteaux | Charles Marie Hippolyte | 1843 | 1869 | 1 |
| Barba | François Joseph | 1860 | 1876 | 2 |
| Baron | Jean | 1861 | 1884 | 1, 2 |
| Bayssellance | Séverin Edmond | 1875 | 1902 | 2 |
| Beaumarchais | Charles Louis Marie Delarue Caron baron de | 1902 | 1911 | 3 |
| Beausire | Lucien Étienne | 1900 | 1914+ | 3 |
| Berrier-Fontaine | Jean-Baptiste Louis Félix Marc | 1860 | 1903 | 1 |
| Bertin | Louis Émile (Émile) | 1860 | 1905 | 1, 2, 3 |
| Bienaymé | Arthur François Alphonse | 1855 | 1903 | 1 |
| Bosquillon de Frescheville | Henri Raymond | 1877 | 1914+ | 2 |
| Bourdelle | Pierre Marc | 1895 | 1909 | 3 |
| Brun | Charles Marie | 1840 | 1883 | 1 |
| Carlet | Marie Pierre Henri Félix | 1847 | 1891 | 1 |
| Cazelles | David Jules Frédéric | 1858 | 1880 | 1 |
| Challiot | Jean Paul | 1860 | 1900 | 1 |
| Chaudoye | Jules Victor Charles | 1862 | 1889 | 1, 2 |
| Clauzel | Gaston | 1866 | 1907 | 1, 2 |
| Clément | Émile Ernest | 1859 | 1897 | 1 |
| Compère-Desfontaines | Théophile Zéphirin | 1846 | 1886 | 1 |
| Courbebaisse | Émile Marie Victor | 1845 | 1890 | 1 |
| Cousin | Victor Louis Félix | 1861 | 1884 | 1 |
| Daymard | Victor André | 1858 | 1885 | 1, 2 |
| De Bussy | Marie Anne Louis | 1845 | 1889 | 1, 2 |
| De Lacelle | Eugène Gaston | 1859 | 1870/1 | 1 |
| De Maupeou d'Ableiges | Gilles Louis | 1861 | 1910 | 1 |
| De Roussel | Anselme | 1842 | 1880 | 1 |
| Delaitre | Pierre | 1868 | 1875 | 1 |
| Delevaque | Charles | 1864 | 1890 | 1 |
| Denis de Senneville | Henri Paul Ernest | 1841 | 1883 | 1 |
| Desdouits | Eusèbe Victor Vincent de Paul | 1865 | 1896 | 1 |
| Doyère | Charles | 1880 | 1914+ | 3 |
| Du Buit | Paul | 1864 | 1878 | 1, 2 |
| Dudebout | Auguste René | 1876 | 1909 | 3 |
| Duplaa-Lahitte | Jean Casimir | 1871 | 1914+ | 1, 2 |
| Dupont | André Simon Eugéne | 1886 | 1911 | 1 |
| Dupuy de Lôme | Stanislas Charles Henri Laur (or Laurent) (Henri) | 1837 | 1869 | 1 |
| Dutard | Louis | 1845 | 1870/1 | 1 |
| Eynaud | Romain Léopold | 1859 | 1904 | 1, 2 |
| Fenaux | Fernand Alphonse | 1899 | 1912 | 3 |
| Ferrand | Charles Pierre Octave Joseph | 1882 | 1912 | 2, 3 |
| Finaz | Joseph Marie | 1869 | 1899 | 1 |
| Finot | Henri Édouard | 1861 | 1890 | 1 |
| Forquenot | Armand | 1840 | 1867 | 1 |

| Last name | First names | Entered Génie | Last active | Part(s) in this book |
|---|---|---|---|---|
| Garnier | Thomas | 1863 | 1907 | 1, 2 |
| Gayde | Numa Émile Prosper | 1879 | 1914+ | 3 |
| Gervaize | Victor Charles Eudore | 1837 | 1881 | 1 |
| Godard | Félix Edmond Théodore | 1878 | 1904 | 2 |
| Godron | Charles Alexandre Paul | 1858 | 1903 | 1, 2 |
| Guesnet | Achille Antoine | 1846 | 1873 | 1 |
| Guichard | Maurice Jules | 1877 | 1903 | 2 |
| Guieysse | Pierre Armand | 1829 | 1876 | 1 |
| Guillaume | Édouard | 1878 | 1907 | 1 |
| Guyot | Georges | 1886 | 1914+ | 1, 2 |
| Hauser | Alphonse | 1867 | 1896 | 2 |
| Huet | Victor Marie Pierre Auguste | 1868 | 1897 | 2 |
| Huin | Charles Ernest | 1857 | 1900 | 1, 2 |
| Hutter | Julien Eugène | 1895 | 1914+ | 3 |
| Jaÿ | Charles Louis | 1846 | 1881 | 1, 2 |
| Joëssel | Joseph | 1856 | 1882 | 1 |
| Korn | Philippe Frédéric | 1854 | 1897 | 1 |
| Lagane | Antoine Jean Amable | 1859 | 1873 | 1, 2 |
| Lamouche | André Pierre Simon | 1910 | 1914+ | 3 |
| Laubeuf | Alfred Maxime | 1885 | 1909 | 3 |
| Layrle | Charles Louis Marie | 1853 | 1886 | 1 |
| Lebelin de Dionne | Alfred François | 1846 | 1882 | 1, 2 |
| Lecointre | Louis Édouard | 1841 | 1867 | 1 |
| Lemaire | Jules Omer | 1860 | 1907 | 2 |
| Lemoine | Nicolas Marie Julien (Nicolas) | 1848 | 1874 | 1 |
| Lévy | André Jacques | 1896 | 1909 | 3 |
| Lhomme | Delphin Albert | 1876 | 1911 | 2, 3 |
| Louis | Àchille François Charles | 1879 | 1914+ | — |
| Lyasse | Léon Alphonse | 1885 | 1911 | 3 |
| Mangin | Amédée Paul Théodore | 1839 | 1877 | 1 |
| Mangini | Louis Léon Lazare André | 1885 | 1894 | 2 |
| Marchal | Théodore Jean Maurice | 1870 | 1897 | 1, 2 |
| Marchegay | Edmond François Émile | 1862 | 1891 | 1 |
| Masson | Paulin Émile Jean François (Paulin) | 1857 | 1886 | 1 |
| Maugas | Gabriel Émile Marie | 1886 | 1914+ | 2, 3 |
| Maurice | Just Lucien | 1883 | 1914+ | 2, 3 |
| Noël | Charles Joseph | 1855 | 1881 | 1 |
| Opin | François | 1863 | 1904 | 1, 2 |
| Orsel | Jules | 1851 | 1873 | 1, 2 |
| Pastoureau-Labesse | Jean-Baptiste | 1840 | 1870/1 | 1 |
| Penelle | Claire Émile | 1862 | 1891 | 1 |
| Peschart d'Ambly | Charles Frédéric | 1847 | 1893 | 1 |
| Petithomme | Emmanuel Marie Victor | 1886 | 1914+ | 3 |
| Picart | Auguste Louis Henri | 1860 | 1900 | 2 |
| Picot de Moras | Paul Marie Étienne | 1835 | 1881 | 1 |
| Rabourdin | Alfred | 1862 | 1895 | 1 |
| Radiguer | Charles Félix Adolphe | 1898 | 1911 | 3 |
| Raymond | Eugène Hippolyte | 1883 | 1895 | 2 |
| Robiou de Lavrignais | Alexandre Auguste Gustave | 1827 | 1873 | 1 |
| Romazzotti | Gaston | 1876 | 1914+ | 2, 3 |
| Sabattier | Victorin Gabriel Justin Épiphanès (Victorin) | 1839 | 1881 | 1, 2 |
| Saglio | Victor | 1859 | 1903 | 2 |
| Schwartz | Frédéric Alfred | 1882 | 1914+ | 2 |
| Silvestre du Perron | Louis Auguste | 1841 | 1867 | 1 |
| Simonot | Jean Ernest | 1889 | 1914+ | 2, 3 |
| Terré | Laurent François Maurice | 1875 | 1902 | 2 |
| Thibaudier | Jules César Claude | 1860 | 1904 | 2, 3 |
| Tissier | Joseph Louis Léon | 1881 | 1914+ | 2 |
| Tréboul | Gaston Denis Alexandre | 1880 | 1914+ | 1, 2, 3 |
| Trogneux | Georges Victor | 1877 | 1902 | 2, 3 |
| Valin | Pierre Gaston Hermann | 1862 | 1888 | 1 |
| Verny | François Léonce | 1859 | 1880 | 1 |
| Vésignié | Louis François Octave | 1853 | 1879 | 1 |

| Last name | First names | Entered Génie | Last active | Part(s) in this book |
|-----------|-------------|---------------|-------------|----------------------|
| Vidal | Albin Abraham | 1847 | 1891 | 1 |
| Villaret | Nathaniel Lucien Louis Jean Jacques (Nathaniel) | 1857 | 1903 | 1 |
| Wahl | Albert | 1883 | 1914+ | 2 |
| Waldman | Albert Max Louis | 1913 | 1914+ | 3 |
| Widmann | Daniel Édouard | 1867 | 1894 | 2 |
| Willotte | Louis Marc Antoine Émile | 1847 | 1880 | 1 |
| Zédé | Gustave Alexandre | 1845 | 1872 | 2 |

**Source:** *Annuaire de la Marine.*

## *Appendix F*

# French Naval Building Programmes, 1857-1912

Shown below are the main building programmes of the French navy between 1857 and 1912. These programmes were the results of efforts by the navy's leadership to determine how many ships of each type the navy needed and to obtain the funds to build them. In some cases, the way in which the naval staff laid out the programmes (reproduced here) also revealed how the ships in the fleet were related to the navy's principal missions. Only the programmes of 1857, 1900, and 1912 were sanctioned by special legislation, but all were used for planning within the Ministry of Marine and for planning and justifying annual budgets.

### THE PROGRAMME OF 1857 (as submitted 8 January 1857)
(Period: 1 January 1857 to 31 December 1869)

*Plan Build*

The Combat Fleet (*Flotte de combat*). Specifications are for the new ships to be built.

| | | |
|---|---|---|
| 25 | 11 | Line-of-battle ships of 90 guns and 900 horsepower (*Vaisseaux de 90 canons*) |
| 15 | 15 | Line-of-battle ships of 70 guns and 700 horsepower (*Vaisseaux de 70 canons*) |
| 20 | 7 | Frigates of 40 guns and 650 horsepower (*Frégates de 40 canons*). |
| 30 | 24 | Corvettes of 14 guns and 400 horsepower (*Corvettes à vapeur*) |
| 30 | 21 | 1st class avisos of 4 guns and 250 horsepower (*Avisos de 1re classe*) |
| 30 | 4 | 2nd class avisos of 4 guns and 150 horsepower (*Avisos de 2e classe*). Included 20 existing gunboats (*Canonnières*) of 110 and 90 horsepower. |

Plus types mentioned but not programmed: 5 floating batteries (*Batteries flottantes*), 8 gun launches (*Chaloupes canonnières*), 1 yacht (*Reine Hortense*), and 34 small avisos.

The Transport Fleet (*Flotte de transport*, to carry 40,000 men).

| | | |
|---|---|---|
| (27) | | Former sail frigates (*Frégates à voiles*, to be converted to screw). |
| (20) | | Former paddle frigates (*Frégates à roues*) |
| 47 | 22 | Screw transports (*Transports à hélice*, new ones to be of 1,200 tons, 4 guns, and 250 horsepower). |

The Transition Fleet (*Flotte de transition*, old types to be maintained but not replaced).

| | |
|---|---|
| (26) | Sail line-of-battle ships converted to steam (*Vaisseaux de 450 à 650 chevaux et de 80 à 114 canons*) |
| ( 3) | Screw corvettes (*Corvettes mixtes de 60, 120, et 200 chevaux*: *Zélée, Sentinelle, Biche*) |
| ( 7) | Paddle corvettes (*Corvettes à roues de 300 à 320 chevaux*) |
| (40) | Paddle avisos (*Avisos à roues de 160 à 220 chevaux*) |

The Sailing Fleet (*Flotte à voiles*, not candidates for conversion and to disappear in eight years).

| | |
|---|---|
| (10) | Line-of-battle ships (*Vaisseaux*) |
| (20) | Frigates (*Frégates*) |
| (14) | Corvettes |
| (32) | Brigs (*Bricks*, plus 2 building) |
| (69) | Other |

*Note:* Unlike in later programmes, the list of ships to be built did not include replacements for existing ships that would reach the end of their useful lives before the end of the programme period, although the programme provided money for such replacements.

### THE PROGRAMME OF 1857 (after revisions up to 1869)

*Plan Completed*

For each programme, the left-hand column of numbers (*Plan*) shows the planned strength of the navy upon completion of the programme. (Numbers in brackets indicate numbers existing rather than planned.) The right-hand column (*Build*) shows the number of ships which would have to be built during the programme period to reach and maintain this planned strength. The programme period upon which these calculations were based is indicated at the top of each programme listing. Note that the programme documents did not always use the nomenclature for ship types in the *Listes de la flotte* that is used elsewhere in this book.

| | | |
|---|---|---|
| 40 | 28 | SHIPS OF THE FIRST RANK (*Bâtiments de 1er rang*) |
| | 17 | Armoured ships of the line and frigates (*Vaisseaux et frégates cuirassés*) |
| | 11 | Unarmoured ships of the line (*Vaisseaux non cuirassés*) |
| 20 | 26 | SHIPS FOR OVERSEAS MISSIONS (*Bâtiments pour missions lointaines*) |
| | 8 | Armoured corvettes (*Corvettes cuirassés*) |
| | 18 | Unarmoured frigates (*Frégates non cuirassés*) |
| 30 | 22 | FAST CORVETTES (*Corvettes rapides*) |
| | 15 | Unarmoured screw corvettes (*Corvettes non cuirassés à hélice*) |
| | 7 | Unarmoured paddle corvettes (*Corvettes non cuirassés à roues*) |
| 60 | 74 | AVISOS |
| | 17 | 1st class screw avisos (*Avisos de 1re classe à hélice*) |
| | 6 | 1st class paddle avisos (*Avisos de 1re classe à roues*) |
| | 19 | 2nd class screw avisos (*Avisos de 2e classe à hélice*) |
| | 10 | 2nd class paddle avisos (*Avisos de 2e classe à roues*) |
| | 22 | Gunboats (*Canonnières*) |

| 72 | 74 | TRANSPORTS |
|---|---|---|
| | 14 | Sail and screw ships of the line (*Vaisseaux mixtes à hélice*) |
| | 12 | Transports with battery decks (*Transports à batteries*) |
| | 16 | Horse transports (*Transports-écuries*) |
| | 24 | Screw transports (*Transports à hélice*) |
| | 8 | Paddle transports (*Transports à roues*) |
| 20 | 19 | COAST DEFENCE SHIPS (*Garde-côtes*) |
| | 4 | Armoured coast defence ships (*Garde-côtes cuirassés*) |
| | 15 | Armoured floating batteries (*Batteries flottantes cuirassés*) |
| 125 | 91 | FLOTILLA CRAFT (*Flottille*) |
| | 11 | Armoured sectional floating batteries (*Batteries cuirassés démontables*) |
| | 15 | Screw avisos (*Avisos à hélice*) |
| | 47 | Screw gun launches (*Chaloupes canonnières à hélice*) |
| | 17 | Paddle avisos (*Avisos à roues*) |
| | 1 | Submarine vessel (*Bâtiment sous-marin*) |
| 2 | 2 | SCHOOL SHIPS (*Bâtiments-écoles*) |
| | 2 | School ships of the line (*Vaisseaux-écoles*) |
| 70 | 80 | SAILING SHIPS (*Bâtiments à voiles*) |
| | 80 | Sailing ships of all types (*Bâtiments à voiles de tout rang*) |
| 439 | 416 | TOTALS (as of 31 December 1869) |

## THE PROGRAMME OF 1872

(Period: 1872-1885)

*Plan Build (1872-81)*

*Combat Ships (Bâtiments de combat)*

| 16 | 7 | Battleships, 1st rank (*Cuirassés de 1er rang*, formerly armoured frigates) |
|---|---|---|
| 12 | 2 | Battleships, 2nd rank (*Cuirassés de 2e rang*, formerly armoured corvettes) |

*Ships for Coastal Defence and Attack (Bâtiments de défense et d'attaque des côtes)*

| 20 | 15 | Coast defence battleships, 1st and 2nd class (*Garde-côtes cuirassés*) (later 10 of each) |
|---|---|---|
| 32 | 20 | Screw gunboats (*Canonnières*, unarmoured, *Crocodile* type) |

*Commerce Raiders (Bâtiments de course)*

| 8 | 7 | Cruisers, 1st class (*Croiseurs de 1er classe*, formerly covered battery frigates and corvettes) |
|---|---|---|
| 8 | 0 | Cruisers, 2nd class (*Croiseurs de 2e classe*, formerly open battery corvettes) |

*Avisos*

| 18 | 1 | Avisos, 1st class (*Avisos de 1ère classe*, later 3rd class cruisers) |
|---|---|---|
| 18 | 14 | Avisos, 2nd class (*Avisos de 2e classe*, later avisos) |

*Steam Transports (Transports à vapeur)*

| 5 | 4 | Large transports for Cochinchina (*Transports pour la Cochinchine*) |
|---|---|---|
| 10 | 10 | Large transports for horses (*Transports-écuries*) |
| 10 | 0 | Transports for matériel (*Transports pour matériel*) |

*Flotilla craft (Bâtiments de flottille)*

| 30 | | Screw or paddle vessels (*Bâtiments à hélice ou à roues*) |
|---|---|---|

*Note:* The total of 157 ships officially in this Programme excluded the 30 flotilla craft. It also excluded the 46 existing *chaloupes-canonnières* (which were no longer considered part of the fleet structure), service craft, and floating school ships, as well as the remaining sailing ships. By 1877 the number of flotilla craft had been increased to 60 and they were included in the programme, giving a total of 217 ships. In addition, there were 7 *torpilleurs à grande vitesse* (probably *Torpilleurs nos 1-7*) not included in the Programme de 1872.

## THE PROGRAMME OF 1879

(Period: 1880-85)

'General condition of the fleet at the end of 1885, indicating at the same time the numbers which it would be appropriate to maintain until further notice.'

*Plan Build*

| 26 | 6 | Squadron battleships (*Cuirassés d'escadre*, including 7 former 1st class coast defence battleships) |
|---|---|---|
| 10 | 0 | Station battleships (*Cuirassés de station*. Includes three of the *Alma* class, six will probably still exist) |
| 12 | 4 | Coast defence ships (*Garde-côtes*. including 8 former 2nd class coast defence battleships and four proposed fast, lightly-protected torpedo vessels (*garde-côtes porte-torpilles*) |
| 10 | 4 | Cruisers, 1st class (*Croiseurs à batterie*). |
| 16 | 0 | Cruisers, 2nd class (*Croiseurs à barbette*) |
| 16 | 0 | Squadron avisos (*Avisos d'escadre*, formerly 3rd class cruisers. Replacement of some of the older ships might become necessary.) |
| 16 | 0 | Station avisos and gunboats (*Avisos et canonnières de station*) |
| 10 | 0 | Large transports (*Grands transports*). |
| 16 | 0 | Transports for matériel and the stations (*Transports pour le matériel et la service des stations*. The station transports soon became *transports-avisos*.) |
| 40 | 0 | Flotilla craft and sailing vessels (*Bâtiments de flottille et bâtiments à voiles*) |
| 60 | 5 | Torpedo boats (*Bateaux torpilleurs pour le service de la défense mobile*) |

Ships of types not to be reproduced that will still exist in 1885.

| 18 | | Gunboats and gun launches for coast defence (*Canonnières et chaloupes-canonnières pour la défense des côtes*). |
|---|---|---|
| 7 | | Floating batteries (*Batteries flottantes*) |
| 8 | | Old armoured frigates of the *Flandre* type (These were considered well suited to protect communications between France and Algeria) |

## THE PROGRAMME OF 1881

(Period: Permanent)

*Note:* The official programme consisted only of the eight primary categories, the subdivisions being considered subject to change as the need arose.

*Plan*

| 28 | BATTLESHIPS (*Cuirassés*). |
|---|---|
| 20 | Squadron battleships (*Cuirassés d'escadre*) |
| 8 | Station battleships (*Cuirassés de station*) |
| 12 | RAMS AND COAST DEFENCE SHIPS (*Béliers et garde-côtes*) |
| 6 | Squadron battleships classified before 1879 as 1st class coast defence battleships (*Cuirassés d'escadre anciens garde-côtes*) |
| 6 | Coast-defence battleships (formerly 2nd class) (*Cuirassés garde-côtes*) |
| 12 | GUNBOATS (*Canonnières*). To be a new type of armoured gunboats. |
| 70 | TORPEDO BOATS (*Torpilleurs*). Torpedo boats and a new type of larger torpedo vessels (*Bateaux et bâtiments torpilleurs*) |
| 24 | CRUISERS (*Croiseurs*) |
| 12 | Cruisers, 1st class (*Croiseurs à batterie*) |
| 12 | Cruisers, 2nd class (*Croiseurs à barbette*) |
| 32 | AVISOS |
| 16 | Squadron avisos (*Avisos d'escadre*) |
| 16 | Station avisos and gunboats (*Avisos et canonnières de station*) |
| 36 | TRANSPORTS |
| 2 | A new type of transports to carry small torpedo boats (*Transports pour l'embarquement de bateaux torpilleurs*) |
| 28 | Transports for matériel and the stations (*Transports pour le matériel et les stations*) |

6     Sail transports (4 *vaisseaux à voiles* and 2 *transports à voiles*)
50    ACCESSORY SERVICES AND FLOTILLA CRAFT IN PEACE-TIME (*Services accessoires et bâtiments de flottille en temps de paix*). Included various auxiliary and small craft: *Bâtiments d'instruction, corvettes et avisos à roues (stationnaires), ateliers flottants, avisos de flottille à hélice, canonnières, chaloupes-canonnières, avisos de flottille à roues, bricks, goëlettes* and *cutters*.

## THE PROGRAMME OF 1890
(As finalized in July 1891. Period: 1892-1901)
*Plan  Build*
*European Waters* (*Mers d'Europe*)

| Plan | Build | |
|---|---|---|
| 24 | 10 | Squadron battleships (*Cuirassés de ligne*) |
| 12 | 1 | Cruisers, 1st class (*Croiseurs d'escadre de 1ère classe*) |
| 12 | 7 | Cruisers, 2nd class (*Croiseurs d'escadre de 2e classe*) |
| 12 | 5 | Cruisers, 3rd class (*Croiseurs d'escadre de 3e classe*) |
| 4 | 3 | Supply transports (*Transports d'approvisionnements*) |
| 4 | 4 | Torpedo-boat transports (*Transports de torpilleurs*) |
| 2 | 2 | Repair ships (*Transports ateliers*) |
| 12 | 5 | Torpedo cruisers acting as squadron torpedo-boat destroyers (*Croiseurs torpilleurs faisant fonction de contre-torpilleurs d'escadre*) |
| 40 | 19 | Seagoing torpedo boats (*Torpilleurs de haute mer*) |
| 45 | 45 | Portable torpedo boats (*Torpilleurs embarqués*) |

*Coast Defence* (*Défense des côtes*)

| Plan | Build | |
|---|---|---|
| 17 | 1 | Coast defence battleships (*Garde-côtes cuirassés*, 17 in programme, 14 on hand, but only one new one planned) |
| 4 | 0 | 1st class armoured gunboats (*Canonnières cuirassés de 1ère classe*) |
| 4 | 0 | 2nd class armoured gunboats (*Canonnières cuirassés de 2e classe*) |
| 10 | 0 | Torpedo avisos (*Avisos-torpilleurs*) |
| 110 | 71 | Torpedo boats, 1st class (*Torpilleurs de 1ère classe*) |
| 110 | 27 | Torpedo boats, 2nd class (*Torpilleurs de 2e classe*) |
| ? | ? | Submarines |

*Overseas Stations* (*Outre-mer*)

| Plan | Build | |
|---|---|---|
| 10 | 8 | Flagship cruisers (*Croiseurs amiraux*, formerly station battleships) |
| 12 | 12 | Station cruisers, 1st class (*Croiseurs de station de 1ère classe*) |
| 12 | 12 | Station cruisers, 2nd class (*Croiseurs de station de 2e classe*) |
| 12 | 8 | Avisos, 1st class (*Avisos de 1ère classe*) |
| 12 | 7 | Gunboats (*Canonnières*) |

## THE PROGRAMME OF 1894
(Period: 1895-1904)
*Plan  Build*
*Fleet for European Waters* (*Escadres des mers d'Europe*)

| Plan | Build | |
|---|---|---|
| 24 | 5 | Squadron battleships (*Cuirassés de ligne*) |
| 12 | 6 | Armoured cruisers (*Croiseurs d'escadre de 1ère classe*), not sheathed. |
| 12 | 0 | Protected cruisers, 2nd class (*Croiseurs de 2e classe*), not sheathed. |
| 12 | 1 | Protected cruisers, 3rd class (*Croiseurs de 3e classe*), not sheathed. |
| 12 | 3 | Torpedo-boat destroyers (*Contre-torpilleurs*), formerly torpedo cruisers and large torpedo avisos, ca. 1,000 tons and no torpedo tubes. |
| 16 | 16 | Seagoing torpedo boats (*Torpilleurs de haute mer*), new type, ca. 220 tons. |

*Coast Defence Fleet* (*Flotte de défense des côtes*)

| | | |
|---|---|---|
| (22) | | Coast defence battleships and armoured gunboats (*Garde côtes* and *canonnières cuirassés*), existing and not to be replaced. |

| Plan | Build | |
|---|---|---|
| 30 | 20 | Torpedo boat leaders (*Chefs de groupes de torpilleurs des défenses mobiles*), ca. 300 tons and 26-27 knots. In the interim, existing small torpedo avisos released from the fleet will be used. |
| 200 | 130 | Torpedo boats (*Torpilleurs des défenses mobiles*). New ones to be ca. 80 tons as recent 1st class boats. |

*Overseas Station Fleet* (*Flotte d'outre-mer*)

| Plan | Build | |
|---|---|---|
| 10 | 7 | Station armoured cruisers (*Croiseurs de station de 1ère classe/croiseurs amiraux*), sheathed. |
| 12 | 8 | Station protected cruisers, 2nd class (*Croiseurs de station de 2e classe*), sheathed. |
| 12 | 12 | Station protected cruisers, 3rd class (*Croiseurs de station de 3e classe*), sheathed. |
| 12 | 9 | Avisos, 1st class (*Avisos de 1ère classe*) |
| 12 | 6 | Gunboats (*Canonnières de station*) |

*Supplementary Programme* (*Programme complémentaire*)

| Plan | Build | |
|---|---|---|
| 2 | 2 | Fast cruisers for commerce-raiding (*Croiseurs rapides*) |

## THE PROGRAMME OF 1896
(Period: 1897-1904)
*Plan  Build*
*Fleet for European Waters* (*Flotte des Mers d' Europe*)

| Plan | Build | |
|---|---|---|
| 28 | 8 | Squadron battleships (*Cuirassés d'Escadre*) (4 squadrons of 6 plus 4 replacements) |
| 12 | 5 | Armoured cruisers (*Croiseurs cuirassés*) |
| 12 | 1 | Protected cruisers (*Croiseurs protégés*), 2nd (and old 1st) class |
| 12 | 1 | Protected cruisers (*Croiseurs protégés*), 3rd class |
| 30 | 16 | Torpedo-boat destroyers (*Contre-torpilleurs*) (ca. 300 tons, as *Durandal*) |
| 30 | 29 | Squadron torpedo boats (*Torpilleurs d'Escadre*) (ca. 150 tons, as *Cyclone*) |

*Coast Defence Fleet* (*Flotte de Défense des Côtes*)
I. *Coast-defence ships that can be formed into another squadron* (*Garde-côtes susceptibles d'être constitués en Escadre*)

| | | |
|---|---|---|
| (9) | | Coast-defence battleships (*Cuirassés garde-côtes*) (*Valmy, Bouvines, Indomptable,* and *Furieux* types; existing and not to be replaced) |
| 3 | 3 | Armoured cruisers (*Croiseurs cuirassés*) |
| 3 | 3 | Protected cruisers (*Croiseurs protégés*), 2nd class |
| 3 | 3 | Protected cruisers (*Croiseurs protégés*), 3rd class |
| 9 | 9 | Torpedo-boat destroyers (*Contre-torpilleurs*) |
| 9 | 9 | Squadron torpedo boats (*Torpilleurs d'Escadre*, formerly *torpilleurs de haute mer*) |

II. *Coast-defence ships assigned to the defensive* (*Garde-côtes attachés à la Défense. Avisos torpilleurs. Torpilleurs des Défenses mobiles.*)

| | | |
|---|---|---|
| (14) | | Coast-defence battleships and armoured gunboats (*Cuirassés et Canonnières garde-côtes*) (existing, not to be replaced) |
| 20 | 10 | Torpedo avisos (*Avisos torpilleurs*) (small, ca. 400 tons) |
| 200 | 62 | Torpedo boats (*Torpilleurs des Défenses mobiles*) (type as recent 1st class) |

*Overseas Station Fleet* (*Flotte d'Outre-Mer*)

| Plan | Build | |
|---|---|---|
| 4 | 3 | Armoured cruisers (*Croiseurs cuirassés*) |
| 2 | 0 | Protected cruisers, 1st class (*Croiseurs protégés de 1ère cl.*) (commerce raiders) |
| 6 | 0 | Protected cruisers, 2nd class (*Croiseurs protégés de 2ème cl.*) |
| 5 | 3 | Protected cruisers, 3rd class (*Croiseurs protégés de 3ème cl.*) |
| 7 | 3 | Avisos (*Avisos*) (1st class) |
| 7 | 0 | Transport avisos (*Avisos-transports*) |
| 10 | 4 | Gunboats (*Canonnières*) |

## THE PROGRAMME OF 1898

This 'programme' consisted of a single but important modification to the programme of 1896: increasing the number of armoured cruisers for European waters from 12 to 18. Including the 3 listed with the coast defence squadron and the 4 on the overseas stations, the total number of armoured cruisers planned for the navy thus rose to 25.

## THE PROGRAMME OF 1900

(Period as approved: 1900-1906)
*Plan Build*
*First-line Fleet*

| | | |
|---|---|---|
| 28 | 6 | Squadron battleships (*Cuirassés d'escadre*) (4 squadrons of 6 plus 4 replacements) |
| 24 | 5 | Armoured cruisers (*Croiseurs cuirassés*) (8 divisions of 3) |
| 52 | 28 | Torpedo-boat destroyers (*Contre-torpilleurs*) |
| 263 | 112 | Torpedo boats (*Torpilleurs*) |
| 38 | 26 | Submarines (*Sous-marins ou Submersibles*) |

*Note:* This programme is the one in the bill submitted by the Government to the Chamber of Deputies on 30 January 1900. The Chamber of Deputies added 50 million francs to the government request, which added an estimated 74 torpedo boats and 18 submarines to the above totals although no new totals were officially set. At the end of the programme period, the navy would also still have numerous ships of types not included in the building programme, notably 14 coast defence battleships and 34 protected cruisers. The programme became law on 9 December 1900.

## THE PROGRAMME OF 1905

(Period: 1906-1919)
*Plan Build*

| | | |
|---|---|---|
| 34 | 11 | Battleships (*Cuirassés de ligne*) (5 squadrons of 6 plus 4 replacements) |
| 18 | 10 | 1st class armoured cruisers (*Croiseurs cuirassés de 1re classe*) (13,500-14,000 tons, 5 divisions of 3 plus 3 replacements) |
| 18 | 6 | 2nd class armoured cruisers (*Croiseurs cuirassés de 2me classe*) (9,000 tons, 12 overseas, 2 replacements, and 4 reserve) |
| 6 | 6 | Scouts (*Éclaireurs*) |
| 109 | 66 | Torpedo-boat destroyers (*Contre-torpilleurs*) |
| 170 | 0 | Torpedo boats (*Torpilleurs*) |
| 49 | 18 | Defensive submarines (*Sous-marins défensifs*) |
| 82 | 72 | Offensive Submarines (*Sous-marins offensifs*) |

*Note:* This programme was quickly updated by the 1906 programme.

## THE PROGRAMME OF 1906

(Period: 1907-1921)
*Plan Build*

| | | |
|---|---|---|
| 38 | 24 | Battleships (*Cuirassés*) (those to be built include two fitting out) |
| 20 | 6 | Armoured cruisers (*Croiseurs cuirassés*) (including 2 *Edgar Quinet* and excluding 2nd class types) |
| 6 | 6 | Scouts (*Éclaireurs*) |
| 109 | 66 | Torpedo-boat destroyers (*Contre-torpilleurs*) |
| 170 | 0 | Torpedo boats (*Torpilleurs*) |
| 49 | 18 | Defensive submarines (*Sous-marins défensifs*) |
| 82 | 72 | Offensive Submarines (*Sous-marins offensifs*) |

*Note:* This programme updated the requirements for battleships and armoured cruisers but accepted the rest of the 1905 programme. The 2nd class armoured cruisers of the *Desaix* class were excluded from this programme along with older station cruisers. The plan was to begin construction of 12 battleships before starting the construction of 6 armoured cruisers and 6 scouts in 1910. The last ships of the programme would be begun in 1919. The *Conseil supérieur* reviewed this programme in

October 1907 while discussing the ships to be laid down in 1909-10 and made no changes.

## THE PROGRAMME OF 1909

(Proposed *Loi organique*. Period 1910-1925)
*Plan*

| | |
|---|---|
| 45 | Battleships (*Cuirassés,* including 5 replacements, service life 25 years) |
| 12 | Fleet Scouts (*Éclaireurs d'Escadre*, including 2 replacements, service life 20 years) |
| 60 | Destroyers (*Bâtiments torpilleurs d'Escadre*, 600 tons or more, including 12 replacements, service life 17 years) |
| 84 | Torpedo boats (*Bâtiments torpilleurs de Flottille*, 300 tons or less, including 12 replacements, service life 17 years) |
| 64 | Submarines (*Bâtiments sous-marins,* including 16 replacements) |
| 3 | Minelayers (*Bâtiments mouilleurs de mines*) |
| 8 | Minesweepers (*Bâtiments dragueurs de mines*) |
| 2 | Repair ships (*Bâtiments ateliers*) |

*The fleet will also include*

| | |
|---|---|
| 10 | Station ships (*Bâtiments de station*), like *Infernet*, not over 3,000 tons. |
| 12 | Avisos and gunboats (*Avisos et canonnières*) |
| 3 | Hydrographic ships (*Bâtiments hydrographiques*) |
| 3 | Coastal transports (*Transports de côte*) |
| 1 | School ship (*Bâtiment école*, the *école d'application des aspirants*, at that time *Duguay-Trouin*) |

*Note:* This programme was a proposed law (not submitted) setting the size of the fleet without planning or authorizing ship construction. The battleships replaced both the battleships and armoured cruisers in previous programmes as a sole type of combatant ship. The fleet scouts were to be as fast as possible, lightly armed and armoured.

## THE PROGRAMME OF 1912

(Naval Law of 30 March 1912)
*Plan Build*

1. The Combat Fleet *(Flotte de combat)*

| | | |
|---|---|---|
| 28 | 13 | Battleships (*Cuirassés d'escadre*, including 4 *escadres* of 6 ships each and 4 replacements) |
| 10 | 6 | Scouts (*Éclaireurs d'escadre*, including 2 *éclaireurs* per *escadre* and 2 replacements) |
| 52 | | Destroyers (*Bâtiments torpilleurs de haute mer*, including 12 per *escadre* and 4 replacements) |

2. Fleet of overseas naval divisions *(Flotte des divisions navales lointaines)*

| | |
|---|---|
| 10 | Ships for overseas naval divisions (*Bâtiments pour divisions navales lointaines*) |
| — | Avisos and gunboats (*Avisos et canonnières*) as needed |

3. Flotillas of submarine defences *(Flottilles des défenses sous-marines)*

| | |
|---|---|
| 94 | Submarines (*Bâtiments sous-marins*) |
| 4 | Mine transports and minelayers (*Bâtiments porteurs et mouilleurs de mines*) |
| — | Minesweepers (*Dragueurs de mines*) as needed |
| — | Torpedo boats (*Torpilleurs*) as needed |

4. Ships for special services *(Bâtiments des services spéciaux)*

| | |
|---|---|
| 3 | Hydrographic ships (*Bâtiments hydrographes*) |
| 3 | Coastal transports (*Transports de côtes*) |
| — | School ships (*Bâtiments écoles*) as needed |
| — | Fishery protection ships (*Bâtiments garde-pêche*) as needed |

*Note:* This programme was first submitted to the Chamber of Deputies as a bill on 9 February 1910 and became law over two years later on 30 March 1912. The number of battleships to be built started with three planned for 1912 (the *Bretagne* class) including one (*Lorraine*) as a replacement for the lost *Liberté*. Four dreadnoughts had already been begun in 1910-11. The six *éclaireurs* to be built were to be begun in 1917-19, four more would have been begun in 1920-21. The law contained no building schedules for other ship types.

## SOURCE NOTES

1. Programme of 1857: *Rapport de son exc. M. le Ministre de la Marine à l'Empereur sur la transformation de la flotte*, Conseil d'Etat, Document No. 657 (8 January 1857), SHD Library, VI-29L41 (marked up printer's proof copy); Franklin Whittelsey Wallin, *The French Navy during the Second Empire: A Study of the Effects of Technological Develpment on French Governmental Policy*, Doctoral dissertation, University of California at Berkeley, 1953, pp. 75-78. An imperial decree of 23 November 1857 implemented the program.

2. Programme of 1857 as revised through 1869: "Extrait de l'exposé de la situation de l'Empire présenté au Sénat et au Corps Législatif le 29 novembre 1869," *Revue maritime et coloniale*, February 1870, pp. 80-81. The same figures were given in the report of Daniel Ancel on the budget for 1871 presented to the Assemblée nationale on 19 August 1871, *Revue maritime et coloniale*, October 1871, pp. 558-559.

3. Programme of 1872: *Budget de la Marine et des Colonies pour l'exercice 1874*, Note préliminaire (March 1873). The headings are from the minutes of the *Conseil d'Amirauté* for 29 August 1871 in the Archives de la Marine, BB8-901. The numbers of ships to be built during the first ten years of the program were calculated from Annexe 7 of the budget submitted by the navy for 1874.

4. Programme of 1879: Minutes of the *Conseil d'Amiraué* (16 August 1879), Supplementary register of secret deliberations (1843-1879), Archives de la Marine, BB8-853.

5. Programme of 1881: Minutes of the *Conseil d'Amirauté* (6 May 1881), Archives de la Marine, BB8-910.

6. Programme of 1890: "Note pour l'Etat-major général" by the Director of Materiel (2 July 1891), Archives de la Marine, BB8-2424/2.

7. Programme of 1894: Minutes of the *Conseil supérieur* (5, 7, 10, and 11 December 1894), Archives de la Marine, BB8-2424/2.

8. Programme of 1896: "Programme adopté pour la constitution de la Flotte" (ca. January 1897), and Minutes of the *Conseil supérieur* (17, 18, and 21 December 1896), Archives de la Marine, BB8-2424/4.

9. Programme of 1898: Minutes of the *Conseil supérieur* (17 January 1898) and supporting papers, Archives de la Marine, BB8-2424/5 and 4.

10. Programme of 1900: Jean-Louis de Lanessan, *Le programme maritime de 1900-1906* (Paris, 1902), especially pp. 188-89 and 259.

11. Programme of 1905: Papers of the *Conseil supérieur* (May 1905), Archives de la Marine, BB8-2424/6.

12. Programme of 1906: Papers of the *Conseil supérieur* (Feb.-Mar. 1906), Archives de la Marine, BB8-2424/8.

13. Programme of 1909: Papers of the *Conseil supérieur* (May-June 1909), Archives de la Marine, BB8-2424/13.

14. Programme of 1912: Archives de la Marine, SS Ed3.

Sunday on board the torpedo aviso *D'Iberville* with the crew posing around the ship's forward 100mm/45 Model 1891(2) Canet QF gun. In the background on each side are two 47mm guns. *(NHHC from ONI, NH-64454)*

# French Naval Shipbuilding Budgets, 1872-1914

This appendix shows the new construction ships contained for the first time in each French naval budget from 1872 to 1914. Ships not in budgets are not listed.

| Type | Designator and name | Later budgets |
|------|---------------------|---------------|
| **Budget 1872. Submitted 9.12.1871, Law of 31.3.1872.** | | |
| Cuirassé de 1er rang | *Redoutable* | 1874-1876 |
| Cuirassé de 1er rang Deferred to 1875 | *N (Unnamed)* | (none) |
| Cuirassé de 2e rang Deferred to 1875 | *N (Unnamed)* | (none) |
| Garde-côtes cuirassé de 1re classe | *Tonnerre* | 1874-1876 |
| Garde-côtes cuirassé de 2e classe | *Tempête* | 1874-1877 |
| Croiseur de 1re classe | *Duquesne* | 1874-1876 |
| Croiseur de 2e classe | *Duguay-Trouin* | 1874-1877 |
| Canonnière de stations | *Bouvet* | 1874-1876 |
| Canonnière de stations | *Parseval* | 1874/1879 |
| Canonnière de stations | *Bisson* | 1874-1875 |
| Canonnière de stations | *La Bourdonnais* | 1874-1875 |
| Canonnière de stations | *Crocodile* | 1874 |
| Canonnière de stations | *Lionne* | 1874 |
| Grand transport | *Annamite* | 1874-1877 |
| Grand transport Late addition | *Mytho* | 1874-1879 |

**Budget 1873. Submitted 14.5.1872, Law of 30.12.1872. (No additional ships).**

**Budget 1874. Submitted 17.3.1873, Law of 30.12.1873. (No additional ships).**

| Type | Designator and name | Later budgets |
|------|---------------------|---------------|
| **Budget 1875. Submitted 12.1.1874, Law of 25.8.1874.** | | |
| Cuirassé de 1er rang | *Foudroyant/Courbet* | 1876/1884 |
| Cuirassé de 2e rang Delayed to 1876, not built | *Condé* | 1876 |
| Garde-côtes cuirassé de 1re classe | *Fulminant* | 1876-1881 |
| Garde-côtes cuirassé de 2e classe | *Vengeur* | 1876-1881 |
| Croiseur de 1re classe | *Tourville* | 1876 |
| Croiseur de 1re classe Not built | *N (Unnamed)* | (none) |
| Croiseur de 3e classe | *Rigault de Genouilly* | 1876-1877 |
| Croiseur de 3e classe | *Éclaireur* | 1876-1877 |
| Canonnière de stations | *Chasseur* | 1876-1878 |
| Canonnière de stations | *Voltigeur* | 1876-1878 |
| Canonnière de stations | *Lutin* | 1877-1878 |
| Canonnière de stations | *Lynx* | 1877-1878 |
| Canonnière de stations Not built | *N (Unnamed)* | (none) |
| Grand transport Delayed to 1876 | *Tonquin* | 1876-1879 |
| Aviso de flottille | *Rôdeur* | 1876 |
| Aviso de flottille | *Furet* | 1876 |
| Aviso de flottille Not built | *N (Unnamed)* | (none) |

| Type | Designator and name | Later budgets |
|------|---------------------|---------------|
| **Budget 1876. Submitted 11.5.1875, Law of 16.8.1875.** | | |
| Cuirassé de 1er rang | *Dévastation* | 1877-1880 |
| Cuirassé de 1er rang | *Amiral Duperré* (*Duguesclin in 1875 fleet list*) | 1877-1880 |
| Cuirassé de 1er rang Delayed to 1878, not built | *N (Unnamed)* | 1877-1878 |
| Cuirassé de 2e rang | *Turenne* | 1877-1881 |
| Cuirassé de 2e rang Delayed to 1877 | *Vauban* | 1877-1884 |
| Garde-côtes cuirassé de 1re classe | *Furieux* | 1877-1885 |
| Garde-côtes cuirassé de 1re classe Delayed to 1877 | *Caïman* | 1877-1885 |
| Garde-côtes cuirassé de 1re classe Delayed to 1877 | *Requin* | 1877-1886 |
| Garde-côtes cuirassé de 2e classe | *Tonnant* | 1877-1883 |
| Croiseur de 2e classe | *Lapérouse* | 1877-1879 |
| Croiseur de 2e classe | *Villars* | 1877-1881 |
| Croiseur de 3e classe Not built | *N (Unnamed)* | (none) |
| Canonnière de stations | *Milan* | (none) |
| Canonnière de stations | *Vautour* | (none) |
| Grand transport Delayed to 1877 | *Shamrock* | 1877-1879 |
| Transport-aviso | *Allier* | 1877-1878 |
| Transport-aviso | *Nièvre* | 1877-1879 |
| Transport-aviso | *Drac* | 1877-1879 |
| Canonnière démontable Delayed to 1877, not built | *N,N,N,N (4 Unnamed)* | 1877 |
| **Budget 1877. Submitted 14.3.1876, Law of 29.12.1876.** | | |
| Cuirassé de 2e rang | *Bayard* | 1878-1881 |
| Cuirassé de 2e rang | *Duguesclin* | 1878-1885 |
| Garde-côtes cuirassé de 1re classe Delayed to 1878 | *Indomptable* | 1878-1885 |
| Croiseur de 2e classe | *D'Estaing* | 1878-1880 |
| Croiseur de 2e classe | *Nielly* | 1878-1881 |
| Croiseur de 2e classe | *Monge/Primauguet* | 1878-1883 |
| Croiseur de 2e classe | *Forfait* | 1878-1879 |
| Croiseur de 2e classe | *Magon* | 1878-1881 |
| Aviso de stations | *Hussard* | 1878 |
| Aviso de stations | *Lancier/Dumont d'Urville* | 1878 |
| Aviso de stations Not built | *N (Unnamed)* | (none) |
| Torpilleur (bâtiment de flottille) | *Torpilleurs nos 1-6* | (none) |
| Grand transport Not built | *N (Unnamed)* | (none) |
| Transport-aviso | *Saône* | 1878-1881 |
| Transport-aviso Delayed to 1878 | *Romanche* | 1878-1879 |
| Aviso de flottille | *Élan* | 1878 |
| Aviso de flottille | *Cigale* | 1878 |

| Type | Designator and name | Later budgets |
|---|---|---|
| **Budget 1878. Submitted 11.1.1877, Law of 30.3.1878.** | | |
| Cuirassé de 1$^{er}$ rang <br> Delayed to 1879 | *Formidable* | 1879-1889 |
| Cuirassé de 2$^e$ rang <br> Not built | *N (Unnamed)* | (none) |
| Cuirassé de 2$^e$ rang <br> Not built | *N (Unnamed)* | (none) |
| Garde-côtes cuirassé de 1$^{re}$ classe | *Terrible* | 1879-1884 |
| Croiseur de 1$^{re}$ classe | *Iphigénie* | 1879-1882 |
| Croiseur de 1$^{re}$ classe | *Naïade* | 1879-1882 |
| Croiseur de 2$^e$ classe | *Roland* | 1879-1883 |
| Croiseur de 2$^e$ classe <br> Not built | *N (Unnamed)* | (none) |
| Canonnière de stations | *Aspic* | 1879-1881 |
| Canonnière de stations | *Vipère* | 1879-1881 |
| Transport-aviso | *Pourvoyeur* | (none) |
| Aviso de flottille | *Mouette* | (none) |
| **Budget 1879. Submitted 2.4.1878, Law of 22.12.1878.** | | |
| Cuirassé de 1$^{er}$ rang | *Amiral Baudin* | 1880/1888 |
| Croiseur de 1$^{re}$ classe | *Aréthuse* | 1880-1883 |
| Canonnière de stations | *Capricorne* | 1880-1882 |
| Canonnière de stations | *Sagittaire* | 1880-1882 |
| Grand transport | *Vinh-Long* | 1880-1881 |
| **Budget 1880. Submitted 23.1.1879, Law of 21.12.1879.** | | |
| Cuirassé de 1$^{er}$ rang | *Hoche* | 1881-1889 |
| Cuirassé de 1$^{er}$ rang | *Magenta* | 1881-1892 |
| Cuirassé de 2$^e$ rang <br> Not built | *N (Unnamed)* | (none) |
| Cuirassé de 2$^e$ rang <br> Not built | *N (Unnamed)* | (none) |
| Garde-côtes cuirassé de 1$^{re}$ classe <br> Not built | *N (Unnamed)* | (none) |
| Garde-côtes cuirassé de 1$^{re}$ classe <br> Not built | *N (Unnamed)* | (none) |
| Grand transport | *Bien-Hoa* | 1881 |
| **Budget 1881. Submitted 30.1.1880, Law of 22.12.1880.** | | |
| Cuirassé d'escadre | *Marceau* | 1882-1891 |
| Cuirassé d'escadre | *Neptune* | 1882-1892 |
| Croiseur à batterie | *Dubourdieu* | 1882-1885 |
| Croiseur à batterie | *Capitaine Lucas* | 1882 |
| Aviso de stations <br> Delayed to 1882 | *Inconstant* | 1882-1885 |
| Aviso de stations <br> Delayed to 1882 | *Papin* | 1882-1886 |
| Grand transport | *Nive* | 1882/1884 |
| Transport-aviso | *Scorff* | 1882 |
| Aviso de flottille | *Écureuil* | (none) |
| Aviso de flottille | *Albatros* | 1882 |
| Aviso de flottille | *Basilic* | 1882 |
| Aviso de flottille | *Oyapock* | (none) |
| **Budget 1882. Submitted 21.1.1881, Law of 29.7.1881.** | | |
| Cuirassé d'escadre <br> Delayed to 1883, reordered in 1888 budget | *Brennus (i)* | 1883-1886 |
| Cuirassé d'escadre <br> Delayed to 1883, not completed | *Charles Martel* | 1883-1885 |
| Cuirassé de 2$^e$ rang <br> Delayed to 1886, not built | *N (Unnamed)* | 1883/1886 |
| Cuirassé de 2$^e$ rang <br> Delayed to 1885, not built | *N (Unnamed)* | 1883/1885 |

| Type | Designator and name | Later budgets |
|---|---|---|
| Croiseur à batterie <br> Not built | *N (Unnamed)* | (none) |
| Éclaireur d'escadre | *Milan* | 1883-1884 |
| Éclaireur d'escadre <br> Not built | *N (Unnamed)* | 1883 |
| Grand transport | *Gironde* | 1883-1884 |
| Transport à voiles (82), <br> transport mixte (83) | *Magellan* | 1883-1884 |
| Transport à voiles (82), <br> transport mixte (83) | *Calédonien* | 1883-1884 |
| Aviso de flottille | *Pluvier* | (none) |
| Aviso de flottille | *Alouette* | (none) |
| Aviso de flottille | *Volage* | (none) |
| Aviso de flottille | *Chimère* | (none) |
| Aviso de flottille | *Fourmi* | (none) |
| **Budget 1883. Submitted 2.3.1882, Law of 29.12.1882.** | | |
| Cuirassé d'escadre <br> Not built | *N (Unnamed)* | 1884 |
| Croiseur à batterie | *Sfax* | 1884-1886 |
| Éclaireur d'escadre <br> Not built | *N (Unnamed)* | (none) |
| Aviso de stations | *Fulton* | 1884-1887 |
| Canonnière de stations | *Comète* | 1884 |
| Canonnière de stations | *Météore* | 1884-1885 |
| Canonnière de stations | *Sirius* | (none) |
| Canonnière de stations | *Gabès* | 1884 |
| Transport-aviso | *Meurthe* | 1884-1885 |
| Aviso de flottille | *Vigilant* | (none) |
| Aviso de flottille | *Goéland* | (none) |
| Aviso de flottille | *Héron* | (none) |
| Aviso de flottille | *Mésange* | (none) |
| Aviso de flottille | *Ardent* | (none) |
| Aviso de flottille | *Brandon* | (none) |
| Garde-pêche | *Mutin* | (none) |
| Garde-pêche | *Railleur* | (none) |
| **Budget 1884. Submitted 3.3.1883, Law of 29.12.1883.** | | |
| Cuirassé d'escadre <br> Not built | *N (Unnamed)* | (none) |
| Canonnière cuirassée de 1$^{re}$ classe | *Achéron* | 1885 |
| Canonnière cuirassée de 1$^{re}$ classe | *Cocyte* | 1885-1889 |
| Canonnière cuirassée de 1$^{re}$ classe | *Phlégéton* | 1885-1892 |
| Canonnière cuirassée de 1$^{re}$ classe | *Styx* | 1885-1892 |
| Canonnière cuirassée de 2$^e$ classe | *Flamme* | 1885 |
| Canonnière cuirassée de 2$^e$ classe | *Fusée* | 1885 |
| Canonnière cuirassée de 2$^e$ classe | *Grenade* | 1885-1888 |
| Canonnière cuirassée de 2$^e$ classe | *Mitraille* | 1885 |
| Croiseur torpilleur | *Condor* | 1885 |
| Croiseur torpilleur | *Épervier* | 1885-1887 |
| Croiseur torpilleur | *Faucon* | 1885-1887 |
| Croiseur torpilleur | *Vautour* | 1885-1889 |
| Canonnière de stations | *Étoile* | 1885 |
| Canonnière de stations | *Lion* | (none) |
| Canonnière de stations | *Scorpion* | (none) |
| Transport-aviso | *Durance* | 1885-1886 |
| Aviso de flottille | *Ibis* | (none) |
| Aviso de flottille | *Alcyon* | (none) |
| Aviso de flottille | *Jouffroy* | 1885-1887 |
| Aviso de flottille | *Pingouin* | (none) |
| Aviso de flottille | *Salamandre* | (none) |
| Aviso de flottille | *Cigogne* | 1885/1888 |
| Aviso de flottille | *Lézard* | 1885/1888 |

| Type | Designator and name | Later budgets |
|---|---|---|
| Frégate à voiles | *Melpomène* | 1885/1889 |
| Frégate à voiles | *Andromède* | 1885/1892 |
| Brick à voiles | *Sylphe* | 1885-1886 |
| Brick à voiles | *Bayonnais* | 1885-1886 |

**Budget 1885. Submitted 28.2.1884, Law of 21.3.1885.**

| Type | Designator and name | Later budgets |
|---|---|---|
| Croiseur à batterie<br>  Delayed to 1886 | *Tage* | 1886-1889 |
| Aviso de stations<br>  Delayed to 1887, not built | *N (Unnamed)* | 1886-1887 |
| Transport-aviso | *Aube* | 1886 |
| Transport-aviso | *Eure* | 1886 |
| Transport-aviso | *Rance* | 1886-1889 |
| Torpilleur-aviso | *Bombe* | (none) |
| Torpilleur-aviso | *Couleuvrine* | 1886 |
| Torpilleur-aviso | *Dague* | 1886 |
| Torpilleur-aviso | *Dragonne* | 1886 |
| Torpilleur-aviso | *Flèche* | 1886 |
| Torpilleur-aviso | *Lance* | 1886 |
| Torpilleur-aviso | *Sainte Barbe* | 1886/1888 |
| Torpilleur-aviso | *Salve* | 1886/1888 |
| Grand transport | *Pacifique* | 1886/1892 |
| Grand transport<br>  Not built | *N (Unnamed)* | 1886 |

**Budget 1886. Submitted 23.3.1885, Law of 8.8.1885.**

| Type | Designator and name | Later budgets |
|---|---|---|
| Croiseur à batterie | *Cécille* | 1887-1889 |
| Transport-aviso | *Manche* | 1887-1891 |
| Canonnière de stations<br>  Not built | *N (Unnamed)* | (none) |
| Canonnière de stations<br>  Not built | *N (Unnamed)* | (none) |
| Canonnière de stations<br>  Not built | *N (Unnamed)* | (none) |
| Torpilleur de haute mer | *Balny* | (none) |
| Torpilleur de haute mer | *Déroulède* | (none) |
| Torpilleur de haute mer | *Doudart de Lagrée* | (none) |
| Torpilleur de haute mer | *Edmond Fontaine* | 1889 |
| Torpilleur de haute mer | *Bouët-Willaumez* | 1889 |
| Torpilleur de haute mer | *Capitaine Cuny* | (none) |
| Torpilleur de haute mer | *Capitaine Mehl* | (none) |
| Torpilleur de haute mer | *Challier* | (none) |
| Torpilleur de haute mer | *Dehorter* | 1889 |
| Torpilleur de haute mer<br>  Not built | *N (funds used for<br>Gabriel Charmes?)* | (none) |
| Torpilleur de haute mer<br>  Not built | *N (funds used for<br>Torpilleur no 150?)* | (none) |

**Budget 1887. Submitted 16.3.1886, Law of 27.2.1887.**

| Type | Designator and name | Later budgets |
|---|---|---|
| Croiseur de 1re classe | *Jean Bart* | 1888-1890 |
| Croiseur de 1re classe<br>  Not built | *Dupuy de Lôme (ii)* | (none) |
| Croiseur de 1re classe<br>  Not built | *Dupuy de Lôme (i)* | (none) |
| Croiseur de 2e classe<br>  Delayed to 1887 extraordinary | *Davout* | 1887-1889 |
| Croiseur de 2e classe<br>  Delayed to 1887 extraordinary | *Suchet* | 1887-1892 |
| Croiseur de 3e classe | *Forbin* | 1888 |
| Croiseur de 3e classe | *Surcouf* | 1888-1889 |
| Croiseur de 3e classe | *Troude* | 1888-1889 |
| Torpilleur de haute mer | *Ouragan* | 1888 |
| Torpilleur de 1re classe | *Torpilleurs nos 75-104* | 1888 |
| Torpilleur de 1re classe | *Torpilleurs nos 105-125* | 1888 |

| Type | Designator and name | Later budgets |
|---|---|---|
| Transport-aviso | *Vaucluse* | 1888/1901 |
| Transport de 3e classe | *Drôme* | 1888 |

**Extraordinary Budget 1887. Submitted ca. late 1886, Law of. 26.2.1887**

| Type | Designator and name | Later budgets |
|---|---|---|
| Croiseur de 1re classe | *Isly* | 1888-1893 |
| Croiseur de 1re classe | *Alger* | 1888-1892 |
| Croiseur de 1re classe<br>  Not built | *Mogador* | (none) |
| Croiseur de 2e classe<br>  Not built | *Chanzy (i)* | (none) |
| Croiseur de 3e classe | *Coëtlogon* | 1888-1891 |
| Croiseur de 3e classe | *Lalande* | 1888-1890 |
| Croiseur de 3e classe | *Cosmao* | 1888-1891 |
| Torpilleur de haute mer | *Coureur* | 1888 |
| Torpilleur de haute mer | *Avant-Garde* | 1888 |
| Torpilleur de 1re classe | *Torpilleurs nos 126-127* | 1888 |

**Budget 1888. Submitted 23.3.1887, Law of 30.3.1888.**

| Type | Designator and name | Later budgets |
|---|---|---|
| Cuirassé d'escadre | *Brennus (ii)* | 1889-1895 |
| Croiseur cuirassé | *Dupuy de Lôme (iii)* | 1889/1895 |
| Aviso de 2e classe | *Bengali* | (none) |

**Budget 1889. Submitted 21.6.1888, Law of 29.12.1888.**

| Type | Designator and name | Later budgets |
|---|---|---|
| Cuirassé de 6,700tx<br>  Delayed to 1890 | *Amiral Tréhouart* | 1890-1896 |
| Croiseur cuirassé<br>  Delayed to 1890 | *Amiral Charner* | 1890-1895 |
| Croiseur torpilleur | *Wattignies* | 1890-1892 |
| Aviso-torpilleur | *Léger* | 1890-1892 |
| Aviso-torpilleur | *Lévrier* | 1890-1892 |
| Torpilleur de haute mer | *Audacieux* | (none) |
| Torpilleur de haute mer | *Agile* | (none) |
| Torpilleur de haute mer | *Alarme* | (none) |
| Torpilleur de haute mer | *Aventurier* | (none) |
| Torpilleur de haute mer | *Défi* | (none) |
| Torpilleur de haute mer | *Téméraire* | (none) |
| Torpilleur de 1re classe | *Torpilleurs nos 128-129* | (none) |

**Budget 1890. Submitted 9.2.1889, Law of 17.7.1889.**

| Type | Designator and name | Later budgets |
|---|---|---|
| Croiseur cuirassé<br>Law of 28.2.1889 | *Latouche-Tréville* | 1891-1894 |
| Croiseur cuirassé<br>Law of 28.2.1889 | *Chanzy (ii)* | 1891-1895 |
| Croiseur cuirassé<br>Delayed to 1891 | *Bruix* | 1891-1897 |
| Croiseur torpilleur | *Fleurus* | 1891/1897 |
| Torpilleur de 1re classe | *Torpilleurs nos 130-144* | 1891 |

**Extraordinary Budget 1890. Submitted 15.7.1889, Law of 26.11.1889.**

| Type | Designator and name | Later budgets |
|---|---|---|
| Cuirassé de 6,700tx | *Bouvines* | 1892-1896 |
| Cuirassé de 6,700tx | *Jemmapes* | 1892-1894 |
| Cuirassé de 6,700tx | *Valmy* | 1892-1896 |
| Aviso-torpilleur | *D'Iberville* | 1892-1894 |
| Aviso-torpilleur<br>  Delayed to 1892. Later M1. | *Cassini* | 1892-1895 |
| Torpilleur de haute mer | *Dragon* | 1892 |
| Torpilleur de haute mer | *Grenadier* | 1892 |
| Torpilleur de haute mer | *Lancier* | 1892 |
| Torpilleur de haute mer | *Turco* | 1892 |
| Torpilleur de haute mer | *Zouave* | 1892 |
| Torpilleur de haute mer | *Éclair* | 1892 |
| Torpilleur de haute mer | *Kabyle* | 1892 |
| Torpilleur de haute mer | *Orage* | 1892 |

| Type | Designator and name | Later budgets |
|------|---------------------|---------------|
| Torpilleur de haute mer | *Sarrazin (Sarrasin)* | 1892 |
| Torpilleur de haute mer | *Tourbillon* | 1892 |
| Torpilleur de 1ʳᵉ classe | *Torpilleurs nᵒˢ 147-149* | 1892 |
| Torpilleur de 1ʳᵉ classe | *Torpilleurs nᵒˢ 152-169* | 1892 |

**Budget 1891. Submitted 22.2.1890, Law of 26.12.1890.**

| Type | Designator and name | Later budgets |
|------|---------------------|---------------|
| Cuirassé d'escadre | *Charles Martel* | 1892-1897 |
| Cuirassé d'escadre | *Lazare Carnot* | 1892-1897 |
| Cuirassé d'escadre | *Jauréguiberry* | 1892-1897 |
| Croiseur de 2ᵉ classe | *Chasseloup-Laubat* | 1892-1895 |
| Croiseur de 2ᵉ classe | *Friant* | 1892-1895 |
| Croiseur de 2ᵉ classe | *Bugeaud* | 1892-1897 |
| Torpilleur de haute mer | *Véloce* | (none) |
| Torpilleur de haute mer | *Grondeur* | (none) |
| Torpilleur de haute mer<br>Late addition | *Archer* | (none) |
| Torpilleur de haute mer<br>Late addition | *Chevalier* | 1893 |
| Torpilleur de haute mer<br>Late addition | *Corsaire* | 1893 |
| Torpilleur de haute mer<br>Late addition | *Mousquetaire* | 1893 |
| Torpilleur de 1ʳᵉ classe | *Torpilleurs nᵒˢ 145-146* | 1892 |
| Torpilleur de 1ʳᵉ classe<br>Late addition | *Torpilleurs nᵒˢ 170-171* | (none) |
| Chaloupe-vedette | *Chéliff* | (none) |
| Chaloupe-vedette | *Seybouse* | (none) |

**Budget 1892. Submitted 17.2.1891, Law of 26.1.1892.**

| Type | Designator and name | Later budgets |
|------|---------------------|---------------|
| Cuirassé d'escadre<br>Later A1. | *A, Bouvet* | 1893-1898 |
| Cuirassé d'escadre<br>Later A2. | *B, Masséna* | 1893-1898 |
| Croiseur de 1ʳᵉ classe<br>Later D1. Delayed to 1894 | *C, Pothuau* | 1893-1897 |
| Croiseur de 3ᵉ classe<br>Later H1. | *D, Linois* | 1893-1895 |
| Croiseur de 2ᵉ classe<br>Later E2. | *E, Pascal* | 1893-1897 |
| Croiseur de 2ᵉ classe<br>Later E1. | *F, Descartes* | 1893-1897 |
| Croiseur porte-torpilleur<br>Later L1. | *G, Foudre* | 1893-1897 |
| Torpilleur de haute mer<br>Later N2. | *H, Flibustier* | 1893-1895 |
| Torpilleur de haute mer<br>Later N3. | *I, Ariel* | 1893-1895 |
| Torpilleur de haute mer<br>Later N4. | *J, Tourmente* | 1893-1894 |
| Torpilleur de 1ʳᵉ classe | *Torpilleurs nᵒˢ 172-181* | 1893 |
| Sous-marin | *Gustave Zédé (ex Sirène)* | 1896-1897 |

**Budget 1893. Submitted 10.3.1892, Law of 28.4.1893.**

| Type | Designator and name | Later budgets |
|------|---------------------|---------------|
| Croiseur de 2ᵉ classe<br>Later G1. | *K, Du Chayla* | 1894-1897 |
| Croiseur de 3ᵉ classe<br>Later H2. The missing 'M' may have been *Lavoisier*, see 1894 | *L, Galilée* | 1894-1897 |
| Croiseur de 1ʳᵉ classe<br>Later C1. Delayed to 1894 | *N, D'Entrecasteaux* | 1894-1899 |
| Croiseur de 1ʳᵉ classe<br>Later C2. Delayed to 1895, not built | *O, Jeanne d'Arc (i)* | 1894-1895 |
| Croiseur de 2ᵉ classe<br>Later E3. Delayed to 1894 | *P, Catinat* | 1894-1897 |

| Type | Designator and name | Later budgets |
|------|---------------------|---------------|
| Croiseur de 2ᵉ classe<br>Later G2. | *Q, D'Assas* | 1894-1897 |
| Aviso-torpilleur<br>Later M2. | *R, Casabianca* | 1894-1896 |
| Canonnière de stations<br>Later T1. | *S, Surprise* | 1894/1897 |
| Torpilleur de haute mer<br>Later N5. | *T, Argonaute* | 1894 |
| Torpilleur de haute mer<br>Later N6. | *U, Averne* | 1894 |
| Torpilleur de haute mer<br>Later N7. | *V, Dauphin* | 1894 |
| Torpilleur de haute mer<br>Later N8. Delayed to 1894 | *W, Aquilon* | 1894-1896 |
| Torpilleur de haute mer<br>Later N9. Delayed to 1896 | *X, Ténare/Cyclone* | 1894-1899 |
| Torpilleur de haute mer<br>Later N10. Delayed to 1895 | *Y, Cerbère/Mangini* | 1894-1897 |
| Torpilleur de haute mer<br>Later N11. | *Z, Forban* | 1894-1896 |
| Torpilleur de haute mer<br>Later N1. Charged to 1890 extraordinary | *Lansquenet* | 1894-1895 |
| Torpilleur de 1ʳᵉ classe | *P1-9, Torpilleurs<br>nᵒˢ 182-191* | 1894 |
| Torpilleur de 1ʳᵉ classe | *P10-19, Torpilleurs<br>nᵒˢ 192-200* | 1894-1895 |

**Budget 1894. Submitted 16.5.1893, Law of 26.7.1893.**

| Type | Designator and name | Later budgets |
|------|---------------------|---------------|
| Cuirassé d'escadre<br>Not funded, not built. See *Iéna*, 1897 | *A3, Henri IV* | (none) |
| Cuirassé d'escadre | *A4, Charlemagne* | 1895-1900 |
| Cuirassé d'escadre | *A5, Saint Louis* | 1895-1900 |
| Croiseur de 2ᵉ classe<br>Delayed to 1895 | *E4, Protet* | 1895-1899 |
| Croiseur de 2ᵉ classe<br>Not funded, not built. Jurien de la Gravière (E5) in 1896 budget bill not approved | *E5 (Unnamed)* | (none) |
| Croiseur de 2ᵉ classe<br>Not funded, not built | *E6 (Unnamed)* | (none) |
| Croiseur de 2ᵉ classe<br>Not funded, not built | *G3 (Unnamed)* | (none) |
| Croiseur de 2ᵉ classe | *G4, Cassard* | 1895-1898 |
| Croiseur de 3e classe | *H3, Lavoisier* | 1895-1898 |
| Torpilleur de haute mer<br>Not funded, not built | *N12 (Unnamed)* | (none) |
| Torpilleur de 1ʳᵉ classe<br>Delayed to 1895 | *P20-21, Torpilleurs nᵒˢ<br>201-202* | 1895-1897 |
| Torpilleur de 1ʳᵉ classe<br>Delayed to 1895 | *P22-24, Torpilleurs nᵒˢ<br>203-205* | 1896-1897 |
| Torpilleur de 2ᵉ classe<br>Not funded, not built | *Q1-Q4 (Unnamed)* | (none) |
| Torpilleur embarqué<br>Ordered in advance | *R1-2, Torpilleurs A - B* | 1895 |
| Torpilleur embarqué | *R3, Torpilleur C* | 1895 |
| Torpilleur embarqué<br>Delayed to 1899 | *R4-9, Torpilleurs D - I* | 1896/1900 |
| Aviso de 2ᵉ classe<br>Not funded, not built | *U1 (Unnamed)* | (none) |
| Chaloupe à vapeur<br>Ordered in advance | *X1, Onyx* | (none) |
| Chaloupe à vapeur<br>Not funded, not built | *X2, X3 (2 Unnamed)* | (none) |

| Type | Designator and name | Later budgets |
|---|---|---|
| Sous-marin | *Goubet* | (none) |
| Payment after cancellation for modifications | | |
| Sous-marin | *Morse* | 1895-1899 |

**Budget 1895. Submitted 17.3.1894, Law of 16.4.1895.**

| Type | Designator and name | Later budgets |
|---|---|---|
| Cuirassé d'escadre | *A7, Gaulois* | 1896-1900 |
| Croiseur rapide | *D'1, Guichen* | 1896-1900 |
| Croiseur rapide | *D'2, Châteaurenault* | 1896/1903 |
| Croiseur de 3e classe | *K1, D'Estrées* | 1898-1900 |
| Delayed, late addition to 1896 | | |
| Croiseur de 3e classe | *K2, Infernet* | 1898-1900 |
| Delayed to 1897 | | |
| Aviso de stations | *S1, Kersaint* | 1896-1899 |

**Budget 1896. Submitted 14.5.1895, Law of 28.12.1895.**

| Type | Designator and name | Later budgets |
|---|---|---|
| Cuirassé d'escadre | *A6, Henri IV* | 1897-1904 |
| Croiseur de 1re classe | *C2, Jeanne d'Arc (ii)* | 1897/1903 |
| Aviso de 1re classe or Contre-torpilleur | *M3, Dunois* | 1897-1900 |
| Aviso de 1re classe or Contre-torpilleur | *M4, La Hire* | 1897-1900 |
| Contre-torpilleur | *m1/M1, Durandal* | 1897-1899 |
| Contre-torpilleur | *M'1, Hallebarde* | 1898-1900 |
| Late addition | | |
| Torpilleur de 1re classe | *P25-26, Torpilleurs nos 206-207* | 1897-1898 |
| Torpilleur de 1re classe | *P27-30, Torpilleurs nos 208-211* | 1898 |
| Late addition | | |

**Budget 1897. Submitted 1.2.1896, Law of 29.3.1897.**

| Type | Designator and name | Later budgets |
|---|---|---|
| Cuirassé d'escadre | *A3, Iéna* | 1898-1901 |
| Croiseur cuirassé | *C3, Dupetit Thouars* | 1898-1905 |
| Croiseur de 1re classe | *D2, Jurien de la Gravière* | 1898-1903 |
| Croiseur cuirassé | *D3, Dupleix* | 1898-1904 |
| Contre-torpilleur | *M2, Fauconneau* | 1898-1900 |
| Contre-torpilleur | *M'3, Espingole* | 1899-1900 |
| Late addition | | |
| Torpilleur de 1re classe | *P31-32, Torpilleurs nos s 223-224* | 1898-1901 |
| Torpilleur de 1re classe | *P33-34, Torpilleurs nos 225-226* | 1898-1900 |
| Torpilleur de 1re classe | *P35-36, Torpilleurs nos 212-213* | 1898-1899 |
| Torpilleur de 1re classe | *P37-45, Torpilleurs nos 214-222* | 1899 |
| Late addition | | |
| Canonnière de stations | *T'1, Décidée* | 1898-1900 |
| Chaloupe à vapeur | *Fourmi* | (none) |
| Late addition | | |

**Supplementary Budget 1897. Submitted 1.4.1897, Law of 9.8.1897.**

| Type | Designator and name | Later budgets |
|---|---|---|
| Croiseur cuirassé | *C5, Gueydon* | 1898-1903 |
| Croiseur cuirassé | *C6, Montcalm* | 1898-1902 |
| Croiseur cuirassé | *D4, Desaix* | 1898-1904 |
| Croiseur cuirassé | *D5, Kléber* | 1898-1904 |
| Contre-torpilleur | *M'4, Pique* | 1898-1900 |
| Contre-torpilleur | *M'5, Épée* | 1898-1900 |
| Contre-torpilleur | *M'6, Framée* | 1898-1900 |
| Contre-torpilleur | *M'7, Yatagan* | 1898-1900 |
| Torpilleur de 1re classe | *P46-54, Torpilleurs nos 227-235* | 1898-1899 |

**Budget 1898. Submitted 18.5.1897, Law of 13.4.1898.**

| Type | Designator and name | Later budgets |
|---|---|---|
| Cuirassé d'escadre | *A9, Suffren* | 1899-1904 |
| Croiseur cuirassé | *C4, Condé* | 1899-1904 |
| Croiseur cuirassé | *C7, Gloire* | 1899-1904 |

| Type | Designator and name | Later budgets |
|---|---|---|
| Croiseur cuirassé | *C8, Sully* | 1899-1904 |
| Torpilleur de haute mer | *N12, Siroco (Sirocco)* | 1899-1900 |
| Torpilleur de haute mer | *N13, Mistral* | 1899-1900 |
| Torpilleur de haute mer | *N14, Simoun* | 1899-1900 |
| Torpilleur de haute mer | *N15, Typhon* | 1899-1900 |
| Torpilleur de haute mer | *N16, Trombe* | 1899-1900 |
| Torpilleur de haute mer | *N17, Audacieux* | 1900 |
| Late addition | | |
| Torpilleur de 1re classe | *P55-60, Torpilleurs nos 236-241* | 1899 |
| Torpilleur de 1re classe | *P61, Torpilleur no 242* | 1900-1902 |
| Late addition | | |
| Torpilleur de 1re classe | *P62, Torpilleur no 243* | 1901/1904 |
| Late addition | | |
| Sous-marin | *Q4, Narval* | 1900 |
| Late addition | | |
| Canonnière de stations | *T'2, Zélée* | 1900 |
| Late addition | | |

**Budget 1899. Submitted 25.10.1898, Law of 30.5.1899.**

| Type | Designator and name | Later budgets |
|---|---|---|
| Cuirassé d'escadre | *A8, République* | 1900-1907 |
| Delayed to 1901 | | |
| Croiseur cuirassé | *C9, Marseillaise* | 1900-1904 |
| Croiseur cuirassé | *C10, Amiral Aube* | 1900-1904 |
| Croiseur estafette | *H4 (Unnamed)* | (none) |
| Not built | | |
| Croiseur estafette | *H5 (Unnamed)* | (none) |
| Not built | | |
| Contre-torpilleur | *M'8, Pertuisane* | 1900-1903 |
| Contre-torpilleur | *M'9, Escopette* | 1900-1903 |
| Contre-torpilleur | *M'10, Flamberge* | 1901-1903 |
| Late addition | | |
| Contre-torpilleur | *M'11, Rapière* | 1901-1903 |
| Late addition | | |
| Torpilleur de haute mer | *N18, Bourrasque* | 1900-1902 |
| Torpilleur de haute mer | *N19, Rafale* | 1900-1902 |
| Torpilleur de haute mer | *N20, Borée* | 1900-1901 |
| Torpilleur de haute mer | *N21, Tramontane* | 1900-1902 |
| Torpilleur de 1re classe | *P63, Torpilleur no 244* | 1900-1902 |
| Torpilleur de 1re classe | *P64-74, Torpilleurs nos 245-255* | 1900-1901 |
| Sous-marin | *Q5, Sirène* | 1900-1902 |
| Sous-marin | *Q6, Triton* | 1900-1902 |
| Sous-marin | *Q7, Farfadet* | 1900-1901 |
| Sous-marin | *Q8, Korrigan* | 1900-1901 |
| Sous-marin | *Q9, Gnôme* | 1900-1901 |
| Sous-marin | *Q10, Lutin* | 1900-1903 |
| Sous-marin | *Q11, Français* | (none) |
| Late addition | | |
| Sous-marin | *Q12, Algérien* | 1901 |
| Late addition | | |
| Vedette-torpilleur | *Libellule* | 1901/1904 |
| Late addition | | |
| Canonnière de rivière | *Argus* | (none) |
| Late addition | | |
| Canonnière de rivière | *Vigilante* | (none) |
| Late addition | | |

**Budget 1900. Submitted 4.7.1899, Law of 13.4.1900.**

| Type | Designator and name | Later budgets |
|---|---|---|
| Cuirassé d'escadre | *A10, Patrie* | 1901-1907 |
| Delayed to 1901 | | |
| Croiseur cuirassé | *C11, Jules Ferry* | 1901-1905 |
| Croiseur cuirassé | *C12, Léon Gambetta* | 1902-1905 |
| Late addition | | |

| Type | Designator and name | Later budgets |
|---|---|---|
| Contre-torpilleur | M'12, Carabine | 1901-1904 |
| Contre-torpilleur | M'13, Sarbacane | 1901-1904 |
| Contre-torpilleur | M'14, Arquebuse | 1901-1903 |
| Contre-torpilleur | M'15, Arbalète | 1901-1904 |
| Contre-torpilleur | M'16, Mousquet | 1901-1903 |
| Contre-torpilleur | M'17, Javeline | 1901-1903 |
| Contre-torpilleur | M'18, Sagaïe | 1901-1903 |
| Contre-torpilleur | M'19, Épieu | 1901-1903 |
| Contre-torpilleur | M'20, Harpon | 1901-1903 |
| Contre-torpilleur | M'21, Fronde | 1901-1903 |
| Torpilleur de 1re classe | P75-84, Torpilleurs nos 256-265 | 1901-1902 |
| Sous-marin   Late addition | Q13, Silure | 1902 |
| Sous-marin   Late addition | Q14, Espadon | 1902 |

**Budget 1901. Submitted 31.5.1900, Law of 25.2.1901.**

| Type | Designator and name | Later budgets |
|---|---|---|
| Croiseur cuirassé | C13, Victor Hugo | 1902-1907 |
| Contre-torpilleur | M'22, Francisque | 1902-1904 |
| Contre-torpilleur | M'23, Sabre | 1902-1904 |
| Contre-torpilleur | M'24, Dard | 1902-1904 |
| Contre-torpilleur | M'25, Baliste | 1902-1904 |
| Contre-torpilleur | M'26, Mousqueton | 1902-1904 |
| Contre-torpilleur | M'27, Arc | 1902-1904 |
| Contre-torpilleur | M'28, Pistolet | 1902-1904 |
| Contre-torpilleur | M'29, Bélier | 1902-1904 |
| Contre-torpilleur | M'30, Catapulte | 1902-1903 |
| Contre-torpilleur | M'31, Bombarde | 1902-1904 |
| Torpilleur de 1re classe | P85-95, Torpilleurs nos 266-276 | 1902-1903 |
| Torpilleur de 1re classe | P96, Torpilleur no 277/8-S | 1902-1904 |
| Sous-marin | Q15-Q22, Naïade to Dorade | 1902-1904 |
| Sous-marin   Late addition | Q23-Q34, Lynx to Truite | 1903-1904 |
| Sous-marin   Late addition | Q35, Sous-marin X | 1903-1904 |
| Sous-marin   Late addition | Q36, Sous-marin Z | 1903-1904 |
| Sous-marin   Late addition | Q37, Sous-marin Y | 1903-1905 |

**Budget 1902. Submitted 29.3.1901, Law of 30.3.1902.**

| Type | Designator and name | Later budgets |
|---|---|---|
| Cuirassé d'escadre | A11, Liberté | 1903-1908 |
| Cuirassé d'escadre | A12, Démocratie | 1903-1907 |
| Cuirassé d'escadre | A13, Justice | 1903-1908 |
| Cuirassé d'escadre | A14, Vérité | 1903-1908 |
| Croiseur cuirassé | C14, Jules Michelet | 1903-1908 |
| Croiseur cuirassé   Delayed to 1903 | C15, Ernest Renan | 1903-1908 |
| Contre-torpilleur | M'32, Stylet | 1903-1907 |
| Contre-torpilleur | M'33, Tromblon | 1903-1907 |
| Torpilleur de 1re classe | P97-111, Torpilleurs nos 278-292 | 1903-1905 |
| Torpilleur de 1re classe | P112, Torpilleur no 9-S | 1903-1904 |
| Submersible   Late addition | Q38, Aigrette | 1904-1905 |
| Submersible   Late addition | Q39, Cigogne | 1904-1905 |
| Submersible   Late addition | Q40, Oméga (Ω) | 1904-1908 |

**Budget 1903. Submitted 14.10.1902, Law of 31.3.1903.**

| Type | Designator and name | Later budgets |
|---|---|---|
| Contre-torpilleur | M'34, Pierrier | 1904-1908 |
| Contre-torpilleur | M'35, Obusier | 1904-1906 |
| Contre-torpilleur | M'36, Mortier | 1904-1907 |
| Contre-torpilleur | M'37, Claymore | 1904-1906 |
| Torpilleur de 1re classe | P113, Torpilleur no 293 | 1904 |
| Torpilleur de 1re classe | P114, Torpilleur no 294 | 1904-1905 |
| Torpilleur de 1re classe | P115-137, Torpilleurs nos 295-317 | 1904-1906 |
| Torpilleur de 1re classe   Delayed to 1904 | P138, Torpilleur no 368 | 1904-1907 |
| Sous-marin | Q41, Émeraude | 1905-1907 |
| Sous-marin | Q42, Opale | 1905-1907 |
| Sous-marin | Q43, Rubis | 1905-1907 |
| Sous-marin | Q44, Saphir | 1905-1909 |
| Sous-marin | Q45, Topaze | 1905-1909 |
| Sous-marin | Q46, Turquoise | 1905-1909 |

**Budget 1904. Submitted 16.6.1903, Law of 30.12.1903.**

| Type | Designator and name | Later budgets |
|---|---|---|
| Croiseur cuirassé | C16, Edgar Quinet | 1905-1911 |
| Contre-torpilleur | M'38, Carquois | 1905-1908 |
| Contre-torpilleur | M'39, Trident | 1905-1908 |
| Torpilleur de 1re classe | P139-188, Torpilleurs nos 318-367 | 1905-1907 |
| Torpilleur de 1re classe | P189, Torpilleur no 369 | 1905-1907 |
| Submersible | Q47, Circé | 1905-1908 |
| Submersible | Q48, Calypso | 1905-1908 |
| Sous-marin   Not completed | Q49, Guêpe Torpilleur no 1 | 1905-1908 |
| Sous-marin   Not completed | Q50, Guêpe Torpilleur no 2 | 1905-1908 |
| Aviso de 2e classe   Late addition | Chamois | 1906 |

**Budget 1905. Submitted 30.3.1904, Law of 22.4.1905.**

| Type | Designator and name | Later budgets |
|---|---|---|
| Croiseur cuirassé | C17, Waldeck Rousseau | 1906-1912 |
| Contre-torpilleur | M'40, Fleuret | 1906-1907 |
| Contre-torpilleur | M'41, Coutelas | 1906-1907 |
| Contre-torpilleur | M'42, Glaive | 1906-1909 |
| Contre-torpilleur | M'43, Poignard | 1906-1909 |
| Torpilleur de 1re classe   Not built | P190-209 (Unnamed) | (none) |
| Sous-marin   Not built | Q59 (Unnamed) | (none) |
| Sous-marin   Not built | Q60 (Unnamed) | (none) |
| Sous-marin   Not in any budget, not completed | Q61 (Unnamed) | (none) |
| Contre-torpilleur   Late addition | M44, Cognée | 1907-1908 |
| Contre-torpilleur   Late addition | M45, Hache | 1907-1909 |
| Contre-torpilleur   Late addition | M46, Massue | 1907-1909 |
| Contre-torpilleur   Late addition | M47, Sabretache | 1907-1908 |
| Contre-torpilleur   Late addition | M48, Oriflamme | 1907-1908 |
| Contre-torpilleur   Late addition | M49, Étendard | 1907-1908 |
| Contre-torpilleur   Late addition | M50, Fanion | 1907-1908 |
| Contre-torpilleur   Late addition | M51, Sape | 1907-1908 |

| Type | Designator and name | Later budgets |
|---|---|---|
| Contre-torpilleur Late addition | M52, Gabion | 1907-1908 |
| Contre-torpilleur Late addition | M53, Branlebas | 1907-1908 |
| Contre-torpilleur Late addition | M54, Fanfare | 1907-1908 |
| Submersible Late addition | Q51, Pluviôse | 1907-1911 |
| Submersible Late addition | Q52, Ventôse | 1907-1911 |
| Submersible Late addition | Q53, Germinal | 1907-1911 |
| Submersible Late addition | Q54, Floréal | 1907-1911 |
| Submersible Late addition | Q55, Prairial | 1907-1911 |
| Submersible Late addition | Q56, Messidor | 1907-1911 |
| Submersible Late addition | Q57, Thermidor | 1907-1911 |
| Submersible Late addition | Q58, Fructidor | 1907-1911 |
| Submersible Late addition | Q59, Vendémiaire | 1907-1911 |
| Submersible Late addition | Q60, Brumaire | 1907-1912 |
| Submersible Late addition | Q62, Frimaire | 1907-1912 |
| Submersible Late addition | Q63, Nivôse | 1907-1912 |
| Submersible Late addition | Q64, Papin | 1907-1909 |
| Submersible Late addition | Q65, Fresnel | 1907-1909 |
| Submersible Late addition | Q66, Berthelot | 1907-1909 |
| Submersible Late addition | Q67, Monge | 1907-1911 |
| Submersible Late addition | Q68, Ampère | 1907-1911 |
| Submersible Late addition | Q69, Gay Lussac | 1907-1911 |

**Budget 1906. Submitted 6.7.1905, Law of 17.4.1906.**

| Type | Designator and name | Later budgets |
|---|---|---|
| Cuirassé d'escadre | A15, Danton | 1907-1911 |
| Cuirassé d'escadre | A16, Voltaire | 1907-1912 |
| Cuirassé d'escadre | A17, Condorcet | 1907 1912 |
| Cuirassé d'escadre Late addition | A15bis, Mirabeau | 1908-1912 |
| Cuirassé d'escadre Late addition | A16bis, Diderot | 1908-1912 |
| Cuirassé d'escadre Late addition | A17bis, Vergniaud | 1908-1912 |
| Contre-torpilleur | M55, Spahi | 1907-1910 |
| Contre-torpilleur | M56, Voltigeur | 1907-1910 |
| Contre-torpilleur | M57, Tirailleur | 1907-1910 |
| Contre-torpilleur | M58, Chasseur | 1907-1910 |
| Contre-torpilleur | M59, Hussard | 1907-1910 |
| Contre-torpilleur | M60, Carabinier | 1907-1910 |
| Contre-torpilleur Delayed to 1907 | M61, Lansquenet | 7.08-1910 |
| Contre-torpilleur Delayed to 1907 | M62, Mameluck | 7.08-1910 |

| Type | Designator and name | Later budgets |
|---|---|---|
| Contre-torpilleur Delayed to 1907 | M63, Janissaire | 7.08-1911 |
| Contre-torpilleur Delayed to 1907 | M64, Fantassin | 7.08-1910 |
| Submersible | Q70, Foucault | 1907-1913 |
| Submersible | Q71, Euler | 1907-1913 |
| Submersible | Q72, Franklin | 1907-1913 |
| Submersible | Q73, Archimède (experimental) | 1907-1910 |
| Submersible | Q74, Mariotte (experimental) | 1907-1913 |
| Submersible | Q75, Watt | 1907-1910 |
| Submersible | Q76, Cugnot | 1907-1910 |
| Submersible | Q77, Giffard | 1907-1910 |
| Submersible | Q78, Faraday | 1907-1912 |
| Submersible | Q79, Volta | 1907-1912 |
| Submersible | Q80, Newton | 1907-1912 |
| Submersible | Q81, Montgolfier | 1907-1912 |
| Submersible | Q82, Amiral Bourgois (experimental) | 1907-1913 |
| Submersible | Q83, Bernoulli | 1907-1913 |
| Submersible | Q84, Joule | 1907-1913 |
| Submersible | Q85, Coulomb | 1907-1913 |
| Submersible | Q86, Arago | 1907-1913 |
| Submersible | Q87, Curie | 1907-1913 |
| Submersible | Q88, Le Verrier | 1907-1913 |
| Submersible | Q89, Charles Brun (experimental) | 1907-1912 |

**Budget 1907. Submitted 26.6.1906, Law of 30.1.1907.**

| | | |
|---|---|---|
| Contre-torpilleur | M65, Cavalier | 1908-1911 |
| Submersible Not built | Q90-Q99 (Unnamed) | 1908-1909 |

**Budget 1908. Submitted 11.5.1907, Law of 31.12.1907.**

| | | |
|---|---|---|
| Contre-torpilleur | M66, Cimeterre | 1909-1911 |
| Contre-torpilleur | M67, Dague | 1909-1912 |
| Contre-torpilleur | M68, Fourche | 1909-1911 |
| Contre-torpilleur | M69, Faulx | 1909-1912 |
| Contre-torpilleur | M70, Boutefeu | 1909-1912 |
| Contre-torpilleur | M71, Bouclier | 1909-1912 |
| Contre-torpilleur | M72, Casque | 1909-1911 |
| Contre-torpilleur Delayed to 1909 | M73, Capitaine Mehl | 1909-1914 |
| Contre-torpilleur Delayed to 1909 | M74, Dehorter | 1909-1913 |
| Contre-torpilleur Delayed to 1909 | M75, Francis Garnier | 1909-1913 |
| Submersible Not built | Q100-Q104 (Unnamed) | 1909 |

**Budget 1909. Submitted 19.5.1908, Law of 26.12.1908.**

| | | |
|---|---|---|
| Contre-torpilleur Delayed to 1910 | M79, Magon | 1910-1914 |
| Contre-torpilleur Delayed to 1910 | M80, Mangini | 1910-1914 |
| Contre-torpilleur Delayed to 1910 | M81, Bisson | 1910-1914 |
| Contre-torpilleur Delayed to 1910 | M82, Renaudin | 1910-1914 |
| Submersible Not built | Q105-110 (Unnamed) | (none) |
| Canonnière à faible tirant d'eau pour le Haut Yang-Tsé | Doudart de Lagrée | (none) |

| Type | Designator and name | Later budgets |
|---|---|---|
| **Budget 1910. Submitted 18.6.1909, Law of 8.4.1910.** | | |
| Cuirassé d'escadre Law of 3.1910. | *A1, Jean Bart* | 1912-1914 |
| Cuirassé d'escadre Law of 3.1910. | *A2, Courbet* | 1912-1914 |
| Contre-torpilleur | *M83, Protet* | 1912-1914 |
| Contre-torpilleur | *M84, Enseigne Henry* | 1911-1912 |
| Contre-torpilleur | *M85, Aspirant Herber* | 1911-1912 |
| Torpilleur de haute mer Not built | *N22-23 (Unnamed)* | (none) |
| Sous-marin | *Q90, Clorinde* | 1911-1915 |
| Sous-marin | *Q91, Cornélie* | 1911-1915 |
| Mouilleur de mines Late addition | *a1, Pluton* | 1912-1913 |
| Chaloupe à vapeur Late addition | *Sonde* | (none) |
| **Budget 1911. Submitted 28.6.1910, Law of 13.7.1911.** | | |
| Cuirassé d'escadre Law of 2.1911. | *A3, France* | 1913-1915 |
| Cuirassé d'escadre Law of 2.1911. | *A4, Paris* | 1913-1915 |
| Sous-marin | *Q92, Gustave Zédé* | 1912-1915 |
| Sous-marin | *Q93, Néréide* | 1912-1915 |
| Mouilleur de mines | *a2, Cerbère* | 1912-1913 |
| **Budget 1912. Submitted 12.7.1911, Law of 27.2.1912.** | | |
| Cuirassé d'escadre Law of early 1912. | *A5, Bretagne* | 1914-1915 |
| Cuirassé d'escadre Law of early 1912. | *A6, Provence* | 1914-1915 |
| Cuirassé d'escadre Law of early 1912. | *A6bis, Lorraine* | 1914-1915 |
| Sous-marin | *Q94, Amphitrite* | 1913-1915 |
| Sous-marin | *Q95, Astrée* | 1913-1915 |
| Sous-marin | *Q96, Artémis* | 1913-1915 |
| Sous-marin | *Q97, Aréthuse* | 1913-1915 |
| Sous-marin | *Q98, Atalante* | 1913-1915 |
| Sous-marin | *Q99, Amaranthe* | 1913-1915 |
| Sous-marin | *Q100, Ariane* | 1913-1915 |
| Sous-marin | *Q101, Andromaque* | 1913-1915 |
| Sous-marin | *Q102, Bellone* | 1913-1915 |
| Transport [du littoral] | *T, Seine* | 1913 |
| **Budget 1913. Submitted 29.3.1912, Law of 30.7.1913.** | | |
| Cuirassé d'escadre Not completed | *A7, Normandie* | 1914-1915 |
| Cuirassé d'escadre Not completed | *A8, Languedoc* | 1914-1915 |
| Cuirassé d'escadre Not completed | *A9, Flandre* | 1914-1915 |
| Cuirassé d'escadre Not completed | *A10, Gascogne* | 1914-1915 |
| Contre-torpilleur | *M86, Mécanicien-Principal Lestin* | 1914-1915 |
| Contre-torpilleur | *M87, Enseigne Roux* | 1914-1915 |
| Contre-torpilleur | *M88, Enseigne Gabolde* | 1914-1915 |
| Sous-marin | *Q103, Hermione* | 1914-1915 |
| Sous-marin | *Q104, Gorgone* | 1914-1915 |
| Sous-marin Late addition | *Q105, Dupuy de Lôme* | 1915 |

| Type | Designator and name | Later budgets |
|---|---|---|
| Sous-marin Late addition | *Q106, Sané* | 1915 |
| Sous-marin Late addition | *Q107, Diane* | 1915 |
| Sous-marin Late addition | *Q108, Daphné* | 1915 |
| Canonnière fluviale | *Balny* | 1914-1915 |
| Aviso Delayed to 1914 | *Flamant/ Quentin Roosevelt* | 1914-1915 |
| Pétrolier (oil tanker) Late addition, to merchant marine | *Meuse* | 1915 |
| Dragueur de mines Late addition | *Herse* | (none) |
| Dragueur de mines Late addition | *Rateau* | (none) |
| Dragueur de mines Late addition | *Charrue* | (none) |
| Dragueur de mines Late addition | *Pioche* | 1915 |
| **Budget 1914. Submitted 4.11.1913, Law of 15.7.1914.** | | |
| Cuirassé d'escadre Completed as aircraft carrier | *I11, Béarn* | 1914 |
| Convoyeur d'escadrilles, ex Éclaireur d'escadre. Not built | *Lamotte-Picquet (ex C1)* | 1915 |
| Convoyeur d'escadrilles, ex Éclaireur d'escadre. Not built | *N (ex C2) (Unnamed)* | 1915 |
| Convoyeur d'escadrilles, ex Éclaireur d'escadre. Not built | *N (ex C3) (Unnamed)* | 1915 |
| Sous-marin | *Q109, Joëssel* | 1915 |
| Sous-marin | *Q110, Fulton* | 1915 |
| Sous-marin | *Q111, Laplace* | 1915 |
| Sous-marin | *Q112, Lagrange* | 1915 |
| Sous-marin | *Q113, Regnault* | 1915 |
| Sous-marin | *Q114, Romazzotti* | 1915 |
| Mouilleur de mines Delayed to 1915, not built | *N (Unnamed)* | 1915 |
| **Budget 1915. Submitted 15.7.1914 (bill not published, no law)** | | |
| Cuirassé d'escadre Not built | *I12, Lyon* | (none) |
| Cuirassé d'escadre Not built | *I13, Lille* | (none) |
| Cuirassé d'escadre Not built | *A14, Duquesne* | (none) |
| Cuirassé d'escadre Not built | *A15, Tourville* | (none) |
| Aviso de stations Not built | *N (Unnamed)* | (none) |
| Sous-marin Not built | *Q115-116 (Unnamed)* | (none) |
| Sous-marin Not built | *Q117-118 (Unnamed)* | (none) |
| Sous-marin Not built | *Q119-120 (Unnamed)* | (none) |

**Sources:** France, Ministère des Finances, *Projet de loi présenté à la Chambre des Deputés portant fixation du budget général de l'exercice* _____ and reports on the annual budgets in France, Assemblée nationale, *Annales de la Chambre des députés, Documents parlementaires.* The draft 1915 budget is from the *Archives de la Défense, Marine* (Vincennes), SS-Ed-3.

# Appendix H

# French Naval Expenditures, 1858-1914

Annual expenditures are shown in millions of francs after final accounting. These figures are from Modelski G., Thompson W.R., *Seapower in Global Politics, 1494–1993* (Palgrave Macmillan, London, 1988), citing for 1858-67 Maurice Block, *Statistique de la France* (Buillaumin, Paris, 1875) and for 1868-1914 the *Annuaire Statistique* of the Ministère du Travail. The authors point out that the main problems with the French data were the use of both ordinary and extraordinary budget accounts and the fact that the colonial administration was funded through the Ministry of Marine until March 1889. The authors were able to combine both ordinary and extraordinary expenditures in most years but were unable to separate the purely naval from the strictly colonial expenses before 1886. The declines in 1886 and 1887 may reflect this adjustment as well as other factors.

| Year | Naval Expenditures | Change from previous year | Year | Naval Expenditures | Change from previous year |
|------|------|------|------|------|------|
| 1858 | 133.43 | — | 1887 | 199.84 | -26.59% |
| 1859 | 293.03 | +119.61% | 1888 | 180.99 | -9.43% |
| 1860 | 241.95 | -17.43% | 1889 | 199.03 | +9.97% |
| 1861 | 206.87 | -14.50% | 1890 | 201.39 | +1.19% |
| 1862 | 218.91 | +5.82% | 1891 | 229.99 | +14.20% |
| 1863 | 137.64 | -37.12% | 1892 | 251.98 | +9.56% |
| 1864 | 193.06 | +40.26% | 1893 | 253.30 | +0.52% |
| 1865 | 192.07 | -0.51% | 1894 | 274.19 | +8.25% |
| 1866 | 179.29 | -6.65% | 1895 | 268.10 | -2.22% |
| 1867 | 159.67 | -10.94% | 1896 | 265.93 | -0.81% |
| 1868 | 155.58 | -2.56% | 1897 | 260.78 | -1.94% |
| 1869 | 163.28 | +4.95% | 1898 | 289.66 | +11.07% |
| 1870 | 195.95 | +20.01% | 1899 | 322.45 | +11.32% |
| 1871 | 167.04 | -14.75% | 1900 | 372.95 | +15.66% |
| 1872 | 143.51 | -14.09% | 1901 | 344.36 | -7.67% |
| 1873 | 151.43 | +5.52% | 1902 | 298.58 | -13.29% |
| 1874 | 152.68 | +0.83% | 1903 | 304.69 | +2.05% |
| 1875 | 155.53 | +1.87% | 1904 | 292.96 | -3.85% |
| 1876 | 170.08 | +9.36% | 1905 | 316.01 | +7.87% |
| 1877 | 192.69 | +13.29% | 1906 | 305.90 | -3.20% |
| 1878 | 197.47 | +2.48% | 1907 | 315.70 | +3.20% |
| 1879 | 194.37 | -1.57% | 1908 | 330.70 | +4.75% |
| 1880 | 193.68 | -0.35% | 1909 | 347.69 | +5.14% |
| 1881 | 207.10 | +6.93% | 1910 | 303.63 | -12.67% |
| 1882 | 222.05 | +7.22% | 1911 | 518.89 | +70.90% |
| 1883 | 259.11 | +16.69% | 1912 | 496.69 | -4.28% |
| 1884 | 298.44 | +15.18% | 1913 | 553.00 | +11.34% |
| 1885 | 309.44 | +3.69% | 1914 | 651.32 | +17.78% |
| 1886 | 272.21 | -12.03% | | | |

The aviso *Kersaint* departing Haiphong between 1899 and 1907. Funding for the overseas station fleets fell off dramatically after the mid-1890s, the only significant ships being this one, the three gunboats of the *Surprise* type, and some river gunboats. *(Detail from a postcard by P. Dieulefils, Hanoi)*

# Appendix I

# Budget and Programme Symbols

In February 1891 the French introduced in the draft 1892 budget the use of different letter designators for individual ships whose construction was planned instead of the traditional 'N' (nouveau) for all of them. Initially each letter was used for a single ship. The 1892 series was extended in the 1893 budget, reaching the letter Z. By May 1893 the system was expanded for both budgets and building programmes to an alfanumeric one in which a letter indicated the ship type and a number indicated the individual ship. This system remained in use, with some changes, until the outbreak of the war in 1914.

**Budget of 1892 (Feb. 1891).**

| | |
|---|---|
| A, B | Cuirassés d'escadre (*Bouvet, Masséna*, later A1, A2) |
| C | Croiseur d'escadre de 1$^{re}$ classe (*Pothuau*, later D1) |
| D | Croiseur d'escadre de 3$^{e}$ classe (*Linois*, later H1) |
| E | Croiseur de station de 2$^{e}$ classe (*Pascal*, later E2) |
| F | Croiseur de station de 2$^{e}$ classe (*Descartes*, later E1)) |
| G | Transport de torpilleurs (*Foudre*, later L1) |
| H, I, J | Torpilleurs de haute mer (*Flibustier, Ariel, Tourmente*, later N3, N2, N4) |

**Budget of 1893 (March 1892).**

| | |
|---|---|
| K | Croiseur de 2$^{e}$ classe (*Du Chayla*, later G2) |
| L | Croiseur de 3$^{e}$ classe (*Galilée*, later H2) |
| M | (not used, possibly for *Lavoisier*) |
| N, O | Croiseurs de 1$^{re}$ classe (*D'Entrecasteaux, Jeanne d'Arc*, later C1, C2) |
| P, Q | Croiseurs de 2$^{e}$ classe (*Catinat , D'Assas*, later E3, G1) |
| R | Aviso-torpilleur (*Casabianca*) |
| S | Canonnière (*Surprise*, later T1) |
| T – Z | Torpilleurs de haute mer (*Argonaute, Averne, Dauphin, Aquilon, Cyclone, Mangini, Forban*, later N5 to N11) |
| (no letters) | Torpilleurs de 1$^{re}$ classe. |

**Programme of 1891 (in use by May 1893).**

| | |
|---|---|
| A | (European fleet) Cuirassés d'Escadre (*Bouvet* was A1). In 1913 the budget designator for contract-built battleships was changed from A to I, for *industrie*. |
| B | (Coastal fleet) Gardes côtes cuirassés |
| C | (Station fleet) Croiseurs de station de 1$^{re}$ classe (changed to D 1896) |
| D | (European) Croiseurs de 1$^{re}$ classe (changed to C 1896) |
| D' | (Station?) Croiseurs rapides (*Guichen* and *Châteaurenault*) |
| E | (Station) Croiseurs de station de 2$^{e}$ classe |
| G | (European) Croiseurs de 2$^{e}$ classe |
| H | (European) Croiseurs de 3$^{e}$ classe |
| K | (Station) Croiseurs de station de 3$^{e}$ classe |
| L | (European) Transports de torpilleurs |
| l | (European) Transports ateliers (lower case letter L) |
| M | (European) Croiseurs torpilleurs ou contre-torpilleurs d'escadre (*Durandal*, M1) |
| m' (M') | (Coastal) Aviso torpilleurs chefs de groupe. (*Hallebarde*, M'1). All destroyers followed here and were called contre-torpilleurs d'escadre. The M-prime programme designator (M') was used for new *contre-torpilleurs* until the 1906 (July 1905) budget when it became MM and the 1907 budget (June 1906) when it became M. |
| N | (European) Torpilleurs de haute mer |
| P | (Coastal) Torpilleurs de 1$^{re}$ classe |
| Q | (Coastal) Torpilleurs de 2$^{e}$ classe. By October 1898 (the 1899 budget) the designator Q had been shifted to submarines. |
| R | (European) Torpilleurs embarqués |
| S | (Station) Avisos de station |
| T | (Station) Canonnières de station (changed to T' 1896 for *Décidée* and *Zélée*) |
| U | (Station) Avisos de 2$^{e}$ classe (adjourned by 11.1894) (V in an early list) |
| X | (Station) Chaloupes à vapeur (*Onyx*) |

**Sources:** As Appendices F and G.

A 356mm torpedo being fired from the starboard torpedo tube of a French torpedo cruiser, probably *Condor*, during the 1890s. The top of the tube is extended in the form of a spoon (*cuillère*) to guide the torpedo in its first moments after launching. (*NHHC from ONI, NH-64386*)

# Appendix J

# French Naval Squadrons (*Escadres*) and Divisions, 1874-1914

The structure of the French Navy's operating forces changed frequently in response to changes in the operational environment and in the Navy's policies. The most significant changes in the Navy's largest operational units, its *escadres* and *divisions navales,* occurred as shown below. Lesser changes during intervening periods are shown in brackets. In general, smaller units like *stations navales* are omitted.

***15 December 1873. État des divisions navales et des stations locales des colonies.***

Escadre d'évolutions
  (1ʳᵉ Division, ended during 1875)
  (2ᵉ Division, ended during 1875)
Station du Levant (added during 1875)
Division navale des Antilles et de Terre-Neuve (later Antilles)
Division navale de l'Atlantique Sud
Division navale de l'Océan Pacifique
Division navale des Mers de Chine et du Japon
Division navale de Cochinchine
Division navale des côtes orientales d' Afrique (previously Station de la Mer des Indes, ended during 1874).
Division navale de la Nouvelle Calédonie
Division du littoral Nord de France (ended during 1874, became the Station de la Manche et de la mer du Nord and the Station de Granville during 1875)
Station de la Mer des Indes (added during 1879, to Division navale during 1883)
Division volante et d'instruction, later Division navale d'instruction (existed during 1880-1881)
Division navale du Tonkin (added during 1883)

***31 January 1885. Table des escadres, divisions, stations navales, etc.***

Escadre d'évolutions
Division cuirassée du Nord (added during 1888)
Division navale de Terre-Neuve
Division navale de l'Atlantique Nord (to 1888)
Division navale de l'Atlantique Sud (to 1888)
Division navale de l'Atlantique (added during 1888 by merger of the above)
Division navale de l'Océan Pacifique
Division navale de l'Extrême-Orient (was the Escadre de l'Extrême Orient in 1885)
Division navale du Tonkin, later de l'Indochine (Tonkin)
Division navale de Cochinchine (from station locale during 1886)
Division navale de l'Océan Indien
Division navale du Levant
Station navale d'Islande

***1 January 1890. Table des escadres, divisions, stations navales, etc.***

Escadre de la Méditerranée occidentale et du Levant
Division navale de réserve de l'escadre de la Méditerranée occidentale et du Levant (added during 1891, became an Escadre during 1892)

Division navale cuirassée du Nord (renamed Escadre du Nord during 1891)
Division navale de l'Océan Pacifique
Division navale de l'Extrême-Orient
Division navale de la Cochinchine (later de l'Indo-Chine)
Division navale de l'Océan Indien
Division navale de l'Atlantique (to 1890, split into south and north units below)
Station navale de l'Atlantique-Sud (added during 1890)
Division navale de l'Atlantique-Nord (added during 1890), became the Division Légère de l'Océan Atlantique during 1891)
Division navale de Terre-Neuve (became the Station navale de Terre-Neuve during 1890)
Division navale du Tonkin (became la station locale du Tonkin et de l'Annam during 1890)
Station navale d'Islande (to 1892)

***1 March 1893. Navires de la Flotte armés, en essais, en montage, et en réserve 1ʳᵉ et 2ᵉ catégories.***

Escadre de la Méditerranée occidentale et du Levant
Escadre de réserve de la Méditerranée occidentale et du Levant
Escadre du Nord
A Division volante et d'instruction was active in 1893-95, followed by a Division navale constituant l'École supérieure de guerre in 1895-96.
Division navale de l'Océan Atlantique
Division navale de l'Océan Pacifique
Division navale de l'Extrême-Orient
Division navale de l'Océan Indien
Division navale de la Cochinchine
Division navale de Terre-Neuve (added during 1895, summer only, to 1896)
Station navale d'Islande (added during 1895, summer only, to 1896)
Division navale de Terre-Neuve et d'Islande (added during 1896 by merger of the above)

***1 January 1899. Navires de la Flotte armés, en essais, en réserve, et en achèvement.***

Escadre de la Méditerranée occidentale et du Levant
Division d'instruction (1898-99 only)
Division de garde-côtes (merged into the Escadre du Nord during 1901)
Division de réserve de l'escadre de la Méditerranée (added during 1901)
Escadre du Nord
Division navale de l'Océan Atlantique (ended during 1907)
Division navale de l'Océan Pacifique
Division navale de l'Extrême-Orient (was an Escadre 1900-06)

497

Division navale de l'Océan Indien
Division navale de la Cochinchine (later de l'Indo-Chine)
Division navale de Terre-Neuve et d'Islande (summer only)
Service des ports et surveillance des pêches, including Algérie (to a
    Division navale during 1907) and Tunisie (which became a Division
    navale during 1899)

### 1 January 1910. Navires de la Flotte armés, en essais, en réserve, et en achèvement.

In 1909 Minister of Marine Boué de Lapeyrère removed the distinction between the Mediterranean and Atlantic fleets, producing the two unnamed Escadres shown in the 1910 list. The second (2º) part of the list, not shown here, was for ships running trials.

**1º Navires armés** (Ships in commission)
1ʳᵉ Escadre
2ᵉ Escadre
Division navale de l'Extrème-Orient
Division navale de l'Indo-Chine
Division navale du Maroc
Division navale de la Tunisie
Division navale de l'Algérie
Station de la côte est d'Amérique et surveillance de la pêche à Terre-
    Neuve (added during 1910)
Islande (summer only)

**3º Navires en réserve** (normale and spéciale)
1º Division de réserve de la 1ʳᵉ Escadre (added during 1910)
2º Division de réserve de la 2ᵉ Escadre (added during 1910)

### 1 January 1912. Navires de la Flotte armés, en essais, en réserve, et en achèvement.

The 1ʳᵉ Armée Navale (fleet) was formed in October 1911 with two battleship escadres (squadrons of large ships) in the Mediterranean and a third at Brest, with attached cruiser light divisions and destroyer escadrilles (squadrons of small ships). The third battleship squadron at Brest with its reserve group remained separate from the Armée Navale.

**1º Navires armés**
1ʳᵉ Armée Navale
    1ʳᵉ Escadre (1ʳᵉ Escadre de ligne, 1ʳᵉ Division légère, 1ʳᵉ Escadrille)
    2ᵉ Escadre (2ᵉ Escadre de ligne, 1ʳᵉ Groupe de disponibilité,
        2ᵉ Escadrille)
    1ᵉʳ groupe de réserve d'escadre (Foudre, for the 2ᵉ Escadre)
    3ᵉ Escadre (3ᵉ Escadre de ligne, 3ᵉ Division légère, 3ᵉ Escadrille)
    2ᵉ groupe de réserve d'escadre (3 cruisers)
Division navale de l'Extrème-Orient
Division navale de l'Indo-Chine

Division navale du Maroc
Division navale de la Tunisie
Station de la côte est d'Amérique et surveillance de la pêche à Terre-
    Neuve
Islande (summer only)

**2º Navires-écoles**
Division des écoles de l'Océan
Division des écoles de la Méditerranée

### 1 January 1913. Navires de la Flotte armés, en essais, en réserve, et en achèvement.

On 1 May 1912 the destroyer squadrons in the Mediterranean were consolidated from the individual escadres into a Flotilla of Destroyers and Submarines of the 1ʳᵉ Armée Navale. The third battleship squadron was moved back from Brest to Toulon in September 1912, joining the 1ʳᵉ Armée Navale and concentrating nearly the whole fleet in the Mediterranean.

**1º Navires armés**
1ʳᵉ Armée Navale
1ʳᵉ Armée de Ligne
    1ʳᵉ Escadre de ligne, 2ᵉ Escadre de ligne, 3ᵉ Escadre de ligne
        (the 3ᵉ Escadre became the Division de complément during 1913)
    1ʳᵉ Escadre légère
    Répétiteur (Jurien de la Gravière) (signal relay ship, added during 1913)
    Flottilles de contre-torpilleurs et de sous-marins
        Flottille de contre-torpilleurs (5 escadrilles, a 6ᵗʰ added during 1913)
        Flottille de sous-marins (2 escadrilles)
    Mouilleurs de mines
    Réserve de la 1ʳᵉ Armée Navale
2ᵉ Escadre Légère
    1ʳᵉ Division légère
    Flottilles de contre-torpilleurs et de sous-marins
        Flottille de contre-torpilleurs (3 escadrilles)
        Flottille de sous-marins (2 escadrilles)
    Mouilleurs de mines
    Réserve de la 2ᵉ Escadre Légère
Division navale de l'Extrème-Orient
Division navale de l'Indo-Chine
Division navale du Maroc
Division navale de la Tunisie (ended during 1913)
Station de la côte est d'Amérique et surveillance de la pêche à Terre-Neuve
Islande (summer only)

**2º Navires-écoles**
Division des écoles de l'Océan
Division des écoles de la Méditerranée

**Source:** Annuaire de la Marine.

# Sources and Bibliography

## ARCHIVAL SOURCES

*Archives de la Défense, Marine (Vincennes)*
*Series BB: General Services.*
**BB4: Bureau des mouvements.**
BB4 2023-28, 2540, 2565-71, and 2635-36: *Feuilles signalétiques* (multi-page technical data sheets on individual ships).
BB4 2546-7: cruisers early 1900s.
**BB8: Records from disparate origins.** These include the personal office of the Minister (1790-1939), the Naval General Staff (1907-1914), the *Conseil d'Amirauté* (1824-1890, 1913), the *Conseil des travaux* (1831-1905), and the *Conseil supérieur de la marine* (1896-1925).
BB8 824-900: *Conseil d'Amirauté.*
BB8-968 Albaret, Jean Rosier, *Documents généraux relatifs aux divers types de bâtiments de la flotte française*, 15 October 1884. An update of his 1881 volume in 0DD1. Nearly all data from devis d'armement before 1885 are taken from this work.
BB8 1106-1165: *Conseil des Travaux*, including detailed minutes of individual sessions and an analytic index for all sessions from 1872 to 1905.
BB8 2344-45: More *Feuilles signalétiques.*
*Series DD: Matériel.*
**DD1: Constructions navales.**
0DD1: *Mémoires* and miscellaneous documents.
0DD1-40, Albaret, Jean Rosier, *Documents généraux relatifs aux divers types de bâtiments de la flotte française*, 1 August 1881. An update of Dislère's 1873 reference for the *Conseil des travaux* of which Albaret was then secretary. See Library, below, and BB8-968, above.
1DD1: Outgoing correspondence of the Direction des constructions navales (1793/1938) and the Service technique des constructions navales (1895- ).
4DD1: Contracts (including hulls and machinery).
7DD1: Files retired when ships were condemned, including *devis d'armement* (commissioning reports), *devis de campagne* (cruise reports), and correspondence and technical reports.
8DD1: Plans of ships and matériel.
*Series SS: World War I.*
SS Ed3 (Etat-Major général, 4e section, forces navales, opérations): Programme and budget documents, 1913-1915.
*Special collection (at Brest).*
9S: Fonds Adam (items collected by Adm. Marcel Adam that include notes taken in the pre-World War II archives at Brest, Lorient, and Rochefort by Pierre Le Conte and Commandant Rouyer).

*SHD Library (Vincennes)*
*Aide-mémoire d'artillerie navale* (1873-1892, passim).
*Bulletin officiel de la Marine* (mainly for strike dates).
Dislère, Paul, 'Documents généraux relatifs aux navires de la flotte recueillis et mis en ordre', Paris, 11 June 1873. *Mémorial du Génie maritime*, N° 7, 1873. This remarkable reference, produced for the *Conseil des travaux* of which Dislère was secretary, was updated and replaced by the two items by Albaret, his successor, in BB8 and 0DD1.
Dislère, Paul, 'Historiques des différents types de la flotte.' Individual historical retrospectives prepared for the use of the *Conseil des travaux* and included in its minutes, then collected into a volume that was deposited in the Ministry's library.
*Listes de la Flotte* (1859-1914, 1920, and 1922-24 plus extracts to 1939).
*Répertoire alphabétique des bâtiments de tout rang armés et désarmés par*

*l'État*, supplements for 1.1.1855 to 31.12.1868 and 1.1.1869 to 31.12.1878, Paris, Imprimerie nationale, 1872 and 1880. The original edition, for 1800 to 1828, was compiled by Baron De Lagatinerie.

*U.S. National Archives*
Record Group 38 (Office of Naval Intelligence), Register 12008A, 25 July 1919, containing *Renseignements sur les Bouches à Feu de l'Artillerie Navale de tous Calibres & Modèles*, forwarded on 17 July 1919 by the *Directeur Central de l'Artillerie Navale* through official channels to the U.S. Naval Attaché. (Appendix A).

## PUBLISHED SOURCES

**Published government documents**
France, Assemblée nationale, *Annales de la Chambre des députés, Documents parlementaires*, 1882-1940 (Library of Congress J341.L4, now on microfilm). There was a similar series for the Senate. These contain the reports of the Budget Commissions and Navy commissions on the annual budgets which often contained the relevant shipbuilding tables (*états*) from the budgets. The debates are in *Annales de la Chambre des députés, Débats* (formerly J341.K2). Both series are also in the *Journal officiel*.
France, Ministère de la Marine et des colonies, *Annuaire de la Marine et des colonies*, annual, 1852-1889, followed by Ministère de la Marine, *Annuaire de la Marine*, annual, 1890-1914. Available for download from the Bibliothéque nationale on www.gallica.fr.
France, Ministère des Finances, *Projet de loi présenté à la Chambre des Deputés portant fixation du budget général de l'exercise ____*, annual 1833-1914 (Library of Congress HJ47.A3). These, the multi-volume budget submissions to Parliament, are the best source for the Navy budgets.
*Répertoire alphabétique des bâtiments de tout rang armés et désarmés par l'État,* Paris, Imprimerie Royale, 4th supplement for 1 January 1855 to 31 December 1868 (1872) and 5th supplement for 1 January 1869 to 31 December 1878 (1880). Series started by Baron De Lagatinerie.

**Selected books and articles, contemporary**
Bertin, Louis-Émile, 'Évolution de la puissance défensive des navires de guerre', *Révue des deux mondes*, 1 December 1905 pp550-568 and 1 January 1906 pp113-144.
Bertin, Louis-Émile, *Notice sur la marine à vapeur de guerre et de commerce depuis son origine jusqu'en 1874*, Dunod, Paris, 1875.
Bertin, Louis-Émile., *La Marine moderne, ancienne histoire et questions neuves*, Flammarion, Paris, 1914.
Dislère, Paul, *La marine cuirassée*, Gauthier-Villars, Paris, 1873.
Dislère, Paul, *Les croiseurs, la guerre de course*, Gauthier-Villars, Paris, 1875.
Renard, Léon, *Carnet de l'officier de Marine*, annual 1879-1898, Berger-Levrault, Paris.

**Books, historical**
Anon, *Chantiers et ateliers de Saint-Nazaire (Penhoët), 1900-1950*, Draeger, Paris, 1950.
Battesti, Michèle, *La marine de Napoleon III*, 2 volumes, Service historique de la marine, Vincennes, 1997.
Belser, Christophe, *Histoire des chantiers navals à Saint-Nazaire*, Éditions Coop Breizh, Spézet (Brittany), 2003.
Bueb, Volkmar, *Die 'Junge Schule' der französischen Marine, Strategie und Politik 1875-1900*, Harald Boldt Verlag, Boppard am Rhein, 1971.
Caresse, Philippe, *Histoire des cuirassés d'escadre Iéna & Suffren: Genèses, Caractéristiques & Carrières,* Éditions Lela Presse, Outreau, France, 2009.

Caresse, Philippe, *Les cuirassés de la classe 'Charlemagne', Programme 1892* with separate volume of plans, Éditions Lela Presse, Outreau, France, 2013.

Clouet, Alain, 'La Flotte de Napoleon III' (website, http://www.dossiersma-rine.org/).

Croguennec, Michel, 1893-1987, *Les chantiers de Normandie, un siècle de construction et de réparation navale en Seine-Maritime*, Gecko Éditions, Rouen, 2008.

D'Arbonneau (ed.), *L'Encyclopédie des sous-marins français. Tome 1, Naissance d'une arme nouvelle*, SPE Barthélémy, Paris, 2009.

de Blois, Hubert, *La guerre des mines dans la Marine française*, Éditions de la Cité - Brest - Paris, 1982.

Demerliac, Alain, *Nomenclature des navires français de 1848 à 1871: La marine de la Deuxième République et du Second Empire*, Éditions ANCRE, Nice, 2013.

Dousset, Francis, *Les navires de guerre français de 1850 à nos jours*, Éditions de la Cité, 1975.

Dumas, Robert and Guiglini, Jean, *Les cuirassés français de 23.500 tonnes* (with separate portfolio of plans), Éditions des 4 Seigneurs, Grenoble, 1980.

Dumas, Robert and Guiglini, Jean, *Les cuirassés français de 23.500 tonnes*, Éditions Lela Presse, Outreau, France, 2005. The *Courbet* and *Bretagne* classes.

Dumas, Robert and Prévoteaux, Gérard, *Les cuirassés français de 18.000 tonnes*, Éditions Lela Presse, Outreau, France, 2011. The *Danton* class.

Estival, Bernard, *Les canonnières de Chine, 1900-1945*, Marines-éditions, Nantes, 2001.

Feron, Luc, Cuirassé d'escadre *Bouvet* de l'ingénieur Huin 1896, EDIMO, Faimes (Belgium), 1996. Monograph with portfolio of plans. Also in *Marines, guerre et commerce*, Nos 42-48 (1996-97).

Frémy, Raymond, and Basili, Georges, *Des noms sur la mer*, ACORAM, Paris, 1990.

Frémy, Raymond, and Basili, Georges, *Des nouveaux noms sur la mer*, ACO-RAM, Paris, 1994. These two volumes reproduce a series initiated in 1973 by Rear Admiral André Huet in the ACORAM journal *Marine* and continued by Francis Dousset and Rear Admiral Frémy.

Friedman, Norman, Naval Weapons of World War One, Seaforth Publishing, Barnsley, UK, 2011.

Gardiner, Robert (ed.), *Conway's All the World's Fighting Ships, 1860-1905*, Greenwich, 1979. French section by N.J.M. Campbell.

Gardiner, Robert (ed.), *Conway's All the World's Fighting Ships, 1906-1921*, Greenwich, 1985. French section by Adam Smigielski.

Garier, Gérard and Croce, Alain, *Les cuirassés 'Échantillons', Tome 01: Brennus, Carnot, Charles Martel*, Éditions Lela Presse, Le Vigen, France, 2020.

Garier, Gérard and Croce, Alain, *Les cuirassés 'Échantillons', Tome 02: Jauréguiberry, Bouvet, Masséna*, et *Henri IV*, Éditions Lela Presse, Le Vigen, France, 2021.

Garier, Gérard, *L'odyssée technique et humaine du sous-marin en France. Tome 1: Du Plongeur (1863) aux Guêpe (1904)*, Marines-édition, Bourg-en-Bresse, undated.

Garier, Gérard, *L'odyssée technique et humaine du sous-marin en France. Tome 2: Des Emeraude (1905-1906) au Charles Brun (1908-1933)*, Marines-édition, Nantes, 1998.

Garier, Gérard, *L'odyssée technique et humaine du sous-marin en France. Tome 3, 1re partie: Des Clorinde (1912-1916) aux Diane (1912-1917)*, Marines-éditions, Nantes, 2000.

Garier, Gérard, *L'odyssée technique et humaine du sous-marin en France. Tome 3, 2e partie: À l'épreuve de la Grande Guerre*, Marines-éditions, Nantes, 2002.

Garier, Gérard, *L'odyssée technique et humaine du sous-marin en France. Tome 4: Des Joëssel (1913-1919) au Jean Corre ex UB-155 (1920-1937)*, Marines-éditions, Nantes, 2004.

Gille, Eric, *Cent ans de cuirassés français*, Marines édition, Nantes, 1999.

Gray, Edwyn, *The Devil's Device, Robert Whitehead and the History of the Torpedo*, revised edition (Annapolis, 1991).

Guiglini, Jean, *Les marques particulières des navires de guerre français (1900-1950)*, Service historique de la Marine, Vincennes, 2002.

Jolly, Jean, *Dictionnaire des parlementaires français*, vol. 1, Paris, 1960. (Tables of all French governments and ministers, 1871-1940.).

Jordan, John and Caresse, Philippe, *French Armoured Cruisers, 1887-1932*. Seaforth Publishing, Barnsley, UK, 2019.

Jordan, John and Caresse, Philippe, *French Battleships of World War One*, Seaforth Publishing, Barnsley, UK, 2017.

Labayle Couhat, Jean, *French Warships of World War I*, Ian Allan, London, 1974.

Langer, William L., *An Encyclopedia of World History*, Houghton Mifflin, Boston, 1972.

Le Conte, Pierre, *Répertoire des navires de guerre français*, Author, Cherbourg, 1932.

Le Masson, Henri, *Histoire du torpilleur en France*, Académie de Marine, undated, for sale by Éditions Maritimes et d'Outre-Mer 1967.

Le Masson, Henri, *Les sous-marins français des origines (1863) à nos jours*, 2nd edition, Éditions de la Cité - Brest - Paris, 1980. The first edition was published by Presses de la Cité, Paris, 1969.

Lecalvé, Frank, *Liste de la flotte de guerre française depuis la naissance de la vapeur à nos jours*, 2 volumes, Author, Toulon, 1990. (Lecalvé also produced a volume going back to 1700 and one on ships requisitioned in the two World Wars.)

*Marine & Technique au XIXe siècle*, Actes du colloque international, Paris, École militaire, les 10, 11, 12 Juin 1987, Service historique de la Marine, 1988. Includes Jean Labayle-Couhat, 'Le torpilleur des origines à 1900'; Philippe Ausseur, 'La Jeune École'; Étienne Taillemite, 'L'opinion française et la Jeune École'; and other papers.

*Marins et navires de la flotte française de guerre d'avant 1914*, SED 4, Paris, 1983. Photographs taken by Cdt. Joseph Wolff.

Masson, Philippe, and Battesti, Michèle, *La révolution maritime du XIXe siècle*, Lavauzelle, Paris, 1987. Based on the colloque international at Paris on 10, 11, 12 Juin 1987.

Michéa, H., Boucheix, P., and Vichot, Jacques, *Répertoire des navires français utilisés en guerre*, 2 volumes, Association des Amis des Musées de la Marine, Paris, 2005.

Modelski G., Thompson W.R., *Seapower in Global Politics, 1494–1993*, Palgrave Macmillan, London, 1988. (For expenditures).

Motte, Martin, *Une éducation géostratéguque, La pensée navale française de la Jeune École à 1914*, Economica, Paris, 2004.

Moulin, Jean, *Tous les porte-aéronefs en France de 1912 à nos jours*, Éditions Lela Presse, Le Vigen, France, 2020.

Olender, Pietr, *Sino-French Naval War, 1884-1885*, MMP Books, Petersfield, Hampshire, UK, 2012.

Peira, M. P., *Historique de la conduite du tir dans la Marine, 1900-1940*, Tome I, édité par le Mémorial de l'artillerie française, 1955. Pages 9-48 cover the period 1900-1918.

Piouffre, Gérard and Simoni, Henri, *3 siècles de croiseurs français*, Marines édition, Nantes, 2001.

Pontoire, Jacques, *Histoire des navires 'Marceau'*, Author, Chartres, 1996.

Prévoteaux, Gérard, *La Marine française dans la grande guerre, Les combattants oubliés*, 2 volumes, Éditions Lela Presse, Le Vigen, France, 2017.

Prévoteaux, Gérard, *Les cuirassés français de 15.000 tonnes*, Éditions Lela Presse, Outreau, France, 2006. The *Patrie* and *Démocratie* classes.

Revault, Hélène, *Le drame du cuirassé Mirabeau en Mer Noire, février-mai 1919*, Author, Angers, 1981.

Robert, Olivier, *L'épopée des transports type Annamite*, Marines éditions, Rennes, 2011.

Roche, Jean-Michel, *Dictionnaire des bâtiments de la flotte de guerre française de Colbert à nos jours. Tome I, 1671-1870* and *Tome II, 1870-2006*. Author (jmroche@netmarine.net), 2005.

Røksund, Arne, *The Jeune École, The Strategy of the Weak*, Brill, Leiden and Boston, 2007.

Ropp, Theodore, *The Development of a Modern Navy, French Naval Policy 1871-1904*, edited by Stephen S. Roberts, Naval Institute Press, Annapolis, 1987.

Saibène, Marc, *Les cuirassés Redoutable, Dévastation, Courbet, Programme de 1872*, Marines éditions, Bourg en Bresse, undated.

Vichot, Jacques, *Répertoire des navires de guerre français*, Association des Amis des Musées de la Marine, Paris, 1967.

Wallin, Franklin W., 'The French Navy during the Second Empire: A Study of the Effects of Technological Development on French Governmental Policy', Ph.D. dissertation, University of California, 1953.

Walser, John Raymond, 'France's Search for a Battlefleet: French Naval Policy, 1898-1914', Ph.D. dissertation, University of North Carolina at Chapel Hill, 1976.

Winfield, Rif, and Roberts, Stephen, *French Warships in the Age of Sail, 1786-1861: Design, Construction, Careers and Fates*, Seaforth Publishing, Barnsley, UK, 2015.

Yakimovich, D. B., 'Eskadrennyy bronenosets Brennus', Nᵒ 12/2012 in the series 'Morskaya Kollektsiya' published by the journal *Modelist-Konstruktor*, Moscow, 2012.

Yakimovich, D. B., 'Eskadrennyy bronenosets Masséna', Nᵒ 2/2009 in the series 'Morskaya Kollektsiya' published by the journal *Modelist-Konstruktor*, Moscow, 2009.

Yakimovich, D. B., 'Plavuchiye «Grand-Oteli»' (2 vols, 4 ships), Nᵒˢ 10-11/2011 in the series 'Morskaya Kollektsiya' published by the journal *Modelist-Konstruktor*, Moscow, 2011.

Zanco, Jean-Philippe, *Le ministère de la marine sous le Second Empire*, Service historique de la marine, Vincennes, c1997.

**Articles, historical**

Key: MGC - *Marines, guerre et commerce*, MFN - *Marines et forces navales* (successor to MGC), N&H - *Navires et histoire*, MM - *Marines Magazine*.

'Dossier l'Amiral Courbet' (9 articles), *Revue historique des Armées*, Nᵒ 3 (1985), pp3-83.

Brunner, Jean-Michel, 'Chaloupes-canonnières coloniales à vapeur. Les bâtiments des chantiers Claparède', *Neptunia* no. 249 (2007), pp5-12.

Buffetaut, Yves, '1918-1937: Le renouveau des sous-marins français', MM Nᵒ 53 (2008), pp14-47.

Buffetaut, Yves, 'D'une guerre à l'autre: les cuirassés de la classe *Bretagne*', MM Nᵒ 51 (2008), pp18-41.

Buffetaut, Yves, 'La marine nationale en 1914-1918', MM Nᵒ 52 (2008), pp18-63.

Buffetaut, Yves, 'La marine nationale en Méditerranée en 1914', MGC Nᵒ 61 (1999), pp35-39.

Buffetaut, Yves, 'Le port de Brest en 1916', MM Nᵒ 37 (2004), pp68-81.

Caresse, Philippe, 'Le garde-côtes cuirassé *Tempête*, ou l'histoire d'un *fer à repasser*', N&H Nᵒ 73 (2012), pp78-85. Translated in 'The "Flat Iron", the coast defence battleship *Tempête*', *Warship 2016* (John Jordan, ed., Conway, 2016), pp161-174.

Caresse, Philippe, 'The battleship *Gaulois*', *Warship 2012* (John Jordan, ed., Conway, 2012), pp113-135.

Caresse, Philippe, 'The battleship *Suffren*', *Warship 2010* (John Jordan, ed., Conway, 2010), pp9-26.

Caresse, Philippe, 'The French Battleship *Brennus*', *Warship 2019* (John Jordan, ed., Osprey, 2019), pp29-46.

Caresse, Philippe, 'The submarine *Mariotte*, known as the Toothbrush', *Warship 2015* (John Jordan, ed., Conway, 2015), pp81-89.

Ceillier, Marie-Raymond, 'Les idées stratégiques en France de 1870 à 1914, La Jeune École', thesis, École supérieure de guerre navale, Paris, 1928. Reproduced in Coutau-Bégarie (ed.), *L'Evolution de la pensée navale* (Paris, 1990), pp195-231.

de Balincourt et Vincent-Bréchignac, Commandants, 'La fin du *Richelieu*', by Vincent-Bréchignac with outline by de Balincourt of projected parts of this series of which only the portions on paddle steamers and vaisseaux mixtes were published, *Revue maritime*, Nᵒ 150 (1932), pp759-761. Drafts of some unpublished articles may be in the Adam collection at SHD Brest.

de Balincourt et Vincent-Bréchignac, Commandants, 'La marine française d'hier, Les Cuirassés, I. Batteries flottantes', *Revue maritime*, Nᵒ 125 (1930), pp577-595.

de Balincourt et Vincent-Bréchignac, Commandants, 'La marine française d'hier, Les Cuirassés, II. Frégates cuirassées', *Revue maritime*, Nᵒ 135 (1931), pp289-317 and Nᵒ 138 (1931), pp776-791.

de Balincourt et Vincent-Bréchignac, Commandants, 'La marine française d'hier, Les Cuirassés, III. Corvettes cuirassées', *Revue maritime*, Nᵒ 143 (1931), pp615-634.

de Balincourt et Vincent-Bréchignac, Commandants, 'La marine française d'hier, Garde-côtes', *Revue maritime*, Nᵒ 143 (1931), pp634-646.

de Balincourt, Commandant, and Le Conte, Pierre, 'La marine française d'hier, V. Navires à roues', *Revue maritime*, Nᵒ 154 (1932), pp472-512 and no. 157 (1933), pp12-54.

de Balincourt, Commandant, and Le Conte, Pierre, 'La marine française d'hier, VI. Vaisseaux mixtes', *Revue maritime*, no. 159 (1933), pp345-362 and Nᵒ 160 (1933) pp483-509.

Estival, Bernard, 'Construction des canonnières en Chine, des bateaux en "kit"', MGC Nᵒ 35 (1995), pp18-22.

Feron, Luc and Roche, Jean, 'The armoured cruiser *Jeanne d'Arc*', *Warship 2018* (John Jordan, ed., Osprey, 2018), pp67-84.

Feron, Luc, '100 ans Marine française: Canonnières, Avisos de station', MM *hors série* Nᵒ 4 (2004), pp4-43.

Feron, Luc, '100 ans Marine française: Croiseurs, Garde-côtes', MM *hors série* Nᵒ 2 (2002), entire issue.

Feron, Luc, '100 ans Marine française: Cuirassés, torpilleurs, contre-torpilleurs, escorteurs', MM *hors série* Nᵒ 1 (2002), entire issue.

Feron, Luc, 'Au sujet du *Suchet*', MM Nᵒ 56 (2009), pp52-79.

Feron, Luc, '*Châteaurenault*, croiseur corsaire', MM Nᵒˢ 44-45 (2006), pp64-81, 66-81.

Feron, Luc, '*Dupleix*, croiseur cuirassé', MFN Nᵒ 168 (2017), pp64-79.

Feron, Luc, 'Émile Bertin et son œuvre', MM Nᵒ 58 (2010), pp64-81.

Feron, Luc, '*Guichen*, croiseur corsaire', MM Nᵒˢ 42-43 (2005-06), pp62-80, 60-81.

Feron, Luc, '*Henri IV*: Premier cuirassé', MFN Nᵒ 164 (2016), pp64-79.

Feron, Luc, 'Il était une petite canonnière (*Zélée*)', MFN Nᵒ 87 (2003), pp60-77.

Feron, Luc, 'L'ingénieur Bertin au secours du Japon', MFN Nᵒ 153 (2014), pp66-79.

Feron, Luc, 'Le *Bruix*', MM Nᵒ 28 (2002), pp70-82.

Feron, Luc, 'Le *Chanzy*', MM Nᵒ 26 (2001), pp76-81.

Feron, Luc, 'Le croiseur *Amiral Charner*', MM Nᵒ 27 (2002), pp74-83.

Feron, Luc, 'Le croiseur cuirassé *Dupuy de Lôme*', MGC Nᵒˢ 56-61 (1998-99), pp55-61, 58-65, 35-44, 51-59, 57-66, and 53-61.

Feron, Luc, 'Le croiseur cuirassé *Jeanne d'Arc*', MFN Nᵒ 157 (2015), pp64-79.

Feron, Luc, 'Le croiseur *D'Entrecasteaux*', MM Nᵒˢ 46-48 (2006-07), pp64-79, 64-79, 64-79.

Feron, Luc, 'Le croiseur *Latouche-Tréville*', MM Nᵒˢ 22-26 (2000-01), pp72-81, 72-81, 72-82, 72-83, 68-75.

Feron, Luc, 'Le cuirassé *Brennus*', MGC Nᵒˢ 14-19 (1991-92), pp43-50, 43-50, 43-51, 43-50, 43-51, 42-50.

Feron, Luc, 'Le cuirassé *Carnot*', MM Nᵒˢ 32, 35, 36 (2003-04), pp64-77, 66-81, 66-81.

Feron, Luc, 'Le cuirassé *Charles Martel*', MGC Nᵒˢ 21-27 (1992-93), pp45-49, 45-51, 45-51, 45-51, 45-50, 45-50, and 45-51.

Feron, Luc, 'Le cuirassé *Hoche*', MGC Nᵒˢ 1-4 (1989), pp38-42, 43-55, 48-57, 42.

Feron, Luc, 'Le cuirassé *Jauréguiberry*', MM Nᵒˢ 49-52 (2007-08), pp64-79, 64-79, 64-79, 64-79.

Feron, Luc, 'Le cuirassé *Magenta*', MGC Nᵒˢ 11-13 (1991), pp41-51, 43-51, 43-49.

Feron, Luc, 'Le cuirassé *Marceau*', MGC Nᵒˢ 4-7 (1989-90), pp42-47, 37-46, 37-48, 26-29.

Feron, Luc, 'Le cuirassé *Masséna*', MFN N$^{os}$ 63-6 (1999-2000), pp48-57, 46-55, 56-65, 58-65, and 54-65.

Feron, Luc, 'Le cuirassé *Neptune*', MGC N$^{os}$ 7-10 (1990), pp30-35, 26-31, 36-45, 41-51.

Feron, Luc, 'Le *Furieux*', MM N$^{os}$ 29-30 (2002-03), pp69-81, 70-82. Translated into English in *Warship International*, Vol. 40, N$^{os}$ 3-4 (2003), pp243-256 and 327-338.

Feron, Luc, 'Le programme de 1890', MGC N$^{o}$ 20 (1992), pp43-51 (Preliminary designs for *Charles Martel*).

Feron, Luc, 'Les atlas de coques', MGC N$^{o}$ 4 (1989), pp38-42.

Feron, Luc, 'Les canonnières *Surprise* et *Décidée*', MFN N$^{o}$ 88 (2003-04), pp56-75.

Feron, Luc, 'Les contre-torpilleurs de 450 tonnes', *MRB* (*Le modèle réduit de bateau*) N$^{os}$ 252-254 (1984), pp6-12, 13-18, 39-44.

Feron, Luc, 'Les contre-torpilleurs de 800 tonnes', MM N$^{os}$ 53-58 (2008-10), pp60-79, 30-45, 32-47, 22-37, 16-31, and 18-35.

Feron, Luc, 'Les cuirassés de la classe *Normandie*', MFN N$^{os}$ 84-86 (2003), pp52-67, 44-59, 56-71.

Feron, Luc, 'Les transformations de la *Lorraine*', MFN N$^{os}$ 71-72 (2001), pp44-57, 54-67.

Feron, Luc, 'The Armoured Cruisers of the *Amiral Charner* class', *Warship 2014* (John Jordan, ed., Conway, 2014), pp8-27.

Feron, Luc, 'The cruiser *Dupuy de Lôme*', *Warship 2011* (John Jordan, ed., Conway, 2011), pp32-47.

Feron, Luc, 'Un marin photographe', MM N$^{o}$ 57 (2010), pp56-79.

Garier, Gérard, 'Les méconnus de la Marine nationale, Les *Quentin Roosevelt*', MFN N$^{o}$ 93 (2004) pp58-64, with supplementary information in MFN N$^{o}$ 102 (2006), pp58-61.

Garier, Gérard, 'Les mouilleurs de mines *Pluton* et *Cerbère*', MGC N$^{os}$ 34-35 (1994-95), pp28-35, 31-39.

Jordan, John, 'From *Danton* to *Courbet*', *Warship 2017* (John Jordan, ed., Conway, 2017), pp38-53.

Jordan, John, 'The battleships of the *Patrie* class', *Warship 2015* (John Jordan, ed., Conway, 2015), pp8-28.

Jordan, John, 'The Semi-Dreadnoughts of the *Danton* class', *Warship 2013* (John Jordan, ed., Conway, 2013), pp46-66.

Le Masson, Henri, 'Des cuirassés qui auraient pu être', *Revue maritime*, N$^{o}$ 204 (1963), pp1291-1309. Also in his *Propos maritimes* pp263-281.

Le Masson, Henri, 'La difficile gestation du croiseur léger français, 1910-1926', *Revue maritime*, N$^{o}$ 199 (1963), pp577-594, and N$^{o}$ 200 (1963), pp747-763.

Le Masson, Henri, 'La politique navale française de 1870 à 1914', in his *Propos maritimes*, Éditions Maritimes & d'Outre-Mer, Paris, 1970, pp181-239.

Le Masson, Henri, 'Les cuirassés du type *Normandie*', *Revue maritime*, N$^{o}$ 203 (1963), pp1172-1191. Also in his *Propos maritimes* pp243-262.

Le Masson, Henri, 'Politique navale et construction de navires de ligne en France in 1914', *Revue maritime*, N$^{o}$ 202 (1963), pp993-1008. Portions used in 'La politique navale française de 1870 à 1914', in his *Propos maritimes*.

Lengerer, Hans, 'The 1884 Coup d'État in Korea, Revision and Acceleration of the Expansion of the IJN', *Warship International*, Vol. 57, N$^{o}$ 4 (2020), pp289-302. Includes a detailed account of Émile Bertin's service in Japan.

Morazzani, A., 'Sous les ponts de Paris avec le *Sabre* et la *Claymore*', *Revue maritime*, N$^{o}$ 208 (1964), pp327-340.

Moulin, Jean, 'Le cuirassé *Bretagne*', MFN N$^{o}$ 67 (2000), pp36-47.

Moulin, Jean, 'Le cuirassé *Danton* retrouvé', MM N$^{o}$ 58 (2010), pp4-17.

Moulin, Jean, 'Les croiseurs français', MFN N$^{o}$ 119 (2009), pp68-79.

Moulin, Jean, 'Les navires français 1914-18', MFN N$^{o}$ 118 (2008-09), pp22-35.

Picard, Claude, 'Le porte-avions *Béarn*', MGC N$^{os}$ 3-5 (1989-90), pp36-44, 20-27, 18-23.

Picard, Claude, 'Les avions du *Béarn*', MGC N$^{o}$ 8 (1990), pp45-50.

Prévoteaux, Gérard, 'Le croiseur de 1$^{re}$ classe *Cecille* (1888-1907)', N&H N$^{o}$ 53 (2009), pp84-89.

Prévoteaux, Gérard, 'Le croiseur de 1$^{re}$ classe *Tage* (1886-1907)', N&H N$^{o}$ 52 (2009), pp.72-77.

Prévoteaux, Gérard, 'Les croiseurs de 1$^{re}$ classe *Châteaurenault* et *Guichen* (1897-1921): *Chateaurenault*', N&H N$^{o}$70 (2012), pp18-29.

Prévoteaux, Gérard, 'Les croiseurs de 1$^{re}$ classe *Châteaurenault* et *Guichen* (1897-1921): *Guichen*', N&H N$^{o}$ 71 (2012), pp18-27.

Prévoteaux, Gérard, 'Les croiseurs de 1$^{re}$ classe type *Alger/Jean Bart* (1889-191): *Alger, Jean Bart, Isly*', N&H N$^{o}$ 54 (2009), pp74-81.

Prévoteaux, Gérard, 'Les croiseurs de 2$^{ème}$ classe *Catinat* et *Protet* (1896-1910)', N&H N$^{o}$ 63 (2010-11), pp86-91.

Prévoteaux, Gérard, 'Les croiseurs de 2$^{ème}$ classe *Davout* et *Suchet* (1889-1910)', N&H N$^{o}$ 55 (2009), pp72-79.

Prévoteaux, Gérard, 'Les croiseurs de 2$^{ème}$ classe *Descartes* et *Pascal* (1894-1920)', N&H N$^{o}$ 62 (2010), pp88-95.

Prévoteaux, Gérard, 'Les croiseurs de 2$^{ème}$ classe type *Bugeaud* (1893-1920): *Bugeaud, Chasseloup Laubat, Friant*', N&H N$^{o}$ 58 (2010), pp72-81.

Prévoteaux, Gérard, 'Les croiseurs de 2$^{ème}$ classe type *Cassard* (1895-1924): *Cassard, Du Chayla, D'Assas*', N&H N$^{o}$ 61 (2010), pp66-77.

Prévoteaux, Gérard, 'Les croiseurs de 3$^{ème}$ classe type *Forbin* (1888-1921): *Forbin, Surcouf, Coetlogon*', N&H N$^{o}$ 56 (2009), pp72-79.

Prévoteaux, Gérard, 'Les croiseurs de 3$^{ème}$ classe type *Troude* (1888-1919): *Troude, Lalande, Cosmao*', N&H N$^{o}$ 57 (2009-10), pp22-28.

Prévoteaux, Gérard, 'Les croiseurs français 1868-1885 (1), Le croiseur *Chateaurenault* (1868-1892)', N&H N$^{o}$ 29 (2005), pp83-86.

Prévoteaux, Gérard, 'Les croiseurs français 1868-1885 (2), Les croiseurs type *Infernet, Sané* (1869-1899)', N&H N$^{o}$ 30 (2005), pp83-90.

Prévoteaux, Gérard, 'Les croiseurs français 1868-1885 (3), Les croiseurs *Duquesne et Tourville* (1869-1899)', N&H N$^{o}$ 31 (2005), pp78-82.

Prévoteaux, Gérard, 'Les croiseurs français 1868-1885 (4), Le croiseur *Duguay Trouin* (1877-1899)', N&H N$^{o}$ 33 (2005), pp88-90.

Prévoteaux, Gérard, 'Les croiseurs français 1868-1885 (5), Les croiseurs *Rigault de Genouilly* et *Éclaireur* (1876-1902)', N&H N$^{o}$ 34 (2006), pp76-80.

Prévoteaux, Gérard, 'Les croiseurs français 1868-1885 (6), Les croiseurs type *Lapérouse* (1877-1902): *Lapérouse, D'Estaing, Nielly, Primaguet*', N&H N$^{o}$ 35 (2006), pp73-79.

Prévoteaux, Gérard, 'Les croiseurs français 1868-1885 (6), Les croiseurs type *Forfait* (1879-1897), (a) *Forfait, Villars*, (b) *Magon, Roland*', N&H N$^{o}$ 36 (2006), pp81-85.

Prévoteaux, Gérard, 'Les croiseurs français 1868-1885 (7), Les croiseurs type *Iphigénie, Aréthuse* (1881-1901): (a) *Iphigénie, Naiade, Dubourdieu* (b) *Aréthuse*', N&H N$^{o}$ 37 (2006), pp86-94.

Prévoteaux, Gérard, 'Les croiseurs français 1868-1885 (8) Le croiseur *Milan* (1884-1908)', N&H N$^{o}$ 39 (2007), pp79-83.

Prévoteaux, Gérard, 'Les croiseurs protégés français (1885-1900) and Le croiseur *Sfax* (1884-1906)', N&H N$^{o}$ 51 (2009), pp68-75.

Roberts, Stephen S., 'The French Coast Defense Ship *Rochambeau*', *Warship International*, Vol. 30, N$^{o}$ 4 (1993), pp333-345.

Roberts, William H., 'Thunder Mountain, The Ironclad Ram *Dunderberg*', *Warship International*, Vol. 30, N$^{o}$. 4 (1993), pp363-400.

Saibène, Marc, 'Les navires hôpitaux français', MGC N$^{o}$ 16 (1991), pp4-8.

Spencer, John, 'Conduite du Tir', part 1, *Warship 2010* (John Jordan, ed., Conway, 2010), pp156-69, and Part 2, *Warship 2012* (John Jordan, ed., Conway, 2012), pp52-64.

Stahl, Frédéric, 'La Marine Nationale en août 1914', N&H N$^{o}$ 81 (2013-14), pp32-71.

Vichot, J., 'Un *compact* documentaire pour ship-lovers et modélistes', *Triton*, N$^{os}$ 36-50 (1956-1959, quarterly). Each issue contained a one-page *fiche* with a plan from the *Album de coque* and basic technical and career data for a single ship.

Wright, Christopher C., 'The French Naval Building Program of 1915', *Warship International*, Vol. 17, N$^{o}$ 1 (1980), pp14-23.

# Index to Named Vessels